# SPECIAL EDUCATION

## Contemporary Perspectives for School Professionals

### Third Edition

## MARILYN FRIEND

University of North Carolina at Greensboro

**PEARSON**

Boston   Columbus   Indianapolis   New York   San Francisco   Upper Saddle River
Amsterdam   Cape Town   Dubai   London   Madrid   Milan   Munich   Paris   Montreal   Toronto
Delhi   Mexico City   Sao Paulo   Sydney   Hong Kong   Seoul   Singapore   Taipei   Tokyo

Vice President and Editor in Chief: Jeffery W. Johnston
Executive Editor: Ann Castel Davis
Editorial Assistant: Penny Burleson
Development Editor: Alicia Reilly
Vice President, Director of Marketing: Quinn Perkson
Marketing Manager: Erica DeLuca
Senior Managing Editor: Pamela D. Bennett
Senior Project Manager: Sheryl Glicker Langner
Senior Operations Supervisor: Matthew Ottenweller
Senior Operations Manager: Laura Messerly
Senior Art Director: Diane C. Lorenzo
Text Designer: Candace Rowley

Cover Designer: Diane Lorenzo
Photo Coordinator: Sandy Schaefer
Cover Image: istock
Permissions Administrator: Rebecca Savage
Media Producer: Autumn Benson
Media Project Manager: Rebecca Norsic
Full-Service Project Management: Carla Kipper,
    S4Carlisle Publishing Services
Composition: S4Carlisle Publishing Services
Printer/Binder: Webcrafters Inc.
Cover Printer: Lehigh-Phoenix
Text Font: Minion

Credits and acknowledgments borrowed from other sources and reproduced, with permission, in this textbook appear on appropriate page within text.

Every effort has been made to provide accurate and current Internet information in this book. However, the Internet and information posted on it are constantly changing, so it is inevitable that some of the Internet addresses listed in this textbook will change.

Photo credits are on page iv.

**Library of Congress Cataloging-in-Publication Data**

Friend, Marilyn Penovich
    Special education : contemporary perspectives for school professionals /
Marilyn Friend. — 3rd ed.
        p. cm.
    Includes bibliographical references and index.
    ISBN-13: 978-0-13-703327-0
        1. Special education—United States. 2. Inclusive education—United States. I. Title.
LC3981.F75 2010
371.9—dc22

                                                                            2010005278

10  9  8  7  6  5  4  3  2  1

www.pearsonhighered.com

ISBN 10:    0-13-703327-3
ISBN 13: 978-0-13-703327-0

# about the author

MARILYN FRIEND has been a professional educator for more than thirty years. She has worked as a general education teacher and a special education teacher, as well as a teacher educator, researcher, and staff developer. Her specific areas of expertise include collaboration among school professionals, inclusive practices, co-teaching, and differentiated instruction. What makes Dr. Friend unique is the balance in her professional activities: Although she is a university faculty member, she maintains close contact with elementary, middle, and high school professionals; and she helps educators in rural, suburban, and urban school districts to refine their practices for meeting diverse student needs. Currently, she is Chair and Professor of Special Education, Department of Specialized Education Services, The University of North Carolina at Greensboro.

# preface

As the first decade of the twenty-first century draws to a close, the pressure on educators has not decreased; if anything, it is greater than ever before. Expectations for improved achievement outcomes for all students continue, and the necessity of basing instruction on careful analysis of frequently gathered data is clear. At the same time, educators must implement the appropriate but complex mandate to ensure that students with disabilities have, like their peers, meaningful access to the general curriculum. All of these elements make information about special education especially important. My goal in *Special Education: Contemporary Perspectives for School Professionals* has been to write a text that provides teacher candidates and other pre-professionals and early career professionals—general educators, special educators, administrators, and related services providers—a solid grounding in today's special education concepts and practices. I wanted to produce an introductory book that clearly relied on the strong research base for our field and that not only aligned with current legislation, but also placed that research and law within the very real and sometimes unclear and challenging world of students and educators, classrooms and schools, families and communities.

## Setting a Context

Two sets of experiences shaped my approach to writing this text. The first is my university work with preservice and practicing teachers in both general education and special education. I've had the privilege of taking a leadership role in developing two undergraduate special education teacher education programs: one that resulted in dual licensure, one a special education major. I've also participated in creating several new graduate special education programs: alternative routes to licensure, master's degrees, and doctoral degrees. In addition, I'm currently engaged in the collaborative, imaginative, and analytical work of re-visioning special education teacher preparation to be responsive to the demands of this twenty-first century society. These experiences inform the goal I have for an introductory special education course: to inspire and foster enthusiasm and yet not shy away from the need to discuss the often complex and occasionally contentious issues that confront the field. We need school professionals who have foundational knowledge, extraordinary assessment and instructional skills, flexible thinking, and an understanding of and respect for the perspectives of colleagues and parents. Those elements are strongly represented in this text. I wanted to draw students into the material, to personalize it so that they feel the book is speaking to them and encouraging them to be the professionals needed for tomorrow's schools.

The second set of experiences reflected in this text is my work in schools. Observing, collaborating with, and teaching educators and administrators as they interact with pupils has taught me that children and youth can accomplish goals that sometimes are difficult even to imagine, as long as their teachers and other service providers believe in them and work together. I am firmly committed to inclusive practices—the way they can and should be. That is, I believe that all learners should be welcomed members of their learning communities. The goal is educating students in typical settings—but not abandoning effective practices or focusing on where students are seated to the exclusion of all other factors. Sometimes decisions for separate instructional settings have to be made, but in inclusive schools they are cautious decisions that take into account both the costs and benefits to students' and are revisited often. And so this textbook also reflects those beliefs: Early career professionals should be optimistic about the potential of their students, but they also should be well schooled in the decision-making processes, settings, and instructional procedures that can best ensure that potential is realized.

## The Plan of the Book

Like any textbook, the overall organization of *Special Education: Contemporary Perspectives for School Professionals* reflects decisions made about how best to capture the essential content that it needs to address and the themes that are emphasized throughout it. Core concepts related to the field of special education are introduced in Chapter One, "Key Concepts for Understanding Special Education," and Chapter Two, "The Personnel and Procedures of Special Education." Chapter Three, "Multicultural and Bilingual Perspectives," explores several essential dimensions of diversity and multicultural issues as they relate to students with disabilities. Chapter Four, "Creating Partnerships through Collaboration," examines the increasingly central role that collaboration plays in the work of all of today's school professionals. Chapters Five through Fifteen comprise the categorical segment of the text, each one devoted to a separate category of disability or special learning need. Each of these chapters goes beyond the mere characterizing of students; the emphasis is on understanding and teaching them.

## Topics Integrated into Every Chapter

The perspectives of *parents and families* are addressed in each categorical chapter in a section designed to address issues pertaining to the overall chapter topic. Likewise, although it is not possible to provide extensive coverage of *instructional practices* in an introductory text, in each categorical chapter a section is devoted to providing examples of *research-based strategies and approaches* in order to give readers a sense of the ways they can have a positive impact on students. An additional example is the topic of inclusion. Each categorical chapter explores *inclusive practices* related to particular groups of students—sometimes to highlight positive practices and sometimes to illustrate that more work is needed. One other topic is addressed in this manner: the *history of the field.* It worries me that in our zeal to prepare professionals who can meet the extraordinarily high expectations set for them today, we sometimes forget to give them a sense of the development of the field of special education and how today's practices are a result of that development.

# New to This Edition

Special education changes rapidly, and in this third edition of *Special Education: Contemporary Perspectives for School Professionals,* great care has been taken to provide new information that reflects the most current research and issues influencing the field. In addition, this edition includes more stories from students, parents, and educators, all designed to give readers a glimpse into the real world of individuals who receive, deliver, and are affected by special education. In addition, each chapter has been carefully reviewed, and updated references, examples, and strategies have been added. These are several of the most significant changes in this edition:

- *Advice from professionals in the field. Speaking from Experience* is a new feature that has been added to every chapter. In it, experienced professionals from across the country like Noel Keener, a special educator who twice has been named her school's Teacher of the Year (Chapter 1), and Jennette Horton, an experienced teacher of high school students with autism spectrum disorders (Chapter 10), offer advice for managing the demands of being a special educator and suggestions for working effectively with students with disabilities, their families, and colleagues.
- *Expanded coverage of response to intervention (RTI).* Since the second edition, more information about response to intervention has become available and more local school districts are implementing this legislatively endorsed and rapidly emerging practice for identifying students as having learning disabilities. As a result, more detailed coverage of RTI is provided in this edition, including its use for students' academic and behavioral problems as well as some of the questions and issues it is raising.

*Issues facing the field of special education* Perhaps because of the complexity of the needs that students with disabilities may have, the field continues to face ongoing and new issues. In this edition, such issues have been embedded in chapters where they are most relevant. For example, recent court cases are addressed in Chapter 1, a discussion of the disproportionate representation of some students in special education is addressed in Chapter 3, and the contentious topic regarding the use of seclusion and restraints with students with challenging behaviors is addressed in Chapter 7.

*The most recent research, data, and thinking about key topics in special education* Up-to-date information is essential for today's professional educators, and this edition provides it. For example, all data related to the numbers of students receiving special education, their placements, their representation in various disability categories, and other facts about them have been updated. In addition, over 600 new references have been added, an indicator of the careful review of each concept presented and the search for the most contemporary thinking available about those concepts.

*New stories about students with disabilities and their families* Professionals who will work with students with disabilities need to understand the perspectives of students and families. Toward that end, new stories about students with disabilities and their experiences in public schools are included.

*More examples of strategies and teaching techniques* Although this book is not intended to comprehensively address teaching methods, each chapter includes research-based, specific strategies that address the learning and behavior needs of students with disabilities. Teacher candidates also are reminded throughout that many of the strategies presented in one chapter are easily and effectively used with students described in other chapters.

*Instructional and assistive technology* Technology seems to change on almost a daily basis, and the technology options included in the third edition have been carefully reviewed and changed to ensure that they reflect those new and improved options. At the same time, dated technology or options that are not longer available have been removed.

*Timelines that provide snapshots of the history of important events* Most professionals agree that teacher candidates should have a perspective on the development of the field of special education. However, they also note the need for such information to be presented in a succinct way. In the third edition, each chapter in which an historical view is appropriate includes a timeline that captures key events in a way that can be quickly scanned and understood. This approach allows for considerable historical detail to be provided in an easily consumed format.

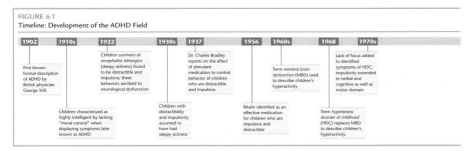

FIGURE 6.1
Timeline: Development of the ADHD Field

*More websites than ever before* The amount and quality of information available to educators through the Internet has exploded. In this new edition, every chapter includes new electronic sources of information, instructional strategies, and tools teachers will find valuable as they gather data, plan instruction, and learn about critical issues in the field.

And those are just a few of the highlights. The third edition of *Special Education: Contemporary Perspectives for School Professionals* reflects along every dimension the most current information about special education.

In addition to presenting the theories, concepts, and realities of the field of special education, I've also attempted to bring to life the experiences and powerful stories of people with disabilities and their parents and families.

## Chapter-Opening Vignettes

**Chapter-Opening Vignettes** describe the experiences of different students as they relate to the topics discussed in each chapter. These individuals' experiences are referenced at key points in the chapter as well. The vignettes can form the basis for applying information and strategies from the chapter, and they can be a launching point for discussions of issues influencing the field, including inclusive practices, collaboration, and response to intervention.

## Firsthand Accounts

**Firsthand Accounts** allow teachers, other school professionals, students, and parents the chance to share, in their own words, their experiences and perspectives about life and learning with special needs. Their words convey the core message of this book—that individuals with disabilities should be thought of in terms of their unique potential and abilities.

## NEW!! Speaking from Experience

**Speaking from Experience** asks teachers practicing in classrooms today for their advice and suggestions for educating students of all abilities, effectively interacting with parents and families, and collaborating with colleagues.

# Evidence-Based Practices

This text emphasizes contemporary information for practicing teachers: teaching approaches, strategies, ideas, and tips that are always based on empirically validated, peer-reviewed research findings.

## Instruction in Action

**Instruction in Action** highlights teaching applications for intensive instruction delivered by special education teachers or other professionals in various educational settings, including teaching examples for individual or small-group situations. The feature provides sample lessons, tips, techniques, ideas, and approaches for working with students with special educational needs, whether in separate setting or general education classrooms.

### Helping Students Succeed in Math

Students struggle in math for many reasons. Wadlington and Wadlington (2008) offer these suggestions for helping students to succeed:

- Address math anxiety
  - Create a safe classroom environment—never criticize or ridicule students struggling with math and expect the same respectful behavior of all students
  - Help a student become an expert in a specific part of math, for example, illustrating word problems
  - Share stories of famous people who have overcome their learning difficulties
  - Use cooperative math games to help students become more comfortable with the language and symbols of mathematics
- Use general instructional strategies that foster math learning
  - Seat students near the focus of instruction
  - Be well-organized in teaching math concepts, and present them in a highly structured and logical order
  - Analyze math skills to be taught, breaking them into small steps and then teaching each step separately

with frequent reviews both during instruction and on subsequent days
  - Use manipulatives, even for older students
  - Provide repeated practice on foundational skills so that they are overlearned
  - Arrange math tutoring for some students, with a classmate, older peer, volunteer, or paraprofessional
- Teach mathematical communication
  - Have students write in a math journal to help them become comfortable with math terms and ideas
  - Model new vocabulary, providing concrete examples
  - Have students create mathematical dictionaries that illustrate key terms and concepts
  - Stress meaning rather than rote memorization
  - If students struggle with reading, be sure math problems are read aloud or are audio-recorded
  - Assess student learning in both formal and informal ways. Use ongoing assessment data to re-teach and group students for instruction
  - Analyze student error patterns; they provide important information about what students do and do not understand

*instruction in action*

## Positive Behavior Supports

**Positive Behavior Supports** illustrates the many positive and proactive ways to address student behavior and social issues as a part of overall classroom teaching and learning.

### Seatwork: Helping Students to Work Independently

Many students with learning disabilities struggle to demonstrate self-control and stay engaged when assigned independent seatwork, especially in general education settings. These ideas can foster student success:

- Involve students in setting classroom behavior expectations. Identify three to five positively worded expectations related to seatwork (e.g., "If you need help, quietly ask a neighbor").
- Create vivid posters that visually depict the expectations and review these with students.
- Model examples and nonexamples of the behavior expectations and provide students opportunities to practice. Give feedback to students and reward appropriate behavior.
- Help students set goals for their seatwork (e.g., "I will complete at least 10 problems during the first 8 minutes," "I will complete two more sentences today than I did yesterday").
- Create a whole-class self-monitoring system. For example, set a timer to go off each 5 minutes. Each time it sounds, all students record the amount of work completed.
- Teach students to self-graph. Students are more likely to persist in their work if they can see their progress. If students graph the number of problems completed, number of sentences written, or other specific data, they may be more motivated to complete work.

- Use effective praise. When a student is working appropriately, quietly and warmly congratulate the student. The more specific the praise the better—for example, "You're staying focused, completing each problem, and raising your hand to ask for assistance. That's great!"
- Use engaging materials and tasks with clear purpose. Adding color, clear directions, and examples can enhance student attention to seatwork.
- Make sure that seatwork is within the student's independent skill level; misbehavior often occurs because the assigned work is too difficult for the student.
- Provide supports by making available word banks, sentence starters, technology, manipulatives, and other accommodations.
- Teach time management. Explicitly teach students how to review assignments, prioritize them, allocate time for each, and make a to-do list.
- Work for real-world connections. Discuss with students how their seatwork assignments relate to their postschool goals.

Source: Rock, M. L., & Thead, B. K. (2009). 20 ways to promote student success during independent seatwork. *Intervention in School and Clinic, 44,* 179–184. Reprinted by permission of SAGE Publications.

*positive behavior supports*

## Technology Notes

**Technology Notes** showcases fascinating new technology applications for teaching students with exceptional needs in special or general educational settings.

*technology notes*

### Brain Research and Learning Disabilities

Advances in medical technology are making it possible for scientists to study the human brain, leading us to a much clearer understanding about the parts of the brain that are most critical for oral language and reading and the differences between the brains of individuals who read fluently and those with reading or learning disabilities (Shaywitz, Lyon, & Shaywitz, 2006; Society for Neuroscience, 2006). Eventually, it may lead to new types of interventions for students.

**Key Regions of the Brain Involved in Reading**

Parieto-temporal **Word Analysis**

Broca's Inferior frontal gyrus **Articulation/Word Analysis**

Occipito-temporal **Word Form**

**Brain Structure**

Three regions of the brain, all located in the left hemisphere as shown in the illustration are involved in reading (Shaywitz & Shaywitz, 2004):

- Broca's region (involved in articulation and word analysis)
- Parieto-temporal region (involved in word analysis)
- Occipito-temporal region (involved in reading fluency)

**Brain Function**

Researchers study how the brain functions through functional magnetic resonance imaging (fMRI), which measures blood flow during brain activity. Results of studies using this approach indicate that the brains of individuals who are dyslexic function differently than the brains of individuals with LD:

# Cutting Edge Information

The field of special education is exciting, fast moving, and continually influenced by new ideas. Teachers and educational professionals of all kinds are encouraged to maintain their connection and to find inspiration from this universe of information.

> ### Understanding Dyslexia
>
> **What is dyslexia?**
> - Dyslexia is a brain-based type of learning disability that specifically impairs a person's ability to read.
> - People with dyslexia typically read at levels significantly lower than expected despite having normal intelligence.
> - Common characteristics among people with dyslexia are difficulty with spelling, phonological processing (the manipulation of sounds), and/or rapid visual-verbal responding.
> - Dyslexia can be inherited in some families, and recent studies have identified a number of genes that may predispose an individual to developing dyslexia.
>
> **What is the treatment?**
> - Early identification for students with dyslexia is particularly urgent given recent studies showing that effective language instruction appears to generate repair in under-activated sections of the brain responsible for this disorder (Shaywitz, 2003).
> - Many students with severe reading disabilities benefit from a beginning reading program that includes the following elements (Friend & Bursuck, 2009, p. 253):
>   - *Direct instruction in language analysis.* For example, students need to be taught skills in sound segmentation or
>
> in orally breaking down words into their component sounds.
>   - *A highly structured phonics program.* This program should teach the alphabetic code directly and systematically using a simple-to-complex sequence of skills
>   - *Writing and reading instruction in combination.*
>   - *Intensive instruction.* Reading instruction for at-risk students should include large amounts of practice in materials that contain words they are able to decode.
>   - *Teaching for automaticity.* Students must be given enough practice so that they are able to read both accurately and fluently.
>
> **What is the prognosis?**
> - For those with dyslexia, the prognosis is mixed.
> - Because dyslexia affects such a wide range of people and produces such different symptoms and varying degrees of severity, predictions are difficult to make.
> - Outcomes generally are positive for individuals whose dyslexia is identified early, who have supportive family and friends and a strong self-image, and who are involved in a proper remediation program.
>
> Source: National Institute of Neurological Disorders and Stroke. (2009, March). *Dyslexia information page.* Bethesda, MD: Author. Retrieved June 10, 2009 from http://www.ninds.nih.gov/disorders/dyslexia/dyslexia.htm.
>
> *professional edge*

## Professional Edge

**Professional Edge** describes conceptual material, cutting-edge information, and contemporary issues relevant to today's teachers. Included are new and sometimes controversial topics that experts in the field are talking about *right now*.

> ### Issues and Trends Affecting Diverse Exceptional Learners
>
> The conditions of urban education disproportionately affect students of color because it is largely these students who populate urban classrooms: Sixty-five of the 100 largest school districts in the United States enroll under 50 percent students who are Caucasian. One-third of these districts have student populations more than 75 percent non-Caucasian (National Center for Education Statistics, 2009a). The following discussion highlights critical issues in this domain.
>
> *Equity Issues*
>
> A number of equity issues arise with respect to urban education. For example, student access to fully credentialed, experienced teachers is a chronic problem (Nieto, 2002–2003). In special education, large school districts are more likely than their smaller counterparts to cite lack of qualified applicants as a significant barrier to filling special education positions. Researchers have suggested that the problem of getting and keeping highly qualified special educators in urban areas is so significant that extraordinary strategies such as offering financial incentives are needed to alleviate the problem (Sindelar et al., 2007). This implies that students with disabilities in urban settings are less likely than other students with special needs to have the benefit of fully prepared teachers (Shaywitz, 2003).

## Current Trends and Issues Sections

**Current Trends and Issues** sections conclude each chapter with a brief look at the most recent developments in the field, and the most interesting—and often still unresolved—questions and dilemmas.

## Margin Notes

**Margin Notes** appear throughout all chapters with a variety of useful information to extend and apply text information.

> ### web link
> www.nabe.org
> The National Association for Bilingual Education is a national organization concerned with the education of language-minority students in U.S. schools.

**Web Link.** Addresses are provided for relevant and useful websites for gaining more information or accessing practical teaching material.

> ### research NOTE
> In commenting on interventions for treating ADHD, Vitiello and Sherrill (2007) note that although research has demonstrated symptoms can be reduced (e.g., less movement, more attention), few studies can directly relate these results to improved academic achievement.

**Research Note.** These summaries of important research studies that have significant and practical impact on the field are concise and free of jargon.

> ### dimensions of DIVERSITY
> Schmitz and Velez (2003) found differences in Mexican, Mexican-American, and Puerto Rican mothers' ratings of their children's ADHD symptoms. They concluded that understanding ADHD must occur within a cultural context.

**Dimensions of Diversity.** Information is given about racial, ethnic, linguistic, gender, and other types of student diversity that teachers will encounter in the classroom.

> ### fyi
>
> Alexander Graham Bell's grandfather and father were both distinguished professionals in the speech and language field. Bell was an expert in his father's phonetic alphabet, a system called *visible speech* that was intended to help people learn to enunciate more carefully but later was used to teach language skills to individuals who were deaf.

**FYI.** The provide high-interest, up-to-the-minute "factoids" related to text discussions.

# Aids to Understanding

## Learning Objectives

**Learning Objectives** begin each chapter to focus your thinking about the main topics to be covered in the upcoming pages. An **Individualized Study Plan** connected to these objectives is included in the book specific resources section of **MyEducationLab**. Each chapter ends with a **Summary** of the main ideas of the chapters.

PEARSON
**myeducationlab**

To check your comprehension on the content covered in Chapter 9, go to the Book Specific Resources in the MyEducationLab (www .myeducationlab.com) for your course, select your text, and complete the Study Plan. Here you will be able to take a chapter quiz, receive feedback on your answers, and then access review, practice, and enrichment activities to enhance your understanding of chapter content.

## Review, Reflect, and Discuss

**Review, Reflect, and Discuss** features conclude each major section of the text, and offer ideas and activities that may by used as organizers for content review and springboards for extended learning.

### REVIEW · REFLECT · DISCUSS

1. Think about the field-independent and field-sensitive cognitive styles. Which most closely describes you? To what extent do you think your cognitive style has been influence by the culture in which you were raised? How does your cognitive style affect your learning habits?

2. As a teacher, how will you distinguish between behavior that is truly inappropriate and that which is associated with culture or alienation? What are the differences in how you might respond to each?

# Supplements

This edition boasts the most comprehensive and integrated collection of supplements to date to assist students and professors alike in maximizing learning and instruction. Together, these materials immerse students in the content of the text, allowing them and their instructors to benefit from a deeper and more meaningful learning experience. All of the instructor supplements are available at the Instructor's Resource Center. To access the Instructor's Resource Manual, the PowerPoint lecture presentation, and the Assessment Package and MyTest software, go to the Instructor Resource Center at www.pearsonhighered.com and click on the "Educators" link. Here you will be able to login or complete a one-time registration for a user name and password.

## Myeducationlab

### *The power of classroom practice.*

"Teacher educators who are developing pedagogies for the analysis of teaching and learning contend that analyzing teaching artifacts has three advantages: it enables new teachers time for reflection while still using the real materials of practice; it provides new teachers with experience thinking about and approaching the complexity of the classroom; and in some cases, it can help new teachers and teacher educators develop a shared understanding and common language about teaching. . . ."[1]

As Linda Darling-Hammond and her colleagues point out, grounding teacher education in real classrooms—among real teachers and students and among actual examples of students' and teachers' work—is an important, and perhaps even an essential, part of training teachers for the complexities of teaching in today's classrooms. For this reason, we have created a valuable, time-saving website—MyEducationLab—that provides you with the context of real classrooms and artifacts that research on teacher education tells us is so important. The authentic in-class video footage, interactive skill-building exercises and other resources available on MyEducationLab offer you a uniquely valuable teacher education tool.

MyEducationLab is easy to use and integrate into both your assignments and your courses. Wherever you see the MyEducationLab logo in the margins or elsewhere in the text, follow the simple instructions to access the videos, strategies, cases, and artifacts associated with these assignments, activities, and learning units on MyEducationLab. MyEducationLab is organized topically to enhance the coverage of the core concepts discussed in the clusters of your book. For each topic on the course you will find most or all of the following resources:

**Connection to National Standards** Now it is easier than ever to see how your coursework is connected to national standards. In each topic of MyEducationLab you will find intended learning outcomes connected to the appropriate national standards for your course. All of the Assignments and Activities and all of the Building Teaching Skills and Dispositions in MyEducationLab are mapped to the appropriate national standards and learning outcomes as well.

**Assignments and Activities** Designed to save instructors preparation time, these assignable exercises show concepts in action (through video, cases, or student and

[1]Darling-Hammond, I., & Bransford, J., Eds. (2005). *Preparing Teachers for a Changing World.* San Francisco: John Wiley & Sons

teacher artifacts) and then offer thought-provoking questions that probe your understanding of these concepts or strategies. (Feedback for these assignments is available to the instructor.)

**Building Teaching Skills and Dispositions** These learning units help you practice and strengthen skills that are essential to quality teaching. First you are presented with the core skill or concept and then given an opportunity to practice your understanding of this concept multiple times by watching video footage (or interacting with other media) and then critically analyzing the strategy or skill presented.

**IRIS Center Resources** The IRIS Center at Vanderbilt University (http://iris.peabody .vanderbilt.edu—funded by the U.S. Department of Education's Office of Special Education Programs OSEP) develops training enhancement materials for pre-service and in-service teachers. The Center works with experts from across the country to create challenge-based interactive modules, case study units, and podcasts that provide research-validated information about working with students in inclusive settings. On your MyEducationLab course we have integrated this content where appropriate to enhance the content covered in your book.

**Teacher Talk** This feature links to videos of teachers of the year across the country discussing their personal stories of why they teach. This National Teacher of the Year Program is sponsored by the Council of Chief State School Officers (CCSSO) and focuses public attention on teaching excellence.

**General Resources on Your MyEducationLab Course** The *Resources* section on your MyEducationLab course is designed to help you pass your licensure exam, put together an effective portfolio and lesson plan, prepare for and navigate the first year of your teaching career, and understand key educational standards, policies, and laws. This section includes:

- *Licensure Exams:* Access guidelines for passing the Praxis exam. The *Practice Test Exam* includes practice questions, *Case Histories*, and *Video Case Studies*.
- *Portfolio Builder and Lesson Plan Builder:* Create, update, and share portfolios and lesson plans.
- *Preparing a Portfolio:* Access guidelines for creating a high-quality teaching portfolio that will allow you to practice effective lesson planning.
- *Licensure and Standards:* Link to state licensure standards and national standards.
- *Beginning Your Career:* Educate yourself—access tips, advice, and valuable information on:
  - Resume Writing and Interviewing: Expert advice on how to write impressive resumes and prepare for job interviews.
  - Your First Year of Teaching: Practical tips to set up your classroom, manage student behavior, and learn to more easily organize for instruction and assessment.
  - Law and Public Policies: Specific directives and requirements you need to understand under the No Child Left Behind Act and the Individuals with Disabilities Education Improvement Act of 2004.
- *Special Education Interactive Timeline:* Build your own detailed timelines based on different facets of the history and evolution of special education.

# Book-Specific Resources

- *Study Plan.* A MyEducationLab Study Plan is a multiple choice assessment tied to chapter learning objectives, supported by study material. A well-designed Study Plan offers multiple opportunities to fully master required course content as identified by the objectives in each chapter:
  - *Objectives* identify the learning outcomes for the chapter and give you targets to shoot for as you read and study.
  - *Multiple Choice Assessment*s assess mastery of the content (tied to text learning objectives) by taking the multiple choice quiz as many times as needed. Not only do these quizzes provide overall scores for each objective, but they also explain why responses to particular items are correct or incorrect.
  - *Study Material: Review, Practice, and Enrichment* gives you a deeper understanding of what you do and do not know related to chapter content. This can be accessed through the Multiple Choice Assessment (after you take a quiz you receive information regarding the module content on which you still need practice and review) or through a self-directed method of study. This material includes text excerpts, activities that include hints and feedback, and media assets (video, simulations, cases, etc.).
  - *Flashcards* help you study the definitions of the key terms within each chapter.

  **Visit www.myeducationlab.com for a demonstration of this exciting new online teaching resource.**

- *Online Instructor's Resource Manual.* The Online Instructor's Resource Manual synchronizes all of the resources available for each chapter. These materials can be used for traditional courses as well as online or online-supported courses. The Instructor's Manual is fully integrated with the MyEducationLab that accompanies this text and includes many ideas and activities to help instructors teach the course. Each chapter of the manual provides a teaching outline, learning activities and handouts, and a guide to MyEducationLab activities.
- *Pearson MyTest.* Pearson MyTest is a powerful assessment generation program that helps instructors easily create and print quizzes and exams. Questions and tests are authored online, allowing ultimate flexibility and the ability to efficiently create and print assessments anytime, anywhere! Instructors can access Pearson MyTest and their test bank files by going to www.pearsonmytest.com to log in, register, or request access. Features of Pearson MyTest include:
- *Premium assessment content*
  - Draw from a rich library of assessments that complement your Pearson textbook and your course's learning objectives.
  - Edit questions or tests to fit your specific teaching needs.
- *Instructor-friendly resources*
  - Easily create and store your own questions, including images, diagrams, and charts using simple drag-and-drop and Word-like controls.
  - Use additional information provided by Pearson, such as the question's difficulty level or learning objective, to help you quickly build your test.
- *Time-saving enhancements*
  - Add headers or footers and easily scramble questions and answer choices—all from one simple toolbar.
  - Quickly create multiple versions of your test or answer key, and when ready, simply save to MS-Word or PDF format and print!
  - Export your exams for import to Blackboard 6.0, CE (WebCT), or Vista (WebCT)!
- *Online PowerPoint slides/Transparency Masters.* These visual aids display, summarize, and help explain core information presented in each module. They can be downloaded from our Instructor's Resource Center. All PowerPoint slides have been updated for consistency and to reflect content in the new edition.

# acknowledgments

Although it is my name that is on the cover of this book, writing and editing is truly a collaborative endeavor. Many people make significant contributions and are involved in the revision—from the first day of discussion until the new book is ready for the field. And so acknowledgements should begin with all of the marvelous professionals at Pearson who offered ideas and insights, politely reminded me of deadlines near and past, and constructively tackled the challenges that invariably arise. Specifically, many thanks are extended to Ann Davis, Penny Burleson, Alicia Reilly, Becky Savage, and Sandy Schaefer.

A second group of professionals who offered their prodigious expertise on this project are those who contributed chapters and other materials. In particular, I want to thank the following individuals: John L. Luckner (University of Northern Colorado)—Chapter Ten, "Students with Deafness and Hearing Loss and June E. Downing and Kathryn D. Peckham-Hardin (both of California State University, Northridge)—Chapter Fourteen, "Students with Severe and Multiple Disabilities."

Reviewers provide invaluable information in preparation for the revision of the textbook. They may never realize how much all their comments, concerns, and suggestions influence decisions made about changes needed. Their reasoned and constructive input—on everything from chapter content through boxed features to formatting and arrangement of the chapter material—were instrumental in shaping the tone of this third edition of the book and ensuring its accuracy and relevance. They are: Martin Dubin, George Mason University; Sharon Gilbert, Radford University; Karen Goodman, Montclair State University; and Kelly O'Neal, Emporia State University.

Yet another group of individuals must be mentioned among those who helped bring this project to fruition: the wonderful people who package the book and turn manuscript into a textbook. I would particularly like to thank the team members at S4Carlisle, especially Carla Kipper, for their meticulous attention to detail.

Special mention must be made of Sonia Martin, administrative assistant extraordinaire in the Department of Specialized Education Services, The University of North Carolina at Greensboro. With a degree in English and technical writing credentials, she remains superbly prepared to help on this project and an integral part of the process from start to finish. More important, though, as she read chapters to ensure they made sense and proofread them for accuracy, as she checked references and compiled glossary entries, and as she copied and express mailed materials and helped resolve queries about missing permission forms and other bits of information, she did so with the combination of seriousness and irreverence that makes her a wonderful colleague even when a book project is not at hand. Graduate assistants Kendra Williamson, Cynthia Shamberger, and Gretchen Smallwood also were collaborators, gathering materials and resources, working on those ever-changing reference lists, and willingly stepping in to resolve whatever timeline-driven crisis happened to arise. Thanks to all.

Finally, these acknowledgments would not be complete without mentioning the other people in my life who support me no matter the projects that I am pursuing. My husband Bruce Brandon truly deserves coauthorship. He listens to me try out new ideas, sends me items from popular media that I might want to use, and patiently helps me work through writer's block and other frustrations of book projects. He has said more than any spouse could ever deserve, "What can I do to help?" His love and patience makes this project possible. The rest of my family—my mom (Mary Ellen Penovich), my sister and brother-in-law (Judy and Conrad Serwatka), and brother and sister-in-law (Dan and Cindy Penovich)—also offered encouragement and sympathy, as did my mother-in-law (Lorena Brandon). I appreciate their support and good-natured teasing about my need to try to save the world.

# brief contents

one      **Understanding Special Education**    2

two      **The Personnel and Procedures of Special Education**    34

three      **Multicultural and Bilingual Perspectives**    66

four      **Collaboration in Special Education**    96

five      **Students with Learning Disabilities**    124

six      **Students with Attention Deficit–Hyperactivity Disorder**    160

seven      **Students with Emotional and Behavior Disorders**    196

eight      **Students with Intellectual and Developmental Disabilities**    232

nine      **Students with Speech and Language Disorders**    264

ten      **Students with Autism Spectrum Disorders**    296

eleven      **Students with Deafness and Hearing Loss**    328

twelve      **Students with Visual Impairments**    366

thirteen      **Students with Physical and Health Disabilities**    398

fourteen      **Students with Severe and Multiple Disabilities**    434

fifteen      **Students Who Are Gifted and Talented**    466

appendix      **CEC Knowledge and Skill Standards Common Core**    498

**Glossary**    503

**References**    512

**Name Index**    579

**Subject Index**    591

# contents

## chapter one

### Understanding Special Education  2

Learning Objectives  2

Concepts That Guide Special Education  4

The Core Provisions of Special Education  4

Special Education  6

  Related Services  6      Supplementary Aids and Services  6

Development of the Special Education Field  7

  Early History  7

Basis for Today's General Education and Special Education System  8

Discrimination and the Beginning of Change  9

  Litigation for the Rights of Students with Disabilities  10

A Federal Response: Laws to Protect Students with Disabilities  11

  Refinements to the Law  11

Federal Special Education Law: Accomplishments and Disappointments  11

  Development of Inclusive Practices  12      Disproportionate Representation  13      An Era of Continuing Improvement  13

Laws for Students with Disabilities  14

Individuals with Disabilities Education Improvement Act (IDEA) of 2004  14

  Zero Reject  14      Free Appropriate Public Education  14 Least Restrictive Environment  14      Nondiscriminatory Evaluation  15      Parent and Family Rights to Confidentiality  15      Procedural Safeguards  15

Other Legislation Related to Special Education  15

  Section 504 of the Rehabilitation Act of 1973  15 Americans with Disabilities Act of 1990  17

Students Who Receive Special Education  17

Prevalence of Students with Disabilities  18

Special Education for Young Children  20

  Students Not Specifically Included in IDEA  20

Recommended Practices for Special Education  21

Inclusive Practices and Access to the General Curriculum  21

  Definitions and Debates  21      Research on Inclusive Practices  22      Inclusive Practices in This Textbook  23

Accountable and Accessible Instruction  24

  Universal Design for Learning  24      Differentiated Instruction  25      Evidence-Based Practices  25 Assistive Technology  26

Positive Behavior Supports  27

Collaboration  27

Parent and Family Perspectives Regarding Their Children with Disabilities  28

Parents and Their Children with Disabilities  28

Parent Participation in Special Education  29

  Barriers to Parent Participation  29      Strategies to Encourage Parent Participation  29

Trends and Issues Influencing Special Education  30

No Child Left Behind Act of 2001  30

  NCLB and Students with Disabilities  31

Special Education Eligibility  31

Summary  32

## chapter two

### The Personnel and Procedures of Special Education  34

Learning Objectives  34

The Professionals Who Work in Special Education  36

Special Education Teachers  36

  Bilingual Special Educator  36      Early Childhood Special Educator  37      Adapted Physical Educator  37

Related Services Professionals  37

  Speech/Language Pathologist  37      School Psychologist  37 School Counselor  38      School Social Worker  38 School Nurse  38      Educational Interpreter  38 Occupational Therapist  38      Physical Therapist  39

Others Who Work in Special Education  39

  General Education Teacher  39      Paraeducator  39 Parents  39      Additional Service Providers  40

Determining Student Eligibility for Special Education Services  41

Initial Consideration of Student Problems  41

  Intervention Assistance  43      Response to Intervention and Three-Tiered Approaches  43      Screening  44

Special Education Referral and Assessment   44

Parents' Rights   45   Assessment Components   45
Assessment Procedures   46

Decision Making for Special Education   47

Preparing the IEP   48   Deciding About Placement   48

Monitoring for Students with Disabilities   48

Annual Review   48   Three-Year Reevaluation   48

Understanding the Individualized Education
Program   49

Members of the IEP Team   49

Required Components of the IEP   51

Present Level of Performance   51   Annual Goals   52
Short-Term Objectives   53   Special Education and Related
Services   53   Supplementary Aids and Services   53
Assistive Technology   53   Participation with Peers Who Do
Not Have Disabilities   53   Accommodations for State and
District Testing   54   Dates and Places   55   Transition
Service Needs and Transition Services to Be Provided   55
Age of Majority   55   Measurement of Progress   55
Other Considerations   55

Placement Options for Students with
Disabilities   56

The Continuum of Special Education Placements   56

General Education   57   Resource Class   57   Separate
Class   58   Separate School   58   Residential
Facility   58   Other Placement Settings   58

Resolving Disagreements Regarding Special
Education   59

Dispute Resolution   59

Mediation   60

Due Process Hearing   61

Issues Related to Special Education Professionals and
Procedures   62

Shortage of Special Education Teachers   62

Response to Intervention   63

Summary   64

## chapter three

## Multicultural and Bilingual Perspectives   66

Learning Objectives   66

Understanding Culture   68

Elements of Culture   68

Macroculture and Microculture   69

Culture and Race   70

Culture and Learning   71

The Content of Instruction   71

Cognitive Styles   72

Field Independence   72   Field Sensitivity   72

Effects of Cultural Dissonance   72

Academic Challenges   73   Behavior Challenges   73

Diversity in Special and Gifted Education   74

Representation in Special Education   74

Continuum of Placements   74   Why Disproportionality
Matters   75

Representation in Gifted Education   76

Factors Contributing to Disproportionate
Representation   76

Poverty   76   Systemic Bias   77

Recommended Practices for Diverse Students with
Special Needs   79

Promising Practices in Referral and Identification   79

Redesigning the Prereferral and Intervention Process   79
Alternative Assessment Strategies   81   Universal Screening
and Early Intervention   81

Promising Practices in Instruction   81

Differentiated Instruction   81   Universal Design   82
Multicultural Education   82

Instruction for English Language Learners   83

Bilingual Education   84   English as a Second
Language   84   Sheltered English   85

Putting It All Together   86

Parents and Families of Diverse Students with
Disabilities   87

Parents of Diverse Learners and Participation in Their
Children's Education   87

Factors Educators Directly Influence   88   Factors beyond
the Direct Influence of Educators   89   Developing
Collaborative Relationships   89

Issues and Trends Affecting Diverse Exceptional
Learners   91

Equity Issues   91

The Standards and Accountability Movement   92

Response to Intervention   92

School Choice Programs   93

Teachers and Their Preparation   93

Summary   95

## chapter four

### Collaboration in Special Education 96

Learning Objectives 96

Understanding Collaboration 98

Understanding Collaboration 99

*Collaboration Is Voluntary 99 Collaboration Is Based on Parity 100 Collaboration Requires a Mutual Goal 100 Collaboration Involves Shared Responsibility for Key Decisions 100 Collaboration Includes Shared Accountability for Outcomes 100 Collaboration Requires Sharing Resources 101 Collaboration Is Emergent 101*

Collaboration within the Context of Contemporary Legislation and Litigation 101

*Collaboration in IDEA 102*

Essential Elements of Collaboration 102

Personal Belief System 103

Communication Skills 103

*Effective Communication Strategies 104 Communication Habits to Avoid 105*

Interaction Processes 106

*Create a Climate for Problem Solving 106 Identify the Problem 107 Generate Alternatives 107 Assess the Potential Solutions, Selecting One or More to Implement 107 Implement the Intervention 108 Evaluate the Intervention Outcome and Decide Next Steps 108 Additional Considerations for Problem Solving 108*

Programs and Services 108

Supportive Context 108

Applications of Collaboration for Schools 109

Teams 110

*Understanding Team Concepts 110 Team Effectiveness 110 Special Education Teams 111*

Co-Teaching 111

*One Teach, One Observe 111 Parallel Teaching 112 Station Teaching 112 Alternative Teaching 113 Teaming 113 One Teach, One Assist 113 Other Co-Teaching Considerations 114*

Consultation 115

Collaboration with Parents and Families 117

Families and Collaboration 117

Building Partnerships with Parents 118

Issues Related to Collaboration in Special Education 119

Working with Paraeducators 119

Time for Collaboration 120

The Effectiveness of Collaboration 121

Summary 123

## chapter five

### Students with Learning Disabilities 124

Learning Objectives 124

Understanding Learning Disabilities 126

Development of the Learning Disabilities Field 126

Definitions of Learning Disabilities 127

*Federal Definition 127 NJCLD Definition 127 Essential Dimensions of a Definition of Learning Disabilities 129*

Prevalence of Learning Disabilities 129

Causes of Learning Disabilities 130

*Physiological Causes 130 Curriculum and Environmental Contributors 132*

Characteristics of Individuals with Learning Disabilities 132

Cognitive Characteristics 133

*Attention 133 Perception 133 Memory 133 Information Processing 133*

Academic Characteristics 134

*Reading 134 Oral Language 134 Written Language 134 Mathematics 136*

Social and Emotional Characteristics 137

*Social Perception and Social Competence 137 Motivation 138*

Behavior Characteristics 139

Identifying Learning Disabilities 140

Traditional Approach to Assessment for Learning Disabilities 140

*Formal Assessments 140 Classroom Assessments 141 Criteria for Eligibility 141*

RTI for Identifying Students Who Have Learning Disabilities 142

*Three-Tiered Models in Response to Intervention 143 Criteria for Eligibility 143*

Educating Students with Learning Disabilities 144

Early Childhood 144

Elementary and Secondary School Services   145

Inclusive Practices   146

Transition and Adulthood   149

Transition Planning   150   Model Transition
Practices   151   Self-Advocacy   151

Recommended Educational Practices for Students
with Learning Disabilities   151

Direct Instruction   152

Strategy Instruction   152

Parent and Family Perspectives   155

Parents as Partners   155

Trends and Issues Affecting the Field of Learning
Disabilities   156

Issues Related to Response to Intervention for Identifying
Students Having a Learning Disability   156

High School and College Students and Learning
Disabilities   157

Summary   158

## chapter six

## Students with Attention Deficit–Hyperactivity Disorder   160

Learning Objectives   160

Understanding Attention Deficit–Hyperactivity
Disorder   162

Development of the ADHD Field   162

Terminology Related to ADHD   163

Definition of Attention Deficit–Hyperactivity
Disorder   163

Prevalence of Attention Deficit–Hyperactivity
Disorder   164

Prevalence Based on Gender   165   Prevalence Based on
Race and Poverty   165

Causes of Attention Deficit–Hyperactivity Disorder   165

Physiological Factors   167   Environmental Factors   168

Characteristics of Individuals with Attention
Deficit–Hyperactivity Disorder   169

Cognitive Characteristics   169

Academic Characteristics   171

Social and Emotional Characteristics   172

Self-Esteem   172   Social Functioning   173

Behavior Characteristics   173

Comorbidity with Other Disorders   174

Identifying Attention Deficit–Hyperactivity
Disorder   175

Initial Referral   175

Assessment   175

Medical Assessment   175   Continuous Performance
Tests   176   Parent Assessment   176   Teacher and
School Assessment   177   Additional Considerations for
IDEA Eligibility   177   ADHD or Gifted   177

Eligibility   177

Educating Students with Attention
Deficit–Hyperactivity Disorder   179

Early Childhood   179

Elementary and Secondary School Services   179

Transition and Adulthood   180

Recommended Educational Practices for Students
with Attention Deficit–Hyperactivity
Disorder   181

Medication   181

Parent and Professional Education   184

Parent Education   185   Professional Education   185

Environmental Supports   185

Behavior Interventions   186

Rewards   186   Low-Involvement Strategies   186
Token Economy   186

Instructional Interventions   188

What Are the Perspectives of Parents and
Families?   189

Parenting Children with ADHD   189

Supporting Students by Supporting Parents   190

Trends and Issues Affecting the ADHD Field   190

Young Children with ADHD   190

The Ethical and Professional Dilemma   191

ADHD in Adolescents and Adults   191

Outcomes for Adults Diagnosed as
Children   191   Identification of ADHD in Adolescents
and Adults   191

The Knowledge Base on Treatment for ADHD   192

Summary   194

## chapter seven

## Students with Emotional and Behavior Disorders   196

Learning Objectives   196

Understanding Emotional and Behavior
Disorders   198

Development of the Field of Emotional and Behavior
Disorders   198

Definitions of Emotional and Behavior Disorders   199

*Federal Definition   199      Criticism of the Federal Definition of Emotional Disturbance   199      Other Considerations in Defining Emotional and Behavior Disorders   200*

Prevalence of Emotional and Behavior Disorders   200

*Prevalence by Gender   201*

Causes of Emotional and Behavior Disorders   202

*Biological Factors   202      Psychosocial Factors   202 Making Sense of the Factors Contributing to Emotional and Behavior Disorders   203*

Characteristics of Individuals with Emotional and Behavior Disorders   203

Behavior and Emotional Characteristics   204

Emotional Characteristics   205

Social Characteristics   208

Cognitive and Academic Characteristics   208

*The Question of Cause and Effect   209*

Emotional and Behavior Disorders and Comorbidity   209

Identifying Emotional and Behavior Disorders   210

Assessment   210

*Formal Assessments   210      Classroom Assessments   210 Other Assessment Strategies   211*

Eligibility   211

*Eligibility Criteria   211*

Educating Learners with Emotional and Behavior Disorders   212

Early Childhood   212

Elementary and Secondary School Services   213

Inclusive Practices   214

Transition and Adulthood   215

Recommended Educational Practices for Students with Emotional and Behavior Disorders   217

The Importance of Prevention   217

*Early Intervention   217      Positive Behavior Supports   217*

The Effectiveness of Collaboration   219

Requirements for Interventions in IDEA   220

*Functional Behavior Assessment   220      Behavior Intervention Plan   221*

Examples of Specific Interventions   222

*Peer-Mediated Instruction   222      Teacher-Led Instruction   223*

Perspectives of Parents and Families   226

The Impact of Having a Child with an Emotional or Behavior Disorder   226

Building Positive Relationships   226

*Parent Education   227      Support Groups   227*

Trends and Issues Affecting the Field of Emotional and Behavior Disorders   227

The Problem of Access   228

Creating a Promising Future   228

Use of Restraints and Seclusion   228

Summary   230

chapter eight

## Students with Intellectual and Developmental Disabilities   232

Learning Objectives   232

Understanding Intellectual Disabilities   234

Development of the Field of Intellectual Disabilities   234

Definitions of Intellectual Disabilities   235

*Federal Definition   236      American Association on Intellectual and Developmental Disabilities Definition   236*

Prevalence of Intellectual Disabilities   236

*Other Prevalence Considerations   237*

Causes of Mental Retardation   237

*Prenatal Causes of Intellectual Disabilities   237      Perinatal Causes of Mental Retardation   239      Postnatal Causes of Mental Retardation   239*

Characteristics of Individuals with Intellectual Disabilities   240

Cognitive and Academic Characteristics   240

*Cognitive Functioning   241*

Social, Behavior, and Emotional Characteristics   243

*Social Characteristics   244      Adaptive Behavior Characteristics   244      Additional Behavior Characteristics   245      Emotional Characteristics   245*

Physical and Medical Characteristics   246

Identifying Intellectual Disabilities   247

Assessment   247

*Assessment of Intellectual Functioning   247      Assessment of Adaptive Behavior   247      Assessment of Medical Factors   248*

Eligibility   248

How Learners with Intellectual Disabilities Receive Their Education   249

Early Childhood   249

Elementary and Secondary School Services   249

*Inclusive Practices   251*

Transition and Adulthood   252

Recommended Educational Practices for Students with Intellectual Disabilities   253

Task Analysis   253

Peer-Mediated Instruction   254

Perspectives of Parents and Families   256

Parent Experiences and Acceptance   256

   Parents' Reactions to Having a Child with an Intellectual Disability   256

Parents' Concerns   257

Professionals' Interactions with Parents of Children with Intellectual Disabilities   258

Trends and Issues Affecting the Field of Intellectual Disabilities   258

Students with Intellectual Disabilities in Today's Schools   258

   Which Curriculum?   259      The Dilemma of High-Stakes Testing   259

Self-Determination: The Potential, Promises, and Practices   259

   Perceptions of Parents and Teachers   260      Implementation of Practices That Foster Self-Determination   260

Summary   262

## chapter nine

### Students with Speech and Language Disorders   264

Learning Objectives   264

Understanding Speech and Language Disorders   266

Development of the Study of Speech and Language Disorders   266

   Emergence of a Profession   266      Contemporary Practices   267

Definitions of Speech and Language Disorders   267

Concepts to Describe Speech and Language Disorders   268

   Elements of Language   269      Language Disorders   270
   Elements of Speech   271      Speech Disorders   273

Prevalence of Speech and Language Disorders   274

   Distinguishing between Speech and Language Prevalence Data   274      Other Prevalence Considerations   274

Causes of Speech and Language Disorders   274

   Biological Causes   275      Environmental Causes   275
   Making Sense of the Factors Contributing to Speech and Language Disorders   276

Characteristics of Individuals with Speech and Language Disorders   276

Cognitive and Academic Characteristics   276

   Academic Characteristics   276      Speech and Language Disorders and Reading   277

Social and Emotional Characteristics   277

Behavior Characteristics   277

Speech and Language Disorders and Other Disabilities   278

Identifying Speech and Language Disorders   279

Assessment   279

   Speech Assessments   279      Language Assessments   280
   Assessment for Students Whose First Language Is Not English or Whose Use of English Is Nonstandard   280

Eligibility   281

How Learners with Speech and Language Disorders Receive Their Education   282

Early Childhood   282

   The Importance of Early Intervention   282      Approaches for Early Speech and Language Intervention   282

Elementary and Secondary School Services   283

   Inclusive Practices   283

Transition and Adulthood   284

Recommended Educational Practices for Students with Speech and Language Disorders   285

Speech/Language Services and Literacy Instruction   285

Communication Using Technology   286

Augmentative and Alternative Communication   286

   Technology for Language Practice   288

Perspectives of Parents and Families   288

Helping Parents to Develop Children's Language Skills   289

Diversity and Speech and Language Interventions   290

Trends and Issues Affecting the Field of Speech and Language Disorders   290

Differences versus Disorders in a Multicultural Society   291

   Language Differences   291      Other Cultural Influences on Communication   292

The Use of Evidence-Based Practices   293

Summary   294

## chapter ten

### Students with Autism Spectrum Disorders 296

Learning Objectives 296

Understanding Autism Spectrum Disorders 298

Development of the Field 298

*Formalizing Understanding 299*

Definitions of Autism Spectrum Disorders 299

*Federal Definition 299      Definitions of the American Psychiatric Association 300      Making Sense of the Definitions 301*

Prevalence of Autism Spectrum Disorders 302

*Other Prevalence Considerations 303*

Causes of Autism Spectrum Disorders 303

*Biological Factors 303      Autism Spectrum Disorders and the Brain 304      Environmental Factors 304      Autism and Immunizations 305*

Characteristics of Individuals with Autism Spectrum Disorders 305

Cognitive and Academic Characteristics 305

*Rote Memory 305      Theory of Mind 306      Problem Solving 306      Motivation 306*

Social and Emotional Characteristics 307

*Language Disorders 308      Communicative Intent 308 Other Language Problems 308      Immaturity 308*

Behavior Characteristics 309

*Self-Stimulatory Behaviors 309      Generalization Difficulties 309      Sensory Issues 309*

Identifying Autism Spectrum Disorders 311

Assessment Practices and Procedures 311

*Assessment Related to Characteristics of Autism 311 Cognitive Ability, Academic Achievement, and Adaptive Skills 311      Developmental Measures 311 Behavior Assessment 311*

Eligibility 312

How Learners with Autism Spectrum Disorders Receive Their Education 312

Early Childhood 312

Elementary and Secondary School Services 313

Inclusive Practices 313

*Exploring the Autism Inclusion Collaboration Model 314*

Transition and Adulthood 314

Recommended Educational Practices for Students with Autism Spectrum Disorders 316

Environmental Supports 317

*Visual Supports 317      Home Base 318*

Assistive Technology 318

Instructional Practices 318

*Priming 318      Discrete Trial Training 320 Prompting 320*

Social Skills Supports 321

*Instruction 321      Social Stories 321 SOCCSS 322*

Perspectives of Parents and Families 323

Family Needs for Information and Support 323

The Roles of Siblings 324

Trends and Issues Affecting the Field of Autism Spectrum Disorders 325

Assessment, Diagnosis, and Prevalence 325

Evidence-Based Interventions 325

Training and Support 326

Summary 327

## chapter eleven

### Students with Deafness and Hearing Loss 328

Learning Objectives 328

Understanding Deafness and Hearing Loss 330

Development of the Field of Deaf Education 330

Definitions of Deafness and Hearing Loss 331

*Federal Definitions 332      Additional Information on Definitions 332      Deaf Culture 333*

Prevalence of Hearing Loss 333

*Hearing Loss and Other Disabilities 333*

Causes of Hearing Loss 333

*Prelingual Causes of Hearing Loss 334      Postlingual Causes of Hearing Loss 334      Types of Hearing Loss 335 Degree of Hearing Loss 336*

Characteristics of Individuals Who Are Deaf or Hard of Hearing 337

Hearing Loss and Child Development 337

*Impact on Communication 337      Experiential Learning 339*

Cognitive Characteristics   339

Academic Characteristics   339

   *Language   339      Reading   341      Written*
   *Language   341      Mathematics   342*

Social and Emotional Characteristics   343

Behavior Characteristics   343

Identifying a Hearing Loss   344

Audiological Evaluation   344

Other Assessments   345

Determination of Eligibility   345

How Learners Who Are Deaf or Hard of Hearing
Receive Their Education   346

Early Childhood   346

Elementary and Secondary School Services   347

   *General Education Classroom   347      General Education*
   *Classroom with Supplementary Instruction   348      Separate*
   *Class for Students Who Are Deaf or Hard of Hearing   348*
   *Other Settings   349      Inclusive Practices   349*

Transition and Adulthood   351

Recommended Educational Practices for Students
Who Are Deaf or Hard of Hearing   353

Integrated Vocabulary and Concept Development   353

Experiential Ladder of Learning   354

Visual Teaching Strategies   356

Accommodations for Students Who Are Deaf or Hard
of Hearing   358

Perspectives of Parents and Families   358

The Voices of Parents   359

Trends and Issues Affecting the Field of Deaf
Education   359

Universal Newborn Hearing Screening   360

Cochlear Implants   360

Bilingual–Bicultural Approach   362

Summary   364

## chapter twelve

### Students with Visual Impairments   366

Learning Objectives   366

Understanding Visual Impairments   368

Development of the Visual Impairment Field   368

   *Early Thinking and Services   369      Residential Schools in*
   *the United States   369      The Emergence of Public School*
   *Programs   369      Other Historical Developments   370*

Definitions of Visual Impairment   370

   *Functional Definitions   370      IDEA Definition   371*
   *Clinical Definitions   371*

Prevalence   372

   *Other Prevalence Information   372*

Causes of Visual Impairment   372

   *Structure of the Eye and How It Works   372*

Examples of Visual Impairments   373

Characteristics of Individuals with Visual
Impairments   374

Cognitive Characteristics   374

Academic Characteristics   375

   *Braille Literacy Skills   375      Print Literacy Skills   377*

Social and Emotional Characteristics   380

Behavior Characteristics   380

Identifying Visual Impairment   381

Assessment   382

Eligibility   382

How Learners with Visual Impairments Receive Their
Education   383

Early Childhood   383

Elementary and Secondary School Services   383

   *Consultant Model   383      Itinerant Teaching Model   383*
   *Resource Model   384      Special Classes and Schools   385*

Inclusive Practices   385

Transition and Adulthood   387

Recommended Educational Practices for Students
with Visual Impairments   389

Instruction in the Expanded Core Curriculum   389

Principles of Special Methods   391

   *Need for Concrete Experiences   391      Need for Unifying*
   *Experiences   391      Need for Learning by Doing   391*

Perspectives of Parents and Families   391

Studying Parent Perspectives   392

Trends and Issues Affecting the Field of Visual
Impairment   393

Shortage of Fully Prepared Personnel   393

Limited Continuum of Placement Options   394

Summary   396

## chapter thirteen

### Students with Physical
### and Health Disabilities   398

Learning Objectives   398

Understanding Physical and Health Disabilities   400

Development of the Field of Physical and Health Disabilities   400

*Increasing Attention for an Ignored Group   401*   *Refining Students' Rights and School Responsibilities   401*

Looking at the Big Picture   402

Key Concepts for Understanding Physical and Health Disabilities   402

Understanding Physical Disabilities   403

*Federal Definition   403*   *Neurological Disorders   404*   *Musculoskeletal Disorders   406*

Understanding Traumatic Brain Injury   406

*Federal Definition   407*   *Types of Traumatic Brain Injury   407*   *The Effects of Traumatic Brain Injury   407*   *Prevalence and Causes   409*

Understanding Other Health Impairments   409

*Federal Definition   409*   *Examples of Health Impairments   409*

Characteristics of Individuals with Physical and Health Disabilities   415

Cognitive and Academic Characteristics   415

Behavior, Emotional, and Social Characteristics   415

*Behavior Characteristics   415*   *Emotional Characteristics   416*   *Social Characteristics   417*

Physical and Medical Characteristics   417

Identifying Physical and Health Disabilities   418

Assessment   418

*Assessment of Medical Condition and Physical Functioning   418*   *Assessment of Intellectual Functioning, Academic Achievement, Language, and Related Areas   418*   *Assessment of Behavior   418*

Eligibility   419

How Learners with Physical and Health Disabilities Receive Their Education   419

Early Childhood   419

Elementary and Secondary School Services   419

*Inclusive Practices   420*

Transition and Adulthood   421

*Postsecondary Education   421*   *Practical Matters of Adulthood   421*   *Career Choice   422*

Recommended Educational Practices for Students with Physical and Health Disabilities   424

Access to Education   424

*Aids for Posture and Mobility   424*   *Aids for Communication   424*   *Aids for Learning   425*   *Related Services   426*

Factors Related to the Illness, Injury, Condition, or Disorder   427

*School Reentry   427*   *Responding to Emergencies   427*

Perspectives of Parents and Families   429

Parent Experiences   429

Advice to School Professionals   430

Trends and Issues Affecting the Field of Physical and Health Disabilities   430

Professionals Prepared to Work with Students with Physical Disabilities   430

Access to Technology   431

Summary   432

## chapter fourteen

## Students with Severe and Multiple Disabilities   434

Learning Objectives   434

Understanding Severe or Multiple Disabilities   436

Development of the Field of Severe and Multiple Disabilities   436

*Emerging Recognition of Needs and Services to Address Them   437*   *A Changing Climate and Advocacy   437*

Definitions of Severe and Multiple Disabilities   437

*Federal Definitions   438*   *TASH Definition   438*

Prevalence of Students with Severe and Multiple Disabilities   439

Causes of Severe and Multiple Disabilities   439

*Labels and Their Limitations   440*

Characteristics of Individuals with Severe and Multiple Disabilities   440

Cognitive Characteristics   441

Educational Implications   441

Academic Characteristics   442

*Literacy   442*   *Oral Language   442*   *Mathematics   443*

Social and Emotional Characteristics   444

Behavior Characteristics   444

*Challenging Behaviors   445*

Assessment of Students with Severe and Multiple Disabilities   446

Assessment for Instruction   446

*Standardized Assessment   446*

Authentic Forms of Assessment   447

*Person-Centered Approach   447*   *Functional–Ecological Assessment   447*   *Portfolio Assessment   448*

How Learners with Severe and Multiple Disabilities Receive Their Education   448

Early Childhood 448

Elementary and Secondary Education 450

Inclusive Practices 451

Partial Participation 451    Paraprofessional
Support 452

Transition and Adulthood 452

Supported Employment 453    Community-Based
Instruction 454

Recommended Educational Practices for Students
with Severe and Multiple Disabilities 454

Meaningful and Individualized Curriculum 454

Making the Core Curriculum Meaningful 455

Collaborative Approaches for Education 456

Active Family Involvement 456    Collaboration on the
Team 457

Positive Behavior Supports 458

Inclusive Education 459

Perspectives of Parents and Families 460

Family Members' Views of Their Children 460

Considering Cultural Diversity 460

Trends and Issues Affecting the Field of Severe and
Multiple Disabilities 462

Accountability of Academic Performance for All
Students 462

The Status of Alternate Assessment 462

Integrated Delivery of Related Services 463

Summary 465

## chapter fifteen

### Students Who Are Gifted and Talented 466

Learning Objectives 466

Understanding Giftedness 468

Development of the Field of Giftedness 468

Emergence of a Profession 468    Recent Changes in the
Field 469

Definition of Giftedness 470

Alternative Conceptualizations of Giftedness 470    A Final
Word on Definitions 472

Prevalence 472

Prevalence, Race, and Gender 473

Determining Factors 474

Characteristics of Individuals Who Are Gifted and
Talented 475

Cognitive Characteristics 475

Ability to Manipulate Abstract Symbol Systems 475
Power of Concentration 475    Unusually Well Developed
Memory 475    Early Language Interest and
Development 476    Curiosity 476    Preference for
Independent Work 476    Multiple Interests 476
Ability to Generate Original Ideas 477

Academic Characteristics 477

Social and Emotional Characteristics 477

Sense of Justice 478    Altruism and
Idealism 478    Sense of Humor 478    Emotional
Intensity 479    Perfectionism 479    High Level of
Energy 479    Strong Attachments and
Commitments 479    Aesthetic Sensitivity 480

Identifying Students Who Are Gifted and
Talented 481

Considerations for Identifying Giftedness 481

Underlying Principles of Effective Assessment 481

Two-Stage Assessment Process 481    Measures to Match
Programs 481    Other Considerations 482
Equity 482

Authentic Assessment 482

Dynamic Assessment 483    Spatial Ability 483

Eligibility 483

How Learners Who Are Gifted and Talented Receive
Their Education 483

Early Childhood Education 483

The Debate on Early Intervention 484

Elementary and Secondary Education 484

Grouping 484    Full-Time and Part-Time Separate
Classes 485    Special Schools 485
Homeschooling 485

Inclusive Practices 485

Transition and Adulthood 485

Special Challenges 486    Supporting Adolescents Who Are
Gifted and Talented 487

Recommended Educational Practices for Students
Who Are Gifted and Talented 487

Curriculum Compacting 488

Acceleration 488

Acceleration in High School 488

Enrichment 489

Differentiation 489

Problem-Based Learning 490

Interventions for Diverse Populations 490

Perspectives of Parents and Families of Students
Who Are Gifted and Talented 491

Parent Strategies for Encouraging Their Children   491

Trends and Issues Affecting Students Who Are Gifted and Talented   492

Talent Development   492

Identification and Programming for Underrepresented Groups   493

*Students Who Are Twice Exceptional*   *493*

Effective Differentiation   494

Alternative Program Models   494

*Technology-Based Options*   *494*        *Opportunities External to Schools*   *496*

Summary   496

appendix    CEC Knowledge and Skill Standards Common Core   498

Glossary   503

References   512

Name Index   579

Subject Index   591

# special features

## firsthand account

A Life of Complexities   5

A Parent's Voice on Having a Child with a Disability   40

Meet the Woods Family   90

A Life with Many Dimensions   99

Michael's Story of Unrealistic Goals . . . and Reaching Them   128

Living with ADHD: Struggles and Success   172

We Did Everything Right, But . . .   206

Eric Has a Contribution to Make . . .   250

Welcome to Holland   257

The Importance of Early Language Intervention   289

A "Quirky Kid" Goes to Middle School   315

Perspectives of an Itinerant Teacher   349

Teaching in a Residential Setting   350

My Daughter Laurel   392

Trae: From a Focus on Limitations to an Emphasis on Possibilities and Potential   408

A Case Study in Determination and Success   410

Our Daughter, Kehaulani   461

Parenting a Gifted Child: A Joy and a Challenge   480

## speaking from experience

Advice for Succeeding as a Special Educator   16

Helping High School Students to Advocate for Themselves   56

A Principal's Perspective on Diversity   80

Co-Teaching Algebra: Leave Your Ego at the Door   114

Being a Special Educator in a Rural Area   148

Students with ADHD: Matching Needs and Strategies   193

Working with Students with Emotional and Behavior Disorders   225

Working with Students with Mild to Moderate Intellectual Disabilities   246

Understanding the Many Roles and Responsibilities of a Speech/Language Therapist   268

Structures for Students, Understanding for Parents   307

Advice for Succeeding as a Special Educator   354

I Knew I Wanted to Teach Children with Visual Impairments   395

Creating Opportunities with Technology   426

My First Year of Teaching: The Dreams and the Realities   457

Managing a Complex Job   458

Students are Gifted All Day Long . . .   486

## positive behavior supports

Setting Classroom Expectations   27

Classroom Strategies That Foster Positive Behavior   60

Cultural Influences on Behavior   73

Consultation in Practice   116

Seatwork: Helping Students to Work Independently   139

Using a Token Economy   187

Implementing a Positive Behavior Support Program   218

Behavior Contracts   222

Using Sociograms to Gather Information About Student Interactions   245

Linking Speech and Language Disorders and Emotional and Behavior Disabilities   278

Power Card: Teaching Appropriate Behavior Using Special Interests   321

Learning Appropriate Behavior with SOCCSS   322

Promoting Alternative Thinking Strategies   345

Infusing Social Skills Instruction in Daily Activities   381

Addressing Behavior for Students with Traumatic Brain Injuries   416

Using Paraprofessionals to Increase Students' Social Interactions   445

Tackling the Challenge of Underachievement   478

## professional edge

Keeping Up with a Rapidly Changing Field   13

Disability Etiquette   18

How Inclusive Is Your School?   23

Preparing Parents for IEP Meetings   50

Involving Students in the IEP Process   51

Parent–School Conflict in Special Education   61

Maximizing Your Listening Skills   105

Finding Time for Collaboration   121

Understanding Dyslexia   135

Michael's Perspectives on His Education   149

ADHD in Girls 167

Teacher Knowledge About Medication and Students with ADHD 184

The Promise of Resiliency 204

Youth Suicide—You Can Make the Difference 207

Self-Determination in Transition Planning 261

Recognizing Language Disorders 271

Interacting with Students Who Stutter 274

Roles and Responsibilities of Speech/Language Pathologists in Schools 279

Understanding Dialects 291

Temple Grandin, A Truly Exceptional Person 302

Keeping Up with Research on ASD 303

Fostering Success for Students Who Are Deaf or Hard of Hearing in General Education Classes 351

Potential Benefits and Barriers of Inclusive Practices for Students Who Are Deaf or Hard of Hearing 352

Common Causes of Childhood Visual Impairment 374

Ensuring a Successful Transition to an Inclusive School Program 387

First Aid for Seizures 411

Universal Precautions for School Professionals 413

Returning to School 428

When a Student Dies 429

Resolving the Pullout Service Dilemma 464

Teaching to Diverse Student Needs Through Multiple Intelligences (MI) 473

Thinking about Girls and Giftedness 474

Students Who Are Twice Exceptional 493

## instruction in action

Ways to Differentiate Instruction 25

Understanding Response to Intervention 44

Universal Design for Learning: Helping Students Participate in General Education 54

Reviewing Children's Literature for Bias 78

Multicultural Teaching: Bringing Learning to Life 84

Response to Intervention and Collaboration 103

Getting Off to a Great Start with Co-Teaching 115

Helping Students Succeed in Math 137

Using Direct Instruction 153

Sample Learning Strategies 154

Executive Functions and Strategies for Learning 171

Teaching to Help Students with ADHD Succeed 188

Social Skills for Classroom Success 208

Teaching Anger Management Skills 216

Numbered Heads Together 224

Using Task Analysis 254

Peer Tutoring 255

Traditional versus Classroom-Based Services for Students with Speech and Language Disorders 284

Getting the Message Across 286

Breaking the Code on Code-Switching 292

Visual Schedules and Task Cards 317

Travel Card 319

Potential Accommodations for Students Who Are Deaf or Hard of Hearing 357

A Unique Application of Differentiation 384

Accommodating Instruction for Students with Visual Impairments 386

Students with Physical and Health Disabilities and Their Needs in General Education Classes 422

Positioning, Seating, and Mobility 425

Functional–Ecological Assessment of Learning Environments 449

When You Can't Plan Ahead: Tricks for Educators in the Inclusive Classroom 455

Ensuring Access to the Core Curriculum 456

Instructional Activities Based on Specific Aptitudes 471

Problem-Based Learning 495

## technology notes

Instructional and Assistive Technology Options for Students with Disabilities 26

SETT the Stage for Success with Assistive Technology 54

Technology and Diversity: The Digital Divide 94

Collaborating Through Technology 109

Brain Research and Learning Disabilities 130

Tools for Students with Learning Disabilities 146

Technology to Help with Daily Tasks 173

Changing Behavior Using Handheld Computers 223

Technology Tools for Real-Life Success 243

Enhancing Students' Speech and Language Skills 287

Teaching by Showing. . . for Real 320

Using Technology to Provide Classroom Supports 348

Using the Telephone—with a Twist 355

Listening to Learn 378

Access to Computers for Students with Visual Impairments 379

Making the Impossible Possible 423

Augmentative Communication Devices 443

Using Switches to Foster Participation and Independence 453

The Power of the Internet 489

## chapter one

# Understanding Special Education

## LEARNING OBJECTIVES

- Explain the fundamental concepts on which special education is based.
- Describe how the history of special education, including key court cases, has shaped its development.
- List the provisions in federal legislation that establish current special education policies and practices.
- Describe the students who receive special education services.
- Outline practices that characterize contemporary special education.
- Explain perspectives and concerns of parents and families of students with disabilities.
- Identify issues influencing the field of special education.

## Elizabeth

Elizabeth is a first-grade student with a completely positive view of life: She loves school, her teachers, her friends, and all the activities that school includes, especially art class. In the morning, Elizabeth usually goes to a special education classroom where she receives highly structured reading instruction from Ms. Hackman, her special education teacher, but she spends much of the school day in Ms. Clark's general education class. One service offered in her general education classroom is speech-language therapy: Ms. Quade, the speech-language therapist, comes to the classroom twice each week for 30 minutes. During that time, she provides services to Elizabeth, but she also assists the other first-graders with their language development. Elizabeth has an intellectual disability, also called *mental retardation*, and learns more slowly than her peers, but she is making strong academic progress. Her goals for the current school year include learning all capital and lowercase letters, at least one hundred sight words, and single-digit math facts; she also has a goal to speak in complete sentences. Ms. Hackman and Ms. Clark meet on a regular basis to discuss Elizabeth's progress and to resolve any problems that occur. Ms. Clark speaks frequently of how much she has learned by working with Elizabeth. She has become a strong advocate of including students with disabilities in general education and points to both the academic and social gains that Elizabeth has made as evidence of the success of this approach.

## Andrew

Andrew is a middle school student who has many dimensions. Ms. Becker, his mother, talks with pride about his extensive knowledge of baseball. Andrew knows detailed statistics of all the major league teams, and he can recite many of the accomplishments of players past and present. She admits, though, that it is becoming a bit tiring as Andrew speaks constantly about this topic, a sentiment echoed by his special education teacher, Ms. Spencer. Andrew spends much of the day in a special education classroom for students with autism. This decision about his education was made because of the extraordinary difficulty he experiences with many school activities and routines. When Andrew has difficulty completing an assignment he often expresses his frustration by loudly and rapidly slapping his hands on his desk. Ms. Spencer is working closely with a behavior specialist to find ways to change this behavior. Andrew also struggles with transitions between activities. If he is working on the computer and it is time to go to lunch, he may refuse to shut down the computer and sometimes tries to hit the paraeducator who assists in the classroom. The professionals who work with Andrew and his parents are in agreement that a major goal is to teach him better ways to deal with frustration and transition so that he can participate more frequently in activities in the general education setting.

## Daniel

Daniel is a sophomore in high school, and he still struggles to understand why he has so much difficulty learning and how his learning disability affects who he is and how others respond to him. As he thinks about his first nine years of school, he cannot remember a time when school was fun. Even in kindergarten, he had difficulty learning his letters and numbers, and he quickly fell behind academically. Though he began receiving special education services at the beginning of third grade, Daniel's reading comprehension is at about the fifth-grade level, and his math skills are at the seventh-grade level. Teachers generally have been supportive, but sometimes even when they mean well, their actions can be hurtful. Daniel remembers one teacher who usually reduced by half the amount of work he had to do—it made him feel as though he was too stupid to learn. For the past two years, Daniel has used recorded books downloaded to his iPod; this has been helpful, as has been accessing a computer when he takes tests. But he'd rather listen to music instead of boring social studies material, and he'd rather take tests like his friends do—not using the computer. As Daniel looks to the future, he is concerned. He cannot earn a regular diploma unless he passes high-stakes tests in five courses. He'd like to go to the community college to train to be an airplane mechanic, but that would require having a diploma, and so the looming tests make him unsure whether he can pursue this goal. He considers himself fortunate to have many good friends who help him with schoolwork, and he readily admits his teachers generally are supportive, but sometimes he is discouraged by the challenges he faces.

research
**NOTE**

In a large-scale survey of teacher candidates, researchers found that educators' perceptions of students with disabilities in general education classes were significantly improved after completing an introductory course in special education (Shippen, Crites, Houchins, Ramsey, & Simon, 2005).

People are interested in learning about individuals with disabilities for many reasons. Some have a child or family member with special needs, and their personal experiences draw them to the field. Others become interested because of volunteer work sponsored by a high school club or a fraternity or sorority. Yet others plan careers in which knowledge of individuals with disabilities and special education is essential—most teachers are in this group. My own interest in pursuing a career working with individuals with disabilities came from several experiences, including volunteering during high school to assist children and adults with disabilities in a recreational program that included dances and bowling; interacting with friends and neighbors whose families included members with disabilities; and meeting a little girl named Ranie, for whom I was asked to take responsibility as a helper in a religious instruction class when it became clear she could smile but not read or write. In college, as a volunteer in a separate school for children with intellectual disabilities, I thought I could do a much better job than the teacher whose primary goal seemed to be occupying his students' days with craft activities. I decided that the students could learn far more than they were being taught, and I wanted to make a difference in such students' lives. What brings you to the study of children and adults with disabilities and other special needs?

In 2007–2008, the most recent year for which data are available, approximately 6.9 million children and youth from birth to twenty-one years of age received special education services as required by federal law (U.S. Department of Education, 2008a, 2008b). Although this law focuses on disabilities, it is more important to remember from the outset of your study of the infants, toddlers, children, youth, and young adults receiving special education that they are individuals for whom special needs are only one small part of their identities. They are preschoolers with mischief in their eyes and insatiable curiosity; they are elementary students who enjoy learning in school and taking swimming lessons and getting to stay up late; they are middle school students grappling with a larger school environment, who sometimes act like children and sometimes act too grown up and who want to fit in with their classmates; and they are high school students who sing in the chorus, like or dislike certain teachers, and worry about what they will do after graduation. They are Elizabeth and Andrew and Daniel and other students just like them—or very different from them.

Whatever brings you to be reading this text—whether you are a special education teacher or related services provider candidate, a general education teacher trainee, the parent of a child with a disability, or someone merely interested in understanding this field— what is most critical is that you learn to look at all individuals, whether they are children or adults, in the context of their strengths and abilities, their value as individuals, and the contributions that they make to your life and that you make to theirs. Your perspective and how you learn to work with children and adults with disabilities as a professional can make all the difference in the world to the individuals about whom this textbook is written.

# Concepts That Guide Special Education

When you think about special education, what images come to mind? A teacher working with a small group of students who struggle to read? A young man in a wheelchair in chemistry class? A student like Neal, whose story appears in the Firsthand Account? All of these images may be part of special education, but it is much more than that. As you explore this complex and rapidly changing field, you quickly will learn that it is characterized by a multitude of technical terms and acronyms. Your interest undoubtedly is in students and learning to work with them effectively, but it is equally important to understand the technical aspects of special education and what it offers to students and their families.

## The Core Provisions of Special Education

Three key concepts form the foundation for all the special services students with disabilities are entitled to receive through public schools, and they are the basis for all the other information you will learn as you read this text.

**ROSIE PARRISH** *is pursuing a doctoral degree in early childhood special education. In sharing her family's story, she offers a perspective that every educator should remember when working with parents of children with disabilities.*

My family's story is overflowing with episodes of hurt, hope, and lots of humor, and it all began with the birth of my son, Neal. After a seemingly perfectly health pregnancy, Neal was born 2 weeks past his due date after an induced labor. To our surprise, he was stillborn and revived after 96 seconds, then underwent multiple tests and operations. At six weeks of age, he was diagnosed with CHARGE syndrome.* This syndrome affects people differently, but my son suffers (yes, suffers) from these specific conditions: congenital heart disease (he's had six heart surgeries and now has a permanent pacemaker), severe/profound deafness, visual impairment, autistic tendencies, frequent bouts of pneumonia due to aspiration, facial paralysis, incontinence, and developmental delays. As the many diagnoses started rolling in over the first few months of his life, each one hit me like a ton of bricks. I knew nothing about raising children, disabilities, or medical care. When I realized that this was to be my new life, I quickly became familiar with these things through research in libraries, on the Internet, and in talking with other families of children with disabilities. For the first several years, I had only one goal—that he would live.

Now Neal is 14 years old and has already lived much longer than we were given reason to believe he would. In many ways, he is a typical teenager and we are a typical family. He has learned the art of manipulating his mother to get what he wants, playing practical jokes, and torturing his younger sister. He has also mastered most PlayStation games. He's doing well in school and gets along with most anybody, for which I am very thankful. As a family, we engage in fun activities like movie and pizza night, swimming, and camping.

Though there is obviously lots of joy in our life, I have spent most every night of his life wondering if he was going to keep on living. I never know if our good-night kiss is going to be our last. Many other mothers of typically developing children tell me they experience the same thing, but I think they probably do not, at least, on the level that I do. I fear his heart will grow tired. He frequently tells me of dreams he has had in which he has visited heaven. He is old enough now to realize that dying is highly possible and to recognize the injustice and to voice his feelings about why he has so many more challenges than other children. Maybe there is a grand master plan of the universe that we simply do not understand. Maybe that plan was that I would go into this field and make a difference somehow in the lives of other families. Or maybe that plan was simply that my son would touch the hearts of everyone he meets . . . that his sweetness, his need for people's compassion would turn their lives around, too. I don't know. I *still* struggle with *why* he was born this way.

Our life is very different from that of our other family members and friends, and "fitting in" is still nearly impossible. There is always some reason Neal can't participate in activities: his heart condition, his pacemaker, his deafness, his visual impairment—all of these things are barriers to his inclusion. Trying to explain to him why the boy next door wants to play with his little sister but *not him* is very hard. I hear lots of talk about community services and other resources available to families like mine, but the truth is there isn't much. After-school activities and summer camps are nearly impossible to find for a child with such an array of disabling conditions. There are no real friends for any of us because our lifestyle choices are so limited.

What bothers me a great deal is other people's inability to understand what it must be like, to put themselves in our shoes for even one day. People hear about an upcoming heart surgery and they think how hard it must be to go through this. They shower me with attention; they come to my house. They don't realize that his being in the hospital is actually valuable respite for me, and I really just want that time alone. They don't realize that the heart is the one thing that can be "fixed." It is the day-to-day living that is the biggest challenge and that's when I need the help.

Fortunately, I have a great relationship with my sister who helps us a lot. I have also been blessed with a daughter who has given me the experience of "typical" parenthood. She's very smart, funny, *and* compassionate. She is my biggest helper. At eight years old, she already knows how to identify when my son is in physical distress and can quickly check his capillary refill while I'm dialing 911. On other days, she treats him just like a brother with all the bickering and tattling. He needs that and so do I. It makes us feel like a normal family.

It's important to all of us that my son enjoys his life because, frankly, the quality isn't that great. One of his favorite things to do is ride on the back of my brother's motorcycle. People have told me I shouldn't let him do that. They think his life is so fragile that I should shelter him from any possible harm. My sister and I laugh about this. We say that one day he might fall off going 60 mph down the road. We'll have to call everyone and say that Neal has passed on. Everyone will respond, "Oh, I'm so sorry. Was it his heart?" And we'll answer, "Heck no! He fell off the back of a Harley!" Life's too short as it is, so we figure "go for it!"

Though I am able to laugh about a lot of things, most days I feel an abundance of sadness and sometimes anger weighing me down. I thought I had gone through the cycle of grief associated with having a child with disabilities, as you frequently see described in textbooks. But I realize now that what I am experiencing is chronic sorrow. And it is not just my sorrow—it's his, his little sister's, and his aunt's. Though there are indeed episodes of joy, the sorrow underlies all of our life experiences. We have just come to a place where we accept that we have fewer choices than most and we instead concentrate on sharing as much love as we can, laughing whenever possible and keeping moving. There's really no other way to do it.

*CHARGE syndrome is a genetic disorder discovered in 1981 and affecting 1 out of 9,000–10,000 births. The letters stand for the original factors thought to comprise the syndrome: Coloboma of the eye, Heart defects, Atresia of the choanae, Retardation of growth and/or development, Genital and/or urinary abnormalities, and Ear abnormalities and deafness. These factors no longer are the basis for the diagnosis of CHARGE, but the name has remained (CHARGE Syndrome Foundation, 2006).

## Special Education

The first term to consider is *special education.* It has a precise definition that comes from the federal law that established it:

> The term "special education" means specially designed instruction, at no cost to parents, to meet the unique needs of a child with a disability, including—
>
> a. instruction conducted in the classroom, in the home, in hospitals and institutions, and in other settings; and
> b. instruction in physical education. (20 U.S.C. §1401[29])

That is, **special education** is the vehicle through which children who have disabilities are guaranteed to receive, within the public education system, an education specifically designed to help them reach their learning potential. We will return later in this chapter to the topic of specially designed instruction as a key part of special education. Special education teachers often have significant responsibility for this specially designed instruction, but general education teachers, paraeducators, specialists, and other professionals also may provide special education. Andrew, the middle school student you read about at the beginning of the chapter, is an example of a student who needs extensive, specially designed instruction and who receives services from a team of professionals.

### Related Services

Two other concepts are companions to special education and further explain it. The first is **related services**:

> The term "related services" means transportation, and such developmental, corrective, and other supportive services (including speech/language pathology and audiology services, interpreting services, psychological services, physical and occupational therapy, recreation, including therapeutic recreation, social work services, school nurse services designed to enable a child with a disability to receive a free appropriate public education as described in the individualized education program of the child, counseling services, including rehabilitation counseling, orientation and mobility services, and medical services, except that such medical services shall be for diagnostic and evaluation purposes only) as may be required to assist a child with a disability to benefit from special education, and includes the early identification and assessment of disabling conditions in children. The term does not include a medical device that is surgically implanted, or the replacement of the device. (20 U.S.C. §1401[26])

This term clarifies the fact that for students with disabilities to succeed in school, they may need one or several additional services—from a bus equipped with a wheelchair lift to individual counseling to physical therapy. As with special education, they are entitled to access these additional supports without cost. The speech/language therapy that Elizabeth receives is an example of a related service.

*After parents and family, educators are usually the most important adults in the lives of their students.*

### Supplementary Aids and Services

The third concept essential to special education, particularly given the current expectation that students with disabilities should be educated in the general education classroom unless data demonstrate this is not possible, is **supplementary aids and services**:

> The term "supplementary aids and services" means aids, services, and other supports that are provided in regular education classes or other education-related settings to enable children with disabilities to be educated with nondisabled children to the maximum extent appropriate in accordance with section 1412 (a)(5). (20 U.S.C. §1401[29])

One example of a supplementary aid or service is access to a computer with software that predicts what the student is likely to type next, thus reducing the amount of typing the student must do. Another example is preferential seating in the classroom (e.g., near the teacher or the blackboard) for a student who has low vision. Yet another example is a teaching assistant or paraprofessional who accompanies a student who requires ongoing adult support in the general education classroom because of challenging behaviors. Take a moment to review Daniel's story at the beginning of the chapter. What supplementary aids and services does he receive?

In the remainder of this chapter and throughout this textbook, many other terms related to special education will be introduced. All of them, however, directly relate back to these three concepts: the provision of special education through specially designed instruction, related services, and supplementary aids and services.

## REVIEW · REFLECT · DISCUSS

1. What are your own experiences with people with disabilities and special education? What have you learned from these experiences?
2. Based on your experiences, what are examples of specially designed instruction, related services, and supplementary aids and services for students with disabilities?

## *Development of the Special Education Field*

Special education is a dynamic field, one with a long and fascinating history, as you can see in the timeline in Figure 1.1, which highlights landmark events. It is a field that is still evolving, and learning the story of its development can give you a perspective on how thinking has changed and services have grown for students with special needs and perhaps even on what might occur in the future.

### Early History

Although much early information about individuals with disabilities focused on adults, attention to children grew in the nineteenth century as pioneering professionals took up their cause. For example, in 1800 French physician Jean-Marc-Gaspard Itard was hired to work with a twelve-year-old child named Victor, who had been found wandering in the woods and was considered a feral child—that is, a human who was living much like an animal. In fact, he was called the "Wild Boy of Aveyron" (Scheerenberger, 1983). Victor was deaf and mute, and professionals disagreed about his potential. Over the next five years, Itard worked with Victor to teach him functional skills (e.g., dressing, personal hygiene), social expectations, and speech, but progress was frustratingly slow. Itard initially considered his efforts with Victor a failure, but he later wrote that Victor could only be compared to himself, and by that measure, he had made great progress. In fact, Victor had learned the letters of the alphabet, the meanings of many words, and self-care. Through Itard's work with Victor, the notion that even children with significant needs could benefit from instruction and were worthy of attention was introduced, as was the concept of communication with children who were deaf and mute (Kanner, 1964).

Another notable development in the field of special education came from France in the mid-nineteenth-century work of Edouard Seguin and his physiological method (Winzer, 1993). Seguin, a student of Itard's, deeply believed that children who were blind, intellectually disabled, or emotionally disabled could be trained to become productive members of society. His method included creating a structured learning environment with attention to developing the senses, learning basic academic skills, and engaging in regular physical activity. Seguin brought several key concepts to the study of educating children with special needs—the positive impact of rewards, the potentially negative impact of punishment, and the importance of structure and clear directions—ideas that today are still integral to effective special education.

In the United States, the idea of providing care and support for children with disabilities emerged slowly during the nineteenth century. The first public school special class was established in Cleveland, Ohio, in 1875 (Scheerenberger, 1983), but it was disbanded shortly thereafter. Another was recorded in Providence in 1896, and others were established by the turn of the twentieth century in cities such as Chicago, Boston, Philadelphia, and New York (Kode, 2002). However, several forces soon led to more rapid growth of such services.

dimensions of
**DIVERSITY**

The Family Village—A Global Community of Disability Related Resources (www.familyvillage.wisc.edu/index.htmlx) provides online information about specific disabilities, adaptive products, and education with resources for people with disabilities, including individuals from different racial and cultural groups.

Do you have a disability? The Educators with Disabilities Caucus of the Council for Exceptional Children (http://www.cec.sped.org/Content/NavigationMenu/AboutCEC/Communities/Caucuses/Educatorswith Disabilities/default.htm) provides important information and resources for educators with disabilities.

FIGURE 1.1

## Timeline of the Development of Special Education Services

This timeline shows some of the most significant events in the history of special education, illustrating how all the various disciplines represented in the field (e.g., the study of deafness and blindness and the study of mental retardation) evolved concurrently and how current practices rely on past events.

| 1817 | 1832 | 1834 | 1848 | 1858 | 1864 | 1884 | 1898 | 1905 | 1910 | 1920 |
|------|------|------|------|------|------|------|------|------|------|------|

**1817** — Connecticut Asylum for the Education and Instruction of Deaf and Dumb Persons opens in Hartford, Connecticut

**1832** — Perkins Institution for the Blind opened by Samuel Gridley Howe

**1834** — Braille code is first published

**1848** — Howe establishes experimental school for feebleminded youth

**1858** — American Printing House for the Blind is established

**1864** — National Deaf Mute College is established, later to be renamed Gallaudet University

**1884** — Formal training for teachers of blind persons begins at Columbia University; Alexander Graham Bell introduces the term *special education*

**1898** — College-level training for teachers of students with mental retardation begins

**1905** — Alfred Binet and Theodore Simon publish their intelligence test, the basis for modern IQ testing

**1910** — Segregated classes in the public schools are established as viable alternatives to instructing children with disabilities; the term *emotional disturbance* comes into use

**1920** — The term *mentally retarded* is introduced; the term *gifted* appears in the professional literature

Source: Based on information in Winzer, M. A. (1993). *The history of special education: From isolation to integration.* Washington, DC: Gallaudet University Press.

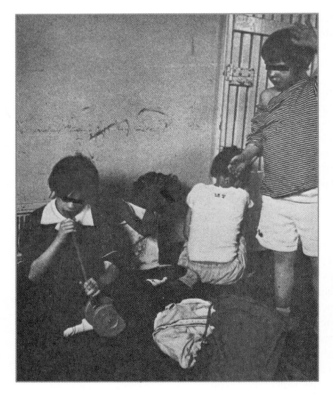

*The history of special education documents periods of deplorable practices that help explain why today's laws must exist to protect students with disabilities.*

## Basis for Today's General Education and Special Education System

During the late nineteenth and early twentieth centuries, urbanization, immigration, and industrialization flourished in the United States (Mondale & Patton, 2001). Large factories were being built in cities, and many people decided to give up the rural life of farming to seek employment in the cities. Waves of immigrants joined them, individuals typically unfamiliar with American culture and language. It was a stressful time in American society: Many middle-class people were fearful of the changes occurring and the impact on their lives, the living conditions for the new city dwellers often were squalid, and governments could not keep up with the demands for social services.

The impact of these social tensions on people with disabilities was unfortunate. Prominent researchers suggested that individuals with intellectual and other disabilities were a threat to society and should not be allowed to have children. They claimed that many immigrants fell into this group; that is, they were "feebleminded" (Smith, 1985). Using this flawed rationale, the *eugenics movement* emerged in which many adults, including those with disabilities, were involuntarily sterilized. In fact, most states had laws to make the practice of sterilization legal when such individuals were judged to be incompetent, and several of these laws were on the books until the 1970s (Fleischer & Zames, 2001). Although the eugenics movement and involuntary sterilization occurred in the past, historians in the field of disabilities argue that the emphasis on curing disabilities—on making people be like everyone else instead of accepting them for who they are—originated during this sad period in history and still dominates thinking in today's society.

For schools, the events of this era altered the face of education and planted the seeds of contemporary special education. First, compulsory public education began to grow, partly as an economic response to the changing society (Osgood, 2008). With few child labor laws in existence at this time, mandatory school attendance functioned as a means of keeping

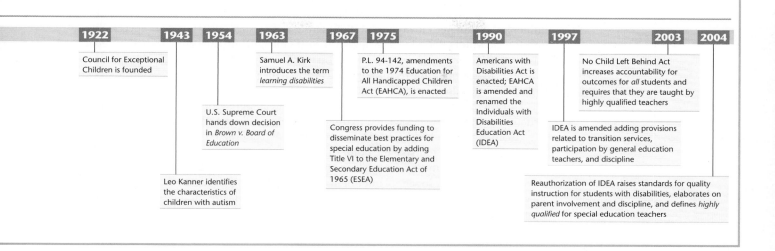

| 1922 | 1943 | 1954 | 1963 | 1967 | 1975 | 1990 | 1997 | 2003 | 2004 |

**1922** Council for Exceptional Children is founded

**1943** Leo Kanner identifies the characteristics of children with autism

**1954** U.S. Supreme Court hands down decision in *Brown v. Board of Education*

**1963** Samuel A. Kirk introduces the term *learning disabilities*

**1967** Congress provides funding to disseminate best practices for special education by adding Title VI to the Elementary and Secondary Education Act of 1965 (ESEA)

**1975** P.L. 94-142, amendments to the 1974 Education for All Handicapped Children Act (EAHCA), is enacted

**1990** Americans with Disabilities Act is enacted; EAHCA is amended and renamed the Individuals with Disabilities Education Act (IDEA)

**1997** IDEA is amended adding provisions related to transition services, participation by general education teachers, and discipline

**2003** No Child Left Behind Act increases accountability for outcomes for *all* students and requires that they are taught by highly qualified teachers

**2004** Reauthorization of IDEA raises standards for quality instruction for students with disabilities, elaborates on parent involvement and discipline, and defines *highly qualified* for special education teachers

children out of the labor force; doing so ensured that jobs would be available for the rapidly growing pool of adults, both immigrants and those moving from farms to cities, who commanded higher wages than youngsters. Second, schools were designed like the most innovative concept of the time, the assembly line. Just as cars and other products were created using piece-by-piece assembly in a standard way, so too were American citizens to be created by moving all children, the "raw material," from grade to grade as they received a standardized education.

However, it soon became apparent that student needs defied standardization. Although children with significant disabilities would not have been accepted in public schools during the first part of the twentieth century, some children who enrolled could not keep up academically with peers, were defiant or belligerent, or had physical disabilities. Consistent with the prevailing belief that de-valued anyone who failed to meet societal expectations of what is "normal," educators decided that these students should be removed from the assembly line of education and offered instruction better suited to their needs (Connecticut Special Education Association, 1936; Winzer, 2007).

With this thinking, separate special classes became increasingly common (Bennett, 1932; Pertsch, 1936). These classes were sometimes called *ungraded classes* because pupils across several grade levels were grouped and taught there (Osgood, 2008). Further, as intelligence testing became popular during this same time period, educators came to believe that they had found a scientific basis for separating learners who would not succeed in typical classrooms. Although not required by federal law, special education classes for students with intellectual disabilities, physical disabilities, and sensory impairments became increasingly common through the first half of the twentieth century.

## Discrimination and the Beginning of Change

Shortly after the advent of the modern civil rights movement in education, with the 1954 **Brown v. Board of Education of Topeka, Kansas** decision clarifying that "separate cannot be equal," some professionals began questioning whether separate classes provided students with disabilities with an appropriate education. For the next decade, researchers explored this issue in a series of studies collectively referred to as the *efficacy studies*. They compared the achievement and social adjustment of students with intellectual disabilities who were enrolled in special classes to that of students of similar abilities who remained in general education settings. The studies tended to find that students with intellectual disabilities (also called *mental retardation*) in general education classes achieved more academically than those in special classes (e.g., Goldstein, Moss, & Jordan, 1965), probably because teachers' expectations of them were higher and because they were learning in the same curriculum as other students. In special classes, emphasis often was placed more on developing manual or job-related skills than on academics, an approach reflecting the beliefs encouraged during the eugenics movement. By the mid-1960s, with the civil rights movement in the headlines, influential researcher Lloyd Dunn (1968) wrote a watershed essay entitled "Special Education for the Mildly Retarded: Is Much of It Justifiable?" Dunn questioned whether separate classes could provide an adequate education for students with disabilities, and he challenged educators to use emerging technology and research on effective teaching to educate students with disabilities along with their peers.

During the same time period, other professionals were looking beyond academic instruction to broader issues related to disabilities, especially the stigmatizing effect of labels (e.g., Goffman, 1963; Hobbs, 1975). For example, Mercer (1973) coined the phrase "the six-hour retarded child" to make the point that some students, often those from nondominant races or cultures or those who spoke a language other than English, were considered disabled while they were in school but not in their neighborhoods. What became clear was that special education was not just a means of assisting children with disabilities; it also had become a means of discriminating against students who might be perceived by educators as more challenging to teach (Rueda, Klingner, Sager, & Velasco, 2008).

## Litigation for the Rights of Students with Disabilities

During the same time that researchers were debating the quality and impact of special education on students, parent groups advocating for the rights of children with disabilities were becoming increasingly vocal (Gallagher, 2006). Parents of children with significant disabilities rightly wanted to know why their sons and daughters could not be educated in the public school system—that is, why they were told to keep their children at home, put them in institutions, or send them to private agencies for their education. Other parents objected to the quality of their sons' and daughters' education. These parents began to win landmark court cases on their children's behalf. For example, in **Pennsylvania Association for Retarded Children v. The Commonwealth of Pennsylvania** *(PARC)* (1972), parents won the guarantee that education did not mean only traditional academic instruction and that children with intellectual disabilities could benefit from education tailored to their needs. Further, children could not be denied access to public schools, and they were entitled to a free public education. In **Mills v. Board of Education** *(Mills)* (1972), a class action lawsuit on behalf of the 18,000 children in the Washington, D.C. schools whose pupils included those with an entire range of disabilities, the court ordered the district to educate *all* students, including these. It also clarified that specific procedures had to be followed to determine whether a student should receive special services and to resolve disagreements between parents and school personnel.

*Special education today is characterized by high standards and increased accountability for student outcomes.*

Other cases highlighted biases against certain students. In **Diana v. State Board of Education of California** *(Diana)* (1970), a Spanish-speaking child was placed in a class for students with mild intellectual disabilities after she scored low on an intelligence quotient (IQ) test because it was administered in English. The public school system was ordered to test Spanish-speaking children in their native language. Finally, **Larry P. v. Riles** *(Larry P.)* (1972) concerned an African American student and discrimination in assessment. The court ruled that schools had to ensure that tests administered to students did not discriminate based on race. The *PARC, Mills, Diana,* and *Larry P.* cases together put a spotlight on the shortcomings and abuses of special education at that time and formed the framework for the legislation that today guides the field (Yell, 2006).

## A Federal Response: Laws to Protect Students with Disabilities

Litigation and legislation for children with disabilities intertwined during the 1960s and early 1970s. As court cases such as those just discussed were clarifying the rights of children with disabilities and their families, legislation was creating mandates to ensure these rights were upheld.

The first federal law to address the education of children with disabilities was the Elementary and Secondary Education Act of 1965 (P.L. 89-750). This law provided funding to states to assist them in creating and improving programs and services for children with disabilities (Turnbull, Stowe, Wilcox, & Turnbull, 2000). In 1974, in the Education for All Handicapped Children Act, Congress further focused its efforts, increasing federal special education funding and charging states with the task of creating full educational opportunities for students with disabilities. That law was amended for the first time in 1975, and that set of amendments, **P.L. 94-142**, the Education of the Handicapped Act, is considered the basis for all subsequent special education practice. This law captured many of the issues that were being addressed in the courts, funded efforts to find children with disabilities who were not in school, and mandated that states follow the law in order to receive federal funding (Yell, Katsiyannis, & Hazelkorn, 2007). The principles of this law are still in force today, and they are so essential to special education that they will be discussed in detail in the next section of this chapter.

### Refinements to the Law

Since 1975, federal special education law has been reauthorized several times. One significant set of changes occurred in 1986, when special education was expanded to include services to infants and young children. In 1990, the amendments renamed the law the **Individuals with Disabilities Education Act (IDEA),** the name by which it is currently known. This legislation also added two disabilities (autism and traumatic brain injury) to those already covered by the law, and it clarified the need for supports for students as they transition to postschool educational or vocational options. In 1997, several significant additions were made when the law was again reauthorized: Procedures for addressing discipline for students with disabilities were included, parent participation was expanded, the roles of classroom teachers in educating students with disabilities were clarified, and assessment of the academic progress of all students with disabilities was mandated. The most recent reauthorization in 2004, formally called the Individuals with Disabilities Education Improvement Act, continued the pattern of refinement and revision: Provisions were added to ensure that IDEA is consistent with other federal education laws, additional strategies were specified to resolve disputes with parents, and evidence-based practices were mandated for student instruction (Yell, Shriner, & Katsiyannis, 2006). As you read this textbook, you will learn more about these and other current provisions of IDEA.

**fyi**

The case *Daniel R.R. v. State Board of Education* (1989) established the guidelines that schools use today to determine the least restrictive environment for students with disabilities (Wright & Wright, 2005).

## Federal Special Education Law: Accomplishments and Disappointments

The passage of federal special education law was revolutionary, and it had many positive effects (Osgood, 2008). Many students who had been completely left out of the public school system were guaranteed an education, decisions about students regarding special education had to be based on unbiased assessment information, and the rights of parents were outlined and clear procedures put in place to ensure that any disagreements with school districts would be addressed in an impartial way. However, the passage of the law did not address all the issues of educating students with disabilities, and it did not mark an end to the debate about appropriate programs and services. Several of the court cases that have shaped special education since P.L. 94-142 was passed in 1975 are listed in Figure 1.2, and some of the unresolved issues are discussed next.

## Development of Inclusive Practices

Soon after the passage of P.L. 94-142, parents of children with significant intellectual disabilities began to express dissatisfaction at the separateness of their children's education (Erwin & Soodak, 2008). Yes, their children were now clearly entitled to access public schools, but they often were housed in separate schools that had no typical learners, or they were placed in a separate wing of a school and not treated as though they were part of the school community. These parents took their cause to court as a civil right rather than an educational issue (Fleischer & Zames, 2001). They argued that separate schools and classes caused their children to miss the full range of school experiences and that this practice was discriminatory. The parents wanted their children included with other students in the school community—and thus the concept of inclusion was introduced to the field of education.

Between 1995 and 2005, the percentage of students with disabilities spending 80 percent or more of the school day in a general classroom showed an overall increase from 45 to 52 percent. Caucasian students were most likely to be educated in that way; African American students were least likely (USDE, 2009).

---

### FIGURE 1.2
### Supreme Court Cases That Have Shaped Special Education

These are significant Supreme Court cases addressing special education issues (Wright & Wright, 2009) that have been particularly influential.

| Court Case | Key Issue | Ruling |
|---|---|---|
| *Board of Education of the Hendrick Hudson Central School District v. Rowley* (1982) | Free Appropriate Public Education (FAPE) | · FAPE provision of IDEA considered met if the IEP, developed through the act's procedures, is reasonably calculated to enable the child to receive educational benefits. |
| *Irving Independent School District v. Tatro* (1984) | Related services | · Health services necessary to assist the student to benefit from special education, when they can be performed by a nonphysician, are considered a related service. |
| *Honig v. Doe* (1988) | Discipline | · Schools must abide by the stay-put provision (during administrative or court proceedings, the student must remain in his present placement). <br> · Students cannot be excluded unilaterally for misbehavior related to their disability. <br> · Excluding students from school for over ten days constitutes a change of placement. |
| *Cedar Rapids Community School District v. Garrett F.* (1999) | Related services | · Health services deemed necessary for a qualified child with a disability by the IEP team must be provided as long as a nonphysician can perform the services. |
| *Schaffer v. Weast* (2005) | Burden of proof | · Parents disputing proposed instructional plans for their children are responsible for proving why the plans are not adequate. |
| *Arlington Central School District v. Pearl Murphy and Theodore Murphy* (2006) | Recovery of fees | · Parents are not entitled to recover the cost of experts who testify for them as part of due process and court cases. |
| *Winkelman v. Parma City School District* (2007) | | · Parents of children with disabilities are entitled to pursue their case in federal court without being represented by an attorney because they have a personal right under IDEA for their children to be appropriately educated. If they only held rights on behalf of their children, this would be prohibited. |
| *Forest Grove School District v. T. A.* (2009) | | · In some situations, parents are entitled to be reimbursed for private school tuition, even when the child has never received special education services from a public school. Prior to this case, the interpretation of law was that public school services had to be accessed or tuition claims would not be considered. |

Source: Katsiyannis, A., Yell, M. L., & Bradley, R. (2001). Reflections on the 25th anniversary of the Individuals with Disabilities Education Act. *Remedial and Special Education, 22,* 324–334. Copyright © 2001 by Pro-Ed, Inc. Reprinted by permission of SAGE Publications.

## Keeping Up with a Rapidly Changing Field

School professionals can keep up with the latest trends and research on practice by accessing a variety of resources. Here are some useful options:

### Websites (U.S. Department of Education)

- Building the Legacy: IDEA 2004

  (http://idea.ed.gov/)

  This website contains key information about IDEA as well as links to related topics and an option for submitting questions you may have about the law.

- What Works Clearinghouse *(WWC)*

  (http://ies.ed.gov/ncee/wwc/)

  Supported by the Institute of Education Sciences, this website documents evidence-based practices that educators should use in teaching all of their students.

- No Child Left Behind

  (http://www.ed.gov/nclb/landing.jhtml)

  This website includes the latest information on implementation of NCLB as well as resources for teachers, parents, and administrators.

- The Access Center: Improving Outcomes for Students K–8

  (http://www.k8accesscenter.org/index.php)

  This website includes information on contemporary, evidence-based practices that can improve outcomes for students with disabilities.

### Professional Journals

*These are some of the most widely read journals that cover a range of topics related to the field of special education:*

- *Exceptional Children*
- *Intervention in School and Clinic*
- *Journal of Special Education*
- *Remedial and Special Education*
- *Multiple Voices*
- *Career Development for Exceptional Individuals*
- *Journal of Disability Policy Studies*
- *Journal of Special Education Technology*
- *Teaching Exceptional Children*
- *Focus on Exceptional Children*

---

In 1986, Madeline Will, then Assistant Secretary for Special Education and Rehabilitation in the U.S. Department of Education, extended this idea to all students with disabilities through the *regular education initiative (REI),* urging general education and special education teachers to work together to educate all their students (Will, 1986). As a result, attention for the past two decades has focused on the rights of students with disabilities to be educated with their peers who do not have identified disabilities, and it forms a major theme for this textbook. However, as you may already know, inclusion remains a source of controversy (e.g., Friend & Shamberger, 2008), and its implementation still varies widely.

### Disproportionate Representation

For more than two decades, it has been apparent that African American students are identified to receive special education services as learning disabled, emotionally disturbed, or intellectually disabled at a disproportionately high rate (Skiba et al., 2008), as are students who are American Indian/Alaska Native (USDE, 2009). At the same time, students who are Hispanic or Asian are underrepresented (USDE, 2009). Whether because of overt or unintentional racial and ethnic biases of educators or factors related to poverty, this issue is one that continues to trouble professionals and is directly addressed in IDEA. It is also a topic that requires extensive discussion, and all of Chapter Three is devoted to it.

### An Era of Continuing Improvement

Special education is a discipline that has evolved rapidly, and change continues today. For example, there is a rapidly increasing expectation that teachers use only strategies and interventions that have been validated through research rather than those that are popular because of tradition or for other reasons, and this expectation will affect how you teach and how your students learn (Zirkel, 2008). As you anticipate your work with students with disabilities, remember that what were common instructional approaches just a few years ago may now be outdated and that effective new practices are constantly being identified. You will need to keep up with such changes and continually examine your knowledge and skills to ensure that they reflect contemporary thinking. The Professional Edge outlines some resources that can help you stay abreast of the ever-changing special education field.

1. When you think about the history of special education, what would you identify as the most important lessons to be learned from it?
2. Why do you think that parents of students with disabilities still need to go to court to preserve their children's right and to obtain the services they want for their children?

**PEARSON**
**myeducationlab**

Go to the Assignments and Activities section of Topic 1: The Law, Least Restrictive Environment, and IEPs, in the MyEducationLab for your course and find several activities related to legal and legislative aspects of special education.

# Laws for Students with Disabilities

In the section you just finished, the laws that govern special education were mentioned briefly. Here, the major provisions of those laws are outlined in detail.

## *Individuals with Disabilities Education Improvement Act (IDEA) of 2004*

Since the first special education law was passed in 1975, legislation has contained core principles to ensure the educational rights of students with disabilities and their parents (Wright & Wright, 2005). These principles include zero reject, free appropriate public education (FAPE), least restrictive environment (LRE), nondiscriminatory evaluation, parent and family rights, and procedural safeguards.

### Zero Reject

The principle of **zero reject** entitles all students with disabilities, even those in private schools, to a free public education regardless of the nature or severity of their disabilities. To accomplish zero reject, each state has in place what is called a **child find** system, a set of procedures for alerting the public that services are available for students with disabilities and for distributing print and electronic materials, conducting screening, and completing other activities to ensure that students are identified. This principle of the law is directly related to the *PARC* and *Mills* cases discussed earlier in this chapter, in which parents won the right for their children to attend public schools.

Today, zero reject also addresses more than finding children with disabilities. It ensures that students with communicable diseases, such as AIDS, cannot be excluded from schools. It also guides school policies related to students who commit serious offenses that might otherwise lead to long-term suspension or expulsion.

### Free Appropriate Public Education

The education to which all students with disabilities are entitled must be a **free appropriate public education (FAPE).** That is, parents and family members cannot be asked to pay for special education services. In fact, if a decision is made that a student needs to be educated outside the student's own school district, the school district bears the cost for that placement, including the expense of transportation. Further, FAPE clarifies that the student's education must incorporate the three concepts that introduced this chapter: special education through specially designed instruction, related services, and supplementary aids and services. These elements are captured in the student's *individualized education program (IEP),* a document described in detail in Chapter Two.

### Least Restrictive Environment

The next principle of IDEA concerns how students receive FAPE. That is, students must be educated in the setting most like that of typical peers in which they can succeed when provided with the needed supports and services, or the **least restrictive environment (LRE).** It is presumed that the LRE for most students with disabilities is the general education setting, and educators must justify any instance in which a student with a disability is not educated there. However, the law spells out additional settings in which students may be educated, including general education with instruction in a special education for a small part of the day, a separate special education classroom where students spend most of the day, a separate school, and others. It is the LRE provision of IDEA and its interpretation that are the basis for most contemporary conversations about inclusion (Epanchin & Friend, 2007; Williamson, McLeskey, Hoppey, & Rentz, 2006). You should realize, though, that IDEA does not use the term *inclusion*.

### Nondiscriminatory Evaluation

**Nondiscriminatory evaluation** is mandated in IDEA. That is, the law outlines the rights of students and their parents to ensure that any assessment completed as part of a special education decision-making process is unbiased. Based on the *Diana* and *Larry P.* court cases already discussed, the law ensures the following:

- Tests are administered in the child's native language.
- Tests are appropriate for the child's age and characteristics.
- More than one test is used to assess the presence of a disability.
- A knowledgeable professional administers and interprets assessment results.
- Assessments occur in all areas of suspected disability (Yell & Dragsow, 2007).

### Parent and Family Rights to Confidentiality

Information regarding a student's disability is highly confidential (Wright & Wright, 2005). IDEA clarifies that such information may be shared only with individuals who are working directly with the student. In fact, a record must be kept of anyone who accesses these student records. Further, parents have the right to request to see and obtain copies of all records kept regarding their child with a disability and to dispute information that they perceive is not accurate. Once records are no longer needed, a procedure must be in place so that they are destroyed within a prescribed timeframe.

### Procedural Safeguards

The final principle in IDEA concerns procedural safeguards (Hazelkorn, Packard, & Douvanis, 2008). Any decisions concerning a student with disabilities are made with parent input and in compliance with all aspects of the law. For example, parents must give written consent for their children to be assessed to determine if they have a disability. Similarly, parents must be invited to attend any meetings regarding their child, and they must give permission for the child to begin receiving special education. When parents and school personnel disagree on any aspect of special education, specific steps must be followed to attempt to resolve the dispute. The procedural safeguards that parents have and how they are incorporated into day-to-day special education in schools will become clearer as you read about the people and procedures in special education in Chapter Two.

These six principles of IDEA inspire special educators to ensure that their students receive the education to which they are entitled. Are you looking forward to joining the ranks of teachers who are passionate about their work students with disabilities? The advice from Noel Keener in Speaking From Experience can help you realize your dream while balancing it with the realities of being a special educator in today's schools.

## Other Legislation Related to Special Education

In addition to IDEA, a law that guarantees *educational rights,* special education is affected by laws that guarantee the *civil rights* of children and adults. These laws are **Section 504 of the Rehabilitation Act of 1973** and the **Americans with Disabilities Act of 1990.**

### Section 504 of the Rehabilitation Act of 1973

When Congress enacted P.L. 93-112, the Rehabilitation Act of 1973, it created the first civil rights legislation in the United States specifically intended to protect individuals with disabilities. As Section 504, the final section of this law, states,

> No qualified handicapped person shall, on the basis of handicap, be excluded from participation in, be denied the benefits of, or otherwise be subjected to discrimination under any

**web link**

At the Circle of Inclusion website (www.circleofinclusion.org/english/books/section1/a.html), you can learn how to review children's books for their treatment of individuals with disabilities. A checklist is included.

Noel Keener came to the field of special education with a degree in psychology and experience in two states working with children and young adults with disabilities and alcohol and drug dependence. Now she has earned teaching licensure and a master's degree. She has taught for 5 years at two large middle schools in the Guilford County Schools (Greensboro, NC) in a self-contained class for students with emotional disabilities and in a resource/inclusive practices program. At each school she was voted teacher-of-the-year by her colleagues. When asked what advice she has for special educators new to the field, her passion for her job instantly came through. Here is what she said:

1. Be compassionate. Some students come from difficult situations. They may be tired or distracted because they didn't have breakfast or a safe place to sleep.

2. Be motivated. Special educators teach many students, and students are at many levels. If the teacher isn't motivated to help students learn, then the students won't be motivated either.

3. Be organized. Even when it's hectic, you have to know where information is kept and that it is secure. You have to be able to pull up students' achievement scores and information about their IEPs. Everything has to be at hand—you never know what you'll need and when you'll need it.

4. Be willing to learn. It's so important to realize that students will learn if you find a way that works for them. For example, one student with an attention problem learned best when I let him alphabetize books on a shelf in the back of the room. He was still listening, but the book task helped him to concentrate. Teachers have to be willing to experiment to find what works for their students.

5. Be thorough. This applies to planning so that all students' needs are met, but it also applies to meetings with parents. They expect me to be an expert on their child's education so I need to have past and current assessments, data about social skills and ability to perform, and other information. They're the experts on their child as a whole, and I always learn from them—for example, they may know a way that I can motivate the child to learn. But I have to be prepared to do my part.

6. Be humble. I've learned that the hard way. You want to prove yourself, prove that you are a good teacher. But it's important to ask lots of questions. Now I'm always the first to tell on myself if I make a mistake. That works better.

7. Be genuine. Students can tell if you're faking it, if you don't really want to be there. So can your colleagues. Especially if you're co-teaching, you have to truly want the partnership. If you do, other teachers will be open to it and it'll work.

8. Be flexible. Things happen. Schedules change. You get students you weren't expecting. That is part of the job. Part of the definition of being a special educator is knowing what's happening now won't last.

9. Be tenacious. I'm always saying, "My students need this" to get equipment and supplies. I can't let down these kids. This is also about teaching. Even when students are disrespectful, you have to stay convinced that they will learn.

10. Be grateful. Every day I have opportunity after opportunity to make a difference in these kids' lives. I know that someday one of them will say, "Ms. Keener told me I needed this for college . . ." and it all will have been worth it. What special educators do really matters.

program or activity which receives or benefits from Federal financial assistance. (Section 504, 29 U.S.C. §794[a])

This law broadly defines *disabilities* as impairments that significantly limit one or more major life activities, including walking, seeing, hearing, and learning. Further, it protects all people with disabilities, not only children, from discrimination in programs receiving federal funding, including all public schools (Guthrie, 2006). Some of the provisions framed in this law that affect children of school age were clarified in IDEA, but this law protects some students who are not eligible for the services outlined in that law (Holler & Zirkel, 2008). An example of a student served through Section 504 might be one who is an average learner but has Type I diabetes. Through Section 504, the school district would ensure that school professionals working with the student understand his needs, that the student has immediate access to snacks and water, and that the student is allowed to use the bathroom whenever requested. This student does not need the educational services of IDEA.

Unlike IDEA, no federal funding is allocated to implement Section 504, so any services or supports provided to students through this law must be paid for by the local school district. You will learn more about Section 504 in Chapter Six in the discussion of attention deficit–hyperactivity disorder (ADHD), another special need sometimes addressed using Section 504 provisions.

### Americans with Disabilities Act of 1990

By far the most comprehensive legislation protecting the rights of individuals with disabilities, no matter their age, is the Americans with Disabilities Act of 1990 (ADA) (Office for Civil Rights, 2009). This more recent legislation uses the same broad definition of *disability* as used in Section 504, but it applies to both public and private sectors, including libraries, state and local governments, restaurants, hotels, theaters, transportation systems, and stores (Fleischer & Zames, 2001). With the exception of public school applications, ADA largely has replaced Section 504. In addition to the other provisions of this law, it directly addresses communication, and so it requires that closed captioning be provided to accommodate individuals who are deaf or hard of hearing. It is the ADA that ensures that buildings have access ramps and that most have elevators, that buses and trains can accommodate wheelchairs, and that employers may not refuse to hire a new employee because that individual has a disability. Mentioning ADA is an opportunity to remind you that many students' disabilities have a lifelong impact, such that these individuals may access certain supports and services even after they leave school.

*Federal special education legislation has guaranteed the right of every student with a disability to a free appropriate public education.*

Taken together, IDEA, Section 504, and ADA ensure that people who have disabilities have the right to fully access throughout their lives all the programs, services, and activities available to other individuals. These laws also clearly establish that civil rights protections specifically include individuals with disabilities and that discrimination will not be tolerated.

## REVIEW · REFLECT · DISCUSS

1. What is an example you might see in schools of each of the six principles of IDEA? How do these principles reflect the history of special education?
2. As a teacher, how might you be affected by *Section 504* and the *Americans with Disabilities Act*?

## Students Who Receive Special Education

Unlike federal civil rights laws for people with disabilities that offer a very broad and functionally based definition of *disability,* as noted previously, IDEA takes the opposite approach. In fact, IDEA specifies thirteen categories of disability, and only students with these disabilities are eligible for special education services:

- Specific learning disabilities
- Orthopedic (or physical) impairments
- Speech or language impairments
- Other health impairments
- Mental retardation
- Autism
- Emotional disturbance
- Traumatic brain injury
- Deaf/blindness (i.e., students who are both deaf and blind)
- Multiple disabilities (i.e., students who have more than one disability)
- Visual impairments
- Developmental delays
- Hearing impairments

## Disability Etiquette

Here are some tips for ensuring that your interactions with students and colleagues with disabilities are respectful and appropriate:

- *Use person-first language.* Say "students with disabilities" or "John, who has a physical disability." Placing the disability first (e.g., "LD students," "special education kids") inappropriately emphasizes the disability instead of the person.
- *Avoid the term handicapped.* Some individuals consider this word derogatory, and it is no longer used in federal special education laws or regulations. The terms *disability* and *special needs* are alternatives. Not even parking spaces should be labeled *handicapped;* they are *accessible.*
- *Avoid the language of pity.* Say "wheelchair user" instead of "wheelchair bound," and do not use words such as *victim, sufferer,* or *afflicted.*
- *Talk to the person.* Be sure to talk directly to the person (whether a student, colleague, or other), as illustrated in the cartoon, rather than to a paraeducator or assistant who is present.
- *Don't make assumptions.* Sometimes people assume that individuals who have significant physical disabilities or sensory disabilities (i.e., blind or deaf) also have intellectual disabilities. It is better to err by presuming competence than lack of competence.

*Source:* Excerpts and cartoons from Cohen, J. (2003). *Disability etiquette: Tips on interacting with people with disabilities* (2nd ed.). Retrieved July 2, 2006, from ww.unitedspinal.org. Copyright 2003 by United Spinal Association and Access Resources. Reprinted with permission.

If you scan the table of contents of this book or preview Chapters Five through Fifteen, you will see that each of these disabilities is discussed in detail, including the definitions as specified by the law, the characteristics of students with these disorders, perspectives of students' parents and families, and research-based instructional approaches best suited for teaching students with these special needs. In Chapter Two you will learn about the detailed set of IDEA-mandated procedures that are followed to determine whether a youngster has a disability and is eligible for special education. The Professional Edge offers reminders regarding disability etiquette for consideration as you begin to think about interacting with people with disabilities, whether they are students, colleagues, or others.

### Prevalence of Students with Disabilities

How many students with disabilities are there? The answer to that question at any point in time is referred to as the *prevalence* of students of disabilities, and information to determine

## FIGURE 1.3

### Students Ages Six Through Twenty-One Served under IDEA
(1987–1988, 1997–1998, and 2007–2008)

| Disability Category | School Year | | |
|---|---|---|---|
| | *1987–1988* | *1997–1998* | *2007–2008* |
| Specific learning disabilities | 1,908,097 | 2,726,930 | 2,563,665 |
| Speech or language impairments | 943,702 | 1,051,607 | 1,137,934 |
| Mental retardation | 521,078 | 588,644 | 487,854 |
| Emotional disturbance | 335,662 | 453,545 | 438,867 |
| Multiple disabilities | 60,940 | 105,533 | 131,347 |
| Hearing impairments | 39,101 | 68,658 | 71,332 |
| Orthopedic impairments | 40,597 | 66,930 | 60,010 |
| Other health impairments | 42,334 | 189,879 | 625,187 |
| Visual impairments | 16,241 | 25,511 | 25,855 |
| Autism[a] | | 42,120 | 256,863 |
| Deaf–blindness | 673 | 1427 | 1310 |
| Traumatic brain injury[a] | | 11,864 | 23,805 |
| Developmental delay[b] | | 1,935 | 88,557 |
| All disabilities | 3,904,425 | 5,343,017 | 5,912,586 |

[a]Reporting on autism and traumatic brain injury was first required in 1992–1993.

[b]Optional reporting on developmental delay for students ages three through seven was first allowed in the 1997–1998 school year. This category now applies to children only to age 9.

Source: U.S. Department of Education. (1989). *11th annual report to Congress on the implementation of the Education of all Handicapped Children Act.* Washington, DC: Author; U.S. Department of Education. (1999). *21st annual report to Congress on the implementation of the Individuals with Disabilities Education Act.* Washington, DC: Author; U.S. Department of Education. (2008a, July). *Children with disabilities receiving special education under Part B of the Individuals with Disabilities Education Act* (Data Analysis System, OMB #1820-0043). Washington, DC: Office of Special Education Programs.

prevalence is gathered each year by the U.S. Department of Education as part of IDEA. As you can see by reviewing Figure 1.3, in 2007–2008, 5.9 million school-age children and youth received special education, or approximately 9 percent of students ages six to twenty-one (U.S. Department of Education, 2008a). Students with specific learning disabilities comprised the largest group of students, accounting for nearly half of all those receiving special education. Students with speech or language impairments formed the next largest group (17.9 percent of the total).

The data in Figure 1.3 demonstrate changes occurring in the students who are identified as having disabilities. During the decade between 1987–1988 and 1997–1998, the number of students identified as having disabilities grew nearly 37 percent while the overall school-age population (that is, the total number of school-age students) grew approximately 14 percent (U.S. Department of Education, 1989, 1999, 2008a). Since 1997–1998, however, the pattern of overall rapid growth is no longer in place. Notice that the number of students identified as having learning disabilities has declined over the past 10 years, and the same is true for students with intellectual disabilities and emotional disturbance. At the same time, the numbers of students identified as having autism or other health impairments (the category that includes many students with ADHD) have skyrocketed. No single explanation can be offered for the fluctuating prevalence rates. The decrease in the number of students with learning, intellectual, and emotional disabilities may be due in part to recent efforts to ensure that students receive early and intensive interventions designed to prevent the need for special education services (e.g., Berkeley, Bender, & Peaster, 2009). The rising number of students with autism is likely influenced by increasing awareness of and attention to this disability (e.g., Coo, Ouellette-Kuntz, & Lloyd, 2008). What other factors do you think might be contributing to changes in the prevalence of students with various disabilities?

dimensions of
**DIVERSITY**

Diversity has many dimensions, including race, culture, gender, and sexual orientation, and one or several of these dimensions may also characterize students with disabilities.

In 2003–2004, a total of 54.5 percent of the students with disabilities ages 14 through 21 who exited school graduated with a regular high school diploma, and 31.1 percent dropped out. The remaining 14.4 percent comprised students in other categories, such as received a certificate of completion, reached maximum age, or died (Planty et al., 2008).

Go to the Assignments and Activities section of Topic 18: Early Intervention, in the MyEducation-Lab for your course and find several activities related to early intervention.

## Special Education for Young Children

Although the primary focus of this textbook is on school-age students with disabilities (ages six to twenty-one), IDEA also includes provisions for young children (ages birth to five). For children birth to two years old, special education is not always required by federal law. However, all states now provide services to these infants and toddlers, and approximately 317,000 children nationwide receive them (U.S. Department of Education, 2008b). For children ages three to five, special education services have been mandated in IDEA since 1986, and in 2007–2008, 700,166 children received these services (U.S. Department of Education, 2008b). As you might guess, some young children who are identified as eligible to receive special education have significant special needs that were identified at a very early age, including physical and sensory disabilities, intellectual disabilities, or autism. However, many young children with disabilities who receive services have milder needs, typically related to language development or motor skills. Because it is often impossible to determine the exact nature of young children's special needs, they may receive services through the IDEA general disability category termed *developmentally delayed.*

### Students Not Specifically Included in IDEA

As you read about the students who receive special education, have you stopped to think about the students whom you might have assumed would be mentioned but who have not been? Because special education as defined through IDEA is available only to the students with one or more of the thirteen disabilities mentioned earlier, some students needing special supports receive them through other means.

**Students Who Are Gifted or Talented.** One group you have not read about is students who are gifted or talented. IDEA does not provide for special education for these students. In fact, although forty-six states define *giftedness,* only eight states mandate education of these students while at the same time providing full funding for it; eight states neither mandate nor fund gifted education; and the remainder of the states have some combination of mandates and partial funding (Davidson Institute for Talent Development, 2009). What are the provisions in your state for students who are gifted or talented? In Chapter Fifteen, you will read more about the characteristics of these students and instructional approaches recommended for them.

It is important to note, too, that some students with disabilities also are gifted or talented, and these students are sometimes referred to as *twice exceptional* or as having *dual exceptionalities* (Johnsen & Kendrick, 2005). These students need a combination of services: They are entitled to special education, related services, and supplementary aids and services to address their disabilities, but they also need enrichment and encouragement to develop their gifts and talents. These students also are discussed in Chapter Fifteen.

**Students with Attention Deficit–Hyperactivity Disorder.** A second group of students not addressed directly in IDEA comprises students with attention deficit–hyperactivity disorder (ADHD) (Mrug, Hoza, & Gerdes, 2009). ADHD is not, by itself, a disability category. Many students with ADHD receive support through the broader provisions of Section 504, introduced earlier in this chapter, and this assistance is largely the responsibility of general education teachers. However, some may receive special education services when identified as *other health impaired (OHI).* Because so many students now are categorized as having ADHD, you will have the opportunity to learn more about this disorder in Chapter Six.

*Many students have diverse learning needs, but these are not necessarily disabilities.*

**Students at Risk for School Failure.** One additional group of students not eligible for services through IDEA is important to mention: students who often are referred to as being *at risk* (O'Connor, Hill, & Robinson, 2009). These students may be homeless, abuse drugs or other substances, live in poverty, or have any of hundreds of other characteristics that can negatively affect their learning. Although students with disabilities also may have these risk factors, the presence of these risk factors alone does not constitute disability. These students need the attention of caring and skillful teachers who can set high expectations, teach in a way that maximizes student potential, and instill in students the love of learning (Miller, 2006). As you work in schools, you are likely to hear professionals mention that a particular student should be in special education but is not eligible. Often they are referring to a student at risk. Students at risk probably need many types of supports and services, but they do not have disabilities and are not eligible for special education.

## REVIEW · REFLECT · DISCUSS

1. Think about the students you plan to teach. Which disabilities might they have? Are these disability labels helpful in thinking about the most effective ways for teaching them? Why? Why not?

2. What do you think is the responsibility of school professionals for supporting students with special needs but who do not have disabilities? Who should provide this support?

## Recommended Practices for Special Education

Although the core legal principles of the special education field have not changed in many years, practices and priorities have. In the following sections, some of the most significant and far-reaching practices that characterize special education today are outlined. As you read subsequent chapters, you also will notice that examples of these practices are highlighted in special sections of each chapter and in boxed features.

### Inclusive Practices and Access to the General Curriculum

No topic related to special education has had as wide an impact or caused as much controversy as inclusion. Even though the term *inclusion* appears nowhere in federal legislation governing the education of students with disabilities, it has been the subject of endless discussion. In this era when pressure is greater than ever before for most students with disabilities to access the general curriculum and reach the same standards as typical learners, the importance of inclusion has continued to grow (Friend & Shamberger, 2008).

#### Definitions and Debates

Many definitions of inclusion have emerged, most focusing on placing students with disabilities in general education settings. However, this book adopts a slightly different view, one emphasizing that **inclusion** is a belief system shared by every member of a school as a learning community—teachers, administrators, other staff members, students, and parents—about the responsibility of educating all students so that they reach their potential. Although the physical location of students in schools and classrooms is one dimension of inclusiveness, inclusion is not about where students sit as much as it is about how adults and classmates welcome all students to access learning and recognize that the diversity of learners in today's schools dictates that no single approach is appropriate for all. Inclusion encompasses students who are gifted and talented, those who are at risk for failure because of their life circumstances, those with disabilities, and those who are average learners. Likewise, it includes all the teachers and other staff members who work in today's schools.

Some would argue that the only way a school can truly demonstrate an inclusive belief system is to place nearly every student in general education full time (Artiles, Harris-Murri, & Rostenberg, 2006; Schwarz, 2007). They point out that public education has two curricula. The first curriculum is *explicit;* that is, it is the curriculum that guides the instruction of typical learners,

research
NOTE

Dyson (2005) found that kindergarten children tend to conceptualize *disability* in terms of physical abilities and that they generally are positive toward people with disabilities; however, only half of the children in the study identified a classmate with a disability as a friend.

PEARSON
**myeducationlab**

Go to the Building Teaching Skills and Dispositions section of Topic 18: Early Intervention, in the MyEducationLab for your course and complete the activity entitled "Making Accommodations and Modifications to Promote Inclusive Practices."

and advocates argue that it cannot truly be accessed by students with disabilities unless they fully participate in general education. The second curriculum is *implicit* and includes social interactions and skills that are best learned with typical peers; again, advocates stress that students with disabilities must be with peers to access this curriculum. These professionals insist that competent teachers, adequate supports and services, and a strong commitment can guarantee any student's success without the need for a separate location.

However, some individuals have grave reservations about the part of inclusive practices related to students being educated in general education classes with typical peers (e.g., Connor & Ferri, 2006; Kauffman, 2005). Some parents fear that their children will be teased or that they will learn inappropriate behaviors in general education settings. They express concern that their children's special needs cannot be met adequately in a general education classroom. Some professionals question whether the general education setting truly can be the least restrictive environment for some pupils, particularly when general education teachers also must meet the needs of twenty, thirty, or even more other students in the class, the pacing of instruction is brisk, and the availability of a special education teacher to provide support may be limited. These professionals suggest that many students need a smaller class size, a higher degree of structure, specialized instructional methods, and, for some, a curriculum that emphasizes life skills that can be delivered most readily in a special education classroom for part or most of the school day.

## Research on Inclusive Practices

Most professionals fall somewhere between these two extremes in their thinking about inclusion (Frattura & Capper, 2006). They strongly support inclusive practices and access to general education for most students. However, they acknowledge that unless careful attention is paid to administrative understanding and support, teacher preparation and commitment, and pragmatic details (such as time for planning and schedules), caution must be advised (e.g., Burstein, Sears, Wilcoxen, Cabello, & Spagna, 2004; Friend & Shamberger, 2008). Research supports these ideas. For example, Praisner (2003) surveyed elementary school principals about their attitudes toward inclusion. She found that only one in five was positive about inclusive practices and that the others were uncertain. In schools in which principals were positive, students were more likely to be educated in less restrictive ways. In a study of teacher attitudes, McLeskey, Waldron, So, Swanson, and Loveland (2001) found that teachers in inclusive schools were more positive toward teachers' roles in inclusion and toward the impact of inclusion than teachers in other schools. Sindelar, Shearer, Yendol-Hoppey, and Liebert (2006) found that inclusive practices were not sustained when school leadership changed, teacher turnover occurred, and emphasis on the assessment of achievement increased.

Of course, any discussion of inclusion needs to examine the impact on students, and these studies generally examine academic achievement and social interactions in general education settings. Many students feel stigmatized when they as assigned to special education settings (Connor, 2006). Some elementary students with significant disabilities have been found to have greater success when they receive their education with their peers, particularly in terms of their social relations and friendships with peers (Meyer, 2001). Older students with intellectual disabilities may realize some academic benefits, but they may remain socially isolated (Doré, Dion, Wagner, & Brunet, 2002).

The picture of academic achievement for students with disabilities is complex and incomplete. For example, Waldron and McLeskey (1998) studied students with learning disabilities (LD). They found that students with mild learning disabilities educated with peers made greater academic gains than did comparable students in special education classes but that the progress of students with severe learning disabilities was the same in both settings. Similarly, Key (2000) found that high school students with disabilities participating in an English class increased their academic achievement. Keefe and Moore (2004) reported that teachers who were interviewed reported higher student achievement in their inclusive classrooms. However, few researchers have been able to directly and meaningfully address the matter of academic achievement of students with disabilities when they are educated in gen-

## How Inclusive Is Your School?

Even though you may not yet have experienced working in a school, you can begin thinking about what it takes to create and sustain inclusive practices. This checklist contains many of the core thinking and practices that characterize inclusive schools.

_____ Do staff members believe that all students truly belong at the school and that the students are the responsibility of everyone who works there?

_____ Have teachers and other staff members recognized that working toward an inclusive environment continues each year—that the process does not end?

_____ Have teachers had opportunities to discuss their concerns about student needs, and have steps been taken to address these concerns?

_____ Has planning to meet all students' needs included classroom teachers, special education teachers, other support staff, administrators, parents, and students?

_____ Have the high expectations for students with special needs who are to be integrated into classrooms been clarified for teachers?

_____ Have shared planning time and possibly shared instructional time been arranged for teams of teachers?

_____ Have staff members received adequate professional development on topics such as collaboration, behavior supports, and instructional interventions?

_____ Are staff members comfortable working collaboratively?

_____ Have start-up resources been allocated for inclusive practices?

_____ Have steps been taken to ensure that teachers will be rewarded for experimentation and innovation, even if efforts are sometimes not successful?

_____ Have students had opportunities to learn about all types of diversity, including individuals with disabilities?

_____ Have parents and families of students with and without disabilities been involved in the development, implementation, and evaluation of the school's inclusive services?

_____ Has a plan been developed for carefully monitoring the impact on student outcomes of approaches for meeting student diversity? Does this plan include strategies for revisions?

_____ Have teachers and other staff identified benchmarks so that they have attainable goals to celebrate after one year? Two years? Three years?

eral education settings (e.g., Idol, 2006). This may be the case because many factors influence the impact of inclusive practices on student outcomes, including the special educator's knowledge of academic content areas, collaboration between teachers, the use of instructional strategies demonstrated through research to be effective, and the emphasis placed on high-stakes testing related to the No Child Left Behind Act (e.g., Scruggs, Mastropieri, & McDuffie, 2007).

The research just described and many other similar studies illustrate that, in today's schools, what is considered inclusive practice varies widely depending on the clarity of state and local policies related to inclusion, the resources available to foster such practices, teacher and administrator understanding and commitment, and parent and community support (Boscardin, 2005; McLeskey & Waldron, 2007). In some schools, inclusive practices are exemplary, and teachers and specialists demonstrate daily how diverse groups of students can learn together and still have their special needs met. In other schools, the term _inclusion_ is used, but the corresponding practices are not in place. The Professional Edge lists items that contribute to inclusive schooling, and you can use it as a way to reflect on inclusive practices at your school or in schools you have visited. What have been your personal experiences related to inclusion? How prepared do you think schools are to welcome and appropriately educate the entire range of diverse learners?

### Inclusive Practices in This Textbook

This discussion of inclusion is intended to help you understand the approach that is taken in this textbook. The viewpoint is that inclusive schools are possible and necessary for twenty-first-century education. This does not mean that every student is educated with peers at all times, but it does mean that the responsibility of discovering effective means for all students to learn together is taken very seriously, and deviations from this approach are made with reluctance and only after careful deliberation. When a decision is reached for any type of separate education, it is based on data about the student's academic and behavior needs, it is monitored carefully to ensure that the cost of this decision to the student is worth

web link

The Council for Exceptional Children (www.cec.sped.org) is the professional organization of teachers, administrators, parents, and other individuals interested in the education of students with disabilities.

the benefit the student is receiving, it is reviewed and revised based on changing needs rather than rigidly scheduled for an entire school year, and it is premised on the goal of reducing the separate service as soon as possible.

## Accountable and Accessible Instruction

Inclusion involves contemporary means of achieving the ultimate end of special education: providing high-quality instruction so that students can reach their potential (Idol, 2006; McLeskey & Waldron, 2007). In today's schools, that instruction is characterized by being more accountable than ever before. For example, IDEA requires that special educators monitor and report their students' progress as often as other students receive progress reports or report cards, usually at least four times during the school year (Wright & Wright, 2005). This approach helps to ensure that students with disabilities are making progress in reaching their educational goals and reaching curriculum standards, and if they are not, it serves as a mechanism for alerting professionals and parents of the need to make changes. Another example of accountability is seen in the IDEA provision that all students with disabilities participate in assessments with necessary accommodations or through alternate assessments (Hyatt, 2007) and that their scores be reported along with those of other students.

### Universal Design for Learning

Instructional accountability and accessibility also is seen in the current emphasis on students' curriculum. Although in the past professionals generally thought that many students with disabilities should have unique curricula designed for their special needs, they now advocate that nearly all students with disabilities should learn from the same curriculum as that used by typical learners, with accommodations or adjustments made as necessary. This logic complements the principles of inclusion: If the goal of education is for students to be successful adults who can live, work, and play in our society, then the way to accomplish this is to ensure that all students have access to the same core learning, beginning as soon as they enter school (Acrey, Johnstone, & Milligan, 2005). If curriculum is not the same, students with disabilities are placed at a disadvantage.

The instructional approach for accomplishing the complex task of ensuring that students with disabilities access curriculum is called **universal design for learning (UDL)**, sometimes also referred to as *universal design for instruction (UDI)*. Universal design originated in the field of architecture, where professionals realized that when access to buildings for people with disabilities was arranged after the building was completed (i.e., retrofitting), the result was often a poorly placed elevator or an awkward or unsightly ramp. However, if access was integrated in the original building design, it could become a seamless part of the structure, often adding to its beauty and enjoyed by many more people than those with disabilities. Applied to education, UDL says that teachers should design instruction from the beginning to meet a wide range of learner diversity rather than try to retrofit, or make adjustments, after they already have created their lessons (Pisha & Stahl, 2005; Jimenez, Graf, & Rose, 2007). If teachers do this, they usually find that most students can benefit from their efforts. Although UDL concepts were first applied to the use of technology to facilitate learning for students with disabilities (e.g., access to learning through means other than print), IDEA now incorporates UDL as it relates to materials, instruction, and assessment (McGuire, Scott, & Shaw, 2006). Elizabeth, whom you met at the beginning of this chapter, is a student for whom UDL is essential. Her teachers are continually examining how they can make the learning that occurs in the first-grade classroom accessible for her.

*Just as universal design in architecture calls for ramps so people can access buildings, universal design in education calls for differentiated instruction so students can access learning.*

## Ways to Differentiate Instruction

Many options can be found to differentiate instruction for students with disabilities and other special needs. How could you apply the following ideas to students like Elizabeth, Andrew, and Daniel, the students you met at the beginning of this chapter?

### Differentiating Based on Content

- Assess students' knowledge prior to instruction so that those who already understand key concepts can be given alternative tasks and those who lack even background knowledge can be readied for the core instruction.
- Select just two or three key concepts to emphasize with students with significant intellectual disabilities from among the twenty that other students are learning.

### Differentiating Based on Process

- Teach all students how to use a Venn diagram to describe how characters in a short story are both similar and different. Students practice using stories of varying levels of difficulty in terms of reading level and character complexity.

- Provide manipulatives or calculators to some students while others complete the math assignment without these tools.

### Differentiating Based on Product

- Offer options for students to demonstrate their knowledge of the novel they just read: Some students make a poster that would advertise the novel if it were made into a major motion picture, some create an alternative ending to the story, and some complete Internet research about the period in history in which the novel occurred.
- Create several ways for students to respond during tests: Some students write essays, some students dictate their answers, and some students make lists of bullet points.

Differentiation can occur in literally thousands of ways. Your challenge as an educator, regardless of the students you teach, is to find those approaches that will have the most positive impact on your students' learning outcomes.

## Differentiated Instruction

One way to operationalize the concept of universal design for learning or instruction is through *differentiation*—the notion that changes can be made in many different aspects of the teaching/learning process to enable diverse student learning needs to be met (King-Sears, 2008). The concept of differentiation originated in the area of gifted education, but it also is employed by special education teachers in their separate classrooms as well as by general and special educators working in inclusive schools. For example, think about the learning environment and how it could be changed to address the needs of different students. Juan, an English language learner, needs to focus his attention as he works on his assignment, and so he uses a cardboard divider on top of his desk to block out visual distractions. Margaret completes her work comfortably slouched in a beanbag chair, while Scott spreads out his materials at a table in the back of the classroom. When the teacher leads instruction, she makes sure that she explains concepts, shows them through the use of pictures or demonstrations, and also has students learn using their bodies (e.g., tracing letters in the air, rapping about the characters in *Hamlet*). The Instruction in Action provides one structure for thinking about differentiated instruction. How does this information apply to the instruction that you will be responsible for providing?

## Evidence-Based Practices

IDEA and the No Child Left Behind Act of 2001 which is the current reauthorization of the Elementary and Secondary Education Act of 1965 (ESEA), (discussed later in this chapter) require that educators use *evidence-based practices* (Council for Exceptional Children, 2006). This means that they must make decisions about what to teach to their students and determine how effective that teaching/learning process has been based on data that they gather. They also must teach using programs, interventions, strategies, and activities that have been demonstrated through research to be effective. Thus, evidence-based practices form a third critical aspect of accountable and accessible instruction. Reading instruction provides a clear example of the use of practices based in research. Many perspectives have been offered on how children learn to read, but not all of them have a research base. For struggling readers, one strongly evidence-based approach is called *direct instruction* (DI). First developed in the 1960s, DI has been demonstrated by decades of research to be effective in helping children, adolescents, and adults learn to read through a fast-paced, highly structured series of lessons (Magliaro, Lockee, & Burton, 2005). DI is considered an evidence-based practice, the first of many such practices you will read about as you progress through this textbook

**web link**

At the IDEA Partnership website (www.ideapartnership.org/ebp2.cfm?ebppageid=5), you can find collections of reports on evidence-based practices.

**research NOTE**

Research on teaching reading has expanded to include students with significant intellectual disabilities. Browder, Ahlgrim-Delzell, Courtade, Gibbs, and Flowers (2008) found that these students could learn early literacy skills that are the basis for later reading fluency.

## Instructional and Assistive Technology Options for Students with Disabilities

As you read this summary of some of the categories of assistive technology devices your students may use, keep in mind how powerful technology can be for facilitating student success and how you, as a professional educator, can integrate it into instruction.

*Technology to assist students with disabilities is common in schools*

| Category | Explanation | Examples | Category | Explanation | Examples |
|---|---|---|---|---|---|
| Sensory enhancers | · Help students with vision or hearing loss access their environments | · Text magnifier<br>· Scanner with speech synthesizer<br>· Communication board | Motivational devices | · Encourage students to interact with their environment | · Spinner operated with a large button switch<br>· Stuffed animal that plays music when squeezed |
| Keyboard adaptations and emulators | · Alternative to standard computer keyboard | · Joystick<br>· Light pen<br>· Touch screen<br>· Touch-sensitive keyboard pad | Mobility devices | · Assist students to get around the school and participate in student activities | · Self-propelled walker<br>· Manual or powered wheelchair<br>· White-tipped cane used by individuals who are blind |
| Environmental controls and manipulators | · Modify operation of a device to facilitate use | · Switch controlled by breath<br>· Telephone with voice dialing<br>· TTY (text telephone) | Self care aids | · Facilitate hygiene and other personal functions | · Adapted eating utensils<br>· Toothbrush with easy-to-grip handle |
| Instructional uses of technology | · Software that facilitates learning | · Software to practice math facts<br>· Computerized remedial reading instructional programs | | | |

*Source:* Virginia Assistive Technology System. (2007). *Assistive technology in the student's Individualized Education Program: A handbook for parents and school personnel.* Retrieved April 9, 2009 from http://www.vats.org/downloads/ATHandbook-rp.doc.

### Assistive Technology

A final dimension of accountable and accessible instruction is the use of instructional and **assistive technology**: the devices, equipment, and services that improve the learning and functional capabilities of students with disabilities (Parette, & Peterson-Karlan, 2007). Many students with disabilities use instructional and assistive technology to facilitate learning. Technology may be low-tech (e.g., a grip to help a student hold a pencil), mid-tech (e.g., an audio recorder used during a class lecture), or high-tech (e.g., an electronic communication board that "talks" for the student when various buttons are pushed). IDEA requires that students have access to the instructional and assistive technology they need. That is, technology must be a significant consideration as a supplementary aid or service, and students' technology needs must be assessed. Appropriate devices need to be provided and the student must be taught how to use them. With each passing year, the technology available to facilitate learning grows exponentially. As you work in schools, you probably will see students using a wide array of such technology. In the Technology Notes, you can begin to learn about the range of instructional and assistive technology available to students.

## Setting Classroom Expectations

For students with disabilities and other special needs, how you state and implement classroom rules can be crucial. Here are some suggestions for creating classroom expectations that are clear, positive, and constructive:

- Phrase rules concisely and in the students' language and post them in a prominent place for frequent review.
- State rules in positive terms (e.g., "Work at your desk" rather than "Don't leave your seat").
- Follow the rules of firmness, fairness, and consistency.
- Discuss negative consequences for breaking rules, rewards for appropriate behavior, and the reasons why classroom rules exist.
- Administer, as promptly as possible, previously agreed-upon rewards and negative consequences.

- Respond to misbehavior in a quiet, slow voice.
- Refrain from becoming visibly irritated to avoid compromising the effect of any consequences.
- Face students when talking to them, as facial expressions will teach students to use and understand proper body language.
- Avoid being trapped into arguments, as this is a no-win situation.

How does each of these suggestions for implementation foster positive behavior in all students?

Source: Duhaney, L. M. G. (2003). A practical approach to managing the behaviors to students with ADD. *Intervention in School and Clinic, 38,* 267–279. Copyright © 2003 by Pro-Ed, Inc. Reprinted by permission of SAGE Publications.

## Positive Behavior Supports

Some students with disabilities have behaviors that are so disruptive or dysfunctional that they interfere with the students' abilities to be with and learn alongside their peers. For example, a student who has difficulty transitioning from one activity to another, like Andrew, the student with autism you met at the beginning of this chapter, might express his frustration by pushing classmates. Too often in the past, such behaviors were addressed through some type of negative consequence, such as taking away computer time or sending the student to the office.

Current practices are very different. Now, professionals use **positive behavior supports** (Chitiyo & Wheeler, 2009). First, they establish schoolwide and classroom standards for behavior so that students understand expectations; examples of such standards are presented in the Positive Behavior Supports. Then, if a problem occurs, they look at student behaviors in the context of the situation in which they occurred, carefully defining what is happening in order to design ways to reduce the negative behavior, increase desired behavior, and help the student have a better academic and social quality of life.

In the example of the student who pushes others, professionals would meet to analyze this serious problem, and once it is better understood, they might then try to prevent some of the student's frustration by ensuring that the work the student is assigned is not too difficult. They might also teach the student a better way to express frustration—perhaps by teaching the student to say "Help me" and rewarding the student for appropriate or acceptable behavior. They would work closely with the family, as well, designing a behavior program with parents so that there could be consistency between the school and home approaches. You will find out more about positive behavior supports and other contemporary practices for responding to student behaviors in Chapter Seven when you learn about students with emotional disabilities.

## Collaboration

Inclusive schools that address diverse student instructional and behavior needs rely on professionals and parents working closely with each other (Cook & Friend, 2010). Not surprisingly, collaboration has become a crucial dimension to the planning, delivery, and evaluation of special education and related services that encompass all of the ideas introduced in this section.

**Collaboration** refers to the way in which professionals interact with each other and with parents or family members as they work together to educate students with disabilities. It concerns the quality of their professional relationships—for example, whether they work as partners in their efforts or whether one or another assumes control while others

research
### NOTE

Baltodano, Harris, and Rutherford (2005) studied nearly 200 adolescents in a long-term youth correctional facility. They found that approximately 30 percent of the youth were eligible for special education services but that academic achievement for the entire group, although lower than average, was not as low as other studies had reported.

acquiesce. Collaboration never exists as a goal in and of itself: It is the means for achieving other goals.

Examples of situations calling for collaboration are almost limitless in today's schools (Friend & Cook, 2010). For example, professionals must work closely with parents and family members, and they may be asked to participate on teams that include teachers and other school personnel (e.g., a speech/language pathologist) as well as representatives from agencies outside the school (e.g., a social worker or representative from the juvenile justice system). In addition, general education and special education teachers or other professionals can work together in general education classrooms instructing all of their students by *coteaching*, a special form of collaboration discussed in detail in Chapter Four. Which of these examples of collaboration might help Daniel, the student you met at the beginning of the chapter, to achieve his goal of earning a high school diploma?

Simply put, the days are gone when an individual could enter the field of education just to work with students. Now a significant part of school professionals' jobs, no matter the setting or type of position, pertains to interacting effectively with other adults. There is too much to know and too much work to be done to have each professional functioning in isolation—to succeed and help students succeed takes the partnership of collaboration.

## REVIEW · REFLECT · DISCUSS

1. Based on your own school experiences, information you have read, and discussions you have had with others, what is your opinion of inclusion? What is the basis for your opinion? How will inclusion affect you as an educator?

2. How do high-quality instruction, assistive technology, positive behavior supports, and collaboration support inclusion?

# Parent and Family Perspectives Regarding Their Children with Disabilities

Parents—including natural, adoptive, and foster parents and guardians and other individuals acting in the parent role—are the strongest advocates that children with disabilities have (Rodgers, 2007). For example, as far back as 1874, a parent went to court to argue that her child with an intellectual disability had a right to be educated in a public school. The courts at that time believed that a free education for all children was not meant to include those thought to be incapable of being educated and ruled against her. Since that time, parents and other advocates have been instrumental in working for the rights of students with disabilities through organizations such as the Council for Exceptional Children, the Arc (formerly called the Association for Retarded Citizens), the United Cerebral Palsy Association (UCP), and hundreds of other disability-specific groups (e.g., the National Association for Down Syndrome). These parents have been instrumental in guaranteeing that their children receive a high-quality education. They have lobbied for strong legislation to protect the rights of their children, and they have taken their cause to court when they believed those rights were not being upheld.

## Parents and Their Children with Disabilities

Entire books have been written, thousands of studies have been conducted, and whole courses have been taught on the relationships of parents and other family members with their children with disabilities. A fairly straightforward conclusion can be drawn from this significant work: Parents and family members see their children primarily as children for whom a disability is only one small part of who they are; they do not make a disability the overriding characteristic of their children. Robert and Timothy and their parents illustrate this point. Robert is highly gifted in a traditional way; he excels in school, and he is a talented pianist. Timothy is gifted, too. He is gregarious and usually surrounded by a set of friends; he is also a star on his Little League baseball team. Robert and Timothy are twins, and their parents have carefully helped each boy to reach his potential and to be proud of his accomplishments. Little attention is paid on a day-to-day basis to the fact that Timothy has an intellectual disability. After a visitor who did not know the boys had listened to Robert play a complex piece of piano music, she asked Timothy what he was really good at. Timothy demonstrated his strong, positive self-concept when he said, "Baseball. I play a million times better than Robert."

Although much has been written about the stress of raising a child with a disability (e.g., Lustig, 2002), professionals increasingly are recognizing that parents and family members also experience positive effects. For example, Taunt and Hastings (2002) interviewed and surveyed 47 parents of children with developmental disabilities. They found that parents reported these positive outcomes of having a child with a disability:

- Positive characteristics of the child, such as a happy disposition
- A changed perspective on life, including not taking things for granted, valuing other people more, and appreciating life
- Increased tolerance of others, sensitivity to others, and patience
- Opportunities to learn about children, disability, self, and other areas
- Improved family dynamics, with the family spending more time together
- Opportunities to meet and share with others and to influence policy makers

To a professional educator, this understanding of positive outcomes is especially important because there is a tendency among school personnel to most often contact parents about problems. If you reflect on the strengths of families of children with disabilities, you will find that you can build strong working relationships with them—relationships based on a multidimensional understanding of your students.

## Parent Participation in Special Education

Parent participation is essential in special education. Research strongly supports the fact that when parents of students with disabilities actively participate in their children's schooling, achievement is higher and fewer behavior problems occur (Salend, 2006). However, it is well recognized that school–home partnerships have not always been easy to build.

### Barriers to Parent Participation

Many factors contribute to parents' occasional reluctance to participate actively in their children's education. For example, time is a critical issue for many parents. Often both parents work, and one or both may have a second job; they have other children who need attention and elderly parents to care for; and they have to manage the innumerable details of supporting their families. They simply may not be able to attend a meeting school professionals schedule at 3:45 P.M. next Thursday or at 7:30 A.M. on Friday.

Many other barriers also exist for families from diverse backgrounds (Matuszny, Banda, & Coleman, 2007). Some families face language barriers in interacting with school professionals; others may lack transportation. Some families, including those of migrant workers, move frequently; thus, developing a close working relationship with a teacher is unlikely. Some parents may be unfamiliar with the customs of U.S. schools or are uncomfortable with them. They also may find teachers and administrators insensitive to their needs.

### Strategies to Encourage Parent Participation

Teachers are well intentioned. They want to welcome parents to school and encourage their participation. Muscott (2002) recommends that you follow these four principles to create school–home partnerships:

1. Use family-centered practices. Emphasize family strengths, not weaknesses, and family choice about services. Think about how you can support the entire family in your interactions, not only one child with special needs.
2. Respect the unique characteristics of each family. Often the most straightforward way to find out what a family needs is to ask. It may be tempting to think that you know what a family is like because you learned about their culture in a course or workshop. That is a common mistake. Remember that no single set of traits can be assigned to any family. Each is different.

**PEARSON**
**myeducationlab**

Go to the Assignments and Activities section of Topic 3: Parents and Families, in the MyEducationLab for your course and complete the activity entitled *Parent Participation in Special Education*.

3. Recognize that families have different understandings of their children's special needs. Whatever your role in the school, your job is not to convince family members that their child has a certain disability or to help them be "realistic." Rather, you are to provide exemplary services and offer assistance to the family, whatever their perception of their child.

4. Match your strategies and resources to family preferences. If you truly understand the first three principles, then this will seem logical. Giving a single parent with several children a book on interventions and advice for using them at home is a strategy that will likely fail. Asking that parent what her concerns and priorities are for her child and offering one specific idea for addressing them will likely be more effective.

Throughout this book, you will learn more about parents of children with disabilities and how you can effectively work with them. Much more than words can convey, parents are your partners in educating your students.

> ## REVIEW · REFLECT · DISCUSS
>
> 1. As a professional educator, what are your responsibilities related to working with the parents and family members of children with disabilities? What ideas do you have for forging strong, positive working relationships with them?

## Trends and Issues Influencing Special Education

You already have learned that special education is a constantly evolving field. Not surprisingly, the rapid pace of change is accompanied by debate over critical concerns. As you read this book, you will learn about many of the most important issues facing the field of special education. Two issues that have particularly widespread implications are (1) the impact of federal education legislation on students with disabilities and (2) the efforts underway to better determine which students need special education.

### No Child Left Behind Act of 2001

You probably have already learned about the **No Child Left Behind Act of 2001** (NCLB, P.L. 107-110). This federal law, the most current reauthorization of the Elementary and Secondary Act of 1965 which provides significant funding for public education, began a sweeping set of education reforms intended to improve the academic achievement of all students, including those with disabilities and other special needs. The law addresses several critical areas (Education Commission of the States, 2004):

1. All students each year in grades three through eight and once in grades ten through twelve are assessed in the areas of reading and math to determine their progress and achievement. Students also must be assessed periodically in the area of science. The results of these assessments must be made available to parents, legislators, and the community and must be reported in a way that allows states to demonstrate overall achievement trends but also to identify gaps in learning that may exist with certain subgroups of students, including, for example, those with disabilities and those who live in poverty.

2. Students for whom English is not their first language must be assessed using tests written in English after they have received three consecutive years of instruction in U.S. schools. A few students are entitled to an additional two years of instruction before this requirement is implemented.

3. By the end of the 2013–2014 school year, schools are required to demonstrate that all their students are academically proficient as measured on a standard assessment or through alternate assessment (allowed primarily for students with significant intellectual disabilities). Each state has gradually increasing yearly targets for student achievement, called *adequate yearly progress (AYP)*, to ensure that this goal can be met.

PEARSON
**myeducationlab**

Go to the Assignments and Activities section of Topic 1: The Law, Least Restrictive Environment, and IEPs, in the MyEducationLab for your course and complete the activity entitled "No Child Left Behind".

4.  Schools in high-poverty areas that fail for two years in a row to make adequate yearly progress are subject to sanctions, including offering tutoring to students, filing a plan for improvement, allowing students to transfer to other schools, and accepting technical assistance from the state. If student achievement does not improve after four years, students may be entitled to transfer to other schools, and additional sanctions may occur.

5.  All students must be taught by highly qualified teachers, and each state is required to set specific criteria by which teacher qualifications are documented. As a teacher candidate, you are directly affected by this element of NCLB.

NCLB includes many other provisions. Some relate to ensuring that schools are safe and drug free. The law also addresses other important matters, including a more flexible use of federal funds for many education programs and services (but not those related to special education).

### NCLB and Students with Disabilities

For students with disabilities and the professionals who work with them, the most significant provision of NCLB pertains to accountability—specifically, the requirement that all schools make adequate yearly progress (AYP) toward the goal of 100 percent student proficiency in reading and math by the year 2014 (Hardman & Dawson, 2008). Data related to AYP are reported by race, ethnicity, and disability, and other indicators, and the implication is that most students with disabilities are expected to reach the same academic achievement goals as other students; if they do not, the schools they attend may face remedial action. Unlike in the past and consistent with the accountability movement discussed earlier in this chapter, most students with disabilities are not exempt from taking the yearly achievement tests on which judgments about progress are made. Only a few students with significant disabilities may take an alternative, functional assessment, and even this is to be aligned with the standards that other students must meet. As you work in schools, you will find that even more than IDEA, NCLB is creating pressure for students' educational goals and objectives to be based on the general education curriculum and for students to access instruction in general education classrooms.

NCLB raises many questions for professionals (Roellke & Rice, 2008): How are academic standards being set and measured, and are the expectations that most students with disabilities be held to these standards reasonable? What are the most effective means for ensuring that students with disabilities can master the curriculum so that they make adequate yearly progress? What if school districts cannot find enough highly qualified special education teachers, especially for urban and other high-need areas? Clearly, questions related to this critical education law will be asked for years to come, and decisions about the application of the law to the field of special education and students with disabilities will be made as policies are created and clarified or as litigation occurs.

## Special Education Eligibility

You learned earlier in this chapter that concern has existed for many years regarding possible bias against some students, especially those who are African American, when decisions are made regarding whether they have disabilities (Skiba et al, 2008). This issue leads to a crucial question: Who should receive special education services? This question does not pertain to students whose disabilities are readily apparent and can directly be assessed—for example, students with hearing or vision loss or those with significant intellectual or physical needs. Instead, it relates to students who might have learning disabilities, mild intellectual disabilities, or emotional/behavior disabilities because determining whether these disabilities exist often includes making judgments about the student's needs.

The apparent bias in deciding who should be called disabled sometimes is just that—deliberate or unintentional discrimination against some students. But it also may pertain to the fact that many students, especially those living in poverty, come to school already at a disadvantage because of their life circumstances and their struggles end up being called disabilities. It also may relate to the fact that some caring educators want to provide help to students such as these who struggle, and they see special education as a way to provide that help, even if they should find other options. No matter why this problem is occurring, a priority in IDEA is addressing this complex issue (USDE, 2009).

**Response to Intervention as a Potential Solution.** A provision in IDEA describes a new approach to determining whether a student who is struggling in school should be labeled as having a disability, and this approach may be contributing to the recent decline in the number of students with a learning disability or an intellectual disability (U.S. Department of Education, 2008a). In **response to intervention** (RTI), when a teacher raises concern about a student who is struggling, a data-based system of increasingly intense interventions is put in place and carefully tracked to see if it might be possible to accelerate the student's learning in order to avoid the need for special education (Berkeley et al., 2009). Using strategies and programs that have been demonstrated through research to be effective in helping students learn, teachers, reading and math specialists, and other professionals make every effort to find the key to unlock the student's potential. If ongoing data collection indicates the student is gradually catching up to peers, professionals know that the student does not have a disability. If in spite of their best efforts they find the student is not making enough progress to eventually catch up, then the professionals may begin the formal procedure of determining whether the student has a disability.

RTI, described in IDEA for determining whether a student has a learning disability, also is being utilized to address serious student behavior issues (McIntosh, Campbell, & Carter, 2009). Regardless of use, its overall goal is to try to effectively address student learning or behavior issues as soon as they occur, rather than delaying until formal assessment procedures indicate that a disability exists. In this way, it is anticipated that some students who might otherwise have been labeled as disabled will instead succeed without the need for that serious, potentially stigmatizing, and possibly inappropriate determination. RTI has many important dimensions, and as you read this textbook, you will learn more about this promising approach.

## REVIEW · REFLECT · DISCUSS

1. What parts of NCLB do you think are especially valuable for students with disabilities? What parts do you think are the most challenging? Discuss with your classmates the pros and cons of setting the same achievement expectations for most students with disabilities as those set for typical learners.

2. Why do you think some students have been possibly misidentified as needing special education services? Why is this such a serious issue?

## Summary

- Special education has three parts: (a) specially designed instruction that meets the needs of students with disabilities, (b) related services, and (c) supplementary aids and services.
- Today's special education is the culmination of efforts by researchers, professionals, parents, and legislators that began prior to the nineteenth century, grew significantly in the United States during the early part of the twentieth century, was questioned and changed as a civil rights issue, and today is guided by federal law (Individuals with Disabilities Education Act) and interpreted by litigation.
- IDEA encompasses six key principles: (a) zero reject, (b) free appropriate public education (FAPE), (c) least re-

strictive environment (LRE), (d) nondiscriminatory evaluation, (e) parent and family rights, and (f) procedural safeguards .
- Section 504 and the Americans with Disabilities Act are additional laws that influence special education.
- IDEA specifies thirteen disabilities that may qualify children, birth through twenty-one years of age, to receive special education: specific learning disabilities, speech or language impairments, mental retardation, emotional disturbance, other health impairments, autism, orthopedic impairments, hearing impairments, visual impairments, deaf/blindness, traumatic brain injury, multiple disabilities, and developmental delays.

- Special education is characterized by inclusive practices, accountable and accessible instruction, positive behavior supports, and collaboration.
- The parents and families of students with disabilities have been their strongest advocates, and their efforts have greatly influenced the field.
- Significant issues shaping special education include the impact of the No Child Left Behind Act of 2001 and initiatives to ensure that only students who truly have disabilities are given that label.

## Council for Exceptional Children — ADDRESSING THE PROFESSIONAL STANDARDS

Council for Exceptional Children (CEC) Common Core Knowledge and Skills addressed in this chapter:

ICC1K1, ICC1K2, ICC1K4, ICC1K5, ICC1K6, ICC1K8, ICC4S4, ICC5K2, ICC5S1, ICC5S3, ICC5S10, ICC7S1, ICC7S9, ICC8S2, ICC9K4, ICC9S5, ICC10K1, ICC10K4, ICC10S1, ICC10S4

Appendix: Provides a full listing of the CEC Common Core Standards, and associated Knowledge and Skill Statements listed here.

## PEARSON myeducationlab

Now go to Topic 1: Law, LRE & IEPs in the MyEducationLab (www.myeducationlab.com) for your course, where you can:

- Find learning outcomes for the broad concepts covered in this chapter along with the national standards that connect to these outcomes.
- Complete Assignments and Activities that can help you more deeply understand the chapter content.
- Examine challenging situations presented in the IRIS Center Resources.
- Apply and practice your understanding of the core concepts and skills identified in the chapter with the Building Teaching Skills and Dispositions learning units.

- Check your comprehension on the content covered in the chapter by going to the Study Plan in the Book Specific Resources for your text. Here you will be able to take a chapter quiz, receive feedback on your answers, and then access Review, Practice, and Enrichment activities to enhance your understanding of chapter content.
- Watch video clips of CCSSO Teacher of the Year award winners responding to the question: "Why I teach?" in the Teacher Talk section.

## chapter two

# The Personnel and Procedures of Special Education

## LEARNING OBJECTIVES

- Describe the roles and responsibilities of the special educators, related services professionals, general education teachers, and other individuals who contribute to the education of students with disabilities.

- Outline the steps that must be followed in order to determine whether a student should receive special education, from a teacher's first awareness that a problem exists through eligibility determination and reviews of the student's educational plan.

- Clarify the purpose of an individualized education program (IEP), and specify the information it must contain.

- Describe the range of services that students with disabilities may access.

- Discuss the options for resolving serious disagreements between school professionals and parents of children with disabilities regarding special education services.

- Outline issues related to special education professionals and procedures.

## Anthony

Anthony is in first grade. His teacher is very concerned about his readiness to learn new skills. Even though Anthony's kindergarten teacher used the district-adopted, highly structured reading and language arts programs (called a *tier 1 intervention*), Anthony struggled to learn his letters and their sounds. During the spring, as classmates made rapid strides in reading and writing, Anthony continued to confuse similar sounds and seemed unable to understand that reading was about attaching meaning to the printed word. Toward the end of the year, Anthony participated in a reading tutorial program (called a *tier 2 intervention*) delivered for 30 minutes three times per week by a specially trained paraprofessional. This year, Anthony is being taught by the school reading specialist for 45 minutes each day using a highly structured, phonics-based reading program (called a *tier 3 intervention*). The team of professionals tracking Anthony's progress and collaborating with his parents concerning his reading difficulties plans to meet at the end of the first grading period to determine the effectiveness of this very intense reading program. If it is found effective, the team may decide to continue it until Anthony's reading skills approach those of his peers. If the reading program is not found effective, the team will consider whether Anthony should be assessed further to determine his eligibility to receive special education services.

## Brianna

Brianna has received special education services since she was a toddler. She uses a wheelchair because she has a physical disability affecting her ability to walk, and she has a mild intellectual disability. She is an outgoing eighth-grade student who attends most classes with her typical peers. She receives assistance from a resource teacher for one class period each day, weekly speech/language therapy, and weekly occupational therapy. She also receives adaptive physical education, but this occurs as she participates in that class with her peers. At this year's meeting to update her individualized education program (IEP), Brianna is going to take a lead role. She has worked with her special education teacher and her mother to learn how to describe her current level of learning, both her strengths and her needs; to state the goals that she has for the next year; and to ask questions about any part of the information being presented that she does not understand. She is a little nervous but also is excited to be treated almost like an adult for this meeting and to have a role in planning her future.

## William

William is in tenth grade. He knows he is at a crossroads, but he is not sure about what to do with his life. Since third grade he has been educated in a self-contained class for students with emotional and behavior disabilities; his opinion is that he never has been able to learn to control his anger and that's why he's there. He despises being called a "retard" by other students—that is the name most kids use for students in any special education class. He has good friends who are already well-established gang members and while he so far has not formally affiliated with the gang, he feels pressured by his friends to join while his grandmother, his legal guardian, pressures him to stay in school and away from gang members. William has had several arrests for misdemeanor crimes, but those are in his juvenile record and so they don't worry him too much. He comes to school about half the time, and his special education teacher, Mr. Powell, has encouraged him to enroll in the new credit recovery program. Mr. Powell is convinced William is bright and has great potential and still has the option to graduate on time with his classmates. William knows Mr. Powell is making extra effort to connect with him, arranging to meet him after school and to help him find job possibilities. But William just doesn't know which path he'll take.

In Chapter One you were introduced to the complex and exciting world of special education. You learned about the development of the field, laws that mandate services for students with disabilities, the students who receive those services, and key issues facing professionals. However, you probably were left with many questions about special education. This chapter provides answers to some of those questions. It overviews the roles and responsibilities of various professionals involved in designing and delivering students' educational programs. It also describes the required procedures that educators follow to determine if a student can receive special education services, and it clarifies the range of services a student with disabilities might receive.

Whether you plan to be a special education teacher or a general education teacher, a school administrator or a teaching assistant, or a professional providing a related service (e.g., counseling, psychological services, speech/language therapy), if you work in a public school setting, you undoubtedly will work closely with other professionals as well as parents and family members on behalf of students with disabilities. Further, you will participate in and perhaps lead meetings at which critical decisions are made regarding whether a student is eligible to receive special education services, what those services should include, whether to continue those services, and how to prepare a student to transition from school into adulthood. The greater your understanding of all the professionals involved in special education and the procedures that must be followed for students to receive those services, the better prepared you will be to make a positive contribution.

## The Professionals Who Work in Special Education

To check your comprehension on the content covered in Chapter 2, go to the Book Specific Resources in the MyEducationLab (www.myeducationlab.com) for your course, select your text, and complete the Study Plan. Here you will be able to take a chapter quiz, receive feedback on your answers, and then access review, practice, and enrichment activities to enhance your understanding of chapter content.

If you think about the broad range of needs of students with disabilities, you will not be surprised to learn that many professionals are involved in providing special education and related services. Some of these individuals work directly with students, some are involved mostly in determining whether a student has a disability, and others offer indirect support.

### Special Education Teachers

**Special education teachers** are the professionals who provide day-to-day instruction and other support for students with disabilities. However, their roles and responsibilities vary considerably (Echaore-McDavid, 2006). They must be highly qualified as established in the No Child Left Behind Act (NCLB) and the Individuals with Disabilities Education Act (IDEA), and if they teach core academic content from the general curriculum (for example, a section of ninth-grade English just for students with disabilities), they usually must be highly qualified in that subject area. Depending on the teacher licensure regulations in their states, these teachers may work with students with only one type of disability (e.g., students with autism), or they may work with students with varying disabilities (e.g., students with mild disabilities, including those with learning disabilities, emotional disabilities, or mild intellectual disabilities). In addition to providing instruction that may be remedial (reteaching), developmental (teaching based on the student's functional learning level), or strategic (teaching tool skills to help the student succeed), special education teachers typically also may prepare materials adapted to meet students' special needs, assess and report student progress in learning, and manage students' overall education programs. Increasingly, special education teachers work in general education classrooms at least part of each day, but they also may work in special education settings such as resource rooms, self-contained classrooms, and separate schools. A special educator who travels from school to school, which is common in rural areas and for those who teach students who have sensory disabilities, sometimes is called an *itinerant special education teacher*.

### Bilingual Special Educator

Students who have disabilities and whose first language is not English sometimes receive their special education services from a **bilingual special education teacher**—that is, a professional who is knowledgeable about both bilingual education and special education. Such a teacher usually has special training in (1) knowledge of language proficiency, (2) appropriate assessment tools and techniques, (3) cultural and linguistic diversity, (4) effective delivery of instruction, and (5) professionalism for working with colleagues, families, and community members (Rodriguez, 2005). Although bilingual special educators are not found in all school districts, where they are available they can provide the dual set of services that some students need.

### Early Childhood Special Educator

Professionals who work with infants, toddlers, and young children with disabilities (ages birth to five years) are called **early childhood special educators** or sometimes *early interventionists*. Generally, they are expected to have knowledge about a wide range of disabilities because distinguishing among young children's specific special needs—particularly for those with speech/language, intellectual, or behavior concerns—often is not possible in early childhood special education programs. These professionals may visit children's homes; teach in a special class that may be housed at a special center or in an elementary school; or work with preschool, kindergarten, or Head Start teachers in general education settings.

### Adapted Physical Educator

Some students with disabilities—like Brianna, described at the beginning of the chapter—cannot safely or successfully participate in a standard physical education program, and they rely on a professional who can adapt exercises, games, and other activities (Akuffo & Hodge, 2008). This professional, an **adapted physical educator**, sometimes works directly with students with disabilities, either during a general physical education class or in a separate special class. However, they also may consult with other physical educators so that those professionals can appropriately address the needs of their students with disabilities. In some school districts, physical educators receive professional development and assist in providing this service to students with disabilities.

## Related Services Professionals

You learned in Chapter One that IDEA mandates both special education and related services (Churchill, Mulholland, & Cepello, 2008). The following sections describe the professionals who provide related services to students with disabilities who are most likely to work with you.

### Speech/Language Pathologist

Many students with disabilities have special needs related to speech or language, and the professionals who diagnose such needs, design interventions to address them, deliver the services, and monitor student progress are called **speech/language pathologists** (Sunderland, 2004). For example, if a kindergarten student is having difficulty correctly making certain sounds (e.g., "wabbit" for "rabbit") or a sixth-grade student cannot form sentences, a speech/language pathologist is likely to provide speech/language therapy. However, speech/language pathologists also have other roles. They may assist students who are deaf or hard of hearing to learn American Sign Language or use their residual hearing to best advantage, and they may teach students who do not have the ability to speak other ways to communicate (e.g., using pictures or a computer system). They may assist students with significant disabilities to learn functional tasks like swallowing and controlling tongue movements.

### School Psychologist

**School psychologists** are professionals who are licensed to administer intelligence tests and other assessments used in determining whether a student is eligible to receive special education services; they also are responsible for communicating this information to parents (Agresta, 2004). In addition, school psychologists are experts in understanding students' social and emotional needs. They often work with other professionals and families to design interventions to help students learn social skills and appropriate behavior. In some school districts, school psychologists work directly with students; in others, they consult with

dimensions of
**DIVERSITY**

In the 100 largest school districts for which data were available, approximately 47 percent of students received free or reduced lunch, 12 percent were identified as having disabilities, and 12 percent were English language learners (ELLs) (National Center for Education Statistics, 2009).

http://www.cec.sped.org/Content/NavigationMenu/ProfessionalDevelopment/CareerCenter/JobProfiles/default.htm
The Career Center at the Council for Exceptional Children website provides profiles of many career paths mentioned in this chapter.

*A speech/language pathologist is a related services professional who assists students in developing their language and other communication-related skills.*

teachers and other professionals who implement the interventions they have recommended to assist particular students.

### School Counselor

Most of the professionals described thus far work primarily with students experiencing difficulties in school and their parents. However, **school counselors** are professionals who work with all students, including those with disabilities, and they generally are considered the problem solvers of a school (Baumberger & Harper, 2007). They may work with individual students to address personal problems; they may conduct lessons for an entire class of students to resolve issues in peer relationships; and they may assist students with disabilities in accessing appropriate high school courses, in locating the right college or university to attend, or in finding a part-time job. School counselors are found in nearly all high schools and middle schools; whether they are assigned to elementary schools depends on state and local practices.

### School Social Worker

As you learn more about the field of special education and students with exceptional needs, you will find that in addition to the instruction and support offered by school personnel, an array of services is available outside of schools. **School social workers** are the professionals who coordinate the efforts of educators, families, and outside agency personnel to ensure that students receive all the supports they need. For example, a school social worker may contact a family when a student has been truant repeatedly, and if the problem persists, this professional will contact the appropriate social agency to ensure that the student's attendance improves (Allen-Meares, 2007). Social workers also might help a family in great need to access charitable organizations that can provide clothing and food or to arrange for counseling. Like school counselors, school social workers often have responsibilities for all the students in a school who need their services, not just those with disabilities.

### School Nurse

The **school nurse** is another professional who usually is responsible for all the students in a school. The school nurse screens children in the areas of vision and hearing, ensures that all students' immunization records are on file, provides routine assistance for students who are ill, educates students about health topics, and manages the distribution of any medications students may take (Bigby, 2004). For students with disabilities, the school nurse also may be called on to interpret medical information, to serve as a liaison between the family physician and school personnel, and to educate staff about medically related issues.

### Educational Interpreter

Some students who are deaf or significantly hard of hearing have an **educational interpreter**—a professional who listens to the words being spoken in school and then translates them into sign language (Seal, 2004). These professionals have to understand the field of deafness and the likely needs of students who are deaf. They also have to be familiar with all aspects of the entire school curriculum. Of course, interpreters provide this service to students accurately and unobtrusively within the general or special education setting as well as during activities such as physical education, art, and assemblies.

### Occupational Therapist

An **occupational therapist** helps students gain independence in school and the community by teaching functional and other living skills such as grasping a pencil, cutting with scissors, buttoning and zipping clothes, and tying shoe laces (Swinth, Chandler, & Hanft, 2004). This individual also might help students learn to feed themselves, wash their faces, use a computer, or cook their own meals. They also are likely to assist students to learn problem-solving and decision-making skills. Occupational therapists often are called upon to determine whether students need adapted equipment (e.g., a spoon with a thick handle; a modified computer keyboard) and to instruct students on how to use such equipment.

### Physical Therapist

If a student's disability affects ability to move, a **physical therapist** might provide services (National Clearinghouse for Careers in Special Education, 2009). This professional deals with students' muscle strength and flexibility, mobility, posture, and positioning (e.g., helping a student sit up in a wheelchair or stand for a while each day to improve circulation). They may help students maintain or improve the use of their large muscles, and they may work with them to increase balance and coordination, such as when students walk using crutches or braces. Physical therapists also may be involved in decisions about the type of wheelchair or other equipment that would best meet students' needs.

## Others Who Work in Special Education

Although special education teachers and key related services personnel provide most of the interventions that students with disabilities receive, several other groups of individuals play pivotal roles in special education.

### General Education Teacher

In the twenty-first century, any discussion of the professionals who work in special education would not be complete without highlighting the role of the general education teacher. More than ever before, students with disabilities receive part or all of their instruction in elementary, middle, and high school classrooms, which makes general education teachers integral members of the special education team (Griffin, Kilgore, & Winn, 2008). They are the professionals who are knowledgeable about the expectations of the curriculum for the grade level or course, they are the ones usually responsible for implementing universal design for learning (UDL) practices that enable their diverse learners to succeed, and they manage the social environment of the typical classroom. Collaboration between general education and special education teachers is critical for student learning.

### Paraeducator

**Paraeducators**—also called *paraprofessionals, teaching assistants, instructional assistants, one-to-one assistants,* and *aides* (although this last term is no longer preferred)—are educators who work under the direction of a teacher or another school professional to help in the delivery of services for students with disabilities (Ghere & York-Barr, 2007). Paraeducators can be assigned a wide variety of tasks, depending on state regulations and local policies. They might tutor a student who is learning to read; accompany a student with an emotional disability from class to class to provide structure and prevent inappropriate behaviors; or serve as a student's personal assistant, pushing a student's wheelchair and helping the student with eating and other personal care activities. Paraeducators work under the direction of professionals who tell them what needs to be done and how to work with students. You will learn more about the roles and responsibilities of paraeducators and your interactions with them in Chapter Four.

### Parents

Of all the individuals with whom you interact on behalf of your students with disabilities, no one is more important than the students' parents or the individuals who serve in that role (e.g., grandmother or grandfather, guardian, foster parents) (Fish, 2008; Harry, 2008). It is the students' parents who have their best interests at heart in a way that no one else can, it is they who advocate for their children no matter the issue, and it is they who can tell you about your students' lives outside the world of school. One of the most important lessons you can learn as a professional educator is to listen carefully, without judgment, to your

**web link**

http://seriweb.com
Special Education Resources on the Internet (SERI) is a collection of Internet-accessible information for those involved in special education and related areas. General information and detailed listings related to a wide variety of disabilities are included.

**WANDRAE** *is a single mother who is also completing college, majoring in accounting and business information systems. She has three children, including Kedric, who is eight years old and identified as having autism. Wandrae has played an active role in his education.*

Kedric is very outgoing; he is always happy, always smiling. My favorite story about him is about how he always took things literally. One time we were driving in the car and he asked, "Can we go to McDonald's?" I told him, "Mommy's *broke—* we can't go." Later that day, we stopped at the ATM. As soon as we got back in the car he said, "Mommy, now you're *fixed,* so can we go to McDonald's now?"

He was almost three years old before I knew what was wrong. He wasn't talking; he wasn't potty trained. He didn't like how the carpet felt on his feet, so he would walk on his toes so he didn't have to touch it. I had some testing done, and he was identified as autistic and started in preschool special education. Once he was in preschool, he suddenly started talking—and reading and writing and everything all at once. He could just look at things and memorize them.

In kindergarten, some people didn't think he could be autistic because he was so smart. He was in a special education class because the other class was too much stimulation, and I worked with the district to change his classroom. In first grade, he was in a regular first-grade classroom, and I had to decide about him taking medication because of aggressive behavior. I was against medication at first but talked with the special education coordinator about it, and we decided to try it. He takes Risperdal—and since then he has been doing really, really well.

I've worked closely with the people at school for Kedric. Like in kindergarten, he kept getting sent to the office for behavior—and the principal's office had all kinds of little knick-knacks and stuffed animals that Kedric loved to play with. So pretty soon, he was misbehaving so he could go play with the toys in the principal's office! Then they started letting him go to the computer lab—they were trying to help him, but he loves computers, too, and he just kept misbehaving. There he would be in the computer lab, typing away, as happy as he could be—instead of being in his class. He was really pulling something on his teacher, and I had to work with her so she would be firm with him. Now I always tell the teachers to let me know if there are any problems.

I've done a lot of research. I figure even if we can't solve all the problems, it helps if I know what is going on. Academically, he's doing really well in school now. He reads everything. He gets especially good grades in math. He got a C+ last year in English, and he was afraid that I was going to be angry with him because his brother, who usually gets all A's, had gotten a C and I had talked to him about it. But I told Kedric how proud I was of him, how hard he worked to earn that C+.

Kedric and his sister are really, really close. Kedric recently got interested in video games because she was interested in video games, and now he and his brother and sister really like to play those games. Kedric's also playing basketball and jogging, and he just had a great soccer season. Soccer is really good for him; it's teaching him to follow directions and to be around other kids.

I just want to say to everyone that almost anything is possible. At the college, I noticed in class that there was a person who was a little different. I suddenly realized that he was my Kedric, all grown up. I tutored him because some of the professors and other students treated him . . . not right. You know, I have a son like that, and someday I hope someone will help my son out, too. And if I have to be there when he's in college, helping him, tutoring him, I will. Kids can do things if they just get the chance.

students' parents and take into account their perspectives on their children's strengths and needs. In the Firsthand Account feature, you can read one parent's perspective on her role in the education of her son.

### Additional Service Providers

This description of individuals who contribute to the work of special education still is not complete. Several other professionals—some with very specialized areas of expertise, whom you may meet only when a student has a particularly unique need—also may contribute to a student's education (e.g., National Clearinghouse for Professions in Special Education, 2009; Dole, 2004; Echaore-McDavid, 2006). Examples of these service providers include the following:

- *Rehabilitation counselor.* This professional helps students, often through special education transition planning, to find and keep appropriate employment upon high school completion. Rehabilitation counselors usually work in a community agency setting.
- *Art or music therapist.* This therapist assists students who are better able to understand their special needs or begin to cope with them through the use of art or music.
- *Orientation and mobility specialist.* This specialist assists students with visual impairments to gain independence by teaching them how to move about confidently in the classroom, the school, and the community.
- *Audiologist.* An audiologist, an expert in diagnosing problems related to hearing and the ear (e.g., loss of balance because of inner-ear problems), may provide services to assess

hearing loss and determine whether it can be addressed with the use of a hearing aid or other device or strategies.

- *Inclusion facilitator.* This individual ensures that students with disabilities receive the supports and services they need to succeed in a general education setting. The inclusion facilitator also answers teachers' questions about working with specific students and helps teachers access resources to foster inclusive practices.
- *Language interpreter.* A language interpreter might be employed to facilitate communication with the student and his or her family in schools with many students whose native language is not English.
- *Special education administrator.* The special education administrator has the responsibility, in many school districts, of ensuring that all the policies and practices related to special education are carried out appropriately.
- *Technology specialist.* A technology specialist is responsible for evaluating whether a student with a disability needs technology support and, if so, what types of support. This is an emerging school position not yet found in all school districts.
- *Therapeutic recreation specialist.* This professional, often working through a community agency or hospital, assists students and families to use recreational activities to improve students' functioning and independence. This specialist may attend IEP meetings to explain services and support family priorities in this domain.
- *Psychometrist or educational diagnostician.* This professional, in some locales, completes the individual assessment of students for special education. The psychometrist or educational diagnostician is specifically trained to administer and interpret tests, but does not have the broad set of skills of a school psychologist.

## REVIEW · REFLECT · DISCUSS

1. Which of the professional roles described in this section were already familiar to you? Which were not? What do you think might be the greatest challenges that occur because so many different professionals contribute to the education of students with disabilities?

2. With which other professionals in special education do you anticipate working most closely? What are questions you still have about the responsibilities of those professionals? How could you learn more about their roles?

# Determining Student Eligibility for Special Education Services

A small percentage of students with disabilities are identified when they are very young. These children often have significant physical or sensory (vision or hearing) disabilities, an intellectual disability (that is, mental retardation), autism, or developmental delays. Brianna, whose story you read at the beginning of the chapter, is an example of a student who began receiving special education services at a very young age. Most students, though, begin school just like their peers, and they are identified as having disabilities only after they experience extraordinary difficulties in school. As a school professional, you have a responsibility to thoroughly understand what happens from the time someone expresses concern about a student struggling in school through the steps of assessment and identification of the student as eligible for special education along with the procedures in place to review the education programs of students with disabilities. This process is outlined in Figure 2.1 and explained in more detail in following sections.

### Initial Consideration of Student Problems

Parents sometimes raise questions about their child's classroom performance, but general education teachers are the professionals most likely to express concern about a student that

PEARSON
**myeducationlab**
Go to the Assignments and Activities section of Topic 5, Assessment Practices, in the MyEducationLab for your course and complete the activity entitled "Assessment for Special Education".

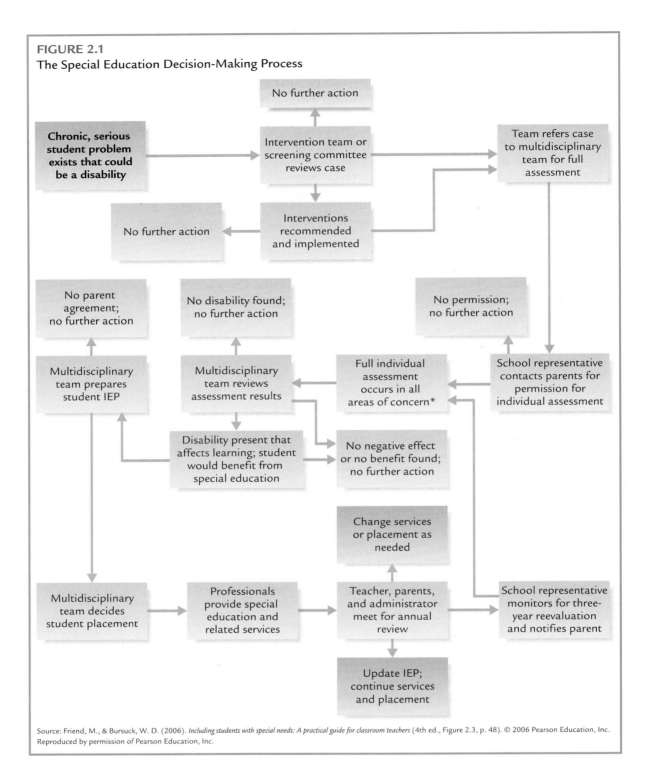

**FIGURE 2.1**
The Special Education Decision-Making Process

No further action

Chronic, serious student problem exists that could be a disability

Intervention team or screening committee reviews case

Team refers case to multidisciplinary team for full assessment

No further action

Interventions recommended and implemented

No parent agreement; no further action

No disability found; no further action

No permission; no further action

Multidisciplinary team prepares student IEP

Multidisciplinary team reviews assessment results

Full individual assessment occurs in all areas of concern*

School representative contacts parents for permission for individual assessment

Disability present that affects learning; student would benefit from special education

No negative effect or no benefit found; no further action

Change services or placement as needed

Multidisciplinary team decides student placement

Professionals provide special education and related services

Teacher, parents, and administrator meet for annual review

School representative monitors for three-year reevaluation and notifies parent

Update IEP; continue services and placement

Source: Friend, M., & Bursuck, W. D. (2006). *Including students with special needs: A practical guide for classroom teachers* (4th ed., Figure 2.3, p. 48). © 2006 Pearson Education, Inc. Reproduced by permission of Pearson Education, Inc.

begins the process of deciding whether that student is entitled to special education services. Usually, the teacher carefully thinks through what the problem might be, tries several strategies to address the problem, discusses the student informally with other teachers and administrators to help determine the seriousness of the situation, and contacts the parents to discover their view of what is occurring (Friend & Bursuck, 2009). The teacher also is likely to gather data to document the concern, including keeping samples of the student's work or keeping a log of behavior incidents that occur in the classroom.

## Intervention Assistance

What if these informal approaches fail to address the teacher's concern for the student? In some states, the next step the teacher takes is to request that the case be reviewed by a team of professionals. These teams have several different names, depending on state and local policy—**teacher assistance team, intervention assistance team,** *student assistance team,* and *instructional consultation team* are a few common ones (Buck, Polloway, Smith-Thomas, & Cook, 2003). The professionals designated to serve on these teams also vary: Some teams are composed exclusively or primarily of general education teachers; some include at least one special education teacher; and some include those two professionals in addition to related services professionals such as the school nurse and the speech/language pathologist. Regardless of the team's name or composition, its goals are to help the teacher problem solve regarding the student, to generate new ideas for helping the student, to consider various explanations for the noted problems, and to prevent—if possible—the need for special education (Prasse, 2006). IDEA now permits school districts to use a portion of their special education funding to provide extra support for such struggling students with this goal of reducing special education referrals in mind.

These teams generally have very precise procedures. For example, the general education teacher usually completes a brief form that provides the team with information about the nature of the concern and the strategies already implemented to help the student. At the team meeting, a specific agenda is followed to discuss the problem, generate some new ideas for intervention, and help the teacher decide which ideas might be effectively implemented. The team also assigns responsibilities for gathering additional information as needed and assisting the teacher in documenting intervention effectiveness. A date is set to review whether the intervention is working and to decide what to do next. Anthony, the first-grader you met in the chapter introduction, might be a student discussed by an intervention assistance team.

## Response to Intervention and Three-Tiered Approaches

The traditional team process for addressing teacher concerns about struggling students is in the midst of a significant change. Specifically, a new option for addressing serious student learning problems that might indicate the presence of a learning disability was approved in the 2004 reauthorization of IDEA. Based on concern that the traditional approach for addressing student learning problems tended to delay systematic and intensive attention to them until the second, third, or even fourth grade or later (Fuchs, Mock, Morgan, & Young, 2003), states now either require or permit alternative systems based on response to instructional interventions (Yell, Katisyannis, & Ryan, 2008; Zirkel & Krohn, 2008). This approach, called **response to intervention (RTI)** (and sometimes *response to instruction*), has two main purposes (Kavale & Spaulding, 2008):

1. To ensure that students receive research-proven remediation and other supports as soon as they are identified as having academic difficulties, even in kindergarten, rather than waiting until the academic gap has grown significantly
2. To ensure that professionals gather high-quality data to document the effectiveness of the remedial strategies that have been implemented

These data, gathered as an ongoing part of instruction, may be used (sometimes in lieu of traditional formal assessment data, discussed later in this chapter) to determine whether a student has a learning disability. This feature of RTI—that is, the ongoing use of data to determine whether a student is responding to the interventions being implemented—is referred to as **continuous progress monitoring.**

RTI usually is based on what is called a **three-tiered approach** to intervention (What Works Clearinghouse, 2009); the experience of Anthony, introduced at the beginning of this chapter, illustrates this approach. Tier 1 is used most often with reading but is sometimes applied to math or behavior concerns, and it generally refers to using research-based approaches for all students so that high-quality instruction is ensured. Students for whom continuous progress monitoring indicates ongoing difficulty despite this instruction move

Go to the Assignments and Activities section of Topic 5, Assessment Practices, in the MyEducationLab for your course and complete the activity entitled "Types of Assessment".

---

dimensions of
**DIVERSITY**

Ortiz, Wilkinson, Robertson-Courtney, and Kushner (2006) reported that English language learners often struggle academically and that teachers could benefit from intervention assistance team support in understanding how to better meet these students' needs.

Although most response to intervention (RTI) research has been conducted in elementary schools, at least some high schools are implementing these increasingly intense instructional procedures as a way to assist struggling learners at that level (Samuels, 2009).

## Understanding Response to Intervention

Although you will learn more about RTI in Chapter Five, you should begin familiarizing yourself with its potential because it is changing the way professionals think about special education eligibility and procedures (Barnett, Daly, Jones, & Lentz, 2004).

### Resources for Exploring RTI

Many resources are available to help you grow in your understanding of RTI. The following websites provide further explanation of the approach and tools for implementing it:

- RTI Wire (www.jimwrightonline.com/php/rti/rti_wire .php)

    This website includes a brief explanation of RTI. It also includes dozens of links to materials related to using RTI, including interventions related to reading, math, and behavior; tools for recording data related to students' re-

sponses to specific instruction; and research-based interventions that might be part of an RTI model.

- National Center on Response to Intervention (RTI) (http://www.rti4success.org/). This U.S. Department of Education-sponsored website has as its goal increasing the capacity of states and districts to effectively implement RTI procedures. It includes a wide variety of materials and a discussion forum, and it includes information on the implementation of RTI with English language learners.

- Wrightslaw (www.wrightslaw.com/info/rti.index.htm)

    The RTI page at this site provides a clear and concise explanation of RTI requirements in the law as well as parent- and family-friendly links to learning more about it.

---

Go to the Assignments and Activities section of Topic 5, Assessment Practices, in the MyEducationLab for your course and complete the activity entitled "Progress Monitoring".

---

to the next tier. Tier 2 generally involves small-group instruction several times each week using more intensive instructional strategies and other supports, such as peer tutoring. The small number of students who still do not respond positively to this more intense instruction after a specified period of time are identified for additional services. Tier 3 is the most intensive level, usually involving one-to-one instruction or small-group instruction outside the classroom. In some systems, tier 3 may include deciding that a student needs special education, a decision-making process that may incorporate some or all of the assessment procedures described later in this chapter. In other systems, tier 3 occurs prior to consideration for special education.

Response to intervention and three-tiered approaches are addressed in more detail in Chapter Five, since they pertain primarily to students who may be identified as having learning disabilities. In the Instruction in Action, however, you can find resources to help you learn more about this new way of thinking for addressing student learning and behavior difficulties.

### Screening

In the few states that do not have a mandated intervention assistance team or response to intervention (RTI) process, some type of screening still must occur when a student is experiencing extraordinary difficulties in school. The school psychologist, the counselor, the principal, or another professional has the responsibility of meeting with the general education teacher(s) to discuss the nature (what is the problem that is occurring?), severity (how intense is the problem?), and persistence (for how long has the problem existed?) of the student's difficulty. This professional also reviews existing information about the student, including report card grades, achievement test scores, examples of classroom work, attendance records, and any other documentation that can clarify the student's past and present performance and inform a decision about whether special education might need to be considered.

### *Special Education Referral and Assessment*

If the intervention assistance team's discussion, response to intervention, or screening process leads to the consensus that a student's difficulties are serious enough that special education should be considered, the student is referred for a full assessment as required by IDEA before any services can be provided. At this point, a **multidisciplinary team** convenes for that purpose. The team may include some of the same team members as the intervention assistance team (e.g., the school psychologist) but not others (e.g., the team usually in-

---

**fyi**

The traditional approach to identifying learning disabilities, which relies on a significant discrepancy existing between ability and achievement, has been criticized as a "wait to fail" approach; RTI is intended to address this criticism.

cludes the student's general education teacher but not several teachers from different grades or departments, as is the case for prereferral or RTI teams); parents also are members of this team. These members and their contributions are described in the section on individualized education programs (IEPs).

When an RTI system is in place, data gathered about the student's academic performance may be integral to this process. These data also may, based on state policies, be used as the primary information in making a decision about the need for special education services, and so the steps described in the following section related to formal assessment may be modified or bypassed.

## Parents' Rights

Before discussing the details of the special education eligibility determination process, it is important to elaborate on the discussion from Chapter One about the rights of parents on behalf of their children in all aspects of special education, beginning at the very first step of student assessment. Parents have these rights:

- To request and give permission for individual testing of their child. IDEA explicitly states that no individual assessment carried out to decide whether a student needs special education can occur without this approval. If the parents disagree with the evaluation results from school, they may seek an independent evaluation.
- To be meaningfully informed, in writing, about the procedures of special education and parent rights, including all procedural safeguards and the way to seek an evaluation of their child that is independent of the school district's evaluation.
- To have their child tested in the language the child knows best. This may include providing an interpreter for a student who is deaf or a test in braille for a student who is blind as well as the administration of tests in the child's primary language.
- To be full members of the team that decides what services a student should get, how often, and how much. Parents must voluntarily approve these decisions. In addition, they may request a review of the IEP at any time, and they may withdraw consent at any time.
- To have their children receive a free appropriate public education. *Free* is defined as at no cost to the parents or student, except for the usual fees associated with attending school. *Appropriate* means the student's educational plan must be tailored to specific needs.
- To have their child educated in the least restrictive environment—that is, to the maximum extent possible with nondisabled peers.
- To be notified in writing whenever the school proposes any of the following: a reevaluation, a change in the student's placement, a decision not to evaluate their child, or a decision not to change a disputed placement.
- To (a) informal dispute resolution, (b) mediation, and (c) an impartial hearing in instances in which a significant disagreement occurs, as long as the request is made within 2 years of the situation at issue. You will learn more about all of these procedures later in this chapter.
- To have access to their child's education records within 45 days of a formal request, to request changes in information they perceive to be inaccurate, and to give permission for anyone other than those working directly with the child to access the student's records.
- To be kept informed of their child's progress at least as often as are parents of other students.

Does it seem as though parents are given many rights? In fact, they are and that is deliberate. If you recall that for most of the twentieth century students were denied their educational rights, it is clear that IDEA is crafted to ensure that such inequities do not happen again.

## Assessment Components

IDEA does not describe the specific domains in which students suspected of having disabilities should be assessed. However, the law does state that students must be evaluated to determine their strengths and also to explore any area of functioning in which a disability

research
**NOTE**

Mothers of children with disabilities reported that teachers' authentic caring about children and parents, clear and frequent communication, and knowledge about children's disabilities significantly affected the level of trust they felt toward these educators (Angell, Stoner, & Sheldon, 2009).

is suspected. For many students, then, the assessment addresses these areas (Pierangelo & Guiliani, 2008):

- *Vision and hearing screening.* If not completed before a formal referral occurs, the school nurse usually checks to be sure that a student's learning difficulties are not the result of a vision or hearing problem. If screening indicates a need in this area, the student's family is referred to the appropriate medical specialist before other types of assessment are undertaken.
- *Intellectual ability.* A student's intellectual ability usually is assessed with an intelligence test, a type of assessment that can only be given by professionals with special training (i.e., a school psychologist or psychometrist). This measure informs the team about the student's capacity to learn.
- *Achievement.* Students who are being assessed to determine eligibility to receive special education services usually complete an individual achievement test. This test might be administered by the school psychologist or psychometrist, a special education teacher, or another professional. This assessment component helps the team to determine the student's present level of learning in school. The results of an individual achievement test are used instead of scores the student may have earned on a group achievement test because the former is likely to be a more accurate estimate of the student's learning than the latter. In RTI systems, the data from the three tiers of intervention would be used for this purpose.
- *Social and behavioral functioning.* Succeeding in school is not only about ability and achievement. Another critical area is how students manage their interactions with peers and adults. Using checklists, questionnaires completed by teachers and parents, observations, and other approaches, the team considers whether a student's social skills or behaviors are part of a suspected disability.
- *Developmental history.* Professionals often are assisted in understanding a student's special needs by learning about the family background as well as any developmental delays, illnesses, or injuries the student experienced as a young child. This information often is obtained by a social worker who may visit the family in their home and request that they complete an inventory covering these topics.
- *Other areas as needed.* Depending on the difficulties the student is experiencing and the suspected areas of disability, other assessments also may be completed. For example, Jasmine's first language is French and her speech is very difficult to understand. Her evaluation would include a specialized assessment completed by a speech/language pathologist. For any student who has been referred by general education teachers, those professionals' input is sought: They might contribute student work samples, complete a social skills inventory, report anecdotal observations, or recount discussions with parents, and the information may cut across the domains just described.

### Assessment Procedures

As you read the chapters in this textbook that describe the disabilities students may have, you will learn more about the specific types of assessments employed to determine whether the disability exists and the procedures used for each. For all assessments, though, IDEA clearly outlines general procedures that must be followed so that the evaluation is nondiscriminatory—that is, accurate and fair (Figueroa & Newsome, 2006). First, any assessment instrument used must be *valid* (i.e., it must measure what it is supposed to measure) and *reliable* (i.e., it must have consistency), and it must be free of racial or cultural bias. Second, the instrument must be administered by a professional trained to do so, and that professional must carefully follow the test's directions. Third, any instrument used must take into account the possible impact of the suspected disability (Cumming, 2008). For example, if a student with limited fine-motor skills is asked to write a response, that response is unlikely to really represent what the student knows because the disability area (motor skill) interferes with the performance.

In addition, if a student's primary language is not English, testing must be completed in the language with which the student is most comfortable to ensure that a language difference is not inadvertently labeled a disability (Pierangelo & Guiliani, 2008). Further, no single test can be used to determine whether a student is eligible for special education. Multiple measures must be used to help the team decide on appropriate services, and several different professionals must be involved in assessment and decision making. Further, if a student transfers to another district during assessment, the sending and receiving districts must coordinate their efforts.

As you can see, many safeguards are in place regarding the assessment of students for possible special education placement. For each of the safeguards just described, what might happen to particular students if it was ignored?

*Part of the process for determining whether a student is eligible to receive special education is an individualized assessment that addresses all areas of potential need.*

## Decision Making for Special Education

Within 60 days of parent consent for evaluation and after a student's comprehensive assessment has been completed, the multidisciplinary team meets to make three critical decisions: (1) whether the student has a disability, (2) whether the disability adversely affects educational performance, and (3) whether the student's needs can be addressed through special education.

For the first decision, the team members review all the data gathered to decide whether the student has one of the disabilities addressed by IDEA. The criteria for making this decision are set by each state based on the disability definitions included in IDEA, but the decision must be made based on the collective judgment of team members, considering all the information gathered and not relying solely on exact test scores. For example, suppose a team is deciding whether a student has an intellectual disability: In most states, the student's intelligence (IQ) test score needs to be below 70 and accompanied by significant difficulties in managing day-to-day tasks. However, a student with a test score of 68 who can make friends, play in the neighborhood, and ride a public bus alone to go shopping might not be identified as disabled. A judgment must be made. The team reviewing the assessment data also must take into account two other factors. If the student's school difficulties are the result of limited English proficiency or a lack of appropriate instruction (Yell & Drasgow, 2007), assistance is needed but a disability probably does not exist.

If the team determines the student has a disability, the second decision to be made is whether the disability is adversely affecting the student's education. This usually is the case—but not always. For example, Shana might have a medical condition that clearly represents a disability, but the condition is controlled with medication that has no significant side effects. Shana has a disability and steps may need to be taken to ensure she takes her medication during the school day, but she does not need special education.

The third decision made by the team is whether the student is eligible to receive special education and related services and can benefit from these services. Usually, if the student has a disability and it is affecting learning, services will be provided based on assessed need—special education, related services, and supplementary aids and services.

All of the decisions just outlined typically are made at a single meeting, and the student's parents participate in making these decisions (Yell, 2006). In addition, they may contribute additional information or evaluation results concerning their child. Consistent with the protection of parent rights, if the student does not have a disability affecting learning, or is not eligible for services, the team must notify the parents of this fact.

### Preparing the IEP

If team members decide that a student is eligible for special education, they then prepare an **individualized education program (IEP).** This document summarizes all the information gathered concerning the student, sets the expectations of what the student will learn over the next year, and prescribes the types and amounts of special services the student will receive (Gibb & Dyches, 2007). The IEP is such a central part of a student's special education that an entire section later in this chapter is devoted to helping you understand what it includes.

### Deciding About Placement

The final decision made by the multidisciplinary team is placement—that is, the setting in which the student will be educated. Placement ranges from full-time participation in general education, through a combination of general education and special education settings, to a full-time special setting, depending on the student's needs. The full range of special education placement options are outlined later in this chapter.

## Monitoring for Students with Disabilities

If you refer back to Figure 2.1 on page 42, you can see that the special education decision-making process does not end with the placement decision. IDEA also includes a clear set of procedures for monitoring student progress after special education services have been implemented to ensure the student's program and placement remain appropriate.

### Annual Review

**research NOTE**

According to the most recent data available, approximately 11.3 percent of the students at U.S. public and private 4-year colleges and universities report having a disability. Approximately 25 percent of those students indicate they have physical or mobility disability, and 22 percent report having an emotional or psychological disability (Ward & Berry, 2005).

The first strategy for monitoring progress is the **annual review.** At least once each year, but more often if necessary, professionals working with the student—often a general education and a special education teacher, a school district administrative representative, and possibly other service providers (e.g., a speech/language pathologist)—meet with parents to review the IEP (Yell, Katisyannis, & Ryan, 2008). During the review, they update information about the student's learning, review the student's progress, and set goals for the upcoming year. After the new IEP is written, parents receive a copy of this document, which guides the student's education for the next year. If minor changes are needed in the IEP during the year, the law allows it to be amended rather than rewritten.

### Three-Year Reevaluation

The second monitoring provision in IDEA takes into account the fact that students with disabilities change over time. At least every 3 years, and more often if the team decides it necessary, the student with a disability is reassessed using many of the same procedures included in the initial assessment process. The purpose of this **three-year reevaluation** is to determine whether the student's program and services remain appropriate or whether they need to change, either to become more or less intensive. However, this reevaluation can be streamlined. If team members and parents decide that no purpose would be served in completing a new assessment, existing information can be used instead (Yell, 2006). This approach makes sense. For example, consider David, a high school student with a moderate intellectual disability who is due for a reevaluation. He was assessed for the first time when he was three years old, and he went through this process again at ages six, nine, and twelve. He has learned a great deal, but his overall ability level has been consistent; the team's focus therefore has been shifting toward vocational skills. David's team members might understandably decide that they can use work samples, teacher-made assessments, and information provided by David and his parents to review his educational plan and create a new one instead of administering tests yet again.

The role of parents in reevaluation is somewhat different than in the initial special education decision-making process. Parents have the right to be informed of the reevaluation and they are encouraged to participate, but school districts are entitled to complete the reevaluation and prepare a new IEP even if parents choose not to participate. In practice, this means that school districts are not required to obtain written parent permission to complete this monitoring step.

## REVIEW · REFLECT · DISCUSS

1. Why might response to intervention (RTI) lead to different outcomes than other procedures in terms of identifying students as having learning disabilities? What are its strengths? What problems might occur with its use? How might such an approach be used with Anthony, the first-grade student you met at the beginning of this chapter?

2. If you were asked to explain to a parent why so many steps are necessary before determining a student is eligible for special education, what would you say?

# Understanding the Individualized Education Program

The individualized education program (IEP), mentioned earlier in the chapter, captures all of the decisions made through the special education assessment, eligibility, and instructional planning procedures. Every student who receives special education services has a current IEP, and as you have learned, the IEP generally must be reviewed and updated annually (Yell et al., 2008), although IDEA has provided for some states to implement IEPs for as long as 3 years before review is required. The IEP serves as a blueprint for the services that a student is to receive, and it clarifies the types and amounts of those supports (Gibb & Dyches, 2007). The guidelines for who participates as members of the IEP team for each student and the elements that must be contained in an IEP are specified clearly in IDEA regulations (20 U.S.C. §320.321).

## Members of the IEP Team

The team that writes the first IEP for a student identified as having a disability often includes all the professionals who participated in assessing the student, and they collaborate so that everyone feels a sense of ownership for the student's education (Wright & Wright, 2006). Thus, IEP teams generally have the following members:

- *Parents.* Clearly, parents are the central members of the IEP team (Fish, 2008), both because it is their right and because they know their child better than anyone else does. Schools are responsible for ensuring that parents can truly be partners in developing their child's IEP. If parents need interpreting service because they are not proficient in English or because they are deaf, that service must be provided. Further, school personnel must explain the results of assessments and any other information pertaining to the student in terms that parents can readily understand. Some school districts help parents prepare for IEP meetings by sending them a set of questions to think about prior to the meeting. A sample of such questions is included in the Professional Edge feature. What questions might you add to this list?

- *Special education teacher.* At least one special education teacher is part of the IEP team because this professional often can best provide information on the day-to-day instructional needs and options for a student with a disability. This professional can offer ideas for modifying the curriculum to meet student needs, identify supplementary aids and services the student may need in the general education setting, recommend testing modifications for the student, and suggest other strategies for individualizing the student's program (Frey & Fisher, 2004).

dimensions of
**DIVERSITY**

Disabled Peoples' International (http://v1.dpi.org/lang-en/index) has as its goals ensuring the rights of the 650 million individuals with disabilities throughout the world and promoting their social and economic integration.

PEARSON

Go to the Building Teaching Skills and Dispositions section of Topic 1: The Law, Least Restrictive Environment, and Individualized Education Programs, in the MyEducationLab for your course and complete the activity entitled "Individualized Education Programs".

## Preparing Parents for IEP Meetings

As a professional educator, you should help parents, especially those who are unfamiliar with special education procedures, to prepare for IEP meetings. Consider providing parents with questions such as these to help them get ready.

### Questions for Parents to Think about Before an IEP Meeting

Before your child's IEP meeting, consider what information you can provide to school professionals to help them better understand your child. Plan to ask questions related to how school staff will provide education services to your child and what you and your child should expect.

- What does my child do well?
- With what does my child struggle?
- What are my long-range goals for my son or daughter?
- What skills would increase the independence of my son or daughter?
- What goals would strengthen us as a family?
- Are there transportation or mobility issues?
- What do I want the school to do for my child?
- What particular things do I want the school to report to me?
- How and when are good times for the school to contact me when this is necessary?
- What if there is an emergency or crisis?
- How can I communicate with the school? Notes? Who and when should I call?
- What information should I give to the school on an ongoing basis?

### Question for Parents to Ask during an IEP Meeting

By the end of your child's IEP meeting, you should be able to answer (*at a minimum*) all of the following questions. If you are unclear about any of these, ask the other members of the child study team to clarify the information for you.

- What is my child's disability?
- What are my child's current strengths and weaknesses?
- What are my child's annual goals (and, if needed, objectives)? How are they being measured?
- What is my child's placement? Is this the least restrictive environment for my child?
- What accommodations and modifications are being made for my child?
- What related services is my child receiving, and what are the times and places for these?
- How will communication between the school and parents be accomplished?
- What do I need to be doing at home to reinforce my child's educational plan?
- How has functional skill development been addressed in this IEP for my child?
- What is the current transition planning for my child?
- What outside agencies, services, and supports should I know about and be looking into?

*Source:* Shea, E. M. (2002, October). *Education advocacy: IEP checklist,* retrieved May 20, 2003, from www.arenj.org. Copyright © 2002 by The ARC of New Jersey. Used with permission from The Arc of New Jersey.

- *General education teacher.* If the student for whom the IEP is being prepared will participate in general education, even on a very limited basis, the team generally must include at least one general education teacher. General educators offer detailed knowledge of the curriculum and contribute a "reality check" on expectations in general education settings; they also may have significant responsibility for implementing parts of the IEP.
- *A school district representative.* As you might expect, providing special programs, services, and instructional and assistive technology to students with disabilities requires a commitment and financial resources from the school district. One person on the IEP team must function as the official school district representative to indicate that such a commitment is being made and that resources will be dedicated to providing the services written into the IEP. Often, a school principal serves in this role. The school psychologist, special education coordinator, or another team member also may be designated as the district representative.
- *An individual who can interpret the results of any evaluations.* Someone on the IEP team must have the expertise to interpret clearly for parents and other team members the results of any evaluations that have been completed. In many cases, the school psychologist or psychometrist has this responsibility.
- *Representatives from outside agencies providing transition services.* Once a student is sixteen years of age or older, plans for the transition to postschool pursuits may include professionals from outside the school. For example, if William, the student who has an emotional disability and who was described in the beginning of the chapter, was entitled to services from the Department of Vocational Rehabilitation after high school, a representative from that agency might attend the IEP meeting to ensure clear communication among all team members about the services that can be provided.

Most professionals agree that students should play an active role in developing their IEPs and participating in their implementation. Here are some ideas for involving students in the IEP process (Konrad, 2008):

- Provide students with materials that teach them about IEPs. One example is *Student-Led IEPs: A Guide for Student Involvement* (McGahee, Mason, Wallace, & Jones, 2002).
- Create an IEP scavenger hunt so that students gather information that will help them participate in the meeting.
- Have students read fiction books about individuals with disabilities to help them voice their own strengths and special needs.
- Involve students in assessment, for example, by having them complete interest inventories.
- Have students send reminders to key participants, either by sending e-mail or (for students who have difficulty writing) composing letters, with assistance as needed.

- Involve students in meeting preparation. For example, they could make name tags for participants.
- Ask students to write a paragraph about their strengths and needs.
- Assist students to draft IEP goals they consider important to their education.
- Ensure that students, even those who are young, attend all or part of the IEP meeting.
- Help students to rehearse parts of the IEP meeting they will lead.
- Teach students self-advocacy skills so that they can communicate their IEP goals to all their teachers.
- Involve students in monitoring their progress in achieving IEP goals, perhaps preparing first-person reports to share with parents.

- *The student.* Increasingly, educators are realizing that students with disabilities should have a voice in the process of planning for their education (Arndt, Konrad, & Test, 2006). A range of options exists regarding student participation: Very young students sometimes do not attend their IEP meetings, or they attend for parts of their meetings. However, older students usually attend their IEP meetings and actively participate in them, even students with significant disabilities. Although not yet a common practice, some professionals are preparing students to lead their IEP meetings (Konrad, 2008), similar to the way that Brianna, whom you met at the beginning of the chapter, will lead hers. The Professional Edge feature provides ideas for increasing student involvement in the IEP process.
- *Other individuals with knowledge or expertise related to the student.* The regulations on who participates in IEP meetings leave open the possibility that one or more individuals beyond those listed previously should attend these meetings because they have valuable information to contribute. Paraeducators, especially those who work one to one with a particular student, may be included in this category.
- *Exceptions to IEP team composition.* If the parents and the school district agree that a particular team member's attendance is not necessary (e.g., a related service professional whose service will not be discussed), that team member can be excused from the IEP meeting (Etscheidt, 2007). In other instances, team members may submit their information in writing instead of attending the meeting in person. In both of these examples, parents must agree in writing to excusing team members from attending.

**web link**

http://www.beachcenter.org/ The Beach Center on Disability, affiliated with the University of Kansas, has as its mission supporting individuals with disabilities and their families and those closely involved with them. The website contains many resources on topics such as inclusion, support for military families, and cultural and linguistic diversity.

## Required Components of the IEP

Although the forms on which IEPs are written vary somewhat across states and local school districts, IDEA spells out clearly the components that must be included in every IEP (Wright & Wright, 2006). As you read the following sections, you might wish to have an IEP form from your state on hand so that you can see how the required components are addressed. (You should be able to download a sample from your state's Department of Education website.)

### Present Level of Performance

A student's IEP must include accurate and current information about any domain in which a concern exists, including academic achievement, social functioning, behavior, communication skills, physical skills, vocational skills, and others as appropriate. Collectively, this information is referred to as the **present level of academic achievement and functional performance** (sometimes shortened to the acronym **PLOP**). This IEP component often comprises individual and group achievement test scores, teacher ratings of student behaviors, and scores on assessments completed by specialists such as speech/language pathologists and occupational therapists. However, present level of performance has another required dimension: The IEP must address how the student's disability affects involvement and progress in the general education curriculum. This requirement is part of the current trend toward increased attention to maintaining high standards for students with disabilities—standards that, in most cases, should not be different from those for typical learners. For example, Carlos is a high school student with an emotional disability. He has difficulty controlling his anger, and he often expresses this anger with loud profanities directed at his teachers. He often refuses to complete assignments. However, Carlos is a very bright young man, and when he is appropriately motivated, he easily masters the high school curriculum. Think about how this aspect of Carlos's disability could affect his involvement and progress in general education.

### Annual Goals

The overall purpose of the IEP process is to ensure that every student with a disability has a carefully designed educational program and that progress within that program can be documented (Bateman & Herr, 2006; Capizzi, 2008). **Annual goals** are statements of the major accomplishments expected for the student during the upcoming 12 months, and they must be able to be measured objectively. An example of an academic goal for Alice, a fifth-grade student who is hard-of-hearing and who currently reads at a beginning third-grade level, might be "Alice will increase her decoding and reading comprehension skills to a beginning fourth-grade level." For Manuel, a middle school student with an intellectual disability, a goal in the social domain might be "Manuel will initiate conversation with classmates at least three times daily." Goals also may address any other areas of need, including the social and behavior domains and self-help skills.

One additional point should be clarified about annual goals: According to IDEA, goals are required only in areas of education affected by the disability. Thus, for many students the IEP represents only part of their education—the areas in which they need specially designed instruction. David's IEP represents an example of this concept. He has a significant learning disability that affects reading. His IEP reflects his disability, and his goals were written to improve his reading skills across the curriculum. However, David's math skills are just about at grade level, and so his IEP does not address math.

*Students should play as active a role as possible in the development and review of their IEPs.*

## Short-Term Objectives

When IDEA was reauthorized in 2004, the requirement for short-term objectives was removed for all students except those few who take an alternate assessment. If your state has implemented this change, annual goals will provide a roadmap for the education of most students with disabilities. However, for all students with the most significant needs (e.g., students with multiple or severe disabilities), the law preserves **short-term objectives,** also called **benchmarks,** which specify the steps, or smaller tasks, that must be accomplished to reach each goal (Gibb & Dyches, 2007). These objectives give parents and educators a way to gauge student progress toward reaching the goals set for them.

For example, what has to happen to get Manuel to initiate conversations? One objective might relate to making eye contact with other people, another might be for Manuel to respond when someone else initiates conversation, and a third might concern Manuel asking others conversation-starting questions such as "How are you today?" Each of these items, along with others, might be incorporated as short-term objectives. Like annual goals, they must be stated in a way that clarifies what is to be measured and how progress can be assessed.

*For most (but not all) students with disabilities, the general education setting is the least restrictive environment.*

## Special Education and Related Services

The components of the IEP build on one another. Present level of performance helps the team to decide appropriate goals (and, for some students, objectives), and the goals lead the team to decide which special education and related services a student needs. For example, Jordan may need small-group instruction supplemented with consultation between the special education teacher and the general education teacher. Richard might need a separate class and speech/language therapy. Emily might need the services of a resource teacher and the assistance of a paraeducator in general education classes as well as transportation in a bus equipped with a wheelchair lift. The number of special education and related services a student receives depends on assessed needs.

## Supplementary Aids and Services

In addition to spelling out special education and related services, the IEP also must clearly outline the supplementary aids and services needed to support the student in general education. Permitting a student to use a calculator in math class, to audiotape answers to assignments instead of writing them, to use a computer to complete writing tasks, and to have modified assignments (e.g., 10 problems to complete instead of 20) are examples of supplementary aids and services.

## Assistive Technology

One important category of supplementary aids and services is *assistive technology.* If the team determines that assistive technology might help the student, the student's needs in that area must be assessed (Marino, Marino, & Shaw, 2006) and the technology provided (Parette & Peterson-Karlan, 2007). The Technology Notes presents a framework for thinking about assistive technology and questions that might be used to guide decision making about it.

## Participation with Peers Who Do Not Have Disabilities

The presumption in IDEA is that students with disabilities should, in most cases, be educated with their peers (Pierangelo & Guiliani, 2007). On the IEP, the team must clearly state the extent to which the student will *not* be in general education, including other activities in that setting (e.g., lunch, recess, and school assemblies), and that decision must be justified. In the Instruction in Action feature, you can find information on universal design for learning, a method that educators are using to think about how to make participation in general education a reality for most students.

If a student needs assistive technology, the IEP may include a provision for the student, parents, teachers, and others to be trained to use the device. However, the school district that purchases the device owns it. If the student moves, the device may stay in the original district.

## SETT the Stage for Success with Assistive Technology

Making decisions about assistive technology is an essential part of IEP meetings. Zabala (1999) proposed the SETT framework, now widely used, to assist professionals in understanding how technology can be considered in the broad context of the student's education.

### Student

· What does the student need to do (e.g., academics, social interactions, mobility)?
· What are the student's special needs?
· What are the student's current abilities?

### Environment

· What materials and equipment are currently available in the environment/classroom/setting?
· What is the physical arrangement? Are there special concerns? If so, what are they?
· What is the instructional arrangement? Will changes likely be made? If so, how might they affect the student and technology-related needs?
· What supports are available to the student (e.g., materials, people, classroom technology)?
· What resources are available to the people supporting the student (e.g., general education teacher, special education teacher)?

### Tasks

· What activities take place in the environment/classroom?
· What activities support the student's curriculum?
· What are the critical elements of the activities?
· How might the activities be modified to accommodate the student's special needs?
· How might technology support the student's active participation in these activities?

### Tools

· What strategies might be used to invite increased student performance?
· What no-tech, low-tech, and high-tech options should be considered when developing a system for a student with these needs and abilities doing these tasks in these environments/classrooms/settings?
· How might these tools be tried out with the student in the customary environments/classrooms/settings in which they will be used?

*Source:* Based on Zabala, J. M. (1999). Get SETT for successful inclusion and transition.

## Accommodations for State and District Testing

Most students in public schools take annual achievement tests that measure their learning in core academic subjects. For each student with a disability, the IEP must indicate any accommodations that the student needs when taking these tests (Elliott & Thurlow, 2006). For example, the student might need to take the test in a small group instead of with an entire general education class. Likewise, the student may need extended time to take the test.

## Universal Design for Learning: Helping Students Participate in General Education

Universal design for learning (UDL) is based on the belief that when educators plan instruction with the needs of all their diverse learners in mind, those students are much more likely to succeed. How could you address each of the following elements in your classroom (Falvey, Givner, & Kimm, 1996)?

1. Physical environment
   * Adjust pacing (e.g., allow for breaks).
   * Make environmental accommodations (e.g., reduce classroom distractions).
2. Organization of the learning environment
   * Vary student grouping arrangements.
   * Vary methods of instruction (e.g., student-led instruction vs. teacher-led instruction).
   * Provide motivation and reinforcement (e.g., point out what students do right).
   * Vary rules.
   * Teach self-management (e.g., give students a picture schedule).
3. Methods of presentation
   * Vary curricular strategies (e.g., provide notes, simplify language).
   * Modify materials.
4. Methods of assessment
   * Use varying testing strategies (e.g., read test to student, use pictures).
   * Use varying assignments (e.g., shorter assignment or simpler assignment).
5. Social interaction support
   * Encourage peer tutoring.
   * Teach friendship.
   * Encourage social communication (e.g., encourage students to say "good morning" or to take turns in a conversation).

*Source:* Falvey, M. A., Givner, C. C., & Kimm, C. (1996). What do I do Monday morning? In S. Stainback & W. Stainback (Eds.), *Inclusion: A guide for educators* (pp. 130–133). Baltimore: Paul H. Brookes. Reprinted by permission of Paul H. Brookes Publishing Co. and Mary A. Falvey.

Achievement tests are not appropriate for a few students with disabilities, and if this is the case, the IEP must include a statement of why the testing is not appropriate and how an alternate assessment of the student's progress will be made (Towles-Reeves, Kearns, & Kleinert, 2009). Each state determines acceptable types of alternate assessments and the procedures for conducting them. For example, for students with multiple disabilities, a portfolio of work, gathered across the school year, may serve this purpose because it can demonstrate learning across time.

### Dates and Places

This component of the IEP is straightforward: The IEP must indicate the date on which it becomes effective and for how long it lasts (i.e., no more than one year unless written as part of the 3-year format mentioned earlier, but it may be less). The IEP also must specify how often services are to be provided and where they are to occur (e.g., in the general education setting or in a special education classroom). This latter IEP component is sometimes referred to as the *placement decision.*

### Transition Service Needs and Transition Services to Be Provided

By the time a student with a disability is sixteen years old, the team writing the IEP must address transition, specifying measurable postsecondary goals based on transition assessments for training, education, employment, and other relevant areas. Transition services on the IEP could include career exploration; participation in a vocational preparation program; training in life skills, such as keeping a budget and writing checks; experience in a work setting; or any other service or activity related to the student's postschool plans (Winn & Hay, 2009).

### Age of Majority

In many states, the rights that parents have had on behalf of their children with disabilities may transfer to the children at the age of majority, usually eighteen years old (National Center on Secondary Education and Transition and PACER Center, 2002). If this is the case, students must be informed at least a year before this transfer of rights as to what those rights are (Wright & Wright, 2006).

### Measurement of Progress

In addition to all the information already described, the IEP includes one more essential element: a statement about how the student's progress in meeting goals and objectives will be measured, including the ways in which this information will be communicated to parents. Some students' progress might be measured by individual testing, and this information might be sent to parents as a supplement to the standard report card each time one is issued.

### Other Considerations

The team preparing the IEP has one final responsibility: Members must consider special situations related to some students. For example, if a student has limited English proficiency, the team must incorporate language needs into the IEP. If the student is blind or visually impaired, provisions for instruction in braille must be part of the IEP, if it is needed. Similarly, for a student who is deaf or hard of hearing, the team must consider language and communication needs, including how the student will interact with school professionals and classmates using her usual method of communication, which might be sign language. Finally, if a student has significant behavior difficulties, the team must identify strategies for addressing them.

Although the process of creating an IEP can appear daunting, school districts have very clear guidelines to guide educators through the process. In the Speaking from Experience feature you also can gain insights on IEP meetings from Matt, a high school special education teacher.

Go to the Assignments and Activities section of Topic 5, Assessment Practices, in the MyEducationLab for your course and complete the activity entitled "Testing Accommodations for Students with Special Needs".

**web link**

http://ncld.softsourcecorp.net/content/view/1360/456252/
The National Center for Learning Disabilities has available podcasts about and a summary of standards-based IEPs, the growing trend to ensure that students' educational plans are based on the general curriculum for their age/grade level, even though deficit areas must be addressed.

## REVIEW · REFLECT · DISCUSS

1. Think about Brianna and William, whom you met at the beginning of this chapter. What are two goals that you might find on each student's IEP?
2. Some educators believe that all students should have an IEP. What do you think of this idea? What might be pros and cons of doing this?

The Personnel and Procedures of Special Education    55

Matt Tucker graduated with a degree in parks and recreation, but after working in a group home for individuals with developmental disabilities he fell in love with the field. After earning teacher licensure in special education, he moved to Alaska and now teaches at Homer High School, where he both co-teaches and offers studies skills classes for students with disabilities. He offers this advice to other special educators concerning working with high school students.

- I encourage students to have as much to do with their IEPs as possible—whether it is tracking their goals with data they're involved in, helping me write their goals, or getting their thinking on their transition plan.
- High school students definitely should participate in their IEP meetings, and a lot of kids are not comfortable with that, so I prep them. We go over their roles, we go through the order of the meeting, I help them practice for places where they should step in. For kids who are more confident, I ask them what they would like me to help them with—giving them the leading role. I've learned the students do better with lots of practice beforehand.
- Beyond the IEP, I encourage kids to make a time to talk with their teachers and offer to go with them as support—or not. We practice, just to have them go over some of their strengths and some challenges. For some it's worked ok and some of the kids just don't want to do it.

- I believe a lot in choice for my students and stress the importance of self-advocacy, especially because they'll be going into the workforce.
- Sometimes helping students means being open and flexible with general education teachers. I feel like once I've bonded with them, they'll accept more of my input and opinion regarding students' needs.
- High school is a very important time in kids' lives, and it's really important to have connections with them as they prepare to go out into the world after school. They especially need positive male role models, but also need good-hearted, positive people around them.
- Some people say "Oh, I wouldn't want to be a high school special ed. teacher, because they're already formed, you can't change them by that time." And I completely disagree with that because I've seen so much amazing growth. Kids in the beginning of the year who were telling me that I was wasting my time with them, that they were going to drop out anyway and they were going to make my life miserable and things like that—now these same kids are coming into school early to have me help them with assignments and staying after school late. Other teachers are amazed at the behavior and the attitude change. I know obviously it's a whole team effort, with support with the parent and everything—but it just tells me that kids are not done changing and they can totally change for the best. And make a huge leap in progress.

## Placement Options for Students with Disabilities

As you have learned, after the IEP has been prepared the team responsible for the student's education must decide the setting in which the student can most successfully be educated. The required components of the IEP establish a clear expectation that most students will be educated completely, or to a significant extent, in general education settings (Reynolds, 2008). However, students' needs vary, and so a continuum of placement options must still be available so that all students receive an appropriate education (Kauffman, McGee, & Brigham, 2004). Figure 2.2 summarizes data on the proportion of all school-age students with disabilities in the United States placed in each educational setting option.

A student's placement can be changed at any time by the student's team and with parental permission, and it must be examined when the IEP review occurs. In addition, if a student commits a zero-tolerance violation (e.g., bringing drugs or a weapon to school), he can be moved for up to 45 days to an interim alternative placement while decisions are made about how best to address this serious situation.

### The Continuum of Special Education Placements

The range of options for educating students with disabilities is called a **continuum of placements** because they range from least to most restrictive. The continuum includes the following settings: (a) general education, (b) resource class, (c) separate class, (d) separate school, (e) residential facility, and (f) home or hospital (U.S. Department of Education, 2008).

## General Education

In 2007–2008, 56.8 percent of school-age students with disabilities spent more than 80 percent of their school time in general education settings (U.S. Department of Education, 2008). Dominic, a sixth-grader with autism, is an example of a student in this group. He spends the entire day with his classmates, except for the check-in session he has each day with Ms. Harrison, his special education teacher, during the 20-minute advisory period that is part of the school's schedule for all students. He also works twice each week with Mr. Wheaton, the speech/language pathologist, but this often occurs during the advisory period as well. Ms. Harrison spends approximately two class periods (English and math) in the general education classroom each day so that Dominic's IEP goals and objectives are addressed, but she does this by working not only with Dominic but with other students as well. Four other students in the classes also have IEPs. In science, a paraeducator is assigned to Dominic's class to assist him as well as the other students.

For a student in high school, placement could include (a) one traditional class period per day in a resource class to learn study and organization strategies and (b) indirect support between general education teachers and the special education teacher. Many, many other types of instructional arrangements fall into this general category. Brianna, whom you met at the beginning of this chapter, participates in general education more than 80 percent of the day.

## Resource Class

Resource support usually is assigned to students who are placed in general education between 40 percent and 79 percent of the school day. Currently, 22.4 percent of students receiving special education services are placed in resource services (U.S. Department of Education, 2008). For example, Tanya has a severe hearing loss. Although her homeroom is a general education class with typical classmates, she spends 2 hours each day with her special education teacher in a resource class for intensive work on vocabulary development and comprehension of her middle school academic courses. She especially needs assistance learning the many abstract concepts taught in her social studies class. Paul also receives resource support. He has a moderate intellectual disability, and he receives his language arts and math instruction from a special education teacher. However, he is assigned to a general education third-grade classroom for science, social studies, and other classes, including art, music, and physical education.

You should be aware that the term "resource" as used here refers just to the amount of time spent outside general education, not the type of instruction that occurs. Resource programs vary widely in this regard. In some locales, resource services are supplemental to core instruction in general education. For example, an elementary, middle, or high school student may have one resource "class" per day during which assistance is provided in whatever academic area the student is experiencing difficulty, and it may include re-teaching, help in completing projects or homework, or extended time for an assessment. In other locales, resource services take the place of general education instruction. That is, a student who has "resource math" receives math instruction from a highly qualified special educator who gives the grade for that subject; the student does not participate in a general education math class.

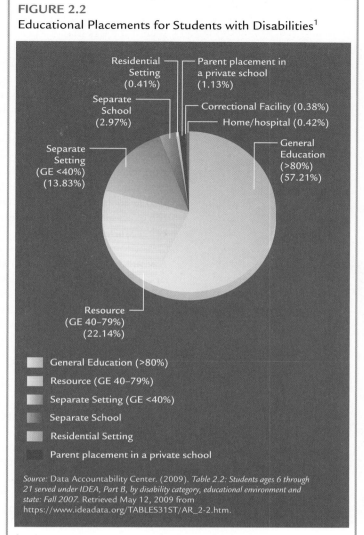

### FIGURE 2.2
### Educational Placements for Students with Disabilities[1]

Residential Setting (0.41%)
Parent placement in a private school (1.13%)
Separate School (2.97%)
Correctional Facility (0.38%)
Home/hospital (0.42%)
Separate Setting (GE <40%) (13.83%)
General Education (>80%) (57.21%)
Resource (GE 40–79%) (22.14%)

- General Education (>80%)
- Resource (GE 40–79%)
- Separate Setting (GE <40%)
- Separate School
- Residential Setting
- Parent placement in a private school

*Source:* Data Accountability Center. (2009). *Table 2.2: Students ages 6 through 21 served under IDEA, Part B, by disability category, educational environment and state: Fall 2007.* Retrieved May 12, 2009 from https://www.ideadata.org/TABLES31ST/AR_2-2.htm.

[1]Students ages six to twenty-one; data are from the 2007–2008 school year

Born in 1870, Elizabeth Farrell grew up to become a teacher in New York City. She created the earliest class placement option for students with cognitive disabilities, called *ungraded classes,* where children across several grade levels were taught practical skills using innovative methods. Farrell was the founder of the Council for Exceptional Children (Kode, 2002).

**research**
**NOTE**

Holzbauer (2008) studied the issue of harassment of students with disabilities. Of 90 teachers surveyed, 87 reported direct observations of harassment, the most common types being epithets, slurs, mimicking, mockery, and staring.

## Separate Class

When students are educated in a general education classroom located within a public school for less than 40 percent of the school day, they are considered to be placed in a separate class. Approximately 15.4 percent of students with disabilities receive their education in this setting (U.S. Department of Education, 2008). Jon, a fourth-grader, is an example of a student in this group. Jon has multiple disabilities, and when he experiences difficulty in communicating what he wants or becomes frustrated with his work, he often is very noisy and rather aggressive, hitting those around him and occasionally trying to bite them. His team has determined that he can be most successful in a small, highly structured classroom with a variety of supports and personnel in place to address his complex intellectual, physical, and behavioral needs. However, Jon's special education teacher ensures that he has contact with students without disabilities. Accompanied by a paraeducator, he usually joins his typical classmates for science, working on alternative goals that are aligned with the general science curriculum. That is, he may not do the exact same activities as other learners, but his goals are directly related to what the other students are studying.

Although separate classes also are still the placement of choice in some school districts for quite a few students with significant intellectual or emotional disabilities or multiple disabilities, this type of placement is being called into question by more and more professionals, as you will see when you learn more about these students in Chapters Seven, Thirteen, and Fourteen. William, whom you read about in the chapter introduction, is educated in a separate setting. What might be opportunities for him to interact with typical peers?

## Separate School

A small number of students with disabilities—3.0 percent—require such specialized services that they attend a public or private separate school (U.S. Department of Education, 2008). In some states, students with vision impairments or severe hearing loss may attend separate schools to receive highly specialized training so that they can go on to lead independent adult lives. Another group that sometimes needs this restrictive placement is students with very serious emotional disabilities for whom a typical public school does not provide enough structure and safety. One other group comprises students with very complex disabilities who require many services that cannot be provided in typical schools. As you might guess, the decision to assign a student to a separate school is a very serious one because this placement usually limits the possibility of contacts with typical peers and does not offer ready access to the general education curriculum. Nonetheless, for a small number of students, this setting does constitute the least restrictive environment.

## Residential Facility

Only 0.41 percent of students with disabilities live in residential settings, where they go to school and live 24 hours a day. In some states, students with visual impairments or those who are deaf or hard of hearing may be placed in such a school. Often, though, students in this placement have very complex needs, such as significant multiple disabilities that include difficult behavior. Sometimes students with emotional disabilities who need the safety and structure of full-time supervision likewise attend a residential facility.

## Other Placement Settings

A small number of students with disabilities are educated in other settings (U.S. Department of Education, 2008). For example, approximately 1.13 percent of students attend a private school based on a parental, rather than a team, decision. An additional .39 percent of students are educated while they are in correctional facilities. Students in parent-determined schools may receive a variety of services based on the school's practices; students in correctional facilities may have a full-time special education teacher who provides services or may receive daily or weekly visits from an itinerant special educator.

Finally, .42 percent of students receive services in either a home or hospital setting, as may happen when a student is suspended or expelled, is receiving extensive medical treatment, or is so medically fragile that coming to school is not possible. For such students, a teacher usually visits the home or hospital setting for a few hours each week, bringing students' work, tutoring them, and providing other services as specified on the IEP.

Remember, even though a full continuum of placement options exists for students with disabilities, more than half spend more than 80 percent of the school day in general education classrooms. That means that regardless of the professional role for which you are preparing, you will likely work with students in that setting and collaborate with others to successfully meet students' needs (Griffin et al., 2008). In the Positive Behavior Supports, you can learn how to assess your own and others' classrooms in terms of their likelihood of facilitating appropriate student behavior and, thus, learning for the many diverse learners who will be educated there.

*Even when students with disabilities are hospitalized, they may continue to receive special education services.*

---

## REVIEW · REFLECT · DISCUSS

1. Make a list of all the placement options for students with disabilities, then describe the students you think might be found in each. Compare your responses with those of your classmates and discuss similarities and differences in your responses. How do your responses compare with the perspectives of your instructor?

2. How can a student be served in the least restrictive environment yet be placed in a setting that seems very restrictive, such as a separate class or separate school?

## Resolving Disagreements Regarding Special Education

Sometimes professionals and parents disagree about what special education programs and services should include, how much service should be provided, or where that service should take place (Zirkel & Gischlar, 2008). When disagreements such as these occur, they must be resolved in a fair and timely manner. Your first approach in solving a disagreement should be to use positive communication strategies, the topic of the Professional Edge feature. However, when an informal approach is not successful, IDEA includes specific provisions for addressing disputes (Wright & Wright, 2006), as long as this occurs within 2 years of the alleged violation.

### Dispute Resolution

The first strategy for addressing complaints is to hold a resolution session. This meeting must occur within 15 days of the notice of complaint having been received by the school district, and it must be attended by individuals who understand the situation, including a school district representative with decision-making authority. The intent is to try to resolve the issues without any further steps. If this is accomplished, the parties sign an agreement

According to IDEA, under certain specific conditions, school districts can seek to recover attorney's fees from parents who have filed frivolous complaints or who have acted with improper purpose.

## Classroom Strategies That Foster Positive Behavior

As you contemplate your responsibilities for fostering positive student behavior, use the following questions to choose classroom practices designed to achieve positive student outcomes.

### Physical Environment

- Are the walls, floors, and furniture clean and in good repair?
- Is the furniture adjusted to the proper size for students? Is it placed to decrease problems with traffic flow?
- Are rules, routines, and procedures posted so that they can be seen and read or understood?
- Are distracting or unnecessary items removed from view and reach?
- Are all materials organized and easily accessible?
- Do students have secure and adequate spaces for personal storage?
- Do instructional areas of the classroom have clear visual boundaries for students?

### Scheduling

- Is the daily schedule of activities posted and reviewed regularly?
- Are the times for transitions and noninstructional activities posted and reviewed regularly?
- Is there a method for posting changes to the schedule?
- Does the schedule provide each student with independent work, one-to-one instruction, small- and large-group activities, socialization, and free time?
- Does each student spend most of the time engaged in active learning activities, with little or no unstructured downtime?
- Are students given opportunities to demonstrate or learn new choice-making skills?

### Instruction

- Are lesson objectives developed based on students' levels of functioning?
- Are assignments relevant and meaningful to students?
- Are materials based on students' academic achievement levels?
- Are timeframes adequate for the tasks planned?
- Are task directions clear and brief?
- Are oral directions paired with pictures, icons, or written words that students can read or understand?
- Is the pace of instruction appropriate for the needs of all students?
- Are nonpunitive provisions made for students who need more time?
- Are student checks for understanding conducted frequently?
- Is specific academic praise provided during instruction?
- Is corrective feedback provided promptly and positively during instruction?
- Is the goal of social acceptance by peers emphasized?
- Is there an emphasis on the development of student autonomy, individual responsibility, as well as interdependence with other students?
- Are mechanisms in place for regular communication between the teacher and families?
- Are skills taught in the settings and situations in which they are naturally needed?
- Are friendships promoted between students with and without disabilities?
- Are classroom assistants actively involved with students to promote independence and peer interactions?

Source: Adapted from Florida Department of Education, Positive Behavior Support Project. *Best Practice Classroom Management Checklist.* Retrieved August 20, 2006, from http://flpbs.fmhi.usf.edu/pdfs/-curriculumtaguide.pdf.

---

that describes the resolution. This option was added for the first time in the 2004 reauthorization of IDEA.

## Mediation

**web link**

www.directionservice.org/cadre/index.cfm
The Center for the Appropriate Dispute Resolution in Special Education (CADRE) is funded by the U.S. Department of Education for the purpose of encouraging parents and educators to find collaborative solutions to their disagreements.

In addition to the informal dispute-resolution meeting, IDEA requires that all states offer **mediation** at no cost to parents as another early formal step in resolving differences. In mediation, an impartial professional meets with each party (i.e., usually the parents and the school district representatives) to try to find a way for the dispute to be resolved (Center for Appropriate Dispute Resolution in Special Education, 2001). The mediator does not make a decision for the parties but helps them find a workable solution.

For example, the parents of a child with autism might be insisting that a specific training program they believe is best be used daily at school. School personnel might maintain that the program has some positive qualities but that it is too intensive and time consuming to be appropriate for the student. The mediator might be able to get the parties to agree to implement parts of the program at school and closely monitor the child's progress. If agreement is reached through mediation, a legally binding document specifying the resolution will be signed by all parties and no additional action is needed.

## Parent–School Conflict in Special Education

Lake and Billingsley (2000) interviewed 22 parents, 16 school officials, and 6 professionals who helped mediate parent–school disagreements. They found that the following factors tend to escalate or de-escalate conflict between school professionals and parents concerning their children with disabilities:

- *Discrepant views of a child.* Parents contend that professionals sometimes do not see their children as individuals and that they tend to think in terms of deficits.

- *Problems related to knowledge.* Parents may lack knowledge about the details of special education laws and procedures, and they may believe that this imbalance puts them at a disadvantage. Professionals may lack knowledge of how to problem-solve with parents.

- *Service delivery.* This category of conflict includes views on inclusion, on the amount of services a student receives, and on the quality of that service.

- *Constraints on resources.* Parents sometimes believe a reluctance to fund services leads to conflict concerning personnel availability to deliver services, time for meetings, and technology availability.

- *Valuation.* When parents sense they are being treated in a condescending manner, conflict is likely to escalate. Similarly, if school professionals perceive that parents are withholding information or not being completely honest, a similar result occurs.

- *Reciprocal power.* Both school professionals and parents use power to address their differences. In difficult situations, each side can "dig in" until relationships may be difficult if not impossible to repair.

- *Communication.* Infrequency of communication, lack of communication, miscommunication, and timing of communication all can cause an increase in the intensity of disagreements.

- *Trust.* When trust exists, parents and professionals often can resolve differences. However, when trust is damaged, parents are less likely to accept school recommendations for their children and more likely to view their work with school professionals as negative.

*Source:* Lake, J. F., & Billingsley, B. S. (2000). An analysis of factors that contribute to parent–school conflict in special education. *Remedial and Special Education, 21,* 240–251. Copyright © 2000 by Pro-Ed., Inc. Reprinted by permission of SAGE Publications.

## Due Process Hearing

From the very beginning of the special education process of referral, eligibility, programming, and placement, parents, on behalf of their children, as well as school districts, have what is called the right to due process. **Due process** refers to a clear set of procedures for making all the critical decisions that are part of special education. All the steps outlined earlier in this chapter that must be taken before a student can receive special education services are part of due process. Typically, parents are more likely to exercise their due process rights than are school districts. Parents do so when they believe the school district is not providing their child with the education to which that child is entitled (Yell, 2006).

The vehicle through which due process rights are addressed is called a *due process hearing.* If informal attempts to resolve disputes (including mediation) fail, then this formal procedure must be followed. In a due process hearing, usually parents make a formal complaint against the school district, and an impartial hearing officer (often an attorney who has been trained for this role) is appointed by a state special education official. This individual acts in many ways like a judge, reading all the documents related to the issue, scheduling and presiding over the hearing, reviewing a transcript of the proceeding, and eventually issuing a written decision based on the evidence provided and the testimony of witnesses at the hearing. If either party disagrees with the decision of the hearing officer, the decision can be appealed to a state-level review hearing officer. This individual reviews all the documents from the initial hearing and writes a decision, either agreeing with the initial decision or overturning it. However, even this is not the end of the process. Either party can still take the issue to court but only after all the steps outlined here have been completed.

Due process hearings usually are held because the needs of students with disabilities are complex and the types, intensity, and quality of services often can be subject to interpretation. Here is an example: The Greens have a daughter, Jessica, who has multiple disabilities. She has a significant intellectual disability, uses a wheelchair, and needs assistance with personal care. Her parents want her to be educated with her peers in middle school. The school district contends that a general education setting is not the least restrictive environment for Jessica and that her education should occur primarily in a self-contained special education class, with opportunities for interacting with typical classmates provided at lunch, assemblies, and in

**research**
**NOTE**

In analyzing why disputes arise between parents and schools, Curtis (2005) found three main causes: (a) inappropriate or insufficient services being provided; (b) lack of services being provided for students who have been overlooked somehow; and (c) parent perceptions of being de-valued or ignored.

http://school.familyeducation.com/special-education/ada/38427.html
The Family Education Network provides a clear explanation of due process hearings, including a brief recap of their development and the current role of mediation in avoiding such hearings.

elective classes such as art. Who is right? What types of information do you think might be presented to help a hearing officer make a decision in such a case?

Many educators complete their careers without ever participating in a due process hearing. If the parents of one of your students disagree with a decision concerning their child, though, you may be asked to testify at a hearing. If this occurs, you usually will meet beforehand with the school district attorney who will help you prepare. Your responsibility will be to answer clearly and honestly the questions you are asked, using objective information you have related to the student (e.g., samples of written work or records of communication with parents). Because a hearing involves conflict, participating in it can be stressful, but your contribution can be important in helping a hearing officer decide what is appropriate for the student.

## REVIEW · REFLECT · DISCUSS

1. Why do you think resolution meetings and mediation were made part of the process for addressing disputes between parents and school professionals for students with disabilities? What advantages do these options have over due process?

## Issues Related to Special Education Professionals and Procedures

In Chapter One, the point was made that special education is a dynamic field that is constantly evolving. This is particularly true of topics that have been addressed in this chapter. The next sections address two of the issues facing the field: (1) a shortage of special education teachers and (2) the implementation of response to intervention.

### Shortage of Special Education Teachers

The number of professionals studying to be special education teachers and working in the field has not kept pace with the number of students who need their services (Nichols, Bi-

*In some parts of the United States, especially urban and rural areas, a critical shortage of special education teachers exists.*

card, Bicard, & Casey, 2008). The data on teacher shortages in special education are sobering. For example, nearly 98 percent of urban school districts have an immediate demand for special education teachers (Center on Personnel Studies in Special Education, 2009). Further, African American male special educators make up less than 2 percent of this professional group (Rice & Goessling, 2005). Cook and Boe (2004) note that the shortage is due largely to the number of special education teachers who leave teaching altogether and who transfer to general education positions; other researchers have demonstrated that another dimension of the problem is that too few teacher candidates select a career in special education (e.g., Billingsley, 2006).

Professionals in the field are scrambling to understand and address the teacher shortage (e.g., Nichols, et al., 2008). Many states now offer some type of intense professional preparation experience, called an *alternative route to licensure* or certification, designed to help individuals who are becoming special educators as a second career do so quickly (Rosenberg, Boyer, & Sindelar, 2007). Some districts are encouraging paraeducators to complete their teaching degrees and partnering with universities to create programs for them. Other initiatives include recruiting retired military personnel to the special education teaching profession and providing incentives for professionals who stay in their jobs for several years.

Are you part of this effort to recruit and keep special education teachers? Perhaps you are a student in an alternative licensure program. Although all students need great teachers, it is especially critical that students with disabilities are taught by professionals who understand their needs, who can provide the specialized instruction that will help them succeed, and who can effectively collaborate with other school professionals.

## Response to Intervention

Response to intervention (RTI) holds great promise for preventing some students from needing special education services by providing them with appropriate instruction as soon as their learning difficulties are noticed. However, a number of questions and concerns surround RTI, and these may affect you. One issue concerns the RTI process: For RTI to be effective, general education teachers must thoroughly understand it. They also must know and able to implement research-based instructional practices and to document their impact on student learning (Kratochwill, Volpiansky, & Clements, 2007). In some locales, special educators play key roles in helping to explain RTI to their colleagues, participating on teams making decisions about interventions for students, and ensuring that the intensive instruction it requires is offered. The dilemma that sometimes occurs relates to workload: How can special educators balance their desire to assist their colleagues and students who struggle (but who have not been identified as having disabilities) with their other responsibilities?

A second RTI issue relates to students with limited English proficiency (Burns, Jacob, & Wagner, 2008), specifically, making sure that RTI does not inadvertently lead to these students being identified as having a disability. For example, some professionals have questioned whether enough is known about effective reading instruction for English language learners and whether current assessment procedures can distinguish between students acquiring language skills from those who possibly have disabilities (Haager, 2007). Such discussions are important reminders to professionals that no single procedure can provide all the answers to understanding student needs and that complex decision-making is part of being a special educator.

**research**
**NOTE**

Zascavage and her colleagues found that contact with and participation in peer-support groups for individuals with disabilities were the most influential factors for college student choosing to major in special education.

**dimensions of**
**DIVERSITY**

http://www.k8accesscenter.org/index.php/category/english-language-learners/
The Access Center focuses on strategies for providing access to the general curriculum for students with disabilities. It includes a special section on English language learners.

## REVIEW · REFLECT · DISCUSS

1. Why have you decided to become a special educator? How would you recruit others to consider this career option? If you are not preparing to be a special educator, what might convince you to become a special education teacher?

2. Think about what you have learned about response to intervention. How would you explain its purpose and procedures to general educators and principals?

# Summary

- Many individuals play key roles in special education. These include special education teachers, related services professionals, and others such as general education teachers, speech/language therapists, school psychologists, paraeducators, and parents.
- Most students are identified as needing special education after they begin school. The general education teacher expresses concern about the student and requests the assistance of a team of colleagues, who problem-solve to determine if the student's needs can be addressed. One recently developed process for addressing student learning deficits in an efficient, effective, and timely manner is response to intervention (RTI).
- If interventions do not ameliorate a student's learning problems, parent permission is obtained for a full, multidimensional assessment of the student's strengths and potential areas of disability, conducted by a team of professionals.
- If the student is eligible for special education, the team prepares the student's individualized education program (IEP) and decides on placement. The IEP must be reviewed at least annually, and the student usually is reevaluated every 3 years.
- The IEP has a number of required components that clarify the student's present level of performance, annual goals, short-term objectives for a few students, special education and related services, participation in general education, accommodations for testing programs, dates for service, placement, transition services, and progress measures.
- Although most students with disabilities receive much of their education in general education settings, resource rooms, separate classes, separate schools, residential schools, and home or hospital options also may be the least restrictive environment for some.
- If disagreements occur between parents and school professionals related to placement or any other part of special education, dispute resolution and mediation are offered, and if agreement is not reached, a due process hearing occurs.
- The field of special education is undergoing rapid changes related to professionals and procedures. Two issues are the shortage of special education teachers and the impact of RTI on special educators.

## Council for Exceptional Children — ADDRESSING THE PROFESSIONAL STANDARDS

Council for Exceptional Children (CEC) Common Core Knowledge and Skills addressed in this chapter:

ICC1K4, ICC1K6, ICC7K5, ICC7S1, ICC7S2, ICC7S7, ICC7S9, ICC8K3, ICC8K4, ICC8S1, ICC8S4, ICC9S12, ICC10S5, ICC10S6, ICC8S6, ICC10K1, ICC10K3, ICC10S2, ICC10S4

Appendix: Provides a full listing of the CEC Common Core Standards, and associated Knowledge and Skill Statements listed here.

**PEARSON**
**myeducationlab**

Now go to Topic 1: Law, LRE & IEPs in the MyEducationLab (www.myeducationlab.com) for your course, where you can:

- Find learning outcomes for the broad concepts covered in this chapter along with the national standards that connect to these outcomes.
- Complete Assignments and Activities that can help you more deeply understand the chapter content.
- Examine challenging situations presented in the IRIS Center Resources.
- Apply and practice your understanding of the core concepts and skills identified in the chapter with the Building Teaching Skills and Dispositions learning units.

- Check your comprehension on the content covered in the chapter by going to the Study Plan in the Book Specific Resources for your text. Here you will be able to take a chapter quiz, receive feedback on your answers, and then access Review, Practice, and Enrichment activities to enhance your understanding of chapter content.
- Watch video clips of CCSSO Teacher of the Year award winners responding to the question: "Why I teach?" in the Teacher Talk section.

## chapter three

# Multicultural and Bilingual Perspectives

## LEARNING OBJECTIVES

- Explain the concept of *culture*.
- Describe how culture affects the learning process.
- Analyze the disproportionate representation of students who are racially and ethnically diverse in special and gifted education, explaining factors that contribute to this situation.
- Identify recommended educational practices for diverse students in special and gifted education.
- Discuss challenges to and opportunities for developing collaborative relationships with racially and ethnically diverse families.
- Summarize issues and trends influencing the education of diverse students in special and gifted education, including those related to the standards and accountability movement, response to intervention, and equity.

### Xiong

Xiong is a first-grade student whose Hmong family came to the United States when he was an infant from the Chinese province of Guizhou through the sponsorship of a local church. He is the youngest member of his family, and he has four older siblings. He lives with his parents, maternal grandparents, and several other extended family members. Xiong's family does not speak English at home, and both his teacher for students learning English as a second language (ESL) and his first-grade teacher are worried about his slow academic progress and classroom behavior. The educators are especially concerned because of their difficulty in communicating with Xiong's family. His parents clearly cherish this youngest child, and they do not seem to believe that a problem exists. Even when the teachers address Xiong's apparent disrespect for others' belongings, his parents do not seem to understand. The teachers are beginning to suspect that Xiong may have a learning or intellectual disability. When they discussed this possibility with their school's response to intervention team, Ms. Klein, the social worker who has worked extensively with community agencies helping families such as Xiong's, explained that some of the concerns may be related to cultural differences. She decided to meet with the teachers and Xiong's parents to facilitate clear communication and understanding.

### Josef

Although Josef is only in eighth grade, he has lived a difficult life. His family is very poor, and they live in a neighborhood with a high crime rate and chronic problems related to gangs and drugs. He did not have the opportunity to attend a preschool program, and so he began his career as a student at a disadvantage, even in kindergarten. At various times he has been determined to be eligible for special education services as having a learning disability, significant ADHD, and an emotional disability, but he currently is receiving services as having a mild intellectual disability. Although in elementary school he received some co-teaching support with limited services in a resource room, in middle school the IEP team determined that he should receive English/language arts, math, and social studies in a separate setting while attending the general education science class. He also interacts with other peers during physical education and exploratory classes (e.g., art, music, technology). All of Josef's teachers describe his learning rate as flat, especially this school year, and they characterize him as unmotivated. He does not complete homework, and when frustrated, he may turn his desk over, throw assigned work in the trash, or refuse to follow teacher directions. When Josef does participate, he often yells out answers and sulks if reprimanded. Josef lives with his mother and grandmother and three younger brothers and sisters, and in settings outside of school, Josef displays a different attitude. He participates enthusiastically in activities that he enjoys, such as playing football with his friends and listening to music. Although he is a high-energy person, his behaviors do not seem to annoy others around him. He also demonstrates problem-solving and memory skills that are not evident at school. For example, he is quite successful in designing and executing plays in football, he knows the statistics about his favorite pro football players, and he creates his own rap lyrics.

### Maria

Maria is a Hispanic American student identified as having learning disabilities. She is a tenth-grader in a large, urban high school and is the oldest of five siblings. Although Maria was born in the United States, her mother and father both came to this country from Mexico as young adults. Spanish is the primary language of Maria's home, but Maria speaks both Spanish and English fluently. She has never received bilingual or ESL services. She was identified as learning disabled as a fifth-grade student, and she has been served primarily through small amounts of resource services combined with some co-teaching. During her elementary and middle school years, Maria did well academically; she is on track for earning a standard high school diploma. During her sophomore year, however, she started to flounder, probably because of several changes in her life. She began a part-time job at nights and on weekends. She also now has a steady boyfriend who is 6 years older than she, and the two have become very close. He is a hard-working young man, and despite the age difference, her family approves of the relationship. Nonetheless, Maria's job and her boyfriend have distracted her from her studies, and her grades reflect this. She is considering dropping out.

**PEARSON**
**myeducationlab**

To check your comprehension on the content covered in Chapter 3, go to the Book Specific Resources in the MyEducationLab (www .myeducationlab.com) for your course, select your text, and complete the Study Plan. Here you will be able to take a chapter quiz, receive feedback on your answers, and then access review, practice, and enrichment activities to enhance your understanding of chapter content.

One of the greatest strengths of the United States is the diversity of its people, and this diversity is reflected in the students that populate today's schools. Racial and ethnic differences constitute one aspect of this diversity, and demographic trends suggest that such diversity has increased considerably in U.S. schools over the past several decades. For example, in 1972 a total of 22.2 percent of public school students were students of color. In 2007, this number had increased to 44 percent (Planty et al., 2009). Although student diversity provides a rich educational resource, in too many instances it is still viewed as a barrier rather than an opportunity.

In Chapters One and Two, you learned many of the fundamental concepts that define the field of special education and that create a systematic and supportive system for educating students with disabilities. In this chapter, you will focus on diverse learners like Xiong, Josef, and Maria in today's schools. In particular, you will consider how educators must take care to ensure that students whose language, learning styles, social interaction skills, and behavior may be somewhat different from those of other students (and teachers) are not inadvertently identified as disabled (Artiles, 2003). As you begin to read this discussion, think about all you have already learned about the procedures through which students become eligible for special education. From the time a teacher first expresses concern about the student until an individualized education program (IEP) is prepared and a placement decision made, how might that student's different cultural background affect the decisions professionals and parents make? As a professional educator, you have the responsibility of being alert for bias. Doing this requires that you think about your own background and experiences and how they have shaped your perceptions.

# Understanding Culture

Have you ever stopped to consider the concept of culture and its impact on our daily lives? **Culture** is a complex system of underlying beliefs, attitudes, and actions that shapes the thoughts and behaviors of a group of people, distinguishing them from other groups (Johnson & McIntosh, 2009). Culture is influenced by the environment and is learned, shared, and constantly changing. We are all cultural beings, but if we have been exposed primarily to only one culture, it is difficult for us to view our own culture objectively or to see it as anything other than "simply the way things are." Pang (2001) has likened culture to the air—always there but not seen by those who live in it. Our culture provides the lens through which we view and interpret the world. It greatly influences our behaviors and our perceptions. Do you think Pang's observations are correct? Think of examples that support or refute her observation about culture.

## Elements of Culture

dimensions of
**DIVERSITY**

*Cultural competence* is a contemporary term for understanding and acting in a way that is respectful of diversity. This term is used in education, health care, business, and many other professions.

Banks (2006) has discussed a number of critical elements of culture, including values and behavior patterns. **Values** are those cultural elements held in great esteem or considered to be important by a society. For example, the **dominant culture,** or the culture of those in power in the United States, values individualism and independence. However, other cultures, including some Native American cultures, place greater emphasis on functioning effectively as a part of a group. These values, in turn, shape behavior patterns, or customary ways of conducting oneself.

For example, children from the dominant American culture are encouraged from the time they are very young to become more and more independent, sleeping over at friends' homes, going to camp, and moving away to attend college. They also learn to value being rewarded for individual accomplishment (e.g., honor roll, medals and trophies for community sports achievement). In contrast, in a culture that values interdependence, far more attention is paid to teaching children about sharing, contributing to the group and helping others to do so, and seeking accomplishment by working with others rather than against them. These patterns are neither good nor bad; the two are simply different.

Language is another element of culture. To some degree, language influences thought. Further, the importance of a concept to a culture often is reflected in how that concept is developed in language. For example, in some languages, including the Alaskan Native language Inuit, as well as English, many words are used to refer to the concept of snow because it is important to the culture (Kaplan, 2003). Conversely, in the language of the Lakota, a Native American people who highly value peace and respect, no word exists to express the concept of war (Marshall & Marshall, 2005). What other examples of language as a critical element of culture can you identify?

Perspectives and worldviews also are important elements of culture. For example, Native Americans may have a different perspective on historical events, such as the 1800s westward expansion of the United States, than is typical of that of the dominant culture. This event may evoke in them feelings of sorrow or resentment. In contrast, for members of the dominant culture it may bring to mind feelings of victory or accomplishment. Likewise, the views Native Americans may hold with respect to concepts such as the ownership of land and the relationship of humankind to the rest of nature also may vary from the views of the dominant culture. Members of the dominant culture embrace the notion of individual ownership of land, but this concept is foreign to traditional Native American cultures. Perspectives and worldviews such as these shape our interactions with others and with our environment.

## Macroculture and Microculture

All members of a society, to some extent, share cultural aspects of that society. For example, in the United States people embrace many democratic ideals. These overarching cultural aspects within a society are referred to as **macroculture.** Macroculture tends to unify the diverse members of a society and define them to others. For example, if you travel to another country, you probably first identify yourself to people you meet as an American. However, within the American macroculture, a number of subgroups form distinct **microcultures—** that is, groups that have distinguishing characteristics with respect to culture, such as language or dialect, values, behaviors, and worldviews. Such microcultures may be based on any of several factors, as illustrated in Figure 3.1, and many microcultures exist within a macroculture. For example, **socioeconomic status (SES)** is a term often used to refer to an individual's educational and income levels, and it may define some microcultures (e.g., working class or middle class). As the figure illustrates, these microcultures also overlap each other, as well as with the macroculture, implying that they share some elements but also maintain distinctions.

As you think about the cultural characteristics associated with various microcultures, you should remember that many factors converge to influence the extent to which individual members of a microculture demonstrate those characteristics. For example, although two individuals may have a common racial or ethnic background, their socioeconomic differences may result in very different cultural profiles. Two individuals may even be demographically identical (e.g., same race or ethnicity, same sex, same SES background, same age), but because of different experiences or life circumstances, they may be very different with respect to cultural characteristics. For example, consider Mary and Alice, who are both white, middle-class females in their twenties. Mary has always lived in an urban, culturally diverse setting and has interacted with and been influenced by peers from many cultures. However, Alice has always lived in a small, homogeneous community and so has had very limited interaction with people from diverse groups. As a result of their life experiences, Mary and Alice may have very different cultural perspectives. How might they differ in their beliefs? How might they be similar? This is why it is often unproductive to make broad assumptions about the cultural characteristics of an individual based solely on demographic factors.

Understanding the concepts of macroculture and microculture is integral to understanding diverse students. Macroculture provides you with a broad awareness of students' likely cultural characteristics. Microculture enables you to recognize that no member of any culture fits a single profile of that culture and that your responsibility is

In 2006–2007, approximately 33 percent of black, 35 percent of Hispanic, and 25 percent of American Indian/Alaska Native students were enrolled in high-poverty schools. In contrast, just 4 percent of white and 13 percent of Asian/Pacific Islander students attended such schools (National Center for Education Statistics, 2009b).

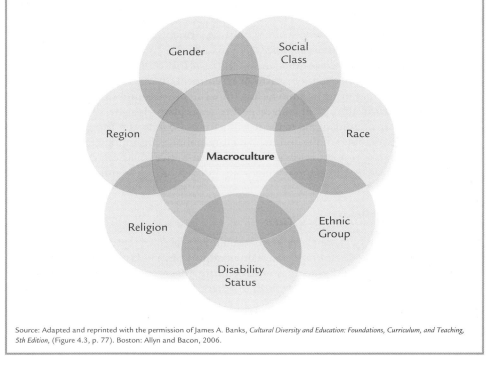

**FIGURE 3.1**

**Understanding Macroculture and Microculture**

*Macroculture* refers to an overarching set of cultural ideas. Being American is an example of macroculture. However, all the factors in the figure can contribute to *microculture*–that is, a subgroup that exists within the macroculture, such as being a southerner, a Protestant, or a gen-xer. One person may belong to several microcultures.

Gender
Social Class
Region
Race
**Macroculture**
Religion
Ethnic Group
Disability Status

Source: Adapted and reprinted with the permission of James A. Banks, *Cultural Diversity and Education: Foundations, Curriculum, and Teaching, 5th Edition,* (Figure 4.3, p. 77). Boston: Allyn and Bacon, 2006.

*What children come to understand and believe about diversity during their school years will directly influence their beliefs and behaviors as adults.*

to respond to the unique microcultural characteristics of students and their families. How do these concepts apply to Maria, the high school student you met at the beginning of this chapter?

## Culture and Race

Race has been a dominant theme in U.S. culture. Because of the historical legacy of segregation in American society, in many instances members of certain racial groups interacted primarily with other members of their racial group in home, school, and community settings. Although legally enforced segregation is no longer practiced, racial isolation is still common. For example, the majority of African American and Hispanic students attend schools that are comprised primarily of students of color (Orfield, Frankenberg, & Lee, 2003). A number of factors contribute to this persisting racial isolation, including socioeconomic disparities and our inclination as humans to seek interaction with those we feel are most like us. This has reinforced cultural differences between racial groups.

The relationship between race and culture is not a simple one. Many other factors influence it. For example, some individuals identify themselves as being members of more than one racial group. According to data from the U.S. Census Bureau (2008), approximately 5 percent of the U.S. population do so. Additionally, individuals vary with respect to the extent to which they adopt characteristics associated with a particular group or internalize values and standards associated with that group (Banks, 2006).

Here is yet another example of the complex relationship between race and culture: Consider a child who was born to parents of one race but raised by individuals from another. This child probably would have been immersed in the culture of the individuals who raised him and would not necessarily have the cultural characteristics associated with the racial background of the birth parents. Keep in mind that racially influenced cultural differences do exist, but they are the result of the interaction of many elements rather than genetics (Bennett, 2003). In other words, just as the concepts of macroculture and microculture illustrate how no individual can be understood based on a superficial understanding of that person's culture, you should not make assumptions about a student or family's culture on the basis of race.

research
**NOTE**

Research in urban settings has shown that teacher trust in students and parents is a positive predictor of student achievement (Goddard, Tschannen-Moran, & Hoy, 2001).

## REVIEW · REFLECT · DISCUSS

1. As you look back at your own experiences of growing up, what factors do you think most affected the development of your cultural identity? How might these factors now influence your views of other cultures?

2. Have you ever been in a circumstance in which you felt culturally different? If so, what was this experience like? Did it have any lasting effect on the way you view cultural differences?

## Culture and Learning

Given how culture strongly influences thought and behavior, it is not hard to imagine that it plays a significant role in the learning process. In fact, almost every aspect of the teaching and learning process is culturally influenced—from decisions about what is important to learn to decisions about how learning is best accomplished and assessed (Nieto, 2002–2003; Warikoo & Carter, 2009).

### The Content of Instruction

If you think about the United States, can you identify the microculture that traditionally has controlled key government decisions? To help your thinking, recall pictures that you have seen of Congress in session. Who is usually portrayed? Now think about education and its leaders—until relatively recently, what group would represent most of the superintendents of local school districts? Did you think of white males? In many aspects of U.S. society, including education, the thinking of this group has been dominant. The implications of this fact are significant: Those who have made decisions about what knowledge is valid and important typically have been white males. Too often, the perspectives, experiences, and contributions of women and people of color have been marginalized. Because school knowledge often has been assumed to be objective and neutral (Banks, 2006), the issue of perspective seldom has been raised and underlying assumptions or biases rarely questioned—until recently.

The **knowledge construction** process—that is, the way in which a particular framework is used to develop, approve, and disseminate new information—generally is not directly examined or studied in school. Thus, students and educators are vulnerable to whatever bias may exist in their curricula and instructional materials. Omissions or distortions can go unchallenged and become ingrained characteristics of the curriculum, proving difficult to eradicate. This circumstance can lead to curriculum content that is incomplete or inaccurate. An example from the recent past illustrates the point: Older textbooks on U.S. history rarely mentioned the roles of women or African Americans. Although this omission would be glaring in the twenty-first century, it took many years for it to be recognized, debated, and eventually addressed.

## Cognitive Styles

Aside from the content of instruction, how students are taught and assessed also is culturally influenced (Bennett, 2003; Guerra & Nelson, 2009). The term **cognitive style** refers to the inclination to take a particular approach or orientation to thinking and learning.

### Field Independence

The cognitive styles of some cultural groups are described as **field independent,** or characterized by the inclination to be analytical in processing information. Students referred to as *field independent* tend to focus on specifics and are not as strongly influenced by surrounding context. These students often learn best when instruction is organized in discrete, incremental steps and geared toward independent work for which individual recognition is received (Bennett, 2003; Klein, 2008). For example, consider the task of learning to write a business letter. A learner who has a field-independent cognitive style might benefit most from a step-by-step explanation of how to write each component of the letter (e.g., inside address, greeting, body), with clarifying examples provided. The teacher might then ask the student to practice individual components of the letter. Finally, the teacher might ask the student to write an example of a business letter independently.

### Field Sensitivity

Unlike field-independent cognitive styles, **field-sensitive** cognitive styles are those that reflect a holistic approach to processing information. Field-sensitive students make use of the context of a learning situation and are said to "require the forest in order to see the trees." These students tend to focus on broader concepts before details, and they may learn best through hands-on, authentic tasks, rather than out of context through books, lectures, and worksheets. Additionally, these students may prefer working in groups instead of alone because they may value interdependence more than independence. They would more quickly learn the causes of World War II by reading biographies of people from that time, interviewing veterans who fought in that war, and working with others to create a story about what caused the war than by reading a chapter from a history book.

Consider again the task of learning to write a business letter. A learner who has a field-sensitive cognitive style might benefit by beginning with an authentic purpose for learning to write business letters (e.g., making a special request of the principal or inviting a guest speaker to class). Field-sensitive learners also may benefit from discussion of situations in which one would write business letters, with examples of business letters presented before individual components are discussed. Although the teacher would point out the standard components of the business letter, the teacher also could show an actual letter and relate it back to the discussion of why business letters are written. Opportunities for practice could be provided by having students critique business letters to determine whether the required components are included and whether these components are in the correct formats. Practice in writing business letters might be provided by pairing or grouping students and having them write letters inviting the principal to a class activity—that is, for a real purpose.

As you look at these two approaches to learning, think about your responsibility to embrace both the field-independent and field-sensitive cognitive styles of your learners within a single lesson. What might be the challenges of accomplishing this?

## Effects of Cultural Dissonance

As might be expected, traditional classrooms typically reflect the dominant culture. As a result, dissonance may be created between the cultural environment of the classroom and that of some diverse learners. **Cultural dissonance** refers to a significant discrepancy between two or more cultural frames of reference. When this happens, academic and behavior problems can result. As you read the following sections, think about how this dissonance may be affecting Josef's performance in school.

## Cultural Influences on Behavior

Teachers should consider cultural influences such as these in their interactions with diverse students (Grossman, 1995):

### Interactional Styles

- *Degree of directness.* In some cultures, it is preferable to get right to the point in the most unequivocal manner possible—without considering how the listener might feel about what you have to say. In other cultures, preference is given to less-direct communication styles—with more elaborate introductory or intervening discourse and greater deference to how the message is received by the listener.
- *Level of emotionality.* In some cultures, a dramatic display of emotions through voice volume and tone, gestures, and facial expressions is typical, while in others this is considered inappropriate.
- *Degree of movement and vocalizations.* In some cultures, it is common for more than one person to speak at a time. In other cultures, this practice is seen as rude. Likewise, in some cultures, a high level of physical activity and verbal exchange may be a natural accompaniment to cognitive activity (e.g., school seatwork), while in others this is not typical.
- *Display of consideration for others.* In some cultures, consideration for others is shown by refraining from behaviors that may offend them. In other cultures, consideration is more often shown by being tolerant of the behaviors of others that one might personally find unpleasant or offensive. For example, in some cultures one may show consideration of others by not playing music loudly (because others may be disturbed by it). In other cultures, the tendency may be to learn to tolerate loud music if someone else is enjoying it.

- *Attitudes toward personal space.* In some cultures, speakers customarily remain at least 2 feet apart when speaking to one another. Failure to recognize this is often interpreted as a desire to seek intimacy or as a prelude to aggression. In other cultures, closer interactions are common and physically distancing oneself might be interpreted as aloofness.

### Response to Authority Figures

- *Perceptions of authority figures.* In some cultures, students may view all adults as authority figures by virtue of their status as adults. In other cultures, position may be a primary determiner (e.g., teachers, police officers). In yet other cultures, designation as an authority figure must be earned by behavior.
- *Display of respect for authority figures.* In some cultures, students show respect for authority figures by not making eye contact; in other cultures, the opposite is true. Likewise, questioning authority figures is considered disrespectful in some cultures; in other cultures, this practice may be valued as an indicator of critical thinking.
- *Response to management styles.* In some cultures, having a permissive management style is viewed as a way to encourage the child's individuality and self-expression. In other cultures, such a management style would indicate weakness or lack of concern.

What examples can you think of that illustrate how these cultural elements might be displayed in classroom behaviors? How can these factors affect your interactions with your students' parents?

Source: Adapted from Grossman, H. (1995). *Special education in a diverse society.* Reproduced by permission of Pearson Education, Inc.

## Academic Challenges

In U.S. schools, many lessons focus on a skill presented in isolation and rely heavily on step-by-step analytical thinking, as was the case in the first business letter example. However, students who have field-sensitive cognitive styles may perform poorly in such lessons—not necessarily because of lack of ability but rather because the instructional approach did not match well with their strengths. If such lessons are the rule rather than the exception, over time the academic performance of the field-sensitive learner may be artificially depressed (Haar, Hall, Schoepp, & Smith, 2002; Klein, 2008).

## Behavior Challenges

Behavior patterns also are culturally influenced (Tyler et al., 2008). For example, some African American students show greater movement, energy, and vitality as a natural course of interacting with others. Their conversations may have features associated with greater exuberance or verve (e.g., louder voices or dramatic gestures) than is typical in the dominant culture. Townsend (2000) also reported that some African American students tend to socialize with others while engaging in school tasks or engage in several activities simultaneously, an example of the cultural value of *communalism*—that is, the valuing of the group over the individual. As you might suspect, teachers often consider these behaviors inappropriate and disruptive. Consequently, students from cultural backgrounds that embrace these behaviors are at greater risk of being punished for them (Connor, 2006). For example, African American males are suspended at two to three times the rate that would be

### dimensions of DIVERSITY

Students who are gay, lesbian, transgender, or bisexual often face multiple forms of bias at school (Hansen, 2007) and even more so when they have disabilities. Educators should ensure a safe and supportive environment for these students (Blanchett, 2002).

suggested by their proportion in the population (Achilles, McLaughlin, & Croninger, 2007). The Positive Behavior Supports feature outlines additional cultural considerations related to student behavior.

Aside from culturally influenced behavioral characteristics, behavior differences also can stem from frustration and feelings of alienation. When a student cannot see herself in the curriculum to which she is exposed, when the teacher's instructional approaches consistently conflict with the way she learns best, and when her behaviors are often misinterpreted negatively by others, this student may understandably feel misunderstood and behave in a way that reflects this (Ishii-Jordan, 1997; Tyler et al., 2008). These behaviors are not evidence that something is wrong with the student; rather, they are a predictable human reaction to negative experiences.

## REVIEW · REFLECT · DISCUSS

1. Think about the field-independent and field-sensitive cognitive styles. Which most closely describes you? To what extent do you think your cognitive style has been influence by the culture in which you were raised? How does your cognitive style affect your learning habits?
2. As a teacher, how will you distinguish between behavior that is truly inappropriate and that which is associated with culture or alienation? What are the differences in how you might respond to each?

The reauthorization of IDEA in 2004 added the requirement that states establish policies and procedures to prevent disproportionate representation.

# Diversity in Special and Gifted Education

Long before special education laws even existed, the percentage of students of color placed in special and gifted education varied significantly from the percentage of these students in the general population. This condition, referred to as **disproportionate representation,** has received significant attention over the past two decades, and the discussion of this issue is likely to continue for years to come (Beratan, 2008; Blanchett, Mumford, & Beachum, 2005; Samson & Lesaux, 2009; Yoon & Gentry, 2009). The following discussion clarifies important dimensions of disproportionate representation.

## Representation in Special Education

Figure 3.2 presents risk ratios that show the likelihood of students ages six through twenty-one in each racial/ethnic group being identified with a given disability (U.S. Department of Education, 2009). An assigned ratio of 1.0 would mean that the group has the particular disability at exactly the rate that would be expected given the entire population. As you can see by reviewing the table, African American students are nearly three times more likely than their non-African American peers to be identified as mentally retarded or intellectually disabled and over twice as likely to be identified as having emotional or behavioral disabilities. For no other racial or ethnic group is disproportionate representation as severe. In contrast, students from the Asian/Pacific Islander group have far less risk of being identified as learning disabled, intellectually disabled, or emotionally or behaviorally disabled than any other group of students.

Go to the Assignments and Activities section of Topic 3: Cultural and Linguistic Diversity, in the MyEducationLab for your course and complete the activity entitled "Cultural Diversity and Special Education".

### Continuum of Placements

Federal data also are gathered on the educational environments that form the continuum of placements in which students with disabilities are served, and these data reveal another interesting trend. All non-Caucasian student groups with disabilities, but especially Hispanic and African American, tend to be served in special education placements that separate them from their nondisabled peers more often than students in other groups (U.S. Department of Education, 2009). As you examine the detailed data in Figure 3.3, consider how the factors already presented in this chapter may affect this troubling pattern related to the environments in which students of different races/ethnicities receive special education.

## FIGURE 3.2

### Risk Ratios for Students with Disabilities Ages 6 to 21, by Race/Ethnicity (Fall 2004)[a]

| Disability[b] | American Indian/ Alaska Native | Asian/Pacific Islander | African American (not Hispanic) | Hispanic | White (not Hispanic) |
|---|---|---|---|---|---|
| Specific learning disabilities | 1.79 | 0.40 | 1.42 | 1.15 | 0.80 |
| Speech or language impairments | 1.33 | 0.71 | 1.06 | 0.90 | 1.07 |
| Mental retardation/intellectual disability | 1.24 | 0.47 | 2.83 | 0.66 | 0.63 |
| Emotional disturbance | 1.55 | 0.28 | 2.24 | 0.54 | 0.85 |
| Multiple disabilities | 1.38 | 0.61 | 1.50 | 0.67 | 1.02 |
| Hearing impairments | 1.31 | 1.22 | 1.12 | 1.24 | 0.78 |
| Orthopedic impairments | 0.97 | 0.77 | 0.99 | 1.08 | 1.00 |
| Other health impairments | 1.18 | 0.35 | 1.15 | 0.46 | 1.52 |
| Visual impairments | 1.27 | 1.00 | 1.24 | 0.94 | 0.91 |
| Autism | 0.71 | 1.26 | 1.03 | 0.55 | 1.30 |
| Deaf–blindness | 1.73 | 1.14 | 0.87 | 1.08 | 0.97 |
| Traumatic brain injury | 1.46 | 0.59 | 1.17 | 0.66 | 1.21 |
| All disabilities | 1.52 | 0.49 | 1.47 | 0.90 | 0.89 |

Source: U.S. Department of Education. (2009). *Twenty-eighth annual report to Congress on the implementation of Individuals with Disabilities Education Act, 2006.* Washington, DC: Author.
[a]A risk ratio of 1.0 indicates no difference between the racial/ethnic groups.
[b]Because the category "developmental delay" is optional and limited to students nine years old or younger, it is not included in this figure.

## Why Disproportionality Matters

Given that placement in special education classes generally includes smaller class sizes, individualized instruction, and greater per-pupil expenditures, you might ask why disproportionate representation is viewed as problematic, at least from the standpoint of those who are overrepresented in such programs. If special education structure and support improve learning, then why would it not be considered a privilege to have greater access to it?

The stigmatization associated with labeling is one reason that disproportionate representation has become an issue. Labels such as *mentally retarded* or *intellectually disabled* and *emotionally disturbed* have inherently negative connotations, and it is inappropriate to apply such labels to students who do not have disabilities merely as a means of giving them access to educational supports (National Alliance of Black School Educators, 2002). Labels

## FIGURE 3.3

### Percentage of Students with Disabilities Ages Six Through Twenty-One Being Educated in Different Educational Environments, by Race/Ethnicity

| Race | <21 percent outside regular class | 21–60 percent outside regular class | >60 percent outside regular class |
|---|---|---|---|
| White (not Hispanic) | 56.85 | 26.14 | 13.26 |
| Hispanic | 47.83 | 26.80 | 22.12 |
| African American (not Hispanic) | 41.00 | 27.23 | 26.23 |
| Asian/Pacific Islander | 50.10 | 22.38 | 23.43 |
| American Indian/Alaska Native | 56.65 | 32.92 | 9.97 |

Source: U.S. Department of Education. (2009). *Twenty-eighth annual report to Congress on the implementation of the Individuals with Disabilities Education Act, 2006.* Washington, DC: Author.

also can inadvertently encourage educators to lower expectations for the labeled students. In an attempt to address learning problems that teachers believe are intrinsic to certain students, they sometimes "teach down" to students who have disability labels (Ferri & Connor, 2005; Harry & Klingner, 2007). This practice can lead to a **self-fulfilling prophecy,** or the idea that students will do or become what is expected of them. Professionals can create or worsen learning problems in students who do not have disabilities by treating them as though they do have disabilities.

Related to the issue of labeling are the liabilities associated with instructional tracking. Students labeled as disabled often have reduced opportunities to interact with typical students. As suggested previously, this may be particularly true for students of color because they are more often placed in educational settings outside the general education classroom. Part of what students learn occurs through their interactions with peers, particularly in areas such as social skill development. If students are segregated in self-contained classrooms, they have fewer opportunities to see typical academic and social behaviors modeled by classmates. Additionally, research has suggested that grouping students homogeneously by ability depresses the academic achievement of students assigned to low-ability groups (Oakes & Lipton, 2003).

## Representation in Gifted Education

Racial and ethnic representation in gifted education is almost a mirror image of representation in special education. That is, African American students tend to appear in gifted education in smaller numbers than would be expected (Ford, Grantham, & Whiting, 2008). These students represent 14.5 percent of the school-age population, but they constitute only 8.4 percent of students served in gifted and talented education programs. Similar figures are found for Hispanic students, who represent 16.2 percent of the school-age population but comprise only 8.6 percent of students served in gifted and talented programs.

Somewhat higher percentages are reported for other racial and ethnic groups. For example, Asian students comprise 2.2 percent of the school-age population but 5.0 percent of students in gifted programs. Caucasian students comprise 71.2 percent of all students and 81.4 percent of students in gifted programs. A review of all these figures indicates that African American and Hispanic students are less than half as likely as white students to be identified as gifted or talented (Donovan & Cross, 2002b). When you reflect on what you have learned about culture and learning, why do you think this underrepresentation might occur?

## Factors Contributing to Disproportionate Representation

No easy answers can be found to the question of what causes the disproportionate representation of students of color in special and gifted education programs and how to reduce it. For nearly 40 years, the field has grappled with this issue (Dunn, 1968), and the discussion continues to receive significant attention today (Artiles, Rueda, Salazar, & Higareda, 2005; Skiba et al., 2008). Two factors that clearly seem to contribute to the problem are poverty and systemic bias.

### Poverty

Poverty is a critical variable that influences the occurrence of disabilities (Artiles & Bal, 2008). Higher poverty rates have been shown to exist among people of color than among people from the dominant culture. Specifically, poverty rates among African American and Hispanic children are more than twice those of their white counterparts (i.e., approximately 23 percent versus 10 percent of the population) (Donovan & Cross, 2002b). Poverty has been associated with factors such as increased childhood exposure to lead, increased prenatal exposure to toxins such as tobacco and alcohol, lack of prenatal care, and poor nutrition, all of which have been associated with increased disability rates.

Undoubtedly, the negative effects of poverty contribute to the disproportionate representation of students of color in special and gifted education (Skiba et al., 2008). However, once socioeconomic differences are accounted for, disproportionality remains significant

*Students of color, especially African American males, are more likely than white students to be identified as having certain disabilities, and they are more likely to be educated in a setting separate from their peers without disabilities.*

(Oswald, Coutinho, & Best, 2000; Skiba et al., 2008). This suggests that in addition to the effects of poverty, other variables contribute to disproportionate representation (Hosp & Reschly, 2004; Salend & Duhaney, 2005).

## Systemic Bias

At least part of the problem of disproportionate representation can be attributed to **systemic bias,** or favoritism toward a particular group that occurs at multiple levels within a society or institution, making such favoritism an implicit part of it. This type of bias can occur in many ways within an educational system. Here are some examples:

- *Curriculum and instruction.* As noted earlier, the content of the curriculum and the instructional approaches teachers use can predispose some students to failure. If only one worldview or cognitive orientation is embraced, some students will be placed at a disadvantage for learning and at greater risk for special education referral (Haar et al., 2002). In the Instruction in Action feature you can see one example of how to avoid this problem—by reviewing children's literature for potential bias.
- *Teacher attitude.* Although the topic makes some professionals uncomfortable, teachers themselves can harbor attitudes and beliefs that do not facilitate the education of culturally diverse students. Negative teacher attitudes and expectations toward students of color have been noted by a number of researchers (Cartledge & Kourea, 2008; Monroe, 2005; Moule, 2009). Classroom observational studies have suggested that teachers tend to have more positive interaction with white students (e.g., praising them or calling on them) than is the case for students of color (Casteel, 1998; Maholmes & Brown, 2002). Negative teacher attitudes also may be reflected in how discipline policies are implemented. Students of color have been found to be more likely than white students to receive harsher punishments for the same rule violations (Fenning & Rose, 2007; Townsend, Thomas, Witty, & Lee, 1997).
- *Special education referral process.* The special education referral process also has been criticized for potential bias (National Alliance of Black School Educators, 2002). Once this process has been initiated, it frequently assumes that any problems that exist are in the child. Professionals often do not critically examine how elements of the classroom

web link

www.nabe.org
The National Association for Bilingual Education is a national organization concerned with the education of language-minority students in U.S. schools.

## Reviewing Children's Literature for Bias

Three decades ago, the Council on Interracial Books for Children (1978) offered the following 10 guidelines as a starting point in evaluating children's books for bias. Because many libraries hold older titles in children's literature as well as newer ones, these guidelines remain valid today in culturally responsive instruction.

1. *Check the illustrations.*
   - Look for stereotypes. Check for oversimplified generalizations about a particular group that may carry derogatory implications.
   - Look for tokenism. Do all people of color look stereotypically alike, or are they depicted as genuine individuals with distinctive features?
   - Who's doing what? Do the illustrations consistently depict females and people of color in subservient or passive roles?

2. *Check the storyline.*
   - Standards for success. Do persons of color or individuals with disabilities have to exhibit superhuman qualities to gain acceptance and approval? In friendships between white and nonwhite children, is it the child of color who does most of the understanding and forgiving?
   - Resolution of problems. Are people of color considered "the problem"? Are problems faced by females, people of color, or people with disabilities consistently resolved through the benevolent intervention of a person who is male, white, or nondisabled?
   - Role of women. Are the achievements of female characters based on their own initiatives and intelligence, or are they a result of their looks or their relationships with male characters in the story?

3. *Look at the lifestyles.*
   - If people of color or people with disabilities are depicted as different, are negative value judgments implied? Look for inaccuracy and inappropriateness in the depiction of other cultures or the portrayal of individuals with disabilities.

4. *Weigh the relationships between people.*
   - Do the white characters in the story possess the power, assume the leadership, and make all the important decisions?

5. *Note the heroes.*
   - Are only "safe" heroes of color depicted—for example, those who have avoided serious conflicts with the white establishment of their time?

6. *Consider the effect on a child's self-image.*
   - What could be the effect on African American children to be continually bombarded with images of the color white as the ultimate in beauty, cleanliness, virtue, and so on and the color black as evil, dirty, menacing, and so on? What happens to a girl's self-image when she reads that boys perform all of the brave and important deeds?

7. *Consider the author's or illustrator's background.*
   - If a story deals with themes related to people of color or people with disabilities, what qualifies the author or illustrator to deal with the subject? What gives him or her credibility in this area?

8. *Check out the author's perspective.*
   - No author can be wholly objective. Read carefully to determine whether the direction of the author's perspective substantially weakens or strengthens the value of his or her written work. Is the perspective patriarchal or feminist? Is it solely Eurocentric, or do diverse cultural perspectives also appear?

9. *Watch for loaded words.*
   - A word is *loaded* when it has insulting overtones. Look for sexist language and words that exclude or ridicule women, people of color, or people with disabilities.

10. *Look at the copyright date.*
    - Nonsexist books, with rare exceptions, were not published before 1973. The copyright date, therefore, can be a clue as to how likely the book is to be overtly racist or sexist. However, a recent copyright date is not a guarantee of a book's relevance or sensitivity.

environment, such as those discussed previously in this chapter, may contribute to the academic or social challenges faced by referred students (Cartledge & Kourea, 2008). The possible contribution of teachers to students' problems likewise is seldom raised. Instruments used in the evaluation process also have been criticized for cultural bias (Salend & Duhaney, 2005), and the use of assessment information obtained from these instruments also has reportedly been tainted by prejudice based on gender, appearance, and socioeconomic status (Artiles & Trent, 1994).

Attention is focused as never before on how to reduce disproportionality, and through IDEA federal funds have been allocated to further study and address it. Among the recommendations for addressing disproportionality are these (Skiba et al., 2008):

- Better teacher preparation regarding cultural differences and potential biases
- Improved strategies for behavior management because discipline is one of the major reasons students are referred for special education services

- Prevention and early intervention, such as those used in RTI, a topic addressed later in this chapter
- Increased attention to possible bias in the assessment process for determining special education eligibility
- Increased family involvement in decision-making regarding strategies and interventions to address student needs

Each of these ideas requires focused and significant effort, and all of them demonstrate the complexity of this issue. Only through such efforts, however, is a more equitable education system likely to emerge—one that results in all students being represented proportionately in both special and gifted education. Several of these recommendations are guiding instruction practice and are discussed in more detail in the following sections.

## REVIEW · REFLECT · DISCUSS

1. Check on data from your local school districts and your state. What is the proportion of students of color in the school-age population? What is their proportion in special education programs? Gifted programs? What do these data imply?

2. Think about a time that you believe you've been treated unfairly in school—perhaps a teacher did not listen to your side of an argument with a classmate, or perhaps your excuse for a late assignment was not considered in assigning a grade for it. How did this experience make you feel? Now think about students from diverse backgrounds in schools. What types of biased treatment might they experience? What should teachers do to ensure all students are treated fairly?

# Recommended Practices for Diverse Students with Special Needs

Given the significant impact that culture plays in the educational process, increasing attention has been given to culturally responsive instruction, one of the topics addressed in the Speaking from Experience feature. Although additional research is needed in this area, several promising practices have been identified with respect to the education of culturally diverse students with disabilities. Two types of practices are important: Some of these practices relate to eliminating bias in the process by which students are determined to be eligible for special education, and others focus on the nature of instruction for diverse learners who have disabilities. Note that recommended practices related to students considered for gifted and talented programs are outlined in Chapter Fifteen.

## Promising Practices in Referral and Identification

As you have learned, the adverse effects of poverty on the learning process and the existence of cultural dissonance between teachers and students can complicate the identification of culturally diverse students with disabilities. For example, students who are preoccupied with satisfying basic needs (e.g., hunger, safety, and a sense of belonging) may not perform well academically and hence may be at increased risk for special education referral. Likewise, students whose cognitive styles or behaviors are not understood or embraced by their teachers also are at increased risk for special education referral (Cartledge & Kourea, 2008; Neal, McCray, Webb-Johnson, & Bridgest, 2003). Several steps can be taken to ensure fairness in the identification process.

### Redesigning the Prereferral and Intervention Process

As you learned in Chapter Two, before a referral for special education is officially made, the educators involved come together as a team to develop a good understanding of the

research
**NOTE**

Students who lack proficiency in both their own language and English are more likely than other students with disabilities to be educated in settings separate from their peers (Artiles, Rueda, Salazar, & Higareda, 2005).

Tanya Green is the principal of the Calverton Elementary-Middle School (pre-K–8) in the Baltimore City Schools. She started out thinking that she would become a doctor and earned her degree in pre-med biology. When her father became very ill, those plans were placed on hold, she took a science teaching position in a middle school not knowing if she had made the right choice, loved it, and decided that education should be her career. Here are her thoughts on leading a school in a way that fosters student success.

We are an unusual school. We have a very large special education population because we have multiple districtwide specialized programs. We have a program for students with emotional disabilities, one for students learning life skills, and a pre-K program for students with autism. Then we have all the other students with disabilities. And we have other children with special needs, too—some who have Section 504 plans, some who just struggle. We have 80 or 85 percent of our students on free or reduced lunch. But we don't even talk about all of that. We are just one school. Here is my advice to new teachers who want to work in an urban setting:

- What's in your heart? That's the first question you have to ask. Because teaching here is all in your heart; you have to believe in your heart for your children and not see a difference between them and other children. You have to believe they can achieve. You have to ask yourself: Is this really for me?
- Read. Learn about what urban schools are like. Learn as many strategies as you can. You'll need all of them to help children succeed.
- Go visit schools so you can learn about the culture of urban schools. It's very different than the culture of suburban schools.

- Don't jump in the field with the preconceived notion that you're going be in a little room with a few kids. That's not the reality. You will co-teach, you will co-plan, you will be that person who has that strategy that another teacher needs.
- It's all about self-reflection. Always think, "Did I say that the right way? Did I do that the best way?"
- Some teachers see the littlest thing, especially with boys, as a behavior problem. You have to bring it back to the reality: This is where the child is cognitively, developmentally. It's ok.
- At my school we use the word "children" instead of "students" because I want to keep in your mind, even if it's an 8th grader, this is a child. They are not adults. The *children* are counting on you. You have to be there for them.

I was a troubled teen, even though academically I was smart. I was constantly suspended. I was constantly cursing at my teachers. I was angry inside, I was poor—had holes in my shoes, I went home eating beans every day, I was happy to get the school lunch every day. For years, no teacher, not one teacher, ever said to me, "Why are you angry? What's wrong?" Then a gym teacher said, "You're a great runner. I saw you running around that track. I want you to come join the track team." And I was shocked, because somebody was saying something good to me. And I ran track, I won all kinds of medals, I went to college on a half track scholarship, half academic scholarship. It changed me, because someone took a second to look at me and say something good to me. Are you going to be that person who noticed me? Because had no one noticed me, where would I be?

---

student's learning or behavior difficulties and to suggest strategies to address these difficulties. In the case of culturally diverse learners, a number of authors have suggested that during the traditional prereferral process or response to intervention (RTI) procedures, the team should carefully examine factors in the student's environment that may influence learning (Atwater, 2008; National Alliance of Black School Educators, 2002). For example, Garcia and Ortiz (1988) recommended systematic examination of classroom and teacher variables, including the following:

- The experience of the teacher in working effectively with multicultural populations
- Evidence that the teacher is knowledgeable with respect to the student's culture
- The extent to which the curriculum incorporates aspects of the student's culture
- The extent to which instruction addresses the student's language characteristics
- The extent to which instruction reflects the student's cognitive style
- The overall quality of instruction and opportunity to learn

Rueda, Klingner, Sager, and Velasco (2008) add that this phase of intervention cannot be presumed to be sensitive to cultural factors that may affect student learning. They note the importance of placing test scores within the context of a student's language proficiency, length of residence in the United States, and the impact of any unusual stressors (e.g., homelessness). What other factors might prereferral teams consider in order to avoid unintended bias in their discussions of students?

## Alternative Assessment Strategies

Beyond enhanced prereferral strategies, others have recommended alternatives to or enhancements of traditional assessment procedures (Fore, Burke, & Martin, 2006; Green, McIntosh, Cook-Morales, & Robinson-Zanartu, 2005). One suggestion has been to make the eligibility determination process less dependent on standardized, norm-referenced assessment instruments because they tend to emphasize verbal skills, analytical thinking, and field-independent cognitive styles—elements that may lead to lower scores for many culturally diverse students. For example, portfolio assessment, performance assessment, and curriculum-based assessment have been offered as effective ways to accurately assess diverse students' capabilities:

- In *portfolio assessment,* examples of students' everyday work are selected to document competence and progress in a certain area. For example, writing samples may be collected over time to show the development of writing skills.
- *Performance assessment* involves evaluating students' skills in a certain area through actual performance of an activity. For example, performance assessment could be used to evaluate scientific knowledge and problem-solving skills by having students perform an experiment.
- *Curriculum-based assessment* specifically targets components of the curriculum actually taught in the students' classroom (as opposed to commercially available standardized tests that may or may not be closely aligned with the school's curriculum). In some applications of curriculum-based assessment, students' performance is compared to that of classroom or school peers, not to a national sample, as is the case for most norm-referenced tests.

Although there is no guarantee that alternative assessment approaches are unbiased or even that these approaches are feasible on a large scale, they do have the potential to create a more culturally responsive process for determining which students have disabilities and need special education.

## Universal Screening and Early Intervention

Universal screening and intensive early intervention for young children, such as RTI (introduced in Chapter Two), also have been proposed as being potentially valuable. Through universal screening and early intervention, students with learning problems receive high-quality interventions targeted to their areas of need in general education beginning early in kindergarten, and so factors that might negatively affect learning can be addressed before they lead to school failure. Only if these interventions fail is a student found eligible for special education. You will learn more detail about this aspect of response to intervention in Chapter Five.

Obviously, one key to the successful implementation of this approach is the broad conceptualization of high-quality interventions. If only one cognitive style is emphasized in generating interventions, students who do not prefer this cognitive style will be at a disadvantage. In this case, the same bias and ultimate outcome could result.

## *Promising Practices in Instruction*

A number of instructional strategies have been found helpful in the education of culturally and linguistically diverse learners with disabilities. These approaches—including differentiated instruction, universal design, multicultural education, and sheltered English—are briefly described in the following sections. The approaches are complementary and often are combined to maximize instructional outcomes for culturally and linguistically diverse learners with disabilities (Van Garderen & Whittaker, 2006; Voltz, Sims, Nelson, & Bivens, 2008).

### Differentiated Instruction

*Differentiated instruction* focuses on designing and delivering effective learning experiences for students, regardless of their unique characteristics. It is intended to allow teachers to more effectively address the learning needs and preferences of individual students (King-Sears, 2008).

**web link**

www.edchange.org/multicultural
The Multicultural Pavilion is a comprehensive source of information related to multicultural education.

Differentiated instruction is integral to teaching diverse students and includes strategies such as learning contracts and tiered lessons (Tomlinson, 2001). Learning contracts allow teachers and students to work together in tailoring the what and how of instruction to student learning needs and preferences. For example, in an instructional unit on poetry that uses learning contracts, individual students may have the opportunity to identify the kind of poetry they wish to target for in-depth study, select the strategies they would like to use to learn about the selected poetry (e.g., Internet research, analysis of the work of famous poets), and determine how they would like to demonstrate what they have learned (e.g., writing original poetry, delivering an oral presentation comparing the writing styles of famous poets). Tiered lessons allow teachers to differentiate instruction within a given skill area based on the prior knowledge and skill base that individual students bring to the learning task. For example, in a tiered lesson on telling time using a standard clock face, three tiers or groups may be used. One group may be doing cooperative learning activities focused on telling time to the nearest quarter hour; another to the nearest 5-minute interval; and yet a third to the nearest minute (Tomlinson, 2001).

### Universal Design

Like differentiated instruction, universal design should be a key dimension of working with diverse learners. In universal design, learning activities provide multiple means of representation or modes of presentation (e.g., auditory, visual, varying levels of complexity). Learning activities also must allow students to respond in various modes and should be designed to engage learners with varying interests and aptitudes (Acrey, Johnstone, & Milligan, 2005). Educators often use instructional or assistive technology in the implementation of universal design to make instruction accessible for a broader array of students (Meo, 2008). For example, electronic books—electronic versions of texts that have been downloaded onto handheld devices—may enable the use of software to translate these print materials into multiple languages. This would be particularly helpful for English language learners with disabilities.

### Multicultural Education

**Multicultural education** is an approach to education that includes perspectives from and content about diverse groups, embraces diverse cognitive styles, and promotes equity in a diverse society. Five major dimensions of multicultural education, also depicted visually in Figure 3.4, are these:

1. *Content integration* implies that the curriculum that students learn should include content about diverse populations and present information from diverse points of view.
2. *Knowledge construction* focuses on how teachers explore with students the influences of culture on (a) the manner in which knowledge itself is constructed and (b) the manner in which decisions are made regarding what does and does not constitute valuable or important knowledge.
3. *Prejudice reduction* refers to activities that are designed to examine and reduce bias in attitudes.
4. *Equity pedagogy* refers to the use of instructional strategies that embrace the learning characteristics and cognitive styles of diverse populations.
5. An *empowering school culture* focuses on eradicating systemic factors such as the negative effects of grouping and tracking practices and disproportionality in achievement and placement in special education (Banks, 2001).

Teaching with a multicultural perspective is a challenging approach that permeates every aspect of instruction. It has implications not only for *what* is taught but also *how* it is taught. Like differentiated instruction and universal design, it seeks to build on the strengths and prior knowledge students bring to the learning context. An example of a multicultural perspective is illustrated in the Instruction in Action feature. It demonstrates how to make a specific lesson plan more culturally responsive.

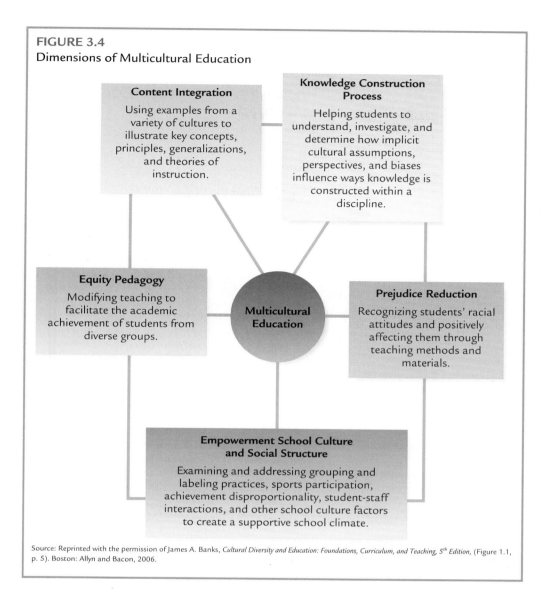

**FIGURE 3.4**
Dimensions of Multicultural Education

**Content Integration**

Using examples from a variety of cultures to illustrate key concepts, principles, generalizations, and theories of instruction.

**Knowledge Construction Process**

Helping students to understand, investigate, and determine how implicit cultural assumptions, perspectives, and biases influence ways knowledge is constructed within a discipline.

**Equity Pedagogy**

Modifying teaching to facilitate the academic achievement of students from diverse groups.

**Multicultural Education**

**Prejudice Reduction**

Recognizing students' racial attitudes and positively affecting them through teaching methods and materials.

**Empowerment School Culture and Social Structure**

Examining and addressing grouping and labeling practices, sports participation, achievement disproportionality, student-staff interactions, and other school culture factors to create a supportive school climate.

Source: Reprinted with the permission of James A. Banks, *Cultural Diversity and Education: Foundations, Curriculum, and Teaching, 5th Edition,* (Figure 1.1, p. 5). Boston: Allyn and Bacon, 2006.

## Instruction for English Language Learners

As you have been reading this chapter, perhaps you have been wondering about students whose primary language is not English. These students are referred to as **English language learners (ELLs).** With the growing number of English language learners in schools has come increased attention. In 2007, 20 percent of school-age students spoke a language other than English at home, up from 9 percent in 1979. Of these, 75 percent (2.1 million) spoke Spanish; 12 percent (320,000) spoke Asian/Pacific Islander languages, 10 percent (287,000) spoke other Indo-European languages, and 3 percent (72,000) spoke another language (National Center for Education Statistics, 2009c). It is estimated that as many as 1 million of these students experience serious learning or emotional disabilities and may be eligible for special education (Hart, 2009).

Given the current and growing number of English language learners in schools, it probably is not surprising that the No Child Left Behind Act requires state and local education agencies to establish English proficiency standards. Although no specific instructional methodology is endorsed, the legislation provides financial assistance to states to support their efforts in helping English language learners meet English proficiency standards. Some

**web link**

www.nameorg.org
Several professional organizations have multicultural education as their primary interest. One example is the National Association of Multicultural Education.

## Multicultural Teaching: Bringing Learning to Life

*Grade Level:* 10–12

*Time:* Five class periods

*Students:* Several Spanish–English bilingual students, a few students with learning disabilities (LD), and a heterogeneous group of typical students

### Objectives

1. Students will identify the main parts of the cardiovascular system and their functions.
2. Students will describe several heart diseases or conditions and their causes.
3. Students will learn a healthy dietary and exercise program.

### Lesson Plan A

**Suggested Procedures**

1. Explain that the class will spend the next few days studying the cardiovascular system, related diseases, and disease prevention.
2. Assign pages in the textbook to read on the structure and function of the cardiovascular system and risk factors.
3. Review the major concepts in a reading assignment, asking questions frequently to check comprehension. Show a video on how the heart works. Encourage students to take notes on the discussion of the textbook assignment and the film.
4. Assign pages in the textbook to read on heart attacks and heart disease.
5. Review the major concepts in the reading assignment; give a mini-lecture elaborating on what physicians do when someone has a heart attack.
6. Invite the school nurse as a guest speaker to talk about how exercise and diet can promote cardiovascular health.

### Evaluation

Evaluate each student's mastery of the objectives using a quiz.

### Resources

Video on how the heart works.

### Lesson Plan B

**Suggested Procedures**

1. Invite students to share the experiences of family members or friends who have heart disease. Explain that the class will study the cardiovascular system, diseases, and disease prevention.
2. Divide the class into three groups based on students' reading levels. Have three sets of reading materials ready. One set, written at the lowest reading level, describes heart diseases. A second set, written at an intermediate level, describes the circulatory system. A third set, written at a more difficult level, describes the parts of the heart. Distribute the appropriate reading materials to each group. Have students read and then quiz each other within their groups until all group members have mastered the material.
3. Regroup the students into four groups; each new group should have two or three members from each of the first groupings. Assign each new group one of the following problems or tasks to complete collaboratively:
   - Explain what types of exercise contribute to the health of the cardiovascular system. Suggest an exercise program for persons ages fifteen to twenty-five that will promote cardiovascular health; give reasons for your suggestions.
   - Explain what cholesterol does to the cardiovascular system. Develop European American and Mexican menus that are low in cholesterol.

---

instructional methods commonly used with English language learners are discussed in the following sections. The Technology Notes feature addresses the specific topic of technology and diverse learners.

### Bilingual Education

For some students, the preferred strategy for reaching English proficiency standards is **bilingual education,** an approach that uses the student's dominant language along with English for instructional purposes. The most common model of bilingual education, the *transitional approach,* uses the student's native language for instruction only until the student has mastered English sufficiently to receive instruction in English only. Because the main goal of these programs is to place students in English-speaking classes as soon as possible, they have been described as programs designed to self-destruct (Winzer & Mazurek, 1998). Students typically exit these bilingual programs within 2 to 5 years. Maintenance bilingual approaches are designed to be longer term and to enhance the development of competence both in the native language and English.

### English as a Second Language

In **English as a second language (ESL)** programs, professionals teach English directly to individuals who speak another language. However, unlike bilingual programs, ESL programs

Go to the Building Teaching Skills and Dispositions section of Topic 3: Cultural and Linguistic Diversity, and Individualized Education Program, in the MyEducationLab for your course and complete the activity entitled "Providing Culturally Responsive Instruction".

- Develop a Spanish–English dictionary that will help Spanish-speaking people with limited English skills to communicate with an English-speaking doctor about common heart problems.
- Determine and describe the functions an artificial heart must perform. Describe the conditions under which one might be helped by an artificial heart.

4. Have each group orally present its completed project to the class. Encourage students to use relevant diagrams, charts, and activities to engage classmates. Make copies of the students' exercise programs, menus, and dictionaries for the entire class.

5. Provide a study guide on the material students should know, as well as additional copies of the first reading assignments for students who wish to read what other groups read. Encourage the students to study together and to quiz each other on the study guide.

### Evaluation

1. Evaluate students' comprehension of main ideas through group projects.
2. Evaluate students' mastery of the objectives using a quiz.

How Do the Revisions Improve the Lesson?

### Learning Style

- Many students tend to learn better through cooperative learning (Lesson Plan B) than through individualistic learning (Lesson Plan A). Cooperative learning also fosters peer tutoring, which helps low-achieving students be successful.
- Many students learn better and achieve more when they actively participate during instruction (Lesson Plan B) rather than being passive recipients of information (Lesson Plan A).

### Relevance

- Little attempt is made in Lesson Plan A to relate the curriculum to these particular students.
- Lesson Plan B includes several attempts: the introductory discussion, the use of the Spanish language in one project, the use of Mexican foods in a group project, and the invitation for students themselves to develop a diet and exercise program.

### Skill Levels

- Lesson Plan A makes no provision for students' diverse skill levels.
- Lesson Plan B does this in two ways: First, reading assignments are made according to students' reading levels, although students later have to teach each other about what they read so no one misses content areas. Second, students are encouraged to study together with a study guide to direct work.

### Language

- The Spanish–English dictionary assignment helps bilingual students learn English words. It can also sensitize English-speaking students to language barriers.

### Boredom

- Lesson Plan B is more interesting than Lesson Plan A without sacrificing integrity. It also encourages more thinking. Students learn better when the lesson itself is enjoyable.

*Source:* Adapted from Grant C.A., & Sleeter, C.E. (1998). *Turning on learning: Five approaches for multicultural teaching plans for race, class, gender, and disability.* Reprinted by permission of John Wiley & Sons, Inc.

do not use the student's native language but instead provide direct instruction on the English language, usually in a setting separate from general education. In ESL programs, no conscious effort is made to maintain or facilitate the development of the student's native language (del Carmen Salazar, 2008).

## Sheltered English

A third instructional approach for students who are not native English speakers uses controlled vocabulary and sentence structure, along with prompting, to facilitate comprehension in English language learners. In these **sheltered English** programs, teachers might use concrete objects and gestures to help convey meaning. Language demands also may be modified by adjusting the rate of speech and providing context clues (e.g., using pictures). As English language competence improves, prompts and controlled vocabulary are gradually removed (Duran, 2006).

When you consider bilingual education, ESL, and sheltered English approaches, you can deduce that each has advantages and disadvantages. Which programs are used in the schools in your geographic region? As you discuss this topic with your classmates, keep in mind and add to your conversation the other cultural components introduced earlier in this chapter.

*Students who are English language learners (ELLs) may receive services through bilingual, English as a second language (ESL), or sheltered English programs.*

## Putting It All Together

There is definitely a lot to think about in planning and delivering instruction for diverse students with disabilities. With this in mind, several authors have integrated aspects of differentiated instruction, multicultural education, universal design, and sheltered English into a single framework. Voltz, Sims, Nelson, and Bivens (2005) developed the M²ECCA framework, which applies the approaches just discussed to the critical aspects of instruction: methods, materials, environment, content, collaboration, and assessment.

- *Methods of instruction.* This is the how of instruction—that is, what teachers do to teach the lesson. Differentiated instruction, universal design, multicultural education, and sheltered English all address this component. The students' strengths, interests, experiential base, cognitive style, and facility with English must be considered in selecting the approach that will be most likely to maximize learning.

- *Materials of instruction.* These are the tangible tools that are used in the instructional process. Differentiated instruction, universal design, and sheltered English all speak to accessibility of instructional materials. For example, universal design encourages the use of instructional and assistive technology as a means of making learning accessible to a broader range of students. Differentiated instruction and sheltered English support the use of materials that reflect the skill level, learning preferences, and facility with English of the students with whom the materials are to be used. Cultural plurality is emphasized in multicultural education and requires that instructional materials reflect ethnic and gender diversity, as well as diversity in disability status.

- *Environment of the classroom.* The physical arrangement, along with other issues that affect the instructional climate (e.g., classroom and behavior management), contribute to this factor. For example, to promote an empowering school culture, multicultural education stresses the importance of creating an environment that values individual differences. This, in turn, creates a climate in which students are more likely to be accepting of differences made in assignments that are a natural outgrowth of differentiated instruction. Differentiated instruction recommends varying the physical arrangement of the class and the rules and routines used to accommodate differences in learning and interaction styles.

- *Content of instruction.* The curriculum is the next part of this model. Multicultural education seeks to enhance the curriculum by integrating content that reflects a variety of cultures, reduces bias, and explores the knowledge construction process. Differentiated instruction, to some degree, also addresses curricular issues. While the basic curriculum itself is held constant in differentiated instruction, the pace at which learners proceed through the curriculum and the depth with which curricular content is explored may vary based on student needs.

- *Collaboration in instruction.* Interactions to promote student success occur among various professionals within schools (e.g., general education teachers, special education teachers, bilingual or ESL teachers, administrators), but they also include the interactions that occur between school professionals and parents and the interactions that occur between school professionals and professionals in nonschool settings (e.g., social service agencies, government agencies). An example from differentiated instruction is co-teaching, an approach discussed in Chapter Four. Multicultural education and sheltered English likewise suggest the need for educators across disciplines to work together and for educators to reach out to families and members of the community in bridging any cultural gaps that may exist between teachers and their students.

- *Assessment process.* Assessment both begins and ends the instructional cycle, providing data on how far students have progressed in the curriculum and what their strengths and needs are. This, in turn, forms the foundation for new instruction. By using principles embodied in multicultural education and universal design, professionals maximize the effectiveness of assessment by reducing the extent to which factors such as cultural mismatches and residual effects of disabilities inappropriately influence students' ability to show what they know.

As you can see, the M²ECCA framework integrates many of the principles of differentiated instruction, universal design, multicultural education, and sheltered English. As a professional educator, you can use this framework to better understand and address the needs of all your diverse learners.

## REVIEW · REFLECT · DISCUSS

1. Review the principles of universal design for learning as outlined in this chapter and also Chapter One. What are examples of these principles in practice for students from diverse groups?
2. Use the M²ECCA model as the basis for discussing how you might design effective instruction for Xiong, Josef, and Maria, the students you met at the beginning of this chapter. How should their teachers use their unique characteristics in planning instruction?

## Parents and Families of Diverse Students with Disabilities

If the mother of one of your students sent you an e-mail each week thanking you for your efforts with her child, asking questions, and offering to volunteer in the class, how would you react? What if that same parent volunteered to bring snacks for a class party or school dance? Or sent her child with a "Teachers Are the Best" coffee mug for you at the holidays? On the other hand, what would you think of a mother who never returned your phone calls (the only number you have for her is at her place of employment)? Who did not return permission forms for school activities? Who failed to come to IEP and other meetings? But then, what if you learned that this mother does not speak English fluently, does not have a phone at home, does not have transportation, and is caring for her elderly grandmother? The point is that biases can exist beyond the immediate classroom when professionals work with families.

Most educators would agree that educational programs are strengthened when families and school personnel work together effectively. Attention to the task of developing effective partnerships with families is important for all students, but it can be particularly critical with families whose cultures differ significantly from the culture of the school (Obiakor, Utley, Smith, & Harris-Obiakor, 2002). Unfortunately, it is with this very population of families that schools have historically been most challenged in developing effective collaborative relationships (Coots, 2007), as may be the case for Xiong's family, introduced at the beginning of the chapter.

### Parents of Diverse Learners and Participation in Their Children's Education

Interesting information regarding parent participation by race and ethnicity is displayed in Figure 3.5. Parents were asked whether they had participated in various school activities during the past school year, including the IEP process. The figure shows little variation across race and ethnicity in the extent to which parents indicated that they had attended an IEP meeting. However, parents of color were considerably less likely than their white counterparts to believe that the level or nature of their involvement in the IEP process was satisfactory. In contrast, Fish (2008) completed a similar study and found a high degree of parent satisfaction, but 80 percent of the parents responding were Caucasian and in a middle- to upper-middle-class socioeconomic area.

## FIGURE 3.5
### Parent Participation in the IEP Process by Race/Ethnicity

These are data from the U.S. Department of Education on the extent to which family members from various racial and ethnic groups participate in the IEP process.

| Percentage of parents reporting... | White | African American | Hispanic | Asian/Pacific Islander | Native American |
|---|---|---|---|---|---|
| Attend IEP meeting | 91.5 | 82.2 | 85.4 | 93.3 | 82.9 |
| IEP goals were created: | | | | | |
| · Mostly by family member(s) | 1.2 | 1.1 | 0.4 | 0.0 | 14.3 |
| · Mostly by school staff | 32.2 | 30.3 | 39.8 | 23.2 | 30.4 |
| · By family member(s) and school staff | 66.3 | 67.0 | 59.7 | 76.5 | 55.4 |
| IEP goals were appropriate and challenging: | | | | | |
| · Strongly agree | 46.4 | 44.0 | 35.2 | 39.9 | 30.1 |
| · Agree | 46.0 | 44.3 | 55.2 | 52.9 | 27.9 |
| · Disagree and strongly disagree | 7.6 | 11.7 | 9.7 | 7.2 | 42.0 |
| IEP services were: | | | | | |
| · Highly individualized | 45.5 | 43.0 | 46.1 | 24.1 | 37.2 |
| · Somewhat individualized | 49.1 | 47.9 | 41.2 | 68.8 | 47.9 |
| · Not individualized | 5.4 | 9.2 | 12.8 | 7.1 | 14.9 |
| Involvement in the IEP process was: | | | | | |
| · Less than desired | 26.4 | 49.7 | 42.0 | 60.5 | 30.4 |
| · About the right amount | 73.3 | 48.8 | 56.3 | 39.5 | 69.0 |
| · More than desired | 0.4 | 1.5 | 1.7 | 0.1 | 0.6 |

Source: U.S. Department of Education. (2001). *Twenty-third annual report to Congress on the implementation of the Individuals with Disabilities Education Act.* Washington, DC: Author.

## Factors Educators Directly Influence

Despite the recognized need for developing educational partnerships with culturally diverse families, educators may engage in a number of practices that are counterproductive to this goal. For example, educators sometimes may believe that families from middle- or high-socioeconomic backgrounds are more concerned about their children's learning and more interested in being involved in their education than are families from low-socioeconomic backgrounds. Based on these preconceived notions, educators may devote greater efforts to working with some parents and family members than others and to value their input more. Some of the variance that may occur in how presumably concerned parents respond to school personnel versus how presumably unconcerned parents respond may be because, in part, of differences in how school personnel interact with them from the outset. A self-fulfilling prophecy can apply to families just as it can apply to students.

Another practice that sometimes thwarts efforts to develop collaborative partnerships with culturally diverse families is the use of a one-size-fits-all approach to family involvement. In such an approach, educators unilaterally expect families to interact with them in a prescribed way. Families whose cultural frameworks and life circumstances are similar to those of school personnel may be more likely to embrace these often unspoken expectations. However, as cultural dissonance increases, so does the likelihood that roles designated by school personnel for family members will be deemed untenable or unproductive by them. If families are uncomfortable with the school's view of family involvement, they may be inclined to avoid it (Harry, 2002). Unfortunately, their actions often are misinterpreted as a lack of interest or lack of caring.

In addition to showing overall respect for diverse cultural groups, teachers must remember that within any group, culturally influenced factors also can affect home–school interactions. For example, conceptualizations of disability are culturally influenced, particularly with respect to areas such as learning disabilities, mild intellectual disabilities, autism, and emotional disabilities (Banks, 2001; Morrier, Hess, & Heflin, 2008; Winzer &

### research NOTE

Subedi (2006) found that pre-service teachers were resistant to learning about religious diversity, and he recommended that this topic become part of teacher education diversity curricula.

Mazurek, 1998). However, conceptions of disability vary according to group norms and expectations (Harry, 2002). In some instances, parents from diverse cultures may hold broader ideas about normalcy than is the case in the traditional school context (Harry, 2002). When the student performs adequately in nonschool settings, parents may reject the idea presented by educators that their child has a disability. This would not be an instance of denial but rather a reflection of dissonance between conceptualizations of disability. Consider Josef, one of the students you met at the beginning of the chapter. Given his competence in home and community environments, it may be difficult for his family to believe that a diagnosis of an intellectual disability is credible.

## Factors beyond the Direct Influence of Educators

*Partnering with diverse families on behalf of their children with disabilities includes building an understanding of their perspectives and priorities.*

Other factors beyond the direct control of educators also can adversely affect interactions with culturally diverse families. For example, family members may harbor unhelpful preconceived notions about schools and school personnel for several reasons. Historically, schools have not served diverse populations well (Bennett, 2003). If family members of culturally diverse students experienced school difficulties themselves, their attitudes toward their children's schools may be influenced by their past negative experiences. Additionally, culturally diverse families may experience feelings of distrust for school personnel that result from the view that the school is merely an extension of a culture that they find oppressive and from which they feel alienated. As you might expect, research has suggested that this distrust is greater in high-poverty schools (Goddard, Tschannen-Moran, & Hoy, 2001). Parents from culturally diverse backgrounds also may be offended by the disproportionate representation of students of color in some areas of special education (Hernandez, Harry, Newman, & Cameto, 2008).

Other socioeconomic realities also can negatively affect the development of partnerships with culturally diverse families. The fact that people of color are disproportionately represented among our nation's poor often means that these families spend a greater proportion of their time, energy, and efforts in meeting basic survival needs than is the case for other families. Additionally, parents of students with disabilities must not only address the everyday stresses of parenting but also must manage stresses associated with having a child with special needs. In the case of culturally diverse parents of students with disabilities, these stresses are further compounded by being culturally different in a society that often views such differences negatively. Given the myriad sources of stress faced by many culturally diverse parents of students with disabilities, it seems reasonable that these parents may not always be physically, emotionally, or psychologically available to participate as vigorously in the education of their children as educators—or they themselves—might desire.

research
**NOTE**

It matters where students with learning disabilities and emotional disorders live: Some states show considerable disproportionality in gender in these two disability categories whereas others do not (Coutinho & Oswald, 2005).

## Developing Collaborative Relationships

Despite the special challenges associated with building partnerships with culturally diverse families, such partnerships can be developed successfully—a fact illustrated in the Woods family story in the Firsthand Account feature. Approaches that encourage educators to personalize interactions with families are helpful in this regard. One approach developed by Shea and Bauer (1993) includes five phases that involve asking parents to identify goals they have for collaborative relationships and activities that may be used productively to accomplish these goals. The five phases include the following:

- *Intake and assessment.* During this phase, interactions occur between family members and educators to determine the needs of each participant regarding the educational relationship. This phase helps answer these questions: What needs of this family hopefully

**ANGIE WOODS**

*is the mother of Junior, an eighth-grader who receives special education services and who recently had the privilege of posing for the pictured poster advertising the United Way fund. Angie works as an employment specialist for the Arc, a national organization that supports individuals with intellectual and developmental disabilities and their families. Angie has always been active in working with school personnel to ensure that Junior receives an appropriate education. Here is their story.*

I need to start with this: I went to the doctor—I had a bad case of bronchitis—and they said they were going to give me a pregnancy test before they could prescribe any medicine. I said, "Fine" because I wasn't pregnant. But the doctor came back and said, "You're six months pregnant," and I started crying. So I immediately got a prenatal doctor and saw him every week. Then they said the baby was in distress, and they took him about three weeks early. They immediately took him to the neonatal intensive care unit, and he was on a ventilator because he couldn't breathe—he was in neonatal intensive care for six months. Then they said he had some birth defects, but there was no name for it. His right foot was clubfoot and his right leg was shorter than his left. He had to be on a ventilator until he was two years old. He had surgeries on both of his eyes for "lazy eye," and he is deaf in one ear. He also had several surgeries for hernia repair, and we've just come back from surgery for scoliosis [curvature of the spine].

Junior started in special education at age three in Head Start. We were so excited that his dad and I had the video camera following him to school that first day. The kids were wonderful; all the teachers were wonderful. They saw Junior as just a little child who needed some help. I was working part time so I started volunteering at his school. That was a great two years.

We had a rough kindergarten year. After the first day, the principal stopped me and complained that Junior had a difficult time finding his way around school. I said, "Well, it's the first day of kindergarten—aren't most of the children like that?" Then he said, "He's not potty trained." I left the office and Junior met me in the hallway and he said, "Mom, I had a good day." And we talked about what he did. He saw my tears and said, "What's the matter? Didn't you have a good day?" All I could tell him was that it really was a good day because he had a good day. I cried all the way home.

Well, we ended up having a meeting and there were lots of people there—all the specialists, the director of Head Start. They just kept bringing in chairs. My husband and I started explaining about Junior. At one point I said, "When you're worried about how to save your child's life, who gives a darn about potty training? If we've gotten through everything else, we'll get through potty training, too." And I understood for the first time about not being wanted, about someone not wanting your child. Well, it all worked out. Junior got an assistant to help him in class—that made a big difference because the teacher had help. Then we could build a relationship with the kindergarten teacher.

By first grade, we only needed the assistant for Junior part of the time, and by the next year we didn't need her at all. And what we learned from all that was that we wanted to work with the teachers. They're professionals, and part of this is my responsibility. I always tell teachers, "If you need something, ask me." I'm a good ally—and now we're looking for solutions together.

Since kindergarten, everything really has been wonderful. Teachers are wonderful, his speech therapist is wonderful. . . . Junior has a learning disability in math. He has a resource teacher at school, and he receives speech services. He also has a tutor who works with him when he's homebound because of surgery. He used to have adaptive physical education, but now he participates in everything and the PE teacher just works around his limitations. Junior is now in the eighth grade and doing well. Last year he was just one "C" away from making the honor roll. He participates in challenger sports and other community activities. As a single mother, I now receive additional financial support that helps me to hire workers to help take care of Junior.

Next year Junior goes to high school—it's going to be a big challenge. But we'll make it. We'll help the teachers and let them know Junior's capabilities so they can push him to his potential. We want to focus on what he can do, not what he can't do.

will be satisfied through the collaborative relationship? What needs of educators hopefully will be satisfied?

- *Selection of goals.* During this phase, specific goals of the collaborative relationship are jointly developed on an individual family basis. These goals are derived from the stated needs of all parties and help to shape the nature of activities that will constitute family involvement.
- *Planning and implementing activities.* This phase involves implementing the activities designed to accomplish the goals outlined in the previous phase.
- *Evaluation of activities.* This phase includes input from families as well as educators. It helps to answer questions such as these: Are we following through with our plan? Is our plan doing a good job of addressing our needs?

- *Review.* This phase allows for a review of the process as well as the product of the collaborative relationship. It helps to answer questions such as these: To what extent have our needs changed? What changes need to be made in the process we use to collaborate?

An approach such as this allows parents to become more active partners in shaping the home–school relationship. It also provides a flexible framework in which the life circumstances and cultural characteristics of individual families can be readily accommodated. Meeting with family members in nonschool settings, such as the local library, church, or fast-food restaurant, are examples of alternative sites that may be mutually agreed on by educators and individual families. Helping families access needed resources such as health care, English language classes, and parent training classes may be a unique way to develop collaborative partnerships designed around needs articulated by some families.

The development of effective collaborative partnerships with families of culturally diverse learners is integral to the task of delivering appropriate educational services to this population of students. Families, regardless of cultural or socioeconomic group, generally are concerned about the educational well-being of their children. It is up to every educator to find ways to connect with families and build effective educational partnerships with them.

http://www.diversitycouncil.org
The Diversity Council website includes activities designed to help elementary, middle, and high school students learn about diversity, bias and racism, and the importance of respecting those different from oneself.

## REVIEW · REFLECT · DISCUSS

1. What school factors do you think could be particularly intimidating for parents who are recent immigrants to this country?
2. What are three specific actions you could take as an educator to facilitate their participation in their children's education?

# Issues and Trends Affecting Diverse Exceptional Learners

The conditions of urban education disproportionately affect students of color because it is largely these students who populate urban classrooms: Sixty-five of the 100 largest school districts in the United States enroll under 50 percent students who are Caucasian. One-third of these districts have student populations more than 75 percent non-Caucasian (National Center for Education Statistics, 2009a). The following discussion highlights critical issues in this domain.

### Equity Issues

A number of equity issues arise with respect to urban education. For example, student access to fully credentialed, experienced teachers is a chronic problem (Nieto, 2002–2003). In special education, large school districts are more likely than their smaller counterparts to cite lack of qualified applicants as a significant barrier to filling special education positions. Researchers have suggested that the problem of getting and keeping highly qualified special educators in urban areas is so significant that extraordinary strategies such as offering financial incentives are needed to alleviate the problem (Sindelar et al., 2007). This implies that students with disabilities in urban settings are less likely than other students with special needs to have the benefit of fully prepared teachers.

Another important equity issue is related to funding (Zhou, 2009). During the 1999–2000 school year, urban districts across the country reported an average expenditure of $11,933 per student for students with disabilities, in comparison to an average of $12,581 per student for students with disabilities in suburban districts (U.S. Department of Education, 2002e). While this discrepancy may not seem large, the magnitude of need also must be considered. Typically, the need for support services of various types is greater in high-poverty schools such as those in urban areas. Consequently, these schools are faced with the task of doing more with less.

Another equity issue concerns the schools themselves. The physical condition of urban schools often compares unfavorably to that of suburban counterparts. For example, inner-city

dimensions of
**DIVERSITY**

Whether parents monitor academic work was the best predictor of academic outcomes for first- and second-generation immigrant high school students, a result that has been reported for other student groups (Plunkett, Behnke, Sands, & Choi, 2009).

*The physical condition of the schools students attend is an equity issue that can affect learning outcomes.*

schools tend to be older and more likely to be severely overcrowded than those in suburban and rural areas (National Center for Education Statistics, 2002a). This factor is significant because greater academic gains have been associated with smaller class size, particularly for students from low-SES backgrounds (Achilles, Finn, & Pate-Bain, 2002; Biddle & Berliner, 2002).

## The Standards and Accountability Movement

Since the passage of the No Child Left Behind Act (NCLB) in 2001, school districts have been held accountable for student progress toward meeting rising achievement standards. This mandate, while affecting education as a whole, is felt with particular force in urban districts, which typically have a large number of students from diverse groups. As you learned in Chapter One, with few exceptions, students with disabilities are required to participate in these high stakes assessments along with their nondisabled peers.

Possible unintended consequences may result from this practice, however. For example, rigid standardization in the curriculum, a possible by-product of accountability and assessment, may conflict with the individualized approach that comprises so much of special education. Additionally, in some cases students must pass state assessments in order to receive a high school diploma or be promoted from grade to grade. Promotion testing is particularly common in urban school districts, even when not required by state policy, and it has been associated with higher rates of retention for students of color. Not surprising is the result: Retention has been associated with dropping out (Heubert, 2003).

The NCLB high-stakes testing for accountability also may encourage the reluctance of general education teachers and administrators to embrace the inclusion of students with disabilities for fear that the scores of these students will depress school or class scores, thereby compounding the tendency for students of color to be placed in self-contained special education classrooms (Morrier et al., 2008). On the other side of the issue, some educators believe that high-stakes testing is forcing the issue of higher standards. By setting high goals and consistently measuring progress toward these goals, these professionals believe that student learning will be enhanced. The inclusion of students with disabilities in these assessments also may increase the likelihood of collaboration between general and special educators because they may perceive benefits that will facilitate the success of learners with disabilities. The concept of shared ownership thus may be reinforced.

## Response to Intervention

Along with higher standards and an increased expectation for accountability, response to intervention is central to current school reform for students at risk of being considered for special education. In many ways, RTI should be a significant part of the response to issues such as disproportionate representation in special education for students of color, because it requires the systemic use of evidence-based interventions that can ensure students

Although there are over 17,000 school districts in the United States, the 100 largest districts (less than 1 percent of all school districts) enroll over 23 percent of all students.

received the instruction that may avoid the inappropriate need for special education eligibility (Skiba et al., 2008).

However, concern has been expressed that RTI is not necessarily a straightforward solution to a complex problem. Klingner and Edwards (2006) noted several factors that must be considered when educators implement RTI related to literacy with students from diverse backgrounds. For example, these authors cautioned that even before professionals consider students' need for increasingly intense interventions, they should review the quality of the overall instruction those students are receiving in their classrooms. That is, if the quality of instruction is a problem, then the teaching should improve before considering the need for additional interventions. Teaching factors may include how teachers motivate students, how they encourage participation, and how they communicate their support of students.

*It is essential that teachers learn strategies and approaches that are culturally responsive as part of their professional preparation.*

Another example concerns the validity of interventions. That is, when specialized interventions are developed, they are tested on groups of students in order to document that they are effective. In some cases, students from diverse backgrounds are not included during this testing, sometimes because they have limited English proficiency. The problem is that whether using such interventions with these students with result in positive outcomes is not known, but if students fail to respond, professionals may use this information as an indication of the need for special education. The assumption may be faulty—it could be that the program is not appropriate for these students. The program approach, for example, may be successful with students who are field independent, a concept introduced earlier in this chapter, but not effective for those who are field sensitive.

## School Choice Programs

As you probably have seen in the popular media, the failure of some large urban school districts to improve student test scores has encouraged efforts to make radical changes in the governing and funding structures that support these districts or select schools within these districts. For example, charter schools, for-profit schools, and vouchers for private schools are receiving ongoing attention as ways to address what is sometimes perceived as the failure of urban schools (Estes, 2006). Public charter schools often are in urban areas where there are higher concentrations of students of color (National Center for Education Statistics, 2007). It is also reported that charter schools employ teachers with fewer years of teaching experience than do traditional public schools. How do you think such a trend affects the education of students with disabilities in the districts most affected by these practices?

The ramifications of various choice programs are quite broad, with possible advantages and disadvantages. However, from the special education perspective, concerns have been raised with respect to students with disabilities being able to have the same degree of access to available options. For example, the enrollment of students with disabilities in charter schools can vary widely, but students with intellectual disabilities tend to be underrepresented. Although recent research suggests that many charter schools are enrolling students with disabilities (Rhim & McLaughlin, 2007), professionals at these schools express concern about being able to adequately meet their needs.

## Teachers and Their Preparation

The preparation teachers receive to work in diverse, urban environments is essential for student success. This may be an area of weakness in both pre-service and in-service teacher

## Technology and Diversity: The Digital Divide

Consider these facts (Fairlie, 2005):

- Just over 50 percent of African American and Latino children have computer access at home, but more than 85 percent of white children have this access.
- These differences hold even when only those children living in families with incomes above $60,000 are considered.
- In homes where English is not the primary language, computer access is especially low.
- Teenagers with computer access at home are 6 to 8 percentage points more likely to graduate from high school than those who do not have computer access at home.

These sobering data demonstrate why teachers should learn more about technology and students from diverse backgrounds and help them access technology. Here are Internet resources that can help:

- http://www.ecs.org/html/issue.asp?issueid=132
  The Education Commission of the States maintains a webpage on technology. By linking to the available readings and research you can find several recent studies of technology access and use for diverse learners.

- http://www.manythings.org/
  At Many Things, you can find a wide variety of simple and interesting activities for English language learners, all designed to help increase language proficiency.

- http://www.colorincolorado.org/afttoolkit.pdf
  *Reaching Out to Hispanic Parents of English Language Learners,* a manual published by the American Federation of Teachers, is a guide for prekindergarten teachers who want to improve their collaborative efforts with parents. The guide offers detailed information on helping these parents to work with their children on reading skills and advice on interacting with these parents.

- http://www.ataccess.org/resources/lowcostnocost/lcncenglish.html
  The Alliance for Technology Access is dedicated to connecting children and adults with disabilities to technology tools. On this webpage you will find a list of no-cost tools, including a magazine for English language learners, translation dictionaries with pictures, and a website for translating documents from English to eleven other languages.

education (Ochoa, Kelly, Stuart, & Rogers-Adkinson, 2004; Trent, Kea, & OH, 2008). Lack of teacher preparedness to address the needs of culturally diverse learners has been cited as a possible contributing factor to the disproportionate representation of these students in some areas of special education (Voltz, 2003).

The diversity of the teaching force also is important to mention. In some school districts, the number of teachers of color is painfully small. For example, whereas African-American males are overrepresented in special education programs, they are severely underrepresented in the special education teaching force, comprising only 0.4 percent of elementary special education teachers and 2.2 percent of secondary special education teachers (Rice & Goessling, 2005). Interestingly, research has shown that as the percentage of minority teachers in school districts increases, the percentage of students of color placed in special education classes or subjected to disciplinary action decreases (Grossman, 1995; Irvine, 1991).

Finally, overall teacher effectiveness should be discussed as an essential component of helping diverse learners to reach their potential. Data from the Tennessee Valued Added Assessment System—a complex procedure used to statistically measure the effectiveness of school systems, schools, and teachers—revealed that teacher effectiveness was the most significant predictor of student achievement (Sanders & Horn, 1998; Stronge & Tucker, 2000). That is, the impact of the teacher's skill in instructing students overcame factors related to race/ethnicity, poverty, and school location. This suggests that teachers really do make the difference in student learning.

Students of color and those who live in poverty are more likely than other students to be taught by less-effective teachers (Haycock & Crawford, 2008).

## REVIEW · REFLECT · DISCUSS

1. What would you say to a colleague who stated that she did not want to have students with disabilities or those who are English language learners in her class because they would lower the average test score, which would, in turn, reflect poorly on her teaching skills?

2. Why might students with disabilities from diverse backgrounds be particularly at risk of performing poorly on high-stakes tests? What could you as a teacher do to help address some of these factors?

# Summary

- Culture provides the lens through which people view and interpret the world. Although culture mediates every aspect of our lives, unless you encounter cultural dissonance you are barely aware that it exists.
- Cultural factors have a great impact on the learning process. If various cognitive styles are not considered in professionals' approach to instruction, students' learning may suffer.
- The disproportionate representation of students of color in special and gifted education has been a lingering challenge to the field. Poverty and systemic bias have been cited as probable contributors to this challenge.
- Practices that may help to address disproportionality begin with improvement in the referral and identification process, including alternative assessment approaches.

- Promising instructional practices for diverse learners include differentiation, universal design for learning, multicultural education, and instruction for English language learners (e.g., bilingual education, English as a second language, sheltered English).
- Promoting collaborative relationships with families is a critical factor in the educational success of culturally diverse students with disabilities. In order to facilitate such relationships, school personnel must be prepared to work with parents as individuals and respect cultural differences.
- A number of issues and trends affect the education of diverse exceptional learners, including the conditions of urban education and the character of urban education reform.

**Council for Exceptional Children**

## ADDRESSING THE PROFESSIONAL STANDARDS

Council for Exceptional Children (CEC) Common Core Knowledge and Skills addressed in this chapter:

ICC1K5, ICC1K8, ICC2K3, ICC3K3, ICC3K4, ICC3K5, ICC4S3, ICC5K8, ICC5K9, ICC5S1, ICC5S13, ICC6K2, ICC6S1, ICC6S2, ICC7S8, ICC8S2, ICC8S4, ICC10K3, ICC10K4, ICC10S3, ICC10S4

Appendix: Provides a full listing of the CEC Common Core Standards, and associated Knowledge and Skill Statements listed here.

## PEARSON myeducationlab

Now go to Topic 4: Cultural/Linguistic Diversity in the MyEducationLab (www.myeducationlab.com) for your course, where you can:

- Find learning outcomes for the broad concepts covered in this chapter along with the national standards that connect to these outcomes.
- Complete Assignments and Activities that can help you more deeply understand the chapter content.
- Examine challenging situations presented in the IRIS Center Resources.

- Apply and practice your understanding of the core concepts and skills identified in the chapter with the Building Teaching Skills and Dispositions learning units.
- Check your comprehension on the content covered in the chapter by going to the Study Plan in the Book Specific Resources for your text. Here you will be able to take a chapter quiz, receive feedback on your answers, and then access Review, Practice, and Enrichment activities to enhance your understanding of chapter content.
- Watch video clips of CCSSO Teacher of the Year award winners responding to the question: "Why I teach?" in the Teacher Talk section.

## chapter four

# Collaboration in Special Education

## LEARNING OBJECTIVES

- Describe what *collaboration* is and why it has become so critical in providing special education services to students with disabilities.
- Identify skills that educators need to collaborate effectively.
- Outline collaborative practices on behalf of students with disabilities that are most common in today's schools, including teams, co-teaching, and consultation.
- Discuss the role of collaboration in working with parents and family members.
- Describe issues related to collaboration in special education.

## Michelle

Michelle is a first-year special education teacher at Washington High School. Her undergraduate degree was in psychology, and she just obtained her teaching credential by completing an alternative licensure program at a local university. She is excited about her new career but a bit anxious as well. One of the most interesting experiences Michelle is having is co-teaching with Kira in algebra. The class includes students who did not take algebra in middle school—generally, students who struggle to learn. Five of the students have individualized education programs (IEPs). Michelle and Kira are developing a strong partnership, but it has taken careful planning and honest communication. For example, the two teachers discussed their respective expectations for sharing instruction in the class, and they also negotiated how to divide the teaching and grading responsibilities. Although Michelle's primary purpose in being in the classroom is to ensure that the students with IEPs receive instructional support, both teachers share the goal of creating an atmosphere in which all the students can succeed. One of the challenges Michelle has faced is making sure that she understands the algebraic concepts well enough to be a teaching partner; she had not thought about the range and depth of curriculum that she would need to understand as part of her job.

## Derek

As an early career special educator, Derek finds his job both rewarding and overwhelming. His greatest concern this year relates to Robert, a sixth-grade student with a moderate intellectual disability who transferred to the school this year. Robert's behavior has become increasingly aggressive as the year has gone by, and Derek asked Mr. Criswell, the district's behavior specialist, to consult with him on how to reduce Robert's inappropriate behavior and increase his appropriate behavior. After meetings, observations, and the implementation of a behavior intervention plan, the problem is not resolved, and now it is time for the annual review of Robert's IEP. Present for the meeting are Mr. Green, the school psychologist; Mr. Criswell; Ms. Adams, the special education administrator; Ms. Taylor, Robert's mother; and Mr. Sanders, the technology teacher in whose class Robert is currently enrolled. Robert is also present. Derek is thinking that it might be best, given the data they have gathered, to have Robert receive all instruction in a special education setting next year, at least until the behavior problems are addressed. Ms. Taylor is opposed. She was anticipating Robert spending more time in general education, perhaps even social studies and science. Mr. Green expresses confidence that additional interventions can be designed, and Mr. Sanders expresses concern on behalf of the general education teachers about safety. Ms. Adams carefully listens to all points of view expressed, and she works diligently to help the team develop an IEP that meets Robert's needs while still ensuring he is educated in the least restrictive environment. Derek appreciates her ability to make sure everyone's ideas are heard and seriously considered.

## Mary Jo

Mary Jo is a teacher for students with visual impairments, but she does not have her own classroom. She is an itinerant teacher who serves 12 students in eight different schools. She usually spends Monday and Wednesday mornings at Kennedy Elementary, which two of her students attend. She sometimes pulls the students from their general education classrooms to check on their learning progress and to monitor the effectiveness of their adaptive equipment. She also touches base with the students' teachers. For example, Ms. Hopewell recently told her that Marcus had broken his glasses and that even though he was using a magnifying glass, he was still having difficulty reading his work. She spoke to Marcus's grandmother and learned that he would be receiving new glasses the next day, and she relayed that information to the teacher, asking that she be notified if Marcus did not come to school with the glasses. Mary Jo also observed Shawn in his fifth-grade class as he worked on a computer with enlarged type. Afterward, she met with Shawn's teacher to discuss his academic work and classroom behavior. She also wanted to be sure that the large-print materials Shawn needs are arriving in a timely manner. Mary Jo finds her job challenging and interesting. She has realized, though, that she has to work diligently to get to know the teachers and administrators in each of her schools, and she sometimes admits that she does not really have a "home" in any single school, a fact that sometimes bothers her.

## fyi

*Collaboration* has another meaning that is far different from the one discussed in this textbook: It is also the situation that occurs when an individual joins with another for a negative purpose, as in collaborating with the enemy!

When you think about being an educator, whatever your role, how do you think you will spend your days? Do you see yourself mostly in terms of your work with students? When you picture your colleagues, do you see them similarly engaged? Many educators think of their roles primarily in terms of their students, and they often consider their interactions with other professionals an add-on or a secondary job responsibility. In fact, teaching has, for many decades, been characterized in just that way—as a profession of isolation and loneliness (Lortie, 1975; Rosenholtz, 1989; Sarason, 1982). This characterization of educators is changing but only gradually (Cullen, 2007), and working with others often is still sometimes more a luxury than a standard of practice (Barth, 2006; Hindin, Morocco, Mott, & Aguilar, 2007; Nieto, 2009).

In contrast to traditional school culture, special education teachers and others who provide services to students with disabilities have long relied on working with others formally or informally (e.g., Armer & Thomas, 1978; Menninger, 1950), and this emphasis continues today (e.g., Kochhar-Bryant, 2008). As an educator in the twenty-first century, your direct work with students is only one dimension—albeit a critical one—of your job (Barth, 2006; Pisha & Stahl, 2005). In many ways, your ability to work with other adults is as important to your success as your knowledge and skills for teaching (Friend & Cook, 2010; Penuel, Riel, Krause, & Frank, 2009). For example, on any given day, in addition to your teaching duties, your schedule might include conferencing with a parent before school begins, sharing teaching responsibilities with a colleague in a class that includes several students who have IEPs, or participating in an IEP team meeting right after the students leave at the end of the day. Collaboration is a central part of special education, a point clearly illustrated in the Firsthand Account.

No matter your planned career as an educator, however, you quickly will learn that collaboration does not occur because of good intentions; it requires learning the skills to make it a reality. As you read this chapter, try to visualize yourself performing your responsibilities and interacting effectively with colleagues, parents, and others. Have you thought about these situations before now? What questions and concerns do you have? One novice special educator recently echoed the sentiments of many when she sighed and commented, "When I began my job, I realized I was very well prepared to meet students' needs. My greatest challenge has been learning how to manage the complexities of working with the other adults."

## Understanding Collaboration

If you peruse almost any publication related to education, you will find the word *collaboration* used often and in many different ways. Sometimes it seems to be a general way of saying "working together," as when teachers are advised that collaboration is an effective means of accomplishing their professional development goals or when principals are admonished to foster collaboration in their schools as a means of raising student achievement (Brownell, Adams, Sindelar, Waldron, & Vanhover, 2006; Dufour, 2007). In some schools, the term *collaboration* appears to be confused with other terms, as when someone notes, "We really believe in collaboration. Almost all of our students are in general education classes for at least part of the day." Collaboration in this example has been used as a synonym for *inclusion*.

As a professional who will need to draw on collaboration expertise every day, you should understand that collaboration is more than simply working together and that it is not at all a synonym for *inclusion*. The technical definition of **collaboration** is that it is "a style for direct interaction between at least two co-equal parties voluntarily engaged in shared decision making as they work toward a common goal" (Friend & Cook, 2010, p. 7). The most critical word in this definition is *style* because collaboration refers to *how* you interact with others, not *what* you are doing. For example, on some teams, everyone present, including the parents, feels free to offer ideas, and all opinions are respected. This is a *collaborative* team. In contrast, on other teams, unwritten rules dictate that certain topics should not be raised or that disagreeing with other team members, particularly when par-

**ANYA LEWIS LOCKHART** *is a parapro-fessional who facilitates in-clusive practices for two students with autism. She is also nearing completion of her special educa-tion teacher preparation program. At the same time, she is the mother of four children, three of whom have special needs. As she shares snippets of her hectic life, she illustrates the importance of strong partnerships in special education and some of the struggles that accompany collaboration.*

My oldest daughter, age 15, has an anxiety disorder. My 12-year-old is abso-lutely typical. Both my 10-year-old and my 8-year-old sons have Asperger syndrome and ADHD, and both have been diagnosed as being bipolar. We've seen a lot of specialists—we have a psychologist, a psy-chiatrist, and of course, a pediatrician—and in some ways all our hard work with them has caused other problems—the profes-sionals at school see how well they're doing and don't think they need support. But that's because of all the outside services. While going through my struggles with di-agnoses, therapies and medications, I really felt like I understood what other parents of children with autism might be going

through. I was receiving only positive feed-back from parents, teachers, and principals about the work that I was doing as a teach-ing assistant. It was then that I thought I could take my assisting to another level. I decided then to go back to school.

I absolutely love being a paraprofes-sional, and the kids are my favorite part of the job. I love working with the kids. With the teachers, though, it changes every year. Sometimes you get a teacher who is willing to let you come in and treats you as part of the classroom. But other teachers want you to sit in a corner working with the students to whom you're assigned—and not helping other students at all.

I'm looking forward to becoming a teacher, but I'm going to miss being a para-professional. As a teacher I'll need to work with teachers across all the grade levels and keep up with all the paperwork. I'll also need to work with the parents, even when there is a problem. Right now, if a parent is concerned, I just let the teacher know. But I'm going to be the teacher; I'll need to find ways to work it out with parents. I know I'll still work with kids, but now that is my whole job and it's very rewarding. When I'm a teacher I'll have all the other things to do, too. It's good that I'm a paraprofessional now before I'm a teacher—I'm getting lots

of experience. Plus, I have the experience from my own children. I wish universities would all have mentoring programs so new teachers would get more support. I'm ready to teach, but I worry that a lot of the other people I'm taking classes with will need help even after they become teachers.

When I'm in classes, I dread working in groups. I'd rather do the work myself than depend on other people. Then it meets my standards. Going to college now is a lot different than when I was eighteen—I know I need to get all the information I can, and I'm still not sure I can rely on other people.

Time is something I never seem to have enough of. I not only have to get my school-work done, I have to make sure my children are getting their homework done, make sure dinner is prepared, and make sure bed-time routines are followed. And I have to do housework, and remember that I have chil-dren with special needs who may require a little more.

So why do I do it? I truly believe that with my talents and ability to work success-fully with children with special needs, there is still work for me to do. My life may be hectic by some standards but I am getting quite good at it.

---

ents are present, is to be completely avoided. The predominant style of this team may be *directive.* In both instances, the interactions relate to working as a team—that is, the meet-ing is the *what.* The factor that varies is the way in which the team approaches its work—that is, the *how* is either collaborative, as on the team that encourages ideas from all parties, or directive, as on the team that avoids certain topics.

## Understanding Collaboration

You can further appreciate what collaboration is and what place it has in your professional role by learning about its characteristics (Friend & Cook, 2010). As you read this section, think about how a collaborative style can positively affect your interactions with colleagues and parents.

### Collaboration Is Voluntary

No matter your role, you might be directed to work with a group of other professionals on a committee or team. You might even be told that you have been partnered to teach with a par-ticular colleague. Neither of these situations feels particularly voluntary. That is partly cor-rect: Being assigned to work in proximity with others is not voluntary, and it is inevitable and appropriate that in schools such decisions will be made, often by an administrator, without your input. However, the choice of whether you and your colleagues use the style of collab-oration remains voluntary. On the committee or team, you and others choose whether to participate as little as possible, thinking of yourselves as a collection of individuals, or to

*When professionals and parents collaborate, parity can be challenging to create and maintain, particularly when cultural differences may be a factor.*

engage fully, recognizing the increased potential of working together—that is, collaborating. Similarly, you and your teaching partner(s) choose whether to divide students and work separately or to blend your talents and create new, shared teaching possibilities. In both cases, proximity is mandated, but collaboration is chosen.

### Collaboration Is Based on Parity

**Parity** refers to the concept that, in collaboration, the contributions of all participants have equal value. For example, imagine that you are at a meeting about a student with very complex needs. Because the other participants casually use medical terms you have never heard, you might believe that you have nothing to offer to the conversation. This would be a breakdown in parity. However, if you realize that you have a unique perspective on how to successfully reach the student in an education setting, you might make a contribution in that area. A sense of parity would exist.

Of course, parity has to be fostered for every person participating in an interaction (Martin, Marshall, & Sale, 2004). In interactions with parents, the vocabulary you use may affect parity. Similarly, if you repeatedly refer to formal reports and other paperwork that the parent does not have, parity may become a problem. How might parity apply to general education teachers in their interactions with you? What might cause a breakdown in parity? It is essential that you work to ensure parity in interactions with both parents and general education colleagues.

### Collaboration Requires a Mutual Goal

One of the greatest challenges of working with other adults in schools can be confirming a shared goal. If a special education teacher is meeting with a general education teacher because a student has been refusing to complete assignments, the special education teacher might assume that the goal is to find out why the behavior problem has been escalating so that it can be addressed and the student maintained in the classroom. However, the general education teacher might have requested the meeting to suggest that the student spend more time away from the general education setting. Clearly, this interaction is not based on having a **mutual goal.** Alternatively, if the teachers decide that their purpose in meeting is to analyze the situation and decide whether to call the parents or request consultation from the school psychologist, they do have a mutual goal. Although it may seem obvious that professionals should ask each other explicitly about the goals of their interactions, often this does not occur. You are far more likely to succeed in collaboration if you make this simple effort.

### Collaboration Involves Shared Responsibility for Key Decisions

When you collaborate, you and your colleagues share the critical decisions related to your goal, but the tasks required to reach that goal usually are assigned to individuals. For example, a special educator and a general education teacher sharing instruction might decide that the students' project will be to dramatize a scene from the literature being read. However, the general education teacher might assume the responsibility of preparing the evaluation rubric for this project while the special educator prepares an organizer to help some students remember all the parts to the assignment and their due dates. In the hectic world of today's schools, not all work can be shared. In collaboration, then, **shared responsibility** for key decisions contributes to parity and mutual goals while allowing professionals to be efficient through a division of labor.

### Collaboration Includes Shared Accountability for Outcomes

Sharing accountability follows directly from sharing responsibility for key decisions. If team members decide to try a behavior intervention plan for a student and it is highly effective, they should share the credit for its success. However, if the plan somehow backfires and causes even further problems, they should avoid trying to assign blame and instead collectively ask, "What should we do now?" In collaboration, **shared accountability** implies that all participants have contributed to planning and implementing a strategy and fully accept the outcomes of those decisions, whether they are positive or a cause for concern.

### Collaboration Requires Sharing Resources

For collaboration to occur, each participant must contribute some type of resource. Perhaps a special educator can offer materials that focus on the same curriculum goals but address them in a simple way or at a lower reading level. That professional also can share technical information about a student's physical, academic, or behavior needs. Perhaps the school psychologist can explain data gathered about a student or group of students and create a system of rewards based on those data. The general education teacher's contribution may be the time to implement the planned intervention and to monitor its impact. By **sharing resources,** everyone engaged in the collaboration shares ownership for the activity or intervention.

### Collaboration Is Emergent

As you have probably surmised, collaboration depends on the development of trust, respect, and a sense of community among participants. However, traits such as these cannot exist, fully developed, at the outset of a working relationship, and so these characteristics of collaboration are referred to as *emergent*. That is, anyone who engages in collaboration begins with a small amount of these characteristics. Would you risk working closely with a colleague if you could not find at least a small amount of trust and respect for that person's knowledge and skills? However, these characteristics become stronger as participants' positive experience in collaboration grows (Brownell, Adams, Sindelar, Waldron, & Vanhover, 2006). For example, at the beginning of the school year, Ms. Galliano, a new special education teacher, learned that she would work closely with Ms. Brighton, the speech/language pathologist, regarding services for Luis. Early in the year, both professionals worked diligently to be respectful, to get to know each other's strengths, and to clearly communicate concerning Luis's program. Later, though, as they became familiar with each other's style, after they jointly and successfully managed a difficult meeting with Luis's parents, and through many lunch periods spent discussing their instructional views, they came to realize that they could rely on each other. They both believed they had Luis's best interests at heart, even when they disagreed, and they both recognized that if a problem occurred, it could be resolved. Their collaborative relationship evolved based on their shared work until they sensed that they were a strong and productive educational team.

Of course, not all efforts that should be collaborative end up that way, and negative experiences, especially early in a partnership, can be difficult to overcome. For example, Mr. Vega, a high school science teacher, and Ms. Hall, a special educator, have been assigned to teach together. Mr. Vega states clearly that he does not need any "help" and tells Ms. Vega that he expects her to remain quiet while he teaches, offering that she has permission to work with struggling students after his instruction has concluded. Even though Mr. Vega admits later that he misunderstood how they could work together and tries to foster a partnership, it takes a long time for Ms. Hall to trust Mr. Vega and believe that he is sincere in his changed view of their shared work.

## Collaboration within the Context of Contemporary Legislation and Litigation

Although collaboration in the field of special education has existed informally almost since its inception, it was during the 1960s that the concept was recognized as a fundamental component of providing special services (Pugach & Johnson, 2002). Several contributing factors can be identified. For example, it was during this time that the role of the school psychologist began to be thought of in terms of working with teachers in order to support students. Tractman (1961) argued that if psychologists taught teachers strategies for effectively reaching their students instead of directly meeting with students individually or in small groups, as was customary, psychologists' influence could be multiplied greatly. During the same era, those developing the principles of *behaviorism* for use with students argued that if specialists would teach these principles to teachers, more students would be reached than if the specialists tried to work directly with students (e.g., Tharp & Wetzel, 1969). These concepts were applied to the work of special education teachers, too. In some programs, special education teachers did not work directly with students. Instead, they were assigned the task of teaching general education teachers to effectively instruct the students in their classrooms who had disabilities by modeling strategies and techniques and providing professional development to the teachers (e.g., McKenzie, 1972).

These predecessors to today's concept of collaboration tended to assume that special educators and other specialists possessed critical knowledge and skills that would benefit general education teachers. That is, the specialists were the "givers" and the general education teachers were the "receivers." However, as federal special education laws were enacted, it became clear that reciprocal sharing was needed: When special education teachers told general education teachers how to better instruct students in their classrooms, the general education teachers often rightfully felt that their own expertise was being ignored. What has evolved is the recognition that everyone involved in designing, implementing, and monitoring the learning of a student with a disability has a contribution to make. Thus, *collaboration* as presented in this chapter has become the contemporary model of school practice for professional interactions (Brownell & Walther-Thomas, 2002; Cook & Friend, in press).

### Collaboration in IDEA

The current provisions of the Individuals with Disabilities Education Act (IDEA) contain the strongest expectations ever for collaboration in special education. As you learned in Chapter Two, collaboration among professionals and between professionals and parents is integral in nearly every dimension of the federal law, including the following:

- Participation of general education teachers on most IEP teams
- Increased parent involvement
- Required conflict resolution efforts when disagreements occur
- Emphasis on educating students in the least restrictive environment
- Consultative special education services

In addition, collaboration is essential for the effective implementation of a response to intervention (RTI) process, the major point of Instruction in Action. When you picture yourself as a school professional, what aspects of your job do you envision as most relying on collaboration?

As you continue to learn about collaboration and its role in the delivery of special services to students with disabilities, keep in mind that collaboration has become increasingly integral to many aspects of society, including business and industry (Ephross & Vassil, 2004; Fullan, 2008; Sawyer, 2007). In fact, a recent ad in a business magazine proclaimed, "Collaborate or die!" Because schools tend to reflect the important trends that shape society (Friend & Cook, 2010), collaboration is likely to become an increasingly larger part of your role as a school professional.

http://www.rtinetwork.org/Connect/Blog/There-Are-All-Kinds-of-Ways-to-Measure-Progress The RTI Action Network includes a concise summary of the crucial role that collaboration plays in effectively implementing RTI procedures.

## REVIEW · REFLECT · DISCUSS

1. Whether through a field placement or observation, group work in your college courses, or other activities, what have been your experiences with collaboration? What has made these experiences positive or negative?
2. How might your collaboration experiences help you to understand the place of collaboration in your responsibilities as a professional educator?

Go to the Assignments and Activities section of Topic 2: Collaboration and Co-Teaching, in the MyEducationLab for your course and complete the activity entitled "Successful Collaboration".

## Essential Elements of Collaboration

As you interact with parents and family members, teachers, administrators, related services professionals, paraeducators, and others, it it not enough to simply hope that collaboration will evolve. You can express your own commitment to collaboration, and you

**Response to Intervention and Collaboration**

Collaboration is integral to response-to-intervention procedures. Here are examples of its use:

Tier 1

- Teachers provide high-quality instruction to all students. This suggests that differentiated instruction, curriculum-based assessment, and positive behavior supports will be provided—all areas in which special educators have highly specialized knowledge to share with their general education colleagues.

Tier 2

- Professionals systematically engage in shared problem solving to design more intensive interventions for students who need them.
- Professional development, consultation, and other collaborative strategies are implemented to assist teachers to assess student needs, implement appropriate interventions, and evaluate student progress.
- As interventions are implemented, the problem-solving team monitors their impact on student learning and behavior.
- Parents are included in the planning, implementation, and monitoring process.

- When Tier 2 is divided into subtiers (that is, multiple interventions), the problem-solving process is repeated, often involving more professionals in the collaboration.

Tier 3

- The multidisciplinary team, which includes the members you read about in Chapter Two, conducts a comprehensive evaluation that includes RTI data along with other measures, follows all requirements for parent participation, and collaborates to determine whether the student has a disability and is eligible to receive special education services.
- Unique to RTI procedures, this team must decide whether standardized test information is needed in addition to the ongoing assessment information gathered during Tiers 1 and 2.

Source: Based on Mellard, D. (2005), *Understanding responsiveness to intervention in learning disabilities determination*, Nashville, TN: National Research Center on Learning Disabilities, Peabody College, Vanderbilt University, retrieved June 24, 2006, from http://nrcld.org/publications/papers/mellard.shtml; Kovaleski, J., & Prasse, D. P. (2004), Response to instruction in the identification of learning disabilities: A guide for school teams, *NASP Communiqué, 32*(5), retrieved June 24, 2006, from www.nasponline.org/publications/cq325instruction.html.

can learn a set of skills that can make the goal of collaboration a reality. These interrelated elements of collaboration (Friend & Cook, 2010) are summarized in Figure 4.1 and described next.

## Personal Belief System

Having read to this point in the chapter, are you convinced that the effort that collaboration requires results in positive outcomes for students and teachers? This consideration, your *personal belief system,* is the first element of collaboration. If you firmly believe that collaboration is worthwhile, you are ready to learn the more technical aspects of this style. If you are uncertain, then you are not likely to embrace collaboration, particularly when it is challenging to accomplish (Griffin, Kilgore, & Winn, 2008).

An example related to your experiences as a student can further illustrate this point. Do you believe that work you do with others is better than what you do alone? Before you quickly say yes, think about the last time you were assigned a group project in one of your courses. Did you mentally groan at the prospect? How might this indicate your readiness and willingness to collaborate? Among all the professionals with whom you will work in schools, the level of commitment to collaboration will vary greatly. Their perspectives, combined with your own viewpoint, will determine whether you will have many opportunities to participate in collaborative activities or whether you will complete much of your work without such support.

## Communication Skills

When coupled with our facial expressions, posture, and other nonverbal signals, the words we choose and the way we express them comprise our **communication skills** (De-Vito, 2009). Communication skills can be taught and learned readily, and entire university courses are devoted to this topic. Communication skills can have a huge effect on the development of collaboration, or they can inhibit it (Gallagher, Vail, & Monda-Amaya, 2008).

research
**NOTE**

Hindin, Morocco, Mott, and Aguilar (2007) studied the collaboration of middle school teachers, including a special educator, regarding literacy instruction. They found that each teacher participated in the learning group that was arranged but that teachers with the most advanced skills shared that expertise in a limited way.

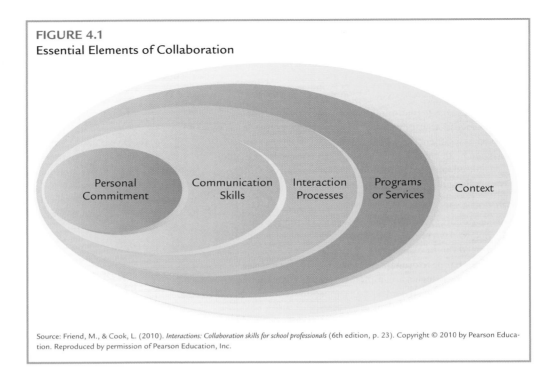

**FIGURE 4.1**
**Essential Elements of Collaboration**

Personal Commitment

Communication Skills

Interaction Processes

Programs or Services

Context

Source: Friend, M., & Cook, L. (2010). *Interactions: Collaboration skills for school professionals* (6th edition, p. 23). Copyright © 2010 by Pearson Education. Reproduced by permission of Pearson Education, Inc.

When all is well and your interactions are positive, you do not necessarily need to have exemplary communication skills. Your colleagues know what you mean, and they do not take offense or read alternative meanings into your words. However, when controversial or awkward situations arise, excellent communication skills are not only helpful but essential (Bradley & Monda-Amaya, 2005). The problem is that if you do not practice these skills when it is easy to do so, you are unlikely to suddenly have them when the situation demands them. Think about the IEP meeting that Derek, introduced at the beginning of the chapter, was attending. How might the communication skills of each participant affect the outcome of the meeting?

Dozens of models of communication and sets of communication skills have been described in the professional literature, and presenting a comprehensive list of them is simply not possible here. However, the following concepts and strategies can be especially helpful to you as an educator and illustrate the importance of these skills for collaboration.

### Effective Communication Strategies

To enhance your communication skills for collaboration, the place to begin is with listening (Johnson, 2009). Even though teachers have been instructing you on effective listening since you were an elementary school pupil, as a school professional you may find that listening is very challenging. You may be distracted because you are thinking about another student or an upcoming conference, you may be so tired that you have difficulty following what the speaker is saying, or you may be confused by the information being presented. The Professional Edge presents information on dilemmas for listening and strategies for improving listening skills.

Another example of effective communication skill occurs when you encourage others to continue speaking through the use of nonverbal signals (Egan, 2001; Johnson, 2009). For example, if a parent is describing her child's favorite play activities at home, your smile is likely to positively influence the parent to tell you more. Similarly, if you sit so that you are leaning forward slightly and nod as a special education colleague describes the job-coaching situation he is helping to resolve with a shared student, he is likely to sense that you understand and want to know more. By communicating with your body, you convey important messages without interrupting the speaker.

A third example of communication skill concerns describing students, situations, and events using nonevaluative language. For example, as you discuss Francis it might be

Friend (2000) has identified four myths that can undermine professional collaboration: (a) Everyone is doing it, (b) more is better, (c) it's about feeling good and liking others, and (d) it comes naturally.

## Maximizing Your Listening Skills

Listening is a critical communication skill, but sometimes being in a hurry or tired, operating on mental overload, daydreaming, or rehearsing what you are going to say can interfere with your ability to listen. Here are suggestions for improving your listening skills:

- *Want to listen.* Remember, there is no such thing as disinterested people—only disinterested listeners.
- *Demonstrate listening behavior.* Be quiet and alert, sit straight, lean slightly forward and make eye contact as appropriate, and let your face radiate interest.
- *React positively.* The only time a person likes to be interrupted is when being "applauded" through nods, smiles, or comments. Be generous with your applause.
- *Empathize with the other person.* Try to put yourself in the other's place so that you can see that point of view.
- *Ask questions.* When you do not understand, when you need further clarification, or when you want to show you are listening, ask questions. Avoid questions that will embarrass or criticize the other person.

- *Leave your emotions behind (if you can).* Try to push your worries, your fears, and your problems away. They may prevent you from listening.
- *Get rid of distractions.* Put down any papers, pencils, and other items you have in your hands.
- *Get the main points.* Focus on the main ideas. Examples, stories, and so on are important, but they usually are not the main points.
- *React to ideas, not to the person.* Do not allow your reaction to the person to influence your interpretation of what is being said. Good ideas can come from people whose skills or personality do not match yours.
- *Do not argue mentally.* When trying to understand the other person, arguing mentally while you are listening sets up a barrier between the two of you.
- *Use the difference in rate.* You can listen faster than anyone can talk (500 words/minute versus 100 to 150 words/minute). Think back over what the speaker has said to remember and reflect on the message.

---

tempting to say something like this: "He's a bad actor. His behavior is too disrespectful to describe, and the rude comments he makes under his breath—but audible enough for everyone to hear—constantly cause a commotion." Notice how these descriptors of Francis are actually evaluations. Instead, suppose you say, "During the past week, Francis has been sent out of class four times by three different teachers, twice for using profanity, once for a comment he made to another student that made her cry, and once for repeatedly refusing out loud to begin work assigned in class." Now you have described accurately what Francis is doing without making judgments about it. Nonevaluative language clearly is preferred.

One final example of effective communication concerns the use of questions that encourage the other person to continue speaking. What is the difference in the way these questions are posed?

- What are his characteristics as a reader?
- Does he read at grade level? Does he understand what he reads? Does he attempt to sound out words that he does not know?

In the first question, the person responding would be free to discuss any of the student's characteristics. The response might include reading level, comprehension, and word attack skills, but it also might include information about the student's fluency and reading interests. In the second example, each question could be answered with a simple yes or no, and the person asking the questions would be largely controlling the types of answers that would likely be given. In your interactions with colleagues and parents, one goal usually is to learn from them. If that is the case for this situation, the first question type generally would be preferred to the latter.

### Communication Habits to Avoid

As you learn communication strategies that foster strong collaboration, you also should know that some communication habits have the potential to undermine your working relationships with colleagues and parents. For example, if a teacher rushes up to you outside the school office, hands you a crumpled piece of paper that looks like it was supposed to be student work, exclaims "Look what Shannon did to her assignment!" and looks at you expectantly, what would your response be? It might be tempting to say, "I'll take care of it," or "She's having a bad day; you can send her down to my room and I'll talk to her," or "What

**fyi**

One of the most effective communication skills you can learn to use is silence. During awkward or difficult interactions, allowing a few seconds of silence can help you to listen more carefully and learn more information by encouraging others to continue speaking and providing you with those seconds to think about your response.

would you like me to do?" All of these responses are quick fixes that indicate you are the person who can remedy the problem—even though you really do not know enough about what happened to respond. Whenever someone is explaining what happened, your reaction should be to seek additional information (Pugach & Johnson, 2002). In this example, a much more appropriate response would be "What happened?" With that information you could gain a better understanding of the situation.

Another example of ineffective communication is the use of questions that actually state your opinions. For example, Mr. Dewey and Ms. Hector are discussing Jamia's behavior plan. Mr. Dewey says, "You're not thinking of using a point system, are you?" Careful consideration of Mr. Dewey's words indicates that he is probably trying to communicate that he is not in favor of a point system, but he uses a question that clearly includes the answer that he wants to hear instead of directly stating his opinion. A far better interaction would have been this: "I'm opposed to the use of a point system with Jamia because.... What is your opinion?" If you find that your communication with others is peppered with questions ending with phrases such as "aren't you?," "can't you?," and "will you?," this might be a communication skill on which you need to work. You will be perceived as far more respectful and honest if you own your opinions and encourage others to express theirs.

One final example of ineffective communication concerns the use of *jargon*. As you learn about the field of special education and become accustomed to the acronyms and expressions associated with it, you may forget when you speak to others, especially parents, that not everyone has this familiarity. If you say to a parent, "Your child's K-TEA and CBA data indicate an independent reading level at 3.5, instructional level at 4.5, and frustration level at 5.0," you have said many words but probably communicated little. To communicate effectively, you need to adjust the words you use depending on the person to whom you are speaking. Remember, too, that the use of understandable language contributes to parity, discussed earlier in this chapter.

It is hoped that these few examples of effective and ineffective communication have piqued your interest in learning more. As you listen to professionals in schools, you can sharpen your own skills by focusing on how they use words that exemplify essential characteristics of collaboration—parity, trust, respect. You can also notice how some communication seems to interfere with the development of collaboration.

## Interaction Processes

An **interaction process** is a set of steps that are followed using effective communication in order to accomplish the mutual goal of collaboration. A number of interaction processes are common in schools, but the one most often used is some form of **interpersonal problem solving** (Bahr et al., 2006; Griffin, Jones, & Kilgore, 2006). In this process, professionals meet as a group to systematically identify and resolve student, service delivery or other professional problems. For example, when you meet with the occupational therapist to devise an alternative way for a student to grip a pencil or crayon, or when you confer with parents to determine how to address a student's behavior challenge, you are problem solving. Likewise, when you meet with a schoolwide team to discuss how to help a struggling student who does not have a disability be more successful in the classroom, you engage in problem solving. If you think about all the roles and responsibilities you may have in school, you can see that most of them can be considered from a problem-solving perspective; this makes it essential that you know and can carry out this key process.

Several authors have proposed interpersonal problem-solving models (e.g., Friend & Cook, 2010; Gravois & Rosenfield, 2006; Lau, Sieler, & Muyskens, 2006). However, all problem-solving models generally incorporate six steps: (1) create a climate for problem solving; (2) identify the problem; (3) generate alternatives; (4) assess the potential solutions; (5) implement the intervention; and (6) evaluate the intervention outcome. Each step is discussed in the following sections.

### Create a Climate for Problem Solving

When you problem solve with others, you need to ensure that all participants are committed to the process. One way to accomplish this is to communicate optimism about success.

For example, if at the beginning of a meeting, a team member says, "Here we go again. I'm getting frustrated that we can't seem to find a way to help Mel learn to communicate his needs," you have a signal that commitment may be wavering. Your response might be, "I've been thinking, though. With all of us here today to discuss this, and with the new ideas we've been researching, I think we have lots of new options to explore." You are trying to help set a positive context for the problem-solving process.

## Identify the Problem

This problem-solving step is deceptively simple. When you work with a group, each person may have a different perspective of the problem. For example, at a team meeting, a general education teacher may perceive that the problem is a student's poor organization skills, while the special education teacher may believe the problem is the other teacher's reluctance to give the student extra time to organize his materials. At the same time, the psychologist may believe that the student possibly has a short-term memory problem, and the principal may think that the student is simply seeking attention. Because the problems you will discuss with others in your collaborative interactions usually are complex and do not have single, clear answers, it is imperative to spend enough time to ensure that all participants share the same understanding of the problem (Brightman, 2002; Welch & Tulbert, 2000).

The complexity of accurately identifying problems can be compounded when the participants represent multiple cultures (Olson, Parayitam, & Bao, 2007); in such instances, clear communication is critical. One effective way of identifying problems is to determine, as objectively as possible, what the current situation is; to describe what the ideal situation would be; and then to describe the problem as a gap between these two circumstances.

## Generate Alternatives

In this step, participants brainstorm ideas for addressing the problem that they have mutually identified. They are careful to avoid evaluating each other's ideas (e.g., "I don't think that will work"), instead trying to encourage expression of as many ideas as possible. Although some options will be discarded later as unrealistic, during this part of problem solving the intent is to generate as many ideas as possible because the quantity of ideas generated tends to increase the overall quality of the solution eventually implemented. Michelle and Kira, whom you met in the chapter introduction, often brainstorm about ways to help make algebra concepts more "alive" for the students in their co-taught class.

## Assess the Potential Solutions, Selecting One or More to Implement

Once a lengthy list of ideas has been compiled, participants eliminate those that are not feasible (e.g., providing a paraeducator for every general education teacher in the school) and those that are unlikely to be implemented or are mostly fanciful (e.g., attaching a student who seems to be in perpetual motion to his seat with Velcro strips sewn to his pants). Each of the remaining ideas is considered carefully (e.g., creating a teacher study group on differentiating instruction; providing teachers with a brief workshop on the student's communication device). Advantages and drawbacks of implementing the idea are noted as well, with a focus on identifying solutions that will reduce the gap between the current and ideal situations. Based on this discussion, the number of ideas is gradually reduced to a few. These are assessed for practical matters, such as cost, time involved, and consistency with student needs, and then one or two ideas are selected for implementation. The final part of this step includes making detailed implementation plans.

*When professionals share in a problem solving process, they are likely to generate many more ideas than any of them would have generated alone.*

### Implement the Intervention

The most straightforward step of problem solving occurs after all the efforts of completing the preceding steps. The intervention or strategy is implemented, and data are gathered so that effectiveness can be measured. One question during implementation usually concerns time: For how many days or sessions should an intervention be implemented before its outcome is assessed?

### Evaluate the Intervention Outcome and Decide Next Steps

After a specified period of time, those involved in problem solving meet to decide whether the solution has been effective. If the intervention has been successful, it may be terminated or continued in its current form. If some difficulties have occurred, it may be modified. If the participants decide that serious problems exist, other ideas are likely to be tried, or the group may decide that the problem needs to be reconceptualized. For example, if a student's behavior plan has corrected the behavior, the plan may be phased out. Or perhaps the special education teacher likes the plan and thinks it is working but finds that it takes up too much time during instruction. In this case, the team might try to streamline the plan or eliminate some parts of it. Finally, if the teacher reports that no improvement in behavior is occurring, even after systemic implementation over a reasonable period of time, the team might decide to try a completely different intervention.

### Additional Considerations for Problem Solving

You might have the impression that problem solving occurs primarily when students have academic or behavior needs. Although this is an important part of the problem solving in which you will engage, it is not *all* of the problem solving. For example, you might problem solve to increase parent involvement at your school (e.g., Murray & Curran, 2008) or to increase all staff members' knowledge about assistive technology (e.g., Judge, Floyd, & Jeffs, 2008). You might even problem solve to figure out a more effective way of having several specialists provide services to a single student in a general education classroom.

As you prepare to become a school professional, you will find that you also need skills for carrying out additional interaction processes that foster collaboration. For example, you will probably practice interviewing parents and conducting conferences with them. You also will discuss how to resolve the conflicts and address the resistance that sometimes occurs in school settings concerning students with disabilities and their services. Finally, you will offer feedback to colleagues and paraeducators. All of these activities are processes because they have steps.

As with communication, you can learn to effectively monitor and follow the steps in problem solving. Both sets of skills are critical: If you have good communication skills but cannot help move an interaction from beginning to end through a series of steps, frustration may occur. Likewise, if you know the steps of problem solving and can implement them from beginning to end but without positive communication skills, participants may see the process as directive, not collaborative.

## Programs and Services

The next element of collaboration is to design programs and services that foster it. Although as an early career educator you may not have significant input into the design of programs and services, your understanding of them can help you make an informed judgment about the potential for collaboration. Later in this chapter you will learn about three programs that rely heavily on collaboration: teaming, co-teaching, and consultation.

## Supportive Context

The fifth and final element that must be in place for collaboration to flourish is a supportive context. As you gain experience as a professional, you may be able to influence the extent to which collaboration is valued in your school and resources are dedicated to fostering it. However, the professional who is most responsible for creating a school culture that encourages collaboration is the principal (Rourke & Boone, 2008; Smith, Wilson, & Corbett,

Go to the Assignments and Activities section of Topic 2: Collaboration and Co-Teaching, in the MyEducationLab for your course and complete the activity entitled "Strengths of Collaboration".

## Collaborating Through Technology

Technology has brought a whole new dimension to professional support and informal collaboration. Here are several websites you might find useful in your work as an early career special educator.

- www.epals.com/
ePALS has as its purpose connecting educators and their students in a safe environment. Winner of many awards, this website brings people from over 200 countries and 500,000 classrooms together as learning partners. The site includes options for joining projects with educators from around the world, exchanging ideas and asking questions of other special educators, and finding e-pals for your students.

- http://teachers.net
Teachers.net contains many discussion boards of interest to early career professionals, including ideas for lesson plans and classroom activities, response to student behavior problems, and other new teacher resources. You also can join a mailring through this website by signing up to receive information from other educators on topics of your choice.

- Teachertube.com/
TeacherTube specializes in videos for educators, and the website has many helpful items related to electronic collaboration. For example, this 5-minute video explains how to use Google Docs and spreadsheets for virtual collaboration: http://teachertube.com/viewVideo.php?video_id=1788&title=Using_Google_Docs___Spreadsheets_for_Virtual_Collaboration.

- pbworks.com and wikispaces.com
PBWorks (formerly PBWiki) and Wikispaces are two sites that provide free wikis to teachers. You can use your wiki for collaboration with colleagues or parents. Not familiar with wikis? You can learn about them in this 4-minute video: http://www.youtube.com/watch?v=-dnL00TdmLY

2009). For example, the principal can ensure that professionals' schedules are arranged to permit them to meet occasionally. This individual also can serve as a facilitator for problem solving (Rafoth & Foriska, 2006). Perhaps most important, the principal can explicitly make collaboration a standard for all the professionals in the school, providing incentives for those working together and directly addressing those who are uncomfortable with the idea. Finally, the principal often can arrange for professional development to help staff members become more aware of the expectations of collaboration and more skillful in implementing collaborative practices (Barth, 2006).

When you put all the elements of collaboration together, you can see that with commitment and understanding, collaboration is a powerful tool for educating students with disabilities. However, you also begin to recognize that it involves far more than simply having conversations with colleagues. As professionals explore the potential of collaboration, they also discover options for interacting with their colleagues in nontraditional formats. The Technology Notes provides examples of electronic communication as part of collaboration.

## REVIEW · REFLECT · DISCUSS

1. Why do you think your own beliefs about collaboration are so important as you prepare for your career? What might happen if your beliefs are different from those of the individuals with whom you may be assigned to work?

2. How is problem solving with others different from problem solving alone? What might be key opportunities and barriers of this common collaborative process?

3. What would you do if you believed that your principal believed collaboration was important but was not offering the support you felt it needed?

## Applications of Collaboration for Schools

Informal opportunities for collaboration occur in schools every day. An occupational therapist and a special educator discuss a problem and devise an accommodation for a student who is having trouble grasping small items. Five teachers explore the possibility of creating a page on the school website to highlight the service activities of all the students in the school. However, formal structures that rely on collaboration also exist. These include teams, co-teaching, and consultation.

## Teams

You learned in Chapter Two that teams play an important role in special education. Through a prereferral or response-to-intervention process, a team designs interventions to help students succeed before consideration for special education services (Bahr & Kovaleski, 2006). A team completes the assessment of a student who might have disabilities, deter-mines eligibility for special education, prepares the IEP, and monitors student progress (Pierangelo & Guiliani, 2009). Now it is time to think in more detail about the team itself and your role as a collaborative team member.

### Understanding Team Concepts

A **team** in education is two or more interdependent individuals with unique skills and per-spectives who interact directly to achieve their mutual goal of providing students with ef-fective educational programs and services (Friend & Cook, 2010). You can see that some of the characteristics of collaboration are embedded in this team definition, including the ex-istence of mutual goals. However, as the definition suggests, teaming is much more.

For example, team members should clearly identify themselves as being part of a team. That is, they should have a sense of affiliation with the intervention assistance team, re-sponse to intervention team, or the IEP team, instead of feeling like a guest or as if the team's business is not truly their own. Team members also abide by a set of formal and informal rules. An example of the former is the procedure the team follows in discussing students. An example of the latter is the group's collective understanding about whether team meetings begin on time or whether being 10 minutes late is acceptable.

Team members also believe that the success of their work is related directly to the suc-cess of the work of all team members (Johnson & Johnson, 2009). For example, after an IEP meeting where Jay's need for instruction related to vocabulary development was carefully addressed, the special education teacher knows he can work with the speech/language pathologist, the paraeducator, and the parents to achieve the goals the team wrote. In addi-tion, team members value their differences; they understand that the professional and per-sonal diversity that they bring to the team enhances the opportunity for collaborative and creative problem solving.

### Team Effectiveness

Think about the teams of which you have been a member through sports, civic groups, or school. What made your team effective? For an educational team, effectiveness depends on several factors. First, team effectiveness can be judged by the quality of the outcomes the team produces (Kovaleski & Glew, 2006). By recommending strong, research-based inter-ventions, was the team successful in reducing the number of students who needed to be re-ferred for full assessment and possible special education placement? In how many instances was the team successful in resolving specific student problems in inclusive classrooms?

A second component of team effectiveness is the clarity of team goals (Snell & Janney, 2005). If all members understand the goals of the group, the team's work will be efficient and student needs will be met; if this does not occur, much valuable time may be spent clar-ifying goals or resolving issues that arise because of the resulting confusion.

A third component concerns team members themselves: On effective teams, members feel that their own needs are being met; that is, even if teamwork is challenging, they believe that its benefits outweigh its costs (Friend & Cook, 2010). However, team members also must be accountable. They need to understand that their contributions, such as getting spe-cific tasks finished on time, affect all team members and that the quality of their work may determine the quality of the team.

Finally, teams are effective when members monitor their own behaviors, offering input but not monopolizing conversations, helping the process of teaming by making suggestions that can resolve emerging conflicts, and encouraging quiet members to offer their comments.

In other words, team effectiveness depends as much on the extent to which each member helps the team accomplish its business as it does on the expertise each member brings to the teaming situation (Fleming & Monda-Amaya, 2001; Martin et al., 2004). How might this element of team effectiveness affect the outcome of Derek's IEP team meeting for Robert?

### Special Education Teams

In Chapter Two, you were introduced to the *multidisciplinary team,* the set of individuals who participate in the special education decision-making process. These professionals tend to coordinate their efforts but keep separate the responsibilities traditionally associated with their roles. This type of team is the minimum acceptable level of partnership for special education procedures, but it is not the only type of special education team (Friend & Cook, 2010). In some schools, team members communicate more and share more discussion about services to be offered, but each professional still delivers services separately. This type of team is referred to as *interdisciplinary.* In a few schools, an even more blended type of teaming is found: On a *transdisciplinary team,* members share their information, skills, and service delivery. For example, a classroom teacher may implement strategies recommended by the speech/language pathologist. The special education teacher may work on cutting and buttoning skills based on consultation with the occupational therapist. The speech/language pathologist may incorporate a reading goal from the special education teacher into her work with a student. Transdisciplinary teams are the most collaborative special education teams, but they also are the most difficulty type of team to create and sustain.

*Whether in other professions or education, teams are most effective when they have clear goals, committed members, and measurable outcomes.*

## Co-Teaching

The rise in inclusive practices has brought about the need for service delivery options that allow students with disabilities to access their education with their peers in general education while also receiving specialized services (Cahill & Mitchell, 2008). One response to this need has been the development of co-teaching (Friend, 2008), the teaching approach that Michelle, whom you met at the beginning of this chapter, is participating in. **Co-teaching** is a service delivery model in which two educators—one typically a general education teacher and one a special education teacher or other specialist—combine their expertise to jointly teach a heterogeneous group of students, some of whom have disabilities or other special needs, in a single classroom for part or all of the school day.

For co-teaching to be effective, the professionals must maximize the benefit of having two individuals with different types of expertise working together (Kloo & Zigmond, 2008; Little & Dieker, 2009). They accomplish this first through clear communication concerning their instructional philosophies, their own strengths and weaknesses as educators, their expectations for themselves and each other, and their preparation for assuming co-teaching roles. Then they decide how to best use their talents in the classroom. Some of the approaches co-teachers might use include (a) one teach, one observe; (b) parallel teaching; (c) station teaching; (d) alternative teaching; (e) teaming; and (f) one teach, one assist (Friend, 2008). Each approach is discussed in the following sections and depicted visually in Figure 4.2.

### One Teach, One Observe

In the one teach, one observe co-teaching approach, one educator manages the instruction of the entire group of students while the other gathers data on one student, a small group of students, or even the entire class. Either teacher may observe, but often special educators know more ways to collect data on students and may need to share that information with general education teachers. If professionals notice that a student seems to be having a great

Go to the Assignments and Activities section of Topic 2: Collaboration and Co-Teaching, in the MyEducationLab for your course and complete the activity entitled "Co-Teaching".

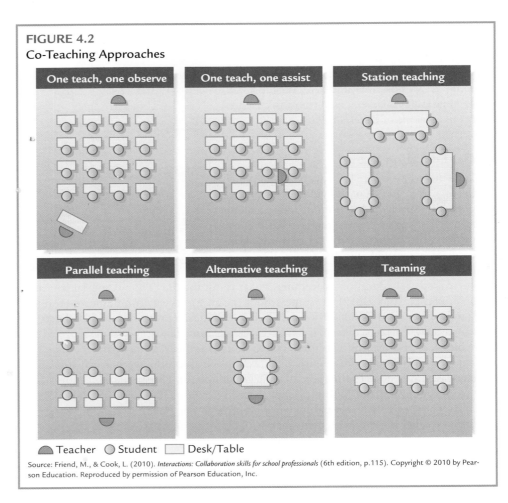

**FIGURE 4.2**
Co-Teaching Approaches

One teach, one observe

One teach, one assist

Station teaching

Parallel teaching

Alternative teaching

Teaming

Teacher   Student   Desk/Table

Source: Friend, M., & Cook, L. (2010). *Interactions: Collaboration skills for school professionals* (6th edition, p.115). Copyright © 2010 by Pearson Education. Reproduced by permission of Pearson Education, Inc.

**research**
**NOTE**

Magiera and Zigmond (2005) found that when professionals co-teach, students with disabilities interact less with the general educator but receive more individualized instruction by interacting with the special education teacher. The researchers concluded that the educators needed professional development and shared planning time to improve their practices.

deal of difficulty transitioning from one activity to the next, they might observe so that they can address this problem. Or they might observe how students approach independent work tasks or for how long they work before becoming distracted. Professionals might also gather data related to a student about whom they are concerned in preparation for an intervention assistance team meeting.

### Parallel Teaching

In some instances, two professionals may decide to split a group of students in half and simultaneously provide the same instruction. This would be appropriate if both teachers were highly qualified in the subject area, or this might occur during discussion so that all students would have more opportunities to participate. In an elementary math class, this approach might be used when some students can work without manipulatives for counting but other students still need them. With middle or high school students, this approach would be helpful for review sessions. With both teachers reviewing, they could more readily address student questions and monitor their mastery of the information. One consideration in using this approach is noise: If two teachers are conducting the same lesson simultaneously in a small classroom, the noise level can become too high. If this is a problem, the teachers might try seating the students on the floor on opposite sides of the classroom or, for middle or high school students, having the student groups face away from each other.

### Station Teaching

In *station teaching*, the teachers divide instruction into two, three, or even more nonsequential components, and each is addressed in a separate area of the room. Each student participates in each station. For example, in an algebra class one group of students might be working with the general education teacher as she introduces systems of equations, the second group might be working with the special educator to review last week's information, and the third group might be working on reports about famous mathematicians. All students would receive the instruction at all three stations. In an elementary classroom, one group might work with the speech/language pathologist on vocabulary and sentences, the second group might discuss the current story with a general education teacher, and the third group might work independently on story writing. With younger students or students who have difficulty working independently, there might only be two stations, each with a teacher. Halfway through the instruction, the groups would simply switch. In a secondary setting, particularly if class periods are relatively short (45 to 50 minutes, for example), a station might last the entire class period. In that case, the lesson plan would have to span two or three days in order for all students to access all the stations.

### Alternative Teaching

In some situations, pulling a small group of students to the side of the room for instruction is an appropriate strategy. When do you think this might occur? If you immediately think about this as a way of providing remedial instruction to students who did not understand a previous lesson, you are thinking like many teachers, and alternative teaching certainly may be implemented for this purpose. But for what else might you use this approach? What about *preteaching*—that is, helping students learn vocabulary words before they are introduced in large-group instruction? What about enrichment? What about teaching several students key concepts that they missed because they were absent? Many professionals appropriately worry that too much alternative teaching, especially for a remedial purpose, can give the impression of having a separate special education class operating within the walls of the general education classroom. This can be stigmatizing for students. However, if the purpose of the group varies and if the teachers take turns working with the small group, this can be a powerful use of two professionals in the classroom.

### Teaming

When teachers have built a strong collaborative relationship and their styles are complementary, they may decide to use a teaming approach to co-teaching—fluidly sharing the instructional responsibilities of the entire student group:

- One teacher begins by explaining the concept of democracy, and then the other teacher gives an example.
- One teacher delivers a brief lecture while the other teacher models note-taking skills for students using the overhead projector.
- One teacher explains a math procedure, and the other teacher interjects questions to ensure that all students understand.
- Two teachers decide to explain latitude and longitude to their students by coming dressed to illustrate the difference: One wears a shirt with vertical stripes and the other a shirt with horizontal stripes.

Some teachers use this approach extensively and find it energizing, as do Hilda and Cheney who are featured in the Speaking from Experience. However, for some teachers the informality and the spontaneity of this approach do not match their styles. Teaming has the potential to capture student attention and so can be an effective way to co-teach, but because the opportunities for dividing students into a variety of groups is powerful, teaming generally should be combined with other approaches, not used exclusively.

### One Teach, One Assist

In this co-teaching approach, one teacher manages the instruction of the entire student group while the other circulates through the classroom, providing assistance. For example, assisting is an accepted co-teaching practice when one teacher is monitoring to ensure all students are completing the math equation correctly. However, assisting has significant drawbacks as well. If teachers, especially special educators, spend too much time assisting, they probably will be bored and feel more like paraeducators than teachers. Also, one person assisting too much can be distracting for students. Finally, if either teacher assists a great deal, some students will come to rely too much on this always-available source of help instead of

*Hilda Wallace and Cheney Jackson have shared instruction in a high school Algebra I class in the Charlotte–Mecklenburg (NC) Public School District for 2 years. Their students include mostly ninth- and tenth-graders. As their comments illustrate, Hilda and Cheney have worked diligently to create an effective partnership and they have valuable advice about making co-teaching successful.*

**Hilda:** To make co-teaching successful, you have to be flexible—you can't think of your partner as your classroom assistant. I can't even tell you how many suggestions Cheney has made that help all the kids, not just the students with disabilities.

**Cheney:** In algebra, I have the experience of taking it in high school and being afraid to raise my hand—I didn't want people to think I was stupid. I know that some of our students feel like that. So in class, sometimes we do things two ways, and the kids can choose the one that makes sense to them.

**Hilda:** Something else. . . We never say, "These are my kids and those are your kids." It's always "our kids." You cannot come into this classroom and identify which kids receive special education. We're that way about being teachers, too, and so are the kids. They just see us as two teachers in algebra.

**Cheney:** We see the results in our achievement testing. When our kids take the district quarterly tests, our scores are among the highest in the county. We have high expectations for all our students—we never lower the standards because the class includes students with disabilities—and we feel like we get the best out of them.

**Hilda:** If I was giving advice to new teachers, I'd tell them to be sure to discuss issues. If one teacher is a control freak, they need to clarify how they're going to run the classroom. They should figure out how to have an equal partnership. For example, they can't say, "You grade those papers and give report card grades to your students, and I'll do mine." If the kids don't see you working together, they'll take advantage of it.

**Cheney:** You have to talk about things. Last year, we had more planning time, but this year, we still meet as much as we can. Sometimes we're on the phone so that we both know what's going on.

**Hilda:** It's especially nice this year because we co-teach in three blocks (out of four). Sometimes after the first block, Cheney will say, "I have an idea about a different way we could do that," and then we try it in second block and do it again if it worked. If there happens to be something she doesn't feel completely comfortable with, she'll hold back the first block, but then she jumps right in during second block.

**Cheney:** We're both kind of easygoing, and so we talk things out and make it work for the kids. We don't disagree; we have different ways of doing things. It's a marriage, and you really have to work together.

*Co-teaching is a powerful and highly collaborative option for providing access to the general curriculum for students with disabilities.*

learning to work independently. This co-teaching model has been criticized for being used too frequently and with too little result, especially in secondary classrooms (e.g., Scruggs, Mastropieri, & McDuffie, 2007).

## Other Co-Teaching Considerations

Co-teaching is a particularly sophisticated type of collaboration that some have likened to a professional marriage. Just as in a personal relationship, great care must be taken in a professional relationship to attend to details, to ensure that communication is clear and direct, to address problems when they are minor so they do not become significant, and to maximize the talents of both participants (Friend, 2007; Stivers, 2008). Further, if one professional is a novice and the other experienced, the co-teachers may have to be especially careful that they build a partnership that is satisfactory to both. In the Instruction in Action you will find a set of questions co-teachers can use to get their partnership started on a strong and collaborative foundation.

## Getting Off to a Great Start with Co-Teaching

The first day of school can set the tone for the entire year of co-teaching. These items— to be discussed with your co-teacher— are examples of elements contributing to co-teaching collaboration. How you address them might determine whether you form a true partnership or whether one person mostly leads and the other person mostly follows.

- Have you set up the classroom to communicate that it has two teachers—for example, two teachers' chairs, both names on the board?

- How have you discussed each person's perception of what co-teaching should look like, what the roles and responsibilities of each person should be?

- How have you made partnership integral to classroom materials—for example, both names on the course syllabus, both names on the newsletter that is sent home to parents?

- What will you and your partner do on the first day so that students understand you have parity in the classroom—for example, how will you introduce yourselves, who will talk about which of the key first-day topics such as classroom expectations and procedures?

- How will you divide students on the first day so that they observe both of you engaged in teaching?

## Consultation

A third application of collaboration for special educators occurs in **consultation,** "a voluntary process in which one professional assists another to address a problem concerning a third party," often a student (Friend & Cook, 2010, p. 85). In many ways, consultation is a specialized form of problem solving (Kampwirth, 2006).

The consultant meets with the other professional, first working to establish a positive relationship. Across several meetings, they jointly identify the problem, brainstorm ideas for addressing it, and select options that seem likely to succeed. The professional receiving consultation support then implements the intervention and reports on its success. Together, the consultant and the other professional decide whether they need to continue to meet, either to revise the intervention or to continue monitoring its effectiveness. In some cases, the consulting relationship ends when the problem is resolved. However, if the consultant has ongoing responsibility for the student in question, consultation might occur for the entire school year. Mary Jo, the teacher for students with visual impairments you met at the beginning of the chapter, provides this type of consultation. As you can see, the overall intent of consulting is to help a professional encountering a problem—often a teacher struggling to address a student need. An additional example of consultation is presented in the Positive Behavior Supports.

For some school professionals, consultation is a typical and significant role responsibility (Brown, Pryzwansky, & Schulte, 2006; Erchul et al., 2007; Vaughn & Coleman, 2004). For example, school psychologists and counselors often have time set aside in their schedules to meet with both special education and general education teachers to discuss how to meet student needs in the classroom. They might work directly with the student on occasion, but they rely on the teachers to implement most of the strategies and to monitor student responses. Special education teachers might or might not have consulting responsibilities. In New York and some other states, certain special educators are assigned to be *consultant teachers.* If you are a consulting teacher or in a similar role, you might model effective ways of working with certain students, meet with teachers to discuss student issues, and observe in classrooms to determine student needs and progress. If you work as a resource or self-contained teacher, particularly in an inclusive school, you might receive or offer consultation (Lamar-Dukes & Dukes, 2005).

Have you noticed that all the examples of consultation in this section imply that the consultant works with other professionals but not with the student? Your observation is correct (Kampwirth, 2006). Consultation is an **indirect service,** not a **direct service.** Consultation is an effective means for professionals to collaborate when the student in question needs only minimal support. It also may be used as a transition strategy for a student who no longer needs special education services. In some cases, as with a student with physical or sensory disabilities, consultation provides an opportunity for teachers to obtain the technical information they need, such as how to use a specialized computer keyboard or a communication device. This is a large part of Mary Jo's job, as you read at the beginning of this

research
**NOTE**

If your career plans include teaching at the high school level, you might enjoy reading Sims' (2008) account of her English co-teaching experience.

## Consultation in Practice

One common use of consultation is for situations in which students are displaying disruptive behaviors for which teachers cannot find effective strategies. Here is a sample of a consultative interaction between behavior specialist Mr. Corlone and beginning special educator Ms. Mitchell concerning Randy, a middle school student with autism. No matter your planned career, this brief interaction illustrates the important contribution of consultation to collaborative school services.

**Mr. C:** I've been looking forward to this second meeting so that we could really start to get at the dilemmas you're seeing for Randy in school.

**Ms. M:** Me, too. It was very helpful last time we met to discuss some of the details about Randy's background and how we would work together, but I'm anxious to address the problems.

**Mr. C:** Let's do it, then. What are the specific concerns that you have about Randy?

**Ms. M:** I don't even know where to begin. At the beginning of the year, Randy had a very difficult time adjusting to this school. He spent a great deal of time rocking and crying, and he refused to do almost everything. We got past all that, but now I see some of those same behaviors returning.

**Mr. C:** How so?

**Ms. M:** Yesterday was a good example. It was time for the students to stop their work to leave for lunch. I had used my usual strategy with Randy of cautioning him ahead of time that a change was coming and of talking to him about the need to begin to put away his materials. He seemed fine at first, but suddenly he swept everything off his desk and began to rock and cry. I have no clue why.

**Mr. C:** What did you do?

**Ms. M:** I gave him a little time to calm down and then started over again. The second time the problems did not occur.

**Mr. C:** What ideas have you had about what might be happening?

**Ms. M:** . . .

### Thinking about the Situation

1. Even if you had not read the introduction to this feature, how would you know which professional is the consultant?
2. These professionals are at what point in the problem-solving process? What part of consulting has already been completed?
3. If you were Ms. Mitchell, what other questions would you like Mr. Corlone to ask?
4. With classmates, take on the roles of these professionals and continue the conversation. Then analyze what is said in terms of the problem-solving process and use of a collaborative style. What communication skills were demonstrated? How did these help or interfere with the consultation?

### web link

http://www.nwrel.org/cfc/frc/collabindex.html
At the website of the Northwest Regional Educational Laboratory you can find discussion of many aspects of collaboration, including activities related to communication skills and ideas for facilitating collaboration with diverse groups of individuals.

chapter. Consultation sometimes is appropriate for other situations, too. For example, a consultant might assist a classroom teacher regarding a student at risk to decide if the student should be referred to the team or response-to-intervention team. Consultation also can have a positive impact on the skills of the professionals who benefit from it. When they learn a new strategy for teaching a student with a behavior disability, they might find that they can use it with other students as well.

As programs and services for students with disabilities become more inclusive and as standards become higher and accountability increases, collaborative options such as teaming, co-teaching, and consulting are likely to expand (Cook & Friend, in press). These formal applications of collaboration will reach their potential for meeting student needs only if you and your colleagues understand how to develop them and carefully continue to refine them.

## REVIEW · REFLECT · DISCUSS

1. Think about a highly effective team that exists in an area other than education (e.g., sports, medical field, faith-based group). What makes this team so effective? How could the same characteristics be applied to a team of which you will be a part?
2. Using a lesson plan developed in another course or a model lesson plan from a website or other source, apply to it each of the co-teaching approaches. Which approaches seem most likely to succeed? Why?
3. If you were told you would be working with a consultant, what would be most important to you in terms of considering the consultation a success? If you were told you were to consult with someone else, what would you do to ensure a successful outcome?

# Collaboration with Parents and Families

**PEARSON**
**myeducationlab**

Go to the Assignments and Activities section of Topic 2: Collaboration and Co-Teaching, in the MyEducationLab for your course and complete the activity entitled "Collaborating and Communicating with Teachers and Parents."

You already are becoming aware that parents and families play a critical role in special education procedures, planning, and programming. The message that accompanies this awareness is that your job includes understanding parents and families in order to collaborate with them (Fraenkel, 2006; Lo, 2005). However, you also have explored in Chapter Three some of the dilemmas of working with families. With increasing diversity in U.S. society, it is risky to assume that you can truly understand families simply because you are a caring educator (Summers et al., 2005). Knowledge and skills must be a companion to your care.

## Families and Collaboration

Many barriers to professional–parent collaboration can arise (Esquivel, Ryan, & Bonner, 2008; Fish, 2008). These are some of the most common (Friend & Bursuck, 2009):

- Parents may have had negative experiences when they were in school, so they may be reluctant to come to school and are uncomfortable interacting with school professionals.
- Some parents who live in poverty or who have come to the United States from another country may view educators as authority figures to whom they must listen. As a result, they may not share information or offer their point of view.
- Parents may encounter logistical problems in getting to school for meetings and conferences. Some lack transportation, some need child care, and some cannot leave their jobs to come to school during the times educators usually wish to meet.
- Some parents are confronted with language barriers in schools and misunderstandings that arise from cultural differences.
- Schools may not make parents feel welcome. Educators may ask them to wait for a lengthy period of time for a meeting to begin, and they may inadvertently ignore or minimize concerns that parents raise concerning their children.
- Some educators believe certain parents are not good parents or that they do not care, and so they may make only minimal effort to interact with those parents.
- Some educators are intimidated by parents, particularly those who are knowledgeable about special education and who insist on particular programs or services. As a result, they may limit communication with these parents.
- Communication from school to home may focus on negatives about the child rather than balancing those with positives.
- Professionals and parents may develop stereotypes of each other, and they may act on those stereotypes instead of on objective information.

*Through collaboration with school professionals, parents can help their children with disabilities reach their potential and realize their dreams.*

When you consider parent interactions with school professionals, would you add other items to this list? In a recent large-scale study in an urban school district, Hernandez, Harry, and Newman (2009) explored factors that influence parent-school relationships as related to special education. They found that the extent to which parents are involved in their children's services and the extent to which they are satisfied with those services were related to these factors:

- *Socioeconomic status.* Families from the lowest income group had the least involvement in their children's services but a high degree of satisfaction with them.
- *Race/ethnicity and primary language.* Although data related to race and ethnicity were difficult to interpret, parents whose primary language was English were more

**research**
## NOTE

Nowell and Salem (2007), after interviewing parents about their experiences with special education mediation, found that whether the experiences were positive or negative depended to a great extent on whether professionals followed up on promises made.

likely to be involved and more likely to indicate their children were not getting required services.

- *Student grade level.* Parents of children in elementary school were more involved and more positive about services than parents of children in upper grades.
- *Nature and severity of the disability.* Parents of children with significant disabilities were more involved in their children's services than other parents, but they also were less satisfied than other parents with those services.

Taken together, all of these barriers should lead you to the conclusion that your responsibilities for working with parents must receive considerable attention, or positive results are unlikely.

## Building Partnerships with Parents

If so many obstacles exist, what can you do to encourage collaboration with parents? The first step is working to understand families' perspectives. In addition, it may be inappropriate to begin by thinking of parents only in terms of collaboration. Although some parents will embrace collaboration and be actively involved working with you on behalf of their child, for others the first step might be to create conditions that encourage meaningful parent participation (Kasahara & Turnbull, 2005). This might be accomplished by providing parents with information about what will occur at a team meeting prior to the meeting date. It could also involve having one person from the school meet separately with the parents prior to a team meeting so that the parents are prepared for what will occur in the larger group. For a few parents, participation might be enhanced by making sure that supplies such as paper, pencils, and folders are available for parents' use; by providing to them samples of their child's work; or by offering to assist with transportation.

To foster participation that might lead to collaboration, you also need to address cultural differences. Lynch (1998) suggests that educators remember three points: (a) Culture is dynamic, and so what you may know of a culture from prior experience may not be valid today; (b) although culture influences people, so do other factors, such as socioeconomic status; and (c) no cultural group is homogeneous. These statements can serve as reminders that as you strive to understand a certain culture and learn to respect its norms, you should avoid treating all members of that cultural group as though they are alike. Developing cultural sensitivity truly is learning to balance knowledge with openness.

dimensions of
## DIVERSITY

Consultants working with migrant families should strive for collaboration by drawing on family strength, seeking language assistance as needed, and learning about family culture (Clare, Jimenez, & McClendon, 2005).

Many other options exist for encouraging parent participation. As noted in the section on communication skills, you should avoid using jargon when interacting with parents. You also can help by asking parents questions about which they have a unique and valuable perspective. For example, you might ask, "What are your child's favorite play activities at home?" or "What are the most important goals that you have for your child for the upcoming school year and after graduation?" When you ask questions that honestly invite parental input, participation is more likely to occur.

Ultimately, perhaps the most important way to increase parent participation is to recognize that unless you have a child with needs very similar to those of the parents with whom you are interacting, you cannot understand those parents' perspective, and you should not expect that you ever will, not in any complete sense. If you can remind yourself of that fact, you will probably remember that listening to the parents' point of view is the first step to fostering parent collaboration (Espe-Sherwindt, 2008; Harry, 2008).

**PEARSON**
## myeducationlab

Go to the Building Teaching Skills and Dispositions section of Topic 3: Parents and Families, in the MyEducationLab for your course and complete the activity entitled "Collaborating with Families".

## REVIEW · REFLECT · DISCUSS

1. Why might cultural differences between a parent and professional negatively affect opportunities for collaboration?
2. What steps can you take to foster positive parent interactions, regardless of whether collaboration is a goal?

# Issues Related to Collaboration in Special Education

dimensions of
**DIVERSITY**
Communication with families is about more than language. Be sure that your questions are respectful. For example, ask "Who reads with Jose?" rather than "Do you read with Jose?" (Rogers-Adkinson, Ochoa, & Delgado, 2003).

Although collaboration is rapidly becoming integral to the roles of professional educators, it is not universally accepted and supported by extensive research. Issues related to collaboration include the extent of its application in special educators' work with paraeducators, the limits to collaboration created by lack of time to meet with colleagues, and the research base for measuring collaboration's effectiveness.

## Working with Paraeducators

Federal special education law acknowledges the importance of paraeducators to the education of students with special needs and notes that they should be trained to carry out their jobs (Jolly & Evans, 2005; McKenzie & Lewis, 2008). In Chapter Two, the roles and responsibilities of paraprofessionals were outlined. However, another dimension in any discussion of paraeducators is the nature of their working relationships with professionals and parents and the place of collaboration in professionals' work with paraeducators (Devlin, 2008).

If you consider the responsibilities that paraprofessionals have in special education and general education settings, what would you say should be the relationship between them and the teachers and other specialists with whom they work? Is collaboration appropriate? The answer to this question is somewhat complicated.

Paraeducators are valuable members of the instructional teams for students, but these staff members do not have the same professional status or job responsibilities as the professionals. Even if paraeducators have a teaching license, they are employed in a nonteaching capacity at a much lower pay scale and generally have responsibilities much more limited than those of professionals. And so, in some cases, collaboration is appropriate, but in others it is not. For example, occasionally a paraeducator will refuse to carry out the directions of the teacher, possibly by "forgetting" them or asserting that they are not best for the student. Once in awhile, a paraeducator will contact the parents and discuss school matters even though the teacher has specifically and appropriately requested that this not occur. How would you handle situations such as these? If the paraeducator is assigned to work under your direction, you are responsible for providing day-to-day supervision for that individual (French & Chopra, 2006). This implies that you appropriately assign work to the paraeducator, meet to discuss plans and problems, and ask for input from others who also observe the paraeducator with students. If a serious problem arises, you are faced with a supervisory matter, not a collaborative one, and you are obligated to meet with the paraeducator to discuss it. Because your principal or another administrator probably has the formal supervision responsibility (i.e., the authority to require changed behavior or to sanction the individual), if you cannot satisfactorily resolve the situation, you should involve your administrator, who will likely request that you keep a record of any negative incidents that occur.

Is it possible for special educators to collaborate with paraeducators? Yes, and most paraeducators are wonderful, caring, and skilled individuals who are true advocates for students and who recognize that teachers and other professionals direct their work (Giangreco, Smith, & Pinckney, 2006). Your collaboration with them is somewhat similar to the possibility of your principal collaborating with you. Just as your

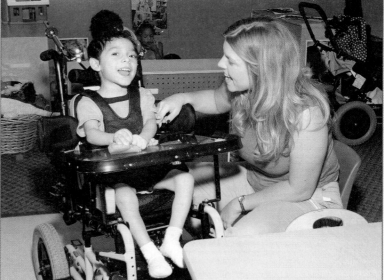

*Paraeducators are valuable school staff members whose work generally is directed and supervised by professionals.*

www.disabilityresources.org/index.
html
Disability Resources is a website
updated monthly that includes
many valuable tools, from details
about specific disabilities to strategies for working with students and
families for professional educators
and families, arranged with an A-
to-Z index.

principal may truly collaborate during a meeting at which a student crisis is discussed, you understand that this does not mean that you and your principal should share all decision making and that your input always will be sought. The same notion holds for paraeducators. You can and should collaborate with your paraeducator as appropriate for the situation, such as to coordinate snacktime or to discuss accommodations that might help a student during world history class. However, at times you will explain to the paraeducator what needs to be done, and it is appropriate to expect the paraeducator to follow your directions—possibly to use a specific computer program to help a student with word attack skills or to position a student in a particular way that encourages better posture and social interactions with other students.

Many professionals have strong working relationships with their paraprofessionals, and together they function as an instructional team (e.g., Malmgren, Causton-Theoharis, & Trezek, 2005). If you communicate clearly with paraprofessionals about their work, invite their feedback and insights, and resolve differences as soon as they arise, you will find that the balance of appropriate supervision and collaboration is easily achieved.

### Time for Collaboration

If you ask any experienced school professional to name the greatest barrier to effective collaboration in schools, you will undoubtedly be told that it is lack of time for shared planning (Horn, 2008; Johnston, Knight, & Miller, 2007). Several issues are involved. First, activities carried out collaboratively take longer to plan and evaluate than activities carried out by individuals. If three people meet to discuss Colby's problems at his community-based job, it undoubtedly will require an hour to discuss and address. If you are working on the problem yourself, you will think about it as you do other tasks, decide on a course of action, and carry it out much more quickly.

The second aspect of time concerns the need for shared time (Kaff, 2004; Khorsheed, 2007). In most schools, special education teachers, general education teachers, and other professionals all have planning time. The dilemma is that they do not have time *together* to discuss shared students. Thus, teams need adequate time to meet when all members can be present and focused on their tasks; co-teachers need opportunities to discuss lessons they have delivered, to plan future lessons, and to assess student progress; and consultants need time to interact with the other professionals. Too often, this time is found during lunch breaks, before or after school, or during evenings and weekends. Many dedicated educators contribute a significant amount of time beyond the school day in order to complete their work, but if they are expected to collaborate, at least some common planning time should be made available during the school day.

A third dilemma related to time concerns the willingness of each participant to collaborate (Friend, 2008). Even when shared planning time is scheduled, in some schools it is not used as intended. A special educator may decide that calling parents and completing IEPs have priority over planning with a general education colleague for the upcoming week. A general education teacher may excuse himself from a planning meeting after just a few minutes, noting that grades are due and no other time is available to finish calculating them. Although all professionals will sometimes find that there are just not enough hours in the day and that they have to make difficult decisions about how to use the time available, if collaboration is not a priority its benefits are unlikely to be seen.

A final time issue concerns a chronic problem for busy educators: running late to arrive at planned times for collaboration. As you walk down the hall or across the courtyard for your meeting, what should you say to the colleague you encounter who says, "I'm so glad I ran into you. I really need to discuss something with you. It'll only take a couple of minutes." If a true emergency exists, of course you will send word to your waiting colleagues and attend to this matter. However, if you stop each time someone asks for your input, you might damage your collaborative relationships with those waiting for you. Your chronic tardiness could be seen as a lack of interest in and respect for the shared work.

Are you wondering how professionals in schools find time for collaboration? You will find several suggestions in the Professional Edge. Which seem feasible to you? As you talk to

http://www.floridainclusionnetwork
.com/page265.aspx
The Florida Inclusion Network
sponsors a website of ideas and resources for including students with
special needs in the general education classroom. It contains ideas
for collaboration among teachers,
paraprofessionals, and
parents/families.

## Finding Time for Collaboration

Professionals have become very creative at finding ways to create time for collaboration. Here are a few of their ideas:

- Other professionals in the school help to cover classes, including principals, assistant principals, counselors, social workers, department chairpersons, psychologists, and supervisors.
- Retired teachers, qualified members of social or civic organizations, and others work as volunteer substitutes (if allowed); they meet the criteria to be employed but refuse the paycheck.
- Co-teaching partners begin each class period with 3 or 4 minutes of instructionally appropriate, independent work time, during which students work alone or with a partner. While students work, the teachers do informal planning.
- Principals and part of the school staff show instructionally relevant videotapes or other programs to groups of students so that other staff members can plan.
- When school-based staff development sessions are scheduled, they begin late or conclude early, with the saved time used for collaboration.

- Teachers come once each month after school for co-teaching planning sessions; they received required staff development credit for doing so.
- When district staff development is scheduled, co-teachers may opt to attend a session that has no speaker or agenda except to provide an opportunity for planning.
- Teachers divide the labor of preparing for instruction to save time. That is, each teacher in a grade level takes the lead for preparing materials for different lessons, making enough copies for all teachers in the grade level.
- If educators can only arrange to meet before or after school for planning, they make their work more enjoyable by bringing favorite snacks or meeting at a coffee shop instead of staying at school.
- Professionals find funds for substitute teachers, possibly through grants or contributions from state or local foundations, parent–teacher organizations, or disability advocacy groups.

practicing teachers and other professionals, explore other ideas for creating time for collaboration by asking them how they manage this chronic education challenge.

### The Effectiveness of Collaboration

As you learned earlier in this chapter, collaboration does not have value unless it is a vehicle for achieving goals for students and their families (Cook & Friend, in press). Thus, it is always a dimension of some other activity. This has made it difficult to study, and the majority of information about collaboration consists of stories of success, reports of perceptions, or advice for accomplishing it in schools (e.g., Cramer & Stivers, 2007; Griffin et al., 2008; Tannock, 2009; van Garderen, Scheuermann, & Jackson, 2009). Further, because collaborative activities tend to be complex—involving several individuals, each of whom has unique contributions to make—trying to study collaboration by comparing the activities of several groups is likewise challenging.

If you look for research that studies only collaboration, you will find that such studies often embed collaboration within broader efforts such as school improvement projects (David, 2008; Goddard, Goddard, & Tschannen-Moran, 2007; Schulte & Osborne, 2003) or inclusive practices (Volonino & Zigmond, 2007). Instead, you also might locate studies about the impact of communication skills on parents' or professionals' sense of collaboration (e.g., McLeskey & Waldron, 2002; Montgomery, 2005). You also might find studies documenting the effectiveness of teaching a specific problem-solving process and implementing it to address student academic and behavior concerns (Ortiz, Wilkinson, Robertson-Courtney, & Kushner, 2006; Santangelo, 2009).

Another way to explore the research related to collaboration is to examine studies about collaborative applications such as teaming, co-teaching, and consultation. More research exists in these areas, but it only indirectly addresses collaboration. For example, teams have been studied in business and education for many years. For schools, data have been gathered concerning the importance of strong team leadership, the impact of clear team procedures on team productivity, and the elements that create the sense of community that maximizes team effectiveness (e.g., Bahr et al., 2006; Esquivel et al., 2008). However, how can collaboration be separated from these elements? Generally, it has not been studied as a discrete part of teams but rather assumed to be the result of other positive team features.

PEARSON **myeducationlab**

Go to the Assignments and Activities section of Topic 2: Collaboration and Co-Teaching, in the MyEducationLab for your course and complete the activity entitled "Challenges of Collaboration".

research
**NOTE**

In proposing a research agenda related to universal design for learning (UDL), McGuire, Scott, and Shaw (2006) emphasized the need for collaboration among educators so that effective practices could be identified.

Consultation also should be considered. Consultation has a considerable research base, mostly in disciplines such as school psychology, counseling, and business; much less research exists related to teacher consultants. Researchers have explored consultants' communication skills, the impact they have on consultation outcomes, and the impact of various consultation models (e.g., Cautilli, Riley-Tillman, & Axelrod, 2006; Wilson, Erchul, & Raven, 2008). Consultation research also has explored teacher and parent perceptions of consultation effectiveness and the extent to which consultants' recommendations are actually carried out (e.g., Sheridan et al., 2004). However, isolating and studying the impact of collaboration on the consultation process has been challenging, and too few studies related to this topic have been completed to reach valid conclusions (Denton, Hasbrouck, & Sekaquaptewa, 2003).

A similar perspective can be offered on co-teaching. Many studies have been completed, but only a handful directly address the collaborative aspect of co-teaching (e.g., Mastropieri, et al., 2005; Murray, 2004; Scruggs, Mastropieri, & McDuffie, 2007). For example, Magiera and her colleagues (Magiera, Smith, Zigmond, & Gebaner, 2005) completed 49 observations of co-teaching in eight high schools. They found that both teachers spent considerable time monitoring student work and that special educators did not usually lead instruction. However, detailed analysis of one of the successful co-teaching partnerships indicated that co-planning and other collaborative activities were integral to positive student outcomes and teachers' satisfaction.

The still-developing status of research related to collaboration does not mean that it is not important or that it should be considered a minor part of your roles and responsibilities. Although it has proven particularly challenging to document that collaboration is an evidence-based practice, it is still true that today's schools rely more than ever on strong collaborative relationships among professionals and others (Barth, 2006; Nieto, 2009). The data that have been gathered related to collaboration suggest it is a powerful approach when used appropriately (Caron & McLaughlin, 2002).

Collaboration as a standard for school professionals is a relatively new idea. It should not be surprising that the research basis for it is still emerging. What is important for special educators to remember is that they should stay abreast of developments related to collaboration, remain open to new ideas about it, and possibly even join with colleagues to read and learn more about it.

## REVIEW · REFLECT · DISCUSS

1. Suppose that you are assigned to work with a very experienced paraeducator in your first year as a teacher, and she seems to want to tell you how students should receive services. What you might do in such a situation? Role-play how you might approach the paraeducator to address this topic.

2. How much planning time do you think educators should have for their collaborative work? How would you go about asking for shared planning time if none was assigned?

3. You read that the research base for collaboration is still emerging. What questions about collaboration would you like to have research answer? Look for a research-based article on that topic, and plan to share your findings with classmates who also have completed this assignment.

# Summary

- Collaboration is a style through which special educators and other professionals can conduct their interactions with each other and parents. It is based on voluntariness, parity, mutual goals, shared responsibility for key decisions, shared accountability for outcomes, shared resources, and the emergence of trust, respect, and a sense of community.
- Collaboration has existed for many years among special educators, but IDEA has bolstered its role in the delivery of services to students with disabilities, especially in general education settings.
- For collaboration to exist, professionals must believe it is valuable, use effective communication skills, follow clear processes (e.g., interpersonal problem solving), create programs and services that support it, and work with administrators to create a culture that fosters it.
- In addition to informal collaboration, three formal applications are common in today's schools: teaming, co-teaching, and consultation.
- Although nearly all professionals would assert that collaboration with parents and family members is critical, accomplishing this can be challenging. Sometimes, a first step is increasing meaningful parent involvement.
- Several issues characterize collaboration, including the complexity of professionals working with paraeducators, the realistic barriers created when shared planning time is not available for collaboration, and the emerging research base for collaborative practices.

## Council for Exceptional Children
## ADDRESSING THE PROFESSIONAL STANDARDS

Council for Exceptional Children (CEC) Common Core Knowledge and Skills addressed in this chapter:

ICC1K1, ICC3K3, ICC5S15, ICC7K5, ICC9S8, ICC9S11, ICC9S12, ICC10K1, ICC10K3, ICC10S3, ICC10S4, ICC10S7

Appendix: Provides a full listing of the CEC Common Core Standards, and associated Knowledge and Skill Statements listed here.

## PEARSON myeducationlab

Now go to Topic 2: Collaboration and Co-Teaching, in the MyEducationLab (www.myeducationlab.com) for your course, where you can:

- Find learning outcomes for the broad concepts covered in this chapter along with the national standards that connect to these outcomes.
- Complete Assignments and Activities that can help you more deeply understand the chapter content.
- Examine challenging situations presented in the IRIS Center Resources.
- Apply and practice your understanding of the core concepts and skills identified in the chapter with the Building Teaching Skills and Dispositions learning units.
- Check your comprehension on the content covered in the chapter by going to the Study Plan in the Book Specific Resources for your text. Here you will be able to take a chapter quiz, receive feedback on your answers, and then access Review, Practice, and Enrichment activities to enhance your understanding of chapter content.
- Watch video clips of CCSSO Teacher of the Year award winners responding to the question: "Why I teach?" in the Teacher Talk section.

## chapter five

# Students with Learning Disabilities

## LEARNING OBJECTIVES

- Define *learning disabilities*, explain their prevalence and causes, and outline the development of the learning disabilities field.
- Describe characteristics of individuals with learning disabilities.
- Explain both traditional and emerging approaches for identifying students with learning disabilities.
- Outline how students with learning disabilities receive their education.
- Describe recommended educational practices for students with learning disabilities.
- Explain the perspectives and concerns that parents and families of students with learning disabilities may have.
- Identify trends and issues influencing the field of learning disabilities.

## Nathaniel

Nathaniel's first grade teacher, Ms. Ivers, was the first to notice that he was not keeping up with his peers, despite the fact that he attended school regularly and fully participated in the basal reading program approved for this grade level. Data gathered on his reading performance confirmed her perception. During the late fall and based on the recommendation of the school's RTI problem-solving team, Nathaniel participated in a reading tutoring program three times per week, but this did not seem to accelerate his learning. During early spring he received 40 minutes per day of small-group, intensive reading instruction from the reading specialist, but the weekly checks on his progress suggested that even this intervention was not proving to be effective. Toward the end of first grade, the multidisciplinary team used the data from the RTI procedures as well as the results of additional assessments to determine that Nathaniel had a learning disability in reading. Now at the beginning of fourth grade, Nathaniel is described as a student of contradictions: When speaking in class it is obvious that he is a bright young man who has many abilities and interests. However, when he attempts to read, he struggles with nearly every word and often does not comprehend what he has read. Writing is also difficult for Nathaniel. His fourth grade teacher often asks him to explain what he has written because the words on the paper are jumbled and difficult to discern. To address his needs, Nathaniel receives supplemental reading instruction from the special education teacher every day, is provided extra time to complete writing assignments, and has permission to ask classmates for assistance. Socially, Nathaniel has many friends among his classmates.

## Danielle

Danielle just started middle school. She likes having several different teachers, but she is having difficulty remembering the locations of all the classrooms and the names of all the teachers. She is finding that she also has to remember to keep all her textbooks with her, take home the right materials to complete her homework, and move promptly from class to class—all tasks involving organizational skills, which are a struggle for her. Danielle is also a little worried about whether she will pass all her classes. She likes her science teacher, and completing all the practical examples and lab activities makes it easy to learn. In her other subjects, though, the amount of reading already seems endless. Danielle reads very slowly and often does not understand what she has read. She is hoping her resource teacher will have tapes of some of the books or study guides similar to those she used in fifth grade. Danielle is glad that her best friend Sophie from elementary school is in her classes; Sophie often helps Danielle indirectly by including her in conversations with other students. Danielle was identified as having a learning disability in third grade, and she has received special education services since then. In middle school, two of her classes will be co-taught, and she can also work with the resource teacher during the advisory period, a time during the day when all students can receive extra assistance from their teachers.

## D'Andre

D'Andre will graduate from high school this year. He was diagnosed with a learning disability early in first grade and has received special education services ever since. During elementary school he attended a special education class that was located in a school across town, receiving all his core instruction there, but in middle and high school he has attended his neighborhood school and participated in an increasing number of general education classes, receiving the supplemental support he needed from a resource teacher. D'Andre now reads at approximately a ninth-grade level, and his math skills are close to average for a senior in high school. However, he continues to experience significant problems in written language; when he was last assessed his writing skills were at an early fifth-grade level. D'Andre is an extremely likable young adult: he volunteers to help adults with disabilities at a local recreation center, and he enjoys talking with both peers and adults. He thrives on outdoor work and can mow a yard, build a fence, or plant a garden as well as anyone. He definitely wants to get a college degree, but he has decided to start by taking two classes next fall at the community college, where he can receive support from the Office of Disability Services. He is not yet sure what he wants to do for a living, but he is thinking of working in the building industry or in landscape architecture.

Have you ever been in a class—perhaps math or a foreign language—and suddenly realized that you had absolutely no understanding of the information being presented? Even after reviewing your notes and asking questions of classmates, you simply did not grasp the concept. Perhaps the experience left you questioning your abilities and feeling incapable of learning. Have you ever become disoriented while driving in an unfamiliar area? Not only did you not know how to get to your destination, but you also were not sure which direction was north or how to get back on your way. Friends may have found your situation funny, but your sense of discomfort was tinged with panic.

Neither of these experiences by itself indicates a learning disability (LD), but it can give you a small insight into what it is like to have a learning disability and how students with learning disabilities often experience frustration and a sense of failure, particularly in school. Their special needs may affect their ability to learn to read, to compute, to speak, to write, or any combination of these. These students may experience difficulty remembering, and they may show gaps in their social skills. Students with learning disabilities sometimes are described as "puzzle children" because they can be highly proficient in one area (e.g., math) and significantly delayed in another (e.g., reading).

# Understanding Learning Disabilities

Compared to other disability areas, the field of learning disabilities has had a relatively brief and intense evolution (Hallahan & Mercer, 2001). The work of medical professionals, psychologists, educators, and parents all contributed to the current understanding of this disorder.

## Development of the Learning Disabilities Field

The study of learning disabilities, displayed in Figure 5.1, began long before the term was introduced. As early as the nineteenth century, researchers were interested in how injuries to the brain affected adults' functioning (Opp, 1994). In the twentieth century, this line of research became more focused when Goldstein (1942) studied brain-injured soldiers returning from World War I (C. R. Smith, 1998). This work eventually was applied to the study of children who were presumed to be brain-injured from unknown causes because they experienced unexplained learning difficulties (Hammill, 1993). Researchers focused on trying to improve these students' learning, not by developing academic interventions, but instead by trying to develop their perceptual skills (e.g., balance, eye–hand coordination, ability to stay within the lines when tracing a line in a visual maze), working from the assumption that the emphasis on perception would eventually lead to improvements in learning (Frostig & Horne, 1964; Kephart, 1960; Strauss & Lehtinen, 1947).

During the 1960s, learning disability was formally established by law as a category of disability (Lerner & Kline, 2006). At the same time, as researchers failed to demonstrate that teaching perceptual skills improved learning, the field shifted from this approach to direct

---

**FIGURE 5.1**

**Timeline: Development of the LD Field**

| 1877 | 1896 | 1905 | 1920s | 1940s | Early 1950s | 1950s |
|---|---|---|---|---|---|---|
| Term word *blindness* introduced by German neurologist Adolf Kussamaul, meaning an inability to read print despite normal vision | Word blindness described in a 14-year-old by ophthalmologist James Hinselwood | | Goldstein (1942) studies of brain-injured soldiers returning from WWI and the impact on functioning | Wayne County Training School in Northville, Michigan applies work with brain-injured adults to children with intellectual disabilities or brain injuries after Werner and Strauss find them similar in functioning | Research coin the term *Strauss syndrome* for children who functioned as though they had brain injuries, where such injury was documented or not | Research and educational practice focuses on students' perceptual skills, assuming that teaching these skills would lead to improved academic functioning |
| | First U.S. report of reading disorder in children published by Dr. W.E. Bruner of Cleveland, OH. | | | | | |

instruction in academics (Hallahan & Kauffman, 1976). Since then, professionals have continued to build a legal and scientific understanding of learning disabilities and to explore alternative instructional methods for students with learning disabilities (e.g., Kavale, Spaulding, & Beam, 2009; Wanzek & Vaughn, 2008; Zirkel, 2009). Michael, whose story is depicted in the Firsthand Account, is an example of a very successful young adult who received special education services for a learning disability throughout most of his school years.

## Definitions of Learning Disabilities

Although the term **learning disabilities** was coined 40 years ago and the study of learning disabilities has been pursued intensely ever since, considerable controversy still exists over what a learning disability really is. The two definitions noted most often that largely shape students' programs and services are (a) the federal definition included in the Individuals with Disabilities Education Act (IDEA) and (b) the definition proposed by the National Joint Committee on Learning Disabilities (NJCLD). Each is explained in the following sections.

### Federal Definition

The federal definition of learning disabilities articulated in P.L. 94-142 in 1975 has changed very little since then. According to IDEA,

> Specific learning disability means a disorder in one or more of the basic **psychological processes** involved in understanding or in using language, spoken or written, that may manifest itself in imperfect ability to listen, think, speak, read, write, spell, or do mathematical calculation, including conditions such as perceptual disabilities, brain injury, minimal brain dysfunction, dyslexia, and developmental aphasia. Specific learning disability does not include a learning problem that arises primarily as the result of visual, hearing, or motor disabilities, of mental retardation, of emotional disturbance, or of environmental, cultural, or economic disadvantage. (IDEA 20 U.S.C. §1401 [2004], 20 C.F.R. §300.8[c][10])

Because states are required to adhere to the provisions of the federal special education law, most of them use either this definition or a variation of it (Reschly & Hosp, 2004). As you would expect, the definition focuses on school tasks and learner characteristics and needs, and it clearly explains that learning disabilities are distinct from other disabilities. What are other important components of the federal definition?

### NJCLD Definition

The **National Joint Committee on Learning Disabilities (NJCLD)** includes representatives from 13 professional and parent organizations concerned about individuals with learning disabilities (National Joint Committee on Learning Disabilities, 2009). This group has expressed concern about the federal definition for several reasons, most of which are related to what the definition does not address: the heterogeneity of students with learning disabilities, the impact of learning disabilities on social perception, the life-span nature of learning

When the Tremaine Foundation conducted a national telephone poll to measure public awareness and understanding of learning disabilities, they found that 75 percent of respondents were somewhat familiar with learning disabilities and nearly all knew students with LD were "just as smart as anyone."

www.teachingld.org
The Division for Learning Disabilities is part of the Council for Exceptional Children. At its website, you can communicate with professionals working with students with learning disabilities, find answers to questions about this disorder, explore tips for teaching these students, and read current news affecting the field.

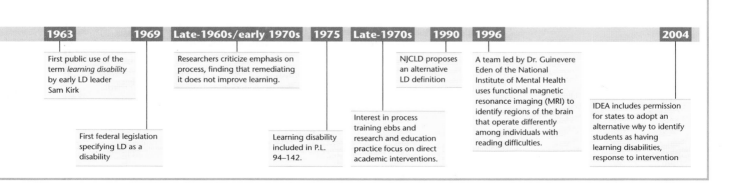

| 1963 | 1969 | Late-1960s/early 1970s | 1975 | Late-1970s | 1990 | 1996 | 2004 |

First public use of the term *learning disability* by early LD leader Sam Kirk

First federal legislation specifying LD as a disability

Researchers criticize emphasis on process, finding that remediating it does not improve learning.

Learning disability included in P.L. 94–142.

Interest in process training ebbs and research and education practice focus on direct academic interventions.

NJCLD proposes an alternative LD definition

A team led by Dr. Guinevere Eden of the National Institute of Mental Health uses functional magnetic resonance imaging (MRI) to identify regions of the brain that operate differently among individuals with reading difficulties.

IDEA includes permission for states to adopt an alternative way to identify students as having learning disabilities, response to intervention

**MICHAEL,** *who earned his bachelor's degree and teaching license in special education from the University of North Carolina at Greensboro, knows firsthand what it is like to be a student with a learning disability. His story explains his passion for making a difference in the lives of students with disabilities.*

I was first identified as having a learning disability in third grade—but by then I had been held back twice. They told my dad that it might be best to send me to a special school because there was not much of a chance that I would learn to read. Later, he told me that he stood up and told them that I would read—within a year. For the next year I remember that every time we were in the car and stopped at a traffic light, my father would show me flash cards. I remember saying to him, "But, Dad, I don't want to look at any more flashcards." He said, "I love you," and kept on doing them. And I did learn to read.

By high school, I was very successful. I also have ADHD so I have lots of energy. I was involved in everything: president of the drama club, very popular, well-liked by my teachers. I had a 3.5 GPA, a very bright future, and high hopes for myself. I was even taking honors and advanced placement classes.

So 11th grade rolled around and it was time to fill out transition paperwork. My parents had to be at the hospital because of my dad, who also has a disability, and so it was just me with the rest of the IEP team. They asked me, "What are your plans for the future?" I told them I wanted to go to college and be a special education teacher. I can still remember this . . . the psychologist was sitting to my right and he said, "We need to start thinking about more realistic goals." Now that took me back, but here's what really kills me: I look around the table and the rest of the teachers, who knew me so well, knew how hard I worked, knew how successful I was . . . were all nodding their heads in agreement. I felt like someone had closed the door on everything I wanted to do. I got very discouraged. My grades started to drop. I was scared to death to turn in any kind of writing assignment because I thought it wasn't good enough.

After my grades started to go down, my dad, still in the hospital, had a meeting with me. I am sitting next to his bed and he asks, "What's going on? You went from an A–B student to making Ds and Fs." So I told him about the IEP meeting and how they had said I should start making more realistic goals for myself. Then my father reminded me about learning to read. What he said to me helped me decide to succeed in spite of what I was told at school.

So let's jump to college. As a special education major, I made the dean's list for the past three years. I was president of our local student chapter of the Council for Exceptional Children and vice president of the North Carolina Youth Leadership Network, an organization connecting youth with disabilities from all over the state. I was also one of twelve members of the Youth Advisor Committee for the National Council on Disabilities, a group that advises the president on legislation pertaining to disability—all this from a person who "realistically" should not have gone to college.

It's important for teachers (and students) to have high expectations. My father had high expectations for me. I think one of the biggest fears of people who work with people who have disabilities is the fear that they will fail. So they lower their expectations for them to be sure they won't fail and so the programs they are in can be called successful. It is true that people with disabilities might fail, but they might not. Young people with disabilities need to know that there are successful people out there. They need to know that they are not struggling alone and that they can make it! I work with hundreds of youth with disabilities in my state and on a national level and I can tell you for every person like me there are more youth who do not make it.

Given the opportunity, youth at risk can achieve great things. I am not saying it is as easy, but we have to make this our core in the field of education. Disability is a natural part of the human experience—it empowers. If we believe that students with learning disabilities can do great things, we will see greater things than we ever believed were possible—and I'm proof of that.

disabilities, and the possibility that learning disabilities can exist concomitantly with other disabilities.

Because of these perceived deficiencies in the federal definition, the NJCLD created its own definition of learning disabilities, which it offers as more accurate and comprehensive:

> Learning disabilities is a general term that refers to a heterogeneous group of disorders manifested by significant difficulties in the acquisition and use of listening, speaking, reading, writing, reasoning, or mathematical abilities. These disorders are intrinsic to the individual, presumed to be due to central nervous system dysfunction, and may occur across the lifespan. Problems in self-regulatory behaviors, social perception, and social interaction may exist with learning disabilities but do not by themselves constitute a learning disability. Although learning disabilities may occur concomitantly with other handicapping conditions (for example, sensory impairment, mental retardation, serious emotional disturbance), or with extrinsic influences (such as cultural differences, insufficient or inappropriate instruction), they are not the result of those conditions or influences. (NJCLD, 1990)

### Essential Dimensions of a Definition of Learning Disabilities

Although discussions about the definition of learning disabilities continue, most professionals seem to agree that learning disabilities include these dimensions (Kavale & Forness, 2000b):

- Learning disabilities comprise a heterogeneous group of disorders. Students with learning disabilities may have significant reading problems (**dyslexia**), difficulty in mathematics (**dyscalculia**), or a disorder related to written language (**dysgraphia**). They may have difficulty with social perceptions, motor skills, or memory. Learning disabilities can affect young children, students in school, and adults. No single profile of a person with a learning disability can be accurate because of the interindividual differences in the disorder.

*Each student with a learning disability has a unique set of characteristics, strengths, and need.*

- Learning disabilities are intrinsic to the individual and have a neurobiological basis. Learning disabilities exist because of some type of dysfunction in the brain, not because of external factors such as limited experience or poor teaching.
- Learning disabilities are characterized by unexpected underachievement. That is, the disorder exists when a student's academic achievement is significantly below her intellectual potential, even after intensive, systematic interventions have been implemented to try to reduce the learning gap. This topic is addressed in more detail later in this chapter.
- Learning disabilities are not a result of other disorders or problems, but individuals with learning disabilities may have other special needs as well. For example, being deaf cannot be considered to be the basis for having a learning disability. However, some students who are deaf also have learning disabilities.

## Prevalence of Learning Disabilities

According to annual data gathered as part of IDEA during the 2007–2008 school year, approximately 2.6 million students between ages six and twenty-one had learning disabilities (U.S. Department of Education, 2009). This number represented about 3.7 percent of the entire school population.

Further exploration of prevalence data reveals several interesting facts. For example, from when the federal law was first passed in 1975 until about 8 years ago, learning disability was the fastest-growing category of special education, growing from only 22 percent of all students receiving special education (Horn & Tynan, 2001) to nearly 50 percent in 2002 (U.S. Department of Education, 2004). Since then, this trend has reversed itself. In fact, the number of students ages six to eleven identified as LD has decreased approximately 24 percent over the past several years, and the growth in the numbers of older students with this disability has leveled off. These data suggest that (a) the use of the relatively new category of *developmentally delayed* is being used for some of these young children and (b) efforts to provide early intervention through RTI procedures are having a positive impact on addressing student achievement problems.

The matter of gender can be raised as a prevalence issue, too. Researchers generally have found that the ratio of boys to girls identified as having learning disabilities is at least 2:1, or perhaps even 3:1 or 4:1 (Coutinho & Oswald, 2005; Siegel & Smythe, 2005). Many explanations have been offered for this phenomenon: Boys might be labeled as having learning disabilities more frequently because of medical factors, such as their greater vulnerability to prenatal and postnatal brain damage; maturational factors, including their documented slower rate of development; sociological factors, such as societal expectations for high achievement from males; and brain organization factors, including the greater likelihood in

dimensions of
### DIVERSITY

The National Association for the Education of African American Children with Learning Disabilities (www. http://www.aacld.org/) was established in 2000 to raise awareness and promote understanding of the unique needs of minority children with learning disabilities.

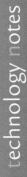

### Brain Research and Learning Disabilities

Advances in medical technology are making it possible for scientists to study the human brain, leading us to a much clearer understanding about the parts of the brain that are most critical for oral language and reading and the differences between the brains of individuals who read fluently and those with reading or learning disabilities (Shaywitz, Lyon, & Shaywitz, 2006; Society for Neuroscience, 2006). Eventually, it may lead to new types of interventions for students.

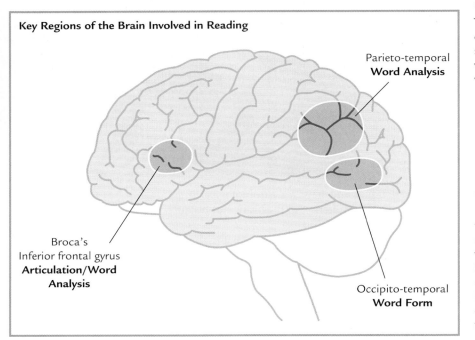

**Key Regions of the Brain Involved in Reading**

Parieto-temporal
**Word Analysis**

Broca's
Inferior frontal gyrus
**Articulation/Word Analysis**

Occipito-temporal
**Word Form**

#### Brain Structure

Three regions of the brain, all located in the left hemisphere as shown in the illustration are involved in reading (Shaywitz & Shaywitz, 2004):

- Broca's region (involved in articulation and word analysis)
- Parieto-temporal region (involved in word analysis)
- Occipito-temporal region (involved in reading fluency)

#### Brain Function

Researchers study how the brain functions through functional magnetic resonance imaging (fMRI), which measures blood flow during brain activity. Results of studies using this approach indicate that the brains of individuals who are dyslexic function differently than the brains of individuals with LD:

boys of genetically based impulsivity (C. R. Smith, 2004). In practice, girls identified as having learning disabilities as a group usually have more severe academic deficits than boys (Lerner & Kline, 2006).

Taken together, these prevalence figures illustrate that learning disabilities represent a complex disorder affecting many students. They also demonstrate that the current definition of learning disabilities probably leads to inconsistency in identifying students as having this special need. In fact, dissatisfaction about who is eligible to receive services due to having this disability is largely what led to the development of response to intervention (RTI) procedures, addressed in more detail later in this chapter.

## Causes of Learning Disabilities

As you might suspect from the preceding discussion about the development of the learning disabilities field and the definition of the disorder, in most cases the cause of a learning disability is simply not known, and it is highly unlikely that a single primary cause will ever be identified. Generally, though, the possible causes of learning disabilities can be divided into two categories: physiological causes and curricular and environmental contributors (Smith, 2004).

### Physiological Causes

Several possible physiological causes of learning disabilities have been identified by education professionals and medical researchers (Gilger & Wilkins, 2008). These include brain injury, heredity, and chemical imbalance.

**web link**

www.ldonline.org
LD Online is one of the best-known sites for teachers and parents of children with learning disabilities. It offers expert advice, contains recent news on learning disabilities, and has a section for children to share their experiences.

- Broca's region is overactivated
- Parieto-temporal region is underactivated
- Occipito-temporal region is underactivated

These differences have been found across cultures and different languages, and they exist in both children and adults who struggle to read.

### Cautions

Although promising, brain research also must be viewed with caution (Bigler, Lajiness-O'Neill, & Howes, 1998; Hudson, High, & al Otaiba, 2007):

- Most of the work has been completed with adults, not children, and although it is assumed that the results are valid for both groups, this is not known for sure.
- The sample sizes in most studies thus far have been very small, and so the reliability of the results and their applicability to others is limited.
- Although the different parts of the brain activated during oral language and reading are being mapped, it is not accurate to assume they function exclusive of each other. The relationships among the parts of the brain used for speaking and reading are not known at this time.
- Most studies have involved reading single letters or words, not paragraphs or passages. Whether brain function during the latter type of activity is different in any meaningful way from the former is not clear.

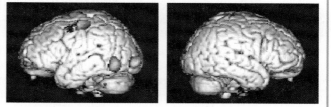

*Brain Activation During Reading.*
*The yellow areas show where typical readers have greater brain activation during word reading, compared to those with LD.*

*Note:* Images above show left and right hemispheres of the brain.

*Source:* Copyright 2001 by Lynn Flowers and Frank Wood. Reprinted with permission from Lynn Flowers and Frank Wood.

- In most studies, the participant pushes a button to indicate the answer to a question read silently (e.g., Do *leat* and *nete* rhyme?). Thus, the research tasks are not at all like a classroom learning environment.
- Information on brain structure and function is not diagnostic; that is, it does not directly tell us the nature of an individual's learning disability or the interventions that might ameliorate or compensate for it.

*Note:* Images above show left and right hemispheres of the brain.

First, as proposed from the earliest work in the learning disabilities field, brain injury probably causes some students' disorders. The injury may occur prenatally, as might happen when a mother consumes alcohol or drugs, contracts measles, or smokes cigarettes. An injury also might occur during the perinatal period, as when a baby is deprived of oxygen during birth. Brain injury also can occur postnatally because of a high fever, a head injury (e.g., falling from a bike or playground equipment), an illness (e.g., meningitis), or an accident (e.g., a near drowning). In the Technology Notes, you can learn more about recent advances in understanding the brain and learning disabilities.

Considerable evidence indicates that heredity is another physiological cause of learning disabilities (National Institute of Child Health and Human Development, 2007; Alarcon, Pennington, Filipek, & DeFries, 2000). Teachers have reported for years that many parents of children with learning disabilities comment, "He's just like his father [or mother]." Now research is supporting those claims. In fact, when one or both parents have a learning disability, their children may have as much as a 30 to 50 percent chance of also having that disorder (Castles, Datta, Gayan, & Olson, 1999). Critics of this research have noted that it does not consider possible environmental factors. That is, perhaps parents and their children share learning disabilities because of similar exposure to allergens or environmental toxins such as lead. However, studies of twins and siblings support the heritability of learning disabilities (Kovas, Haworth, Dale, & Plomin, 2007). The reading level of one identical twin is very likely to predict the reading level of the other, even when they are reared apart, and this holds true when one has been identified as having a learning disability. In contrast, a non-twin sibling's reading level is much less likely to predict the reading

**research**
**NOTE**

The National Institutes of Health indicates that about 8–10 percent of all school-age students have some type of a learning disability, but just 4–5 percent receive services in this category through special education.

level of the other sibling when they are reared separately. This line of research provides evidence of a genetic link.

A third physiological cause of learning disabilities sometimes mentioned is biochemical. For some children, learning disabilities seem to be related to significant attention problems, which may be the result of chemical imbalances in the brain. This topic is explored in more depth in Chapter Six on students with attention deficit–hyperactivity disorder (ADHD).

You should be careful in attributing learning disabilities to physiological causes. Just because a child has a head injury does not mean that a learning disability is inevitable. Likewise, just because one child has a learning disability does not mean his sibling will have the disorder. Perhaps in the future, emerging medical technology will provide scientists and researchers with new tools for studying the relationship between the brain and individuals' patterns of learning. In the meantime, professionals should consider such information intriguing but somewhat speculative.

### Curriculum and Environmental Contributors

For some children, learning disabilities are caused by the situations in which they live (Fletcher, Lyon, Fuchs, & Barnes, 2007). For example, children who have poor nutrition may develop learning disabilities, as may those who live for an extended period of time in a highly adverse emotional climate. Some students have learning disabilities because of toxins in their environments, as might happen to children who develop lead poisoning because of the use of lead-based paint in older homes. Yet other children may have too little stimulation (e.g., adults who fail to model language, lack of access to books, few experiences such as visits to the zoo) (Rashid, Morris, & Sevcik, 2005). When you think about all these factors, can you identify a single group of youngsters who might be most expected to have learning disabilities because of environmental causes? If your response is children who live in poverty, you are correct. These children also may be placed at greater risk of having learning disabilities because of poor medical care or low parent education level (Skiba et al., 2008).

One other environmental cause of learning disabilities should be mentioned. Although in an ideal world this paragraph would not need to be written, some students have learning disabilities because of poor instruction (Haycock & Crawford, 2008). When teachers use outdated instructional practices, do not consider the differences in students' maturational levels, and ignore students' learning styles, they can cause some students to display characteristics of learning disabilities. This cause of learning disabilities is one of the most controversial. IDEA specifically prohibits students who receive poor instruction from being identified as having this or any other disability on that basis. However, some professionals argue that if teaching has been so inadequate that a learning disability has been created in a student, then that student should receive the benefit of a specialized education to remediate the problem.

## REVIEW · REFLECT · DISCUSS

1. What are the critical differences between the federal and NJCLD definitions of learning disabilities? How might school practices change if the latter definition were adopted in federal law?

2. Why are researchers so interested in determining the causes of learning disabilities? How might some of the areas of research explored in this chapter influence future practices for educators?

Go to the Assignments and Activities section of Topic 8: Learning Disabilities, in the MyEducation-Lab for your course and complete the activity entitled "Characteristics of Learning Disabilities".

## Characteristics of Individuals with Learning Disabilities

Individuals with learning disabilities are an extraordinarily heterogeneous group, with different areas of strengths and special needs in the cognitive, academic, social-emotional, and behavior domains. The following sections highlight some of the most common characteristics.

## Cognitive Characteristics

Although students with learning disabilities typically have average or above-average intelligence, they usually display weaknesses in one or more areas of cognition, including attention, perception, memory, and thinking/processing.

### Attention

Students with learning disabilities may have poor selective attention (Mayes, Calhoun, & Crowell, 2000; Zera & Lucian, 2001). One way to illustrate what this means is to think about the setting you are in as you read this paragraph. Stop to listen and look around. Is someone nearby typing on a computer or texting from a phone? Is there noise in the hallway or on the street? Is there a pile of other reading material right beside you? Until you were directed to notice items such as these, you likely ignored them because your attention was devoted to reading your textbook. Students with learning disabilities may have extraordinary difficulty attending to only the important stimuli in their environments. The other reading material may be as captivating as the book in front of them; the plane overhead is as noticeable as the teacher's voice.

### Perception

Many students with learning disabilities exhibit perceptual problems (Lerner & Kline, 2006; Silver, 2004). *Perception* does not pertain to whether a student sees or hears but rather to how her brain interprets what is seen or heard and acts on it. For example, a student with a visual perception problem may see perfectly well the words on a page. However, when asked to read the words, the student may skip some of them. Other symptoms of visual perception difficulties include spatial orientation and judgment (e.g., bumping into things; knowing how to safely get from one point to another); the ability to distinguish right from left; labored handwriting; and overall clumsiness or awkwardness in walking, skipping, balancing, and other large-motor activities (C. R. Smith, 2004). Problems in auditory perception often include difficulties with perceiving sounds that are not attributable to a hearing loss (Kruger, Kruger, Hugo, & Campbell, 2001). For example, some students may have trouble understanding whether the word spoken was *team* or *teen, odor* or *over, pet* or *bet.* Of course, the result can be misunderstood directions, poor communication, and awkwardness in social interactions.

www.ldanatl.org
The website for the Learning Disabilities Association of America contains numerous links and resources for individuals with disabilities and their families, including information about rights and recent legislation regarding learning disabilities.

### Memory

In addition to problems related to attention and perception, students with learning disabilities may experience problems with memory (Fletcher et al., 2007; Swanson, Zheng, & Jerman, 2009). Everyone has two types of memory: short term and long term. **Short-term memory** is the mechanism by which a person holds information in the mind for a brief amount of time—less than a minute. Unless it is acted on in some way, it is gradually lost. One simple example is when you look up a phone number. You remember it long enough to dial it, but if you delay dialing you probably have to look up the number again unless you have consciously taken steps to remember it (e.g., by repeating it several times). **Long-term memory** is the permanent storage mechanism in the brain, and information to be remembered generally has to be transferred from short-term to long-term memory. An example might be verses from a favorite childhood song: Even if you have not recalled them for many years, you can still sing the words as soon as you hear the title "If You're Happy and You Know It" or "The Barney Song." Students with learning disabilities may have difficulty with either short-term memory or long-term memory or both.

### Information Processing

Finally, students' general information-processing or thinking skills may be deficient (Schiff, Bauminger, & Toledo, 2009). Students with learning disabilities may have difficulty with **metacognition**, or thinking about thinking. They may lack the ability to actively consider how new information they are learning relates to other information already stored or how to apply that knowledge in a novel learning situation. For example, as you read this chapter, you probably are actively relating the concepts to people you know who have learning disabilities or perhaps to knowledge you acquired in a course in psychology. You might also be using a strategy to help you remember information that may be on a test—for example, by repeating key ideas aloud. These are all metacognitive activities. Some students with learning disabilities will not use such strategies to foster their learning without explicit training (discussed in a later section of this chapter).

## Academic Characteristics

By far the most commonly noted characteristic of students with learning disabilities is their struggle with school learning. Their difficulties may occur in reading, spoken language, written language, mathematics, or any combination of these. Academic difficulties comprise the most likely reasons for classroom teachers to suspect a student has a learning disability, and such difficulties often are emphasized in the services provided by special education teachers.

### Reading

Most students with learning disabilities experience significant problems in reading (Falk-Ross et al., 2009; Vaughn & Edmonds, 2006). For example, many students struggle with *phonological awareness*, which is the ability to make the connection between letters and the sounds they stand for. This skill is essential for developing reading proficiency. These students are not able to sound out words, and they often rely on visual cues or the context in which a word is used to determine what the word is.

Other students struggle with *oral fluency* (Therrien & Kubiana, 2006). They may read aloud in a word-by-word manner without appropriate inflection or rhythm, unable to relate the patterns of spoken language to the printed word. Students with weakness in this area often dread being asked to read aloud in class.

One other typical reading problem for students with learning disabilities is *comprehension* (Faggella-Luby & Deshler, 2008). Unlike the student previously described who labors to say each word, some students are able to read a passage so fluently that you might assume they are highly proficient readers. However, when they are asked questions about what they have read, these students may have little or no understanding of the words. Not surprisingly, students who have difficulty with phonological awareness and oral fluency also are likely to experience weakness in reading comprehension.

You might find that some people refer to reading problems of all sorts as *dyslexia* (e.g., Mortimore, 2008). The Professional Edge clarifies the meaning of this term and strategies for addressing dyslexia.

### Oral Language

Another academic area that can be a significant problem for students with learning disabilities is oral language. Problems usually fall into the areas of phonology, morphology, syntax, and pragmatics.

Students may have difficulties with *phonology*—that is, using the correct sounds to form words. They may struggle with *morphology*, the study of the smallest meaningful units of language (e.g., that *-ed* denotes past tense or that *pre-* means "before"). Likewise, students may have problems with *syntax*, the rules of grammar, or with *semantics*, the meanings of words or phrases. Finally, *pragmatics*—the ability to successfully participate in interactions with others—may be a weakness.

If you think about all these elements of spoken language, you can begin to see how pervasive the effects of this type of learning disability can be. For example, a student with poor oral language skills may miss subtle meanings of words during conversations or fail to understand the punch line of a joke based on word meanings. Such a student also may have difficulty participating in conversations with classmates or adults.

### Written Language

For some students, learning disabilities are manifested in written language (Brice, 2004; Graham, Harris, & Fink-Chorzempa, 2003; McCurdy, Skinner, Watson, Shriver, 2008). For example, the motor coordination required for handwriting can be overwhelming for

In the future it may be possible to relate reading disabilities to specific genes, thus making it possible to identify individuals at-risk for reading problems and to develop interventions tailored for them.

some students. As shown in the sample in Figure 5.2, it is nearly impossible to determine what these students have written even though the words form complete sentences and are spelled correctly. For other students, the deficiency is spelling. Not only do these students labor to discern the sounds comprising words, but they also may be unable to distinguish between appropriate uses of homonyms (e.g., meet–meat; there–their) or to recognize when they have written a misspelled word (e.g., *seperate* instead of *separate; advise* instead of *advice*). Students also may have difficulty knowing when and how to punctuate the sentences they write, struggling not only with the appropriate application of periods and commas but also with the use of apostrophes (e.g., *it's*—it is instead of *its*—possessive form). Finally, they may also be uncertain about capitalizing words (e.g., *My Brother likes mexican food*).

In an era when spelling, punctuation, and many other conventions of written language can be corrected with computer software and other electronic tools, perhaps the most serious issue for students with learning disabilities in written expression is composition skill. In order to write effectively, students need to be able to organize their thoughts, present them in some type of logical order, and provide enough details to convey the intended message to readers (Espin et al., 2008; Williams & Ward-Lonergan, 2001). These tasks can be exceedingly difficult for students with learning disabilities like D'Andre, who was described at the beginning of the chapter. When telling a story, they may make assumptions about what the reader knows (e.g., not explaining who a main character is but writing as though the reader is familiar with this character) or jump from topic to topic (e.g., mixing together information about the causes, battles, and outcomes of World War II instead of presenting them as categories of information). Because of their disability, these students sometimes struggle with using adjectives to enrich their writing (e.g., *The meal was good. We had lots of stuff.* Instead of *Thanksgiving dinner was delicious. We devoured turkey roasted to a golden brown, fluffy mashed potatoes, crunchy green bean casserole, and pecan pie.*). As these students move through school, they will likely find it difficult to succeed in the many school tasks that rely on clear written expression.

### dimensions of
### DIVERSITY

When Hispanic American students in the primary grades were provided with supplemental reading instruction (e.g., word attack skills), their overall fluency and literacy increased. This result occurred regardless of the students' initial levels of English proficiency (Gunn, Smolkowski, Biglan, & Black, 2002).

## FIGURE 5.2
### Writing Sample from a Student with Learning Disabilities

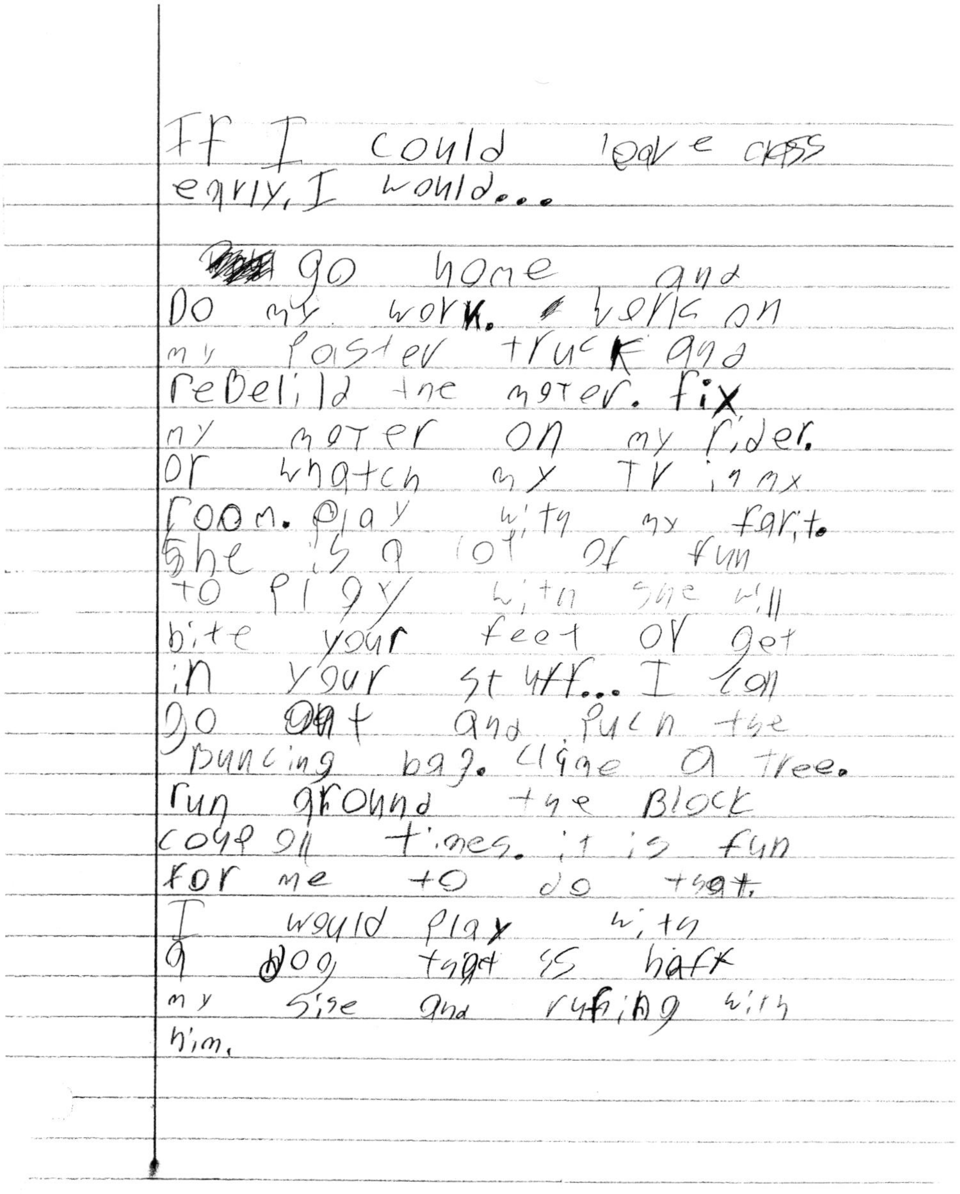

> If I could leave class
> early, I would...
>
> go home and
> Do my work. work on
> my faster truck and
> rebelild the moter. fix
> my moter on my rider.
> or whatch my TV in my
> room. play with my farit.
> She is a lot of fun
> to play with she will
> bite your feet or get
> in your stuff... I can
> go out and puch the
> puncing bag. clime a tree.
> run around the Block
> coup on times. it is fun
> for me to do that.
> I would play with
> a dog that is haft
> my size and rufing with
> him.

## Mathematics

A final domain in which students with learning disabilities may experience difficulty is mathematics (Bryant & Bryant, 2008; Swanson & Jerman, 2006), a disorder sometimes referred to as *dyscalculia*. Some students are not able to learn basic math facts or fundamental computational skills. Others cannot grasp the principles of estimation, mental calculation, and probability. Yet others find mastery of fractions or decimals difficult. For some students, learning various types of measurement or concepts related to time is extraordinarily challenging. Geometry is a weakness for others. One other area that may cause difficulty is problem solving. Whether because of the reading requirement or the inability

## Helping Students Succeed in Math

Students struggle in math for many reasons. Wadlington and Wadlington (2008) offer these suggestions for helping students to succeed:

- Address math anxiety
  - Create a safe classroom environment—never criticize or ridicule students struggling with math and expect the same respectful behavior of all students
  - Help a student become an expert in a specific part of math, for example, illustrating word problems
  - Share stories of famous people who have overcome their learning difficulties
  - Use cooperative math games to help students become more comfortable with the language and symbols of mathematics
- Use general instructional strategies that foster math learning
  - Seat students near the focus of instruction
  - Be well-organized in teaching math concepts, and present them in a highly structured and logical order
  - Analyze math skills to be taught, breaking them into small steps and then teaching each step separately

with frequent reviews both during instruction and on subsequent days
  - Use manipulatives, even for older students
  - Provide repeated practice on foundational skills so that they are overlearned
  - Arrange math tutoring for some students, with a classmate, older peer, volunteer, or paraprofessional
- Teach mathematical communication
  - Have students write in a math journal to help them become comfortable with math terms and ideas
  - Model new vocabulary, providing concrete examples
  - Have students create mathematical dictionaries that illustrate key terms and concepts
  - Stress meaning rather than rote memorization
  - If students struggle with reading, be sure math problems are read aloud or are audio-recorded
  - Assess student learning often, in both formal and information ways. Use ongoing assessment data to reteach and group students for instruction
  - Analyze student error patterns; they provide important information about what students do and do not understand

to understand the mathematical concepts that underlie the problem, students may be unable to sort relevant from extraneous information, to recognize the correct computational procedure, or to determine whether the answer they obtain is reasonable (Fletcher, 2005; Montague, 2008). The Instruction in Action provides further information about students with learning disabilities and helping them to learn mathematics.

## Social and Emotional Characteristics

Understanding the social and emotional characteristics of students with learning disabilities is as important as understanding their cognitive and academic traits. How students perceive themselves and others and how adept they are in social situations can significantly affect their learning success (Lackaye, & Margalit, 2006). Further, their accomplishments in life may depend on this ability to interact effectively with others. Two areas are particularly relevant: social perception and motivation.

*In addition to experiencing difficulties with reading, writing, math, and other academic areas, students with learning disabilities also may struggle in their social interactions with peers.*

### Social Perception and Social Competence

Many students with learning disabilities may have some type of deficit in the area of social skills (Burden, 2008; Gumpel, 2007; Lane, Carter, Pierson, & Glaeser, 2006). When compared to peers without disabilities, these students tend to have lower self-esteem. They often are less accepted by their nondisabled peers than are other students, and they are more likely than typical peers to be rejected by classmates (Pavri & Luftig, 2000). Danielle, the middle school student discussed at the beginning of this chapter, experiences such difficulties.

Studies of teachers' ratings also suggest that students with learning disabilities have lower social status than other students (Al-Yagon & Mikulineer, 2004; Wiener & Tardif, 2004), a fact that may be explained in two ways. First, among nondisabled peers who value school and proficiency at school-related tasks, students with learning disabilities may be viewed as less-desired classmates because of their academic struggles. Second, the status of students with learning disabilities may be related to their *social competence*—that is, their ability to accurately receive, interpret, and respond to the subtleties of interpersonal interactions (Murray & Greenberg, 2006). Seth exemplifies problems in social competence. He was seated on the floor of the office in his middle school with several of his peers, waiting to be seen by the principal about an altercation that occurred during lunch. The boys were discussing a variety of topics including who had won the cafeteria shoving match and who had bragging rights for the lowest grades on their recently issued report cards. In the middle of this conversation, Seth chimed in, "I'm going to see my grandma next weekend." Even though the other boys' topics of conversation may not have been those preferred by an adult, Seth's comment illustrates his obvious lack of awareness of the nuances and expectations of him in this social situation. The other boys immediately began making fun of him. As you might expect, students with learning disabilities who have poor social skills often are reported to have difficulty making and keeping friends (Pavri & Monda-Amaya, 2001), and they may feel lonely and depressed, especially through adolescence and adulthood (Maag & Reid, 2006).

It is important to note, however, that some students with learning disabilities are well adjusted and well liked by their peers and teachers (Meadan & Halle, 2004). One explanation for this finding concerns the learning environment. When teachers value and respect students, focus on their abilities, and create a supportive social environment, students thrive. Conversely, when too much emphasis is placed on students' problems, they become negative about themselves and are viewed in this way by peers.

Another explanation is offered by those who hypothesize that students with learning disabilities and poor social competence form a distinct subgroup who have **nonverbal learning disabilities (NLDs)** (Semrud-Clikeman & Glass, 2008). These students may read and speak fluently, but because of a dysfunction in the part of the brain that controls nonverbal reasoning, they are unable to accurately interpret nonverbal communication (e.g., facial expressions, posture, eye contact), and they fumble in social interactions. For example, a student with this disorder might not recognize that he is receiving "the look" from a teacher or parent and thus may not change the behavior at issue. Likewise, this student might keep talking during a conversation, failing to understand the signals from others that they would like to talk, too.

## Motivation

Many special education and general education teachers, especially those in middle and high schools, comment that students with learning disabilities are not motivated to learn, and research suggests that this is a common characteristic (Banda, Matuszny, & Therrien; 2009; Sanacore, 2008). *Motivation* is the desire to engage in an activity. This desire can be **intrinsic** (e.g., out of curiosity, as when you complete a crossword puzzle simply to see if you can) or **extrinsic** (e.g., for payment, as when you agree to help a neighbor with chores to earn money for a planned vacation). Ideally, all students would be intrinsically motivated to learn, but many students with learning disabilities are not. This could be due to what is called their *locus of control*, which is their belief about whether their life experiences are determined by internal (e.g., personal effort and skill) or external (e.g., luck) factors. Students with learning disabilities often attribute academic success to external factors and failure to internal factors. For example, if a student with learning disabilities does well on a test, he may comment that it is because of "good luck" or "an easy test." If the student does not pass it, he may say, "I'm dumb." You can easily see how this would eventually lead to a low level of motivation.

However, it is difficult to determine whether motivation is a characteristic of some students with learning disabilities because of neurological dysfunction or an effect of students' school experiences. For example, some students demonstrate **learned helplessness** by giving up on a task before they even try. They may do this because they have failed at so many

## web link

www.dyslexia.com
At The Gift: Dyslexia website you can find a discussion board and links to additional information as well as a bookstore and other aids, all related to dyslexia.

## Seatwork: Helping Students to Work Independently

Many students with learning disabilities struggle to demonstrate self-control and stay engaged when assigned independent seatwork, especially in general education settings. These ideas can foster student success:

- Involve students in setting classroom behavior expectations. Identify three to five positively worded expectations related to seatwork (e.g., "If you need help, quietly ask a neighbor").
- Create vivid posters that visually depict the expectations and review these with students.
- Model examples and nonexamples of the behavior expectations and provide students opportunities to practice. Give feedback to students and reward appropriate behavior.
- Help students set goals for their seatwork (e.g., "I will complete at least 10 problems during the first 8 minutes," "I will complete two more sentences today than I did yesterday").
- Create a whole-class self-monitoring system. For example, set a timer to go off each 5 minutes. Each time it sounds, all students record the amount of work completed.
- Teach students to self-graph. Students are more likely to persist in their work if they can see their progress. If students graph the number of problems completed, number of sentences written, or other specific data, they may be more motivated to complete work.

- Use effective praise. When a student is working appropriately, quietly and warmly congratulate the student. The more specific the praise the better—for example, "You're staying focused, completing each problem, and raising your hand to ask for assistance. That's great!"
- Use engaging materials and tasks with clear purpose. Adding color, clear directions, and examples can enhance student attention to seatwork.
- Make sure that seatwork is within the student's independent skill level; misbehavior often occurs because the assigned work is too difficult for the student.
- Provide supports by making available word banks, sentence starters, technology, manipulatives, and other accommodations.
- Teach time management. Explicitly teach students how to review assignments, prioritize them, allocate time for each, and make a to-do list.
- Work for real-world connections. Discuss with students how their seatwork assignments relate to their postschool goals.

Source: Rock, M. L., & Thead, B. K. (2009). 20 ways to promote student success during independent seatwork. *Intervention in School and Clinic, 44*, 179–184. Reprinted by permission of SAGE Publications.

---

school tasks that they would rather not begin the work than fail again, or they may have discovered that if they say they cannot do a task, the teacher or a peer will help them do it.

## Behavior Characteristics

If you think about the possible results of having deficits in academic subjects, selective attention, social competence, and motivation, you probably will conclude that a significant number of students with learning disabilities (although not all) also have behavior problems (Kortering, & Christenson, 2009). You are correct. However, whether the behaviors are part of the learning disability or a result of the frustration that many of these students experience is unclear. For some students, difficulties in communicating with others may lead to inappropriate behaviors (Vallance, Cummings, & Humphries, 1998). For others, the prospect of not being able to complete an academic task might cause them to act out in a sort of learner "road rage." Examples of behavior problems that have been studied for students with learning disabilities include excessive out-of-seat behavior, talk-outs, and physical and verbal aggression.

One of the difficulties in discussing the behavior characteristics of students with learning disabilities is the fact that a significant number of these students have comorbid (i.e., occurring simultaneously) learning disabilities and **attention deficit–hyperactivity disorder (ADHD)**. For example, a recent study found that 28 percent of students diagnosed with one of these disorders had also at some point been diagnosed with the other (Pastor & Reuben, 2008); other estimates have been as high as 70 percent (Forness & Kavale, 2001a; Mayes, Calhoun, & Crowell, 2000). This comorbidity factor raises the possibility that the behavior problems of some students with learning disabilities are, in fact, symptoms of a second disorder. Details about the characteristics of students with ADHD are covered in Chapter Six. The Positive Behavior Supports provides one example of educators' efforts to help students with learning disabilities learn appropriate classroom behavior.

Go to the Assignments and Activities section of Topic 11: Attention Deficit Hyperactivity Disorder, in the MyEducationLab for your course and complete the activity entitled "Self-Monitoring".

## REVIEW · REFLECT · DISCUSS

1. Think about the cognitive, academic, social and emotional, and behavior characteristics of students with learning disabilities. Which do you think might most affect students' learning? As a special educator, how would you explain each of these areas to a general education colleague?

2. Using the story about one of the students you met at the beginning of the chapter—Nathaniel, Danielle, and D'Andre—discuss which of the characteristics of LD the student has and how those characteristics might be shown in schoolwork. Do you think the characteristics of LD would change as students move from elementary to middle to high school? How so?

research
**NOTE**

Swanson (2008) reviewed the observational research on reading for students with learning disabilities, reporting that their reading instruction generally was of low quality and conducted in large groups, with little explicit instruction in phonics or comprehension.

# Identifying Learning Disabilities

In order for students to receive special education services to address their learning disabilities, they must be identified as being eligible for them. This involves assessments to determine the existence of learning disabilities. Based on the information derived from these assessments, the multidisciplinary team must decide that the disability exists and that students are eligible for services (if the disability negatively affects educational performance).

IDEA 2004 made dramatic changes to the basis on which students may be identified as having a learning disability. The law still permits traditional assessment procedures based on identifying discrepancies between ability and achievement, and these procedures are still used in some locales. However, it also explicitly introduced and gives permission for *response to intervention (RTI)*, the procedure you have learned about in earlier chapters that is based on the extent to which a student's learning does not improve when specific interventions are implemented. Both the traditional and RTI procedures are explained in the following sections.

## Traditional Approach to Assessment for Learning Disabilities

In Chapter Two, you learned that all students who receive special education services first go through a careful process of assessment. For students with learning disabilities being assessed in the traditional way, this process includes both formal and informal assessments. These assessments are designed to create a picture of a student's learning capacity, academic achievement in reading and mathematics, social and emotional skills, and behavior patterns.

### Formal Assessments

In many school districts, the formal assessments used to determine whether a student has a learning disability are either norm-referenced or criterion-referenced tests. **Norm-referenced tests** are those in which the student taking the test is being compared to a large number of students, or *norm group*. Examples of norm-referenced tests used to identify learning disabilities include intelligence tests, such as the Wechsler Intelligence Scale for Children–IV (Wechsler, 2003), and achievement tests, such as the Woodcock–Johnson III-NU (Woodcock, McGrew, Schrank, & Mather, 2007). Another example is the Learning Disabilities Diagnostic Inventory (LDDI) (Hammill & Bryant, 1998), which was designed specifically to assist professionals in identifying in school-age children intrinsic processing problems related to listening, speaking, reading, writing, mathematics, and reasoning. Unlike other assessments that compare the achievement of students to all other students, the LDDI compares the learning patterns of the student only to those of students known to have learning disabilities.

**Criterion-referenced tests** are another type of formal assessment that may be used during this type of evaluation for learning disabilities. These tests are designed to determine whether a student has learned a specific body of information, so they represent an absolute standard rather than the comparative standard of norm-referenced tests. One example of a criterion-referenced test nearly everyone has experienced is a driver's test. This test is designed to determine whether you have learned enough to drive an automobile safely; comparing you to other test-takers is not relevant. Examples of criterion-referenced tests to assess for learning disabilities include the Stanford Diagnostic Reading Test-4 (Karlsen & Gardner, 1995) and the Brigance Comprehensive Inventory of Basic Skills-Revised (e.g., Brigance, 1999).

### Classroom Assessments

Classroom assessment information, usually considered informal, is the second type of data gathered to determine whether a student has a learning disability. Three types of classroom assessments are most often used: (a) curriculum-based measurement, (b) portfolio assessment, and (c) observation.

**Curriculum-based measurement (CBM)** is designed specifically to supplement information obtained from formal assessments by sampling a student's understanding of the classroom curriculum (Stecker, Lembke, & Foegen, 2008). CBM may include having a student read short passages from books in the district language arts or English curriculum and answer comprehension questions. By comparing the student's reading rate (i.e., correct words read per minute) and comprehension to a sample of other students in the classroom or the district, a determination can be made about the student's learning progress.

Teachers may complete a portfolio assessment as another type of classroom assessment. A *portfolio* is a purposeful collection of a student's work that demonstrates the quality and progress of her learning (Jochum, Curran, & Reetz, 1998). For a student being assessed for learning disabilities, a portfolio might include drafts and final versions of writing assignments, a list of books read, an audiotape of the student reading, samples of assignments and problems solved in mathematics, and some type of student self-evaluation. The intent of a portfolio is to capture a snapshot of the student's performance in the reality of the classroom, and it usually supplements other data gathered in the assessment and identification process.

A third form of classroom assessment is observation. For a student to be identified as having a learning disability, federal law requires that he be observed in the general education classroom or, for young children, in a school-like environment, such as a preschool. Observation often involves getting a general sense of the student's academic and behavioral functioning in the classroom. It may also include tabulating information of interest—how often the student leaves his seat, how often the student blurts out answers instead of raising his hand, and how the frequency of such behaviors compares to that among other students in the class.

### Criteria for Eligibility

In schools using a traditional approach to identifying learning disabilities, the multidisciplinary team convenes once assessment data have been gathered. Using all of the assessment information, the team then uses the following questions to determine if a student meets the eligibility criteria for having a learning disability:

1. *Does a significant gap exist between the student's ability and academic achievement?* Although a number of methods can be used for determining the presence of a learning disability and IDEA explicitly states that school districts do not have to find a severe ability–achievement discrepancy, a common method is to compare the student's scores on an individual intelligence test with his scores on the individual norm-referenced or criterion-referenced achievement measures and then to consider curriculum-based measures and portfolio information. For example, if a student's measured intellectual ability (i.e., IQ) is 100 but his equivalent reading score is 80, a decision might be made that a learning disability exists. However, if the intelligence score is 90 and the reading score is 88, no significant discrepancy and, hence, no learning disability exists. Any other related information (e.g., information from parents or teacher records) also can be used in answering this question. Keep in mind, too, that a discrepancy may be found between ability and any area of academic achievement, including thinking skills, oral expression, listening comprehension, written expression, basic reading skills, reading comprehension, mathematics calculation, and mathematics reasoning.

2. *Is the learning problem the result of a disorder in an area of basic psychological processing involved in understanding language?* These processes are included in the definition of

**PEARSON**
**myeducationlab**
Go to the Assignments and Activities section of Topic 5, Assessment Practices, in the MyEducationLab for your course and complete the activity entitled "Curriculum Based Assessment".

web link

www.cldinternational.org
The International Council for Learning Disabilities is an organization for professionals interested in learning disabilities; its website addresses current issues regarding this disorder.

learning disabilities that you learned earlier and in the description of student characteristics. They include sensory-motor skills, visual or auditory processing, and cognitive skills, such as attention and memory. As the team looks at all the assessment data, it must consider whether such processing problems are present.

3. *Can other possible causes of the learning problem be eliminated?* As noted earlier, the IDEA definition of a learning disability includes the provision that the discrepancy cannot be the result of other factors, including environmental factors (e.g., an unsatisfactory home or school situation), poor teaching, poverty, and poor school attendance. Similarly, learning disabilities cannot be the result of other disabilities (e.g., intellectual disability, vision or hearing disability, behavior disability) or a language difference. This requirement to eliminate possible alternative explanations for a student's learning problems is called the *exclusionary clause*.

If the student's learning problems are serious enough, the other criteria are met, and the team determines the student would benefit from special education, the student is eligible to receive services as having a learning disability.

## RTI for Identifying Students Who Have Learning Disabilities

As you learned in Chapter Two, the traditional approach to identifying the presence of learning disabilities as just described has been criticized as a "wait to fail" model because students must progress far enough in school and experience significant academic frustration to even be considered as having learning disabilities (Lyon et al., 2001). Professionals also have speculated that practitioners sometimes ignore the traditional diagnostic standards for learning disabilities in order to provide services to students without having to use more potentially objectionable labels (e.g., mental retardation or intellectual disability) and in order to provide help to those students sometimes referred to as "slow learners," who exhibit overall marginal achievement but otherwise would not be eligible for special education.

Response to intervention (RTI) was added to IDEA 2004 specifically to address these concerns about the identification of students as having learning disabilities (Kavale & Spaulding, 2008). Although RTI is permitted, but not required, in the law, it is being developed or implemented in nearly all states (Berkeley, Bender, Peaster, & Saunders, 2009). It in-

**PEARSON**
**myeducationlab**

Go to the Assignments and Activities section of Topic 8: Learning Disabilities, in the MyEducationLab for your course and complete the activity entitled "Progress Monitoring for Students with Learning Disabilities".

*In response to intervention, educators use increasingly intense, research-based interventions to accelerate students' rate of learning as soon as a problem is identified; only if these efforts fail is the presence of a disability considered.*

cludes these principles, which illustrate how distinct it is from traditional assessment and identification procedures:

1. It replaces the ability–achievement discrepancy criteria with a simple direct assessment of the extent of a student's underachievement. This solves the problem of identifying young children and providing early intervention because it eliminates the need to wait for a discrepancy to emerge.

2. It removes the provision that inadequate instruction, emotional disturbance, and cultural or social issues make a student ineligible for services as learning disabled. In RTI, if learning problems are extreme, the reasons for them are not as important as providing assistance to the student.

3. It requires measures of a student's achievement on well-designed early instructional interventions (especially in prekindergarten through second grade) as part of the assessment process. Doing so ensures that the quality of instruction will be high as well as provides clear documentation of efforts to address student learning problems (Lyon et al., 2001).

### Three-Tiered Models in Response to Intervention

The most common procedures being used to implement the RTI approach address reading problems, and they are outlined in three-tiered models of intervention (Fuchs, Compton, Fuchs, Bryant, & Davis, 2008; Fuchs & Fuchs, 2006). Nathaniel, whom you met at the beginning of the chapter, has experienced the three-tier approach. Here is an explanation of each tier:

- *Tier 1.* Most students should succeed when they are taught to read using practices that have been demonstrated through research to be effective. All students participate in tier 1, and educators are responsible for implementing proven instructional methods, including differentiation, and closely monitoring the progress of students in the core reading curriculum.

- *Tier 2.* For approximately 20 to 30 percent of students, tier 1 instruction is not enough. That is, the gap between their skills and what would be considered average progress is significant, and it is likely, based on the data, to get worse. Based on diagnostic data gathered, students in tier 2 receive supplemental instruction that might include structured tutoring by a trained assistant or peer, additional opportunities to practice skills, and individually paced instruction. The interventions are research based, and they are in addition to the core reading instruction being delivered in the classroom.

- *Tier 3.* If diagnostic data indicate that a student still is not making adequate progress in acquiring essential reading skills when tier 2 interventions are being implemented, even more intensive interventions are initiated. For the few students who need this intensive assistance (i.e., usually no more than 5 to 10 percent of all students), instruction usually is delivered by a reading specialist or even a special educator and often occurs outside the general education classroom. The instruction might include a specific reading program (e.g., Wilson Reading, Corrective Reading), but it is primarily characterized by its intensity, its repeated opportunities for practice and review, its reliance on carefully analyzed and sequenced instruction, and its use of frequent data collection for continuous monitoring of progress. In some but not all applications, this tier is considered special education service.

### Criteria for Eligibility

When RTI is the approach used to assess students for the possible presence of learning disabilities, decision making is slightly different from that in traditional approaches. The multidisciplinary team still convenes and considers the available data, but its focus is on the following:

1. Even though research-based, individually designed, systematically delivered, and increasingly intensive interventions have been implemented, is the student still exhibiting significant gaps in learning compared to what would be expected? Is it likely that, despite the interventions, the gaps will stay the same or increase instead of decrease?

dimensions of
**DIVERSITY**

Denton, Wexler, Vaughn, and Bryan (2008) provided ELL middle school students with severe reading disabilities 40 minutes per day of intensive reading instruction for a 13-week period. They reported that students did not show significant growth in word recognition, comprehension, or fluency. The authors concluded the students needed even more intense interventions.

In some states, even when RTI procedures are fully implemented, traditional achievement data, classroom observation data, other curriculum-based measures, and even measures of ability (all described in the preceding section) also may be considered in making a decision about eligibility. However, emphasis remains on the existence of a significant learning gap that, without additional support, will worsen over time.

2. If the team decides that the student is *nonresponsive to intervention*, he may be determined to have a learning disability.

Notice that this approach completely eliminates an ability–achievement discrepancy. It also takes out issues related to psychological processing, environmental factors, and quality of instruction. You should note, though, that RTI has raised many questions related to specific guidelines for use, including the length of time each tier should be implemented before it is determined to be inadequate, the way that RTI applies to mathematics, and the types of research-based practices teachers should be using.

Perhaps the most important question related to RTI concerns whether it is a valid approach to identifying students with learning disabilities or rather an indirect means of ensuring high-quality instruction for all students. Controversy is growing on this topic. You can read more about this rapidly evolving debate in the last section of this chapter.

**fyi**

During the late 1960s and early 1970s, an assessment to determine whether a learning disability existed had to include a statement from a physician because a learning disability was considered a physiologically based disorder.

## REVIEW · REFLECT · DISCUSS

1. Response to intervention (RTI) is a significant departure from traditional approaches to identifying students as having learning disabilities. Do you think this approach will lead to more students being identified? Fewer? What might be the direct impact of RTI on you as a professional educator?

2. In using traditional assessment strategies to identify learning disabilities, why is it helpful to have both formal and informal assessment data?

## Educating Students with Learning Disabilities

Students with learning disabilities are educated in a range of settings. However, strong emphasis is placed on ensuring that these students are held to the same academic expectations as are typical learners. Federal law outlines the basic requirements for how all students with disabilities receive their education. Within those guidelines, though, many options exist.

### Early Childhood

Young children generally are not diagnosed as having learning disabilities for several reasons. First, the indicators of learning disabilities (e.g., problems related to reading, math, oral and written language) usually are not apparent in preschool children. Second, because the possibility of misdiagnosis is so high, professionals are reluctant to risk the negative impact on child self-perception and teacher expectations that might occur if the learning disability label is applied in error. Overall, the considerable normal differences in rates of development among young children make formal identification inappropriate; what might appear to be a learning disability could easily turn out to be a developmental difference well within the normal range.

Programs for young children with *developmental delays* (the general term you have learned, often given when young children receive special services) usually address areas indirectly related to learning disabilities. For example, such programs focus on improving children's gross-motor skills (e.g., hopping) and fine-motor skills (e.g., using scissors or crayons), their expressive language skills (e.g., naming objects, asking questions to indicate need) and receptive language skills (e.g., following simple directions), their attention (e.g., persisting in a task for several minutes), and their social skills (e.g., taking turns, playing in a group). Interventions in all of these areas help create a solid foundation for later academic tasks, and students with significant delays in these areas may or may not later be identified as having learning disabilities.

## Elementary and Secondary School Services

Ninety-eight percent of school-age students with learning disabilities receive their education in a typical public school setting (U.S. Department of Education, 2008). As you can see from the information presented in Figure 5.3, approximately 59 percent of today's students with learning disabilities spend nearly their entire school day in general education settings with their peers. These statistics illustrate the strength of the trend toward inclusive practices introduced in Chapter One. Only 20 years ago, just 15 percent of students with learning disabilities spent this much time in general education settings (U.S. Department of Education, 1988). However, these data vary greatly from state to state, with Alabama and North Dakota educating 80 percent or more of their students with learning disabilities primarily in general education and Hawaii and the District of Columbia educating fewer than 20 percent of their students in this setting (U.S. Department of Education, 2009). What do the data for your state suggest about how students with learning disabilities receive their services? Consider the implications for students of having such large discrepancies across states regarding placement options for students with learning disabilities.

Knowing the proportion of time students spend in general education versus special education settings does not adequately convey what an individual student's services might involve. In schools using best practices, a student in general education—whether for a large or small part of the day—would use materials adjusted for his reading level and other

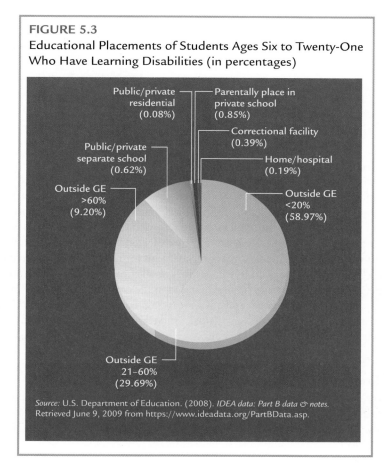

**FIGURE 5.3**

**Educational Placements of Students Ages Six to Twenty-One Who Have Learning Disabilities (in percentages)**

Public/private residential (0.08%)

Parentally place in private school (0.85%)

Correctional facility (0.39%)

Public/private separate school (0.62%)

Home/hospital (0.19%)

Outside GE >60% (9.20%)

Outside GE <20% (58.97%)

Outside GE 21–60% (29.69%)

*Source:* U.S. Department of Education. (2008). *IDEA data: Part B data & notes.* Retrieved June 9, 2009 from https://www.ideadata.org/PartBData.asp.

## Tools for Students with Learning Disabilities

Current instructional and assistive technology provides many tools to help students with learning disabilities take in information, organize their thinking, and demonstrate their learning. Here are several excellent examples:

### Text to Speech Software

A number of free software programs for Windows-based computers make it possible to have the computer read text to students (this software is built into the most recent Mac operating system). Depending on the software, you may be able to change the reading voice, increase or reduce the reading speed, and use the software for websites as well as documents such as worksheets and tests. Examples include these:

- Read Please (http://www.readplease.com/english/products/)
- NaturalSoft (http://www.naturalreaders.com/?gclid=CPig0tCHh5sCFRabnAodLEmxow)
- Acrobat Reader 9 (only for .pdf files) (http://www.adobe.com/products/reader/)

### Electronic Learning Assistants

A variety of types of hardware are available to facilitate student reading and writing. A quick exploration of assistive technology on the Internet will lead you to find many options in addition to the ones listed here:

- Reading Pens are small devices that, when

*Reading Pen*

passed over a word or line of text, scan, define, translate, and pronounce it. Reading pens come in simple or advanced versions, the former usually for elementary students and the latter, with larger vocabulary and more options, for high school students. Two samples of reading pens are

- Readingpen (http://www.readingpen.com/)
- Quick-pen (http://www.quick-pen.com/index.php)

- Neo 2 Classroom Computing Device

The Neo 2, the latest version of what many educators first knew as an *Alphasmart*, is designed to facilitate student writing, especially those reluctant to compose by handwriting. This latest version is lightweight (under 2 pounds) and battery operated rather than using wires. It is both much more rugged and much less expensive than a portable computer. It offers wireless printing, word prediction options, text-to-speech availabil-

*Alphasmart Neo 2*

special needs and access a computer and other appropriate assistive technology, as illustrated in the Technology Notes. Peer supports, such as peer tutoring or a buddy system, would be in place, and a special educator might co-teach in the classroom for part of the day (Friend, 2008). In the resource setting (the typical arrangement when students leave the classroom for part of the day), the student would receive intense, individually designed, and closely monitored instruction in any academic area affected by the learning disability. A student who is away from the general education classroom for more than 60 percent of school time is in a self-contained program in which most or all core academic instruction is delivered by a special education teacher highly qualified in the core content areas. However, students in such settings often join general education classmates for some instruction, as well as for related arts and electives such as art, music, and technology. In middle and high school settings, students might take exploratory classes, electives, or study skills training with other students.

### Inclusive Practices

As you know, decisions about where students receive their education are determined on the IDEA principle of *least restrictive environment (LRE)* and the specific needs identified in their IEPs. Within this context the issue of whether inclusive practices are the best edity, and the ability to add other popular software (e.g., *Accelerated Reader* quizzes; *Co-Writer*, a word prediction software package). It even has a way to practice math facts.

### Software to Facilitate Learning

- *Inspiration Software (http://www.inspiration.com/)* produces a suite of tools (Inspiration, Kidspiration, Inspiredata) that provide visual learning tools for students. For example, they can create webs or concept maps that enable them to see a visual organization of information they are learning. They also can convert information they have put into tables into clear visual representations. The software can be an integral part of brainstorming ideas for a project or for prewriting activities. Versions of this program exist for younger or older students.

- *Write:OutLoud (http://www.donjohnston.com/products/ write_outloud/index.html)* is a talking word processor software package designed for students across grade levels and reading abilities who experience difficulties writing. As the student types, it can say each letter, word, or sentence, thus providing constant feedback about what is being written. The program also has a talking spell checker. It can read information to the student that has been accessed from the Internet or another source, so it can be used to assist poor readers in preparing reports.

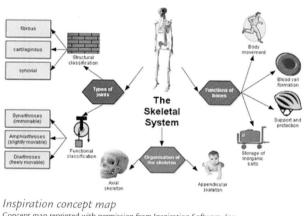

*Inspiration concept map*

Concept map reprinted with permission from Inspiration Software, Inc., www.inspiration.com.

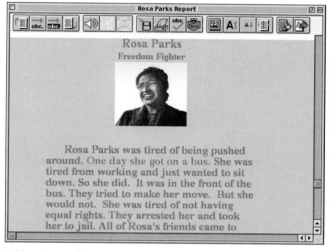

*Write:OutLoud® story*

Source: Write:OutLoud®, http://www.donjohnson.com. Reprinted with permission from Don Johnson, Inc.

---

ucational approach for students with learning disabilities was debated for many years (e.g., Carlberg & Kavale, 1980; De Simone & Parmar, 2006; McPhail & Freeman, 2005; Volonino & Zigmond, 2007). In the early twenty-first century it appears that fundamental questions about whether students with learning disabilities should receive at least some services with their peers are largely answered, but many questions regarding the best combinations of support in general education settings and special education settings remain. In the Speaking from Experience you can learn how Robanne, a teacher in a rural Alaska school district, balances the many needs of her students and the range of supports and services they need.

It is important to remember the premise of this book—that inclusion is about how the adults and students in any particular school think about teaching and learning for all the students who go there. Being inclusive does not mean that students never leave the general education setting. Instead, it means that consideration is given to how a student's needs can be met within the classroom context before resorting to instruction in a separate setting. If the latter is considered in the student's best interest, it is provided for as long as it is warranted. Within that framework, professionals in the field now are thinking about the outcomes for students who receive an inclusive education versus those who receive more traditional services. The data are mixed.

www.ldresources.com
The LD Resources website contains published resources and materials for individuals with learning disabilities.

*Robanne Stading contemplated a career in journalism and began college in Oklahoma. But after a summer spent in Alaska, she fell in love with the state and a man she met there, and she decided that she should become a teacher. She quickly finished her journalism degree, married, and returned to Alaska, where she worked in a daycare program in Barrow. Eventually, she earned general education teacher licensure through a distance education program and then special education teacher licensure in her master's degree program. She now teaches at Nikolaevsk School, a K–12 school with 75 students, 75 percent of whom are from a Russian background. She provides services to 10 students, most with learning disabilities in reading or written expression, but also works as the Title I reading teacher and migrant teacher.*

Here is what my typical day looks like. There are two elementary teachers, two secondary teachers, and the principal teaches half-time. Early in the day I co-teach language arts in high school. But I had to split that time because there was a younger child who needed more support than he was getting—so I also do late-third-grade math. It worked out ok because there is a student on my caseload who is in sixth grade who also is in that group (he's very small so he doesn't look out of place). But I don't just co-teach. I also pull students out, especially in the elementary grades. My whole day is like that. We do a lot of different things here and I love it.

- In a rural setting, the scope of what has to be done is always a concern. I work with a first grader, but I also have an eleventh grader on my caseload and other students in-between. It's always busy, but I worry about the services the students receive—whether it's enough.

- Co-teaching is the best part of my job, especially co-teaching with one of the secondary language arts teachers. She's a little bit more experienced than I am, but I do enjoy collaborating with her when I get a chance to, or you know, even popping in and bouncing ideas off her: 'Okay, what are we doing? Okay, this sounds cool. Hey, I'll take over that, not a problem.' Then when we're in class together we do try to use the different approaches.

- The hardest part about my job is all the paperwork, especially this year because I had all the special ed. paperwork and all the Title I paperwork. Seven students received title services.

- I think that flexibility and a willingness to do almost anything is the key to being successful in a rural setting. If what I'm doing isn't perfect, as long as I know I'm making a good effort and trying to be sure students get their services, I don't beat myself up about it. I'm willing to try. That really is the key.

- You also have to realize that you can't expect to have everything. We have a speech therapist half a day per week. Our school psychologist is out here maybe twice a month. That's how they're scheduled, but when meetings come up at other times, they often cannot be here. This year both are here the same day, so I made sure I didn't have any extra duties then so I could meet with them.

- Everyone here—the students—are more or less related to each other. I see nearly all of the parents of my students at one time or another in the building. Lots of it is informal and the parents are very supportive. No one's saying, 'Oh, why aren't you doing this with my child.' They're all really happy with what's going on.

- The biggest thing that appeals to me is that K-12 community, family, being able to be with all sorts of different kids throughout the day. You know, I find that when I go to other sites and see people working with just young children or just high school students, I keep thinking how much I'd miss the other kids.

- The hardest thing about working in a rural school is learning to say 'no.' It's so easy to end up doing too much, spending too much time at school, especially when you see the kids need you. It's like a big family. That's one of the best parts of working in a rural school.

For example, Idol (2006) studied inclusive practices at eight elementary, middle, and high schools. She generally found positive results related to teacher perceptions and student outcomes. Rea, McLaughlin, and Walther-Thomas (2002) reported similar results for students in middle schools. They found that the students with learning disabilities in inclusive programs earned higher grades, scored at comparable or higher levels on achievement tests, and attended school more days when compared to students with learning disabilities in resource programs.

Not all the results are clearly positive, however. For example, Magiera and Zigmond (2005) explored the question of whether co-taught versus solo-taught middle school classes had differential effects on students with learning disabilities. They found no significant differences except that general education teachers interacted less often with the students with learning disabilities when the special educator was present. Vaughn and her colleagues (e.g., Klingner, Vaughn, Hughes, Schumm, & Elbaum, 1998; Vaughn, Elbaum, Schumm, & Hughes, 1998; Vaughn & Klingner, 1998) examined the locations in which services are delivered and the academic and social outcomes of inclusion. They found that

## Michael's Perspectives on His Education

Have you ever wondered what students with learning disabilities think of their services? Connor (2006) reported on his study of Michael, a young adult with learning disabilities who is also African American and living in poverty. Here are excerpts from Michael's story:

The kids who are placed in that special ed. classroom,
They don't want to learn.
Most of the kids act like they don't care.
They destroy the rooms, they play around, make jokes, throw stuff. . . .
But once you're placed in an environment with regular ed. kids, they sit there. . . .
A totally different person, coz they don't want to embarrass themselves.
When you're placed in a room with people who they claim that is your kind,
You don't care.
*"Oh, we all special ed., so we can all act the same way."*
*"You're here, I'm here. So something's wrong with all of us."*
*"He's stupid, I'm stupid, we're all in special ed."*
When it starts at a young age, when it goes up, it just gets more corrupt.
*"I'm special ed. I'm slow in all these classes. I don't need to do none of the work."*
They don't think they're good in anything.
It seems like teachers have pity on the special ed. kids.

*"He can't pass the test, but he's a good boy so let's just pass him"*
I used to sit in the corner and like, *"This work, Oh, my God, might as well go to sleep."*
When you're in regular ed., everyone loves you and adores you.
In special ed., you're treated differently.
They have mercy on you.
When you do special ed. work, they try to help you too much.
Special class work was easy.
Basically special ed. kids only stick with special ed. kids.
Coz, at the lunch table if they find out that you're in special ed;
No one's gonna hang out with you—you might as well hang out with your own kind.
You're just lost, labeled as a reject. . . .
In high school, no one ever really knew I was in specialed.
Coz I'd sit there and carry myself like a regular kid.
I'd come to all my classes. Just to make sure the hall is clear,
I'd go into the classroom and hide in the corner, coz you don't want people to know.
Once they find out, girls don't want to date you . . . No one wants to talk to you.
I kept it to myself, I still do keep it to myself.

*Source:* Connor, D. J. (2006). Michael's story: "I get into so much trouble just by walking": Narrative knowing and life at the intersections of learning disability, race, and class. *Equity & Excellence in Education, 39,* 154–165. Reprinted by permission of Taylor & Francis Group, http://www.informaworld.com.

students have better social outcomes when in-class services, such as co-teaching, are available on a part-time rather than a full-time basis, and they found that both social and academic outcomes vary based on individual student characteristics. Dyson (2007) reported that parents of students with LD being educated in general education settings experience frustration and stress and find they have to frequently advocate for their children with school professionals. Ultimately, whether this approach is successful depends largely on the quality of the instructional practices in general education classrooms, including implementing universal design for learning (UDL) and differentiation; the availability of supports such as assistive technology; and the provision of intense, separate instruction as it is needed (Sapon-Shevin, 2003).

The discussion of inclusive practices often overlooks the perspectives of students. In the Professional Edge, read the poetry of Michael, a young adult with a learning disability who received special education through junior high and high school. What does Michael's experience tell you about students' perspectives on special education and learning environment?

## Transition and Adulthood

The outcomes for students with learning disabilities as they move into adulthood are as varied as the individuals who comprise this group. Some of these young adults successfully complete high school and move into postsecondary options—vocational training, college, and employment—with confidence and success. However, the majority of young adults experience difficulties (Lindstrom, Doren, Metheny, Johnson, & Zane, 2007). For example, Murray, Goldstein, Nourse, and Edgar (2000) followed the progress of two cohorts of high school graduates with and without learning disabilities for up to 10 years. They found that the graduates with learning disabilities were significantly less likely to have participated in any form of postsecondary education, and if they did participate, they were more likely than

*Students with learning disabilities may attend college and receive supports there through the Americans with Disabilities Act.*

other students to have attended a training school or vocational program than a college or university. Others have found that adults with learning disabilities are more likely to be employed in part-time jobs, to have lower occupational status, and to earn lower wages (Collett-Klingenberg, 1998; Luftig & Muthert, 2005).

## Transition Planning

Why do many students with learning disabilities who are acknowledged to have at least average intelligence continue to have various difficulties as they become adults? Consider the traits and skills students need to go to college or to obtain and keep a job, including an ability to work independently and to seek assistance as needed; to be organized; to focus attention for long periods of time; to listen, speak, read, write, and compute effectively and efficiently; to problem solve; and to handle social situations with competence. These are the precise areas in which students with learning disabilities may be deficient. And because these students may demonstrate a slower rate of career maturity, poor ability to advocate for themselves, and low self-esteem, they may have unrealistic job expectations in terms of how to juxtapose their strengths and weaknesses with vocational choices (Bear, Kortering, & Braziel, 2006). Think about D'Andre, the high school student introduced at the beginning of this chapter. How might his learning disabilities affect his selection of a postschool option?

Since transition planning was added to federal special education law in 1990, increased attention has been paid to issues such as those just outlined by preparing students with learning disabilities for life after high school. As you know, a transition plan includes a statement of needs that begins at age sixteen and is updated annually. The statement pertains to the student's course of study and puts forth a specific plan with measurable goals and an explanation to the student of his rights.

However, the quality of transition plans and services is still not fully established (Carter, Lane, Pierson, & Glaeser, 2006). Researchers studying students in the transition process have reported disappointing results (Agran & Hughes, 2008; Hitchings et al., 2001): Of the students who had received special education services during their elementary or secondary school years, only one could recall participating in a meeting specifically to plan transition. Many of the students had difficulty explaining the nature of their disabilities and the impact their disabilities might have on career choice, and few reported taking an active role in transition planning. As you might suspect, the quality of students' transition is significantly influenced by their parents (Lindstrom et al., 2007).

research
**NOTE**

School professionals now are required to use research-based practices in their interventions with students. You can read more about this very important topic at the U.S. Department of Education website: www.ed.gov/rschstat/research/pubs/rigorousevid/index.html.

## Model Transition Practices

Model practices for transition for students with learning disabilities in one high school were found to include these features (Collett-Klingenberg, 1998):

- Inclusion of career awareness and exploration activities beginning in the freshman year and continuing through high school
- Instruction related to skills needed for successful transition, including problem solving, organization, self-advocacy, and communication
- Transition-planning activities for school professionals and community members regarding the next steps that might be needed to improve activities and services

In addition, students and parents were integrally involved in transition planning, and transition-planning teams included community representatives as appropriate. Academics were given priority; however, work experiences were increasingly being incorporated into student plans, and linkages were created between students and their parents and postschool services, such as the Division for Vocational Rehabilitation.

## Self-Advocacy

One other topic needs to be considered in a discussion of students with learning disabilities and transition: **self-advocacy** (Carter et al., 2006; Madaus & Shaw, 2006). This topic often relates to the transition from high school to college. First, students need to be willing to identify themselves as having a disability. Some students are reluctant to do this on college applications because they fear it will affect their admission status; others have been advised by school counselors to drop their learning disability designation prior to applying for college (Hitchings et al., 2001). In addition, students need to research and access the supports available to them from the college or university campus office designed to provide such assistance (Lock & Layton, 2001). These supports might include tutors, note-takers, and audiotaped textbooks. Finally, students need to be confident enough to articulate their needs to professors and negotiate accommodations, such as extended time for tests, so that they can compensate for their learning disabilities. Unless students learn and use strong self-advocacy skills, they are likely to drop out of college or to remain underemployed or unemployed (Trainor, 2005). If they have these skills, they are likely to complete college and enter the workforce much like other young adults (Anctil, Ishikawa, & Tao Scott, 2008).

## REVIEW · REFLECT · DISCUSS

1. If you are currently participating in a practicum or field experience, compare with classmates the ways in which students with learning disabilities receive their services. Are the schools inclusive? How common are resource programs? Do any students receive most of their core instruction in a special education classroom?

2. Do you know someone with a learning disability who is attending college? If so, what is this person's perspective on the quality of supports and services available to students with learning disabilities as they leave high school for college?

## Recommended Educational Practices for Students with Learning Disabilities

Go to the Building Teaching Skills and Dispositions section of Topic 8: Learning Disabilities, in the MyEducationLab for your course and complete the activity entitled "Scaffolding Learners".

For more than two decades, professionals have been investigating which techniques and methods are most effective for addressing the academic, cognitive, social, and behavioral needs of students with learning disabilities. A wealth of research information now is available to guide teachers' practices (e.g., Jitendra, Edwards, Sacks, & Jacobson, 2004; Rupley, Blair, & Nichols, 2009; Schumaker & Deshler, 2009; Vaughn & Linan-Thompson, 2003). These data indicate that two methods, used in combination, are highly effective for most

## web link

www.jimwrightonline.com/php/rti/rti_wire.php
At the RTI Wire website, you can learn details about implementing this alternative approach to identifying learning disabilities and also access helpful tools, such as templates for gathering data.

**PEARSON**
**myeducationlab**

Go to the Assignments and Activities section of Topic 8: Learning Disabilities, in the MyEducation-Lab for your course and complete the activity entitled "Direct Instruction for Students with Learning Disabilities".

students, regardless of age or specific type of learning disability: direct instruction (DI) and strategy instruction (SI).

## Direct Instruction

**Direct instruction (DI)** is a comprehensive, teacher-led approach based on decades of research. Direct instruction emphasizes maximizing not only the quantity of instruction students receive but also the quality (National Institute for Direct Instruction, 2006; Rupley et al., 2009). This approach includes clear demonstrations of new information in small segments, practice that is teacher guided, and immediate feedback to students on their work (Henley, Ramsey, & Algozzine, 2001). Direct instruction is based on these guiding principles:

1. Present lessons in a well-organized, sequenced manner.
2. Begin lessons with a short review of previously learned skills necessary to begin the lesson.
3. Begin lessons with a short statement of goals. Provide clear, concise explanations and illustrations of what is to be learned.
4. Present new material in small steps with practice and demonstrations at each step. Provide initial guidance through practice activities.
5. Provide students with frequent opportunities to practice and generalize skills.
6. Ask questions to check students' understanding, and obtain responses from everyone (Mather & Goldstein, 2001, p. 146).

The Instruction in Action illustrates the use of direct instruction in a sample lesson plan.

## Strategy Instruction

One of the overall goals for all students' education is independence. Because of students' learning disabilities, achieving academic independence can be particularly difficult. Some students cannot write essays because they do not know the components of an essay and what content goes in an introduction, body, and conclusion. Others do not comprehend their textbooks because they do not have a plan for processing and remembering the information presented. Yet others struggle to take notes because they cannot decide what information is essential or how to organize it. **Strategy instruction (SI)**, a highly

*Research suggests that students who struggle with reading are most likely to succeed when they receive early, intense phonologically-based instruction.*

Direct instruction (DI) is one of the most recommended approaches for teaching students with learning disabilities. Here is a sample lesson plan based on DI principles:

### Title of Lesson: Contractions (e.g., *he's, she's, it's, that's*)

### Classroom Management: (1–2 minutes)

*Grading Criteria:* 15 percent reading sentences correctly, 35 percent generation of new sentences with learned contractions, 25 percent completed worksheet, and 25 percent slate writing activity.

*Contingency:* If the entire class's criterion level performance is at or better than 85 percent correct, students qualify for extra slate time (i.e., free choice to write or draw on their slates).

### Specific Learning Outcomes: (1–2 minutes)

"Today, we are going to learn about contractions. You will learn to read a contraction alone and in a sentence. You will also learn to correctly write a contraction when given two words, and use the newly learned contraction in a sentence."

### Anticipatory Set: (3 minutes)

*Focus Statement.* "Most often when we speak, we shorten a word or phrase by omitting one or more sounds. Listen to this sentence, 'It is raining.' Now listen again as I omit a sound, 'It's raining.' What two words did I shorten by omitting a sound?" (Students respond.) (Repeat with other examples such as "He's going to the store" and "She's at the mall.")

"When we shorten a word or phrase by omitting one or more sounds or letters, it is called a contraction."

*Relevance of the Lesson.* "It is important to learn how to read contractions because they are often used in storybooks, newspapers, magazines, and most material that you read. Also, you need to learn how to write contractions to use in your own writing."

*Transfer of Past Learning.* "We learn many new words in reading. A contraction is a special word because it is written differently than a regular word. Learning how to read and write contractions will make you a better reader and writer."

### New Vocabulary Terms: (1–2 minutes)

Contraction—shortening of a word or phrase by omitting one or more letters or sounds.

Apostrophe—a mark that takes the place of the missing letter(s) in the contraction; it looks like a comma but is placed at the top of the line.

### Teaching (10–12 minutes)

1. Review decoding words in isolation and in sentences: *he, she, it, that, is.* Have students use words in their own sentences.

   **Questions**
   "What is this word?"
   "Read this sentence."
   "Use this word in your own sentence."

2. Define a contraction and an apostrophe.

   **Questions**
   "When a word or phrase is shortened by omitting one or more letters or sounds, it is called a _____."

   "What is the name of the visual mark used to take the place of the missing letters?"

3. Present examples and nonexamples of contractions and have students identify them.

   **Examples:**
   *he's, she's, it's, that's.*

   **Nonexamples:**
   *cat, drum, bell.*

   **Questions**
   "Is this a contraction? Why or why not?"

4. Model the sequence of steps for forming contractions.

   **Example:** *It is*

   a. Write the two words together without a space between them.

   b. Erase the letter *i* in *is* and put an apostrophe in its place.

   c. Read the new word by blending the sounds. Point out that the apostrophe doesn't make a sound. Have students read the word, spell it, and repeat the word again.

   d. Write sentences:
   *It is hot today.*
   *It's hot today.*
   "Do these two sentences mean the same thing? How do you know?"
   Have students read sentences with the teacher.
   Have students use the contraction in a new sentence.

   e. Repeat steps a–d with other examples (e.g., *he, she, that*) using simple sentences.

5. Do a discrimination test of irregular words and previously known words. Call on students as a group to read words by randomly pointing to each word several times.

6. Test individual students on reading contractions.

### Guided and Independent Practice: (5–8 minutes)

1. Students first complete a worksheet with teacher direction and then do similar exercises independently. Students match the contraction with the two words that it is composed of.

2. The teacher provides guided and independent practice in writing the contractions on slates when the two words that make up the contraction are presented on the board.

3. Examples on board: *He is, she is; it is; that is*

4. Students will correctly write the contractions in newly generated sentences and share sentences with the class.

### Closure: (3 minutes)

"Today, we learned about contractions and the apostrophe. We also learned that contractions have the same meaning as the two words that make them up. What is a contraction? What is an apostrophe? What word means the same as *it is*? What two words make up *he's*?"

*Source:* Jitendra, A. K., & Torgerson-Tubiello, R. (1997). Let's learn contractions! *Teaching Exceptional Children, 29*(4), 16–19. Copyright © 1997 by the Council for Exceptional Children. Reprinted with permission.

## Sample Learning Strategies

Here are two examples of learning strategies to help students with learning disabilities succeed in a wide variety of tasks.

### The AWARE Strategy for Note-Taking

The AWARE strategy is designed for high school and college students who need a systematic way to remember to take notes effectively during lectures and other instruction.

1. **A**rrange to take notes.
   Arrive early.
   Take a seat near the front or center.
   Obtain a pen and notebook.
   Note the date.
2. **W**rite quickly.
   Indent minor points.
   Record some words without vowels.
3. **A**pply cues.
   Attend to accents and organizational verbal cues.
   Record cued lecture ideas.
   Make checkmarks before cued ideas.
4. **R**eview notes as soon as possible.
5. **E**dit notes.
   Add information you forgot to record.
   Add personal details.
   Supplement notes with details from readings.

### TREE for Writing

TREE is designed for elementary school students as a way to assist them in learning how to write persuasive essays.

1. **T**opic sentence.
   Tell what you believe.
2. **R**easons
   Tell three or more reasons: Why do I believe this?
   Will my readers believe this?
3. **E**nding
   Wrap it up!
4. **E**xamine
   Ask myself: Do I have all my parts?

Keep in mind that students need to be taught how to use strategies. They should see the importance of the strategy, discuss it, watch you model it, and memorize it. You should provide ongoing support until students can use a strategy independently.

*Sources:* Based on Hughes, C. A., & Suritsky, S. K. (1993). Notetaking skills and strategies for students with learning disabilities. *Preventing School Failure, 38*(1), 7–11; Harris, K. R., Graham, S., & Mason, L. H. (2003). Self-regulated strategy development in the classroom: Part of a balanced approach to writing instruction for students with disabilities. *Focus on Exceptional Children, 35*(7), 1–16.

recommended method for students with learning disabilities, addresses these types of problems. *Strategies* are techniques, principles, and rules that guide students to complete tasks independently (Friend & Bursuck, 2009). Strategies outline the steps students can take to accomplish learning tasks and provide some type of memory assistance (often an acronym) so that students can easily recall them. Teachers usually introduce strategies by helping students realize an instructional dilemma (e.g., a challenge students encounter with word problems in math) and then explaining why the strategy will help them overcome the dilemma. In the Instruction in Action, you can see a specific example of a learning strategy for writing.

Many research-based strategies have been described in the professional literature (e.g., Schumaker & Deshler, 2009; Flores, 2009; Friend & Bursuck, 2009), from those for enhancing writing skills (e.g., Deatline-Buchman, & Jitendra, 2006) to those for learning social studies (e.g., Fontana, Scruggs, & Mastropieri, 2007) to those for solving algebraic equations (e.g., Van Garderen, 2007). You are likely to find a strategy that can assist a student with learning disabilities regardless of her age or specific needs.

## REVIEW · REFLECT · DISCUSS

1. Using a lesson that you have developed or read about in another course, use the information on direct instruction to modify the original lesson plan so that it is more effective for students with learning disabilities. What did you learn by doing this? What aspects of the modification were challenging? Straightforward?

2. Think about strategies and students with learning disabilities. How does strategy instruction address some of the characteristics they have?

# Parent and Family Perspectives

Unlike the parents of students with significant sensory, cognitive, or physical disabilities, who may learn of their child's disabilities soon after birth, parents of children with learning disabilities often are not aware of their child's special needs until the child is enrolled in school and experiences frustration and failure in academic tasks. Parents may be surprised when they are informed about their child's disability, relieved to hear an explanation for their child's struggles to learn or concerned about the time lost in finding effective interventions. As Mary, a college-educated professional and the mother of first-grader Guy, told school professionals as they conducted the initial eligibility and IEP meeting:

> Stop. Wait. You're saying my son has a disability—a disability. You've just changed my whole world and how I think about Guy. You can't just say, "He's learning disabled. Let's write a plan for his education." I need to think about this. I need to understand better what this means. It may be routine to you, but he's my son. I can't sit here right now and make decisions. It's his life we're talking about. I wouldn't sign a contract to buy a car without a lot of thought and some careful research. How can you expect me to sign these papers about Guy's life without even knowing what I'm signing? I need to know what this means and what I'm agreeing to before I can sign anything.

Although not all parents can express their sentiments in such an articulate manner, it is important to remember that the disability label often affects parents of students with learning disabilities in ways that school professionals cannot completely understand (Heiman, Zinck, & Heath, 2008). Many parents will have to redefine their image of their child. Some parents may blame school personnel for their child's problems, especially if the child is identified during middle or high school. Other parents may believe that they have failed their child and that they should have been able to prevent the disability. Special education teachers and other school professionals need to be aware that their attitudes toward parents, their communications with them, and their openness to parent and family perspectives can affect greatly the quality of the student's education and support received from home. In fact, one of the most common concerns expressed by parents of students with learning disabilities about school services is the frequency (i.e., too little) and focus (i.e., negative instead of positive) of communication from teachers and other professionals.

## Parents as Partners

Many parents of students with learning disabilities take active roles in their children's education. For example, Munk and Bursuck (2001) took a collaborative approach that involved students with learning disabilities, their parents, general education teachers, and special education teachers to create personalized grading plans. They found that the team effort resulted in a greater sense of fairness regarding grading students with learning disabilities and that students reported trying harder with this coordinated effort. Similarly, Bryan and Burstein (2004) reviewed the research on improving the homework completion of students with learning disabilities. They noted that a key factor in successful efforts was parent involvement, even though such assistance was sometimes inconsistent because of disruptions in evening routines.

Although parent involvement is preferred, sometimes it can be a challenge. For example, Hughes, Schumm, and Vaughn (1999) examined Hispanic parents' perspectives on home reading and writing activities. They found that many parents of Hispanic children with learning disabilities provided books to their children, took them to the library, and read to them. However, some parents reported that they did not receive enough communication from school regarding how to help their children, and others indicated that their own difficulty with the English language constrained their ability to provide assistance. In another study, Starr, Foy, Cramer, and Singh (2006) compared the experiences of parents of students with learning disabilities to those of parents of students with other, more apparent disabilities (e.g., Down syndrome). They found that the former group of parents generally was less satisfied than the latter group with their interactions with school professionals and the

web link

www.matrixparents.org
An excellent website for parents, the Matrix Parent Network for Parents of Children with Learning Disabilities includes a discussion board for parents to exchange ideas.

services their children received. The authors cautioned that their data suggest the importance of educating teachers about forming partnerships with parents and ensuring that promised supports and services are implemented. Clearly, working closely with parents should be a top priority for professionals who teach with students with learning disabilities.

## REVIEW · REFLECT · DISCUSS

1. If you were talking to a parent whose child had just been identified as having a learning disability, how would you describe the disorder in a way the parent could understand?
2. Why is such emphasis placed on forming partnerships with parents of students with disabilities?

## Trends and Issues Affecting the Field of Learning Disabilities

Controversy has characterized the field of learning disabilities almost since its inception, and that trend continues today. In this era in which standards are rising and accountability for education outcomes is increasing, it is not surprising that many aspects of learning disabilities continue to be examined under a critical lens.

### Issues Related to Response to Intervention for Identifying Students Having a Learning Disability

Earlier in this chapter, you learned how response to intervention is being implemented as a procedure for identifying students as having learning disabilities in a way significantly different from traditional approaches. RTI has many benefits, including its reliance on data directly related to instruction and its potential for heading off serious learning problems through early intervention (Berkeley et al., 2009; Fletcher, Denton, & Francis, 2005). A rapidly growing body of professional literature is exploring both the applications and the viability of RTI. Not surprisingly, a number of questions are being raised regarding its use (Holdnack & Weiss, 2006; Johnson, Mellard, & Byrd, 2005; Kavale & Spaulding, 2008).

First, some professionals are concerned that RTI may not adequately and fairly address the diversity of students who may have learning disabilities (Wilkinson et al., 2006). For example, students who are gifted and who also have learning disabilities may be able to compensate enough for their areas of deficiency that they will not be identified using an RTI model, even though a traditional approach would have highlighted a discrepancy between these students' potential and their achievement (National Joint Committee on Learning Disabilities, 2005). A possible result is that RTI would under-identify students who are gifted and learning disabled. Conversely, preliminary research has raised concern regarding RTI for students who live in poverty and other high-risk situations. For these students, a real risk of overidentification may exist (Skiba et al., 2008).

A second area of concern has to do with the specific procedures that comprise response to intervention and the ways these procedures are implemented (Gerber, 2005; Mastropieri & Scruggs, 2005). Some of the questions being raised are these:

- For how long should an intervention be implemented before it is determined to be ineffective?
- How often and for how long should students receive tier 2 and tier 3 interventions (Fuchs, 2003; Speece, 2005)?
- Which research-based interventions should be used at each tier (Deshler, 2003; Semrud-Clikeman, 2005)?
- Is a three-tier model the best approach, or might four- tier or other models, as are being designed in some states, be more effective?

dimensions of
**DIVERSITY**

Haager (2007) cautions that the effectiveness of RTI procedures with English learners is unknown because of the lack of research concerning reading practices in general for this group, the unique characteristics of each ELL group and community, and the quality of the tools for assessing reading performance for these students.

*Some professionals see RTI more as a means of ensuring that all students receive high quality instruction rather than an assessment approach for identifying students as having learning disabilities.*

A third set of concerns pertains to the resources required to effectively and fully utilize RTI models. For example, implementing RTI requires that educators understand research-based interventions and strategies for data collection related to screening, diagnostics, and progress monitoring (Vellutino, Scanlon, Small, & Faneule, 2006). The implication is that considerable professional development is needed, and resources must be committed for that purpose. In addition, professionals need appropriate materials for assessment and instruction; again, resources must be allocated for the purchase of such items.

Yet another area of concern relates to the emerging implementation of RTI in states and local school districts (Berkeley et al., 2009). Although intended to directly address problems in the identification of students as having learning disabilities, in many locales RTI has become a renewed and more data-driven way to providing high-quality instruction to any struggling learner. Kavale and Spaulding (2008) note this is a positive step, but that it calls into question whether RTI is truly being used as a means of determining the presence of learning disabilities. This point of view is bolstered by the fact that most states require at least some traditional assessment procedures to be followed, even when an RTI system is in place.

Response to intervention has the potential to significantly change how students who struggle to learn receive their education (Francis et al., 2005; Gibbons, 2008). However, most professionals agree that far more information is needed before RTI can be considered valid and well established (Fuchs, Mock, Morgan, & Young, 2003). Whatever your planned role as a professional educator, you should anticipate that you will be affected by RTI, and you should closely watch for developments related to its implementation.

### High School and College Students and Learning Disabilities

As the field of learning disabilities has matured and services have improved for older students, more and more students have successfully completed high school and continued on to college. In fact, students with learning disabilities now make up the largest single group of students with disabilities at the college level (Henderson, 2001; Scott, McGuire, & Shaw, 2003). However, challenges accompany what seems like a strongly positive trend: First, some students are being identified for the first time as having learning disabilities during the high school years (U.S. Department of Education, 2004). Advocates applaud this as evidence of a deeper understanding among professionals about what learning disabilities are and how

**web link**

www.interventioncentral.org
The Intervention Central website is designed to help educators find and implement research-based practices. Reading, writing, math, behavior, and motivation are among the areas addressed.

the increased demands in high school for student independence and responsibility expose previously unidentified learning disabilities. Critics claim that many students thus identified in high school are hoping to take advantage of the testing accommodations they may be able to obtain to improve their scores on SATs and other college entrance exams and to parlay a disability label into special treatment while they are in college (Siegel, 1999). The increase in students identifying themselves as having learning disabilities late in their school careers has led colleges and universities to outline more carefully the documentation necessary to be eligible for services and the types of supports that can be provided (Madaus & Shaw, 2006).

A second issue for these students concerns the transition from high school to college. The National Joint Committee on Learning Disabilities (2007) reported that the inconsistent requirements across colleges and universities for documentation of a learning disability, as well as the differences in the laws governing the K–12 system versus the higher education system, can lead to problems for students. The Committee recommended that professionals assist students and their families in gathering needed documentation, explain the differences in the laws to them, and educate students and families on making early contact with prospective colleges and universities.

## REVIEW · REFLECT · DISCUSS

1. You have now read a considerable amount of detail about response to intervention. What is your opinion of this alternative approach to identifying students as possibly having learning disabilities? Do you think RTI is valid for this purpose, or do you believe that it is more a way to encourage general educators to use effective instructional strategies? Defend your answer.

2. What types of supports do you think students with LD in college should receive? Why? How should these supports be similar to or different form the supports they received in kindergarten through twelfth grade?

## Summary

- The origin of the learning disabilities field can be traced to nineteenth-century research on the brain, but recognition of learning disabilities as a discrete category occurred in the 1960s.

- The definition of *learning disability* that guides most school practices was included in the first federal special education law in 1975, and it has changed little since.

- Nearly 50 percent of all students receiving special education services are identified as having learning disabilities, which may be caused by physiological factors or curriculum and environmental influences. Students with learning disabilities may experience problems in cognition (e.g., perception or memory), one or more academic areas, social or emotional functioning, and behavior.

- Students are assessed for learning disabilities through one of two approaches: traditional formal and informal assessments or response to intervention (RTI). Eligibility is determined either by a failure to improve significantly or by the presence of a discrepancy between ability and achievement.

- Most students with learning disabilities receive their services in general education settings with some type of special education assistance there or in a separate setting.

- Recommended instructional practices for students with learning disabilities include direct instruction, which is a highly structured, teacher-led approach for teaching students across academic areas, and strategy instruction, which includes steps to guide students so that they can achieve independence for completing common academic tasks.

- Parents of students with learning disabilities often are highly involved in their children's education, but sometimes barriers to participation occur, especially for parents from nondominant cultures and those who live in poverty.

- Two important issues currently facing the learning disabilities field are (a) the validity of response to intervention as a method for identifying the presence of learning disabilities and (b) whether high school and college students should be identified as having learning disabilities for the first time.

Council for Exceptional Children (CEC) Common Core Knowledge and Skills addressed
in this chapter:

ICC1K5, ICC1K6, ICC1K8, ICC2K1, ICC2K2, ICC2K5, ICC2K6, ICC3K1, ICC3K2,
ICC4S2, ICC4S3, ICC4S4, ICC4S5, ICC4S6, ICC5K4, ICC5S8, ICC5S9, ICC8K2, ICC8K3,
ICC8S2, ICC8S4, ICC8S6, ICC10K3, ICC10S4

Appendix: Provides a full listing of the CEC Common Core Standards, and associated
Knowledge and Skill Statements listed here.

**PEARSON** **myeducationlab**

Now go to Topic 8: Learning Disabilities, in the
MyEducationLab (www.myeducationlab.com) for your
course, where you can:

- Find learning outcomes for the broad concepts covered in
  this chapter along with the national standards that connect
  to these outcomes.
- Complete Assignments and Activities that can help you
  more deeply understand the chapter content.
- Examine challenging situations and cases presented in the
  IRIS Center Resources.

- Apply and practice your understanding of the core concepts and skills identified in the chapter with the Building
  Teaching Skills and Dispositions learning units.
- Check your comprehension on the content covered in the
  chapter by going to the Study Plan in the Book Specific Resources for your text. Here you will be able to take a chapter quiz, receive feedback on your answers, and then access
  Review, Practice, and Enrichment activities to enhance
  your understanding of chapter content.
- Watch video clips of CCSSO Teacher of the Year award
  winners responding to the question: "Why I teach?" in the
  Teacher Talk section.

# Students with Attention Deficit–Hyperactivity Disorder

## LEARNING OBJECTIVES

- Define attention deficit–hyperactivity disorder (ADHD), explain its prevalence and causes, and outline its development as a recognized special need.
- Describe characteristics of individuals with attention deficit–hyperactivity disorder.
- Explain how ADHD is identified.
- Outline how learners with attention deficit–hyperactivity disorder receive their education.
- Describe recommended educational practices for students with ADHD.
- Explain the perspectives and concerns that parents and families of students with attention deficit–hyperactivity disorder may have.
- Identify trends and issues influencing the field of ADHD.

## Cedric

Cedric has always been an active child. He has the dubious distinction of having been asked not to return to two different preschool programs because of his behavior; concerns were raised about his safety and that of other students after several incidents of running away from teachers, climbing on classroom furniture, and pushing and repeatedly hitting other children. One of the preschool teachers used the word *whirlwind* to describe Cedric. Cedric's parents report that he prefers games and activities that include lots of movement, and he most enjoys swimming at the neighborhood pool. Cedric's pediatrician diagnosed him with ADHD when he was four years old, and he has taken medication since that time. His mother also has attended a variety of parent education classes to learn how to better understand and respond to Cedric's attentional problems. At home he follows a highly structured routine each morning and evening, and he earns rewards (such as extra swimming time) for positive behavior. In first grade, Cedric has difficulty with the necessary classroom structure and procedures, as well as the expectation for focusing attention, remaining seated for some activities, and taking turns. Cedric's teacher often is surprised by what he has learned: She sometimes assumes that he is not listening because he so often is moving, but she is gradually recognizing this is not always the case. The school's intervention team has discussed Cedric's academic and behavior needs. For now, since he is making appropriate learning progress, they are focusing on helping his teacher address behavior concerns. Cedric says of his behavior, "Sometimes I just do things and can't stop," a description his teacher would consider very accurate. Cedric has a Section 504 plan that addresses his medication and behavior plan. He does not receive special education services, nor does that seem likely to happen at this point. Although he experiences difficulties, he does not have a disability as defined by IDEA.

## Louis

Louis began middle school last fall, and he and his family soon learned how different it would be from the smaller and more structured experiences of elementary school. With six class periods on an alternating-day schedule, a locker, and multiple teachers, Louis was overwhelmed. He frequently forgot exactly where his locker was, and he came to class late at least eight times during September because he either took a wrong turn in the school hallway or got distracted by conversations with his classmates. He often came to class without his supplies and without his homework. His teachers asked his parents, Mr. and Mrs. Deffenbaugh, to come to school for a conference. At that meeting the teachers explained that Louis clearly was capable of the higher expectations of middle school but that his poor organizational skills and resulting frustration were interfering with his school success. The Deffenbaughs related that Louis already "hated" middle school, reported that he felt "stupid," and stated that he had refused to complete homework that he found difficult. After the meeting, Mr. and Mrs. Deffenbaugh revisited yet again the decision they made several years ago to address Louis's ADHD without medication. After the school conference, discussions with Louis and his pediatrician, and some Internet research, they agreed that Louis should take Ritalin. After one adjustment in the dosage and several meetings with teachers to work on other supports for Louis, they noticed that he seemed to be able to concentrate on his work more readily. His teachers remarked on the improvement, too. School still was challenging for Louis, but as the spring approached he was passing in all subjects, had changed his mind about middle school and now liked it, and was planning to try out for the football team in the fall. His teachers nominated Louis for the "greatest learning growth" award for the third grading quarter.

## Marcus

Marcus will graduate in one more year from M. L. King High School, and with this major milestone in sight he knows he will make it. He believes he has had to work harder than most other students—not only to learn but also to do all the other things related to attending school. He includes on this list activities such as remembering to take books and assignments home; remembering to do homework, especially long-term projects; getting everything back to school; and turning in his assignments instead of leaving them in his locker. He writes *everything* down, and he has learned a few techniques to assist him. For example, when he has an assignment due, he pictures a huge billboard (i.e., "a-sign" for "as-sign-ment") with the project described on it. He also relies on a close friend to help him keep track of the details of being a high school student. At home Marcus tries to follow a routine and to go to bed at a reasonable time, but he keeps two alarm clocks set and places them across the room from his bed because he tends to oversleep. Marcus has encountered several teachers who were unwilling to accommodate his special needs, maintaining that he could pay attention if he tried. In those situations Marcus has had some behavior issues, including storming out of a classroom and using profanity after arguing with one teacher. Most teachers have been understanding, though. He is especially grateful that his high school resource teacher Mr. Lewis encouraged him to think about his future. Because of his dual interests in working outdoors and outdoor sports, Marcus plans to attend a two-year community college program in turf-grass management technology while he decides whether to continue his education with a degree in business administration. Marcus knows that adults with attention problems often have difficulty selecting a major and sticking with the demands of postsecondary education, and he is determined to avoid these problems. Marcus is identified as having both a learning disability and other health impairments (for his ADHD), but his parents, and now Marcus himself, are adamant that he can manage his special needs through structure and behavior supports rather than relying on medication as an intervention.

When you were in school, did you have classmates like Cedric, Louis, and Marcus who could not seem to focus on their schoolwork, who were constantly getting out of their seats and distracting other students from learning? Even as a child, you realized that the active behaviors of those classmates were unusual. Have you ever had a friend who always was thinking about something other than the situation at hand? Did it seem that every time you asked that friend a question, you had to ask it again, even after you were sure he or she was paying attention to you? Perhaps you are one of the students who displayed such behaviors, and you are reading this paragraph thinking that you could have contributed your own story to begin this chapter.

Students who have attentional problems have received extensive consideration during the past two decades, both among the scholars who have made great strides in understanding the nature of this disorder (e.g., Fasbender & Schweitzer, 2006; Houghton, 2006; Vaughn, Wetzel, & Kratochvil, 2008) and in the popular press through newspaper and magazine articles (e.g., Mahr, 2007; Rubin, 2009). A positive result is that parents and professionals now better understand that attention deficit–hyperactivity disorder (ADHD) is a lifelong and chronic disorder. It can profoundly affect students' early childhood and school careers as well as their adjustment during adulthood (National Institute of Mental Health, 2008; Toner, O'Donoghue, & Houghton, 2006). Although it should be clearly noted that ADHD is not a disability category directly addressed by the Individuals with Disabilities Education Act (IDEA), this disorder often occurs simultaneously with learning, emotional, and other disabilities. If ADHD is significant, a student also may qualify for services as other health impaired (OHI), as Marcus did. However, many students with ADHD are served through Section 504 of the Vocational Act of 1973. These topics are explored in greater detail later in this chapter.

**PEARSON**
**myeducationlab**

To check your comprehension on the content covered in Chapter 6, go to the Book Specific Resources in the MyEducationLab (www.myeducationlab.com) for your course, select your text, and complete the Study Plan. Here you will be able to take a chapter quiz, receive feedback on your answers, and then access review, practice, and enrichment activities to enhance your understanding of chapter content.

# Understanding Attention Deficit–Hyperactivity Disorder

The fact that some children are so extraordinarily active that adults take notice and view them as having behavior problems has been recognized for many years. Today's thinking about these students and best practices for effectively working with them comes from decades of research and discussion.

## Development of the ADHD Field

The first known formal description of ADHD was reported by British physician George Still in 1902, attributing some children's unexplained misbehavior and impulsivity to an unknown medical condition (Rafalovich, 2001). As you can see through the information pre-

*Although some students with ADHD are often in motion, others are inattentive and may appear forgetful and disorganized.*

sented in the timeline in Figure 6.1, interest in understanding and treating attentional problems continued through the twentieth century, with physicians and psychologists first studying children's *hyperactivity* (excessive movement) but shifting their research in the 1970s to children's *cognitive impulsivity*—that is, their difficulties focusing. This latter line of research eventually led to exploration of the brain's role in ADHD, and work in that area dominates the field today (e.g., Krain & Castellanos, 2006; Weyandt, 2006).

### Terminology Related to ADHD

The language used to describe attentional problems has reflected the evolving thinking about their origins and characteristics. In the early part of the twentieth century, children were called *hyperkinetic* and were referred to as having minimal brain dysfunction (MBD) (Rafalovich, 2001). Later they were called *hyperactive* (Renshaw, 1974). In 1980, the *Diagnostic and Statistical Manual of Mental Disorders–III (DSM-III)* introduced the term **attention deficit disorder (ADD)** to describe this group of children, and it noted that the condition could exist with or without hyperactivity (American Psychiatric Association, 1980). Several years later that term was redefined to encompass both types of the disorder and was called attention deficit–hyperactivity disorder (ADHD). In yet another revision, the fourth edition of the *DSM (DSM-IV)* retained the ADHD term but reverted to distinguishing whether hyperactivity was present (American Psychiatric Association, 1994). Even though you might still hear some professionals and parents use the term ADD, the most recent and currently accurate term to describe this disorder is attention deficit–hyperactivity disorder (ADHD).

## *Definition of Attention Deficit–Hyperactivity Disorder*

**Attention deficit–hyperactivity disorder (ADHD)** is considered a psychiatric disorder with symptoms occurring before age seven. As already noted, it is not one of the disability categories specified in IDEA. According to the Diagnostic and Statistical Manual of the American Psychiatric Association (4th ed., text revision) *(DSM-IV-TR)*, ADHD is

> a pervasive pattern of inattention, impulsivity, and/or hyperactivity–impulsivity that is more frequent and severe than is typically observed in individuals at a comparable level of development. (American Psychiatric Association, 2000, p. 78)

## FIGURE 6.1
Timeline: Development of the ADHD Field

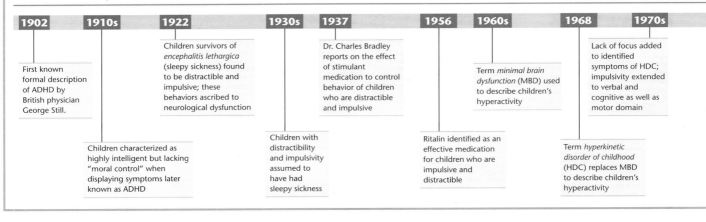

A complete description of ADHD is presented in Figure 6.2. It contains these elements:

- For some students with ADHD, inattention is the primary symptom. These students might skip important parts of an assignment, may appear to be daydreaming during large-group instruction, cannot seem to get organized, and generally seem forgetful both in school and at home. This variation of the disorder is called **ADHD–predominantly inattentive type**.
- For another group of students with ADHD, the primary symptom is a combination of hyperactivity—high amounts of movement, and impulsivity—and inability to "put on the brakes" before acting. Students who have this type of ADHD tap their desks and wiggle in their seats, often run instead of walking, appear to have an internal engine that does not stop, and may talk a lot. This form of the disorder is called **ADHD–predominantly hyperactive–impulsive type**.
- Some students with ADHD have symptoms suggesting that both inattention and hyperactivity–impulsivity are part of their disorder. These students are referred to as having **ADHD–combined type** (*DSM-IV-TR*).

The terms for and descriptions of ADHD can be a bit confusing. This list summarizes the key elements of ADHD:

1. ADHD is considered *neurobiological* (i.e., originating in the brain), and it is developmental, beginning before the age of seven.
2. ADHD is chronic, long term, and not acutely acquired (i.e., not the immediate result of an accident or injury).
3. The primary trait is an inability to attend beyond what is typical for peers of comparable age. Significant impulsivity also may be characteristic.
4. ADHD is not situational; that is, it affects the children and adults who have it across all settings. However, their symptoms may be most apparent at school because of the structure and expectations there.
5. Students with ADHD are more likely to have a *production* deficit rather than an *acquisition* deficit. That is, they may take information in and sometimes surprise their teachers by what they know, as in the case of Cedric, who was described at the beginning of the chapter. Their greatest difficulty often lies in production—that is, in completing their work.
6. ADHD is not caused by environmental situations or other disabilities, but it may be present with them.

### Prevalence of Attention Deficit–Hyperactivity Disorder

Discussing the prevalence of ADHD is not straightforward. Some professionals maintain that ADHD simply does not exist—that it has been created by parents who want an explanation for

ADHD is considered a mental health disorder. At the federal level, it is studied by the Centers for Disease Control and Prevention as well as the U.S. Surgeon General and the National Institute of Mental Health.

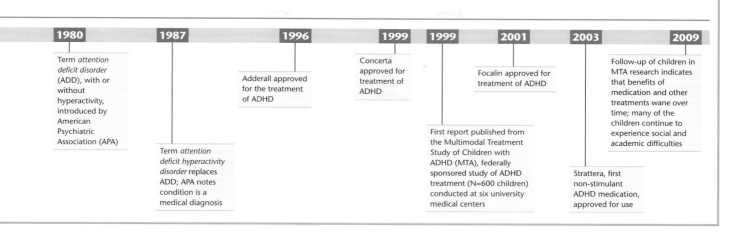

| 1980 | 1987 | 1996 | 1999 | 1999 | 2001 | 2003 | 2009 |

Term *attention deficit disorder* (ADD), with or without hyperactivity, introduced by American Psychiatric Association (APA)

Term *attention deficit hyperactivity disorder* replaces ADD; APA notes condition is a medical diagnosis

Adderall approved for the treatment of ADHD

Concerta approved for treatment of ADHD

First report published from the Multimodal Treatment Study of Children with ADHD (MTA), federally sponsored study of ADHD treatment (N=600 children) conducted at six university medical centers

Focalin approved for treatment of ADHD

Strattera, first non-stimulant ADHD medication, approved for use

Follow-up of children in MTA research indicates that benefits of medication and other treatments wane over time; many of the children continue to experience social and academic difficulties

their children's difficult behaviors and by pharmaceutical companies that want to sell medication for both children and adults with attentional problems (e.g., Cohen, 2006; Parens & Johnson, 2009). However, several major organizations, including the National Institutes of Health (NIH) and the American Medical Association (AMA), as well as the U.S. Surgeon General, have concluded that the disorder is real and that it occurs across the life span (Barkley et al., 2002).

Currently, ADHD is one of the most commonly diagnosed childhood psychiatric disorders (Salend & Rohena, 2003). Most professionals estimate that 3 to 5 percent of the population has ADHD (National Institute of Mental Health, 2006). Among children, the prevalence is estimated at 3 to 7 percent (Centers for Disease Control and Prevention, 2009). Although it used to be believed that ADHD gradually disappeared in adulthood, recent research suggests that slightly more than 4 percent of adults exhibit the characteristics of this disorder (National Institute of Mental Health, 2008).

### Prevalence Based on Gender

Would you guess that boys or girls are most often identified as having ADHD? Early research suggested that boys might be up to nine times more likely than girls to have this disorder (Arnold, 1995), but recent studies suggest that the ratio is closer to two or three to one (Pastor & Reuben, 2008). Even these figures are tentative. Although girls and boys may exhibit the same symptoms of ADHD, research suggests that girls may display lower levels of these symptoms (Zambo, 2008) and so are not identified as often. You can learn more about ADHD in girls by reviewing the Professional Edge feature.

### Prevalence Based on Race and Poverty

One other dimension of ADHD prevalence is important to consider: differences that may exist based on race/ethnicity and poverty. Data generally do not suggest that ADHD occurs significantly more or less frequently in any particular racial or ethnic group. However, differences may exist in terms of treatment (Miller, Nigg, & Miller, 2009; Pastor & Reuben, 2005). For example, using a large sample of health interview data from parents, Pastor and Reuben (2005) found that African American and Hispanic children were less likely than Caucasian children to receive medication for ADHD, even when factors such as income level and insurance were accounted for.

### *Causes of Attention Deficit–Hyperactivity Disorder*

The causes of attention deficit–hyperactivity disorder have been debated for many years. In the past, some professionals claimed that ADHD was the result of permissive parenting, that children's apparently uncontrolled behavior occurred because no limits were placed on them. Other professionals proposed that ADHD was caused by diet—either food allergies or the consumption of too much sugar—or by other allergies. Although parenting skills certainly influence children's behaviors and a few children do have reactions to certain foods

**web link**

www.help4adhd.org
The National Resource Center on AD/HD is a clearinghouse for both technical information and helpful resources concerning this disorder. It is funded by the Centers for Disease Control and Prevention.

FIGURE 6.2
*DSM-IV-TR* Criteria for ADHD

**I.** Either A or B

  **A.** Six or more of the following symptoms of inattention have been present for at least six months to a point that is disruptive and inappropriate for developmental level:

    **Inattention**

    **1.** Often does not give close attention to details or makes careless mistakes in schoolwork, work, or other activities.

    **2.** Often has trouble keeping attention on tasks or play activities.

    **3.** Often does not seem to listen when spoken to directly.

    **4.** Often does not follow instructions and fails to finish schoolwork, chores, or duties in the workplace (not due to oppositional behavior or failure to understand instructions).

    **5.** Often has trouble organizing activities.

    **6.** Often avoids, dislikes, or doesn't want to do things that take a lot of mental effort for a long period of time (such as schoolwork or homework).

    **7.** Often loses things needed for tasks and activities (e.g., toys, school assignments, pencils, books, or tools).

    **8.** Is often easily distracted.

    **9.** Is often forgetful in daily activities.

  **B.** Six or more of the following symptoms of hyperactivity–impulsivity have been present for at least six months to an extent that is disruptive and inappropriate for developmental level.

    **Hyperactivity**

    **1.** Often fidgets with hands or feet, or squirms in seat.

    **2.** Often gets up from seat when remaining in seat is expected.

    **3.** Often runs about or climbs when and where it is not appropriate (adolescents or adults may feel very restless).

    **4.** Often has trouble playing or enjoying leisure activities quietly.

    **5.** Is often "on the go" or often acts as if "driven by a motor."

    **6.** Often talks excessively.

    **Impulsivity**

    **1.** Often blurts out answers before questions have been finished.

    **2.** Often has trouble waiting one's turn.

    **3.** Often interrupts or intrudes on others (e.g., butts into conversations or games).

**II.** Some symptoms that cause impairment were present before age seven years.

**III.** Some impairment from the symptoms is present in two or more settings (e.g., at school/work and at home).

**IV.** There must be clear evidence of significant impairment in social, school, or work functioning.

**V.** The symptoms do not happen only during the course of a pervasive developmental disorder, schizophrenia, or other psychotic disorder. The symptoms are not better accounted for by another mental disorder (e.g., mood disorder, anxiety disorder, dissociative disorder, or a personality disorder).

**Based on these criteria, three types of ADHD are identified:**

    **1.** ADHD—*combined type:* if both criteria IA and IB are met for the past six months

    **2.** ADHD—*predominantly inattentive type:* if criterion IA is met but criterion IB is not met for the past six months

    **3.** ADHD—*predominantly hyperactive–impulsive type:* if criterion IB is met but criterion IA is not met for the past six months

Source: DSM-IV TR Diagnostic Crieteria for ADHD, p. 92–93 from *The Diagnostic and Statistical Manual of Mental Disorders, Text Revision,* Fourth Edition, (Copyright 2000).

## ADHD in Girls

The symptoms of ADHD in girls may be subtly different from those in boys. Nadeau and Quinn (2004) prepared the following checklist for girls to complete if they are concerned they may have ADHD. Nearly all girls will check some of the items, but a professional assessment might be warranted if many are checked.

### ADHD Checklist for Girls

**Please place a check mark beside each item that you feel describes you.**

☐ 1. It's very hard for me to keep track of homework assignments and due dates.

☐ 2. No matter how hard I try to be on time, I am usually late.

☐ 3. I have trouble getting to sleep at night.

☐ 4. I have trouble getting up in the morning.

☐ 5. I jump from one topic to another in conversation.

☐ 6. I interrupt other people when they're talking, even though I try not to.

☐ 7. Even when I try to listen in class my thoughts start wandering.

☐ 8. I have difficulty remembering what I've read.

☐ 9. I can't seem to get started on school assignments until the last minute.

☐ 10. My room is very messy.

☐ 11. My friends say I'm "hyper."

☐ 12. My friends call me "spacey."

☐ 13. I forget to do things my parents ask me to do.

☐ 14. I frequently lose or misplace personal items.

☐ 15. My parents and teachers tell me I need to try harder in school.

☐ 16. I am distracted easily by sounds or by things I see.

☐ 17. My parents tell me that I overreact to things.

☐ 18. I feel anxious or worried a lot of the time.

☐ 19. I feel moody and depressed, even for no reason.

☐ 20. My moods and emotions are much more intense during the week before my period.

☐ 21. I am easily frustrated.

☐ 22. I'm pretty impatient and hate to wait.

☐ 23. I feel different from other girls.

☐ 24. I wish my parents understood how hard high school is for me.

☐ 25. I feel mentally exhausted when I get home from school.

☐ 26. It takes me longer to get assignments done compared to my classmates.

☐ 27. Even when I study hard I can't seem to remember things when I'm taking an exam.

☐ 28. It's so hard for me to stay organized.

☐ 29. I only make good grades in the classes that really interest me.

☐ 30. I have trouble completing papers and projects on time.

☐ 31. The only way I can really study for a test is to stay up late the night before.

☐ 32. I sometimes eat to calm down.

☐ 33. It seems like I'm always messing up.

☐ 34. I fidget or doodle in class because it's hard for me to sit still and listen.

☐ 35. I blurt things out without thinking.

*Source:* From Nadeau, K. G. & Quinn, P. (2004). *ADD (ADHD) self-report questionnaire for teenage girls.* Used with permission from ADDvance, www.addvance.com.

and other environmental elements, research on these factors indicates that neither is a cause of ADHD, nor is too much television watching or poor schooling (National Institute of Mental Health, 2009). However, research into these and other causes of ADHD continues.

Perhaps you are wondering what *does* cause ADHD and why some students in almost every school have this disorder. Recent research indicates that attention deficit–hyperactivity disorder is the result of a disorder of the brain (Fischer et al., 2005; Weyandt, 2006), but other factors also probably contribute to the severity and persistence of the symptoms, including physiological and environmental factors.

### Physiological Factors

Many medical and educational professionals have studied physiological causes of ADHD. One significant factor is *heredity*. Researchers have explored characteristics of the parents, siblings, and other close relatives of individuals with this disorder (e.g., Joseph, 2000) and often found that individuals with ADHD are much more likely than other individuals to have a family pattern of ADHD (e.g., Levy, Hay, & Bennett, 2006). In fact, 25 percent of the relatives of individuals with ADHD also have ADHD, compared with 5 percent of individuals in the typical population (National Institute of Mental Health, 2009).

Such studies can be flawed, though, because of environmental factors. For example, all members of a family may live in such a chaotic setting that they appear to have attentional problems. As an alternative, some researchers have studied fraternal and identical twins—those

## web link

http://www.nimh.nih.gov/health/publications/attention-deficit-hyperactivity-disorder/index.shtml This NIMH website provides a downloadable, detailed booklet on the symptoms, causes, and treatments for ADHD; it addresses children as well as adults and describes current research on this disorder.

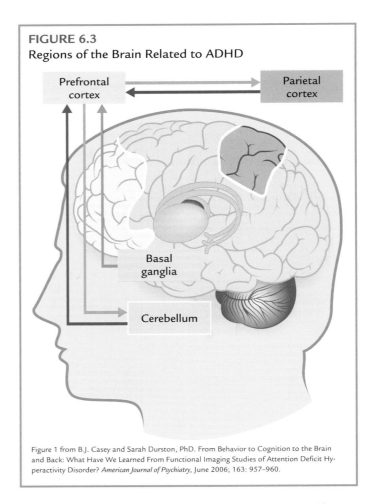

**FIGURE 6.3**
Regions of the Brain Related to ADHD

Prefrontal cortex

Parietal cortex

Basal ganglia

Cerebellum

Figure 1 from B.J. Casey and Sarah Durston, PhD. From Behavior to Cognition to the Brain and Back: What Have We Learned From Functional Imaging Studies of Attention Deficit Hyperactivity Disorder? *American Journal of Psychiatry*, June 2006; 163: 957–960.

**web link**

http://www.addresources.org/ adhd_websites.php
The Attention Deficit Disorder Resources website provides a page of links to helpful information about ADHD, including sites with basic information, information in Spanish, and information for parents and teachers.

raised in the same household and those raised in two different households—as might happen with adoption. Using this approach, researchers can better separate the effects of heredity from those of environment. In this line of research the most convincing studies are those of identical twins: They are highly likely to share the disorder, whether they have been raised in the same household or in different households (Levy, Hay, & Bennett, 2006).

Some of the most contemporary and exciting research related to ADHD concerns the differences in the brains of those with this disorder. For example, several studies have found that certain regions of the brains of individuals with ADHD are slightly smaller than is typical (Brieber et al., 2007). Other differences can be understood by referring to the illustration of the brain in Figure 6.3. Using magnetic resonance imaging (MRI) and other technology you learned about in Chapter Five, scientists have found that three parts of the brain—the frontal region, the basal ganglia, and the cerebellum—often function differently in individuals with ADHD than in other people (Barkley, 2006). Specifically, for children and adults with ADHD, the level of blood flow is lower than typical in those regions of the brain. In addition, some researchers have found that some individuals with ADHD may show less electrical activity in certain brain regions than is typical, but other researchers have found just the reverse—that is, increased electrical activity (Weyandt, 2006). Finally, the brains of some individuals with ADHD appear to metabolize glucose at a lower rate than is typical. Of course, professionals who are studying these neurological causes of ADHD hope that their work will lead to more effective treatments, a topic addressed later in this chapter. This area of study is rapidly changing, and far more detailed and definitive information about the brain and ADHD probably will be learned in the next few years.

### Environmental Factors

Most current work investigating ADHD emphasizes physiological causes, and environmental factors generally are seen as primarily contributing to the severity of the symptoms (National Institute of Mental Health, 2008). For example, if a young child with attention deficit–hyperactivity disorder is raised in a highly structured home in which clear rules are in place and appropriate behavior is emphasized, that child is likely to display a milder set of ADHD characteristics than is a similar child raised in a home with little structure.

However, researchers are finding that environmental factors might actually contribute to the development of ADHD for some children. In particular, a significant correlation seems to exist between children with high levels of lead in their blood during the first 2 or 3 years of life and ADHD (Agency for Toxic Substances and Disease Registry, 2007). Similarly, maternal prenatal smoking and alcohol consumption are correlated with an increase of ADHD in children.

## REVIEW · REFLECT · DISCUSS

1. Review the chapter opening descriptions of Cedric, Louis, and Marcus. Which type of ADHD does each seem to have? On what characteristics and behaviors do you base your decisions?

2. What are the possible reasons why ADHD is identified so much more often in boys than in girls? How do you think race or culture affects the identification and treatment of ADHD?

## Characteristics of Individuals with Attention Deficit–Hyperactivity Disorder

Learning about the causes of ADHD provides you with a perspective on why some students experience difficulty in school. However, you also need to recognize the typical characteristics of these students. Although generalizing about students is risky, by learning about the cognitive, academic, social/emotional, and behavior characteristics of students with ADHD, you will be prepared to more thoroughly understand, plan for, and address their needs.

### Cognitive Characteristics

The cognitive characteristics of students with ADHD are thought to be directly related to the unusual features of their brains. Interestingly, the parts of the brain that are different in individuals with ADHD are those known to regulate attention. Barkley (2006) considered this fact as well as all the research describing the behavior of individuals with ADHD. Using this substantial set of information, he proposed that the primary deficit in individuals with ADHD is not really attention; rather, it is **behavior inhibition** and self-regulation problems related to these neurological factors. In other words, it is not that students with ADHD cannot pay attention; it is that they cannot regulate where their attention is directed, how often it switches to other areas, or how to redirect their attention when it wanders. These problems with behavior inhibition set the stage for dilemmas related to the **executive functions**, or the mental activities that help them regulate their behaviors. Barkley (2006) suggests that executive functions can be classed into these four mental activities that operate interactively:

*Research suggests that ADHD has a genetic component and includes differences in the size and functioning of the brain.*

1. **Working memory** is the mental activity that enables students to remember events and use hindsight and foresight based on that memory. For example, if a student has been corrected previously for leaving his seat during large-group instruction, a typical student would remember the teacher's words as he began to stand again—and probably would sit back down. However, a student with ADHD probably would not recall the teacher's instructions or consequences for

the behavior and would get out of his seat again. In fact, this might happen repeatedly, which explains the often-heard comment that students with ADHD do not seem to learn from experience. Cedric, the elementary student discussed at the beginning of the chapter, might have difficulty in this area.

2. **Self-directed speech** is that little voice in your head that keeps you thinking about the topic at hand instead of allowing your thoughts to wander. This mental activity, sometimes called *self-talk*, is the mechanism students use to reflect on how they are doing, to problem solve, and to follow instructions. Although young children might vocalize their self-talk as they develop this skill, by the time children are school age they usually carry out this mental activity privately. Louis, the student introduced in the chapter opening, probably has difficulty with self-directed speech.

3. **Control of emotions and motivation** involves setting aside frustration and other emotions to complete a task as well as generating emotions internally and taking the perspectives of others. For example, have you ever been faced with an extraordinarily frustrating task? It could have been academic, such as solving a complex math problem, or it could have been a daily activity, such as replacing the tiny screw that holds your eyeglasses together. To accomplish the task, you probably took a deep breath to calm down and persisted until you succeeded. Some students with ADHD are not able to manage their emotional responses, and so when faced with frustrating tasks, they may have temper tantrums or storm out of the room. The outbursts that Marcus, the high school student introduced at the beginning of the chapter, sometimes experiences are evidence of this problem.

4. **Reconstitution**, or *planning*, refers to the ability for both analysis and synthesis. *Analysis* is the skill of breaking down what is observed into component parts; *synthesis* is the skill of combining parts in order to perform new actions. Reconstitution enables educators to teach students key skills but not to have to directly teach every example of every skill: Students can put similar pieces together themselves. Thus, when students learn the parts of a sentence, they usually can write longer and shorter sentences, add adjectives to the nouns in their sentences, and recognize sentences in many contexts. Students with ADHD may, academically or behaviorally, have difficulty with this activity. They may not recognize the similarity of one academic task to another; they may not realize that the rules for conduct in the classroom are similar to the rules that one should follow in the lunchroom.

According to this model of ADHD, as most children develop and their behavioral inhibition increases, the executive functions increasingly control motor behavior (Barkley, 2006). That is, behavior becomes more planful and deliberate because children increasingly are able to implement the executive functions to think before they act, to remember consequences and thus change their behavior, to persist at a task even when it is difficult, and to realize on their own what behaviors might be considered appropriate in new situations. In children with ADHD, problems in behavioral inhibition contribute to problems in the development of executive functions. The result is poor motor control—distractibility and/or impulsivity.

Barkley (2006) notes that ADHD is, in many ways, a problem of internal time management. Students cannot slow down the sequences of internal mental activities that would let them better manage their behaviors. This model of ADHD has direct applicability for teachers. If you can identify the type of problems a student is having related to behavior inhibition and the executive functions, then you can implement teaching strategies to address the problem or work around it, as illustrated in the Instruction in Action feature.

In addition to Barkley's explanation of the cognitive functioning of students with ADHD, brief mention should be made of these students' intellectual abilities. If you review the diagnostic criteria for ADHD, you will see that no mention is made of a range of intellectual ability for students who have this special need. In fact, students who have ADHD may be gifted, average, or struggling learners (Schuck & Crinella, 2005). In some cases, students with intellectual disabilities also may be identified as having ADHD (Hastings, Beck, Daley, & Hill, 2004). ADHD is not directly related to intelligence (Dillon & Osborne, 2006).

## Executive Functions and Strategies for Learning

Students with ADHD have difficulty with behavior inhibition because of problems related to the executive functions. Here are several specific strategies that can help address the dilemmas these students may face in completing common school tasks and activities:

- *Calendar and buddy review.* If students are given a calendar for keeping track of homework each week, many frustrations will be relieved. Teachers may pair students, giving each student a support person who ensures that the correct information is written on the calendar and that the appropriate books are packed to go home.

- *Color-coded notes.* Adapt notes such that different aspects of the content (e.g., vocabulary, key ideas, supporting details, tools) are highlighted with different colors. This may help students who have difficulty organizing and understanding notes or text.

- *Organizational system.* A student with executive control difficulties may have trouble keeping up with important supplies, assignments, books, and other necessary school materials. Providing an organizational system—such as a notebook with color-coded dividers for different subjects, homework, and assignments—may allow the student to experience more success.

- *Metacognitive strategies.* Often students must be taught strategies to use when trying to learn new material, when studying, or when completing classwork. Metacognitive strategies help make the student aware of the mental processes she is using to learn or rehearse information.

- *Student evaluation of work progress.* For the student who is often off task, some instruction may be beneficial to teach him to monitor when he is and is not doing what he is supposed to be doing. This awareness could be the first step in teaching the student what to do when he finds that he is not on task.

- *Graphic organizers.* Graphic organizers are available for many different forms of content, problem-solving techniques, relationships, and information formats. They are excellent tools for lecture guides, study guides, and class activities because they help students understand how their ideas relate to one another.

- *Model note taking.* Students may benefit from the teacher demonstrating how to take notes on the board, including an explanation of abbreviations and symbols.

- *Student evaluation of overall progress.* A student with executive control difficulties may benefit from learning how to properly edit her writing. The teacher should provide a consistent guide for completing this process.

*Source:* North Carolina Partnership Training System for Special Education. (1997). *Special needs, special teaching: Teaching students with disabilities in your classroom.* Chapel Hill, NC: Author.

## *Academic Characteristics*

Because ADHD is not related to intellectual ability, it is not surprising that the academic characteristics of students with ADHD can vary tremendously (Volpe et al., 2006). For example, some students with ADHD also are gifted or talented, and educators may find that they need both to challenge these students and to assist them to focus their unique abilities (Flint, 2001). DuPaul and Weyandt (2006) have reviewed recent research on this topic and argue that these students need diverse instructional interventions and other supports to help them reach their potential.

Many students with ADHD can be successful in school, particularly if effective interventions are put in place, a point illustrated in Louis's story at the beginning of the chapter. They achieve at or near grade level, complete high school and postsecondary education, and generally are able to overcome or compensate for the symptoms of ADHD that could have negatively affected their education. One example of a student for whom this is true is Abigail Zureich, the young adult described in the Firsthand Account feature. Her story illustrates how students with ADHD have to work diligently to learn but also how their persistence pays off.

The majority of students with ADHD experience great difficulty with the academic structure and demands of school, and they consistently achieve below their potential (Owens, Hinshaw, Lee, & Lahey, 2009; Schultz, Evans, & Serpell, 2009). Not surprisingly, there appears to be a correlation between the severity of the symptoms of ADHD and achievement: The more severe the symptoms, the greater the negative impact on school performance (DeShazo-Barry, Lyman, & Klinger, 2002). For some students, their academic self-concept is an important contributing factor; that is, when they view themselves as being not very capable of succeeding at schoolwork, they are more likely to stop trying and to develop behaviors that lead to further academic failure (e.g., Pisecco, Wristers, Swank, Silva, & Baker, 2001; Tabassam & Grainger, 2002). Conversely, if they are successful, they develop a positive academic self-concept and are more likely to keep trying, even when schoolwork is difficult.

**ABIGAIL ZUREICH** *finished a double major in psychology and humanities with a minor in dance at Saint Mary's College. She earned good grades. She is interviewing for a human resources job in Chicago and plans to attend law school in a year. What's more, she has attention deficit–hyperactivity disorder.*

Even as early as kindergarten, school was a struggle for the Dallas native. In grade and middle schools, she'd put in hours and hours of work and get C's at best. Then, when she was a freshman in high school, she read an article in *Seventeen* magazine about ADHD. "I said, This is what I have," she recalled. A specialist diagnosed her with ADHD, and she began taking Ritalin, a stimulant drug. For the first time, Zureich was able to focus, and her grades went from C's and D's to A's and B's. "It was like a light was turned on," she said. Ritalin acts as a filter, she said. "People with ADHD are overloaded with stimuli. You don't know what to focus on." If she doesn't take her medication, "every little thing distracts me," she said. "If I didn't take it before I went to class, I couldn't really tell you what we talked about."

Although the Ritalin helped, she still had to work extra hard for the grades she wanted.

Over the years, Zureich, who also was diagnosed with dyslexia and dyscalculia (difficulty with numbers), has devised ways to work around her problems. She schedules her time strictly, and when she studies for a test, she rewrites all her notes while reading them out loud. She can't compose term papers at the word processor, so she writes them out on paper before typing them.

### Recognizing Strengths

"People with ADD and ADHD have their challenges, but they also have their strengths," said Catherine Pittman, chairwoman of the psychology department at Saint Mary's College. "They are creative, they can deal with complexity, their entrepreneurial skills are excellent, they have energy you can't exhaust, and they can juggle many tasks," she said.

Pittman, who facilitates a resource group for Saint Mary's students with learning disabilities, said young people who struggled in the classroom often feel confident and competent once they are out in the real world where the demands are different. For example, when Zureich took an internship in the admissions office at Saint Mary's, she learned that there's a wonderful world beyond exams and term papers. "I really love interacting with students and families," she said. "I have a lot of independence, which is great." Designing a web-based recruitment program, for example, was a pleasure.

Pittman tells students who struggle with academics that their whole life won't be like this. When they leave school and enter a new environment, they may find themselves doing much better, she said. "You can have a very fulfilling life."

That's what Zureich envisions for herself. She knows that in law school she'll have to work harder than her classmates—but that's OK, she says.

People with attention deficit-disorders shouldn't give up, Zureich said. "It isn't something that will defeat you. It is a roadblock you can walk around."

*Source:* Johnson, N. (2002, July 17). Those with attention-deficit disorders zoom in on developing strengths, ADHD: From keyed up to keyed in. *South Bend Tribune,* p. A1. Reprinted by permission of the *South Bend Tribune.*

The more you keep students active, the more likely they will attend to instruction. Use choral responding—that is, having all students call out the answers to simple questions. Give students small whiteboards so that they can write down answers, hold them up for your inspection, and then erase them. After you ask a question during large-group instruction, have students trade answers with a partner before calling on someone in the large group.

Some students with ADHD can be helped in developing a positive academic self-concept through the use of technology. As outlined in the Technology Notes feature, readily available technology can help students be successful in organizing and completing school tasks.

## Social and Emotional Characteristics

The social and emotional characteristics of students with ADHD have been the focus of extensive research. This research has emphasized students' self-esteem and overall social functioning and the likelihood that they will experience depression.

### Self-Esteem

*Self-esteem* refers to a person's overall regard for himself or herself as a person. If you have positive self-esteem, you perceive yourself as having many strengths; if you have negative self-esteem, you sense in yourself many weaknesses. Whether students with ADHD have positive or negative self-esteem is not clear. Some researchers (e.g., Cukrowicz, Taylor, Schatschneider, & Iacono, 2006; Slomkowski, Klein, & Mannuzza, 1995) have found that students with ADHD have much lower self-esteem than typical peers of the same age. Others have found few differences. For example, in a large-scale study of elementary school students, Eisenberg and Schneider (2007) found that the self-perception of students with ADHD toward their math and reading achievement was similar to that for students without this disorder, the exception being that boys with ADHD were somewhat more negative about their math skills than were other boys. It should be noted, though, that parents and teachers were more negative about students, especially girls, with ADHD than about other students.

### Social Functioning

In contrast to the somewhat contradictory data about self-esteem, information about the social functioning of students with attention deficit–hyperactivity disorder is clear. Students with ADHD often experience challenges in coping with social demands at school, at home, and in other settings (Owens et al., 2009). For example, these students might not recognize that they need to behave differently in different types of social situations (Lee, Lahey, & Owens, 2008). They may not realize that there are particular ways to act when in school and talking to their teachers that are different from the ways they act when playing with their friends on the playground. Students with ADHD also are not particularly accurate at judging their own social abilities, tending to overestimate them (Kellner, Houghton, & Douglas, 2003).

Given these difficulties with social functioning, you can probably guess that students with ADHD are more likely than their peers to have problems in developing and maintaining friendships. For example, adolescents with ADHD report that they have fewer close friendships than do those without ADHD (Bagwell, Molina, Pelham, & Hoza, 2001). Students with ADHD also are more likely than other students to be seen as both victims of bullying and bullies themselves (Wiener & Mak, 2009). Their parents confirm this finding. Research also suggests that children with ADHD are more likely than other children to be rejected by their peers (Mrug et al., 2009). Studies that have focused on girls with ADHD have found similar results. Girls with ADHD have fewer friends than do peers without ADHD, or they have no friends at all; they have difficulty maintaining any friendships they do form; and they are more likely to have conflicts with their friends (Blachman & Hinshaw, 2002). These difficulties likely are related to their aggressive behavior, as described in the next section.

### *Behavior Characteristics*

The frequency and severity of behavior problems for students with ADHD vary widely, a fact that you can easily understand by reviewing the diagnostic criteria for the disorder.

research
**NOTE**

When Hosterman, DuPaul, and Jitendra (2008) compared teachers' ratings of the behavior of Caucasian, African-American, and Hispanic students to actual classroom observation data, they found that the teachers were more accurate for the latter two groups of students than the former, thereby contradicting other studies that have found teachers biased in their assessments of minority students.

Students who have the hyperactive–impulsive or combined type of ADHD usually have behavior problems that are immediately apparent to their teachers and other school personnel. Those who have inattentive ADHD may not have many outward behavior symptoms of their disorder, but they may be disruptive in the classroom when they try to find their misplaced materials or need ongoing teacher assistance to stay focused on their work.

Students with ADHD exhibit an array of disruptive behaviors well known to educators. Reis (2002, p. 175) includes these:

- Failure to closely attend to details or making careless mistakes in schoolwork
- Failure to complete schoolwork
- Failure to listen when spoken to directly
- Difficulty organizing tasks and activities
- Avoidance of, dislike of, or reluctance to engage in tasks that require sustained effort, such as schoolwork or homework

Students with ADHD also may have difficulty working alone or in large groups (Zentall, Moon, Hall, & Grskovic, 2001). In one study teachers reported feeling significantly more stressed when teaching students with ADHD, particularly those with behavior problems, than when teaching their other students (Greene, Beszterczey, Katzenstein, Park, & Goring, 2002).

## Comorbidity with Other Disorders

Any discussion of the characteristics of students with ADHD would be incomplete without mention of **comorbidity**, or the simultaneous occurrence of two or more disabilities or disorders. Although estimates vary widely, one study found that approximately 26 percent of students who were identified as having learning disabilities also were diagnosed with ADHD (Forness & Kavale, 2001a). Marcus, the high school student described at the beginning of this chapter, has both a learning disability and ADHD. The number is even higher for students with emotional disabilities: Approximately 43 percent of these students also have ADHD. In addition, approximately 40 percent of students receiving special education services as other health impaired have been diagnosed as having ADHD, and some of these students also have a health impairment in addition to significant ADHD. ADHD also has been studied as comorbid with intellectual disabilities (Hastings et al., 2004), emotional disabilities (Dietz & Montague, 2006), autism, and traumatic brain injury (Slomine et al., 2005).

In addition to comorbidity with disabilities as defined in IDEA, researchers have studied the extent to which ADHD exists with psychiatric disorders listed in the latest edition of the *Diagnostic and Statistical Manual of Mental Disorders* (*DSM-IV-TR*) (National Institute of Mental Health, 2009). Estimates of this type of comorbidity range from 30 to 60 percent (Fowler, 2002; U.S. Department of Education, 2008). Students with ADHD also may have mood disorders such as depression (15 to 38 percent); disruptive behavior disorders, including oppositional defiant disorder (ODD; 40 to 60 percent); and anxiety (23 to 30 percent). (The symptoms of these disorders are presented in Chapter Seven.) These students also may have serious sleep disorders and might be at higher risk for substance abuse (including nicotine, alcohol, and caffeine) (e.g., Biederman, Ball, & Monuteaux, 2008; Zaff, Calkins, Bridges, & Margie, 2002).

These comorbidity statistics have several implications. First, the high rate at which ADHD occurs simultaneously with IDEA disabilities partly explains why so much overlap seems to occur in the characteristics of these groups. Second, the simultaneous occurrence of ADHD with other serious disorders should serve as a caution to educators that interventions that address only the visible symptoms of ADHD may not truly address all the critical areas of student need. Finally, a discussion of comorbidity serves as a reminder that school professionals should stay in close contact with parents and medical personnel regarding students with ADHD.

1. What are additional examples of each of the four types of executive functions? How might each type of executive function affect classroom behavior and academic performance?

2. Think about a child with whom you have interacted who has been diagnosed as having ADHD. Which of the cognitive, academic, social/emotional, and behavior characteristics described in this chapter does that child display? How might these characteristics influence the instructional decisions you would make as this child's teacher?

3. What is *comorbidity*? Why might it be particularly challenging to design effective instruction for a student with ADHD as well as a comorbid disorder? What other dilemmas might an educator face in working with these students?

# Identifying Attention Deficit–Hyperactivity Disorder

Because attention deficit–hyperactivity disorder is primarily a psychiatric rather than an educational disorder, deciding whether a student has ADHD requires close collaboration among physicians, psychiatrists, and other medical personnel, as well as school professionals and parents. The procedures to determine whether the diagnosis can be made medically have been outlined by the American Academy of Pediatrics (2000), and the steps outlined in Chapter Two must be followed to determine whether a student is eligible for services through IDEA. The following is a summary of how both sets of procedures typically are implemented.

## Initial Referral

Some parents will already have discussed their child's behavior with their physician or pediatrician during the child's preschool years, and so some students will already have been diagnosed as having ADHD when they begin school, as was the case for Cedric. However, most referrals occur when children are faced with the structure and need for sustained attention required for success in elementary school. When children encounter difficulty in the school setting, some parents will ask their doctor if their child's behavior might signal ADHD and request that an evaluation for this disorder be completed. General education or special education teachers also may suggest to parents that they discuss their children's behavior with a physician, but because they are not qualified to make a diagnosis, they may not in any way suggest that they suspect the child has ADHD. In addition to primary care or family practice physicians and pediatricians, pediatric neurologists, psychiatrists, and psychologists also may diagnose ADHD.

## Assessment

No single test can reliably indicate whether a student has attention deficit–hyperactivity disorder. Therefore, an assessment for ADHD requires input from medical professionals, parents and family members, and school personnel.

### Medical Assessment

In considering whether a child has ADHD, the physician first tries to eliminate other problems that might have similar symptoms. Thus, routine vision and hearing screening and a thorough physical examination typically are completed (Mercugliano, 1999). The doctor

**myeducationlab**

PEARSON

Go to the Assignments and Activities section of Topic 11: ADHD, in the MyEducationLab for your course and complete the activity entitled "Assessment of Students with Special Needs".

dimensions of
**DIVERSITY**

Schmitz and Velez (2003) found differences in Mexican, Mexican-American, and Puerto Rican mothers' ratings of their children's ADHD symptoms. They concluded that understanding ADHD must occur within a cultural context.

usually asks the parents about the pregnancy and developmental history of the child. In addition, parents are asked questions such as these:

- When did you first notice that your child seemed to have more behavior problems than other children? What types of problems is your child experiencing?
- How is your child doing in school?
- Is there a family history of ADHD, or did anyone in your family experience behavior problems during the school years?
- How does your child get along with other children? Siblings? How easily does your child make friends?
- In what situations do you observe your child experiencing behavior problems? Home? School? Church? Activities such as scouting, dance lessons, or music lessons? In a child care setting?
- What do you find are the most effective means for disciplining your child?
- What are your child's interests? Hobbies? In what areas does your child excel?

*ADHD is diagnosed by a pediatrician or other physician, with input from parents and teachers.*

The intent of such questions is to determine whether the child meets the criteria for ADHD as described in *DSM-IV-TR* and outlined in Figure 6.2. To gain an even better understanding, the physician also may interview the child about his perception of the problems being experienced and what is causing them. The doctor supplements the information obtained from parents and children with input from teachers and other school personnel.

## Continuous Performance Tests

Some professionals who evaluate children for ADHD use **continuous performance tests (CPTs)**, assessment instruments designed to require a student to sustain attention in order to respond correctly to the test items. These instruments usually take advantage of computer technology. For example, the Conners' Continuous Performance Test–II (version 5) (Conners, 2003) requires the student taking it to watch the computer screen for a single letter to appear. If the letter is an *X*, the student does not press the space bar; the student does press the space bar for any other letter. Other similar tests include the Integrated Visual and Auditory Continuous Performance Test + PLUS (IVA+PLUS) (Sanford & Turner, 2006) and the Test of Variables of Attention Continuous Performance Test (TOVA) (Greenburg, 1999). Although continuous performance tests have appeal because they seem to directly assess the key characteristics seen in students with ADHD, to date research has not supported their ability to differentiate between students with ADHD and those without. Moreover, CPTs cannot distinguish students who do not respond quickly because of ADHD from those who are slow at processing because of a learning disability. Given these problems, CPTs generally are not considered appropriate by themselves for making a diagnosis of ADHD, although information from them is sometimes used to supplement other assessment information (American Academy of Pediatrics, 2000).

## Parent Assessment

Whenever children are being evaluated for ADHD, their parents provide critical information to inform medical and education professionals. In addition to questionnaires and interviews that are used to gather general information, parents usually complete a behavior rating scale. Examples of such scales are the Conners' Parent Rating Scale–Revised (CPRS-R) (Conners, 1997b) and the Child Behavior Checklist for Ages 4–18, Parent Form (CBCL/4–18-R) (Achenbach, 1991a).

The American Academy of Pediatrics (2000) has issued policies for pediatricians regarding the diagnosis and treatment of ADHD. The recommendations for treatment include helping families with children who have ADHD link to other families for support, collaborating with school personnel, and using stimulant medication and/or behavior therapy to improve outcomes for children.

### Teacher and School Assessment

After parents and close family members, teachers typically are the most significant adults in children's lives. Children most often are diagnosed with ADHD when they are in elementary school, spending most of each day with one teacher (Kos, Richdale, & Hay, 2006). This teacher provides a valuable perspective on the child's functioning in the school environment and is usually asked to complete a behavior checklist similar to that for parents. Two examples of such a checklist are the Conners' Teacher Rating Scale–Revised (Conners, 1997a) and the Child Behavior Checklist, Teacher's Report Form (Achenbach, 1991b). When doctors receive completed copies of these checklists from both parents and teachers, they not only can use the information as one dimension of the diagnostic process, but they also can judge whether there are significant discrepancies between parents' and teachers' perceptions of the child.

Teachers also may provide other types of information regarding students who might have ADHD, including samples of students' work that illustrate attention to detail, ability to complete work, and ability to follow instructions. Teachers also might contribute anecdotal information that helps describe in detail what students are like while they are at school. Teachers may be asked to collect data about students' behaviors. For example, a teacher might record for a one-hour period how often a student inappropriately left her seat or tally how many times during a week a student had tantrums.

### Additional Considerations for IDEA Eligibility

The information gathered by medical personnel can assist school professionals in making a decision about whether a student with ADHD is eligible for services through IDEA, but additional steps are needed. For example, a psychologist usually administers an individual intelligence test and an individual achievement test—assessments discussed in Chapter Five. Additional information also may be gathered about the student's behavior, often by having a psychologist, counselor, special educator, or other school professional observe the student in the general education classroom. Once these data have been collected, the team meets to continue the special education decision-making process, about which you already have learned.

### ADHD or Gifted

One additional topic should be mentioned in discussing the identification process: Some professionals believe that students who are gifted and talented (a topic addressed in detail in Chapter Fifteen) sometimes are misdiagnosed as having ADHD (e.g., Rinn & Nelson, 2009). In fact, many behaviors associated with ADHD also are associated with giftedness. Examples include poor sustained attention, impulsivity, higher than typical levels of activity and restlessness, and difficulty adhering to rules. However, distinctions do exist: While students with ADHD experience difficulty in attending in nearly all situations, those who are gifted are inattentive only in specific situations, such as when they are bored. Impulsivity characterizes students with ADHD, but for students who are gifted, it often is a signal that good judgment is lagging behind intellectual development. In addition, students with ADHD may not follow rules because of their inability to regulate their behaviors; those who are gifted may deliberately question rules and create their own.

The possibility for misdiagnosing students who are gifted as ADHD illustrates the importance of the assessment process. By observing students in several settings, listening carefully to parent and teacher perceptions of students, and gathering other detailed medical, family history, and achievement information, professionals can accurately identify students' needs and develop options to help them succeed.

### *Eligibility*

Whether a student is determined to have ADHD is a decision made by a pediatrician or family physician. If a student does have ADHD, the doctor discusses with parents the options for treatment, including medication and behavior interventions. The doctor and parents also develop a follow-up plan to monitor the child's progress. The school team decides whether the ADHD is adversely affecting the student's educational performance (U.S.

Stormont (2008) suggests that sticky notes are a versatile tool for helping students with ADHD in the classroom: Have students use them to mark the place in students' books, jot questions, make lists of tasks to do, and write down homework assignments.

## FIGURE 6.4
### Comparing Section 504 and IDEA

| Component | Section 504 | IDEA |
|---|---|---|
| Requirements of the law | · Any school receiving federal financial assistance must provide students covered an education comparable to that provided to other students. | · Students with disabilities must have available a free appropriate public education with special education related services and supplementary aids and services designed to address their individual needs. |
| Individuals protected | · All school-age children who have a physical or mental impairment that substantially limits a major life activity, have a record of such an impairment, or are regarded as having such an impairment. Major life activities include walking, seeing, hearing, speaking, breathing, learning, working, caring for oneself, and performing manual tasks. | · Children age 3 through 21 (or graduation) who have one of the 13 disabilities specified in the law and whose educational performance is adversely affected by the disability. States may also serve infants and toddlers ages birth through 2. |
| Funding | · Does not provide additional funds. IDEA funds may not be used to serve students protected only under Section 504. | · School districts receive additional federal funding for students identified as having disabilities |
| Evaluations | · Parent notice (but not consent) is required for initial evaluation. Requires periodic reevaluations and reevaluation before a significant change in placement. Evaluation must occur at no expense to parents. | · Parent consent required before initial evaluation. Reevaluation required at least every three years. Provision for independent evaluations. Evaluation must occur at no expense to parents. |
| Placement | · Placement is general education classroom with supports in place to facilitate access to the educational experience. Parent participation not mentioned (but strongly advised). | · Placement must be in the least restrictive environment (LRE), which is most often the general education setting but also could be a parttime or fulltime separate special education classroom, separate school, or specialized setting (e.g., residential, hospital). Parent participation required. |
| Documentation | · Section 504 plan that specifies accommodations to be provided and related details. | · Individualized education program (IEP) with components specified in the law. |
| Services | · Eliminates barriers that would prevent a student from full participation in programs and services available to all students. | · Special education, related services, and supplementary aids and services to enable student participation in all the programs and services as well as extracurricular activities (e.g., field trips) available to all students |
| Due process | · Impartial hearing must be conducted when disagreements occur and cannot be resolved. Requires notice, the right to inspect records, the right to participate in a hearing and to be represented by counsel, and a review procedure. Complaints are filed with the Office of Civil Rights. | · Impartial hearing must be conducted when disagreements occur and cannot be resolved and mediation and conflict resolution are not successful. Due process procedures outlined in the law. Complaints are filed with the state. |
| Enforcement | · U.S. Office for Civil Rights, U.S. Department of Education. | · Office of Special Education and Rehabilitative Services promulgates IDEA regulations, U.S. Department of Education |

Department of Education, 2008). If they determine this to be the case, they have the option of identifying the student as eligible for IDEA services as other health impaired (OHI). Not all students with ADHD are eligible, however. Many students with ADHD who receive medication can be successful in school when minor accommodations are made in their general education classrooms. Such students may be eligible for a Section 504 plan that outlines the needed classroom supports but does not include special education services. A comparison of IDEA and Section 504 requirements is outlined in Figure 6.4. A third option is possible as well. As you learned earlier in this chapter, a significant number of students assessed for

ADHD are found also to have learning, emotional, or other disabilities. These students are eligible for IDEA services because of their other disabilities, regardless of whether their ADHD is determined to be a disability.

## REVIEW · REFLECT · DISCUSS

1. Consider two students with ADHD. A team decides that one should be served as other health impaired but the other should have a Section 504 plan. What differences can you identify in terms of the needs that led to these different decisions and the types of support each student would receive? Use information from both Chapter Two and this chapter in developing your response.

2. What do you think are the ethical dilemmas teachers face when parents ask them whether their child has ADHD? How do you think teachers should respond?

## Educating Students with Attention Deficit–Hyperactivity Disorder

How students with ADHD receive their education depends on many variables, including when they are diagnosed, whether they are eligible for special education services, and whether they have other disabilities.

### Early Childhood

Although most students with ADHD are diagnosed after they enter elementary school, children as young as two years of age have been identified as having this disorder (Harvey, Youngwirth, & Thakar, 2009). Considerable difficulty exists in making an accurate diagnosis at an early age because formal assessment instruments generally are not designed for very young children, development may vary considerably among children, and some of the behaviors associated with ADHD may be appropriate in toddlers and preschoolers. Very young children who are diagnosed as having ADHD often have sleep problems, difficulty bonding, difficulty taking turns or sharing, more accidents than would be expected, an inability to remain still for even a few minutes, difficulty following directions, repeated instances of inappropriately intruding into others' space, and forgetfulness (Stormont & Stebbins, 2005).

For children who exhibit these symptoms to an excessive degree and who have been diagnosed with ADHD, early intervention is crucial. Young children with ADHD are at risk, like Cedric, for being expelled from daycare and preschool settings, the places they are most likely to receive their education prior to kindergarten. Further, without early intervention their behaviors are likely to continue and escalate as they move to elementary school (Deutscher & Fewell, 2005; McGoey, Eckert, & DuPaul, 2002). Few studies of intervention effectiveness have been completed with young children. McGoey and her colleagues (McGoey et al., 2002) completed a literature review on this topic and found that although medication, parent training, and behavior interventions all were effective, so few studies have been completed that the results must be viewed with great caution. These researchers recommended that preschool classrooms provide a highly structured environment emphasizing consistent and immediate feedback to young children accompanied by clear, age-appropriate rewards (e.g., the opportunity to play with a particular toy). However, the best combination of interventions has yet to be determined for young children with ADHD.

### Elementary and Secondary School Services

School-age students with ADHD receive their education based on their needs. Because ADHD is not by itself a disability in IDEA, the federal government does not gather and publish information regarding the locations where these students are educated. Even if students are eligible as other health impaired (OHI), because this disability category includes children with other disabilities it is not possible to identify where students with ADHD receive their education using data from this disability group. Finally, students who have both ADHD and a learning or emotional disability are served in accordance with the least restrictive environment provision of IDEA, but the application of this dimension of the law for these students cannot be discerned from the annual reports issued about IDEA implementation.

Given the nature of ADHD, the fact that many students with ADHD receive accommodations through Section 504 plans, and the emphasis on inclusive practices for students with learning and emotional disabilities (who may also have ADHD), you can probably safely assume that most students with ADHD receive their education in a general education classroom (U.S. Department of Education, 2008). This means that general education teachers, with support from special education teachers and other school professionals, must focus their efforts on collaborating with parents to find effective means for helping students with ADHD to compensate for their special needs in order to succeed in their schoolwork (Rogers, Wiener, Marton, & Tannock, 2009).

## Transition and Adulthood

Although professionals used to believe that ADHD was a disorder that most students outgrew by adolescence, this view is no longer considered accurate (Evans, Serpell, Schultz, & Pastor, 2007; Harty, Miller, Newcorn, & Halperin, 2009). In fact, up to 80 percent of students diagnosed with ADHD during elementary school or before continue to have symptoms in their teenage years, and 66 percent of these students continue to have the disorder in adulthood (Kessler et al., 2006). Older students with ADHD show a decline in hyperactivity and inattention, but so do students who do not have ADHD, and so the gaps between the two groups remain.

A description of young adults with ADHD must be considered tentative because extensive research on the impact of this disorder after the school years has been conducted only recently (Houghton, 2006). Many adults with ADHD are disorganized and impulsive and have poor work skills. They tend to be disorderly and impatient and may become bored easily. They often lose their belongings, and they may have difficulty forming relationships. Many adults with ADHD change jobs frequently and express dissatisfaction with their jobs (Painter, Prevatt, & Welles, 2008; Wasserstein, Wasserstein, & Wolf, 2001). However, many others complete college degrees or programs at technical schools (Wirt et al., 2003), find employment in occupations where their characteristics do not leave them at a disadvantage (e.g., a doctor in an emergency room; a CEO with a skillful administrative assistant), and learn to compensate for their special needs (Reitman, 2003).

Whether students with ADHD successfully transition into postschool options can depend heavily on their understanding of their disorder, their skills for advocating for themselves, the support they receive during high school, and their overall ability to cope with their symptoms. Having a supportive family is also crucial (Robin, 1998). Finally, adults with ADHD have a better chance of being satisfied with their lives if they have received supports for any comorbid conditions and, for many, if they take some type of medication (Davidson, 2008).

research
**NOTE**

By teaching students social skills, addressing organizational skills, and responding constructively to inappropriate behaviors, educators, working closely with counselors and families, can help middle school students with ADHD experience success (Evans et al., 2006).

## REVIEW · REFLECT · DISCUSS

1. Because students with ADHD are educated in general education settings, do you think that special education teachers have any responsibility to assist them or their teachers? If not, why? If so, how?

2. Do you know someone in your university or college who has ADHD? If so, what is that person's perspective of his or her school experiences? What types of support services does this individual access in order to succeed in higher education?

# Recommended Educational Practices for Students with Attention Deficit–Hyperactivity Disorder

Go to the Assignments and Activities section of Topic 11: ADHD, in the MyEducationLab for your course and complete the activity entitled "Instructional Strategies for Students with ADHD".

Recent progress in understanding the causes of ADHD, coupled with research on treatment effectiveness, provides a wealth of information for special educators and other school professionals who work with students with this disorder (Dawson, 2007). Perhaps the most comprehensive study of interventions for students with ADHD is the Multimodal Treatment Study of Children with ADHD (MTA), a federally funded research project conducted by eighteen leading experts in the field of ADHD (National Institute of Mental Health, 2002). The following description of effective interventions draws heavily from that project and follow-up reports on the students who participated (Miranda, Jarque, & Tárraga, 2006).

## Medication

Although not universally supported, according to the MTA and related research (e.g., Davidson, 2008) the most clearly effective, short-term intervention for students with ADHD is medication. As you begin to learn about this information, keep the following points in mind:

- *The use of medication is controversial.* Some parents and professionals believe that too many students are declared to have ADHD and given medication as a sort of quick fix for their challenging behaviors at school and at home (Advokat, 2009; Lloyd, Cohen, & Stead, 2006). In contrast, data from the MTA study suggest that medication for this group of students can be highly effective in controlling symptoms (Biederman, 2003), although recent reports acknowledge that the appeal of medication diminishes over time (National Institute of Mental Health, 2009) and many families decide to discontinue its use. Some parents also have expressed concern about the side effects of medication (e.g., loss of appetite) and the potential for later substance abuse. Researchers have found, though, that side effects related to growth tend to be mild and seldom pose serious problems if medication is properly matched to the child and monitored closely (Zachor, Roberts, Hodgens, Isaacs, & Merrick, 2006). Concerning substance abuse, one study found that students with ADHD who took medication were at less risk for later substance abuse than similar students who had not taken medication (Biederman, Wilens, Mick, Spencer, & Faraone, 1999), although others have noted that when ADHD exists with other disorders (such as learning disabilities or emotional disabilities), risk for substance abuse may increase (e.g., Latimer, Ernst, & Hennessey, 2004). Children who take medication have a slight risk of other complications, and medications for ADHD contain warnings concerning these risks (National Institute of Mental Health, 2008).

- *The decision to prescribe medication only indirectly involves school professionals.* Clearly, school personnel observe their students daily and form opinions about the seriousness of their behaviors and what might help them, but school personnel *do not* have the expertise to recommend to parents that medication be considered. As you learned earlier in this chapter, pediatricians and other medical personnel usually ask for educators' input as they evaluate a student for ADHD, and they also may request that teachers and other school personnel periodically report on the apparent effects of medication on a student's school performance. In fact, educators are explicitly prohibited from directly or indirectly telling parents that a student should take medication for ADHD.

- *Medication is helpful in ameliorating the symptoms of ADHD in 70 to 80 percent of the students for whom it is prescribed.* Slightly more than half of all students diagnosed as having ADHD take some type of medication, the most common age range for this being between nine and twelve years (Centers for Disease Control and Prevention, 2009). Taking medication usually reduces significantly the amount of daydreaming or disruptive behaviors that students display. However, it is critical to recognize that students taking medication do not automatically improve in terms of academic achievement. Additional interventions, including educational and behavior strategies such as those already described, usually are needed, thus making the expertise of teachers and other educators a

**fyi**

Many alternative treatments have been proposed for ADHD. These include herbal formulas, vitamin regimens, special diets, and biofeedback. To date, none of these treatments has been demonstrated through research to be widely effective.

*Parents often struggle to decide whether medication is an appropriate intervention for their child with ADHD.*

critical companion to medication as an intervention. Further, the MTA study demonstrated that when systematic behavior interventions were used in conjunction with medication, lower doses of medication were found to be effective (Forness & Kavale, 2001a; Pelham et al., 2000).

Three different types of medication are commonly used to reduce the symptoms of ADHD. Approximately 80 percent of students for whom medication is prescribed take **stimulant medication** (Kollins, Barkley, & DuPaul, 2001), including Ritalin, a medication first introduced for students with ADHD in 1956 (Eli Lilly, 2003). Other stimulant medications include these trade names: Dexedrine, Cylert, Adderall, and Focalin. Antidepressants and antihypertensives account for an additional 17.2 percent of the medication prescribed. Antidepressant medications include Norpramin, Tofranil, Prozac, and Zoloft. Antihypertensive medications, also used to lower blood pressure, include Clonidine and Tenex. The chart in Figure 6.5 provides additional details about the names, side effects, benefits, and precautions concerning these and other medications students with ADHD may be taking. Kollins and his colleagues (2001) have suggested several factors to examine when medication is considered:

- The child's age
- Prior attempts at other interventions and their impact on the behaviors of concern
- Parent and child attitudes toward using medication
- Presence in the household of substance abusers (stimulant medications are controlled substances)
- Severity of symptoms
- Availability of adults in the household to supervise use of medications, ensuring that medications are taken regularly and as prescribed
- Participation in sports or the likelihood of enrollment in the military (in some cases, students can be banned from either of these activities if they are taking medication)

The controversy over the appropriateness of using medication for treating students with ADHD probably will continue for the foreseeable future (Swanson et al., 2008) as researchers learn more about the causes and preferred treatments for this disorder. For ex-

## FIGURE 6.5
## Medications Prescribed for Students with ADHD

| Drug | Common Side Effects | Duration of Behavioral Effects | Pros | Precautions |
|---|---|---|---|---|
| **Concerta** (methylphenidate) | Insomnia, decreased appetite, weight loss, headache, irritability, stomachache | About 12 hours | Works quickly, lasts for 12 hours. No need for second dose during school or third after-school dosing | Use cautiously in patients with marked anxiety, motor tics, or family history of Tourette syndrome |
| **Ritalin** (methylphenidate) | Insomnia, decreased appetite, weight loss, headache, irritability, stomachache | About 3 to 4 hours | Works quickly (within 30 to 60 minutes); effective in 70 percent of patients; good safety record | Use cautiously in patients with marked anxiety, motor tics, or family history of Tourette syndrome |
| **Ritalin-SR** (methylphenidate) | Insomnia, decreased appetite, weight loss, headache, irritability, stomachache | About 7 hours | Particularly useful for adolescents with ADHD to avoid noontime dose; good safety record | Slow onset of action (1 to 2 hours); use cautiously in patients with marked anxiety, motor tics, or family history of Tourette syndrome |
| **Focalin** (dextro-methylphenidate) | Insomnia, decreased appetite, weight loss, headache, irritability, stomachache | About 4 to 5 hours | Works quickly; only half the dose of Ritalin needed | Use cautiously with patients who cannot take Ritalin, including those with anxiety, motor tics, or family history of Tourette syndrome |
| **Dexedrine** (dextroamphetamine) | Insomnia, decreased appetite, weight loss, headache, irritability, stomachache | About 3 to 5 hours (tablet); about 7 to 10 hours (spansule) | Works quickly (within 30 to 60 minutes); may avoid noontime dose in spansule form; good safety record | Use cautiously in patients with marked anxiety, motor tics, or family history of Tourette syndrome |
| **Adderall** (mixed salts of a single-entity amphetamine product) | Insomnia, decreased appetite, weight loss, headache, irritability, stomachache | About 3 to 6 hours | Works quickly (within 30 to 60 minutes); may last somewhat longer than other standard stimulants | Use cautiously in patients with marked anxiety, motor tics, or family history of Tourette syndrome |
| **Adderall XR** (mixed salts of a single-entity amphetamine product) | Insomnia, decreased appetite, weight loss, headache, irritability, stomachache | About 12 hours | Works quickly (within 30 to 60 minutes); avoid needing a noontime or afternoon dose | Use cautiously in patients with marked anxiety, motor tics, or family history of Tourette syndrome |
| **Tofranil** (imipramine, hydrochloride) **Norpramin** (desipramine, hydrochloride) | Dry mouth, decreased appetite, headache, stomachache, dizziness, constipation, mild tachycardia, tremor | 12 to 24 hours | Helpful for ADHD patients with comorbid depression or anxiety; lasts throughout day | May take 2 to 4 weeks for clinical response; to detect preexisting cardiac conduction defect, a baseline ECG may be recommended; discontinue gradually |
| **Metadate CD** (methylphenidate) | Insomnia, decreased appetite, weight loss, headache, irritability, stomachache | About 8 to 10 hours | Particularly useful for adolescents and adults to avoid needing a noontime dose; good safety record | Use cautiously in patients with marked anxiety, motor tics, or family history of Tourette syndrome |
| **Catapres** (clonidine, hydrochloride) | Sleepiness, hypotension, headache, dizziness, stomachache, nausea, dry mouth, localized skin reaction with patch | 3 to 6 hours (oral form); 5 days (skin patch) | Helpful for ADHD patients with comorbid tic disorder or severe hyperactivity and/or aggression | Sudden discontinuation could result in rebound hypertension; to avoid daytime tiredness, starting dose given at bedtime and increased slowly |
| **Strattera** (atomoxetine HCl) | Decreased appetite, insomnia, nausea and vomiting, fatigue, dizziness, mood swings | About 8 to 10 hours | Not a controlled substance; works quickly (1 to 2 hours) | Long-term effects for children are not yet known; some indication of increased suicidal thinking; not indicated for patients with heart problems, liver problems, or high blood pressure |

Sources: Parker, H. C. (2003, April 3). *Medication chart to treat attention deficit disorders*. Retrieved May 1, 2003, from www.ldonline.org/ld_indepth/add_adhd/add_medication_chart.html; Healthplace.com. (2002, November). *Atomoxetine HCl*. Retrieved June 15, 2003, from http://healthplace.com/medications/strattera.htm; Novartis Pharmaceuticals US. (2001, November 15). *FDA grants marketing approval for Focalin, The first chemically advanced form of Ritalin for ADHD—New drug for ADHD contains only the effective isomer of Ritalin*. Retrieved July 3, 2003, from www.pharma.us.novartis.com/newsroom/pressReleases/releaseDetail.jsp?PRID=165. Novartis Pharmaceutical material used with permission.

## Teacher Knowledge About Medication and Students with ADHD

Nearly all teachers will, at some point, teach students who are identified as having ADHD, and so teachers need to be knowledgeable about the disorder and the effects of medication on students.

Here is the true-false quiz that 59 general education and 86 special education teachers were given. The teachers taught in elementary, middle, and high schools, and they averaged 16.5 years of experience. Take the quiz to check your own knowledge concerning ADHD and medication, and then continue reading to see how the teachers performed.

_____ 1. ADHD is the most commonly diagnosed psychiatric disorder of childhood.

_____ 2. Data indicate that ADHD is caused by a brain malfunction.

_____ 3. ADHD symptoms (e.g., fidgeting, not following through on instructions, being easily distracted) may be caused by academic deficits.

_____ 4. Stress and conflict in the student's home life can cause ADHD symptoms.

_____ 5. Diagnosis of ADHD can be confirmed if stimulant medication improves the child's attention.

_____ 6. Stimulant medication use may decrease the physical growth rate (e.g., height) of students.

_____ 7. Stimulant medication use may produce tics in students.

_____ 8. Adderall, Ritalin, and Dexedrine have abuse potential similar to Demerol, cocaine, and morphine.

_____ 9. The long-term side effects of stimulant medications are well understood.

_____ 10. Over time, stimulant medication loses its effectiveness.

_____ 11. While on stimulant medication, students exhibit similar amounts of problem behaviors as their normally developing peers.

_____ 12. Short-term studies show that stimulant medication improves the behaviors associated with ADHD.

_____ 13. Studies show that stimulant medication has a positive effect on academic achievement in the long run.

The researchers who gave teachers this quiz were somewhat surprised by the results. Only 5 of the 13 quiz items were answered correctly by more than half of the general education and special education teachers. As you can see if you look at the following responses, the teachers knew about long-term effects of medication but not about potential risks. They also misunderstood the fact that the effect of medication on behavior is a signal that the ADHD diagnosis was correct; in fact, this medication improves the behavior of other students as well.

### Teachers' Responses

Percentage of teachers answering the item correctly (correct response):

1. 58 (true)
2. 10 (false)
3. 63 (true)
4. 71 (true)
5. 33 (false)
6. 38 (true)
7. 45 (true)
8. 46 (true)
9. 67 (false)
10. 46 (true)
11. 27 (false)
12. 86 (true)
13. 6 (false)

_Source:_ Snider, V. E., Busch, T., & Arrowood, L. (2003). Teacher knowledge of stimulant medication and ADHD. _Remedial and Special Education, 24,_ 46–56. Copyright © 2003 by Pro-Ed, Inc. Reprinted by permission of SAGE Publications.

---

Go to the Building Teaching Skills and Dispositions section of Topic 11: ADHD, in the MyEducationLab for your course and complete the activity entitled "Using Self-Regulation Strategies".

ample, a relatively new medication—atomoxetine (trade name, Strattera)—currently is receiving considerable attention, and its use has both advantages and drawbacks. It is not a stimulant and thus does not have some of the potentially negative side effects of stimulant medications. However, it may lead to an increase in suicidal thoughts. As an educator, your responsibility is to have an accurate understanding of what medication can and cannot accomplish (Snider, Busch, & Arrowood, 2003). Teachers must recognize their roles in enhancing the success of students taking medication for ADHD by designing effective instruction for them and collaborating with parents in monitoring students' progress and any problems that arise when medication has been prescribed.

Are you prepared to work with students with ADHD and to understand how their medication can affect their learning and behavior? If so, take the quiz in the Professional Edge feature and discuss your answers with your classmates.

### Parent and Professional Education

In addition to medication, researchers have found that effectively educating students with ADHD requires that their parents and teachers understand the disorder and develop effective strategies for responding to the symptoms children are likely to display (Chako, Wymbs, & Flammer-Rivera, 2008; Wagner & McNeil, 2008).

## Parent Education

Although parent and student education programs are not sufficient by themselves to address the symptoms of ADHD, in conjunction with other interventions they can help a family to better understand and respond to the child's special needs. Regularly scheduled group parent education sessions should first address behavior management skills, including how to set consistent expectations and limits, create an effective discipline system that includes rewards and negative consequences, develop a strategy to address serious behavior problems, and identify the child's strengths to build positive self-esteem. In addition, parents need to learn techniques for stress and anger management to use with their child and in other aspects of their lives, strategies for assisting their child in making and keeping friends, and skills for working with school personnel on behalf of their child (Wells et al., 2000). Other topics for parent education include up-to-date information about ADHD and research-supported interventions, appropriate evaluation and treatment procedures, and advocacy skills, including knowledge of IDEA and Section 504 (Chako et al., 2008).

## Professional Education

Although many teachers and other educators have accurate general knowledge about students with attention deficit–hyperactivity disorder, they also have many misconceptions (Kos et al., 2006). They generally know the classic symptoms of ADHD but may not realize that students with ADHD often can perform better in a novel situation than in a familiar one or that students may respond in a more compliant way to their father's directions when compared to their mother's. Similarly, teachers often know more about the diagnosis and characteristics of ADHD than about effective interventions (West, Taylor, Houghton, & Hudyma, 2005). Staff development sessions can increase professionals' knowledge of these students and how to reach them (Jones & Chronis-Tuscano, 2008). The researchers in the MTA study found that it also was beneficial to assist the teachers in developing effective home-school communication systems, establishing appropriate classroom rules and behavior management systems, responding quietly to student behavior disruptions or ignoring them when possible, and differentiating instruction (Wells et al., 2000).

## *Environmental Supports*

Most students with ADHD are fully capable of learning what is being taught in their classrooms. However, they need assistance to access that learning and to complete it. One way for professionals to provide that assistance is through environmental supports—that is, the arrangement of the learning setting so that it supports students with attention disorders. Here are some examples of environmental supports for students with ADHD:

1. The classroom physical space should be organized and free of distractions. Students should be able to work without looking at or bumping into classmates. In a crowded classroom the use of desk carrels may help. A desk carrel is a three-sided piece of cardboard, about 15 inches in height, that can be placed on a student's desk to shield her from other classroom activity. Desk carrels can be purchased or made.

2. Physical space considerations also should include the number and intrusiveness of decorations. Although decorations are not usually a problem in middle school and high school, they may be in elementary school. Some elementary teachers pride themselves on having brightly colored bulletin boards and intricate art projects suspended from the classroom ceiling. Such displays should be kept out of the direct line of sight of students with ADHD.

3. In Chapter One you learned about the importance of posting clear classroom rules and discussing expectations for students. This environmental support is particularly important for students with ADHD.

4. Teachers should post and follow classroom routines. If a change in the schedule is necessary, a student with ADHD should be warned of the change. The teacher should then plan to stay close to the student with ADHD because even with a warning, the change may cause the student to have behavior difficulties.

Color can be an effective tool for helping students to focus their attention. Try highlighting keywords on printed materials in yellow or green, and consider using several colors when writing on a whiteboard or printing transparencies.

5.  Another type of environmental support concerns pacing of instruction. Teachers help students with ADHD when they mix difficult or tedious tasks with those that are more stimulating. Teachers also can build into their instruction opportunities for student movement. For example, in secondary classrooms, students who think they know an answer can be told to stand or to turn around in their seats. Younger students can transition between activities by clapping to music, marching around the classroom, or playing Simon Says.

Environmental supports are very much part of universal design for learning. They do not harm any students, they enhance learning for many of them, and they can be incorporated into classroom procedures and activities at the elementary, middle, and high school levels.

## Behavior Interventions

Because of problems with behavior inhibition, students with ADHD may display challenging behaviors. As you might expect, a cornerstone of effective education practices for these students is systematic behavior intervention.

Many of the behavior interventions that you learn to assist students with disabilities can be implemented for students with ADHD (Wells et al., 2000). For example, in Chapter Five you learned about self-management as a positive behavior support for students with learning disabilities. Many students with ADHD can be taught to use this strategy as a way of reducing inappropriate behavior, such as calling out answers, and increasing appropriate behavior, such as working on assignments until they are completed. The following sections provide a few additional examples of behavior interventions (Jones & Chronis-Tuscano, 2008; Pfifner, Barkley, & DuPaul, 2006).

### Rewards

Providing rewards for appropriate behaviors is a common behavior intervention. In one study (Wells et al., 2000), these common behaviors were identified as important for students: getting started; interacting with others in a polite way; following classroom rules, including those about being quiet and remaining seated; completing assigned work; stopping when directed to prepare for the next activity or class; and following directions. For each student, a small subset of these behaviors was selected. Students were rewarded with points or tokens for performing the identified behaviors. They could then trade in their points or tokens for rewards. Over time, students had to display more correct behaviors for longer periods of time in order to earn rewards. Remember that if you use rewards, you should use them in combination with praise, and you should give them for behaviors that help students (e.g., completing work) instead of only for compliance (e.g., not getting out of their seats).

### Low-Involvement Strategies

For some students with ADHD, if you can intervene to stop an inappropriate behavior when it is minor or just beginning, you can avoid the need for more intense interventions. For example, if Calvin is beginning to talk to a classmate when there should be silence, making eye contact with him may cause him to stop speaking. If that is not effective, proximity control might work: Physically move toward Calvin and stand near his desk or table, placing your hand on his shoulder if necessary to gain his attention. For a few students, you may have private signals. If Calvin is getting too loud in a group discussion, two taps on his desk may serve as a reminder to use an "indoor" voice. Finally, if Calvin is struggling, you might create a break for him by asking him to help you with a chore. Can you think of similar low-involvement behavior strategies that might help students such as Calvin with ADHD? Although these low-involvement strategies may not be effective for all students, they can help reduce the amount of time you spend addressing student behavior, leaving more time for teaching and student learning.

### Token Economy

Another behavior intervention that can assist students with ADHD and other behavior disorders is a token economy. Some students enjoy participating in this type of behavior

## Using a Token Economy

A token economy is an in-class system for rewarding students for appropriate behavior. Here are the steps for creating a token economy, whether in a general education or a special education setting:

1. *Identify the behaviors for which students can earn credit.* You might select completing and turning in work, keeping hands to oneself, talking in a classroom voice, bringing to class all needed (and specified) learning supplies, returning homework, or exhibiting other behavior that can be clearly observed. Students can be involved in deciding what behavior(s) to include.

2. *Decide on the classroom "currency."* You could use points, punches on a card, X's on a recording sheet, poker chips or other tokens, play money, or any other system. In choosing a currency, keep in mind that you need to efficiently award it and monitor its use.

3. *Assign a value to each target behavior.* Simple behaviors should have a lower value. More difficult behaviors should have a higher value. In a very simple system, you would assign the same value (for example, one point) for each target behavior on a daily basis.

4. *Decide on the privileges or rewards students can earn.* Having variety in the possible "purchases" students can make helps maintain interest in the system (e.g., make-your-own-homework-assignment privilege; lunch with the teacher). Include on the reward list at least one item that costs the minimum amount of currency a student might earn (for example, one point) so that all students have the opportunity to participate in the economy.

5. *Assign purchase "prices" to the privileges and rewards.* In general, if a reward is readily available and not limited in quantity, its purchase price should be lower (e.g., sticker). Items that are tangible (and perhaps literally cost more), limited in supply, or time consuming should have a higher cost (e.g., lunch with a friend and the teacher).

6. *Explain the economy to students.* Demonstrate the economy with several examples to ensure that students understand it. You might give your system a name. For example, you could call it *Cougar Cash* or *Bulldog Bucks,* reflecting the name of the school mascot. When the economy is new, student participation should be carefully monitored to check that students are earning and receiving token and spending them as intended.

7. *Establish a systematic way for students to exchange their currency for privileges or rewards.* In most classrooms, it is effective to allow students to use their currency once a week or once every two weeks on a particular day. By having a consistent time and a system for the exchange, you avoid a constant stream of student requests for privileges or rewards and the aggravation of the constant monitoring this would require.

Keep token economies simple for young students and more complex for older students, and let students help select the rewards and assign values for them. You also may need to adjust the behaviors being targeted and the rewards being offered as time passes.

Source: Friend, M., & Bursuck, W. (2009). *Including students with special needs: A practical guide for classroom teachers* (5th ed., pp. 447–449). Copyright © 2009 by Pearson Education, Inc. Reprinted with permission of Pearson Education, Inc.

*Students with ADHD thrive when instruction is structured and brisk with many opportunities for active participation; otherwise, students may lose focus and display behavior problems.*

## Teaching to Help Students with ADHD Succeed

Universal design for learning (UDL) indicates that educators should anticipate the needs of all their students as they plan instruction. The following principles can guide you in developing effective teaching strategies for students with ADHD:

- Use more rewards for students with ADHD than may be necessary for other students. If consequences are necessary because of inappropriate behavior, they should occur immediately.

- Change the rewards used for students with ADHD more frequently than those for other students. For example, let students select a reward from a menu that includes eight or ten choices.

- Plan ahead. Especially when transitions are about to occur or on days when the schedule is disrupted, remind students of changes, ask them to review rules or procedures, and prompt them to recall rewards and consequences for classroom behavior.

- Students with ADHD often need more external cues to help them regulate their behavior. Reminders, pictures, signals, and other approaches are helpful.

- Any intervention that addresses behavior needs to be continued only if data suggest it is effective; most interventions should be modified as time goes by to sustain their usefulness.

- During instruction, use brief periods of large-group instruction characterized by a businesslike tone and fairly rapid pace. Change activities relatively often, alternating between those that are likely to require higher and lower levels of attention.

As you think about these principles, how might they affect how you manage your classroom? Which of the principles might be beneficial for nearly all learners with special needs? Which seem unique to students with ADHD? Think about what challenges might occur in using these principles and how you could overcome them.

*Source:* Pfiffner, L. J., Barkley, R. A., & DuPaul, G. J. (2006). Treatment of ADHD in school settings. In R. A. Barkley (Ed.), *Attention-deficit hyperactivity disorder: A handbook for diagnosis and treatment* (3rd ed.). New York: Guilford Press.

management program because it involves all the students in the class. Others are likely to improve their behavior because of the positive peer pressure the system can foster. In a token system, you distribute to students physical tokens (e.g., stickers, poker chips, craft sticks) or points for appropriate behavior. The tokens can be redeemed for rewards that are "priced" based on their popularity. You can learn how to create such a classwide reward system by reviewing the Positive Behavior Supports feature.

The examples presented here illustrate only a few of the many strategies available to special educators, general education teachers, and others who work with students with ADHD. You will learn about other behavior interventions that also are effective for students with ADHD in the Chapter Seven discussion of students with emotional disabilities.

### Instructional Interventions

Instructional interventions are likely to be effective with many students with ADHD (Barkley, 2007; Trout, Lienemann, Reid, & Epstein, 2007), and they should be designed to provide structure, quick pace, and variety. Several examples are provided in the Instruction in Action feature. Here are several more:

- *When giving directions, be sure the instructions follow the three Cs: clear, concise, and complete.* After introducing the activity, say, "Take out one sheet of paper. Put on the heading. Write three sentences to describe the main character's feelings." Avoid saying things such as "OK. Let's get going. Take out some paper—does everyone have paper? Regular paper . . . no, regular with the holes punched. Got it? OK. Now put the heading on your paper, you know, name. . . . No, don't number your paper. Not for this. It's really nice outside— if we get finished early we might end class out on the benches."

- *When giving directions, have students repeat the directions back to you.* Doing this will ensure that everyone hears the directions twice, and more students will be likely to remember them.

- *When older students have a lengthy or complex assignment, break the assignment into several short tasks.* Consider giving students a deadline for each of the segments to help them stay organized.

- *Use as much active responding during instruction as possible.* For example, use a strategy called "One Say, All Say": When one student gives a correct response, have all the students repeat it. If the student's response is not correct, call on other students until the correct response is given and then have classmates repeat it. What other ideas do you have for increasing students' active responding during instruction?

Are you looking for additional ideas for working with students with ADHD? In the Speaking from Experience feature on page 193, Kelly Stalcup, an experienced special educator, shares her favorite simple strategies.

## REVIEW · REFLECT · DISCUSS

1. Many educators have a limited understanding of the variety of medications available for students with ADHD, their effects on students, and their side effects. What are your responsibilities as a teacher related to knowing about student ADHD medication? How might such knowledge influence how you interact with students with ADHD?

2. Among the various types of interventions that can help students with ADHD, which do you consider most important? Why? What difference do you see in interventions for students with learning disabilities and those with ADHD?

# What Are the Perspectives of Parents and Families?

School professionals need to work effectively with parents on many issues related to students with ADHD. These include participating in assessment, coordinating interventions between school and medical professionals, monitoring medication (both its effect and whether it is being taken as prescribed), planning and implementing any needed behavior strategies, and managing homework.

## Parenting Children with ADHD

Being the parent of a child with ADHD can be exhausting and extraordinarily stressful (Wymbs et al., 2008). Even when these children are very young, they may not sleep as long or as often as other children, they may seem to move without stopping, and their behaviors may seem unfocused. One set of parents described their daughter's preschool escapades as including climbing into the cupboards over the kitchen counters, dangling from a shower curtain rod, and hiding in the oven during a game of Hide and Seek (McCluskey & McCluskey, 1999). As children with ADHD grow older, the problems do not necessarily end. Children's disruptive or inattentive behaviors may worsen with increased freedom (Evans, Sibley, & Serpell, 2009). Parents may be faced with decisions about whether to use medication to treat their children, and they need to build positive relationships with the teachers and other school personnel educating their children.

Parents of children with ADHD also face the same dilemmas as those whose children have other special needs, and so they may experience phases of anger, denial, grief, and adjustment (Colson & Brandt, 2000). In addition, they have to deal with the reactions of family members such as grandparents, as well as those of neighbors. These parents may at times also feel like they are referees between the child with ADHD and siblings.

At school, parents may face an array of challenges. In one study, parents of students with ADHD reported that their children were from three to seven times more likely than other children to be receiving special education, to have been expelled or suspended, and to have repeated a grade (LeFever, Villers, Morrow, & Vaughn, 2002). Not surprisingly, these parents may come to view their children as being at high risk for school failure.

## Supporting Students by Supporting Parents

General education teachers and other school professionals can take many practical steps to enhance their interactions with parents of students with ADHD. Here are several points to keep in mind to foster collaboration (Fad, 1998):

1. *Be realistic in your expectations of parents.* If a parent is struggling to keep a family together because of a child's disruptive behavior, suggesting complex interventions probably will not work. Instead, try suggesting only one or two simple ideas that can be implemented easily.

2. *Encourage the parent to be a good role model for the student.* If you can compliment the parent on keeping a sense of humor, on responding calmly to the child, or on other positive behaviors, you may encourage the parent to keep using those helpful approaches.

3. *Help parents to be realistic in their expectations for their child.* Although parents certainly understand their children better than educators do, you can suggest limiting the amount of time students should spend on homework. Also be sure to tell parents about their children's successes.

4. *Make related resources available to parents.* Although school professionals do not identify students as ADHD, once a child has been diagnosed parents may seek information, and educators can help them meet that need. By keeping a list of websites, contact information for local support groups, and copies of brochures and other information created in your school district, you can empower parents to find answers to their questions and concerns.

## REVIEW · REFLECT · DISCUSS

1. Review the information in this chapter concerning parents' perspectives of ADHD and the information on cultural diversity in Chapter Three. How might cultural differences influence how family members respond to their child with ADHD and affect their preferences for different types of interventions?

2. If a parent asked you for advice concerning how to help a child with ADHD, what would you say?

# Trends and Issues Affecting the ADHD Field

The field of ADHD has evolved very rapidly, particularly during the past decade. Educators and parents alike have difficulty keeping up with the changes in thinking about the causes, prevalence, and interventions for students with this disorder. Three significant issues to consider are (1) the identification of very young children as having ADHD and appropriate treatment for them, (2) the identification and treatment of individuals with ADHD in high school and adulthood, and (3) the status of knowledge on effective treatment of ADHD.

## Young Children with ADHD

Although many parents of children with ADHD will tell you that they knew that their child was different at a very early age, only recently has formal diagnosis of ADHD for young children become common. There is a problem with this development, however: Little information can be found to inform professionals regarding this important topic. For example, the MTA studies focused on students ages seven through fourteen, not younger students. Few studies of ADHD have addressed preschoolers directly, leaving pediatricians uncertain about the use of medication and other interventions, preschool educators unclear on addressing behavior issues, and parents concerned about the stigma of labeling their toddlers.

The largest study to date of young children with ADHD, the Preschool ADHD Treatment Study (PATS), was undertaken by the National Institute of Mental Health (2006). One finding of this study is that preschoolers can benefit from stimulant medication such as Ritalin™, but that it should be given in low doses and that each child's reaction should be closely monitored since one in 10 children may have side effects so serious that the medication should be stopped (National Institute of Mental Health, 2006).

### The Ethical and Professional Dilemma

One result of the increasing recognition of ADHD as a disorder that can exist even in very young children is heated discussion about the appropriateness of labeling and medication for them (as well as other students with ADHD). Should preschool children be given stimulant medication to address attentional problems? Leo (2002) noted that the question should not be whether drugs are safe for young children but whether drugs should even be considered an option when young children's behavior do not conform to predetermined norms. In contrast, Greenhill and his colleagues (2006) found that appropriate medication significantly reduced the symptoms of ADHD in young children and so enabled them to better benefit from early educational experiences. Discussion concerning the use of the ADHD label and the appropriateness of various interventions for young children who have the characteristics of this disorder is likely to continue as the knowledge base increases and outcomes are studied for children first diagnosed with ADHD at a very young age.

**web link**

http://www.healthcentral.com/ adhd/c/1443/12022/ 12-things-high-school On this page of the ADHD Central website, you can read a list of 12 things high school students with ADHD want their teachers to know. The last one is this: *Although I have ADHD, I am not ADHD. I am a person.*

## ADHD in Adolescents and Adults

For many years ADHD was thought to be a disorder of childhood that was outgrown during adolescence. However, with increased understanding of the causes of ADHD and more attention to long-term prognosis of children identified with the disorder, interest is growing in exploring ADHD in adolescents and adults (Barkley, 2006). Moreover, the use of medication among adults with ADHD has grown dramatically over the past several years (Adler, Spencer, & McGough, 2009).

### Outcomes for Adults Diagnosed as Children

One area of interest involves what happens to children with ADHD when they grow up (e.g., Lee et al., 2008; Seidman, 2006). To date, very few studies have carefully followed a group of students who received medication or another intervention as they left high school for postsecondary education or work. Some information is available, but it is based on individual reports. For adults who do not continue treatment, the outcomes are not very positive (Casey, 2003; Owens et al., 2009). These adults are at higher risk for substance abuse, for problems at work, and for family difficulties. They may have problems keeping a job, trouble keeping up with life routines, and difficulties with self-discipline (Wasserstein et al., 2001). They also are more likely to engage in criminal activity than those without ADHD. Of adults who do continue treatment, medication seems to be effective in the same way that it is for children (Advokat, 2009). Few other interventions have been systematically explored, but most professionals also recommend therapy to address how ADHD and any co-morbid disorders are affecting the individual's life, education about the disorder, and information about tools that can be helpful such as computer scheduling software and day planners (Bramham, Young, & Bikerdike, 2009).

*ADHD often continues into adulthood and can affect success at college, on the job, and in social relationships.*

### Identification of ADHD in Adolescents and Adults

A second area of concern related to adolescents, adults, and ADHD is late identification (Young, Gray, & Bramham, 2009). Some adults recall the difficulties they experienced as children in school, and they seek assistance when they recognize similar problems in adulthood. While adolescents with ADHD are not as likely as their younger counterparts to be hyperactive, they are at high risk for school failure, for suspension, for retention, and for behavior problems such as defiance and noncompliance (Stringaris & Goodman, 2009), and it is essential that they seek or continue treatment.

For an adult seeking identification, an extensive developmental, family, and school history will likely be taken, and the individual will be asked to respond to survey or interview questions concerning current functioning. If a decision is made that ADHD is present, a physician will prescribe medication and help the individual to access other support resources.

For an adolescent, identification follows the same procedures used for other school-age students. In addition, an increased emphasis on careful transition planning can be particularly helpful for these students (Dowdy, Patton, Smith, & Polloway, 2000). Because many adolescents with ADHD should be able to succeed in higher education, transition planning might include learning study and organizational strategies, self-advocacy skills, ways to access services for students with special needs at college, and time management.

## The Knowledge Base on Treatment for ADHD

Earlier in this chapter you read about treatments for addressing the needs of students with ADHD. However, clear evidence that any single approach is more effective than another or that particular combinations of treatments will lead to the best long-term outcomes still does not exist. For example, the National Institute of Mental Health (2007; 2009, March) reported that in follow-up studies of the students—now in high school—from the original sample from the MTA research project, results were mixed:

- Nearly all the students in the original studies showed sustained improvement in functioning when follow-up data were gathered.
- No differences were found in symptoms or functioning among students who had been assigned to different treatment groups, leading researchers to conclude that neither type nor intensity of a one-year treatment approach can predict long-term outcomes.
- Students still had academic and social problems, including more conduct problems, more depressions, and more psychiatric hospitalizations than other students.
- Students who had responded well to treatment in the original study were functioning best at the 8-year follow-up.
- Sixty-one percent of students no longer were taking medication at the follow-up, and these students were functioning as well as those still taking medication. Researchers reported that different students seemed to respond differently to medication, with some students gradually improving in response to medication, some quickly improving and sustaining those improvements, and some improving but then losing that improvement.

One dilemma in attempting to study treatment effectiveness is the number of factors that can affect results. For example, some families may decide to give their children medication at a very early age and at the same time provide behavioral and other supports. Other families may decide to use the same interventions, but they do so when the child is older. Yet other families may emphasize behavioral and academic interventions and decline the use of medication or use it for a very short period of time. Each of these scenarios may result in different outcomes, and these and other variations in treatment and child characteristics makes predicting the long-term benefit of treatments exceptionally challenging.

What is clear is that the symptoms of ADHD are persistent and require a long-term perspective on treatment. Both teachers and professionals must keep in mind that interventions effective for young children may need to be re-evaluated and possibly changed as students approach adolescence. Further, the increasing academic and social demands students face as they progress through school should be kept in mind: Without careful attention to them, students may lose whatever gains they have made. Ultimately, as a teacher you should keep abreast of the continuing development of knowledge concerning this complex but relatively common childhood disorder so that you are prepared to assist students to reach their potential.

*Kelly Stalcup is a resource teacher in the Charleston County School District who has achieved certification by the National Board of Professional Teaching Standard. She has taught students with disabilities from preschool through grade 8 and in self-contained and resource settings. She also has served as her district's inclusion facilitator. Here is her advice on working with students with ADHD.*

Students with ADHD can present unique challenges. Strategies like these can help both the teacher and students manage behaviors.

- Educators often favor extra time as an accommodation for students with ADHD. This sounds helpful but, in practice, it gives students more time to be off-task. Instead of extended time, students often need assignments chunked into pieces with short breaks between work sessions.

- One way to help students persist or manage time is to use a timer. The teach timer I have found to be the most effective operates this way: When it is set, the selected amount of time appears red. As the time elapses, it turns white. When time is over, the entire face of the clock is white. It provides a good visual and does not disturb other students with audible signals.

- To discourage unwanted behaviors by replacing those behaviors with a desired behavior, use a positive reinforcement system. One of the most effective systems I have found requires only an index card and a variety of hole punchers. Simply write one to three wanted behaviors on the card. Each time the student exhibits the behavior, punch the card. After a set number of punches, the student receives an agreed upon re-

ward such as computer time or helping younger students. This strategy can be used with multiple students at once or even as a whole-class system.

- Students with ADHD often have difficulty skimming and scanning large amounts of text. When asking students to answer questions from a text after reading, it can be beneficial to write the page number where the answer can be found in the text by the question and the number of the question in the text where the answer can be found. This strategy is not 'cheating.' It is intended to assess the student's comprehension, not the student's ability to skim and scan text.

- Help students organize. Use color coding to help students with ADHD manage papers and materials for various subjects—red folder for math, blue for English language arts, yellow for social studies, and so on. Papers and materials are placed in the correct folder. For other students, a three ring binder with pocket protectors and a section for each subject seems to work to help keep students organized.

- Many students with ADHD cannot stay seated; they need to move in some way. Allowing these students to stand at their desks when working can be effective. Some students may 'tap' frequently which can be distracting to other students in the classroom. Have students tap on their legs or attach a small sponge to the desk where students can then tap the pencil with little noise. If you model how to tap and clarify your expectations, students will use this strategy appropriately.

- If a student needs to move frequently, find errands the student can complete: taking notes to other teachers, taking items to the office, taking the lunch count to the cafeteria.

## REVIEW · REFLECT · DISCUSS

1. Why has attention only recently been focused on attention deficit–hyperactivity disorder in young children and adults? What is your opinion about the existence of ADHD for these two groups and appropriate interventions?

2. What does the existing research on interventions for students with ADHD tell you? How can you reconcile the sometimes confusing and contradictory results that are reported?

# Summary

- ADHD is not a disability category in IDEA, but it is defined in the *DSM-IV-TR* (i.e., predominantly inattentive, predominantly hyperactive–impulsive, and combined type) and affects 3 to 7 percent of the school-age population.
- ADHD generally is believed to be caused by neurobiological problems resulting in deficient behavior inhibition, but it also is influenced by environmental factors.
- Students with ADHD vary widely in their cognitive, academic, social/emotional, and behavior characteristics, and some students with this disorder have comorbid learning, emotional, and other disabilities.
- Because ADHD is a medical condition, a doctor must make the diagnosis based on a comprehensive evaluation of the student and include input from school personnel and parents. To be considered for special education services (usually as other health impaired), students who are ADHD also must be assessed. Decisions made about these students must follow IDEA guidelines.
- Some students receive services through Section 504 plans, depending on their needs.
- Medication is recommended for many students with ADHD; other interventions, often used in combination with medication, include parent and professional education, environmental supports, behavior interventions, and instructional interventions.
- Parents of students with ADHD vary in their responses to their children and their perceptions of the effectiveness of interventions, partly based on cultural differences.
- Issues related to ADHD concern the prescribing of medication for very young children, the persistence of ADHD past the school years, and the uncertain knowledge base on effective treatments and interventions for students with ADHD.

## ADDRESSING THE PROFESSIONAL STANDARDS

Council for Exceptional Children (CEC) Common Core Knowledge and Skills addressed in this chapter:

ICC1K5, ICC1K8, ICC2K1, ICC2K2, ICC2K3, ICC2K6, ICC2K7, ICC3K1, ICC4S6, ICC5S3, ICC5S8, ICC5S10, ICC5S11, ICC8K2, ICC8S3, ICC8S6, ICC9S2, ICC10K3, ICC10S2, ICC10S3

Appendix: Provides a full listing of the CEC Common Core Standards, and associated Knowledge and Skill Statements listed here.

**PEARSON**
# myeducationlab

Now go to Topic 11: ADHD, in the MyEducationLab (www.myeducationlab.com) for your course, where you can:

- Find learning outcomes for the broad concepts covered in this chapter along with the national standards that connect to these outcomes.
- Complete Assignments and Activities that can help you more deeply understand the chapter content.
- Examine challenging situations and cases presented in the IRIS Center Resources.
- Apply and practice your understanding of the core concepts and skills identified in the chapter with the Building Teaching Skills and Dispositions learning units.

- Check your comprehension on the content covered in the chapter by going to the Study Plan in the Book Specific Resources for your text. Here you will be able to take a chapter quiz, receive feedback on your answers, and then access Review, Practice, and Enrichment activities to enhance your understanding of chapter content.
- Watch video clips of CCSSO Teacher of the Year award winners responding to the question: "Why I teach?" in the Teacher Talk section.

## chapter seven

# Students with Emotional and Behavior Disorders

## LEARNING OBJECTIVES

- Define emotional and behavior disorders (EBD), explain their prevalence and causes, and outline the development of the EBD field.
- Describe characteristics of individuals with emotional and behavior disorders.
- Explain how emotional and behavior disorders are identified.
- Outline how students with emotional and behavior disorders receive their education.
- Describe recommended educational practices for students with emotional and behavior disorders.
- Explain the perspectives and concerns that parents and families of students with emotional and behavior disorders may have.
- Identify trends and issues influencing the field of emotional and behavior disorders.

## Krystal

Krystal was identified as having an emotional disability early in third grade. The decision was made after consistent efforts by Krystal's kindergarten, first, and second grade teachers, with input from the school team, to help Krystal learn to deal appropriately with the tremendous anger she seems to hold. Repeated meetings with family members, support from the school counselor, and counseling from community mental health services did not seem to have any significant positive effect. Several serious incidents in which Krystal attacked other students and teachers resulted in a team decision that, at least for now, she is best educated in a separate special education classroom. Krystal's life circumstances contribute to the situation. Krystal was given up for adoption at birth by her fifteen-year-old mother. Krystal was removed from her adoptive family, however, when a child abuse charge was made concerning another child in the home. Since then Krystal has lived in three foster homes—two families decided that they could not manage her behavior. When Krystal is observed playing alone, she often stages violence. She crashes two cars together and talks to herself about the people inside dying. Or she draws people stabbing or shooting each other and always labels at least one as dead. Krystal's special education teacher comments that she has tremendous potential and really should achieve at grade level, but she also notes that Krystal's behavior outbursts and their consequences interfere with her learning. Krystal's IEP goals include achieving grade-level curriculum competencies in all academic areas as well as learning skills to address her anger in appropriate ways.

## Garrett

Garrett is a challenge for his teachers, and they are very concerned about his well-being. Garrett's physical appearance is consistent with his emotional response to others: He is a somewhat overweight sixth grader, large for his age, with a noticeably pale complexion and long, thin, often dirty hair plastered to his scalp. His face is expressionless, and he often sits motionless for long periods. Unless coaxed, he does not speak in class or for that matter in the halls or the cafeteria. His special education teacher describes him as always being in "emotional neutral"; he does not laugh at jokes or other students' antics and he does not appear to be motivated by any system of rewards that school personnel have designed for him, even with his input. His general education teachers comment that he does not participate in class discussions or activities; does not complete in-class or homework assignments; and seems content to simply sit, almost as though he is letting all the instruction and interactions of middle school classes roll right over him. Academically, Garrett is barely passing his core classes, but his teachers are not sure that this is an accurate reflection of his ability. Garrett lives with his grandmother, who is his legal guardian. She is reluctant to come to school to discuss Garrett's problems. She describes Garrett as well behaved and much less of a burden to raise than his older brother. She explains that Garrett spends most of his time at home in his room, watching television, mentioning only that he is not much help with household chores.

## Carlos

Carlos has had a difficult life. His father was killed before he was born, and his mother has serious alcohol and drug problems. He spent much of his childhood in six different foster homes. Of his three older siblings, two are in state prison. Carlos was retained in first grade and again in fifth grade, and his clearest memories of elementary school include feeling dumb and fighting classmates who called him names. While in middle school, Carlos was arrested for setting fires in neighbors' trash cans; after that he attended an alternative school for students with significant behavior and academic problems. According to Carlos, the school was "like prison, with guards all over the place and someone always in your face." He completed his first year of high school in his neighborhood in a self-contained program for students with emotional disabilities, but he missed 30 days of school that year. Carlos began his sophomore year but dropped out last month. Asked why, he describes high school as a waste of his time. He also admits that he had a shouting match with a security guard and was probably going to be suspended again anyway. Carlos has been arrested twice since he began high school: once for stealing a car and once for drug possession. He has no specific plans for getting his high school diploma. When asked what type of job he would like to have, he brightens and says that he would like a job where he would sit at a desk and have a secretary to take his calls and greet his visitors.

Of all the school-age students who have disabilities, few can be as puzzling as those who have emotional and behavior disorders. As you can tell from the vignettes about Krystal, Garrett, and Carlos, these students defy simple description, and at times it is difficult to understand how they can be grouped into a single disability category. When compared to other students with disabilities, these students are more likely to have attended multiple schools, and they are four times more likely to have been suspended or expelled from school (Wagner, Kutash, Duchnowski, Epstein, & Sumi, 2005). Their teachers often report feeling unprepared to work with them (Liljequest & Renk, 2007; Wagner et al., 2006). These students pose unique challenges to school personnel because they often need structure and therapeutic intervention strategies that are difficult to provide. At the same time, successful outcomes for students with emotional and behavior disorders rely on those interventions.

## Understanding Emotional and Behavior Disorders

The study of emotional and behavior disorders has gone on for centuries. Contemporary practices for students in public schools have their foundation in the work of early physicians and psychologists and their efforts to treat adults with mental illness.

### Development of the Field of Emotional and Behavior Disorders

Fascination with insanity and mental illness can be found throughout history (Kauffman & Landrum, 2006), but it was not until the very late nineteenth century that emotional problems in children were considered a valid topic for study. G. Stanley Hall was one of the first psychologists to specialize in the study of these children, publishing a two-volume book on adolescent psychology in 1904.

Several factors made it challenging to study children with emotional and behavior disorders (Winzer, 1993). First, no consistent set of terms existed to describe these children. Their disorders were called such intimidating names as *dementia praecox, catatonia, paranoia, childhood schizophrenia,* and *juvenile insanity.* Second, in many cases, mental illness and mental retardation were still confused and addressed as though they were a single disorder. Third, professionals were reluctant to openly admit that children could have mental illness because this view contradicted the long-held perspective that only adults were affected. Mental illness also was still sometimes associated with evil or satanic possession, making it seem unethical to assign this diagnosis to children.

As you can see in the timeline in Figure 7.1, an understanding of emotional disabilities as they pertained to children gradually developed and services to address these students' needs eventually emerged. Particularly since the passage of federal special education laws, professionals in the area of emotional and behavior disorders have been researching factors that cause these disorders, studying effective interventions, and striving to ensure that all students who have these disorders are identified and educated appropriately. These topics are addressed later in this chapter.

### FIGURE 7.1
Timeline of the Development of the Emotional and Behavior Disorders Field

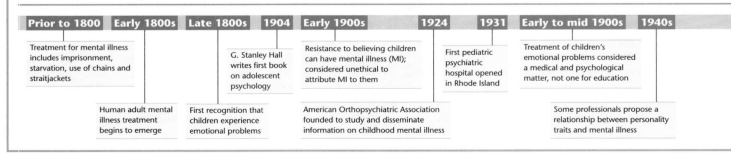

## Definitions of Emotional and Behavior Disorders

The very language used to describe the students about whom this chapter is written requires explanation. For example, the Individuals with Disabilities Education Act (IDEA) uses the term *emotional disturbance (ED)* to identify this population. Many professionals in the field object to that term, noting that it carries a strong negative connotation. They advocate for the alternative—**emotional and behavior disorder (EBD)**—the term used throughout this chapter. However, other terms also are assigned to describe this group of students, including *emotionally disabled (ED)*, *behavior disordered (BD)*, *emotionally impaired (EI)*, and *seriously emotionally disturbed (SED)*. What terminology is used in your state to describe this disability?

Like the language used to describe students with emotional and behavior disorders, the definition of this disability category is somewhat controversial (Mathur, 2007). The definition most often applied is the one found in IDEA. However, critics have pointed out major problems with that definition.

### Federal Definition

As noted, the term used in IDEA for emotional and behavior disorders is **emotional disturbance (ED)**, which the law defines as

> a condition exhibiting one or more of the following characteristics over a long period of time and to a marked degree that adversely affects a child's educational performance:
>
> a. An inability to learn that cannot be explained by intellectual, sensory, or health factors.
> b. An inability to build or maintain satisfactory interpersonal relationships with peers and teachers.
> c. Inappropriate types of behavior or feelings under normal circumstances.
> d. A general pervasive mood of unhappiness or depression.
> e. A tendency to develop physical symptoms or fears associated with personal or school problems.

The term includes schizophrenia. The term does not apply to children who are socially maladjusted, unless it is determined that they have an emotional disturbance. (IDEA 20 U.S.C. §1401 [2004], 20 C.F.R. §300.8[c][4])

For a student to qualify for services through this definition, three sets of factors must be taken into account: First, the student's problem has to occur for a long period of time, to a marked degree, negatively affecting educational performance. Second, only students meeting one or more of the five listed criteria are considered to have this disability. Third, like the definition of learning disabilities, this definition contains an exclusionary clause; that is, some students are explicitly prohibited from being identified as having emotional disturbance. Students who are **socially maladjusted** (i.e., those who intentionally act out or break rules) are not considered to have this disability unless they also meet one of the other criteria.

### Criticism of the Federal Definition of Emotional Disturbance

Almost since the passage of P.L. 94-142, professionals have criticized the federal definition of emotional and behavior disorders. For example, a group of 30 professional organizations

**fyi**

Although the link between television violence and violent behavior in children is still being debated, the American Psychological Association, the American Academy of Child and Adolescent Psychiatry, and other professional groups have reported that television violence can cause children to become less sensitive to others' pain and suffering, more fearful, and more likely to behave in aggressive or harmful ways.

| 1940s | 1950s–60s | 1960s | 1975 | 1984 | 1997 | 1999 |
|---|---|---|---|---|---|---|
| Some professionals propose all mental illness is the result of neurological dysfunction or disease | Behaviorists propose that emotional or behavior problems are learned and can be changed by teaching other more appropriate behaviors | Medical focus for treating children with emotional and behavior problems criticized and role of education begins to increase | P.L. 94–142 includes students with emotional and behavior disorders in the category *severe emotional disturbance* | National Center for School Safety established by the U.S. Departments of Justice and Education to focus on the prevention of school violence through positive strategies | Term in IDEA for this disability is changed from *seriously emotionally disturbed* to *emotionally disturbed* | Center for Positive Behavioral Interventions and Support (PBIS) established by the U.S. Department of Education to build the capacity of schools to effectively address student behavior in positive, systematic, and differentiated ways |

joined together as the National Coalition on Mental Health and Special Education to lobby for change to the definition, contending that the federal definition had several significant problems (Forness & Knitzer, 1992). First, they argued that the five criteria in the definition were not supported by research. Second, they noted that the reference to educational performance too narrowly focused on academic learning, excluding the important but indirect social curriculum of education.

A third criticism of the federal definition was particularly significant. The coalition maintained that the exclusionary clause concerning social maladjustment was unnecessarily confusing and that the intent was to exclude only juvenile delinquents, not all students with this disorder. They illustrated this point by describing students with **conduct disorders**, which are emotional and behavior problems involving aggression, destruction of property, lying or stealing, or serious rule violation (e.g., running away). The coalition reported that conduct disorder is the most common type of social maladjustment, that most states include social maladjustment in their educational definition of emotional disabilities, and that this group of students in fact makes up the largest single group of students included in this category. The coalition proposed this alternative definition (Forness & Knitzer, 1992, p. 14):

> The term emotional or behavioral disorder means a disability characterized by behavioral or emotional responses in school so different from appropriate age, cultural, or ethnic norms that they adversely affect educational performance. Educational performance includes academic, social, vocational, and personal skills. Such a disability
>
> a. is more than a temporary, expected response to stressful events in the environment;
> b. is consistently exhibited in two different settings, at least one of which is school-related; and
> c. is unresponsive to direct intervention in general education or the child's condition is such that general education interventions would be insufficient.

Emotional and behavioral disorders can co-exist with other disabilities. This category may include children or youth with schizophrenic disorders, affective disorders, anxiety disorders, or other sustained disorders of conduct or adjustment when they adversely affect educational performance in accordance with section (i).

As you compare the two definitions, what do you notice? Do you think the coalition definition enhances your understanding of this disorder? Although the coalition was not successful in getting this definition incorporated into federal law, professionals who work in this field generally prefer the latter definition and use it to guide their work, contending that it does not violate the federal definition but rather provides a clearer basis for school practice.

### Other Considerations in Defining Emotional and Behavior Disorders

One more topic should be mentioned before concluding this discussion. Because children's emotional and behavior disorders are a focus of treatment in the medical and mental health fields as well as the educational field, the disorders also have been defined by medical professionals. The *Diagnostic and Statistical Manual of Mental Disorders* (fourth ed., text revision) (*DSM-IV-TR*) (American Psychiatric Association, 2000), a publication you learned about in the Chapter Six description of attention deficit–hyperactivity disorder (ADHD), contains a classification system and definitions of emotional disorders among children. This classification system, which refers to these conditions as **mental disorders**, includes disorders that you have probably heard of but that are not explicitly defined in special education law. Examples include conduct disorders such as **oppositional defiant disorder (ODD)**, **mood disorders** such as depression, and eating disorders such as anorexia nervosa. Brief explanations of these and other *DSM-IV-TR* disorders are outlined in Figure 7.2.

### *Prevalence of Emotional and Behavior Disorders*

Controversy over the definition of emotional and behavior disorders and differences across school, medical, and mental health settings related to who is considered emotionally and behaviorally disordered contribute to uncertainty in estimating the prevalence of this disability among school-age children and young adults. According to the federally collected IDEA data (U.S. Department of Education, 2008), 438,867 students ages six to twenty-one received special education services as emotionally disturbed during the 2007–2008 school year, mak-

## FIGURE 7.2

### Examples of Emotional and Behavior Disorders from a Medical Perspective

Unlike the general definition of emotional and behavior disorders in IDEA, the definition provided by the medical community has identified many specific disorders. These are included in the *Diagnostic and Statistical Manual of Mental Health (DSM-IV-TR)* where they are referred to as *mental disorders*. The following list includes examples of mental disorders that educators would consider emotional and behavior disorders:

- *Anxiety disorders.* An anxiety disorder occurs when a student experiences an overwhelming sense of fear or dread. One example is obsessive–compulsive disorder (OCD) in which the student cannot stop worrying excessively about a specific concern (e.g., germs). Other examples include phobias such as fear of specific items (spiders) or certain activities (going to school), and posttraumatic stress disorder (PTSD) in which the student re-lives in nightmares or flashbacks a traumatic event that was witnessed.

- *Disruptive behavior disorders.* This category includes three types of disorders:
  1. *Attention deficit–hyperactivity disorder (ADHD),* as you learned in Chapter Six, is characterized by inattention, a high level of activity and impulsivity, or a combination of these.
  2. *Oppositional defiant disorder (ODD)* is diagnosed when a student is defiant with adults and vindictive or blaming with peers to an excessive degree over a long period of time.
  3. *Conduct disorder* is diagnosed when a student fights, bullies, displays cruelty to animals or people, or otherwise repeatedly breaks serious rules.

- *Eating disorders.* The most common eating disorder is *anorexia nervosa*, in which the student believes she is overweight and refuses to eat, even when near starvation.

- *Mood disorders.* Also called *affective disorders*, this group includes depression (discussed elsewhere in this chapter) and bipolar disorder (also called *manic depression*), in which the student's moods swing from extreme highs (manic) to extreme lows (depression).

- *Tic disorders.* Tics are involuntary, rapid, stereotyped movements of specific muscle groups. A student with tics may blink his eyes or repeatedly sniff. The most well-known tic disorder is *Tourette syndrome*, which ranges from mild to severe and includes both facial and other physical tics as well as vocal tics (often barking or profanity).

ing this the fifth-largest disability category. This group of students comprised approximately 7.5 percent of all students receiving special education and .67 percent of all students in schools, a prevalence rate that is a slight decline from a decade ago. As you learned in Chapter Three, African American students are overrepresented in this category of disability. They are half again as likely as students in any other racial/ethnic group to receive special education services for this disability (U.S. Department of Education, 2009).

Data on prevalence from schools is only one source of information concerning this group of youngsters. Prevalence estimates using data from mental health clinics, private practitioners, and other community sources indicate that many more children and youth than are recognized in schools have emotional and behavior disorders. In fact, the federal Substance Abuse and Mental Health Services Administration (SAMHSA) (2003) estimates that one of every five children and adolescents has a mental health disorder requiring treatment. This difference in prevalence reports probably occurs because many children receive counseling or services in those settings even though they do not meet IDEA eligibility criteria. Considering prevalence data from any sources, professionals in the field suggest that 3 to 6 percent of school-age children have some type of significant emotional or behavior disorder (Blanchard, Gurka, & Blackman, 2006).

### Prevalence by Gender

As with both learning disabilities and ADHD, far more males than females are diagnosed as having emotional and behavior disorders. Although precise statistics are not available, researchers estimate that these disorders are found in boys three or more times more often than in girls (Wagner et al., 2005). Some professionals argue that these differences are inflated

**web link**

www.samhsa.gov
At the website of the Substance Abuse and Mental Health Services Administration, an agency of the U.S. Department of Health and Human Services, you can find information on many topics related to emotional and behavioral disabilities, including descriptions of children's mental health disorders, strategies for the prevention of school violence, and strategies to share with parents.

because of basic differences in teachers' reactions to students. They hypothesize that teachers are more likely to rate the same behavior displayed by boys and girls as more disturbing in boys. Further, they suggest that as boys move into adolescence, they tend to increase their acting-out behaviors while girls tend to turn inward. The boys' behaviors are more disturbing to teachers, and so boys are more likely to be identified as having these disorders.

## Causes of Emotional and Behavior Disorders

Emotional and behavior disorders include a wide variety of complex problems, and seldom can any single, clear cause be identified for them. Two types of factors are most likely to contribute to the development of emotional and behavior disorders: biological factors and psychosocial factors.

### Biological Factors

As is true for learning disabilities and attention deficit–hyperactivity disorder, research suggests that at least some emotional and behavior disorders are the result of a physiological problem. One consideration in this category is genetics and whether these disorders are inherited. In at least some instances, research supports this possibility (Kopp & Beauchaine, 2007). For example, between 20 and 60 percent of children who have depression, a disorder recently receiving considerable attention, have at least one parent who has this disorder. Similarly, children with one parent who has schizophrenia, another adult mental illness, are much more likely than other children to develop this disorder by early adulthood (Sullivan, 2005). The rate is even higher if both parents have schizophrenia. As with learning disabilities and attention deficit–hyperactivity disorder, data such as these come from studies of siblings, especially twins, raised apart.

A second area examined as a biological influence is brain injury. Children whose mothers abused alcohol or drugs during pregnancy are more likely than other children to develop emotional and behavior disorders. Brain injury also can be related to environmental toxins. Again, children diagnosed with lead poisoning or exposed over time to other chemicals in their homes and neighborhoods are at risk for developing these disorders. Poor nutrition is yet another factor that can affect neurological development and contribute to the development of emotional and behavior disorders. Finally, some children have neurologically based emotional disabilities as a result of an accident (e.g., falling from a bicycle) or illness (e.g., high fever).

### Psychosocial Factors

Children are influenced in their psychological and social development by the people around them, the events they experience, and their living conditions. Collectively, these are considered **psychosocial factors**. The following psychosocial factors are associated with emotional and behavior disorders in children (U.S. Department of Health and Human Services, 1999; Wagner, Kutash, Duchnowski, Epstein, & Sumi, 2005):

- *Chronic stress.* Some children grow up in home and community settings characterized by stress. Perhaps the child's parents fight frequently, sometimes physically assaulting each other. Perhaps the family does not have enough income for even a marginal existence, and so there are frequent moves to avoid eviction or periodic stays in a homeless shelter. In some families with many children, even caring parents simply cannot divide their attention among everyone needing it, and this functions as a stressor for the children competing for that attention. Finally, chronic stress may come from

*Children who live in extreme poverty are at risk for developing emotional and behavior disorders.*

the community—for example, when shootings, drug dealing, and gang activities are common occurrences.

- *Stressful life events.* A second group of psychosocial factors includes intense life events. Two of the most common examples are the death of a parent or primary caregiver and divorce. However, other stressful life events also can affect children. One common example is when children witness violence in homes or their communities.

- *Childhood maltreatment.* Reports on television and in newspapers are a constant reminder that child abuse is a very real health concern in the United States. According to the Children's Bureau (2009), in 2007 approximately 794,000 children were victims of abuse or neglect. Most professionals consider this figure to be a significant underestimate of the situation. In 73.4 percent of cases reporting abused or neglected children, the perpetrator is one or both of the parents (Children's Bureau, 2009). Children who are physically or psychologically abused are at greater risk of developing emotional or behavior disorders.

- *Additional family factors.* Other family problems also can influence youngsters and possibly cause emotional and behavior disorders. For example, research suggests that when a parent is depressed, he or she may lack the motivation and energy to use effective child-rearing practices, and the children in the household thus will be at risk. Peers may also play a role; if extreme sibling rivalry develops, emotional problems can result.

### Making Sense of the Factors Contributing to Emotional and Behavior Disorders

Clearly, many different factors, alone or in combination with others, can lead to emotional and behavior disorders. The current thinking is that biological and psychosocial factors probably interact. That is, some children may have a genetic predisposition to have a disorder, and when they live in a situation that includes one or more of the other risk factors, they are more likely to develop a disorder. A related line of thinking addresses **correlated constraints**. It proposes that when children's lives are permeated with risk factors, those factors collectively promote maladaptive behavior patterns and subsequently constrain the development of positive adjustment (Farmer, Farmer, Estell, & Hutchins, 2007).

However, you should keep in mind that children tend to have **resilience**; that is, they tend to be able to recover and not experience long-term harm from brief episodes of stress or single negative experiences (Abelev, 2009; Martinez-Torteya, Bogat, von Eye, & Levendosky, 2009). And so many children, even those who might be at risk for developing emotional disabilities, do not experience these disorders. Resilience is explained more fully in the Professional Edge feature.

## REVIEW · REFLECT · DISCUSS

1. What is your opinion of the current federal definition of emotional disturbance? Given criticism about it, do you think it should be changed? If so, how?

2. What is the value for educators of understanding that both biological and psychosocial factors may contribute to the development of emotional and behavior disorders? Explain your response using specific examples.

# Characteristics of Individuals with Emotional and Behavior Disorders

The characteristics of students with emotional and behavior disorders vary so much that it is almost impossible to provide a comprehensive list. Instead, in this section you will learn about some of the most common behavior and emotional, social, and cognitive, and academic qualities of these learners.

## The Promise of Resiliency

*Resiliency* is the ability to bounce back from adversity, frustration, and misfortune. Research suggests that when schools, families, and communities help to build resiliency in children, those children are capable of becoming healthy, competent adults, in spite of the life stresses they may experience (Abelev, 2009). Here are some ways that you can foster resiliency in students:

1. Practice unconditional positive acceptance. When begun from an early age, unconditional positive regard increases the likelihood of positive social development.

2. Establish close, supportive relationships. In addition to parents, educators and other professionals help children develop trust.

3. Communicate high but realistic standards. Students need to know that you expect their best and that you believe they can achieve it.

4. Be sure that students know the important rules and limits. Depending on age, students should be involved in developing the rules.

5. Use warm, positive instruction and as little criticism as possible.

6. Focus on frequent, concrete praise. By telling students what they are doing right, you are helping to clarify expectations and increasing the likelihood that appropriate behavior will be repeated.

7. Help children learn how to persist in reaching their goals by clearly identifying a goal, deciding why it is important, thinking about the best ways to reach the goal, and taking action.

8. Celebrate efforts. Acknowledge efforts and successes. This helps students to develop confidence.

9. Provide opportunities for children to delay gratification. This builds a sense of control and confidence. It also helps students to decrease impulsiveness.

10. Teach students survival and life skills including assertiveness, conflict resolution, refusal skills, stress management, coping techniques, and decision making.

11. Develop students' competencies based on their interests, increasing the complexity of student activities to enhance their self-esteem.

12. Be aware of gender differences. Research suggests that boys often respond to structure, organization, and rules to a greater degree than girls do. Girls may need more support to take risks.

13. Arrange for students to participate in service activities. When students give of themselves, they can develop confidence, self-esteem, and feelings of accomplishment.

14. Motivate students with stories about characters who have risen above adversity to find their own paths to success and achievement.

15. Share your humor. Humor is an effective coping strategy, and when students observe adults responding to challenges with humor and a willingness to try again, they will do the same.

*Source:* Janas, M. (2002). Twenty ways to build resiliency. *Intervention in School and Clinic, 38*(2), 117–121. Copyright © 2002 by Pro-Ed, Inc. Reprinted with permission of SAGE Publications.

*Although professionals may first think of students who act out as having emotional disabilities, some students have internalizing disorders such as anxiety or depression.*

## Behavior and Emotional Characteristics

The behaviors of students with emotional and behavior disorders often are not completely different from those of other students. Rather, they occur more often, with more intensity, for a longer time, and they have a significantly negative impact on student learning. Further, the behaviors of these students cover an entire spectrum. One of the most common ways of conceptualizing these behaviors is to think of them as being either internalizing or externalizing. **Internalizing behaviors** are those characterized as withdrawn or directed inward. Garrett, the sixth-grader described at the beginning of this chapter, exhibits internalizing behaviors. Additional examples of these behaviors can be found in Figure 7.3. Not surprisingly, because students with internalizing behaviors often do not disrupt the classroom, their needs can be overlooked by busy educators unless they are particularly vigilant.

**Externalizing behaviors** are those characterized as directed toward others; when students display these behaviors, they generally bother both teachers and other students. Krystal and Carlos, students whose stories began this chapter, both display externalizing behaviors. They are aggressive, they violate school rules and commit crimes, and they might be described as acting out. As you might expect, students with externalizing behaviors are very likely to be identified by their teachers as needing assistance, and teachers' perceptions of these children can be negative (Cavell, Elledge, Malcolm, Faith, & Hughes, 2009). Figure 7.3 includes examples of externalizing behaviors.

Thinking about students having internalizing or externalizing behaviors is a convenient way to illustrate the diversity comprising emotional disabilities, but such a simple frame-

## FIGURE 7.3

**Examples of Internalizing and Externalizing Behaviors for Students with Emotional and Behavior Disorders**

Students with emotional and behavior disorders may display two types of behaviors that cause concern. *Internalizing behaviors* are characterized by withdrawal, and *externalizing behaviors* are characterized by acting out. Here are examples of both types of behavior.

*Internalizing Behaviors*

- Exhibits sad affect, depression, and feelings of worthlessness
- Cannot get mind off certain thoughts, ideas, or situations
- Cannot keep self from engaging in repetitive and/or useless actions
- Suddenly cries, cries frequently, or displays totally unexpected and atypical affect for the situation
- Complains of severe headaches or other somatic problems (stomachaches, nausea, dizziness, vomiting) as a result of fear or anxiety
- Talks of killing self—reports suicidal thoughts and/or is preoccupied with death
- Shows decreased interest in activities that were previously of interest
- Is excessively teased, verbally or physically abused, neglected, and/or avoided by peers
- Shows signs of physical, emotional, and/or sexual abuse

*Externalizing Behaviors*

- Displays recurring pattern of aggression toward objects or persons
- Argues excessively
- Forces the submission of others through physical and/or verbal means
- Is noncompliant with reasonable requests
- Exhibits persistent pattern of tantrums
- Exhibits persistent patterns of stealing, lying, and/or cheating
- Frequently exhibits lack of self-control and acting out behaviors
- Exhibits other specific behavior(s) that intrudes on other people, staff, self, or the physical environment to an extent that prevents the development or maintenance of satisfactory interpersonal relationships

Source: Kentucky Department of Education and Department of Special Education and Rehabilitation Counseling at the University of Kentucky. (1999, December). Behavioral examples. Retrieved August 14, 2003, from www.state.ky.us/agencies/behave/EBD%20TA%20Manual/beexaman.html.

work can be misleading. In fact, a single student may display both types of behaviors. For example, Hector is a middle school student who usually keeps to himself. He may even be the victim of others' bullying. However, Hector may suddenly lash out at other students, hitting and cursing about what may seem to an observer to be a minor incident—for example, a classmate bumping into his desk.

## Emotional Characteristics

Students' behaviors often are indicators of their emotions. Some students identified as having emotional disturbance experience anxiety as the result of excessive fears. They may be afraid of going to school, afraid of enclosed spaces or other specific types of physical environments (e.g., stairways), afraid of potential catastrophic events (e.g., hurricanes or terrorist attacks), or afraid of becoming ill. Fears such as these are intense and quite real to the students.

Other students with emotional and behavior disorders, like Krystal, may feel anger. They may respond to your request for them to complete an assignment by refusing to work at all. They may perceive that a classmate who smiles at them is making fun of them. They may run from the classroom when corrected for using profanity. Often when students feel

**web link**

www.ccbd.net
The Council for Children with Behavior Disorders is a division of the Council for Exceptional Children. Its website includes a discussion forum, links to professional materials and conferences, and the organization's policy statements on topics related to students with emotional and behavior disorders.

**ROBIN ROBERTS** *is a special educator who understands her students better than many people because she also is the mother of Jensen, her daughter who has an emotional disability.*

Jensen was a very happy young lady. I noticed a change when she got to 7th grade. It started with her wanting to fit in with everybody. I tried to impress upon her that she had her own individual talents, tried to get her involved in sports and other things, but things just started falling apart. I realized it when we were in the car one day and she started screaming, "I want to die, I don't want to live, I'm going to jump out of the car." My youngest son leaned over from the back seat to hold her while I was hanging on to the door to keep it from flying open. During this same time, she was texting, and the texting was becoming very mean and hateful. It was so severe at that point that I reported it to the police and the school board. It was bullying on the internet, and then she would fall apart.

I already knew she had a learning disability, and she received some resource classes, but this was something else. When the problems got more frequent, lasted longer, and were so intense, I chose to move

from that district to another district trying to "band aid" the problem as any parent would. It didn't work. She ended up hospitalized twice, and she has been hospitalized three more times since then. That's because I would call the police because I was afraid she was going to commit suicide, and she would end up in the hospital. I know from my training if somebody says they're going to commit suicide, you don't hesitate—you take it seriously.

I tried to find counseling for her, hoping she'd get better. I tried counseling through the church, through the school, through outside services. Outside school, it was very expensive, and I couldn't afford it. Then for awhile, she was in a good program, but we moved again. And during this time Jensen played sports. In ninth grade she started softball; she was awesome at it. But her self esteem never would go up, and I was baffled by that. People around her would tell her how much talent she had, that she was loved. And it just didn't click. Nothing seemed to click, and even now she feels like she has no talents. She dropped out of school in the 10th grade. We tried half days, we tried homebound—it didn't help. By then she had gotten in with so many different kids, making wrong choices, doing wrong things. She ran away once and became sexually active, and we ended up going to a psychiatrist. That's when she was

put on medication. And she's been on and off meds since then. She got pregnant, had a baby, again on and off meds, and now I'm raising her baby.

She still gets very angry. She just loses control. I try to calm her down, but it escalates. And at this point I'm too close to the situation, I believe, for me to make any difference. I start arguing with her and I realize arguing accomplishes nothing, but I can't seem to not; I just want to shake her. Right now, her diagnosis is that she is bipolar, and she has ADHD, and she has a learning disability—she is dyslexic. I want her to get her GED, but she wants me to do the work of setting it up, and she needs to do that. I can't do it all for her.

This has been an experience I would not want anybody to go through. I love my daughter, but I don't like her sometimes at all. I don't like her choices, I feel like . . . we went to church every week, we were involved in church, she went to camps. We did everything right . . . I don't really know what I could have done differently. And I don't know if I've done any good for her or not.

I see some of these families of the students who I teach and at least I can understand and empathize with them because I know what it's like to be single. And I know what it's like to raise a child with ED. And I think that makes me a better teacher. A better parent, I don't know . . . I don't know.

such anger, they display it through the externalizing behaviors of aggression (e.g., hitting, spitting, fighting).

Yet other students have very low self-esteem. They see only their negative characteristics instead of their positive traits, and they may describe themselves as worthless. When such feelings are chronic, these students may be identified as having **depression**, a mental illness that includes clusters of these symptoms persisting for more than 2 weeks (National Institute of Mental Health, 2009a):

- Frequent sadness, tearfulness, crying
- Hopelessness
- Decreased interest in activities, or inability to enjoy previously favorite activities
- Persistent boredom, low energy
- Social isolation, poor communication
- Low self-esteem and guilt
- Extreme sensitivity to rejection or failure
- Increased irritability, anger, or hostility
- Difficulty with relationships
- Frequent complaints of physical illnesses such as headaches and stomachaches
- Frequent absences from school or poor performance in school

## Youth Suicide—You Can Make the Difference

Youth suicide is preventable, if professionals, parents, and community members take seriously warning signs such as the following:

- Belief that a person goes to a better place after dying
- Tendency to be impulsive (i.e., acting before thinking about consequences)
- Tendency to be a perfectionist
- Family history of suicide attempts
- Hopelessness, feeling that things will never get better

### Verbal and Behavior Clues

Here are specific verbal and behavior clues that should cause you to seek assistance for a student identified as high risk for suicide:

| *Verbal Clues* | *Behavior Clues* |
|---|---|
| "I shouldn't be here." | Talking or joking about suicide |
| "I'm going to run away." | Giving possessions away |
| "I wish I were dead." | Being preoccupied with death or violence in television, movies, drawings, books, playing, or music |
| "I'm going to kill myself." | Displaying risky behavior such as jumping from high places, running into traffic, and self-cutting |
| "I wish I could disappear forever." | Having several accidents resulting in injury, including close calls |
| "If a person did _____, would he or she die?" | Being obsessed with guns and knives |
| "The voices tell me to kill myself." | Previously having suicidal thoughts or attempts |
| "Maybe if I died, people would love me more." | |
| "I want to see what it feels like to die." | |

### Tips for School Professionals

Here are things that you can do if you suspect a student is at high risk for suicide:

- Know the warning signs.
- Know the school's responsibilities. The courts have held schools liable for not notifying parents in a timely fashion of a suicide threat or adequately supervising the suicidal student.
- Encourage students to confide in you. Encourage them to come to you if they or someone they know is considering suicide.
- Listen without being accusatory or judgmental and reassure students that help is available.
- Refer students immediately. You should escort a student you suspect is suicidal to the appropriate person, possibly the principal, psychologist, counselor, or social worker.
- Help to form a school crisis team and participate on it. If educators are prepared in advance, they are better able to respond to students' crises.
- Advocate for the child. If an administrator or other professional minimizes the warning signs, represent the student's interests until you are satisfied the student is safe.

*Sources:* Suicide Awareness Voices of Education (2003, August), Suicide: Identifying high risk children and adolescents. Retrieved August 12, 2003, from www.save.org/Identify.shtml; and National Association of School Psychologists (2009), Preventing youth suicide—Tips for parents and educators. Retrieved July 2, 2009, from http://www.nasponline.org/resources/crisis_safety/suicideprevention.aspx

---

- Poor concentration
- A major change in eating and/or sleeping patterns
- Talk of or efforts to run away from home
- Thoughts or expressions of suicide or self-destructive behavior

Approximately 5 percent of children and adolescents in the United States experience depression (American Academy on Child and Adolescent Psychiatry, 2009). The risk of depression is approximately equal for boys and girls during childhood, but during adolescence girls are twice as likely as boys to develop this disorder. If you understand the symptoms of depression in children and are vigilant as you interact with students, you can play an important role in urging parents to seek assistance for their children and in alerting counselors and other school professionals about students who may have this mental illness.

Sadly, when children's depression is untreated it can lead to suicide, the third-leading cause of death among children ages ten to fourteen, adolescents ages fifteen to nineteen, and young adults ages twenty to twenty-four (National Institute of Mental Health, 2009b). Most students who commit suicide give clear signals before they take their lives, and you should be alert to these warning signs. They are outlined in detail in the Professional Edge feature.

**Fyi**

More than one million children come into some type of contact with the juvenile justice system each year. As many as 60 to 75 percent of these youths have mental health disorders. However, more than 50 percent of incarcerated youths avoid recidivism (i.e., being a repeat offender) if they are provided with highly structured, intensive, and long-term treatment programs that teach them specific skills such as anger management and self-control (National Mental Health Association, 2006).

## Social Skills for Classroom Success

For students with emotional and behavior disorders to succeed in general education settings, they must have key social skills. Lane, Pierson, and Givner (2004) surveyed 240 middle and high school teachers who identified the following social skills as most essential:

- Responds appropriately to aggression from peers
- Politely refuses unreasonable requests
- Responds appropriately to teasing by peers
- Accepts peers' ideas for group activities
- Receives criticism well
- Attends to instructions
- Controls temper with peers
- Listens to classmates when they present work
- Controls temper with adults
- Complies with directions
- Responds appropriately to peer pressure
- Initiates conversations with peers
- Introduces self to new people without being told to do so
- Appears confident in social interactions with opposite-sex peers
- Invites others to join in activities
- Gives compliments to members of the opposite sex

Schoenfeld, Rutherford, Gable, and Rock (2008) proposed the ENGAGE model for embedding instruction in social skills into daily instruction:

E   Examine the demands of the curriculum, looking for ways to incorporate social skills instruction into other learning and avoiding the excuse that there is not enough time to teach these skills because of pressure to teach academic content.

N   Note essential social skills, prioritizing these and planning how to address them.

G   Go forward and teach skills in small time increments, with expectations for gradual improvements for students.

A   Actively monitor student social skills development, preferably involving them in this process.

G   Gauge progress, keeping aware that you may need to provide intensive individual social skills instruction for some students.

E   Exchange reflections, involving all students in constructive conversations about social skills and keeping a positive note.

*Source:* Lane, K. L., Pierson, M. R., & Givner, C. C. (2004). Secondary teachers' views on social competence. *Journal of Special Education, 38,* 174–186. Reprinted with permission of SAGE Publiations, Inc. and Schoenfeld, N. A., Rutherford, R. B., Gable, R. A., & Rock, M. L. (2008). ENGAGE: A blueprint for incorporating social skills training into daily academic instruction. *Preventing School Failure, 52*(3), 17–28. Reprinted by permission of Heldref Publications, www.heldref.org.

## Social Characteristics

Students with emotional and behavior disorders experience significant challenges in establishing and maintaining social relationships with peers and adults. For example, in one large study, teachers rated students who were receiving special education services for emotional disabilities and also those not labeled as having emotional and behavior disorders (Cullinan, Evans, Epstein, & Ryser, 2003). The identified students were rated as having significantly more relationship problems than other students. This was true for both boys and girls, and it was true for both African American and Caucasian students. In fact, professionals generally agree that lack of social skills is one of the primary reasons that students are identified as having emotional and behavior disorders (Jones, Dohrn, & Dunn, 2004).

Some students have problems in their social interactions because they live in situations in which adults and other children model inappropriate social skills (Wagner et al., 2005). For example, if the expectation in a student's home is that children should be quiet, that student may not know how to join peers in a game or activity or to ask a teacher for assistance. The message for educators is this: When students do not have the social skills necessary for them to interact effectively with peers and adults, they need to be taught those skills (Cook et al., 2008), a topic addressed in the Instruction in Action feature.

## Cognitive and Academic Characteristics

The first step in understanding the cognitive and academic characteristics of students with emotional and behavior disorders is to recognize the guidelines that are used in identifying these students. If a student's cognitive ability is below a certain level—usually an IQ of about 70—he generally will be considered to have an intellectual disability, and any behavior problems he displays will be thought of as secondary to or caused by his primary disability. The

## web link

http://www.mentalhealthamerica.net/

The website of the Mental Health America includes pages on topics specifically for students, parents, and educators, including tips about bullying, eating disorders, and depression. Other topics are building respect for diversity and appreciating differences in people.

student generally will not be identified as having an emotional or behavior disorder. Thus, you might think that students with emotional and behavior disorders could have a cognitive ability from a low-average to a gifted range because there is no direct relationship between intelligence and emotional problems. Although this is true, most of these students have been found to have low-average to average intellectual ability (Sabornie, Evans, & Cullinan, 2006; Wagner et al., 2005).

The academic difficulties that students with emotional and behavior disorders experience are significant. They range from low grade point averages to high risk for retention to high risk for dropping out of school (Vannest, Temple-Harvey, & Mason, 2009). Many authors have documented that students with emotional and behavior disorders fail to achieve in school and that their academic problems occur across subject areas. For example, Nelson, Benner, Lane, and Smith (2004) examined the academic achievement of a sample of students with emotional and behavior disorders spanning kindergarten through twelfth grade. They found that the students had significant academic problems across all content areas.

*Students with emotional and behavior disabilities often have difficulty learning to work or play with peers.*

### The Question of Cause and Effect

Many professionals have considered this question: Do emotional and behavior disorders cause academic problems, or do students' chronic and significant academic problems cause emotional and behavior disorders? No clear answer to this question can be found. However, it is likely that both parts of the question contain some truth. Because of emotional difficulties, some students cannot adequately focus on schoolwork. At the same time, repeated failure in schoolwork contributes to some students' emotional and behavior disorders. What is most important for educators to keep in mind is that effective services for these students address both academic and emotional and behavior needs.

### *Emotional and Behavior Disorders and Comorbidity*

In Chapter Six you learned that many students with ADHD also have other disabilities. The same point must be made for students whose primary disability is emotional disturbance. Many students who are identified as having an emotional or behavior disorder have comorbid, or additional, disabilities (National Institute of Mental Health, 2006; Wagner et al., 2005). Some also have a learning disability, and others have ADHD. In addition, many of these students have more than one emotional or behavior disorder—for example, both depression and a disruptive behavior disorder. For school professionals, recognizing comorbid disorders is essential so that all the needed interventions can be implemented to help the student succeed.

According to the Centers for Disease Control and Prevention (2008), illicit drug use has declined among youth, but the rate of non-medical use of prescription medications (e.g., pain relievers, tranquilizers, stimulants, depressants) remains high. In 2006, 2.1 million teens abused prescription drugs.

## REVIEW · REFLECT · DISCUSS

1. What does it mean to say that a student has internalizing or externalizing behaviors? What is the relationship between these types of behaviors and the emotional and social characteristics of students with emotional and behavior disorders?

2. Academically, students with emotional disabilities generally are capable of reaching the same level of achievement as other students. How does this relate to the skills teachers need for these students and inclusive practices? What dilemmas might be created?

# Identifying Emotional and Behavior Disorders

Before special education services are considered for students with emotional and behavior disorders, professionals already have tried to assist them in many ways. General education teachers have implemented behavior reward systems and other strategies that have been successful with other students. In most schools, educators also have requested input from a prereferral team. In some school districts, response to intervention procedures are being implemented to address student behavior problems (Cheney, Flower, & Templeton, 2008). If that is the case, a series of increasingly intense, evidence-based interventions also probably have been tried. If none of these efforts is successful in addressing student needs, a referral is made to determine whether an emotional or behavior disorder exists, whether special education services are needed, and whether those services would benefit the student.

## Assessment

Although the areas of assessment for emotional and behavior disorders are similar to those for learning disabilities and intellectual disabilities, the emphasis for the former is on emotional, behavior, and social concerns. As for all students, the assessment must address all pertinent aspects of student functioning, use multiple measures, and be nondiscriminatory.

### Formal Assessments

Several types of formal assessments may be completed to help professionals decide whether a student has an emotional or behavior disorder. First, rating scales may be used to determine the nature and extent of a student's problems. For example, the Scale for Assessing Emotional Disturbance (SAED) (Epstein & Cullinan, 1998) is a norm-referenced instrument that teachers can complete in just a few minutes. It includes a subscale for each dimension of the federal definition: inability to learn, relationship problems, inappropriate behavior, unhappiness or depression, and physical symptoms or fears. An additional subscale addresses social maladjustment. Other rating scales that are to be completed by professionals and parents include the Behavior Assessment System for Children (BASC-2) (Reynolds & Kamphaus, 2004) and the Behavior Rating Profile (BRP-2) (Brown & Hammill, 1990).

In addition to assessments regarding emotional and behavior factors, cognitive ability and achievement levels also are measured. An intelligence test such as the Wechsler Intelligence Scale for Children–IV (WISC–IV) (Wechsler, 2003) usually is administered to decide whether a student's cognitive level might be affecting her emotions and behavior. An achievement test such as the Woodcock–Johnson Psychoeducational Battery–III (Tests of Achievement) (Woodcock, McGrew, & Mather, 2001) helps the team decide the extent to which the emotional and behavior disorders are affecting the student's educational performance.

### Classroom Assessments

An essential part of an assessment for emotional and behavior disorders is systematic observation in the classroom, lunchroom, physical education class, and other school and possibly home environments. Professionals need to see exactly what students do or do not do in a variety of activities and settings, they need to analyze what might trigger inappropriate behavior, and they need to consider the context in which the student is expected to function—the level of structure in the classroom, the number of adults with whom the student interacts, and so on. Rating scales measure what teachers, parents, and others perceive the student is doing. *Observations* of actual behavior provide confirmation of those perceptions and more detail about the student's strengths and problems.

Classroom assessments also can include curriculum-based measurements that demonstrate how the student is achieving in day-to-day schoolwork in core academic areas. This information supplements the standardized achievement data gathered as part of the formal assessment.

Go to the Assignments and Activities section of Topic 10: Emotional/Behavioral Disorders, in the MyEducationLab for your course and complete the activity entitled "Assessment of Behavior".

dimensions of
**DIVERSITY**

Hosp (2008) noted that although Latino youth are underrepresented in the IDEA category of emotional disturbance, they are two and a half times more likely than Caucasian youth to be in juvenile correctional facilities, concluding that many of these students are not receiving needed behavioral interventions in school.

## Other Assessment Strategies

Several other assessment strategies usually are included in deciding whether a student has an emotional or behavior disorder. A family history is obtained by interviewing parents and other key family members; this information can help to explain whether genetic and/or environmental factors might be affecting the student. The developmental history of the student in question, also obtained through parent interviews, provides professionals with information on whether the problem has been evident for some time or has recently emerged. For example, family members might be asked whether their child tended to dislike adult attention as an infant or toddler, whether the child began speaking at a later rather than an earlier age, and whether the child played with other children in age-appropriate ways.

In many cases a psychologist or counselor also will interview the student who is being assessed. Using nonthreatening approaches, these professionals seek to hear from the student his perspective on what is occurring and the reasons for his problems. Think about this component of assessment. What information might be obtained directly from the student that would not otherwise be considered?

**Medical Information.** If a student is under the care of a physician or psychiatrist, school professionals, with parental permission, will request pertinent information from those medical professionals. For example, a student might be taking a medication related to depression, and school professionals need to know this information. Alternatively, a student might be receiving intensive therapy from a private clinic. Again, school professionals obtain appropriate details so that they can be considered in their evaluation of the student.

**Strengths-Based Assessment.** Most of the assessments for emotional and behavior disorders are designed to discover details about the student's problems and to thoroughly explore the nature and severity of those problems. However, professionals also advocate assessing student strengths and assets. **Strengths-based assessment** refers to measuring students' social and emotional strengths, the characteristics that give them confidence, and the traits that help them cope with adversity. Epstein (2004) has developed a strengths-based assessment instrument, the Behavioral and Emotional Rating Scale (BERS–2nd ed.), which gathers information on interpersonal strength, family involvement, intrapersonal strength, school functioning, and affective strength. Why is it particularly important to include strengths-based assessment information in the evaluation process for students with emotional and behavior disorders?

## Eligibility

Once assessment data have been gathered, the multidisciplinary team, including the parents, meets to make the critical decisions regarding eligibility.

### Eligibility Criteria

The team must address the following questions in deciding whether a student has an emotional or behavior disorder and should receive special education:

1. *Does the student have one or more of the characteristics in the definition of emotional disturbance?* If you refer back to the federal definition of this disability earlier in this chapter, you will see that the characteristics include unexplained difficulties in learning, unsatisfactory interpersonal relationships, a pervasive mood of unhappiness, and physical symptoms associated with personal or school problems. If a student is to receive special education, one or more of these characteristics must be documented through the information that has been gathered.

2. *Do the student's characteristics, as assessed, adversely affect educational performance?* Special education services are designed only for students whose education is being limited by their disabilities. Professionals look at cognitive ability and achievement data to make this decision. For students with emotional and behavior disorders, the concern is whether the emotional or behavioral difficulties prevent them from learning at a level consistent with their ability.

According to the Office of Juvenile Justice and Delinquency Prevention (Snyder, 2008), 2.2 million arrests were made in 2006 of persons under age eighteen. These individuals account for 17 percent of all violent crime arrests and 26 percent of all property crime arrests for that year.

3. *Can social maladjustment be eliminated as the sole cause of the student's behavior problems?* As you have learned, the federal definition of emotional disturbance contains an exclusionary clause: If a student is socially maladjusted and no other emotional disability exists, she is not eligible for services. Recall, though, that many states do not use this clause in their definitions, and so for those states this question would not be necessary.

If the multidisciplinary team answers yes to the preceding questions, the student is identified as having an emotional and behavior disorder and can begin to receive services if it is determined they would be beneficial. However, if the team's decision is that a disability does not exist or that the student is not eligible for special education services, the members might decide to recommend that a Section 504 plan be prepared to provide support to the student. Alternatively, they may assist the general education teachers working with the student to design interventions to address the emotional or behavior problems that prompted the initial referral.

## REVIEW · REFLECT · DISCUSS

1. What is a strengths-based assessment? Why is it gaining importance in the assessment of students with emotional and behavior disorders? How does a strengths-based assessment help professionals in working with these students?

2. How might assessment procedures that are supposed to be objective result in the over-identification of African American students as emotionally disabled? How could this problem be addressed by professionals? What is your role in addressing this problem?

# Educating Learners with Emotional and Behavior Disorders

Because students with emotional and behavior disorders typically are capable of learning the same curriculum as their peers without disabilities, you might think that they are likely to be in general education settings. However, this often is not the case. These students are educated in the entire range of educational environments outlined in federal law—from general education through part-time special education to self-contained classes to separate educational facilities and homebound services. In fact, some data suggest that they are educated in separate settings more than most other students with disabilities (Wagner et al., 2006).

## Early Childhood

As you know, young children are not usually assigned specific disability labels. When the disability under consideration is an emotional or behavior disorder, the reluctance to assign a label is particularly strong, for several reasons. One is that when a child is young, judgments about the presence of emotional and behavior disorders are particularly difficult to make because of developmental differences. Another reason is that all the labels related to emotional and behavior disorders are viewed as having a strong negative stigma, one that professionals are uncomfortable assigning to young children.

Despite this uneasiness about labeling, however, professionals have for many years been concerned about the mental health of infants, toddlers, and preschoolers (Egger & Angold, 2006; Mayr & Ulich, 2009). This concern is based on two related factors. First, professionals are strongly committed to addressing the risk factors discussed earlier in this chapter for young children so that they are less likely to develop emotional and behavior disorders. In particular, professionals focus their efforts on educating young women about the risks associated with prenatal alcohol, nicotine, and drug use; teaching new mothers parenting skills; and improving parent–child relationships. Second, early interventionists know that young children who already are displaying behaviors known to be associated with later se-

**research NOTE**

Frey (2002) found that teachers who were most confident of their behavior management skills recommended less restrictive placements for students with emotional and behavior disorders, including general education. Students with low socioeconomic status were likely to be recommended for more restrictive placements. No placement differences were found based on race/ethnicity.

rious emotional and behavior disorders must receive intensive intervention at a very early age in order to change the course of their lives (Brauner & Stephens, 2006; Conroy, Sutherland, Haydon, Stormont, & Harmon, 2009; Morgan, Farkas, & Wu, 2009). Thus, they have developed a number of programs designed to help young children at risk for emotional and behavior disorders as well as their families.

Effective early intervention for children at risk of developing emotional and behavior disabilities includes several components (Conroy et al., 2009). These include the following:

- Precorrrection (that is, teaching appropriate behavior for particular situations before misbehavior has a chance to occur) combined with close supervision of students and monitoring of their behavior so that problems can be averted whenever possible
- Increased instructional pacing by increasing students' opportunities to respond during classroom instruction
- Increased rate of praise for students when they behave as expected
- Specific feedback to children about their behavior and error correction by teaching acceptable behavior
- Development and implementation of clear classroom rules
- Collaboration between professionals and parents
- Home–school communication.

These elements are similar to those advocated for school-age groups, but they are not all necessarily emphasized in traditional early childhood programs. In addition, families often play a more central role in addressing their children's needs in these programs, and interventions are more likely to be designed for implementation across home and daycare/preschool settings.

## Elementary and Secondary School Services

Students with emotional and behavior disorders in elementary, middle, and high school receive their education in all the settings described in IDEA, more so than almost any other group of students with disabilities. As Figure 7.4 shows, 37.3 percent of these students are in general education for 80 percent or more of the school day. Approximately 24 percent of them attend self-contained special education classes, and nearly 20 percent are educated in separate schools or other facilities (U.S. Department of Education, 2008). Compare these data to the comparable information for students with learning disabilities in Chapter Five. Why do you think the figures are so different?

Placements for students with emotional and behavior disorders also vary considerably across states (U.S. Department of Education, 2008). In Alabama, nearly two-thirds, and in North Dakota, approximately 71 percent, of these students are in general education settings at least 80 percent of the day. In contrast, New York places 40 percent of these students in a special education setting for most of the day, and Hawaii follows closely at 38 percent. Think about the practical and potential lifelong implications for students of these wide differences in placement decisions: If you were a student with an emotional or behavior disorder and you lived in Alabama, you would have a very good chance of being educated beside your peers without disabilities. However, if your family moved to New York, you probably would spend much of the day in a special education classroom, interacting primarily with other students with emotional and behavior disorders, excluded from

### web link

http://cecp.air.org
The Center for Effective Collaboration and Practice facilitates the production, exchange, and use of knowledge about effective practices for students with emotional and behavior disorders. The center's website includes information on critical issues (e.g., juvenile justice), opportunities for discussions, and resources for developing behavior intervention plans.

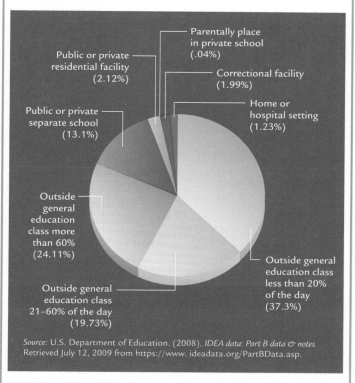

**FIGURE 7.4**

**Educational Placements of Students Ages Six to Twenty-One Who Have Emotional or Behavior Disorders (in percentages)**

- Parentally place in private school (.04%)
- Correctional facility (1.99%)
- Home or hospital setting (1.23%)
- Public or private residential facility (2.12%)
- Public or private separate school (13.1%)
- Outside general education class more than 60% (24.11%)
- Outside general education class 21–60% of the day (19.73%)
- Outside general education class less than 20% of the day (37.3%)

*Source:* U.S. Department of Education. (2008). *IDEA data: Part B data & notes.* Retrieved July 12, 2009 from https://www. ideadata.org/PartBData.asp.

*Increasingly, professionals are stressing that very early and intensive intervention is essential for improving outcomes for students with emotional and behavior disorders.*

many of the typical social lessons learned in the general education environment. Do you think such differences should exist? Why or why not?

The types of services students receive may vary somewhat based on the setting in which they are educated. In a general education classroom, a student may be expected to meet most of the same expectations as other students, but the teacher probably will pay closer attention to effective instructional approaches and interventions that can reduce inappropriate behavior. In a resource room, students may receive instruction from a highly qualified special educator in a single academic subject such as reading or English, or they may get assistance with organizational skills, general learning and study strategies, and self-management techniques. The special educator in this setting also will manage various types of behavior intervention programs designed to help students display appropriate classroom behavior. In a self-contained special education classroom, a small group of students may spend the day with a single teacher or move as a group among several special education teachers, with limited amounts of time spent with peers either in academic or related arts classes.

Students in a self-contained level of service often are working on highly structured point systems that move students through various levels of privileges based on their behavior. For example, leaving the classroom unaccompanied might be a reward earned by displaying appropriate in-class behavior.

For students needing an even more restrictive placement, alternatives may include day treatment or residential programs (Gagnon & Leone, 2005; Kalke, Glanton, & Cristalli, 2007). **Day treatment programs** are special schools that include special education in small classes and place a strong emphasis on individualized instruction. They usually also include individual and group therapy, family counseling, vocational training, crisis intervention, positive skill building, and other services such as recreational, art, and music therapy. **Residential programs**, usually attended by students with the most serious or dangerous emotional problems, are just what the name suggests: Students live at these schools, attending classes and participating in therapeutic and recreational activities. The school services may look much like those in a day treatment program.

## Inclusive Practices

Given the data about educational placements for students with emotional and behavior disorders, it is clear that inclusive practices are an issue for these students (Johns & Guetzloe, 2004; Visser & Stokes, 2003). In fact, the debate about inclusion for students with emotional and behavior disorders has been particularly contentious. Coleman and Webber (2002) have identified these areas of concern:

1. *Curriculum.* With today's academic standards, general education classrooms establish high expectations for students. This pressure may cause students with emotional and behavior disorders to develop further problems. At the same time, these classrooms often do not emphasize social skills development, anger management, and other topics that may be crucial for students with emotional disabilities. Unless these concerns are directly addressed, students may be inadvertently set up for failure (Fitzpatrick & Knowlton, 2009).
2. *Social rejection.* Students with emotional and behavior disorders often have difficulty making friends, or they make friends with students who have similar problems. Just as important, general education teachers are more negative about students with these dis-

orders than about any other group of students with disabilities. They often note that they feel ill prepared to work with these students (Wagner et al., 2006). As a result they often do not have a sense of ownership for the students or feel responsible for their success or failure. This concern implies that teachers need professional development to learn how to support students in the social domain.

3. *Mental health treatment.* Students with emotional and behavior disorders often need comprehensive services that include a strong mental health component in addition to academic supports (Gudino, Lau, Yeh, McCabe, & Hough, 2009). Although general education classrooms address academic and social domains, they are not structured to incorporate mental health services, such as counseling. However, it should be noted that the provision of mental health treatment can be problematic in any school setting, whether inclusive or more restrictive.

Two important points should be made in thinking about the inclusion of students with emotional and behavior disorders. First, the concerns just mentioned are based on the assumption that inclusion is mostly about where students sit. The view of this textbook is that inclusion is about welcoming all students to their learning community—that is, their school. Thus, in inclusive schools, students with emotional disabilities might spend most (or all) of the day in a general education classroom, or a small part of the day, or they might have the option of leaving that classroom if it becomes too stressful. In addition, students without disabilities might tutor students with emotional and behavior disorders in the special education classroom, and they might also serve as buddies for these students. In other words, students can be included even if they do not sit in a general education classroom for the entire day.

Second, with careful planning and preparation, school professionals are succeeding in supporting some students with emotional and behavior disorders in their general education classrooms (Heineman, Dunlap, & Kincaid, 2005; Kaff, Zabel, & Milham, 2007). For example, one group of researchers provided staff development for school professionals in the best practices for supporting students with emotional disabilities in general education settings (Shapiro, Miller, Sawka, Gardill, & Handler, 1999). By providing this training and offering intensive consultation designed to help the general educators problem solve about specific students and implement the interventions they had learned, inclusionary practices were successful for these students.

Thus, to say that inclusion for students with emotional and behavior problems is not possible is an overstatement: It is more accurate to say that it requires strong administrative support; a plan for implementation that addresses academic, behavioral, and emotional needs; attention to enhancing the knowledge and skills of general education teachers as well as other school professionals; and the option for alternatives for students who need them. How might these concepts apply to Krystal, Garrett, and Carlos, the students whose stories appeared at the beginning of this chapter?

## Transition and Adulthood

The outcomes for students with emotional and behavior disorders have been disappointing (Samuels, 2008). For example, it is estimated that between only 35 and 44 percent of students with these disorders graduate from high school while 56 percent drop out. Although some of these students later earn their high school diplomas through GED programs, those who do not are especially at risk for poor adult outcomes. In addition, students with emotional and behavior disorders have difficulty finding and keeping jobs (Carter & Wehby, 2003).

Most professionals agree that improving outcomes for students with emotional and behavior disorders is quite feasible (Carter, Lane, Pierson, & Glaeser, 2006). The key is to translate the knowledge base for effective interventions into widespread practice. For example, students with these disorders should be served through family-centered approaches that coordinate school and community assistance (Test, Fowler, White, Richter, & Walker, 2009). Better access to mental health services for students and their families is needed. These students should be taught specific skills that will help them pursue postschool options. An example is anger management, a skill described in the Instruction in Action feature. Focused transition programs with measurable goals that provide

**research**
**NOTE**

In a study of 99 third- through eighth-grade students reported to social workers for excessive absences from school (Dube & Orpinas, 2009), it was found that 60 percent of the students received parent attention or other reinforcements for absences. This suggests that most students miss school to gain something outside of school rather than to avoid something at school.

## Teaching Anger Management Skills

Research has demonstrated that students can be taught anger management strategies that help them to reduce their anger and to display anger more appropriately (e.g., Kellner, Bry, & Salvador, 2008).

Anger management programs usually include

- recognition that anger is normal
- understanding of individual responses to anger
- identification of anger triggers
- awareness of degrees of anger

- tools for anger management—cognitive and behavioral
- practice of anger management strategies.

The accompanying figure illustrates an anger log used by students in middle and high school after they had completed an anger management program. In what types of situations might such a log be helpful for students in monitoring and refining their anger management skills?

*Source:* Kellner, M. H., Bry, B. H., & Colletti, L. A. (2002). Teaching anger management skills to students with severe emotional or behavioral disorders. *Behavioral Disorders, 27*, 400–407. Reprinted by permission of the Council for Children with Behavioral Disorders.

---

### Final Anger Log

**Name** _____    **Date** _____

*What was your trigger?*

- ❑ Somebody started fighting with me.
- ❑ Somebody teased me.
- ❑ Somebody insisted I do something.
- ❑ Somebody took something of mine.
- ❑ Somebody did something I didn't like.
- ❑ Other _____

*Where were you when you got angry?*  ❑ School    ❑ Neighborhood    ❑ Home    ❑ Other _____

*How angry were you?*

| 1 | 2 | 3 | 4 | 5 |
|---|---|---|---|---|
| not angry | mildly angry | moderately angry | really angry | burning mad |

| | | How did you handle your anger? | How will you handle your anger next time? |
|---|---|---|---|
| *Inappropriate responses* | Yelling | ❑ | ❑ |
| | Throwing something | ❑ | ❑ |
| | Cursing | ❑ | ❑ |
| | Threatening someone | ❑ | ❑ |
| | Breaking something | ❑ | ❑ |
| | Hitting someone | ❑ | ❑ |
| | Other _____ | ❑ | ❑ |
| *Appropriate responses* *Physiological tools* | Counting to 10, 20, 30 | ❑ | ❑ |
| | Taking deep breaths | ❑ | ❑ |
| | Relaxing my muscles | ❑ | ❑ |
| | Other _____ | ❑ | ❑ |
| *Thinking tools* | Using self-think/self-statement | ❑ | ❑ |

*Write down what you thought or said to yourself.*

_____

_____

| | | | |
|---|---|---|---|
| *Behavioral tools* | Talking it out | ❑ | ❑ |
| | Ignoring it | ❑ | ❑ |
| | Going for a run | ❑ | ❑ |
| | Walking away | ❑ | ❑ |
| | Other _____ | ❑ | ❑ |

*Did you make your anger work for you?*

- ❑ Yes    I stayed in control, respected people and property, and had positive results.
- ❑ No    I lost control, hurt people or property, and/or had negative results.

*How did you handle the situation?*

| 1 | 2 | 3 | 4 | 5 |
|---|---|---|---|---|
| poorly | not so well | OK | well | great |

*Source:* Reprinted from *In control: A Skill-Building Program for Teaching Young Adolescents to Manage Anger* (p. 91) by M. H. Kellner (2001).Champaign IL: Research Press. Copyright 2001 by M. E. Kellner. Reprinted by permission.

vocational training and on-the-job training also can help outcomes (Corbett, Clark, & Blank, 2002) as can specific training in self-determination skills (Carter et al., 2006). Finally, better training for school professionals is necessary so that all the other elements of transition can be implemented.

## REVIEW · REFLECT · DISCUSS

1. What are the likely critical factors that teams discuss when deciding on the appropriate educational placement for a student with an emotional disability? How might these factors change across grade levels?

2. What are the arguments for and against inclusion of students with emotional and behavior disorders? What can educators do to increase the success of inclusive practices for these students?

# Recommended Educational Practices for Students with Emotional and Behavior Disorders

Over the past 25 years, a strong base of research has developed that can guide school professionals in their work with students with emotional and behavior disorders. Effective practices include prevention, collaboration, procedures required by IDEA, and specific interventions.

## The Importance of Prevention

Because of highly publicized incidents of school violence and research demonstrating poor outcomes for students with emotional and behavior disorders, the prevention of these disorders has in recent years become one of the highest priorities among school and community agencies concerned about children (Masia-Warner, Nangle, & Hansen, 2006; Reddy, Newman, DeThomas, & Chun, 2009; U.S. Department of Health and Human Services, 1999).

### Early Intervention

Prevention has several components. As you have read, one component is early intervention. Professionals agree that if early interventions could be implemented with young children who are at risk for developing behavior disorders, some children would not experience later problems. This type of early intervention may address young children's behavior. It also may address the development of their language and other communication skills because of the evidence already discussed suggesting that one factor that may contribute to the development of emotional and behavior disorders is the frustration that results from poor communication skills (Benner, Nelson, & Epstein, 2002; Ritzman & Sanger, 2007).

### Positive Behavior Supports

Another focus for prevention in elementary and secondary schools involves implementing schoolwide **positive behavior supports (PBS)**. Schoolwide PBS includes these elements (U.S. Department of Education, 2003):

1. An approach to discipline that is agreed on by all the administrators, teachers, and other professionals in the school
2. A positive statement of the purpose of the PBS
3. A small number of rules for students and staff, worded in positive ways
4. Clear procedures for teaching behavior expectations to students
5. A set of procedures for encouraging students to display appropriate behaviors
6. A set of procedures for discouraging inappropriate behaviors and rule breaking
7. A clear plan for monitoring the schoolwide PBS and for evaluating its effectiveness

dimensions of
**DIVERSITY**

Studying African American students in kindergarten through grade 3 in an urban setting, Sanchez Fowler, Banks, Anhalt, Hinrichs Der, and Kalis (2008) found that student-teacher relationships became more negative across the grades and that students who had prosocial behaviors in addition to behavior problems had better relationships with their teachers than those with few prosocial skills.

## Implementing a Positive Behavior Support Program

These questions can help you to understand how PBS is implemented at the individual, classroom, and school levels.

| Question | Individual | Classroom | Schoolwide |
|---|---|---|---|
| Who should be involved in the process and how? | Must include student, parents, teacher, and other direct support providers, but may include friends, extended family, administration, specialists, and community members. | Must include teacher, administration, and paraprofessionals, but may include related service providers, specialists, student/parent representatives, and other teachers. | Must include administration, grade-level, and discipline- specific representatives, but parents, community members, and students are recommended participants. |
| How do we identify the variables affecting student behavior? | Identification of contexts (setting, events, antecedents) and functions (maintaining variables) of individual student behavior (e.g., obtained via functional behavioral assessment) | Inventory of classroom features and management (including disciplinary procedures) and identification of problematic routines that affect the behavior and academic performance of students in the classroom(s) | Multilevel site analysis (incorporate classroom, individual students), surveys, observations, patterns in discipline referrals, and organizational features that affect all of the students in a school |
| How do we identify and implement effective strategies? | · Modifying the circumstances associated with the problem behaviors (e.g., difficult tasks)<br>· Teaching replacement behaviors (e.g., asking for breaks)<br>· Providing functional consequences for behavior (e.g., earning free time)<br>· Addressing lifestyle supports (e.g., peer buddy, medical evaluation) | · Modifying classroom management structure (e.g., rules, routines, arrangement of physical environment)<br>· Modifying instructional methods to engage participation and address social–personal skills<br>· Implementing rewards and in-class discipline methods (e.g., time-out) | · Redesigning the school environment (e.g., increased supervision)<br>· Establishing, teaching, and rewarding adherence to schoolwide expectations<br>· Implementing a continuum of consequences for infractions<br>· Addressing staff incentives and organizational changes (e.g., revised policies and procedures) |
| What systems will be used to measure desired outcomes? | Increases/decreases in specific target behaviors, including development of skills to replace problem behaviors, and quality of life changes (e.g., improved relationships, participation in integrated activities) | Increases in academic engagement (e.g., assignment completion, grades) reductions in disruptive behavior, and enhanced classroom functioning (e.g., fewer referrals, time-outs, more rewards/points earned) | Improvements in overall social and academic environment (e.g., grades, attendance, school climate); fewer discipline referrals and crisis procedures as well as diminished need for individual plans |

Source: Heineman, M., Dunlap, G., & Kincaid, D. (2005). Positive support strategies for students with behavioral disorders in general education settings. *Psychology in the Schools, 42*, 779–794. Reproduced with permission of John Wiley & Sons, Inc.

**PEARSON**
## myeducationlab

Go to the Building Teaching Skills and Dispositions section of Topic 10: Emotional/Behavioral Disorders, in the MyEducationLab for your course and complete the activity entitled "Establishing Classroom Rules and Routines".

In schools using PBS, all students and teachers are clear about the expectations for behavior in all common use areas of the school—hallways, gym, cafeteria, and so on. Students are rewarded for knowing and following these rules. In addition, behavior expectations are set at the classroom level. That is, teachers arrange the physical space of the classroom, establish expectations with students, and arrange rewards tailored to the specific group of students. For students whose behavior is not addressed with these schoolwide and classroom strategies, often a team meets and creates an individualized behavior plan using the procedures for functional behavior assessment and behavior intervention plans outlined in the next section. Key questions that guide this contemporary approach to behavior management are outlined in the Positive Behavior Supports.

Research on the effects of schoolwide PBS is encouraging. Professionals in schools using this approach report that they are more effective and that they are motivated to continue using PBS (Oswald, Safran, & Johanson, 2005; Sadler & Sugai, 2009). In middle school, this approach has led to fewer office discipline referrals, fewer suspensions, and an increase in math and reading achievement scores that could be directly attributed to fewer behavior problems (Lassen, Steele, & Sailor, 2006). Why do you think that schoolwide PBS can have such positive effects?

*Positive behavior supports that are schoolwide, classwide, and individual can assist students with emotional and behavior disabilities to succeed in inclusive settings.*

## The Effectiveness of Collaboration

A second element of effective practice for students with emotional and behavior disorders is *collaboration,* a topic that was introduced in Chapter Four. For students with emotional and behavior disorders, however, collaboration takes on an added dimension. Professionals have increasingly come to agree that because the needs of students with emotional and behavior disorders are so complex and addressed by so many different agencies and organizations, the only way to ensure effective services is to create systems for effective interagency collaboration—that is, collaboration that spans school and nonschool agencies (Anderson, 2000; Worcester, Nesman, Raffaele Mendez, & Keller, 2008). These agencies might include the school, a community mental health agency, a family social services agency, the juvenile justice system, a state hospital or other residential facility, and so on.

Many examples of this type of interagency collaboration have now been documented, and collectively they are sometimes referred to as **wraparound services** (Quinn & Lee, 2007). Most of these collaborations are based on a **system of care** (Stroul, 1996), an approach to interagency collaboration based on a coordinated network of service providers that is child and family centered, community based, and sensitive to cultural diversity. The system of care approach is guided by these principles:

1. Children with emotional disabilities should have access to a comprehensive array of services that address their physical, emotional, social, and educational needs.
2. Children with emotional disabilities should receive individualized services in accordance with their unique needs and potential and guided by individualized service plans.
3. Children with emotional disabilities should receive services within the least restrictive, most normative environment that is clinically appropriate.
4. The families and surrogate families of children with emotional disabilities should be full participants in all aspects of the planning and delivery of services.
5. Children with emotional disabilities should receive services that are integrated with linkages between child-serving agencies and programs and mechanisms for planning, developing, and coordinating services.
6. Children with emotional disabilities should be provided with case management or a similar mechanism to ensure that multiple services are delivered in a coordinated and

### fyi

Educators should remind themselves to tell students what they are doing that is right. By saying "Thanks for putting your assignment in the in-box," "It was very nice of you to apologize when you bumped into Jerry," and similar comments, you help students understand your expectations. This is much more effective than simply telling students what not to do.

therapeutic manner and that they can move through the system of services in accordance with their changing needs.

7. Early identification and intervention for children with emotional disabilities should be promoted by the systems of care in order to enhance the likelihood of positive outcomes.

8. Children with emotional disabilities should be ensured a smooth transition to the adult service system as they reach maturity.

9. The rights of children with emotional disabilities should be protected, and effective advocacy efforts for children and youth with emotional disabilities should be promoted.

10. Children with emotional disabilities should receive services without regard to race/ethnicity, religion, national origin, sex, physical disability, or other characteristics, and services should be sensitive and responsive to cultural differences and special needs.

As you might expect, the outcomes of such shared work can vary significantly depending on the level of participation of each agency, the amount of coordination in their work, and the intensity of the interventions employed (Copp, Bordnick, Traylor, & Thyer, 2007; Stambaugh et al., 2007). In essence, success of the system of care approach relies on the understanding that meaningful collaboration among families, professionals, and community services is the most effective way to address the multiple and complex needs of students with emotional and behavior disorders.

## Requirements for Interventions in IDEA

IDEA requires that school professionals use very systematic procedures to document the behavior problems that students display, to analyze the reasons those behaviors occur, and to develop and systematically implement interventions intended to reduce inappropriate behaviors while increasing appropriate behaviors. Two specific procedures—functional behavior assessment (FBA) and the development of a behavior intervention plan (BIP)—are required for all students with disabilities who experience behavior problems, regardless of whether their identified disability involves emotional disturbance. For example, Renée is a student with autism. When she gets upset she tries to bite her teachers and herself. The team making educational decisions for Renée would need to complete a functional behavior assessment and a behavior intervention plan for her, even though she is not identified as having an emotional or behavior disorder. However, these procedures are particularly applicable to students with these disorders.

### Functional Behavior Assessment

When a student misbehaves, school professionals are faced with the challenge of finding an effective way to respond. **Functional behavior assessment (FBA)** is a multidimensional problem-solving strategy for analyzing the student's behavior within the context of the setting in which it is occurring. The purpose is to decide the function of the behavior and determine how to address it (Erickson, Stage, & Nelson, 2006; Scott, Anderson, & Spaulding, 2008).

FBA is based on two assumptions (Ryan, Halsey, & Matthews, 2003). The first is that challenging behavior occurs in context; that is, it is influenced by the setting in which it occurs. Thus, the setting must be considered when trying to change a behavior. The second assumption underlying FBA is that challenging behavior serves a function for the student. Educators need to identify that function in order to change the behavior. Functional behavior assessment involves these five steps:

1. *Identify the problem behavior.* Carefully describe the behaviors in observable ways and prioritize them. For example, instead of stating that Tate sulks when work is assigned, the team would specify that four out of five times when Tate is given a written assignment by the general education teacher, he puts his head down on his desk, covers his face, and does not respond to teacher requests that he begin his work.

2. *Describe in detail the settings in which the behavior occurs.* In the example of Tate, the setting of concern is the general education classroom. The team might further note that

Some students with emotional and behavior disorders can be helped by proximity control. In this simple technique, a professional observing student misbehavior moves toward the student in a nonthreatening manner, often making direct eye contact, with the intent of getting the student to stop the behavior in question.

Tate is seated in the front of the room, that the class includes 27 other students, and that the desks are arranged in rows with aisles.

3. *Gather information about the behavior using interviews, rating scales, observation, review of student records, and other techniques.* One common observation technique is called an ABC approach. ABC stands for *antecedents* (what comes immediately before the behavior that causes it to happen), *behaviors,* and *consequences* (what happens as a result of the behavior). For Tate, the antecedent is his teacher giving him an assignment. The behavior is what Tate does. The consequence is that his teacher asked him again to do the work. After several cycles of asking and refusing, the teacher sent Tate with a discipline referral to the office. One other element might be considered: setting events. These are things that may have happened earlier in the day that could be affecting the situation. For Tate, a setting event might be his working in the evenings at a fast-food restaurant and not getting enough sleep.

4. *Review the data.* The team would examine the observational data; they probably would also have information from the teacher, from Tate, and possibly from Tate's parents. They might compare what was observed to Tate's perception of his behavior and to his teacher's views (Kinch, Lewis-Palmer, Hagan-Burke, & Sugai, 2001).

5. *Form a hypothesis about the function of the behavior based on the data gathered.* If you were going to make an educated guess about what function Tate's behavior is serving, what would you say? One reasonable hypothesis is that Tate's behavior is his way of avoiding difficult assignments. By refusing to do the work, he gets sent to the office and does not have to complete the work. In other situations, behaviors could serve other functions (Frey & Wilhite, 2005), such as the following:
   - For some students, behaving inappropriately is a way to get adults to pay attention to them, something they may crave.
   - For other students, behaving inappropriately may be a means for ending a social interaction with a classmate.
   - For yet other students, behaving inappropriately may help them to get items or activities that they want (e.g., having a tantrum results in being taken to the special education classroom, where the student can play with colored chalk on the blackboard).

   What other functions can you think of that behaviors might address? If you think about Krystal, Garrett, and Carlos, introduced at the beginning of the chapter, what functions might their behaviors have?

### Behavior Intervention Plan

Based on the hypothesis the team makes, the next task is to create a **behavior intervention plan (BIP)**, a set of strategies designed to address the function of the behavior in order to change it (Killu, 2008; Wright-Gallo, Higbee, Reagon, & Davey, 2006). For Tate, the team decided to change the antecedent by arranging for Tate temporarily to be partnered with a classmate whenever lengthy written assignments were given. In addition, the team developed a *contract.* A contract is a behavior intervention strategy that clearly spells out expectations, rewards, and consequences for students, as illustrated in the Positive Behavior Supports feature. For Tate, the contract rewarded him for completing work. It also included an extended deadline so that he could work on such assignments in parts. The setting event of working in the evenings is one that the team decided it would not be able to address. Data were gathered to determine whether the assignment partner and contract with rewards and extended time were effective. In this case, the BIP was successful: It addressed the behavior so that learning could occur. If it had not been a success, the team would have been responsible for reanalyzing the information it had gathered about the problem, possibly looking for additional information, and designing another intervention. The new intervention also would be evaluated to check its effectiveness.

If you review all the Positive Behavior Supports features in the chapters that you have read as well as those in the chapters that follow this one, you will see that the strategies and interventions could be parts of BIPs. In fact, the expectation today for students experiencing behavior problems is to teach them appropriate behaviors that will help them succeed not

research
NOTE

Are functional behavior assessments and the resulting behavior intervention plans effective? Van Acker, Boreson, Gable, and Potterton (2005) examined FBAs and BIPs from trained professionals. They found that those who had at least two days of intensive training on these topics were most successful in using these procedures.

## Behavior Contracts

Behavior contracts, often used as one means of achieving IEP goals for students with serious behavior problems, can address a wide array of behaviors and can be used with elementary, middle school, and high school students. Here is one example of a behavior contract.

---

**Behavior Contract**

**Effective dates: March 1, 2010, to March 15, 2010**

**I,** _____Doug_____ **, agree to do the following:**
Begin assignments when they are given to me.
Ask for help by raising my hand if I am stuck.
Put completed assignments in the "Completed Work" tray.

**I,** _____Ms. Coble_____ **, agree to do the following:**
Check with Doug to be sure he understands the assignment.
Alert Doug when the time for completing an assignment is nearly up.
Give Doug 2 points for beginning his work, one point each time he asks for help by raising his hand, and one point for putting work in the "Complete Work" tray. Doug may accumulate up to 6 points per class period.

**Reward**

Each time Doug accumulates 10 points, he may spend them on 10 minutes of computer time.

**Bonus**

If Doug accumulates 25 points for two weeks in a row, he may assist Mr. Ames in the computer lab for one class period.

**Penalty**

If Doug does not attempt an assignment, he will be asked to complete it at home that evening.
If Doug calls out instead of raising his hand for help more than two times in a class period, this information will be shared with his mother.

**Signatures**

_____          _____

**Doug Shoales**                                             **Ms. Coble**

_____

**Mrs. Shoales**

---

only in school but also later in life. Negative consequences, or punishment, although not eliminated completely, usually are employed only in partnership with positive behavior supports and only if no other effective approaches can be found.

## Examples of Specific Interventions

In addition to interventions that are incorporated into the FBA and BIP procedures, general education teachers, special education teachers, and other professionals working with students with emotional and behavior disorders can use a wide variety of strategies to enhance student learning while fostering appropriate behaviors. For example, many students need assistance in recording their assignments, remembering when assignments are due, and dealing with the mechanics of completing them, including checking spelling and grammar. Others may benefit by learning how to use technology to self-monitor their learning behaviors, the topic of the Technology Notes.

### Peer-Mediated Instruction

The goal for many students with emotional and behavior disorders is to learn to participate in groups with other students without disruption. Some teachers use peer-mediated

Self-monitoring is a research-based intervention for helping students to improve behavior. It involves these three steps:

1. Teach the student to discriminate occurrences versus non-occurrences of the target behavior (e.g., on-task versus off-task; attending versus not attending).
2. Teach the student to self-record the behavior (e.g., Am I on-task? Am I attending?).
3. Teach the student to graph the behavior.

Although in the past, teaching self-monitoring generally involved written descriptions of the behavior and paper-and-pencil recording and graphing forms, technology now offers more efficient, effective, and motivating strategies to accomplish the same goals.

Gulchak (2008) used a Palm™ device and software from HanDBase™ to teach self-monitoring to an eight-year-old student identified as having an emotional disability. Here is the procedure Gulchak followed:

1. Create a simple 3-part description of on-task behavior (1. Keep hands away from face; 2. Complete work assigned; 3. Raise hand to ask questions) and used the software to enter this description on the handheld computer.
2. Create a simple data form that the student completed each 10 minutes during the 60-minute reading instructional period in the self-contained classroom.

3. Create a simple report procedure using the software that allowed the student to summarize the data and produce a graph at the end of each session.
4. Set the device's alarm to sound a tone every 10 minutes to remind the student to decide whether he was attending and record yes/no on the device.
5. Teach the student how to recognize the desired behavior, to operate the device, to record data, and to produce summary reports and graphs.

After gathering observational data demonstrating the student's rate of being on-task was 64 percent without using the handheld computer, the student was given the device to use during reading instruction. His rate of being on-task jumped to 90 percent, and he used the device as instructed every single day.

If you think about it, this approach to teaching self-monitoring has tremendous potential:

- Handheld computers are inexpensive, especially when compared to laptop or desktop computers.
- The software also is inexpensive.
- Use of a handheld computer is motivating for the student.
- The handheld computer has far less stigma than paper-and-pencil recording; in fact, it may give a student improved social status with peers.

instruction, a collection of programs and interventions for which a long history of research has demonstrated success (e.g., Kroeger, Burton, & Preston, 2009; What Works Clearinghouse, 2007), to accomplish this goal. Two examples of peer-mediated instruction are peer tutoring and cooperative learning. In peer tutoring each student works with one other student to practice math facts, review vocabulary, or complete another instructional task. One student is the tutor, or the student responsible for acting as the peer teacher; the other student is the tutee, or the student answering the questions. In one successful peer-tutoring approach, called *reciprocal tutoring*, both students take both roles in a single tutoring session.

In cooperative learning, students work in groups of three or four. They have a specific task to complete, play assigned roles (e.g., notetaker), and take accountability for the learning. One cooperative learning method, called Numbered Heads Together, combines the skills and learning efforts of students with a bit of luck. Numbered Heads Together is described in the Instruction in Action feature.

For peer tutoring and cooperative learning to be effective with these students, teachers must implement it carefully, following methods that have been demonstrated through research to produce positive outcomes (Bowman-Perrott, 2009). In addition, students should receive instruction in appropriate leadership, communication, decision-making, and trust-building skills (Sutherland, Wehby, & Gunter, 2000). Finally, teachers or others implementing peer tutoring and cooperative learning should assess its impact on student achievement and monitor student behavior in these instructional arrangements.

### Teacher-Led Instruction

One final area of intervention should be mentioned. Students with emotional and behavior disorders clearly struggle with academic achievement, and evidence increasingly points to the importance of using specific programs and procedures to help them learn (e.g., Carroll et al., 2005; Nelson, Benner, & Gonzalez, 2005; Vannest, Temple-Harvey, & Mason, 2009). In addition, many of the strategies that make instruction effective for all

# Numbered Heads Together

Numbered Heads Together is one example of a research-based cooperative learning approach that can be effective for teaching academic content and social interaction skills to students with emotional and behavior disabilities (Maheady, Harper, & Mallette, 2001). Here are the steps to follow to implement Numbered Heads Together:

1. Assign students to groups of three or four. These groups should be heterogeneous, including students at various achievement levels. Students should be seated near one another when the approach is used.

2. Have students assign themselves numbers from one to three or four.

3. Ask the class a question.

4. Have students "put their heads together" so that they determine the correct answer or several answers, depending on the type of question asked. Students are instructed to be sure that every member of their group knows the answer(s).

5. Call the groups back together. Call a number (one to three or one to four) and have the students in the class with that number stand.

6. Call on one of the standing students to answer the question. If there is more than one correct answer, continue to call on students.

7. Ask the rest of the class to agree or disagree with the stated answer.

8. Award points or rewards. This can be done in several ways. Some teachers use a positive approach: As long as each student called on gets an answer, all teams are rewarded. Other teachers give each team one "pass" so that if a member does not answer correctly the team still has an opportunity to be rewarded.

Keep in mind that while this strategy is effective for students with emotional and behavior disorders, it is also successful with many other groups of students, with or without disabilities.

*Source:* Based on Maheady, L., Harper, G. F., & Mallette, B. (2001). Peer-mediated instruction and interventions and students with mild disabilities. *Remedial and Special Education, 22*(1), 4–14. Copyright © 2001 by Pro-Ed, Inc.

students are particularly important for these students, including the following (Quinn et al., 2000):

- Keep lesson objectives clear.
- Deliver lessons in a lively manner, and make sure that students are engaged.
- Use concrete vocabulary and clear, succinct sentences.
- Give all students immediate encouragement and specific feedback.
- Use meaningful materials and provide examples to which students can relate.
- Have students recite in unison.
- Prompt student answers after allowing an appropriate amount of wait time (i.e., to encourage participation, which may vary for each student).
- Break long presentations into shorter segments that include student responding.
- Break down a large assignment into smaller ones. As students finish each mini-assignment, build in reinforcement for task completion.
- When students make mistakes, help them to learn from those mistakes. Be careful not to overcorrect, and praise any progress toward the desired behavior change.
- Follow low-interest activities with high-interest activities so that students get occasional breaks from difficult or less-interesting activities.
- Build on student interests. Students often learn by relating material to real-life situations that they find interesting.
- Allow students to make choices. Let them decide between two tasks or select the order in which they complete assigned tasks.
- Employ appropriate technology applications that can engage student interest and increase motivation.
- Use hands-on, experiential learning activities to enable students to apply learning to the real world. This is one of a teacher's most powerful tools.

A discussion of instructing students with emotional and behavior disorders would not be complete without mentioning the importance of one additional topic: the qualities, abilities, and perspectives of the teacher. Perhaps more so than for any other group of students with special needs, teachers of students with emotional disabilities must have a strong sense of confidence in their ability to help these students and the capacity to care deeply even when students' behavior make it difficult (Mihalas, Morse, Allsopp, & McHatton, 2009).

*Mackenzie Benson was always drawn to working with children, especially concerning their emotions. With a nearly-completed degree in applied behavior analysis and a father in ill health, Mack completed his professional preparation at North Texas State University, elected to become a special education teacher, and began his teaching career in the Pasadena (TX) Independent School District working in an elementary self-contained unit for students with severe emotional and behavior problems. Although he has since become an elementary school counselor in a nearby district, he offers important insights on working with these students. Here are his thoughts on working with students with emotional and behavior disorders.*

- A lot of the kids with emotional disturbances, their parents have emotional or other issues, too—like one parent was abusing the child's meds [medications]. Not all of them, but a lot of them do. And so you're trying to form this foundation with students of this behavior they should exhibit at school, but when they get home the parents have their own issues and everything you've done that day kind of gets trumped. So you're just always hoping that one thing that I taught them today kind of sticks with them so they can work their way through situations when they need to.

- I think the most rewarding thing about working with these students is to see them exhibit a behavior. . .you've been working so hard with them, and you watch them finally do something like raise their hands and ask for something. Or instead of hitting someone they actually just walk away from them. It's small things but it's huge when you look at the big picture. And that's my mantra with the kids: Just remember one thing that I've taught you. Just one thing. Maybe that will keep you out of a world of trouble.

- Do not get into a power struggle with kids. I think so many teachers get into this thing of I'm the teacher, I'm always right. Sometimes you do have to lose a little bit with the kids, and sometimes you can lose a little bit with saving face. And so I think it's all about the compromise and the way you do it, like giving choices to a kid, especially a kid with emotional disturbance.

- This is related. You've got to check your ego at the door. Kids will try to find any button they can to push. You just can't let an eight-year-old upset you to the point that you'd lose control. What sense does that make?

- You just can't take it home with you. There were times when my wife would say that I grit my teeth when I sleep. That's bad. You've got to find an outlet; you can't just take it home with you. Some of the kids have problems you can't even imagine . . . a student whose parents didn't want him, whose adoptive parents were sexually abusing him, and in the foster home he was being cruel to animals, horrible things. If you don't learn to let it go, and it's hard, you'll wind up taking it home and you'll destroy the relationships you have with the people in your own family. Go work out, go run, go do something. You give 110% at work, and then when you leave work you have to let it go. That doesn't mean you don't care.

- I thought that in my first couple of weeks or months their behavior was going to change because of what I did, and so I kind of felt like a failure my first couple of months with them because they were not getting better. A lot of these kids have had these issues for years, and you're not going to cure the problem. You can make it better, but I don't think you should take it to the point of thinking you're not doing a good job. Some things are just going take a while, more than the time you have with them. Sometimes you're fighting an uphill battle. I think the minute that you think you've lost, or are not being consistent, you lose it. The kids need consistency so much in their lives because lots of things in their life are so inconsistent. So they need to you come in every day with a straight face. We're all going have difficulties in our lives, but they don't need to see it from you because they'll pick up on it. Some of the kids are so in tune to people's emotions.

- Anything I do I can credit to two really good teachers I had. They could teach a child to do anything. And I had good mentors as a new teacher. It's good to learn all you can from people like them and then turn around and mentor someone behind you.

Mack Benson, a former teacher for students with emotional disabilities and now a counselor, eloquently addresses this topic in Speaking from Experience.

## REVIEW · REFLECT · DISCUSS

1. Why do some professionals consider collaboration more important in designing programs for students with emotional and behavior disorders than for any other group of students with disabilities?

2. Think about a student with problematic behavior you have known or observed (or use a case study from another source or think about a child who is a neighbor or relative). What function might this student's behavior be serving? Given the function of the behavior, what interventions in a behavior intervention plan (BIP) might help to address it?

# Perspectives of Parents and Families

Have you considered what it might be like to be the parent of a child with an emotional or behavior disorder? What do you think might be the greatest challenges you would face? The greatest joys? One report summarized in its title the experiences of these students and their families: "blamed and ashamed" (U.S. Department of Health and Human Services, 2003).

## The Impact of Having a Child with an Emotional or Behavior Disorder

The parents and family members of students with emotional and behavior disorders face several unique challenges in working with school professionals (Taylor-Richardson, Heflinger, & Brown, 2006). First, these families are more likely than families of other students to have a low income and to be headed by a single parent with a less-than-average amount of education (Mundschenk & Foley, 2000). These demographic characteristics by themselves form a barrier to partnership because many school programs assume the existence of a nuclear family.

Second, students with emotional and behavior disorders are at high risk of having at least one parent who also has an emotional, behavior, or other psychosocial disorder. For example, in a series of studies looking at predictors of such problems in over 2,300 children ages nine to seventeen, Copeland, Shanahan, Costello, and Angold (2009) found that those at highest risk were likely to have parents or a step-parent who were diagnosed as having mental illness, abused drugs or alcohol, or engaged in criminal activity. These data suggest that working with these parents may, in some cases, be complicated by parents' needs and the extent to which they are being addressed. If a parent is abusing drugs or alcohol, she is less likely than another parent to be able to actively participate in her child's education and the decisions to be made regarding programs and services.

A third barrier for these families is the often negative set of interactions that occur regarding their children. Teachers frequently are frustrated with students with emotional and behavior disorders; this emotion may lead teachers to have an overall negative perception of the student and the family. Teachers may then contact the family to enlist its help in addressing school problems, too often asking the parents to punish the student for behavior problems at school and too seldom involving the parents in reward systems. The parents may not be able to carry out the requests made by the teachers, or the parents' efforts may not be successful. The result may be additional frustration on the parts of teachers and parents alike (Fox, Vaughn, Wyatte, & Dunlap, 2002).

The negative interactions between school professionals and family members sometimes are highlighted during meetings. Parents may be anxious about working with school personnel, worried about the behaviors of their child, and concerned that any meeting will be an opportunity to learn about yet another issue related to their child that they may feel powerless to address (Jones et al., 2004). Parents' behaviors at meetings may be viewed as combative or disruptive. Unless school professionals recognize the reasons for these behaviors, they may form even more negative opinions about the student and family.

One other challenge faced by families of students with emotional and behavior disorders concerns advocacy (Mundschenk & Foley, 2003; Murray, 2005). Many disability groups are represented in schools and the community by advocacy groups that are led by parents. These groups often can collectively ensure that their children's rights are upheld and foster positive perceptions of their children's special needs by educating professionals, other parents, and students and by seeking positive publicity concerning individuals with disabilities. Such advocacy generally does not exist among parents of students with emotional and behavior disorders (Knitzer, 2005).

## Building Positive Relationships

More than anything else, families need professionals to genuinely care about their children (Fox et al., 2002). And so for educators working with families of students with emotional

### research NOTE

Zigmond (2006) found that 61 percent of students who had attended a separate day-treatment school (N = 97; 57 had graduated and 40 had dropped out) held jobs, most of which were minimum wage and part-time. This result was comparable to the rate reported for students who had been placed in less restrictive settings.

and behavior disorders, it is essential to diligently strive to form strong partnerships using a collaborative focus such as that outlined earlier in this chapter and to be flexible in terms of expectations for family involvement. Efforts also may involve parent education and support groups.

### Parent Education

In some cases, schools can offer assistance to parents by teaching them strategies that might help them to address their children's behavior at home (de Graaf, Speetjens, Smit, de Wolff, & Tavecchio, 2008). Parent education also can address topics such as how to help their children with homework, how school services for their children are structured, how to access community resources, and how to advocate for their children (Anderson & Matthews, 2001).

Of course, parent education programs that require struggling parents to come to school at times that are convenient only for teachers and administrators are not likely to be successful. A variety of options should be considered, including offering programs at times that are convenient for parents; locating programs in community centers, libraries, or other settings possibly more comfortable for parents than the school; and creating options such as packets of print or electronic materials that can be accessed by parents (e.g., information sent home; information on a school or teacher website; information that can be disseminated by school social workers through home visits).

### Support Groups

For some families, one of the most helpful options is a support group that includes the parents of other students with emotional and behavior disabilities (Kratochwill, McDonald, Levin, Scalia, & Coover, 2009). In support groups, parents share information about local resources and services, trade ideas for addressing specific problems, and obtain the reassurance of knowing that they are not alone in dealing with day-to-day challenges. Although school professionals might arrange to start a support group, parents take the lead and give the group its identity and direction. Even more common are support groups that exist outside school in the local community. Teachers can help parents access this type of assistance by keeping at hand details about such groups or knowing who at school (such as the counselor or social worker) can provide the needed information.

## REVIEW · REFLECT · DISCUSS

1. What are the greatest barriers that parents of students with emotional and behavior disorders perceive in their interactions with school and other professionals? What should you as a professional do to reduce these barriers as much as you can?

2. Think about the Firsthand Account of Robin and her daughter Jensen. If you had been one of Jensen's teachers, how would you have tried to establish a relationship with her? What advice would you have given her mother regarding addressing Jensen's behavior?

## Trends and Issues Affecting the Field of Emotional and Behavior Disorders

Many trends and issues related to the field of emotional and behavior disorders have been introduced elsewhere in this chapter. For example, you have learned about the controversy that exists about the definition of this disability and concerns about inclusive practices. However, if you asked experienced professionals to name the most important issues, they probably would include these two topics as significant for the field: (a) the difficulty that students and their families face in obtaining essential mental health services and (b) the controversy surrounding the use of seclusion and restraint with students with emotional and behavior disabilities.

Go to the Building Teaching Skills and Dispositions section of Topic 10: Emotional/Behavioral Disorders, in the MyEducationLab for your course and complete the activity entitled "Discouraging Bullying at School".

*Without early, intense, and ongoing intervention, outcomes for students with emotional and behavioral disabilities have not been positive.*

**web link**

http://www.nlm.nih.gov/medline-plus/childmentalhealth.html Medline Plus, sponsored by the National Institutes of Health, contains a wealth of information on topics and issues related to children and emotional and behavioral disorders, ranging from descriptions of common mental health disorders, through information about medications used to treat children's mental illness, to commonly asked questions.

## The Problem of Access

Professionals generally agree that the number of students with emotional and behavior disorders in the United States has risen during the past decade and that the nature and severity of these students' disorders have become more serious (Walker et al., 2005). However, the first problem related to access concerns identification: Whether considering schools or community services, far fewer students receive treatment than the number of students who need it. In fact, it has been estimated that less than 20 percent of the approximately 14 million youth who have mental illness receive treatment and that 90 percent of those who commit suicide have an untreated emotional or behavior disorder (Zionts & Villiers, 2003). The National Alliance on Mental Illness (2007) estimates that half of all serious mental illness begins by age fourteen, but that years and even decades go by before many of these individuals access treatment. This group also notes that up to 70 percent of youth in correctional facilities have some type of mental disorder, and 20 percent of incarcerated youth have a very serious mental illness. This situation has been referred to by advocates as a "hidden conspiracy" (Sachs, 1999).

For some families, access requires unthinkable sacrifices. In order to access Medicaid services that can provide mental health interventions, families that make enough money to survive but too much to be eligible must relinquish custody of their children. In one study, 23 percent of parents reported that they had been told by public officials that they should give up custody so that their children could get the care they needed (Collins, 2003; Friesen, Giliberti, Katz-Leavy, Osher, & Pullmann, 2003).

### Creating a Promising Future

To address the problem of access, professionals, parents, and community agency personnel are lobbying politicians to pass legislation to expand and strengthen services for students with emotional and behavior disorders and their families (Gruttadaro, 2008; Zionts & Villiers, 2003) by emphasizing better health care coverage that includes coverage for these disabilities and providing funding for families that cannot afford services. The importance of these efforts has been punctuated by several events of the twenty-first century that have been extraordinarily stressful for children, including the attack on the World Trade Center in 2001; Hurricanes Katrina, Rita, and others; and the wars in Iraq and Afghanistan. Each of these has taken a toll on the emotional well-being of untold numbers of students (Burnham, 2009).

For school professionals, emphasis is on recognizing students' emotional and behavioral disorders, responding to them appropriately, and providing access through the use of best practices (LaRusso, Romer, & Selman, 2008; Maggio, 2009; Scheuermann & Johns, 2002). Instead of punishing students for misbehaviors, educators need to identify and implement programs and interventions that have been demonstrated to help students learn appropriate behaviors. Administrators, teachers, other school professionals, and even school board members should understand and observe the results that can be obtained using positive behavior supports. They also need to emphasize the prevention of these disorders by using schoolwide systems, as outlined earlier in this chapter.

## Use of Restraints and Seclusion

When students with emotional and behavior disorders exhibit behaviors likely to result in serious harm to themselves or others, emergency measures are sometimes employed. Two such measures are the use of (a) physical restraint and (b) seclusion. The value and appropriate use of both of these procedures are vigorously debated in the field.

**Physical restraint** occurs when a teacher or another professional restricts a student's freedom of movement, physical activity, or access to his body (Council for Children with Behavior Disorders (2009a). For example, Lucas believes he has been treated unfairly by his teacher. As the teacher tries to talk to him in a way designed to calm him, he instead speaks in a louder and louder voice. He suddenly moves toward the teacher with fists up, screaming that he will show her what is fair, flipping desks over and swinging at other students. Another teacher, trained in a specific and safe procedure for restraining students in such situations, prevents him from harming himself or others.

**Seclusion** occurs when a student is involuntarily confined to a room, left alone, and prevented from leaving. For example, in one morning Beverly has repeatedly bullied others in her class by hitting them, grabbing items on their desks, and threatening them with harm after school. After several other interventions, the teacher tells Beverly that she will be placed in seclusion if she continues this behavior. Beverly's response is to turn to the nearest classmate and hit him. Using restraint, Beverly is placed in a seclusion room. An assistant monitors her through a glass window, at the same time preventing Beverly from leaving the room. Ten minutes after Beverly stops pounding on the door and after speaking with her teacher, she is released from the room to re-join her peers.

Many concerns exist regarding the use of physical restraint and seclusion in schools. These are some of the issues:

- Few states or local districts have clear policies on when these procedures should be used or how they should safely be carried out (Rozalski, Yell, & Boreson, 2006). Such policies need to address student safety and emergency procedures, parent notification, alternatives to these procedures, and requirements for de-briefing and follow-up after they are employed.
- Although many professionals claim that physical restraint and seclusion can benefit students, no research base exists to document the effects of them on students' behavior and learning (Fogt, George, Kern, White, & George, 2008). Kutz, 2009).
- Some educators believe that the use of restraint and seclusion is increasing in schools. They suggest that the return of students with emotional disabilities to their local schools and the increased effort to include them in general education settings may be resulting in increased behavior incidents resolved through these procedures (Council for Children with Behavior Disorders, 2009a, 2009b).
- Many professionals question whether restraint and seclusion should even have a place in school settings, noting that if they are used repeatedly, they may indicate a failure in instruction (Council for Children with Behavior Disorders, 2009a, 2009b).

Discussions about restraint and seclusion are likely to continue for several years (Ryan, Peterson, & Rozalski, 2007). As a teacher of students with disabilities, your responsibility is to stay informed of the emerging knowledge base on this topic and consider carefully the legal, educational, and ethical impact of using these procedures with students.

## REVIEW · REFLECT · DISCUSS

1. In this chapter you learned that one of the most critical issues facing professionals and families of children and youth with emotional and behavior disorders is the lack of mental health services. What could be the impact of this dilemma for you as an educator? What steps could educators take to reduce this problem?

2. Under what conditions do you think restraints or seclusion should be used with students with emotional disabilities? What do you see as the benefits or risks? What training would you want before being asked to restrain student?

# Summary

- The study of children with emotional and behavior disorders began at the beginning of the twentieth century in the fields of medicine and psychology, and it continues today.
- The current definition of emotional and behavior disorders—called *emotional disturbance* in IDEA—and their prevalence continue to be debated, but professionals agree that both biological and psychosocial factors are contributing causes of these disabilities.
- Students with emotional and behavior disorders display internalizing and externalizing behaviors, and their emotional difficulties often lead to problems in social relationships. Typically, these students have low-average to average ability, but their achievement is below expected levels.
- Formal and informal assessment instruments and procedures used to identify whether students have emotional and behavior disorders include behavior checklists; interviews with professionals, parents, and students; observations; ability and achievement testing; and medical information.

- Most students with emotional disabilities spend a significant amount of time in special education settings, a fact supported by the widely acknowledged difficulty of implementing inclusive practices for these students.
- Best practices for students with emotional and behavior disorders include prevention, particularly with early intervention; collaborative efforts on the part of school and community personnel; functional behavior assessments and behavior intervention plans; and classroom instruction designed to provide structure and engagement.
- The parents and families of students with emotional and behavior disorders often feel isolated from others and struggle to find appropriate services to help their children.
- One of the most serious issues facing the field of emotional and behavior disorders today is the lack of mental health services for children and youth.

## ADDRESSING THE PROFESSIONAL STANDARDS

Council for Exceptional Children (CEC) Common Core Knowledge and Skills addressed in this chapter:

ICC1K2, ICC1K5, ICC1K6, ICC1K8, ICC2K1, ICC2K2, ICC2K3, ICC2K4, ICC2K5, ICC2K6, ICC3K1, ICC4S6, ICC5K2, ICC5K6, ICC5S4, ICC5S5, ICC5S10, ICC7S7, ICC8K4, ICC8S1, ICC8S2, ICC8S4, ICC8S6, ICC8S8, ICC9K3, ICC10K2, ICC10K3, ICC10S3, ICC10S6

Appendix: Provides a full listing of the CEC Common Core Standards, and associated Knowledge and Skill Statements listed here.

**myeducationlab** PEARSON

Now go to Topic 10: Emotional/Behavioral Disorders in the MyEducationLab (www.myeducationlab.com) for your course, where you can:

- Find learning outcomes for the broad concepts covered in this chapter along with the national standards that connect to these outcomes.
- Complete Assignments and Activities that can help you more deeply understand the chapter content.
- Examine challenging situations and cases presented in the IRIS Center Resources.

- Apply and practice your understanding of the core concepts and skills identified in the chapter with the Building Teaching Skills and Dispositions learning units.
- Check your comprehension on the content covered in the chapter by going to the Study Plan in the Book Specific Resources for your text. Here you will be able to take a chapter quiz, receive feedback on your answers, and then access Review, Practice, and Enrichment activities to enhance your understanding of chapter content.
- Watch video clips of CCSSO Teacher of the Year award winners responding to the question: "Why I teach?" in the Teacher Talk section.

## chapter eight

# Students with Intellectual and Developmental Disabilities

## LEARNING OBJECTIVES

- Outline the development of the field of mental retardation, now often called intellectual disabilities; define current terminology, including *developmental disabilities*; and explain the prevalence and causes of this disability.
- Describe characteristics of individuals with intellectual disabilities.
- Explain how intellectual disabilities are identified.
- Outline how learners with intellectual disabilities receive their education.
- Describe recommended educational practices for students with intellectual disabilities.
- Explain the perspectives and concerns that parents and families of students with intellectual disabilities may have.
- Identify trends and issues influencing the field of intellectual disabilities.

## Hope

Hope is in the fifth grade. If you observed her for only a few minutes in the classroom with her peers, you would say she seems like a typical student. She chats with classmates whenever the opportunity arises. She is at that in-between age: not quite a child and not quite an adolescent. However, if you observed Hope over time, you would understand why she is identified as having an *intellectual disability,* also called *mild mental retardation.* Academically, she is doing quite well, reading at a second-grade level, but she simply does not learn at the rate of her classmates. Mr. Rosen, Hope's resource teacher, works closely with fifth-grade teacher Ms. Moretti to identify the most important concepts for Hope to learn from the curriculum. Hope receives reading instruction in the resource room four times per week, which she attends with four other students (one from sixth grade and three from fourth grade) reading at approximately her level. Hope's special needs are especially apparent at this age in her social skills and interactions with classmates. The other girls are beginning to worry about their hair, think about boys, and read fashion magazines; Hope still has a favorite doll that she sometimes brings to school. Hope's classmates sometimes become impatient with her increasing differences from them, and she is puzzled by their negative comments.

## Anthony

Anthony is still a little overwhelmed at the middle school he attends as a sixth grader, but even so, he likes it. In elementary school, he spent about half the day in the special education room with his teacher Mr. Reynolds, and when he was in a general education class, he was accompanied to the room either by a paraeducator or a peer buddy. His school was also much smaller. In middle school, Anthony has a locker that he practiced learning to open over the summer, and he changes classes with other students, moving from one room to another, also practiced before the school year began. He receives reading, English, math, and social studies instruction from two special educators. The teachers are careful to align their teaching with the district curriculum and state learning standards, but they empha-size the vocabulary, reading, math, and other skills Anthony and his classmates need for daily living. Anthony receives science instruction and his elective classes (e.g., art, music, technology, Spanish) in general education. Anthony is required to take a high-stakes test each year, just like most students, but his alternate assessment is based on a portfolio of samples of his work rather than a traditional paper-and-pencil test, and it is scored using a rubric. Anthony has Down syndrome; he also has several heart problems and already has had two surgeries to correct them. Anthony is very positive about his future, as is his family. He anticipates that he will work in the family's printing business once he finishes school.

## Jack

Jack is nineteen years old, and he is a student at Lincoln High School. He attends classes for part of the day, and then he participates in a vocational training program. Jack takes part in one general education class—an art class that has only nine other students. He is assisted in the class by Ms. Russo, a special education paraprofessional. Jack has a moderate intellectual disability that is the result of a disorder called *Fragile X syndrome,* but his most significant challenges concern behavior. For example, he tends to be distracted by nearly any small noise or movement in the classroom. When he is upset, he sometimes chews on the neck band of his T-shirt. One thing that disturbs Jack is change in routine such as last week's shortened class schedule on an early-release day. Jack has just begun a new job. He is working two hours per day in the small business of a friend of his family, and his responsibilities include making copies, shredding documents, and helping to distribute and organize supplies. With the help of a job coach and this rather structured environment, Jack is quickly learning to work independently. Although Jack does not speak very often, he has communicated that he wants to work in a full-time job after high school. Jack's stepmother and father concur that Jack should work after high school, and they hope he can achieve his goal of living in an apartment. Even so, they are planning for him to live at home at least for the next few years, and they also are meeting with an estate planner to ensure that Jack has what he needs after they die.

For most of the history of public schools, students with intellectual disabilities, also called *mental retardation,* have been characterized primarily by the word *can't*—what they can't do, what they can't learn, what they can't participate in. For example, in my own late-1970s classroom for students with mild intellectual disabilities, no books were provided because of the strongly held belief that these students could not learn to read. As these students became adults, the emphasis on their limitations continued. Except for those individuals who blended into society and shed their disability labels, most people with mental retardation lived with their parents, were placed in residential facilities, or resided under close supervision in group homes with several other adults with disabilities.

Although the past sometimes still influences professionals in today's schools, contemporary thinking about individuals with intellectual disabilities now is based on much higher expectations and a world of possibilities, not limitations. This has meant rethinking beliefs about these students' academic potential and the priorities they may have for their lives beyond the school years. As you read this chapter, continue to think about your own beliefs about children and adults with intellectual disabilities, including the stigma associated with the term *mental retardation* and the influence your perceptions can have on these students' lives.

You will notice that the focus of this chapter is on students with mild or moderate intellectual disabilities or mental retardation. That is deliberate and based on the tremendous diversity of students who may have this disability. You will learn about students with autism who may have intellectual disabilities in Chapter Ten, those with traumatic brain injury who may have intellectual disabilities in Chapter Thirteen, and those with multiple and severe disabilities who also have intellectual disabilities in Chapter Fourteen.

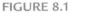

To check your comprehension on the content covered in Chapter 8, go to the Book Specific Resources in the MyEducationLab (www.myeducationlab.com) for your course, select your text, and complete the Study Plan. Here you will be able to take a chapter quiz, receive feedback on your answers, and then access review, practice, and enrichment activities to enhance your understanding of chapter content.

# Understanding Intellectual Disabilities

Contemporary perspectives on intellectual disabilities are a response to past views and practices. By understanding how this field developed and was shaped by societal trends, you can better appreciate the significance of today's changing vocabulary and rising expectations for students with this disability.

## Development of the Field of Intellectual Disabilities

Focused study of and interest in individuals with intellectual disabilities began in the early nineteenth century, earlier than the study of people with most other disabilities (Hickson, Blackman, & Reis, 1995). As the timeline in Figure 8.1 illustrates, the field evolved for the next hundred years, with an optimistic emphasis on care and treatment and a belief that many individuals would be "cured" (Hickson et al., 1995).

The turmoil in American society at the beginning of the twentieth century that you read about in Chapter One led to a radical shift in thinking about individuals with intellectual disabilities. Optimism was replaced by pessimism. Prominent physicians and psy-

**FIGURE 8.1**
**The Development of the Field of Intellectual Disabilities**

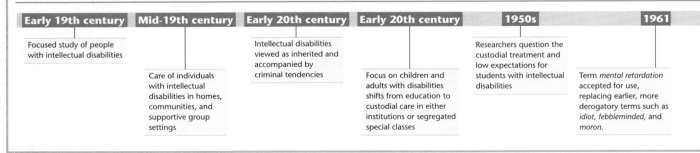

| Early 19th century | Mid-19th century | Early 20th century | Early 20th century | 1950s | 1961 |
|---|---|---|---|---|---|
| Focused study of people with intellectual disabilities | Care of individuals with intellectual disabilities in homes, communities, and supportive group settings | Intellectual disabilities viewed as inherited and accompanied by criminal tendencies | Focus on children and adults with disabilities shifts from education to custodial care in either institutions or segregated special classes | Researchers question the custodial treatment and low expectations for students with intellectual disabilities | Term *mental retardation* accepted for use, replacing earlier, more derogatory terms such as *idiot, febbleminded,* and *moron.* |

chologists theorized that intellectual disabilities—called *mental deficiency* at that time—were inherited, that they were accompanied by criminal tendencies, and that allowing people with these disabilities to have children would undermine the strength of American society (Kanner, 1964). As a result, professionals gradually abandoned efforts to educate these children and adults, and they became satisfied with providing custodial care for them, either in institutions or segregated special classes (Winzer, 1993). Most experts agree that the early twentieth century was the lowest point in the modern history of education for individuals with intellectual disabilities (Wehmeyer & Patton, 2000).

By the middle of the twentieth century, beliefs were beginning to change (Hickson et al., 1995), and for the next two decades, the efforts of researchers, social reformers, and parents guided the field toward major reform. The result of their diligence was the litigation that eventually formed the basis for Public Law (P. L.) 94-142, the federal special education law now called IDEA (the Individuals with Disabilities Education Act).

## Definitions of Intellectual Disabilities

As is true for some other students with disabilities, the language that describes students with intellectual disabilities requires clarification (Switsky & Greenspan, 2006). You may already have noticed that the terms *intellectual disabilities* and *mental retardation* are being used interchangeably in this chapter. Here is the explanation why: The term used in IDEA is *mental retardation,* and many (but not all) states still use it. However, this term often is considered offensive and stigmatizing, partly because of the negative connotations assigned to it at the beginning of the twentieth century (Akrami, Ekehammar, Claesson, & Sonnander, 2006). Many professionals and parents now use the term **intellectual disabilities**. In fact, in January 2007 the American Association on Mental Retardation (AAMR), the leading professional organization addressing the needs of these individuals throughout the life span, changed its name to the **American Association on Intellectual and Developmental Disabilities (AAIDD)**. The second part of the new name—**developmental disabilities**—is a broad term that is usually used in reference to chronic and significant impairments such as cerebral palsy and autism that result in intellectual disabilities.

You may find that your state uses yet other terms to refer to students with intellectual disabilities. For example, you may hear the term **cognitive impairment** or **cognitive disability** or *mental impairment, mental disability, or mental handicap.* Over the next several years, continued changes in the language used for students with this disability are likely. These changes will reflect a positive step in transforming understanding about these students and their potential.

*Although in the past many children with intellectual disabilities were sent to institutions, professionals and families now stress helping them to reach their potential and function successfully in society.*

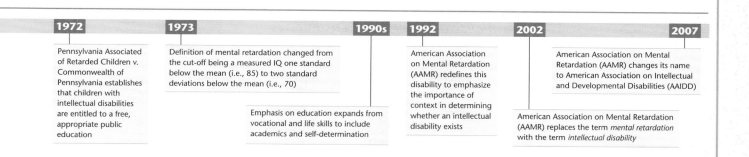

**1972**
Pennsylvania Associated of Retarded Children v. Commonwealth of Pennsylvania establishes that children with intellectual disabilities are entitled to a free, appropriate public education

**1973**
Definition of mental retardation changed from the cut-off being a measured IQ one standard below the mean (i.e., 85) to two standard deviations below the mean (i.e., 70)

Emphasis on education expands from vocational and life skills to include academics and self-determination

**1990s**

**1992**
American Association on Mental Retardation (AAMR) redefines this disability to emphasize the importance of context in determining whether an intellectual disability exists

**2002**
American Association on Mental Retardation (AAMR) replaces the term *mental retardation* with the term *intellectual disability*

**2007**
American Association on Mental Retardation (AAMR) changes its name to American Association on Intellectual and Developmental Disabilities (AAIDD)

## Federal Definition

The definition generally used by educators is the one in IDEA. This definition for mental retardation is based on one developed in 1982 by the AAMR (now AAIDD). It states that **mental retardation** is

> significantly subaverage general intellectual functioning, existing concurrently with deficits in adaptive behavior and manifested during the developmental period, that adversely affects a child's educational performance. (IDEA 20 U.S.C. §1401 [2004], 20 C.F.R. §300.8[c][6])

This definition illustrates the important fact that the mental retardation designation is assigned only when a student demonstrates both low intellectual ability and significant problems with **adaptive behavior**—that is, the day-to-day skills that are necessary for independence (e.g., self-care, the use of money). The third part of the definition clarifies that the identification of mental retardation is made only if the condition is present by the time the student is eighteen years old—the generally accepted definition of the phrase "during the developmental period." If an adult was injured or experienced an illness that resulted in a significant reduction in intellectual ability, a term such as *cognitive impairment* might be used, but the term *mental retardation* usually would not be applied.

## American Association on Intellectual and Developmental Disabilities Definition

In 1992 the AAMR revised its definition on which federal special education law was based. It reaffirmed the use of this new definition in 2002, even though the group has not yet been successful in changing the IDEA definition. This newer definition states the following:

> Mental retardation is a disability characterized by significant limitations both in intellectual functioning and in adaptive behavior as expressed in conceptual, social, and practical adaptive skills. This disability originates before age eighteen.

The following five assumptions are essential to this definition:

1. Limitations in present functioning must be considered within the context of community environments typical of the individual's age, peers, and culture.
2. Valid assessment considers cultural and linguistic diversity as well as differences in communication, sensory, motor, and behavioral factors.
3. Within an individual, limitations often coexist with strengths.
4. An important purpose of describing limitations is to develop a profile of needed supports.
5. With appropriate personalized supports over a sustained period, the life functioning of the person with mental retardation generally will improve. (Luckasson et al., 2002, p. 1)

This definition does not so much contradict the IDEA definition as extend it. Specifically, it stresses the importance of context in considering intellectual disabilities (Gross & Hahn, 2004; Harries, Guscia, Kirby, Nettelbeck, & Taplin, 2005). Some students are eligible for the designation only while they are in the intensive academic environment of public schools. When they leave school and find employment that does not rely heavily on specific academic skills, the label may no longer apply. The definition also emphasizes strengths and the need for supports for helping individuals to succeed, a dimension that includes assistance in social skills, life skills, and health and medical matters. As you compare the older and newer definitions of intellectual disabilities, would you support adoption of the latter in IDEA? Why or why not?

## *Prevalence of Intellectual Disabilities*

During the 2007–2008 school year, 0.74 percent of all children ages six through twenty-one, or 487,854 students, received special education because they were identified as having mental retardation (U.S. Department of Education, 2009). An additional 0.13 percent, or 88,557 students, in this age group were served with the general label *developmentally delayed*, the alternative federal disability category for students ages three through nine that includes some students with mental retardation.

The prevalence of mental retardation as reported in IDEA dropped off dramatically between the 1970s and 1980s, and it has continued a slow decline for the past decade. Some of the decline in prevalence may be attributable to better differentiation between these students and those with other disabilities, including learning disabilities and autism. However, some professionals also propose that the recent trend in the figure reflects the strong stigma associated with mental retardation terminology and an increasing reluctance to avoid assigning it to students (Cooney, Jahoda, & Gumley, 2006; Hourcade, 2002).

Because the decision to identify an individual as having an intellectual disability involves professional judgment, no single prevalence estimate is considered definitive. For example, the American Association on Intellectual and Developmental Disabilities (Luckasson et al., 2002) estimates that 2.5 percent of the population has this disability. The Arc (2004), an organization for professionals and parents supporting children and adults with intellectual disabilities, estimates prevalence at 3 percent. These data suggest that school-age children with intellectual disabilities are possibly underidentified.

## Other Prevalence Considerations

Little research has explored the prevalence of intellectual disabilities in boys versus girls or based on age. Generally, boys are thought to have intellectual disabilities at a slightly higher rate than girls (1.5:1). In addition, some specific syndromes that include intellectual disability (topics addressed later in this chapter) affect boys and girls at different rates (Koenig & Tsatsanis, 2005).

The aspect of prevalence and intellectual disability that has received the most attention among educators is the disproportionate representation of African American students, especially boys, in this group (Skiba et al., 2008). As you learned in Chapter Three, the reasons for this situation include teacher expectations for student classroom behavior and academic performance, racial/ethnic bias, bias in assessment, and risk factors such as living in poverty. Presently, African American students are nearly three times more likely than other students to be identified as having an intellectual disability, based on their overall representation in the population (U.S. Department of Education, 2009). These data indicate that despite widespread attention to disproportionate representation, the issue still exists.

## Causes of Mental Retardation

For most students with intellectual disabilities, especially those with mild impairments, the cause of the disability cannot be determined. Hope, the elementary student introduced at the beginning of this chapter, is in this group of students. A mild intellectual disability for which a specific cause cannot be identified but that is presumed to be attributable to living in a disadvantaged environment is sometimes referred to as **cultural familial retardation**. This term is a remnant of early-twentieth-century thinking in that it implies that intellectual disabilities occur in certain family groups and are related to the ways in which they live.

For students with more significant intellectual disabilities, the causes usually are considered in terms of when they occurred: during the *prenatal* (before birth), the *perinatal* (during or immediately after birth), or the *postnatal* (after birth) period. The following examples illustrate the types of conditions that can lead to intellectual disability and the extent to which scientific knowledge about this disability has progressed.

## Prenatal Causes of Intellectual Disabilities

Intellectual disabilities sometimes are caused by factors at play before birth. For example, they may be the result of chromosomal abnormalities such as these:

**Down Syndrome.** Probably the most well known of all the genetic disorders that can result in intellectual disabilities is **Down syndrome (DS)**. One in every 733 children is born with DS (National Down Syndrome Society, 2006), and this syndrome occurs in both sexes and across racial/ethnic groups. The cause of DS is clear: Individuals typically have 46 chromosomes—23 contributed each by one's mother and father. In individuals with Down syndrome, an extra chromosome is present in the twenty-first chromosome pair, and so the syndrome is sometimes called **trisomy 21**. Scientists have not yet discovered why this extra chromosome develops, but it is this extra genetic material that causes children with this syndrome to have easily identified characteristics.

When these children are young, they often have poor muscle tone and may be called "floppy" babies. They also have eyes that slant upward and small ears, and their tongues may seem somewhat large for their mouths. About half of these children have vision

dimensions of
**DIVERSITY**

Some disorders that result in intellectual disabilities are linked to gender. For example, Rett syndrome is found only in females. It is characterized by handwringing and deteriorating cognitive ability.

www.nads.org
The National Association for Down Syndrome (NADS) provides counseling and support to families of children newly diagnosed with this syndrome. It also advocates for the rights of individuals with Down syndrome and provides news related to this disorder.

impairments or hearing loss, and approximately the same number have heart defects that may require medication or surgery (March of Dimes, 2006). Students with this syndrome usually have mild or moderate intellectual disabilities. Anthony, the middle school student described at the beginning of this chapter, has Down syndrome.

Although Down syndrome can occur in any expectant mother, there is a correlation with age. Mothers who are twenty-five years old have a 1 in 1,250 chance of having a baby with Down syndrome. Those who are forty years old have a 1 in 100 chance of having a baby with DS (National Institute of Child Health and Development, 2007).

**Fragile X Syndrome.** The most common form of inherited intellectual disability is **fragile X syndrome**, sometimes called Martin-Bell syndrome. Both men and women may carry the disorder, but only mothers transmit the disorder to their children. This syndrome develops when a mutation occurs in one of the genes in the X chromosome. The mutation occurs in a gene segment that is repeated in most people about 30 times. In those with this disorder, the segment is repeated from 55 to 200 times, causing the gene to turn off—that is, to stop producing a chemical present in the cells of people who do not have this disorder (Fast, 2003). Full fragile X syndrome (gene repeated 200 times) is seen in approximately 1 in every 1,200 males and 1 in every 2,500 females (National Institute of Child Health and Human Development, 2008), although far more individuals have what is called *premutation*—that is, gene repetition between 55 and 200 times (National Institutes of Health, 2008). Males with this disorder usually have significant intellectual disabilities (Roberts et al., 2005; Schwarte, 2008); females usually have much milder impairments.

Individuals with fragile X syndrome tend to have long faces, large ears, and poor muscle tone, but generally they are healthy. They often display characteristics similar to those in students with attention deficit–hyperactivity disorder (ADHD), including distractibility, and they may share some characteristics with students who have autism, including hypersensitivity to certain stimuli (e.g., the sound of a doorbell, the feel of certain types of clothing) and a tendency to say or do the same thing over and over again (Symons, Clark, Roberts, & Bailey, 2001). Students with this syndrome also are likely to become anxious when routines are changed, and they often have poor social skills. You might recall that Jack, described in the chapter opening, has fragile X syndrome.

**Prader-Willi Syndrome.** **Prader-Willi syndrome** is much less common than Down syndrome and fragile X syndrome, occurring in about 1 of every 15,000 babies (Prader-Willi Association, 2009). It is caused by any of several types of mutation on chromosome 15 (e.g., the father's chromosome is missing in the child; the mother contributes both chromosome 15s instead of one coming from the father). It occurs equally in boys and girls and occurs in individuals from any race/ethnicity.

Children who have Prader-Willi syndrome may have mild or moderate intellectual disabilities, and some have abilities in the low-average to average range (Prader-Willi Syndrome Association, 2009). Research on the specific cognitive characteristics of these individuals is just beginning (Kundert, 2008).

These children typically are happy as toddlers, and their behavior is similar to that of their peers. As they reach school age, though, they begin to have significant behavior problems, including stubbornness, problems switching from one activity to another, and resistance to changes in routines. However, the primary characteristic of this disorder is insatiable appetite and compulsive eating, and this symptom generally begins between the ages of two and four. Students with this disorder may steal food or eat discarded food, and educators working with these students must ensure that all food is kept locked away. Obesity occurs in 95 percent of these students if food intake is not carefully controlled. Families who have children with Prader-Willi syndrome often are under a great deal of stress because of the need to provide constant control and extensive behavior interventions (Kundert, 2008).

The technical information in the preceding paragraphs may leave you thinking that most intellectual disabilities are caused by chromosomal problems. This is not the case. There are many other prenatal causes of mental retardation, including those described in the following sections.

**Fetal Alcohol Syndrome.** The potentially harmful impact of maternal alcohol consumption on the unborn child has been known for many years, but it was not until 1973 that the term

**fetal alcohol syndrome (FAS)** was first used. The prevalence of FAS generally is believed to be significantly underreported and ranges from .2 to 1.5 cases per 1,000 babies born, with some regional variation in rate (National Center on Birth Defects and Developmental Disabilities, 2009). Some experts have proposed that as many as two-thirds of all students receiving special education services in the area of intellectual disabilities may be affected by this disorder, or its less severe form, **fetal alcohol effect (FAE)**. FAS is considered the leading cause of intellectual disabilities and the only one that is clearly preventable (Burd, 2004; Miller, 2006), but it must be remembered that not every student with FAS has an intellectual disability.

Students with fetal alcohol syndrome usually are somewhat small and slower in their development than other children. Their eyes may be small with drooping eyelids, the groove between the upper lip and nose may be absent, and the lower part of the face may seem flat. These students often have mild or moderate intellectual disabilities, and they also are likely to have very short attention spans and hyperactivity, learning disabilities, and poor coordination (Dybdahl & Ryan, 2009; Edmonds & Crichton, 2008).

**Phenylketonuria.** Phenylketonuria (PKU) is an inherited metabolic disorder that leads to intellectual disabilities if it is untreated. It affects 1 out of every 10,000–15,000 babies (Genetics Home Reference, 2009). PKU occurs when the body is unable to produce the chemicals needed to convert other toxic chemicals into harmless products. Children inherit PKU only if both parents carry the defective gene that causes it, and it affects boys and girls equally. PKU is mentioned here because you have undoubtedly seen a warning about it: If you look at the small print on a diet soft drink can, you will see a warning to "phenylketonurics" that the product contains phenylalanine, the chemical they cannot metabolize. All states now mandate that newborns be tested for PKU.

The treatment of PKU can begin even before a baby is born; when a mother known to carry this gene controls her dietary intake of phenylalanine, prenatal harmful effects can largely be avoided. Treatment for the child begins as soon as the disorder is detected, and it consists of a carefully planned diet low in foods containing phenylalanine (National Institutes of Health, 2006). For example, certain high-protein foods such as meat, fish, and poultry are not allowed. Although it was once believed that the special diet could be discontinued around age six, lifelong control of diet is the current recommended practice (National Institutes of Health, 2006). When the diet is followed and chemical levels in the blood are carefully monitored, students with this disorder experience no significant effects on intellectual ability or learning.

**Toxoplasmosis.** Toxoplasmosis is an infection caused by a parasite, and more than 60 million people in the United States carry it (Centers for Disease Control and Prevention, 2008), including 10 to 15 percent of women of childbearing age (fifteen years to forty-five years old). It usually is harmless because the body's immune system prevents it from causing illness. However, an expectant mother who becomes infected with the parasite for the first time can pass it on to her unborn child. The baby may seem fine at birth, but an intellectual disability or blindness may develop later in life. It is important to know that this parasite is spread through cat fecal matter. Thus, expectant mothers are cautioned to have someone else clean the litter box.

## Perinatal Causes of Mental Retardation

In some instances, a problem that occurs during or immediately after the birth of a child leads to an intellectual disability. For example, premature babies weighing less than 3.3 pounds have a 10 to 20 percent risk of having an intellectual disability (Beers & Berkow, 2003). Birth injury is another category of causes of intellectual disabilities during the perinatal period. For example, if a baby is deprived of oxygen as she is born or if the infant is hurt by the incorrect use of forceps or procedures followed during birth, an intellectual disability may result.

## Postnatal Causes of Mental Retardation

Children who are born without disabilities sometimes develop an intellectual disability as a result of an accident or illness that occurs during childhood. Examples include the following:

**Encephalitis.** Inflammation of the brain, or encephalitis, can be caused by any viral infection. Vaccinations have reduced the chances of most children getting certain viral infections

*Fetal alcohol syndrome (FAS) is a completely preventable cause of intellectual disabilities.*

Genetic research currently under way could have far-reaching implications for the field of intellectual disabilities. For example, gene therapy—in which a donor provides a complete healthy gene to a person who has a known genetic problem—could someday eliminate PKU and other genetic disorders.

(e.g., measles, mumps, chickenpox), but this disease also can be carried by certain types of mosquitoes and animals that have rabies. In some cases, encephalitis results in intellectual disabilities.

**Lead Poisoning.** You already have learned that young children exposed to lead are at higher risk for developing learning disabilities, emotional and behavior disorders, and ADHD. Lead poisoning can lead to intellectual disabilities as well. It is estimated that nearly more than 250,000 children ages one through five have raised levels of lead in their blood (Centers for Disease Control and Prevention, 2009). Even though lead-based paint was banned in 1978, it is the primary source of childhood lead exposure and is found in more than 4 million buildings in which young children live. Like fetal alcohol syndrome, lead poisoning is a completely preventable cause of intellectual disabilities. Eradication of lead poisoning in children by 2010 is part of a set of federal priorities to improve the health of people in the United States.

**Brain Injury.** Although many children have accidents and experience no long-term negative effects, any event that causes injury to the brain can be a cause of intellectual disabilities. Examples include falls from bicycles or playground equipment, auto accidents, near drowning, child abuse, and severe malnutrition.

Does it seem that the causes of intellectual disabilities are a little overwhelming? Remember that the preceding discussion includes only a few of all the causes and that advances in medical technology are providing additional information every year. These advances someday may help prevent some types of intellectual disabilities from ever occurring and minimize the impact of those that cannot be prevented.

## REVIEW · REFLECT · DISCUSS

1. The early twentieth century is considered a low point in the history of educating individuals who have intellectual disabilities. How are the events and decisions from that era still influencing the perceptions and treatment of these individuals today?

2. How are the IDEA and AAIDD definitions of mental retardation similar? Different? What are the implications for educators of the assumptions that are included in the AAIDD definition?

3. Some causes of intellectual disabilities in children are preventable. What role should educators play in helping to eliminate these causes?

## Characteristics of Individuals with Intellectual Disabilities

As you read about the causes of intellectual disabilities, you learned some of the specific characteristics associated with individuals who have well-known syndromes and disorders. In this section the emphasis is on a more general picture of the cognitive, academic, social, behavior, emotional, and physical/medical characteristics of this group of students.

### Cognitive and Academic Characteristics

A student is identified as having mental retardation only if his IQ score places him at approximately 2 standard deviations or more below the mean or average score of 100. And even though IDEA does not draw these distinctions, in traditional classification systems individuals are grouped based on the extent of their cognitive impairment:

| | |
|---|---|
| Mild mental retardation | IQ = 55–69 |
| Moderate mental retardation | IQ = 40–54 |
| Severe mental retardation | IQ = 25–39 |
| Profound mental retardation | IQ = below 25 |

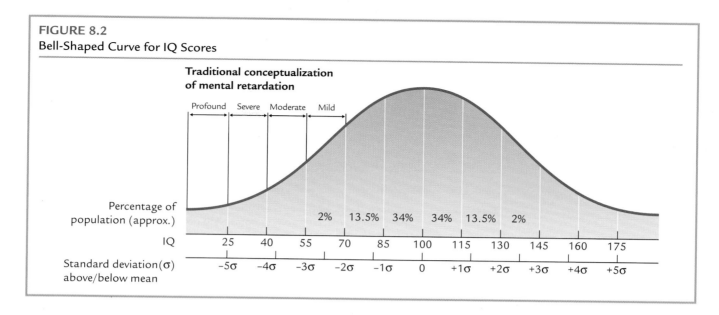

**FIGURE 8.2**
Bell-Shaped Curve for IQ Scores

What does all this mean? Perhaps you have seen a diagram like the one presented in Figure 8.2—a *bell-shaped curve*. It demonstrates how these concepts relate to one another. The average IQ score is considered 100. Most people—approximately 68 percent of them—have an IQ score that falls between 1 standard deviation (i.e., 15 points) below the mean and 1 standard deviation above the mean, or between 85 and 115. As you can see from the figure, the IQ scores for students with intellectual disabilities fall significantly below this range.

Keep in mind that IQ scores are approximations that guide professionals in making decisions about students' needs, but the scores should not by themselves dictate decisions regarding students. A student with an IQ slightly above 70 could be identified as having an intellectual disability if he was experiencing many problems in adaptive skills. Likewise, a student with a score slightly below 70 might not be identified if she seemed to be functioning well.

Although some variation of this classification system of mild, moderate, severe, and profound is used in most states, it has bothered professionals for many years because of its emphasis on limitations and its tendency to relate specific scores to highly stigmatizing labels. In 1992, the American Association on Mental Retardation (now AAIDD) proposed an alternative classification system based on the **levels of support** that individuals with intellectual disabilities may need. Figure 8.3 provides a summary of this support–need approach to thinking about and planning for individuals with intellectual disabilities—one that classifies students based on whether they need intermittent, limited, extensive, or pervasive support. This system was praised because it deemphasized reliance on IQ scores in program planning and stressed assisting individuals to reach their potential (Wehmeyer, Chapman, Little, Thompson, Schalock, & Tassé, 2009). Although not commonly used in schools, this system enables professionals to look in a constructive way at arranging services so that individuals with intellectual disabilities can reach their potential.

### Cognitive Functioning

The cognitive characteristics of students with intellectual disabilities have a significant impact on several dimensions of cognitive functioning (Bergeron & Floyd, 2006), including memory, generalization, metacognition, motivation, language, and academic skills.

**Memory.** In some respects, students with intellectual disabilities have cognitive functioning difficulties similar to those of other students about whom you have already learned. One example concerns working memory. Do you recall that students with ADHD have difficulty with working memory, or the ability to remember what needs to be done and how much time there is to do it? Students with intellectual disabilities also experience these problems.

http://www.thearc.org/ NetCommunity/ Page.aspx?pid=183
The Arc is the world's largest organization of and for children and adults with intellectual and developmental disabilities. Its goal is to improve supports and services for these individuals. You might find your community has a local chapter.

> **FIGURE 8.3**
> **AAIDD Classification System Based on Levels of Support Needed**
>
> | Level | Support Needed |
> |---|---|
> | Intermittent | Supports provided on an as-needed basis. Characterized by episodic nature, person not always needing the support(s), or short-term supports needed during life span transitions (e.g., job loss or an acute medical crisis). |
> | Limited | An intensity of supports characterized by consistency over time and time limited but not of an intermittent nature; may require fewer staff members and cost less than more intense levels of support (e.g., time-limited employment training or transitional supports during the school-to-adult period). |
> | Extensive | Supports characterized by regular involvement (e.g., daily) in at least some environments (such as work or home) and not time limited (e.g., long-term home living support). |
> | Pervasive | Supports characterized by constancy, high intensity, and provision across environments; of a potential life-sustaining nature. Pervasive supports typically involve more staff members and intrusiveness than do extensive or time-limited supports. |
>
> Source: Luckasson, R., et al. (2002). *Mental retardation: Definition, classification, and systems of support* (10th ed., p. 152). Washington, DC: American Association on Mental Retardation. Reprinted with permission.

dimensions of
**DIVERSITY**

Based on population data, Hispanic students are underrepresented in the category of intellectual disabilities. If a risk of 1.0 means that the proportion of students is exactly what would be predicted, these students are represented at the 0.66 level, just two-thirds of the number expected.

They are likely to forget what they are supposed to do, particularly if a task involves many steps. However, technology is helping to address this dilemma. The Technology Notes explains how personal digital assistants (PDAs) are being used to help these students overcome limitations in working memory.

**Generalization.** The ability to learn a task or idea and then apply it in other situations is called **generalization**. When a student learns in language arts or English to use adjectives to make her writing more interesting and then uses adjectives when she is writing an essay in a social studies class, generalization has occurred. Students with intellectual disabilities have difficulty with generalization of academic tasks, of behavior expectations, and in social interactions. For example, if a student who tends to speak loudly is being taught to keep his voice at an acceptable classroom level, the skill may need to be taught in general education classrooms, in the music room, and in the cafeteria.

**Metacognition.** Another challenge for many students with intellectual disabilities is metacognition, or the ability to "think about thinking," which was introduced in Chapter Five in the discussion of students with learning disabilities (Erez & Peled, 2001). Students with intellectual disabilities are most successful when they are not expected to make judgments about what to do next; otherwise, they may struggle. For example, Anthony, the student you met at the beginning of the chapter, has learned how to move from class to class in his middle school. One day, however, his usual route is disrupted: A corridor is closed because of a water problem. Although other students easily divert to an alternative hallway, Anthony becomes confused and requires assistance to find his way to his next class.

**Motivation.** Some students with intellectual disabilities share another characteristic with students with learning disabilities. They experience problems with motivation and learned helplessness—that is, the tendency to give up easily. For students with intellectual disabilities, however, learned helplessness may not be a result of frustration with the task at hand. It sometimes develops because professionals and classmates, in attempts to be helpful, are too eager to offer assistance. Some students soon learn that if they simply wait, someone will help out. Professionals are working to teach students with intellectual disabilities skills such as self-management so that they learn to begin and complete the school tasks (King-Sears, 2008).

**Language.** As you might expect, many students with intellectual disabilities have delays in the development of language. For example, it may take longer for them to learn concepts

## Technology Tools for Real-Life Success

Technology that is available in nearly any electronics store can help students with intellectual disabilities succeed both in school and in the community. Here are examples:

### Personal Digital Assistants

Do you use a PDA or Smartphone to help keep you organized? Students with intellectual disabilities can do the same thing. Gillette and DePompei (2008), drawing on research on adults, taught 35 students with mild to moderate intellectual disabilities or traumatic brain injury to use such devices. They found that:

- Electronic devices that beeped to remind students of scheduled tasks were more effective than paper-and-pencil options.
- A single morning reminder helped the students using the PDAs, but teachers reported this was significantly less intrusive than the frequent reminders that had to be given before.
- The devices were not distracting.
- Some students began on their own to use the PDAs to remind them of tasks not part of the study.
- Many of the students began to explore other functions and options on the PDAs.
- The PDAs, especially when compared to specialized devices developed primarily for the use of people with disabilities, were very inexpensive.

### Presentation Software

Many teachers use presentation software (e.g., PowerPoint, Impress, Keynote) when they teach groups of students but also when they design work students will complete on computers in-dividually or in small groups. Here are options that exist within such software that can facilitate learning for students with intellectual disabilities (Doyle & Giangreco, 2009):

- Use the various print options to produce hard copies of slides for students to use as notes (e.g., print full-page slides, or half-page slides with space for note-taking). Consider providing slides to other teachers or parents so they can review with students.
- Let students know which slides are especially important for them to learn from by designating them in a special way; for example, using a different background color. Although the student will see all the slides, those with the special color are the ones they should emphasize.
- On a computer the student accesses, provide the highlighted slides or a shortened version of the presentation. This is easily accomplished by using the "hide" function in the software and permits the student to review key ideas easily and repeatedly.
- Activate the text-to-speech function in your software so that students can review slides by listening to them. Consider creating your own simple narration and adding it to the presentation so that students can independently review what they have learned.

How else could you use these two technologies to facilitate the learning of students with intellectual disabilities? What other readily available technologies might also enhance your teaching and students' learning?

*Source:* Based on Doyle, M. B., & Giangreco, M. F. (2009). Making presentation software accessible to high school students with intellectual disabilities. *Teaching Exceptional Children, 41*(3), 24–31;. Gillette, Y., & DePompei, R. (2008). Do PDAs enhance the organization and memory skills of students with cognitive disabilities? *Psychology in the Schools, 45,* 665–677.

---

such as *up/down* and *over/under*. These students also may struggle with words that are abstract in meaning and benefit when professionals can make those words more concrete. Here is an example: A middle school student with an intellectual disability was in a social studies class learning about democracy, a very abstract concept. By using discussions and examples, the student was able to learn what democracy means. When other students wrote essays on the subject, she compiled pictures and described them to her classmates. For example, she held up a picture of a protest rally and explained that in a democracy people can say things that other people do not like and the people saying the things cannot be put in jail for saying them. No one doubted that she grasped the essential meaning of democracy.

**Academic Skills.** Students with intellectual disabilities usually have to work harder and practice longer than other students in order to learn academic skills (Bertella et al., 2005). In times past, assumptions were made about the so-called ceilings that these students would reach in learning. Now, however, professionals are balancing the realistic understanding that learning is difficult for these students with the conviction that they may learn more than anyone ever thought they could—if they are only given the opportunity. For example, Cole, Waldron, and Majd (2002) reported that when students with mild intellectual disabilities are educated in general education classrooms with peers, they often make more academic progress than similar students who are taught in special education classes.

## Social, Behavior, and Emotional Characteristics

The social, behavior, and emotional characteristics of students with intellectual disabilities can vary as much as those of students without disabilities (Freeman, 2000). Stereotypes that

*Many students with intellectual disabilities need assistance in developing friendships with their peers.*

assign specific characteristics to particular groups of children generally are not accurate unless a specific behavior is associated with a particular disorder, such as those you read about earlier in the chapter.

## Social Characteristics

Many students with intellectual disabilities have difficulties in social relationships (Addeduto et al., 2006), as does Hope, the student you met at the beginning of this chapter. They tend to be less accepted by their peers and more likely to be rejected by them, although inclusive practices may help students to be more positive about their peers with disabilities (Krajewski & Hyde, 2000; Krajewski, Hyde, & O'Keefe, 2002). Students with intellectual disabilities also have few friends outside school (Matheson, Olsen, & Weisner, 2007).

Several reasons can be offered for these difficulties in social relationships. First, many students with intellectual disabilities have immature behaviors that make other students want to avoid them. Second, their ways of dealing with social situations may be inappropriate (Angell, Bailey, & Larson, 2008). For instance, a student with an intellectual disability may walk up to a group of students engaged in conversation and elbow his way in; those students then may form a negative perception of him. Finally, students with intellectual disabilities may have difficulty picking up subtle social cues, and so they may misinterpret other students' actions (Leffert, Siperstein, & Millikan, 2000). One way that school professionals measure the social relationships among students in their classrooms, including those with intellectual disabilities, is to use sociograms, as explained in the Positive Behavior Supports feature.

## Adaptive Behavior Characteristics

To be identified as having an intellectual disability, a student must display deficits in adaptive behavior. These are some of the skills that are included in the area of adaptive behavior:

- *Communication*—the ability to exchange thoughts, messages, or information with other people through speaking, sign language, or other means
- *Self-care*—the ability to tend to personal hygiene, eating, and other related tasks
- *Social skills*—the ability to interact appropriately with others
- *Home living*—the ability to manage the day-to-day tasks of living in an apartment or house
- *Leisure*—the ability to use free time productively
- *Health and safety*—the ability to take precautions and act in ways that do not endanger oneself or others
- *Self-direction*—the ability to make and implement decisions
- *Functional academics*—the reading, writing, math, and other skills needed for independence
- *Community use*—the ability to identify and access services and activities in the neighborhood or area
- *Work*—the ability to obtain and keep employment

In very young children, adaptive behavior might include learning to crawl and then walk and learning to speak. In elementary school, adaptive behavior includes taking turns, following directions, and moving safely around the school and its grounds. For middle and high school students, adaptive behavior includes going to the mall, dining out with friends, changing classes at school, and preparing for employment. Students with mild intellectual disabilities may experience delays in a few areas of adaptive behavior. Students with more significant disabilities are likely to have difficulties in many of these domains.

### research NOTE

In interviews about friendship with 27 adolescents with mild to moderate intellectual disabilities, Matheson, Olsen, and Weisner (2007) found that (a) companionship (i.e., someone to do things with) and (b) the ability to transcend contexts (e.g., going to school, the mall, church) were the most consistent elements these students included in their descriptions of friends.

## Using Sociograms to Gather Information about Student Interactions

One concern about students with disabilities in inclusive settings is their acceptance by peers. You can get a sense of the patterns of friendships and social interactions in a classroom by using a *sociogram,* a teacher-made survey intended for this purpose. Students respond to teacher-provided items such as these:

- "List the two classmates with whom you would most like to sit."
- "Write the name of the person with whom you would enjoy working on a project."
- "If you were going on a vacation, which of your classmates would be nice to have along, and why?"

The responses are then compiled to create a social snapshot of the class group.

### How to Make and Use Sociograms

1. Devise one or several questions depending on the ages and abilities of students. State questions in easy-to-understand language. Word questions to be consistent with the information you wish to obtain (e.g., who to assign as field trip partners; who is unpopular and in need of social skills instruction).

2. Have students write their answers to your questions. Allow and encourage your students to make their choices privately. Clearly explain any limitations on choices (e.g., number of choices, classmates only). Some students may need assistance writing down their responses.

3. On a class list, tally next to each student's name the number of times she was selected by another student.

4. You can analyze the data in several ways. One way is to make a large diagram of concentric rings so that it looks like an archery target. Have one more ring than the greatest number of times any student was chosen. Start outside the last ring and number the spaces from the outside toward the inside starting with zero. Write each student's name inside the ring space corresponding to the number of times he or she was chosen. Draw arrows from each student to the student(s) they selected.

5. A simple strategy is to draw a bar graph, in which one bar represents each student and the number of times she was selected.

6. Survey your results to assess popularity and interaction preferences. Of course, you should keep this information confidential.

In the sample below, ten students were asked who they would like to sit next to. What does the chart tell you about student social status?

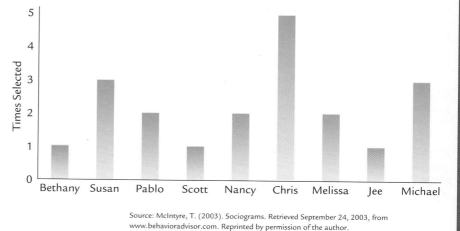

Source: McIntyre, T. (2003). Sociograms. Retrieved September 24, 2003, from www.behavioradvisor.com. Reprinted by permission of the author.

### Additional Behavior Characteristics

Some types of intellectual disabilities are related to specific behaviors. Prader-Willi syndrome, with its compulsive eating, is one example. However, many students with intellectual disabilities do not display extraordinary behaviors. Rather, they need rewards and consequences much like those needed by other students, perhaps with a greater emphasis on the use of tangible rewards (e.g., stickers, small prizes) used in a very systematic way. A few students may have self-injurious behaviors such as pulling their hair out or biting others. When such behaviors are present, the services of a behavior specialist will likely be needed to design interventions to reduce or eliminate the behaviors.

### Emotional Characteristics

A relatively new topic being explored in relation to school-age students with intellectual disabilities is these students' mental health (Dudley, 2005). Researchers have found that students with intellectual disabilities experience more loneliness than do students without disabilities (Howell, Hauser-Cram, & Kersh, 2007), and these feelings may persist into adulthood (McVilly, Stancliffe, Parmenter, & Burton-Smith, 2006). Clearly, valuing individuals with intellectual disabilities includes understanding that they experience the same emotions

*Kathy Grossnicklaus is the director of special education for O'Neill (NE) Public Schools, a district of about 850 students, 100 of whom have disabilities. In her role, she observes teachers and works with families, and she has a broad perspective on what it takes to succeed as a teacher of students with mild to moderate intellectual disabilities. Here is her advice.*

- Teachers need to really understand what a mild or a moderate intellectual disability is. They're going to talk to parents, they're going to talk to general education teachers about their students, and many people don't really understand what this disability is. That includes understanding how a diagnosis was made, understanding the testing that is part of determining this disability. Teachers will have to explain at nearly every IEP meeting what it means to have this disability, the problems, the challenges and do it in language that parents understand. The same is true for talking to general education teachers; they have to explain so that the student receives work at the right level.

- It's also very important to understand the family, that is, to learn about the family's functioning, what the child brings to school. Some families are strong, but in some families, the parents may have problems, maybe mental health problems, and that may affect the student. You have to understand student academic needs but also the social and emotional piece, and often that includes the family.

- The next advice I would give to new teachers is to know about the materials available to help these students and what the expectations are regarding what these students should learn. Sometimes, you will need to ask to order some items because what is already in the classroom isn't appropriate for the students you are teaching. Many of these students take the same [high stakes] tests as other students, and you have to get them ready. As a teacher, you'll need the tools so that you can match your students' learning needs to the expectations and assessments.

- Technology is very important in working with these students. There is so much software available now that can help students learn. Teachers have to educate themselves about what's available to address learning problems, and ask to get that software. Each student has unique needs, and technology has to be matched to those needs.

- New teachers also have to know the situation at their school . . . what has happened in the past in terms of services for students and what everyone is used to. As a new teacher, you'll have lots of great techniques and you'll be enthusiastic, but in some schools if you move too fast, the culture of the school may not be ready for your ideas.

- When I'm interviewing someone for a position to work with students with mild or moderate intellectual disabilities, I want to be sure the person can get along and work effectively with parents, colleagues, and others; that they can work with children who live in difficult situations—some teachers just aren't prepared for that; that they know special education, including information about disabilities but also writing IEPs and things like that; and that they have ways to relax because that is also important.

as others and that they have mental health needs (U.S. Department of Health and Human Services, 2001; Lorenzi, Horvat, & Pellegrini, 2000).

## Physical and Medical Characteristics

Most students with mild intellectual disabilities do not have any extraordinary medical conditions. However, some researchers have found them to be more likely than other students to be obese and not physically fit (Frey, Stanish, & Temple, 2008; Waldman & Perlman, 2007).

As a student's cognitive impairments become more pronounced, the likelihood of having serious physical problems and medical conditions needing intervention increases. Examples were provided earlier in the descriptions of specific causes of intellectual disabilities; for example, children with Down syndrome likely will have vision or hearing loss or heart problems requiring surgery. For educators, knowing about students' health and medical needs is important for several reasons. First, if a student's medical condition is fragile or changing, educators need to know whether an emergency might occur and how to respond. Second, if a student should be wearing glasses or using a hearing aid or another medical device, educators need to be prepared to monitor this. Finally, some students may miss significant amounts of school because of surgery or illness; in these cases, professionals are responsible for working with parents to minimize the impact on student learning.

## REVIEW · REFLECT · DISCUSS

1. Explain the traditional and AAIDD systems of classifying intellectual disabilities. What are the advantages and drawbacks of each? How can each help you as a professional educator in your work with students with intellectual disabilities?

2. Review Figure 8.1. The lower range of average intelligence, which is part of the definition of learning disabilities, generally is considered to be an IQ of 85 or so. Mild intellectual disability generally is identified at an IQ of 70 or so. These ranges indicate that a group of students whose intellectual abilities are in the 71 to 84 IQ range generally are not eligible for services. Whose responsibility is it to provide assistance to these students who struggle to learn? Do you think they should they have been included in IDEA?

## Identifying Intellectual Disabilities

For students with intellectual disabilities to receive special education services, they must go through the formal process of identification. For some students, this will have occurred when they are very young, even as infants, using assessment methods designed just for that age group. Other students are identified when they enter kindergarten and cannot manage the academic, social, and other expectations of the school setting, and yet others are identified sometime during the elementary school years.

### Assessment

For students who may have intellectual disabilities, assessment focuses on intellectual functioning and adaptive skills, as stressed in the definitions presented earlier. However, medical and other information also is assessed as appropriate.

**Assessment of Intellectual Functioning**

You already have learned that one common test used to assess intellectual functioning in students being considered for special education services is the Wechsler Intelligence Scale for Children (WISC–IV) (Wechsler, 2003). Another test sometimes used is the Stanford–Binet (Roid, 2003). These tests tend to measure a student's overall abilities and predict school achievement. They are individually administered only by professionals specially trained to do so.

You should keep in mind that no single test can measure all aspects of intelligence. Moreover, intelligence tests tend to ignore what some people consider key components of intelligence such as creativity and humor. Most professionals also acknowledge that no single, universally accepted definition of *intelligence* exists. And so, although intelligence tests and the scores they produce are integral to the procedures of special education, they should be treated as valuable information, not as a prescription of a student's abilities and limitations.

**Assessment of Adaptive Behavior**

The assessment of adaptive behavior is completed through interviews or surveys with parents, teachers, and others and with direct observation of the student. The goal is to obtain an accurate description of how well the student is functioning across school, home, and community settings.

One common assessment instrument used for this area is the AAMR Adaptive Behavior Scale (2nd ed.) (Lambert, Nihira, & Leland, 1993). It is available in a school form and a form for individuals in residential or community settings. This instrument considers a student's abilities to independently perform daily-living skills that are age appropriate and situation appropriate. It also evaluates inappropriate behaviors, including self-injurious behaviors (e.g., biting oneself when anxious). A teacher or another professional completes the scale for a student who has been referred, rating her adaptive behaviors.

**fyi**

Special Olympics is an organization that provides sports training and competition to more than one million people with intellectual disabilities in 150 countries. Competitions occur at the local, state, national, and international levels.

As students with intellectual disabilities approach adulthood, the emphasis in their education usually shifts toward learning job skills that will enable them to be successful members of their community.

Another measure of adaptive behavior is the Vineland Adaptive Behavior Scales (2nd ed.) (Sparrow, Balla, & Cicchetti, 2005). This instrument is based on interviewing, and it must be administered by a psychologist, social worker, or other appropriately trained professional. The scales address communication, daily-living, socialization, and motor skills, and they include an assessment of motor skills for children younger than six years old and an optional behavior assessment for children older than five.

On these and other adaptive behavior instruments, a student's current level of functioning is compared to that of typical children. The student's score provides an estimate of whether he is functioning at the expected level, above the expected level, or below it.

### Assessment of Medical Factors

For students with medical considerations, school team members may seek input from appropriate medical professionals concerning medications being taken, health risks for or limitations needed on physical activities, chronic conditions that school professionals should be aware of, and anticipated medical procedures that may affect school attendance or performance. These factors may be found to be integral to students' disabilities and services they may need at school.

## Eligibility

The decision to identify a student as having an intellectual disability must be based on the assessment information that has been gathered. The essential questions that are asked include these:

1. *Does the student's intelligence, as measured on a formal individual assessment, fall at least 2 standard deviations below the mean? That is, is the student's measured IQ approximately 70 or below?* The federal definition of mental retardation refers to significantly subaverage intellectual functioning, and the IQ scores mentioned earlier represent the operational definition of that term. However, as noted earlier, no cutoff score is considered absolute, and students with scores slightly above 70 might still be considered in this disability category.
2. *Does the student display deficits in adaptive behavior?* For this decision, team members review data from the adaptive behavior scales used in the assessment as well as observational data and anecdotal information offered by teachers, parents, and others. In many ways, answering this question relies on making a judgment call. Although the scales provide scores that indicate a student's functioning level in the adaptive domain, the team must consider the school and home context and the student's overall success in each. If clear and persistent deficits are noted, the decision is straightforward. However, for some students whose skills are marginal, discussion might be needed about the scores obtained versus observed student functioning. As with intelligence measures, a test score is considered a guideline.
3. *Do the student's characteristics adversely affect educational performance?* Federal special education law is premised on the adverse effect of disabilities on student learning and behavior, and so the team must consider this question as well as the others.

If the multidisciplinary team finds that the student meets the criteria to be identified as having an intellectual disability and would benefit by receiving special education, the remaining special education procedures are followed, and an individualized education program (IEP) is prepared so that the student receives an appropriate education. Some of the options for education are outlined in the following section.

## REVIEW · REFLECT · DISCUSS

1. What areas of functioning are included in the assessment of adaptive behavior? How do professionals assess adaptive behavior in order to determine whether a student has mental retardation?

2. Why do you think the cutoff score for determining the presence of an intellectual disability is left as a guideline rather than an absolute? How might the judgment call required by professionals assist or potentially hurt students being assessed for this disability category?

# How Learners with Intellectual Disabilities Receive Their Education

Students with intellectual disabilities access the same sets of services in the same settings as other students with disabilities. However, because of the nature of their special needs and the importance of both early intervention and transition from school to adult life activities, their education often includes some specialized options.

## Early Childhood

Young children who have clearly recognizable disorders that include an intellectual disability sometimes are identified as needing special services shortly after birth, and these babies may begin their education during the first few months of life. For these very young children, services often are based in the home and have an emphasis on helping family members learn how best to teach their children (McIntyre, 2008). Both parents and early childhood professionals view this type of service as highly valuable in fostering children's development and learning and increasing parent confidence in working with their young children (Dunst & Bruder, 2002). This type of early intervention usually includes an early interventionist who consults with the family, but it also could involve a physical therapist, speech/language pathologist, and other specialists. Services for these infants and toddlers may include medical and health professionals as well (Beirne-Smith, Ittenbach, & Patton, 2002).

These young children move into preschool programs at age three, where they may be joined by children who recently have been identified as having developmental delays or other disabilities. Preschool programs have been demonstrated to have strongly positive effects on the language skills, motor development, and pre-academic skill development of children with intellectual disabilities (e.g., Berglund, Eriksson, & Johansson, 2001; Roberts, Hatton, & Bailey, 2001; T. Smith, Groen, & Wynn, 2000). Both professionals and families continue to strongly support such programs (Delgado, Vagi, & Scott, 2006), and attention on them has shifted to improving the services offered (e.g., Mogharreban & Bruns, 2009; Watson & McCathren, 2009).

## Elementary and Secondary School Services

Students with intellectual disabilities in elementary, middle, and high school are entitled to receive their education in the least restrictive environment just like other students with disabilities. However, if you review the information included in Figure 8.4, you can see that only a small proportion of students identified with this disability spend more than 80 percent of their time in general education classrooms. In fact, the most common setting for these students is a special education classroom for more than 60 percent of the day. Sandy Baker, an experienced special educator, is the mother of Eric, a student with an intellectual disability. Her perspective on her son's life and potential, found in the Firsthand Account, can help you understand some of the issues related to the education of these students.

When students with intellectual disabilities are in general education classrooms with their peers, the extent to which they participate in exactly the same activities and the amount of support they need depends on the student's level of functioning (Fox, Farrell, & Davis, 2004). In one first-grade classroom, Jasmine—who has a moderate intellectual disability—was participating in a review of consonant blends. The chart being used contained nearly two dozen blends, but when it was Jasmine's turn to pronounce a blend and include it in a word, she always was given the blend *fr*, the one that happened to be at the beginning of her family name, *Franklin*. No special accommodations were needed.

research
**NOTE**

A nationwide study indicates that general education teachers perceived the placement to be very appropriate for 46 percent of their secondary students with mild intellectual disabilities, somewhat appropriate for 33 percent, and not appropriate for 21 percent of these students (U.S. Department of Education, 2009).

dimensions of
**DIVERSITY**

Ly (2008) studied the perceptions of Asian American and European American parents of children with Down syndrome, finding that the former parents judged their children as being less successful and having less potential for future success than the latter parents, even though the children's performances on a puzzle completion task were similar.

**SANDY BAKER** *has been a special education teacher in western Michigan since 1987, working with students with significant disabilities. Her son Eric was born in 1992. Because she had had a completely normal pregnancy, even teaching aerobics classes during this time, she and her husband had no idea that there was any problem until after Eric was born.*

After the pediatrician checked Eric over, he told us that he saw several signs that caused him concern: The bridge of Eric's nose was very flat, his ears were set lower than is typical, his lip seemed a little droopy, and his eyes were shaped like half moons. The doctor said he thought it might be Down syndrome, and he took blood from Eric's heel and sent it for testing. It took 23 days. I had gone grocery shopping. I came home and my husband's demeanor had completely changed. He said, "They called." Until then I think I had been in denial. In a heartbeat our lives changed. We cried and cried. We started calling family members, and I think it was the only time I heard my father cry. We had the test done again to be sure. The results came back the same.

I was devastated and went through a range of emotions, but there was nothing to do but move on. My husband relied on me for understanding because I was the one with special education background. There were lots of struggles. Before he was born everyone was volunteering to babysit; afterwards, everyone got really quiet. The school district was notified immediately and be-

cause in Michigan services are offered birth to age 26, Eric began receiving services that first summer, even before I returned to work the fall after he was born. He has received special services ever since.

Eric struggled with health issues that resulted in eye surgery to remove a cataract at 11 months of age. They don't do lens transplants on young children, and so they wanted me to put a contact lens in his eye every day. He'd fight it. Imagine what that was like! Then at 18 months we found out he had a hole in his heart and unless he had heart surgery he would die. And then at 36 months his tonsils and adenoids were removed. Since then, no major surgeries, thank goodness.

In kindergarten, Eric was in a special education classroom. He was six years old and we had to get the potty training done. Then we moved, and I took the opportunity to slow down the educational timetable, and so he was in kindergarten again. Then he went to first grade with a combination of being in both the general education and the special education classroom. We did that until second grade. I realized the socialization was great, but that to get the education he needed it was going to be the special education classroom. And since then that has been how he has been educated. But not all the time. He would be general education for PE and art, for example.

Now Eric is 17. In high school he spends about 80 percent of the day in special education. But he's also the guy on the sidelines with the clipboard at the football and basketball games. The coach also

teaches a year-long course on CPR and first aid, and Eric is in that class. He also works with the drama teacher in a class once a week to build sets and do things like that. An assistant principal also took him under his wing and every Friday, instead of the usual announcements, the school has the Big E show. Eric does the morning news and announcements (but it's the AP who is helping him the whole time). The other kids really got behind it, and they sold T-shirts that say "The Big E show," and Eric signed them. The local newspaper and radio picked up on it—it's gotten a lot of publicity, and the AP says the kids actually pay attention to support Eric.

I'm very proud of Eric. He's an acolyte at our church, and he likes to be active at church. He'd wear a suit every day if I'd let him—he loves wearing suits. He's very social. What I want for Eric's future is for his teachers to have higher expectations. I do. I want high school for Eric to be like college for other students. I want him to get as many employability/job readiness skills as he can and as many socialization skills as possible. He may need to start by living in a group home, but I want him eventually to have a condo or a duplex with a roommate. I may have to hire someone to check on him, clean the house, do laundry, but that would be ok. He has something to offer to the community, and with help he'll be able to contribute.

I believe Eric was put in my care for a purpose. There is a reason for everything.

**PEARSON**
# myeducationlab

Go to the Assignments and Activities section of Topic 9: Intellectual Disabilities, in the MyEducationLab for your course and complete the activity entitled "Functional Curriculum: An Integrated Lesson".

Some students need alternative activities based on the general education curriculum. For example, the students in a sixth-grade social studies class were studying cultures, and they had reached the study of ancient Egypt. As part of the unit students were given the assignment of creating a magazine that ancient Egyptians would have wanted to read. Some students applied their new knowledge to produce magazines that contained references to Egyptian recreation, politics, and religion. Chase, a student with a moderate intellectual disability, created a picture magazine that incorporated artifacts from ancient Egypt for which he would see references in the normal course of life, including pharaohs and pyramids.

Other students with intellectual disabilities are supported in general education settings through the use of paraprofessionals (Broer, Doyle, & Giangreco, 2005; Carter, Sisco, Brown, Brickham, & Al-Khabbaz, 2008), but many students spend at least part of the day receiving specialized academic instruction in a special education setting. For example, in Ms. De-Cuir's classroom of middle school students who take an alternate assessment, the goal of the math program is to assist students to learn the skills they will need in order to shop, order in a restaurant, and possibly work in a fast-food restaurant. For some students the concept of a budget and saving money also is a priority. This is part of a **life skills curriculum**, a plan for students' education that stresses skills they need throughout life. In several lessons, the middle school students review coins and paper currency using real coins and facsimiles of bills, and they practice at their own skill levels how to make change—an **applied academic skill**. On Friday, Ms. DeCuir plans to take the students to the Dollar Store so they can make small purchases and put their skills into action. The outing will conclude with a stop at a fast-food restaurant where students will practice ordering food items based on how much money they have. The outing is part of **community-based instruction (CBI)**—that is, experience in applying skills learned in the classroom within the larger context of the community in which they live.

High school students are more likely than younger students to be educated primarily in special education settings, although in some communities inclusion is emphasized (Williamson, McLeskey, Hoppey, & Rentz, 2006). Andrew, a student with a mild intellectual disability, exemplifies a blended approach to education. As a sophomore he decided to take the introductory Spanish class. Although you might find his decision surprising, there is a reason. He lives in a community with many Spanish-speaking residents and wants to know about their language. No Spanish instruction was available in a special education class. With a strongly supportive Spanish teacher, Andrew learned basic Spanish. However, Andrew's English and math classes were taught by special education teachers. Three afternoons each week Andrew went to a local nursing home with his **job coach**, Ms. Hickman. There he learned how to change bed linens, check that supplies such as tissues and towels were available in each room, and assist residents with tasks such as eating. Ms. Hickman's role was to analyze the skills that Andrew needed, help him learn them, and ensure that he could carry out his responsibilities independently. Andrew hopes to enroll in a nurse's assistant program after leaving high school.

A few students with intellectual disabilities attend separate schools or live in residential facilities that include academic programs. Usually, these are students who have complex medical needs requiring the on-call availability of nursing or medical staff, or they are students who have very serious behavior problems in addition to intellectual disabilities. In some regions of the United States, the separate schools for students with moderate intellectual disabilities that were built around the time the first federal special education law was passed are still in place. They are becoming less and less common, though, as access to the general education curriculum and emphasis on an academically and socially integrated education have become priorities.

### Inclusive Practices

Despite the fact that the parents of children with intellectual disabilities were leaders in the educational movement that greatly increased inclusive practices, the preceding discussion indicates that this goal has been only partially achieved. Why are so many students with intellectual disabilities still separated for instruction?

The answer to this question is complex (Clegg, Murphy, Almack, & Harvey, 2008). One factor affecting the education of these students is traditional thinking. Many educators still believe that the best instructional arrangement for these students, particularly as they move

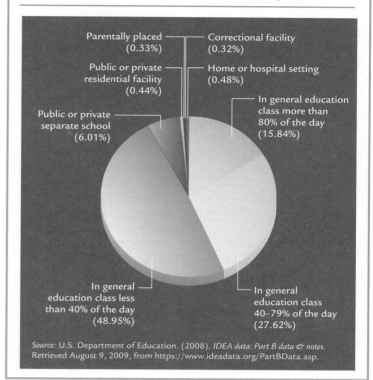

**FIGURE 8.4**

Educational Placements of Students Ages Six to Twenty-One Who Have Intellectual Disabilities (in percentages)

Parentally placed (0.33%)

Correctional facility (0.32%)

Public or private residential facility (0.44%)

Home or hospital setting (0.48%)

In general education class more than 80% of the day (15.84%)

Public or private separate school (6.01%)

In general education class less than 40% of the day (48.95%)

In general education class 40–79% of the day (27.62%)

*Source:* U.S. Department of Education. (2008). *IDEA data: Part B data & notes.* Retrieved August 9, 2009, from https://www.ideadata.org/PartBData.asp.

dimensions of
**DIVERSITY**

The transition goals and experiences of girls are different from those of boys and are influenced by their families, other mentors, opportunities to learn about post-school options, and peers (Hogansen, Powers, Geenen, Gil-Kashiwabara, & Powers, 2008).

from elementary to middle and high school, is a special education classroom. Many high school special education teachers for students with mild intellectual disabilities have asked, "Why would I support putting my students into classrooms where they don't know what is being taught and can't keep up with the pace? They need the practical skills that I give them." Their concern for their students is understandable and their advocacy for their education is important, especially given the current climate of accountability and the resulting pressure on secondary teachers to ensure students are successful on high-stakes tests.

However, the belief that only special educators can give the students what they need and that the entire high school curriculum is irrelevant for these students is troublesome (Carter, Sisco, Brown, Brickham, & Al-Khabbaz, 2008). It reflects the thinking of the past and raises another point: Inclusive practices do not mean that a student's only option is to attend general education classes for the entire school day without necessary supports. For example, in some high schools, part of the move toward inclusiveness is a peer-buddy program in which students without disabilities receive an elective credit to assist students with cognitive and other disabilities in their general education classes (Copeland et al., 2002). This highly successful arrangement has many benefits: Students with intellectual disabilities receive the support they need to succeed in general education classes, general education teachers are satisfied that the problem of not being able to get to all the students who need assistance is being addressed, and the peer-buddies are exploring career options related to special education. In other high schools, too, students with intellectual disabilities participate in general education academics and electives while receiving the supports they need (Yu, Newman, & Wagner, 2009).

More and more questions are being raised about appropriate educational options for students with intellectual disabilities (Browder, Wakeman, Spooner, Ahlgrim-Delzell, & Algozzine, 2006; Clayton, Burdge, Denham, Kleinhart, & Kearns, 2006), and some of the factors prompting these questions are reviewed in the section on issues later in this chapter. Few educators would argue about the need for a continuum of services for students with intellectual disabilities, but how decisions are made regarding where student are educated and how often and why those decisions are re-visited have not been adequately addressed. Further, no one would argue about a continuing priority to carefully coordinate all the various special education, related, and community services these students require in order to create flexible models that address students' needs while providing them access to the general curriculum and extracurricular activities, and all the academic, emotional, behavioral, and social benefits resulting from that access. As educators create additional options for successful inclusion (e.g., Carter, Hughes, Guth, & Copeland, 2005; Maroney, Finson, Beaver, & Jensen, 2003), the ways in which students with intellectual disabilities receive their education are sure to change.

## Transition and Adulthood

As students with intellectual disabilities reach adolescence, emphasis usually shifts to helping them make a successful transition from school to adulthood. Some students will leave school at about age eighteen with their peers. Others are entitled to receive services through age twenty-one. For students with mild intellectual disabilities, transition may emphasize learning tasks that foster independence, including planning and using a household budget, searching for and finding employment, using resource tools such as the phone book and Internet, and developing hobbies and recreational skills. For students with more significant intellectual disabilities, the same types of preparation may be emphasized but on a somewhat more limited basis. Instead of budgeting, for example, math activities may focus on making wise choices about using spending money. The vehicle through which this type of planning occurs is the transition plan that is required by federal special education law, and it is a collaborative effort on the part of parents, the student, and professionals (Test, Fowler, White, Richter, & Walker, 2009). The importance of transition planning for these students and the concept of **self-determination**—that is, students' rights to make plans that reflect their wishes, not only the ideas of professionals and parents—is addressed in detail in the final section of this chapter as a critical issue for the field.

## Which Curriculum?

One question concerns the curriculum that is appropriate for students with intellectual disabilities (Bouck, 2008; 2009). In the past these students often followed a curriculum that was different from that of typical learners. It usually emphasized life skills and adaptive behavior, and it could be offered in a special education classroom. Skills such as counting money and personal care (e.g., brushing teeth) were not simply occasional topics for elementary students; they were of central concern. As students got older, cooking tasks and household chores (e.g., changing bed linens, doing laundry) were emphasized. Increasingly, however, most students with intellectual disabilities are being expected to learn in the same curriculum as other students, whether in a general education or a special education setting.

Some see this change as positive, enabling students to have true educational access and to learn as much of that curriculum as possible. Proponents of this thinking argue that it is unethical for professionals to decide that students with intellectual disabilities should not have the same learning opportunities as other students. They maintain that although some variations in activities and assignments will be needed, these students are capable of learning far more than those supporting alternative curricula have assumed. Opponents argue that many topics in the general education curriculum simply are not important for students with intellectual disabilities, especially when viewed in the context of all the survival skills these students need to learn before adulthood. These critics contend that students with intellectual disabilities, even mild cognitive impairments, too often attend general education classes where they understand little of the instruction, even when accommodations are provided. The content is too abstract; the pace is too fast.

### The Dilemma of High-Stakes Testing

A discussion of curriculum expectations can be related directly to the accountability for that curriculum as measured on high-stakes tests (Bouck, 2009). As you learned, few students with disabilities can be exempt from such tests, and some students with mild intellectual disabilities are being expected to complete them.

Some professionals applaud this strong initiative to ensure that high standards are maintained for all students with disabilities. They point to student success stories and argue that over time, as an increasing number of students with intellectual disabilities access the general education curriculum from the beginning of their school careers, more and more students will learn more and more of that curriculum. Opponents to the current requirements for high-stakes testing tell stories as well. They describe tearful children being asked to take tests that are beyond their capabilities. They contend that few students with intellectual disabilities should participate in high-stakes testing, noting that the current assessment systems seems to emphasize "equal" rather than "equitable." They contend that legislation demanding students' participation does not make it correct. Critics further point out that in some communities, students with disabilities are blamed for causing schools' failure to achieve federally mandated goals of adequate yearly progress. Finally, some professionals support the participation of all students in assessment, but they strongly support using tests that are appropriate for the students' levels of learning (Council for Exceptional Children, 2003).

As you read about the No Child Left Behind Act and the focus on accountability in your professional preparation courses, keep both of these perspectives in mind. Think about the possibilities of helping more students to master the core curriculum as well as the pitfalls of setting standards at too high a level. How can these two points of view be reconciled?

**PEARSON** **myeducationlab**

Go to the Assignments and Activities section of Topic 5: Assessment Practices, in the MyEducationLab for your course and complete the activity entitled "High-Stakes Testing".

## Self-Determination: The Potential, Promises, and Practices

The topic of self-determination was mentioned as becoming particularly important for students with intellectual disabilities as they make the transition from school to adulthood (Jones, 2006). It is included here as an issue, not because of professional sentiment about its importance but because of the difficulties in making the concept of self-determination a reality in the transition process (Carter et al., 2008).

## Perceptions of Parents and Teachers

Parents' views of self-determination seem to be unequivocally positive: They strongly believe that their nearly adult children should be directly taught self-determination skills and fully participate in transition planning (Grigal, Neubert, Moon, & Graham, 2003; Lee, Palmer, Turnbull, & Wehmeyer, 2006). However, it also has been reported that parents do not seem to deliberately assist their children to use self-determination skills (Thoma, Rogan, & Baker, 2001). For example, they do not seem to know how to go about preparing their children to participate in their IEP meetings, which offer natural opportunities for self-determination.

Another dimension of ensuring that students learn self-determination skills relates to teachers: How familiar are they with self-determination, how supportive are they of it, how well prepared are they to teach self-determination skills, and are they doing so? Fiedler and Danneker (2007) surveyed the professional literature related to these topics and found that teachers know that current legislation and policy stress self-determination, and they recognize its importance. However, the authors also found that teachers spend far too little time teaching self-determination because of these and other barriers:

- Traditional special education instructional models place students in relatively passive roles with teachers responsible for decision-making. Many special educators believe that the decision-making that occurs during IEP and transition meetings is too complex for students.
- The expectations set by NCLB and IDEA for access to general curriculum and the requirement for assessment at grade level for most students is in conflict with the design of programs individualized to their needs. A result is that students do not have enough opportunities while they are at school to practice self-determination skills.

And so, even when teachers recognize the importance of self-determination skills, they do not necessarily make teaching these skills to their students a priority.

However, another study suggests a positive trend in thinking about and teaching self-determination. Carter, Lane, Pierson, and Stang (2008) surveyed a large sample of both special and general education high school teachers, asking them about the importance of various self-determination skills (e.g., problem solving, self-advocacy) and the amount of class time spent instructing students on those skills. They found that both general education and special education teachers viewed self-determination skills as highly important and spent time in class addressing self-determination skills. These authors concluded that their results are promising in this era in which most students spend a significant part of the day in general education settings.

## Implementation of Practices That Foster Self-Determination

As some professionals have been exploring the beliefs of parents and teachers regarding self-determination, others have been reviewing their practices. For example, when Zhang and Stecker (2001) interviewed teachers about self-determination, the teachers reported that students had a low level of participation in transition meetings, particularly in activities that were implemented after the meetings. Observational studies support this view. Thoma and her colleagues (Thoma et al., 2001) observed transition IEP meetings for students with intellectual disabilities and found that while students were physically present, the adults in the meetings talked about the students rather than with the students. The adults also tended to ignore ideas expressed by the students during the planning process.

Clearly, the positive impact of teaching students to act on their own behalf is that they will be able to advocate for themselves throughout life (Palmer & Wehmeyer, 2003).

**research**
**NOTE**

Here is an example of self-determination: When secondary students, including those with intellectual disabilities, were taught how to lead their IEP meetings, they were significantly more likely than other students to start, talk at, and lead their meetings (Martin et al., 2006).

**PEARSON**
**myeducationlab**

Go to the Assignments and Activities section of Topic 5: Assessment Practices, in the MyEducationLab for your course and complete the activity entitled "Self-Determination".

## Self-Determination in Transition Planning

Self-determination skills can be taught beginning in elementary school, but they are particularly important as students make the transition from school to adulthood. Here are some activities that foster self-determination.

### Professionals' Activities: Before Developing a Transition Plan

- Listening to the student/family share their future vision regarding the student's life after high school
- Identifying the student's interests and preferences
- Identifying the student's needs
- Incorporating the student's family's needs, interests, and preferences into a draft transition service plan

### Professionals' Activities: During Transition Planning Meetings

- Helping the student identify available choices
- Facilitating the student in making his or her own decisions
- Allowing the student to take charge of some or all parts of the transition planning meeting
- Providing the student/family opportunities to review the developed transition plan
- Providing the student/family sufficient time for asking questions
- Responding to the student/family questions
- Having the student and/or family sign the transition plan after they understand and agree with the plan

### Students' Activities

- Before the meeting, talking with teacher and/or parents in order to be prepared
- Before and during the meeting, expressing ideas about preferences
- During the meeting, actively participating in discussions
- After the meeting, meeting with school personnel to discuss the transition plan
- During the academic year following the meeting, asking questions about the plan and wanting to know about progress related to the plan

*Source:* Zhang, D., & Stecker, P. M. (2001). Student involvement in transition planning: Are we there yet? *Education and Training in Mental Retardation and Developmental Disabilities, 36,* 293–303. Reprinted with permission.

---

Further, programs have been developed to teach specific self-determination skills to students (Konrad, 2008; Konrad & Test, 2007). What remains are questions about how to better prepare teachers and other professionals to teach these skills to students and how to ensure that students have opportunities to learn and practice them, whether in a special education setting, a general education setting, or the community (Lee, Wehmeyer, Palmer, Soukup, & Little, 2008; Steere & Cavaiuolo, 2002). The Professional Edge contains some important aspects of self-determination that can be addressed as part of transition.

## REVIEW · REFLECT · DISCUSS

1. How should the positive trend of raising expectations for students with intellectual disabilities be balanced against some educators' concerns that the current requirements for academic achievement for these students are too high? How can high academic expectations and the need for vocational preparation be reconciled?

2. What is *self-determination*? Why is self-determination an important yet somewhat controversial topic in considering best practices for students with intellectual disabilities?

# Summary

- The treatment of children and adults with intellectual disabilities, called *mental retardation* in IDEA, has been strongly influenced by societal views and currently can be characterized by rising expectations and a focus on abilities instead of limitations.
- Although the causes of most students' intellectual disabilities are unknown, some prenatal causes (e.g., chromosomal abnormalities, toxoplasmosis, alcohol use), perinatal causes (e.g., lack of oxygen, low birth weight), and postnatal causes (e.g., illness, brain injury) have been identified.
- Students with intellectual disabilities usually have a cognitive functioning level at least 2 standard deviations below the mean of 100 on an IQ test; they have significant problems in carrying out the day-to-day life activities, referred to as *adaptive behavior*; and they also may have physical and health problems.
- All the procedures outlined in IDEA must be followed in identifying students as having intellectual disabilities, with the emphasis on assessing intelligence level and adaptive behavior.
- Students identified as having intellectual disabilities are likely to receive a significant amount of their education in special education classrooms, although parents and other advocates continue to promote a more inclusive education for them.
- Because of these students' characteristics, recommended instructional strategies stress repetition, small increments of learning, and the use of concrete materials, as well as peer-learning strategies such as cooperative learning and peer tutoring. Assisting students to prepare for independence after school also is essential.
- Parents may learn of their children's intellectual disabilities when they are infants or toddlers, or not until learning difficulties are encountered in school. Their ability to adapt and to normalize family functioning often relies on their system of supports.
- Two issues facing the field today are (a) students' participation in high-stakes testing and other accountability systems in today's public schools and (b) options available for these individuals in adulthood.

 **Council for Exceptional Children**  ADDRESSING THE PROFESSIONAL STANDARDS

Council for Exceptional Children (CEC) Common Core Knowledge and Skills addressed in this chapter:

ICC1K5, ICC1K6, ICC1K8, ICC2K1, ICC2K5, ICC2K6, ICC3K3, ICC4S4, ICC4S5, ICC4S6, ICC5S3, ICC7K2, ICC7S1, ICC7S5, ICC7S7, ICC8K2, ICC8S6, ICC10K1, ICC10K3, ICC10S4

Appendix: Provides a full listing of the CEC Common Core Standards, and associated Knowledge and Skill Statements listed here.

**PEARSON**
**myeducationlab**

Now go to Topic 9: Intellectual Disabilities in the MyEducationLab (www.myeducationlab.com) for your course, where you can:

- Find learning outcomes for the broad concepts covered in this chapter along with the national standards that connect to these outcomes.
- Complete Assignments and Activities that can help you more deeply understand the chapter content.
- Examine challenging situations presented in the IRIS Center Resources.

- Apply and practice your understanding of the core concepts and skills identified in the chapter with the Building Teaching Skills and Dispositions learning units.
- Check your comprehension on the content covered in the chapter by going to the Study Plan in the Book Specific Resources for your text. Here you will be able to take a chapter quiz, receive feedback on your answers, and then access Review, Practice, and Enrichment activities to enhance your understanding of chapter content.
- Watch video clips of CCSSO Teacher of the Year award winners responding to the question: "Why I teach?" in the Teacher Talk section.

## chapter nine

# Students with Speech and Language Disorders

## LEARNING OBJECTIVES

· Outline the development of the study of speech and language disorders, define speech and language disorders, and explain their prevalence and causes.

· Describe characteristics of individuals with speech and language disorders.

· Explain how speech and language disorders are identified.

· Outline how learners with speech and language disorders receive their education.

· Describe recommended educational practices for students with speech and language disorders.

· Explain the perspectives and concerns that parents and families of students with speech and language disorders may have.

· Identify trends and issues influencing the field of speech and language disorders.

## Andrew

Andrew's second-grade teacher describes him as a very quiet child who rarely speaks unless asked to do so—a student she worries about overlooking. His academic performance in math is nearly average, but he seems to be struggling more and more with reading. When he is observed on the playground, he is by himself most of the time. Andrew's mother explains that he always has had difficulty pronouncing certain words and that she and her husband did not worry too much about what they thought were minor developmental problems, thinking that he would "grow out of it" as many children do. However, Andrew still is substituting the sound /t/ for /k/ and the sound /f/ for /th/. Andrew might say "tite" when he means "kite," "tountry" when he means "country," and "fink" when he means "think." Andrew began receiving assistance from a speech/language therapist soon after he enrolled in kindergarten, and he now works with this professional twice each week for 30 minutes. In addition, his teacher helps him in the classroom setting to practice the sounds he is learning.

## Jade

Jade appears to be an average middle school student, a girl who seems most interested in boys, music, and the current pop icons. She is a below-average student but attends school regularly and sincerely tries to complete her work. However, Jade has rather complicated special needs. After she received a gunshot wound to her head as an innocent bystander in a gang incident, she was diagnosed with traumatic brain injury and also has a learning disability. The physical effects of her injury have long since healed, but Jade now receives special education services both in her English and math classes as well as in a resource room. Jade also receives services twice each week from Ms. Ochoa, a speech/language therapist. Ms. Ochoa is working with Jade in several areas. For example, it sometimes is clear that Jade knows what she wants to say but cannot seem to get her brain to instruct her throat, jaws, mouth, and tongue to form the words she needs. Ms. Ochoa is helping Jade to relearn these skills, working closely with her special education teacher and meeting regularly with her general education teachers. Ms. Ochoa also assists Jade in areas that might traditionally be considered language arts—that is, developing vocabulary and writing. A key component of Jade's services is restoring her confidence in her communication skills.

## David

David is an eleventh-grade student at Walt Whitman High School. He is enrolled in a program with a vocational emphasis, learning important skills for getting and keeping a job when he leaves school at age twenty-two. He spends part of the day in special education classes, part of the day in general education classes such as physical education, and part of the day in a vocational school where he is learning skills to work as a data entry specialist. David has received speech-language services since he was a toddler, but the types of services have changed over time. When he was young, his speech-language therapist emphasized proper use of his lips and tongue to accurately produce sounds. Gradually, emphasis shifted to language skills such as vocabulary development. As he enters this final part of his schooling, focus now is on assisting David to initiate conversations and ask questions and to understand idioms that he may encounter in the workplace (e.g., "That was a piece of cake." "Let's get this up and running."). Another priority is making sure that David appropriately makes eye contact with teachers, work supervisors, and peers. David's speech-language therapist consults with the professionals working with David so that they also emphasize these skills.

To check your comprehension on the content covered in Chapter 9, go to the Book Specific Resources in the MyEducationLab (www .myeducationlab.com) for your course, select your text, and complete the Study Plan. Here you will be able to take a chapter quiz, receive feedback on your answers, and then access review, practice, and enrichment activities to enhance your understanding of chapter content.

At some point in your life, you may have experienced a speech or language problem. Perhaps your parents have a recording of your preschool rendition of a favorite song in which you say "wabbit" for "rabbit" or "tate" for "cake." Everyone who hears the tape now chuckles at the mispronunciations that you have long since outgrown. More recently, you may have encountered a momentary problem in recalling a particular word you wished to write on your exam answer, probably because of fatigue or stress. You knew you knew the word, but you simply could not bring it to mind when you needed it. If you are uncomfortable speaking to groups, you might have found that giving presentations to classmates made you feel as though you could not coherently string words together into sentences or smoothly transition from one topic to another. The 15 minutes you spoke felt like 15 hours.

The speech and language challenges that many individuals have faced are brief episodes—unsettling but temporary. As such, they provide no more than a glimpse of what it is really like to have a speech or language disorder. Imagine sitting in an elementary classroom and not being able to pronounce common words. Imagine being in high school and having difficulty grasping verbal directions and expressing your thoughts aloud. What might be the impact of these chronic problems on academic achievement? On interactions with peers and adults? On behavior? These are some of the topics considered in this chapter.

## Understanding Speech and Language Disorders

Today's practices in the field of speech and language disorders are based on work that began nearly two centuries ago. This discipline has been influenced by research in medicine, psychology, and education, and it has progressed from simple approaches to complex understandings.

### Development of the Study of Speech and Language Disorders

As you can see in the timeline in Figure 9.1, some of the earliest work related to speech and language disorders was undertaken in Europe at the beginning of the nineteenth century on behalf of individuals who were deaf (Duchan, 2008). In the United States, the first textbook on speech disorders was published in 1802 by S. C. L. Potter. The rest of that century was characterized by the use of unproven treatments—for example, improving speech by placing rolls of linen under the tongue.

#### Emergence of a Profession

Although much early work was completed by medical specialists, by the beginning of the twentieth century it was clear that a new group of professionals called *speech clinicians* was emerging to address speech and language disorders. Most of the interventions these professionals provided for children with speech or language disorders took place in public

**FIGURE 9.1**

Timeline of the Development of the Field of Speech and Language Disorders

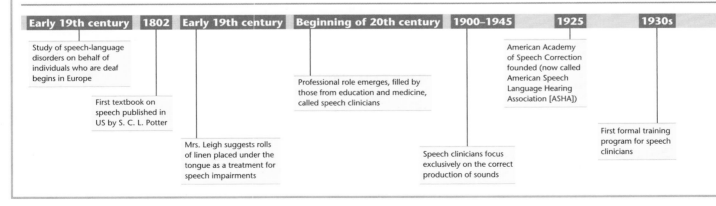

schools (Duchan, 2008). However, the emphasis on speech-language therapy gradually shifted from exclusive attention to the correct production of speech sounds to children's overall ability to use language to communicate.

### Contemporary Practices

Strongly influenced by the passage of federal special education law in 1975, the profession of speech-language therapy has continued to evolve. For example, in the past two decades, conceptualizations of speech and language disorders have expanded yet again to stress the role of communication. That is, professionals now acknowledge that not only is it important to recognize whether students can produce complete sentences using the correct tense, but it is also essential to think about what students are trying to express and to whom (Duchan, 2008). This most recent thinking—including the communication context—is particularly significant for addressing the needs of students with disabilities. Read the Speaking from Experience to learn more about a speech/language therapist's view of the field and the work of these professionals.

## Definitions of Speech and Language Disorders

The number of terms and concepts associated with the field of speech and language disorders reflects the wide range of conditions it encompasses. In this chapter the term **speech and language disorders** is used to refer to all the disorders that can occur within this disability category. However, you also may come across the term **communication disorders**. It, too, is a global term for all the conditions that comprise this disability, but it sometimes is used to include difficulties with communication that arise from hearing loss whereas the other term sometimes excludes those individuals.

In IDEA, the term **speech or language impairment** is used, and it is defined as

> a communication disorder such as stuttering, impaired articulation, language impairment, or a voice impairment that adversely affects a child's educational performance (IDEA 20 U.S.C. §1401 [2004], 20 C.F.R. §300.8[c][11])

This definition is far less detailed than the definitions of most of the other disabilities covered by IDEA, but it is deceptively simple. Combining speech and language problems into a single definition allows considerable variation to exist among states in terms of which students receive services and how they receive services. In all states, students whose primary disability is a language disorder are served within this category. However, because IDEA

*The most critical period for learning language is during the first few years of life.*

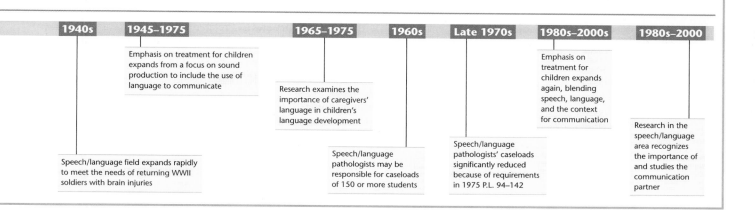

| 1940s | 1945–1975 | 1965–1975 | 1960s | Late 1970s | 1980s–2000s | 1980s–2000 |

Emphasis on treatment for children expands from a focus on sound production to include the use of language to communicate

Research examines the importance of caregivers' language in children's language development

Emphasis on treatment for children expands again, blending speech, language, and the context for communication

Research in the speech/language area recognizes the importance of and studies the communication partner

Speech/language field expands rapidly to meet the needs of returning WWII soldiers with brain injuries

Speech/language pathologists may be responsible for caseloads of 150 or more students

Speech/language pathologists' caseloads significantly reduced because of requirements in 1975 P.L. 94–142

# speaking from experience

*Jennifer Santangelo is a speech/language therapist who works in a small district about 75 miles from New York City. She has a total of 8 years of experience. Her description of the many dimensions of her job can help you to understand the valuable role such professionals play in meeting the needs of students with speech, language, and communication disorders.*

I always knew I wanted to do *something* with children. As I was growing up I had the opportunity to observe a master speech/language therapist at the preschool where my mother worked. She got the kids so engaged and it was amazing what she got them to do; that's how I chose being a speech/language therapist as *exactly* what I wanted to do with children.

What I do as a therapist varies all the time—and includes augmentative communication, communication boards, social skills—along with therapy. My first year, I had five elementary schools that I traveled to. And then another year I worked in only one school. One year I was doing an intervention program for kindergarten. I went into nine different kindergarten classes to teach the children listening skills, comprehension skills, language development, and vocabulary—depending on their needs.

Right now, I also go into self-contained special education classrooms in order to do language lessons. What I'm saying is that I don't just stay in my therapy room. I like to be in classrooms a lot. Of course, I also pull students out. I go to a smaller building (which means I'm there for a very limited amount of time), and don't have the option to schedule going into classrooms, even though that is where I'd rather be. When I do pull students out, I try to connect what we're doing with the classroom. For example, a fourth-grade teacher gives me review materials for tests. When I work with the students I'll use those materials to also teach them strategies to be successful. That way they see that what I'm doing with them is really related to what they are doing in fourth grade.

Another part of my job is working with teachers. For example, with a student getting articulation therapy I'll go into the classroom to observe. Sometimes I'll remind the teacher to say to the student, "I know you can say the sound the way Ms. XXX taught you . . ." instead of saying "Say the sound the 'right' way. . . ." I don't want kids to feel like they are doing something "wrong" and I have to count on the teacher to help on that.

Working with parents is important, too. Sometimes parents don't really want their children to get speech therapy or to leave the classroom to go to the therapy room. You have to convince them. Or, sometimes we have to get them what they need in other ways. The reading teacher came to me and asked me to teach her how to help a student make certain sounds. The parent wouldn't let the child receive speech therapy but would agree to reading instruction. Now I'm teaching the reading teacher strategies to help the child, and the parents are fine with it because it is taught as part of reading.

Other parents are completely the opposite. The other day I had a parent call me concerned that her son could not say the /r/ sound. I explained that we had been working on it in therapy and that I could send some information home so that the parent could practice with him correctly (how to move his lips, what to do with his tongue) at home for about five minutes each night. She was so grateful to know what to do to help him. She asked about other concerns, but I told her just to work on one sound at a time, that we would eventually address all the areas of need.

My job involves both articulation therapy and language therapy, and they intertwine all the time. I usually don't focus just on articulation because you can do it through language activities like reading stories. You can go through a story and identify the sounds that students need to work on and stress those sounds as you go. Another type of therapy I sometimes do is called *oral-motor*. This year, for example, there is a student who has feeding goals. During lunch time, you teach the student how to take a fork, put it in his mouth, take the food off the fork, and then chew it. Sometimes I also help students learn how to swallow because that could affect their articulation.

When I think about advice I would give to professionals new to the field, I know that I was lucky to have had a wonderful mentor. If you can form a relationship with another therapist or a classroom teacher, you can learn so many strategies that you never would learn in school. I think it's also important to stay flexible when you work in schools because your job probably is going to change—from year to year, but also from session to session.

---

## web link

http://www.asha.org/default.htm
The American Speech-Language-Hearing Association is the professional organization for audiologists, speech/language pathologists, and other professionals concerned with speech and language disorders in children and adults. Its website includes articles on many topics and information about specific disorders.

includes speech services both within this category and as a related service, states vary in their regulations. In some states, students can have IEPs that are "speech only"; that is, the primary disability is considered the speech disorder, and special education services are offered for it even if those are the only services needed. In other states, students can only receive services for speech disorders as a related service—that is, only if the students have been identified as having other disabilities under IDEA. In those states, if speech therapy is the only special need, students are not eligible for special education.

## Concepts to Describe Speech and Language Disorders

To appreciate the scope of special needs addressed in this disability category, more explanation is needed than is offered in the IDEA definition. A beginning point for exploring speech and language disorders is an overview of human communication.

**Communication** is the exchange of information and knowledge among participants (Lue, 2001), and it is a basic and critical human need (Peets, 2009; Romski, Sevcik, Adamson, & Bakeman, 2005). Communication requires a *message* (the information or knowledge), a *sender* (the person who transmits the message), and a *receiver* (the person who grasps the message). It also involves a *channel*, or a route through which the message travels. Finally, communication involves a sort of volleyball game, in which the sender and receiver send messages back and forth. For example, when a friend says to you "Are you ready to go?" while looking at his watch, standing in the doorway with his coat on, and fidgeting, the friend is the sender, you are the receiver, and the message concerns being late. The channel is both *verbal*—the words he spoke—and *nonverbal*—the glance at his watch and the posture of fidgeting while standing in the doorway. The back-and-forth of communication would continue when you responded to your friend.

### Elements of Language

**Language** is the system of symbols, governed by complex rules, that individuals use for communication, and it is based on their culture (Newman, 2006). More than 6,800 languages are spoken across the world (Anderson, 2004; National Virtual Translation Center, 2006), but not all languages rely on speaking. The clearest example of a nonspoken language is American Sign Language (ASL), the language used by some individuals who are deaf.

Language also must be thought of in terms of its application. **Expressive language** refers to the ability to produce language. **Receptive language** refers to the ability to comprehend language. If you have studied Spanish, Urdu, Mandarin, or any language that you did not speak as you were growing up, you are very familiar with the difference between these two concepts. You probably gained skill in comprehending the language when it was spoken to you or when you read it (receptive language) faster than you acquired the skills necessary to accurately speak the language or write it (expressive language).

When language is spoken, it has five components, any of which can be the source of problems for a student with a disability. The first three components—phonology, morphology, and syntax—give language its form; the next component, semantics, refers to a language's content. Pragmatics, the last component, refers to the function or use of the language.

- *Phonology.* Every spoken language includes a set of sounds, called **phonemes**, on which the language is based. For example, English includes the phoneme /ae/, but it is spelled in several ways (e.g., p*ai*n, b*ay*, g*a*m*e*, n*a*ture). Further, rules govern which sounds may be combined and where they may be used in words. Thus, it is acceptable to blend the letters /n/ and /d/ to form /nd/, as in the words *sand* and *window*, but that combination of letters never appears at the beginning of a word. **Phonology** is the ability to hear the sounds used in a language and to use them correctly in words. Perhaps you have heard that one effective strategy for helping struggling readers is by improving their **phonemic awareness**. As you might guess, this refers to assisting them to make the fine discriminations among the sounds that make up the English language, as is illustrated in the words *hat, him, and hint*. **Phonological awareness** is the ability to identify those sounds and to manipulate them, for example, by rhyming.

- *Morphology.* **Morphemes** are the smallest units of a language that have meaning, and they are composed of phonemes. English has two types of morphemes. The first is called a *free morpheme*, meaning that it can exist without being attached to any other morpheme. Examples of free morphemes include many basic words such as *child, pretty, to*, and *run*. The second type is a *bound morpheme*. This type of morpheme has meaning, but it must be attached to another word according to the rules of the language. For example, when you see the suffix /-ed/, you know that generally it means past tense. You also know that this set of letters must be attached to another word. Other examples of bound morphemes include /-s/ and /pre-/. What are other examples? **Morphology**, then, is the ability to form words using one or more morphemes within the rules of the language.

- *Syntax.* Every language has a set of rules that determine the order in which words are used. The ability to recognize and follow these rules is what is meant by **syntax**. For example, in English adjectives generally precede the nouns they describe, and so *The clear blue sky* is correct but *The sky blue clear* is not. Young children who are learning to speak often

**PEARSON myeducationlab**

Go to the Assignments and Activities section of Topic 12: Communication Disorders, in the MyEducationLab for your course and complete the activity entitled "Describing Language Impairments".

**fyi**

Approximately 7.5 million Americans have difficulty using their voice, between 6 and 8 million have some type of language disorder, and 3 million stutter (National Institute on Deafness and Other Communication Disorders, 2009).

experience difficulty with syntax. They might say something such as *I car go* instead of *I'm going in the car* and *Cookie me* instead of *I want a cookie.*

• *Semantics.* As mentioned at the beginning of this section, **semantics** pertains to the content of one's language, or to the meaning and precision of the words selected. Think about the differences in these two sentences: *It was bad outside* and *The temperature was below zero, the heavy, wet snow was accumulating quickly, and the wind was howling.* Which presents a more accurate description that clearly communicates what was meant? Another example is common in day-to-day interactions: Have you ever known a person who peppers conversation with words such as *things* or *stuff?* This is an example of a semantics problem related to precise word selections.

• *Pragmatics.* The fifth and final component of language concerns **pragmatics**, the function or use of language within a social context (Brice, Franklin, & Ratusnik, 2008). Each language has a unique set of rules that govern pragmatics. In English, for example, the rules include these: Only one person speaks at a time; everyone contributes to the conversation; interruptions usually are to be avoided; and topics generally are introduced, explored, and then completed (Owens, Metz, & Haas, 2003). Pragmatics is important because the primary purpose of language is to communicate with others. Even if individuals have mastered all the other components of language, they are at a disadvantage if they cannot put the language to effective use in interactions with others.

### Language Disorders

Students with language disorders may have significant and chronic problems related to any one of the discrete components of language outlined, or they may have disabilities that encompass several of these components. When students have language disorders that cannot be explained by physical disabilities, intellectual disabilities, hearing loss, or other disabilities, they are referred to as having **specific language impairments (SLIs)** (Pickles et al., 2009; Pratt, Dotting, & Conti-Ramsden, 2006). For example, some students are not able to clearly distinguish among the words being spoken because they cannot discriminate among similar sounds. When a teacher, referring to a page in the social studies text, says "Let's look at the map," the student may focus her attention on the picture of a famous explorer (man) on the opposite page because she did not correctly hear the ending sound /p/. This is a language disorder related to phonology. Some students make errors in forming words, perhaps saying "I getted three book at the library," a disorder related to morphology. Yet others experience challenges in forming sentences, saying "I overslept because I was late" instead of "I was late because I overslept," a syntactical error.

Students who have difficulty finding correct words or understanding the nuances of language (e.g., not understanding the expression *It's raining cats and dogs* or *You're trying to butter me up*) have problems with semantics, a problem being addressed with David, the high school student you met at the beginning of the chapter. Finally, some students experience difficulty participating in the social aspect of communication (Volden, Coolican, & Garon, 2009). They might monopolize a conversation, unaware that others would like to speak as well. Or they might start talking about a topic unrelated to the one currently being discussed, causing peers or adults to look at them questioningly. These are issues related to pragmatics.

The Professional Edge includes many additional examples of student behavior that might signal the presence of language disorders. As you look at this list, which behaviors might you expect to see in Jade, the middle school student introduced at the beginning of the chapter?

Many language disorders cannot be characterized based on a single dimension. These are some examples of language disorders that have several components:

• Some students acquire language at a rate slower than is typical (Hoff & Shatz, 2007). This is referred to as a **language delay**. Some of these students eventually will catch up, and their language skills will be comparable to those of their peers. Others may always lag behind, but they may continue to make progress. For a few students, the delay can be significant, and the students do not progress. Early intervention, a topic introduced later in this chapter, is particularly helpful for students with language delays (Suarez & Daniels, 2009).

- **Aphasia** refers to loss of language after it has developed. Although this term is most commonly applied to adults, children can become aphasic as a result of a traumatic brain injury (TBI), as might occur after an accident or an injury such as the one experienced by Jade, whom you met in the chapter opening. Aphasia includes difficulty in using language, receptively or expressively, and it can range from mild to severe. Examples include difficulty in recalling the words that describe common objects (e.g., *chair, glass*), forming sentences, and listening and reading with understanding (Shames & Anderson, 2006).

- In order to use speech and language, the ears and their related structures and the brain must take in and interpret auditory information. Students who have **central auditory processing disorders (CAPDs)** do not have hearing loss, but for some reason their brains do not effectively interpret the auditory information that comes from their ears (Heine & Slone, 2008). They may have difficulty in several related areas, including listening and speaking using the rules of the language. It should be noted, though, that professionals disagree about whether CAPD is a unique disorder (MacFarland & Cacace, 2006); some view it instead as related to attention deficit–hyperactivity disorder (ADHD), learning disabilities, or specific language impairment (Bailey & Snowling, 2002).

### Elements of Speech

**Speech** is the use of the oral channel for exchanging information and knowledge. Hundreds of muscles and structures can be involved in speech (Shames & Anderson, 2006), and some of these are highlighted in Figure 9.2. First, breath has to be expelled from the lungs using the muscles of the rib cage and the diaphragm. This air has to be forced through the larynx (also called the *voice box*), which includes structures and muscles in the neck. Here the muscles control the amount of air flowing out at one time, causing the vocal folds (also called the *vocal chords*) to *vibrate* and produce sound. Professional singers provide an example of how important this part of speech production can be. They have learned to control these muscles precisely so that they can make exactly the correct pitch at exactly the correct loudness. Finally, the structures and muscles in the head, including the lips, jaws, tongue, teeth, and soft palate, provide for the fine-tuning of speech. Think about what you do to form the

**PEARSON**
**myeducationlab**

Go to the Assignments and Activities section of Topic 12: Communication Disorders, in the MyEducationLab for your course and complete the activity entitled "Describing Speech Impairments".

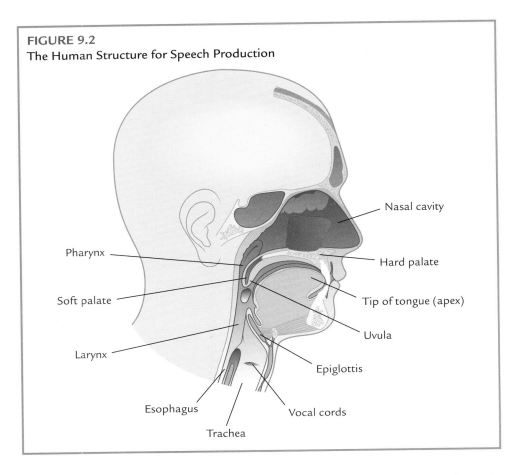

**FIGURE 9.2**
**The Human Structure for Speech Production**

Nasal cavity

Pharynx

Hard palate

Soft palate

Tip of tongue (apex)

Uvula

Larynx

Epiglottis

Esophagus

Vocal cords

Trachea

Alexander Graham Bell's grandfather and father were both distinguished professionals in the speech and language field. Bell was an expert in his father's phonetic alphabet, a system called *visible speech* that was intended to help people learn to enunciate more carefully but later was used to teach language skills to individuals who were deaf.

highlighted sounds in these words: *bond, pond.* You rely mostly on your lips to form the sounds correctly. Here is another example. Say these words: *this, think.* These sounds require touching the tip of the tongue to the upper teeth. If you have ever been to the dentist for work that involved numbing your mouth, you know exactly how much clear speech relies on controlling your lips, teeth, and tongue.

Speech has these dimensions (Lue, 2001): voice, resonance, articulation, and fluency.

- **Voice** includes three components: (1) *Pitch* is the highness or lowness of the sound; (2) *intensity*, or loudness, is the perceived volume of speech; and (3) *quality* concerns the extent to which speech would be characterized as smooth or hoarse. Spoken language requires voice, but voice also is used for laughter, singing, and crying. The air exhaled from the lungs may be voiced by the vibration of the vocal folds within the larynx. In contrast, whispered sounds are not voiced, nor are a few speech sounds such as /p/, /t/, and /k/.
- The nasal or oral aspect of spoken sound is called **resonance**, and it sometimes is considered part of voice (Lenden & Flipsen, 2007). It is the component of speech that is determined by the balance of sound vibration in the mouth, nose, and throat. Resonance can be affected by the physical make-up of these structures or by problems in using them (Kummer, 2006). You can think of resonance in terms of people's voices: Some people have rich and full voices, but others have voices that might be considered weak or reedy.
- Of all the dimensions of speech, school professionals often are most familiar with articulation. **Articulation** involves the movement of the tongue, teeth, lips, and palate to produce the sounds of a language. In the examples given previously (*bond, pond; this, think*), it is articulation skills that enable a person to say each word correctly.
- It is not enough to be able to voice the sounds of our language. **Fluency** refers to the ability to speak without hesitations that interfere with clear communication. Children are considered fluent when they can produce speech smoothly, making words, sentences, and paragraphs that follow the cadence of English, with pauses for taking breaths.

## Speech Disorders

Just as with language disorders, students who have **speech disorders** may have problems in any of the four components (voice, resonance, articulation, or fluency) of speech or in a combination of them. **Voice disorders** occur when students have difficulty with pitch, intensity, vocal quality, or resonance. For example, Evelyn is a student with a voice disorder. When she speaks, she breathes very shallowly and her voice seldom reaches above a whisper. Brittany also has a voice disorder; if you heard her speak, you would describe her voice as having a harsh, rough quality. Judd's voice is muffled. He sounds as though he has a cold even when he does not. Some voice disorders are caused by physical disabilities such as cleft lip and palate, discussed later in the chapter.

Many young children experience **articulation disorders**, including **omissions** (*bo* for *boat*), **substitutions** (*wan* for *ran*), or **additions** (*ammaminal* for *animal*). **Distortions** are yet another articulation disorder. They occur when a sound not found in the child's language is used for another sound. For example, if *soup* was said with air escaping from the side of the mouth, a distortion would have occurred. These errors are considered disorders only when they persist beyond the typical developmental period, as illustrated in Figure 9.3. Andrew, the student introduced at the beginning of this chapter, has an articulation disorder.

The most common of **fluency disorders** is stuttering (Proctor, Yairi, Duff, & Zhang, 2008). **Stuttering** occurs when a person's speech is broken by sound repetitions (e.g., *w-w-want*), prolonged sounds (e.g., *wwwant*), or unanticipated stoppages of sound (Venkatagiri, 2005). Some individuals who stutter also make unusual facial expressions or body movements as they struggle to speak. Interventions such as those outlined in the Professional Edge can have a strong positive impact when you work with students who have this disorder (e.g., Blomgren, Roy, Callister, & Merrill, 2005; Prins & Ingham, 2009; Weiss, 2004).

Another fluency disorder, **cluttering**, occurs when an individual speaks in bursts or pauses in unexpected places during speech. The rhythm of speech may be described as jerky when a person clutters, and that person may not be aware that this is a problem.

An example of a particularly complex speech disorder is called *apraxia of speech* (American Speech-Language-Hearing Association, 2007). This disorder exists when an individual has extra-ordinary difficulty in producing speech that other people manage easily. When a child has this disorder, it is called **childhood apraxia of speech**. No matter how hard the child may try, she cannot put together the movements and patterns required to speak. Her lips, tongue, and other speech mechanisms seem to be unable to do what her brain is telling them to do. Students with apraxia usually understand language very well; the disorder is one of expression. As a result of apraxia of speech, some students' words are unintelligible. Many students with this disorder speak as little as possible, and so they often are perceived as being very shy or quiet. Some peers and adults may perceive them as

**fyi**

Tiger Woods, Bruce Willis, James Earl Jones, Shane Yellowbird, and Julia Roberts are all famous people who overcame stuttering difficulties.

**web link**

http://www.mnsu.edu/comdis/ kuster/stutter.html
The Stuttering Homepage was developed by a specialist at Minnesota State University. The site contains a wide variety of resources for children and adolescents, parents, teachers, and other professionals.

---

**FIGURE 9.3**

**Mastery of English Speech Sounds**

Although most children master vowel sounds by two to three years of age, it takes several additional years to learn consonant sounds and blends and to use them in the beginning, middle, and end of words.

| Student Age | Sounds Typically Measured |
|---|---|
| 2 | p, h, n, b, k |
| 3 | m, w, g, f, d |
| 4 | t, S ("sh"), j, ("y") |
| 5 | s, v, n, ("ng"), r, l, T ("ch"), z, D ("j") |
| 6 | q ("th" in "thin"), D ("th" in "the"), ("zh" in "measure") |
| 8 | Consonant blends and clusters |

Source: Adapted from Owens, R. E., Metz, D. E., & Haas, A. (2003). *Introduction to communication disorders: A life span perspective* (2nd ed., p. 107). Boston: Allyn & Bacon.

## Interacting with Students Who Stutter

More than anything, students who stutter need a communication environment that is supportive. Professionals can help by following these guidelines:

- Don't tell the child "slow down" or "just relax."
- Don't complete words for the child or talk for him or her.
- Help all members of the class learn to take turns talking and listening.
- All children—and especially those who stutter—find it much easier to talk when there are few interruptions and they have the listener's attention.
- Expect the same quality and quantity of work from the student who stutters as the one who doesn't.
- Speak with the student in an unhurried way, pausing frequently.

- Convey that you are listening to the content of the message, not how it is said.
- Have a one-on-one conversation with the student who stutters about needed accommodations in the classroom. Respect the student's needs, but do not be enabling.
- Don't make stuttering something to be ashamed of.
- Talk about stuttering just like any other matter.

You can watch a video about stuttering or download a handbook with additional valuable information about stuttering from the website of The Stuttering Foundation at http://www.stutteringhelp.org/Default.aspx?tabid=519.

*Source:* From Scott, L., & Guitar, C. (2008). *Stuttering: Straight talk for teachers, 3e* [Publication No. 0125]. Memphis, TN: The Stuttering Foundation, www.stutteringhelp.org.

lazy or unmotivated; others sometimes mistakenly assume that they lack the ability to achieve (Lewis, Freebairn, Hansen, Iyengar, & Taylor, 2004).

## Prevalence of Speech and Language Disorders

According to recent figures from the U.S. Department of Education (2009), approximately 1.14 million students ages six to twenty-one received services for a speech or language disorder as their primary area of disability. This group constitutes approximately 1.7 percent of all school-age students. However, these data do not provide a complete picture of the number of students who receive speech and language services because, as noted earlier, they do not include students whose needs are addressed by related services.

### Distinguishing between Speech and Language Prevalence Data

An additional dilemma exists in considering the prevalence of speech and language disorders. IDEA reports data only for the combined prevalence for these disorders, not for each separately. However, several studies have examined prevalence of speech and language disorders individually. Overall, researchers estimate that 5 percent of all children in first grade have a speech disorder and that nearly 6 percent of children in the primary grades have a language disorder not caused by a physical or sensory disability (National Institute on Deafness and Other Communication Disorders, 2009). Recognize, though, that even this information does not necessarily provide a clear picture of prevalence. As you learned in the section outlining the numerous types of speech and language disorders, some students have disorders that affect more than one area of speech or language, and many students have combinations of both speech and language disorders.

### Other Prevalence Considerations

Several studies have examined whether speech and language disorders occur among boys and girls at approximately the same rate. Generally, boys are more likely than girls to be identified as having speech disorders in a ratio of approximately 2:1 (National Institute on Deafness and Other Communication Disorders, 2009). Boys are more likely than girls to be identified as having language disorders in a ratio of approximately 1.75:1. Prevalence related to race or ethnicity is difficult to estimate because of the many complicating factors that can arise in evaluating these students' speech and language skills, a topic addressed later in this chapter.

## Causes of Speech and Language Disorders

Speech and language disorders are caused by many different factors. The following section highlights some of the most common biological and environmental causes.

## Biological Causes

Some speech and language disorders are the result of problems related to the central nervous system or to the structure and functioning of other systems within the body. For example, many individuals who have intellectual disabilities also have speech and language disorders, and so intellectual disability is considered a biological cause of the related speech or language disorder. Other disabilities or special needs that involve the central nervous system, including the brain, also are part of this category—for example, autism and attention deficit–hyperactivity disorder. Likewise, hearing loss or deafness and vision loss or blindness can be causes of speech and language disorders. When students have physical disabilities that include muscle weaknesses as occurs in the disorder cerebral palsy (discussed in Chapter Thirteen), they may not be capable of producing the sounds needed for speech and language. Emotional disabilities also can cause speech and language disorders. Think about a young child with an internalizing disorder, who is focused inward and who largely ignores other children and adults. The child's inattention to the speech and language occurring in the environment can lead to delays or disorders.

Many students with disabilities have speech and language disorders, including those with autism, intellectual disabilities, learning disabilities, emotional disabilities, and hearing loss.

Many other types of biological causes of speech and language disorders also can be identified. For example, some of these disabilities may be the result of a specific brain injury, as is the case with aphasia, a disorder described earlier. Other biological causes may be related to heredity (Bishop, 2002; DeThorne, Petrill, Hayiou-Thomas, & Plomin, 2005).

Yet another cause of speech and language disorders is referred to as *congenital*, meaning the disorder is present at birth as a result of a known or unknown cause. One example of a congenital disorder is **cleft lip and/or palate**, the most common birth defect in the United States, affecting one out of every 600 newborns (Cleft Palate Foundation, 2007). A child born with a *cleft lip* has a separation between the two sides of the lip that often also involves the upper jaw. In a *cleft palate*, an opening exists in the roof of the mouth. Some children have cleft lips, some have cleft palates, and some have both conditions.

As is occurring in several other disciplines, professionals who study individuals with speech and language disorders are exploring whether and how their brains may be different from those of other individuals (e.g., Arbib, 2009; Helenius, Parviainen, Paetau, & Salmelin, 2009), and this research may in the future provide insights and new approaches to interventions. For now, though, this work generally is considered preliminary, and the results should be treated with caution.

## Environmental Causes

A second group of causes of speech and language disorders relates to a child's environment. For example, some disorders occur because of repeated ear infections that interfere with hearing and eventually affect speech and language development (DeThorne et al., 2005; National Institute on Deafness and Other Communication Disorders, 2009). Another example of an environmental cause is neglect or abuse. Perhaps a young child is left alone much of the time without peer or adult language models. Alternatively, perhaps the child is punished for being noisy—for experimenting with speech sounds as all babies do, or for talking as a toddler. In either case, a negative impact on speech and language development is likely.

The activities in which students engage comprise another environmental cause of speech and language disorders. Some students abuse their voices. They scream or yell too frequently, causing problems that may lead to hoarseness or an inability to speak loudly enough. Others damage their speech structures by speaking in a way that stresses the muscles involved in producing speech. In addition, some students have significant allergies that, when aggravated, may affect their speech.

**web link**

http://www.cleftline.org/
The Cleft Palate Foundation website provides easily understood information about this congenital disorder as well as links to many related websites. It also has a list of suggestions for teachers working with children with cleft palate.

An additional environmental factor that can lead to speech and language disorders is one that you have read about in other chapters—poverty (Bond & Wasik, 2009; Nancollis, Lawrie, & Dodd, 2005). Children who live in poverty are more likely to be malnourished, possibly leading to brain damage and a variety of disabilities, including speech and language disorders. These children also are less likely than others to receive adequate medical care, and so illnesses such as ear infections and allergies are more likely to go untreated. Once again, speech and language disorders can be the outcome.

### Making Sense of the Factors Contributing to Speech and Language Disorders

This discussion of causes of speech and language disorders could leave you with the impression that each cause is distinct and that identifying a cause is essential to intervention. This is not the case. As you learned in the discussions about learning disabilities, emotional and behavior disorders, and intellectual disabilities, in many cases the cause of a disability is unknown; the same is true for speech and language disorders. For example, a child's mother might have been a substance abuser, and during the birth process a brief period of anoxia may have occurred. The child may have a slight hearing loss, a fact that goes undetected until the student reaches kindergarten. Although the child then receives services at school, the family is not able to provide reinforcement at home and so progress is slow. Often no single cause is identified, and in many cases, identifying a cause is not particularly helpful for planning the child's instruction.

In 1996 the American Speech-Language-Hearing Association published its conclusion that central auditory processing disorder (CAPD), a source of considerable controversy in the field, is a distinct disorder requiring specific interventions to address it.

## REVIEW · REFLECT · DISCUSS

1. Why is the definition of speech and language impairments included in IDEA generally considered inadequate for understanding the types of needs students with these disabilities may have?

2. On a piece of paper list each of the five elements of language. Then, with classmates, generate at least three examples of each element. To check your understanding, try to make your examples very different from one another.

3. Why is it difficult to estimate the prevalence of speech and language disorders among all students? What additional factors have to be considered for students with other disabilities?

# Characteristics of Individuals with Speech and Language Disorders

Students who have speech and language disorders are a diverse group, and any discussion of what they are like cannot completely describe them. However, in the following sections, some of the most common cognitive and academic, social and emotional, and behavior characteristics of these students are outlined.

## Cognitive and Academic Characteristics

No generalizations can be made concerning the cognitive characteristics of students with speech and language disorders. These students may be academically gifted, they may be average in their cognitive ability, or they may struggle to learn and understand. In addition, many students who have intellectual disabilities also have speech and language disorders.

### Academic Characteristics

Although the academic achievement of some students with speech and language disorders is comparable to that of their peers, these disorders often have a profound impact on students' ability to learn (Shapiro, Hurry, Masterson, Wydell, & Doctor, 2009). From the day that children begin to comprehend language, it is an essential means through which they explore their world and come to understand it. When they enter school, the importance of language is magnified. Early school learning relies largely on the sharing of information using oral language. At the same time, students begin to learn how to use language for reading and writing. As students progress through school, they are expected to have an increasingly sophisticated vocabulary, spoken and written, to compose stories and essays and to comprehend complex written materials such as those found in textbooks. No matter what age, students also need speech and language skills for communication and learning in all their other subject areas as well as during nonacademic activities such as lunch and after-school programs.

### Speech and Language Disorders and Reading

Most of the research on the influence of speech and language disorders on student learning focuses on reading, and the available information is sobering (Al Otaiba & Smartt, 2003). Children who have significant speech or language delays are at high risk for reading difficulties (e.g., Koutsoftas, Harmon, & Gray, 2009; Shapiro et al., 2009; Wolter, Wood, & D'zatko, 2009), a problem that Andrew, the first-grade student you met at the beginning of this chapter, is experiencing. Further, children with speech and language disorders often are unable to benefit from the early literacy experiences that are common in kindergarten, and so they are at an academic disadvantage almost from the time they begin school.

The types of reading difficulties students encounter are directly related to their speech and language problems. Some students have difficulty learning to sound out words they read because they cannot distinguish among similar sounds. Others do not understand how to add prefixes or suffixes to words or to recognize compound words. Some students do not hear the rhythm of language in their heads as they read, and this interferes with comprehension. If you review all the elements of speech and language that have already been presented, you probably can list reading problems likely to be related to each.

## Social and Emotional Characteristics

Many students with speech and language disorders struggle socially and emotionally (Tommerdahl, 2009). First, they must deal with their own self-concepts and their perceptions of how others interact with them. Students with fluency disorders, for example, may be the targets of peer teasing as described by this student:

> I like participating in class, but when I'm answering questions (and stutter) I always hear whispers of people imitating my stuttering and giggling. Even when I'm not stuttering I can hear them imitate me in a stuttering voice. The other day this kid named Scott says, "It's funny when you stutter." When I tried to tell him to buzz off, he imitated me with every word, even though I hardly stuttered.

When students have negative experiences such as these, they may need assistance maintaining positive views of themselves.

In addition to teasing, students with speech or language impairments may experience difficulty in social situations in any number of ways. If they mispronounce words, others may have difficulty understanding them. If they cannot find the word they need during a conversation or if they do not use the conventions of grammar, they cannot fully participate in the interactions. In addition, some students face challenges because they do not understand how to participate in conversations, and so they may become socially isolated. The problem can be compounded by adults who form negative opinions about students with speech and language disorders and their ability to achieve (e.g., Overby, Carrell, & Bernthal, 2007).

## Behavior Characteristics

Young children who cannot express their needs in words sometimes resort to inappropriate behaviors, as in the example of a toddler who bites a playmate in order to get a desired toy. A similar pattern can be seen among school-age students who have speech and language disorders. Some evidence is emerging to indicate that students with speech and language disabilities are at high risk for behavior problems and even for being identified as having emotional and behavior disorders (Nelson, Benner, & Cheney, 2005; Rescorla, Ross, & McClure, 2007). This relationship is explored in more detail in the Positive Behavior Supports.

research
**NOTE**

With second-grade teachers listening to intelligible and moderately unintelligible student speech, Overby, Carrell, and Bernthal (2007) found the majority of teachers had a negative attitude regarding academic expectations for the latter student.

www.apraxia-kids.org/index.html
Apraxia-Kids is the website of the Childhood Apraxia of Speech Association of North America. The website includes information about this disorder, links to many other resources, FAQs, and stories about children with this disorder and their families.

## Linking Speech and Language Disorders and Emotional and Behavior Disabilities

Have you ever observed a young child whose language skills are just developing try to get a toy from a shelf that is out of reach? First, the child may go to an adult and point at the shelf. Then he may make a noise that might be an approximation of the desired toy (/kee/ for *kitty*). If the adult does not get the message, the child may become frustrated, crying and possibly hitting the adult in an attempt to make her understand. When language fails, children use behaviors, often disruptive ones, in their efforts to communicate. Although this dilemma is common among young children, it usually resolves itself as children's language skills improve. However, for some school-age students, the problem may persist.

Researchers have clearly demonstrated that a link exists between emotional disabilities and speech and language disorders (Long, Gurka, & Blackman, 2008; Rescorla, Ross, & McClure, 2007). In a review of pertinent studies, nearly nine out of every ten students with emotional disabilities in public schools also had language disorders. Among more specific findings were these

- Students with language deficits are at substantially higher risk for antisocial behavior than students with speech disorders.
- Students with receptive language problems often are undiagnosed, and these students have higher rates of behavior problems than other students.
- The coexistence of language problems in students with emotional disabilities is ten times higher than it is in the general population.

- Language disorders significantly and negatively affect interpersonal relationships, often leading to antisocial behavior.

It is not clear which problem comes first. That is, do the speech and language impairments cause the emotional problems, or do the emotional disabilities lead to the communication disorders? It really does not matter. Instead, this information suggests that educators should be alert for the simultaneous presence of both disabilities so that appropriate assessment, diagnosis, and intervention can be implemented as follows:

- Students with emotional and behavior disorders should be screened for the presence of language disorders. This type of screening often is skipped with this group of students because of the immediate need to address their behaviors.
- Appropriate language interventions should be designed with input from speech/language pathologists for students needing these services.
- Screening and intervention should occur as early as possible. Students benefit from language instruction primarily when they are very young, and missing this opportunity is likely to lead to later emotional and behavior problems. A proactive approach emphasizing prevention is far superior to later attempts at remediation.

Source: Based on Benner, G. J., Nelson, J. R., & Epstein, M. H. (2002). Language skills of children with EBD: A literature review. *Journal of Emotional and Behavioral Disorders, 10*, 43–59. Copyright © 2002 by Pro-Ed., Inc.

## *Speech and Language Disorders and Other Disabilities*

You have already learned that the term *comorbidity* refers to the simultaneous existence of two or more disabilities. As mentioned earlier in this chapter, students with many different disabilities often have a comorbid speech or language disorder. In addition to students you have already learned about (i.e., those with learning disabilities, emotional disabilities, or intellectual disabilities), students with hearing loss, autism, physical or health disabilities, as well as multiple disabilities also may have a speech or language impairment.

Think about the issue of comorbidity as it is related to speech and language disorders. What might be the implications for students who have these disorders as well as another disability in terms of learning and behavior? Think, too, about the professionals who work with these students—whether they are general education teachers, classroom teachers, or speech/language pathologists. How would the presence of two disabilities affect their work with students?

## REVIEW · REFLECT · DISCUSS

1. Review each of the major types of speech and language disorder that may affect a student. How might each of these have a direct effect on a student's academic achievement?

2. Think about the relationships between language skills and behavior. What examples can you think of to illustrate that relationship?

# Identifying Speech and Language Disorders

The procedures used to evaluate students with possible speech or language disorders and to determine if they are eligible for special education services are similar to those for identifying other students with disabilities. Intellectual ability is assessed using formal testing instruments, and overall school achievement is considered. Screening is completed to determine whether a vision or hearing loss is present. In this section, emphasis is placed on the evaluation strategies that directly address the speech or language disorder. Keep in mind that speech/language pathologists play a key role in assessing students with possible speech and language needs. You can review the scope of their responsibilities in the Professional Edge.

## Assessment

A hallmark of assessment for speech and language disorders is the importance of integrating information obtained from formal assessments, data gathered from students' spontaneous conversations, and the contributions made by teachers and parents.

### Speech Assessments

Several types of assessments may be completed to help professionals decide whether a student has a speech disorder. For many students, the speech/language pathologist administers a standardized test to determine whether a problem with articulation is present. Common tests include the Goldman–Fristoe Test of Articulation 2 (Goldman & Fristoe, 2000) and the Fisher–Logemann Test of Articulation Competence (Fisher & Logemann, 1971). Although the tests used for this purpose vary, they all have the common goal of detecting errors in articulation that are not expected given the child's age. By asking a child to finish sentences or to name pictures that are part of the test, the speech/language pathologist can determine whether he is omitting certain sounds, substituting one sound for another, adding sounds, or distorting the way a sound is made.

---

## Roles and Responsibilities of Speech/Language Pathologists in Schools

Here is a summary of the roles and responsibilities speech/language pathologists have in ensuring that students with speech and language disorder receive appropriate services. These may vary slightly from state to state because of regulations, policies, and preferred practices.

| Role | Examples of Responsibilities | Role | Examples of Responsibilities |
|------|------------------------------|------|------------------------------|
| Prevention | Providing staff development for school personnel, consulting with teachers | Transition | Facilitating the move from preschool to school, elementary to middle school, middle school to high school, and high school to postschool; fostering less restrictive placements |
| Identification | Screening for hearing, speech, and language disorders; participating in the pre-referral process | Dismissal | Determining if a student no longer needs services based on federal and state regulations |
| Assessment/ eligibility/IEP | Collecting assessment data, interpreting data, contributing to the determination of whether a disability exists, developing appropriate sections of the IEP | Supervision | Supervising practicum students and volunteers |
| Caseload management | Scheduling, creating service options for students, managing caseload | Documentation/ accountability | Creating all required documentation of assessments and services, including progress reports, treatment outcome measures, and paperwork required by federal and state regulation |
| Intervention | Designing and implementing interventions, arranging for technology support as needed | | |
| Counseling | Setting goals, making referrals as needed | | |
| Reevaluation | Participating in annual, triannual, and ongoing assessment activities | | |

*Source:* Adapted from American Speech-Language-Hearing Association. (2000). *Guidelines for the roles and responsibilities of school-based speech-language pathologist* (pp. 258–259). Rockville, MD: Author. Copyright © 2000 by the American Speech-Language-Hearing Association. Reprinted with permission.

professional edge

However, formal tests are not enough because they do not capture the way a student speaks in day-to-day activities. Speech/language pathologists also gather a spontaneous language sample that can help them to assess whether a student has an articulation disorder, a problem with voice or fluency, or a combination of disorders. They may ask a young student to talk about a toy or a game. They may engage an older student in a conversation about school, friends, or any other topic that seems likely to encourage him to provide several paragraphs of conversation. In addition, the professional likely will ask parents to provide a history of the student's development related to speech and ask teachers to describe the student's strengths and problems.

Speech/language pathologists also examine the student's physical structures for producing speech. They may observe whether a student's teeth are aligned well enough for sounds to be produced correctly. They also may look for abnormalities in the student's hard palate (i.e., the roof of the mouth). Other items assessed include the student's ability to easily use the lips and tongue to produce speech sounds. Finally, the speech/language pathologist notes whether the student's breathing patterns are typical. How might each of these areas affect a student's ability to produce speech?

### Language Assessments

Students with specific language impairments may experience difficulty in any of several areas, and the assessment must address each of these. Examples of language components that might be assessed include the following:

- Receptive and expressive vocabulary
- Ability to retrieve words as needed (sometimes called *word finding*)
- Comprehension and processing of sentences
- Correct use of the rules of grammar
- Comprehension of stories and other narratives
- Ability to produce language, whether to tell a story or to participate in a conversation

To gather information about these areas, the speech/language pathologist uses both formal and informal measures. Tests such as the Comprehensive Assessment of Spoken Language (CASL) (Carrow-Woolfolk, 1999), the Clinical Evaluation of Language Fundamentals 3 (CELF-3) (Semel, Wiig, & Secord, 1995), and the Test of Adolescent and Adult Language 3 (TOAL-3) (Hammill, Brown, Larsen, & Wiederholt, 1994) are used to systematically assess the student's language production. Additionally, samples of the student's written schoolwork are reviewed, the student is observed in the classroom setting as well as in less structured environments (e.g., the lunchroom or playground), and parents and teachers are interviewed.

### Assessment for Students Whose First Language Is Not English or Whose Use of English Is Nonstandard

One common dilemma faced by speech/language professionals is evaluating a student whose native language is not English or who speaks a variation of English that is considered nonstandard. In such a case, many precautions must be taken so that the assessment is accurate and fair (Brice, 2001; Kohnert, Windsor, & Yim, 2006). For example, in the use of standardized tests, speech/language pathologists must ensure that the test was developed for use with the students to whom it is being administered (Shames & Anderson, 2006). They also must ensure that directions and other aspects of the test are not confusing to individuals who do not speak standard English; this may lead to incorrect re-

*When students' native language is not English, professionals must be careful that assessment results accurately reflect students' abilities and skills.*

sponses, not because of language problems but because of the style in which the directions are given.

Other general factors also must be reviewed in this type of assessment. The testing situation itself may be particularly stressful for a student who is not a native English speaker. The expectation for the student to participate in a conversation with the professional administering the assessment may violate some students' cultural norms (e.g., children should not speak at length to an adult who is an authority figure). Can you identify other dilemmas that might arise in assessing students whose native language is not English or whose language is not standard English?

Later in this chapter, additional information is provided on language differences or variations and speech/language services. For now, it is important to remember that the assessment of students from diverse backgrounds poses challenges to the speech/language pathologist as well as to the team making a decision about eligibility for special education.

## Eligibility

Along with data regarding cognitive ability, achievement, and other domains, the information about a student's speech and language skills is considered by a team that includes the parents, the student (if appropriate), general and special educators, an administrator, specialists such as the speech/language pathologist, and others as needed. They respond to these questions:

Gottardo and Mueller (2009) found in studying English language learners from first to second grade that English oral proficiency and skill in word reading were the strongest predictors of English reading comprehension.

1. *Given the student's age, does the student have a significant delay or difference in speech or language that would be considered a speech or language impairment?* As noted in the preceding section, the professionals addressing this question must take into account whether the assessment data suggest a true disorder or a language difference because of native language or culture.

2. *Does the student's speech or language impairment adversely affect educational performance?* As you know, this question must be asked because IDEA stipulates that special education services can be offered only if the disability negatively affects educational performance.

3. *Can the student benefit from special education intervention?* Although the answer to this question generally would be yes, if that has been the case for the other questions, sometimes the issue is not completely clear. For example, it may be doubtful that special education services can address certain speech disorders, particularly for a student who is older—perhaps a high school student. Issues such as these must be considered.

Based on the answers to these questions, the multidisciplinary team determines whether the student needs special education. However, keep in mind the fact that in some states, students are eligible for services because of their speech or language disorders alone, whereas in other states, services in this area are provided only if students also have other disabilities. In the latter case, the student would have been evaluated for speech and language services to be provided as a related service, not as special education.

## REVIEW · REFLECT · DISCUSS

1. How are the procedures for determining whether a student is eligible for services as having a speech or language disorder similar to or different from the procedures used in identifying other disabilities? What do you think are issues that have to be carefully considered for this disability, more so than for others?

2. How do speech/language pathologists ensure that assessments of students who are not native English speakers are unbiased? What are some of the special challenges of determining whether these students are eligible to receive special education services for speech and language disorders?

# How Learners with Speech and Language Disorders Receive Their Education

Students with speech and language disorders receive their education in the setting most appropriate for them based on their special needs. If the speech or language disorder is the primary disability, emphasis is placed on providing services in general education with peers. If other disabilities also exist, the team that makes the decision about placement will take these into account.

## Early Childhood

Most young children are not given a specific disability designation because of the difficulty of completing an accurate assessment and the resulting risk of misidentification. However, the most critical time in life for speech and language development is early childhood, and much is known about typical speech and language development and problems that can occur for very young children (e.g., Paden & Yairi, 1999). In fact, of the approximately 693,000 children ages three to five who received special education services through IDEA in 2004–2005, nearly 327,000 were identified as having speech or language impairments as the primary disability (U.S. Department of Education, 2009).

### The Importance of Early Intervention

The rationale for providing intensive speech and language intervention for young children can be justified in several ways. First, research suggests that when a problem exists, the earlier an intervention is begun and the longer it is implemented, the more likely the problem will be addressed effectively. Second, when early intervention is undertaken, services can be intense; that is, they can involve a speech/language pathologist, a teacher, and the child's family. By involving all the important adults in the intervention process, more services can be delivered and more positive results can be expected. The final justification also is related to the notion of intensity. Specifically, the progress that young children make in overcoming speech and language disorders will more likely be maintained if support is provided during these critical years across settings and across time. In recognition of this, there has been an increase in the extent to which speech/language therapists work even with children between birth and age three.

### Approaches for Early Speech and Language Intervention

Traditionally, speech/language services were offered in a *pullout model*, even for very young children. That is, the speech/language pathologist would come to the home or preschool classroom to get the child to receive services; take the child to a separate room, classroom, or office; provide intervention individually or in a small group; and then return the child to the parent or classroom. This approach had the benefit of eliminating distractions for the child, but it removed the child from the natural setting in which speech and language occur and had the potential for stigmatizing the child.

Although a traditional approach sometimes is still appropriate, other options can be implemented as well. Some young children receive their speech/language services in the context of the early childhood center, preschool setting, or kindergarten classroom. The advantage of this approach is that the speech/language pathologist can observe the child's ability to function in the natural environment. However, the presence of an additional adult in the classroom can be distracting to a group of young children, and some youngsters with speech or language problems may dislike being singled out for intervention in the presence of their peers.

One additional option is an approach that combines separate service, in-class service, and indirect service. In some cases, the speech/language pathologist periodically may work directly with a child in a separate setting, often to check on progress, to address particularly complex problems, and to make decisions about subsequent steps in intervention. However, at least some of the services are offered within the classroom context. The final component of this approach is consultation. The speech/language pathologist meets with the early childhood specialist or special educator to problem solve about the child's needs and to discuss interventions. The goal is for classroom personnel to play significant roles in helping the child's skill development; this is an important factor because the speech/language pathologist may only be available for direct services on a limited basis.

## Elementary and Secondary School Services

Nearly all school-age students who have been identified as having speech or language disorders receive their education in a typical school setting. In fact, as you can see by reviewing Figure 9.4, approximately 87 percent of students with this disability are educated in general education classrooms more than 80 percent of the school day (U.S. Department of Education, 2009).

The way in which speech/language services are implemented depends on the nature of the student's disability. For example, many elementary students receive speech/language therapy services once or twice each week, usually for 30 minutes per session. In this model, the speech/language pathologist is likely to provide direct services in a separate setting. You may hear this service model referred to by children as "going to speech." When this approach is employed, the general education teacher and speech/language pathologist stay in touch so that the teacher knows which skills should be reinforced and the specialist knows what topics form the focus in the classroom language arts program as well as other areas of the curriculum. Keep in mind that in many school districts, speech/language pathologists work in two or more schools, and so their time to meet with teachers and to attend critical team meetings sometimes is limited.

For students who have disabilities in addition to speech or language disorders, services are part of their overall education program. Some of these students receive services in a pullout model similar to that previously described. For other students, a speech/language pathologist may provide services in the special education classroom. For example, if a student has a significant hearing loss that is affecting the clarity of her speech and receives special education services in a separate setting for 2 hours per day, the speech/language pathologist may provide services in the special education classroom. A similar approach might be employed for students with significant intellectual disabilities. Sometimes both in-class and pullout services are delivered.

### Inclusive Practices

If you think about the nature of speech and language disorders and the impact they can have on all aspects of students' lives—their academic performance, their relationships with peers and teachers, and their interactions in the family and community—it really is not surprising that inclusive practices are readily supported for students with this disability. The most appropriate setting in which nearly all students can learn and practice speech and language skills is general education. One relatively new role for professionals working there with students with speech and language disorders is co-teaching (Boswell, 2005), a service delivery option you learned about in Chapter Four. When this inclusive approach is used, speech/language pathologists and general education teachers design and deliver language-based interventions to all the students in a class. For example, students may be divided into three groups. One group works with the general education teacher on a comprehension activity related to the story being read. The second group works with the speech/language pathologist on vocabulary related to the story. The third group works independently to write a different ending for the story or to draw pictures to illustrate their favorite scenes.

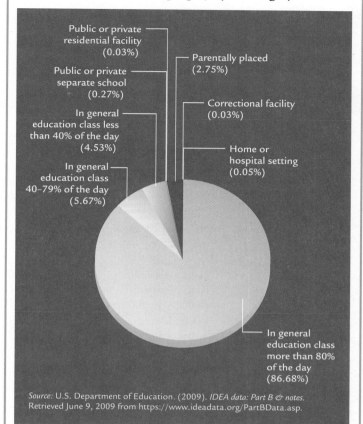

**FIGURE 9.4**

**Educational Placements of Students Ages Six to Twenty-One Who Have Speech and Language (in percentages)**

- Public or private residential facility (0.03%)
- Parentally placed (2.75%)
- Public or private separate school (0.27%)
- Correctional facility (0.03%)
- In general education class less than 40% of the day (4.53%)
- Home or hospital setting (0.05%)
- In general education class 40–79% of the day (5.67%)
- In general education class more than 80% of the day (86.68%)

*Source:* U.S. Department of Education. (2009). *IDEA data: Part B & notes.* Retrieved June 9, 2009 from https://www.ideadata.org/PartBData.asp.

Go to the Building Teaching Skills and Dispositions section of Topic 12: Communication Disorders, in the MyEducationLab for your course and complete the activity entitled "Collaborating with the Speech Language Pathologist".

## Traditional versus Classroom-Based Services for Students with Speech and Language Disorders

Increasingly, speech/language services are being delivered in close collaboration with special educators, classroom teachers, and parents. These are some of the most significant differences between the two approaches, although the precise roles of these professionals may vary somewhat state by state.

| | Separate Pullout Services | Classroom-Based Services |
|---|---|---|
| Intervention contexts | Isolates students from authentic contexts, presents intervention in a separate room | Includes students in authentic social situations, presents intervention in functional contexts (classroom, playground, lunchroom) |
| Role of the SLP* | Serves as primary service provider, presents the intervention | Plans an intervention program (decides where, when, and who will facilitate language) |
| Relationship of the SLP to parents and teachers | Serves as the expert, engages teachers and parents as helpers | Collaborates with and values the expertise of parents and teachers, draws upon parents and teachers as change agents |
| Goals and objectives | Selects goals on the basis of test measures and language analyses, determines contents and tasks arbitrarily, without regard to curriculum | Bases goals on curricular content and tasks, individualizes expectations, determines need for adaptations or supports |
| Language focus | Addresses components of language removed from real discourse events | Focuses on language components as they relate to functioning in whole discourse events, integrates language parts |
| Assessment mechanisms | Relies on standardized measures, identifies students' weaknesses—what they can't do, compares students' performance to test norms | Assesses performance within curricular tasks, identifies abilities and influence of supports, determines functioning relative to curricular demands |
| Evaluation methods | Readministers tests periodically, charts attainments of specific targets | Monitors outcomes continually, assesses functioning in context, analyzes products |
| Student roles | Places students in structured one-on-one interactions, leads to limited, passive roles | Draws upon an array of communicative events, permits active social roles and varied types of participation |
| Communicative options, demands | Limits or structures response options and participation in types of communication events | Requires flexible use of communication skills, leads to participation in a variety of "whole" communicative events |

*Speech/language pathologist

Source: Adapted from Culatta, B., & Wiig, E. H. (2002). Language disabilities in school-age children and youth. In G. H. Shames & N. B. Anderson (Eds.), *Human Communication Disorders: An Introduction* (7th ed. pp. 218–257). Copyright © 2006 by Pearson Education Adapted and reprinted by permission of Pearson Education, Inc.

Each group eventually completes all three activities. The Instruction in Action highlights how the trend over the past decade to provide more and more support for students with speech and language disorders in general education settings has positively affected those services.

### Transition and Adulthood

Some of the needs of students with speech and language disorders who are transitioning from childhood to adulthood are similar to those of other students with disabilities. These needs include the ability to self-advocate, the importance of making wise choices regarding higher education and careers, and the skills to function successfully in a job and the community. Some students also may need assistance in building self-esteem so they leave school with a true appreciation of their strengths and talents in addition to an understanding of their special needs (Blood, Blood, Maloney, Meyers, & Qualls, 2007; Conti-Ramsden, Botting, & Durkin, 2008). Although fewer students receive speech/language services as they continue through school, some receive services until they graduate, as does David, the high school student introduced at the beginning of this chapter.

One indicator of the challenges faced by adolescents and young adults with speech and language disorders is found by looking at information about behavior. Experts esti-

research
**NOTE**

A study that queried employees with communication disorders and their employers found that noise, tasks that required speed, jobs that included speaking to groups, and co-worker attitudes all were barriers that had to be overcome (Garcia, Laroche, & Barette, 2002). Issues such as these should be considered in transition planning for students with speech and language disorders.

mate that the prevalence of language disorders among female juvenile delinquents is three times greater than in the rest of the population (Castrogiovanni, 2002). Most researchers agree that speech and language disorders are far more prevalent among juvenile offenders than among other young adults (Snow & Powell, 2004). As with young children, professionals clearly find that students who experience difficulty in communicating with words may turn to aggression or other inappropriate behavior as an alternative. This issue must be addressed or students will be unlikely to make a smooth transition from school to adulthood.

## REVIEW · REFLECT · DISCUSS

1. Think about inclusive practices and students with speech and language disorders. Why might a general education setting be the least restrictive environment for many of these students? In what situations should some services be offered outside that setting? Why?

2. Which students do you think would benefit from speech/language therapy in high school? As a special educator, what would your role be in working with a speech/language pathologist to deliver these services?

# Recommended Educational Practices for Students with Speech and Language Disorders

Students with speech and language disorders may benefit from the academic and behavior interventions that are effective for students with learning and behavior problems, but specialized interventions are needed as well. Some students receive articulation therapy, others are assisted to use their physical speech apparatus correctly, and yet others benefit from intensive programs that increase phonemic awareness. In the Instruction in Action, you can learn about general interventions that teachers and other educators may use on a day-to-day basis. In the sections that follow, you can learn about two areas of particular interest: (1) the integration of speech and language services with literacy instruction and (2) augmentative and alternative communication.

## Speech/Language Services and Literacy Instruction

Throughout this chapter, emphasis has been placed on how speech and language disorders can affect students' achievement and behavior. This relationship is widely recognized among school professionals, and as a result speech/language pathologists increasingly are partnering with general education teachers, special education teachers, bilingual educators, and others to ensure that all students receive the early communication assistance needed to develop crucial language and literacy skills (Boswell, 2005; Gillon, 2005).

According to the American Speech-Language-Hearing Association (Kamhi, 2003), speech/language pathologists can reinforce relationships between spoken language and preliteracy skills, provide interventions related to phonemic awareness and memory, analyze the language demands found in textbooks and other school materials and media, and analyze student language so that interventions can be tailored to students' needs. Speech/language pathologists also can play roles in prevention, early intervention, assessment, therapy, program development, and documentation of outcomes. Finally, they can help to advocate for literacy programs at the local and state levels. How might some of these strategies assist Jade, the middle school student you met in the beginning of this chapter?

A strong implication of this educational practice relates to collaboration (Gardner, 2006). It is essential that school professionals recognize that their efforts are far more effective if they blend their expertise (Kassini, 2008). This means that general and special education teachers need to keep speech/language pathologists informed about critical curriculum topics being addressed and problems that they observe in students. Conversely,

research
**NOTE**

Catts, Adlof, and Weismer (2006) examined the language abilities of eighth-grade students who had poor comprehension as measured on standardized reading tests. Not surprisingly, they found that these students had problems in overall language comprehension. However, they did not have deficits in phonological processing.

Go to the Building Teaching Skills and Dispositions section of Topic 12: Communication Disorders, in the MyEducationLab for your course and complete the activity entitled "Collaborating with the Speech Language Pathologist".

## Getting the Message Across

The severity of students' speech or language disorders can range from mild to extensive. These ideas can help school professionals communicate clearly with these students:

- Before giving the message, say the student's name and wait for the student to look at you.
- Speak slowly, clearly, and loudly enough to be heard. If possible, use hand gestures, too.
- Keep instructions short. Give several sets of short instructions rather than a single long list.
- Emphasize important words. Do not use adverbs and adjectives unless the student knows the meaning of these words.
- Keep the ideas in messages simple. Use one sentence for each idea. For example, say, "I like the way you finished your work." "Now go get your science book." This form is better than putting the two messages into a single sentence.
- If you want to give a multistep instruction, use visual reminders with the instructions. Use pictures, symbols, or written words to depict each part of the instruction.

- If you want to give an if–then instruction, say, for example, "We will go to lunch after you put away your materials." That is, give the instruction in "then–if" order with emphasis on what is required by the student.
- If a student does not respond, wait at least ten seconds, get his or her attention, and give the message again using fewer words with emphasis on the important words.
- If the student responds incorrectly, get his or her attention and repeat the message using different words.
- If the student consistently responds incorrectly, teach the student by using modeling and feedback to follow the instruction.
- Remember to keep your "cool." Sometimes the easiest message to convey is anger.

How could you apply each of these ideas to the professional role that you plan to have? How might these strategies vary depending on whether you work in an elementary, a middle, or a high school?

*Source:* Adapted from Saunders, M. D. (2001). Who's getting the message? Helping your students understand in a verbal world. *Teaching Exceptional Children, 33*(4), 70–74. Copyright 2001 by the Council for Exceptional Children. Reprinted with permission.

*Augmentative and alternative communication (AAC) devices can provide a means for students with speech and language disorders to interact more easily with people inside and outside school.*

speech/language pathologists must initiate conversations with teachers to discuss student needs and plan subsequent steps for interventions. For all, clear and frequent communication is essential (Mroz, 2006).

## Communication Using Technology

Many students with speech and language disorders can be helped tremendously through technology (Light & McNaughton, 2008; Mechling & Cronin, 2006). In addition to the examples provided in the Technology Notes, computer hardware and software, personal digital assistants (PDAs), smartphones, and options now available via the Internet can help students communicate effectively and practice the skills they are learning.

## Augmentative and Alternative Communication

**Augmentative and alternative communication (AAC)** comprises strategies that compensate for an individual's communication limitations or disabilities. AAC strategies usually are divided into two categories: (1) *unaided*, or those that do not require the use of special equipment or materials (e.g., sign language) and (2) *aided*, those that depend on some type of equipment or materials. Because sign language is addressed in Chapter Eleven, it is not considered here. Instead, the emphasis is on aided communication options. AAC can greatly benefit students with speech and language disorders (Binger & Light, 2006; McNaughton, Rackensperger, Benedek-Wood, Krezman, Williams, & Light, 2008).

One example of an AAC device is a communication board. This device uses pictures, symbols, or printed words to facilitate student communication, and it can be low tech or high tech. For example, for a young student whose communication needs are fairly simple, a communication board might consist of small pictures arranged in rows and columns on

## Enhancing Students' Speech and Language Skills

Many students with speech and language disorders—regardless of whether they have other disabilities as well—can learn new skills and practice emerging skills with the assistance of computer technology (Kelley-Smith, 2000). Here are some examples of this type of software:

### TypeIt4Me (version 4.1.1)

www.typeit4me.com

- Macintosh computer software works with most other programs, including word-processing and database software.
- Students create lists of words they are likely to use, categorize them, and then click to bring up the category. By clicking on the desired word, they do not have to type it out or know exactly how to spell it.
- Students also store other information that they may need. For example, students can type their initials and their name will appear on-screen. They also can create abbreviations for long words to facilitate composition.

### textHELP! Read & Write (version 9.0)

www.texthelp.com/page.asp?pg_id=10060

- Designed for students over the age of seven, this Windows-based software is in essence a floating toolbar that provides tools for reading and writing, running concurrently with other computer programs.

- The software can read back to the student text that has been composed.
- Spell-checking can occur as the student types or after he composes; spell-check includes phonetic analysis.
- Words easily confused are highlighted so students can check for correct word use (e.g., *there, their; here, hear*).
- Other features include a built-in dictionary, thesaurus, and calculator and an Internet site for teachers using the software.

### The Talking Series by Laureate Learning Systems

http://www.enablemart.com/Catalog/Laureate-Learning-Systems/Talking-Sterling-Edition

- This interactive software is designed to encourage students to develop expressive language skills and skills for using augmentative and alternative communication.
- Three programs focus on the uses of nouns and verbs.
- Activities include the computer speaking the words to students, picture matching, picture identification (i.e., finding the word that corresponds to the picture), and finding nouns that all belong to a single category.

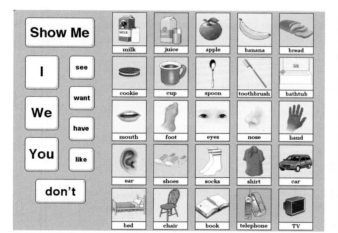

**A Communication Board**
*Source:* Used with permission from Laureate Learning Systems, Inc.

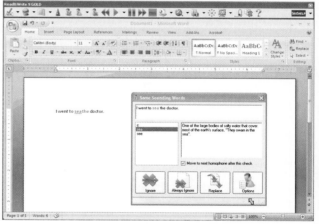

**textHelp! Software**
*Source:* Reprinted with permission from Texthelp Systems, Inc.

a flat display. The student points to the picture that displays the desired message (e.g., "I want a drink" by pointing to a glass or "I'm hungry" by pointing to a dish). Many far more sophisticated versions of communication boards exist as well. These boards may be computerized and include a synthesized speech component. Software also exists that professionals can use to tailor the images on a communication board to a student's precise needs. Communication boards also exist for adolescents and adults that incorporate many symbols and permit communication about highly technical topics. Also available are communication boards that appear on computer monitors. When used with a touch screen, this option eliminates the need for a separate board.

research
**NOTE**

Nippold, Ward-Longergan, and Fanning (2005) studied the development of persuasive writing skills in children, adolescents, and adults. The researchers used their findings to make recommendations concerning how speech/language therapists and teachers could help students develop syntactic, semantic, and pragmatic skills in this important communication style.

Word prediction software is another type of AAC tool. For students who have difficulty writing, this software guesses at the current word being typed and offers suggestions in a list. The student can select an option and avoid having to type the entire word, and the software ensures that words are spelled correctly. Word prediction software also serves to help composition skills. It predicts what the student's next words will be, and the student can either accept the prediction or substitute the intended word. One recent advance is the development of this type of software for personal digital assistants and smartphones. This innovation can help older students communicate, even without their voices, in a way that is very much accepted in today's society.

## Technology for Language Practice

Technology also assists students in skill development. Perhaps you have observed students in an elementary school using a computer program to practice their knowledge of letters and sounds. Alternatively, they may have been learning how to make new words by combining various letters. Such technology is becoming commonplace and can be valuable for students who need extensive practice on basic speech and language skills. One example of such software is Fast Forword (Scientific Learning), a set of programs for students in kindergarten through twelfth grade that includes intensive skill development (from phonemic awareness to listening comprehension) using game-like exercises and immediate feedback.

Technology for students with speech and language disorders continues to advance. In some classrooms, the teacher wears a microphone and the students wear or sit near receivers so that they clearly hear the teacher's voice during instruction. This technology is referred to as a *soundfield amplification system*. Technology also is emerging to help students who stutter speak more slowly to avoid hesitations and to produce natural-sounding synthetic speech for those who cannot use their own voices. Certainly, one defining feature of schools of the very near future will be the use of technology to help students communicate and learn. School professionals should stay abreast of developments in these areas, and if they are working with students using unfamiliar technology, they should seek input from specialists so that they can better interact with students and recognize if problems are occurring. At the same time, teachers should constantly monitor to ensure that technology is supporting students' communication, not interfering with it.

### REVIEW · REFLECT · DISCUSS

1. Why does speech/language therapy now often incorporate helping students to develop literacy skills? What implications might this have for you if you plan to be a special educator? A general educator?

2. What are questions you have about the use of technology to facilitate communication with students with disabilities? Whether your goal is to work with students with mild disabilities or students with more complex needs, what types of technology do you think should be available to your students? How would you make it an integral part of your classroom routines?

## Perspectives of Parents and Families

The importance of parents' participation in their young children's development is universally acknowledged, and it is the premise on which early intervention services for children with disabilities are based. When attention turns to children's speech and language development, parents' roles become, if anything, even more crucial (Guralnick, Connor, Neville, & Hammond, 2002; Thomas-Stonell, Oddson, Robertson, & Rosenbaum, 2009). Children acquire speech and language skills by observing language models, by experimenting in communication with others, and by refining their language skills based on feedback from others. Katie Dwiggins, a special educator, knows this well. She shares the story of her son Mason in the Firsthand Account.

**KATIE DWIGGINS** *is a special educator in Camdenton, Missouri. She and her husband are the adopted parents of Mason, who is about to turn four years old. Katie shares their experiences in learning that Mason has a language delay.*

We got Mason when he was three months old, and we were finally able to adopt him last year. We know that his mother was a drug addict, but we don't know whether she used drugs while she was pregnant. Anyway, I'm a special education teacher, and we've done everything right for Mason. I've read to him from the beginning. We've also made sure to use lots of language with him. We've done everything you're supposed to do. I didn't want to come home from work every night and be his teacher, but I began to notice that he wasn't talking the way he should be. A lot of his language was gibberish, and it still is today. He kept getting bigger, and his language wasn't getting better. I took him to Parents as Teachers [a parent support group operated through the local schools and designed to help new parents be sure their children are reaching important developmental mile-stones]. The people there wanted a formal assessment of Mason's language. When that came back, he was diagnosed as being language delayed.

And so I went to his IEP meeting. Even as a teacher, I don't like having to tell parents things they don't want to hear. As a parent, hearing it, I cried through the whole meeting, and sometimes I still cry. They took him into the preschool a little early as an intervention. He loves school. He wants to go every day even when he's not feeling well! It's an integrated program—children with disabilities and children without disabilities. He loves to read; he's happy and energetic, and he seems perfectly fine.

He still mixes up his words. He'll say "I want to push you" when he means that he wants to push the cart at the store. Or he uses words backwards or the words don't make sense at all for what he's talking about. At home I end up being his interpreter because my husband doesn't understand him. I'm so used to interpreting children's language from being a special education teacher that it comes easily. Actually, I think it took me longer to realize Mason had a problem because I was used to working with children every day who talked that way.

Sometimes, there is frustration. My husband gets frustrated when Mason doesn't understand a direction or something else said. I try to tell him that he needs to be shown. And sometimes Mason gets what we call "sassy pants." Even when it's gibberish, I can tell he is saying something not appropriate, and I send him to timeout. My husband says, "But you don't even know what he said," and I say, "It doesn't matter what he said, it's how he said it: Timeout." I can tell by how he's talking that it's not appropriate . . . hand on his hip, the tone of his voice . . . And that is not allowed.

At school, Mason receives language services. We could do some of the things at home, but it's better for him to go to language group at school. He also is receiving occupational therapy—he still has some balance problems. At home those aren't a big deal, and they're less noticeable when he has his shoes off. With shoes on at school, he falls sometimes. Again, as a parent I was trying not to see those things, but eventually I had to.

I tried to do everything, and it didn't matter. I mean, I'm sure it helped . . . the problem could have been much worse, I suppose. What I hope is that someday he won't have to cope with this at all. He's improved a lot even in the past six months, and maybe by later in elementary school he won't need services.

## Helping Parents to Develop Children's Language Skills

Have you ever observed parents with their young children? They talk to them, repeat their youngsters' words, and elaborate on their children's attempts to communicate (e.g., Child: "Me go." Parent: "Oh, do you want to go?"). Most parents intuitively interact with their young children in ways that foster speech and language development. Even so, enhancing parents' awareness and understanding of speech and language development and helping them learn how to foster it can be very beneficial, especially for children with delays or disorders.

One example of educating parents comes from a summer "sound camp" for children with speech disorders (Al Otaiba & Smartt, 2003). Parents were taught about the concept of phonemic awareness and given simple activities to help their children practice at home the skills being learned at camp. When parents were asked about their perceptions of the camp and the parent education component of it, they reported that the camp was very helpful for their children. In addition, they commented that they had a much better understanding of the concepts related to speech and language development and that they could thus better help their children at home and advocate for them at school. The parents also appreciated learning how to teach their children—for example, using small steps and occasionally repeating or reviewing skills already learned. They stressed the importance of home-based activities being family friendly, too.

research
### NOTE

Although young children with significant disabilities could benefit from the literacy instruction in a kindergarten classroom, their success may be limited by access barriers (e.g., ability to produce intelligible speech) and opportunity barriers (e.g., lack of collaboration among general education and special education professionals) (Pufpaff, 2008).

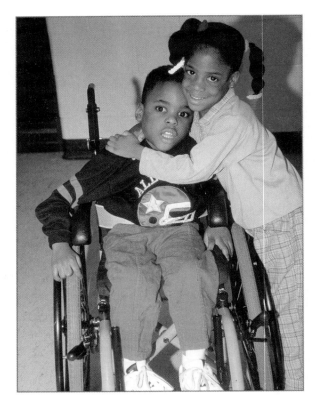

*Parents play a critical role in helping their children to acquire key speech and language skills.*

## Diversity and Speech and Language Interventions

Because language is a core element in every culture, speaking with parents from diverse groups about students' speech and language needs can be particularly difficult. For example, parents who do not speak English fluently may have difficulty helping their children to make sounds correctly and blend them into words. If English is not spoken in the home but school professionals are teaching it at school, students may not have enough opportunities to practice emerging skills and so may be at a disadvantage (Swanson, Hodson, & Schommer-Aikins, 2005). Based on what you have read in this chapter and your own experiences, what other issues can you identify that might occur with parents from nondominant cultures of students with speech and language disorders?

Significant differences may exist between Western cultures and other cultures. Think about augmentative and alternative communication. Most school professionals applaud the emerging technologies that facilitate student communication, give them greater independence, and assist them in their learning (Grether & Sickman, 2008). School professionals not only encourage parent participation in choosing and using AAC devices, but they also rely on it. Not everyone shares this view, however. In some families, AAC might be seen as unnecessary or even detrimental because it can be intrusive in terms of family interactions (Huer, Parette, & Saenz, 2001; Huer, Saenz, & Diem, 2001). Its benefit of providing independence may be viewed as a reason to avoid it (Parette & Huer, 2002). For example, some Asian families may want AAC options that do not detract from the family's traditional caregiving role. These families also may presume that AAC options are the responsibility of school professionals, not families. They may even delay approving of AAC devices for their children until they observe that such technology is accepted and used by other children.

## REVIEW · REFLECT · DISCUSS

1. Imagine being a parent and learning that your child has a speech or language disorder. What types of questions would you want to ask school professionals? What is your role as a professional related to understanding parents' beliefs about the reasons for their child's speech or language disorders and preferences for treating them? What should you do if you think parents are misinformed or that they do not understand?

2. If you know a family with a young child, observe the parents as they interact with their infant or toddler. Based on your observations and the information you learned in this chapter, what are the most important roles that parents play in the development of children's speech and language skills? How does the family's culture affect speech and language development?

## Trends and Issues Affecting the Field of Speech and Language Disorders

The complexity of the field of speech and language disorders guarantees that it is characterized by rapidly changing practice and controversy (e.g., Harris, Prater, Dyches, & Heath, 2009). Two important topics for professionals who work with students with speech and language disorders are (a) identifying and addressing these disabilities in a multicultural society and (b) basing student interventions on evidence-based practices.

## Differences versus Disorders in a Multicultural Society

Diversity is a defining characteristic of the U.S. population. Given this, school professionals who address students' speech and language needs must recognize how diversity affects their efforts (Griffer & Perlis, 2007; Kennedy, 2006; Whitney, 2005).

### Language Differences

Speech and language professionals are careful to distinguish between **language differences**—variations from standard speech and language that are considered normal—and **language disorders**—impairments that interfere with language comprehension and use (Roseberry-McKibbin & O'Hanlon, 2005). One example of a language difference is an **accent**, a variation in the surface characteristics of language. If you have friends from different parts of the country,

*It is essential that professionals distinguish language differences from language disorders.*

you may comment that one of them has a Boston accent or a Southern accent. You are referring to the way they pronounce words or make particular sounds, but you are not implying that their language is disordered. If you know individuals who learned English after learning another language, you may notice that they, too, speak English with an accent.

A somewhat different example is a **dialect**, which refers to the structure of language and the rules that govern it (Shames & Anderson, 2006). One dialect that has received considerable attention is African American Vernacular English (AAVE), sometimes called *Black-English* or *Ebonics*. It is spoken by many (but not all) working-class African American families, and it includes differences in some of the sounds made (*dis* for *this*) and

---

### Understanding Dialects

Many misconceptions exist regarding dialects. Here are some of the most common:

*Myth:* A dialect is something that someone else speaks.

*Reality:* Everyone who speaks a language speaks some dialect of the language; it is not possible to speak a language without speaking a dialect of the language.

*Myth:* Dialects always have highly noticeable features that set them apart.

*Reality:* Some dialects get much more attention than others; the status of speaking a dialect, however, is unrelated to public commentary about its special characteristics.

*Myth:* Only varieties of a language spoken by socially disfavored groups are dialects.

*Reality:* The notion of dialect exists apart from the social status of the language variety; there are socially favored as well as socially disfavored dialects.

*Myth:* Dialects result from unsuccessful attempts to speak the correct form of a language.

*Reality:* Dialect speakers learn their language by imitating members of their speech community who speak the same variety, not by failing to mimic speakers of the standard variety.

*Myth:* Dialects inherently carry negative social connotations.

*Reality:* Dialects are not necessarily positively or negatively valued; their social values are derived strictly from the social position of their speech community.

As you work with students, you can help all of them to understand how language differences such as dialects are part of the diversity and richness of today's society. Here are some suggestions for helping students to understand dialects:

- Use literature written in various dialects (e.g., short stories, poems, dialogue). Students can read passages out loud, compare ways people talk with ways they write, and discuss spelling variations.

- Play music with lyrics in various dialects. Have students write out lyrics and discuss the language used (e.g., its authenticity).

- Recognize and respect student dialects by allowing their use without correction during classroom discussions, when they are writing in journals, or acting out plays with dialogue.

- Have students explore the grammatical rules of a dialect. They might try to create lessons for teaching the dialect to others or try translating a poem in standard English to a dialect.

*Sources:* Adapted from Newton, D. W. (2004), *The reality of dialects*. Retrieved January 31, 2004, from www.westga.edu/~dnewton/engl2000/dialects.html (Originally in Wolfram & Schilling-Estes, 1998); and Language Varieties Network (2004), *Pidgins, creoles, and other stigmatized varieties*. Retrieved February 7, 2004, from www2.hawaii.edu/~gavinm/home.htm.

## Breaking the Code on Code-Switching

Code-switching occurs when an individual switches from one language or dialect to another. It also can occur within a language, as when you speak differently (e.g., more formally, using or excluding particular words) to your grandmother than to your close friends. Here are three examples of code-switching:

### Language Code-Switching

Students who are bilingual may switch between languages, either within a sentence or between sentences. Although this could indicate a problem in language proficiency, it may also have other purposes, such as these (Sayer, 2008):

- A student whose first language is not English uses phrases or sentences in that language, especially to express complex ideas, emphasize a point, or convey nuances of emotion.
- A student speaks English to teachers but immediately switches to her first language in interactions with peers who also speak that language.

### Dialectical Code-Switching

Dialects differ from standard patterns of English. AAVE is one common dialect that has its own grammatical rules and patterns. Professionals recommend that teachers not treat this dialect as a set of errors but rather explicitly teach their students how to code switch by showing them the differences,

helping them to master these differences, and providing opportunities to practice code-switching (Wheeler, 2008). Here are examples:

- Subject-verb agreement (*John come [versus comes] to school every day.*)
- Possessives (*My brother [versus brother's] coat got torn.*)
- Past tense: (*Joe finish [versus finished] his paper yesterday.*)

### Digital Language Code-Switching

The abbreviated language forms students use for texting, e-mail, social networking, and instant messaging may show up in students' written work. As with dialects, it may be more effective to teach students to switch between text speak and standard English than to convey to students that the former is inferior and incorrect (Turner, 2009). Here are examples:

- Use of phonetic or shortened spellings (e.g., *u, r, cuz*)
- Omission of capital letters at the beginning of sentences and in proper names
- Omission of apostrophes in contractions (e.g., *wont [versus won't], cant [versus can't]*)

Which of these types of code-switching affect your own language use? Which might you encounter with your students? How could you teach code-switching to them?

---

words used (*Where is my paper at?* instead of *Where is my paper?*). The Professional Edge outlines myths and realities related to dialects and provides suggestions for addressing dialects in the classroom. Keep in mind that dialects are differences, not disorders. In fact, in recent years professionals have worked diligently to stop the practice of trying to change students' dialects. Instead, they have focused on helping students learn to *code switch*, or to use standard English when it is important to do so and their dialect in the family, community, and other appropriate settings. The Instruction in Action explains more about code-switching.

### Other Cultural Influences on Communication

Accent and dialect are not the only cultural factors that may affect language. Students who are English language learners may experience difficulty in learning how to begin or finish a conversation, may have to learn to take turns during conversations, may not understand subtle humor, and may struggle to pronounce some words correctly. Likewise, they may be reluctant to initiate conversations or to contribute to them.

### dimensions of
### DIVERSITY

Would you like to learn more about AAVE? This website—http://www.une.edu.au/langnet/definitions/aave.html—provides information on its history and grammar as well as links to explore other dialects.

The examples that have been provided in this section are intended only to illustrate some of the issues related to speech and language and diversity. Comparable comments could be made for the many other cultural groups that comprise the population of this country (e.g., Laing & Kamhi, 2003; Poon-McBrayer & Garcia, 2000). All school professionals need to be aware of their students' language differences and learn how to work appropriately with students who do not speak standard English. Further, they need to recognize the risk of mistaking a language difference for a language disorder and seek input from speech and language professionals when they have concerns regarding a particular student's speech and language skills.

## The Use of Evidence-Based Practices

Throughout education, including special education and the field of speech and language services, a significant trend is the identification of *evidence-based practices* and their use in schools (American Speech-Language-Hearing Association, 2005; Brackenbury, Burroughs, & Hewitt, 2008). That is, speech/language therapists are emphasizing that the interventions used with students should only be those for which high-quality, multiple research studies have demonstrated effectiveness and systematic use by clinicians has supported their use. The trend toward the use of evidence-based practices is a direct result of the accountability movement in today's schools, prompted by the No Child Left Behind Act and its requirements as well as a trend toward improving the quality of research that is used to justify various interventions (Justice & Fey, 2004).

The implications of using evidence-based practices in speech-language services are far reaching. Here are some examples:

- *Collection of data.* Speech/language therapists are expected more and more to gather systematic data that can be used to judge the effectiveness of their strategies for preventing the development of speech and language problems, their diagnostic procedures, and their methods for intervening to address student speech and language difficulties (Brackenberry et al., 2008; Joint Coordinating Committee on Evidence-Based Practice, American Speech-Language-Hearing Association, 2005).

- *Use of data for decision making.* Although decisions regarding speech and language services have always relied on data, the focus on evidence-based practices strengthens the expectation that interventions should be attempted or continued based on specific data related to the students with whom they are used and large-scale studies that document their impact. Conversely, strategies that are not supported by research or not demonstrated to be positively influencing students' skills should be discarded. An example concerns assessment tools: Hundreds of these instruments are advertised to professionals each year, and some of them lack reported research about their accuracy. Only the instruments with a strong set of data demonstrating their validity for particular groups of students and the reliability of the information they gather should be used (Research and Scientific Affairs Committee, 2004).

- *Professional education.* Clearly, speech/language therapists need to be educated about the importance of evidence-based practices and the ways in which they should guide practices in public schools (Nail-Chiwetalu & Ratner, 2006). At the same time, teachers and other educators need to know why these practices should be central to speech/language therapists' work, how teachers can participate in further developing evidence-based practices, and what these practices imply for students and their families.

It will take time to document through scientific research the effectiveness of interventions used for students with speech and language disorders (Coyle, Easterling, Lefton-Greif, & Mackay, 2006; Kent, 2006). However, these efforts can help ensure that the time available to improve outcomes for students will be spent as wisely as possible.

PEARSON
**myeducationlab**

Go to the Assignments and Activities section of Topic 12: Communication Disorders, in the MyEducationLab for your course and complete the activity entitled "Instructional Accommodations for Students with Communication Disorders".

## REVIEW · REFLECT · DISCUSS

1. What are *language differences?* How do they differ from *language disorders?* Why is the distinction between these concepts especially important for school professionals? Why should you teach students about code-switching?

2. How does the concept of evidence-based practices pertain to speech and language services? How might evidence-based practices change the approaches used by speech/language pathologists? How might these practices affect your collaborative work with speech/language pathologists?

# Summary

- Speech and language disorders have been a professional area of study since the beginning of the nineteenth century, and understanding of students with these disorders has progressed from an emphasis on the production of speech to the use of language to a comprehensive view based on the purpose of communication.

- Although IDEA provides a simple definition of speech and language impairments, many specific disorders are encompassed by this disability category, including receptive and expressive language disorders (i.e., those related to phonology, morphology, syntax, semantics, pragmatics) and speech disorders (i.e., those related to articulation, fluency, voice). These disorders can result from biological or environmental factors.

- Students with speech and language disorders vary widely in terms of their cognitive ability and academic achievement as well as in their social or emotional status and the likelihood of their displaying behavior problems.

- Speech/language pathologists are the specialists who evaluate students using formal and informal means to determine whether these disorders are present, but as for all students, a team determines eligibility for special education services.

- Most students with speech and language disorders receive their education in typical schools and participate in general education for most of the school day.

- Increasingly, interventions for these students focus on blending the skills that speech/language pathologists can bring to the overall instructional program and the use of augmentative and alternative communication strategies, if needed.

- The parents and families of students with speech and language disorders are as diverse as the students themselves, and their preferences and concerns may, in part, be culturally determined.

- Issues facing the field include differentiating between language differences and language disabilities in an increasingly diverse student population and the importance of implementing evidence-based practices.

 **Council for Exceptional Children**

## ADDRESSING THE PROFESSIONAL STANDARDS

Council for Exceptional Children (CEC) Common Core Knowledge and Skills addressed in this chapter:

ICC1K5, ICC1K6, ICC1K8, ICC2K1, ICC2K2, ICC2K3, ICC2K4, ICC2K6, ICC3K1, ICC3K3, ICC4S5, ICC5S1, ICC6K4, ICC7K1, ICC7S2, ICC7S9, ICC8S2, ICC8S5, ICC8S8, ICC9K4, ICC9S7

## PEARSON myeducationlab

Now go to Topic 12: Communication Disorders, in the MyEducationLab (www.myeducationlab.com) for your course, where you can:

- Find learning outcomes for the broad concepts covered in this chapter along with the national standards that connect to these outcomes.
- Complete Assignments and Activities that can help you more deeply understand the chapter content.
- Examine challenging situations presented in the IRIS Center Resources.
- Apply and practice your understanding of the core concepts and skills identified in the chapter with the Building Teaching Skills and Dispositions learning units.

- Check your comprehension on the content covered in the chapter by going to the Study Plan in the Book Specific Resources for your text. Here you will be able to take a chapter quiz, receive feedback on your answers, and then access Review, Practice, and Enrichment activities to enhance your understanding of chapter content.
- Watch video clips of CCSSO Teacher of the Year award winners responding to the question: "Why I teach?" in the Teacher Talk section.

## chapter ten

# Students with Autism Spectrum Disorders

## LEARNING OBJECTIVES

· Outline the development of the field of autism spectrum disorders, define these disorders, and identify their prevalence and causes.

· Describe the characteristics of individuals with autism spectrum disorders.

· Explain how autism spectrum disorders are identified.

· Discuss how students with autism spectrum disorders receive their education.

· Outline recommended educational practices for students with autism spectrum disorders.

· Summarize the perspectives and concerns of parents and families of students with autism spectrum disorders.

· Identify issues and trends affecting the field of autism spectrum disorders, including assessment, diagnosis, and prevalence; the evidence base for interventions; and the lack of adequate professional preparation programs.

Written by Marilyn Friend, based on an earlier chapter by Brenda Smith Myles (Autism Asperger Publishing Company) Taku Hagiwara (Hokkaido University of Education, Asahikawa, Japan), and Melissa Trautman and Elisa Gagnon (Blue Valley Public Schools, Overland Park, Kansas).

## Lance

Lance is a fifth-grade student at Southwest Elementary School. He has received special education services since he was three years old when he was diagnosed as having a pervasive developmental disorder. Lance's pediatrician explained to his parents that his language delays, his heightened sensitivity to certain noises, and his difficulties with certain sensations (for example, the feel of grass on his bare feet) suggested autism spectrum disorder (ASD), a disability later confirmed by school professionals. Lance generally has spent much of his time in school in a separate special education setting, but for the past two years one of his IEP goals has been to increase participation in general education. Although Lance now participates in science and social studies with typical peers, some of his behaviors can be a bit disruptive. For example, every day when he enters class he says to Mr. Beck, the science teacher, "When's your birthday?" He does this in a monotone—that is, without inflection and in a way that sounds robotic. Mr. Beck has learned that he should not repeatedly answer this question, and he instead asks Lance a question about a readily understood topic—Lance's choice of a shirt, the weather, activities in science class, and the like. Lance's parents want him to be able to live independently when he is an adult, and the IEP team is already working to make this a reality by emphasizing the development of social skills and including plans to help Lance overcome behaviors that interfere in his interactions with classmates and adults.

## Geneva

Geneva is a seventh-grade student who has faced many challenges in her life. She was identified as having an intellectual disability and autism when she was only a year old. Her parents describe how difficult it was to get her to sleep as a young child and how worried they are about her future. In elementary school, Geneva spent most of her time in a separate classroom for students with significant disabilities. This decision was made because of her strong need for structure and order and her tendency to hit others or bite them when she was frustrated. With intensive intervention and the guidance of a paraprofessional, she gradually began to spend small amounts of time in general education classrooms with peers.

Now in middle school, Geneva participates in general education science and art classes, but she still requires a small-group, structured learning setting for much of the school day. Her general education teachers have learned to follow a clear schedule in their classrooms, and if a change is planned, they remind Geneva often, as does the special education teacher and Geneva's parents. Geneva is learning from a modified curriculum; that is, she is not expected to complete the high-stakes testing that her peers must take, and so her teachers work on her IEP goals and objectives in both general education and special education settings. One goal for Geneva this year is to walk unaccompanied from class to class. Although she cannot yet complete this task, she is usually able to accurately lead the paraprofessional who accompanies her. The next step is for the paraprofessional to trail behind Geneva, and then the team is planning, as another step in learning, to ask a peer to accompany Geneva.

## Casey

Casey, a fifteen-year-old boy with autism, attends a large suburban high school. He is enrolled in a drama course, and some of the students in the course have befriended him, including Matt. On entering the classroom one day, Matt walked up to Casey and said, "What's up, dog?" a common greeting among the popular group at the high school. However, Casey did not understand and proceeded to become quite upset, repeatedly yelling "Don't call me *dog!*" Even though Matt tried to explain that it was a greeting, Casey did not understand. The special education teacher wrote a social story (explained later in this chapter) to help Casey understand that "What's up, dog?" is a greeting and does not mean that Matt is calling him a *dog.* It is just a funny way to be friendly and say "Hi." The social story was done with words and icons because Casey enjoys picture books. After the special educator introduced the story to him he understood and even began using the expression himself. Casey's parents own a popular local restaurant, and they anticipate that Casey will work in the family business. They are working closely with school professionals to address situations that cause misunderstandings for Casey and to identify and teach him the skills he'll need after he graduates.

If you watch the popular media for information about individuals with autism, you might wonder whether some professionals are making mistakes: In newspaper stories, magazine articles, movies, and novels, individuals with autism sometimes are portrayed as brilliant but eccentric, sometimes as significantly impaired, and sometimes as turned almost completely inward, as though incapable of dealing with the realities of day-to-day living. In fact, all of these descriptions could be based in truth. Autism, today often referred to as **autism spectrum disorders (ASD)**, has been described as an enigma because individuals identified as having this disability may have widely different characteristics that set them apart from typical peers and from peers with other disabilities (Simpson & Myles, 1998).

## Understanding Autism Spectrum Disorders

The study of autism spectrum disorders is relatively new in the field of special education, as can be seen in the timeline of its development in Figure 10.1. However, the evolution of understanding about these disabilities has been rapid, and today's practices for students with autism spectrum disorders are informed by considerable research about students' characteristics and needs.

### Development of the Field

In 1943, psychologist Leo Kanner described a unique group of 11 children whose very unusual behaviors made them qualitatively different from children with other disabilities. According to Kanner (1943), these children's special needs were apparent even in early childhood and included the following:

- An inability to relate typically to other people and situations
- Delayed speech and language development, failure to use developed language for communication purposes, and other speech and language abnormalities, such as extreme literalness
- Typical physical growth and development
- An obsessive insistence on environmental sameness
- An extreme fascination and preoccupation with objects
- Stereotypic or repetitive behavior and other forms of self-stimulation

The characteristics of autism as first described by Kanner more than half a century ago have been revised, refined, and broadened in recent years. Nonetheless, today's definitions and conceptualizations of autism continue to reflect many of Kanner's original observations.

**PEARSON**
**myeducationlab**

To check your comprehension on the content covered in Chapter 10, go to the Book Specific Resources in the MyEducationLab (www.myeducationlab.com) for your course, select your text, and complete the Study Plan. Here you will be able to take a chapter quiz, receive feedback on your answers, and then access review, practice, and enrichment activities to enhance your understanding of chapter content.

### FIGURE 10.1
#### Timeline for the Development of the Field of Autism Spectrum Disorders

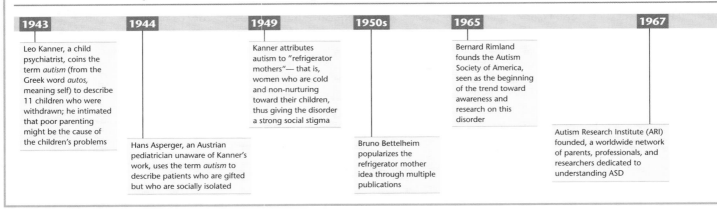

**1943** — Leo Kanner, a child psychiatrist, coins the term *autism* (from the Greek word *autos*, meaning self) to describe 11 children who were withdrawn; he intimated that poor parenting might be the cause of the children's problems

**1944** — Hans Asperger, an Austrian pediatrician unaware of Kanner's work, uses the term *autism* to describe patients who are gifted but who are socially isolated

**1949** — Kanner attributes autism to "refrigerator mothers"— that is, women who are cold and non-nurturing toward their children, thus giving the disorder a strong social stigma

**1950s** — Bruno Bettelheim popularizes the refrigerator mother idea through multiple publications

**1965** — Bernard Rimland founds the Autism Society of America, seen as the beginning of the trend toward awareness and research on this disorder

**1967** — Autism Research Institute (ARI) founded, a worldwide network of parents, professionals, and researchers dedicated to understanding ASD

Other developments in the field quickly followed, including the identification of Asperger syndrome as a disorder potentially distinct from autism and a belief, held by many professionals, that autism was caused by detached, non-nurturing mothers—sometimes called "refrigerator mothers" (Janzen, 2003). This misconception persisted until the 1970s and 1980s when published studies of twins demonstrated a genetic basis for autism (Rutter, 2000).

### Formalizing Understanding

With continued research in the 1980s, the knowledge base about the wide range of disorders called autism quickly grew as did interest in finding effective treatments (e.g., Wing, 1991). Autism was identified as a separate category of disability in the Individuals with Disabilities Education Act (IDEA) beginning in 1990.

## Definitions of Autism Spectrum Disorders

As is true for many other disabilities, the language related to autism requires a brief explanation. The traditional term used for this group of students is *autism*, and that is the term used in IDEA and many state special education laws. The term *autism spectrum disorders (ASD)* is used in this textbook because it clarifies that these disorders occur in many forms and cannot be described in any one way; ASD is rapidly becoming the term of choice among professionals in the field. Finally, as you will learn later in this chapter, in medical circles both autism and Asperger syndrome are considered part of a disability called *pervasive developmental disorder (PDD)*.

### Federal Definition

According to IDEA, autism is defined as follows:

  i. Autism means a developmental disability significantly affecting verbal and nonverbal communication and social interaction, generally evident before age three, that adversely affects a child's educational performance. Other characteristics often associated with autism are engagement in repetitive activities and stereotyped movements, resistance to environmental change or change in daily routines, and unusual responses to sensory experiences.
  ii. Autism does not apply if a child's educational performance is adversely affected primarily because the child has an emotional disturbance.
  iii. A child who manifests the characteristics of autism after age three could be diagnosed as having autism if the criteria in paragraph (c)(1)(i) of this section are satisfied. (IDEA 20 U.S.C. §1401 [2004], 20 C.F.R. §300.8[c][1][i–iii])

This definition follows the pattern of IDEA, specifying some essential characteristics of students with the disorders, excluding other disabilities, and identifying the necessity of impact on educational performance. However, it does not provide much detail in terms of understanding the many types of students who might have these disorders.

**web link**

www.autism-society.org
The Autism Society of America was founded in 1965 by a small group of parents. Today, with more than 20,000 members, it is a leading source for information about autism spectrum disorders, and it calls itself "the voice and resource of the autism community."

research
**NOTE**

Safran (2008) analyzed IDEA data related to students with autism from the past several years. He concluded that the number of students receiving special education in this disability category was far fewer than would be expected, with those under-identified being students who have higher abilities.

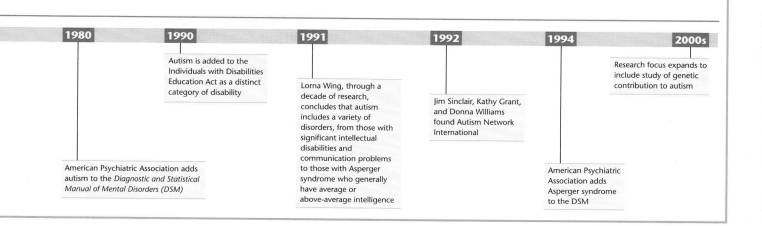

| 1980 | 1990 | 1991 | 1992 | 1994 | 2000s |

**1990** — Autism is added to the Individuals with Disabilities Education Act as a distinct category of disability

**1991** — Lorna Wing, through a decade of research, concludes that autism includes a variety of disorders, from those with significant intellectual disabilities and communication problems to those with Asperger syndrome who generally have average or above-average intelligence

**1992** — Jim Sinclair, Kathy Grant, and Donna Williams found Autism Network International

**2000s** — Research focus expands to include study of genetic contribution to autism

**1980** — American Psychiatric Association adds autism to the *Diagnostic and Statistical Manual of Mental Disorders (DSM)*

**1994** — American Psychiatric Association adds Asperger syndrome to the DSM

### Definitions of the American Psychiatric Association

Because autism spectrum disorders generally are diagnosed by the medical community using criteria set forth in the *Diagnostic and Statistical Manual of Mental Disorders* (*DSM-IV-TR*; American Psychiatric Association, 2000), it is important for special educators to understand these definitions as well as the one provided in IDEA. As noted earlier, the *DSM-IV-TR* classifies autism as a type of **pervasive developmental disorder (PDD)**, a term in which children and youth "are characterized by severe and pervasive impairment in several areas of development: reciprocal social interaction skills, communication skills, or the presence of stereotyped behavior, interests, and activities" (p. 69). Subcategories of pervasive developmental disorders include autistic disorder, Asperger syndrome, and pervasive developmental disorder not otherwise specified (PDD–NOS); each of these disorders is briefly explained below.

The diagnosis of **autistic disorder** is reserved for individuals who display social interaction and communication impairments, as well as repetitive, stereotypic, and restricted interests and activities prior to thirty-six months of age. This disorder often is accompanied by a moderate or severe intellectual disability. The specific diagnostic criteria for this disorder are outlined in Figure 10.2.

**fyi**

Autism-Europe prepared a Charter of Rights for People with Autism, and in 1996, a written declaration of their rights was approved by the European Parliament. This document states that people with autism have the same rights enjoyed by all European Union citizens.

---

**FIGURE 10.2**
*DSM-IV-TR* Criteria for Autism Disorder

---

**A.** A total of six (or more) items from (1), (2), and (3), with at least two from (1), and one each from (2) and (3):

**(1)** qualitative impairment in social interaction, as manifested by at least two of the following:

  **(a)** marked impairment in the use of multiple nonverbal behaviors such as eye-to-eye gaze, facial expression, body postures, and gestures to regulate social interaction

  **(b)** failure to develop peer relationships appropriate to developmental level

  **(c)** a lack of spontaneous seeking to share enjoyment, interests, or achievements with other people (e.g., by a lack of showing, bringing, or pointing out objects of interest)

  **(d)** lack of social or emotional reciprocity

**(2)** qualitative impairments in communication as manifested by at least one of the following:

  **(a)** delay in, or total lack of, the development of spoken language (not accompanied by an attempt to compensate through alternative modes of communication such as gesture or mime)

  **(b)** in individuals with adequate speech, marked impairment in the ability to initiate or sustain a conversation with others

  **(c)** stereotyped and repetitive use of language or idiosyncratic language

  **(d)** lack of varied, spontaneous make-believe play or social imitative play appropriate to developmental level

**(3)** restricted, repetitive, and stereotyped patterns of behavior, interests, and activities, as manifested by at least one of the following:

  **(a)** encompassing preoccupation with one or more stereotyped and restricted patterns of interest that is abnormal either in intensity or focus

  **(b)** apparently inflexible adherence to specific, nonfunctional routines or rituals

  **(c)** stereotyped and repetitive motor mannerisms (e.g., hand or finger flapping or twisting, or complex whole-body movements)

  **(d)** persistent preoccupation with parts of objects

**B.** Delays or abnormal functioning in at least one of the following areas, with onset prior to age three years: (1) social interaction, (2) language as used in social communication, or (3) symbolic or imaginative play.

**C.** The disturbance is not better accounted for by Rett's disorder or childhood disintegrative disorder.

Source: Reprinted with permission from the *Diagnostic and Statistical Manual of Mental Disorders, Text Revision*, Fourth Edition, (Copyright 2000). American Psychiatric Association.

The second disorder included in autism spectrum disorders is **Asperger syndrome**. The essential feature of Asperger syndrome is an impairment in social interaction. Children with this disorder usually speak fluently by age five, but their language may be unusual (e.g., mixing up the pronouns *I* and *you*) (Frith, 1991). They also are able to demonstrate interest in other people but often are challenged to act appropriately in social situations. The specific *DSM-IV-TR* criteria for Asperger syndrome are outlined in Figure 10.3. One well-known and accomplished individual with ASD is Temple Grandin. A brief biography of her life is included in the Professional Edge.

The third category of exceptionality included as part of pervasive developmental disorders, **pervasive developmental disorder not otherwise specified (PDD–NOS)**, including atypical autism, is described as follows in the *DSM-IV-TR:*

> This category should be used when there is a severe and pervasive impairment in the development or reciprocal social interaction association with impairment in either verbal or nonverbal communication skills or with the presence of stereotyped behavior, interests, and activities, but the criteria are not met for a specific Pervasive Developmental Disorder. (p. 84)

For example, a child who seems to meet the criteria for autistic disorder but who did not display those characteristics until school age might receive a PDD–NOS classification.

## Making Sense of the Definitions

The number of terms associated with autism spectrum disorders can be confusing. Figure 10.4 demonstrates the relationship among the various terms to help you see how they relate to one another. Keep in mind that IDEA definitions are the ones generally used

---

**FIGURE 10.3**

*DSM-IV-TR* Criteria for Asperger Disorder

**A.** Qualitative impairment in social interaction, as manifested by at least two of the following:

  **(1)** marked impairment in the use of multiple nonverbal behaviors such as eye-to-eye gaze, facial expression, body postures, and gestures to regulate social interaction

  **(2)** failure to develop peer relationships appropriate to developmental level

  **(3)** a lack of spontaneous seeking to share enjoyment, interests, or achievements with other people (e.g., by a lack of showing, bringing, or pointing out objects of interest to other people)

  **(4)** lack of social or emotional reciprocity

**B.** Restricted, repetitive, and stereotyped patterns of behavior, interests, and activities, as manifested by at least one of the following:

  **(1)** encompassing preoccupation with one or more stereotyped and restricted patterns of interest that is abnormal either in intensity or focus

  **(2)** apparently inflexible adherence to specific, nonfunctional routines or rituals

  **(3)** stereotyped and repetitive motor mannerisms (e.g., hand or finger flapping or twisting, or complex whole-body movements)

  **(4)** persistent preoccupation with parts of objects

**C.** The disturbance causes clinically significant impairment in social, occupational, or other important areas of functioning.

**D.** There is no clinically significant general delay in language (e.g., single words used by age two years, communicative phrases used by age three years).

**E.** There is no clinically significant delay in cognitive development or in the development of age-appropriate self-help skills, adaptive behavior (other than in social interaction), and curiosity about the environment in childhood.

**F.** Criteria are not met for another specific pervasive development disorder or schizophrenia.

Source: Reprinted with permission from the *Diagnostic and Statistical Manual of Mental Disorders, Text Revision,* Fourth Edition, (Copyright 2000). American Psychiatric Association.

## Temple Grandin, A Truly Exceptional Person

*Temple Grandin is one of the most famous individuals with autism. She is the author of two books about autism and has also written an autobiography. Now at Colorado State University, she is an associate professor who designs livestock facilities.*

Temple Grandin, Ph.D., is a truly accomplished professional. She is associate professor of animal science at Colorado State University. She is known worldwide for her work related to the humane handling of cattle at meat plants, work designed to reduce animal fear and pain. Nearly half of all cattle handling in the U.S. is based on equipment that she designed, and she has consulted on this topic with huge corporations such as McDonald's and Burger King and others worldwide. In 2009, she was named a fellow of the *American Society of Agricultural and Biological Engineers*.

What makes Dr. Grandin's accomplishments even more remarkable is that she has autism. Born in 1947, she did not speak until she was three years old. At about that time she was labeled *autistic*, and her parents were advised to place her in an institution. However, her mother enrolled her in a highly structured nursery school and also hired a nanny who spent many hours playing games with Dr. Grandin that emphasized turn-taking. Dr. Grandin recalls middle school and high school as painful, full of teasing and name-calling. But she persisted and after graduation, she began her college career in the field of psychology, switching to animal science for her master's and doctoral degrees.

Dr. Grandin is a strong advocate for individuals with autism, and she has appeared on many network television shows and specials and has been featured in several major national magazines. She is also a best-selling author on this topic, and HBO has made a movie of her life. She believes that too many people believe that the individuals with autism cannot achieve success, and she is committed to changing that perception.

You can read more about this extraordinary individual at these websites:

- http://www.templegrandin.com/templehome.html
- http://www.grandin.com/

*Source:* Grandin, T. (2002, May 6). Myself. *Time*. Copyright 2002 Time Inc. Reprinted with permission.

---

in public schools. However, the added detail of the *DSM-IV-TR* definitions provides a deeper understanding of these students. Taken together, the definitions should lead you to conclude that if you learn you will be working with students with autism, you need to ask many questions before you can understand their strengths and needs.

## Prevalence of Autism Spectrum Disorders

The prevalence of autism spectrum disorders is hotly debated. IDEA provides an estimate of the prevalence of autism as 0.25 percent of all students ages six to twenty-one (U.S. Department of Education, 2009), or about 165,552 students. However, that estimate is based on school data, which are usually incomplete. The *DSM-IV-TR* reports a prevalence rate of autism of 5 per 10,000, but these data do not address Asperger syndrome or PDD–NOS. Upon studying the children in one town, Scott, Baron-Cohen, Bolton, and Brayne (2002) found that 57 in 10,000 had what they termed *autistic spectrum condition*, which included autism, atypical autism, PDD–NOS, and Asperger syndrome. Most recently, Kogan and his colleagues (2009), using data from the *National Survey of Children's Health*, estimated that approximately 1 percent of all children ages three to seventeen have an autism disorder, or

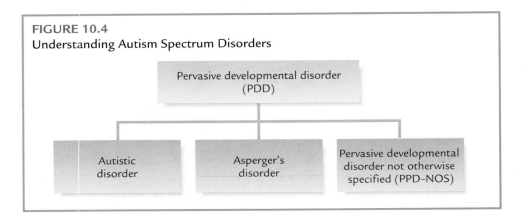

**FIGURE 10.4**
**Understanding Autism Spectrum Disorders**

approximately 673,000 children. As you can see from these estimates, no consensus exists on the prevalence of this disability.

### Other Prevalence Considerations

According to IDEA data, autism exists at approximately the same level in all racial and ethnic groups (U.S. Department of Education, 2009), although students who are Asian/Pacific Islander are identified at a slightly higher frequency than students in other racial groups (.31 percent). Students who are Hispanic have the lowest reported prevalence (.15 percent). In terms of gender, the rate of autism is four to five times higher in males than in females (Kogan et al., 2009), and the rate of Asperger syndrome is more than five times higher in males (*DSM-IV-TR*). Scott and his colleagues (2002) reported a 4:1 ratio. Agreement seems to exist that autism spectrum disorders are more common in boys than girls, but no single, clear conclusion has been reached to date on the extent of the difference.

## Causes of Autism Spectrum Disorders

As with many disabilities, the specific causes of autism spectrum disorders are not truly understood. Professionals generally agree that symptoms of these disabilities are triggered by genetic differences or other malfunctions in the brain (National Institute of Neurological Disorders and Stroke, 2009) and that trauma related to abuse or neglect by caregivers is not a cause (Gillberg & Coleman, 2000), although environmental factors may contribute to the disorders. Research on the causes of ASD is leading to rapid changes in the field. To learn about how to find the most current information, access the resources summarized in the Professional Edge.

**fyi**

Research conducted over the past several years indicates that a diagnosis of autism can be reliably made before children are three years old (Charles et al., 2008).

### Biological Factors

Researchers currently are focusing on genetic factors related to autism spectrum disorders, speculating that DNA might be responsible for causing developmental dysfunction in the brains of individuals with these disabilities. Simple logic based on this hypothesis is that parents with autism spectrum disorders are likely to have a child with ASD. However, such cases are very rare. Extensive genetic research has shown that as many as 10 genes may contribute to the development of ASD and various specific characteristics of these disorders (National Institute of Child Health and Human Development, 2005), but the degree of exhibited symptoms varies across family structure (e.g., Smith et al., 2009). For example, the father of a child identified with an autism spectrum disorder might have subtle characteristics (e.g., relatively intense concentration when working on a favorite project) compared with others

---

### Keeping Up with Research on ASD

As you read this chapter, you probably are noticing that many topics related to autism spectrum disorders are changing rapidly. More students are being identified with ASD, medical studies are increasing knowledge about the causes of this disability, and research is under way to identify treatments and interventions that would be most beneficial to students. If you are interested in keeping up with research related to autism, here are resources to use:

- The Collaborative Programs of Excellence in Autism (CPEA) network is supported by the National Institutes of Health. Its purpose is to conduct research on the causes of autism, and studies underway address genetics, environmental contributions, and immunological factors. The CPEA network also is charged with examining the diagnosis of autism, including early detection, the characteristics of individuals with autism with an emphasis on

behavior and communication, and treatments. You can learn more about this project, visit websites of the participating universities, and learn about recent research results at this website: www.autismresearchnetwork.org/AN/wfCPEA.aspx.

- The Studies to Advance Autism Research and Treatment (STAART) network also is supported by the National Institutes of Health as part of the Children's Health Act of 2000. This project includes eight centers, and each one is conducting at least three research projects. Like the CPEA network, STAART is exploring the causes, diagnosis, and treatment of autism. However, this network also is researching prevention. You can read about the university members of this network and their recent research results at www.autismresearchnetwork.org/AN/wfSTAART.aspx.

*professional edge*

http://autismresearchinstitute.com
The Autism Research Institute provides a comprehensive and well-
organized bank of research-based
information for professionals and
parents. The links to information
on a variety of hot topics are particularly useful.

or odd social skills but function in an acceptable manner in his social life. Evidence also suggests a high frequency of autism spectrum disorders among siblings when compared to
other disabilities (Yirmiya, Shaked, & Erel, 2001). Research to date, though, suggests that no
single genetic factor is responsible for causing autism spectrum disorders. Rather, multiple
genetic factors seem to intricately connect to form a wide range of developmental malfunctions (National Institute of Child Health and Human Development, 2005).

### Autism Spectrum Disorders and the Brain

If genes are the cause of autism spectrum disorders, what symptoms are found in the brain?
Recent technology, such as magnetic resonance imaging (MRI), enables researchers to obtain accurate information about the brain, and a number of brain functions that may trigger autistic symptoms have been observed. For example, individuals with autism spectrum
disorders have been found to have abnormalities in the cerebellum, the part of the brain that
controls motor coordination, balance, and cognition (Courchesne et al., 2001). Similarly, research has surveyed the frontal and temporal lobes: The frontal lobe manages social and
cognitive functions (Klin, Jones, Schultz, & Volkmar, 2003; Pierce & Courchesne, 2001),
whereas the temporal lobe is involved in understanding facial expressions and in social cues
and memory (Hubl et al., 2003; Itier & Taylor, 2004; Passarotti et al., 2003). Researchers generally have found that in these parts of the brain, individuals with autism spectrum disorders have fewer cells, higher cell density, or less volume than in typical individuals (e.g.,
Williams, 2008).

### Environmental Factors

Although the early belief that autism spectrum disorders were caused almost exclusively by
environmental factors such as maternal neglect has long been proven untrue, most professionals agree that these factors can influence the number and intensity of symptoms (London & Etzel, 2000). For example, the quality of care by family members and professionals
plays an important role in the development of children with autism spectrum disorders
(Simpson & Zionts, 2000). A positive, structured environment can significantly improve behavior problems often displayed by these children and youth. In many cases, positive supports, unconditional family love, and similar factors probably have a positive effect on how
the symptoms of autism spectrum disorders occur.

*An area of challenge for most students with autism spectrum disorders is understanding how to
interact in social situations.*

## Autism and Immunizations

One of the most controversial causal issues related to autism spectrum disorders is immunization, especially that given for measles, mumps, and rubella (MMR). However, findings to date on the causal relationship between MMR shots and autism spectrum disorders do not warrant stopping these immunizations (Charles, Carpenter, Jenner, & Nicholas, 2008). For example, most of the authors of a key study on this topic have retracted their original conclusions, now indicating that no causal link was established (Centers for Disease Control and Prevention, 2004a), a position that is also supported by experts from the Institute of Medicine and the American Academy of Pediatrics. Further, several studies have completely refuted the autism–MMR vaccination link (Dales, Hammer, & Smith, 2001; Stratton, Gable, Shetty, & McCormick, 2001).

## REVIEW · REFLECT · DISCUSS

1. Create a Venn diagram or another type of visual aid that explains how the IDEA and American Psychiatric Association definitions of *autism* and associated disorders relate to each other. How are the concepts similar and different?

2. What factors can you identify that make it difficult to get an accurate picture of the prevalence of autism spectrum disorders? Briefly explain how each factor you name affects this issue.

# Characteristics of Individuals with Autism Spectrum Disorders

Beginning at an early age and typically continuing throughout the life span, individuals with autism spectrum disorders have difficulty relating appropriately to others. They usually have a wide range of language and communication disorders. Many have an obsessive insistence on environmental sameness and are well known for their atypical and often difficult-to-understand behaviors, including stereotypic, repetitive, and self-stimulatory responses (e.g., Lee, Odom, & Loftin, 2007). However, each student with these disabilities may have a unique combination of strengths and needs.

## Cognitive and Academic Characteristics

Children and youth with ASD often have irregular patterns of cognitive and educational strengths and deficits, with the majority of individuals with autism disorder having some level of intellectual disability and those with Asperger syndrome having average to above-average ability (Barnhill, Hagiwara, Myles, & Simpson, 2000; Mayes & Calhoun, 2008). Although children and youth with autism share some characteristics with students with other disabilities, their unique features set them apart and sometimes create significant challenges for those who serve them. These distinguishing characteristics include overreliance on rote memory, problems with theory of mind, and problem-solving challenges.

### Rote Memory

**Rote memory** is the ability to easily remember things without necessarily knowing what they mean. Have you ever memorized a phrase in a different language or a mathematical formula so that you could say it or write it when you needed to—even if you did not understand what it meant? Those are examples of rote memory. Although rote memory usually would be considered an asset, it can be a great liability for students with autism spectrum disorders. Because they have well-developed rote memory skills, students with these disabilities can give the impression that they understand certain concepts when in fact they do not (Gabig, 2008). For example, a student with autism may hear certain words or phrases in conversation and then use them in a rote manner that mimics comprehension.

This parroting gives the inaccurate impression that the student has well-developed, higher-level comprehension skills.

Rote memory may be a disadvantage for students with autism spectrum disorders in another way, too. Adults often assume that having strong rote memory skills means that students can remember, at any time, pieces of information or events. But this is not true for many individuals with autism spectrum disorders. Although chunks of information are stored in memory, students with this exceptionality may have trouble retrieving them. Often, a question worded in a specific manner must be used to prompt retrieval from memory. For example, Devon, a twelve-year-old boy with autism, has memorized all of the menu items at a fast-food restaurant. However, unless the server asks "May I take your order?" Devon cannot recall what he wants to order and may repeat all the items on the menu. The server's words need to be precise in order for Devon to access the information he has memorized.

### Theory of Mind

One of the core cognitive deficits of autism spectrum disorders concerns **theory of mind**. This relatively new explanation of autism is based on the belief that people with these disorders do not truly understand that others have their own thoughts and points of view and that people with autism face challenges in understanding others' beliefs and emotions (Perra et al., 2008; Peterson & Slaughter, 2009). Difficulties with theory of mind can be seen when individuals with autism spectrum disorders have difficulty explaining their own behaviors, predicting others' emotions or behaviors, comprehending others' perspectives, understanding how behavior affects others' thoughts and feelings, participating in conversations, and distinguishing fact from fiction (Myles & Southwick, 2005).

Some professionals contend that it is theory-of-mind deficit that sets individuals with autism spectrum disorders apart from those with other disabilities. For example, Robert, a high school sophomore with Asperger syndrome, could not understand why he was in trouble for loudly announcing that his history teacher had bad breath. In his mind, he was only telling the truth.

### Problem Solving

Many students with autism spectrum disorders have access to only one problem-solving strategy for a particular situation and use it consistently, regardless of whether it is successful and even if the situation changes. Difficulty retrieving information or strategies may make problem solving even more challenging (Scheuermann & Webber, 2002b). For example, when Alex could not find his toothbrush, he discontinued brushing his teeth. It did not occur to him to ask his mother to purchase a new toothbrush or to help him to find the old one. Although learners with autism spectrum disorders may be able to recite several problem-solving strategies and verbally report that they can be generalized, often they are not able to recall any of these strategies when needed. That is, Geneva, who was introduced at the beginning of the chapter, has learned that if she is not sure how to find her classroom, she can ask another student or an adult, or look to see if she is near the office and ask someone there. When she suddenly becomes disoriented, though, she cannot remember what to do and begins screaming and thus still needs to be accompanied from class to class.

Problem solving becomes even more difficult if abstract concepts or interpersonal interactions are involved (Goddard, Howlin, Dritschel, & Patel, 2007). The problem-solving deficits of some students, particularly those with Asperger syndrome, may not be recognized easily, thus making the situation even more complex. Their pedantic style, advanced vocabulary, and grammatically perfect responses often mask their skill levels. For these reasons, by the time they realize that a problem exists, they often are so confused or angry that their reactions are inappropriate, often involving tantrums or withdrawal.

### Motivation

In addition to the other cognitive and academic difficulties that students with autism spectrum disorders face, motivation can be a serious issue. Students with these disabilities gen-

*Jennette Horton's undergraduate degree (from Miami University of Ohio) and master's degree (from Xavier University in Cincinnati) are in the area of moderate, severe, and multiple disabilities. She is also certified by the National Board for Professional Teaching Standards as an Exceptional Needs Specialist, early childhood through young adult. She has 13 years of experience teaching students with special needs, and most recently taught high school students with autism spectrum disorders. Here is her advice on working with these students and their families.*

- *Establish clear routines and rules within your classroom from the first day.* Students with autism have a difficult time anticipating what will happen next, which can cause a lot of anxiety. If the school day follows a predictable pattern (even if each day is different, but Mondays are always the same), transitions are easier to predict and expectations are known.

- *Visually structure the physical layout of the classroom.* Students need to know where they should be to perform different classroom tasks. Use a carpet to delineate the group area, bookshelves to section off the reading area, label individual work space, and so on.

- *Provide visual schedules to increase understanding.* Some students need schedules to be broken down within activities (Math class – listen to the teacher and watch examples on the board, work at desk finishing problems #1–5, turn in work to teacher, select quiet folder activity from those in red bucket on counter); others are fine just knowing that after group we have math then morning break.

- *To increase and support language, provide scripts, sentence starters, and other visuals to cue responses.* It's important to remember that students with autism tend to be very visual learners. Language processing is difficult so providing visual cues to jump start this processing can be very powerful. If every morning at group each student greets another, provide pic-

tures of the other students with names to increase the likelihood of interaction. As the student learns this routine, levels of visual cues can be faded or new scripts can be introduced.

- *Raising a child with special needs is tough enough, but many parents of children with autism feel judged across environments.* For example, many parents fear going to the grocery store for fear their child will have an outburst and another parent will judge their parenting skills. Offer to help the parent create visual cues, schedules, social stories, or whatever they are ready to introduce at home. Don't force strategies on families, but provide examples of those that work at school and could translate well into the home.

- *Parents of children with autism tend to be very well educated in their legal rights and school responsibilities.* Don't take this personally; it's their job to advocate for their child. Make the parent an active member of the IEP team, carefully listening to her concerns and suggestions.

- *Sit next to the parent or caregiver when having an IEP meeting.* Many parents report feeling like they were up against a jury with the school team on one side of the table and the family on the other. Sitting next to parents creates a warmer climate, a sense that you want to work with them and are all equal members of the team.

- *Remember that the grieving process can be cyclical.* Many parents go through sadness, denial, and anger before accepting a new diagnosis when their child is young. It is common for parents to experience many of these feelings again when their child reaches high school and they realize that graduation, college, and a job aren't going to be the norm. It is hard to be at the receiving end of angry emails, but I would always rather a parent be angry with me about what the child is or isn't doing than be upset with the child. Try to see the parent's perspective.

erally are interested only in a small number of activities or rewards. Sometimes professionals and parents struggle to figure out what these interests are, but without warning, these students also may completely change their preferences. Taken together, these factors make motivating students with autism spectrum disorders an ongoing challenge (Carnahan, Musti-Rao, & Bailey, 2009; Vismara & Lyons, 2007). In the Speaking from Experience, Jennette Horton, an experienced special educator who most recently has taught high school students with autism, talks about matching classroom practices to the complexities of working with these students and supporting their parents, who may themselves be struggling.

## Social and Emotional Characteristics

The social and emotional challenges that students with autism spectrum disorders encounter are directly related to their other special needs. In particular, language disorders, unconventional language use, and immaturity often characterize these students.

**PEARSON**
**myeducationlab**

Go to the Assignments and Activities section of Topic 13: Autism, in the MyEducationLab for your course and complete the activity entitled "Communication and Social Skills of Students with Autism Spectrum Disorders".

## Language Disorders

Many students with autism spectrum disorders have extraordinary difficulties in language development (Solomon, 2008; Tager-Flusberg et al,, 2009). This, in turn, has a significant negative impact on their abilities to interact successfully with others. For example, they may experience delays in developing language. In addition, they may fail to use language to communicate, or they may lack the desire to interact with others.

Several examples of language disorders can clarify how important this area is for students with autism spectrum disorders. Students may have problems with **proxemics**—that is, knowing the socially acceptable distance to maintain between people during conversation. These students may stand closer to or farther away from another person than is customary. They also may stare intensely at another person while interacting, making that person very uncomfortable. In contrast, some students may fail to make any eye contact at all, looking to the side or up or down during conversation. This makes it difficult for the other person to judge whether the student is engaged in the topic being discussed. In addition, students may fail to understand or respond to others' gestures and facial expressions during communication. As a result, they may not notice that the other person is bored or that the person wants to ask a question.

### Communicative Intent

One characteristic that is somewhat unique to individuals with autism spectrum disorders concerns problems with **communicative intent**. That is, these students often do not communicate in order to obtain the attention of others, and they may not communicate for social purposes (Scheuermann & Webber, 2002a). Approximately 50 percent of individuals with autism are nonverbal; that is, they have few or no verbal language skills.

Those who do have verbal skills often engage in **echolalia**, repeating words and phrases that have been uttered by someone else with little or no understanding of their conventional meanings. Students also may have problems with pronoun reversals, using *you* for *I* and vice versa. They also may lack voice tone or inflection. Individuals with autism may have **prosody** problems—use of a monotone or sing-song tone of voice, regardless of the intended message (Chevallier, Noveck, Happe, & Wilson, 2009).

### Other Language Problems

Students at the higher end of the autism spectrum—those with Asperger syndrome—often have unusual traits in their language skills (Janzen, 2003; Saalasti et al., 2008; Wing, 1981). For example, Louise, a six-year-old with Asperger syndrome, told her mother that she "waved" her clothes on the bathroom floor. She was using the word *waved* instead of *left*. Her reason was that you "wave when you leave."

Many students cannot comprehend language related to abstract ideas such as democracy and justice. They also may struggle with understanding and correctly using figures of speech such as metaphors, idioms, parables, and allegories and grasping the meaning and intent of rhetorical questions. For example, when Rick was told, "Put your best foot forward," he looked down and asked which foot was his best foot!

Students with Asperger syndrome also may have good structural language skills, such as clear pronunciation and correct syntax, but poor pragmatic communication abilities. For example, some students—like Lance, whom you met at the beginning of the chapter, may repeat the same phrase over and over, talk with exaggerated inflections or in a monotone and droning style, discuss at length a single topic that is of little interest to others, or experience difficulty in sustaining a conversation unless it focuses exclusively on a particular narrowly defined topic. These communication problems are not surprising, given that effective communication requires that individuals have mutually shared topics to communicate about and are willing to listen as well as to talk.

### Immaturity

When you think of an individual whom you consider mature, what characteristics come to mind? Maturity is often assessed by actions in social situations. To be socially adept, people must be able to perceive and understand social cues such as frowns, smiles, boredom, and other expressions of emotion. They must be able to think clearly about their own behaviors and the behaviors of others. Because of the many language disorders and communication challenges experienced by students with autism (including those with Asperger syndrome), they often make statements that do not make sense or give inappropriate responses to others' questions. They also experience frustration when their communication does not accomplish its purpose. As a result, these students often seem extraordinarily naïve or immature.

## Behavior Characteristics

A final domain to consider in characterizing students with autism spectrum disorders is behavior. Some of the challenges these students may have include self-stimulatory behaviors, difficulty with generalizations, and sensory responses.

*A goal for most students with autism spectrum disorders is learning communication and social skills that enable them to interact effectively with peers, teachers, family members, and others.*

### Self-Stimulatory Behaviors

**Self-stimulatory behaviors** may involve rocking, hand flapping, and any other repetitive, stereotyped behavior patterns that appear to have no apparent function (Cunningham & Schreibman, 2008). These behaviors, common for students with autism, tend to stigmatize them, interfering not only with social acceptance and integration but also with learning. Other similar behavioral challenges, such as self-injurious behaviors (e.g., biting, head banging), also can be serious issues; however, such behaviors are relatively uncommon.

### Generalization Difficulties

A major challenge facing educators and others who work with students with autism spectrum disorders relates to their difficulty in transferring information to new settings, individuals, and conditions. As a result, a student who is able to perform a written task in one classroom cannot be assumed to be able to perform the same task correctly in another classroom. To address generalization, professionals must spend considerable time developing strategies for enabling students to use information and skills flexibly. These strategies may include practicing skills in community and general education classroom settings (Simpson & Myles, 1998).

### Sensory Issues

Students with autism spectrum disorders experience a myriad of sensory processing issues (Wiggins, Robins, Bakeman, & Adamson, 2009). That is, they have difficulty with the (a) tactile, (b) vestibular, (c) proprioception, (d) visual, (e) auditory, (f) gustatory, and (g) olfactory senses. Figure 10.5 provides an overview of each of the sensory systems, including its location and function. The figure also provides examples of how students with autism may experience difficulties related to the senses. For example, you may know a person with autism who can hear sounds that are not discernible to those without autism or who finds the feeling of a tag inside a shirt very painful. Because the visual perception area tends to be a strength for students with autism spectrum disorders, visual supports often are used to assist in learning (Odom et al., 2003).

Sensory difficulties affect all areas of learning. Many students with autism spectrum disorders receive occupational therapy to address these issues and to receive the maximum benefit from instruction. All professionals who work with students with autism spectrum disorders should be aware of the impact of sensory issues on behavior and achievement (Myles, Cook, Miller, Rinner, & Robbins, 2000).

## FIGURE 10.5

### Understanding Sensory Systems and Autism

This figure explains each of the sensory systems in which students with autism may experience difficulties, its location, and its functions. It also provides examples of the common sensory problems.

| System | Location | Function | Example of Sensory Problems |
|---|---|---|---|
| Tactile (touch) | · Skin—density of cell distribution varies throughout the body. Areas of greatest density include mouth, hands, and genitals. | · Provides information about the environment and object qualities (e.g., touch, pressure, texture, hard, soft, sharp, dull, heat, cold, pain). | · Feel of fabric texture on skin may be painful; student may not feel heat or cold and so is more at risk for injuries. |
| Vestibular (balance) | · Inner ear—stimulated by head movements and input from other senses, especially vision. | · Provides information about where our body is in space and whether we or our surroundings are moving. Tells about speed and direction of movement. | · Student may lose balance more easily than classmates or experience difficulty in some games or activities (e.g., jumping rope, playing basketball). |
| Proprioception (body awareness) | · Muscles and joints—activated by muscle contractions and movement. | · Provides information about where a certain body part is and how it is moving. | · Student may seem clumsy, bumping into desks in narrow aisles or knocking crayons off a table. |
| Visual (sight) | · Retina of the eye—stimulated by light. | · Provides information about objects and persons. Helps us define boundaries as we move through time and space. | · Student may be very sensitive to bright lights such as those found in classrooms. |
| Auditory (hearing) | · Inner ear—stimulated by air or sound waves. | · Provides information about sounds in the environment (loud, soft, high, low, near, far). | · Certain sounds (e.g., fire alarm) may be too loud for the student; student may focus on sounds others do not attend to (e.g., electrical hum from classroom equipment). |
| Gustatory (taste) | · Chemical receptors in the tongue—closely associated with the olfactory (smell) system. | · Provides information about different types of taste (e.g., sweet, sour, bitter, salty, spicy). | · Student may refuse to eat anything except certain preferred foods. |
| Olfactory (smell) | · Chemical receptors in the nasal structure—closely associated with the gustatory system. | · Provides information about different types of smell (e.g., musty, acrid, putrid, flowery, pungent). | · Student may have a strong reaction to certain scents (e.g., perfume, materials used in a science experiment). |

Source: Myles, B. S., Cook, K. T., Miller, N. E., Rinner, L., & Robbins, L. A. (2001). *Asperger syndrome and sensory issues: Practical solutions for making sense of the world* (p. 5). Shawnee Mission, KS: Autism Asperger Publishing. Reprinted with permission from Autism Asperger Publishing Co.

## REVIEW · REFLECT · DISCUSS

Go to the Assignments and Activities section of Topic 13: Autism, in the MyEducationLab for your course and complete the activity entitled "Behavior Characteristics of Students with Autism Spectrum Disorders".

1. What are at least four examples of sensory issues that students with autism spectrum disorders may experience? How might each of these affect students' educational experiences?

2. You already have learned that deafness and hearing loss often are most accurately described in terms of communication challenges and that speech and language disorders can significantly affect many students. In this chapter, considerable attention is focused on the communication needs of students with autism. How are these three groups of students similar? Different? Why do you think that so many challenges related to disabilities turn out to be about communication?

# Identifying Autism Spectrum Disorders

The definition of autism in IDEA is very general, and so it is common for this disorder to be diagnosed using the criteria in *DSM-IV-TR*. However, identifying these students is rather complex because the symptoms occur in so many different ways. As for all students, a team, including the parents, must participate in the assessment and eligibility determination process.

## Assessment Practices and Procedures

Many students are identified as having an autism spectrum disorder before they enter school. Assessing for this disability usually includes checking whether a student displays the characteristics known to be associated with autism spectrum disorders. In addition, information is gathered concerning the child's cognitive, academic, and adaptive behavior skills. Finally, the child's developmental history is reviewed and observations of behavior are assessed.

### Assessment Related to Characteristics of Autism

Deciding whether a student has the characteristics of an autism spectrum disorder involves both formal and informal assessment. Psychologists and psychiatrists may use standardized instruments that are designed just for this purpose. One example is the Autism Diagnostic Interview–Revised (ADI–R) (Le Couteur, Lord, & Rutter, 2003). However, teachers and other professionals also may be asked to complete rating scales designed to screen students for the disability. Two examples of these rating scales are the Modified Checklist for Autism in Toddlers (M-CHAT) (Robins, & Dumont-Mathieu, 2006; Barton, Robbin, & Fein, 1999) and the Asperger Syndrome Diagnostic Scale (ASDS) (Myles, Bock, & Simpson, 2001).

One additional evaluation informs professionals about whether a student has an autism spectrum disorder: sensory assessment. Usually administered by a trained professional, an instrument such as the Sensory Profile (Dunn, 1999) can be used to pinpoint specific sensory problems such as the ones about which you have already read.

### Cognitive Ability, Academic Achievement, and Adaptive Skills

Part of the assessment for autism spectrum disorders is similar to the assessments completed for students who may have other disabilities. That is, individual intelligence tests are administered, as are both formal and informal assessments of academic achievement using standardized achievement tests and curriculum-based measures. Language assessment often is part of this process because most students with autism spectrum disorders have language-related delays or problems. In addition, students' adaptive behaviors are measured, including tasks related to self-help (e.g., dressing, brushing teeth) and functioning in the community (e.g., ordering in a fast-food restaurant, riding a bus).

### Developmental Measures

Because autism spectrum disorders are considered developmental disabilities, comprehensive assessment also must explore developmental characteristics. Using an instrument such as the Psychoeducational Profile 3 (PEP 3) (Schopler, Lansing, Reichler, & Marcus, 2005), a professional can ask parents about their child's fine- and gross-motor skill development, language development, and related areas. For older students, questions may be asked concerning vocational skills, independent functioning, leisure activities, functional communication, and interpersonal behavior.

### Behavior Assessment

Students with autism spectrum disorders nearly always have behavior problems. These behaviors usually are assessed by asking parents, teachers, and others who interact with the student to complete a behavior checklist, a procedure you learned about in Chapter Seven regarding students with emotional disabilities.

Rodriguez (2009) found that culturally and linguistically diverse (CLD) students with autism may not be receiving needed special education and other services due to factors such as cultural differences, socioeconomic status, lack of awareness and sensitivity of professionals, and lack of information available to CLD families in their language.

**fyi**

Autism spectrum disorders may occur simultaneously with other disabilities, including intellectual disabilities (Chapter Eight), physical or health disabilities (Chapter Thirteen), and learning disabilities (Chapter Five).

In addition, a functional behavior analysis also may be helpful for determining the relationships between behavior and the environment for students with autism. As you may recall, the functional behavior analysis usually involves investigating antecedent events and their consequences based on a previously developed hypothesis about what is causing a behavior. Through this process, environmental, social, and communicative factors that might trigger problem behaviors are revealed and interventions can then be planned (Aspy & Grossman, 2006).

## Eligibility

research
**NOTE**

Sleep disturbances are part of the complexity of autism spectrum disorders and increase with the severity of autism. Predictors of sleep disorders included parent reports of autism severity, hyperactivity, mood variability, and aggression (Mayes & Calhoun, 2009).

After assessment data are gathered, the team of educators, medical professionals, parents, and related services personnel address the questions that guide special education decision making:

- Does a disability exist?
- Does it have a negative impact on educational performance?
- Is the student eligible for special education services?
- Will the student benefit from those services?

As for all students with disabilities, the most important part of the identification process is not what label is assigned but what services are provided to meet the student's needs. Continuous data collection, monitoring, and analysis through assessments and flexible interventions are essential to effectively educate such a student.

## REVIEW · REFLECT · DISCUSS

1. How is assessment for students with autism spectrum disorders similar to and different from assessment for other students who might have a disability?
2. Why do you think many of the instruments used to determine whether a student has this disability are checklists of behaviors rather than traditional tests?

# How Learners with Autism Spectrum Disorders Receive Their Education

Because children and youth with autism spectrum disorders differ greatly in their skill levels, their educational options vary as well. Generally, however, early and intensive education provides the best outcome.

## Early Childhood

The National Research Council (2001) studied educational programs that provide early intervention services to young children with autism. It found many instructional approaches and many variations regarding the setting in which the program was offered. For example, one program used the home as the instructional setting, and one used a school-only model. The programs shared the following features:

- Intervention prior to age three
- Twenty to forty-five hours of intervention per week
- Active family involvement
- Highly trained staff providing services to children with autism and their families
- Ongoing assessment of children's progress
- A systematically implemented curriculum
- A highly supportive teaching and learning environment
- A focus on communication goals and other developmental areas

*Strong visual supports help students with autism spectrum disorders to understand classroom expectations and routines.*

students, and many of the practices benefit other students with disabilities as well. Similarly, many of the academic interventions introduced for students with learning disabilities, emotional disabilities, intellectual disabilities, and communication disorders also enhance learning for students with autism spectrum disorders.

## Environmental Supports

**Environmental supports** are changes in a student's surroundings that are considered key to effective programming. Some of the most common environmental supports include visual supports, a home base, and assistive technology.

### Visual Supports

Students with autism spectrum disorders benefit from visually presented information because it is more concrete than auditory information and allows for greater processing time. One example for younger students involves labeling items (e.g., *desk, door, table*) in the general or special education classroom in order to help expand these students' vocabularies. Another example is a *visual schedule*, which presents a list of activities using a combination of

### Visual Schedules and Task Cards

Students with autism spectrum disorders often benefit by having tasks, schedules, and activities clearly explained to them ahead of time. Using words, pictures, or a combination of both, professionals can prepare students for the school day, help them know what happens next, clarify expectations, and foster independence. Two examples of visual supports are given here. Try making a simple visual support for one of the students described at the beginning of the chapter or another student with whom you are familiar.

**Today Is Monday, April 16, 2000**

| | |
|---|---|
| Attendance | 8:15 |
| Math | 8:20–9:00 |
| Reading and Centers | 9:00–10:00 |
| Spelling | 10:00–10:15 |
| Writing | 10:15–10:45 |
| *Assembly* | 10:45–11:30 |
| Lunch and Recess | 11:30–12:15 |
| Music | 12:30–1:15 |
| Science | 1:15–1:50 |
| Read Aloud | 1:50–2:20 |
| Journal | 2:20–2:25 |
| Get Ready to Go | 2:25 |
| Bell Rings | 2:30 |

*Sometimes the schedule changes*

**Get Ready for Lunch**

1. Put books in desk _____
2. Put math papers in blue folder _____
3. Put pencils in pencil case _____
4. Get lunch from backpack _____
5. Sit at desk _____
6. Look at teacher and wait _____
7. When the teacher calls my name, give her this paper and get in line _____

*Source:* S. T. Moore. (2002). *Asperger syndrome and the elementary school experience: Practical solutions for academic and social difficulties.* Shawnee Mission, KS: Autism Asperger Publishing. Reprinted by permission of Autism Asperger Publishing Co.

icons, photographs, words, or clock faces to help students anticipate upcoming events and activities, develop an understanding of time, and predict change.

*Task cards* are similar. They help students with Asperger syndrome recall academic content, routines, or social skills. Typically presented on business-card-size paper, the task card lists the steps the student must follow in a series of directive statements, expressed in concise language. For adolescents, task cards can provide an overview of the routines and teacher expectations in each class. For younger children, a task card may outline four conversation starters that can be used with peers during lunch. Examples of visual schedules and task cards that special education teachers or general education teachers might use are included in the Instruction in Action.

The *travel card* is yet another type of visual support for students with autism spectrum disorders in middle or high school settings (Carpenter, 2001). This type of card provides an efficient and effective means for dealing with the complex scheduling and shortage of time for personalized communication that characterize secondary schools. As you read about travel cards in the Instruction in Action, think about how they would be helpful to parents, teachers, and students.

### Home Base

*Home base* is a place students can go when they are beginning to feel anxious or upset and need to calm themselves (Myles & Adreon, 2001; Myles & Southwick, 2005). For example, students with autism spectrum disorders can go to a home base to (a) plan or review the day's events; (b) escape the stress of the classroom; (c) prevent a "meltdown"; or (d) regain control if a tantrum, rage, or meltdown has occurred. A resource room or counselor's office commonly is used as the home base. When a student feels the need to leave the classroom, whether general education or special education, she can take assignments to the home base and work in that less stressful environment.

School personnel frequently schedule the school day of students with autism spectrum disorders so that they begin at the home base and have frequent stops there throughout the day. This creates a consistent student–teacher relationship and specifies a place to go when the need arises. It also can help students participate in general education by providing them with breaks from the social stress of the classroom.

## Assistive Technology

You have learned about the importance of assistive technology for many students with disabilities, and you probably can surmise that students with autism spectrum disorders access technology, too. These students may use items that other students with disabilities use such as adapted eating utensils, talking calculators, pencil grips, voice output devices, audible word-scanning devices, and talking word processors with text.

Yet another increasingly popular use of technology for students with autism is video-based intervention (VBI) (Rayner, Denholm, & Sigafoos, 2009). For example, Hagiwara (1998) created a multimedia program that successfully taught students self-help and on-task skills. Specifically, the program contained video-taped segments that showed students engaging in appropriate target behaviors as well as a story-type format that told the students the steps and outcomes for completing their individually targeted skills. Others have implemented VBI approaches to teach social skills (e.g., Scattone, 2008; Nikopoulos, & Nikopoulou-Smyrni, 2008) and early literacy skills (e.g., Biederman, & Freedman, 2007). You can read more about this innovative assistive technology in the Technology Notes.

## Instructional Practices

Many instructional strategies have been demonstrated to be effective with students with autism spectrum disorders. Three examples that illustrate successful strategies are priming, discrete trial training, and prompting.

### Priming

Wilde, Koegel, and Koegel (1992) devised priming to familiarize students with academic material prior to its use in school, reduce stress and anxiety by bringing predictability to new

## Travel Card

As students move from elementary school to middle and then high school, ensuring clear communication becomes more difficult. More teachers work with the students, the schools are larger, and maintaining close communication with parents can become more challenging. A travel card is designed to support students with autism spectrum disorders who are in middle schools or high schools. It is designed to:

- Increase appropriate student behavior across environments
- Facilitate collaboration among teachers
- Increase awareness among teachers of the academic, behavior, and social goals on which the student is working
- Improve home–school communication (Carpenter, 2001; Jones & Jones, 1995)

As you can see by looking at the accompanying figure, the travel card lists four or five of a student's target behaviors across the top and the classes the student attends along the left side. Classes include reading, science, social studies, and others. At the end of each period, the teacher indicates whether the student performed the desired behaviors by marking a + (yes), 0 (no), or NA (not applicable) on the card. At the end of the day, the positive notations are tallied and graphed. Points are accumulated toward a menu of rewards that have been negotiated by the student and the professionals responsible for the travel card.

### Travel Card
### Rocky

Date_____

**Key**    + = Yes    0 = No    NA = Not applicable

| | Did student follow class rules? | Did student participate in class? | Did student complete assignments? | Did student turn in homework? | Teacher's initials |
|---|---|---|---|---|---|
| Reading | | | | | |
| Science | | | | | |
| Social Studies | | | | | |
| Study Skills | | | | | |
| English | | | | | |
| Spanish | | | | | |
| Bonus Points | Went to nurse after getting off bus? | | | Has assignment book? | |
| Total | + | 0 | | | |

*Teacher Comments/Suggestions/Announcements:*

*Source:* Travel card from Myles, Brenda S., & Adreon, D. (2001). *Asperger syndrome and adolescence: Practical solutions for school success.* Shawnee Mission, KS: Autism Asperger Publishing. Reprinted by permission of Autism Asperger Publishing Co.

tasks, and increase student success. **Priming** occurs when a parent, paraprofessional, teacher, or trusted peer previews with a student the actual materials that will be used in a lesson or activity the day, the evening, or the morning before that lesson or activity occurs (Gately, 2008). In some instances, priming occurs just prior to an activity. Priming is most effective when it is built into the student's routine. It should occur in a relaxed environment and be facilitated by a primer who is both patient and encouraging. Finally, priming sessions should be short, providing a brief overview of the day's tasks in 10 or 15 minutes (Myles & Adreon, 2001).

## Teaching by Showing . . . for Real

Through video modeling, professionals can take advantage of the strong visual learning tendencies of many students with autism spectrum disorders and at the same time provide very concrete and specific skill instruction. This readily available technology is being used to teach skills such as these (Baker, Lang, & O'Reilly, 2009):

- Appropriate classroom behavior (and reduction of inappropriate behavior)
- On-task and other learning behaviors
- Peer interactions
- Job related skills

Several approaches to video modeling have been developed, usually based on who is selected to demonstrate on a video recording the skill being taught. These are the most common options (McCoy & Hermansen, 2007):

- Adult models, usually someone familiar to the student such as a parent or teacher
- Peer model, usually someone of the same age and gender as the student, or perhaps a classmate or sibling
- Self, when the student is "caught on camera" appropriately demonstrating the skill being taught and is

then shown that video in order to increase his use of the skill

- Point-of-view, in which the image shown is what would be seen if the participant was actually engaged in the behavior. For example, a camera might be held over the shoulder of a peer stuffing an envelope which would show the student with autism what he would see when completing the task
- Mixed model, using more than one of the above approaches

Students often view such videos on a computer, but they also can be placed on smartphones so that students can view them as they move from place to place. Teachers usually combine this learning experience with other techniques, including behavior plans that provide reinforcement.

Research on the effectiveness of video modeling is still emerging, and so more information on how to best utilize it is like to come in the near future. How else do you think this technology could be applied to improve learning for students with autism spectrum disorders?

### web link

www.asperger.org
The Asperger Syndrome Coalition of the United States is a national nonprofit organization focusing on Asperger syndrome. The site includes links to books, articles, and other resources.

### Discrete Trial Training

Unlike most of the practices outlined so far that might be implemented by general education teachers, special education teachers, or others working with students with autism spectrum disorders, **discrete trial training** (DTT) is a highly specialized approach that requires a significant time commitment and often is supervised by a special educator or sometimes a parent (Leaf & McEachin, 1999; Ghezzi, 2007). Most commonly implemented with preschool children, this practice follows a basic pattern in which the teacher gives a prompt (i.e., cue) to which the student attends, a command for the student to perform, and finally a reward to the student for the desired behavior (Lovaas, 1987).

For example, the student could be given a prompt such as "Look at me" or a nonverbal cue such as pointing to the teacher's eyes. Once this command is given, the teacher waits for the student to focus attention as directed. In some instances, the teacher may need to guide the child physically through the desired behavior, such as lifting the child's chin so her eyes focus on the teacher when the command "Look at me" is given. In addition, the teacher may decide to reward behavior similar to or leading toward the desired behavior, a technique referred to as *shaping the behavior*. For example, when the command "Look at me" is given, a reward would be given if the student lifted her head briefly, even if she did not maintain eye contact. Of course, the goal is for students to be able to use the skills they learn in the discrete trial training across settings and situations.

### Prompting

As you just learned, a **prompt** is a cue designed to get a student to perform a specific behavior, and it is effective in promoting student achievement. Prompts frequently are used by professionals working with students with autism spectrum disorders, and prompts vary based on their intrusiveness. For example, a physical prompt is very intrusive, with the teacher physically engaging the student (e.g., moving the student's hand to the pencil or turning the student's head toward the task). Somewhat less intrusive are gestures, such as pointing or signing, guiding the student where to look or move. Verbal questions or statements are even less intrusive prompts, involving no physical prompting at all. Finally, a written prompt, such as a cue card or keyword taped to the student's desk, is the least intrusive

### dimensions of
**DIVERSITY**

At least one study (Mandell, Listerud, Levy, & Pinto-Martin, 2002) has found that African American children receiving Medicaid benefits tend to be diagnosed with autism approximately 2 years later than comparable white children.

prompt. Prompts help students to learn without repeatedly making mistakes. How might you use prompts if you were working with students like Lance, Geneva, or Casey, the students introduced at the beginning of the chapter?

## Social Skills Supports

Perhaps the most important area of intervention for students with autism spectrum disorders is social skills (White, & Roberson-Nay, 2009). Social skills interventions generally are positive behavior supports designed to enhance opportunities for social interaction, reduce problem behaviors, and build new competencies that have a positive impact on quality of life (Gutstein & Whitney, 2002; Myles et al., 2000). Specific issues that can be addressed include understanding the thoughts and feelings of others, following social rules, and learning self-monitoring (Barnhill, Cook, Tebbenkamp, & Myles, 2002; Leaf et al., 2009).

### Instruction

Unlike many typical learners, students with autism spectrum disorders must be directly taught the social skills they need to be successful. One example of an intervention for this purpose is the *power card strategy*, a visually based technique that uses a student's special interests to facilitate understanding of social situations, routines, and the meaning of language (Gagnon, 2001). This intervention contains two components: a script and a power card. A teacher, therapist, or parent develops a brief script, written at the child's comprehension level, detailing the problem situation or target behavior. It includes a description of the behavior and describes how the child's special interest has addressed that social challenge. The power card, which is the size of a business card or trading card, contains a picture of the special interest and a summary of the solution. The power card can be carried; attached to the inside of a book, notebook, or locker; or placed on the corner of a child's desk (Gagnon, 2001). The Positive Behavior Supports provides an example of this technique.

*Some students with autism learn more effectively when teachers prompt them using physical assistance, gestures, or questions.*

### Social Stories

A **social story** is an individualized text or story that describes a specific social situation from the student's perspective. The description may include where and why the situation occurs, how others feel or react, or what prompts their feelings and reactions (Chan & O'Reilly,

---

### Power Card: Teaching Appropriate Behavior Using Special Interests

Professionals sometimes use the special interests of students with autism to help them learn appropriate ways to behave in particular situations. For example, for Cheyenne, a student who was fascinated with Elvis Presley, the following story was written. Then it was summarized, incorporating an appropriate picture, onto a power card that Cheyenne could keep on her desk or carry in her backpack.

#### Elvis and His Fans

Elvis Presley loves being the king of rock-and-roll, but sometimes it is difficult for him to be nice to everyone. At the end of a long day in the recording studio or after a concert, he is often tired, and it is difficult for him to be nice to fans and friends. Elvis has learned, however, that it is important to smile at people he meets and say nice things to everyone, even when he is tired. He

has learned that if he can't say something nice, it is better to just smile and say nothing at all. He stops and thinks about comments he makes before he says anything.

Just like Elvis, it is important for young people to think before they talk. It would make Elvis proud when preteens and teenagers remember to do the following:

1. Think before you say anything. Say it in your head first before saying it out loud.
2. If you can't think of anything nice to say, don't say anything.
3. You do not have to say every thought out loud that you think.

When kids who love Elvis remember these three things, Elvis says, "Thank you, thank you very much!"

## Learning Appropriate Behavior with SOCCSS

SOCCSS (situation, options, consequences, choices, strategies, simulation) is a strategy for helping students with autism spectrum disorders to understand cause and effect and to plan how to respond in certain situations. These are the six steps to SOCCSS:

1. *Situation.* The teacher and student identify what happened or what could happen using questions such as these: What was the problem? What is the goal to prevent a problem?

2. *Options.* Brainstorming is the next step: What are things to do to reach the goal? Note that at this step the teacher accepts all the student's responses.

3. *Consequences.* For each option, possible consequences are identified. The purpose of this step is to help the student understand cause and effect.

4. *Choices.* With teacher guidance, the student prioritizes the choices, selecting the one with the most positive consequences.

5. *Strategies.* The teacher and student develop a plan of action for the choice selected. The goal is for the student to feel a sense of ownership of the plan.

6. *Simulation.* The student role plays the situation, incorporating the selected choice, or writes out the plan in order to be prepared to respond to the situation.

The accompanying SOCCSS worksheet illustrates how the steps are implemented. What are the advantages of implementing the SOCCSS strategy with students with autism spectrum disorders? What challenges might occur? For what types of classroom situations might it be valuable?

| *SOCCSS* **Worksheet** | | |
|---|---|---|
| **Situation** | | |
| Who | What | |
| When | Why | |

| Options | Consequences | Choices |
|---|---|---|
|  |  |  |
|  |  |  |
|  |  |  |

| Strategies |
|---|
|  |

| Simulation Type | Simulation Outcomes |
|---|---|
|  |  |

| Follow-Up |
|---|
|  |

Source: From Myles, B. S., & Simpson, R. L. (2001). *Intervention in School and Clinic 36*, pp. 279–286. Copyright © 2001 by SAGE Publications Inc. Reproduced with permission of SAGE Publications, Inc.

2008; Gray, 2000; Reynhout & Carter, 2009). Social stories may be written documents, or they can be paired with pictures, audiotapes, or videotapes. They may be created by any professional or the parent, often with student input. Casey, the student you met in the chapter introduction, was provided with a social story to help him understand his peers' meaning in calling him a dog.

### SOCCSS

The *situation, options, consequences, choices, strategies, simulation (SOCCSS)* strategy helps students with social disabilities understand social situations and develop problem-solving skills by putting social and behavioral issues into a sequential form (Roosa, 1995). Specifically, this teacher-directed strategy helps students understand cause and effect and realize that they can influence the outcomes of many situations with the decisions they make. The

**fyi**

Ivor Lovaas and colleagues introduced intensive behavioral programs for children with autism spectrum disorders in 1966. Today, you may still hear people refer to *Lovaas treatment.*

strategy can be used with an individual student or as a group activity, depending on the situation and students' needs. Although this strategy is designed to be interpretive, it also can be used as an instructional strategy. That is, teachers can identify problems students are likely to encounter and address them using SOCCSS so that students have a plan prior to a situation occurring. More detail on this strategy can be found in the Positive Behavior Supports.

research
**NOTE**

Starr, Szatmari, Bryson, and Zwaigenbaum (2003) compared students with autism and Asperger syndrome. They found that the latter group displayed fewer and less severe symptoms of the disorder and that these results were stable across time.

---

## REVIEW · REFLECT · DISCUSS

1. Identify a common challenge faced by students at the level you are interested in (elementary, middle school, high school). It could concern teasing, forgetting assignments, or being respectful of others. Create a social story to help students successfully face the challenge. What did you learn by completing this exercise?

2. Take one of the students (Lance, Geneva, Casey) you met at the beginning of the chapter. Imagine what his or her school day might include and create a visual schedule that would help that student learn and follow daily routines.

## Perspectives of Parents and Families

dimensions of
**DIVERSITY**

Overton, Fielding, and Alba (2007), when clinically assessing 28 Hispanic children thought to have autism, found that 18 of them had the disorder, with four having a comorbid disorder. They concluded the clinical and cultural complexities of identifying children in this area may affect their representation in this disability category.

Parents of children with autism spectrum disorders usually are the first to recognize that their youngsters are responding differently to the world than are typically developing children. Some parents have reported that as an infant, their child was perfectly content to lie quietly in the crib staring at toys. The infant appeared to be a "good baby." One mother was convinced that her toddler was gifted because before the age of two, he recognized all of the letters of the alphabet and could read several sight words. However, the child seldom initiated interactions with those in his environment.

Many parents of children with autism spectrum disorders begin to suspect that something is different in their child's development sometime after the child's first birthday. For example, the child may become attached to an object such as a stuffed animal and tantrum uncontrollably when the object is not in sight, or the child may show no interest in play, preferring to watch videos for hours on end. Initially, the pediatrician may assure worried parents that there is nothing to be concerned about, but usually nagging doubts persist.

### Family Needs for Information and Support

Following diagnosis, parents may become frustrated because even though they have a name for their child's unique differences, they have little idea what to do about them. Many families of children with autism have found that early intervention, often with an intensive one-to-one home program, enables their children to make progress in the areas of behavior, communication, socialization, and self-help. This type of program, although beneficial to many children with autism spectrum disorders, requires a time commitment of 30 or 40 hours per week and can be emotionally and financially taxing for families.

Parents of children with autism spectrum disorders may find themselves forced to play demanding roles in the lives of their children. In order to provide appropriate education, parents need to be familiar with the latest research on autism, understand special education law, and know how to be effective advocates for their children. Many parents have learned how to collaborate effectively with the professionals who provide services to their children and are valuable members of the school's educational team. These parents understand the value of knowing the characteristics of autism and effective educational practices. Parents of children with these disorders also need skills related to resolving differences within a constructive atmosphere and providing support for the professionals who work with their children.

*Families of children with autism spectrum disorders cannot be described in any single way: They may experience joy, but they also often face many challenges.*

Like parents of children with other disabilities, parents of children with autism spectrum disorders often feel concern about their children's welfare in the years ahead, their children's ability to function independently at some point, and the community's acceptance of their children. Mothers of children with autism also report more stress in their lives than do mothers of children with other disabilities.

Parents of children with autism spectrum disorders benefit from the availability of both formal and informal social support, but such support must be individualized to meet the needs of each family. Potential sources of support include classroom teachers, IEP team members, pediatricians and other health professionals, and other families of children with autism. Families often find that attending a local support group provides much-needed information and support.

A recent study by Myers, Mackintosh, and Goin-Kochel (2009) affirmed the complexity of parenting a child with autism. In an on-line survey of nearly 500 of these parents, they found that parents described their experiences through five major themes with both positive and negative examples. The themes related to stress; the child's behavior; parents' well-being, including the impact on work and marriage; family impact; and social isolation. Here is an example of a parent's positive comments:

> He has made us 'see the light' and reprioritize. Things we used to think were important are no longer important. Our goals are no longer career oriented. We enjoy life a little more. Our biggest priorities are being happy, having fun, and doing whatever it takes to make sure that E will be a happy and self-sufficient adult (p. 678)

Here is an example of a parent quote expressing the negative impact of having a child with autism:

> I have 3 other children who are often embarrassed by their brother and often hear others laughing at him. It is difficult to go anywhere as a family. His brothers have no privacy, have had many of their possessions broken, have been physically hurt by their brother, and, of course, must 'stand in line' for their needs. (p. 679)

## The Roles of Siblings

Siblings often play important yet demanding roles in the lives of their brothers or sisters with autism spectrum disorders, often believing that they need to assume parental roles for them, even as youngsters (Bleach, 2001). For example, they may be required to take on additional responsibilities in the home and serve as care providers in the absence of a parent. Despite having demands placed on them, siblings' knowledge of the disability may be limited. They should have access to resources appropriate to their developmental levels and be as well educated as their parents in the area of autism (Glasberg, 2000). Many nondiagnosed siblings feel that they frequently are ignored in day-to-day family life. They may exhibit more difficulties in emotional, behavioral, and social adjustments and with peer interactions (Hastings, 2003), although many establish strong, positive relationships with their sibling with autism spectrum disorder (Orsmond, Kuo, & Seltzer, 2009). It is vital that parents help siblings pursue their own interests and spend time with them away from the sibling with autism.

**web link**

www.autism-pdd.net
The Autism–PDD Resources Network includes information especially designed for parents and children. Topics range from basics about special education through planning for college to estate planning.

## REVIEW · REFLECT · DISCUSS

1. Think about your current family or the family in which you grew up. How would having a child or sibling with an autism spectrum disorder affect it? How can you use this information to help you appreciate the complexities families of these students may experience?

2. Parents of children with autism often need assistance in learning how to respond to their children's behaviors and how to advocate for their children at school. How can professionals help ensure that collaboration occurs with these parents?

## Trends and Issues Affecting the Field of Autism Spectrum Disorders

research
**NOTE**

Robertson, Chamberlain, and Kasari (2003) studied the relationship between general education teachers and elementary students with autism. An inverse relationship was found—that is, teachers' perceptions were more positive when students exhibited lower levels of behavior problems.

The field of autism spectrum disorders is still relatively young, yet it is faced with several significant issues. Among those issues are those related to more accurate information on assessment, diagnosis, and prevalence; the need for research to identify effective interventions; and the lack of adequate professional preparation programs for teachers for these students.

### Assessment, Diagnosis, and Prevalence

One dilemma for the field of autism is the difficulty of early identification (Williams, Atkins, & Soles, 2009). Many parents of young children who eventually are diagnosed as having autism spectrum disorders initially are told that nothing is amiss. Given that the most positive outcomes tend to accrue to children who begin interventions at the earliest ages, it is imperative that better assessment procedures be identified for use with young children, that pediatricians become more sensitive to the possibility of autism being present, and that efforts be made to more accurately identify the prevalence of these disorders.

In addition, a research agenda is needed that will lead to a greater understanding of the neurological, behavioral, and developmental characteristics of autism spectrum disorders. This, in turn, might help professionals identify key indicators of autism much earlier in a child's life.

As you learned earlier in this chapter, the prevalence estimates for autism spectrum disorders vary significantly. Does this matter? Yes. Resources often are allocated to study a disorder and to provide innovative treatments based on its prevalence, and so more accurate prevalence estimates of autism, especially those published by federal agencies such as the National Institutes of Health, might lead to more resource allocation.

### Evidence-Based Interventions

Just as for other disability areas, concern exists in the field of autism spectrum disorders to find effective and research-based approaches for teaching students (Simpson, 2008). This view is held by researchers, practitioners, and parents (Simpson, McKee, Teeter, & Beytien, 2007). At the same time, some professionals who work with individuals with autism spectrum disorders advocate for particular intervention approaches with good intentions, but their preferences sometimes are based on personal experience and not on research. In fact, many debates about the effectiveness of interventions for students with autism spectrum disorders rely more on emotion than on data. Some of the interventions that have been recommended for which researchers have not been able to independently replicate the claims of those advocating the treatments include the following (Schectman, 2007): auditory integration training, facilitated communication, use of secretin (i.e., a hormone aiding digestion that sometimes is given therapeutically to children), use of vitamin B6 and magnesium, dietary interventions (e.g., eliminating gluten and casein), chelation therapy (a detoxification procedure designed to address the concern that mercury poisoning is the cause of autism), and hyperbaric oxygen therapy (breathing extra oxygen in a pressurized chamber). A Web search would yield many sites related to these unproven approaches.

To address treatments such as these, studies that compare their impact on students need to be undertaken and the results shared with practitioners and parents. In the meantime, you may find that parents insist on the effectiveness of particular treatments or interventions, and you should be prepared to seek out accurate information about them. You also may need to consider the complex ethical issues that may be raised: You should not advocate such treatments, and although you can discuss your concerns with parents, you may not be able to convince them of your views.

## Training and Support

Before autism was included as a separate disability category in IDEA in 1990, students with these disorders often received services from professionals prepared to work with students with severe and multiple disabilities or intellectual disabilities. Since 1990, the number of students identified with ASD has grown quickly, but far too few university programs provide coursework to prepare professionals to work with these students (Hess, Morrier, Heflin, & Ivey, 2008). Further, regional resource and training centers and local agencies still are unable to adequately support the needs of local schools and families for information and skills (Lerman, Vorndran, Addison, & Kuhn, 2004). For example, teachers have to become familiar with rapidly changing theories and approaches, they need to clearly understand behavioral techniques, they have to know how to select and use appropriate assistive technology, and they must have considerable knowledge of language acquisition and use and understand how to foster language development in their students. In addition, they have to be adept at creating needed adaptations in the environment, gathering data, and working collaboratively with parents, paraprofessionals, and colleagues (National Research Council, 2001). The need for school personnel and families to receive accurate and up-to-date information remains a challenge for this field.

## REVIEW · REFLECT · DISCUSS

1. Do you think it is a positive or a negative that some professionals are working to ensure that more children with autism are identified at very young ages? Defend your answer.
2. Using the websites provided throughout this chapter, look for information about the research base for interventions for students with autism. What did you find? That is, what are points being made by experts in the field? What interventions seem to definitely be research-based?

# Summary

- The study of autism spectrum disorders is relatively young, having begun with Kanner's work published in 1944. Today, these disorders are understood to have a biological rather than an environmental basis.
- At least two distinct groups of students with these disabilities have been identified: those with autism and those with Asperger syndrome. Although the term *autism spectrum disorders (ASD)* is not used in federal special education or American Psychiatric Association definitions, it now is used to convey the heterogeneity of individuals with these disabilities.
- Students with autism spectrum disorders may experience difficulties in cognitive and academic functioning, social and emotional abilities, and appropriate behavior. They also may experience a variety of sensory challenges.
- These students usually are identified at a young age with input from education, medical, family members, and others.

- Students with autism are entitled to the same special education services and supports as other children with disabilities, although they are less likely than many other students to be placed in general education for most of the school day.
- Interventions for students with autism spectrum disorders can be grouped into these categories: environmental supports, assistive technology, instructional supports, and social skills supports.
- Parents of children with autism spectrum disorders often need information about how to work with their children and support for themselves. Siblings, too, may need assistance.
- Issues facing the field of autism include the need for better assessment and identification procedures, more accurate prevalence estimates, more and better quality research on the effectiveness of interventions, and additional resources for preparing professionals to work with these students.

Council for Exceptional Children

## ADDRESSING THE PROFESSIONAL STANDARDS

Council for Exceptional Children (CEC) Common Core Knowledge and Skills addressed in this chapter:

ICC1K5, ICC1K6, ICC1K7, ICC1K8, ICC2K1, ICC2K2, ICC2K4, ICC2K6, ICC3K2, ICC3K3, ICC3K4, ICC4S3, ICC4S6, ICC5K4, ICC5K8, ICC5S3, ICC6K4, ICC7K1, ICC7S2, ICC8K1, ICC8S2, ICC8S6, ICC10K3, ICC10S4

Appendix: Provides a full listing of the CEC Common Core Standards, and associated Knowledge and Skill Statements listed here.

## PEARSON myeducationlab

Now go to Topic 13: Autism, in the MyEducationLab (www.myeducationlab.com) for your course, where you can:

- Find learning outcomes for the broad concepts covered in this chapter along with the national standards that connect to these outcomes.
- Complete Assignments and Activities that can help you more deeply understand the chapter content.
- Examine challenging situations presented in the IRIS Center Resources.
- Apply and practice your understanding of the core concepts and skills identified in the chapter with the Building Teaching Skills and Dispositions learning units.

- Check your comprehension on the content covered in the chapter by going to the Study Plan in the Book Specific Resources for your text. Here you will be able to take a chapter quiz, receive feedback on your answers, and then access Review, Practice, and Enrichment activities to enhance your understanding of chapter content.
- Watch video clips of CCSSO Teacher of the Year award winners responding to the question: "Why I teach?" in the Teacher Talk section.

## chapter eleven

# Students with Deafness and Hearing Loss

Written by John L. Luckner, University of Northern Colorado, and Marilyn Friend

## LEARNING OBJECTIVES

- Outline the development of the field of deaf education, define *deafness* and *hearing loss,* outline their prevalence, and explain their causes and types.
- Describe characteristics of individuals who are deaf or hard of hearing, including the impact of hearing loss on language and academic skills, social interaction opportunities, and career attainment.
- Discuss how hearing loss is identified.
- Identify the educational settings in which students who are deaf or hard of hearing may receive services, and describe the advantages and disadvantages for them in general education classrooms.
- Outline recommended educational practices for students who are deaf or hard of hearing.
- Discuss the perspectives of the parents and families of a child who is deaf or hard of hearing.
- Identify trends influencing the field of deaf education.

## Paige

Paige is seven years old. She has a profound bilateral sensorineural hearing loss which occurred when she contracted cytomegalovirus (CMV) as an infant. At the age of three, Paige received a cochlear implant in her left ear. She wears a behind-the-ear hearing aid in her right ear. She lives with her mother and five-year-old sister and visits her father on weekends. The family first used *contact signing* (i.e., a combination of vocabulary and grammar from both English and American Sign Language) to communicate with Paige, but they stopped signing after she received her cochlear implant. From the ages of three to five, Paige attended a general education preschool in her neighborhood where she received support from a teacher of students who are deaf or hard of hearing and a speech language pathologist. She currently rides a bus a short distance daily to attend a local elementary school that has a center-based program for students who are deaf or hard of hearing. At school, she spends the majority of her day in a general education second grade classroom. Because she is delayed in her vocabulary; use of grammatical markers such as plurals and past tense markers; and use of articles, pronouns and prepositional phrases, she also spends an hour a day in the resource room for students who are deaf or hard of hearing for additional instruction and practice. Paige also works with the speech language pathologist for 30 minutes, twice a week. Paige wears her cochlear implant and hearing aid at school and home. The general education classroom is equipped with a sound-field amplification system. The teacher believes that many students who do not have an identified hearing loss also benefit from the system. Paige has both hearing and deaf friends and loves to tell stories about her pets and her little "troublemaker" of a sister.

## Zachary

Zachary is a seventh-grade student at Morehead Middle School. He has a moderate hearing loss as a result of an illness he contracted at the age of 18 months. Zachary is also identified as having an intellectual disability. Zachary spends each morning in his special education classroom, where Mr. Reynolds, his special education teacher, helps him and his classmates with their reading, language arts, and math skills. In the afternoon, Zachary participates in the science class with his peers without disabilities, accompanied by a teaching assistant who supports the science teacher by assisting Zachary and three other students with disabilities in the class.

Zachary also participates in exploratory classes with his classmates; during this quarter of the school year, they have an occupational exploration class where they are learning about careers. Zachary communicates using some signs, some spoken words, and some gestures. His individualized education program (IEP) goals for this year include reading and math goals but also asking for assistance before becoming frustrated as well as participating appropriately in small-group activities with his peers. Mr. Reynolds is concerned about Zachary. Twice recently, the science teacher asked the assistant to escort Zachary from the room after he became very upset when he did not understand the teacher's directions. Mr. Reynolds is planning to meet with the teacher and the school psychologist after school tomorrow to discuss exactly what happened and then to consider whether Zachary might benefit from a behavior intervention plan.

## JJ

JJ is a nineteen-year-old high school senior. He has a severe hearing loss affecting both ears. He was born in Guadalajara, Mexico and moved to the United States when he was three years old. He was identified as having a hearing loss at the age of six by an educational audiologist. He lives with his parents, maternal grandparents, a younger sister, and twin brother, who does not have a hearing loss. The family communicates using predominately monolingual Spanish, but JJ's primary method of communicating is sign language. He has been fitted with hearing aids but refuses to wear them. JJ spends the majority of his school day in the special education room at the secondary center-based high school program in the town where he lives. He spends very little time in the general education classroom because of the difficulties he has with receptive, expressive, and written language. In his classroom, he works with a teacher of the deaf on academics and life skills. He is well behaved, respectful of teachers, and interested in learning and completing his assignments. However, he becomes easily frustrated because of his language and literacy deficits. At lunch and during breaks he interacts with other students who are deaf or hard of hearing, but he does not usually socialize with hearing students. Since JJ's twin brother graduated from high school a year ago, JJ has been talking about quitting school so he can work and earn money. However, his mother insists that he stay in school. He likes working on automobiles and hopes to help his father fix cars when he leaves high school.

I magine how your life might be different if you faced situations such as these on a daily basis:

- Being unable to use the drive-through at a restaurant because it requires the use of a speakerphone
- Needing to rely on another person, an interpreter, to talk to teachers, friends, and others
- Thinking that you have vacuumed the entire room before realizing the plug was pulled out

As you walk across campus, drive around town, or go shopping, you see many people talking on their cell phones or listening to music on their personal stereo systems. We live in a sound-oriented society, and it is through sound that extensive amounts of information are conveyed, either deliberately or incidentally, through conversation (Scheetz, 2001). Family members discuss the events of the day, work through problems, and talk about upcoming activities, all within the earshot of children. By listening to these conversations and interacting through language with parents, neighbors, and others, children acquire and refine their communication skills, learn concepts, and develop social skills. Individuals who are deaf or hard of hearing often are cut off from such direct and incidental communication experiences. This not only affects their ability to develop communication and language skills, but it also negatively affects their experiential background as well as their knowledge of the world (Stewart & Kluwin, 2001).

## Understanding Deafness and Hearing Loss

The long history of specialized education for students who are deaf or hard of hearing, illustrated in Figure 11.1, still strongly influences contemporary understanding of these individuals and how they are educated. However, evolving priorities in federal special education law and advances in technology are now changing professionals' understanding of these students and their needs.

### Development of the Field of Deaf Education

Many professionals agree that the earliest special education in the United States began when Thomas Hopkins Gallaudet opened the American Asylum for the Education of the Deaf and Dumb (now the American School for the Deaf) on April 15, 1817, in Hartford, Connecticut (Winzer, 1993). This model, a residential school away from populated areas, became a national standard and was often the only option available to these children until the middle of the twentieth century (Stewart & Kluwin, 2001) when attitudes toward individu-

**PEARSON**

**myeducationlab**

To check your comprehension on the content covered in Chapter 11, go to the Book Specific Resources in the MyEducationLab (www .myeducationlab.com) for your course, select your text, and complete the Study Plan. Here you will be able to take a chapter quiz, receive feedback on your answers, and then access review, practice, and enrichment activities to enhance your understanding of chapter content.

**FIGURE 11.1**
**Timeline for the Development of the Field of Deafness**

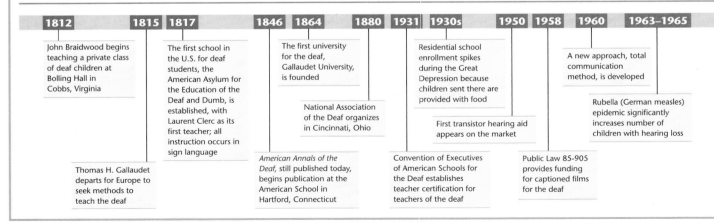

als with disabilities began to shift. Especially during the 1960s, after the number of children who were deaf or hard of hearing increased significantly as a result of the rubella (i.e., measles) epidemic, residential schools were inundated. As a result, more local schools were forced to begin providing education to students who could not be accommodated in residential settings.

Another aspect of the history of the field of hearing loss is communication method. During the late nineteenth century, debate erupted about whether students who were deaf or hard of hearing should use sign language or oral language. The latter view prevailed and it profoundly affected the American field of deaf education for many years (Zapien, 1998). Students in the residential schools were prohibited from signing; it was believed that if students signed, they would not learn to speak. Many students who had never heard or used oral language were very frustrated, as were their teachers. Although this extreme view was eventually modified, controversy about communication methods is still characteristic of the field of deaf education today.

When Public Law (P.L.) 94-142 (now the Individuals with Disabilities Education Act, or IDEA) was passed in 1975, a wider variety of educational options for children with hearing loss became available for the first time. Since then, emphasis has centered on the appropriate and least restrictive settings for educating students who are deaf or hard of hearing and researching the most effective communication methods (Gallaudet Research Institute, 2008). Consequently, most residential schools for the deaf, once these students' most likely educational option, have experienced a decline in enrollment, and several have closed.

## Definitions of Deafness and Hearing Loss

Although the treatment of individuals who are deaf is much better today than in the past and far more educational options exist, disagreement continues about what it means to be deaf or hard of hearing. The three most frequently discussed views of deafness suggest that it is (a) a disability, impairment, disorder, or ailment; (b) a logistical problem, especially in terms of contact with the hearing community; or (c) a social community/culture in its own right (Freebody & Power, 2001). Although each perspective is discussed in more detail later in the chapter, now is a good time for you to think about how deafness may be perceived from each viewpoint.

Many terms are used to describe an individual who has a **hearing loss,** which is the general term used in this chapter to distinguish among various types of hearing disorders. People may describe themselves as being deaf, Deaf, hard of hearing, hearing impaired, or having a hearing disorder. Initially, you might think that deafness would be a simple concept describing a condition that could be diagnosed through administration of a hearing test. However, the psychological, cultural, and educational issues that are unique to

Alexander Graham Bell, the inventor of the telephone, proposed legislation that would prohibit congenitally deaf individuals from marrying each other.

Go to the Assignments and Activities section of Topic 15: Sensory Impairment, in the MyEducation-Lab for your course and complete the activity entitled "Hearing Impairment".

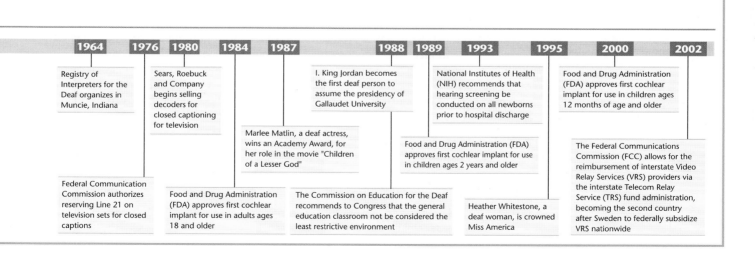

Timeline:

**1964** — Registry of Interpreters for the Deaf organizes in Muncie, Indiana

Federal Communication Commission authorizes reserving Line 21 on television sets for closed captions

**1976** — Sears, Roebuck and Company begins selling decoders for closed captioning for television

**1980** — Food and Drug Administration (FDA) approves first cochlear implant for use in adults ages 18 and older

**1984** — Marlee Matlin, a deaf actress, wins an Academy Award, for her role in the movie "Children of a Lesser God"

**1987** — The Commission on Education for the Deaf recommends to Congress that the general education classroom not be considered the least restrictive environment

**1988** — I. King Jordan becomes the first deaf person to assume the presidency of Gallaudet University

**1989** — Food and Drug Administration (FDA) approves first cochlear implant for use in children ages 2 years and older

**1993** — National Institutes of Health (NIH) recommends that hearing screening be conducted on all newborns prior to hospital discharge

Heather Whitestone, a deaf woman, is crowned Miss America

**1995** — Food and Drug Administration (FDA) approves first cochlear implant for use in children ages 12 months of age and older

**2000** — The Federal Communications Commission (FCC) allows for the reimbursement of interstate Video Relay Services (VRS) providers via the interstate Telecom Relay Service (TRS) fund administration, becoming the second country after Sweden to federally subsidize VRS nationwide

**2002**

*Early, consistent communication is essential for optimal development.*

## web link

www.agbell.org
The Alexander Graham Bell Association for the Deaf and Hard of Hearing is an international organization and resource center on hearing loss and spoken language approaches and related issues.

## fyi

An alarming number of young people, ranging in age from six to nineteen, have reported some degree of hearing loss resulting from exposure to excessive noise from rock concerts, personal listening devices, lawn mowers, snowmobiles, and other sources.

individuals who have a hearing loss make it more difficult to define; it is not a simple matter of saying that an individual has a particular percentage of a hearing loss. Examples of considerations include the age of onset of the hearing loss, the cause of the hearing loss, the age at which intervention began, the family response, the hearing status of the family, the presence of additional disabilities, and the type of education program attended.

### Federal Definitions

A starting point for precise definitions is the federal law. It uses two terms related to hearing loss, **hearing impairment** and **deafness**:

> Hearing impairment means an impairment in hearing, whether permanent or fluctuating, that adversely affects a child's educational performance but that is not included under the definition of deafness in this section. (IDEA 20 U.S.C. §1401 [2004], 20 C.F.R. §300.8[c][5])

> Deafness means a hearing impairment that is so severe that the child is impaired in processing linguistic information through hearing, with or without amplification, [and] that adversely affects a child's educational performance. (IDEA 20 U.S.C. §1401 [2004], 20 C.F.R. §300.8[c][3])

Some of the technical aspects of these definitions (e.g., fluctuating hearing loss) are addressed later in the chapter. What you can see is that these definitions are based on the first perspective mentioned—the one focusing on disability or impairment. Note that, as for all disabilities, the hearing loss must negatively affect educational performance. Finally, you might wonder about one related term discussed in Chapter One: *deaf–blindness.* Students who have both of those disabilities are not considered in this chapter; their extraordinary special needs are addressed in Chapter Fourteen.

### Additional Information on Definitions

The federal definitions related to hearing loss are not particularly controversial, but they are somewhat incomplete. Although still not representing consensus among all those in the field, the National Center for Education Statistics (2002c) has extended the federal definitions:

> *Hearing impairment*—An impairment in hearing, whether permanent or fluctuating, that adversely affects a child's educational performance, in the most severe case because the child is impaired in processing linguistic information through hearing. (p. 546)

*Deafness*—Having a hearing impairment which is so severe that the student is impaired in processing linguistic information through hearing (with or without amplification) and which adversely affects educational performance. (p. 546)

*Hard of hearing*—Having a hearing impairment, whether permanent or fluctuating, which adversely affects the student's educational performance, but which is not included under the definition of "deaf." (p. 546)

If you compare the two sets of definitions, you will notice that although the definitions of *deafness* are virtually identical, the definition of *hearing impairment* is clarified in the second set and a definition for **hard of hearing** is added.

### Deaf Culture

In considering definitions, it is also important to recognize use of the term *Deaf* with a capital *D*. This term is used to refer to members of the **Deaf community** who embrace **Deaf culture,** a unique subset of American society (Padden & Humphries, 1988). Membership in the Deaf community varies from place to place. Factors often mentioned as important for Deaf culture identity include (1) being deaf; (2) using **American Sign Language (ASL)** as a primary means of communicating, which is a visual-gesturing language that has its own rules of grammar distinct from English; and (3) attending a residential school for the deaf (Lane, Hoffmeister, & Bahan, 1996).

However, the fundamental value of Deaf culture is that deafness is not a disability—that is, it is not a condition that needs to be "fixed." Instead, deafness is viewed as an identity with its own rich history, traditions, and language (Obasi, 2008). The Deaf community often organizes local, regional, state, national, and international events such as conferences, athletic competitions, art shows, plays, and pageants.

## *Prevalence of Hearing Loss*

No single set of data can adequately convey the prevalence of hearing loss. For example, the National Center for Health Statistics (n.d.) reports that more than 34 million persons in the United States have a hearing loss. As you might suspect, the highest prevalence is among individuals who are sixty-five years of age and older. For students in public schools, the National Association of State Directors of Special Education (2006) reports that approximately 1.5 out of every 1,000 school-age children have an educationally significant hearing loss. Included in this group are children who are deaf and hard of hearing, as well as those who have a hearing loss in one ear, called a *unilateral hearing loss.* The U.S. Department of Education (2009) reports that approximately 1.3 percent of all school-age students ages six to twenty-one who receive special education services are served under the disability category of hearing impairment. This represents a total of 71,112 students in American public schools.

### Hearing Loss and Other Disabilities

Research suggests that approximately 40 percent of all students who are deaf or hard of hearing have one or more additional, educationally significant disabilities, similar to Zachary, whom you met at the beginning of this chapter (Gallaudet Research Institute, 2008). The most frequently reported conditions include intellectual disabilities, learning disabilities, attention deficit–hyperactivity disorder (ADHD), and other health impairments. These students also may have cerebral palsy, a physical disability described in Chapter Thirteen. These students are unique (Vernon & Rhodes, 2009), and decision making regarding their education should emphasize looking at their strengths and preferences as a basis for instructional planning and meaningfully engaging families as participants in that planning (Guardino, 2008; Jones, Jones, & Ewing, 2006).

## *Causes of Hearing Loss*

A hearing loss can occur before or after birth. A loss that is present at birth is referred to as a **congenital hearing loss.** One that develops after birth is referred to as an **acquired,** or **adventitious, hearing loss.** Most education professionals are less interested in whether a hearing loss is congenital or acquired than they are in whether the loss was **prelingual,** prior

**web link**

www.deaflinx.com
Deaf Linx was established to provide factual information and resources in support of a Deaf-friendly world.

**fyi**

Between 50 and 85 percent of adults in the United States are infected with *cytomegalovirus,* a member of the herpes virus family (as are chickenpox and fever blisters). Although this virus usually is not a cause for concern, when a pregnant woman contracts it for the first time and transmits it to her unborn child, the child is at high risk for hearing loss (as was Paige at the beginning of the chapter), vision loss, or intellectual disabilities.

*Many, but not all, students with hearing loss also have other disabilities.*

to speech and language development, or **postlingual,** after speech and language have developed. Generally, professionals agree that the longer children have had normal hearing, the greater the chance that they will maintain the knowledge and ability to use the language and communication skills they have developed (Schwartz, 2007).

### Prelingual Causes of Hearing Loss

Do you remember reading about genetic causes of other disabilities, including intellectual disabilities? In the field of deaf education, more than half of all hearing losses in children are believed to have genetic causes (National Institute on Deafness and Other Communication Disorders, 2000). A **genetic hearing loss** is one caused by the presence of an abnormal gene within one or more chromosomes. Either one or both of the parents may have passed on this abnormal gene, or it may have developed as the result of a spontaneous mutation or change during fetal development.

Approximately 95 percent of children who are deaf or hard of hearing have hearing parents because most genetic hearing loss is the result of a recessive genetic trait rather than a dominant genetic trait (Mitchell & Karchmer, 2004). That is, both parents must have the trait before it can be transmitted, and even then the probability of the child being deaf is only one in four. Similarly, most deaf parents have hearing children.

Prelingual causes of hearing loss that are not hereditary include prenatal infections, illnesses, or conditions occurring at the time of birth or shortly thereafter. Examples include these:

- Intrauterine infections, including rubella (i.e., German measles), cytomegalovirus, and herpes simplex virus
- Prematurity
- Maternal diabetes
- Toxemia during pregnancy, a condition that includes dangerously high blood pressure in the mother
- Anoxia (i.e., lack of oxygen) before, during, or after birth
- Malformation of ear structures

### Postlingual Causes of Hearing Loss

A postlingual hearing loss usually happens as the result of a disease or an injury. Examples of conditions that can cause acquired hearing loss in children and youth include the following:

- Bacterial meningitis—an infection of the fluid of a person's spinal cord and the fluid that surrounds the brain
- Otitis media—ear infections that often are caused when bacteria related to a child's cold or other illness get inside the ear and produce fluids and mucus that are trapped there; these infections affect three out of four children by the time they are three years old
- Ototoxic drugs—medications that can cause hearing loss
- Measles
- Encephalitis—an inflammation of the brain caused by a virus that, in severe cases, is accompanied by high fever, severe headache, nausea and vomiting, stiff neck, double vision, drowsiness, and disorientation
- Chicken pox
- Influenza (i.e., the flu)
- Mumps
- Head injury
- Repeated exposure to loud noise

Many of these causes have been introduced in other chapters, and they demonstrate how single illnesses or injuries can result in several types of disabilities.

## Types of Hearing Loss

In the deaf and hard-of-hearing field, the causes of hearing loss are closely related to the type of hearing loss that a person has. In order to understand the different types of hearing loss that individuals' experience, it is useful to understand the process of hearing. As you can see by examining Figure 11.2, hearing occurs when sound waves enter the outer ear and travel through the auditory canal to the *eardrum*, where tiny bones vibrate to amplify the sound and send it into the inner ear. There, the **cochlea,** a fluid-filled hearing organ that contains thousands of tiny cells with hairlike projections, experiences wavelike motions. These movements prompt the hair cells—the sensory organs that allow us to hear—to send messages to the brain, where they are translated into what we recognize as sound.

Hearing loss can be classified into three basic types, depending on the location of the impairment within the ear:

**1. Conductive hearing loss.** A conductive hearing loss occurs when a problem of the outer or middle ear prevents sound from being conducted to the inner ear. This type of hearing loss can exist if part of the external or middle ear is not fully developed or if it develops abnormally. A conductive hearing loss also can be caused by disease within the external ear or the middle ear that leaves fluid or causes wax buildup, leading to improper movement of the eardrum, or **ossicles,** the three small bones in the middle ear. Conductive hearing losses often can be improved through surgery, medication, and **amplification**—that is, personal hearing aids or other **assistive listening devices,** hard-wired or wireless transmitting and receiving instruments that send sound from a microphone directly to the listener, minimizing the effect of distance, noise, and reverberation on clarity.

**2. Sensorineural hearing loss.** A sensorineural hearing loss is caused by a problem in the inner ear or along the nerve pathway to the brain stem. As a result, the sound that travels

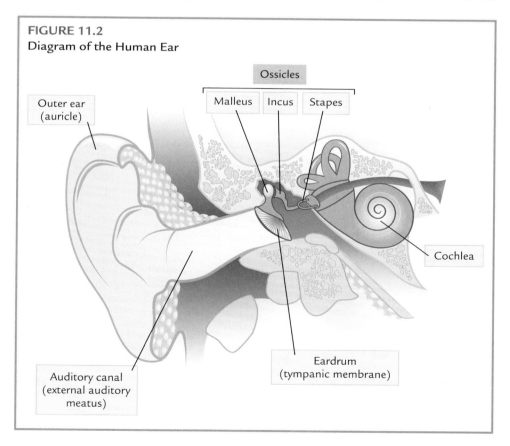

**FIGURE 11.2**
**Diagram of the Human Ear**

Ossicles

Malleus  Incus  Stapes

Outer ear
(auricle)

Cochlea

Auditory canal
(external auditory
meatus)

Eardrum
(tympanic membrane)

to the inner ear and brain stem is not delivered at all or is much softer or distorted. JJ, one of the students you met in the chapter opening, has sensorineural hearing loss.

**3. Mixed hearing loss.** A mixed hearing loss involves both a conductive and a sensorineural loss.

Two important additional factors in the discussion of types of hearing losses concern whether the hearing loss is bilateral or unilateral and whether the hearing loss fluctuates. A **bilateral hearing loss** is a loss in both ears; a **unilateral hearing loss** refers to a loss in only one ear. An individual with a unilateral hearing loss may experience difficulty localizing sound and listening in noisy settings. An individual with a **fluctuating hearing loss** may function differently from day to day because of periodic ear infections or a buildup of fluid or earwax.

### Degree of Hearing Loss

One additional concept usually considered when discussing causes of hearing loss is the degree of loss—that is, the quantity and quality of sound that individuals with a hearing loss are able to process that affects their ability to understand and produce spoken language. Hearing loss is measured in **decibels (dB)**, a measure of the intensity or loudness of sound. Whispering is about 20 to 25 dB; normal conversation is about 60 dB; a child screaming is about 90 dB. More important than the cause or type of hearing loss is the amount of residual hearing that an individual has and can use. As you can see by examining Figure 11.3, the degree of hearing loss usually is explained by the use of seven classifications that can be arranged along a continuum that runs from normal hearing to a profound hearing loss. Mitchell (2004) reports that approximately 60 percent of children receiving special education services have mild to moderate hearing losses and approximately 40 percent have severe or profound hearing losses.

Keep in mind that this is a very general classification system. The ability to use residual hearing varies from individual to individual and is affected by additional variables, such as age of identification, use of amplification, the auditory environment, and cultural identity.

Hearing ear dogs are trained to assist people who are deaf or hard of hearing. The dogs are trained to distinguish among sounds such as a siren, a crying baby, a car horn, and a ringing telephone and to alert their owners.

## REVIEW · REFLECT · DISCUSS

1. Have you ever heard about Deaf culture? As you think about it, what similarities can you draw between your own cultural background and Deaf culture? Consider looking for other resources about Deaf culture to learn more about it.

2. Three diverse perspectives of deafness were introduced in this chapter: (a) as a disability or impairment; (b) as a logistic problem, especially in contact with the hearing community; and (c) as a social community/culture in its own right. How might each of these perspectives influence educators' beliefs about students with hearing loss and their approach to teaching these students? What is the basis for your thinking?

# Characteristics of Individuals Who Are Deaf or Hard of Hearing

As you might expect, the population of individuals who are deaf or hard of hearing is very diverse. Hearing losses range from mild to profound. Some individuals with a hearing loss use American Sign Language (ASL) and identify with the Deaf community. Other people who are deaf or hard of hearing use both sign language and spoken language to communicate, and they have friends who are deaf, hard of hearing, and hearing. In addition, some individuals who are deaf or hard of hearing prefer to communicate using speech, are able to use their residual hearing, and function primarily in the general hearing society.

## Hearing Loss and Child Development

A hearing loss may alter a student's development in two specific ways: (a) in the area of communication, which in turn influences many other areas of development; and (b) in the area of experiential learning.

### Impact on Communication

The first point to remember in a discussion on the importance of communication is that children who are deaf or hard of hearing and have parents with a hearing loss differ in many respects from children who are deaf or hard of hearing and have hearing parents. Parents who are deaf or hard of hearing themselves often are able to communicate with their children sooner and with greater facility than hearing parents. As a result, research suggests that children who are deaf with parents who are deaf develop ASL skills at a similar rate as the spoken English skills of same-age hearing peers (Newport & Meier, 1985).

Like breathing, food, water, and sleep, communication is a basic human need. Communication is fundamental to everything we do every day: It defines and gives meaning to our emotions, beliefs, hopes, imaginations, and life experiences (California Department of Education, 2000; Siegel, 2000). Human infants are uniquely born with the ability to interact with their caregivers (Schore, 2000). Communication between infants and their caregivers is essential for two reasons. First, communication develops emotional bonds between children and their caregivers. Second, children acquire language as a result of early conversations with their caregivers. Through these interactions children learn the underlying rules of the language used by the adults in their lives (Schirmer, 2001).

For children who are deaf or hard of hearing, the quality and quantity of interactions and communication partners tend to differ significantly from those of other children (Brasel & Quigley, 1977; McGowan, Nittrouer, & Chenausky, 2008). As noted earlier, most children who are deaf or hard of hearing are born to hearing parents who generally use spoken language as their primary means of communicating with others. In addition, because hearing loss is a low-incidence disability—that is, one that is far less common than learning and behavior disabilities—most parents have never come into contact with a person who is deaf or hard of hearing. Consequently, they have a limited understanding of what it is like to have a hearing loss. Further, families with a child who has a hearing loss face the additional burden of having to decide what communication approach they will use with their child. Take the time to review the options in Figure 11.4, and you will see why this is often a difficult decision for many families.

Go to the Assignments and Activities section of Topic 15: Sensory Impairment, in the MyEducation-Lab for your course and complete the activity entitled "Life with Hearing Loss".

research
**NOTE**

The earlier a child is identified as having a hearing loss and the earlier the family accesses resources to support it, the more the child's language development will be comparable to that of hearing children (Yoshinaga-Itano, 2003).

## FIGURE 11.4
### Communication Options for Individuals Who Are Deaf or Hard of Hearing

| | Spoken English | Cued Speech | Signing Exact English (SEE2) | Signed English | Contact Signing/ Pidgin Sign English (PSE) | American Sign Language (ASL) |
|---|---|---|---|---|---|---|
| Description | Individual taught to use residual hearing as effectively as possible through the use of hearing aids, cochlear implants, FM systems, or other assistive listening devices, while simultaneously developing speech skills. | Sound-based visual communication system using eight hand shapes in four different locations ("cues") in combination with the natural mouth movements of speech; supplements speechreading and aided residual hearing. | An invented system developed to visually represent morphemes of English. Used while simultaneously speaking. Approximately 65% of SEE signs are borrowed from ASL. Others adapted using initialized forms (e.g., b hand shape for band). Also, prefixes (e.g., im, dis) and suffixes (s, ed, ing) are added. For example, the word unbelievable would be signed UN-BELIEVABLE-ABLE. | Users speak and sign at the same time, using English word order. Some signs borrowed from ASL while others borrowed from SEE. A more simple sign system than SEE2 because there are only 14 grammatical markers used (i.e., affixes). Does not have firm rules about signing literally or conceptually. | Viewed as a "bridge" between native ASL users and native English speakers. ASL signs usually used in English word order. Certain elements of English, such as function words, articles, pronouns, and prepositions omitted to speed up communication. | A visual-gestural language recognized as a true language in its own right. Does not follow the grammatical structure of English; it has its own grammar and syntax. You cannot sign ASL and speak simultaneously. The grammar of ASL is expressed through body movement and facial expression. Used extensively within the Deaf community, a group that views itself as having a separate culture and identity from mainstream hearing society. |
| Potential Strengths | Speech is the primary mode of communication worldwide for social exchanges and provides the basis for the development of literacy skills. | System can be learned quickly, about 20 hours, although proficiency takes longer. English grammar is learned; and reading and writing skills develop approximately at the same rate as hearing peers. | Considered easier to learn than ASL for hearing individuals because it follows English word order. | Considered easier to learn for individuals who have already internalized English. Shows the use of verb tense markers, articles and prepositions of English. | Like ASL, this is a visual/conceptual system of communication. Individuals can voice and sign simultaneously, but it is not always used that way. | A beautiful language. Many deaf people consider ASL to be the most natural and accessible language for them because of its visual properties. |
| Potential Limitations | Learning spoken English can be frustrating for those who do not benefit from amplification or were late identified. If this approach is not successful, individuals may have limited ways to communicate with others and experience language development delays, adversely affecting learning and social-emotional development. | Not used as commonly as other approaches; consequently, the number of people who cue is very limited. It is not truly a communication system since it is used to enhance receptive language skills; generally, individuals do not cue to express themselves. | Not a true language. Often described by native ASL users as artificial and cumbersome. Takes longer to convey messages. SEE2 is signed literally, not conceptually like ASL. | Not a true language. Cannot show every aspect of spoken English since there is no sign equivalent for many affixes. No community of adult users exists. | Not a true language—it is not ASL, nor is it English. Varies widely depending on communication partners' linguistic background and competence. | Can be challenging to make the transition from ASL as the first language to English as the second language through reading and writing. Can be difficult to develop speech and audition skills. A shortage of native ASL users makes it difficult for some schools to implement a true bilingual/bicultural program. |

**Experiential Learning**

The second way that a hearing loss may alter an individual's development concerns the reduction in quantity and quality of direct and vicarious experiences. Learning is experiential in nature. We learn the characteristics of a concept as a result of numerous experiences with it. As a child's world of experience expands, deeper understandings are constructed. For example, think about your own ability to manage and use money. You began by being able to identify coins and bills. Education and experience helped you develop the skills to make purchases and count your change. Through additional training and practice, you learned how to use a checking account and an ATM. Figure 11.5 illustrates the potential differences in communication patterns, as well as overall opportunities for direct and incidental learning, that may exist for individuals who are hearing as compared to individuals who are deaf or hard of hearing (Scheetz, 2001).

Life experiences and concepts are stored and organized in memory structures called *schemata*. A schema (the singular of schemata) is a framework that enables us to organize a large amount of information into a unit of knowledge (Borich & Tombari, 1997). For example, each of us has schemata for topics such as clothing, sports, insects, and music. Yet it is likely that we have slightly different schemata for the same concepts based on our individual interests and experiences. The more knowledge we acquire, the more elaborate our schemata become, and having more knowledge helps us organize information into accessible pathways. Conversely, the lack of experiences and/or the inability to access enough information creates gaps in pathways, making access more difficult. As a result of the gaps in experiential background, students who are deaf or hard of hearing may lack the schemata needed for following some abstract conversations, being able to comprehend what is happening in a story, understanding current events, or solving multistep problems (Stewart & Kluwin, 2001).

As you can see, children with hearing loss often do not bring to their educational experience the same extensive language, conceptual, and experiential knowledge that their hearing peers do. These deficits greatly affect most aspects of their educational process.

**web link**

http://www.pepnet.org/
PEPNet is a national network of regional centers that provides resources, information, in-service training, and expertise to enhance educational opportunities for individuals who are deaf or hard of hearing and their families.

## Cognitive Characteristics

Early research on the cognitive skills of individuals who were deaf or hard of hearing routinely found them to lag behind their hearing peers. The tests used in those studies often required comprehension of English and spoken language. Thus, many researchers were confusing cognitive ability with language ability. More recently, a variety of tests of cognitive ability have been developed that include nonverbal performance measures, such as tracing from a starting point to a stopping point on an increasingly complex maze and identifying the correct geometric form to put next in a sequence. The results of these studies indicate that a hearing loss in and of itself imposes no limitation on the cognitive capabilities of an individual (Moores, 2001; Scheetz, 2001). For example, Braden (1994) conducted a meta-analysis (i.e., a study that examines the results of other studies) of the research literature on the effect of hearing loss on intelligence. He reported similar IQ distributions between the hearing and deaf/hard-of-hearing groups.

## Academic Characteristics

The discussion earlier in this section regarding the presence or absence of early communication has important consequences for the children's development of academic skills. During the first years of life, basic language skills are acquired. Children who do not acquire age-appropriate language skills face both immediate challenges in being able to communicate with others as well as long-term struggles to acquire information. Simply stated, a hearing loss presents a potential barrier to communication, which in turn influences most areas of development, including those related to academic achievement. This central point is explained later in greater detail.

### Language

Language is central to everything that we do because it is the means for communicating with others, thinking, and learning (Schirmer, 2001). Even though children who are deaf or hard

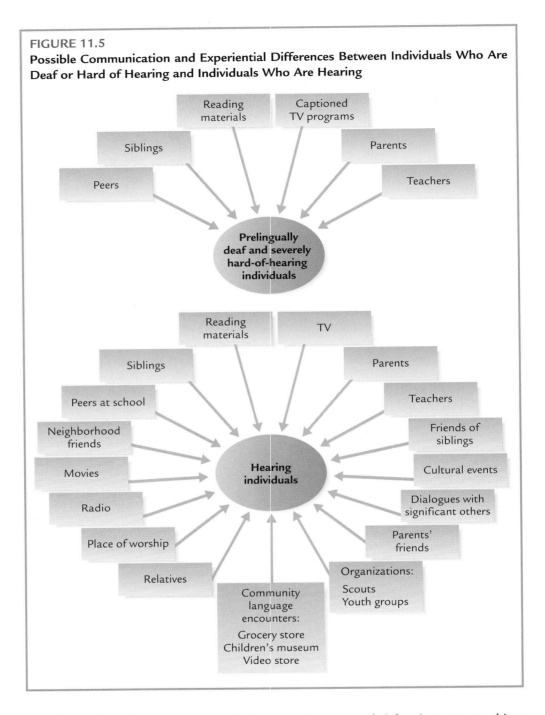

**FIGURE 11.5**

**Possible Communication and Experiential Differences Between Individuals Who Are Deaf or Hard of Hearing and Individuals Who Are Hearing**

of hearing have the same cognitive ability to learn language as their hearing peers, to achieve their linguistic potential they need to interact with adults and other children who consistently talk and/or sign with them. The experience of seeing, hearing, and forming words stimulates brain development in ways that help the child communicate more effectively (Diamond & Hopson, 1998). Consequently, a clear relationship exists between children's progress in language learning and the amount of conversation they have with sophisticated language users (Hart & Risley, 1999; Wells, 1986).

Communicating with others enables children to plan, explore, problem solve, question, and discuss. Unfortunately, many children and adolescents who are deaf or hard of hearing do not engage in conversations with family members, peers, or professionals (Tye-Murray, 1994). When they do have conversations, those interactions often are controlled by adults

**fyi**

In 1886, William Hoy became the first deaf person to play major league baseball. Hoy is credited with creating the hand signals still used in baseball today to indicate balls and strikes.

and consist of question-and-answer interchanges that are linguistically simple, concrete, and literal (Wood & Wood, 1997). This pattern of limited conversations can have negative long-term effects on the ability of individuals who are deaf or hard of hearing to acquire reading skills, access the curriculum, relate cause and effect, solve problems, and make thoughtful decisions about behaviors.

## Reading

You might assume that reading would not be a problem for students who are deaf or hard of hearing because hearing is not needed to read. That is not the case. Reading is a complex skill that challenges most students with a hearing loss, primarily because of the communication and language development connection. Acquisition of a first language and ongoing language development throughout early childhood and elementary school are necessary for individuals to become skilled readers (Goldin-Meadow & Mayberry, 2001). Sadly, many students who are deaf or hard of hearing are learning to read at the same time that they are learning to communicate and use language, and difficulties result.

Research on the performance of students who are deaf or hard of hearing using standardized tests of reading comprehension suggests that, on average, they encounter great difficulty in processing standard English in print. For example, Traxler (2000) presented achievement data for students who are deaf or hard of hearing for the ninth edition of the Stanford Achievement Test. She reported that for eighteen-year-old students, the median grade level for reading comprehension was just below the fourth grade. She also found a median score of fourth-grade level for vocabulary.

One additional factor makes the acquisition of reading skills difficult for students who are deaf or hard of hearing. Many children with a hearing loss do not have books read to them by adults, which has been determined to be an essential component in literacy development (Adams, 1990; Aram, Most, & Simon, 2008). Adults often do not read books to children who are deaf or hard of hearing because they feel uncomfortable signing, have a limited sign vocabulary, or find it difficult to find a comfortable way to seat the child and hold the book to accomplish satisfactory visual contact (Paul, 1998; Stewart & Kluwin, 2001).

Although the majority of students who are deaf or hard of hearing struggle to become fluent readers, some of these students perform on grade level when compared to their hearing peers (Erickson, 1987; Geers & Moog, 1989). The factors suggested to explain these students' success include the quality and quantity of interactions with significant others, parent participation in their education, supportive early educational environments, and high-quality educational programs (Donne & Zigmond, 2008; Marschark, Convertino, & LaRock, 2006; Paul, 1998).

## Written Language

Like reading, writing can pose challenges for students who are deaf or hard of hearing. In fact, research suggests that the problems faced by these students in mastering written English are even more formidable than those they encounter in developing reading skills (Moores, 2001).

The problems that students who are deaf or hard of hearing often experience with writing have to do with the fact that writing is considered a secondary form of linguistic expression, and thus it is highly dependent on a primary language system, such as speech or sign, as a foundation. Additionally, many students who are deaf or hard of hearing struggle with the mechanical as well as the organizational aspects of writing. In general, researchers find that

Steinberg, Bain, Yuelin, Montoya, and Ruperto (2002) studied the decisions that Hispanic families made regarding their children identified as deaf or hard of hearing. The researchers found that language barriers made it more difficult for these parents to obtain information about options available. These parents also tended to be dissuaded from investigating cochlear implants as an option for their children.

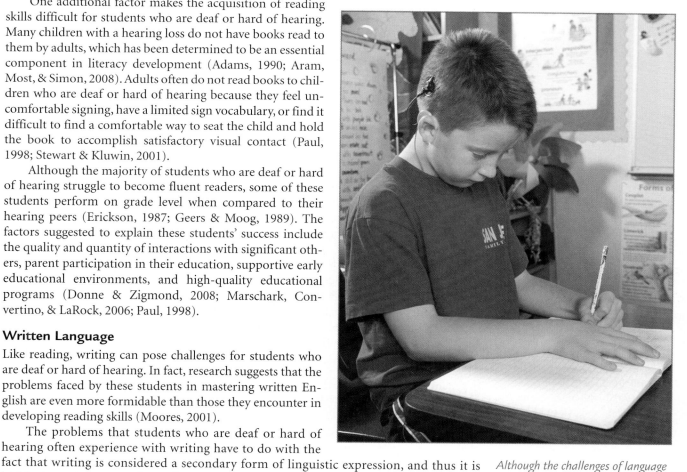

*Although the challenges of language development can create difficulty in reading, some students with hearing loss read at grade level.*

Sample from a teenager who is deaf and experiencing difficulty acquiring written language skills

### Coyote

My Dad hunt Coyote. coyote almost kill my Dog. My Dog are OK now My dad said not Dead I am glad of them. My DaD took my dog to Dr Because I need white to make Better on friday night. Dad Said My Dad will watch coyote. Coyote will not Come here at 3:30 am at morning my Dad Said oh hunt Dog My Dog are sick I will move my Dog in mollys house I have more to hunt to Coyote for Coloardo Sping to Dr my Shop name is S.p.zazzephanie.

the end

Sample from a twelve-year-old who is deaf and has developed many written language skills

### Hiking. The good points and the bad.

Hiking can be easy and fun. Mostly though it is hard. The good points are, I like to eat with my friends and walk with them in the mountains. I never get bored. I like to swin in Prarie mountain lake, and have a picnic, and have some fun.

My favorite exercise is walking on trails, and walking up White Chuck mountain. I would like to hike in warm weather, not too hot, and no rain.

The bad points are no bathroom. I have to find a secret place to go the bathroom. I hate bugs. The mosquitoes are the worse and I hate falling in the mud, because it is dirty, wet, and no change of clothes.

The bad weather includes lightning. It is dangerous. If I were to be hit by lightning I would be shocked. Bad weather also includes rain. Hard and soft and often it is cold. Wild animals can be dangerous. Bears, Bigfoot and mountain lions. I would be very scared to be lost in the woods. That is why I hike with my Dad and my brother. Sometimes with Mom also.

The mountains are wonderful. Dangerous only to the unprepared.

students who are deaf or hard of hearing continue to make slow improvement in written language throughout their educational programs (e.g., Woblers, 2008; Yoshinaga-Itano & Downey, 1996). In Figure 11.6, the first written language sample is from a thirteen-year-old girl with a profound, bilateral, sensorineural hearing loss. It illustrates how some skill deficits compromise a student's ability to successfully communicate using written language.

As noted in the research on reading, students who are deaf and hard of hearing comprise a highly heterogeneous group of writers. Many students have become successful (Aram, Most, & Simon, 2008; Schirmer, Bailey, & Fitzgerald, 1999), and some even have become award-winning journalists (e.g., Kisor, 1990). If you examine the second sample in Figure 11.6 and compare it to the first sample, you can see that these two students with similar hearing losses have vast differences in their writing abilities.

## Mathematics

In general, students who are deaf or hard of hearing achieve at a higher grade level in mathematics than in reading or writing, although their achievement level generally still is problematic. For example, Traxler (2000) reported that the median grade level in mathematics for eighteen-year-old students who were deaf or hard of hearing was just below a sixth-grade level for computation and a fifth-grade level for problem solving.

Pagliaro (2006) has identified three primary factors that cause students who are deaf or hard of hearing to perform poorly in mathematics:

1. *Experiential deficits*—Lack of incidental mathematics learning negatively affects the building of schemata. Unlike their hearing peers, these students do not get opportuni-

**web link**

http://center.uncg.edu
The Collaborative Early Intervention National Training e-Resource (CENT-eR) is designed to inform and support graduate-level professionals serving families with infants and toddlers who are deaf or hard of hearing through web-based training. You can sample the training modules at the CENT-eR website.

ties to overhear adults talking about such topics as 20 percent discounts, buy-one-get-one-free sales, and increased gas prices.

2. *Language difficulties*—As in other areas, mathematics uses specialized language such as conditionals, comparatives, negatives, inferentials, abbreviations, and symbols that combine to create barriers to mathematical concepts for students who are deaf or hard of hearing.

3. *Traditionally based instruction*—Rote memorization of facts, formulas, and algorithms through drill-and-practice and worksheets filled with computation exercises sometimes are used instead of opportunities to engage in problem solving and conceptual development.

To address these problems, educators must raise their expectations for students who are deaf or hard of hearing in the area of mathematics, present experiences that build students' background mathematical knowledge, teach the language of mathematics as well as the application, and integrate mathematics throughout the curriculum (Pagliaro 2006; Stewart & Kluwin, 2001).

## Social and Emotional Characteristics

The manner in which each of us understands others, our culture, and ourselves is strongly influenced by direct interactions as well as incidental learning. For many children and youth who are deaf or hard of hearing, both of these areas often are compromised. For example, their impoverished diet of early conversations often continues into the preschool years, where they have fewer interactions as well as less exposure to social and emotional language. This lack of interaction and limited opportunities to observe proficient users of social skills negatively affects the social and emotional development of these students.

As a result of these challenges, children and youth who are deaf or hard of hearing tend to have fewer friends, parents who have more restrictive rules for behavior, and parents who are unable to communicate expectations about social interactions (Marschark, 1997). When parents and adults cannot fluently communicate with the child who is deaf or hard of hearing, they are unable to explain the causes of other people's social and emotional behavior and cannot provide feedback about the child's behavior. Similarly, when adults are unable to communicate well with children who are deaf or hard of hearing, they tend to solve the children's problems for them rather than explain what to do, offer assistance, or give feedback. Thus, the linguistic and cognitive complexity of tasks often is reduced for these students (Greenberg & Kusché, 1993).

Socialization in educational settings is an area of particular concern for students who are deaf or hard of hearing. Some proponents of educating these students in general education settings contend that this is the best environment for developing social skills because the students have opportunities to interact with peers who are both hearing and deaf or hard of hearing. However, research has demonstrated that students who are deaf or hard of hearing are unlikely to form positive relationships with hearing peers unless efforts are made by professionals to bridge the communication barrier and to structure situations where positive interactions can occur (e.g., Antia, Kreimeyer, & Eldredge, 1994; Coyner, 1993; Maxon, Brackett, & van den Berg, 1991).

## Behavior Characteristics

To behave in socially appropriate ways, children and youth have to consider alternatives in social situations. Students who are deaf or hard of hearing often lag behind their hearing peers in recognizing the reasons for other people's behaviors, in part because they are less likely to receive or overhear explanations for those behaviors. As a result, students who are deaf or hard of hearing may not understand why people act or react the way that they do (Marschark, 1997). In addition, most of us learn to understand our emotions and the subtle differences between emotions (e.g., anger, frustration, disappointment) by interacting with others, who explain how they are feeling or who describe how we might be feeling. Again, as a result of limited conversational partners, many students who are deaf or hard of hearing have a limited vocabulary of emotional language that helps them understand

research
**NOTE**

Titus, Schiller, & Guthmann (2008) found that youth with hearing loss who were admitted to substance abuse treatment facilities reported similar rates of marijuana and alcohol use, but they had a more severe level of involvement and were more likely to have been victims of abuse.

their own feelings or those of others (Greenberg & Kusché, 1993; Schirmer, 2001). One successful approach for addressing the behavior problems that students who are deaf or hard of hearing may experience is called PATHS. The Positive Behavior Supports describes this approach.

## REVIEW · REFLECT · DISCUSS

1. What are examples of experiential learning that children with typical hearing go through in their preschool years that children with significant hearing loss may not encounter? How might these differences affect these children's learning when they reach school age?

2. If you had a child who was identified as having a severe hearing loss at birth, would you teach her sign language? Why or why not? What factors would influence your decision?

# Identifying a Hearing Loss

For a student to receive services as deaf or hard of hearing through IDEA, the formal procedure for assessment, identification, and eligibility must be followed as it is for all students who might be eligible. The central concern is the student's capabilities and limitations related to hearing. However, as demonstrated in the following discussion, other areas of assessment also must be addressed.

## Audiological Evaluation

A hearing loss is identified through the process of a hearing screening and/or an audiological evaluation. Hearing screenings are often conducted on newborns before they leave the hospital, a topic discussed later in the chapter. In most states, this procedure is now a common practice.

The purposes of an **audiological evaluation,** a specialized series of hearing tests, are to determine if a hearing loss exists and to quantify and qualify hearing in terms of the degree of hearing loss, the type of hearing loss, and the configuration of the hearing loss. Degree and type of hearing loss have already been discussed. To determine the *configuration* of the hearing loss, the audiologist looks at qualitative attributes such as bilateral versus unilateral hearing loss, high-frequency versus low-frequency hearing loss, and flat versus sloping and stable versus fluctuating hearing loss. The audiologic evaluation consists of a battery of tests, including the following:

- A case history
- A physical examination of the outer ear, the ear canal, and the eardrum
- A pure-tone audiometry test of hearing that is recorded on a graph called an **audiogram**
- Tests of middle ear function

After the test battery has been completed, the audiologist reviews each component to obtain a profile of hearing abilities and needs.

Audiological evaluations also are carried out to periodically check the status of an individual's hearing loss. Specifically, professionals are interested in finding answers to these questions:

- Has the hearing loss improved as a result of medical intervention?
- Does the hearing loss fluctuate?
- Is the hearing loss progressively getting worse?

Simultaneously, it also is important to monitor whether students are benefiting from the use of amplification (e.g., personal hearing aids or assistive listening devices). Professionals want answers to questions such as these:

- Does the amplification work correctly?
- Does the hearing aid fit well?

## Promoting Alternative Thinking Strategies

The Promoting Alternative Thinking Strategies (PATHS) Curriculum (Kusché & Greenberg, 1993) is a comprehensive program for promoting emotional and social competencies and reducing aggression and behavior problems in elementary school-age children. PATHS consists of approximately 130 lessons initially developed for students who are deaf or hard of hearing, but it is currently being used with hearing students as well as with other students with special needs.

The authors recommend that the PATHS Curriculum be taught three times per week for a minimum of 20 to 30 minutes per day. The curriculum provides teachers with systematic, developmentally based lessons, materials, and instructions for teaching their students emotional literacy, self-control, social competence, positive peer relations, and interpersonal problem-solving skills. A key objective of promoting these developmental skills is to prevent or reduce behavioral and emotional problems. PATHS lessons include instruction in many areas:

- Identifying and labeling feelings
- Expressing feelings
- Assessing the intensity of feelings
- Managing feelings
- Understanding the difference between feelings and behaviors
- Delaying gratification
- Controlling impulses

- Reducing stress
- Practicing self-talk
- Reading and interpreting social cues
- Understanding the perspectives of others
- Using steps for problem solving and decision making
- Having a positive attitude toward life
- Developing self-awareness
- Learning nonverbal and verbal communication skills

Research examining the effectiveness of using the PATHS Curriculum with students who are deaf or hard of hearing has demonstrated significant improvements for program youth compared to control youth in the following areas (e.g., Greenberg & Kusché, 1993):

- Self-control
- Ability to tolerate frustration
- Social problem solving
- Recognition and understanding of emotions
- Social/emotional adjustment

As you review the topics included in PATHS, which do you think might be most appropriate for all students? Which would pertain primarily to students who are deaf or hard of hearing? What is your opinion about incorporating such a program in general education programs and special education programs?

- Is the power setting on the hearing aid set properly?
- Should a different type of hearing aid be tried?

## Other Assessments

Although hearing is the primary consideration for eligibility for services in this disability category, other areas are not ignored. For example, the multidisciplinary team checks the student's vision and requests information about the student's overall health. An intelligence test is administered, as is an individual achievement test. These assessment procedures enable the team to determine whether the student is achieving at an expected level. Remember that measuring intelligence for students who have significant hearing loss usually involves the use of special tests that do not depend on the student's language skills. These students also complete an assessment of their specific communication skills, and teachers and parents may be asked to complete inventories regarding students' social and emotional functioning as well as their school and home behavior. For older students, an assessment related to transition goals is included.

## Determination of Eligibility

The multidisciplinary team considers all the information gathered about the student in deciding whether the hearing loss constitutes a disability that requires providing special education services. Although federal law does not specify a minimum threshold of hearing loss that would make a student eligible for services and some states do not set forth more specific guidelines, the following student characteristics, measured through formal tests, often are considered:

- Inability to recognize most words spoken at a conversational level in a quiet room without the use of assistive devices
- A significant receptive or expressive language delay
- Impairment of speech articulation, voice, or fluency

- A significant discrepancy between verbal and nonverbal performance on an intelligence test
- Significant delay in the development of reading skills because of language deficit or overall significantly lower than expected academic achievement
- Inattention or serious behavior problems related to the hearing loss

If the multidisciplinary team determines that special education is appropriate, members then prepare the IEP and make decisions about communication methods and the need for language support (e.g., the need for interpreter services). Then the team members determine the educational setting in which the student's needs can best be met.

## REVIEW · REFLECT · DISCUSS

1. In addition to assessments related to audiology, what other domains are considered in deciding whether a student should be eligible to receive special education services as deaf or hard of hearing? How might hearing loss affect the assessment?

2. Why might parental input be particularly important in assessing a student with a hearing loss for possible special education services?

# How Learners Who Are Deaf or Hard of Hearing Receive Their Education

The overriding concern in determining the appropriate and least restrictive educational environment for children who are deaf or hard of hearing was addressed by the U.S. Department of Education in 1992. In a document titled "Deaf Students Education Services Policy Guidance," five considerations were listed for determining appropriate educational placements and IEP development for students who are deaf or hard of hearing:

1. Preferred communication needs of the child and family
2. Linguistic needs
3. Severity of hearing loss and potential for using residual hearing
4. Academic level
5. Social, emotional, and cultural needs, including opportunities for peer interactions and communication (U.S. Department of Education, 1992a)

These factors are used to help shape today's educational options for students who are deaf or hard of hearing.

PEARSON
**myeducationlab**

Go to the Assignments and Activities section of Topic 15: Sensory Impairment, in the MyEducationLab for your course and complete the activity entitled "The Inclusion of Students with Hearing Loss".

## Early Childhood

Early childhood services can begin as soon as a baby has been identified as having a hearing loss. Services usually are provided by a state's department of health or department of education. The goals of early intervention are these:

1. To help the family understand hearing loss and gain confidence as parents of children who are deaf or hard of hearing
2. To help the baby who is deaf or hard of hearing learn to communicate, to use any available hearing, and to interact socially
3. To help the baby become a fully participating member of the family (Boys Town National Research Hospital, n.d.)

An early intervention specialist for these children has knowledge about hearing loss and its effect on development. The family works closely with the specialist to identify needs, set priorities, help locate resources, and get questions answered. The specialist schedules regular visits to the family's home or another natural environment such as a daycare setting or to a place where the child spends a majority of time.

*The majority of students who are deaf or hard of hearing attend general education classes with their hearing peers.*

The early intervention specialist also serves as the central point of contact between the family and the school program and/or other professionals. The specialist works with the family to identify and meet the baby's needs by coordinating both formal and informal supports. An example of a formal support is the coordination of the multidisciplinary team to work with the family to determine strengths, needs, and resources. Examples of informal support include helping families participate in a parent group; organizing social gatherings and play groups; and introducing the family to deaf adults or to organizations such as the American Society for Deaf Children (ASDC), Hands and Voices, and Hearing Loss Association of America (HLAA).

## Elementary and Secondary School Services

Elementary and secondary school services for students who are deaf or hard of hearing tend to occur in a variety of educational placements. As shown by the data presented in Figure 11.7, a large majority of these students are enrolled in typical public schools, but just slightly more than half participate in general education nearly all day (U.S. Department of Education, 2009). Many receive resource or self-contained classroom special education support. The placements that most school districts and states provide for students who are deaf or hard of hearing usually include those described in the following sections.

### General Education Classroom

Students who are deaf or hard of hearing may receive their entire educational program with their hearing

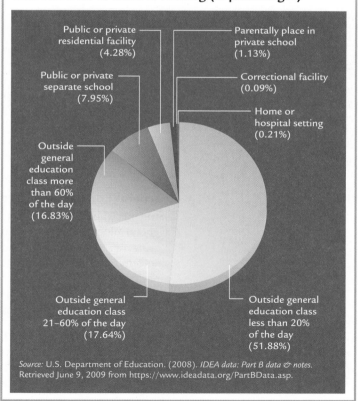

**FIGURE 11.7**

**Educational Placements of Students Ages Six to Twenty-One Who Are Deaf or Hard of Hearing (in percentages)**

- Public or private residential facility (4.28%)
- Parentally place in private school (1.13%)
- Public or private separate school (7.95%)
- Correctional facility (0.09%)
- Home or hospital setting (0.21%)
- Outside general education class more than 60% of the day (16.83%)
- Outside general education class 21–60% of the day (17.64%)
- Outside general education class less than 20% of the day (51.88%)

*Source:* U.S. Department of Education. (2008). *IDEA data: Part B data & notes.* Retrieved June 9, 2009 from https://www.ideadata.org/PartBData.asp.

## Using Technology to Provide Classroom Supports

### C-print

*C-print* is a computer-aided, speech-to-print transcription system developed as a classroom support service for students who are deaf or hard of hearing in general education classrooms.

- A typist called the *C-print captionist* types the teacher's lecture as well as students' comments into a laptop computer that has word-processing and abbreviation software.
- The typed information is simultaneously displayed on a second laptop computer or television monitor for students who are deaf or hard of hearing to read during the lecture or discussion.
- The captionist uses a computerized abbreviation system to type the words of the teacher and students as they are spoken. The text display of the message appears approximately three seconds after the words are spoken and remains on the screen for approximately one minute.
- The text files are saved and can be used by students, tutors, and instructors after class by reading them on a monitor or from a printed copy (Elliot, Stinson, McKee, Everhart, & Francis, 2001).

The system was developed by researchers at the National Technical Institute for the Deaf (NTID) to improve the classroom experiences for secondary and college students who are deaf or hard of hearing. It also can be used in other settings, such as community and business meetings.

Research indicates that many students who are deaf or hard of hearing prefer C-print to using an interpreter and that the C-print real-time display enables them to achieve a high level of comprehension of lecture material (e.g., Stinson & McKee, 2000). Limitations of C-print include the lag time between what is said and what appears on the screen, the captionist's possible difficulty in capturing other students' comments, and C-print's inability to capture visual material, such as illustrations and mathematical formulae.

### Sign Language Software

Vcom3D (www.vcom3d.com/Profile.htm) has developed animated GIFs (graphical interchange formats) and movies of signs that focus on vocabulary and concepts covered in the curriculum of early education classes (i.e., pre-kindergarten through third grade). This company also has developed an educational software product called Reading Power, which focuses on storytelling, conversation, and tools to build comprehension and vocabulary.

In addition, Vcom3D has collaborated with TERC to develop an interactive three-dimensional (3D) sign language dictionary of science terms and definitions to support access to standards-based science content for elementary- and middle-grade students. Each product uses animated 3D characters, called *signing avatars*. The characters can produce movements of the fingers and hands, facial gestures, body movements, and co-signs, in which two different words or ideas are signed at the same time. The characters can be programmed to communicate in either ASL or signed English.

---

## fyi

In addition to laws and policies that encourage educating students who are deaf or hard of hearing in general education, the increasing use of cochlear implants also is contributing to this trend (Miller, 2008).

peers. They may be accompanied by an **interpreter** (i.e., a person who helps someone with hearing loss to communicate by translating what is said into signs or words with cues) in order for the students to meet their communication needs. Alternatively, they may use technology for this purpose as explained in the Technology Notes. In many instances, though, a teacher of students who are deaf or hard of hearing monitors the academic and social progress of these students and consults with general education teachers to make appropriate accommodations and modifications. In some areas, this consultation model is used when one teacher for students who are deaf or hard of hearing is responsible for students in several schools (Foster & Cue, 2009), as Amy Sinclair describes in the Firsthand Account.

### General Education Classroom with Supplementary Instruction

Students who are deaf or hard of hearing may receive the majority of their instruction from general education teachers and also be provided direct instruction, additional practice, tutoring, or specialized skills instruction by a teacher of students who are deaf or hard of hearing and/or a speech/language pathologist. These services often are arranged during a specific block of time each week, and the instruction can occur in the general education classroom or in a resource room. This service relies on effective collaboration among all the professionals working on behalf of the student.

### Separate Class for Students Who Are Deaf or Hard of Hearing

Slightly less than one in five students who are deaf or hard of hearing receive most or all of their instruction from a teacher of students who are deaf or hard of hearing in a special education classroom. These students are most likely to interact with their hearing peers during lunch, recess, art, library, physical education, extracurricular activities, and other school functions.

**AMY SINCLAIR** *is a deaf educator who works with students in several schools. Here, she describes the many experiences she has already had in this role.*

I am an itinerant teacher for students who are deaf or hard of hearing. My job requires daily travel to a variety of schools and working with students, classroom teachers, and other support staff to best help students to succeed in the general classroom setting. It really varies as to how much time I spend with each of the 20 students on my caseload. It depends on the specific needs of each student. The student I work with who has the most needs is profoundly deaf and has an interpreter who accompanies her to all of her classes. I see this student an hour a day to reinforce concepts learned in academic areas where I have observed gaps due to her lack of language acquisition. I work with the lowest-needs students on a consultative basis. I visit these students once a week for fifteen to thirty minutes and consult with the general education teacher or the special educator to make sure the appropriate accommodations and modifications are being carried out. The needs of each student are carefully evaluated among the educational team members and parents to develop a supportive educational program for each student.

There are many aspects of my job as an itinerant teacher that I enjoy. I am able to make my own schedule in deciding when I work with students according to the IEP requirements for each student. On a typical day, my planning time consists of preparing for IEP meetings; planning for students; checking auditory training equipment; consulting and meeting with teachers, parents, and other professionals; and, of course, handling emergencies. All in all, I very much enjoy the freedom that working as an itinerant teacher gives me. The job has also been an incredible learning experience in the area of working with a variety of people and in facilitating IEP meetings for students.

Some of my greatest challenges are motivating the students themselves and dealing with the politics around the unrealistic expectations of parents and other team members. The parents, as well as the teachers, are all here to make a concerted effort to help each student move into adulthood, and sometimes there are varying opinions as to how this should be carried out. A further reality of this job is making sure I present parents and others involved in the student's life with all options available, while keeping my personal philosophy of teaching students who are deaf or hard of hearing out of the equation.

Another challenge for an itinerant teacher is how to connect with the students. I work with many students for only a half hour each week. This makes it difficult to feel like I am truly helping these students to succeed in school. I feel as though I am doing more paperwork and participating in more meetings than doing actual planning and teaching, and this is both positive and negative. Finally, as a first-year teacher, I am very lucky to be working with a group of professionals who are willing and open to helping me. I have gained and continue to gain insight from colleagues who assist me to address sensitive situations and to deal effectively with challenging students.

One of my greatest challenges in this job is also one of my best learning experiences. This is learning how to work with a variety of people in a variety of settings. Every day I meet secretaries, speech/language pathologists, general education teachers, audiologists, special education teachers, students, administrators, psychologists, and parents. In addition, it is very important that I make sure that the students who are deaf or hard of hearing feel comfortable and accepted among their hearing peers. If there is a concern in this area, I will go into the classroom and provide an in-service to the entire class so that they are aware of exactly what it means and what it is like to have a hearing loss.

Of utmost importance in my job is the fact that not only am I a source of knowledge on deafness, but I am also the student's advocate. When I walk into a meeting concerning a student, my main thought is, "What will be the best decision on how to best help this student now to later become a productive member of society, one who is able to support oneself, be part of a community, know self-empowerment, and advocate for oneself?"

## Other Settings

Almost 14 percent of students who are deaf or hard of hearing attend a special school that serves only students with significant hearing loss (U.S. Department of Education, 2009). Teachers of students who are deaf or hard of hearing provide instruction. These schools may be either public or private day schools, to which students commute from home each day, or public or private residential schools at which students live during the week, as Sherry Humphries describes in the Firsthand Account. A few students—those with serious health problems, for example—may be served in home or hospital settings.

## Inclusive Practices

The meaning of the least restrictive environment (LRE) for students who are deaf or hard of hearing is a source of ongoing debate (e.g., Johnson & Cohen, 1994; Snider, 1995). Supporters of inclusion contend that students who are deaf or hard of hearing should be integrated into general education settings and that all or most of their services can be provided in general education classrooms. They maintain that general education is the least restrictive environment for these students (Nowell & Innes, 1997; Ryndak & Alper, 1996;

Powers (2003) studied the family and environmental factors that had positive effects on secondary school performance. Later onset of deafness and high family socioeconomic status were the two strongest predictors of secondary school success. What does this imply for professionals and students?

**SHERYL HUMPHRIES**

*teaches middle school students who are deaf at a state residential school. Her classes typically have 5–9 students. Students who live more than 20 miles away live at the school; those who live closer commute daily.*

The students I work with vary in their experiences, language, and abilities. Students' hearing losses can range from mild to profound. The students may or may not use hearing aids, and we are teaching increasing numbers of students who have cochlear implants. The students come from families with deaf parents and families where the student is the only deaf person. Our school provides academic, modified, and special needs classes. I work with students who are gifted and who have learning disabilities, behavior concerns, mental impairments, and attention deficit disorder.

My classroom is much like a general education classroom. The curriculum is based on the state standards but I incorporate modifications depending on the students' abilities. While many of the students can understand grade level concepts, their English language delays make it difficult for them to comprehend written text. I often re-write information and make my own materials to enhance my lessons. I also use inquiry methods, visuals, and experiential learning to support the concepts I am teaching.

I am able to take on a variety of responsibilities outside of the classroom. Each year I lead a four-day outdoor education trip for the eighth grade students. I coach the MathCounts club and I take the students to a national deaf math competition. I also coach the fingerspelling spelling bee contestants to prepare for the state competition.

Each teacher in the building where I work is assigned an average of eight students to oversee as the IEP case manager. I am responsible for writing the IEP with input from the team and running the annual IEP meeting. In addition, some of the students may have a three-year evaluation review. I write the classroom teacher report and attend the meeting for the students on my case load. I also provide information for other teachers writing three-year evaluation reports for the students I teach.

The school has adopted a communication philosophy using bilingual–bicultural methods. The staff is encouraged to separate ASL and English during instruction and communication.

There are many aspects of working at a residential school that I enjoy. The environment of a residential school fosters the development of the whole child—academically and socially. The students have access to communication at all times. They have deaf role models via teachers, dorm staff, coaches, and more. Most importantly, the students have numerous peers that they can communicate with, in contrast to being the only student who is deaf or one of a few students with a hearing loss as often occurs in inclusive settings. There is a common understanding on campus about the communication needs of the students.

Due to the nature of the school, field trips are encouraged. Administrators recognize the importance of providing deaf students with experiences that can't be replicated in the classroom. I've been able to provide students with both day and overnight trips to enhance their learning. Our school has its own busses and vans so transportation is rarely an issue.

One challenge of working at a residential school is the fact that the majority of the students do not live at home. As a science teacher, I assign projects to be done inside or outside of class. Getting materials necessary for projects can be cumbersome because students do not have the same access to materials as they would if they lived at home (e.g., art supplies, common household items, tin cans). Students at home also have parent help if needed but may have difficulty getting one-on-one time with the dorm parents to assist them with the projects.

Getting to know the parents of the dorm students is also more difficult. I may only see the parents once a year at the IEP meeting, and that would only be for some of my students. This makes it difficult to get to know the parents. Luckily, technology has been helpful with the increased use of email and video phones. However, sometimes the face-to-face contact is nice.

Living away from home can also be difficult for students. Every year when we receive first year students we deal with homesickness and getting them used to dorm life. At times, it is too much for students, and they return home. Those who stay soon become acclimated to dorm and campus life.

Another challenge is to not get caught up in the contained environment of a residential school and to be sure to be a part of the education world as a whole. On the one hand, the focus on ASL and Deaf culture leads to an enhanced educational experience for the students. On the other hand, as a classroom teacher, I am responsible for academic content, state learning standards and state testing. A college program in deaf education generally does not prepare a preservice teacher to teach the content subjects of math, science, and social studies. How can a teacher be expected to teach students who are deaf, especially at the middle or high school level, at the same level as their hearing peers if the teacher is not knowledgeable in the subject matter and methods? It is easy to be focused on only the deaf aspect at a residential school because that is one of the primary reasons that students attend. But to be the best overall teacher for these students, it is necessary to continue to participate in professional development by attending classes and conferences and participating in experiences that help you teach the content.

Previously, I worked as an itinerant teacher and as a self-contained teacher in a general education school. When I compare this to those experiences, I don't ever see myself leaving a residential setting. Here, I am able to work with the students for three years. I see them mature from gangly sixth graders into confident young adults. I watch them interact with their peers, join clubs, play sports, and participate in class because no matter the situation, the students do not have to worry about communication. It is exciting to work with the students in a nurturing, accessible environment.

## Fostering Success for Students Who Are Deaf or Hard of Hearing in General Education Classes

Luckner and Muir (2001) reported the results of a qualitative research study of 20 successful students who were deaf and received the majority of their educational services in general education settings. They interviewed (a) the successful students; (b) the deaf education teacher, the educational interpreter, and/or the paraprofessional note-taker of the successful students; (c) a general education teacher who worked with the successful students; and (d) parents of the successful students. In addition, they observed the students in one of their general education classrooms. The following 10 factors were identified as being important for promoting the students' success:

1. Family involvement
2. Self-determination
3. Extracurricular activities
4. Social skills/friendships
5. Self-advocacy skills
6. Communication with and support for general education teachers
7. Content and vocabulary being learned in the general education classroom being pretaught and posttaught
8. Collaboration with early identification and early intervention service providers
9. Reading
10. High expectations

How could school professionals work to ensure that all these factors are deliberately fostered when a decision has been made to include a student who is deaf or hard of hearing in general education classes? What challenges might professionals face in accomplishing this goal?

Source: Luckner, J. L., & Muir, S. (2001). Successful students who are deaf in general education settings. *American Annals of the Deaf*, 146, 450–461.

Salend, 1998). In the Professional Edge, you can read about the characteristics of students who succeed in general education settings.

Although there are many advantages to educating students who are deaf or hard of hearing in an inclusive environment, a variety of challenges exist as well, including issues related to the development of communication competence, the availability of social interactions, exposure to role models, and other areas already outlined. The Professional Edge lists some of the potential benefits and barriers to providing services in general education for students who are deaf or hard of hearing (Nowell & Innes, 1997; Stinson & Liu, 1999). However, keep in mind that implementing inclusive practices does not necessarily mean full-time participation in general education.

Professionals developing educational plans and considering appropriate settings for students who are deaf or hard of hearing should ask these questions:

- Is this student developing age-appropriate communication skills?
- Is this student making satisfactory academic progress?
- Does this student have friends?
- Does this student have access to all components of the educational process, including lunch, recess, and extracurricular social and athletic activities?

If the answer to any of these questions is no, then it may be necessary to explore ways of providing increased support for the student or different placement options while still ensuring interactions with hearing peers.

### research NOTE

Reed, Antia, and Kreimeyer (2008) reported that student self-advocacy, motivation, high family and student expectations, good communication between professionals, and family ability to assist with homework facilitated the success of students who were deaf or hard of hearing and attending general education classes.

## Transition and Adulthood

Successful adults who are deaf or hard of hearing can be found in almost every profession (Schroedel & Geyer, 2000). A variety of stories about the lives of successful individuals who are deaf or hard of hearing have been published and are available and enjoyable to read (e.g., Carroll & Mather, 1997; Moore & Panara, 1996; Podmore, 1995; Robinette, 1990; L. A. Walker, 2001).

Even though many students who are deaf or hard of hearing find high school to be academically challenging, they are significantly more successful at completing high school when compared to students who do not have disabilities and to other students with disabilities (Wagner, Newman, Cameto, & Levine, 2005). What might explain this? One possibility is that in school, students who are deaf or hard of hearing can find adults and other students with whom they are able to communicate and socialize.

The National Longitudinal Transition Study-2 (NLTS-2) (Wagner et al., 2005) reports that significantly more students who are deaf or hard of hearing attend 2- and 4-year

## Potential Benefits and Barriers of Inclusive Practices for Students Who Are Deaf or Hard of Hearing

Professionals and parents continue to discuss the benefits and barriers to the participation of students who are deaf or hard of hearing in general education classrooms. Here are some of the points they make.

### Potential Benefits

1. Students can live at home with their families instead of having to attend a special school and live there throughout the week.

2. Students who are deaf or hard of hearing are exposed to and required to communicate and interact with skilled language users.

3. Continual social interactions in the classroom with other students who live in the same vicinity provide opportunities for social contacts in and out of school.

4. Students can observe, imitate, and receive feedback from age-appropriate peers about acceptable and unacceptable behaviors.

5. Students are taught the general education curriculum and expected to participate in the standard learning tasks and assessments with individualized adaptations.

6. Students who are hearing have a variety of opportunities to interact with their classmates who have a hearing loss. As a result, hearing students have the opportunity to learn that disability is a form of diversity and that individuals with disabilities are people with whom they can learn and share.

7. By living, learning, and socializing in settings with hearing people, students who are deaf or hard of hearing will be ready to live and work in the community after completing their formal educations.

### Potential Barriers

1. General education teachers may not want to teach students who are deaf or hard of hearing, which may be detri-

mental to the students who are deaf or hard of hearing and also could negatively affect the attitudes of hearing classmates.

2. General education teachers and teachers of students who are deaf or hard of hearing may not have the necessary interpersonal communication and planning skills needed to work together to create an educational environment that addresses the academic and social needs of these students.

3. Most general education teachers have little experience working with students who are deaf or hard of hearing. Consequently, they may lack the ability to directly communicate with these students, may not know how to or want to use an interpreter, and may lack the skill or desire to make adaptations needed for students to succeed.

4. Educational interpreters may not have the skills needed to model language or express content material (Schick, Williams, & Bolster, 1999). When educational interpreters are not qualified, students miss a great deal of information and are effectively denied equal access to the formal and informal interactions that occur.

5. Students' access to the information transmitted during classroom discourse can be reduced significantly because of the rapid rate of discussions, continuous turn taking, quick change of topics, and high number of speakers involved in a discussion, as well as more than one student talking at a time.

6. Students who are deaf or hard of hearing may experience feelings of loneliness and isolation if they are unable to participate in social activities with peers because of communication difficulties.

7. Students who are deaf or hard of hearing may lack opportunities to interact with successful deaf adults as well as to gain access to the Deaf community.

---

postsecondary education programs when compared to students with other types of disabilities or students without disabilities. Unfortunately, most of these students—approximately 71 percent—drop out prior to receiving a degree (English, 1997; Walter, Foster, & Elliot, 1987). One reason so many of these students do not succeed in postsecondary education is that they have not acquired the necessary knowledge or skills to be responsible for themselves or to learn independently (Luckner, 2002)—essential elements for succeeding in postsecondary education and adulthood. Individuals who do complete postsecondary programs most often are awarded a degree at the 2-year level (Schroedel & Watson, 1991). A reasonable conclusion to draw from this information is that many adults who are deaf or hard of hearing are not educated to the level of their capability, and so they may be at a disadvantage in addressing the demands of adulthood.

Many youth who are deaf or hard of hearing receive Supplemental Security Disability Insurance (SSDI) (Danek & Busby, 1999). The Social Security Administration (2004) indicates that 46,921 individuals in the United States who are deaf or hard of hearing collect SSDI. Whereas NLTS-2 (Wagner et al., 2005) suggests that an increasing number of individuals who are deaf or hard of hearing find employment after completing high school, other studies indicate that a large number of students who are deaf or hard of hearing are not prepared for the world of work. For example, in a national follow-up study of such students, Macleod-Gallinger (1992) found that one year after graduation from high school, 53 percent of the respondents were unemployed. However, by 10 years after graduation, the

## web link

www.deafed.net
The Deaf Education Network is a website focused on the preparation of new teachers as well as support for the ongoing professional development of existing teachers.

situation had improved considerably, with almost 81 percent of the respondents who were deaf or hard of hearing reporting employment.

Underemployment is also an area of concern. Workers who are deaf or hard of hearing are employed in blue-collar jobs more often than their hearing peers. They receive fewer promotions and, as a result, 10 years after high school graduation they have an occupational profile that is similar to that of hearing workers in their early years of employment. Similarly, workers who are deaf or hard of hearing earn significantly less than their same-age hearing peers (Macleod-Gallinger, 1992).

For students who are deaf or hard of hearing, the transition planning process and the transition component of the IEP should be considered capacity-building activities that bring together the resources of the students, families, professionals, adult service agencies, and community members and organizations. Sample activities to promote the process of transition for students who are deaf or hard of hearing, as suggested by Luckner (2002), are as follows:

- Teach a unit on and reinforce responsible and independent behaviors.
- Take career field trips.
- Read books with students about the work that people do.
- Have students complete interest inventories to help them think about career options.
- Set up job-shadowing opportunities for students.
- Provide self-determination and self-advocacy training.

Students who are deaf or hard of hearing have great potential—potential that too often goes untapped. Their prospects for successful adult lives are enhanced when educators realize the scope of their possible needs and enlist the widest array of resources to help them accomplish their dreams. Such resources might include recent advances in technology (e.g., Crow, 2008), as you can read about in the Technology Notes. Considering a student such as JJ, introduced in the beginning of the chapter, what might those resources be?

**fyi**

Most people who are deaf or hard of hearing are not good lip readers because only 30 percent of all spoken sounds are visible on the lips.

---

## REVIEW · REFLECT · DISCUSS

1. If a student who is deaf was in your class, whether in special education or general education, how would you help him develop friendships with his hearing peers?

2. What are the advantages and disadvantages of educating students who are deaf or hard of hearing in general education classrooms with their hearing peers? How might the principles of universal design for learning help you to accommodate the needs of students like Paige, Zachary, and JJ?

# Recommended Educational Practices for Students Who Are Deaf or Hard of Hearing

As you have learned, one result of the No Child Left Behind Act has been increased attention on the use of scientifically based research as a means of selecting instructional strategies for students. Unfortunately, the field of deaf education lacks much research to guide it. The information presented in this section is based on the research that does exist, as well as the literature on best practices. It describes examples of approaches that promote the academic and social development of these students. In the Speaking from Experience, Susan Elliott, an experienced teacher of students who are deaf or hard of hearing, offers valuable insights on implementing techniques such as these.

## Integrated Vocabulary and Concept Development

Many students who are deaf or hard of hearing have limited and/or delayed receptive and expressive vocabulary, and this negatively affects comprehension (Traxler, 2000), especially as concepts and vocabulary become more abstract. Thus, to make academic progress in the content areas of the curriculum, these students require additional support (Brackett, 1997).

Susan Elliott has been a teacher of students who are deaf or hard of hearing for the past 32 years. She has taught students from kindergarten through high school. She is a National Board Certified Teacher. She was recently named the *Colorado Teacher of the Year 2009* and was also selected as one of the four candidates for National Teacher of the Year 2009. These are her suggestions for succeeding as a special educator.

1. *Build elasticity into your program*—Structure your program in a way that values individual differences. Assure that the program will have the capacity to fit every child rather than demanding that every child fit the predetermined program. Embrace the concept that every IEP is a work in progress to be fine-tuned throughout the year to promote students' achievement in every domain as they grow and mature.

2. *Teach students to work in teams*—Using cognitive coaching techniques, posture yourself as a guide by their side. Teach students active listening, communication, problem-solving, and group participation skills. Develop a supportive sense of 'family' in your classroom where students feel safe to take risks. Foster the development of a strong group identity, rich with 'inside' humor. Positively recognize the diverse personality traits and differences among group members.

3. *Focus on the curriculum-instruction-assessment cycle*—Identify the information students must absolutely know, then determine *how* to teach those essential learnings effectively. Begin with the 'big picture' by giving students the broader context for learning. Students who understand why they are learning a particular topic and who can see their learning targets will demonstrate higher levels of engagement. Guard your instructional time. Literally days and weeks of class time can be lost to unnecessary disruptions. Demonstrate technology integration in your lessons and pledge to keep homework meaningful. Last, determine a variety of ways students can demonstrate what they know and can do relative to the essential learnings. Engage students in project based learning where technology is used as a tool for research, explication, and creativity.

4. *Create a culture of thinking*—Actively promote and value the collective thinking of groups and individuals as a regular day-to-day practice in your classroom. Take care to monitor the types of questions you ask in class. Pose questions that require students to synthesize information and promote higher-order thinking.

5. *Collaborate and reflect*—Become a member of a professional learning community (PLC). Seek opportunities to work in groups with staff members. Most schools have annual improvement goals. Find out how you can participate. Take time to reflect regularly both privately and with your team. Invite feedback from others and ask for suggestions for improving any aspect of your program.

6. *Build team capacity*—Foster the development of a strong team. Recognize and value each member's input. Job titles should not get in the way of everyone trying to create a harmonious educational experience for the students you serve. Recognize that parents are also members of your team and are a critical component of your work. Take care to actively listen to parents and include their thinking in your work with their children. Even those who have a history of being 'difficult' will become your greatest allies if they know that they are *heard* and their opinions are respected. Remember that routine communication goes a long way.

7. *Respect privacy*—Assure that team members respect the privacy of each student. Remember that students who have an IEP have many eyes on them throughout the day and this can be stifling. General education students have opportunities to interact in the school environment without being scrutinized by adults. Part of growing up is being allowed to make mistakes. Remember that sometimes there is a fine line between assisting students and policing them.

8. *Make learning a habit*—Model the love of learning at every opportunity both in and outside of your classroom. Engage in personal learning opportunities and make them public. Share new understandings that pique your curiosity and compel you to engage in further investigation. Students will naturally emulate this behavior. In this way learning can and should become *generative*. Celebrate curiosity and imagination. Professional growth is the fuel for constant renewal in your classroom.

---

### research
#### NOTE

In Guteng's (2005) study of beginning teachers of students with hearing loss, he found that administrative support generally was perceived as lacking, particularly for itinerant teachers.

That support can come in a variety of forms. One approach that was beneficial for students in a study reported by Luckner and Muir (2001) was the use of pre- and postteaching activities to supplement daily lessons and help make the content accessible. Pre-teaching essential vocabulary and concepts assisted the students in establishing the knowledge base needed to understand new information. Post-teaching was used to review key concepts, clarify misconceptions, organize information, and expand students' knowledge of the content or skills emphasized during the lesson.

## Experiential Ladder of Learning

How did you learn to ride a bike? To operate a computer? To tell someone that you cared about him or her? To cook a meal? Most of these skills are acquired through direct experience. Central to learning is the quantity and quality of experiences that we have in childhood

## Using the Telephone—With a Twist

If you are deaf or hard of hearing, the telephone is not a particularly useful tool—at least not when viewed in the traditional way. However, technology has created opportunities for the telephone to be a valuable resource for individuals who are deaf or hard of hearing. Here are some of the options currently available.

### TTY

TTY stands for *text telephone;* this device also is sometimes called a *TDD,* or *telecommunication device for the deaf.* A TTY is a special device that permits individuals who are deaf or hard of hearing to use the telephone by typing messages instead of speaking. To use a TTY, each party must have the device. It "rings" via a flashing light. The telephone handset is placed onto the TTY, and the individuals who use it simply type on the device's keyboard, sending their messages back and forth.

TTY users rely on abbreviations similar to those used by computer users and in text messaging. Some examples include these:

| | |
|---|---|
| GA | "Go ahead" |
| CUL | "See you later" |
| R | "Are" |
| SK | "Send kill" (stop the call) |
| UR | "Your" or "You are" |

TTY technology continues to evolve. Some models now include a wristband that vibrates to signal an incoming call. Others have printer options, and yet others come equipped with an answering machine.

### Telecommunications Relay Service (TRS)

If a hearing person does not have a TTY or a person who is deaf wants to contact someone who does not have this device, communication is still possible. The Americans with Disabilities Act (ADA) requires all phone companies to provide telecommunications relay service (TRS) 24 hours a day, 7 days a week, at no additional cost to consumers. With TRS, you dial a special phone number that is answered by a communications assistant, who provides the link between the two parties. Using a TTY, this person types the message of the hearing person for the person who is deaf or hard of hearing and then speaks the typed mes-

sage of the deaf person back. The communications assistant speaks/types exactly what each person is communicating (including slang and profanity) and is required to keep all communication confidential.

### Video Relay Service (VRS)

Webcam technology has made it possible to send and receive video images through the Internet. Video relay service (VRS) provides ASL users with a way to communicate with hearing individuals by videoconferencing using their native language. VRS allows individuals who are deaf or hard of hearing to communicate with a live video interpreter via a computer with a video camera. The video interpreter signs the telephone conversation with the ASL user and voices to a hearing person via a standard telephone. According to Communication Services for the Deaf (CSD) (2001), the benefits of using VRS include the following:

1. Enabling ASL users to communicate in their native language
2. Increased communication speed
3. Enhanced communication with use of facial expressions and body language cues
4. Removal of communication barriers for slow typists and/or exclusive ASL users

VRS is supported by federal funds administered by the National Exchange Carriers Association (NECA), which funds traditional TRS. The ADA, which requires functional equivalency in telecommunications access, makes these funds available.

*The principles of universal design for learning and instructional differentiation are clearly beneficial for students who are deaf or hard of hearing.*

and throughout life. Those experiences help shape our intelligence, character, and interests. Many students who are deaf or hard of hearing grow up in homes where they are overprotected, and so they miss mediated experiences (Marschark, 1997; Stewart & Kluwin, 2001). In view of the limitations placed by a hearing loss on vicarious learning, it is important to structure authentic experiences for children and youth who are deaf or hard of hearing.

Bruner, Oliver, and Greenfield (1966) suggest that humans represent the experience of the world through three modes: (a) *symbolic* (words, language), (b) *iconic* (pictures, charts, graphs), and (c) *enactive* (experiences). Depth and breadth of knowledge about individual concepts and procedures comes from learning that involves all three modes (Luckner & Nadler, 1997). A useful framework for planning units of study and learning activities, suggested by Luckner (2002), is the *experiential ladder of learning*. It is presented in Figure 11.8. The ladder offers alternatives to using lecture, discussion, or assigned reading for assisting students to understand concepts and course content.

### Visual Teaching Strategies

Given the auditory limitations that accompany a hearing loss, many researchers and educators have suggested that educators establish a visually rich learning environment for students who are deaf or hard of hearing (e.g., Nover & Andrews, 1998; Reeves, Wollenhaupt, & Caccamise, 1995). Professionals in these environments use (a) sign, finger-spelling, and **speech reading** (i.e., watching another person's face and mouth as she forms words); (b) equipment such as overhead projectors, bulletin boards, computers, and televisions; and (c) materials including pictures, illustrations, artifacts, slides, computer graphics, and films with captions.

Although there has been an increase in the use of interpreters and ASL features in educational settings, signing, like speech, provides a transient signal. The signal moves—it is there and then it is gone. Visual teaching strategies can be more permanent and can be used to help students focus on important information, see how concepts are connected, and integrate prior knowledge with new knowledge. Examples of visual aids that can be

---

**FIGURE 11.8**

The Experiential Ladder of Learning
**This organizer can help educators plan lessons that integrate more visual and hands-on learning in day-to-day instruction.**

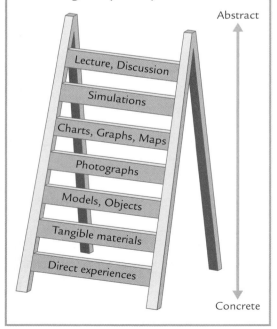

Abstract

Lecture, Discussion

Simulations

Charts, Graphs, Maps

Photographs

Models, Objects

Tangible materials

Direct experiences

Concrete

# Potential Accommodations for Students Who Are Deaf or Hard of Hearing

Many students who are deaf or hard of hearing can be supported in general education classrooms using accommodations (Antia, Jones, Reed, & Kreimeyer, 2009). In addition to ideas that assist all students, try the strategies listed here.

## Environmental

- Seat the student in the best place to enhance attending and participation.
- Give the student a swivel chair on casters.
- Use a semicircular seating arrangement.
- Reduce noise and reverberation with carpeting, draperies, acoustic ceiling tile, and acoustic wall treatments.
- Use flashing lights along with bells for signaling events in the class schedule.
- Use flashing lights for safety alarms (e.g., fire, tornado).

## Input

- Use a radio frequency transmission unit (FM) system.
- Use a sound-field amplification system.
- Stand in a place from which the student can read your lips.
- Face the student when talking.
- Use an overhead projector.
- Employ an educational interpreter.
- Co-teach: general education teacher with a teacher of students who are deaf or hard of hearing.
- Provide a copy of your notes to the student.
- Supplement the lesson with visual materials (e.g., real objects, pictures, graphic organizers, photographs, charts, videos).
- Provide manipulatives for multisensory, hands-on instruction or activities.
- Provide a note-taker for the student.
- Cue the student visually to indicate that someone is talking during class discussions or intercom messages.
- Repeat information that has been expressed by a person who is out of view or delivered over the intercom.
- Use captioned movies and television programs.
- Demonstrate directions to clarify what to do.
- Check for understanding by having the student restate the directions.
- Break long-range projects into short-term assignments.
- Post the date on the board when assignments and projects are due. Give frequent reminders.
- Shorten the lengths of assignments, and provide additional opportunities for practice.
- Teach organizational skills and assist the student to generalize these skills.

## Output

- Allow more time to complete assignments.
- Allow the student to make models, role-play, develop skits, and create art projects to demonstrate understanding of the information.
- Allow a written or drawn response to serve as an alternative to an oral presentation.
- Allow the student to use a computer or word processor.

## Social

- Teach hearing students to sign.
- Make books about hearing loss and deafness available.
- Invite adults who are deaf to come to school and share stories.
- Structure activities and experiences so that students who are deaf and hearing students work together.
- Teach units on social topics (e.g., friendship, avoiding fights, emotions, stealing, dating, dealing with divorce).
- Provide direct instruction on specific social skills (e.g., starting conversations, giving compliments, responding to criticism).

## Behavioral

- Place general rules and behavior expectations on charts displayed in the room or on a sheet of paper placed on the student's desk.
- Provide regular feedback and check progress often.
- Develop a home–school contract with the student's family, whereby the student receives a specified reinforcer at home when he demonstrates a specific behavior in school.
- Use corrective feedback (e.g., "I would like you to take out a book and read when you finish your work, rather than bother the person sitting next to you.").
- Increase the frequency of descriptive praise (e.g., "You really paid attention and stayed in your seat for the past 15 minutes.").
- Limit the number of distractions by establishing an isolated work/study area.
- Teach the student anger control strategies.

## Evaluation

- Have test items signed to the student, and allow the student to respond in sign.
- Allow tests to be taken with the teacher of students who are deaf or with a paraprofessional.
- Provide extra time to complete tests and quizzes.
- Modify the vocabulary used in test items to match the student's abilities.
- Give shorter tests on a more frequent basis.
- Use projects or portfolios in lieu of tests.
- Provide graphic cues (e.g., arrows, stop signs) on answer forms.
- Give alternative forms of the same test (e.g., matching, multiple-choice questions, fill-in-the-blank questions, true–false questions, short-answer questions, essay questions).
- Teach test-taking skills.

## Grading

- Use IEP goals and objectives as the criteria for grades.
- Write descriptive comments and give examples regarding student performance.
- Use a checklist of competencies associated with the course, and evaluate according to mastery of the competencies.

used in the classroom to enhance the communication and learning processes include classroom rule charts, job and choice menus, transition time cards and charts, task organizers, daily schedules, and the Internet (Luckner, Bowen, & Carter, 2001). In addition, visual representations of knowledge—referred to by a variety of names, including *graphic organizers, semantic maps, webs, semantic organizers, story maps,* and *Venn diagrams*—can be used to provide a framework to make thought and organization processes visible (Tarquin & Walker, 1997). These visual teaching techniques allow professionals to omit extraneous information while emphasizing important concepts and demonstrating their connections to each other. Also, these visual representations of information are easier for students to remember than extended text (Bromley, Irwin-DeVitis, & Modlo, 1995).

### Accommodations for Students Who Are Deaf or Hard of Hearing

Because most general education teachers have limited training or experience in working with students who are deaf or hard of hearing, they depend heavily on teachers of students who are deaf or hard of hearing to help them identify and implement ways to make the curriculum and social interactions accessible, as well as to ensure that the processes of assessment and grading are valid and reliable. The decisions about what specific accommodations to use depend on the goals for the student, the needs of the individual student, and the instructional style of the teacher. The Instruction in Action highlights some of the potential accommodations as described by Luckner and Denzin (1998) for students who are deaf or hard of hearing. As you can see by examining the list, many of the accommodations for students who are deaf or hard of hearing also are appropriate for students with other special needs.

## REVIEW · REFLECT · DISCUSS

1. Examine the writing sample titled "Coyote" in Figure 11.6. What are some of this student's strengths? What are some areas needing instructional attention?
2. What are examples of each of the "steps" on the experiential ladder of learning presented in Figure 11.8? Why are the items on the upper steps more challenging for students who are deaf or hard of hearing?

## Perspectives of Parents and Families

**web link**

http://clerccenter.gallaudet.edu
The mission of the Laurent Clerc National Deaf Education Center is to develop, evaluate, and disseminate innovative curricula, instructional techniques and strategies, and materials for children and youth who are deaf or hard of hearing.

When hearing parents learn that their child has a hearing loss, they usually experience a range of reactions and emotions and face a variety of challenges (Lane, Bell, & Parson-Tylka, 1997). Some of those challenges include understanding the impact of a hearing loss, finding appropriate services and support, and developing communication strategies. Parents also have to deal with the reactions of family and friends. Whether the family chooses to use an oral approach, a sign language system based on the English language, or American Sign Language to communicate with their child, they have to make significant changes in how they interact with her. They must choose either to learn and use sign or to use amplification, optimizing residual hearing and speaking directly to the child.

In contrast, many parents who are deaf or hard of hearing themselves and involved in the Deaf community would prefer to have a child who is deaf or hard of hearing (Lane et al., 1996; M. S. Moore & Levitan, 1993). Like most parents, parents who are deaf look forward to having a child who is a reflection of themselves. They bring their baby home to an environment where they will all share the same mode of communication—ASL or one set up to provide visual cues to environmental signals, such as doorbells and text telephones that flash lights rather than make noise. These parents are able to communicate with their child immediately, and the child is able to access incidental interactions that occur among family members because ASL is being used around them (Lane et al., 1996). Yet, as previously noted, only 5 percent of children who are deaf or hard of hearing have parents who both have a hearing loss (Mitchell & Karchmer, 2004).

Thus, parents often feel alone and in need of support as they adjust to their child's special needs. At the same time, they want information in order to make the right decisions for him and to become advocates for the services he needs immediately as well as in the years to come. That support and information can be provided by an early intervention specialist, other parents who have gone through similar experiences, and parent organizations.

## The Voices of Parents

As part of a larger study focusing on successful students who were deaf or hard of hearing, Luckner and Muir (2001) interviewed 19 parents to explore their perceptions of the factors that contributed to their child's success. They reported the following factors:

- Skilled and caring professionals
- Family support
- Early identification and early intervention
- Involvement in extracurricular activities
- The value of reading
- Perseverance

Parents were also asked "What advice do you have to help other students who are deaf to become successful?" The following quotes exemplify what many parents shared (pp. 439–440):

- "Don't let deafness hold you back."
- "You just have to keep your child's best interests at heart."
- "Before you make any decision about how you're going to educate or how you're going to allow your deaf child to live, you make sure you get as much information as you possibly can."
- "I would go back and do less worrying and relax a little bit more and have a little bit more fun with him."

As a school professional, a key to working with parents of students who are deaf or hard of hearing is to remember that unless you have a significant hearing loss or are the parent of such a child, you do not understand their experience. You should look to the parents to help develop your own understanding of the child, the family, and their hopes and needs.

## REVIEW · REFLECT · DISCUSS

1. Compared to the other families you have read about thus far in this textbook, what makes the parents and families of students who are deaf or hard of hearing unique? How might working with them be unique as well?

2. What is one strategy you might use to foster clear communication with the parents of a student who is deaf? How would this strategy be similar to or different from your communication with the parents of a student with a learning disability? An intellectual disability? An emotional or behavior disorder?

## Trends and Issues Affecting the Field of Deaf Education

The field of deaf education is being affected by advances in science and technology and also shifts in thinking about appropriate communication options for students who are deaf or hard of hearing. Three trends illustrate these changes: (a) universal newborn hearing screening, (b) the increasing use of cochlear implants, and (c) the bilingual–bicultural approach for educating these students.

*Many adults who are deaf or hard of hearing are active in the Deaf community.*

### web link

www.babyhearing.org
The Boys Town National Research Hospital website has a wealth of information focusing on early identification and answers for families whose child has recently been identified with a hearing loss.

## Universal Newborn Hearing Screening

Professionals in the field of deaf education have known of the advantages of identifying a child's hearing loss at an early age for more than half a century. Recent research has substantiated this perception by demonstrating that children identified with congenital hearing loss prior to six months of age acquire age-appropriate language skills by thirty-six months of age (Mayne, Yoshinaga-Itano, Sedey, & Carey, 2000; Moeller, 2000; Yoshinaga-Itano, Sedey, Coulter, & Mehl, 1998).

Yet, until recently, most children with a congenital hearing loss were not identified until they were nearly two years of age (Stein, Jabaley, Spitz, Stoakley, & McGee, 1990), old enough to take a formal hearing test. Now hospitals and agencies use two simple, inexpensive tests to screen babies for hearing loss. Both tests are safe, comfortable, and pose no risks to the infant. The screening measures include *otoacoustic emissions (OAEs)* and *auditory brainstem response (ABR)*. Many professionals refer to the screening programs by the name *Early Hearing Detection and Intervention (EHDI)*. This is an appropriate title because detecting a hearing loss is only the first step. Collectively, this notion of screening infants for hearing loss is referred to as **universal newborn hearing screening.** Currently, 48 states plus the District of Columbia and Guam have EHDI laws or voluntary compliance regarding screening the hearing of newborns (Centers for Disease Control and Prevention, 2009). As a result, 94.4 percent of infants born in 2007 in the United States had their hearing screened before being discharged from the hospital (National Center for Hearing Assessment and Management, 2009). Many children with significant hearing loss are identified within the first few months of their lives because of this screening.

## Cochlear Implants

### PEARSON myeducationlab

Go to the Assignments and Activities section of Topic 15: Sensory Impairment, in the MyEducation-Lab for your course and complete the activity entitled "The Cochlear Implant".

A **cochlear implant** is an electronic device that directly stimulates the hearing nerve in the cochlea, or the inner ear. This stimulation is designed to allow individuals with severe to profound hearing loss to perceive sound. A cochlear implant consists of three parts. The *receiver* is the part that is surgically implanted. It looks like a magnetic disk and is about the size of a quarter. It is placed under the skin behind one ear. Tiny wires that extend from it, called *electrodes,* are surgically inserted into the cochlea. A small headpiece is worn just behind the ear, and it contains the microphone, which picks up sound in the environment,

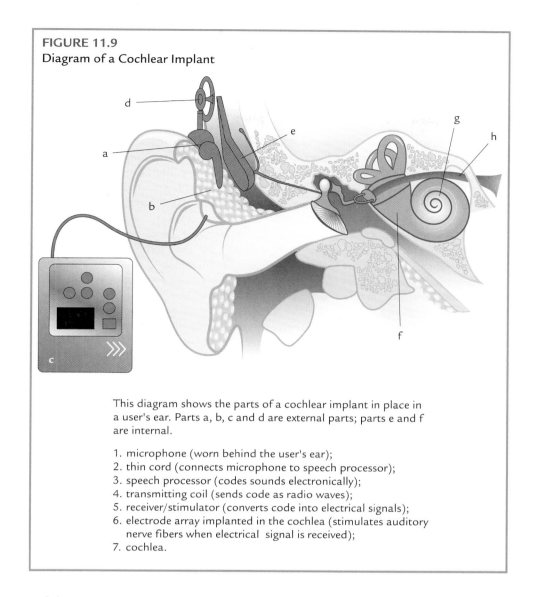

**FIGURE 11.9**
Diagram of a Cochlear Implant

This diagram shows the parts of a cochlear implant in place in a user's ear. Parts a, b, c and d are external parts; parts e and f are internal.

1. microphone (worn behind the user's ear);
2. thin cord (connects microphone to speech processor);
3. speech processor (codes sounds electronically);
4. transmitting coil (sends code as radio waves);
5. receiver/stimulator (converts code into electrical signals);
6. electrode array implanted in the cochlea (stimulates auditory nerve fibers when electrical signal is received);
7. cochlea.

and the transmitter, which sends sound through the system. The speech processor is worn on the body, either behind the ear or on a belt. It is attached to the transmitter by a special cord. The cochlear implant converts sound energy into electrical signals. The signals are delivered to the electrodes in the cochlea, which in turn stimulate the auditory nerve fibers. The resulting information is sent to the brain. Figure 11.9 includes a diagram of a cochlear implant.

The U.S. Food and Drug Administration (FDA) first approved cochlear implant devices for adults in 1985 and for children in 1990. Current FDA guidelines permit cochlear implantation in children with profound deafness as young as twelve months of age and in children with severe to profound hearing loss at age two years and older.

While it still is not possible to predict exactly which students will benefit from receiving a cochlear implant, McClatchie and Therres (2003) report that the Cochlear Implant Team at Children's Hospital and Research Center in Oakland, California, has identified specific intrinsic and extrinsic factors that affect outcomes. Positive outcomes are predicted for individuals who are implanted early, have an intact cochlea, do not have additional disabilities, attend an educational program that promotes auditory oral/verbal development, and have a family actively involved in promoting their listening and communication skills.

**web link**

http://www.bionicear.com/ UserFiles/Media/ How%20a%20CI%20works% 202008%20web.wmv
Advanced Bionics provides an animated video of how a cochlear implant works.

One of the primary reasons for choosing a cochlear implant is for the individual to develop spoken language and listening skills; however, children still may use alternative communication strategies. For example, some children may employ simultaneous communication in which sign language and spoken language are used at the same time. Other children may use *cued speech,* explained earlier in Figure 11.4, in which eight hand-based cues, placed in four locations around the face, are combined with spoken language to help distinguish among similar sounds (e.g., /b/ and /p/) as speech is read.

Keep in mind, too, that controversy about cochlear implants arises in relation in several areas. For example, questions arise regarding whether children who have had a cochlear implant should learn oral communication or also manual communication (e.g., Moores, 2009). Other issues relate to Deaf culture. Some individuals who strongly identify with Deaf culture view having a cochlear implant as an intrusive and inappropriate intervention for people who are deaf or hard of hearing. They point out that the very nature of the cochlear implant implies that deafness is a condition that needs to be "cured," a view strongly opposed by Deaf individuals. They also point out that the use of cochlear implants may threaten Deaf culture, as parents who encourage their children to have an implant will, in effect, be excluding them from that culture. Individuals who take a moderate view note that this is not an "either–or" matter—that individuals with cochlear implants may still identify with and participate in Deaf culture (Tyler, 1993).

Finally, you should be aware that problems can arise related to cochlear implants. Some individuals have contracted bacterial meningitis after the surgery, and a few individuals have lost what remaining hearing they had (U.S. Food and Drug Administration, 2006). Even though these risks and the other controversy surrounding cochlear implants may be considered strong deterrents to receiving them, many children are currently being implanted, and more will continue to be implanted in the future because the research indicates that early implantation reduces or prevents the language and speech delays that often exist for children with severe to profound hearing losses (e.g., Schorr, Roth, Froma, & Fox, 2009; Svirsky, Robbins, Kirk, Pisoni, & Miyamoto, 2000).

## Bilingual–Bicultural Approach

In the past decade, a variety of residential schools and charter schools have adopted a **bilingual–bicultural (Bi–Bi) approach** to educating students who are deaf or hard of hearing. This means that ASL is the primary language of instruction and that English is taught as a second language through reading and writing print. The goal of bilingual–bicultural programs is for students to learn two languages (ASL and English) and to be able to function in two cultures (Deaf and hearing). Figure 11.10 provides a sample of some common ASL signs, but because ASL includes facial expressions and a unique grammatical structure, these examples cannot capture the richness of this distinct language.

Bilingual–bicultural programs support instruction in Deaf culture—that is, the history, contributions, values, and customs of the Deaf community. Supporters of Bi–Bi contend that when children who are deaf are able to establish a strong visual first language, ASL, they then have the tools they need for thinking and learning and to develop a healthy sense of self through connections with other deaf people (Gallimore & Woodruff, 1996). The principles of the Bi–Bi approach for students who are deaf or hard of hearing, as suggested by Lane, Hoffmeister, and Bahan (1996), are as follows:

- Respect for the language of the student (ASL)
- Incorporating Deaf heritage information into teaching
- Using ASL to increase understanding of content information
- Increasing the complexity and metalinguistic knowledge of ASL students
- Developing transfer strategies from ASL to English to gain information
- Developing a strong metalinguistic awareness of English and how it is used in different settings and situations

## FIGURE 11.10

Examples of American Sign Language Signs

**These ASL signs can be helpful for school professionals working with students who are deaf or hard of hearing.**

Hello, hi

Yes

No

Friend

Think

Bored

Understand

Oh, I see

Don't know

Professionals who do not support using the Bi–Bi approach often express these concerns:

- Limited attention is given to the development of speech and auditory training.
- Most parents of children who are deaf or hard of hearing are not fluent in ASL.
- Problems in successfully transitioning students from conversing in ASL to reading and writing in English have not been thoroughly explained.
- To date, little published research has demonstrated the effectiveness of this approach.

**research NOTE**

In one study of 71 day and residential schools for students who are deaf or hard of hearing, 19 identified themselves as proponents of bilingual–bicultural (Bi–Bi) approaches (LaSasso & Lollis, 2003).

## REVIEW · REFLECT · DISCUSS

1. Think about students who have a profound hearing loss. What might be the advantages or disadvantages of them receiving a cochlear implant?
2. What is your opinion of the Bi–Bi approach to educating students who are deaf or hard of hearing? What is the basis for your opinion?

# Summary

- Concern for the education of individuals who are deaf or hard of hearing has existed for centuries in the United States.
- A hearing loss is considered a low-incidence disability and affects approximately 1.5 in 1,000 school-age children.
- Children and youth who are deaf or hard of hearing represent a very diverse group of individuals. Some use speech, some use sign, and some use both speech and sign to communicate.
- A hearing loss often affects the development of communication skills, which in turn often negatively affects language development, academic progress, socialization, and career attainment.
- Assessment for eligibility for special education services for students with hearing loss focuses, of course, on the extent of the loss and the impact that has on education, but it also incorporates ability, achievement, and social/emotional/behavioral domains.

- Most students who are deaf or hard of hearing receive all or part of their education in general education settings, and this approach has many advantages. However, because of the diverse needs and preferences of students who are deaf or hard of hearing and their families, a variety of educational placement options must be available for them.
- Recommended instructional practices for students who are deaf or hard of hearing focus on ways to increase students' vocabulary, concept knowledge, and experiential backgrounds.
- The majority of students who are deaf or hard of hearing are born into hearing families, who are required to make a variety of difficult choices about how to communicate with and educate their child.
- Issues currently affecting the field of deaf education include newborn hearing screening, cochlear implants, and bilingual–bicultural educational approaches.

**Council for Exceptional Children**   ADDRESSING THE PROFESSIONAL STANDARDS

Council for Exceptional Children (CEC) Common Core Knowledge and Skills addressed in this chapter:

ICC1K5, ICC1K6, ICC1K7, ICC1K8, ICC2K1, ICC2K2, ICC2K4, ICC2K6, ICC3K2, ICC3K3, ICC3K4, ICC4S3, ICC4S6, ICC5K4, ICC5K8, ICC5S3, ICC6K4, ICC7K1, ICC7S2, ICC8K1, ICC8S2, ICC8S6, ICC10K3, ICC10S4

Appendix: Provides a full listing of the CEC Common Core Standards, and associated Knowledge and Skill Statements listed here.

**PEARSON**

# myeducationlab

Now go to Topic 12: Sensory Impairments, in the MyEducationLab (www.myeducationlab.com) for your course, where you can:

- Find learning outcomes for the broad concepts covered in this chapter along with the national standards that connect to these outcomes.
- Complete Assignments and Activities that can help you more deeply understand the chapter content.
- Examine challenging situations presented in the IRIS Center Resources.
- Apply and practice your understanding of the core concepts and skills identified in the chapter with the Building Teaching Skills and Dispositions learning units.

- Check your comprehension on the content covered in the chapter by going to the Study Plan in the Book Specific Resources for your text. Here you will be able to take a chapter quiz, receive feedback on your answers, and then access Review, Practice, and Enrichment activities to enhance your understanding of chapter content.
- Watch video clips of CCSSO Teacher of the Year award winners responding to the question: "Why I teach?" in the Teacher Talk section.

## chapter twelve

# Students with Visual Impairments

## LEARNING OBJECTIVES

· Outline key events in the history of educating students with visual impairments, define terms related to visual impairment, and describe the causes and prevalence of visual impairments.

· Describe characteristics of students with visual impairments.

· Explain the unique aspects of assessment and the identification process for students with visual impairments.

· Explain the ways in which students with visual impairments receive their education.

· Describe best practices in educating students with visual impairments.

· Explain concerns typically faced by parents and families of students with visual impairments.

· Identify significant issues in educating students with visual impairments.

## Jonas

Jonas is in the fifth grade. A year ago, after frustrating experiences with several ophthalmologists, Jonas was diagnosed with Cone-Rod dystrophy, an inherited, progressive, and incurable disease that is usually not diagnosed until the early teen years. Although there is a blank spot in the center of his field of vision, Jonas can see large items and reads with a magnifier or with the font set at a very large size on a computer. Jonas is rather sensitive to light, and he wears sunglasses while he is in any type of light. Jonas spends most of his time in his fifth-grade classroom, but he is receiving instruction in braille twice each week, delivered by the district itinerant vision specialist. Jonas also is learning skills for moving about school, his home, and his neighborhood. These services are in anticipation of a time when Jonas is likely to lose his functional vision. At the present time, Jonas is an average student, and he is eager to finish elementary school and move to middle school. However, concerns are arising about his social interactions. His mother reports that when he invites friends over, the boys are happy to come, and they play appropriately, but he is not invited to others' homes to play. She explains that several times recently, Jonas's feelings have been hurt when invitations were given to others—right in front of him. His IEP addresses this area, and his special education and fifth-grade teachers are collaborating to help Jonas with social skills while also educating other students about friendship and reciprocity.

## Anna Marie

Anna Marie has a small amount of vision in a limited field in one eye and is blind in the other eye. She lives in a rural area. In elementary school, she was bused to a special class for students with visual impairments in a neighboring district, but she wanted to go to school with her friends, and so she began sixth grade at Madison Middle School. Her special education teacher Ms. Barich does not have a background in working with students like Anna Marie; her teaching license is in the area of mild disabilities. Ms. Barich had a long list of questions for the vision specialist who consulted with her right before school began, but even so, the beginning of the school year was rather difficult. First, Anna Marie was not prepared for the challenges of moving from class to class for most of the day; assigning a peer buddy helped with that problem. Second, each of the four general education

teachers had different questions about working with Anna Marie: "If she cannot complete a lab because she cannot safely use the equipment, how should she be graded?" "In math, nearly everything is written on the board; how will she be able to keep up?" "If she composes in braille, how will I grade her work?" Ms. Barich has been trying to be sure that all the teachers' questions are addressed while also working with Anna Marie to advocate for herself by asking for assistance when she needs help but being as independent as possible. Ms. Barich recently commented to a colleague that Anna Marie has caused her to look at the entire educational process in a new way—one that requires success without relying on sight.

## Thomas

Thomas is a high school senior enrolled in a specialized school. When he was a ninth grader, he was diagnosed with a progressive eye condition that typically results in blindness sometime in early adulthood. At first, he only had difficulty seeing during the evening and at night. But after a couple of years, the condition began to affect his schoolwork. During his sophomore and junior years, services from a teacher of students with visual impairments and an orientation and mobility specialist were provided in his neighborhood school. However, the demands of learning the new skills he would need as a person who is blind, along with making progress in all of his academic subjects, proved overwhelming. To get a boost on learning new technology and braille skills, Thomas attended a summer program just for this purpose. For the first time since his eye condition was diagnosed, Thomas received specialized instruction daily, starting in the morning and continuing into the evening. He began to feel a sense of empowerment as he learned alternative techniques for activities that he had once completed visually, and his interactions with peers and teachers who also were visually impaired helped him to envision his future with optimism. Although he made excellent progress during the summer program, both Thomas and his parents realized the need for the same level of intensity of specialized instruction for a longer period of time. They decided that he would spend his senior year at the school. Continued emphasis on braille literacy, safe travel, independent living, technology, and other skills, along with his academic subjects, would prepare him to meet his next goal of attending college to study computer programming.

You probably have had the experience of being at home when the electricity goes off at night during a storm. You moved cautiously, occasionally bumping into furniture and walls as you tried to find a candle and matches or a flashlight. Your usually familiar home was turned temporarily into something of an obstacle course. You also probably have experienced the disorienting effect of driving a car in dense fog or a bad storm when you could see only a small portion of the otherwise familiar road and scenery at any given time. Even though traffic was moving slowly, objects appeared to move very quickly into and out of view.

Experiences such as these may provide an analogy for what blindness or visual impairment may be like, but they are not entirely accurate. These experiences are temporary, unlike most visual impairments, which last throughout a person's life. Also, blindness is not about seeing blackness, as the examples convey; it is about seeing nothingness, as though you shut your eyes and try to see the back of your head. In addition, you have had the benefit of a wealth of visual experiences that help you understand your environment and that assist you during times when your vision is temporarily restricted or unavailable. Finally, and perhaps most importantly, you have not learned skills to compensate for a lack of vision or reduced vision.

Students with visual impairments comprise a very diverse group. Their vision loss may vary from mild to severe, but in addition, they may or may not have additional disabilities that affect learning. As you learn about these students and their needs, keep in mind that their uniqueness makes generalizing about them difficult. As you meet students with visual impairments during your career, the input of specialists in this area will be invaluable in helping you understand these students and assist them to learn.

## Understanding Visual Impairments

Some background information can help you to begin to understand the unique field of educating students with visual impairments. A brief look at its history demonstrates how thinking has changed regarding these students, while current approaches to defining visual impairment and estimating its prevalence provide a snapshot of the current status of the field. In addition, by learning about the structure and function of the eye, you can better understand some of the most common causes of visual impairment in school-age children.

### Development of the Visual Impairment Field

For centuries, professionals have recognized that individuals with visual impairments need specialized schooling. However, the way that instruction is provided has evolved significantly.

### FIGURE 12.1

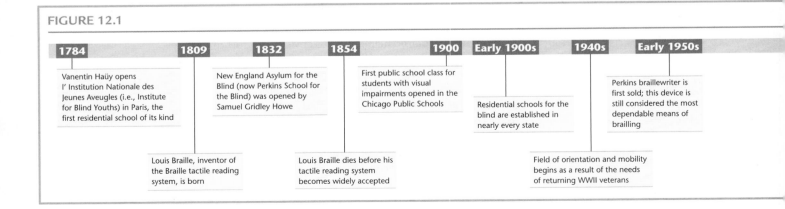

| 1784 | 1809 | 1832 | 1854 | 1900 | Early 1900s | 1940s | Early 1950s |

Vanentin Haüy opens l' Institution Nationale des Jeunes Aveugles (i.e., Institute for Blind Youths) in Paris, the first residential school of its kind

New England Asylum for the Blind (now Perkins School for the Blind) was opened by Samuel Gridley Howe

First public school class for students with visual impairments opened in the Chicago Public Schools

Residential schools for the blind are established in nearly every state

Perkins braillewriter is first sold; this device is still considered the most dependable means of brailling

Louis Braille, inventor of the Braille tactile reading system, is born

Louis Braille dies before his tactile reading system becomes widely accepted

Field of orientation and mobility begins as a result of the needs of returning WWII veterans

### Early Thinking and Services

As shown on the timeline in Figure 12.1, the history of visual impairments begins in France. There, Louis Braille, born in 1809 and blinded at the age of three by an accident in his father's workshop, developed the dot-based system of reading and writing known today simply by his last name, *braille*. It was not until after Braille's death in 1854 that his system became widely accepted.

### Residential Schools in the United States

Services for children with visual impairments began to develop in the United States during this same time period. In 1832, the New England Asylum for the Blind (now Perkins School for the Blind) was opened, led by noted philanthropist Samuel Gridley Howe (Roberts, 1986). Howe believed that educational programs should follow three principles: (a) Pay attention to each student's individual needs; (b) provide a curriculum similar to that for sighted students; and (c) expect students to integrate into their communities. Even though Howe was a pioneer in the residential school movement in the United States, he also was one of its earliest critics, publicly opposing the segregation of these students and advocating for public day school education for them (Roberts, 1986).

### The Emergence of Public School Programs

In 1900, the first part-time class for students with visual impairments was established on an experimental basis in the Chicago Public Schools. Students spent most of the day in general education classes and received instruction in braille and typing from a special teacher. These new classes were designed specifically for students with low vision who were not blind; the intent was to rely on oral instruction as a means of saving their residual sight, an approach referred to as *sight saving*.

The next significant change came in the 1950s when a dramatic increase occurred in the number of babies who were visually impaired because of a condition called *retrolental fibroplasia (RLF)*. This condition developed when premature babies were placed in newly available incubators and given uncontrolled amounts of oxygen to assist their breathing. The high oxygen levels caused underdeveloped blood vessels to grow into the retinas of the eyes, causing retinal damage and detachment and often leading to severe visual impairment. This disease, now called **retinopathy of prematurity,** sometimes still causes visual impairments in 400 to 600 premature babies per year (National Eye Institute, 2009).

The sheer number of students with visual impairments at that time gave parents the impetus and support they needed to advocate for establishing programs for these students in their local schools, and this created a revolution in their education. By the mid-1960s, schooling for students with visual impairments had largely moved from residential to local schools (Hatlen, 2000), a trend that continues today (U.S. Department of Education, 2008).

http://www.nei.nih.gov/health/examples/index.asp
At the website of the National Eye Institute you can see simulations of common disorders related to visual impairments.

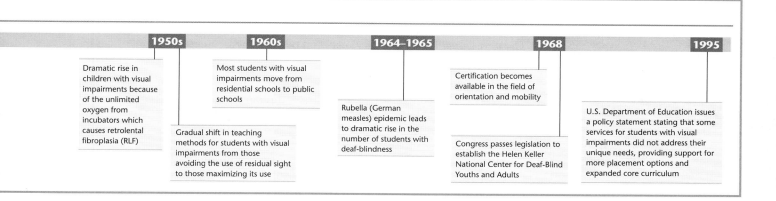

| 1950s | 1960s | 1964–1965 | 1968 | 1995 |
|---|---|---|---|---|
| Dramatic rise in children with visual impairments because of the unlimited oxygen from incubators which causes retrolental fibroplasia (RLF) | Most students with visual impairments move from residential schools to public schools | Rubella (German measles) epidemic leads to dramatic rise in the number of students with deaf-blindness | Certification becomes available in the field of orientation and mobility | U.S. Department of Education issues a policy statement stating that some services for students with visual impairments did not address their unique needs, providing support for more placement options and expanded core curriculum |
| | Gradual shift in teaching methods for students with visual impairments from those avoiding the use of residual sight to those maximizing its use | | Congress passes legislation to establish the Helen Keller National Center for Deaf-Blind Youths and Adults | |

*Many students with visual impairments also have other disabilities.*

## Other Historical Developments

Two other major historical developments shaped the provision of educational services to students with visual impairments in the latter half of the twentieth century. The first development was a radical shift in the methods used to teach students who were partially sighted. In contrast to the earlier practice of sight saving for these students, research indicated that using residual vision could actually improve visual efficiency (Ashcroft, Halliday, & Barraga, 1965; Barraga, 1964; Holmes, 1967), and so sight-saving classes were disbanded in favor of programs that emphasized using available vision.

The second development was a dramatic increase in the number of students with visual impairments who had additional disabilities—the result of a rubella epidemic in 1964 and 1965 that left 30,000 infants born with deaf–blindness and other health conditions (Hatlen, 2000). In addition, advancements in medical interventions for premature infants increased their survival rate dramatically, but these infants often had multiple disabilities, including visual impairments (Pogrund & Fazzi, 2002). Today, about 65 percent of students with visual impairments have additional disabilities (Kirchner & Diament, 1999b).

## Definitions of Visual Impairment

A variety of terms are used to describe visual impairment. Functional definitions are most often used in schools because they describe the impact of the vision loss on the student. Clinical definitions describe the clarity of a person's vision, and these definitions generally relate to legal matters and entitlement to special services beyond public schooling.

### Functional Definitions

The term **visual impairment** is perhaps the most commonly accepted general term to describe people with decreased vision, regardless of the severity of the vision loss (Huebner, 2000). Students with mild visual impairments may function visually with little impact on their daily lives. Students with moderate to severe visual impairments experience a greater impact on performing daily tasks. They may need to use large print for reading, strong magnifying devices, and other adaptations. Some students in this group also may learn to read braille and use tactile and auditory approaches to complete tasks. For example, they might learn to sprinkle salt into their hand before placing it on food or to listen to books on tape to supplement print or braille reading. Students who have profound visual impairments or who have no vision complete most or all tasks primarily using touch and hearing. They learn to read and write in braille and use many day-to-day adaptive techniques (e.g., folding money in ways to denote various denominations, labeling clothes to facilitate proper matching).

The term *visual impairment* is global, and two subcategories generally are recognized within it: low vision and blindness.

**PEARSON**
**myeducationlab**

Go to the Assignments and Activities section of Topic 15: Sensory Impairment, in the MyEducation-Lab for your course and complete the activity entitled "Defining Visual Impairments".

1. People with **low vision** have some vision but have difficulty accomplishing typical visual tasks. Using compensatory strategies, technology, and environmental modifications, these individuals can enhance their ability to accomplish these tasks (Corn & Koenig, 2002). Students who were just described as having mild to severe visual impairments have low vision.

2. **Blindness** refers to having no vision or only light perception, or the ability to determine the presence or absence of light (Huebner, 2000). The students just described as having profound visual impairment or no vision are blind. The terms **functionally blind** and **educationally blind** are used sometimes in schools to further describe these students.

Two other general terms are used to describe visual impairment: congenital and adventitious. A **congenital visual impairment** refers to a condition that is present at or near the time of birth, while an **adventitious visual impairment** is a condition that is acquired after birth, either in childhood or at some later point in life (Huebner, 2000). As you might expect, the age when a visual impairment occurs often has implications for education. Students with congenital visual impairments need access to alternative instructional approaches from the earliest age. For example, they develop an understanding of their environment by smelling, touching, and moving. Students with adventitious visual impairments may use their prior visual experiences for continued learning and for understanding alternative approaches to tasks. For example, these students may know the layout of the school grounds from when they could see it, and this helps to facilitate learning to move around those grounds with a long cane.

## fyi

In Chapter Ten, you learned that hearing loss also is categorized as congenital or adventitious.

### IDEA Definition

The Individuals with Disabilities Education Act (IDEA) uses a functional definition of *visual impairment:*

> Visual impairment including blindness means an impairment in vision that, even with correction, adversely affects a child's educational performance. The term includes both partial sight and blindness. (IDEA 20 U.S.C. §1401 [2004], 20 C.F.R. §300.8[c][13])

This definition stresses the point already introduced: Students' visual impairments cover an entire range, from mild to blindness. It also includes the provision that is common to all IDEA definitions: a negative impact on educational performance.

One more point should be mentioned regarding terminology. Although the federal government generally has chosen to use the term *disabilities* throughout IDEA and the Americans with Disabilities Act (ADA), the term *visual disabilities* rarely is used among professionals who work in educational settings with students with visual impairments. Professionals in the field generally use the term *visually impaired* (Rosenblum & Erin, 1998), and so that term is used in this chapter.

### Clinical Definitions

Clinical definitions of blindness rarely are used for determining eligibility for special education, but they are used to qualify persons for Social Security benefits, federal tax exemptions, and other services. These definitions are based on clinical measures of **visual acuity,** the clarity or sharpness of vision, and **visual field,** the range in which objects can be seen centrally or peripherally (Koestler, 1976).

**Legal blindness** refers to the condition in which central visual acuity is 20/200 or less in the better eye with corrective glasses or central visual acuity is more than 20/200 if a visual field defect exists so that it is 20 degrees or less in each eye (Koestler, 1976). Think back to your most recent eye exam. On a standard eye chart, the large letter at the top is used to determine if a person has 20/200 vision. If a person cannot identify that letter, then he is considered legally blind. A central field of 20 degrees can be simulated (roughly) by getting a large piece of poster board, cutting a hole in the middle about the size of a typical dinner plate, and then holding the poster board at arm's length. If a person sees only what is in the center hole of the poster board or less, regardless of visual acuity, he also would be considered legally blind based on visual field restrictions. Remember, though, that a person who cannot read the top letter of an eye chart or who has a restricted visual field still may use vision for reading and other daily tasks, and so the legal definition of blindness is not especially helpful in determining educational needs. From the discussion of functional definitions, students who were legally blind might have moderate, severe, or profound visual impairments.

Low vision typically is defined as visual acuity of 20/70 to 20/200 in the better eye with correction or a visual field of 20 to 40 degrees or less in the better eye with correction (Brilliant & Braboyes, 1999, as cited in Huebner, 2000). Some states use a visual acuity of 20/70 (or sometimes 20/60 or better) to provide a minimal level of acuity restriction for the purposes of qualifying for special services. Students who have a visual acuity between 20/70 and 20/200 typically would be considered to have mild or moderate functional visual impairments.

## Prevalence

Visual impairment is considered a low-incidence disability because it occurs infrequently in the general population and in less than 5 percent of all children with disabilities (Mason, Davidson, & McNerney, 2000; Multiethnic Pediatric Eye Disease Study Group, 2009). This means that compared to other categories of disabling conditions, the number of students with visual impairments is relatively low.

A precise prevalence figure for students with visual impairments in the United States is difficult to confirm because no single registry of students with visual impairments exists; moreover, various databases use different definitions for visual impairment and collect data on different age groups (Kirchner, 1999). For example, according to the U.S. Department of Education (2008), a total of 28,855 students with visual impairments and 1,600 students with deaf–blindness between the ages of six and twenty-one years received special education services during the 2007–2008 school year. However, these figures dramatically underestimate the total number of students with visual impairments because students who are visually impaired and have other disabilities often are reported in another category (Mason et al., 2000). Because they can only be included in one primary category, their visual impairments are not tallied.

### Other Prevalence Information

The American Foundation for the Blind (AFB) (2006) estimates that 10 million people in the United States are blind or visually impaired, with just 1.8 million of these being legally blind. The American Printing House for the Blind (APH) (1999) further reports that there are 55,200 legally blind children between the ages of zero and twenty-one. These figures also underestimate the number of students who receive special education services because only legally blind students can be registered (Mason et al., 2000). The APH figure does include students with additional disabilities, and so it provides a more accurate accounting of students who fall into the legal blindness category. However, because not all students with visual impairments are legally blind, the APH prevalence estimate is still not comprehensive. One other estimate from the National Dissemination Center for Children with Disabilities (2004) places the overall prevalence of students under age eighteen with visual impairments at 12.2 per 1,000 and those legally or totally blind at .06 per 1,000. Clearly, estimating the number of students with visual impairments is problematic.

## Causes of Visual Impairment

Visual impairments result when problems exist in the structure or functioning of the eye or when the eye is damaged through illness or injury. The first step in understanding these causes of visual impairment is to briefly review the structure of the eye and how it works (Ward, 2000).

### Structure of the Eye and How It Works

As shown in Figure 12.2, the eyeball is an incredibly complex organ composed of three layers. The first layer is protective and includes the **cornea,** the transparent structure that both protects and has a major role in the process of bending the light rays entering the eye—a process called **refraction.** This layer also includes the white portion of the eye, called the **sclera,** which helps the eye maintain its shape.

The second layer of the eyeball is called the **uveal tract,** and it provides nutrition to the eye. It includes the **iris,** the colored portion of the eye with a hole in the middle called the **pupil.** Behind the iris and pupil is the **lens,** the part of the eye that changes shape to focus light at the appropriate place at the back of the eye. The middle layer also includes the **ciliary body,** the part of the eye that produces a clear fluid called **aqueous humor** to nourish the eye. The **choroid,** the structure that carries a rich supply of blood to vital parts of the eye, is also part of this middle layer.

The third and innermost layer of the eye is known as the **retina.** The retina is the light-sensitive membrane that covers the back wall of the eyeball. It connects the rest of the eye to the **optic nerve,** which allows the brain to process the visual information it receives. Various parts of the retina help people do close, detailed work; to see colors; and to see in low

*Retrolental fibroplasia (RLF)* literally means "fibrous plate behind the lens of the eye." The fibrous plate results from the rapid growth of blood vessels in the retinas of the eyes because of uncontrolled exposure to oxygen. This condition now is called *retinopathy of prematurity.*

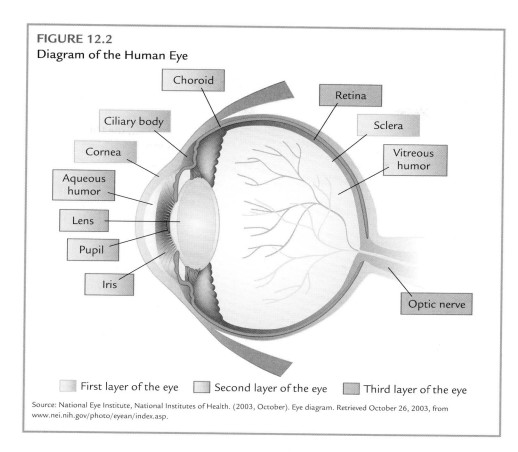

**FIGURE 12.2**
Diagram of the Human Eye

Choroid

Retina

Ciliary body

Sclera

Cornea

Vitreous humor

Aqueous humor

Lens

Pupil

Iris

Optic nerve

☐ First layer of the eye  ☐ Second layer of the eye  ☐ Third layer of the eye

Source: National Eye Institute, National Institutes of Health. (2003, October). Eye diagram. Retrieved October 26, 2003, from www.nei.nih.gov/photo/eyean/index.asp.

light and detect motion. And finally, the space between the lens and retina is filled with a transparent gel called **vitreous humor.** It keeps the eyeball from collapsing.

Each eyeball lies in a pear-shaped, bony cavity known as the *eye socket,* and it is attached by six muscles. Two corresponding sets of muscles allow both eyes to move in a coordinated fashion, some contracting while others relax. Other structures outside the eyeball include the eyelids and tear ducts, which work together to protect the eyeball.

Now you can understand the very complex process of what happens when a person sees. Light rays enter the eye, traveling through the cornea where they are refracted. They continue traveling through the aqueous humor to the iris, which ensures that only the appropriate amount of light goes to the interior part of the eye. At this point, the lens bends the rays again to make finer adjustments. They land on the retina where they come together, focused. They are then turned into electrical signals that travel along the optic nerve to the brain. The brain's interpretation of those electrical signals is what we know as sight.

## Examples of Visual Impairments

A visual impairment can result from any number of problems with the anatomical structure of the eye or with the process of transmitting light rays to the brain and interpreting their meaning. Here are a few examples of conditions that can affect vision:

- **Strabismus**—The muscles of the eyes do not hold both eyes in proper alignment.
- **Amblyopia**—One eye does not develop vision or loses vision because of nonuse, possibly caused by strabismus.
- **Cataract**—The lens is cloudy and cannot transmit light rays properly to the retina.
- **Aniridia**—The iris is missing, so too much light enters the eye.
- **Glaucoma**—Damage to the optic nerve is caused when the aqueous humor does not flow properly.
- **Cortical visual impairment**—Damage to the part of the brain dealing with sight means that the images received in the eyes are not interpreted correctly.

**web link**

www.aerbvi.org
The Association for Education and Rehabilitation of the Blind and Visually Impaired is the primary professional organization for those who work with children or adults with visual impairments.

## Common Causes of Childhood Visual Impairment

The eye is small and complex, and not surprisingly, it can be harmed in many different ways. These are some of the most common causes of vision loss for children and young adults (Erin, Fazzi, Gordon, Isenberg, & Paysse, 2002):

- *Retinopathy of prematurity*—A disease that occurs in premature babies in which damage is caused to the retina when abnormal blood vessels form there
- *Optic-nerve hypoplasia*—A condition in which the optic nerve fails to develop fully
- *Microphthalmia*—Congenitally small eyes
- *Anophthalmia*—Congenitally absent eyes
- *Retinoblastoma*—A tumor in the eye resulting in blindness when the eye is removed
- *Myopia*—Nearsightedness occurring when light entering the eye focuses in front of the retina to the extent that it cannot be corrected with conventional lenses

- *Albinism*—A lack of pigment in eyes and/or skin, resulting in underdeveloped retinas
- *Nystagmus*—Involuntary jerky eye movements resulting in reduced acuity
- *Hyperopia*—Farsightedness occurring when light entering the eye focuses behind the retina
- *Retinitis pigmentosa*—A group of diseases that include the deterioration of the retina, leading to problems with peripheral vision and night vision
- *Diabetic retinopathy*—A leading cause of blindness that is a complication of diabetes; occurs when diabetes damages blood vessels inside the retina

These conditions represent only a small portion of the hundreds of causes of visual impairments. Several additional common causes of visual impairment among children in the United States are presented briefly in the Professional Edge.

## REVIEW · REFLECT · DISCUSS

1. What problems may result from the variety of definitions that are used to describe students with visual impairments and to determine their eligibility for special education services? Think about this question in terms of which students are identified, who provides services to them, and how supports are arranged for general education teachers.

2. Why do you think it is so difficult to establish reliable prevalence rates for visual impairments among children? As you review the rates from IDEA and other sources described in this section, what do you think the implications are for you as a professional educator?

# Characteristics of Individuals with Visual Impairments

Think about how vision allows even the youngest children to move around freely in the environment, to find toys and friends with whom to play, and to observe and imitate their parents in routine activities. Children with visual impairments miss such incidental learning, which may have a significant impact on their development, learning, social skills, and behavior.

## Cognitive Characteristics

Visual impairment directly influences development and learning in a variety of significant ways. Lowenfeld (1973) has described the impact of blindness or low vision on cognitive development by identifying basic limitations on the child in the following three areas:

1. *Range and variety of experiences*—When a child has a visual impairment, experiences must be gained by using the remaining senses, especially touch and hearing. However, these senses do not compensate entirely for the quick and holistic information provided by vision (e.g., size, color, and spatial relationships). Unlike vision, exploring objects by touch is a part-to-whole process, and the person must be in contact with the object being explored. Some objects are too far away (e.g., stars, horizon), too large

(e.g., mountains, skyscrapers), too fragile (e.g., snowflakes, small insects), or unsafe (e.g., fire, moving vehicles) to be examined tactilely.

2. *Ability to move around (i.e., mobility)*—Vision allows for early and free movement within the environment, but blindness or severe visual impairment restricts such movement (Houwen, Visscher, Lemmick, & Hartman, 2009). This restriction limits the person's opportunities for experiences and also affects social relationships. Children with visual impairments, unlike other children, must learn to travel safely and efficiently in the environment using a variety of **orientation and mobility skills** (i.e., competencies for traveling safely and efficiently through one's environment) and tools, such as the long cane (McAllister & Gray, 2007).

3. *Interaction with the environment*—Because vision allows for quick gathering of information at a distance, people with typical vision have immediate and direct control of the environment. For example, if you walk into a crowded party, you can quickly scan the room, find someone or someplace to go to, and then move freely to that location. People who are blind or severely visually impaired do not have this same control of the environment. Even with effective mobility skills, they still have some level of detachment from the environment.

When the absence of experiences such as those just described is combined with the lack of opportunity to observe and imitate other children and adults, the effect on all areas of development can be significant (Cho & Palmer, 2008). For example, children with typical vision play interactive games before ten months of age, but those with visual impairments do so two months later (Ferrell, 2000; Pogrund & Fazzi, 2002).

As a group, students with visual impairments will exhibit a wide range of cognitive and intellectual abilities. Some students with visual impairments fall into the gifted range, and many students have average intellectual abilities. Still others experience some level of cognitive disability, particularly if they have more than one identified disability. That is, among students with multiple and severe disabilities (the focus of Chapter Fourteen), the incidence of visual impairment is quite high.

### research
### NOTE

Among students with visual impairments ages 6–21, 54 percent receive orientation and mobility services. No differences exist across gender or family income, but not surprisingly, students who are blind rather than low vision are most likely to participate in this critical training.

## Academic Characteristics

The impact that visual impairments have on cognitive development likewise affects the development of academic skills, particularly in the areas of reading and writing (Bosman, Gompel, Vervloed, & van Bon, 2006; Steinman, LeJeune, & Kimbrough, 2006). For example, when you read or write, you rely, without realizing it, on your ability to distinguish the fine details of letters and words—something most students with visual impairments cannot do because of problems with acuity. These students instead use a variety of alternative media and tools for reading and writing, depending on their individual needs. They may use braille or an alternative form of print (Emerson, Corn, & Siller, 2006). With appropriate assessment and instruction, students with visual impairments who do not have additional disabilities develop reading and writing skills commensurate with their peers with typical vision, as is true for Jonas, who was introduced at the beginning of this chapter (Clark & Stoner, 2008; Eisenbraun et al., 2009). For students with multiple disabilities, especially intellectual disabilities, academic instruction may emphasize function skills rather than the traditional curriculum (e.g., Durando, 2008).

### Braille Literacy Skills

Students who are functionally blind typically learn to read and write braille, as do some students with low vision. **Braille** is an efficient and practical means of written communication based on the 26 letters of the alphabet, as shown in Figure 12.3. Capital letters are designated with a dot in the lower right-hand position preceding the letter to be capitalized. Another

*Students who are functionally blind need to acquire braille literacy skills in the same way that other students acquire print literacy skills.*

**FIGURE 12.3**
Braille Alphabet and Example of Its Use

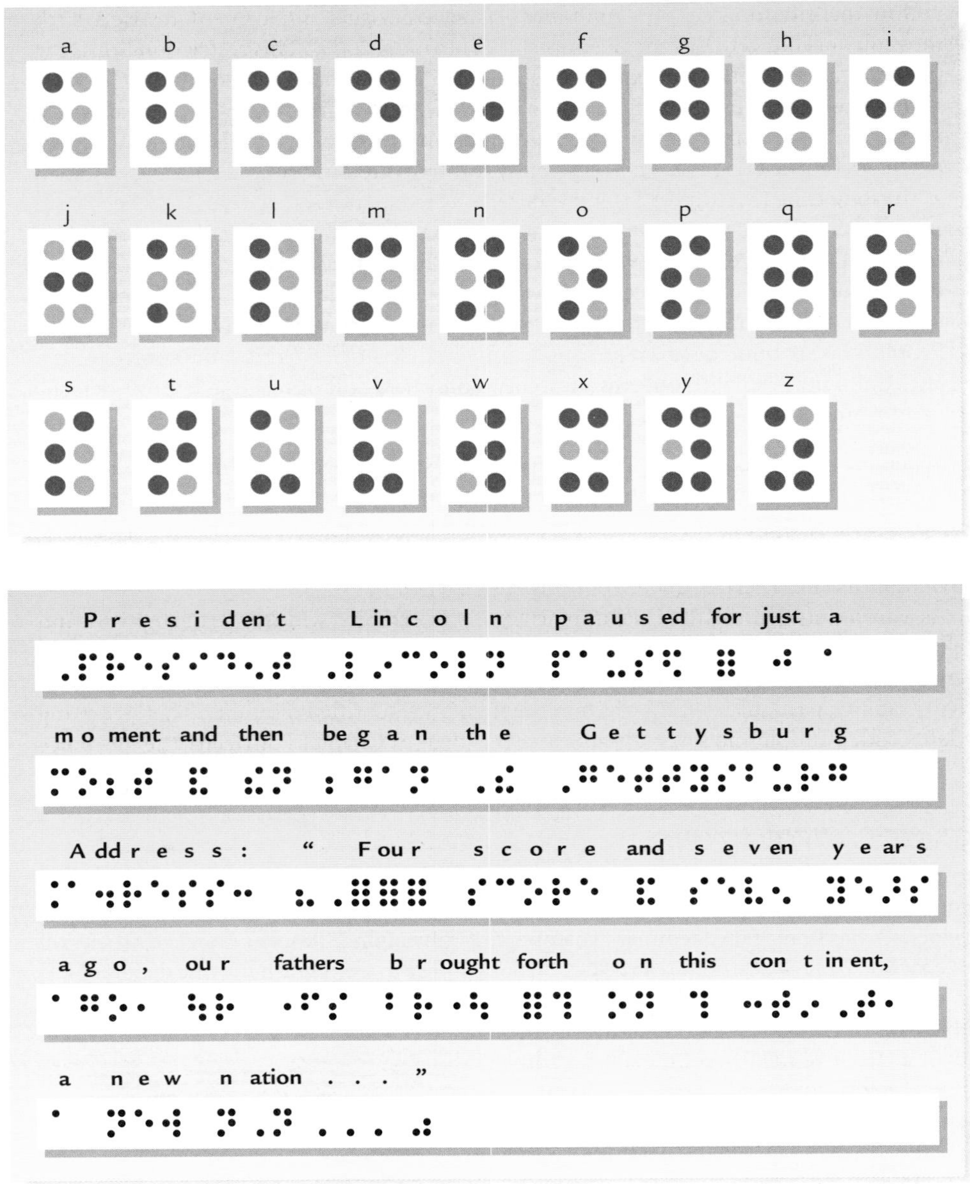
a b c d e f g h i
j k l m n o p q r
s t u v w x y z
P r e s i den t Lin c o l n p a u s ed for just a
m o ment and then be g a n th e G e t t y s b u r g
A dd r e s s : “ F ou r s c o r e and s e v en y e ar s
a g o , ou r fathers b r ought forth o n this con t in ent,
a n e w n ation . . . ”

sign (the upper and lower dots on the right-hand side of the cell) designates italicized words. Also, various configurations are assigned to punctuation marks.

In addition to the 26 letters of the alphabet and the various punctuation marks, the literary braille code includes 186 contractions and short-form words (Day, McDonnell, & O'Neill, 2008). For example, the word *for,* or the individual letters *f-o-r,* are represented by all of the dots in the braille cell. Also, most letters are assigned a whole-word meaning; for example, when *j* stands alone (i.e., with a space before and after), it is read as the word *just.* As another example, some short-form words are formed with a few letters from the entire word; the letters *abv* represent the word *above.* Beyond the literacy braille code, other codes are used to represent mathematics and science, music, and computer symbols.

Students learn to read braille by moving the fingers of both hands smoothly across the lines of braille words from left to right. Students learn to write first with a *braillewriter*—a mechanical device with six keys corresponding to each dot in the braille cell—generally starting in preschool or kindergarten. The writer presses various combinations of these six keys simultaneously to write the various configurations in each cell. Other keys allow the writer to space, backspace, and change lines. Students also learn to write braille with a *slate and stylus,* a portable device containing a template of braille cells (the slate) arranged in several lines. The writer uses the stylus, a pointed device with a blunt tip, to press each dot separately within each cell. Because the dots are being pressed through the paper, writing proceeds from right to left (rather than left to right). Students typically learn the relatively simple process of writing with a braille slate in late primary or middle school.

Braille reading rates tend to be slower than print reading rates. Although current research on braille reading is sparse, a rate of about 100 to 125 words per minute is considered typical for students in high school (Heinze, 1986). In contrast, adolescents who read print average 140 to 150 words per minute. Braille reading rates can be even slower when students are required to read critically and answer comprehension questions and faster when they are reading aloud and not paying attention to the details of the passage (Wetzel & Knowlton, 2000).

Because the reading rate for braille readers generally is slower than that for readers with typical vision, students with vision impairments need additional tools for gathering information (e.g., Ely et al., 2006). For example, they may listen to books on tape using sources such as those illustrated in the Technology Notes. Alternatively, they may use a live reader or access synthesized speech from a computer. Finally, they may use computers for word processing, database management, and other applications to help them manage the extensive amount of written information required in school and adult life.

To teach braille, **visual impairment (VI) specialists** (i.e., teachers specially trained to work with students with visual impairments) work with young children to ensure that they have a wide range of experiences and develop the unique perceptual and hand movement skills needed for braille reading. Then, typically in kindergarten, VI specialists provide direct instruction in braille literacy skills, often using an approach and materials that parallel those used by general education teachers (Crawford & Elliott, 2007). Some of this instruction may occur in the general education classroom setting, and so it requires appropriately adapted reading materials and close collaboration between the VI specialist and the general education teacher (Koenig & Holbrook, 2000). The VI specialist also provides instruction in the special braille symbols that are used in mathematics, science, and other nonliterary applications.

### Print Literacy Skills

Many students with low vision can use compensatory strategies and tools so that print is their primary literacy medium. Some students will use large-print materials (Lussenhop & Corn, 2002), but then they can read only when such materials are available. Instead, most students are taught to use optical **low-vision devices.** For example, a magnifier, either handheld or spectacle mounted, makes reading print possible for some students. This option provides maximum flexibility because a magnifier is portable and can be used in almost any situation. Some magnifiers even have built-in light sources.

Electronic devices also can enlarge materials. The most common is the closed-circuit television (CCTV). This device has a camera that transmits an enlarged image of the reading material to a screen. The user moves the material back and forth below the camera to follow the lines of text, thereby creating a moving image on the screen. The CCTV user can control the size of the letters on the screen and can select either black letters on a white background or vice versa, depending on which format can be seen more easily. Some CCTV models provide true color images of the materials being viewed.

An alternative to devices like CCTV is the Kurzweil–National Federation of the Blind reader (National Federation of the Blind, 2006). The user holds this hand-sized equivalent of a talking digital camera over print material and snaps a picture of it; then within a few seconds, the print is read aloud in synthetic speech. The device allows storage of files, exchanges files with a computer, and can be used with an earphone. Thus, it provides access to print even to students who are blind. Think of how such a device could assist a student like Anna Marie, whom you met at the beginning of this chapter.

dimensions of
**DIVERSITY**

African American students with oculocutaneous albinism have light-colored skin and hair and are visually impaired. Although educators have long been concerned that these students' self-esteem may suffer, one study found that it did not seem to be affected (Gold, 2002).

www.acb.org
www.nfb.org
The American Council of the Blind and the National Federation of the Blind are the largest organizations of consumers with visual impairments.

## Listening to Learn

For many individuals who are visually impaired, alternatives to using braille include recorded books and other learning materials. Here are examples of organizations that provide these services.

### Recording for the Blind & Dyslexic (RFB&D)

Started in 1948 by the New York Public Library's Women's Auxiliary for World War II veterans who had lost their sight, RFB&D currently has more than 7,700 volunteers who upload digital recordings of books. It serves more than 237,298 members (kindergarten through adult) worldwide, circulating 533,938 titles in 2008.

Visit the RFB&D website (http://www.rfbd.org/index.htm) to learn more about this organization and the work it does.

### National Library Services for the Blind and Physically Handicapped (NLS)

This federally funded program, which is part of the Library of Congress, provides braille and recorded materials for individuals who are blind or who cannot read because of other physical limitations. It was established in 1931 for adults, expanded to include children in 1952, and expanded yet again in 1966 for individuals with other physical disabilities. This program offers full-length books and magazines that are distributed to a cooperating network of regional and local libraries and circulated to eligible borrowers using postage-free mail. Many materials also are available on the Internet through Web-Braille. Since 1966, the program also has included music.

Any resident of the United States, as well as a citizen living abroad, can access NLS materials, and the program is used by many. The most popular items tend to be best-selling books, other fiction, biographies, and how-to books. Some titles are available in Spanish. Approximately 70 magazines also are offered. The brailling and recording of the materials is completed mostly by volunteers and the organization is beginning the move toward digital recordings. You can learn more about the NLS at http://www.loc.gov/nls/index.html.

### BookShare

Bookshare™ provides the world's largest online library of accessible reading materials for people with visual impairments and other print disabilities. Members have unlimited access to digitally recorded books, magazines, and newspapers that can be downloaded and accessed through readily available text-to-speech software. Through a grant award from the U.S. Department of Education, materials from Bookshare™ can be obtained free of charge for eligible students in public schools. Learn more details at http://www.bookshare.org/.

---

Students with low vision demonstrate a wide range in reading efficiency and proficiency, depending on factors related to their eye condition and personal characteristics such as motivation, experiential and conceptual background, and level of reading skill (Bailey et al., 2003). One comprehensive study of reading proficiency among students with low vision was conducted by Corn and her colleagues (Corn et al., 2002). These researchers studied the reading skills of 185 fifth-grade students with low vision in Tennessee. One goal of the study was to compare the students' reading skills in the fall, when low-vision devices were not used, with their reading skills in the spring, after instruction in the use of low-vision devices had been provided. When all of the students' reading rates were included, regardless of their level of comprehension, the average silent reading rate was 45.5 words per minute in the fall and 107.4 words per minute in the spring. The authors concluded that learning to use a low-vision device for reading was critically important for such students.

Students with low vision share with students who are blind the need for acquiring additional tools to facilitate schoolwork and written communication. They may learn keyboarding skills, skills to use speech output devices and screen enlargement programs on the computer, and other **access technologies**—that is, high- and low-tech options to help access computers and other sources of information. The Technology Notes provides additional information on the range of technological options to assist students with low vision. Finally, some students with low vision learn to read and write braille as a supplement to or replacement for print.

The six-dot code developed by Louis Braille forms the basis of the braille code used today in North America. Braille authorities in English-speaking countries later added the letter *w*, which is not part of the French alphabet.

## Access to Computers for Students with Visual Impairments

A variety of tools provide students with visual impairments access to the wealth of digital information available on computers, CDs, DVDs, and the Internet. The key is to match the student's sensory capabilities with specific access tools, whether focusing on auditory, visual, or tactile options or a combination of these.

### Auditory Tools

- *Synthetic speech.* Using a combination of screen-reading software and a speech synthesizer, a student who is visually impaired can access what is presented on the computer screen. The screen reader converts the characters or words into spoken language, whereas the synthesizer produces the sound. The user can control the speed of the speech as well as navigate the screen.

- *Optical character recognition (OCR) with speech and scanner.* OCR devices convert printed text into electronic files and serve as reading machines for users who are visually impaired. These devices use scanners to input text and OCR software to convert the text into electronic formats that the user can then access in a variety of formats, such as braille and synthetic speech.

### Visual Tools

- *CCTV.* A CCTV system uses a video camera to project an image onto a television screen or computer monitor. A student can use a CCTV to read regular-print books and maps at greatly enlarged sizes and to do written assignments using a pen, pencil, or computer.

- *Screen-enlargement software.* Screen-enlargement software increases the sizes of images on computer screens.

### Tactile Tools

- *Braille translation software.* This software converts print into braille (forward translation) and braille into print (backward translation), enabling students to output braille translations of text from the computer and print versions of their written braille work.

- *Braille printer.* An electronic braille printer (also called an *embosser*) connects to a computer and embosses braille on paper to provide hard copy. It functions like a standard printer.

- *Refreshable braille displays.* This output device is connected to a computer, often in front of or under the keyboard, and the characters on it can be felt in braille. The braille display consists of pins arranged in the shape of braille cells that raise and lower to form braille characters. Software converts the characters from the computer into the braille on the refreshable display.

- *Audible and braille notetakers.* Notetakers provide some of the capabilities of computers in a small, portable device. They offer a variety of software and hardware functions and features, such as synthetic speech output, refreshable braille, a choice of keyboards (braille or standard), and braille translation. A notetaker usually can interface with a regular computer.

  - *Electronic braillewriter.* This device produces braille but also has special features, such as synthetic speech, braille and print translation, automatic erase and correction, and a memory for storing files. It also can interface with a computer.

  - *Tactile graphics maker.* This device enables the automatic production of tactile graphics material using heat-sensitive paper.

*Source:* Text from Spurgin, S. (Ed.). *When you have a visually impaired student in your classroom: A guide for teachers* (pp. 72–74). Copyright © 2002 by AFB Press. Adapted with permission of AFB Press, American Foundation for the Blind. All rights reserved.

## Social and Emotional Characteristics

Think for a few moments of the social skills that you use on a daily basis. Did someone teach you how to look at the people to whom you are talking, how to wave good-bye when you depart, how to take turns when having a conversation, and how to use facial expressions to communicate nonverbally? In each of these situations, the answer is probably no. We typically develop social behaviors by observing social events and customs and imitating them (Ophir-Cohen, Ashkenazy, Cohen, & Tirosh, 2005). Refinement occurs through repeated use of social behaviors and, if needed, indirect feedback from socially competent persons. Because a visual impairment restricts incidental learning through observation and imitation, students with visual impairments often have difficulties demonstrating socially appropriate behaviors (Celeste, 2006; Correa-Torres, 2008; Shapiro, Moffett, Lieberman, & Dummer, 2008).

The dilemma of developing social interaction skills extends even to other types of interactions. In a recent study drawing on data from students with disabilities from across the country, Kelly and Smith (2008) compared the use of the computer (e-mail and chat rooms) and telephone for students with visual impairments ages six to sixteen to that for other students with disabilities. They found that both preadolescents and adolescents with visual impairments used electronic communication more than students with disabilities that may have affected the ability to access this technology (i.e., students with intellectual disabilities, students with autism). However, just 23 percent of preadolescents and 38 percent of adolescents with visual impairments had ever used computer-based social interaction options. Although assistive technology might facilitate these students' access to these social interactions that are so central to today's youth, apparently its use is limited.

Given the impact of having a visual impairment on the development of social skills, students with visual impairments—like Jonas, whom you met at the beginning of this chapter—must receive direct and systematic instruction in areas such as these (Ophir-Cohen et al., 2005; Sacks & Silberman, 2000):

- developing friendships
- promoting risk taking and decision making
- maintaining eye contact and facial orientation
- demonstrating confident body postures
- using appropriate gestures and facial expressions
- using appropriate voice tone and inflection
- expressing feelings
- timing messages during communication
- demonstrating appropriate assertiveness

The Positive Behavior Supports presents examples of goals and activities for teaching social skills to students with visual impairments.

## Behavior Characteristics

Visual impairment alone does not cause a student to have significant behavior problems or disorders, although it does generally have some subtle influences on behavior. For example, students with visual impairments may be socially immature, more isolated, and less assertive than other children (Bishop, 2004; Krebs, 2006), topics that were addressed earlier in this chapter as developmental issues and that may continue throughout childhood and adolescence. Additionally, students with visual impairments sometimes are viewed as less capable of taking care of daily needs, and so others tend to do things for them (Shapiro, Moffett, Lieberman, & Dummer, 2005). When this happens, students can become even more passive.

Some students with visual impairments demonstrate **stereotypic behaviors,** or repeated behaviors that serve no apparent constructive function. Examples include eye pressing, finger flicking, head or body rocking, and twirling (Silberman, 2000). A variety of theories exist as to why students with visual impairments sometimes develop stereotypic behaviors. They may occur because of restricted activity and movement in the environment,

www.napvi.org
The National Association for Parents of the Visually Impaired is an organization of parents who have children with visual impairments. This group's website provides a wealth of information on blindness and visual impairment.

## Infusing Social Skills Instruction in Daily Activities

Social skills typically are developed and refined through observation and imitation of socially competent individuals using various social manners, customs, and nuances in daily life. Because students with visual impairments have difficulty learning by observation, social skills must be taught directly and then reinforced in meaningful, applied contexts. The following are two examples of specific goals for developing social skills in young children with visual impairments, along with strategies for infusing instruction in these skills into daily activities.

**Goal:** The child will maintain appropriate eye contact when engaged in interactions with adults and peers.

- Hold the child in your arms, and encourage him to face adults when they are talking.
- Get down close to the child's level when talking to him. Verbally or physically prompt the child to turn his body toward you when you are speaking.
- Encourage the child to turn his body and head toward a person who is speaking. Reinforce verbally throughout

the day when the child spontaneously looks and faces a person.

- Encourage the child to maintain appropriate eye contact throughout a conversation or interaction.

**Goal:** The child will initiate appropriate and positive comments during social interactions.

- Model specific positive feedback (e.g., "Marc, you're sitting up straight!" "Michelle, I like your new dress!").
- Model appropriate times to say "Please," "No, thank you," "You're welcome," "I'm sorry," and "Excuse me." Reinforce the child and her peers when they approximate and/or spontaneously use these amenities.

Source: Sacks, S. Z., & Silberman, R. K. (2000). Social skills. In A. J. Koenig & M. C. Holbrook (Eds.), *Foundations of education: Instructional strategies for teaching children and youths with visual impairments* (2nd ed., pp. 616–652). New York: American Foundation for the Blind Press. (Original source: McCallum, B. J., & Sacks, S. Z. [1993]. *The Santa Clara County social skills curriculum for children with visual impairments.* Santa Clara, CA: Santa Clara County Schools.)

---

social deprivation, or the absence of sensory stimulation (Scholl, 1987). Usually, professionals try to reduce or eliminate these behaviors by helping the student increase activity or by using behavior change strategies such as those mentioned throughout this textbook (e.g., rewards and teaching alternative, more positive behaviors).

## REVIEW · REFLECT · DISCUSS

1. Review the three limitations imposed by a visual impairment as described by Lowenfeld (1973). What educational strategies and techniques— including those outlined for other students throughout this textbook— could be used to overcome these limitations?

2. This chapter noted that many students with visual impairments have difficulties in social interactions, as did Jonas, the student you met in the chapter introduction. As a teacher, what would your responsibilities be for helping students in social interactions? For helping students who do not have disabilities to include students with visual impairments in the friendship circles?

## Identifying Visual Impairment

The initial identification of a congenital visual impairment generally occurs by an eye care specialist early in a child's life. When an **ophthalmologist,** a physician specializing in the care of the eyes, or an **optometrist,** a professional trained to identify eye problems and to prescribe corrective lenses, detects a visual impairment that cannot be corrected by regular eyeglasses, that professional generally advises the parents to contact their local school regarding special education services. Other young children may be initially identified through child-find activities sponsored by local, regional, or state educational agencies (Pogrund & Fazzi, 2002). For a student with an adventitious visual impairment, initial identification may occur when the student's classroom performance or visual behaviors change, through regular vision screenings offered by local school districts, or by an ophthalmologist or optometrist. Once an initial identification has been made, a determination must be made as to whether the eye condition adversely affects the student's learning. This process involves a comprehensive educational assessment, followed by a determination of eligibility (Lewis & Allman, 2000).

## Assessment

According to regulations in IDEA, students who may have a disability must be assessed in areas related to the suspected disability. A unique focus in assessing students with visual impairments is to determine the extent, if any, to which an eye condition affects learning. Because psychologists and other professionals who usually carry out assessment procedures typically are not specialists in visual impairment, the assessment team should include the VI specialist. This individual often serves as the coordinator of the assessment team and plays a central role in interpreting the student's needs and planning the student's education (Lewis & Allman, 2000). For example, the VI specialist can help other team members know what accommodations are needed so that the assessment is accurate. Some students might need braille materials, others large-type materials, and yet others extended testing time.

Two functional assessments generally are conducted to determine the impact of the eye condition and to provide information for the assessment team. The **functional vision assessment** is designed to directly evaluate the student's efficiency in using her vision. The VI specialist observes the student's basic visual skills, including tracking items with the eyes as they are moved, shifting attention, and reaching for objects. The teacher also observes the student completing a variety of tasks using vision up close (e.g., reading books, writing, and working on a computer) and at a distance (e.g., reading the chalkboard, observing demonstrations, and watching sports events). Observations are made in a variety of environments, especially in those with low, typical, and high levels of light. The **learning media assessment** examines a student's overall approach to using sensory information for learning (i.e., visual, tactile, and auditory) and identifies the kinds of literacy media (e.g., braille, large type, or regular type with low-vision devices) that a student needs in school (Koenig & Holbrook, 1995). The functional vision assessment typically is administered just to students with low vision, and the learning media assessment is administered to all students with visual impairments.

In addition, a **clinical low-vision evaluation** typically is conducted for a student with low vision, either during the comprehensive individual assessment or as a result of a recommendation from that assessment. This involves deciding whether the student could benefit from **optical devices, nonoptical devices,** or other adaptations. This evaluation is conducted by an ophthalmologist or an optometrist who specializes in low vision, ideally one who has had training and experience in working with children.

## Eligibility

After completing the comprehensive educational assessment, the team shares the findings and determines whether a student has a visual impairment that adversely affects learning. At this point, the team examines the assessment results in light of the criteria established by its state to determine whether the student is eligible to receive special education services as a student with a visual impairment. In many states, functional characteristics alone are used to determine eligibility. In other states, both functional and clinical criteria must be satisfied. If you check the website of your state's department of education, you can find these criteria.

**web link**

www.aph.org
The American Printing House for the Blind offers a wide variety of products for persons with visual impairments and professionals who provide educational and rehabilitation services. It has been in existence for more than 150 years.

## REVIEW · REFLECT · DISCUSS

1. What basic considerations must be addressed in order for a student with a visual impairment to receive a fair and unbiased educational evaluation?
2. What are the contributions made by the functional vision assessment and the learning media assessment in determining whether a student has a visual impairment? How do these assessments help professionals in designing educational services?

# How Learners with Visual Impairments Receive Their Education

Students with visual impairments are educated in a variety of educational settings, ranging from home environments to general classrooms to specialized schools (Ajuwon & Oyinlade, 2008). The complexity of individual student needs, coupled with the low incidence of visual impairments, presents challenges to administrators and educators in providing each student with an appropriate education.

## Early Childhood

Young children with visual impairments usually receive educational services in two types of programs (Correa, Fazzi, & Pogrund, 2002). For infants and toddlers (through age two), the most common type of service delivery is similar to the type you have learned about for other young children: a home-based program. Home-based services focus on working with families to optimize their children's development. Early interventionists often model appropriate strategies for working with young children, answer parents' questions, and provide resources. Such programs are offered by a variety of agencies—local school districts, special regional state education agencies, and private agencies—depending on the state or local organizational structure.

For preschool students with visual impairments (those ages three to five), a center-based preschool is a common service delivery option. The focus of center-based programs is on direct and consistent teaching of specific developmental skills (e.g., fine-motor, gross-motor, and language) (Brambring, 2007; Celeste, 2007; Clark & McDonnell, 2008). Again, these programs may be offered through public school districts, private agencies, and other organizations, and they may be special programs for students with visual impairments, general programs for young children with special needs, or, increasingly, inclusive settings which provide early education to students with disabilities and nondisabled peers (Watson & McCathren, 2009).

## Elementary and Secondary School Services

Students with visual impairments generally receive elementary and secondary school services in one or a combination of the following options: consultant model, itinerant services, resource model, or specialized school settings (Lewis & Allman, 2000).

*Visual impairments often are identified at a very young age, and these children begin learning important compensatory skills in home-based or center-based programs.*

### Consultant Model

The consultant model is most appropriate for students who require few or no direct services related to their visual impairments. These students are involved in all activities of the general classroom, and the general education teacher provides primary direct instruction. The VI specialist collaborates closely with the general education teacher to plan appropriate adaptations and modifications of learning activities (e.g., describing pictures, having the student participate in a demonstration, or pairing a student with a partner for a science experiment) and to provide adapted learning materials (e.g., large type, adapted measuring devices, or tactile maps). This approach also may be used to address the vision needs of students with additional disabilities, such as learning disabilities and intellectual disabilities (Erin, 1988; Lewis & Allman, 2000), regardless of the other services they receive.

### Itinerant Teaching Model

The itinerant teaching model is perhaps the most widely used option for delivering specialized services to students with visual impairments. In this model, students attend their

Go to the Assignments and Activities section of Topic 15: Sensory Impairment, in the MyEducationLab for your course and complete the activity entitled "Educational Considerations for Students with Visual Impairments".

local schools, and general education teachers provide most of the instruction. A VI specialist travels from school to school to provide specialized instructional programs. The skills taught by an itinerant teacher specifically target areas of the curriculum that are unique to students with visual impairments, such as braille reading and writing skills, technology skills, independent living skills, and career education skills (Correa-Torres & Johnson, 2004). Also, the VI specialist provides specialized assessments, consults with classroom teachers and others on the educational team, and provides adapted classroom materials. The critical distinction between the itinerant model and the consultant model is that the VI specialist is providing consistent, direct instruction as an itinerant teacher; this does not occur under the consultation model. In reality, VI specialists often serve as both consultants and itinerant teachers.

The itinerant teaching model works well for students who have mild to moderate needs for instruction in specialized skills and are generally independent in the classroom. In addition to the services provided by itinerant VI specialists, orientation and mobility specialists also work on an itinerant basis teaching students to travel safely in the school and community. Examples of how such services can be successful are provided in the Instruction in Action.

### Resource Model

The resource model is ideal for students with visual impairments who have more intense needs than can be met with the itinerant teaching model. In the resource model, a classroom is designated in the school district to serve elementary or secondary students. It is equipped

## instruction in action

## A Unique Application of Differentiation

Providing support for students with visual impairments requires professionals to extend their thinking about differentiation. Consider Mitch, a twelve-year-old with deaf-blindness. Mitch is totally blind in both eyes and has a moderate to severe hearing loss, conditions that were present in infancy. He received early intervention and preschool services and participated in a regular kindergarten program with support from specialists. He attends a fifth-grade class in an elementary school in his home school district, where he receives supplemental support and instruction from special educators, orientation and mobility spe-

cialists, and consultants from a regional special education agency.

In reviewing Mitch's program, team members identified a number of critical factors they believed to be essential for his success. These factors, along with examples of outcomes, are provided in the accompanying chart. As you examine these factors, consider how each is important to Mitch's overall success in school. What are other examples of actions or outcomes for addressing each of the critical factors? Who might be responsible for ensuring that each factor is addressed?

| Critical Factors | Examples of Actions or Outcomes |
| --- | --- |
| Adaptation of materials and activities | Make a tactile tic-tac-toe board for Mitch to use during recess |
| Administrative involvement | Purchase assistive equipment, such as a brailler and a computer<br>Allot time for periodic team meetings |
| Alternative communication | Teach peers to identify themselves by name when approaching Mitch |
| Attitude of belonging | Emphasize social learning and interaction with peers |
| Effective teaming | Ensure parents participate as members of the educational team<br>Identify outside consultants for assistance and resources (e.g., equipment decisions) |
| Instructional strategies | Implement cooperative learning activities |
| Peer involvement | Shift the quality of interactions with Mitch from assistive to social |
| Physical environment | Put braille signs in the hallways, on doors, and in bathrooms<br>Occasionally change the seats of all students to promote interaction and participation |
| Problem-solving skills | Desensitize Mitch to the sound of hallway bells |
| Role release and flexibility | Increase peer interaction by reducing the physical proximity of adults |
| Social expectations | Help Mitch learn how to talk about his feelings instead of crying |
| Students' respect | Ensure peers note Mitch's need for privacy during lunch |
| Support services | Provide orientation and mobility and braille instruction before school |

Source: Adapted from Sall, N., & Mar, H. (1999). In the community of a classroom: Inclusive education of a student with deaf-blindness. *Journal of Visual Impairment and Blindness, 93*, 197–210. Copyright © 1999 American Foundation for the Blind. All rights reserved.

with special materials, resources, and technology, and it is staffed full time by a VI specialist. Students participate in general classroom instruction to the extent determined appropriate by the educational team, with support available throughout the day from the VI specialist. In addition, students needing more intense support go to the resource room for that specialized instruction.

Although students in this type of program may not attend their neighborhood schools, the resource model provides options for students who have instructional needs that can only be met through consistent, often daily, service delivered by a highly trained VI specialist (Lewis & Allman, 2000).For example, students who are beginning to learn braille reading and writing skills need to receive an hour or more of instruction per day simply to address their literacy needs (Koenig & Holbrook, 2000). A similar intensity level likewise would be necessary for older students who have acquired visual impairments and must learn an alternative to print reading.

### Special Classes and Schools

Some students with visual impairments need more than a resource program. They may be educated in full-time special classes offered in local school districts, special day schools, or private schools and specialized schools with residential options (often referred to as *residential schools for the blind*). Day classes or day schools are available primarily in large cities, and many of them include specialized programs to meet the needs of preschool students with visual impairments and students with multiple disabilities (Lewis & Allman, 2000). Most states have a residential school for students with visual impairments.

Students in specialized schools have intense needs that cannot be addressed appropriately through other program options, as was the case for Thomas, who was described in the introduction to this chapter. These students receive all of their instruction from teachers who are specifically prepared to teach students with visual impairments. Specialized instruction is offered throughout the day and, in the case of students in residential schools, during the mornings and evenings as well. Although the environment of the specialized school is typical of most schools, its setting and resources are specifically geared to the needs of students with visual impairments, including accessible computers and other forms of assistive technology; library and media resources; tactile teaching aids and devices; adapted physical education equipment; and so forth.

One concern often leveled at specialized schools is that they provide an isolated, segregated environment. This is rarely true today. Most specialized schools offer a range of options for providing inclusion in the city, town, or neighborhood through community-based instruction as well as local events, clubs, and other activities. Also, many specialized schools offer options for students to attend some classes in the local school district with the assistance of an itinerant teacher who is on the special school faculty (Lewis & Allman, 2000).

Many specialized schools today are developing new options for addressing the needs of students with visual impairments. Most adhere to a so-called revolving-door approach, encouraging short placements for students of one or a few years at a residential school to gain needed compensatory and disability-specific skills while recommending attendance at a local school during the rest of their academic careers (Zebehazy & Whitten, 2003). Also, many schools are offering targeted summer school programs or intensive, short-term instruction during the school year for students enrolled in local school programs. For example, students might attend an intensive, short-term session for two weeks at a specialized school to learn technology skills that will allow more efficient access to information when they return to their local schools.

### Inclusive Practices

Most students with visual impairments are educated in neighborhood schools with peers without disabilities (Conroy, 2008). However, two factors must be considered. First, a general education setting is appropriate for many, but not all, students with visual impairments and, as for all students with disabilities, its appropriateness must be determined by a team and on an individual basis. Second, specific and planned intervention from a professionally prepared VI specialist and other specialists is of paramount importance. These specialists must carry

## Accommodating Instruction for Students with Visual Impairments

### Use of Chalkboards and Overhead Projectors

- Say aloud everything that is being written or presented on the chalkboard or overhead.
- Provide a copy of the information to be written or presented on the chalkboard or overhead to the student in her preferred reading medium.
- Encourage a student with low vision to move closer to the chalkboard or overhead or to use low-vision devices if appropriate.
- Use preferential seating, if appropriate, to allow a student with low vision to have ready access to information presented on the chalkboard or overhead.
- Encourage the student to ask for clarification or more information if something is missed from the chalkboard or screen.

### Demonstrations

- Allow the student to participate in the demonstration if possible, or to explore the materials in advance of the lesson.
- Try to reduce glare and visual confusion by moving away from windows to an uncluttered wall.

- Allow the student with low vision to stand close to the demonstration and to use low-vision devices if appropriate.

### Modeling

- Allow the student with low vision to stand close to the model and to use low-vision devices if appropriate.
- Talk through the steps of the activity.
- Allow the student to touch your hands as you model the activity.
- Provide physical guidance to allow the student to move through the steps of the activity being modeled.

### Field Trips

- Discuss the field trip with the VI specialist in advance to determine the types of adaptations or modification that will be needed.
- Provide printed materials in accessible media and, if appropriate, scale or full-size models for tactilely inaccessible items.

*Source:* Adapted from Holbrook, M. C., & Koenig, A. J. (2000). Basic techniques for modifying instruction. In A. J. Koenig & M. C. Holbrook (Eds.), *Foundations of education: Instructional strategies for teaching children and youths with visual impairments* (2nd ed., pp. 173–193). New York: AFB Press.

---

out a range of activities to ensure that appropriate accommodations and modifications are made in the learning environment and instructional materials and that supplemental instruction is provided as needed (Bardin & Lewis, 2008; Bishop, 2004). If participation in a general classroom setting is deemed most appropriate, the VI specialist works collaboratively with the educational team to accomplish the following:

1. Ensure that all educational materials are provided in appropriate media (e.g., large print, regular print with use of optical devices, braille, recordings), new technologies are making it relatively easy for educators some of these tasks themselves, sometimes more quickly than they could be completed by the VI specialist (Farnsworth & Luckner, 2008)
2. Ensure that the student is instructed in the use of appropriate devices and technology and that these devices are available in the learning environment
3. Provide specialized instruction related to compensating for the visual impairment
4. Recommend seating requirements and other environmental modifications (e.g., lighting control, glare reduction, reading boards)
5. Ensure that teachers and other professionals who provide direct instruction understand the unique needs of students with visual impairments
6. Recommend modifications, if appropriate, in assignments or testing procedures
7. Collaborate with members of the educational team on methods and techniques for including students with visual impairments in routine learning experiences
8. Provide opportunities for students without disabilities to better understand visual impairment (Spungin & Ferrell, 1999)

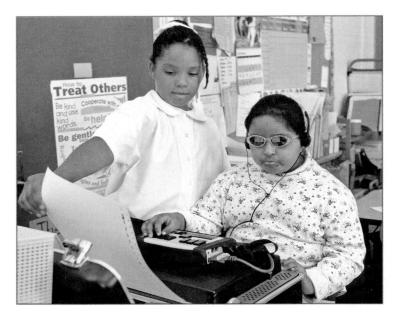

*Students with visual impairments may receive their education in a general education settings, a special education setting, or a combination of the two, depending on their individual needs.*

### Ensuring a Successful Transition to an Inclusive School Program

Planning for a student with a visual impairment to participate in a general education setting requires teamwork. Kevin was born with cerebral palsy, an intellectual disability, severe visual impairment, and other health conditions. When his parents and IEP team decided he should be educated in his neighborhood school instead of the special school he had attended previously, they included these items in planning the transition (Muhlenhaupt, 2002):

**Curriculum, Instructional Methods, and Materials**
- Need for preteaching and reteaching strategies
- Use of highlighted visual material and other visual aids
- Use of word processor and other technology support
- Use of braille materials
- Large print
- Enlarged worksheets
- Use of audiotaped books and videotapes
- Oral or pictorial directions
- Oral responses; need to allow audiotaped assignments
- Brightly colored markers, crayons, and pencils
- Resources from community agencies (community-based associations, federations for people who are blind, committees)

**Environment**
- Preferential seating (bus, classroom, cafeteria, other areas)
- Presence of stairs
- Special lighting
- Need for Kevin to regain familiarity following environmental changes
- Room arrangement (definition of areas; location of supplies, materials, personal belongings)

- Distances to travel on the school campus (safety and efficiency)
- Negotiating the school bus
- Playground opportunities and safety
- Wheelchair availability
- Use of a mobility cane in new surroundings

**Pacing of Work/Activity**
- Reduced amount of copying
- Need for breaks in activities
- Shortened assignments

**Peer Relations and Social Interactions**
- Use of small groups for instruction
- Role of Kevin as a peer and a student
- Use of peer assistance, advocacy
- Role of Kevin's siblings

**Administrative Support**
- Advanced and ongoing training to increase the building staff members' knowledge and confidence
- Ongoing school–family communication
- Coordinating interagency resources
- Plan for on-site medication needs and emergency procedures (seizures, apnea, building evacuation)
- Flexibility in scheduling and providing related services support
- Methods to evaluate the implementation and outcomes of the program

*Source:* Muhlenhaupt, M. (2002). Family and school partnerships for IEP development. *Journal of Visual Impairment and Blindness, 96,* 175–178. Reprinted with permission.

The Instruction in Action provides a summary of the common accommodations and modifications made by VI specialists to allow students with visual impairments to benefit from instruction in general education settings.

In considering which setting is the most appropriate placement for a student, the educational team must consider the individual student's needs. Sometimes a short-term placement in a more specialized setting may offer a better match for a student's learning needs at a given period in his school career. Then, after the student attains appropriate compensatory skills, placement in an inclusive setting may be a valuable and lifelong option. The case study of Kevin in the Professional Edge shows how one educational team worked collaboratively to ensure a successful transition from a specialized school to an inclusive setting.

### Transition and Adulthood

Children with visual impairments have limited opportunities to learn about jobs and workers through observation and incidental experiences. Therefore, the transition to adulthood for these students actually must begin in preschool with a systematic and organized career education program. This effort must continue throughout the school years with a coordinated transition-planning process beginning in high school (Wolffe, 2000).

Students with visual impairments have a very high graduation rate (73.4 percent), higher than that for students in any other disability category (U.S. Department of Education, 2008). However, adults with visual impairments still experience a high level of

A review of 50 years of research on teaching mathematics to students with visual impairments found that only four studies met federal standards for adequate research quality, and none of these have been replicated, calling into question the basis for current practices (Ferrell, Buettel, Sebald, & Pearson, 2006).

**FIGURE 12.4**

**Career Education Competencies throughout the School Years**

| Level in School | Competencies |
|---|---|
| Preschool | Learning to listen |
| | Learning to follow directions |
| | Learning to be responsible |
| | Learning basic organizational skills |
| | Fantasizing about adult roles |
| | Learning to play |
| Elementary school | Learning to follow more complex directions |
| | Learning to work individually and in a group |
| | Learning to respond appropriately to adults and peers |
| | Learning to be responsible for actions |
| | Learning to organize work–school materials |
| | Assuming responsibilities at home and at school |
| | Identifying work roles and assuming them in fantasy and play |
| | Recognizing different community workers |
| | Understanding the rewards of work |
| | Learning to solve problems |
| | Developing good communication skills |
| | Developing basic academic skills |
| Middle school | Meeting increased demands for organizing time |
| | Meeting increased responsibilities at home and in the community |
| | Meeting increased demands for skills development |
| | Showing a full understanding of the work performed by adults |
| | Showing a beginning notion of preferred work for adulthood |
| | Investigating identified areas of interest |
| High school | Showing well-developed academic skills |
| | Showing well-developed thinking skills |
| | Showing well-developed work behaviors |
| | Participating in work activities |
| | Planning for life beyond high school |

Source: Adapted with permission from Wolffe, K. E. (2000). Career education. In A. J. Koenig & M. C. Holbrook (Eds.), *Foundations of education: Instructional strategies for teaching children and youths with visual impairments* (Vol. 2, 2nd ed., pp. 679–719). New York: AFB Press. Copyright © 2000 American Foundation for the Blind. All rights reserved.

unemployment (approximately 74 percent) (American Foundation for the Blind, 2004; Kirchner & Smith, 2005). These two disparate facts demonstrate that students' educational success does not ensure later success in employment, and so improving and strengthening career education programs and transition services clearly must be a priority. Furthermore, the skills addressed through such programs change with increasing age and skill development levels. Wolffe (2000) has identified general career education competencies for students in preschool, elementary school, middle school, and high school, as presented in Figure 12.4. A key element of a student's career education is actual, community-based work experiences (Oddo & Sitlington, 2002).

As with all students who have identified disabilities, the formal transition planning process for students with visual impairments should begin as early as age sixteen with a formal *individualized transition plan (ITP)*. For these students, additional members of the team who assist with developing the transition plan may include representatives from the state's commission or department of services for persons who are blind or the state's rehabilitation agency. Many states have rehabilitation services that are specialized for persons with visual impairments, and professionals from these agencies should participate in developing the transition plans for these students. After graduation from high school, some students may continue in a postsecondary program at a residential school for the blind to gain additional

dimensions of
**DIVERSITY**

Teachers of English language learners who are also visually impaired use real objects to present language to students. In addition, the total physical response approach (e.g., saying stand up and then physically helping the student to stand) may facilitate learning (Conroy, 2005).

skills needed either for employment or to enter a vocational school or a community or four-year college. Other students may enter a vocational rehabilitation program, either one specifically designed for persons with visual impairments or one designed for all persons with disabilities. There they will learn specific vocational skills or receive on-the-job training and support. The elements of a student's postsecondary program, if desired by the student, are specified in a document called the *individual plan for employment* (Moore & Wolffe, 1996). This document is not part of IDEA, but in many ways it is like a postschool transition plan. It delineates the postschool goals of vocational rehabilitation services, outlines the training and other supports that are to be offered, and specifies the timeframe for these services.

The career options for persons with visual impairments are extensive. With appropriate accommodations on the part of the employer and preparation on the part of the individual, almost all jobs available for persons with typical vision are also available to those with visual impairments. Persons with visual impairments include lawyers, teachers, farmers, psychologists, cooks, computer programmers, businesspersons, sociologists, musicians, college professors, and gardeners (Wolffe & Spungin, 2002), to name only a few. The role of the educational team is to help the student explore her individual interests and abilities, provide adequate career education during the school years, ensure a coordinated and effective transition plan, and facilitate the transition to adult services and adult life. How might these ideas be applied as professionals help Thomas, whom you met at the beginning of the chapter, plan for his life after school?

*With appropriate accommodations, the career opportunities for students with visual impairments are nearly limitless.*

## REVIEW · REFLECT · DISCUSS

1. Most students with visual impairments receive some of their education in a general education setting. What questions do you anticipate a general education teacher might have regarding supporting such students?

2. What are the advantages and limitations, both educationally and philosophically, of placing students with visual impairments in specialized school settings? How can you reconcile a belief in inclusive practices with specialized schooling?

3. Recall that individuals with visual impairments usually graduate from high school but have a high unemployment rate. What role might attitudes and employers' unwillingness to provide accommodations have in influencing these data? How might professionals help students transitioning from high school to postschool options to advocate for themselves?

# Recommended Educational Practices for Students with Visual Impairments

Best practices for students with visual impairments center around what, how, and where disability-specific skill instruction is provided for them. As an overview, the areas in which students need specialized instruction constitute *what* is taught, and the principles of special methods offer a framework for *how* instruction is provided. Finally, determining an appropriate educational placement to address each student's identified needs addresses *where* instruction takes place.

## Instruction in the Expanded Core Curriculum

Professionals recognize that students with vision impairments have two sets of curricular needs. First, they must access the existing core curriculum, as required of all students and

research
NOTE

Bruce, Godbold, and Naponelli-Gold (2004) found that teachers of students who are deaf-blind need to learn effective communication techniques—techniques that address just one message at a time and that permit students time to respond.

including, for example, language arts, math, and science. Of course, for most students this includes reaching the high standards mandated in the No Child Left Behind Act (Ferrell, 2005; West, 2005). Second, they must access the **expanded core curriculum** that uniquely addresses visual impairment—for example, compensatory skills, social interaction skills, and career education skills (George & Duquette, 2006; Lohmeier, Blankenship, & Hatlen, 2009). The elements of the expanded core curriculum and specific examples in each skill area are provided in Figure 12.5.

VI specialists, especially those who provide support and instruction to students in inclusive settings, may struggle over the dilemma of what to teach in the limited amount of time available. The pressing demands of the day may force the teacher to focus on tutoring or other activities related to maintaining progress in the general classroom. Despite this challenge, professionals have affirmed that direct teaching of the disability-specific skills of the expanded core curriculum is essential for success in school and adult life and therefore should be considered a cornerstone of best professional practices (Lohmeier, 2007, 2009).

---

### FIGURE 12.5
### Areas of the Expanded Core Curriculum and Examples of Specific Skills

| Expanded core area | Points of Interest | Examples |
|---|---|---|
| Compensatory access skills | Skills that students who are visually impaired need to access all areas of the core curriculum in a manner equal to that of his or her sighted peers. | Concept development, communication modes (calendar systems, braille, print), organizational skills, needed accommodations |
| Social interaction skills | Individuals who are visually impaired cannot learn social interaction skills in a casual and incidental fashion. They learn them through sequential teaching and modeling. | Social concepts, physical skills, social integration, parallel and group play, eye contact, tone of voice |
| Recreational and leisure sills | These skills must be deliberately planned and taught and should focus on the development of lifelong skills. | Hobbies, sports, games, orientation, physical fitness |
| Assistive technology and technology skills | Assistive technology devices provide access to the general learning environment to enhance communication and learning. It makes information that is typically inaccessible readily available. | Media literacy, technical concepts, selection of appropriate assistive devices, media needs, accessibility to information |
| Orientation and mobility skills | O&M emphasizes the fundamental need and basic right of people who are visually impaired to travel as independently as possible, enjoying and learning to the greatest extent possible from the environment through which they are passing. | Body image, travel, spatial awareness, safety, directionality |
| Independent living skills | This area, often referred to as daily living skills, consists of all the tasks and functions that people perform, according to their abilities, to live as independently as possible. | Hygiene, food preparation or retrieval, money management, time monitoring, dressing |
| Career education | Career education is vital because general instruction assumes a basic knowledge of the world of work that is based on prior visual experiences. | Exploring interests, areas of strength, job awareness, planning, preparation, placement, work ethic |
| Sensory efficiency skills | Systematically training students to use their remaining functional vision and tactile and auditory senses better and more efficiently is vital. | Visual, auditory, and tactile learning: environmental cues and awareness, personal attributes, sensory attributes, use of low vision devices |
| Self-determination skills | This area is based on the premise that students who are visually impaired must acquire specific knowledge and skills and have many opportunities to practice them to become successful. | Sense of self, decision making, problem solving, goal setting, personal advocacy, self-control, and assertiveness training |

Source: From Lohmeier, K., Blankenship, K., & Hatlen, P., (2009). Expanded core curriculum: 12 years later. *Journal of Visual Impairment & Blindness, 103,* (102–112). Copyright 2009 by American Foundation for the Blind (AFB). Reproduced with permission.

## Principles of Special Methods

Go to the Building Teaching Skills and Dispositions section of Topic 15: Sensory Impairments, in the MyEducationLab for your course and complete the activity entitled "Using Technology to Support Learning in Students with Visual Impairments".

How students with visual impairments are taught should reflect their unique learning needs (Lohmeier, 2009). For example, general education teachers often rely heavily on demonstration and modeling to deliver instruction, which clearly is not particularly helpful for students with visual impairments. More than 35 years ago, Lowenfeld (1973) described three principles of special methods that help to overcome the limitations imposed by visual impairment. These principles—the need for concrete experiences, the need for unifying experiences, and the need for learning by doing— still guide the field today.

### Need for Concrete Experiences

First, teachers should provide early and ongoing opportunities for students to learn about their environments through tactile exploration of real objects and situations as well as through other available senses. For students with low vision, such experiences should be supplemented, but not replaced, by visual exploration. When actual objects are not available, models may be useful.

### Need for Unifying Experiences

Because a visual impairment limits the ability to perceive the wholeness of objects and events, teachers should provide opportunities for students to integrate parts into wholes. Developing study units, where connections among academic subjects and real-life experiences can be enhanced (e.g., studying community workers in social studies by visiting those workers in their workplaces), is an important way to provide unifying experiences.

### Need for Learning by Doing

Finally, teachers should provide opportunities for students with visual impairments to learn skills by actually doing and practicing those skills. For example, one can easily see the value of teaching a student to bowl by actually going to a bowling alley, renting shoes, selecting a ball, exploring the lane and return mechanisms, using a guide rail to deliver the ball, and keeping score on an adapted score sheet. However, one can quickly understand the absurdity of providing a verbal description of bowling without the actual event to make it meaningful. Most of the areas of the expanded core curriculum lend themselves very readily to a learning-by-doing approach.

All students, regardless of whether they are visually impaired, would benefit from instruction based on these three principles of special methods, and using methods such as these is integral to the concept of universal design for learning (UDL) that has been mentioned throughout this textbook. However, for students with visual impairments, the use of a concrete, activity-oriented approach is a necessity and must be an integral part of teachers' plans for differentiation.

## REVIEW · REFLECT · DISCUSS

1. What elements of the principles of special methods for students with visual impairments may be beneficial for all students? Provide examples to justify your responses.

2. Why do you think the various areas of the expanded core curriculum for students with visual impairments are not addressed in the core curriculum for all students? If you were asked to help a school incorporate the expanded core curriculum into general education classes so that students with visual impairments could be successful, what would you recommend the professionals do?

## Perspectives of Parents and Families

To understand the perspectives of parents of children with visual impairments, you must take the time to listen to their words and, to the greatest extent possible, try to understand

**JAMIE** *is the parent of a daughter with congenital blindness. She describes their experiences here.*

My daughter, Laurel, was born with facial congenital anomalies including a right eye that was small and deformed and a left eye that was missing. I will never forget the doctor's words when he told us that she would never see anything. After several surgeries to fix the obstruction in her nose, we began to focus on the fact that our daughter was blind. I began a search for information, which I devoured as it trickled in. We didn't have regular services from a teacher of the visually impaired, so I began planning our own lessons to help Laurel develop the skills she needed. Everything was a lesson. Laurel didn't learn to reach for a toy or object by happenstance—everything was "taught." I remember working on rolling over, crawling, and reaching. Each step was like climbing a mountain, and just as we mastered one skill, another challenge followed.

Laurel was blessed to have a wonderful educational team that worked with her in elementary school. She did very well in each class setting, participating fully with her peers in projects, classwork, homework, and extracurricular activities. One of my joyous moments came the day I learned that Laurel had been "in trouble" on the playground during recess. Apparently, she would not let the boys into the tunnel that she and the other girls were playing in and someone tattled on her. Her first-grade teacher was perplexed at my joy when she told me of the incident. I explained that I was pleased that she was treating my daughter like any other child in her class and not giving her special privileges just because she was blind. I was relieved to know that the teachers and school personnel saw my daughter as a child first and as a child with special needs second. Laurel's peers soon realized this, too, as they saw the school staff treating Laurel just like everyone else. It has been quite a journey!

This year Laurel made the transition to middle school. The day I dropped her off might have been more difficult than the first day of first grade. I left Laurel at the curb and watched her use her cane to find the sidewalk and make her way to the school building. I knew that if the other students observed her independence, they would begin to develop ideas about how a blind child is just as capable as anyone else in the school. Laurel travels independently and participates in the school choir. Today as I write this, she is taking her first comprehensive semester exams in braille.

I sometimes worry that there are too many skills to learn. Laurel is learning the general education curriculum, but she is also learning the additional compensatory skills needed by visually impaired persons, including technology, orientation and mobility, and daily living skills. I sometimes feel that her life is too full of "lessons" and "assessments." There are some days when she spends excessive amounts of time on homework, and I just wish that she could have time to play and relax like her friends do. We make adjustments, but I worry that she is overloaded. I know that our journey is not over. But, with determination, planning, and hope, we will move on to the next challenges whatever they may be.

their dreams and concerns from their individual points of view (Ulster & Antle, 2005). The Firsthand Account was written by the mother of a sixth grader who is blind. Her words offer glimpses of what it is like to be the parent of a child with a visual impairment: shock at hearing the news from a doctor, thirst for information, concerns over lack of educational services, joy at having a supportive educational team, the satisfaction of knowing her child is accepted by teachers and peers, concerns over the present time demands for developing unique skills, and optimism for the future. Although other parents share similar feelings and perspectives, remember that the individual circumstances of each family, the characteristics of the child, the support received from family and friends, cultural beliefs and customs, and a multitude of other factors influence and continually shape those feelings and perspectives.

## Studying Parent Perspectives

To gain a general notion of the perspectives of parents with children with visual impairments, Leyser and Heinze (2001) conducted a survey of 130 randomly selected parents in Illinois. These parents completed a questionnaire and responded to a series of open-ended questions. The written comments were divided into general themes and further subdivided into specific concerns. Here are the major findings:

- *Concerns and situations that caused stress:* the future, providing for their child's needs, finances, adequate services, effects on siblings, social concerns, and limited information and assistance available to help parents
- *Impact of the child's disability on family and changes over time:* becoming happier over time, changing attitudes toward persons with visual impairments, becoming more com-

passionate, stronger family relationships, increased worrying, and need to plan more for the future

- *Strategies and supports that assisted parents in coping with concerns:* actively helping their child, reading information, discussions with professionals, enjoying recreation and leisure activities, and praying

Additionally, parents commented on their experiences with schools and inclusive practices. The parents generally were supportive but expressed concern about their child's social isolation, limited opportunities for participation in extracurricular and community activities, and classroom teachers' lack of knowledge about visual impairments or unwillingness to make needed accommodations (Leyser & Heinze, 2001).

All of the participants in the Leyser and Heinze study were parents of children who attended public school programs. Other research has focused on the perceptions of similar families but compared them to families whose children attend specialized schools. For example, Ajuwon and Oyinlade (2008) surveyed 220 families across the country. They found that parents selecting between public and special schools made their decisions based on child-related factors, including the child's specialized needs, the availability of knowledgeable professionals, and opportunities for social interactions and friendship with peers with similar disabilities. Parent needs, including a reasonable distance between home and school and parent convenience, generally ranked much lower for both parent groups.

Viewed collectively, the perceptions of parents of students with visual impairments represent themes mentioned throughout this textbook: Parents want what they view as best for their children and what is best depends on their children's characteristics and needs. And, ultimately, parents are willing to do whatever is necessary to ensure successful outcomes for their children.

## REVIEW · REFLECT · DISCUSS

1. Think about all that you have learned about parents' rights related to special education. What role should special educators play in discussing placement options with the parents of students with visual impairments, particularly when one option being addressed is a residential school?

2. How might working with the parent of a student who has a visual impairment be different from working with the parent of a student with a visual impairment as well as physical or intellectual disabilities? How might a situation change again if the parent was from a nondominant culture?

# Trends and Issues Affecting the Field of Visual Impairment

More than 200 years of program development, trial and error, research, and legislative mandates have transformed educational services for students with visual impairments from those that started exclusively in residential schools to those that now are based largely in neighborhood schools. The population of students has also changed from one in which visual impairment was a sole disability to one in which more than half of all students with visual impairments have additional disabilities. As the field continues to develop, professionals face a growing number of issues to address and trends to facilitate, including the personnel shortage and the limited range of placement options for students with visual impairments.

## Shortage of Fully Prepared Personnel

As described elsewhere in this book, shortages of qualified personnel are occurring in many areas of special education. Perhaps now more than at any time in history, the field of visual impairment is facing a particularly severe shortage of qualified personnel to deliver

research
**NOTE**

Suvak (2004) found that teachers of students with visual impairments spent the largest proportion of their time teaching braille reading and writing. The next most frequently completed tasks were adapting materials and working on the deaf–blind curriculum.

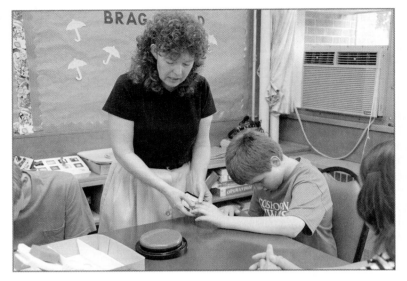

*The shortage of vision specialists has led to the development of innovative teacher preparation programs.*

special education services to students. The issue is so critical that the U.S. Department of Education funded a 2-year project specifically to study the personnel shortage and to generate recommendations for preparing adequate numbers of teachers and other professionals (Mason et al., 2000). Other personnel studies also have focused on this area (Corn & Spungin, 2003). Studies such as these have indicated that just 34 programs are available nationwide to prepare vision specialists (Smith & Kelly, 2007), and of these, some do not have even one full-time faculty member. Similarly, just 17 programs prepare orientation and mobility instructors, and only 10 programs prepare specialists to work with students who are deaf–blind. Using these data and other data regarding the number of students needing services as visually impaired, and based on a best-practices ratio of eight students to one teacher, researchers estimate an immediate need across the United States for 5,000 VI specialists and more than 10,000 orientation and mobility specialists (Corn & Spungin, 2003).

Personnel issues in the field of visual impairments are compounded by other factors. For example, because visual impairment is a low-incidence disability, university programs tend to enroll small numbers of teacher candidates. Economic pressures result when teacher education courses have low enrollments and do not produce very many credit hours; some programs are being forced to reduce or close preparation programs in this area, thus making the personnel shortage even worse. In addition, the number of professionals reported as needed is probably an underestimate because some school districts with students needing services know that they simply will not be able to find the appropriate specialists and so do not even list such positions as unfilled (Mason et al., 2000). Finally, anticipated retirements among professionals in the field may make the problem of finding qualified personnel even more severe.

Think about the implications of this information: If insufficient numbers of teachers are providing services to students with visual impairments, then existing teachers have much higher caseloads than the recommended 8:1 student–teacher ratio. In fact, in a survey of itinerant teachers in North America, an average caseload size of 22 students was found among respondents (Griffin-Shirley et al., 2003). Further, if some vacancies are left unfilled, students will be left without adequate specialized support. At least some students with visual impairments are not receiving appropriate educations under IDEA, though the true magnitude of the impact is not known fully.

The field is taking direct steps in response to the personnel shortage. University programs have started offering distance-based personnel preparation programs using web-based instruction, interactive television, and other approaches (Ajuwon & Craig, 2007; DeMario & Heinze, 2001). Some states have initiated approaches for entering the profession in other than a university-based education, although such options have not met with widespread approval among professionals in the field. Also, some states are developing innovative programs. For example, the state of New Mexico contracted with a university in Texas to prepare 100 new VI specialists and 30 orientation and mobility specialists over a 5-year period (Griffin-Shirley, personal communication, 2003).

### Limited Continuum of Placement Options

A second significant issue facing the field is the limitation in the continuum of educational placement options for students with visual impairments that exists in most parts of the

*Katherine Brittain recalls how she chose to work in the field of visual impairments: "Honestly, in sixth grade I read the book 'Helen Keller' and it was at that point that I knew that I wanted to teach children with visual impairments!" She earned her undergraduate in that area, began her career teaching students with visual impairments in rural West Virginia, and then added a master's degree in special education. She returned to her home state of Pennsylvania, working with students with visual impairments as well as other students with disabilities. She earned certification in orientation and mobility in 1996, and now works as an itinerant vision specialist for the Westmoreland Intermediate Unit in Greensburg, PA. Here is the advice she offers to special educators and other professionals entering their careers:*

- If you have students with visual impairments, establish an open line of communication with the teacher of the visually impaired (TVI). Your cooperative working relationship is the key to success.

- Ask the TVI about the student's eye condition and its impact in the classroom. For example, is one eye stronger than the other? This would affect where you seat the student. Is glare an issue? This might suggest avoiding the use of laminated items. Is lighting a consideration? Does the student experience difficulties copying items from the board? Does the student have specialized equipment that will be used? Allow the TVI to spend as much time as needed in your classroom so that the compensatory skills taught outside of the class (e.g., braille, orientation and mobility, utilization of hand-held magnifiers, skills associated with assorted assistive technology devices) can be integrated directly into the classroom en-

vironment. With NCLB this is essential: I spend at least half of my scheduled time with each student in their actual classroom so the student with a visual impairment can make the transfer of an acquired skill into the daily routine and it becomes a functional skill.

- Foster self-advocacy for visually impaired students. One young student, who couldn't read the words high on the classroom's word wall, asked his teacher, "When it is my turn, can you just point to one that is lower and I can then get as close as I need to read it?!" Students need to be part of the solution at all ages.

- When you work with families, you should ask whether there are visual issues at home. Visual fatigue? Is adequate lighting available?

- Many accommodations used for other students with disabilities are also helpful for the student with a visual impairment, including these: give a copy of the information being written on the board; supplement visual information with auditory input; use manipulatives; use peer buddies; stress organizational skills; and enable student to demonstrate mastery in ways other than paper-and-pencil tasks.

- When planning a class trip, be aware of any difficulties the student may have adjusting to changes, for example, in lighting (bright sunlight to a dark theater).

- Allow for additional storage for the student's materials. They may take up a lot of space!

- If you re-arrange your classroom, be sure to orient the student to the new arrangement. Teach other students to keep belongings off the floor so that the student with a visual impairment can travel safely and efficiently around the room.

---

United States. Although best educational practices, federal law, and federal policy uphold the need for multiple options based on student needs, such placements tend to exist only in large cities and metropolitan areas. In many cases, services in suburban and rural areas are limited to consultant or itinerant teaching in local school programs or specialized schools, as you learned when you read about Anna Marie at the beginning of this chapter. These options do not benefit students who require support throughout the day, such as that provided by resource classes. In some communities, the only viable option is to seek placement in a residential specialized school.

Unfortunately, the field has made slow progress in exploring innovative options for providing a full array of services to students with visual impairments who live in rural areas and other geographic areas facing this challenge. In some cases, school districts have hired paraeducators to provide ongoing services when a VI specialist is not available (Forster & Holbrook, 2005). However, as described earlier, these personnel often are not qualified to teach students and may even hamper students' progress toward independence (Giangreco & Broer, 2007; Lewis & Allman, 2000). The shortage of teachers makes this problem worse. Now that agreement has been established and accepted on principles of best practice, professionals in the field of visual impairment need to turn their attention to the critical issue of expanding the range of placement options for students with visual impairments.

1. How do you think the outcomes for students with visual impairments are affected by the availability or lack of availability of placement options? What options do you think policymakers should explore to address this serious issue?

2. How might the shortage of VI specialists and the limited range of placement options affect you as a special educator who does not have expertise in the area of visual impairments? What would you do if you were assigned a student with a visual impairment, either for direct services or consultation?

## Summary

- The field of educating students with visual impairments has a long history that progressed from the founding of residential schools in most of the United States to the current practice of educating most students in general education classrooms.

- Although definitions of *visual impairment* vary widely, educational definitions focus on eye conditions that have an adverse effect on progress in school and include students who are functionally blind and those with low vision.

- About 1 in every 1,000 students of school age has a visual impairment that influences learning, and about 60 percent of those students have additional disabilities. Visual impairments are caused by a wide variety of conditions related to the eye or to the part of the brain that interprets visual signals.

- Development, learning, behavior, and social and emotional domains are affected significantly by a visual impairment and, as a result, students with this disability have educational needs that are unique.

- Students with visual impairments generally are identified early in life by an eye care practitioner, but eligibility for special education services must be established through individualized assessments that determine the impact of the visual impairment on learning.

- Educational placements are the same as those for other students with disabilities, although specialized residential options are more often considered than for most students with disabilities.

- Best practices for students with visual impairments include the provision of instruction in the expanded core curriculum, use of disability-specific principles of special methods, and decisions on appropriate educational placements.

- The views of parents and families of children with visual impairments vary based on the nature of the visual impairment, the presence of additional disabilities, and the appropriateness of educational placements.

- The field of educating students with visual impairments is facing a severe personnel shortage and a limited range of placement options. These factors have the potential to hamper appropriate services for these students.

Council for Exceptional Children (CEC) Common Core Knowledge and Skills addressed in this chapter:

ICC1K5, ICC1K6, ICC1K7, ICC1K8, ICC2K1, ICC2K2, ICC2K4, ICC2K5, ICC3K2, ICC4S3, ICC4S4, ICC4S5, ICC4S6, ICC5K5, ICC5S3, ICC5S11, ICC7S7, ICC7S9, ICC8S2, ICC9K4, ICC9S2, ICC9S5, ICC10K3, ICC10S6

Appendix: Provides a full listing of the CEC Common Core Standards, and associated Knowledge and Skill Statements listed here.

**PEARSON**
**myeducationlab**

Now go to Topic 15: Sensory Impairments, in the MyEducationLab (www.myeducationlab.com) for your course, where you can:

- Find learning outcomes for the broad concepts covered in this chapter along with the national standards that connect to these outcomes.
- Complete Assignments and Activities that can help you more deeply understand the chapter content.
- Examine challenging situations presented in the IRIS Center Resources.
- Apply and practice your understanding of the core concepts and skills identified in the chapter with the Building Teaching Skills and Dispositions learning units.

- Check your comprehension on the content covered in the chapter by going to the Study Plan in the Book Specific Resources for your text. Here you will be able to take a chapter quiz, receive feedback on your answers, and then access Review, Practice, and Enrichment activities to enhance your understanding of chapter content.
- Watch video clips of CCSSO Teacher of the Year award winners responding to the question: "Why I teach?" in the Teacher Talk section.

## chapter thirteen

# Students with Physical and Health Disabilities

## LEARNING OBJECTIVES

· Outline the development of understanding and services for physical and health disabilities.

· Define *physical disabilities*, other *health impairments*, and *traumatic brain injuries*, and explain their prevalence and causes.

· Describe characteristics of individuals with physical and health disabilities.

· Explain how physical and health disabilities are identified.

· Outline how students with physical and health disabilities receive their education.

· Describe recommended educational practices for students with physical and health disabilities.

· Explain the perspectives and concerns that parents and families of students with physical and health disabilities may have.

· Identify trends and issues influencing the field of physical and health disabilities.

## Ryan

Ryan began kindergarten right on schedule at age five, and he enjoyed school, made new friends, and learned beginning reading and math skills along with his classmates. In April of Ryan's kindergarten year, however, his mother and teacher noticed that he seemed to tire easily. He also had several bouts with unexplained fever. Worried, his mother took him to the family pediatrician. After a series of tests and referral to a specialist called a *pediatric oncologist*, Ryan was diagnosed with leukemia. Chemotherapy was started soon after that, and Ryan missed the final 3 weeks of kindergarten. Now beginning first grade, Ryan has completed his first round of chemotherapy, but he will undergo another cycle of this treatment later in the school year. He attends school for the entire day, but he does not participate in physical education and also has permission to go to the nurse's office for a nap if he is tired. His mother sends him to school with snacks that he eats as he wishes; with little appetite, his doctors are concerned about increasing his caloric intake. Ryan is now bald, so he always wears a baseball cap. His friends at school are jealous since they are not permitted such headwear; one classmate asked if he could wear a cap if he got his dad to shave his head. Ryan's reading skills have not kept pace with those of his classmates, and Ms. Turner, a resource teacher, spends an hour each day in Ryan's classroom, assisting him and two other students with disabilities to improve their skills. Ms. Turner and Ms. Campbell, Ryan's first-grade teacher, are keeping in very close contact with Ryan's mother because his condition and needs can change rapidly.

## Aponi

Aponi is a fourteen-year-old eighth-grade student whose favorite subject is science. She has cerebral palsy and a mild intellectual disability, likely the result of being born 12 weeks premature. She uses a motorized wheelchair to get around her school, and her communication board usually is on its tray. To help Aponi's circulation, she is sometimes placed in a prone stander, a piece of equipment that supports her body so that she can stand with her classmates as they complete a lab during science class. Aponi participates in general education classes for four class periods—English, science, social studies, and one elective, currently technology. She receives reading instruction in a resource class, and she receives consulting services from a physical therapist and an occupational therapist. Aponi also receives speech/language therapy twice each week. Because Aponi has complex physical needs, her IEP team has decided that when she is in general education, she needs a personal assistant to be able to truly participate. The assistant also helps her in moving from place to place, using the restroom, and eating. All of the general education teachers attended a staff development session about working with Aponi, and they know that she needs to learn independence. The result is that the assistant spends less and less time hovering near Aponi and more time working with all the students in Aponi's classes.

## Jeffrey

Jeffrey is eighteen years old and a high school senior. He is looking forward to graduation and is anxious to go to college. However, about 10 months ago, Jeffrey's plans changed radically. Until then, he and his family had assumed he would attend college on a football scholarship. He had been on the varsity team since his tenth-grade year, and his coach frequently commented on his skill and determination, a combination sure to lead to success. Jeffrey had been contacted by several good schools, his grade point average was strong, and he had performed well on the SAT. That all changed during the first home game of the season. When tackled, Jeffrey remembers thinking, "Uh-oh. That was serious." and then remembering nothing else for two weeks. Jeffrey's neck had been broken, leaving him a quadriplegic, that is, with no ability to move either his arms or legs. After a lengthy hospitalization and a month in a rehabilitation facility, partnered with unwavering support from family and friends, Jeffrey regained his strength. With special education services he has been able to complete his remaining courses, and he has learned to use a variety of assistive technology devices so that he can "type" by voice and operate lights and other devices using the small amount of control he has in his left ring finger. What has been a more difficult part of the recovery has been regaining confidence, and Jeffrey has received extensive counseling. One day his blog entry read, "Why did this happen to me? I had everything going for me and I didn't do anything to deserve this. It's not fair; I'll never be a whole person again. Some of my friends won't even talk to me now." However, Jeffrey slowly has realized that he now has new friends, and he will soon graduate with his classmates. One of his graduation surprises, one he already has received, is a service dog. Thunder is trained to open doors, retrieve items that fall, and even to put Jeffrey's arm back on the wheelchair armrest when it slips off. Jeffrey and Thunder plan to spend the summer getting to know each other. Jeffrey's parents, although concerned, are committed to helping him achieve his goal of going away to college. They are counting on Thunder and a personal assistant to provide the supports Jeffrey needs.

Most people know someone who has a physical or health disability. Perhaps as you were growing up, a friend was injured in a car accident and became physically impaired. Perhaps you had a classmate who had juvenile diabetes. Do your own experiences suggest to you that you already know quite a bit about people with physical and health disabilities? If so, caution is in order. Some students with health or physical conditions do not need special education at all—their special needs do not affect their education. Some students, though, have disabilities that are significant and immediately apparent—for example, those who need assistance with mobility, such as using a walker or wheelchair, or those who need help with fine-motor skills, such as holding a pen. This group also includes students who may have illnesses or disorders that you cannot see but whose disabilities still affect their strength, their memory and ability to complete schoolwork, and their behavior. The focus of this chapter is on students with physical and health disabilities who need special education. They are so unique that making general statements about them, while necessary in this overview, includes the risk of creating inaccurate impressions.

## Understanding Physical and Health Disabilities

Interest in the characteristics and needs of people with physical and health disabilities certainly is not new, but early work emphasized medical needs and options for care. As you can see by reviewing the timeline in Figure 13.1, only during the past century did education gradually become a priority.

### Development of the Field of Physical and Health Disabilities

Accounts of people with physical and health disabilities have existed since ancient times, but it was not until the late 1600s that physicians and other prominent professionals advocated for the treatment of these disorders. Even in the nineteenth century, medicine was advancing, but options for assistance still were very limited (Winzer, 1993). The most common recommendation to parents of children with these disabilities was institutionalization. Families who kept their children at home did not have access to programs or services, and whether a child thrived often depended on the family's support network and community assistance (Longmore & Umansky, 2001).

**FIGURE 13.1**
**Timeline of the Development of the Field of Physical and Health Disabilities**

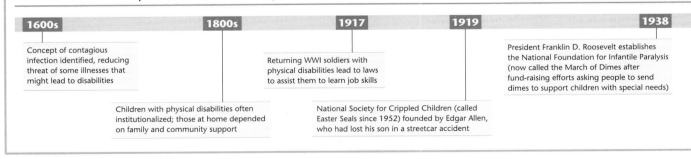

| 1600s | 1800s | 1917 | 1919 | 1938 |

Concept of contagious infection identified, reducing threat of some illnesses that might lead to disabilities

Children with physical disabilities often institutionalized; those at home depended on family and community support

Returning WWI soldiers with physical disabilities lead to laws to assist them to learn job skills

National Society for Crippled Children (called Easter Seals since 1952) founded by Edgar Allen, who had lost his son in a streetcar accident

President Franklin D. Roosevelt establishes the National Foundation for Infantile Paralysis (now called the March of Dimes after fund-raising efforts asking people to send dimes to support children with special needs)

## Increasing Attention for an Ignored Group

Early in the twentieth century, the needs of war veterans forced increasing attention on people with physical and health disabilities, and this attention contributed to a gradual increase in concern about children. Two organizations still active today that you probably are familiar with were founded during this era: Easter Seals and the March of Dimes. Organizations such as these helped keep attention focused on the needs of children with physical and health disabilities. Eventually, with the legal cases of the late 1960s and 1970s and the passage of the federal special education law (now called the Individuals with Disabilities Education Act, or IDEA) in 1975, these children claimed their rights along with other children with disabilities.

## Refining Students' Rights and School Responsibilities

In the years since IDEA was first implemented, two court cases have been particularly significant for students with physical and health disabilities. First, in *Irving Independent School District v. Tatro* (468 U.S. 883), an eight-year-old girl with spina bifida (a condition discussed later in this chapter) needed **clean intermittent catheterization (CIC)** every 3 or 4 hours to help her relieve her bladder, and she could not attend school if this procedure was not performed. Her parents believed the school district was responsible for providing this service, but the district considered it a medical procedure not covered by IDEA. The U.S. Supreme Court supported the parents' view, identifying this procedure as a *related service*—that is, one needed by the child in order to attend school (unlike procedures needed just once a day that could be performed during nonschool hours). The court ruled that because the procedure could be performed by a school nurse or anyone else who attended a brief training session, it was not a *medical service*—that is, one that had to be completed by a physician (Vitello, 1986).

The second court case, *Cedar Rapids Community School District v. Garrett F.* (19 S. Ct. 992), further clarified schools' responsibilities for providing health-related services (Katisyannis & Yell, 1999). Garrett F. was paralyzed from the neck down at age four as a result of a motorcycle accident, and his parents had ensured that his many physical needs were met in the classroom by providing a nurse for him. However, when Garrett was in fifth grade, his parents requested that the school district take over paying for this intensive support. The school district maintained that this was a medical service not required through IDEA. The U.S. Supreme Court ruled against the school district, stating that the only services considered medical were those that could only be performed by a physician. It established that the nursing care needed by Garrett was a related service under IDEA and that schools were obligated to provide it if required for students to attend school.

These two cases made it clearer than ever before that students with physical and health disabilities—those who have disorders such as those summarized in Figure 13.2—have as much right as other students to access education. This is the case even if their needs require professionals to offer highly specialized services.

www.marchofdimes.com
The March of Dimes supports a wide range of research and advocacy activities, all designed to promote the health of babies. This group also partners with organizations throughout the world to expand its mission for infants everywhere.

dimensions of
**DIVERSITY**

Overrepresentation, an issue that is central in considering learning and intellectual disabilities, is generally not a significant factor when prevalence rates are considered for physical and health disabilities.

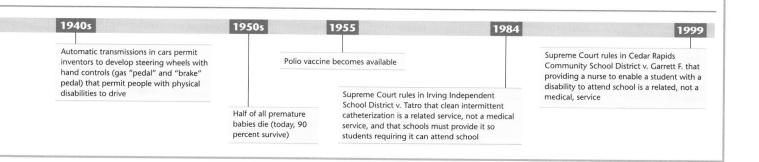

**1940s** Automatic transmissions in cars permit inventors to develop steering wheels with hand controls (gas "pedal" and "brake" pedal) that permit people with physical disabilities to drive

**1950s** Half of all premature babies die (today, 90 percent survive)

**1955** Polio vaccine becomes available

Supreme Court rules in Irving Independent School District v. Tatro that clean intermittent catheterization is a related service, not a medical service, and that schools must provide it so students requiring it can attend school

**1984**

**1999** Supreme Court rules in Cedar Rapids Community School District v. Garrett F. that providing a nurse to enable a student with a disability to attend school is a related, not a medical, service

*Stephen Hawking is an eminent British theoretical physicist who was diagnosed more than 40 years ago with a neuromuscular disorder.*

## web link

http://www.youtube.com/
watch?v=fAdEOXD9Tvk
You can see Ellen, a bright young woman who has cerebral palsy, demonstrating her use of assistive technology at this youtube address.

## Looking at the Big Picture

Before exploring specific examples of the physical disabilities, traumatic brain injuries, and health impairments that school-age students may have, it may be helpful to step back for a moment to keep the following information in perspective. First, review the information on the prevalence of these disorders in Figure 13.3. Two points should be apparent. First, considering that nearly 6 million U.S. students ages six to twenty-one are eligible for special education (U.S. Department of Education, 2008), the total number of students in these groups is very small. If you are a general education teacher, you probably will teach students with one or more of these illnesses or conditions but probably not every year. If you are a special services provider, you are more likely to work with students in these groups, but unless you specialize in this area, you, too, may find that these students are only periodically among those you serve. Second, the data indicate that the categories *other health impairment* (OHI) and *traumatic brain injury* (TBI) have grown dramatically over the past 10 years. For OHI, this growth may in part be attributable to the increase in students identified as ADHD being included in it, a topic addressed in Chapter Six. For TBI, the growth undoubtedly reflects the fact that this disability was added to IDEA in 1990, and it took several years for this identification to be utilized as a label for eligible students.

Most importantly, remember that students with these disabilities have many different needs, and their illnesses and conditions can have many different influences on their learning. Your first need in educating them is to educate yourself about their unique strengths and challenges. Your responsibility is to find out what you need to know to work with them effectively and to ensure that they participate as fully as possible in school experiences (Giangreco, 2001; Myers, 2007).

## Key Concepts for Understanding Physical and Health Disabilities

As you learn about students with physical and health disabilities, several concepts can help your understanding. First, the conditions and disorders described in the following sections can be thought of in terms of how they affect the individual student. Some conditions are **chronic**; that is, they exist all the time, typically change very little, and currently have no known cure. Cerebral palsy is one example. Others are **acute**; they are serious but can be treated and possibly cured. Childhood cancer falls into this group. A third group of disor-

---

**FIGURE 13.2**
**Examples of Physical and Health Disabilities**

| IDEA Disability Category | Examples |
|---|---|
| Orthopedically Impaired (Physically disabled) | · Neurological Disorders<br>· Cerebral palsy<br>· Spina bifida<br>· Spinal cord injury<br>· Musculoskeletal Disorders<br>· Duchenne muscular dystrophy<br>· Juvenile rheumatoid arthritis |
| Traumatic Brain Injury | No separately named examples |
| Other Health Impaired | · Asthma<br>· Epilepsy<br>· HIV/AIDS<br>· Cancer<br>· Sickle cell disease<br>· Diabetes |

ders is **progressive**; they get worse over time and may lead to death. Muscular dystrophy is an example of a progressive disorder. Finally, some conditions and disorders are **episodic**; they occur with intensity but at times are dormant. Epilepsy is an episodic disorder. As you read about the many disorders described in the following pages, see if you can identify into which group each might be placed.

A second set of concepts related to these disabilities pertains to causes. Some physical and health disabilities are *congenital,* or present at birth. These disorders may occur because of a genetic problem or heredity, or they could be the result of an environmental influence (e.g., drug or alcohol use by the mother, injury to the mother or child) during pregnancy. In many cases of congenital disabilities, the cause simply is not known. Other physical and health disabilities are *acquired.* They occur during or shortly after birth (perinatal causes), possibly because of trauma during delivery, or later as a result of an accident, illness, injury, or environmental factor (e.g., a severe allergy).

Finally, as you read this chapter, keep in mind that for some students with physical and health disabilities, no need exists for special education services because the condition is mild or readily treated with medication. These students may receive support through a Section 504 plan, a topic addressed in Chapter Six. For other students, their education will be successful only if special education and significant accommodations are made.

## Understanding Physical Disabilities

Physical disabilities are conditions that affect movement—that is, an individual's gross-motor control or mobility (e.g., walking, standing) and fine-motor control (e.g., writing, holding or manipulating small objects using the hands, oral–motor skills). These disabilities may be mild, moderate, or severe, but in this discussion, the focus is on physical disabilities that have a significant effect on students' lives and educational needs. Aponi, one of the students introduced at the beginning of the chapter, has a physical disability.

### Federal Definition

Although most educators refer to students as having *physical disabilities*, in IDEA this disability category is called *orthopedic impairments.* Throughout this chapter, the former term is used as a synonym for the latter. According to the IDEA definition, an orthopedic impairment is

> a severe . . . impairment that adversely affects a child's educational performance. The term includes impairments caused by congenital anomaly (e.g., clubfoot, absence of some member, etc.), impairments caused by disease (e.g., poliomyelitis, bone tuberculosis, etc.), and impairments from other causes (e.g., cerebral palsy, amputations, and fractures or burns that cause contractures). (IDEA 20 U.S.C. §1401 [2004], 20 C.F.R. §300.8[c][8])

You can tell by the definition that this disability category includes students with many types of disorders. As illustrated in Figure 13.4, some of those disabilities (e.g., those with a neurological basis, such as cerebral palsy) are described in terms of the parts of the body that are affected (Bigge, Best, & Heller, 2000). Specifically, **monoplegia** is the term used when only one limb is involved. **Hemiplegia** occurs when the arm, leg, and trunk of the body on the same side are affected. **Paraplegia** occurs when only the legs are affected. **Tetraplegia**

---

**FIGURE 13.3**

**Prevalence of Physical and Health Disabilities**

| | Number of Students Identified | | |
| --- | --- | --- | --- |
| | *1992–1993* | *2007–2008* | *Percentage Change* |
| Physical disabilities | 52,854 | 60,010 | 13.5 |
| Other health impairments | 65,943 | 625,187 | 948.1 |
| Traumatic brain injury (TBI) | 3,887 | 23,805 | 612.4 |

Source: Figures are from Data Accountability Center. (2009), *Part B data and notes,* Washington, DC: U.S. Department of Education; and U.S. Department of Education (1994), *Sixteenth annual report to Congress on the implementation of IDEA,* Washington, DC: Author.

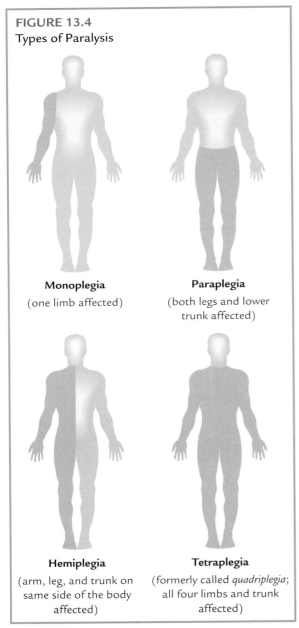

**FIGURE 13.4**
Types of Paralysis

**Monoplegia**
(one limb affected)

**Paraplegia**
(both legs and lower trunk affected)

**Hemiplegia**
(arm, leg, and trunk on same side of the body affected)

**Tetraplegia**
(formerly called *quadriplegia*; all four limbs and trunk affected)

(formerly called *quadriplegia*) involves both arms and both legs, the trunk of the body, and the neck. **Diplegia** occurs when both legs or both arms are involved. At the same time, some physical disabilities do not fall into this categorization scheme. As you read about each disorder, think about why this approach is helpful for thinking about some students but is not relevant for others.

### Neurological Disorders

One group of physical disabilities comprises **neurological disorders** (Bowe, 2000). These conditions occur because of a problem in the central nervous system—that is, the brain, the spinal cord, and their nerve endings. Examples of neurologically based physical disabilities students may have include cerebral palsy, spina bifida, and spinal cord injury.

**Cerebral Palsy.** The term **cerebral palsy** literally means "paralysis of the brain." This disability is a group of conditions involving muscle control, posture, and movement that is not progressive, meaning that it does not get worse over time. The problem that occurs for students with cerebral palsy is not in the muscles themselves. It is in the brain's ability to consistently tell the muscles what to do (Bigge, Best, & Heller, 2000). The most common type of cerebral palsy in children, affecting approximately two-thirds of those with this neurological condition, is called **spastic cerebral palsy** in which students' muscles are stiff (a condition referred to as *hypertonia*) and their movements are awkward. In **athetoid cerebral palsy**, students cannot control their muscles, and so they may have sudden and unexpected twisting motions or other movements. In **ataxic cerebral palsy**, a rare disorder, balance and motor coordination are affected, and students may seem very clumsy, misjudging when they reach for objects and struggling to keep their balance. Finally, students may have cerebral palsy that involves several of these characteristics. This is referred to as **mixed cerebral palsy**.

When cerebral palsy is present at birth, its causes are usually unknown. However, any factor that can damage the developing baby's brain can increase the risk. For example, a genetic abnormality affecting the brain may result in cerebral palsy. Likewise, premature babies are at risk as are those who have other medical conditions (e.g., heart problems, kidney problems) (Adams-Chapman, 2009). Newborns whose mothers abused alcohol or drugs, smoked cigarettes, contracted rubella or other serious infections, or experienced serious malnutrition during pregnancy also are at increased risk. After birth, children may develop cerebral palsy as a result of asphyxia—for example, by choking on toys or food or nearly drowning. Cerebral palsy also can occur when a child has been abused. Finally, severe infections such as meningitis can lead to cerebral palsy.

Because cerebral palsy involves a malfunction in the brain, students with this condition often have other disabilities as well (Kilincaslan & Mukaddes, 2009). This is true for Aponi, the student who has both cerebral palsy and an intellectual disability, whose story begins the chapter. These students also may have vision or hearing loss, learning disabilities, receptive and expressive communication disorders, or seizure disorders. Their physical limitations also may affect their ability to complete daily activities that you take for granted, including swallowing, controlling the bladder and bowels, and even breathing. But keep in mind that these students are unique (Davis et al., 2009): A student who has significant cerebral palsy may be academically gifted. Professionals need to be sure that they do not let the overall physical limitations of these students influence their perceptions of the students' abilities.

The total number of children with cerebral palsy can only be estimated because they may be counted for IDEA purposes in the very broad category of **orthopedic impairments**.

Alternatively, they may be included as having an intellectual disability, traumatic brain injury, or multiple disabilities. Professionals estimate that between 5,000 and 10,000 babies each year are born with cerebral palsy and that another 1,500 preschool children acquire it through illness or injury (Centers for Disease Control and Prevention, 2004; National Dissemination Center for Children with Disabilities, 2004).

**Spina Bifida.** When some children are born, the bones of the spinal column are not closed properly. This condition is called **spina bifida** (literally meaning "a split or divided spine"), and it also is a physical disability with a neurological basis (National Dissemination Center for Children with Disabilities, 2002; Sandler, 1997). Two types of spina bifida generally do not lead to significant disabilities: *spina bifida occulta* and *meningocele* (Singh, 2003). The third type, **myelomeningocele**, occurs when the spinal cord and its covering protrude from the opening in the spine. This type of spina bifida is nearly always severe. Students with this condition usually are paralyzed in their lower bodies and legs. They often have *hydrocephalus* (an accumulation of cerebrospinal fluid in the brain), a condition that can be relieved by inserting a *shunt,* a small plastic tube that drains the fluid (Marlin, 2004). They also are likely to have various seizure disorders as well as bladder and bowel problems. Infants with severe spina bifida usually undergo surgery shortly after birth to close the opening in the spine, but this does not eliminate the effects of the condition.

Professionals agree that 75 percent or more of the cases of spina bifida are preventable (Center for the Evaluation of Risks to Human Reproduction, 2003; Spina Bifida Association of America, 2009). In particular, studies have suggested that women of childbearing age who eat a diet rich in folic acid are at much less risk for having a baby with spina bifida than are other women (Brent & Oakley, 2006), and the National Institutes of Health (1997) recommend that all women ages fifteen to forty-four take a folic acid supplement. Further, since 1996, the Food and Drug Administration (FDA) has recommended that breads and similar foods be fortified with folic acid (Kurtzweil, 1999). These public health actions had a positive effect: The incidence of spina bifida has fallen significantly (Boulet, Gambrell, Shin, Honein, & Mathers, 2009).

Currently, professionals estimate that slightly less than 18 out of every 100,000 children born have spina bifida. In 2002, that meant that only approximately 700 cases were reported (Mathews, 2009). The hope is that with continued education of women across all socioeconomic and ethnic groups and ongoing folic acid research, this number will drop even more.

**Spinal Cord Injury.** **Spinal cord injuries** are an increasingly common source of neurological physical disabilities, particularly among adolescents. These injuries occur when there is a break, severe bruise, or other damage to the spinal cord that affects motor and sensory functions. It is through the spinal cord that most messages are carried from the brain to various parts of the body and from various parts of the body back to the brain. With a spinal cord injury, the brain cannot communicate with the body, and the result is paralysis. The type and extent of paralysis is determined by where the injury occurs; the higher up the spinal cord toward the neck, the more extensive the paralysis. Jeffrey, the student you met at the beginning of this chapter, experienced a sports-related spinal cord injury.

The causes of spinal cord injuries are ones that may have affected you, a family member, or a friend. They include automobile accidents (approximately 42 percent of cases), acts of violence (15 percent), falls (27 percent), sports injuries (7 percent), and other injuries (9 percent) (National Spinal Cord Injury Statistical Center, 2009). Among the injuries from violence, most result from gunshot and knife wounds, and the victims are likely to be from racial or ethnic minority groups. Among the injuries caused by sports, two-thirds are diving accidents.

Other data on spinal cord injuries also are important (National Spinal Cord Injury Statistical Center, 2009). Approximately 80 percent of all spinal cord injuries happen to males and only 20 percent to females. The age range of those who have suffered these injuries has been changing—over the past several years, the average age of injury has increased from nineteen years old to twenty-eight years old. These injuries are almost entirely preventable. Wearing a seatbelt, avoiding diving in shallow water, and using protective gear during sports are only three examples of how the incidence of spinal cord injuries could be greatly reduced.

**web link**

www.cerebralpalsyfyi.com/index
.html
At the website for Cerebral Palsy FYI, you can learn more about this physical disability. The site also contains links to several other national organizations dedicated to the study of cerebral palsy and to the support of individuals affected by it.

Go to the Assignments and Activities section of Topic 14: Physical and Health Impairments, in the MyEducationLab for your course and complete the activity entitled "Raising a Child with Spina Bifida".

**web link**

www.spinalcord.org
The National Spinal Cord Injury Association includes information about adults and children with these injuries. The site has an index that covers many related topics.

*Rapid advances in technology are creating new opportunities for students with physical disabilities.*

Physicians can test to see if a child has muscular dystrophy even before the baby is born.

www.arthritis.org/communities/ juvenile_arthritis/ children_young_adults.asp
The Arthritis Foundation website has pages that explain this disorder as it occurs in children. Included are tips for parents, information about medication, and several types of information specifically for teachers.

## Musculoskeletal Disorders

A second group of students with physical disabilities have **musculoskeletal disorders** (Bowe, 2000); that is, their disabilities are the result of problems related to the skeleton or muscles. Two of the most common disorders are Duchenne muscular dystrophy and juvenile rheumatoid arthritis.

**Duchenne Muscular Dystrophy.** Muscular dystrophy is actually an entire group of genetic disabilities, but the most common and most severe form of it is called **Duchenne muscular dystrophy**, named for the French neurologist Guillaume Benjamin Amand Duchenne who first described it in the 1860s (Muscular Dystrophy Association, 2000). Duchenne muscular dystrophy occurs when a protein called *dystrophin*, used by the body to keep muscles working properly, is missing or significantly deficient. The first symptoms of muscular dystrophy usually occur when children are toddlers. They may seem awkward, and they may walk later than their peers. By the elementary years, these children's muscles begin to deteriorate, and usually by age eleven or twelve, they need a wheelchair for mobility. The deterioration of muscles continues through adolescence, eventually affecting the lungs and heart. Individuals with this disorder typically die by the time they are in their late teens or early twenties (National Institute of Neurological Disorders and Stroke, 2009).

Duchenne muscular dystrophy is a genetic disorder that occurs only in boys. It is carried on the X chromosome, and if a woman transmits the chromosome to her son, that child has a 50 percent chance of having the disease. Because fathers give their sons a Y chromosome, they cannot transmit the disease. If a girl inherits the defective X chromosome, she becomes a carrier of the disorder, but she usually does not develop muscular dystrophy. Approximately 1 in every 3,500 to 5,000 boys have muscular dystrophy; that means about 15,000 school-age children have Duchenne or a milder form of this disorder.

**Juvenile Rheumatoid Arthritis.** Arthritis is characterized by inflammation of the joints, and it exists in more than 100 forms, making it the most common chronic health condition in all people over the age of fifteen (Arthritis Foundation, 2006). **Juvenile rheumatoid arthritis (JRA)** is a form of this disease that is diagnosed when symptoms last for more than 6 weeks in children who are sixteen years of age or less. The symptoms of the disorder are redness, swelling, and soreness in one joint or several joints. Students with this disorder may limp in the morning, they may sometimes have limited mobility, and they may develop eye inflammations. The symptoms vary from student to student, and some students may have periods when no symptoms are present at all.

The exact cause of juvenile rheumatoid arthritis is not known. It is an *autoimmune disorder,* in which the body mistakenly responds to some of its own cells as though they are foreign and should be fought off. The symptoms of JRA occur when the immune system attacks these healthy cells. Researchers speculate that juvenile rheumatoid arthritis is a genetic disorder that is then triggered by a factor in the environment, perhaps a virus. Juvenile rheumatoid arthritis occurs in approximately 50 of every 100,000 births (Harold, 2009). Professionals estimate that between 150,000 and 200,000 children now have the disorder. This disorder is found more often among girls than boys, in a ratio of approximately 2:1. Some children outgrow JRA, but most continue to have some types of symptoms throughout their lives.

## Understanding Traumatic Brain Injury

A second group of students with physical and health disabilities have a brain injury. The IDEA definition of this disorder refers to it as **traumatic brain injury (TBI)**, the result of a sudden and significant insult to the brain. You will find, though, that brain injury caused by other factors such as near drowning, diseases, or electrical shock is sometimes referred to as **acquired brain injury (ABI)** (Brain Injury Association of America, 2009), and this group of injuries is not directly addressed in IDEA.

### Federal Definition

According to IDEA, *traumatic brain injury* is defined as

> an acquired injury to the brain caused by an external physical force, resulting in total or partial functional disability or psychosocial impairment, or both, that adversely affects a child's educational performance. The term applies to open or closed head injuries resulting in impairments in one or more areas, such as cognition; language; memory; attention; reasoning; abstract thinking; judgment; problem solving; sensory, perceptual, and motor abilities; psychosocial behavior; physical functions; information processing; and speech. The term does not apply to brain injuries that are congenital or degenerative, or to brain injuries induced by birth trauma. (IDEA 20 U.S.C. §1401 [2004], 20 C.F.R. §300.8[c][12])

This disability category was added to IDEA in 1990, and so educational information about students with TBI is still emerging. Nearly all students who are identified as having traumatic brain injuries will have been hospitalized, making medical information integral to understanding these students.

### Types of Traumatic Brain Injury

In some cases, traumatic brain injury is caused by a direct blow to the head, as might happen during a sports activity or in a fall. Other causes include physical violence and automobile accidents. When the brain is injured by bouncing around inside the skull but there is no physical damage to the skull itself, the injury is referred to as a **closed head injury**. When the skull is fractured and the membrane surrounding the brain is penetrated, resulting in the brain being directly injured, the injury is referred to as an **open head injury** (Michaud, Semel-Concepcíon, Duhaime, & Lazar, 2002).

Sometimes a mild brain injury is referred to as a *concussion;* this type of injury accounts for the majority of brain injuries. Usually, a child who receives a concussion does not lose consciousness. However, as you may know, a concussion is a serious injury that requires medical attention (Youse, Le, Cannizzaro, & Coelho, 2002). Professionals fear that many children's injuries are never brought to anyone's attention and that some children who would benefit from treatment do not receive it (Hux, Marquardt, Skinner, & Bond, 1999).

### The Effects of Traumatic Brain Injury

Nearly any domain of functioning can be affected by traumatic brain injury (Arroyos-Jurado & Savage, 2008; Keyser-Marcus et al., 2002). These are some of the areas that may be significantly affected when students experience traumatic brain injuries:

- *Cognitive skills.* Students may experience difficulty with reasoning, problem solving, memory, and organization.
- *Processing ability.* A traumatic brain injury can affect the speed at which a student can interpret information received through all the senses. For example, if someone is speaking to a student while music is playing, this may cause confusion and frustration.
- *Language.* Depending on the part of the brain that is injured, some students may experience speech and language disorders. In particular, they may have difficulty comprehending language and speaking fluently.
- *Academic achievement.* Many students with traumatic brain injuries regress in their levels of achievement and may struggle to regain lost skills and learn new ones.
- *Emotions.* Students who have experienced traumatic brain injuries often are characterized as having a changed personality. In many cases, they have difficulty controlling their emotions, and they may become frustrated, angry, or upset with an intensity that surprises their teachers and other professionals and often leads students to experience difficulties with peers (Yeates et al., 2007).
- *Behavior.* Students with traumatic brain injuries may have behavior problems similar to those of other students (e.g., refusing to work, leaving the classroom without

PEARSON
**myeducationlab**

Go to the Assignments and Activities section of Topic 16: Multiple Disabilities and Traumatic Brain Injury, in the MyEducationLab for your course and complete the activity entitled "Traumatic Brain Injury".

Students with Physical and Health Disabilities    **407**

**DAVID AND MELONIE** *are the parents of Trae and his three siblings. In this blended family, the emphasis has shifted from what Trae cannot do to what he can do now and probably will be able to do in the future.*

**Melonie:** Trae was a victim of shaken baby syndrome at ages nine, ten, and eleven weeks. Although he survived, for the first three years of his life he was medically fragile and identified as having traumatic brain injury. He began receiving early intervention services at about eighteen months and started in the school district at age four.

I was extremely protective of him because of what had happened. When Trae was five, I was finally told, "Back off, Mom."

In school, Trae was in a special education class with students with physical disabilities and cognitive impairments. The only class he went to with other students was art, but the stipulation was that if other kids were ever making fun of him or if the assistant left his side, then he was to be pulled back to the special education setting.

Then I was accepted in Partners in Policymaking [a national program to train parents of children with disabilities in leadership skills]. They told me that whenever I talked about Trae, I introduced him as a victim of shaken baby syndrome, who did not talk, had trouble walking, had trouble learning, and had a visual impairment. What the director told me is that I did not have any of those things—what I had was a little boy. I came home crying; I said I was going to quit. And then it got worse. I went to a seminar and the speaker said, "We're doing an injustice to our children if we keep them segregated, separated." And I raised my hand and said to him, "Who are you to

come in here and tell us what to do with our children?" I was afraid Trae would be hurt again. And the speaker said, "But you're the one hurting him."

**David:** At this time, we were dating. Melonie had told me all the things Trae couldn't do. Initially, watching him play videogames, I was thinking, "He's a mama's boy." I was able pretty quickly to see past the disabilities and could help her get through this. I went to some school meetings and was appalled at how they were set up. A lot of things had to change to make good things happen.

**Melonie:** And then I got it. I understood what was possible.

**David:** And another thing was that at this point we were married or about to be married and so he got new siblings. The competitiveness and all that brought him up to another level of wanting to excel, wanting to compete. That, coupled with inclusion, and he just took off.

**Melonie:** And so it started with art, music, and PE. And I said that wasn't enough, and so science and social studies were added. And he had the best special education teacher ever—working on her master's degree and full of energy, ready to do anything for the children. When Trae was in special education, it was different than before. In his earlier classes, it was stacking blocks, more like daycare. But in third grade, this new teacher said, "Oh, my gosh, this little boy has everyone fooled. He is so smart. It's amazing what he knows." She had them learning content; it was hard to tell her room from the general education classroom.

Now, in fourth grade, we have a little boy who, instead of stacking blocks, just got a 93 percent on a test on the layers of the earth. He's got a memory like a steel trap. Once we found out how to help him communi-

cate (gestures and a communication board), it definitely helped. We're still convincing some people of what he can do. For example, we were told he had no fine-motor skills. The assistive technology person came to our home with his teachers to watch him manipulate through video games—with no problems. And they couldn't do what he did because it was too many buttons!!! They were forgetting that he tends to do things—but only when he's motivated.

Trae just turned eleven, and he's all boy. He loves trains and basketball, and he's taking an interest in girls. He's also very independent now. He has friends, and when I want to give him a kiss now, he's like, "Yuck!"

From an academic standpoint, we know we have to stay on top of things. Everyone else's dreams for their children are to be a doctor or lawyer. All I ask is that he have a job, that he be a contributor, and that he be accepted in the community. From what teachers tell us, the other kids, even those who at first did not want Trae in their class, now encourage him. At the field day, one little boy who was very competitive even helped Trae—jogging backwards to tell Trae to hurry. He helped Trae to finish even though it meant the boy didn't win. Trae benefited, but we've got a little boy who's changing other people's lives. What more of a contributor could you ask to be?

Trae and his parents have truly made a difference. The individual who abused Trae was never prosecuted because the statute of limitations ran out before he was charged. Melonie advocated for a change in the law on behalf of Trae and all other abused children. As a result of her efforts, Trae's Law lengthened the statue of limitations in Texas for causing injury to a child—as well as individuals who are disabled or elderly—to ten years.

permission, hitting others), but their problems may be more intense and more difficult to address because of the other cognitive difficulties caused by the injury (Bullock, Gable, & Mohr, 2005).

### Prevalence and Causes

The statistics on traumatic brain injury are sobering. This condition is the most common cause of disability and death among individuals in the United States under the age of twenty-one, resulting in 37,000 hospitalizations and 435,000 emergency room visits each year (Centers for Disease Control and Prevention, 2006). The two age groups at highest risk for TBI are children ages zero to four and young adults ages fifteen to nineteen; and boys are about twice as likely as girls to experience a brain injury. The causes of TBI are, for the most part, preventable (Centers for Disease Control and Prevention, 2006). TBI occurs in automobile and motorcycle accidents (20 percent of all TBI), especially when children are not wearing seatbelts or are not otherwise properly restrained or protected. It also results from children falling (28 percent), for example, from their bicycles when they do not have on protective headgear or from playground equipment. Assaults (e.g., firearms use) also are a major cause of TBI (11 percent). One final cause is referred to as struck by/against (19 percent) and includes child abuse, especially shaken baby syndrome. Trae is a child with a traumatic brain injury as a result of child abuse. You can read about his challenges and accomplishments in the Firsthand Account.

## Understanding Other Health Impairments

Some students have disabilities that cannot be seen but relate to health conditions. In IDEA, students with these disabilities are categorized as having **other health impairment**, the term *other* separating this group from students with intellectual or other disabilities that also may affect health.

### Federal Definition

The IDEA definition for this disability category is as follows:

> Other health impairment means having limited strength, vitality or alertness, including a heightened alertness to environmental stimuli, that results in limited alertness with respect to the educational environment, that—
>
> i. Is due to chronic or acute health problems such as asthma, attention deficit disorder or attention deficit hyperactivity disorder, diabetes, epilepsy, a heart condition, hemophilia, lead poisoning, leukemia, nephritis, rheumatic fever, and sickle cell anemia; and
>
> ii. Adversely affects a child's educational performance. (IDEA 20 U.S.C. §1401 [2004], 20 C.F.R. §300.8[c][9])

### Examples of Health Impairments

Hundreds of health impairments that may affect children have been identified, but only a small sample of these disorders can be addressed here. If you read Brittany Matthews's story in the Firsthand Account, you can see just how complicated issues related to health impairments can become. Keep in mind, too, that students with attention deficit–hyperactivity disorder (ADHD) may receive special education services through this disability category, and so some of the students labeled with this disability were discussed in Chapter Six. Other types of health impairments are described in the following sections.

**Asthma.** The most common chronic illness among children is **asthma**, a lung disease that causes episodes of extreme difficulty in breathing (Gabe, Bury, & Ramsay, 2002). For some children, asthma may be fairly benign; for example, they have coughing spells when they laugh too hard. For other students, the condition is much more serious. When exposed to certain triggers, these students' airways swell and they produce mucus that makes it difficult for them to breathe (Lim, Wood, & Cheah, 2009). These students may require emergency medical intervention. Asthma has a clear hereditary basis—if one parent has asthma, his or her child has a 50 percent chance of also having this disease (Lemanek & Hood, 1999). However, it often is triggered by allergens, including tree and grass pollen, dust, molds, animal

**fyi**

Children who experience mild brain injuries may not be able to articulate what they are feeling. Some signs of a potential problem include listlessness, irritability, a change in eating or play habits, and loss of balance.

research
**NOTE**

Nowicki and Sandieson (2002) completed a meta-analysis (i.e., a study of studies) of students' attitudes toward people with physical and intellectual disabilities. They reported that children tend to prefer other children without disabilities over those with disabilities, suggesting that teachers have a significant responsibility to foster positive interactions among students with and without disabilities.

**BRITTANY MATTHEWS**

*is 19 years old and a sophomore at the University of North Carolina at Greensboro where she is pursuing a double major in communication studies and recreational therapy. But she's not just any student; she has overcome daunting health obstacles to pursue her dreams.*

When I was 13 months old I was diagnosed with a condition called common variable immune deficiency—CVID for short—which means I don't have an immune system and am very susceptible to infections. I have Evans syndrome, an autoimmune disorder where my body attacks itself–red blood cells, white blood cells, and platelets. There are only a few hundred cases in all of North America. Everything in my body turned against itself and created this complete devastation. I was in the hospital from the time I was diagnosed until I was about 2 1/2 years old. I'd come out for the weekend and I'd be right back in three days later. The hospital became my second home. It was hard for my parents, hard for my family.

Then they found out I have idiopathic thrombocytopenic purpura (ITP), where not only was my body attacking itself, but I also had an abnormally low number of platelets. There was nothing they could do. So all the way through preschool, elementary school, and middle school I couldn't play any physical contact sports. All the other girls were in there doing cheerleading and volleyball, softball, whatever. And I couldn't do that because it was life threatening to me. And people didn't understand that, teachers didn't understand it. They said, "She doesn't look sick." I know I don't look sick, but if you could see those lab reports, if you could see the doctor's reports, you'd understand what's going on.

I had to repeat kindergarten because I missed so many days. It was baffling. My mom asked about guidelines for kids who had illnesses and disabilities. They didn't tell us about that until my mom brought it up. And then they wrote at IEP, but it was after that year. I had an IEP until I was in the 7th grade. I also had a cleft palate that was corrected with surgery when I was in the first grade, and so I needed speech therapy, but then I didn't need that anymore. They switched me to a Section 504 plan at that point.

In middle school I was teased so much. I didn't know people could be this mean, but in the cafeteria one day I went to sit down at a table and these girls wouldn't let me sit there because they said I was a freak. I was on steroids all the time for my illness, and they make you blow up really big. They would tell me I was a freak; they would call me blowfish, Ms. Piggy, all these names. What hurt me most was that they were excluding me from their group just because I wasn't pretty enough to sit with them.

In 8th grade, the Evans syndrome, which had been in remission for six years, came back in full force. I missed the second half of my 8th grade year and the beginning half of my 9th grade year. I got really depressed because all my friends went through the 8th grade graduation, they were hanging out with each other over the summer getting ready for high school . . . and I was in the hospital. I was home-schooled for the spring semester of 8th grade and when 9th grade started I begged my doctors, "Can I please go back?" They kept telling me, "No, you're too weak, you're too sick." A home teacher would come in and I'd do my work, I'd do my tests. She'd take it back to school, and then she'd come back and bring more. I was kind of teaching myself a little bit, and having her teach me, but it wasn't the same as being in school. I had been schooled this way for three or four months in third grade when they did surgery to repair my webbed fingers, and my platelets hadn't come back the way they should; they wouldn't let me return to school until I was healthier.

I got to back to school second semester of 9th grade. Now going to 9th grade was hard enough, but going 2nd semester, when everybody's been there for a semester, made it doubly challenging. Thankfully, my brother was a junior at the time, and his friends were there, and they didn't let anybody pick on me. I really got into debate in high school, speech and debate, and people in that were a lot more understanding. And they became my group of friends. I didn't care what everybody else thought–I just really wanted to have friends.

I had an awesome counselor named Ms. Brown. She helped me get a scholarship to go to college. It surprised everyone because I was always ill and the scholarship included helping others. But I always tried to do that, whenever I could. I also had a great hospital teacher named Ellen. My mom called her my guardian angel. She has known me since I was in kindergarten, and she is the one who made sure everything got done—letters from the doctors for school, schoolwork help, and on and on.

Ultimately, I'm comfortable with my illness. People are going to ask about it, and it's easier to tell them about it than to have them making up their own stories.

dander, and food allergies to eggs, seafood, and other items, as well as by strenuous physical activity (Greiling, Boss, & Wheeler, 2005). Fortunately, for most students asthma usually can be controlled through medication and attention to environmental triggers (Cates, 2009; Taras & Potts-Datema, 2005).

Asthma affects approximately 9.4 percent of all children in the United States, or about 7 million students (Centers for Disease Control and Prevention, 2009a). Further, the number of cases of asthma has been rising, and the severity has been increasing. Experts in this field advise parents to protect their children from known triggers such as tobacco smoke, outdoor allergens, certain foods (e.g., nuts) as one means of addressing this problem (Cates, 2009). Only students who have severe asthma are likely to be entitled to special education services.

## First Aid for Seizures

Everyone should know how to respond if someone (child or adult) is having a seizure. The following first aid procedures are recommended Epilepsy Foundation of America, 2009).

### First Aid for Generalized Tonic-Clonic (Grand Mal) Seizures

- Keep calm and reassure other people who may be nearby.
- Don't hold the person down or try to stop his movements.
- Time the seizure with your watch.
- Clear the area around the person of anything hard or sharp.
- Loosen ties or anything around the neck that may make breathing difficult.
- Put something flat and soft, such as a folded jacket, under the head.
- Turn the person gently onto one side. This will help keep the airway clear. Do not try to force the mouth open with any hard implement or with your fingers. It is not true that a person having a seizure can swallow his tongue. Efforts to hold the tongue down can injure the teeth or jaw.
- Don't attempt artificial respiration, except in the unlikely event that the person does not start breathing again after the seizure has stopped.
- Stay with the person until the seizure ends naturally.
- Be friendly and reassuring as consciousness returns.
- Offer to call a taxi, friend, or relative to help the person get home if he seems confused or unable to get home by himself.

### First Aid for Nonconvulsive Seizures

You don't have to do anything if a person has brief periods of staring or shaking of the limbs. If someone has the kind of seizure that produces a dazed state and automatic behavior, then do the following:

- Watch the person carefully, and explain to others what is happening. Often people who don't recognize this kind of behavior as a seizure think that the dazed person is drunk or on drugs.
- Speak quietly and calmly in a friendly way.
- Guide the person gently away from any danger, such as a steep flight of steps, a busy highway, or a hot stove. Don't grab hold of her, however, unless some immediate danger threatens. People having this kind of seizure are on "automatic pilot" as far as their movements are concerned. Instinct may make them struggle or lash out at the person who is trying to hold them.
- Stay with the person until full consciousness returns, and offer to help her return home.

*Source:* Adapted from Epilepsy Foundation, (2005a, 2005b). First aid for generalized tonic clonic (grand mal) seizures and first aid for non-convulsive seizures. Used with permission of the Epilepsy Foundation, www.epilepsyfoundation.org, 1-800-332-1000.

---

**Epilepsy.** A second example of a health impairment, one that is the result of a central nervous system problem, is **epilepsy**, sometimes called a **seizure disorder**. Epilepsy is a neurological condition in which damage to the brain leads to periodic sudden, uncontrolled bursts of electrical activity that may be seen as seizures (Michael, 1995).

Epilepsy occurs in two major categories: partial and generalized (Weinstein, 2002). **Partial seizures** occur when the electrical discharge affects only part of the brain. Partial seizures may involve involuntary twitching of muscles or rapid eye blinks. You may be more familiar with **generalized seizures** (Avoli, Rogawski, & Avanzini, 2001), the most well known of which is the **tonic-clonic seizure** (formerly called a *grand mal seizure*). Sometimes this type of seizure is preceded by an *aura,* or warning, in which the person senses an odd smell, taste, or sound. Usually the person soon stiffens, loses consciousness, and falls (the tonic phase), and then the person's arms and legs jerk (clonic phase) or contract. This type of seizure lasts several minutes but usually does not require medical intervention. You can read more about how to respond if a student has a seizure in the Professional Edge.

A second type of generalized seizure is referred to as an **absence seizure** (pronounced "ab-SAWNCE" and formerly call a *petit mal seizure*). This type of seizure usually lasts for only a few seconds, and educators may mistake it for daydreaming or an attentional problem. Some children can have as many as 100 absence seizures per day. This type of seizure disorder usually disappears by adolescence, but students with this type of epilepsy may develop other types of seizures.

In 70 percent of all cases of epilepsy, no specific cause can be identified. When a cause is known, only rarely is it related to a genetic disorder. Instead, it is likely to be the result of a head injury, as caused by an auto accident, fall, or extreme child abuse (e.g., shaken baby syndrome). High fevers, poisoning, and brain tumors also can cause epilepsy. When a student has epilepsy, environmental factors can contribute to a seizure occurring. For example, sleep deprivation can serve as a trigger, as can flashing lights and loud or monotonous noise.

Did you know that cancer kills more children than any other disease and more children than asthma, diabetes, cystic fibrosis, and AIDS combined?

As is the case with other physical disabilities, assigning prevalence is difficult because no central registry exists. The Epilepsy Foundation (2009) estimates that 326,000 U.S. school-age children through the age of fifteen have epilepsy. The foundation also reports that African Americans and students from socially disadvantaged groups are at higher risk for this disorder than are Caucasians, and males are slightly more likely than females to develop epilepsy. Epilepsy also is comorbid with other disorders. For example, half the children who have both cerebral palsy and an intellectual disability also have epilepsy.

**HIV and AIDS.** HIV and AIDS were unknown in humans until the second half of the twentieth century. HIV stands for *human immunodeficiency virus,* a virus that can take over a cell's own genetic material and then produce more diseased cells. This virus attacks the body's own immune system, making individuals with HIV more susceptible to illnesses. AIDS stands for **acquired immune deficiency syndrome**, and it is a collection of illnesses, including some cancers, that only individuals who have HIV can contract. HIV is transmitted through contact with infected blood or other body fluids, as occurs with unprotected sexual contact and sharing of needles. Most students who have AIDS became infected during their mothers' pregnancies, and mothers abusing drugs and those with HIV who have complications during delivery are most likely to transmit the disease to their babies (DePaepe, Garrison-Kane, & Doelling, 2002). However, an increasing number of youth are becoming infected through their own unprotected sexual activity (Donenberg & Pao, 2005; Silver & Bauman, 2006).

Precise data on the prevalence of HIV and AIDS are difficult to obtain. According to the Centers for Disease Control and Prevention (2009b), in 2007 approximately 2,000 new cases of HIV/AIDS were reported for children and adolescents through age nineteen. However, many other adolescents are probably infected with HIV but have not yet developed AIDS and so have not been diagnosed. A 36-state study indicated that 58 percent of the adolescents were male and 42 percent female; in addition, 28 percent were Caucasian, 50 percent were African American, and 20 percent were Hispanic (Body Health Resources, 2005).

Although great strides are being made in treatments for HIV and AIDS, no cure exists. Students with AIDS may have to take medications in school, and they may have increasing absences if their health deteriorates. They may or may not require special education. One fact to keep in mind is that confidentiality policies about HIV and AIDS vary from locale to locale, and professionals may not know whether a student has this disorder (Sileo, 2005). For that reason, it is imperative that all school professionals use what are called *universal precautions* in addressing an illness or injury that may include blood or other body substances. You can read more about this important topic in the Professional Edge.

**Cancer.** Cancer, an uncontrolled division of abnormal cells, is relatively rare among children, but it does occur. The two most common types, accounting for more than half of all cases, are leukemia (i.e., blood cell cancers) and brain tumors (National Cancer Institute, 2008). Prior to the early 1960s, the mortality rate for some forms of pediatric cancer, including leukemia, was 100 percent (R. T. Brown & Madan-Swain, 1993). By the late 1970s, the situation had changed significantly such that the survival rate for all childhood cancers had risen to 55 percent. In the twenty-first century, the survival rate has climbed to 79 percent (National Cancer Institute, 2005).

Students who are diagnosed and treated for cancer are at risk for a variety of learning problems (Gartin & Murdick, 2009), just like Ryan, the student introduced at the beginning

*Professionals have a responsibility to help students with physical and health disabilities to focus on and celebrate their abilities, not their disabilities.*

## Universal Precautions for School Professionals

What would you do if one of your students suddenly had a bloody nose? What if a student fell in the hallway and knocked a tooth loose or badly scraped a knee or elbow? No matter what your role in the school and no matter who your students are likely to be, you should be aware of *universal precautions* for dealing with blood and other body fluids that may carry bloodborne pathogens—that is, microorganisms that can cause disease and illness. These microorganisms can be transmitted when blood or another body fluid from an infected individual comes into contact with an open cut, a skin abrasion, acne, or the mucous membranes of the mouth, eyes, and nose. The most common bloodborne pathogens are HIV/AIDS, hepatitis B, and hepatitis C.

### Staying Healthy

To avoid the risk of being exposed to disease, all educators should be familiar with these universal precautions (Edens, Murdick, & Gartin, 2003):

- Wear disposable gloves and other protective equipment (e.g., a protective jacket or face mask) when performing tasks that involve risk of exposure, such as assisting a student with personal hygiene or responding to a student injury.
- In an accident or situation where no gloves are available, place another barrier (e.g., an article of clothing) between yourself and the blood or body fluid.

- Notify a custodian if there is a blood spill. Custodial staff should use a hospital disinfectant or bleach solution to clean up blood spills and disinfect potentially contaminated surfaces.
- Pick up potentially contaminated sharp objects (e.g., needles, knives, broken glass) with a tool such as pliers or tweezers. Never pick up such objects with your hands.
- Discard any articles contaminated with blood or body fluids in a leak-resistant container, and if the objects are sharp, use a puncture-proof container.
- When you are ready to remove your gloves, turn them inside out as you do to avoid contact with blood.
- Discard gloves in a leak-resistant container.
- Use soap and warm water to thoroughly wash hands and any skin that may have been contaminated. Flush with water if the eyes, nose, or mouth has come into contact with blood.
- If you had significant contact with a student's blood, seek medical attention.

School districts generally have specific policies in place for universal precautions. If you have questions, your school nurse or principal should be able to answer them.

*Source:* Adapted from Grosse, S. J. (1999). Educating children and youth to prevent contagious disease [ERIC Digest]. ERIC Clearinghouse on Teaching and Teacher Education. Retrieved March 1, 2004 from www.ericfacility.net.

---

of the chapter. Radiation may lead to problems in cognitive functioning. Students have been identified as having difficulties in mathematics, attention, and memory as well as behavior problems and social skills deficits. Some students in this group first may be identified as other health impaired because of the cancer. Later, they may be identified as learning disabled, intellectually disabled, or behavior and emotionally disabled because of the lasting effects of their illness.

In 2008, 10,730 children were diagnosed with cancer, which is one to two children per every 10,000 in the United States (National Cancer Institute, 2008). Diagnoses for some cancers have risen slightly over the past 30 years, but those for leukemia have dropped.

What do you think is the most common cause of cancer? If you said it is unknown, you are correct. A few conditions have genetic links, but many suspected causes have not been verified. Among the areas studied and to date not found to cause cancer are these: ultrasound use during pregnancy, low-level radon exposure, magnetic field exposure from power lines, maternal cigarette smoking, and exposure to specific viruses (National Cancer Institute, 2005). Research continues to focus on prenatal factors and environmental factors that could make children susceptible to cancer.

**Sickle Cell Disease.** One health impairment about which considerable information is available is **sickle cell disease**, a disorder that affects the part of the red blood cells that carries oxygen from the lungs to other parts of the body (Dooley & Perkins, 1998). Normally, red blood cells are round and soft, and they can fit through small blood vessels. In sickle cell disease, these cells become sickle shaped and inflexible, and they block small blood vessels. This causes the flow of oxygen to be slowed or stopped. When this happens, individuals with this disease experience pain (the most common symptom), their bodies can be damaged (e.g., kidneys, lungs, bones), and they may become anemic. Educators may need to help students avoid extreme heat and cold, drink enough fluids, and use relaxation strategies to help avoid or cope with pain (DePaepe et al., 2002).

dimensions of
**DIVERSITY**

Although sickle cell disease is usually thought to affect only African Americans, it also is found in people from Mediterranean, Caribbean, South and Central American, Arabian, and East Indian descent (Bonner, Gustafson, Schumacher, & Thompson, 1999).

Students with a severe form of sickle cell disease may miss school frequently. They also may experience problems in learning and memory as well as in the behavior and social domains (Daly, Kral, & Brown, 2008; Koontz, Short, Kalinyak, & Noll, 2004). These students may have sudden crises, and educators who work with them need to be alert to the need to contact parents so that medical attention can be sought. Keep in mind, though, that most students with this disorder lead full and productive lives, and with early identification many of the potential complications of the disease can be prevented.

Sickle cell disease affects one in every 500 African American newborns (Taras & Potts-Datema, 2005). One in 12 individuals of African descent carries the recessive gene for this disorder, but most never develop symptoms. However, sickle cell disease also affects Hispanic Americans, occurring in about 1 in every 1,000 to 1,400 births for that group (Human Genome Project, 2005).

**Diabetes.** One additional health impairment to mention is diabetes, a metabolic disorder in which the body cannot properly break down sugars and store them (National Diabetes Information Clearinghouse, 2003). Because of this problem, children with the disorder must carefully monitor their diets and also receive injections of insulin. Approximately 136,000 children and young adults under the age of twenty have diabetes (National Diabetes Information Clearinghouse, 2008).

There are two types of diabetes. The first is Type I diabetes, which most often is diagnosed during adolescence. The period following diagnosis can be particularly difficult for students: They have to change their eating habits, they may be embarrassed or upset by the diagnosis, they have to learn to monitor their blood sugar levels and find a time and place to do so, and they may have to face teasing from peers. Students who have **juvenile diabetes** often can be successful without any specific school intervention. However, they may need a Section 504 plan to accommodate their needs (e.g., procedures to monitor their glucose and for insulin injection; procedures for responding to high or low blood sugar). Some students need assistance only at particular times. For example, Ginger plays on the girls' junior varsity basketball team. During practices and games, her coach monitors her carefully to be sure she drinks enough fluids and does not ignore warning signals that she needs to rest. Approximately 35 children are diagnosed as having juvenile diabetes every day, and approximately 125,000 children have the disorder (DePaepe et al., 2002). If you work with students with diabetes, your school nurse can be an important source of information for helping these students to manage their disease.

Type II diabetes, which is preventable, has quadrupled among children over the past 15 years, and it now accounts for 16 percent of all childhood diabetes (American Obesity Association, 2005). Consider this information: Nearly half (46 percent) of U.S. children ages six to nineteen are either overweight or obese. This is more than double the rate from 20 years ago. Not surprisingly, the alarming increase in Type II diabetes is causing health and school professionals to focus their attention on helping students and their families to understand the importance of healthy eating habits and adequate physical activity (Winter, 2009). It also is prompting these professionals to provide healthier foods at school and to limit students' access to soft drinks and other high-calorie food from vending machines (LaFee, 2005; Schantzenbach, 2009). Not all of these students may be entitled to special education, but the number who need these services is likely to continue to grow.

## REVIEW · REFLECT · DISCUSS

1. What would you say to someone who presumes that students with physical or significant health disabilities are best educated away from other students? Justify your responses.

2. If you were told that you would be working with a student who has a physical or health disability, what could you presume about the student? What would you not know? Generate a set of questions that you think any professional working with a student with a physical or health disability should ask.

# Characteristics of Individuals
# with Physical and Health Disabilities

It is difficult to apply generalities to students who have physical and health disabilities because their strengths and needs can range immensely within a single domain as well as across domains. Some information about these students' characteristics was embedded in the descriptions of their disorders, but additional details can help you to understand how you can best meet their needs.

## Cognitive and Academic Characteristics

Students with physical and health disabilities have cognitive and academic abilities that range from extraordinary giftedness and special talents to significant intellectual disability. Students' abilities in this domain often are related to the nature of the disorder, the severity of the disorder, and the effects of treating the disorder (e.g., Daly et al., 2008; Kennedy, 2008; Lehmkuhl et al., 2008; Wolters, Brouwers, & Perez, 1999). For example, Edgar was in a farming accident in which he lost one arm just above the elbow and three fingers on his remaining hand. He also experienced serious internal injuries that required hospitalization. After being released from the hospital, he spent time in a rehabilitation facility while he adjusted to his injuries and was assessed for a prosthetic arm. Edgar was a high-achieving student before his accident, and he probably will continue at this level when he returns to school. In contrast, Marcy has cerebral palsy that has caused her to have diplegia. She has epilepsy as well, but it is usually controlled through medication. Marcy also has a moderate intellectual disability, which is not particularly surprising, given that she has two other conditions that are directly related to neurological functioning. Her curricular objectives are adjusted to take into account her current learning level.

As a professional educator, your responsibility is to get to know the cognitive and academic characteristics of your students with physical and health disabilities (Cunningham & Wodrich, 2006). Even more important, it is essential that you not presume that students who have limited ability to move or difficulty communicating have limited intellectual ability—a common error, even in the twenty-first century.

## Behavior, Emotional, and Social Characteristics

Although students with physical and health disabilities do not always have special needs in the behavioral, emotional, and social domains, these areas can be particularly important for them. The reasons for this become clear when you understand all the information you have just read about the various conditions.

### Behavior Characteristics

Some physical and health disabilities are associated with the presence of behavior problems. Perhaps the clearest example occurs among students with traumatic brain injuries (Arroyos-Jurado & Savage, 2008). These students often cannot make judgments about appropriate behaviors, and they become anxious and frustrated when they are not told exactly what to do. They need exceptionally clear rules to follow, and they need reminders about those rules because they may have problems with memory. In addition, students with traumatic brain injuries may require very specific behavior intervention plans that have extensive rewards built in for appropriate behaviors. These students also may become aggressive as a means of expressing their frustrations. They need consistency, a topic addressed in the Positive Behavior Supports. However, students with traumatic brain injuries represent only one group with behavior problems. Many students who have health disorders, including sickle cell disease and asthma, also may display inappropriate behaviors. Some of these behaviors relate to students' discomfort or irritability resulting from their disorders. Alternatively, some inappropriate behaviors represent the frustration of students who have limited ways to communicate. As you have learned in earlier chapters, teachers need to be aware of and respond to behavior as communication, and they should address the underlying issue, not only the behavior as a symptom of the issue.

The Juvenile Diabetes Foundation Research International is predicting that a cure for juvenile diabetes is not only possible but also likely to be found within a few years.

Most traumatic brain injuries on playgrounds occur when children fall from swings, monkey bars, and slides.

## Addressing Behavior for Students with Traumatic Brain Injuries

Students with traumatic brain injuries often develop serious behavior problems. They may take medication to help control difficult behaviors, and they may need counseling that includes peers to learn to manage their behaviors. Here are some essential elements related to consistency and communication for addressing these students' behavior needs (Kay, Spaulding, & Smerdon, 2004):

### Consistency within the school.

- All of the professionals at the school should be aware of the student's strengths and needs.
- Professionals should develop a highly detailed behavioral care plan consistently implemented across settings. Example: Brian responds best when given a choice in activities. School staff members all use this information. The media teacher asks Brian to choose from among three library books; the art teacher asks Brian to choose between two colors of paper; and the language arts teacher has Brian decide whether to create a poster about the short story just read or to audiotape a summary of it.

### Communication within the school.

- All the professionals working with the student should meet regularly to share information and report progress and problems.
- Formal communication should be supplemented with an informal dialogue about day-to-day events.
- If anyone at school notices a change in the student's behavior, a meeting should be called to discuss what is occurring and how to respond.

### Consistency between school and home.

- Different responses to the same behavior may confuse a student.

Example: Teachers respond to a student's frustration-based crying by matter of factly saying to him, "Take a break" and leaving him alone for three minutes. His parents respond by holding him and distracting him with a toy or game. The inconsistency may result in increased rather than decreased behavior problems.

### Communication between school and home.

- Clear communication between school professionals and parents is imperative.
- A daily behavior log can be exchanged in which parents and educators jot down notes about student successes and questions or concerns.
- Written communication can be supplemented with phone calls and e-mail.
- More formal interactions may occur when parents meet with school representatives because their child's conditions and needs may be changing rapidly and they need to update the professionals. Depending on the situation, the student also may attend all or parts of these meetings.

### Communication among community professionals, school, and family.

- Open lines of communication among medical and community services professionals, the school, and the family are crucial to ensure that all the professionals working with the student across all settings are consistent in their approach.
- Multiple, fragmented, and inconsistent interventions can significantly limit student recovery and may even create additional behavior problems.

## Emotional Characteristics

One widely reported characteristic of students with physical and health disabilities is poor self-esteem (Antle, 2004; Sze & Valentin, 2007; Turkstra, Williams, Tonks, & Frampton, 2008). Students who have cerebral palsy, spina bifida, or asthma may ask why they had to be born with their condition, and they may think of themselves as being less valuable than others (e.g., LeBovidge, Lavigne, Donenberg, & Miller, 2003). Students who experience a spinal cord injury, cancer, traumatic brain injury, or another sudden-onset condition may experience a wide range of emotional problems, including anger at their situation; rejection of the support offered by families, friends, and educators; and poor images of themselves as valuable people.

An example from students with leukemia can illustrate how school professionals must keep in mind these students' emotional status. Sullivan, Fulmer, and Zigmond (2001) studied the role of school as a normalizing factor for children who had leukemia. They found that maintaining contact with the school during absences helped these students feel connected to their classmates and reminded students and their families that the "other life," without hospitals and treatments, was still there. More than anything, attending school, even sporadically, and participating in school activities, even in a limited way, helped the children and their families feel a sense of normalization.

Professionals working with students with physical and health disabilities may encounter a perplexing problem: It may be difficult to assess the emotional strengths and

**research NOTE**

In a survey of 393 pediatricians and pediatric residents, Sneed, May, and Stencel (2000) found that approximately 75 percent believed that they were inadequately prepared to treat children with physical and health disorders.

*Students with physical or health disabilities should have access to the full range of school activities, including field trips and extracurricular programs.*

needs of students with limited abilities to communicate. As for all needs related to communication, the use of assistive technology and input sought from parents and school staff working closely with students can help ensure this critical dimension of growth is not overlooked.

### Social Characteristics

Students with physical and health disabilities also frequently need interventions related to interacting with their peers (e.g., Reiter-Purtill, Gerhardt, Vannatta, Passo, & Noll, 2003; Yeates et al., 2007). For some students, this need relates to explaining their conditions to peers and responding when others tease or bully them. However, for others, the need is for social skills training to learn or relearn how to communicate with their classmates. For example, a student with muscular dystrophy may need to learn how to join games or discussions with classmates within the context of his changing physical abilities. Students with traumatic brain injuries may have to learn how to interact without becoming aggressive.

Perhaps the most critical element of these students' social relationships is having access to them. Teachers and other professionals, including counselors and social workers, play a central role in facilitating interactions among students with physical and health disabilities and their peers (Harrison, 2007). These professionals may need to create opportunities for students to interact in meaningful and positive ways, to use student grouping and cooperative class activities for this purpose, and to model for students how to interact appropriately.

## Physical and Medical Characteristics

Some mention must be made of the physical characteristics of students in these groups. Many students with physical and health disabilities are more knowledgeable about hospitals, medications, and emergency procedures than adults. Some must take medication during school hours, and some must monitor the foods they eat and the activities in which they participate. No single statement can be made about their physical and medical needs except to mention that this domain is the one that probably is the basis for special education eligibility. Given this, professionals working with students in these groups should learn as much as they can about each student's conditions, risks, and needs.

1. Think about students with the types of disabilities described in this chapter. Why do you think it would be easy to underestimate these students' abilities? How could you as a school professional work to avoid this type of bias? What could you do to help others understand students with physical or health disabilities?

2. Why is it particularly important to understand the domain of social and emotional characteristics in relation to students with physical and health disabilities?

**PEARSON**
# myeducationlab

Go to the Building Teaching Skills and Dispositions section of Topic 14: Physical Disabilities and Health Impairments, in the MyEducation-Lab for your course and complete the activity entitled "Identifying and Responding to the Needs of Students with Physical Disabilities".

## Identifying Physical and Health Disabilities

For students with physical and health disabilities, the decision about eligibility for special education may be made at a very early age or during the school years. A medical assessment that is completed outside the school setting usually is a primary consideration for a student in this group.

### Assessment

Most of the assessment procedures for students with physical and health procedures are identical to those for other students with potential disabilities. However, their physical functioning also must be evaluated.

#### Assessment of Medical Condition and Physical Functioning

Each disorder or condition that was briefly described in an earlier section of this chapter usually is diagnosed by a pediatrician or pediatric specialist using many different types of procedures. For example, blood tests are used to determine whether a child has sickle cell disease, juvenile diabetes, HIV or AIDS, or cancer. A student who may have a brain tumor or traumatic brain injury is likely to have a CAT scan (i.e., a specialized, three-dimensional X-ray) or an MRI (i.e., a procedure in which magnetic field and radio signals are used to construct images of the brain). A student with a spinal cord injury, cerebral palsy, or another physical disability probably was assessed by a medical professional using a standardized instrument to determine how much the student can move and how well. School professionals who may contribute to this type of assessment include physical therapists and occupational therapists.

#### Assessment of Intellectual Functioning, Academic Achievement, Language, and Related Areas

research
**NOTE**

Innes and Diamond (1999) studied how mothers talked to their young children about physical disabilities and Down syndrome and the relationship between parents' comments and children's ideas about disabilities. They found that mothers talked more during a storytelling activity about children with physical disabilities than about Down syndrome and that the children's comments were positively related to teachers' ratings of how the children interacted with classmates with disabilities.

You already have learned about the procedures used to assess a student's ability, achievement, language, and communication skills. These formal assessments (e.g., IQ tests, achievement tests, inventories) and informal assessments (e.g., observations of the student, interviews and checklists completed by parents and teachers, curriculum-based assessments) also are used to assess a student with physical or health disabilities. These assessments are important because they provide information on whether the student is struggling to learn—one of the conditions that must be met in order for the student to be eligible for special education services. However, for some students, measuring cognitive capability and achievement can be difficult because of the nature of the physical disability. If a student experiences difficulty communicating and also has limited movement ability, special care has to be taken so that ability is not underestimated.

#### Assessment of Behavior

You also have learned about the methods for assessing student behavior, and again, these measures often are used with students with physical and health disabilities. Parents and teachers may be asked to rate a student's behaviors, and if the student has an intellectual disability, an assessment of adaptive behavior also is likely.

## Eligibility

The critical question for eligibility of a student with physical or health disabilities concerns whether the student's disability has a significant, negative effect on educational performance. If it does, the student is eligible for special education services, and an IEP will be prepared and services implemented. If it does not, the team considers other options. For some students in this group, including students with ADHD and physical conditions that result in limited energy but no other direct educational impact, a Section 504 plan may be sufficient. For yet other students, the decision will be made that no services are warranted.

### REVIEW · REFLECT · DISCUSS

1. How is the assessment process for students with physical and health disabilities similar to and different from those procedures for other students suspected of having a disability?

2. You've learned a lot about assessment and special education throughout this book. Why might traditional approaches to assessment be inadequate in identifying the strengths and needs of students with physical or health disabilities?

## How Learners with Physical and Health Disabilities Receive Their Education

In the past, students with physical and health disabilities identified as needing special education were likely to be educated primarily in a separate classroom or school so that their medical and physical needs more easily could be met. Today, it is clear that decisions should never be made based on the disability identified; instead, decisions should be based on the team's assessment of the specific educational needs of the student. As a result, students with physical and health disabilities now appropriately access a full range of placements.

PEARSON
**myeducationlab**

Go to the Assignments and Activities section of Topic 14: Physical and Health Impairments, in the MyEducationLab for your course and complete the activity entitled "Physical Disabilities in School-Age Children".

### Early Childhood

Students with significant physical and health disabilities may begin to receive special education services when they are still infants, following referral for services by social workers or early interventionists assigned to work with hospital personnel. At such an early age, most services are offered in the home, with early intervention specialists, physical and occupational therapists, and other professionals as needed coordinating their efforts to work with the family. During this time and continuing through the in-home, center-based, or preschool program that a student accesses upon turning age three, services clearly are intended to help the child, but the relationship with family members also is essential (Murray & Mandell, 2004). Many parents during this time are seeking information and services, trying to learn about their children's special needs, coping with possible increased medical expenses and difficulties in arranging child care, and wondering if other families have had similar experiences. Early intervention professionals can be instrumental in helping family members to locate and access the resources that they need.

### Elementary and Secondary School Services

When students with physical and health disabilities reach school age, several factors determine how they receive services. The presumption of IDEA is that the general education setting is preferred, and so a primary concern is how students' needs—including the academic, physical, and behavioral domains—can be supported to ensure students' success. As shown in Figure 13.5, nearly half of all students with physical disabilities and health impairments are educated primarily in general education classrooms, but less than one-third of students with traumatic brain injury are placed in that setting. Many students in all three groups still spend a significant amount of time in special education classrooms, in residential facilities, and at home or in hospitals.

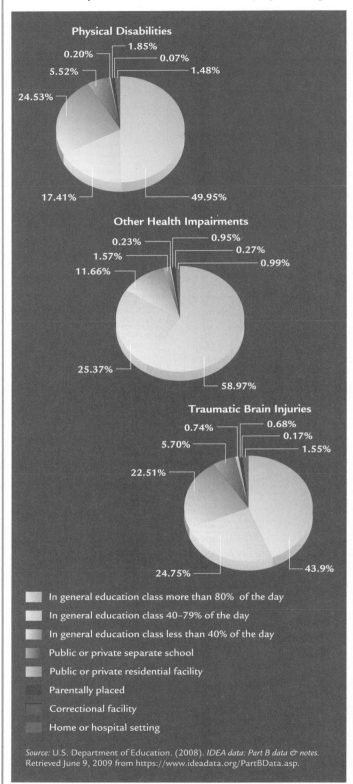

**FIGURE 13.5**

Educational Placements of Students Ages Six to Twenty-One Who Have Physical and Health Disabilities (in percentages)

**Physical Disabilities**

1.85%
0.20%
0.07%
5.52%
1.48%
24.53%
17.41%
49.95%

**Other Health Impairments**

0.23%
0.95%
0.27%
1.57%
0.99%
11.66%
25.37%
58.97%

**Traumatic Brain Injuries**

0.74%
0.68%
0.17%
5.70%
1.55%
22.51%
24.75%
43.9%

- In general education class more than 80% of the day
- In general education class 40–79% of the day
- In general education class less than 40% of the day
- Public or private separate school
- Public or private residential facility
- Parentally placed
- Correctional facility
- Home or hospital setting

*Source:* U.S. Department of Education. (2008). *IDEA data: Part B data & notes.* Retrieved June 9, 2009 from https://www.ideadata.org/PartBData.asp.

Some students with physical and health disabilities appropriately receive services in a resource room or separate setting for part of the school day (Kulik, 2001), usually because the nature of their needs requires it. For example, a student who is learning how to chew and swallow food may need privacy while learning this essential skill because it is difficult to master and involves a high degree of concentration. Practice may occur during lunch, but additional assistance may be provided in the special education setting.

In some communities, students with significant physical disabilities are educated in separate classes or separate schools. Often these are students with significant intellectual disabilities as well as physical disabilities. Many reasons—some valid, some not—are given for these decisions on placement. Some professionals still believe that these students should learn daily living skills from an alternative curriculum beginning at an early age in a special education classroom. Some mention easier accessibility to nursing assistance, the availability of specialized equipment and related services personnel, and the sense of family or community. Even when students are placed in these settings, school professionals have an obligation to ensure that these students have opportunities to participate in general education whenever possible—in core content classes, in related arts classes (e.g., music and technology), and in extracurricular activities.

However, in more and more communities, students with physical and health disabilities are placed in general education classrooms. Support is provided in a separate setting only if the team decides that a student's educational and behavioral needs cannot be met completely in the general education setting, even with extensive supports. This is the decision that was reached for Ryan, whom you met at the beginning of this chapter.

One placement option for a small number of students with physical and health disabilities is a hospital school program. This type of placement typically is reserved for students who need repeated treatments or surgeries or who miss many school days because of illness. In a small community, a hospital school program may be part of the responsibility assigned to a special education teacher. This professional serves as a liaison between the teachers at school and the student, teaching the student either in the hospital room or, if the student is at home for an extended period of time, in that location. In a larger community, a hospital school program may have several staff members—teachers and related services providers—who teach their pupils in a classroom in the hospital, in a student's hospital room, or in the home.

## Inclusive Practices

For some students with physical and health disabilities, no discussion of inclusion is needed at all. Their special needs relate to their health or physical capabilities, and few other accommodations are needed, except perhaps the need for physical access to the classroom and instructional materials, provision of a paraprofessional to assist with personal care at certain times of the day, or flexibility because of absences. There is no reason to segregate these students from their peers.

The issue of inclusion is more likely to be raised regarding students who have significant or multiple disabilities, especially those with physical, medical, and intellectual disabilities. For these students, the team must address the same questions that have been raised in regard to other students with disabilities: What are the goals and objectives for the student within the context of the curriculum that all students follow? To what extent can appropriate supports and services be provided in the general education setting to ensure that the student progresses on IEP goals and objectives? Do any of the student's needs make education in the general education setting inappropriate (e.g., aggressive behavior or issues related to medical needs, such as unusual allergies)? One other factor to consider in making a placement decision is student voice. The Instruction in Action highlights the opinions of students and their families regarding their needs in inclusive settings. In many cases, effective use of universal design for learning, particularly through the use of technology and instructional differentiation, can make access to general education quite feasible.

## Transition and Adulthood

The decisions that students with physical and health disabilities and their families face as they look toward the transition from school to postschool can be particularly complex (e.g., MacLennan & MacLennan, 2008; Stumbo, Martin, & Hedrick, 2009). They must consider whether postsecondary education is the best option, address practical matters such as transportation and living arrangements, and think about career choices. They also must think about and access all the agencies that might provide support in adulthood and all the professionals who should be part of the transition-planning process for these students (Roberts, 2007). What decisions might Jeffrey and his family, introduced at the beginning of the chapter, face once he graduates from high school? Think about him as you read the following sections.

### Postsecondary Education

One consideration for students with physical and health disabilities concerns whether postsecondary education is the right choice (Stumbo et al., 2009). For some students, this decision relates more to their academic abilities and interests than to their special needs. For others, though, factors such as stamina, the need for surgeries and other hospital procedures, resistance to illness, and other issues related to their illnesses or conditions must be considered. For these students, online learning might be a possibility. For a few students, yet another factor may be important. One young man with physical disabilities who had just completed high school made this comment: "I began school before I was two years old, and so I had been in school for four years before any of the other kids started. I already have more than sixteen years of education, and I need a break before I go to college—it's time for everyone else to do that other four years, but not me."

### Practical Matters of Adulthood

Regardless of whether students and their families decide that a college or university is the best choice, other very practical matters have to be considered, at least for some students (Kraska, Zinner, & Abebe, 2007). For students who cannot drive, how will their transportation needs be met as they move toward adulthood? For students with significant physical limitations, what type of personal assistance will be necessary? What provisions can be made so that this assistance will be affordable? Living arrangements also can be a concern. Do family members prefer that their child live at home for several years? Is a supported living arrangement—perhaps an apartment shared with another person with physical limitations plus an attendant—the best choice? What options are available in the local community? Financial concerns also may need to be raised. What options exist through insurance or

dimensions of
**DIVERSITY**

Among U.S. female youth, the highest rates of being overweight and obese are found in African American girls. Among U.S. male youth, the highest rates are found in Mexican American boys.

web link

http://www.youtube.com/
watch?v=OCDDCI87iMo
The Internet includes valuable information on first aid for seizures. You can listen to helpful information from a safety and rescue captain at youtube.com.

## Students with Physical and Health Disabilities and Their Needs in General Education Classes

Students with physical and health disabilities and their parents report that the following supports are needed to foster student success in general education settings (Mukherjee & Lightfoot, 2000):

- *Clear information for teachers concerning the student's health and physical problems.* When such information was not provided, support varied considerably, with some teachers refusing to allow students to use the restroom as needed and others refusing to believe that a student felt ill.

- *A system for sending work home.* Students often had difficulty keeping up with assignments and other homework because of frequent absences.

- *A system for helping students catch up when they returned to school.* Students did not want to be on their own. They also asked teachers to keep in touch during long absences because this decreased the students' sense of isolation.

- *Adaptations for physical education and extracurricular opportunities (e.g., clubs).* Students wanted teachers to take seriously their desire to participate in all school activities.

- *Discussion of the condition.* Students requested that teachers check with them as to whether to discuss their medical condition with other students, especially in their presence.

- *Attention to social interactions.* Students appreciated it when teachers made sure that a friend could stay with them while others completed an activity beyond their abilities.

- *Supportive climate.* Students wanted to be able to discuss with teachers their worries about their physical and health disorders. Students were appreciative when teachers were willing to listen and offer support.

Taken together, these findings suggest how important it is for educators to be sensitive to student preferences and to be aware of how their own actions can either support students or interfere with their participation in instruction and school activities.

*Today's technology offers many options to facilitate communication for students with physical disabilities.*

Social Security benefits to cover medical needs such as hospitalization, medication, and equipment? What about needed assistive technology?

Many individuals with physical and health disabilities live in complete or near independence as adults. The options for achieving this independence have been enhanced tremendously by technology. The Technology Notes provides a wide range of resources to illustrate how children and adults find and use assistive technology.

### Career Choice

Students with physical and health disabilities have many, many career choices, but they may need more help than other students in thinking carefully about their options (Stewart-Scott & Douglas, 1998). For example, a military career may not be possible for a student with sickle cell disease or severe asthma. A sales position that requires long days and extended travel may not be a choice for a student who is a recent cancer survivor. School professionals who help students make career choices should focus on students' abilities—what they *can* do. What are their strengths and interests? For students with these and intellectual disabilities, another option may be supported employment in which the individual learns job skills with careful coaching from a school professional or a co-worker. You will learn more about supported employment in Chapter Fourteen when you read about students with severe and multiple disabilities.

### REVIEW · REFLECT · DISCUSS

1. For what reasons might students with physical and health disabilities appropriately need to receive some of their services in a setting other than a general education classroom?

2. What would you place on a list of items that students with physical disabilities leaving high school should keep in mind when they consider options for going to college or for entering the workforce?

## Making the Impossible Possible

Many of the examples of instructional and assistive technology you've learned about elsewhere in this book also might be used by students with physical or health disabilities. Here is a list of additional websites that provide a wealth of information about assistive technology for these students:

- Alliance for Technology Access (http://www.ataccess.org/) ATA has as its mission increasing the technology use of children and adults with disabilities and other functional limitations. At its website you can find a variety of information to help you further understand the use of assistive technology, including
  - a link to a video that shows assistive technology examples
  - stories highlighting the successful use of technology
  - a page describing No Child Left Behind requirements and their relationship to the use of assistive technology
- Abledata (http://www.abledata.com/) Abledata is a national data base that includes detailed descriptions of more than 27,000 assistive technology products. It also has a searchable list of literature related to assistive technology. Because Abledata does not sell any products or produce any products, it offers objective information about products listed.
- Dreamms for Kids (http://www.dreamms.org/) Dreamms (Developmental Research for the Effective Advancement of Memory and Motor Skills) for Kids is a non-profit organization dedicated to the use of assistive technology for children. The site includes a link to a clear explanation of assistive technology, many links to information about assistive technology, and information about laws that govern the provision of assistive technology.

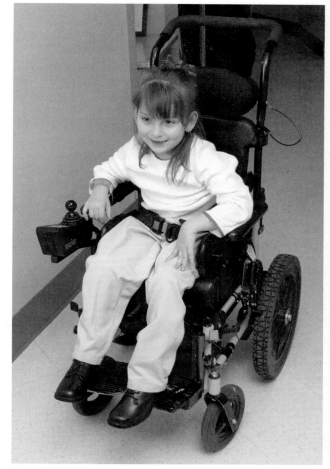

- Cerebral Palsy and Technology (http://www.computers-technology-cerebralpalsy.com/index.html) This website offers straightforward information and examples about technology to assist children and adults with cerebral palsy. The site is divided into sections on communication, mobility, and links to technology products and information. Within each section are descriptions, photos, and other information to explain the use of technology.

# Recommended Educational Practices for Students with Physical and Health Disabilities

For students who have physical and health disabilities and also experience learning or intellectual disabilities, emotional or behavior disorders, or attention deficit–hyperactivity disorder, the instructional strategies that you have already learned about are appropriate. However, while you are implementing these instructional approaches, you also have to take into account two issues for these groups of students: (a) accessibility, so that they can benefit from your instruction, and (b) factors that are directly related to students' physical and health needs (Closs, 2000).

## Access to Education

When typical learners and those with high-incidence disabilities come to school each day, they race or saunter through the classroom door, put their books and materials away, slip into their seats, chat with their friends, and begin their written or reading assignments. For students with physical and health disabilities, every one of these small activities may need an accommodation. Students in these groups usually need assistance in accessing their education (Myers, 2007). Part of this accessibility is related to physical accessibility— wheelchair ramps, elevators, wide doorways—but this type of access generally is straightforward. The access that is more challenging to accomplish, but critical, is access to instruction.

### Aids for Posture and Mobility

Is there a position that you like to be in when you study? Seated at a desk with your materials around you? Sprawled on your bed? Propped up in a lounge chair? Students with physical disabilities may not be able to make choices such as these, at least not without assistance. Further, their posture and the position in which they sit or sometimes lie can have an impact on their ability to breathe as well as their comfort and their long-term health. Sometimes these students need to be physically moved into the positions that are recommended for them.

A second concern is how students move around the classroom and school. Wheelchairs have been mentioned to provide mobility for students, but these are not the only options. Some children may have IEPs calling for instruction in mobility skills. In these cases, mobility equipment—such as gait trainers and adaptive walkers that help students maintain their balance and support their weight—are used to teach standing and walking skills (Barnes & Whinnery, 2002). Yet others need braces and similar devices, collectively called **orthoses**, that stabilize their legs so that they can walk. You can read more about aids for posture and mobility by reading the Instruction in Action. No matter what devices are used, students need to learn how to use them effectively.

### Aids for Communication

Like students with communication disorders, some students with physical and health disabilities require assistance to communicate with their teachers and peers. Some use communication devices and other technology to convey their thoughts and needs. However, if students do not have the use of their hands to type or to point to pictures on a communication device, they have to look for other options. Some communication devices are made with larger sections that are edged with raised rims; for students who can touch the board but have some limitation in fine-motor control, this provides assistance in reaching and touching the correct icon or picture. Some students may not use their hands at all. Such a student might wear a pointing wand attached to his head to touch items on the board. For all professionals working with students using aids to communicate, some adjustment during instruction might be needed. For example, some students may need additional time to respond to teacher questions. Others may need the teacher to ask questions that require pri-

## Positioning, Seating, and Mobility

Students with physical and health disabilities may need changes in instruction, but they also may require special attention to positioning, seating, and mobility (Best, Heller, & Bigge, 2010).

### Positioning

*Positioning* refers to keeping a student's body supported so that posture is maintained in a healthy way. For example, some students may slump over the side of the wheelchair if they are tired. Others may not be able to sit on the floor unless supported by a bolster. Yet others may need to change their position (e.g., sitting versus standing, sitting versus lying on their sides) several times during the day.

Positioning can help students to maintain muscle tone and posture, especially those whose conditions include a neurological element. For example, if Joan—who has cerebral palsy—is seated correctly in her wheelchair, it prevents her muscles from tightening further. Positioning also can help students use their upper bodies (i.e., the head, arms, hands) more effectively. If they are supported so that their bodies are stable, writing or pressing a switch will be accomplished much more easily. Finally, positioning makes the student feel safe and secure.

### Seating

A student should be seated in a wheelchair with the same good posture that you probably heard about while you were growing up: pelvis in a neutral position, back straight, chin slightly tucked in. In addition, the feet need to be supported so that they are level. Foot support helps with overall body stability, and a safety factor comes into play, too.

If a student cannot hold his body in a healthy position while seated in the wheelchair, assistance is provided. Wedges may be placed around the student, a tray placed high enough so that it can be used to support the upper body, and straps or headrests may be included. If seating is not managed properly, the consequences for the student can be serious—a rounded back, sliding out of the wheelchair and risking injury, or having the head or body lean uncomfortably.

### Mobility

Students with physical and health disabilities use many different types of aids for mobility. Some students will use a manual wheelchair which is lightweight and durable. However, the energy required to move such a wheelchair may be beyond a student's ability. An alternative is a wheelchair that is electric and motorized. Such a chair can be operated with a joystick or simple controls.

Some students use a walker, a rigid frame with wheels. It may be designed to provide support from the front, so that the student is pushing it. However, some walkers support from behind, helping the student to stand straight. Younger students also may use a travel stroller that is pushed by an adult. This stroller is similar to the type used for infants and toddlers but is designed with more support. Finally, some students may use a tricycle or go-cart, particularly during play periods. These mobility options help students to participate in typical, age-appropriate activities.

*instruction in action*

marily yes/no or one-word answers to facilitate communication, particularly during group instruction.

Some students communicate with multiple types of technology. Garry has cerebral palsy and epilepsy. He can speak, but he is difficult to understand. He cannot control his arms, hands, and fingers well enough to type or write. However, Garry is an above-average student. At school, he uses a communication board to talk to his classmates and teachers. He also uses voice recognition software to write papers and assignments. He uses the same software to communicate via e-mail with his cousins and grandmother who live in another state. The assistive technology that Garry is learning gives him communication access. You can learn more about the opportunities technology can create and the challenges special educators sometimes face with its use in the Speaking from Experience.

### Aids for Learning

Whether students with physical and health disabilities learn easily or struggle, they may need special consideration related to schoolwork. For example, some strategies accommodate student absences and fatigue. You might need to let students make up missed schoolwork without a penalty for lateness. You also might need to assist them in learning concepts and skills they missed while they were absent.

In general education classrooms, you might find that many of the instructional strategies presented throughout this textbook will be helpful. In addition, some students with physical and health disabilities may benefit from *curriculum overlapping*. In this approach, students participate in the same activities as typical classmates, but they may have different goals. For example, as students work in cooperative groups to learn about causes of the

Samantha Fecich obtained her bachelor's degree from California University of PA in 2001, earning licensure in elementary education (K-6) and special education (K-12). In her special education master's degree program at Pennsylvania State University, she specialized in augmentative and alternative communication. After working for DynaVox Technologies where she was an educational consultant and created software applications for that company's communication systems, she became a teacher for students with multiple disabilities. She now is a technology teacher, ensuring that technology is used to support students with disabilities in their classrooms. Here is the advice she offers to educators on using technology to help students reach their potential.

- Sometimes because of a student's outward appearance or assumed cognitive level, your colleagues may think that the student is not capable of much. Your role is to be a catalyst of change for that student, encouraging him to try his very best, whether it be answering a math problem correctly or raising his eyes to indicate "yes." Show other teachers and professionals that this student is capable of so much. Encourage them to just look past the physical or medical limitations, and treat the student like a regular kid!

- A challenge in the field of assistive technology is cost. Once a piece of equipment has been selected for a student, you may need to ask questions about how it is going to be funded. Is it the responsibility of the school district? Is the equipment something that should be provided by the parent? Private insurance? Medicaid? Medicare? Payment for such equipment and questions about its use at home as well as at school may get complicated, and you may need input from an administrator who has the authority to decide about and potentially commit funds.

- Another challenge you might face is adapting technology used in the classroom to fit the needs of students with disabilities. For example, if a classroom is equipped with an interactive whiteboard which is frequently used by the teacher, how can you adapt that piece of technology for a student with limited mobility in her arms? One option might be to create an adapted pointer that she is able to grasp or to secure the pointer to her wrist. Another option might be to make the targets on the interactive whiteboard larger to accommodate the student's field of motion.

- Another challenge you might face if working with a student using assistive or augmentative technology is the maintenance and care of equipment. Questions that need to be asked include these: Who will be the provider of maintenance on the device? Who will pay the fees for maintenance? Do I have any responsibilities related to equipment care or maintenance?

- Occasionally, parents or caregivers do not wish to use technology with their child at home. One way to help change their mind regarding the technology is to take pictures or video of the child using the technology successfully in the classroom. Another is to provide parents and caregivers with information regarding the equipment purchased for their child. Give them details about training sessions (offered by the company or at the school) so they can attend them and learn more. This is especially helpful when many students use the same type of device. A professional might hold a workshop on that specific device to many parents and family members.

Vietnam conflict, a student with physical and intellectual disabilities may be working toward the goal of responding to classmates when asked a question. You will learn about other approaches for fostering access to learning in Chapter Fourteen in the discussion of students with multiple and severe disabilities.

Another type of access to instruction may relate to assistive technology. Some students may need materials to be adapted so that they can be used. For example, the small counters being used by some students may need to be much larger for a student with limited motor control to be able to move them around. A beaker in the science class may need a handle so that the student can grasp it. Think about lessons you are likely to teach. What other accommodations might be needed to help students access learning?

### Related Services

Access to education for some students relates to procedures that enable them to attend school. In addition to clean intermittent catheterization, as resolved in the *Tatro* case discussed earlier in this chapter, some students may not be able to chew or swallow food and so might receive nourishment through a tube that leads directly to the stomach. The procedure, called *tube feeding,* might be carried out by a speech/language pathologist, a special education teacher, a paraprofessional, or a school nurse. Yet another student may need a constant supply of oxygen, and school professionals may need to ensure that the oxygen equipment is operating properly. Only a few students are medically fragile, and they may at-

**myeducationlab**

Go to the Assignments and Activities section of Topic 14: Physical and Health Impairments, in the MyEducationLab for your course and complete the activity entitled "Accommodations for Students with Health Impairments".

tend school accompanied by a nurse who can respond to medical emergencies.

Keep in mind that related services also pertain to other areas. Students with physical and health disabilities may need services from a speech/language pathologist, a physical therapist, an occupational therapist, or an adaptive physical educator. These professionals help students access education by addressing their communication needs, their large- and small-motor needs, and their needs for recreation and physical skill building, often within the context of the general education classroom. Yet other students need specialized transportation, and this must be provided. An example is a student whose school bus must be equipped with a wheelchair lift.

## Factors Related to the Illness, Injury, Condition, or Disorder

The specific physical and health needs that students have also affect their access to education. Two areas for attention are school reentry and responses to crises or episodes related to students' disabilities.

### School Reentry

Many students with physical and health disabilities miss a lot of school. They may be especially susceptible to illnesses and infections, they may require prolonged hospital stays, or they may have to make many trips to the doctor's office. The more school students miss, the more difficult it is for them to feel connected to their learning, their classmates, and their teachers. They often have to adjust to changes that occurred while they were absent and to their own changing physical status and emotional needs. For students with traumatic brain injuries, an additional consideration is that their personalities, behaviors, and learning abilities may have changed significantly as a result of the injuries, and school professionals and classmates need to be prepared for those changes.

School reentry usually involves a representative from the medical community, school personnel who specialize in some of the services that the student may need (e.g., the related services previously explained), other members of the IEP team (e.g., an administrator, special and general educators), and the parents (Deidrick & Farmer, 2005; Harris, 2009). Parents often play a central role in the school reentry process. Because they are their child's best advocates, parents bring information from the medical community to school professionals and carry school information back to physicians and other medical personnel. Parents also ensure that lines of communication stay open and that any problems encountered are resolved quickly. Finally, parents focus attention on the matter of acceptance—that is, ensuring that the returning student is welcomed by peers and adults at school (Roberts & Smith, 1999). You can read more about school reentry and parent roles in the Professional Edge.

You will find that some school districts have clearly outlined procedures and checklists that are followed for school reentry. Others manage this process on a case-by-case basis. As a school professional, your responsibility is to make the contributions that you can, depending on your role, and to help the parents and student make the transition as smoothly as possible (Lemanek, 2004; Moore, Kaffenberger, Oh, Goldberg, & Hudspeth, 2009).

### Responding to Emergencies

Students with physical and health disabilities sometimes experience crises, episodes, and emergencies at school, and school professionals need to know how to respond. Using universal precautions and responding to student seizures (both explained earlier in this chapter) are

*Related services professionals, including occupational therapists, play key roles in educating students with physical and health disabilities.*

### web link

http://www.compassionatefriends.org/Resources/Available_Brochures.aspx Compassionate Friends offers brochures on death and dying, including information for parents, siblings, classmates and friends, and one specifically about children with disabilities.

### research
#### NOTE

Nabors, Iobst, Weisman, Precht, Chiu, and Brunner (2007) surveyed 82 children ages six to eighteen regarding their juvenile rheumatoid diseases (e.g., arthritis). They found that 70 percent reported that they had trouble concentrating when they experienced pain at school. More than classmates, teachers, or nurses, the students stated that they most need help from good friends while at school.

## Returning to School

Many parents of students with physical and health disabilities have dealt with the stress of wondering whether their child would survive a medical crisis. Once the crisis has passed, the child's reentry to school becomes the focus. This process can be successful only with careful collaboration. Here are some of the barriers that can occur as part of reentry and the solutions for addressing them:

### Problem

Poor communication, including teacher lack of awareness, unclear or incomplete information provided to the teacher, and miscommunication because of jargon

### Solutions

- Use of a structured form for communication
- Use of videotapes as a basis for discussion of the student's needs
- Scheduled visit of school professionals to the rehabilitation facility
- Specific dates for communication established

### Problem

Knowledge gaps and attitudinal barriers (e.g., parents and professionals failing to recognize the importance of the reentry process), professional misinterpretation of student behaviors, and lack of parental knowledge about the special education system

### Solutions

- Training for professionals
- Identification and distribution of user-friendly materials for professionals and parents
- Information about special education and parent roles in advocating for their children

### Problem

Peer understanding, including fears and misconceptions about their classmate's condition

### Solution

- Emphasis on facilitating interactions between the student and classmates during the transition

### Problem

Systems issues, including those related to time, resources related to rehabilitation, and budget for needed services

### Solutions

- Emphasis on collaboration as part of training for professionals
- Careful scheduling of meetings so that school professionals can attend
- Use of videocams and other technology to eliminate the need for travel to meetings between school and medical personnel
- Training for school administrators on the need for flexibility and frequent updates for students reentering school

Many essential topics should be discussed at reentry, including these:

- The student's health status and its probable effect on attendance
- Whether the student can participate in physical education, recess, and other physical activities
- Any changes in the student's physical appearance
- The student's feelings about returning to school
- Any anticipated behavioral changes resulting from the student's medication or treatment
- The possible effect of medications on the student's academic performance
- Whether any medications or other health services need to be given at school
- Any special considerations the student may need, such as extra snacks, more rest periods, or extra time to get from class to class
- Concerns about others' exposure to communicable disease
- Signs and symptoms requiring parent notification (e.g., fever, nausea, pain, swelling, bruising, nosebleeds)
- Clarification that the teacher's job is to teach and that the parents and nurse will take care of all medical issues

If you were asked to attend a reentry meeting about a student with whom you have worked in your first year as a professional educator, what types of questions would you want to ask? Why?

*Source:* Deidrick, K.M., & Farmer, J.E. "Table 4 Barriers to School Reentry and Potential Solutions: School reentry following traumatic brain injury." *Preventing School Failure: Alternative Education for Children and Youth, 49*(4) (2005): 30–31. Reprinted by permission of Heldref Publications, www.heldref.org.

---

two examples of responses that are well prescribed and should be in place in every school. In addition, parents can provide additional information about their children and answer questions you may have. However, you also should check with a school district representative. Some districts have policies about how teachers and other school professionals are to respond to certain situations, and you should be aware of and follow those policies.

Professionals who work with students with physical and health disabilities also should think about the possibility of a student death. What might you need to do to help your other students cope with a classmate's death? How might you respond, and what assistance might you need for your students and yourself? How could you assist a colleague dealing with a student's death? These are topics addressed in the Professional Edge on the next page.

## When a Student Dies

Some children come to school with life-threatening conditions; others experience sudden illnesses or accidents. Educators know intellectually that sometimes students die, but few consider this sad topic in terms of how to react.

### Helping Students

When a classmate dies, students may express their feelings in many ways, including anger, withdrawal, aggression, anxiety, fear, guilt, or physical symptoms. Here are a few suggestions for helping students cope with the death of a classmate:

- Be honest in explaining to students what happened, keeping in mind their developmental stages and ability to understand. Sometimes, especially for younger students, it might be better to say that "Joe was very sick and the doctors could not make him better" than to discuss abstract concepts about death.
- Understand that students may express grief in many different ways and for different lengths of time. Some students may joke about death; that is sometimes their means of coping with something difficult to understand. Some students may be very sad or angry for a brief time, then seem to have recovered, and then show symptoms of grief again. Such a cycle may be repeated a number of times.
- Find a way for students to express their grief and their thoughts about their classmate. Students may wish to draw what they're thinking. They may want to make cards to give to the classmate's family, and they may wish to talk about their classmate. Teachers should create a safe environment for these activities.

- Students also may have questions and misunderstandings about the classmate's death. These should be addressed in a straightforward way.
- A school counselor may be able to assist in helping you respond to classmates' grief.
- Keep in touch with parents, alerting them to the classmate's death and communicating with them about your plan for helping their child through this difficult experience.

### Helping Yourself

Teachers need to grieve, too. Here are some considerations for you:

- Acknowledge that your grief will not likely follow precise stages or last for only a specified period of time.
- Learn about the tasks of grieving—understanding, grieving, commemorating, going on.
- Use experiences with loss—not just death—to know what you need.
- Develop rituals to say goodbye to the student, such as creating a memory book.
- Ask colleagues for assistance.
- Be aware of your personal signs of stress; don't ignore them.
- Give yourself time and permission to grieve.
- Create a period for rest and renewal.

*Source:* Munson, L. J., & Hunt, N. (2005), Teachers grieve! What can we do for our colleagues and ourselves when a student dies?, *Teaching Exceptional Children, 37*(4), 48–51.

## REVIEW · REFLECT · DISCUSS

1. What strategies can be used to ensure that students with physical and health disabilities have access to learning? Which of these strategies might be used by each of the students introduced at the beginning of this chapter (i.e., Ryan, Aponi, Jeffrey)?
2. Think about what it would have been like to miss a month or more of school when you were in elementary, middle, or high school. What concerns might you have had? How can you use this understanding to help a student reenter school after a prolonged absence? What might such a student have experienced for which your own perceptions could not prepare you?

## Perspectives of Parents and Families

Parents of children with physical and health disabilities usually have become experts on their children's special needs. They often have spent hours, days, and weeks beside their children's hospital beds; they have rushed their children to emergency rooms; and they have taken notes, visited websites, read books, attended support groups, and otherwise educated themselves about their children's conditions and their rights and needs.

### Parent Experiences

When parents find out that their child has a potentially life-threatening condition, a life-changing chronic disorder, or a serious injury, they first deal with the immediate matter at hand—survival. This is a stressful time (Carnes & Quinn, 2005). Parents in this situation have reported that they focus on getting the care that is needed, making it through one day at a time, and not thinking too much about the future (Mason, O'Sullivan, O'Sullivan, & Cullen, 2000).

As their child's condition stabilizes—and perhaps as they also become accustomed to the procedures and routines of having a child with a physical or health disability—the parents' attention often turns toward educating themselves and beginning to advocate for their child (Taub, 2006). They also may question why their family was given this challenge. As time goes by, and depending on the severity of the disability, they may begin to explore education and career options for their child and perhaps even advocate on behalf of all families whose children have similar conditions. Of course, these reactions and families' specific actions and priorities may be heavily influenced by culture and education.

Siblings also may be affected by a brother or sister with a physical or health disability (Dew, Balandin, & Llewellyn, 2008). Although research does not indicate that siblings perceive the other child as a stressor, at times the child with special needs requires full parental attention, which means time is taken away from the other children (Shepard & Mahon, 2002). Siblings also may not understand why the illness or condition occurred, and they may imagine that they are to blame or that the disorder is contagious when, in fact, it is not. Interestingly, siblings usually recognize the positive effects of having a brother or sister with a disability as well as the challenges.

### Advice to School Professionals

Lee and Guck (2000) offer extensive advice to professionals working with the families of children with physical and health disabilities. Among their suggestions are these:

- Help parents to develop an optimistic but realistic view of their child's illness.
- Encourage parents to maintain involvement with relatives and neighbors as well as immediate family.
- Help parents to ask questions of and continue communication with medical personnel.
- Know helpful materials that parents can access related to their child's condition.
- Ensure that the child's return to school is based on a comprehensive plan that is closely monitored. (p. 272)

## REVIEW · REFLECT · DISCUSS

1. What are the greatest concerns that parents of children with physical and health disabilities are likely to have? What is the responsibility of school personnel to help them address these concerns?
2. Review the list of suggestions for teachers on working with parents of students with physical or health disabilities. What are examples of how you could turn each concept into a reality for the students introduced at the beginning of the chapter (Ryan, Aponi, Jeffrey)?

## Trends and Issues Affecting the Field of Physical and Health Disabilities

Advances in medical and computer technology have had a far-reaching impact on the field of physical and health disabilities. However, these developments also have raised questions: How prepared are teachers to work with students with physical and health disabilities? How available is technology to students who are not affluent?

### Professionals Prepared to Work with Students with Physical Disabilities

Both general education teachers and special education teachers have expressed concern about their preparation to adequately teach students with physical disabilities. Heller and

Swinehart-Jones (2003) are particularly concerned about the latter group of teachers because they often have the responsibility of providing information to the former group. These authors note that professionals need to understand students' functional limitations in several areas (e.g., motor, health), related psychosocial and environmental factors (e.g., motivation, social competence), and the details of students' physical impairments (e.g., neurological). Heller and Swinehart-Jones acknowledge that a team of professionals addresses all these areas, but they assign these six sets of standards to special education teachers: (a) physical and health monitoring, (b) adapted assessment, (c) modifications and assistive technology, (d) specialized instruction, (e) disability-specific curricula, and (f) ensuring an affective and learning environment. They also note that if licensure patterns that prepare teachers in broad areas instead of specialized areas are to be the norm, then perhaps technical assistance options, offered through regional consultants, should be encouraged. Their analysis is supported in the profession (Baldwin, 2007), and increased attention to professional preparation standards for these students has grown.

## Access to Technology

Technology of all sorts—including the examples you have read about in this chapter and the high- and low-technology examples from other chapters—significantly enhances the lives of individuals with physical and health disabilities. In some cases, technology is essential for enabling these individuals to learn effectively in school and live independently as adults (e.g., DePompei et al., 2008). However, have you ever stopped to ask yourself who has access to technology such as computers and specialized devices and how these items are funded?

Part of the answer lies in the provisions of IDEA—the law requires that assistive technology for education be provided when needed. However, most professionals believe that many students and adults lack access to all the technologies they need (Lee & Templeton, 2008). Two groups that are not necessarily distinct from one another illustrate the problem: students who live in rural areas and those who live in poverty. Students who live in rural areas may have less access to computers, few options for transportation, an increased likelihood of being served by personnel who are not fully qualified (and who may lack skills for obtaining technology), and more barriers for mobility (e.g., lack of sidewalks, absence of curb cuts). Students who live in poverty, whether in rural, suburban, or urban areas, may encounter many similar barriers, and they may not even be aware of some of the technology options that exist (Jans, 2000).

Access to technology is an ethical dilemma that school professionals face every day. IDEA may fund a communication board that a student uses at school but not fund a similar device for home. In some communities, extraordinary justification is required before technology can be accessed because, even if mandated by law, it takes resources from other programs and services. When technology involves an item that is tailored to a student's needs (e.g., a motorized wheelchair), consideration has to be given to replacement cost when the item no longer fits, and money has to be set aside for repairs. As an educator, you may find yourself participating in discussions of this important topic.

research
NOTE

DePompei, Gillete, Goetz, Xenopoulos-Oddsson, Bryen, and Dowds (2008) found that PDAs and smartphones were very helpful for students with traumatic brain injury, including as an aid for organization and scheduling.

## REVIEW · REFLECT · DISCUSS

1. What type of professional preparation program are you pursuing? When you complete your program, how prepared do you believe you would be to provide support to a student with a physical or health disability? What is the basis for your opinion? What resources could you access to enhance your knowledge and skills if you are concerned, especially given that many professionals are asked to support students outside their specific areas of expertise?

2. Not all students can easily access the technology needed to facilitate their learning. What is your role in addressing this issue? How might you help make technology more available to all students?

# Summary

- Individuals with physical and health disabilities have been known throughout history, but their treatment has been based on changing beliefs, from pessimism and isolation to optimism and opportunity.
- Students receiving special education because of physical or health disabilities include the following: those with physical disabilities, called *orthopedic impairments* in IDEA (e.g., students with cerebral palsy, spina bifida, spinal cord injuries, muscular dystrophy, arthritis); those with traumatic brain injuries; and those with other health impairments (e.g., students with asthma, epilepsy, HIV or AIDS, cancer, sickle cell disease, diabetes).
- Students with physical and health disabilities vary tremendously in cognitive ability, social and emotional needs, and behavior. What they have in common are medical or physical needs that may affect all other areas of their education.
- Many students with physical and health disabilities are identified before they reach school age. Identification includes assessment of all critical areas, including information about any medical or health conditions.
- Students with physical and health disorders receive their education based on the decisions made for them by the team preparing the IEP. They often receive early intervention, and in elementary and secondary schools they may spend little time in a separate setting or nearly all their time there. Inclusive practices apply to these students as to all others receiving special education. As students transition to adulthood, they often need assistance in considering postsecondary education, dealing with practical matters such as transportation, and selecting careers.
- Recommended educational practices for these students include ensuring access through aids for mobility and posture, communication, and learning as well as addressing highly specialized needs such as school reentry and responses to emergencies.
- The parents and families of students with physical and health disabilities often have dealt with medical and health crises, and they may have questions and concerns regarding access to services, the financial stress of having a child with physical or health needs, and options for their child's future.
- Trends and issues facing the field of physical and health disabilities include teacher preparation and the rapidly developing options of technology and their availability to students.

 ADDRESSING THE PROFESSIONAL STANDARDS

Council for Exceptional Children (CEC) Common Core Knowledge and Skills addressed in this chapter:

ICC1K5, ICC1K5, ICC1K7, ICC2K1, ICC2K6, ICC3K1, ICC3K3, ICC4S3, ICC5K4, ICC5K6, ICC5S3, ICC5S10, ICC5S16, ICC6S1, ICC7S1, ICC7S7, ICC7S9, ICC8S2, ICC10S1, ICC10S6

Appendix: Provides a full listing of the CEC Common Core Standards, and associated Knowledge and Skill Statements listed here.

**PEARSON**
**myeducationlab**

Now go to Topic 14: Physical Disabilities and Health Impairments, and Topic 16, Multiple Disabilities and Traumatic Brain Injury, in the MyEducationLab (www.myeducationlab.com) for your course, where you can:

- Find learning outcomes for the broad concepts covered in this chapter along with the national standards that connect to these outcomes.
- Complete Assignments and Activities that can help you more deeply understand the chapter content.
- Examine challenging situations presented in the IRIS Center Resources.

- Apply and practice your understanding of the core concepts and skills identified in the chapter with the Building Teaching Skills and Dispositions learning units.
- Check your comprehension on the content covered in the chapter by going to the Study Plan in the Book Specific Resources for your text. Here you will be able to take a chapter quiz, receive feedback on your answers, and then access Review, Practice, and Enrichment activities to enhance your understanding of chapter content.
- Watch video clips of CCSSO Teacher of the Year award winners responding to the question: "Why I teach?" in the Teacher Talk section.

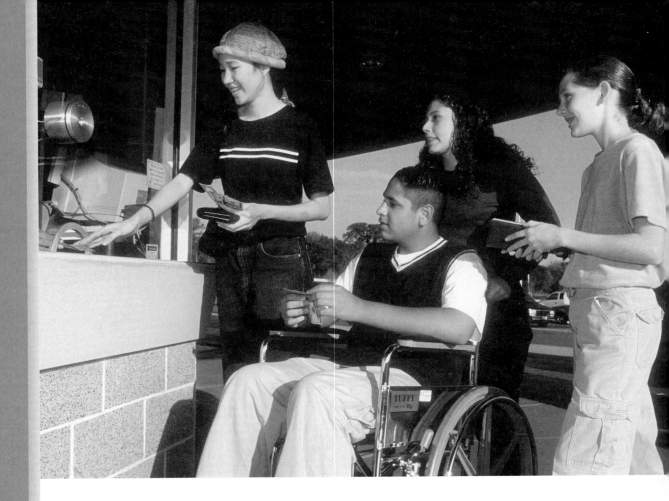

# Students with Severe and Multiple Disabilities

## LEARNING OBJECTIVES

- Summarize the development of the field of severe and multiple disabilities, explain what severe and multiple disabilities are, and outline their prevalence and causes.
- Describe characteristics of students with severe and multiple disabilities.
- Explain key concepts related to identifying students with severe and multiple disabilities that go beyond using labels to characterize this population.
- Outline how students with severe and multiple disabilities receive their education and how inclusive practices have significantly changed these approaches.
- Discuss recommended educational practices for students with severe and multiple disabilities.
- Explain the perspectives and concerns that parents and families of students with severe and multiple disabilities may have.
- Outline trends and issues affecting the field of severe and multiple disabilities.

Written by June E. Downing and Kathryn D. Peckham-Hardin, both of California State University, Northridge, and Marilyn Friend

## Sergio

Sergio is a seven-year-old second grader who has multiple impairments, including a mild physical impairment, communication delays, a moderate intellectual impairment, and challenging behaviors. Sergio uses speech, but it is often unintelligible. He also struggles to find the right words to use, especially when he is upset. When he cannot communicate effectively with speech, Sergio will yell, spit, kick, hit, bite, or try to leave the area to get his message across. Sergio is very interested in learning and loves to be on a computer, which can be incorporated into everyday lessons to increase his motivation. Sergio also loves to be at the front of the classroom, writing on the dry-erase board. He can read and write a few simple words, and he takes every opportunity to show off his skills to his classmates. Sergio can be a very engaging young boy, but he finds it quite challenging to sit at his desk for very long; he much prefers to be up and moving about the room. The second-grade teacher was initially challenged by some of Sergio's behaviors, but she learned how to address them by working in collaboration with his family and the special education teacher. Aspects of the curriculum were adapted to be made more relevant to Sergio's life, and he was provided with alternative ways to express his frustration (e.g., through the use of picture symbols). In addition, multiple opportunities were provided throughout the day so that Sergio could get up, move around the room purposefully (e.g., hand out worksheets, throw away trash), and act as a leader for his class (e.g., help out with demonstrations). His interest in the computer gave him an alternate way of completing work at his level and helped to bypass his frustration with paper-and-pencil tasks. Essentially, the team used Sergio's strengths and interests to improve his educational performance and support his learning in the least restrictive environment.

## Sasha

Sasha is an eighth-grade student with multiple disabilities who spends approximately two-thirds of her day in general education classes and the remaining third of the day in a special education setting. Sasha has a severe cognitive delay and a visual impairment. With the aid of glasses, she can discriminate among enlarged images (pictures and print) when placed on contrasting backgrounds (e.g., yellow flower on black paper). Objects are also used to help her understand her world. For example, rocks of different sizes, textures, weight, etc. are used during science to help her better understand the different forms of rock while simultaneously teaching related vocabulary (e.g., small/big, heavy/light). Similarly, Sasha uses a tactile schedule to navigate her day. For example, since she often listens to audio books during English, a CD is used to represent this class. Sasha's IEP goals and objectives include (a) using pictures, objects, and a voice-output communication device to answer content-related questions, respond to peers' and adults' questions and comments, and request assistance; (b) counting objects, associating numbers with quantity, and using an enlarged and talking calculator to complete modified math work; and (c) using her daily schedule to transition from class to class. Sasha's general education teachers were initially apprehensive when they learned Sasha would attend their classes, but they now comment that with the appropriate supports (e.g., professional development, support from a teaching assistant, and consultation with special education staff members), everything has worked out. They add that other students also have benefited from getting to know Sasha and often volunteer to assist Sasha during class activities.

## Cassie

Cassie is sixteen years old. She has long blond hair that she likes to streak with red. Like many girls her age, Cassie enjoys spending time with boys and actively seeks their attention by sitting next to them in class. She also likes to shop, watch music videos (especially those with a lot of visual effects and dancing), and take pictures of herself and others. She wants a job that involves photography when she graduates from high school. Cassie is a junior and participates in assemblies and other school events. Cassie also has severe and multiple disabilities. She has cerebral palsy that primarily affects her lower body, making it difficult for her to walk. She uses a wheelchair to get from one class to another and sometimes relies on a walker. For example, during photography Cassie uses her walker while working in the darkroom so she can stand to watch the pictures develop. Cassie also has a significant hearing loss. She relies on her vision to keep aware of what is going on around her. Because of Cassie's severe cognitive delay, she needs accommodations to facilitate learning.

For example, during her Spanish class students are learning new vocabulary and how to speak, read, and write these in sentences. Cassie works with a peer buddy in class to learn pictorial vocabulary in English that her peer then translates into Spanish and uses in sentences. Because Cassie does not speak, she communicates through alternative means. She sometimes gestures, she knows several signs, and she also uses a picture board, pointing to pictures to communicate (e.g., a photo of a glass of water to indicate that she wants a drink).

Students with severe and multiple disabilities are boys and girls who, despite the complexity of their serious disabilities, are quite capable of learning and want to be as much like their peers without disabilities as possible. Most of these students struggle to communicate to make their needs and thoughts known and find learning abstract material quite difficult. However, given the right amount and types of supports, these students can acquire important skills that will greatly improve their daily lives and interactions with others.

Keep in mind as you read this chapter that the characteristics and needs of the students described overlap somewhat with students already discussed; you will notice references to those students as you read. This chapter considers students who have severe or profound intellectual disabilities, those who are both deaf and blind, and those who have two or more disabilities, usually from among these categories: autism, intellectual disability, communication disorders, vision or hearing loss, physical disabilities, traumatic brain injury, or other health impairments.

## Understanding Severe or Multiple Disabilities

Many misconceptions exist concerning students with severe and multiple disabilities. This is due in large part to the small number of these students and to the fact that, until relatively recently, they did not attend public schools.

### Development of the Field of Severe and Multiple Disabilities

Many of the historical developments in the field of severe and multiple disabilities have paralleled those in other disability areas, as you can see in the timeline in Figure 14.1. For example, you learned that during the nineteenth century, children with intellectual disabilities or hearing loss often were institutionalized. The same was true for children with multiple or severe disabilities. The focus of these early institutions was education and rehabilitation, but by the late 1800s, the goal changed from education to custodial care (Gardner, 1993). This trend continued until the mid-1900s when families and profession-

**FIGURE 14.1**
**Severe and Multiple Disabilities**

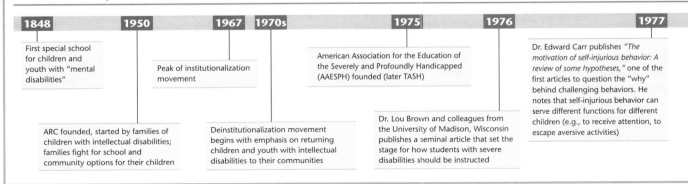

| 1848 | 1950 | 1967 | 1970s | 1975 | 1976 | 1977 |

First special school for children and youth with "mental disabilities"

Peak of institutionalization movement

American Association for the Education of the Severely and Profoundly Handicapped (AAESPH) founded (later TASH)

Dr. Edward Carr publishes "The motivation of self-injurious behavior: A review of some hypotheses," one of the first articles to question the "why" behind challenging behaviors. He notes that self-injurious behavior can serve different functions for different children (e.g., to receive attention, to escape aversive activities)

ARC founded, started by families of children with intellectual disabilities; families fight for school and community options for their children

Deinstitutionalization movement begins with emphasis on returning children and youth with intellectual disabilities to their communities

Dr. Lou Brown and colleagues from the University of Madison, Wisconsin publishes a seminal article that set the stage for how students with severe disabilities should be instructed

als in the field began to advocate for the closure of institutions. Today, the vast majority of individuals with severe and multiple disabilities do not live in institutions but rather in homes with their families.

### Emerging Recognition of Needs and Services to Address Them

It is important to remember that many children who thrive today because of advanced medical technology might not have survived to school age during the first half of the twentieth century. During that time, many children with severe disabilities were simply kept at home by their families; they learned basic life skills by helping out at home and relying on those around them to teach and support them. However, outside support for children with severe disabilities was beginning to emerge. For example, the National Society for Crippled Children was established by 1921, and private schools gradually became available for children with significant disabilities in some parts of the United States. Public schools, however, did not offer education to these students.

### A Changing Climate and Advocacy

Landmark decisions during the late 1960s and early 1970s paved the way for the federal special education laws that now ensure all students the right to education, regardless of the severity of their disabilities. Initially, students with severe and multiple types of disabilities were placed in special schools and educated apart from peers, but increasingly they are receiving educational services in general education schools and classrooms. For example, in 1990–1991, just 6.6 percent of students with multiple disabilities were educated primarily in general education, but by fall 2004, this percentage had risen to 13 percent (U.S. Department of Education, 1993, 2009).

In 1975, a small group of professionals and advocates formed the American Association for the Education of the Severely and Profoundly Handicapped (AAESPH), an organization whose purpose was to draw national attention to the status of individuals having severe and profound disabilities. In 1980, it was renamed The Association for the Severely Handicapped, or **TASH**, and today, to reflect the wishes of those it represents, the acronym TASH is used as the name of the organization. References to *severe* and *handicaps* have been dropped. TASH continues to represent the interests of those with the most challenging disabilities and leads the field in advocating for full rights, inclusion, and empowerment of this group of individuals.

## Definitions of Severe and Multiple Disabilities

Students with severe disabilities quite simply are, first and foremost, students. Although they may have a wide range of significant special needs, their disabilities do not prevent them from having most of the same needs and desires as others their age. These students' similarities with their peers should be emphasized and considered well before the focus is

One of the most famous individuals with multiple disabilities was Helen Keller (1880–1968). Both deaf and blind, she was taught by Anne Sullivan and became a world traveler, lecturer, and author of 12 books.

www.tash.org
TASH is an international advocacy organization for people with disabilities. Its tagline is "equity, opportunity, and inclusion for people with disabilities since 1954."

| 1989 | Late 1980s/early 1990s | 1992 | 1997 | 2004 |
| --- | --- | --- | --- | --- |

*Timothy W. v Rochester, New Hampshire School District, 875 F. 2nd 954 (1st Cir.1989)* A 9-year-old boy with severe and multiple disabilities was denied an education by the Rochester, New Hampshire School District. The district felt he was unable to benefit from an education. The US Court of Appeals reverses a lower court's decision, requiring the school district to provide FAPE for Timothy

Inclusive education gains recognition as a preferred learning environment for students with severe disabilities

*Board of Education, Sacramento city Unified School District v. Holland, 14 F. 3d 1398 (9th Cir. 1994).* Results in four factors to consider when determining LRE for a student: educational benefit is equal to or better than a specialized setting, social benefits are equal to or better than a specialized setting, impact of student on other students in class, and cost of inclusion versus segregation

Amendments to the IDEA required that all students, including students with the most significant needs, participate in state and district-wide testing and all states are required to develop an "alternate" assessment for them

Individuals with Disabilities Education Improvement Act (IDEIA) amendments to the IDEA further reinforces the mandate that students with disabilities—including those with the most significant needs—have access to and progress in the core curriculum

shifted to their disabilities and the descriptors that are attached to them. For example, Sergio may have several severe disabilities that interfere with his learning, but instead of focusing on these challenges, emphasis shifts to his love of the computer and its motivating potential to help him achieve. However, in order to be eligible to receive special education services, students must meet specific eligibility criteria as specified in IDEA.

### Federal Definitions

Students with severe and multiple disabilities are described in several categories in the Individuals with Disabilities Education Act (IDEA); no single category exists that is labeled *severe and multiple disabilities*. First, this group includes students with severe and profound intellectual disabilities, terms introduced in Chapter Eight and for which no separate federal definition exists.

Second, this group comprises students who are both deaf and blind. In IDEA, these students are given a separate category because of the extraordinary nature of their needs, and this category is defined as follows:

> Deaf-blindness means concomitant hearing and visual impairments, the combination of which causes such severe communication and other developmental and educational needs that they cannot be accommodated in special education programs solely for children with deafness or children with blindness. (IDEA 20 U.S.C. §1401 [2004], 20 C.F.R. §300.8[c][2])

A third group of students also is included in this chapter. They have multiple disabilities, defined in IDEA as follows:

> Multiple disabilities means concomitant impairments (such as intellectual impairment-blindness, intellectual impairment-orthopedic impairment, etc.), the combination of which causes such severe educational needs that they cannot be accommodated in special education programs solely for one of the impairments. The term does not include deaf-blindness. (IDEA 20 U.S.C. §1401 [2004], 20 C.F.R. §300.8[c][7])

These disability definitions are consistent with the others included in IDEA. They stress the impairments that students have, and they emphasize that the disabilities must have a negative educational effect for students to receive services.

### TASH Definition

Many professionals find the definitions provided in IDEA inadequate. These definitions tend to focus on deficits and lead professionals to emphasize students' challenges. This in turn can lead to negative portrayals of these students as individuals with severe and multiple disabilities having limited skills and abilities, and therefore, as people who cannot learn. These views are inaccurate and serve to further perpetuate harmful and nonconstructive stereotypes (McDonnell, Hardman, & McDonnell, 2003). As you can see from reading about Cassie in the chapter opening, such an approach would be quite limiting. Cassie's biography demonstrates that she has interests, strengths, and desires, in addition to having special needs. The point is this: Students with significant disabilities can and do learn many skills (Hunt & Goetz, 1997; Westling & Fox, 2009). Consistent with this change in emphasis, TASH defines persons with severe disabilities as

> individuals with disabilities of all ages, races, creeds, national origins, genders and sexual orientation who require ongoing support in one or more major life activities in order to participate in an integrated community and enjoy a quality of life similar to that available to all citizens. Support may be required for life activities such as mobility, communication, self-care, and learning as necessary for community living, employment, and self-sufficiency (TASH, 2000).

This definition emphasizes that persons with severe disabilities can represent all types of individuals from all walks of life. For the purpose of this chapter, students with severe and multiple disabilities are defined as individuals who require ongoing and highly specialized support to participate fully in typical home, school, work, and community activities, regardless of the specific disability label(s) applied to them.

## Prevalence of Students with Severe and Multiple Disabilities

The population of students having severe and multiple disabilities represents a low-incidence category comprising approximately 0.1 to 1 percent of the general school-age population and approximately 2 percent of the total population of students having special education needs (U.S. Department of Education, 2009). Consequently, based on natural proportion, it is not likely that more than one student with severe and multiple disabilities would be enrolled in any given general education classroom. Although relatively few students have this identification, their needs are significant, and they may require substantial supports and services to benefit from their special education programs.

## Causes of Severe and Multiple Disabilities

Several causes of severe and multiple disabilities are known. These known causes can be divided into three categories, determined primarily by when they occur. Some disabilities can originate prenatally, some occur perinatally, and some happen postnatally (Batshaw, Pellegrino, & Roizen, 2007). The causes of severe and multiple disabilities are similar to those for intellectual impairment, as discussed in Chapter Eight. In case you need to review these causes, they are summarized in Figure 14.2. Keep in mind, though, that in many cases, a specific cause for the disabilities is not known.

The severity and complexity of the resulting disability varies depending on the genetic abnormality, the amount of actual damage done to the brain, and the cultural and physical environments in which the child is raised. In general, the more severe the genetic abnormality or the more pervasive the damage to neural cells in the brain, the more severe the impact. However, a supportive environment that includes expectations for the child to learn can have a positive impact on overall development. Children who are not developing normally or whose normal development has been interrupted by an accident or a viral or bacterial infection typically struggle to learn incidentally (i.e., through observation) and require more direct intervention to understand their world. Some families are able to provide the needed stimulation and structured guidance to help their children acquire information, but others are not able to offer this type of assistance. As a result, two children with the exact same diagnosis may appear quite different in skill level and behavior.

---

**FIGURE 14.2**

**Causes of Severe and Multiple Disabilities**

Many of the causes of severe and multiple disabilities, summarized below, are similar to those for intellectual impairment, although often a specific cause for the disability cannot be identified.

| Prenatal (before birth) | Perinatal (during birth) | Postnatal (after birth) |
|---|---|---|
| Chromosomal abnormalities | Lack of oxygen supply to the baby's brain (e.g., prolonged labor, disconnect of umbilical cord, cord wrapped around child's neck) | Infections (e.g., meningitis, encephalitis) |
| Viral infections (e.g., rubella, German measles) | | Traumatic brain injury (e.g., fall, car accident, near drowning, child abuse) |
| Drug/alcohol intake, especially during early months of pregnancy | Physical injury to the brain during birth | Lead poisoning |
| Malnutrition | Contracted infections during birth (e.g., syphilis) | Reaction to medication |
| Physical trauma to the mother | | Environmental conditions (e.g., exposure to toxins) |

Source: U.S. Department of Education. (1993). *Fifteenth annual report to Congress on the implementation of the Individuals with Disabilities Education Act.* Washington, DC: Author; and U.S. Department of Education. (2003). *Twenty-fifth annual report to Congress on the implementation of the Individuals with Disabilities Education Act.* Washington, DC: Author.

*Students with severe and multiple disabilities benefit from the same activities as other students, and they enjoy friendships with their classmates.*

Darrow (2009), writing for music educators, notes that for inclusive practices to succeed, professionals must overcome organizational barriers, attitudinal barriers, and knowledge barriers. Her words apply to all of education, not just music.

## Labels and Their Limitations

Labels are very common in special education and are used to categorize groups of students who presumably share a set of characteristics. However, labels are rarely informative when it comes to determining educational intervention. The phrase *severe and multiple disabilities,* although convenient to use for collectively discussing students with significant special needs, does not provide a meaningful description of particular students. The same problem exists when a student is referred to as intellectually disabled or mentally retarded, autistic, or any other categorical label. Labels do not explain the most important aspects of a student. They do not help a teacher or an educational team determine the most effective ways to communicate with a student or how best to help a student learn, nor do they describe the individual strengths and goals of a student. Labels oversimplify the complexity of individual students and detract from viewing them as complete individuals, with likes and dislikes (Fewell, 2000; Smith & Polloway, 2008).

### REVIEW · REFLECT · DISCUSS

1. Students with severe and multiple disabilities used to receive their education at home, in private schools designed just for them, or in institutions. What are some of the factors that have led to their participation in public schools and their inclusion in typical schools and classrooms?
2. How do labels influence thinking about individuals with disabilities? When you think about individuals with severe or multiple disabilities, what comes to mind? What might be your biases toward these students?

## Characteristics of Individuals with Severe and Multiple Disabilities

Understanding the characteristics of students with severe and multiple disabilities is important. First, exploring their characteristics can highlight ways in which you can work effectively with students. In addition, by thinking about these students' characteristics, you can see how they are in many ways similar to students who have milder disabilities and students who are typical learners.

## Cognitive Characteristics

When students with severe and multiple disabilities are tested using typical standardized assessments such as IQ tests, they typically will score within the severe or profound range of cognitive delay due to the heavy emphasis on verbal skills and the unfamiliar and out of context environment. While IQ scores in the range of 85 to 115 are considered average and characterize more than two-thirds of all students, IQ scores for students with severe and multiple disabilities tend to fall within the following ranges: 25 to 40 for students with severe intellectual disabilities and 0 to 25 for those with profound levels of intellectual disabilities (Grossman, 1983). While testing of this sort is typically done to provide evidence for eligibility to receive special education services, these assessments are not particularly helpful in determining who the student is, what skills are most critical to teach, or how best to provide instruction. Additional assessment information is needed. For example, some students may not be able to respond to a question about a complex concept such as death or dying, but they can identify a picture of dead plants from pictures of live ones because of a particular interest in this area. That is, additional effort must be taken to tap into these students' creativity and understanding.

**web link**

www.disabilityisnatural.com
Disability Is Natural is a user-friendly website that provides a contemporary way of thinking about individuals with significant disabilities.

## Educational Implications

Because these students experience significant cognitive limitations, they need more time to learn new things and many opportunities to practice new skills. For example, John is learning to point to pictures to communicate interests and preferences, as well as to demonstrate knowledge. The more opportunities throughout the day in which John can use pictures to communicate these needs, the more quickly he is likely to learn this skill. In this example, John is learning more than just communication skills: He is learning a *strategy* of using pictures to communicate. An advantage of teaching strategies is that the student can use this skill to communicate a variety of things (e.g., interests, preferences, knowledge, joy, frustration, agreement, disagreement). Further, because communication is needed continuously throughout the day, numerous opportunities arise for practice. Another example of teaching a larger strategy is teaching students to follow step-by-step pictorial directions/instructions when they are completing multi-step tasks. The larger skill is following directions—if students can learn to use such a format, then the number of tasks they can complete with greater independence increases. And since students are likely to experience many multi-step tasks throughout the day, many teaching opportunities occur. Although students with severe and multiple disabilities do learn at a slower rate, they can and do learn. Professionals' task is to select important and meaningful skills that can be taught under typical conditions throughout the school day.

Because of cognitive delays, students with severe and multiple disabilities usually have difficulty understanding abstract concepts. To address this issue, information needs to be presented in concrete ways. For instance, during a lesson on fractions, Sandra's teacher uses pictures of pizza slices to help her understand the concept of larger or more instead of the specific fractional pieces. As another example, to understand "the passage of time," a relatively abstract concept, students may need pictorial representations showing how trees grow from seedling to large trees or how babies become toddlers.

Finally, like many learners, these students experience difficulty generalizing information or skills learned to different settings, tasks, materials, and people. Although Sandra, who is learning about less/more during a class lesson on fractions, may learn to identify which of several pieces of the pizza is bigger or more, she may not generalize this knowledge when asked to give her classmate the container holding more liquid as part of a science experiment. To address these needs, educators use approaches such as these:

- Teach a specific skill in a direct and systematic way by breaking it into very small steps as part of meaningful activities.
- Prompt students; that is, provide assistance to them using words, demonstrations, and even physical guiding, such as placing a hand under the student's hand to teach the use of a switch.
- Immediately reward correct responses.

- Teach within the natural context.
- Teach across as many settings, tasks, and people as possible so that the students can use what they learn in any appropriate situation (Downing, 2008; Ryndak & Alper, 2003).

## Academic Characteristics

Even though less emphasis traditionally has been placed on academics for children with severe and multiple disabilities, they can and do learn important skills in this domain. However, the depth of what they learn is likely to be different from that of their peers without disabilities. In science, a student may learn that electrical outlets are needed to operate certain appliances while other students are working to understand ohms, watts, and voltage. The key to designing academic instruction for students with severe and multiple disabilities is setting aside biases about their learning capability while recognizing the importance of making learning relevant and meaningful.

### Literacy

Students with severe and multiple disabilities often have been thought of as being incapable of acquiring literacy skills and, therefore, were provided with limited, if any, literacy instruction (Browder, Wakeman, Spooner, Ahlgrim-Delzell, & Algozzine, 2006). However, these students should learn as many literacy and literacy-related skills as possible. For example, Browder, Mims, Spooner, Ahlgrim-Delzell, and Lee (2008) taught three students with profound and multiple disabilities to respond to simple questions during shared stories by touching the objects related to the stories. The focus in this instruction is on how best to ensure meaningful access (Browder et al., 2008). Some students may learn to recognize certain letters, such as the letters in their names; familiar and frequently used words (e.g., *girls, boys, lunch*); and favorite words (e.g., *Taco Bell, TV, ball*). Students may use pictures to help them recognize words and may write or sequence their thoughts using pictured information. For students with limited or no vision, objects or parts of objects can be attached to pages in specially designed books to help them understand what is read to them. A simplified text also can be added in both braille and print (Downing, 2005b; Lewis & Tolla, 2003).

Motivation plays a key role in teaching literacy skills to students with severe and multiple disabilities, and so building learning activities based on student interests is important (Koegel, Openden, Fredeen, & Koegel, 2006). For example, Mandy had a strong fascination with the aquarium in her first-grade class. At every opportunity, she went to the aquarium to stare at the fish. Mandy was nonverbal and did not know the letters of the alphabet, and so picture and word cards were created to take advantage of her interest. When Mandy went to the tank, she was asked to read the words on the cards (*fish, orange, black, white, striped*) and to find the fish in the tank that each word described. This activity addressed her IEP goal of learning vocabulary within the context of her interests.

### Oral Language

Communicating with speech may be particularly difficult for students with severe and multiple disabilities because of intellectual and physical disabilities. Students may not rely on speech to communicate their needs, or their speech may be difficult to understand. Students may use a few words that are intelligible, especially to family members and friends, but many students will use other forms of **nonverbal communication**— facial expressions, body gestures, manual signs, pictures, and objects (Beukelman & Mirenda, 2005; Downing, 2005a). For example, Hatias, who is essentially nonverbal, was outside with his high school earth science classmates, monitoring the growth of their plants. To express his desire to get the large watering can, he tried to verbalize the word *can* while pointing to the shed where it was kept, vocalized several words that were unintelligible, signed *water*, and used gestures to indicate *big*. He increasingly exaggerated his communication until his message was understood. The use of multiple modes of communication is a frequent and positive approach when speech is not present or not effective by itself.

Receptive language also may be compromised for these students. They may have extreme difficulty processing oral language, and they often benefit when teachers, parents, and

**web link**

www.isaac-online.org
Many students with severe and multiple disabilities use augmentative and alternative communication. You can learn more about this topic at the website of the International Society for Augmentative and Alternative Communication (ISAAC), which lists resources, publications, and events and includes an idea exchange.

## Augmentative Communication Devices

Assistive technology plays a major role in ensuring the full and active participation in school of students with severe and multiple disabilities (Cosbey & Johnston, 2006; Lancioni et al., 2002). Of critical importance is its application in the area of communication (Cosbey & Johnston, 2006; Downing, 2000). Many students with severe and multiple disabilities find it difficult to communicate using the speech mode. These students can benefit significantly from the use of augmentative communication devices.

**Augmentative communication devices (ACDs)** are adapted aids that provide students with alternatives to speech to convey their messages; you were introduced to a few examples of these devices in Chapter Nine on communication disorders. Here are some points to keep in mind about ACD and students with severe or multiple disabilities:

- ACDs can range from highly technological (computerized systems) to very light- or low-technological accommodations, such as picture boards and books.
- These devices can be developed to meet the unique needs of students with severe and multiple disabilities, providing

graphic symbols, voice output, or written display as needed (Beukelman & Mirenda, 2005).

- ACDs for students with severe and multiple disabilities typically are easy to use, depict a visual symbol, and offer a relatively small number of individual messages.
- Because students need to communicate in all environments, ACDs also must be readily available and easily portable. One student may have several different devices to use for different purposes and in different situations.

Several examples of ACDs are displayed in the accompanying photos.

classmates present oral information in small segments, clarifying their words with gestures, pictures, and objects (Beukelman & Mirenda, 2005; Downing, 2005a). In the Technology Notes, you can read about some of the alternative communication options available for these students, including Cassie, who was introduced at the beginning of the chapter.

### Mathematics

If you were teaching students who could learn only the most essential math skills, which skills would you emphasize? Why? Students with severe and multiple disabilities demonstrate mathematic skills in various ways. Some students learn to recognize or match

*Students with significant disabilities demonstrate their learning through the use of portfolios and other authentic assessments.*

numbers. They may learn one-to-one correspondence through such activities as handing out materials and setting the table. All students, including those with severe and multiple disabilities, learn math more readily when they can see its application in their daily lives. For example, students may learn to recognize numbers in order to use a calculator or perform steps in a numbered task. Students may learn to identify certain times of day (e.g., 8:00 to start school, 10:00 for recess, 12:00 for lunch, and 3:00 to go home) by reading the daily schedule and matching it to clock time. Another example involves learning the concepts of *more* and *less* as they relate to money for making purchases.

Learning mathematics skills that have direct application to everyday activities can have a substantial impact on a student's quality of life and so should be an integral component of any meaningful curriculum (Browder, Ahlgrim-Delzell, Pugalle, & Jimenez, 2006; Downing, 2008; Westling & Fox, 2009). A recommended practice is to use math content standards for a specific grade level and identify the basic skills within these standards that are meaningful to students with significant disabilities (Collins, Kleinert, & Land, 2006). For instance, in an algebra class students may learn to identify the single-digit numbers and letters in the equation and use pictures of preferred items to learn the amounts of the numbers.

## Social and Emotional Characteristics

Students with severe and multiple disabilities typically display social and emotional skills that lag far behind those of other students their age. Limitations in communication skills and language development contribute to these challenges. For example, children typically use language to indicate interests in others' activities or to express their ideas about a current topic or project. These skills tend to develop naturally as children begin to understand the purpose of language through their day-to-day interactions with and observations of parents, family members, and friends. However, students with severe and multiple disabilities are not as likely to acquire these skills on their own. Instead, they usually require direct instruction in how and when to use language or alternative forms of communication to initiate and respond to others. In addition, what they eventually learn is not likely to be at the same level of sophistication as their typically developing peers.

Despite difficulties in developing communication and social skills, students in this group still desire and benefit from social relationships, and the Positive Behavior Supports shows how paraprofessionals can assist in this area. Friendships are particularly critical for these students, and friendships between children with and without severe disabilities are not unusual (e.g., Fryxell & Kennedy, 1995; Werner, Vismara, Koegel, & Koegel, 2006). Although some professionals question the ability of students with severe and multiple disabilities to truly make friends, considerable research indicates this is a real possibility and provides information on the means to facilitate it (Carter & Hughes, 2005; Downing & Peckham-Hardin, 2007; Downing, Spencer, & Cavallaro, 2004).

## Behavior Characteristics

Students with severe and multiple disabilities share behavioral characteristics common for students without disabilities. For example, some students may be outgoing and very animated while others may be reserved and shy. These students may also display behavioral characteristics that are less common. For example, students with physical and sensory impairments may engage in behaviors that seem highly unconventional and inappropriate. But understanding the disability helps in better understanding the different behaviors the stu-

## Using Paraprofessionals to Increase Students' Social Interactions

Students with significant disabilities may have difficulty in their social interactions with peers, and this dilemma sometimes is compounded when the paraprofessionals assigned to assist these students become a barrier to social interactions rather than a facilitator of them. However, paraprofessionals can be taught to change their behavior in order to help students with severe disabilities.

Causton-Theoharis and Malmgren (2005) decided to address this matter. They provided four one-hour training sessions for four paraprofessionals working with students with severe disabilities in two elementary schools. The training included topics such as the importance of peer interactions and paraprofessionals' roles in fostering those interactions. The students, who spent nearly all day in general education, interacted 25 times more frequently with peers after the paraprofessionals received training. Here are examples of the ways the paraprofessionals were observed to facilitate social interactions between the students with severe disabilities and their peers:

- Ensure that the student is in close physical proximity to peers.
- When peers ask questions about the student, redirect the classmate to ask the student directly.
- Partner the student with typical peers during academic tasks, even if the student's version of the task is adapted.

- Verbally highlight similarities between the student and peers (e.g., "David really likes that show, too").
- Directly teach peers how to interact with the student.
- Use interactive technology to foster communication (e.g., a tape player with two headsets).
- Use rewards that encourage interactions (e.g., lunch with a friend, puzzle time with a classroom peer).
- Arrange for the student to have classroom responsibilities that foster interactions (e.g., handing out papers or collecting homework).
- As peers become more comfortable interacting with the student, gradually become less and less involved so that the interactions are less arranged and more spontaneous.

Think about the critically important impact that these simple strategies could have on students' social interactions. Which strategies seem most feasible to you? Which are most likely to have a positive impact? How could you help paraprofessionals incorporate these strategies and others into their work with students?

Source: Adapted from Causton-Theoharis, J. N., & Malmgren, K. W. (2005). Increasing peer interactions for students with severe disabilities via paraprofessional training. *Exceptional Children, 71*(4), Figure 1, p. 436. Reproduced with permission of Council for Exceptional Children.

dent may display. Thomas, a young man of sixteen who is deaf and blind, illustrates this concept. Thomas has very limited communication ability and is quite isolated from the world, and so he amuses himself with the stereotypic behaviors of spinning around in tight circles and tapping his forehead with the back of his hand. Without understanding the complexity of Thomas's disabilities and his difficulty in obtaining sensory input, one might misjudge him and consider his behavior strange. However, when compared to others his age who also engage in self-stimulatory types of behaviors (e.g., doodling, pen clicking, paperclip tapping, hair twirling), the reason for the behavior becomes more apparent. Unfortunately, due to his visual impairment, Thomas cannot observe these more accepted forms of self-stimulatory behavior performed by others his age, and so he created his own.

### Challenging Behaviors

Students with severe and multiple disabilities also can engage in behaviors that are disruptive to others, destructive of property, or harmful to themselves or others (Westling & Fox, 2009). These behaviors can range in severity and intensity from minor off-task behaviors to loud crying/screaming or hitting others or themselves. For example, Aaron is an eight-year-old with a severe intellectual disability who does not speak and at times struggles to understand the expectations of others. He dislikes tasks that are repetitive in nature (e.g., writing his name over and over again), that require him to sit and listen for long periods of time, and that involve handling sticky or gooey materials (e.g., paints and glue). When asked to do such tasks, Aaron tears the paper, throws the pencil, and sometimes hits his head with his hand. Such behaviors are clearly not appropriate and can be challenging for teachers, parents, and others on the team to address, but they can understand these challenging behaviors, and Aaron can learn alternative behaviors. Aaron engages in these behaviors to communicate his dislike of such activities. Once the purpose behind the challenging behavior is understood, educators can implement strategies to reduce these behaviors while simultaneously teaching appropriate behaviors. When students lack efficient means of self-expression and find it difficult to understand the messages of others, they may resort to challenging behaviors to bring attention to what they need. Therefore, understanding the

**research NOTE**

Providing students with the opportunity to control their world through the use of choice has been shown to be a relatively simple and effective strategy to reduce challenging behaviors (Shogren, Faggella-Luby, Bae & Wehmeyer, 2004). It also promotes self-determination and enhanced quality of life. Examples include choosing what questions to answer or what writing instrument to use.

meaning behind these behaviors and providing the student with alternative means of meeting her needs is a critical consideration in addressing these needs. For the previous example of Aaron, can you imagine what he was trying to convey through his seemingly aggressive behavior? What might you do to prevent this type of behavior?

## REVIEW · REFLECT · DISCUSS

1. In considering the characteristics of students with severe and multiple disabilities, many professionals maintain that these students cannot participate in general education because of their cognitive and academic characteristics. What is your own perspective on this topic? What is your justification for your view?
2. Many students with severe and multiple disabilities experience problems in the area of behavior. Why? What should educators remember about this characteristic of these students?

# Assessment of Students with Severe and Multiple Disabilities

Determining eligibility for services is not the primary reason for assessing students who have severe and multiple disabilities. Typically, identification occurs at birth, during infancy, or after some specific trauma, and the need for special education services is obvious (La Paro, Olsen, & Pianta, 2002). Rather than using tests to determine eligibility, assessment focuses on developing quality educational programs for these students.

## Assessment for Instruction

Assessment should help educators understand how their students learn and what motivates them. Knowing this information can help teachers select the most appropriate teaching strategies for each student. As you might imagine, students with severe and multiple disabilities do not perform well in formal assessment situations. They often do not understand what is expected or why it is important to respond as desired. As a result, alternatives to formal and norm-referenced assessments generally are recommended. You can read about the advantages and disadvantages of different types of assessment for students with severe and multiple disabilities in the following sections.

### Standardized Assessment

As you know, *norm-referenced assessments* are standardized tests that delineate specific skills that most students should demonstrate at certain ages or stages of development. Students typically are assessed in an artificial environment (e.g., the office of the psychologist or psychometrist), and they may not understand why they should do as requested. This type of testing is especially difficult for students with severe or multiple disabilities. For instance, Brian is eleven years old and has developed several important skills including grasping objects of interest (a red marker), following directions when getting ready to eat, and looking for a favorite magazine when it is out of sight. However, in a formal testing situation, he does not always grasp items presented to him (e.g., blocks, beads), may not follow simple directions to stack blocks or put objects into a container, and does not search for a toy that has been hidden from view. The lack of context or meaning interferes with Brian's ability to adequately demonstrate his knowledge. Consequently, Brian scores poorly on this test, ending up with an IQ score of 25 and a developmental age of one year or younger. This score does not reflect what Brian is capable of accomplishing.

Standardized assessments are problematic for students with severe and multiple disabilities for an additional reason: The results of such tests fail to help teachers decide what to teach or how (Brown, Snell, & Lehr, 2006; Heward, 2006). Because students with severe and multiple disabilities experience significant cognitive and language impairments, they are likely to score very low in every area being tested (Campbell, Reilly, & Henley, 2008; Westling & Fox, 2009). This can make it difficult to determine what skills are critical to learn. Some teachers may believe that they should teach students the items failed on a given test without considering student age, interests, and skill relevance. Doing so can lead to instruction in age-inappropriate and nonfunctional skills, such as teenagers being taught to engage in activities typical of a preschool or kindergarten classroom (e.g., coloring, playing with blocks), not in activities that will help them as adults.

Finally, low test scores can lead some to conclude that students with significant disabilities are not capable of learning higher-order skills. For example, Samantha, an adolescent with severe cognitive delay, may not be able to discriminate between coins and dollar bills. Based on this finding, one might conclude that Samantha could not learn how to make purchases or manage a checking account. However, with the appropriate supports, she can learn that in order to get a desired item, she must give the cashier money. The amount of money in her wallet can be predetermined, or she can be given only dollar bills so that she learns to wait for change before taking her purchase. If modified and supported correctly, the activity does not require Samantha to have a full understanding of the value of the individual coins and bills; she needs to comprehend only cause and effect. What other activities could Samantha also engage in, even though she does not have typical prerequisite skills?

## Authentic Forms of Assessment

Authentic assessment enables students with severe and multiple disabilities to more accurately demonstrate their skills and abilities. **Authentic assessment** is an ongoing assessment process that occurs within the student's natural environment and includes observation of a student's performance as well as the necessary supports for the student (Kleinert & Kearns, 2001; Snell, 2002).

### Person-Centered Approach

A key characteristic of authentic assessment is making decisions about what to assess based on input from family members, friends, teachers, paraprofessionals, and others who know the student's abilities, strengths, and goals. In particular, those closest to the student—usually family members—are asked what they believe the student should learn so that the assessment considers the student's personal, cultural, and religious beliefs. This **person-centered approach** focuses the student's assessment and education plan on his unique characteristics and interests (O'Brien, O'Brien, & Mount, 1997; Wehmeyer, 2002) and not on any predetermined set of skills, such as those on a formal assessment. Once the team has this information, professionals and family members can use it to guide their observations of the student. The observational data are more meaningful than traditional test data in setting appropriate goals for the student.

### Functional–Ecological Assessment

Another form of authentic assessment is a **functional–ecological assessment**, which provides a means of organizing information from written observation notes and video or digital recordings (Downing, 2008; Siegel & Allinder, 2005). A functional–ecological assessment analyzes the typical demands of the environment (e.g., what steps others typically engage in to complete activities) and the natural cues in the environment that exist to prompt the expected behavior. The student's performance is noted (what she can and cannot do), and the discrepancy between what is expected and how the student performs is analyzed.

As part of this type of assessment, professionals note how they can help the student complete a task, which helps them plan how to teach the student specific skills. The Instruction in Action provides an example of functional–ecological assessment of a spelling lesson. The outcome of such assessment is to discover skills that the student needs to learn and adaptations that need to occur to help the student be actively involved and successful in meaningful and frequently occurring activities. Results from this type of assessment, instead of an IQ score or a developmental level, lead to ideas for direct intervention.

**fyi**

Remember that the students addressed in this chapter might have other disabilities including intellectual disability (Chapter Eight), hearing or vision loss (Chapters Eleven and Twelve), autism (Chapter Ten), or physical and medical disabilities, including other health impairments and traumatic brain injury (Chapter Thirteen).

dimensions of
**DIVERSITY**

African American parents of children with severe disabilities are satisfied with professionals' cultural sensitivity when they perceive that they are being treated with respect (Zionts, Zionts, Harrison, & Bellinger, 2003).

**Portfolio Assessment**

In addition to observational information, authentic assessment also includes examples of student work, such as an adapted geometry assignment in which the student matches by shape and color. Explanations of the adaptations used and how the student was supported accompany the samples. Videotaped segments or digital video recordings of the student learning in different activities and situations can be collected to document learning style. Such examples of student performance are maintained in a student portfolio that clearly creates a record to show a student's progress over time (Kleinert & Kearns, 2001; Siegel-Causey & Allinder, 1998). Student portfolios can be an effective alternative to standardized educational assessments for students with severe and multiple disabilities. Student artifacts can be aligned with grade-level content standards to demonstrate student progress and accountability (Kearns, Burdge, Clayton, Denham, & Kleinert, 2006).

Authentic assessment—with a focus on person-centered planning, functional–ecological assessment, and portfolio assessment—provides teachers with accurate information about students' abilities and guides the development of meaningfully individualized programs. Further, such assessment provides clear information for future teachers to use as the students transition from grade to grade. Given the value of these approaches for students with severe and multiple disabilities, what might be the benefit of using authentic assessment for students without disabilities?

## REVIEW · REFLECT · DISCUSS

1. Tara, a ten-year-old student, has been identified as having severe and multiple disabilities based on an IQ score of 20. To what extent does this information provide the educational team with what they will need to develop a high-quality individualized program for this student? What else is important to know about Tara?

2. A common means of assessing students with severe disabilities is a portfolio. Why might this approach be preferred to other options? What are the drawbacks of portfolios?

**research**
**NOTE**

Dunst and Trivette (2009) stress the importance of using research-based practices to educate young children with disabilities. Their review of the literature revealed that many practices used regularly in early childhood special education settings, including infant massage, therapeutic electrical stimulation, oral-motor stimulation, and vestibular stimulation, lack data that support their continued use.

## How Learners with Severe and Multiple Disabilities Receive Their Education

Several different options exist for educating students with severe and multiple disabilities. These options vary depending on the age of the student, the geographical area in which the student lives, and the preference of family members. As you have learned, IDEA clearly states that students with disabilities should be educated with their peers without disabilities to the maximum extent possible.

### Early Childhood

The importance of early intervention for children with severe and multiple disabilities cannot be stated strongly enough. These children, because of the complexity of their disabilities, enter preschool without the basic skills that most children acquire without effort. Their communication skills may be severely delayed. Some children may be learning to walk, and others may exhibit difficulties with sitting, crawling, or standing (McDonnell, Hardman, & McDonnell, 2003). Many children without disabilities enter preschool with basic literacy skills, and they can sit quietly listening to stories, understand those stories, and respond to questions. Children with severe and multiple disabilities typically display few literacy skills and thus enter preschool considerably more disadvantaged than their peers without disabilities (Kliewer & Biklen, 2001).

Young children with severe and multiple disabilities may have had limited opportunities to interact with other children their age; given this, they may demonstrate minimal so-

## Functional–Ecological Assessment of Learning Environments

*Setting:* Third-grade classroom
*Activity:* Writing assignment using spelling words.

**Key**

| | |
|---|---|
| + | Does all parts of step independently |
| 0 | Doesn't complete step or does it incorrectly |
| P | Does some parts of the step |

| Nondisabled Peer Inventory | Natural Cues | Student Performance | Discrepancy Analysis | Plan to Intervene (what to teach, accommodations, partial participation) |
|---|---|---|---|---|
| Get out paper and pencil. | Teacher instruction; other students doing this. | 0 | Still working on previous assignment (math); did not appear to hear teacher instruction. Does not have the physical ability to do this. | Reduce number of problems so assignments can be completed within typical timeframe. Teach student how to use daily schedule to prepare him for upcoming events. Teach him to request help getting materials. |
| Put name on paper. | Teacher instruction; blank paper and pencil on desk. | 0 | Can grasp pencils/pens but cannot write name. Learning to recognize some letters. Cannot keep up with fast pace. | Provide different way to write using labels or name stamp; present two different names and have him select his name and indicate where it should be put on paper. |
| Write spelling words in sentences. | Teacher direction and example on the board. Past experience doing this. | 0 | Does not write. | Modify task demand. Student finds the picture that matches the word and indicates the line that is blank within a prewritten sentence that also contains pictures. A peer or adult support pastes in the picture. |
| Turn paper in when finished and get out book to read. | Teacher instruction; students finishing and handing in their papers and getting books to read. Finished with assignment. | P | Cannot physically do this. Doesn't understand the need to go on to another task. | Peer in front of student will ask him if he wants help turning in his paper. Teach student to use a device to respond or make this request. Teach him to check his daily schedule to see what's next. Offer choices of books to read. |

cial skills. Picture three-year-old Belinda, who is blind and nonverbal. She also has difficulty moving her body and holding objects, and she has a severe intellectual disability. Belinda has not been able to learn much about objects in her life because she cannot see them at a distance; even when they are within her reach, she has great difficulty grasping and exploring them. She does not understand basic concepts because she cannot learn incidentally and is unable to ask questions about things she encounters. Belinda relies on the interactions of her peers without disabilities to keep her motivated to learn. Since it is difficult for Belinda to initiate interactions, her peers have been taught to approach her, place toys in her hands, and talk to her about them. They have learned to offer her two play items to touch and choose from. Belinda responds well to her peers' efforts to engage her, and they have the opportunity to learn about differences in a very positive way.

Unfortunately, most preschool children with severe and multiple disabilities have limited access to peers without disabilities (Etscheidt, 2006). Although young children with disabilities have access to free and appropriate public education, those without disabilities do not have this legal guarantee. Therefore, the majority of typical preschoolers either stay at home or attend a private preschool. Finding ways to educate young children with severe

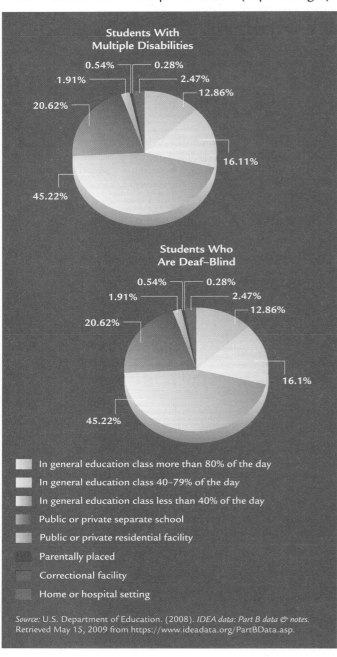

**FIGURE 14.3**

Educational Placement of Students Ages Six to Twenty-One Who Have Severe and Multiple Disabilites (in percentages)

**Students With Multiple Disabilities**

0.54%    0.28%
1.91%    2.47%
20.62%    12.86%
45.22%    16.11%

**Students Who Are Deaf–Blind**

0.54%    0.28%
1.91%    2.47%
20.62%    12.86%
45.22%    16.1%

- In general education class more than 80% of the day
- In general education class 40–79% of the day
- In general education class less than 40% of the day
- Public or private separate school
- Public or private residential facility
- Parentally placed
- Correctional facility
- Home or hospital setting

*Source:* U.S. Department of Education. (2008). *IDEA data: Part B data & notes.* Retrieved May 15, 2009 from https://www.ideadata.org/PartBData.asp.

disabilities with their nondisabled peers is an ongoing challenge that requires planning and creativity (Cavallaro & Haney, 1999; Downing & Demchak, 2008; Purcell, Horn, & Palmer, 2007). For example, instead of placing children with severe disabilities in specialized settings during their preschool years, in some communities, needed support is provided to the child in more typical settings, such as Head Start programs and private preschools.

## Elementary and Secondary Education

Many students with severe and multiple disabilities receive their education in segregated programs with an emphasis on life skills, a fact illustrated in the data presented in Figure 14.3. However, this trend is changing. Consistent with IDEA, students with severe and multiple disabilities, like other students with more mild disabilities, must have access to the core curriculum.

The literature is clear regarding the benefits of placing these students in general education classes with their peers without disabilities (Fisher & Meyer, 2002; Foreman, Arthur-Kelly, Pascoe, & King, 2004; Hunt & Goetz, 1997). Practices that foster success for other students with disabilities are effective for students with severe and multiple disabilities, too. Universal design for learning (UDL), cooperative learning, active and hands-on learning, and instructional differentiation are helping to open doors for students traditionally excluded from the general education environment (Eichinger & Downing, 2008; Katz, Mirenda, & Auerbach, 2002; McGuire, Scott, & Shaw, 2006). In many schools, these students are spending at least a significant part of their day in a general education setting.

Regardless of the program in which students participate, professionals agree that students with severe and multiple disabilities should be assigned to the same grade level as their chronological peers, not a grade level according to ability. The logic for this should be clear: These students are not going to catch up in any traditional sense, so assisting them to learn as much as possible while moving through the years of their public school education is the preferred strategy. The alternative might result in students who are fifteen, sixteen, or seventeen years old and still assigned to elementary school.

Within an age-appropriate placement, specific accommodations are made across subject matter to enable students to access and participate in the core curriculum as much as possible. For example, during a study of the planets, one fourth grader with severe and multiple disabilities—Stephen—may not be learning all the facts about the planets that his classmates are learning, but he is practicing finding certain colors by pointing, counting the planets to nine, and recognizing which of three different numbers is the numeral *9.* He also may be learning to distinguish a circle (the shape of a planet) from a square or another shape.

As students move from elementary school through middle school and into high school, the type of setting in which they are educated often changes. Even students who were members of general education classrooms in elementary school are very likely to attend self-contained special classes or separate schools for their secondary education. The logic for this approach concerns the difficulty of the curriculum and teachers' and parents' concerns that these students' time is better spent learning functional skills. However, learning with nondisabled peers is as important for secondary-age students with severe and multiple disabilities as it is for younger students. For example, students can learn about social and cultural expectations from their peers such as age-appropriate activities for teenagers, styles for dress and hair, and mannerisms that enable them to function more like their peers. Further, the curriculum offered to all students can provide meaningful learning opportunities in terms of vocabulary building and understanding the big ideas of lessons when teachers adapt the material as needed.

## Inclusive Practices

You have already learned that students with severe and multiple disabilities, to a large extent, have remained segregated from their peers (Fisher & Meyer, 2002; Fisher & Ryndak, 2001; Hunt & Goetz, 1997). However, inclusive practices have benefits for these students as well as for their peers and teachers (Downing et al., 2004; Fisher, Sax, & Grove, 2000). Benefits for students with severe and multiple disabilities include improvements in academic skills, social skills, motor skills (e.g., walking), communication skills, and appropriate behavior skills (Fisher & Meyer, 2002; Hunt, Soto, Maier, & Doering, 2003). Logan and his colleagues (1998) reported increased measurements of happiness of students with profound and multiple disabilities as a result of time spent with their nondisabled peers. The many benefits of inclusive practices extend to students without disabilities. Peck, Staub, Gallucci, and Schwartz (2004) analyzed responses from 389 parents of children with no disabilities who had classmates with severe disabilities. Parents reported that their children were more accepting and understanding of individual differences. Cole, Waldron, and Majd (2004) found that students without disabilities made significantly greater gains in reading and math when learning in inclusive classrooms than their peers in noninclusive rooms. Likewise, Carter and Kennedy (2006) found that when at-risk students supported students with severe disabilities in a classwide peer tutoring program, their academic skills increase.

### Partial Participation

When students are not able to fully perform an activity or project on their own, they often succeed with **partial participation**. This term refers to engaging in some parts of an activity with supports as needed. For example, when Sergio's class is engaged in learning to add two-digit numbers, the teacher asks him to find a particular one-digit number from among three different numbers in front of him. She does this twice and then uses Sergio's correct answers to

research
**NOTE**

Carter and Pesko (2008) surveyed high school general educators, special educators, and paraprofessionals about the effectiveness of various strategies for fostering social interactions with students with significant disabilities. These educators perceived that peer-mediated strategies such as peer-buddy programs were highly effective.

*Students with disabilities are entitled to access all school activities such as class field trips.*

form two-digit numbers that she uses in her demonstration to the entire class. Sergio is learning to identify single-digit numbers in the same lesson on addition that the teacher gives to the rest of the class. While they practice adding the two-digit numbers, he works on counting small items to find the answer to addition of two of the single-digit numbers he identified.

Assistive technology, such as the use of switches, can play a major role in allowing students to partially participate in a variety of meaningful and age-appropriate activities. These devices are explained in the Technology Notes. For instance, during eleventh-grade English class, Lindsey, who cannot speak and has severe physical and intellectual disabilities, uses a simple switch to activate a random spinner that can point to class members' names or questions on a study guide. Her teacher calls on her whenever she intends to randomly call on a student in the class or to choose a question at random to quiz the class. In using the spinner, Lindsey partially participates in her English class and meets her IEP goal of activating the switch and responding to the direction of her teacher.

**Paraprofessional Support**

Paraprofessionals have come to play a critical role in the inclusion of students with severe and multiple disabilities in general education classrooms. These individuals often provide the necessary added support for a student to ensure meaningful access to the core curriculum and to provide individualized instruction. These students may need extra adult support on a fairly regular basis, but a problem exists when paraprofessionals are left without instruction or supervision (see Etscheidt, 2005 for an analysis). Paraprofessionals tend to be the least-trained members of the team, yet they are asked to assist students with the most challenging educational and behavioral needs. These individuals need to receive ongoing training and monitoring by general and special educators as they support different students with severe and multiple disabilities in a variety of classrooms and grade levels.

Increasingly, experts in the field have begun to question the potential over-reliance on paraprofessionals to maintain inclusive programs for students with severe and multiple disabilities (Giangreco, 2003; Giangreco & Broer, 2005; Giangreco & Doyle, 2002). Without appropriate training, paraprofessionals may not implement programs effectively and may hinder students' progress by remaining too close to them, overassisting and interfering with their interactions with other students. In fact, researchers are increasingly looking at how peers can provide more natural support to relieve an overreliance on paraprofessionals (Carter, Sisco, Melekoglu, & Kurkowski, 2007).

General and special educators need to collaborate in their work with and supervision of paraeducators. Determining when, where, and how to assign these school staff members ensures high-quality support for students. Paraeducators supporting students with severe and multiple disabilities in general education classrooms should follow guidelines such as these:

- Interact with all students in the room, based on teacher directions.
- Teach small groups of children.
- Facilitate interactions among all students.
- Avoid hovering around the student with significant needs.
- Share information with general and special educators regarding the student's performance.
- Collect data on IEP objectives. Ask for guidance to do this properly.

## Transition and Adulthood

Upon graduating from high school, students with severe and multiple disabilities should have adult options similar to those of their peers without disabilities. Unfortunately, fears and low expectations combine to limit adult goals for these students. However, families and educators are beginning to consider new options for these students, such as home ownership with support, active participation in typical activities in the community, and postsecondary options (Carroll, Blumberg, & Petroff, 2008).

Some students with severe and multiple disabilities leave school to work in a job in the competitive marketplace (Parsons, Reid, & Green, 2001; Wehman & Sherron Targett, 1999). They might work at a store bagging groceries or stocking shelves; as an office assistant, de-

## Using Switches to Foster Participation and Independence

Simple technological devices such as switches allow students with physical and cognitive limitations to play a more active role in numerous academic and nonacademic activities (Bryant & Bryant, 2003; Lancioni et al., 2002; Reed, 1998).

- Switches offer students control over physical items that would typically be much too difficult for them to use.
- Using a switch, the student can watch and listen to a story on a computer and keep the story moving by activating the switch.
- A student without the physical means to cut can use a switch connected to battery-operated scissors to cut out shapes or pictures to be used in an assignment. A peer or adult would hold the scissors and guide it, while the student with severe disabilities would access the switch to provide the power.
- A student can also use a switch to turn on a slide projector or other equipment used by the teacher during classroom instruction. For example, as directed by a teacher during a science demonstration, a student activated a switch to power a fan that represented wind power. A control unit bypasses the normal electrical route of plugging a device into an outlet and makes it switch-dependent instead. As a result, almost anything that is electrical or battery operated can be used with a switch to

place greater control in the hands of the student with limited physical and cognitive skills and add to the learning of the entire class.

Switches come in a variety of different forms to meet the needs of students with severe physical limitations:

- A flat-plate switch can be touched with any part of the body over which the student has control (e.g., hand, elbow, knee, foot, head).
- A Mercury or gravity switch can be used to encourage a student to move a certain body part, such as an arm, the head, or a leg, in a controlled fashion to activate a given device.
- A puff switch works when the student blows a puff of air.
- A toggle switch requires any movement from any direction to activate a device.
- A light or vibratory switch adds an additional sensory input to encourage the student to activate them.

Determining the best switch or switches to use for an individual student is a team effort and depends on the student's physical abilities, demands of the task, physical situation, and positioning needs of the student. Occupational and physical therapists can be particularly helpful in determining the type(s) of switches to use and the best position for the student.

---

livering mail, duplicating materials, and shredding unneeded documents; or in the kitchen at a hotel restaurant, filling and emptying the dishwasher. They also may share an apartment with a person without disabilities who offers valuable support. Other students are not employed; instead, they may live in a separate residential setting, attend a special adult day activity center, or work in a sheltered workshop, where they complete repetitive or made-up tasks for little or no pay. Whether students achieve the former or are limited to the latter often largely depends on the quality of the transition assistance they receive while they are in school.

### Supported Employment

Clearly, the preferred and more progressive trend is to support individuals to work in real jobs that meet specific needs in the workforce, whether it is through employment in hotels, retail stores, restaurants, or offices (Mautz, Storey, & Certo, 2001; Parsons, Reid, Green, & Browning, 1999). **Supported employment** is the practice of assisting adults with disabilities to obtain jobs in the competitive market and providing them with the necessary physical, instructional, and social support to ensure success for the employee and satisfaction for the employer. One strategy for supported employment involves co-workers helping to teach young adults the skills required in their jobs and helping them practice until they are proficient in carrying out their job responsibilities (Hartman, 2009; Ohtake & Chadsey, 2001). This type of support is referred to as a **natural support**. Nearly everyone uses such supports, at least temporarily, when they begin a new job. For students with severe and multiple disabilities, this type of support is particularly helpful. If students need additional support, specialists called *job coaches* sometimes accompany them to their workplaces to do just what the job title implies: coach students as they master the requirements of the job and make sure that the job is completed satisfactorily. The goal is to gradually remove this intrusive support, but this may not always be possible or appropriate.

web link

www.inclusion.org
The Inclusion Network is an information-rich resource on inclusive education with related links. At this website, you can e-mail your questions about inclusion and receive a personal response.

**Community-Based Instruction**

To ease the transition from school to work, students with severe and multiple disabilities need to experience instruction in the community where they can sample different types of jobs and become accustomed to accessing community facilities. Such instruction, referred to as community-based instruction (CBI), is highly individualized, reflecting the interests of students while helping them to explore new possibilities. Students in high school may take some classes with their peers and then spend one or two periods each day in the community, either working at a particular job or learning to access community resources (e.g., use a grocery store, post office, laundromat). Because students with severe and multiple disabilities have considerable difficulty generalizing skills learned in one environment to another, teaching students within the natural environment of the community (whether a vocational or recreational setting) reduces this problem with transfer of skills (Westling & Fox, 2009).

Keep in mind that students with severe and multiple disabilities usually attend school until they are twenty-two years old, an option included in IDEA. In addition, they are able to access financial support after they leave school for vocational training, housing, and other needs. Because of their extraordinary needs, they usually require some type of support for their entire lives. However, their school experiences should help to prepare them for a life with as much independence as possible.

## REVIEW · REFLECT · DISCUSS

1. What benefits can all students, those with and without severe disabilities, gain from inclusive educational opportunities?

2. What is community-based instruction? What is its importance in the education of students with severe and multiple disabilities?

# Recommended Educational Practices for Students with Severe and Multiple Disabilities

For students with severe and multiple disabilities to receive the most appropriate education, professionals must use the practices that can have the greatest positive impact for them. A sample of recommended educational practices includes meaningful and individualized curriculum, collaborative approaches for educating students, positive behavior supports, and inclusive education.

## *Meaningful and Individualized Curriculum*

Because of the tremendous diversity among students with severe and multiple disabilities, they cannot be expected to fit into pre-existing curricula. Instead, the team members responsible for designing students' education must work together to determine what will best meet the specific needs of different students. **Meaningful curriculum** is relevant curriculum provided for each student according to interests, personal goals, and limitations in reaching those goals. The curriculum also must be age appropriate and not reflect the activities of much younger children. Using age-appropriate activities, expectations for performance will be modified to address the skill level and needs of the student.

Students who have been identified as having severe disabilities often are relegated to a life skills curriculum that consists of only nonacademic skill instruction such as grooming skills (e.g., handwashing, teethbrushing), socialization skills (waving "hi" to someone, making eye contact), food preparation skills, dressing skills, and home care. Although these skills are important, they can be addressed as they occur naturally throughout the day, not as isolated lessons. For example, dressing skills can be targeted when young children take off their shoes for playing in sand or when they don painting shirts for art. For older students, these skills can be addressed during physical education class when other students are also changing their clothes. Devoting the entire curriculum to such life skills is inappropriate and deprives students of rich learning opportunities. It also denies access to the core curriculum as mandated by law. However, for these students to benefit from more academic activities, adaptations and accommodations must be present.

## Making the Core Curriculum Meaningful

As you have learned, students with severe and multiple disabilities need to experience the same curriculum as their peers with no disabilities (Browder & Spooner, 2006; Downing, 2008; Fisher & Frey, 2001; Smith, 2006). Without exposure to a curriculum that may appear beyond their ability level, these students are further penalized in their education. However, the curriculum must be made relevant and meaningful to the individual student to motivate that student to learn, the topic in the Instruction in Action. Here is an example of making the curriculum meaningful: Nine-year-old Trevor participates in daily journal writing in his third-grade class by choosing from several different photographs and sequencing them in such a way that they tell about his weekend. After affixing the photos to his paper, Trevor chooses his name from among three different names written on sticky labels and attaches it to his paper. Trevor is learning to write using photographs to express himself, and he is also learning to recognize his name and add that to all of his work. When he is finished with his journal entry, his classmate Peter writes the words beneath Trevor's picture so that the meaning is clear, and then Peter reads the story back to Trevor.

Depending on the student's individually determined goals and objectives, the educational team members work together to analyze the activities of the curriculum and to determine ways to make the material meaningful for the student. Sometimes, advanced preparation is not possible, and teachers must be very flexible and creative when developing accommodations. The Instruction in Action gives some general ideas of possible adaptations that can be implemented at the spur of the moment to effectively include a student in a learning activity.

**PEARSON myeducationlab**

Go to the Building Teaching Skills and Dispositions section of Topic 16: Multiple Disabilities and TBI, in the MyEducationLab for your course and complete the activity entitled "Making the Core Curriculum Meaningful".

### When You Can't Plan Ahead: Tricks for Educators in the Inclusive Classroom

Although collaboration between special and general educators is a recommended practice to achieve effective inclusive instruction, sometimes for very good reasons this planning may not occur. All educators should be prepared to make adaptations on short notice, even if they are not as extensive as they would otherwise be.

Here are materials teachers and paraprofessionals keep on hand (Downing & Demchak, 2008):

- index cards
- felt-tip markers of different colors
- consumable pictures grouped by category
- highlighters of different colors
- a glue stick
- sticky notes in various colors
- blank white labels
- scissors
- extra batteries for switches and switch-activated devices

With these materials, sufficient accommodations can quickly be made as the general education teacher is giving directions to the class. For example, a special educator had adapted materials for a fifth grader with severe disabilities so that she could participate in a creative writing activity that involved students writing their autobiographies. Because the student she was supporting did not speak or write, the special educator had obtained photographs from the student's family. The student was to sequence these in a specific order to "write" about herself. However, the classroom teacher decided to postpone this activity for a later date and instead directed the class to write about whether or not they would want to join the circus. This assignment was related to a story that the class had just finished and a recent field trip to see Cirque du Soleil. Using some brochures from this performance, pictures from her picture library, and a glue stick, the special educator had the student determine which pictures were associated with a circus (learning vocabulary). The pictures were labeled and color-coded using highlighters. The student then was given choices of what she preferred: a picture of a circus performer or a picture of a completely unrelated field (e.g., police officer, cook). She was asked simple yes–no questions regarding why she liked a particular picture (occupation), which the teacher recorded next to the pictures. Although the special educator was not as prepared as she would have been if the lesson had been discussed in detail in advance, this simple adaptation using materials that accompanied the student created meaningful participation and an appropriate learning task for her.

instruction in action

## Ensuring Access to the Core Curriculum

In the not-so-distant past, students with severe disabilities were considered unable to benefit from grade-level curriculum (Orelove, 1991). More recent thinking reflects higher expectations with energies being used to determine how best to ensure access (Downing, 2008; Downing, in press).

### Teaching the Big Ideas

One strategy is to identify the big ideas of the lesson and related vocabulary to make the information relevant to the student. Students with severe disabilities and multiple disabilities may not learn exactly the same information at the same level of understanding, but they can learn valuable skills during the same lesson.

For example, in Cassie's English class, students are reading Mark Twain's *Huckleberry Finn* to understand the satire in the writing given the political issues of the day. While Cassie may not be expected to understand Twain's satire, she is expected to understand some of the story line and several vocabulary words. Working with a peer tutor, Cassie learns vocabulary words such as boy, Black, White, friend, paint, work, bad, good, and like. While the class is discussing racial issues and the literary conventions Twain uses when he addresses these topics, Cassie is using pictured information to understand the differences in skin colors and learn the signs for *White, Black, boy, men, bad,* and *good.* The peer tutor acts out some of the big ideas that address the Black/White issues, using the signs and pictures to support the concepts. Cassie uses a pictorial adaptation of the book that is written at approximately a first-grade level and so is acquiring basic reading and vocabulary skills to aid her communication efforts. To keep her actively involved in the group discussion, the teacher asks her a simple question (*Which one is the White boy?*). Cassie differentiates between two or three pictorial options, and the teacher uses her answer to ask the entire class a more in-depth question (e.g., What type of character is Huck Finn?).

Teachers decide what the big ideas are and what vocabulary can be used to describe these ideas, they gather the needed materials, and decide how to use the materials, incorporating them into the whole-class lesson. Finally, they decide how the students will demonstrate acquisition of the targeted skills.

### Applying the Big Idea Approach

When teaching a high school lesson on World War II, the big idea is that war is fighting and fighting hurts people. This can be related to fighting that can occur between students and the importance of talking things through versus fighting. Vocabulary to be taught would include fight, hurt, people (or men and women), talking, airplanes, bad, and good. Pictures are pulled from the textbook as well as other books and from the Internet. Unrelated pictures also will be used as distracters so that the student must demonstrate the ability to differentiate between the pictorial information based on the information presented. While the class discusses certain turning points of the war, the adult support (paraprofessional or special educator) asks the student to identify the target vocabulary from two or three pictorial options. The lead teacher routinely asks the student a simple question (e.g., *Which picture is of men negotiating or talking?* or *Which picture shows the use of airplanes in warfare?*). The adult support repeats and simplifies the question stressing the key vocabulary words and assisting the student to make the appropriate selection. The lead teacher then praises the student and asks a nearby classmate to read the question on the back of the picture selected. This question in turn leads the class into more discussion of critical points. In this way, students of quite different ability levels will have the same access to the core curriculum, but with very different outcomes.

---

**research**
**NOTE**

Hunt, Soto, Maier, and Doering (2003) investigated the impact of collaborative teaming for students with significant disabilities. They found that when all team members consistently implemented the plans that had been formulated, students experienced success in academic skills, peer interactions, and other classroom activities.

## *Collaborative Approaches for Education*

Collaboration has been stressed as important for many aspects of special education. For students with severe and multiple disabilities, collaboration with families and collaboration among the professionals and staff providing services on a day-to-day basis are both imperative, a lesson Sheri describes in Speaking from Experience.

### Active Family Involvement

A critical aspect of educational programming necessarily involves family members and significant others. Those who know the student the best—the family—have the information needed to guide the team in the development of an effective and individualized program. Unique cultural considerations, beliefs, and religious preferences are best obtained from the family (Thousand, Villa, & Nevin, 2002; Turnbull, Turnbull, Erwin, & Soodak, 2006). In addition, family members know their child's unique styles of communication (e.g., that rocking her head from side to side means that Brittany wishes to get out of the wheelchair) and what seems to be most effective in helping their child to understand others. Family members know what has and has not worked for their child, and they can be strong advocates for ensuring the most appropriate program that meets their child's needs.

*Like many new teachers, Sheri learned that she had to balance what she hoped to accomplish with the real limitations of time and energy.*

The first year I taught special education was one of the most rewarding and, at times, most frustrating experiences I have ever known. I currently teach and support high school students with severe, multiple, and physical disabilities. I strongly believe in including students with disabilities in general education classes with their same-age peers. I also feel it is very important to provide learning opportunities for students with disabilities so they can actively participate in the classroom setting.

That year, I decided to set weekly goals for myself. These goals included meeting with every teacher three days a week, working with each student on his or her individualized goals every day, adapting all curriculum two or three days in advance, organizing every student's weekly agenda, and meeting with every teaching assistant on a daily basis. What I was trying to do was conquer the world in one day. What I realized is that my goals just were not realistic. I was unable to meet with every teacher three times a week, nor could I work on every student's goals daily. I was not able to find out what the students were going to be working on the week prior to instruction, nor even the day before instruction, and I was not able to meet with every teaching assistant. I began to focus on what really mattered. I wanted to learn from my fellow teachers by collaborating and possibly co-teaching with them. I wanted to establish rapport and facilitate students' learning. Finally, I wanted to create a sense of teamwork among the teaching assistants, the general education teachers, and me. Here is what I learned:

- To be flexible, understanding, and extremely positive when advocating for the students with severe and multiple disabilities in the general education environment.

- To reassure teachers and point out the benefits that students with severe disabilities can bring to general education settings.
- To listen very carefully to teachers' and assistants' concerns in order to find a positive result to the problem at hand. Remaining positive helps a situation, even when times are tough, and a little "schmoozing" doesn't hurt either.
- To explore all students' interests and strengths and recognize their growth.
- To set high yet realistic expectations. I always told the students that I knew they could complete an assignment or make a choice.
- To understand a student's form of communication and find ways for some students to communicate their wants and needs. I would present pictures, offer choices using objects, and use some manual signs in order to help the students communicate.
- To provide a break if I noticed a student becoming agitated and then present the task again.
- To recognize that challenging behavior is not necessarily intended to frustrate or possibly injure someone; it is the only way some students have learned to express themselves.

The important elements of becoming a teacher are compassion, tolerance, patience, collaboration, flexibility, and the desire to make a difference in all of the students' lives—whether they are students with or without disabilities. Thinking back, I would have never thought of myself as becoming a special educator. Today, I understand why I love to teach, and I would never give that up for anything in the world.

## Collaboration on the Team

Because students with severe and multiple disabilities often have complex needs, it is impossible for one person to know everything necessary to best address those needs. Instead, the most effective approach is to call on the collective knowledge and expertise that various team members bring to the educational planning process (Hunt et al., 2003; Thousand et al., 2002). Family members, of course, are central team members, providing relevant and meaningful assessment information that helps to identify critical educational goals. Special educators have expertise in the area of individualizing instruction (e.g., curricular modifications) and related services professionals (e.g., speech pathologists, physical and occupational therapists) can provide more in-depth knowledge in their areas of specialization (e.g., suggestions regarding communication devices, positioning equipment, use of assistive technology).

Finally, the general education teacher brings to the team expert knowledge of the core curriculum. This person also provides information about how the day is organized, which helps to identify natural opportunities for peer interaction (e.g., during cooperative groups) and can help to highlight potentially difficult times (e.g., periods that require extensive sitting, listening, or note-taking) so additional support can be put in place (e.g., use of a paraprofessional).

**web link**

www.enablingdevices.com
Enabling Devices is a company dedicated to making assistive technology (AT) available to all ages of individuals who have disabilities. At the company's website, you can see a wide array of AT supports for students with severe and multiple disabilities.

*Susie knew in third grade that she wanted to be a teacher. She has taught fifth grade on the Navajo Reservation and GED on the Havasupai Reservation; at a private, alternative school with her husband; at the elementary level for 13 years; and after earning a master's degree in special education at the University of Arizona, as a teacher at an inclusive school in Tucson for 18 years. Susie received the AZTASH Legacy Award in 2009 for recognition of her impressive efforts to include students with severe disabilities in general education classrooms. Here is her advice to fellow special educators:*

- Keep your heart open to everyone. You are interacting with so many different people, each and every day, from students to parents, educational assistants to classroom teachers, and related service providers to itinerant teachers. Each has their own view and way of doing things. If you keep your heart open (that doesn't mean you have to agree!) the struggles and interactions you have will be less confrontational.

- Focus on the kids. Help the peers of the students with disabilities understand that everyone needs friends. Help the peers learn how to use communication devices and computer programs. Have lunch bunches so kids can get to know each other in a nonacademic setting.

- Get a good line of communication going with the general education teachers and the specialists (music, art, PE) so that you can have modifications and accommodations ready. When the general education teachers do their weekly plan-

ning, sit in on that and then you get firsthand what the next week will bring.

- Have a home-school communication notebook for each student. That way you can write about the student's day and the family can write to you information that might be helpful for the day. Use it only for sharing the student's day and activities coming up. Don't use to tell parents or families what they need/should be doing.

- Be flexible because things change, and you have to be ready to modify on the fly, too. And so do your educational assistants—so train them well.

- Don't "assign" one person to one student. Rotate the support instead. I rotate staff every hour or two. But it is good to have the same person every day with a student, say for science, because then he knows what is happening and can help keep you informed on upcoming projects. This helps students learn to work with different people and it helps adults not feel like they are the only one who knows a particular student.

- Be compassionate and nonjudgmental to everyone you have contact with. We do not always know the whole story.

- We are the teachers of the students, not their parents. It can be easy to fall into a parent type role with a student. Remind them that they are the teacher and that is a different role than parent. The students, most of the time, already have parents or guardians.

- Have fun! For me, it is so much fun being with students for six hours a day.

---

*For students who experience difficulty communicating their needs, pictorial and other supports can facilitate communication and prevent behavior problems resulting from frustration.*

Collaborative planning is critical for bringing together everyone's expertise in support of an effective program for a student (Friend & Cook, 2010). This is a key point made in Susie's advice to special educators in the Speaking from Experience.

## Positive Behavior Supports

As you learned in the discussion of the characteristics of students with severe and multiple disabilities, these students often have great difficulty communicating. This challenge can produce a great deal of frustration, leaving the student to convey intent through unconventional and undesired behaviors (Moes & Frea, 2002; Scotti & Meyer, 1999). Imagine how you would react if you could no longer express yourself through speech and could not tell others about your feelings, needs, and desires. How would you want others to respond? Understanding the limitations that students with severe disabilities must cope with on a daily basis can help others respond in a positive and supportive manner versus a critical and punitive one.

Positive behavior supports for students with severe and multiple disabilities are not significantly different from those for other students. However, particularly careful attention is needed because of the complexity of these students' needs. A functional behavior analysis should be completed and a behavior intervention plan designed, implemented, and evaluated. Within the plan, the goal should be to enable students to get their needs met in appropriate ways (Carr et al., 2002; Scotti & Meyer, 1999).

Sergio, who was introduced at the beginning of the chapter, exemplifies the importance of using positive behavior supports with students with severe and multiple disabilities. By providing him with opportunities to move around the classroom and ways to appropriately express his frustration using picture symbols, his behaviors became more appropriate. The focus of the behavior support plan is to modify the environment while simultaneously teaching prosocial and other adaptive skills. For example, if a difficult task is likely to elicit challenging behaviors, then efforts should be made to modify the task by either making it easier or breaking it into small and discrete skills and providing pictorial cues to help the student understand what he is to do. Similarly, by teaching positive and adaptive skills, the student can get his needs met in a socially acceptable manner. When challenging behaviors are associated with difficult tasks, the student might be taught either to ask for help as a way to lessen the frustration associated with the task or to ask to take a break as a way of temporarily avoiding the task altogether.

The way the student with severe or multiple disabilities asks or communicates these needs will vary. Some students may have adequate verbal language, and thus the focus of the intervention will be on teaching them to make requests at appropriate times. For students without verbal speech, alternative forms of communication—such as gestures, pictures, objects, and augmentative communication devices—may be used.

Functional behavior assessment was discussed in detail in Chapter Seven in relation to students with emotional and behavior disabilities. Those principles are the same ones applied in addressing the behavior of students with severe and multiple disabilities.

## Inclusive Education

If you remember that inclusion is an increasingly research-based practice with numerous benefits for students, you can understand its importance for students with the most significant disabilities and the reasons why it is so stressed in this chapter. That is, inclusive education for students with severe disabilities does not refer only to the physical placement of students in age-appropriate general education classrooms. It also holds the expectation of systematic instruction, numerous support services, curricular adaptations, and differentiated outcomes. It also encompasses the firm commitment by all staff members in a school to share the responsibility for educating all students and that it is their efforts that make the difference. Think about how each of the students introduced at the beginning of this chapter—Sergio, Sasha, and Cassie—are meeting success as educators address their IEP goals and objectives in the general education setting.

When students with significant disabilities participate in inclusive schooling, benefits accrue to teachers and other students, as well (Downing & Peckham-Hardin, 2007; Downing et al., 2004; Fisher & Ryndak, 2001). Teachers gain the ability to learn together about the curriculum and individualizing instruction. More support is available to all students in a given classroom as special educators and related services provide support to all children. Students without disabilities (and their families) gain a greater understanding and acceptance of those who have disabilities and learn ways of providing natural supports in a variety of contexts.

## REVIEW · REFLECT · DISCUSS

1. Use a lesson plan that you are creating for another course or one provided by your instructor. Pick one of the students introduced at the beginning of this chapter, and make four recommendations about how you can make your lesson meaningful for that student. What parts of this task were simple to accomplish? Which parts were challenging?

2. What do you think would be the challenges of collaborating with all the professionals who provide services to students with severe or multiple disabilities? What ideas do you have for how to overcome those challenges?

# Perspectives of Parents and Families

As you might imagine, families' perceptions regarding their children with severe or multiple disabilities vary considerably. Some families view having a child with severe disabilities as a gift, but others may express more negative perceptions (Turnbull et al., 2006). Regardless, just as most parents have an unconditional love for their children, so, too, do parents of children with severe disabilities.

## Family Members' Views of Their Children

dimensions of
**DIVERSITY**

In some cultures based on Catholicism, including that of Puerto Rico, a mother having a child with severe disabilities may be perceived to have sinned, with the child representing her penance (Rogers-Adkinson, Ochoa, & Delgado, 2003).

Most parents eagerly seek out and highlight their children's gifts and talents. We all have experienced proud parents who eagerly share photos, newspaper clippings, or report cards that highlight their child's accomplishments. Families of children with severe and multiple disabilities also are able to quickly identify and share their children's gifts. For example, Celese, a thirteen-year-old with cerebral palsy, is very good at making quick decisions. Having noted this as one of her strengths, her family calls on Celese whenever there is a family conflict (e.g., what movie to see, what restaurant to go to). However, sometimes it is difficult for families of children with severe and multiple disabilities to see their positive attributes. Such a family may only see what the child cannot do. Such a narrow view of the child may in turn limit the opportunities the family provides. For example, if parents think their child cannot make choices, then the family will not include the child in the decision-making process.

Other factors influence how families come to perceive and thus accept a child with severe and multiple disabilities. The extent to which the family has the financial resources to pay for medical and other expenses associated with the disabilities can influence how it views the child. Similarly, access to extended family to help provide support could matter. Finally, the severity of a disability, the presence of challenging behavior, the quality of the child's educational program, and other external factors all can influence the family's perceptions. Clearly, this is a complex issue that requires that educators approach families as unique, bringing with them their own values, beliefs, and experiences that guide their perceptions and their behaviors. The Firsthand Account demonstrates one family's experiences with a child with severe and multiple disabilities.

## Considering Cultural Diversity

The way we are raised—specifically, the values and beliefs of our family, culture, religion, and community—influences our perceptions, including our views toward disabilities (Callicott, 2003). Mainstream U.S. culture historically has viewed disabilities from a deficit orientation (Chen, Downing, & Peckham-Hardin, 2002; Orelove, 1991). However, not all families approach disabilities with a deficit approach, and this directly affects their children and their education. Specifically, families of different cultures may define disabilities differently (Rogers-Adkinson et al., 2003). For example, some families see the birth of a child with a disability as a "gift from God," but families from other cultural and religious backgrounds may see the child's birth as punishment for some past indiscretion (Chen et al,, 2002; McCabe, 2008). One view results in a goal of "fixing" the disability, the second results in a celebration, and the third results in feelings of shame and guilt.

Similarly, in mainstream U.S. culture, educational programs for students with severe and multiple disabilities tend to focus on promoting independence and self-sufficiency (Chen et al., 2002). For example, self-care, home care, academic skills, community access, vocational skills, and independent-living skills are typical targets. However, not all families share these values. Some traditional Latino families place less emphasis on acquiring self-help skills (Zuniga, 1998). Their children may enter school still reliant on others to help with feeding, dressing, and toileting. If educators fail to take the time to understand the family context, they may mistakenly conclude that the student is less capable than she really is. Also, because students with severe and multiple disabilities often experience deficits in these areas, the teacher is likely

**LYNN AND GARY** *have many experiences to share concerning their daughter Kehaulani.*

Inclusion was the furthest thing from our minds as the doctor stood over me in the recovery room when our daughter was born and counted on each of his 10 fingers all the things that he felt were "wrong" with our daughter. I still recall our shock and devastation as he recommended that we institutionalize her. As she grew, professionals around us felt that her needs were best served in special schools, and our social worker still recommended that we place her in a special home. I once inquired about having Lani attend a local school but was told that they could not accommodate her because she was not potty trained and she was too severely disabled. I passively accepted that, and instead of having her spend her days with other children with severe disabilities, I finally took Lani out of school when she was six and educated her at home with her four-year-old sister. Then we learned of another special school, this time in Bakersfield, California, that offered a unique program called Mobility Opportunities Via Education (M.O.V.E.).

Moving to Bakersfield was a major turning point in our lives. Not only did our ten-year-old Kehaulani learn to walk there, but the attitude of the professionals was refreshingly contagious. Their mottos of "All children can learn" and "Some things must be believed before they can be seen" empowered all of us and gave us renewed strength. More importantly, it was at this time that my friend took me to hear a man speak about something called inclusion.

This speaker explained how he and his wife stopped trying to "fix" their daughter since she wasn't "broken" and how they just accepted her value as an individual with her unique gifts. What amazed me was that his daughter sounded like she was nonverbal and like Kehaulani. He described how she had real friends among her classmates who spoke up on her behalf. These friends also spent time with her outside of school. He had me agreeing wholeheartedly, and I wanted the same for Kehaulani. How could she have normal friends if she was constantly segregated? He planted the dream of inclusion within us.

How can our society be expected to live with differently abled people if we are not taught that in our formative years? It was as if someone had turned on the light for us. Accepting her value and unique gifts lifted some of that guilt burden I had been carrying. Inclusion seemed so logical. Why hadn't we thought of it ourselves since we saw how Kehaulani enjoyed the company of her own two younger siblings? We soon discovered, though, that it was not just our own ignorance that kept Lani segregated, but that there was ignorance and prejudice against inclusion among professionals and even among our own family and friends. To describe the difficulty we encountered in achieving that inclusion for Lani would take up an entire chapter, but it has totally been worth the struggle.

Kehaulani first attended fifth grade at our neighborhood school when she was eleven, repeated fifth grade when we moved to a different county, and has since spent all her days in regular classes with her peers. She has since been diagnosed with Rett syndrome, and this disorder includes lack of functional use of her hands, seizures, erratic breathing and extreme mood changes,

drooling, and blowing raspberries. She also is legally blind and has other neurological problems. With minimal self-care skills, Lani must be fed and physically prompted through everything, and we are extremely fortunate today to have an amazing one-on-one instructional assistant to help her. Lani's success in school can best be attributed to the collaboration of her great team that includes her assistant, special and general education teachers, therapists, and some of her classmates.

It is still difficult whenever Lani is disruptive, or if we have a new teacher who is new to the idea of inclusion. Overall, however, we feel that being around these other students has been a mutually beneficial experience. Lani has had some great friendships, and she has taught other severely normal kids to be more tolerant and accepting of those who have different abilities. We have seen kids with low self-esteem and reading difficulties suddenly blossom and improve their own skills as they have helped to read to Lani, thereby helping themselves. In turn, these kids teach the adults about tolerance and acceptance. I shall never forget the overwhelming gratitude and joy I felt the first time I experienced the fruits of our decisions for Lani: I went to the market, as usual with Lani, prepared to have people stop and stare whenever Lani made her raspberries sounds or other vocalizations, but this time a girl suddenly came running toward us calling out "Lani! I thought I heard you over here!" She introduced herself as a classmate of Lani's and then proceeded to introduce Lani to her family. Everything just seemed so normal. I no longer needed to feel so defensive and wary, and Lani no longer needed to be "fixed."

---

to identify instruction in self-help skills as a priority, even though family members may view the acquisition of academic, social, and communication skills as having greater importance.

Here is another example: In traditional Asian families, adult children are not encouraged to move from the family home and, in fact, often do not leave the family home as early as do children from mainstream U.S. culture (Groce & Zola, 1993). For these families, community-based instruction and job training may be a lower priority than for families of European descent. In these situations, it is important for special educators to be aware of cultural factors that influence what families view as important and to work with families to develop educational plans that are consistent with those goals.

dimensions of
**DIVERSITY**

When determining what types of augmentative communication devices to use with a particular student, make sure you consider family preference, language, and culture.

*Parents of students with significant disabilities have the same hopes and dreams for their children as parents of nondisabled students do.*

## REVIEW · REFLECT · DISCUSS

1. What roles should family members play in the education of their child with severe and multiple disabilities? Why is parent involvement particularly important for students with these disabilities?
2. If you were discussing IEP goals related to increasing student independence with parents of a child from a cultural background that did not prioritize such goals, how would you proceed? Is it your responsibility to convince the parents or to respect parent preferences and write goals based on those preferences?

# Trends and Issues Affecting the Field of Severe and Multiple Disabilities

From the previous information provided on students having severe and multiple disabilities, you may be able to discern that several critical issues face professionals in this field. The practice of educating these students with their nondisabled peers is very much a trend as well as a critical issue. Two issues yet to be considered are accountability in assessment and integrated related service delivery.

## Accountability of Academic Performance for All Students

Schools increasingly are being held accountable to ensure that all students learn and acquire basic skills and knowledge. Statewide tests are used to gauge schools' abilities to meet this charge. Since the 1997 reauthorization of IDEA, students with disabilities have been required to be included in any statewide testing process. This requirement was reaffirmed with the No Child Left Behind legislation, and the U.S. Department of Education must approve each state's assessment plan to ensure that it is comprehensive and valid for all students.

### The Status of Alternate Assessment

Although most students with disabilities can participate in standard statewide tests with the use of proper accommodations (e.g., large print, extended time), these tests are not appropriate for students with the most significant needs. Instead, IDEA requires that each state develop an alternative assessment process to ensure that schools are meeting the needs of this group of students. That is, states must consider not only how to assess students but also what to assess. Specifically, the assessment must be directly linked to age-appropriate, grade level content standards that apply to all students, but it also must incorporate a more functional set of learning outcomes. As for other students, the data from these assessments must be reported each year.

Approaches to alternate assessment are evolving rapidly. They generally blend the expectation that all students access the academic curriculum to the extent they can with the need to incorporate functional skills (Browder et al., 2004). For example, in New York, students with significant disabilities are assessed using what is called a *datafolio*. Using key ideas directly related to the core curriculum in each academic area and specific performance indicators, students are assessed on related tasks. An illustration of this process is the area of English/language arts. In this subject area, one standard states that students will "read, write, listen and speak for literary response and expression" (New York State Department of Education, 2009), and the alternate standard of speaking and writing includes reacting to the content and language of text by (a) presenting a personal response to literature and (b) communicating about literature on a literal level. Students may demonstrate they have met this standard by acting out stories, drawing characters from literature, or creating picture books.

## Integrated Delivery of Related Services

A recommended practice in the area of severe and multiple disabilities is the integration of related services within the student's natural learning environment (Anderson, Hawkins, Hamilton, & Hampton, 1999; Cloninger, 2004). This approach exists in contrast to *isolated service delivery*, a traditional approach in which specialists remove the student from a classroom and provide the service in a specialized environment, which tends to fragment understanding of the student into various deficit parts and does not lead to the development of a holistic program. Further, removing the student from a classroom means that he is missing valuable instructional time. Not only does the student miss instruction, but he also must generalize what was worked on in isolation with a specialist in a unique setting to the natural environment where it is most needed. These concepts apply whether the student is being educated in a special education or a general education classroom. For example, fifteen-year-old Derrick really enjoys his music class, where he has many opportunities to interact with his classmates. However, twice each week, the speech/language pathologist pulls him from this class to work on articulation goals in her office. Derrick misses out on the social interactions with his nondisabled peers as well as what the class is practicing for an upcoming recital. Although he likes the speech/language pathologist, he is not very responsive during this speech therapy time and obviously does not like working on pronouncing words that are difficult for him—words that he usually does not use when speaking to friends. At the same time, his music teacher and his peers are not learning ways of helping him to articulate his words because they never witness the techniques that the speech/language pathologist recommends.

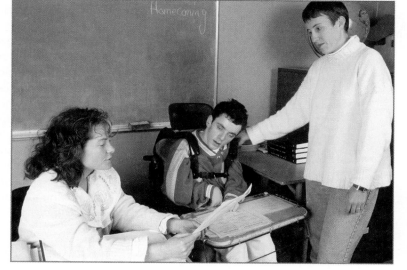

Kari's experiences, described in the Professional Edge, are completely different from those just described and illustrate **integrated service delivery**. In integrated related service delivery, instead of removing the student from the classroom, specialists in various related services disciplines (e.g., occupational therapists, physical therapists, adaptive physical educators) bring their knowledge and skills to the student's learning environment. They use their expertise as well as an understanding of the student's overall program to assist the student in reach-

*When professionals and families collaborate to design seamless educational options, less fragmentation occurs and students are more likely to be successful.*

## Resolving the Pullout Service Dilemma

This is the story of Kari, a child with severe disabilities who, for the first time ever, was to attend a third-grade general education classroom. Prior to this, Kari had received special education services in a special day class for students with needs similar to hers. While in this class, she was often pulled out to receive specialized services (e.g., speech therapy, occupational therapy). Because this approach was fairly common at this school, being pulled away from ongoing instruction was not perceived as problematic. In fact, Kari's family members had fought hard for her to receive these services, and they insisted that these services be provided in a consistent manner. The method in which special and related services were being delivered had not been an issue.

However, attitudes changed once Kari became a member of the general education classroom. First, one of the reasons the family wanted Kari to be a member of a general education class was to provide her with the opportunity to have access to the core curriculum. Being pulled out to receive services from the special education teacher often resulted in missed instruction. In addition, Kari often returned from the special education classroom in the middle of a lesson, requiring that she try to catch up so she could participate with her peers. Another reason the family wanted Kari in the general education setting was to help her establish friendships with peers without disabilities. Being pulled out for services not only interfered with this, but the purpose of the speech therapy sessions was to learn social skills, such as how to initiate and maintain social interactions and how to read social cues. Although the intent of the therapy sessions was good, the lack of context and unique stimuli of the

special room made learning and generalizing these skills difficult. Finally, the instruction Kari was receiving from the adaptive physical education teacher failed to help her in her ability to play games at recess or during physical education class. Overall, the goals the family had envisioned for their daughter were not being realized. Not only did she not have friends, but also she began to actively resist (e.g., crying, refusing to get out of the car) going to school. For the first time, the issue of both where and how special and related services were being provided became a focus of attention.

This realization posed a dilemma for all of Kari's team members. The parents understandably were hesitant to give up some of these services, and some team members found it difficult to consider other ways of doing things. In the end, the amount of time Kari was being pulled out was reduced from more than 300 minutes per week to less than 60 minutes per week. This outcome came as a result of compromise. The family agreed to give up some services, and professionals agreed to provide direct services within the general education classroom as well as during recess and physical education class. The positive outcomes are clear: Kari's mother reports that for the first time, her daughter has friends. Furthermore, she no longer resists going to school. Through collaboration that kept the best interests of the student firmly in mind, this dilemma was resolved.

If you were part of Kari's team, what would you list as benefits of having Kari remaining with her peers while receiving additional support services? Dilemmas? What are the drawbacks of removing Kari from her general education classroom to receive these related services? Possible benefits?

ing individual goals (Thousand et al., 2002). By applying their expertise to meaningful student activities, preferably within typical environments, other members of the collaborative team are able to learn directly from the specialists. After watching how the specialist works with the student on specific goals, teachers, paraprofessionals, and other related services specialists thus are better able to model effective strategies. They can receive feedback from specialists on techniques to use while working with the student throughout the day. For example, in the situation described earlier with Derrick, the speech/language pathologist would arrange to come into his classes at the high school to see where he is having difficulty making himself understood. She would work with him to more clearly pronounce the words that he is singing and suggest alternative strategies for him to use with his peers when communication breaks down.

Students with severe and multiple disabilities often receive services from several professionals. They also may receive support from community agencies. If each service is treated as a distinct program component and each service provider works with the student in a separate setting, the fragmentation does not help the student's education—it hinders it. Integrating services, both into the classroom and across providers, prevents fragmentation and is consistent with recommended practices of inclusive education.

## REVIEW · REFLECT · DISCUSS

1. Why is it important that all students be included in local and state assessment systems? Why should assessments for students with severe or multiple disabilities be linked to the same curriculum standards for which all students are accountable?

2. How does integrated service delivery differ from the traditional pullout model of service delivery for related services providers?

# Summary

- The study of students with severe and multiple disabilities shares a history with other disciplines within special education, and this area includes students classified as having severe or profound intellectual disabilities as well as those identified through IDEA as having multiple disabilities and those who are deaf and blind.
- The disabilities these students have may be caused by factors that appear before, during, or after birth. Overall, this group of students is the smallest among all students with disabilities.
- These students are limited in their cognitive ability, academic achievement, social and emotional development, and behavior skills, but with support from professionals and parents, expectations for them can be kept high and they can be educated with their peers largely in general education settings. Because these students usually are identified as needing special education services very early in life, the preferred assessment tools are informal assessments such as person-centered planning, functional–ecological assessment, and portfolio assessments that focus on identifying student strengths, designing appropriate instructional activities, and monitoring progress.
- While many students with severe and multiple disabilities spend their preschool, elementary, and secondary years of school in separate special education environments, this trend is changing. A growing number of these students are being educated at all levels of schooling with their typical peers, a trend that assists students as they leave school for employment.
- The best educational practices for this diverse population include meaningful and individualized curriculum, collaborative approaches to education, positive behavior supports, and inclusive education.
- When educating students with severe and multiple disabilities, addressing the perspectives of family members is necessary for effective assessment, planning, and intervention, particularly because cultural, religious, and personal beliefs play a role in family preferences and involvement.
- Trends for this field include (a) accountability and the need to demonstrate effective teaching practices and positive outcomes for students often accomplished through the use of portfolio assessment approaches; (b) integration of the expertise of various service providers into a meaningful and unified service delivery system; and (c) efforts to ensure that these students are treated with the dignity and respect they deserve, which includes exploring creative ways of supporting them to be active members of their homes, schools, and communities.

## Council for Exceptional Children ADDRESSING THE PROFESSIONAL STANDARDS

Council for Exceptional Children (CEC) Common Core Knowledge and Skills addressed in this chapter:

ICC1K5, ICC1K8, ICC2K4, ICC2K5, ICC3K5, ICC4S3, ICC4S4, ICC4S6, ICC5S1, ICC5S2, ICC5S3, ICC5S15, ICC6S1, ICC7K2, ICC7S1, ICC7S5, ICC7S7, ICC7S9, ICC8K2, ICC8K4, ICC8S2, ICC8S4, ICC8S6, ICC10K2, ICC10K4, ICC10S6

Appendix: Provides a full listing of the CEC Common Core Standards, and associated Knowledge and Skill Statements listed here.

## PEARSON myeducationlab

Now go to Topic 16: Multiple Disabilities & TBI in the MyEducationLab (www.myeducationlab.com) for your course, where you can:

- Find learning outcomes for the broad concepts covered in this chapter along with the national standards that connect to these outcomes.
- Complete Assignments and Activities that can help you more deeply understand the chapter content.
- Examine challenging situations presented in the IRIS Center Resources.

- Apply and practice your understanding of the core concepts and skills identified in the chapter with the Building Teaching Skills and Dispositions learning units.
- Check your comprehension on the content covered in the chapter by going to the Study Plan in the Book Specific Resources for your text. Here you will be able to take a chapter quiz, receive feedback on your answers, and then access Review, Practice, and Enrichment activities to enhance your understanding of chapter content.
- Watch video clips of CCSSO Teacher of the Year award winners responding to the question: "Why I teach?" in the Teacher Talk section.

## chapter fifteen

# Students Who Are Gifted and Talented

## LEARNING OBJECTIVES

· Outline the development of the field of gifted education, define *giftedness*, and explain the prevalence and determining factors of giftedness.

· Describe the intellectual, academic, social, and emotional characteristics of individuals who are gifted and talented.

· Explain how students who are gifted and talented are identified.

· Outline how learners who are gifted and talented receive their education.

· Describe recommended educational practices for students who are gifted and talented.

· Explain the role of parents and families of students who are gifted in their talent development.

· Identify trends and issues influencing the field of gifted education.

## Warren

Warren is just turning nine years old and is in the fifth grade. He is young to be in that grade—he was moved up from third to fourth grade when his parents, school professionals, and Warren himself decided he would do better if he advanced a grade. Warren attends a magnet school for students who are academically gifted; he was admitted because of his past academic performance, testing completed by the school districts, and teacher recommendation. At his school, Warren is following the same curriculum that students in other schools use, but Warren and his classmates generally are assessed for each unit of instruction, and they do not spend time on topics they have already mastered. Instead, under the guidance of the teacher, they have opportunities to select special projects in which to participate. Warren has chosen a community project that involves completing research on the status of a local landfill. He meets with community members to discuss the potential for water pollution from household chemicals and other items likely dumped there, and composes letters to local authorities recommending ideas for addressing the problem. Six weeks ago, Warren spoke to the town council to convince it to take action. Now he is reflecting on his project, analyzing its effectiveness and impact, and proposing next steps. Warren's father explains that Warren has always been described as precocious and has always championed causes (whether defending younger children against bullies, rescuing animals in distress, or trying to right a wrong). Warren does not have many friends, but he is tremendously loyal to those he does have. Warren plans to be an environmental engineer when he grows up and is already talking about the college he would like to attend.

## Kimberly

Kimberly wakes up every school day with a knot in her stomach. She thinks a lot about what is going on and tries to analyze what is occurring, but she does not see any way to change things. When she recalls elementary school, her memories are filled with friendly teachers, interesting activities, and pride in her rapidly growing knowledge and skills. Now, though, she dreads school. She already knows most of what is being taught, and she feels as if doing assignments is surrendering when she would prefer to rebel. In addition, if she does well on the work, it humiliates her classmates because many of them do not learn easily, and it humiliates her because they tease her about being too smart. To her, being called "Einstein" is the ultimate insult. Kimberly's father has been threatening to take away her after-school computer privileges if her grades do not improve, but she just cannot seem to make that happen. Her parents act as though she is doing this deliberately to hurt them. She would never, ever do that, but she still just cannot seem to do what they ask. Her grades are not so bad that she won't be promoted to eighth grade, but she clearly will not make the honor roll—and that upsets her parents, too. Kimberly is tired of being nagged by teachers and parents, tired of not wanting to achieve, and tired of worrying about everything.

## Steven

Steven is a sixteen-year-old high school junior who is gifted and also has a learning disability. He enjoys skateboarding, playing in the jazz band, and downloading the latest music to his iPod, but he tends to be a loner. His favorite subjects in school are math and Mandarin Chinese, but he dislikes and does rather poorly in English and social studies. His teachers encourage Steven and support his interests. However, they are somewhat concerned about his future. At Steven's last (IEP) meeting, he indicated that he does not plan to apply to a university or the community college; he hopes to form his own band and earn his living as a musician. His mother has been trying to change his mind and get him to select colleges to visit, but Steven keeps making excuses to avoid thinking about his options after high school. His mother is not a college graduate, and she hopes Steven will be the first in the family to earn a degree. Recently, he visited his school counselor, Mr. Davis, who also enjoys the arts and has been a mentor to him. Mr. Davis and Steven discussed many postschool choices that Steven could make, but he is hesitant to make a decision that includes additional schooling. He knows his mother has hopes of him becoming a doctor, and that just is not going to happen.

When you were in school, did you have classmates whose academic abilities were astounding? Whose scores on tests always made those of the rest of the class appear mediocre? Perhaps you knew someone who did not excel academically but who had extraordinary ability in dance, music, drama, or art. You might also have had a friend who kept her abilities well hidden, a friend who was a strong leader away from school but quiet and unmotivated in the classroom. All of these descriptions apply to students who are gifted and talented—students who clearly have extraordinary abilities or who seem to have great potential to develop their abilities.

# Understanding Giftedness

To check your comprehension on the content covered in Chapter 15, go to the Book Specific Resources in the MyEducationLab (www .myeducationlab.com) for your course, select your text, and complete the Study Plan. Here you will be able to take a chapter quiz, receive feedback on your answers, and then access review, practice, and enrichment activities to enhance your understanding of chapter content.

The study of giftedness has been marked by an evolution in definitions, programs and services, and professional interest. Today, new conceptualizations of giftedness are bringing renewed attention to the needs of students who have extraordinary abilities.

## Development of the Field of Giftedness

Societal interest in extraordinary ability has existed for centuries (Jolly, 2005). As shown in Figure 15.1, it was the work of Lewis Terman and his colleagues (Jolly, 2008; Terman & Oden, 1959) that laid the groundwork for efforts in U.S. schools to identify and nurture students who are gifted. In a longitudinal study begun in 1921 and continuing until 2020, Terman and his successors have debunked myths about social and emotional abnormalities of students who are gifted. Their research has shown that a large number of these individuals have accomplished significant achievements but not eminence and suggested that success generally is associated with a lifelong high degree of motivation or persistence.

Other researchers during the first half of the twentieth century (e.g., Havighurst, Stivers, & DeHaan, 1955; Hollingworth, 1926, 1942; Passow, Goldberg, Tannenbaum, & French, 1955; Witty, 1951) also provided insights into the characteristics of students who are highly gifted. They suggested that giftedness should be defined more broadly than what can be measured on an intelligence test and led efforts to develop specialized programs for these students.

### Emergence of a Profession

The 1959 launch of the Soviet space capsule *Sputnik* was perceived by many Americans as an embarrassing educational failure, especially those in the scientific, engineering, and mathematical fields. As a result, a flurry of publications offered guidance to teachers on how to teach and counsel gifted students, but gifted education remained optional in public schools. Eventually, understanding of giftedness broadened to include more than high intelligence, a development outlined in Figure 15.2.

**FIGURE 15.1**

**Timeline of the Development of the Field of Gifted Education**

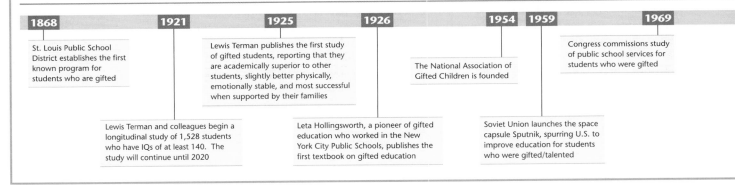

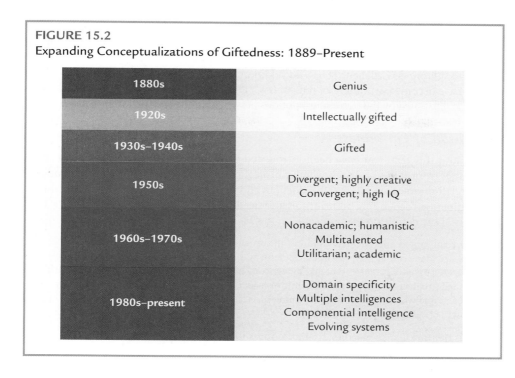

**FIGURE 15.2**

**Expanding Conceptualizations of Giftedness: 1889–Present**

| | |
|---|---|
| 1880s | Genius |
| 1920s | Intellectually gifted |
| 1930s–1940s | Gifted |
| 1950s | Divergent; highly creative<br>Convergent; high IQ |
| 1960s–1970s | Nonacademic; humanistic<br>Multitalented<br>Utilitarian; academic |
| 1980s–present | Domain specificity<br>Multiple intelligences<br>Componential intelligence<br>Evolving systems |

Throughout the 1970s and 1980s, programs for students who were gifted grew and prospered, supported increasingly by state educational funding. This era in the field of gifted education culminated in 1988 when Congress passed the Jacob K. Javits Gifted and Talented Students Education Act. This law focused on identifying and serving students who were gifted and from culturally diverse groups, those living in poverty, and those with disabilities. However, no funding accompanied the law until 1994.

### Recent Changes in the Field

In the 1990s, federal support for gifted education emphasized serving educationally disadvantaged students (Castellano & Díaz, 2002). For example, publication of *National Excellence: A Case for Developing America's Talent* (U.S. Department of Education, 1993), a report that updated the definition of giftedness, noted the importance of nurturing gifts and talents in all students and renewed attention on the need to identify and serve students from diverse groups.

As the field of gifted education has matured in the twenty-first century, it has been characterized by an increase of collaborative services and inclusion of students in general education

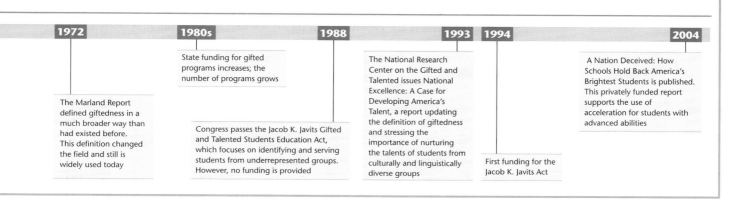

**1972** — The Marland Report defined giftedness in a much broader way than had existed before. This definition changed the field and still is widely used today

**1980s** — State funding for gifted programs increases; the number of programs grows

Congress passes the Jacob K. Javits Gifted and Talented Students Education Act, which focuses on identifying and serving students from underrepresented groups. However, no funding is provided

**1988** — The National Research Center on the Gifted and Talented issues National Excellence: A Case for Developing America's Talent, a report updating the definition of giftedness and stressing the importance of nurturing the talents of students from culturally and linguistically diverse groups

**1993**

**1994** — First funding for the Jacob K. Javits Act

**2004** — A Nation Deceived: How Schools Hold Back America's Brightest Students is published. This privately funded report supports the use of acceleration for students with advanced abilities

settings (e.g., Callard-Szulgit, 2005; Reis, 2003; Rogers, 2007). The No Child Left Behind Act of 2001 has raised issues for gifted education similar to those raised for special education, such as the possible negative impact of high-stakes testing on students who are gifted and talented (Moon, Brighton, & Callahan, 2003). In addition, efforts to expand enrichment to whole schools have become part of school reform (e.g., Eckstein, 2009; Renzulli & Reis, 2002). This concept is illustrated by the curriculum options presented in the Instruction in Action.

Go to the Assignments and Activities section of Topic 17: Gifted and Talented, in the MyEducationLab for your course and complete the activity entitled "Definitions of Giftedness".

## Definition of Giftedness

Throughout this text, you have been introduced to definitions of various exceptionalities with quotes from IDEA and authoritative professional organizations. For *giftedness*, no single clear definition can be cited; IDEA does not address it (Johnsen, 2009; Zirkel, 2009). States define giftedness depending on priorities and needs. However, one definition used is a 1978 variation of the definition that appeared in the *Marland Report* (Stephens & Karnes, 2000):

> The term "gifted and talented children" means children and, whenever applicable, youth, who are identified at the preschool, elementary, or secondary level as possessing demonstrated or potential abilities that give evidence of high performance capability in areas such as intellectual, creative, specific academic or leadership ability or in the performing and visual arts and who by reason thereof require services or activities not ordinarily provided by the school. (P.L. 95-561, Title IX, [a])

This definition also clarified that giftedness includes these areas:

- General intellectual ability
- Specific academic aptitude
- Creative or productive thinking
- Leadership ability
- Visual and performing arts

The most recent federal definition of giftedness is included in the Jacob K. Javits Gifted and Talented Students Education Act of 1988, which was reauthorized in 1994:

> Children and youth with outstanding talent who perform or show the potential for performing at remarkably high levels of accomplishment when compared with others of their age, experience, or environment. These children and youth exhibit high performance capability in intellectual, creative, and/or artistic areas, possess an unusual leadership capacity, or excel in specific academic fields. They require services or activities not ordinarily provided by the schools. Outstanding talents are present in children and youth from all cultural groups, across all economic strata, and in all areas of human endeavor. (P. L. 100-297 §4130)

Although NCLB includes a definition of giftedness, its use is not mandated by the legislation.

Another source for definitions of giftedness is the field, including professional organizations. For example, a third definition of giftedness is offered by the National Association for Gifted Children (NAGC) (2009):

> A gifted person is someone who shows, or has the potential for showing, an exceptional level of performance in one or more areas of expression.

As you look at the older but still widely used *Marland* definition, the more recent Javits definition, and the broad NAGC definition, what differences do you see? In many ways, the definitions capture the evolution of thinking about giftedness: the shift from using the term *gifted* to using the term *talented*, the recognition that extraordinary ability may exist in one or several areas, and the acknowledgment that giftedness exists across the diversity of today's students.

Generally, then, and based on these definitions, **giftedness** is evidence of advanced development across intellectual areas, within a specific academic or arts-related area, or unusual organizational power to bring about desired results. **Talent** sometimes is defined as extraordinary ability in a specific area, but it also now is used interchangeably with *giftedness.*

### Alternative Conceptualizations of Giftedness

Many other conceptualizations of giftedness have been developed by professionals in this field. For example, Renzulli (2002) proposed that giftedness includes three related dimen-

## Instructional Activities Based on Specific Aptitudes

These are ideas for teaching students with talents in particular areas. Many of the ideas represent exemplary teaching ideas that can be implemented in some form for all learners.

### Reading

- Select biographies and books in the content areas (including subjects dealing with multicultural issues) for supplemental reading.
- Provide literature that is broad based in form (myths, nonfiction, biography, poetry, etc.), rich in language, and that provides role models for emulation.
- Use children's literature that involves finding solutions to scientific, environmental, and mathematical problems or mysteries.

### Writing

- Use a writing program that encourages incorporation of ideas from literature into stories.
- Encourage extracurricular experiences that are language based, such as involvement in the school paper or yearbook.
- Encourage personal journal writing.

### Verbal Expression

- Include experiences in foreign language in the curriculum.
- Help students develop word relationship skills (e.g., analogies, antonyms, homonyms).
- Provide opportunities for students to speak in public settings.
- Teach oral presentation and debating skills.

### Math

- Focus on developing spatial skills and concepts through geometry and other media.
- Focus on logic problems that require deductive-thinking skills and inference.
- Emphasize mathematical concepts more and computational skills less.
- Emphasize applications of mathematics in the real world through creation of special projects.
- Focus on the use of probability, estimation, statistics, and computer technology.
- Apply mathematical concepts across the curriculum—for example, by having students read and report on a book about a famous mathematician, assess the mathematical challenges of planning a Civil War battle, or study a unit on the history of mathematics.

### Science

- Provide reading material that suggests experiments students can try, and provide a balance between text and activities.
- Help students develop a scientific hobby, such as bird watching, shell collecting, gardening, or electronics.
- Provide opportunities for naturalistic observation at the beach, the mountains, or a local pond.
- Provide basic tools such as a magnifying glass, binoculars, and a camera.

### Social Studies

- Encourage understanding of cultures.
- Study the development of cities.
- Encourage development of geography skills and mapmaking.
- Encourage development of cultural literacy based on important historical events in U.S. history and world history.
- Help students develop an understanding of global interdependence.

### Creativity/Aesthetics

- Provide art appreciation opportunities.
- Provide music opportunities.
- Provide dramatic instruction.
- Provide opportunities for dance and movement.
- Consider providing an artist mentor.
- Provide unstructured activities, allowing students to choose the medium of expression.

### Leadership and Social Skills

- Encourage leadership skills through work with student government, the safety patrol, and other school organizations and community groups, such as Scouts, book clubs, or church.
- Have students explore leadership training programs for precollegiate students at local colleges and universities.
- Assist students in selecting biographies and autobiographies about high achievers.
- Provide monitored opportunities for involvement in volunteer and social service work in the community or at school.

*Source:* Based on VanTassel-Baska, J. (1998). *Excellence in educating the gifted* (3rd ed.). Denver, CO: Love.

---

sions: (a) above-average ability; (b) task commitment or motivation; and (c) **creativity,** or the capacity for innovation, originality, expressiveness, and imagination and the ability to manipulate ideas in fluent, flexible, elaborate, and original ways. Renzulli's model has been foundational for professionals seeking ways to broaden the concept of giftedness and expand opportunities for students from diverse groups. Tomlinson (Tomlinson et al., 2002) contributes the notion that giftedness is not static but rather influenced greatly by opportunity and environment. She argues that schools should create opportunities and environments to maximize every student's potential, a topic addressed in more detail later in this chapter. Yet

*In the twenty-first century, professionals recognize that giftedness has many dimensions.*

The states with the highest percentage of students identified as gifted are Kentucky (16.1%) and Oklahoma (13.7%); those with the lowest percentage are Massachusetts (.2%) and Vermont (.8%) (National Center for Education Statistics, 2008).

another conceptualization of giftedness is based on Gardner's work in the area of multiple intelligences (Christodoulou, 2009; Gardner, 1983). Gardner argues that intelligence cannot be reduced to a single dimension reported by a test score. He notes that at least nine types of intelligence can be identified and that students may excel in any one or several of these: verbal/linguistic, visual/spatial, logical/mathematical, bodily/kinesthetic, musical, intrapersonal, interpersonal, naturalist, and existential. The Professional Edge provides more information about each of these intelligences. Gardner notes that many students have relative strengths; that is, in a self-comparison they have more ability in some intelligences than in other intelligences. However, he defines *giftedness* as an absolute strength or having significantly more ability in any or all of the intelligences when compared to other individuals.

### A Final Word on Definitions

Taken together, the definitions can be a little confusing. If you think about the purpose of defining an exceptionality such as giftedness, though, you can make sense of them. Definitions are important because they help professionals pinpoint who they are studying in their research, and they help clarify who is entitled to special programs and services. When viewed this way, then, the definitions just outlined represent an accurate picture of thinking about giftedness. They recognize the traditional perspective of high academic ability, but they also stress the importance of nurturing the talents of a diverse group of students (Callahan & Miller, 2005; Coleman, 2004).

## Prevalence

Because so many definitions of giftedness have been offered and so little agreement exists on exactly what giftedness and talents are, estimates of the prevalence of students who are gifted and talented vary considerably (Bélanger & Gagné, 2006). One way of looking at prevalence is to examine data gathered by each state. Of course, these data can be misleading, because each state sets its own definition for giftedness and uses its own procedures for identifying students who are gifted (Johnsen, 2009). Currently, depending on the state, anywhere from 2 to 22 percent of students may be served in a program for students who are gifted and talented (Council of State Directors of Programs for the Gifted, 2001). One estimate indicates approximately 3 million students currently receive services as gifted or talented (Council of State Directors of Programs for the Gifted, 2007).

Go to the Assignments and Activities section of Topic 17: Gifted and Talented, in the MyEducationLab for your course and complete the activity entitled "Multiple Intelligences in the Classroom".

Prevalence is another indicator of the changes in this field over the past four decades. The 1972 *Marland Report* specified that 3 to 5 percent of the school population was an appropriate number of students to identify for gifted and talented programs. As more recent and inclusive definitions have been operationalized, up to 20 to 25 percent of the school population might be eligible for these services.

### Prevalence, Race, and Gender

In several chapters of this book, you have read that students from minority groups are overrepresented as having disabilities. Here, the opposite is true. Although specific statistics are difficult to find because no single federal agency gathers the data, professionals unanimously acknowledge that students from minority groups are significantly underrepresented in programs for those who are gifted and talented (Ford, Grantham, & Whiting, 2008; Gordon & Bridglall, 2005). For example, in a national report on minority students in special and gifted education, Donovan and Cross (2002a) reported that in many states, Caucasian students were three to four times more likely than African American students to be identified as gifted. Similar data were reported when Caucasian and Hispanic students were compared. A concerted effort now is under way to ensure that students from these and other minority groups are not overlooked (Henfield, Moore, & Wood, 2008; Yoon & Gentry, 2009).

Girls are another group underrepresented among students identified as gifted and talented (Navan, 2009). This fact can be illustrated by examining specific content areas. For example, girls are less likely than boys to be identified as mathematically gifted (Gavin & Reis, 2003). When they are identified, they are less likely to develop their talent by enrolling in related advanced courses in math or science during high school (Heilbronner, 2009).

## fyi

Federal funding for gifted education comes from the Jacob K. Javits Gifted and Talented Students Education Program, funded in 2008 for approximately $7.5 million.

## Thinking About Girls and Giftedness

Girls who are gifted often face unique challenges in developing their potential. First, they may face external barriers, such as these:

- Parents who send subtle but conflicting messages, setting expectations for high achievement but also preferring appropriately feminine, demure behavior
- Bias in school, particularly in math and science classes
- Advertising that presents stereotyped and unrealistic images of ideal women that focus on physical appearance

    In addition, girls also may face internal barriers:

- A loss of self-confidence as they grow older
- A sense that being gifted is a social disadvantage in interactions with peers
- Perfectionism that leads to setting unreasonable goals and unhealthy work habits in trying to achieve them

The combination of external and internal barriers often leads to underachievement. An example can be drawn from schools: In too many cases bright boys who are highly verbal, who like to debate, and who frequently express curiosity are considered precocious, while girls with the same traits are considered aggressive. Other research has found that boys vocally dominate classrooms and receive more attention than girls.

Here are profiles of three women who rose above challenges to become eminent in their fields.

- Dr. Maya Angelou is a poet, educator, author, and civil rights activist who has influenced people all over the world with the beauty and wisdom of her words.

- Judge Sonia Sotomayor is the third woman and the first Hispanic in history appointed to the U.S. Supreme Court. Although she grew up in public housing projects and her father died when she was nine, with her mother's support she attended Princeton University and later Yale Law School.

- Dr. Barbara McClintock was an American geneticist. In 1983, she became the first woman ever to receive an unshared Nobel Prize for her discovery of genetic transdisposition.

*Sources:* Based on TwiceGifted.net (2004). Gender issues: Gifted girls, Retrieved February 27, 2004, from www.twicegifted.net/gender.htm; and Reis, S. M. (2002), Social and emotional issues faced by gifted girls in elementary and secondary school, *SENG Newsletter, 2*(3), 1–5.

### dimensions of
### DIVERSITY

Examining Office of Civil Rights data across 3 years, Yoon and Gentry (2009) found that the proportion of students from various racial and cultural groups in gifted programs varied tremendously across states, but that Asian students generally were overrepresented.

Although the reasons for these differences are not entirely clear, contributing factors may include parents' beliefs and treatment of their daughters and teachers' biases about boys excelling in math and science while girls excel in English. The Professional Edge explores issues regarding giftedness in girls.

## Determining Factors

Giftedness generally is considered to be the result of a combination of genetic and environmental factors. The interaction can be highlighted by a single fact about giftedness: Although firstborn children are most likely among all children in a family to be gifted, if one child is gifted, chances are that other children in the family will be gifted, too. Firstborn children often receive considerable adult attention, and this environmental factor can help to maximize their potential. However, the fact that other children in the same family often are gifted suggests that heredity also may play a role.

## REVIEW · REFLECT · DISCUSS

1. Do you think that it would be better if students who are gifted or talented were protected by the Individuals with Disabilities Education Act? What might be the advantages and disadvantages of having such protection?
2. Why do you think that professionals in this field have failed to agree on a single definition of giftedness? What is the impact of this disagreement? What do you think the definition of giftedness should include? Why?

# Characteristics of Individuals Who Are Gifted and Talented

Programs and services for students who are gifted and talented are based on studies of these students' characteristics, including cognitive, academic, and social/emotional (e.g., Callahan & Miller, 2005; Reis & Sullivan, 2009). As you read about each characteristic, think about students with whom you have worked, either as a student or as a preservice professional. Have you known someone who displayed any of these characteristics?

## Cognitive Characteristics

Students who are gifted often display advanced behaviors in the cognitive domain from an early age, and when they are nurtured, these characteristics continue to develop. As you read about these students' cognitive traits, keep these ideas in mind:

1. Not all students who are gifted display all of the characteristics or at the same level.
2. These characteristics may be viewed as developmental in the sense that some students may display them at early stages of development while others may not display them until later stages.
3. Many students who are gifted have particular clusters of these characteristics.
4. These characteristics may be evident only when students are engaged in an area of interest and aptitude.

### Ability to Manipulate Abstract Symbol Systems

A student who is gifted may understand language and mathematics at an earlier age than is typical and may have unusual abilities for solving puzzles. With support, such skills will continue to grow. Prodigies such as Bobby Fisher, who benefited from mentoring at the Manhattan Chess Club, and Wolfgang Mozart, who inherited a genetic predisposition for music from Leopold Mozart, are examples of people for whom talent and a supportive environment resulted in **eminence,** or adult achievement of a high level in a particular field after years of productivity.

### Power of Concentration

A student who is gifted and absorbed by a particular project or topic may be somewhat like an absent-minded professor. Both display a high degree of concentration and an ability to focus on a problem for a considerable period of time. For example, Julia became interested in horticulture at the age of seven. She found books about plants at her local library and spent most of her free time reading and studying about them. By the age of eleven, she knew the names and growing conditions of all of the trees, shrubs, and flowers in her community.

### Unusually Well Developed Memory

Memory, the ability to retain and recall past experience, is essential for acquiring knowledge and skills. Even from an early age, many students who are gifted have a phenomenal memory

**web link**

www.nagc.org
The National Association for Gifted Children (NAGC) has as its purpose addressing the needs of children and youth who are gifted and talented, including students who may have untapped potential. The organization includes parents, teachers, administrators, and other professionals. The website includes links to many private, government, and service organizations related to giftedness.

for information they have seen only once. One young boy at age three had memorized all the license plates, house numbers, and telephone numbers in his neighborhood. Another young girl at age four could recite Clement Moore's *A Visit from St. Nick* in its entirety after only one practice session. A third preschooler knows all the presidents of the United States and a few facts about each.

Although memory is a central aspect of intelligence, it can be trivialized into spelling contest activity and other demonstrations and feats that have few long-term implications and little usefulness. However, the ability to recall military events, battle strategies, and their historical significance is an example of acquired information that can be used to understand and connect to other disciplines.

### Early Language Interest and Development

Students who are gifted often exhibit precocious language development and an early strong interest in reading. Although early reading for all young children is more common today than it was several decades ago—probably because of the influence of smaller families, educational television, and other societal changes—it is still moderately predictive of later advanced reading behavior (Mills & Jackson, 1990; Olson, Evans, & Keckler, 2006).

### Curiosity

Students who are gifted usually display curiosity—a strong need to know and to understand how the world works. From early childhood on, they crave making sense of the world. Adults who treat their questions with respect and provide information appropriate to the needs of these students will help build in them a personality orientation that seeks to discover the world. Warren, from the beginning of the chapter, displays this characteristic.

Curious children ask questions frequently, and often these questions are on adult subjects fundamental to the large issues of life, such as "How was the world created?" "Where did I come from?" and "Why do people die?" This type of questioning illustrates the advanced level of thought in which such students engage, an important indication of advanced development.

### Preference for Independent Work

Students who are gifted often prefer working alone, figuring things out for themselves. This trait reflects their enjoyment in constructing an internal schema to solve problems rather than a tendency toward antisocial behavior. After eighth grade, Robert attended a special summer program at a major university and told the instructor that his goal was to complete algebra and trigonometry so that he could take Advanced Placement (AP) calculus in the fall. The instructor replied that all Robert needed to do was finish two math books, whereupon Robert said, "Give me the books." He reached his goal, and he began high school enrolled in the calculus class.

### Multiple Interests

Students who are gifted have large storehouses of information and good memory skills. This combination often leads to these children having a wide range of interests. For example, Latasha was a five-year-old child in first grade who appeared highly able, and the teacher decided to mention to her the concept of birds as linear descendants of dinosaurs. Even so, the girl's response, "Oh, you mean like *Archaeopteryx*," came as a surprise to the teacher. When asked about favorite books, Latasha spoke of an interest in science fiction and in H. G. Wells's *War of the Worlds*, which she had read four times. Latasha's story illustrates that having multiple interests may be missed or go unappreciated in students who are gifted if the activities used with them do not allow for open exploration in a variety of areas. Further, multiple interests also can create frustration when a student is required to focus on a single and unpreferred area of study.

*With a sense of social justice, high energy, and multiple interests, students who are gifted or talented may find themselves overwhelmed with lessons, activities, and volunteer work.*

### Ability to Generate Original Ideas

Students who are gifted can generate novel ideas alone or in collaboration with others. For example, John was a published poet in fourth grade partly because of his teacher's encouragement and partly by virtue of the writing talent search in his large school system. In another example, Lien, identified with a learning disability, and Phillip, identified as having an emotional disability, collaborated successfully as gifted ten-year-olds on building a model city, complete with electricity.

## Academic Characteristics

The academic abilities of students who are gifted and talented often reflect their intellectual skills. Figure 15.3 presents some of the most common academic characteristics of these students, although unless students are academically gifted across all areas, they may not have all the characteristics listed. Steven, whom you met in the introduction to this chapter, is an example of this type of student. He is talented in mathematics and music but not in English and social studies. Students such as Steven sometimes have problems with motivation. The Positive Behavior Supports looks more closely at this topic.

## Social and Emotional Characteristics

Students who are gifted and talented often display social and emotional characteristics that are somewhat different from those discussed in relation to other students. As you read about

**research**
**NOTE**

In a longitudinal study, Gottfried, Cook, Gottfried, and Morris (2005) found that motivation could be distinguished from intelligence, and they proposed that *gifted motivation,* or superior determination and persistence, should be considered a type of giftedness.

---

**FIGURE 15.3**

**Academic Characteristics of Students Who Are Gifted and Talented**

Reading Behaviors
- Has early knowledge of the alphabet
- Often reads early or unlocks the reading process quickly and sometimes idiosyncratically
- Reads with expression
- Has a high interest in reading; reads voraciously

Writing Behaviors
- Displays early ability to make written sound–symbol correspondence
- Exhibits fluency and elaboration in story writing
- Uses advanced sentence structure and patterns
- May show an interest in adult topics for writing, such as the state of the environment, death, war, and so on
- Writes on a topic or story for an extended period of time
- Generates many writing ideas, often of a divergent nature
- Uses precise, descriptive language to evoke an image

Speaking Behaviors
- Learns to speak early
- Has a high-receptive vocabulary
- Uses advanced sentence structure
- Uses similes, metaphors, and analogies in daily conversation
- Exhibits highly verbal behavior in speech (i.e., talks a lot, speaks rapidly, articulates well)
- Enjoys acting out story events and situations

Mathematical Behaviors
- Has early curiosity and understanding about the quantitative aspects of things
- Is able to think logically and symbolically about quantitative and spatial relationships
- Perceives and generalizes about mathematical patterns, structures, relations, and operations
- Reasons analytically, deductively, and inductively
- Abbreviates mathematical reasoning to find rational, economical solutions
- Displays flexibility and reversibility of mental processes in mathematical activity
- Remembers mathematical symbols, relationships, proofs, methods of solution, and so forth
- Transfers learning to novel situations and solutions
- Displays energy and persistence in solving mathematical problems
- Has a mathematical perception of the world

## Tackling the Challenge of Underachievement

Underachievement in academic settings is a major problem among some students who are gifted. Underachievement usually is the result of a lack of motivation, which may be caused by any of the following:

- General boredom
- Depression
- Another disability (e.g., ADHD or a learning disability)
- Fear of failure
- Lack of challenging work
- Lack of meaningful work
- Lack of study skills
- Lack of family support for learning

Teachers can use these strategies to help to address motivation problems among students who are gifted:

- Counseling students individually on issues that may be affecting their achievement
- Using mastery learning strategies based on assessing student skills in order to assign work at appropriate levels; this approach needs strong teacher oversight to monitor for potential learning problems
- Conferencing with parents on how the motivation problem is displayed in school with dialogue on how to collaborate between home and school for improvement
- Teaching students metacognitive strategies directly related to planning, monitoring, and assessing learning progress

- Setting motivation "traps" by designing high-interest activities that will draw students into learning activities (e.g., having them write letters to their heroes or design advertising for a popular movie)
- Employing a tutorial model of instruction to assess the nature and extent of the problem
- Clustering students with motivation problems for instruction
- Encouraging student inquiry, hands-on work, and discussion activities
- Allowing students variety and choice in classroom and homework activities
- Providing extra encouragement based on praising specific accomplishments when performance standards are met
- Asking students to consider seriously the implications of not succeeding in their classes using items such as these:
  a. If I do poorly in this class, then ____;
  b. This class is important because ____; and
  c. The thing that I am most interested in learning more about is ____.
  (Siegle & McCoach, 2005, p. 24)

Keep in mind that the extent to which you consistently communicate to students, including those who are gifted, that you believe in their ability to achieve even when they appear uninterested, you can help them to reach their potential.

---

these characteristics, think about how they might affect these students' interactions with classmates, teachers, and others.

### Sense of Justice

Many students who are gifted display a strong sense of justice in their relationships. At later ages, they generally are attracted to causes that promote social equality and activities that reflect their concern for a humane world. For example, at age six, Renee wanted to protest the nuclear waste dump disposal procedures in her community. She created signs, organized her friends, and held a kids' march.

### Altruism and Idealism

Consistent with their sense of social justice, students who are gifted also often display a helping attitude toward others. They may want to volunteer at a hospital or a senior center in the community. They may become very supportive of parents or older adults in their neighborhoods, taking on a caregiving attitude. This **altruism**—unselfish concern for the welfare of others—and **idealism**—the act of envisioning things in an ideal form—frequently lead to student involvement in service organizations or leisure activities that can consume large amounts of energy but become a basis for later career decisions. One risk can be identified with these characteristics, however. Although students with special gifts and talents sometimes appropriately are asked to assist classmates, they should not spend so much time assisting classmates that their own learning is affected.

### Sense of Humor

Have you ever known someone who could easily recognize or appreciate the inconsistencies and incongruities of everyday experience? Students who are gifted often have this ability, and it gives them a keen sense of humor. However, humor also may signal difficulties. It

Go to the Assignments and Activities section of Topic 17: Gifted and Talented, in the MyEducationLab for your course and complete the activity entitled "Cultural Influences on Students' Attitudes Toward School".

sometimes is used to defuse painful experiences such as being the victim of teasing or bullying (Peterson & Ray, 2006). It also can be used for self-deprecation and self-defense, leading some students who are gifted to become known as class clowns or stand-up comics. Humor also may mask a sense of alienation. For all these reasons, humor from these students should be analyzed carefully.

### Emotional Intensity

Just as students who are gifted are more able cognitively, they frequently experience emotional reactions at a deeper level than their peers, showing a capacity for **emotional intensity,** or the ability to focus emotions for long periods on a single subject or idea (Van Tassel-Baska, Cross, & Olenchak, 2009). For example, the death of a pet caused prolonged grieving for Dylan. His emotional intensity was later apparent in his support for animal rights and his volunteer work at a local animal shelter. For some students, emotional intensity leads to a career or hobby in theater where their other skills—particularly in the nuances of language—also can be highlighted. This characteristic, though, sometimes can make students who are gifted targets of bullying (Peterson & Ray, 2006). Think of how Kimberly, the middle school described at the beginning of the chapter, is reacting to what some might consider typical transition stresses as she moves from elementary to middle school.

### Perfectionism

Students who are gifted may display characteristics of **perfectionism,** or striving for a self-imposed advanced goal or unrealistic standard. These students focus undue energy on doing everything exactly so, and they dislike it if they or others make mistakes. Sally became incensed when she received a score of 98 percent on her paper because of a punctuation error. She immediately asked the teacher if she could redo the paper. Ed reacted by sulking when members of his group could not answer the quiz bowl questions he considered easy.

As you encourage students to do their work, you should be aware of the risk of crossing a line that causes them to internalize unhealthy perfectionist tendencies. A realistic acceptance of error in people, in the world, and in oneself should temper the judgments students are likely to make. Growth should be toward excellence, not perfection. Teachers and parents must appreciate this subtle distinction when working with learners who are gifted.

### High Level of Energy

Students who are gifted often display high energy in the conduct of play and work; this high energy can be observed in their ability to accomplish a great deal in a short time. For example, in fourth grade, Lenore decided on her own to work on homonyms one weekend after having been introduced to them in school on Friday. Through careful dictionary work, she discovered more than 450 homonyms and proudly brought her list to school on Monday.

As you learned in Chapter Six, some teachers can misinterpret the high energy level that students who are gifted bring to school tasks as hyperactivity. Using students' energy for productive purposes requires channeling it into meaningful tasks and encouraging persistence in working toward short- and long-term goals, which in turn will enhance students' motivation and success.

### Strong Attachments and Commitments

Students who are gifted and talented often form strong attachments to one or two friends who may be a few years older or to an adult figure. As adults, they may develop equally strong attachments to their work. Laurel's life patterns illustrate this point. At age twelve, she had maintained only two strong friendships, but those friendships were begun before she entered school and continued into adulthood. In her career as a teacher, she works tirelessly. She comments that it is not really like a job because she loves what she does. Teachers and mentors often are valuable for students who display strong attachments. They provide positive role models and can guide students in career choices.

**fyi**

Some parents and educators think that students who are gifted and talented are just like other children—except for their special abilities. This is not the case. Students who are gifted and talented sometimes may seem like many individuals—that is, like an elementary student when riding a bike, like a teenager when reading, and like an adult when debating about an issue of interest. This notion is referred to as *asynchronous development.*

**ELISSA**

*is the mother of Rose, a child who was identified as gifted when she was in first grade. Elissa has experienced an entire range of emotions as she has raised her daughter.*

Rose has never afforded me the luxury to "let my guard down." The energy it takes to be her mother, to try to stay one step ahead of her, is a test of both endurance and strength of character. (At this point, with Rose as a sixteen-year-old, I'm not sure who is in the lead.) Rose's thought processes, like those of other highly gifted children, flow much quicker than her hand can write or her mouth can speak. This mismatch between the rapidity of thoughts and the ability to articulate them in writing or in speech often leads to a high frustration level.

Because she can hold multiple thoughts on a variety of topics at any given time, but then is required in the classroom to narrow the scope of her thoughts to the topic at hand and come up with a simplistic answer, such as the date of the Battle of Saratoga, she has difficulty maintaining sustained focus if the topic at the moment is not mentally stimulating. She loves to learn but does not like playing school.

Rose will be the first to tell you that she has difficulty with authority if she intuitively senses that the individual does not thoroughly know the subject matter, whether it is in academics, athletics, or another area of expertise. She challenges the ideas, not the individual, but unless the person has a healthy self-esteem, he or she often will be intimidated. Heaven help the individual who falters, stumbling around to find an answer to Rose's conceptual questions. Rose, like a hungry lion, will go for the jugular. This has been going on since she was in kindergarten. Rose's adjustment period during each new school year is more for the teacher than for herself. On one occasion, Rose decided to take on the position of coach when her losing junior varsity basketball team was down twenty points. At the time, she was team captain. She started arguing with the adult coach over plays he should tell the team to do and which players should be in the game. That went over like a lead balloon. She lost her captain status and was benched for the rest of the season.

My approach to Rose has always been direct and with as much information on any given topic as I could gather. I have found that because she intellectualizes things, this approach has worked better than a parental response of "because I said so." She likes to debrief topics orally, and often conversations are lengthy but engaging. I have had to balance being a friend and mother. One caution that I have to keep in mind in raising her is that while I am tempted to speak to her intellect, I cannot neglect her emotional side. She acts so mature that it is easy to forget that she is struggling with teen acceptance, peer pressure, and independence. Frequently, by giving her a gentle hug or brushing her hair, I can emotionally connect with her.

As a mother, I applaud her individuality, her tenacity to take a stand, her assertiveness to speak out, and her ability to challenge the system—especially because she's often right. Yet, I also understand from experience the need to play the game, get along with others even when they are wrong, and sometimes accept the inevitable mediocrity that exists on a daily basis. I suspect that I'll continue to face questions as she moves from adolescence to adulthood: How do I counsel her? How can she remain true to herself and fit within a context that sometimes does not reward, support, or respond to her intellectual prowess?

## Aesthetic Sensitivity

Some students who are gifted have extraordinary **aesthetic sensitivity,** which is a keen perception of the characteristics and complexity of the arts and the interrelationships of the arts with other domains. For example, Leonard has been composing music since he was in elementary school. Now in high school, he also writes lyrics. His next planned project is to produce a musical, and he plans to choreograph it himself. He is planning the performance for the residents of a local elder care facility as well as the district's elementary schools. Leonard is not talented in just one area; he has the capacity to blend an understanding of several arts in a way that few can accomplish.

As you think about all the characteristics of students who are gifted and talented, keep in mind that exploring them separately is less powerful than seeing them merged into an integrated understanding of these students. In the Firsthand Account, you can see how Rose displays many of the characteristics of being gifted.

## REVIEW · REFLECT · DISCUSS

1. Review the characteristics of students who are gifted and talented. In each domain, create a list of possible ways you might see the characteristic displayed by students.

2. How might the characteristics of students who are gifted and talented look different for students who also have disabilities, for girls, and for those from nondominant cultures?

# Identifying Students Who Are Gifted and Talented

The procedures required by federal special education law for identifying students with disabilities do not apply in the area of giftedness; rather, each state sets its own criteria for identifying these students (Johnsen, 2009). Some states use traditional definitions of giftedness and limit the number of eligible students to a small percentage. Others use more contemporary definitions and offer services to many students.

## Considerations for Identifying Giftedness

Before looking at best practices for identifying students as gifted and talented, some issues should be addressed. First, look at the types of instruments shown in Figure 15.4 that generally are used in traditional and nontraditional assessments. The instruments can influence whether giftedness is found. For example, some students do not do well on traditional tests but excel if they perform (e.g., problem solving, music). One result of this recognition is that in recent years, the use of both performance-based and portfolio approaches have gained favor and are included in several states' and school districts' identification guidelines (Baldwin, 2002; Bracken & Brown, 2006).

A second issue related to assessment concerns students who are gifted across many areas versus those with talents in specific areas (Joseph & Ford, 2006; Renzulli, 2005; Schroth & Helfer, 2008). The latter group of students is much larger than the former, and assessment procedures need to take this fact into account. If assessment only identifies students with general giftedness, many students with special abilities may be missed. This also is the point at which assessment and programs intersect. If programs are designed only for the first group of students, the potential of students who need specialized opportunities in a specific area cannot be realized.

### web link

http://www.gifted.uconn.edu/nrcgt.html
Sponsored by the U.S. Department of Education, the National Research Center on the Gifted and Talented (NRC/GT), a partnership between the University of Connecticut and University of Virginia, investigates and develops new methods of identifying and teaching gifted students. The center produces a wide variety of research-based and practical materials.

## Underlying Principles of Effective Assessment

Regardless of the definition of giftedness used in a school district, several principles should guide student assessment.

### Two-Stage Assessment Process

Assessment for gifted education should rely on a two-stage process. First, students should be screened using a traditional achievement or aptitude test. Many students may score near perfect on such a test. These students then may participate in *off-level testing;* that is, they take a more advanced test in order to obtain a better description of their abilities. Examples of instruments used for this type of assessment are the School and College Ability Test (SCAT) and the Sequential Tests of Educational Progress (Benbow & Stanley, 1996).

### Measures to Match Programs

As you might guess, the use of measures that are relevant to program emphasis is also a crucial consideration. If the program emphasis is writing, a writing sample should be included in the identification process. If the program emphasis is science, an assessment related to

---

**FIGURE 15.4**

**Assessment Tools Often Used to Identify Students as Gifted and Talented**

| Traditional | Contemporary |
| --- | --- |
| Intelligence tests | Nonverbal ability tests |
| Achievement tests | Creativity tests |
| Aptitude tests (domain specific) | Student portfolios or performance by audition |
| Grades | Performance-based assessment |
| Teacher recommendations | Parent, peer, or community recommendations |

*Authentic assessment is an important companion to traditional assessments for identifying students as gifted or talented.*

science concepts or perhaps a science project portfolio should be incorporated into the assessment procedures. Kimberly, the middle school student introduced at the beginning of the chapter, probably would benefit from this approach to assessment.

### Other Considerations

Assessment for giftedness and talents also must consider several other factors. For example, checklists that are **domain specific**, describing abilities or interests in a particular area, such as mathematics or music, can help professionals pinpoint student strengths. In addition, most professionals agree that high ability alone does not constitute giftedness. Motivation, personality, persistence, and concentration also are essential. Assessment procedures need to take those factors into account.

### Equity

Once assessment information has been gathered, *equity* becomes a concern. Rather than rely only on cutoff scores or particular sets of information, professionals need to rely on their judgment of individual student profiles to make decisions about eligibility for programs and services. This principle is important for two reasons. First, it is consistent with the understanding that giftedness has many dimensions. Second, it addresses concerns about students who have potential that has not been developed (King, Kozleski, & Landsdowne, 2009).

## Authentic Assessment

A recent shift in thinking has occurred regarding identifying students who are gifted and talented. Professionals now call for a variety of measures with a strong emphasis on authentic assessment, or assessment that more clearly resembles the actual curriculum and instruction students experience in schools, including writing essays, debating, and creating portfolios (Moon, Brighton, Callahan, & Robinson, 2005). Instead of relying solely on intelligence and achievement test scores for identification, multiple criteria are used. Authentic assessment helps address the serious matter noted earlier of recognizing gifts and talents in minority students and girls (Callahan, 2005). Two examples of second-stage authentic assessment practices are dynamic assessment and assessment of spatial ability.

## Dynamic Assessment

The assessment of giftedness also involves trying to tap into fluid rather than static abilities (Brown et al., 2005; Feng & Van Tassel-Baska, 2008). **Dynamic assessment,** which is ongoing identification of student learning needs and ability, is one approach used to assess cognitive abilities that often are not apparent when most forms of standardized tests are used. Dynamic assessment usually consists of testing students, teaching skills to them, and then testing them again. The measure of giftedness is how much students improve based on the skill instruction (VanTassel-Baska, Johnson, & Avery, 2002). This is a promising approach because disadvantaged learners who may be overlooked on traditional tests perform well on this type of task.

## Spatial Ability

Spatial ability is the capability to mentally visualize and manipulate objects. As with dynamic assessment, an assessment approach with a strong spatial component can greatly reduce the disparities between scores from students of various socioeconomic status (SES) levels and racial or ethnic groups. Examples of instruments that assess spatial ability include the Matrix Analysis Test, the Ravens Matrices, and the UNIT test (Bracken & McCallum, 1998).

## *Eligibility*

The specific ways eligibility decisions are made for students who are gifted and talented vary widely across states and school districts. Often, an eligibility committee is formed at the school level. It may include a specialist in gifted education, an administrator, and at least one teacher with experience in teaching students who are gifted and talented. Committee members review student profiles and make final decisions about students eligible for program placement. However, in some small districts, decisions about participation may be made at the district level.

## REVIEW · REFLECT · DISCUSS

1. Think of someone you've known who you considered gifted or talented. Would traditional assessment approaches have been appropriate for identifying this person's abilities? Why or why not?
2. Think of the three students you met at the beginning of this chapter—Warren, Kimberly, and Steven. Which types of assessments would best highlight their talents? Why?

# How Learners Who Are Gifted and Talented Receive Their Education

Students who are gifted and talented receive their education in a variety of settings. No data are available to indicate the amount of time they spend in a particular setting, and decisions about placement often depend on the breadth and level of a student's abilities as well as on the program options generally available based on local and state policies.

## *Early Childhood Education*

With the exception of children who are prodigies—that is, those who have abilities so remarkable that they come to the attention of researchers and the media at an early age—relatively little attention has been paid to young children who are gifted and talented (National Association for Gifted Children, 2008a). In fact, in most school districts, students are not identified to receive services as gifted until they are in the middle elementary grades. However, some professionals are urging that this custom be rethought and that young children be identified to receive services (Chamberlin, Buchanan, & Vercimak, 2007). For example, in one early study (Fowler, Ogston, Roberts-Fiati, & Swenson, 1995), enrichment was offered to children ages two to three. While it would be expected that approximately 5 percent of children of university faculty members would be identified as gifted, in this study 68 percent of those children were later identified. Among parents who had not completed high school, far less than 1 percent might be expected to be identified as gifted. In this study, 31 percent were later identified. This research suggests that early intervention could be a key component for encouraging students' gifts and talents, and similar research continues to emerge (Harrison, 2004).

### The Debate on Early Intervention

The thought of providing programs and services for young children who are gifted and talented raises many points of view. Advocates argue that the developmental benefits for all young children would likewise be available to young children who are gifted and talented if they received specialized instruction at the preschool level. They also note that even if programs began in kindergarten or first grade instead of later, children would be afforded greater benefits. Advocates also suggest that students in this age group tend to be particularly lonely because they have few agemates who share their abilities, unlike older students who can access a greater range of peers in special programs and classes.

Those opposed to early gifted education programs state that all children should receive early intervention and that a special program for children who are gifted cannot be justified when every child would benefit from an enriched early childhood intervention. They also question the potential drain on financial resources from such programs, particularly in light of the budget constraints that most school districts experience. Finally, critics express concern at the potential negative consequences of labeling young children, possibly segregating them and sending messages to them and others that they should not be part of typical early intervention programs.

Although no resolution to the questions about early childhood gifted education programs is likely in the near future, one compromise is to identify students not in preschool but in kindergarten or first grade. They then could be served using approaches that foster inclusive practices, approaches outlined in the next section. This would permit children's talents to be developed while avoiding the stigmatizing effects of separating them from their peers.

## web link

http://cty.jhu.edu/
The Johns Hopkins University Center for Talented Youth (CTY) is dedicated to identifying students with exceptional ability. This center conducts an annual talent search, and students selected through its testing program are eligible to participate in online and summer programs as well as conferences.

## Elementary and Secondary Education

When children who are gifted or talented enter the public schools, several placement options may exist to meet their needs. These include within-class grouping, full-time and part-time special programs, separate schools, and homeschooling.

### Grouping

In most elementary and middle schools, students who are gifted and talented are educated with their typical peers. A variation is to place students in skill groups for part or all of the school day (e.g., for reading instruction or math instruction). **Ability grouping** is a characteristic of any program in which school personnel use test scores or school performance to assign same-grade students to groups or classes with markedly different levels of academic preparation. The most common type of group assigns several students who are gifted to a single, otherwise heterogeneously grouped class.

*Within-class grouping* is part of the concept of universal design for learning (UDL), and it can be effective at all levels of schooling and for students with many types of special needs. At the elementary level, it creates opportunities for students who already have mastered material being addressed to work on alternative and challenging assignments with peers. For students struggling to learn, it allows time for more practice or review. At the secondary level, it allows the teacher to plan to meet the tremendous range of student ability that may exist even in honors or Advanced Placement courses. Examples of how within-class grouping works include these: In one class, students were grouped by reading ability. They all read folktales, but each group was assigned tales at the appropriate level. In an English class, groups were assigned different topics for their papers, thus permitting some students to pursue complex topics with added depth and breadth.

### Full-Time and Part-Time Separate Classes

At the elementary level, some school districts offer completely separate classes for students who are gifted. This practice is based on evidence that many teachers fail to differentiate for the students in their classes, spending the vast majority of the time on whole-group activities aimed at meeting the needs of average students. Another common approach is to group students for a specified period of time each week, perhaps for two hours each Tuesday and Friday morning. This arrangement sets aside time to nurture student talents. Of course, in most high schools, such classes already exist through special programs such as Advanced Placement (AP), International Baccalaureate (IB), and dual enrollment (DE)—programs addressed in more detail later in this chapter.

### Special Schools

Although far from common, a few residential public high schools have been developed for students who are gifted (e.g., Coleman, 2005; National Association for Gifted Children, 2008b). Moreover, governors' schools—special regional schools created and funded by the state (e.g., a state school for the arts, a state school for math and science)—are popular options when they exist, particularly since they usually offer academic-year as well as summer opportunities. Other specialized day schools, public and private, have emerged in response to the needs of these learners and the doctrine of parental choice. These schools, usually available only to the most highly gifted students, serve as immersion programs. They enable students to explore their areas of interest, develop their own skills, and accomplish their goals in a strongly supportive environment.

### Homeschooling

One additional emerging educational option for students who are gifted and talented is homeschooling (Kunzman, 2008). For example, in Williamsburg, Virginia more than 100 families homeschool their children identified as gifted. This option is one parents may select when they have strong concerns about the quality and availability of options in local schooling or when they have a child who is so gifted or talented that attention to that child's abilities makes traditional schooling impossible (e.g., a skater who needs to practice during school hours).

## Inclusive Practices

Clearly, students who are gifted and talented should be part of an *inclusive* school community, in the way that the term has been defined for this textbook (Callard-Szulgit, 2005). However, some professionals in the field of gifted education are skeptical that these students receive the education they need when they spend their days with peers in general education. Concerns include teachers' inability or unwillingness to provide differentiated instruction for these students, resulting in boredom and lack of motivation, and even more important, the failure to maximize these students' potential (VanTassel-Baska & Stambaugh, 2005).

In some ways it helps to think of students who are gifted and talented just like you think of other students with exceptional needs. No single answer is always correct. When principles of universal design for learning are established and differentiation is commonplace, the needs of many students can be met in the classroom, at least much of the time (Smith, 2006). For students whose needs are extraordinary, additional options may be appropriate, as they are for students with disabilities. You can read about the application of these ideas in the Speaking from Experience, where Denise DiGiovanni, High Ability Learner Director, discusses several of her favorite ideas for teachers and her beliefs about appropriate educational practices for these students.

## Transition and Adulthood

Some people mistakenly assume that adolescents who are gifted and talented avoid the stresses and uncertainties that usually accompany the teenage years. After all, they are academically high achievers, or have the potential to be high achievers, or they are obviously

Some gifted children come to school knowing how to read or learn to read very rapidly during kindergarten and first grade; others may display early nonverbal strengths but be delayed slightly in learning to read.

*Denise DiGiovanni is the High Ability Learner Director for the North Platte (NE) Public School District. In that role, she is responsible for ensuring that the gifts and talents students in grades kindergarten through tenth grade are nurtured and expanded. Here are her words of wisdom to teachers and other educators.*

- Students who have high abilities have those abilities all day long. Although our program began with pullout services, I really thought about it and decided that I needed to work with the teachers to be sure student needs were met throughout the day. Now I operate before- and after-school seminars, but during the day I work with teachers on differentiating to reach all learners.

- It's important to remember that giftedness isn't just the students who demonstrate their abilities. Some students may not be typical; they have a different way of looking at things.

- There are many simple strategies that teachers can use to differentiate; they're low work but high impact for students. One popular option is called think-tac-toe [see a set of power point slides that clearly explain this technique at http://daretodifferentiate.wikispaces.com/Choice+Boards]. Another is cubing [go to www.teach.virginia.edu/files/nagc_**cubing**__think_dots.pdf for an explanation and examples of cubing]. I also like to help teachers create learning contracts for students and set up learning centers that are based on differentiation.

- Technology also is a great tool for students who are gifted and talented (and other kids, too). I keep accumulating more and more resources from the Internet. There is something about technology that inspires these kids. I think it's because there are always things to figure out, and they can manipulate it, and there are lots of variations. Here is an example: In seminar, I was helping students to use voki.com, where you can create avatars. The students could write things for them to say. They loved it. I also used moodle.com to create some advanced math options for some students

who were several grade levels ahead of their classmates in math. One student commented, "I don't feel like I'm sitting in math class looking out the window because I already know everything we're doing." Technology lets us reach and challenge all the students.

- A key to working with students who are gifted and talented is pre-assessment. Why don't we all do that for everything we're planning to teach? We can't plan instruction without it. We can't assume students who are gifted know everything to be taught, nor can we assume students who are more typical don't know it. We need to have data to back up our decisions, but then we need to move students along if they already know what is to be taught.

- Some students are twice exceptional. I think it's very important to use their strengths to get at the areas where there is a struggle—strengths can be motivators.

- I'm definitely in favor of inclusive programs. That has taken a lot of work with parents, who were comfortable with their children being pulled to a special program during the day. But I think they're starting to understand it.

- We do offer other options for a few students. We had a first grader who skipped a grade, and some high school students go to college courses in the afternoon. It depends on what the students need.

- I work hard to get teachers to avoid having students who are gifted just do more. Sometimes they ask me for worksheets or brainteasers. That's a sure way for students to shut down. They know that if they show they're smart they're going to get extra work. Students should do something different, not more of the same.

- At the same time, all the students and all the parents should know that differentiation is part of the classroom. It would be like a doctor giving a cough drop to everyone who came to the office, regardless of their ailments. I tell students that teachers are like doctors; they have to figure out what is needed and then provide it, and it's different for different students. Students understand that, and so do parents.

talented in an area such as art, music, drama, or sports and so have a direction for their lives—right? Evidence suggests that for many students, this is not the case, as certainly is true for Steven, whom you met at the beginning of this chapter. These students experience the same changes and challenges that all adolescents face—seeking personal relationships, developing a sense of ethics, and thinking about complex social issues such as poverty. They, like their peers, have to struggle to develop their identities and to make choices about their futures.

### Special Challenges

In addition to typical adolescent problems, students who are gifted and talented also may experience difficulties such as these (Buescher & Higham, 2001):

- *Ownership of their abilities.* These students know they have special abilities, yet they may also express disbelief about them. They may feel like impostors, waiting for someone to tell them that they are not that special after all.
- *Dissonance.* These students often have set very high standards for themselves. When they do not always achieve those standards, they may be dissatisfied with the gap between what

they had expected of themselves and what they accomplished, even if others do not ever think a gap existed.
- *Competing expectations.* Adolescents who are gifted and talented often receive advice from parents, teachers, friends, grandparents, counselors, university representatives, and others. They may feel pulled in many directions, wanting to please everyone but also themselves.
- *Premature identity.* Because of all the pressures they may experience, some adolescents take on an adult identity too soon. They may make career choices prematurely, decide on educational options before they should, and then experience frustration with their choices.

All these dilemmas, combined with these students' tendencies to be extraordinarily sensitive to the people and world around them, can lead to increased risk for problems with motivation and a high degree of anxiety.

### Supporting Adolescents Who Are Gifted and Talented

The outlook for students who are gifted and talented when they leave high school is not necessarily negative, but it is complex. These students need to work closely with counselors, mentors, and understanding teachers who can help them process the feelings they experience and carefully think through the important decisions they must make (Wood & Gavin, 2009). Educators can assist these students by helping them to set priorities and avoid overcommitment, understand their own strengths and weaknesses, reframe mistakes as learning experiences, and identify sources of stress so that they can be addressed (Fleith, 2001). In addition, schools should make it possible for these students to discuss their needs without fear of ridicule and without the risk of sensing their concerns are being devalued (e.g., "What do you have to worry about? You have everything going for you!").

**web link**

www.cectag.org
The Association for the Gifted (TAG) is a division of the Council for Exceptional Children (CEC). Its goal is to foster the welfare and education of students who are gifted and talented. On the TAG website you can find links to related organizations, summaries of articles from the organization's journal, and updates regarding legislation.

## REVIEW · REFLECT · DISCUSS

1. What are the options for providing appropriate services to students who are gifted and talented in elementary and secondary schools? Which option do you think would have the greatest likelihood of success? Why? Which, if any, do you think might not be beneficial for students? Justify your response.
2. Why do you think that not all gifted learners are good students or end up as eminent individuals? What other factors may intervene?

# Recommended Educational Practices for Students Who Are Gifted and Talented

In planning instructional programs for students who are gifted or talented, the National Associated for Gifted Children (2000) recommends these guiding principles:

1. Differentiated curriculum for the gifted learner must span grades pre-K–12.
2. Regular classroom curricula and instruction must be adapted, modified, or replaced to meet the unique needs of gifted learners.
3. Instructional pace must be flexible to allow for the accelerated learning of gifted learners as appropriate.
4. Educational opportunities for subject and grade skipping must be provided to gifted learners.
5. Learning opportunities for gifted learners must consist of a continuum of differentiated curricular options, instructional approaches, and resource materials.

Based on those principles, several practices are recommended for effectively educating these students, including curriculum compacting, acceleration, enrichment, differentiation, and interventions for diverse populations.

## Curriculum Compacting

Some students who are gifted and talented often already are familiar with the concepts being taught in their classrooms, or they can master the concepts in a fraction of the time that it takes their classmates. If these students' needs are not addressed, they can become frustrated. A solution to this problem is **curriculum compacting,** in which the goals of an instructional unit are identified, student mastery of all or part of the goals is documented, and alternative instruction is provided as appropriate (Reis & Renzulli, 2004). With the instructional time gained using curriculum compacting, options such as acceleration and enrichment, described next, can be employed. Warren, one of the students you met at the beginning of the chapter, might benefit from curriculum compacting.

## Acceleration

One important option for students who are gifted and talented is acceleration. **Acceleration,** advancing learners through levels of curriculum and programs according to individual achievement and performance, assumes that different students of the same age are at different levels of learning within and across learning areas (Chapman, 2009). Acceleration can occur in many ways. For some students, acceleration refers to allowing them to begin school before the age established through district policies. For other students, acceleration might mean moving through two grade levels in a single year, skipping a grade level altogether, or entering high school or even college before the age typically permitted.

Another type of acceleration is content based. That is, some students may need to advance quickly in math or English but not in other subject areas. This practice, referred to as **curriculum flexibility,** makes learning options responsive to learner needs and contextual demands by offering content-based acceleration practices at all levels of schooling and in all subject areas. For learners who are gifted with precocious abilities in the verbal, scientific, and artistic areas, such flexibility is crucial.

Acceleration is one option for serving students with a wide array of talents in a low-cost but direct way (Howley, Rhodes, & Beall, 2009). Advocates note that it promotes high achievement for students, but it does not require designing or implementing new instructional programs, nor does it require hiring new personnel. Opponents express concern about cross-age grouping of students, the impact on the self-identity of students who are gifted, and the likelihood of these students being stigmatized and bullied.

### Acceleration in High School

You may already be familiar with options for acceleration in high school, or perhaps you participated in them. Examples include the College Board Advanced Placement (AP) program and the International Baccalaureate (IB) program. Both of these programs offer students the opportunity to earn college credit while they are in high school.

Another high school option is *dual-enrollment courses* in which students take courses at local community colleges or universities or arrangements are made for these courses to be offered on the high school campus. Students earn college credit that then counts toward an undergraduate degree. Currently, 40 states have dual-enrollment policies, encouraging local districts to take advantage of the opportunity for students to gain access to higher education while still in high school (Mokher & McLendon, 2009). In rural areas, where AP and IB options may not be feasible, dual enrollment is an attractive alternative.

One additional acceleration option found primarily in high schools, often in rural areas, is the use of telecommunications. Advanced courses are made available through inter-

*In many locales, students who are gifted and talented receive services in a separate classroom, either fulltime or several times each week.*

## The Power of the Internet

The Internet has been called "the most significant technology available" to students who are gifted and talented (Siegle, 2005, p. 30) because it provides depth, breadth, and complexity at the touch of a few keys. However, especially for elementary and middle school students, their often self-taught strategies leave them using the Internet inefficiently and ineffectively. Here are some websites that can assist learners with advanced ability to learn effective search strategies:

- **Ask for Kids** (www.askforkids.com)
  This search engine enables students to narrow their search by subject area and by approximate age group. Students also may type in a complete question (e.g., What causes hurricanes?).

- **KidsClick!** (kidsclick.org)
  This search engine is arranged on its homepage by topics. It is not intended to filter sites. Rather it points students' searches to 6,400 high-quality sites. It is operated and maintained by the School of Library and Information Science (SLIS) at Kent State University.

- **Awesome Library** (www.awesomelibrary.org)
  This private database of 37,000 sites is designed for K–12 students, teachers, and parents. The principles applied to the sites included are these: child-safe links, useful information, "real stuff," current items that load quickly, and the best version available.

- **Kid's Search Tools** (http://www.rcls.org/Ksearch.htm)
  This website has on a single page several search tools for students, including a means of searching student-created websites and a link to FirstGov for Kids, federal government websites for children.

- **TekMom** (http://www.tekmon.com/search)
  This website has easy links to several of the sites already mentioned. It also offers other electronic resources, including links to biographies, an encyclopedia, and dictionaries. The site has other tools as well, including instructions for students on how to cite the sources they use.

*Source:* Based on, J. (2009). Besides Google: Guiding gifted elementary students onto the entrance ramp of the information superhighway. *Gifted Child Today, 32*(1), 27–31. Used with permission of Prufrock Press.

---

active video, on-line formats, or similar mechanisms. This increasingly feasible option enables students to access learning opportunities that nurture their talents that otherwise would not be possible because of the cost of hiring a teacher for just one or a few students.

### Enrichment

Another instructional approach to meeting the needs of students who are gifted and talented is **enrichment,** the extension of regular curriculum with different examples and associations that build complex ideas (McAllister & Plourde, 2008). For example, in a middle school social studies class, students are learning about the causes of the American Revolution. Zeta is already familiar with most of the material. To provide enrichment, Ms. Baldwin, her teacher, asks her to explore the causes of several major wars in which the United States has participated and to create a visual that demonstrates their similarities and differences. Zeta completes this assignment in lieu of the activities assigned to her classmates.

In some school districts, curriculum compacting may occur but not acceleration. For students in these districts, enrichment can be a valuable option. Enrichment can encourage student creativity and the development of critical-thinking skills, and it can be an appropriate substitute for material that is too basic for some students' skill levels. Of course, if enrichment is practiced only for students considered gifted and not as a part of classwide differentiation, it can lead to student isolation and feelings of being different.

One strategy for enrichment (as well as for differentiation, explained next) is the use of technology. As illustrated in the Technology Notes, teachers can help students become skilled Internet researchers so that they can explore curricular topics in more depth, breadth, and complexity.

### Differentiation

You have been reading about universal design for learning and differentiating throughout this textbook in the context of meeting the diverse student needs in general education classrooms, yet the term was first used in educational settings in gifted education. **Differentiation** for students who are gifted, as for all students, refers to an instructional approach that assumes that students need many different avenues to reach their learning potential (Cox,

research
**NOTE**

Jolly and Kettler (2008) reviewed 80 years of research on gifted education. They concluded that most of the research has been on the description of what constitutes giftedness and issues related to underserved populations rather than on topics related to high-quality instruction.

www.nku.edu/~mathed/gifted.html The University of Northern Kentucky hosts a website on mathematics resources designed for parents, teachers, and students who are gifted. The site includes hundreds of web links at many levels of complexity.

**myeducationlab**

Go to the Assignments and Activities section of Topic 17: Gifted and Talented, in the MyEducationLab for your course and complete the activity entitled "Differentiated Instruction".

2008; Tomlinson, 2001). It can address the content students are learning, the assessment tools through which learning is measured, the tasks students complete, and the instructional strategies employed (Tomlinson et al., 2002).

Curriculum design is one major component of differentiation for students who are gifted (Brown & Abernethy, 2009). What is important for these students to know and be able to do at what stages of development? How do planned learning experiences focus on meaningful experiences that provide (a) *depth,* exploration of a topic or concept beyond what is normally addressed, and (b) **complexity,** exploration of multiple perspectives, issues, variables, and relationships, at an appropriate pace? Related to curriculum design is materials selection. In classrooms serving these students, materials should go beyond a single textbook, also including advanced readings that present interesting and challenging ideas, treat knowledge as tentative and open ended, and provide a conceptual depth that allows students to make interdisciplinary connections.

Above all, keep in mind that differentiation can benefit all the students in a classroom. When teachers use large-group, small-group, individual, and student–teacher conference grouping strategies and take into account student interests, cultural uniqueness, and learning styles, their classrooms can become exciting places where all students are meaningfully engaged in learning. Differentiation is the foundation of inclusive education practices—those that truly address the entire diversity of the student population.

### Problem-Based Learning

Differentiation encompasses instruction that is inquiry based, is open ended, and employs flexible grouping practices. One example is *problem-based learning (PBL),* in which students encounter a real-world problem designed by the teacher to address key concepts (e.g., Tennison, 2007). The students explore the problem, gather research data about it, and design interventions to solve it. The instructional techniques needed by the teacher include high-level questioning skills, listening skills, conferencing skills, and tutoring in order to guide the process. PBL also incorporates flexible team grouping and whole-class discussion. Problem resolution usually involves student-initiated projects and presentations, guided by the teacher. You can learn more about problem-based learning, an approach highlighted for students who are gifted but applicable to all students, in the Instruction in Action.

In classrooms using problem-based learning, performance-based assessment is typical. Having students create products or critique their work provides a detailed picture of individual progress toward specific education goals. In fact, for students who are gifted and talented, the quality of performance on such measures may be a better indicator than paper-and-pencil measures of skills and concepts deeply mastered.

## Interventions for Diverse Populations

General interventions that have been documented as successful with learners identified as gifted and economically disadvantaged include early attention to needs, family involvement, use of effective instructional and leadership strategies in the school, experiential learning approaches, encouragement of self-expression, community involvement, counseling efforts, and building on strengths (Moore, Ford, & Milner, 2005). As you have learned throughout this text, it also is important to be sensitive to cultural values. For example, some students who live in poverty may mask their giftedness because of issues related to social acceptance. The following guidelines have been found effective in teaching students from nondominant cultures who are gifted and talented:

1. Provide separate instructional opportunities for students with the same developmental profiles. Students from diverse groups need to have opportunities to interact with students similar to themselves. Students should be grouped by critical variables—for example, by gender or social background.
2. Use technology, especially computers, to aid in transmission of learning. Although applications of technology have evolved for students who have disabilities, it holds promise for targeted use with other learners, as well.

**research NOTE**

*A Nation Deceived: How Schools Hold Back America's Brightest Students*, a 2004 report on services for students who are gifted and talented, noted that unfounded bias against acceleration unnecessarily limits education options for these students (Colangelo, Assouline, & Gross, 2004). The report has received worldwide attention and is translated into seven languages.

3. Provide small-group and individual counseling, mentorships, and internships, all of which make possible individual attention to affective as well as cognitive issues of development.

4. Focus on the arts as a therapeutic intervention as well as a creative and expressive outlet. Whether it be in art, music, drama, or dance and whether targeted students have high academic ability or a particular talent, the arts provide an outlet that fosters creativity and encourages higher-level functioning.

5. Use materials rich in ideas and imagination coupled with an emphasis on higher-level skills. Both self-concept and motivation are jeopardized when students overuse basic materials, as sometimes happens for English language learners. Challenging content with attention to ideas and creative opportunities is essential to avoid boredom and withdrawal.

## REVIEW · REFLECT · DISCUSS

1. What is your opinion of acceleration as a recommended instructional practice for students who are gifted or talented? What are the potential opportunities and drawbacks for students who are accelerated during their school careers?

2. What might differentiation look like for a student who is gifted and talented in your classroom or the classroom of a colleague? How does this type of differentiation compare to that for a student with disabilities who is not gifted or talented? How could teachers integrate both applications of differentiation?

## Perspectives of Parents and Families of Students Who Are Gifted and Talented

The role of families in the development of giftedness and talent has been well documented in the literature (Hertzog & Bennett, 2004; Matthews, Foster, & Gladstone, 2007). Parents typically have been key influences in their children's progress in specific talent areas as well as in generally nurturing the learning process. Parents of these students often decide to make personal sacrifices to further their children's skills—for example, moving to place the child in a better school or with a master teacher or coach. Even parents who do not make such efforts still nurture their children's talent development. Families of high-achieving students who are gifted often are characterized as intact, and they tend to place high values on education and hard work (Schilling, Sparfeldt, & Rost, 2006).

### Parent Strategies for Encouraging Their Children

Parents of children who are gifted often want advice on ways to nurture their children's abilities in the home. Some important approaches include these:

- Reading to the child at all ages
- Providing educational puzzles and games
- Holding dinner table discussions on issues of the day
- Having the child interact with adult friends, who may serve as role models or mentors
- Providing trips to the local library for books and research
- Traveling to interesting places and even having the child plan the trip
- Viewing films and special television programs together and discussing them
- Encouraging the child to be creative and expressive in the arts areas in which she shows a sustained interest

With the advent of so many educational alternatives outside schools for students who are gifted, parents have been forced to become analysts of educational services, often

**web link**

http://www.sengifted.org/
At Supporting Emotional Needs of the Gifted (SENG), an organization dedicated to ensuring that students who are gifted accepted themselves and are accepted and valued by others, you can find a library of articles on these students' social and emotional needs and other related topic.

Go to the Building Teaching Skills and Dispositions section of Topic 3: Parents and Families, in the MyEducationLab for your course and complete the activity entitled "An Extended Family".

*Many eminent individuals credit their success to the support provided by their parents.*

having to make choices among attractive options. For example, one option parents may consider is homeschooling, introduced earlier in this chapter. Usually the decision to homeschool emerges out of both a strong parental value system about the importance of individualized education and the characteristics of a child who is gifted that may suggest unevenness in ability and development. Frequent concerns of homeschooling parents of children who are gifted include what to do at home, how to select challenging educational content, how to keep a child who is gifted motivated and committed to learning, and when to opt for a more formal educational setting for their child.

Parent support frequently is cited by eminent individuals as having been critical to their success. Author Robert Penn Warren credited his literary talent to his father's reading him the classics until he went off to college. Robert Root Bernstein, a Nobel Prize-winning chemist, cited his mother's interest in his science projects as crucial to spurring him on to compete for a Westinghouse scholarship. These are but two of many examples of the positive outcomes of parent encouragement for children who are gifted and talented, and they suggest that, as for other students, working closely with parents is central to education success.

## REVIEW · REFLECT · DISCUSS

1. Think about working with parents of students who are gifted and talented. What do you think might be their concerns? How are these concerns similar to and different from those of parents of students with disabilities who are not gifted and talented? What lessons have you taken from this book regarding working with parents of children with special needs?

2. How would you go about convincing the parents of a student who has great potential but is underachieving to enroll their child in a talent program? What questions might they ask? To what extent do you think the student should make this choice? Why?

# Trends and Issues Affecting Students Who Are Gifted and Talented

Many contemporary issues in gifted education have been hinted at elsewhere in this chapter. As you read the synopsis of several of these issues in the following sections, consider these questions: What are the implications of these topics for me as a professional educator? How might these topics affect the students with whom I may work?

## Talent Development

The case could be made that all of education is about talent development—that is, nurturing one, several, or many abilities of students, a view of schooling at its best. For students who are gifted and talented, though, this topic has recently become a focus. Whole schools have been founded and many schools reorganized around the talent development concept. Specialized searches for finding precocious talent in children identify and serve more than 200,000 students per year through national searches. Talent development efforts in the arts, especially through private lessons and tutorials, continue to thrive. Parents, too, are integral to this trend; they are seeking opportunities for their children and ensuring that their potential is reached.

Talent development is premised on the belief that many individuals may possess special abilities, even if they do not have overall high abilities. The trend toward talent development is likely to continue because it addresses in an equitable way the increasing diversity of today's students.

## Identification and Programming for Underrepresented Groups

No one would question that giftedness and talent exist in all segments of the population, yet students from minority groups and those who live in poverty remain underrepresented (King et al., 2009; Obiakor & Ford, 2002). This situation exists despite more than 30 years of efforts to address this problem. In the 1990s, major national emphasis was given to this area through a priority assignment when federal funding in the Javits Act was allocated to explore this issue. Today, nearly every publication related to gifted education acknowledges the need to maintain focus on identifying students from underrepresented groups (e.g., Jolly & Kettler, 2008).

### Students Who Are Twice Exceptional

Students with disabilities who also are gifted and talented sometimes are referred to as *twice exceptional*, and they are receiving more attention than ever before (Pereles, Omdal, & Baldwin, 2009). Students who have learning disabilities, ADHD, autism spectrum disorder, a vision or hearing loss, emotional disabilities, physical or health disabilities, or other special needs often are inadvertently excluded from programs serving those who are gifted, even though they may qualify when appropriate accommodations are made during the assessment process (e.g., Besnov, Manning, & Karnes, 2006; Reis & Ruban, 2005; Tomlinson, 2004). In the Professional Edge you can read more about students who are twice exceptional—and ideas for successfully instructing them.

research
**NOTE**

When 64 experts on gifted education were asked about issues in the field, they identified the most pressing topics as the need to clarify the definition of giftedness and procedures for identifying students who are gifted and talented, the underrepresentation of minority students among those identified as gifted, and moving research in the field to classroom practice (Pfeiffer, 2003).

---

**professional edge**

### Students Who Are Twice Exceptional

When students have special gifts and talents as well as disabilities, finding effective ways to teach them can be a challenge. Here is a summary of characteristics of twice exceptional students (Colorado Department of Education, 2009):

| Strengths | Challenges |
| --- | --- |
| · superior vocabulary | · easily frustrated |
| · highly creative | · stubborn |
| · resourceful | · manipulative |
| · curious | · opinionated |
| · imaginative | · argumentative |
| · questioning | · problems in written expression |
| · problem-solving ability | · highly sensitive to criticism |
| · sophisticated sense of humor | · inconsistent academic performance |
| · wide range of interests | · lack of organization and study skills |
| · advanced ideas and opinions | · difficulty with social interactions |
| · special talent or consuming interest | |

Teaching strategies for working with these students include these:

1. Use key learning principles that apply to all students.
   * Build on student knowledge.
   * Nurture students' deep understanding of factual knowledge in order to prepare them for further and richer inquiry.
   * Help students to learn metacognitive strategies—that is, to have an awareness of their own learning and how it occurs.
2. Vary student instructional activities across these four factors, based on student needs:
   * *Time.* Use dynamic assessment to judge student work, often providing extended periods so that they can complete projects.
   * *Structure.* Identify big ideas that you would like students to learn so that you can prioritize activities. Relate new learning to knowledge and skills that students already possess (e.g., by using visual organizers to point out connections to students). Arrange the classroom so that there are quiet areas, areas for discussion, and areas with comfortable furniture.
   * *Support.* Create a classroom climate that is respectful and welcoming of all students. Provide the assistance students need (but not more than they need) in order to succeed. Advocate for students, and encourage them to become self-advocates.

*Source:* Based on Coleman, M. R. (2005). Academic strategies that work for gifted students with learning disabilities. *Teaching Exceptional Children, 38*(1), 28–32; and Colorado Department of Education. (n.d.). Twice-exceptional students: Gifted students with disabilities, an introductory resource book. Denver: Author. Retrieved September 11, 2009 from http://www.cde.state.co.us/gt/publications.htm.

*Some students who are extraordinarily gifted benefit by acceleration, sometimes even enrolling in college courses at a very early age.*

## Effective Differentiation

Although presented as a recommended practice, differentiation also is an issue in the field of gifted education because it has been perceived by educators in very different ways. One common misunderstanding of the term implies that students who are gifted receive a totally different program from other students. That is, average students take subject matter courses while students who are gifted learn higher-order skills, with the strong implications that students who are gifted do not need content and that other learners do not need higher-level skills. Obviously, this is not true, yet the debate continues. For some researchers, the heart of differentiated practice rests with students engaging in independent project work (Ozturk & Debelak, 2008; Renzulli, 2002). For others, differentiation is best satisfied through individualized approaches within the general education classroom (Heacox, 2002; Tomlinson & McTighe, 2006). For still others, differentiation requires an integrative and comprehensive set of experiences conducted in a separate setting with intellectual peers (Robinson, 2003).

Each of these points of view has some validity, and the challenge facing school professionals is to recognize and act on all of them. One reason for these various points of view relates to the students who are being considered. If the programs respond primarily to **precocity**—that is, demonstrating early development or maturity in such ways as early language development, rapid learning ability, or unusual attention span—then advanced content is the logical form of differentiation. However, if professionals emphasize complexity of thought as a student characteristic, then a differentiated set of experiences that provides real-world problems to solve becomes the differentiated response.

Another source of disagreement on this issue relates to the level at which differentiation should occur. For some educators, the focus is on the individual student, with the program always responding to the interests and abilities present at a given point in time. For other educators, differentiation occurs through changes in curriculum goals and outcomes for groups of learners. For still other educators, it is implemented in a more general way through mentorships or chess clubs, for example. Perhaps a next step for the study of differentiation is one that simultaneously considers it from all these perspectives.

## Alternative Program Models

In addition to the options available through university coursework and weekend or summer university programs for students who are gifted and talented, several other education options are becoming more common. These include technology use and opportunities external to schools.

### Technology-Based Options

Some students participate in acceleration through technology as a delivery system for a high-powered curriculum (Roschelle, Pea, Hoadley, Gordin, & Means, 2000). Stanford University's Education Program for Gifted Youth (EPGY) is a prime example. Begun in 1963 when computers were a brand new idea, this program has kept as its goal making available to students who are gifted and talented advanced learning opportunities through distance education. More than 50,000 students from 35 countries have completed on-line courses since the programs' inception. Other similar innovative uses of technology for gifted programming are also growing. What might be the advantages and disadvantages of this option for students with special gifts and talents?

## Problem-Based Learning

In problem-based learning, students are given realistic problems that are open ended and challenging. The problems do not have single correct answers. Students systematically problem solve using a wide variety of resources to find solutions. In a health class, one teacher proposed these problems to students:

*Group 1:* As a sports nutritionist, create a menu plan for a week for a female athlete who weighs 130 pounds; is 5 feet, 5 inches tall; and plays on a soccer team.

*Group 2:* As a diet expert, create a menu plan for a week for a fifteen-year-old boy who wants to build muscle and put on weight before football season.

This approach to instruction can help all students to make connections between what they are learning and school and real-world situations, but it is particularly effective with students who are gifted and talented because it encourages creativity, enables them to research problems in depth, and fosters skills for working independently of the teacher. The diagram summarizes the steps used in problem-based learning. How might you use such an approach as you work with students?

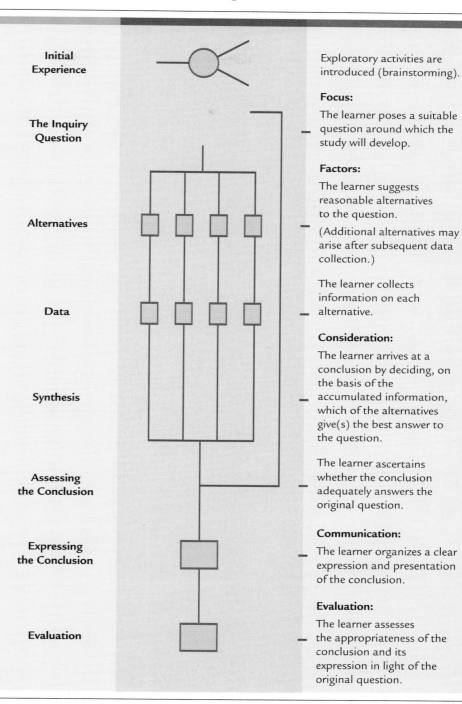

**Initial Experience**
Exploratory activities are introduced (brainstorming).

**The Inquiry Question**

**Focus:**
The learner poses a suitable question around which the study will develop.

**Alternatives**

**Factors:**
The learner suggests reasonable alternatives to the question.

(Additional alternatives may arise after subsequent data collection.)

**Data**
The learner collects information on each alternative.

**Synthesis**

**Consideration:**
The learner arrives at a conclusion by deciding, on the basis of the accumulated information, which of the alternatives give(s) the best answer to the question.

**Assessing the Conclusion**
The learner ascertains whether the conclusion adequately answers the original question.

**Expressing the Conclusion**

**Communication:**
The learner organizes a clear expression and presentation of the conclusion.

**Evaluation**

**Evaluation:**
The learner assesses the appropriateness of the conclusion and its expression in light of the original question.

*Source:* Adapted from Gregory, G. H., & Chapman, C. (2002). *Differentiated instructional strategies* (pp. 126–130). Thousand Oaks, CA: Corwin.

instruction in action

### Opportunities External to Schools

Although local schools play critical roles in educating students, schools can be even more effective when coupled with outside community resources that supplement learning. One program model includes Saturday or summer enrichment programs offered by local universities. These programs allow students who are gifted to use their leisure time pursuing a topic of academic interest, such as poetry, chemistry, or architecture, under the direction of a highly qualified instructor. Because such programs usually charge tuition, though, they may not be feasible for students who live in poverty. Another example of university programming includes a talent search, usually targeted to academically able middle school students who qualify based on SAT scores (Stanley, 2005). Many of these programs, which are offered during the summer and include a residential component, provide accelerated content equivalent to high school coursework.

Other external activities that involve the community include mentorships and internships. The former involves selecting a **mentor,** an individual who serves as a role model to a student and establishes a one-to-one relationship. This connection helps a student understand how an adult experiences and processes the world; the relationship typically is built on some area of mutual interest. Internships and job-shadowing opportunities involve placements in community settings, usually for a period from 2 weeks to a full semester. The purpose is to help the student explore the real world and to see the work habits and task demands that accompany certain professions. Both of these alternatives are highly relevant for students who are gifted, particularly those who feel very different from the norm and may have time available as a result of program or content acceleration to explore different work environments and career options.

## REVIEW · REFLECT · DISCUSS

1. Should gifted programs exist to serve children at preschool age? What should such an educational option include? How would it be different than early education for other students with or without disabilities? If you think that it should not exist for preschool, at what age do you think it should begin? Why?

2. The trend of talent development implies that many students, including girls and individuals from diverse groups, should be identified as gifted. What is your opinion on this trend? What is its impact for funding and serving this group of students? If you could propose legislation to address the needs of this group, how would you prioritize the needs?

## Summary

- The past century has seen many developments in the field of gifted education, including a broader definition of giftedness and attention to inequities in identifying and serving students who are gifted and talented. Giftedness is not addressed in IDEA.

- Although estimates of the prevalence of students who are gifted and talented vary dramatically based on state definitions and priorities, professionals generally agree that it is the interaction of genetic predisposition and environmental support that determines whether students develop the characteristics of giftedness.

- Students who are gifted have common cognitive, academic, and social/emotional characteristics, including the ability to manipulate abstract symbol systems, intense power of concentration, and early language interest and development; specific behaviors in reading, writing, speaking, and mathematics; a strong sense of justice, altruism, and idealism; a sense of humor; emotional intensity; and strong attachments and commitments.

- Although identification criteria and procedures vary by state and locality, most professionals use a two-stage assessment process. Best practices recommend the use of

- authentic assessment, including dynamic assessment, and nonverbal spatial ability assessments.
- Students who are gifted and talented receive services based on local policies. Options include grouping, part-time and full-time separate classes, specialized schools, and homeschooling.
- Recommended practices for these students include curriculum compacting, acceleration, enrichment, differentiation, and specific strategies for diverse student groups.

- Parents need to be aware of the characteristics and needs of their children who are gifted and talented and the options and opportunities available both within and outside school.
- Examples of trends and issues affecting gifted education include talent development, identification of and programming for underrepresented groups, debates about effective differentiation, and alternative program models.

## ADDRESSING THE PROFESSIONAL STANDARDS

Council for Exceptional Children (CEC) Common Core Knowledge and Skills addressed in this chapter:

ICC1K4, ICC1K5, ICC1K7, ICC1K8, ICC2K4, ICC2K5, ICC2K6, ICC3K1, ICC3K2, ICC3K4, ICC4S3, ICC5K3, ICC5S2, ICC7S1, ICC7S9, ICC8S4, ICC8S5, ICC8S6

Appendix: Provides a full listing of the CEC Common Core Standards, and associated Knowledge and Skill Statements listed here.

## PEARSON myeducationlab

Now go to Topic 17: Gifted & Talented in the MyEducationLab (www.myeducationlab.com) for your course, where you can:

- Find learning outcomes for the broad concepts covered in this chapter along with the national standards that connect to these outcomes.
- Complete Assignments and Activities that can help you more deeply understand the chapter content.
- Apply and practice your understanding of the core concepts and skills identified in the chapter with the Building Teaching Skills and Dispositions learning units.

- Check your comprehension on the content covered in the chapter by going to the Study Plan in the Book Specific Resources for your text. Here you will be able to take a chapter quiz, receive feedback on your answers, and then access Review, Practice, and Enrichment activities to enhance your understanding of chapter content.
- Watch video clips of CCSSO Teacher of the Year award winners responding to the question: "Why I teach?" in the Teacher Talk section.

# CEC Knowledge and Skill Standards Common Core

### Standard I: Foundations

ICC1K1:  Models, theories, and philosophies, and research methods that provide the basis for special education practice.

ICC1K2:  Laws, policies, and ethical principles regarding behavior management planning and implementation.

ICC1K3:  Relationship of special education to the organization and function of educational agencies.

ICC1K4:  Rights and responsibilities of students, parents, teachers, and other professionals, and schools related to exceptional learning needs.

ICC1K5:  Issues in definition and identification of individuals with exceptional learning needs, including those from culturally and linguistically diverse backgrounds.

ICC1K6:  Issues, assurances, and due process rights related to assessment, eligibility, and placement within a continuum of services.

ICC1K7:  Family systems and the role of families in the educational process.

ICC1K8:  Historical points of view and contributions of culturally diverse groups.

ICC1K9:  Impact of the dominant culture on shaping schools and the individuals who study and work in them.

ICC1K10:  Potential impact of differences in values, languages, and customs that can exist between the home and school.

ICC1S1:  Articulate personal philosophy of special education.

### Standard II: Development and Characteristics of Learners

ICC2K1:  Typical and atypical human growth and development.

ICC2K2:  Educational implications of characteristics of various exceptionalities.

ICC2K3:  Characteristics and effects of the cultural and environmental milieu of the individual with exceptional learning needs and the family.

ICC2K4:  Family systems and the role of families in supporting development.

ICC2K5:  Similarities and differences of individuals with and without exceptional learning needs.

ICC2K6:  Similarities and differences among individuals with exceptional learning needs.

ICC2K7:  Effects of various medications on individuals with exceptional learning needs.

### Standard III: Individual Learning Differences

ICC3K1:  Effects an exceptional condition(s) can have on an individual's life.

ICC3K2:  Impact of learner's academic and social abilities, attitudes, interests, and values on instruction and career development.

ICC3K3:  Variations in beliefs, traditions, and values across and within cultures and their effects on relationships among individuals with exceptional learning needs, family, and schooling.

ICC3K4:  Cultural perspectives influencing the relationships among families, schools, and communities as related to instruction.

ICC3K5:  Differing ways of learning of individuals with exceptional learning needs including those from culturally diverse backgrounds and strategies for addressing these differences.

## Standard IV: Instructional Strategies

ICC4K1:   Evidence-based practices validated for specific characteristics of learners and settings.

ICC4S1:   Use strategies to facilitate integration into various settings.

ICC4S2:   Teach individuals to use self-assessment, problem-solving, and other cognitive strategies to meet their needs.

ICC4S3:   Select, adapt, and use instructional strategies and materials according to characteristics of the individual with exceptional learning needs.

ICC4S4:   Use strategies to facilitate maintenance and generalization of skills across learning environments.

ICC4S5:   Use procedures to increase the individual's self-awareness, self-management, self-control, self-reliance, and self-esteem.

ICC4S6:   Use strategies that promote successful transitions for individuals with exceptional learning needs.

## Standard V: Learning Environments and Social Interactions

ICC5K1:   Demands of learning environments.

ICC5K2:   Basic classroom management theories and strategies for individuals with exceptional learning needs.

ICC5K3:   Effective management of teaching and learning.

ICC5K4:   Teacher attitudes and behaviors that influence behavior of individuals with exceptional learning needs.

ICC5K5:   Social skills needed for educational and other environments.

ICC5K6:   Strategies for crisis prevention and intervention.

ICC5K7:   Strategies for preparing individuals to live harmoniously and productively in a culturally diverse world.

ICC5K8:   Ways to create learning environments that allow individuals to retain and appreciate their own and each other's respective language and cultural heritage.

ICC5K9:   Ways specific cultures are negatively stereotyped.

ICC5K10:  Strategies used by diverse populations to cope with a legacy of former and continuing racism.

ICC5S1:   Create a safe, equitable, positive, and supporting learning environment in which diversities are valued.

ICC5S2:   Identify realistic expectations for personal and social behavior in various settings.

ICC5S3:   Identify supports needed for integration into various program placements.

ICC5S4:   Design learning environments that encourage active participation in individual and group settings.

ICC5S5:   Modify the learning environment to manage behaviors.

ICC5S6:   Use performance data and information from all stakeholders to make or suggest modifications in learning environments.

ICC5S7:   Establish and maintain rapport with individuals with and without exceptional learning needs.

ICC5S8:   Teach self-advocacy.

ICC5S9:   Create an environment that encourages self-advocacy and increased independence.

ICC5S10:  Use effective and varied behavior management strategies.

ICC5S11:  Use the least intensive behavior management strategy consistent with the needs of the individual with exceptional learning needs.

ICC5S12:  Design and manage daily routines.

ICC5S13:  Organize, develop, and sustain learning environments that support positive intracultural and intercultural experiences.

ICC5S14: Mediate controversial intercultural issues among students within the learning environment in ways that enhance any culture, group, or person.

ICC5S15: Structure, direct, and support the activities of paraeducators, volunteers, and tutors.

ICC5S16: Use universal precautions.

### Standard VI: Communication

ICC6K1: Effects of cultural and linguistic differences on growth and development.

ICC6K2: Characteristics of one's own culture and use of language and the ways in which these can differ from other cultures and uses of languages.

ICC6K3: Ways of behaving and communicating among cultures that can lead to misinterpretation and misunderstanding.

ICC6K4: Augmentative and assistive communication strategies.

ICC6S1: Use strategies to support and enhance communication skills of individuals with exceptional learning needs.

ICC6S2: Use communication strategies and resources to facilitate understanding of subject matter for students whose primary language is not the dominant language.

### Standard VII: Instructional Planning

ICC7K1: Theories and research that form the basis of curriculum development and instructional practice.

ICC7K2: Scope and sequences of general and special curricula.

ICC7K3: National, state or provincial, and local curricula standards.

ICC7K4: Technology for planning and managing the teaching and learning environment.

ICC7K5: Roles and responsibilities of the paraeducator related to instruction, intervention, and direct service.

ICC7S1: Identify and prioritize areas of the general curriculum and accommodations for individuals with exceptional learning needs.

ICC7S2: Develop and implement comprehensive, longitudinal individualized programs in collaboration with team members.

ICC7S3: Involve the individual and family in setting instructional goals and monitoring progress.

ICC7S4: Use functional assessments to develop intervention plans.

ICC7S5: Use task analysis.

ICC7S6: Sequence, implement, and evaluate individualized learning objectives.

ICC7S7: Integrate affective, social, and life skills with academic curricula.

ICC7S8: Develop and select instructional content, resources, and strategies that respond to cultural, linguistic, and gender differences.

ICC7S9: Incorporate and implement instructional and assistive technology into the educational program.

ICC7S10: Prepare lesson plans.

ICC7S11: Prepare and organize materials to implement daily lesson plans.

ICC7S12: Use instructional time effectively.

ICC7S13: Make responsive adjustments to instruction based on continued observations.

ICC7S14: Prepare individuals to exhibit self-enhancing behavior in response to societal attitudes and actions.

ICC7S15: Evaluate and modify instructional practices in response to ongoing assessment data.

## Standard VIII: Assessment

ICC8K1:   Basic terminology used in assessment.
ICC8K2:   Legal provisions and ethical principles regarding assessment of individuals.
ICC8K3:   Screening, prereferral, referral, and classification procedures.
ICC8K4:   Use and limitations of assessment instruments.
ICC8K5:   National, state or provincial, and local accommodations and modifications.
ICC8S1:   Gather relevant background information.
ICC8S2:   Administer nonbiased formal and informal assessments.
ICC8S3:   Use technology to conduct assessments.
ICC8S4:   Develop or modify individualized assessment strategies.
ICC8S5:   Interpret information from formal and informal assessments.
ICC8S6:   Use assessment information in making eligibility, program, and placement decisions for individuals with exceptional learning needs, including those from culturally and/or linguistically diverse backgrounds.
ICC8S7:   Report assessment results to all stakeholders using effective communication skills.
ICC8S8:   Evaluate instruction and monitor progress of individuals with exceptional learning needs.
ICC8S9:   Develop or modify individualized assessment strategies.
ICC8S10:  Create and maintain records.

## Standard IX: Professional and Ethical Practice

ICC9K1:   Personal cultural biases and differences that affect one's teaching.
ICC9K2:   Importance of the teacher serving as a model for individuals with exceptional learning needs.
ICC9K3:   Continuum of lifelong professional development.
ICC9K4:   Methods to remain current regarding research-validated practice.
ICC9S1:   Practice within the CEC Code of Ethics and other standards of the profession.
ICC9S2:   Uphold high standards of competence and integrity and exercise sound judgment in the practice of the professional.
ICC9S3:   Act ethically in advocating for appropriate services.
ICC9S4:   Conduct professional activities in compliance with applicable laws and policies.
ICC9S5:   Demonstrate commitment to developing the highest education and quality-of-life potential of individuals with exceptional learning needs.
ICC9S6:   Demonstrate sensitivity for the culture, language, religion, gender, disability, socioeconomic status, and sexual orientation of individuals.
ICC9S7:   Practice within one's skill limit and obtain assistance as needed.
ICC9S8:   Use verbal, nonverbal, and written language effectively.
ICC9S9:   Conduct self-evaluation of instruction.
ICC9S10:  Access information on exceptionalities.
ICC9S11:  Reflect on one's practice to improve instruction and guide professional growth.
ICC9S12:  Engage in professional activities that benefit individuals with exceptional learning needs, their families, and one's colleagues.
ICC9S13:  Demonstrate Commitment to engage evidence-based practice.

### Standard X: Collaboration

ICC10K1: Models and strategies of consultation and collaboration.

ICC10K2: Roles of individuals with exceptional learning needs, families, and school and community personnel in planning of an individualized program.

ICC10K3: Concerns of families of individuals with exceptional learning needs and strategies to help address these concerns.

ICC10K4: Culturally responsive factors that promote effective communication and collaboration with individuals with exceptional learning needs, families, school personnel, and community members.

ICC10S1: Maintain confidential communication about individuals with exceptional learning needs.

ICC10S2: Collaborate with families and others in assessment of individuals with exceptional learning needs.

ICC10S3: Foster respectful and beneficial relationships between families and professionals.

ICC10S4: Assist individuals with exceptional learning needs and their families in becoming active participants in the educational team.

ICC10S5: Plan and conduct collaborative conferences with individuals with exceptional learning needs and their families.

ICC10S6: Collaborate with school personnel and community members in integrating individuals with exceptional learning needs into various settings.

ICC10S7: Use group problem-solving skills to develop, implement, and evaluate collaborative activities.

ICC10S8: Model techniques and coach others in the use of instructional methods and accommodations.

ICC10S9: Communicate with school personnel about the characteristics and needs of individuals with exceptional learning needs.

ICC10S10: Communicate effectively with families of individuals with exceptional learning needs from diverse backgrounds.

ICC10S11: Observe, evaluate, and provide feedback to paraeducators.

From *CEC What Every Special Educator Must Know*. Copyright 2009 by The Council for Exceptional Children. Reprinted with permission.

# glossary

**ability grouping** Characteristic of any program in which school personnel use test scores or school performance to assign same-grade students at similar levels to groups or classes with markedly different levels of academic preparation.

**absence seizure** Type of generalized seizure usually lasting for only a few seconds and sometimes mistaken for daydreaming or inattention; formerly called petit mal seizure.

**acceleration** Practice of advancing learners through levels of curriculum according to individual achievement and performance.

**accent** A normal variation in the surface characteristics of a language.

**access technology** High-tech and low-tech devices and software that allow persons with impairments to gain access to computers and other forms of information.

**acquired brain injury** Injury that occurs after birth as a result of accidents, illness, injuries, or environmental factors (e.g., severe allergies).

**acquired hearing loss** Hearing loss that develops after a baby is born; also called adventitious hearing loss.

**acquired immune deficiency syndrome (AIDS)** Collection of illnesses, including some cancers, that only individuals who have human immunodeficiency virus (HIV) can contract; most children become infected during mothers' pregnancies.

**acute condition** Medical disorder that is serious and requires immediate attention, but that can be treated and probably cured.

**adaptive behavior** Day-to-day knowledge and skills necessary for independence, including communication, self-care, social skills, home living, leisure, and self-direction. Deficits in adaptive behavior comprise one component of identifying students with mental retardation.

**additions** Articulation disorder in which a person inserts extra sounds in words spoken.

**ADHD–combined type** Subtype of ADHD in which individuals have symptoms of both inattention and hyperactivity–impulsivity.

**ADHD–predominantly hyperactive–impulsive type** Subtype of ADHD in which individuals have as a primary symptom a high amount of movement and an inability to "put on the brakes" before acting.

**ADHD–predominantly inattentive type** Subtype of ADHD in which individuals' inability to attend is a primary symptom.

**adventitious hearing loss** Hearing loss that develops after birth; also called acquired hearing loss.

**adventitious visual impairment** A visual condition that is acquired after birth.

**aesthetic sensitivity** A keen perception of the characteristics and complexity of the arts and the interrelationships of the arts with other domains.

**altruism** Unselfish concern for the welfare of others, a characteristic of many students who are gifted and talented.

**amblyopia** Reduced vision in an eye that did not receive adequate use in early childhood.

**American Association on Intellectual and Developmental Disabilities (AAIDD)** Oldest interdisciplinary organization providing leadership to the field of mental retardation, particularly in the areas of definitions and classification systems (formerly called American Association on Mental Retardation or AAMR).

**American Association on Mental Retardation (AAMR)** Oldest interdisciplinary organization providing leadership to the field of mental retardation, particularly in the areas of definitions and classification systems.

**American Sign Language (ASL)** Visual-gesturing language that has its own rules of grammar distinct from English; used primarily by culturally Deaf people.

**Americans with Disabilities Act (ADA) of 1990** Federal law protecting the civil rights of individuals with disabilities that applies to public and private sectors and addressing matters such as transportation, public accommodations, and telecommunications.

**amplification** Use of hearing aids and other electronic devices to increase the loudness of sound and reduce background noise so that select sounds may be received and understood more easily.

**aniridia** Rare genetic eye condition in which the iris is missing.

**annual goals** IEP component that consists of statements of the major accomplishments expected for the student during the upcoming twelve months; must be able to be objectively measured.

**annual review** Required meeting of parents and school professionals, occurring at least once each year, to review a student's IEP and set goals for the next year.

**aphasia** Any language impairment, receptive or expressive, that is caused by brain damage.

**applied academic skill** Skill taught to students that has immediate applicability to day-to-day life. An example is making change for a dollar.

**aqueous humor** Clear fluid between the cornea and the lens that provides nourishment to the eye.

**articulation** Movement of the tongue, teeth, lips, and palate to produce the sounds of a language.

**articulation disorder** Speech disorder involving the abnormal production of sounds, including additions, omissions, substitutions, and distortions.

**Asperger syndrome** A pervasive developmental disorder that is considered part of autism spectrum disorders and characterized by impairment in social interactions.

**assistive listening devices** Hard-wired or wireless transmitting and receiving instruments that send sound from a microphone directly to the listener, minimizing the effect of distance, noise, and reverberation on clarity.

**assistive technology** Devices and services that improve the functional capabilities of students with disabilities.

**asthma** Lung disease that causes episodes of extreme difficulty in breathing; most common chronic illness among children.

**ataxic cerebral palsy** Rare type of cerebral palsy in which balance and fine-motor skills are affected, often causing individuals to seem clumsy.

**athetoid cerebral palsy** Type of cerebral palsy in which individuals cannot control their muscles and so they may have sudden and unexpected twisting motions or other movements.

**attention deficit disorder (ADD)** 1980 term to describe individuals with the disorder now called attention deficit–hyperactivity disorder; it noted the condition could exist with or without hyperactivity.

**attention deficit–hyperactivity disorder (ADHD)** Psychiatric disorder with symptoms occurring before age seven that includes a pervasive and significant pattern of inattention, impulsivity, and/or hyperactivity–impulsivity.

**audiogram** Graph on which a person's ability to hear different pitches (frequencies) at different volumes (intensities) of sound is recorded.

**audiological evaluation** Specialized series of hearing tests to determine if a hearing loss exists as well as to quantify and qualify hearing in terms of the degree of hearing loss, the type of hearing loss, and the configuration of the hearing loss.

**augmentative and alternative communication (AAC)** Strategies for compensating for an individual's communication limitations or disabilities.

**augmentative communication devices (ACDs)** Adapted high- or light-technological aids that provide students with alternatives to speech to convey their messages.

**authentic assessment** Ongoing assessment process that occurs within the student's natural environment and includes observation of a student's performance as well as the necessary supports for the student. Authentic assessment also includes work samples that the student has produced.

**autism spectrum disorders** Contemporary term used to speak collectively about autism.

**autistic disorder** A pervasive developmental disorder that is considered part of autism spectrum disorders. This diagnosis is reserved for individuals who display social interaction and communication impairments, as well as repetitive, stereotypic, and restricted interests and activities prior to thirty-six months of age; often accompanied by moderate or severe mental retardation.

**autonomy** State of being self-sufficient and self-reliant.

**behavior inhibition** The ability to regulate one's attention and how often it switches, and the behavior that accompanies this ability; students with ADHD have difficulties with behavior inhibition.

**behavior intervention plan (BIP)** Set of strategies designed to address the function of a student's behavior in order to change it.

**behavior patterns** Customary ways of conducting oneself.

**behaviorism** Theory that all behaviors are learned, including those that are inappropriate, and that such behaviors can be addressed by teaching other, more appropriate behaviors.

**benchmark** A type of short-term objective included on the IEP.

**bilateral hearing loss** Hearing loss in both ears.

**bilingual–bicultural (Bi–Bi) approach** Teaching students ASL as the primary language of instruction and English as a second language for reading and writing print; its goal is for students to function in both the Deaf and hearing cultures.

**bilingual education** An approach that is often used with English language learners (ELLs) in which the student's dominant language is used along with English for instructional purposes.

**bilingual special education teacher** Professional who is knowledgeable about both bilingual education and special education.

**blindness** Disability in which an individual has no vision or has only the ability to detect the presence or absence of light.

**braille** System of tactile reading and writing that uses various combinations of six embossed dots, arranged in a pattern with two dots across and three dots down, to denote letters, numbers, contractions, punctuation marks, and special symbols.

***Brown v. Board of Education of Topeka, Kansas*** Supreme court case that clarified that "separate cannot be equal," leading to racial desegregation of public schools.

**cataract** Condition in which the lens of the eye is cloudy and cannot transmit light rays properly to the retina.

**central auditory processing disorder (CAPD)** Condition in which the brain of a person who has normal hearing does not effectively interpret the auditory information that comes from the ears.

**cerebral palsy (CP)** Group of nonprogressive conditions involving muscle control, posture, and movement; literally means brain paralysis.

**child find** State systems that support zero reject goal by alerting the public that services are available for students with disabilities and otherwise ensuring that students are identified.

**childhood apraxia of speech** Expressive speech disorder in which a child is unable to use the tongue, lips, and other speech structures to easily produce the sounds for language.

**choroid** Part of the eye between the retina and sclera composed of layers of blood vessels that nourish the back of the eye.

**chronic condition** Medical disorder that exists all the time, does not change significantly, and cannot be cured.

**ciliary body** Component of the middle layer of the eye that produces aqueous humor.

**clean intermittent catheterization (CIC)** Health service procedure that enables individuals to relieve their bladders.

**cleft lip and/or palate** Fourth most common birth defect; a separation between the two sides of the lip that often involves the upper jaw and palate such that an opening exists in the roof of the mouth.

**clinical low-vision evaluation** Examination performed by an optometrist or ophthalmologist who specializes in low vision to determine whether an individual with a visual impairment would benefit from the use of optical devices, nonoptical devices, or other strategies to enhance visual functioning.

**closed head injury** Injury in which the brain is damaged by bouncing around inside the skull without physical damage occurring to the skull itself.

**cluttering** Fluency disorder that occurs when an individual speaks in bursts or pauses in unexpected places during speech.

**cochlea** Part of the inner ear that is shaped like a snail shell and contains thousands of tiny hair cells that vibrate in response to sound. These vibrations are converted into electrical signals that are carried to the brain by the auditory nerve to be interpreted and given meaning. Damage to these hair cells can be a cause of sensorineural deafness.

**cochlear implant** Electronic device surgically implanted to stimulate nerve endings in the inner ear (cochlea) in order to receive and process sound and speech.

**cognitive disability** Term sometimes used synonymously with mental retardation, although it also may include other conditions (e.g., autism).

**cognitive impairment** Term sometimes used synonymously with mental retardation and often considered a newer, less stigmatizing description of this disability.

**cognitive style** Inclination to take a particular approach or orientation to thinking and learning.

**collaboration** Style for direct interaction between at least two coequal parties voluntarily engaged in shared decision making as they work toward a common goal.

**communication** The exchange of information and knowledge among participants that is a basic human need. It requires a message, a sender, a receiver, and a channel.

**communication disorder** Term sometimes used synonymously with speech and language disorders, but also likely to be used in discussing individuals who have hearing loss.

**communication skills** Words chosen and the way they are expressed, coupled with facial expressions, posture, and other nonverbal signals.

**communicative intent** Characteristic of many students with autism in which they do not seek to obtain the attention of others and do not communicate for social purposes.

**community-based instruction (CBI)** Highly individualized instruction in the community where students can sample different types of jobs and become accustomed to accessing community facilities. This instruction reflects the interests of students, while helping them to explore new possibilities.

**comorbidity** The simultaneous occurrence of two disabilities, disorders, or conditions.

**complexity** A feature of curriculum that requires exploration of multiple perspectives, issues, variables, and relationships.

**conduct disorder** The most common type of social maladjustment, described in the *Diagnostic and Statistical Manual of Mental Disorders,* that includes aggression, destruction of property, lying or stealing, or serious rule violation (e.g., running away).

**conductive hearing loss** Hearing loss caused by the failure of sound waves to reach the inner ear through the normal air conduction channels of the outer and middle ear. In children, conductive loss often is medically correctable.

**congenital hearing loss** Hearing loss that is present at birth.

**congenital visual impairment** Visual condition that is present before or at birth.

**consultation** Voluntary process in which one professional assists another to address a problem concerning a third party; in schools, consultants often are psychologists or other specialists, consultees often are teachers, and clients usually are students.

**continuous performance tests (CPTs)** Assessment instruments designed to require a student to sustain attention in order to respond correctly to test items.

**continuous progress monitoring** Data gathered as an ongoing part of instruction, often part of response to intervention (RTI).

**continuum of placements** The range of settings in which students with disabilities receive their education.

**control of emotions and motivation** Mental activity that involves setting aside frustration or other emotions in order to complete a task.

**cornea** The transparent outermost layer of the eye that both protects it and has a major role in the process of refraction.

**correlated constraints** When children's lives are permeated with several risk factors, those factors constrain the development of positive adjustment.

**cortical visual impairment** Condition in which damage to the part of the brain dealing with sight results in the images received in the eyes not being interpreted correctly.

**co-teaching** Service delivery model in which two educators, one typically a general education teacher and one a special education teacher or other specialist, combine their expertise to jointly teach a heterogeneous group of students, some of whom have disabilities or other special needs, in a single classroom for part or all of the school day.

**creativity** Capacity for innovation, originality, expressiveness, and imagination and the ability to manipulate ideas in fluent, flexible, elaborate, and original ways.

**criterion-referenced test** Assessment designed to determine whether a student has learned a specific body of information against an absolute standard rather than a comparative standard.

**cultural dissonance** Significant discrepancy between two or more cultural frames of reference.

**cultural familial retardation** Dated view of mental retardation, usually mild, for which a specific cause could not be identified, and so it was assumed to be a result of the family's characteristics and living conditions.

**culture** Complex system of underlying beliefs and attitudes that shapes the thoughts and behaviors of a group of people.

**curiosity** Strong need to know and to understand; a characteristic of many students who are gifted and talented.

**curriculum-based measurement (CBM)** Approach to assessment that measures achievement by sampling a student's understanding of the classroom curriculum.

**curriculum compacting** Educational practice in which the goals of an instructional unit are identified, student mastery of all or part of the goals is documented, and alternative instruction is provided as appropriate.

**curriculum flexibility** A combination of learning options responsive to learner needs and contextual demands; options include acceleration through grade skipping, scaling of objectives, enrichment options, and out-of-school options.

**deaf** Hearing loss that is so severe that the student has difficulty processing linguistic information through hearing (with or without amplification) and that adversely affects educational performance.

**Deaf community** The lives and activities of a group of people who have shared experiences relating to deafness and who use American Sign Language as their primary means of communication.

**Deaf culture** The history, contributions, values, and customs of the Deaf community.

**decibel** Logarithmic measure of the intensity or loudness of sound; commonly expressed as dB.

**depression** Mental illness with symptoms that include chronic and significant feelings of sadness and hopelessness, and may include thoughts of death.

**depth** A feature of curriculum that allows for exploration of a topic or concept beyond what is normally addressed.

**developmental disability** Term sometimes used synonymously with *mental retardation.*

**developmentally appropriate practices** Use of strategies and approaches based on day-to-day decisions about individual students within the context of their families and cultural and social values.

**dialect** The structure of language and the rules that govern it.

**differentiation** Modifying curriculum and other services to meet specific needs of individual learners.

**diplegia** Paralysis of both arms or both legs.

**direct instruction (DI)** A comprehensive, highly structured, teacher-led instructional approach that emphasizes maximizing not only the quantity of instruction students receive but also the quality.

**discrete trial training (DTT)** Highly specialized intervention for young students with autism spectrum disorders in which the teacher gives a prompt to which the student attends, a command for the student to perform, and finally a reward to the student for the desired behavior.

**disproportionate representation** Instances in which a particular group is represented significantly more or less than would be expected based on the percentages of those who comprise that group in the general population.

**distortions** Articulation disorder that occurs when a sound not found in the individual's language is used in place of another sound.

**domain-specific** An ability or intense interest in a particular area of inquiry such as mathematics or music.

**dominant culture** Culture of those in power.

**Down syndrome** Genetic cause of mental retardation in which an extra chromosome is present in the twenty-first chromosome pair. Individuals with Down syndrome are usually short in stature, have straight hair and slanting eyelids, and may have hearing disabilities or heart conditions.

**Duchenne muscular dystrophy** One type of a group of progressive genetic disorders involving a deficiency in the protein dystrophin that results in muscle degeneration; death usually occurs early in adulthood.

**due process** Procedures specified in IDEA for making all the critical decisions that are part of special education.

**dynamic assessment** Ongoing identification of student learning needs and ability.

**dyscalculia** An impairment in the ability to solve mathematical problems or to comprehend mathematical concepts.

**dysgraphia**   An impairment in the ability to produce written language.

**dyslexia**   An impairment in the ability to read or comprehend written language.

**early childhood special educator**   Professional who works with children with disabilities ages birth to five years old, including kindergarten; also called early interventionist.

**echolalia**   Behavior of some individuals with disabilities in which they repeat words and phrases that have been uttered by someone else with little or no understanding of their conventional meanings.

**educational blindness**   Disability in which the auditory and tactile senses generally are used for learning during the school years, often including the use of braille.

**educational interpreter**   Professional who translates spoken words into sign language for students who are deaf or significantly hard of hearing.

**eminence**   Adult achievement of a high level in a particular field after years of productivity.

**emotional and behavior disorders (EBD)**   Term preferred by professionals to describe emotional disabilities.

**emotional disturbance (ED)**   Term used in IDEA to describe the disability that students with emotional and behavior disorders have.

**emotional intensity**   Capacity to focus emotions for long periods on a single subject or idea.

**English as a second language (ESL)**   Practice of directly teaching English to individuals who speak another language.

**English language learners (ELLs)**   Students who are learning English as a second language.

**enrichment**   Extending normal curriculum with different examples and associations that build complex ideas on the basis of the general curriculum.

**environmental supports**   Changes to students' surroundings that help them function successfully.

**epilepsy**   Neurological condition in which damage to the brain leads to sudden, uncontrolled bursts of electrical activity that may be seen as seizures.

**episodic condition**   Medical disorder that periodically occurs with intensity but that at other times is dormant; an example of an episodic condition is asthma.

**executive functions**   The mental activities that help individuals regulate their behaviors.

**expanded core curriculum**   Curriculum encompassing the range of skills that address disability-specific needs of students' visual impairments, including communication skills, social skills, daily living skills, and orientation and mobility skills.

**expressive language**   An individual's ability to produce language.

**externalizing behaviors**   Behavior excesses displayed by students with emotional and behavior disorders in which actions are directed at others (e.g., hitting, shouting).

**extrinsic motivation**   Reason to act on the basis of an incentive separate from the individual (e.g., money or a prize).

**fetal alcohol effect (FAE)**   Mild form of fetal alcohol syndrome (FAS).

**fetal alcohol syndrome (FAS)**   Prenatal, preventable cause of mild to moderate mental retardation resulting from maternal alcohol consumption. FAS is considered the leading cause of mental retardation.

**field independent**   Inclination to be analytical in processing information, such that consideration of surrounding context is not requisite to understanding.

**field sensitive**   Inclination to take a holistic approach to processing information, such that consideration of contextual variables becomes paramount to developing understanding.

**fluctuating hearing loss**   Hearing loss that varies from day to day. Some days a student may hear better or worse depending on a variety of factors (e.g., colds and allergies).

**fluency**   Ability to speak without hesitations that interfere with clear communication.

**fluency disorder**   Speech disorder in which hesitations during speech interfere with communication.

**fragile X syndrome**   Most common form of inherited mental retardation, transmitted from mother to child and causing a mutation in one of the genes in the X chromosome. Also called Martin-Bell syndrome.

**free appropriate public education (FAPE)**   Core principle in IDEA specifying that students with disabilities are entitled to receive an education designed to address their special needs, at no cost to parents.

**functional academics**   The reading, writing, math, and other related skills needed for independent living.

**functional behavior assessment (FBA)**   Multidimensional problem solving strategy required in IDEA for students experiencing serious behavior problems. It includes analyzing a student's behavior within the context of the setting in which it is occurring for the purpose of deciding the function the behavior is serving and a way to address it.

**functional blindness**   Disability in which the auditory and tactile senses generally are used for gathering information, often including the use of braille.

**functional–ecological assessment**   Form of authentic assessment that analyzes the typical demands of the environment (what steps others typically engage in to complete activities), identifies natural cues in the environment that exist to prompt expected behavior, documents student performance during meaningful activities, and specifies the discrepancy between expected behavior and student performance. Supports provided to the student are documented and initial considerations are explored that would facilitate more competent performance in meaningful activities.

**functional vision assessment**   Evaluation process to determine whether a student with a visual impairment can use vision for accomplishing daily tasks and to ascertain the student's potential to increase the use of vision.

**generalization**   Ability to learn a task or idea and then apply it in other situations.

**generalized seizure**   Seizure that involves the entire body and may be one of two types: tonic-clonic or absence.

**genetic hearing loss**   Hearing loss caused by the presence of an abnormal gene within one or more chromosomes.

**giftedness**   Advanced development across intellectual areas within a specific academic or arts-related area or unusual organizational power to bring about desired results; also, outstanding abilities capable of leading to high performance.

**glaucoma**   Disease in which damage to the optic nerve occurs when the aqueous humor does not flow properly.

**hard of hearing**   Hearing loss, whether permanent or fluctuating, that adversely affects a student's educational performance but that is not included under the definition of "deaf."

**hearing impairment (HI)**   Term that refers to any degree of hearing loss, from mild to profound, encompassing the terms *deaf* or *hard of hearing*. This term is losing acceptance by deaf persons because the word *impaired* has a negative connotation.

**hearing loss**   General term used when a distinction among various types of hearing impairments is not critical to make.

**hemiplegia**   Type of paralysis involving the arm, leg, and trunk of the body on the same side.

**hyperopia**   Visual impairment that occurs when light entering the eye focuses behind the retina causing individuals to have difficulty seeing items that are close; also called farsightedness.

**idealism** Act of envisioning things in an ideal form; pursuit of one's ideals.

**inclusion** Belief system shared by every member of a school as a learning community, often based on a mission statement or vision, emphasizing the commitment to educate *all* students so they can reach their potential.

**indirect versus direct service** Intervention offered to students by special service providers versus intervention arranged among special service providers and general educators, but implemented by general educators or other school staff. Consultation is an example of an indirect service.

**individualized education program (IEP)** Document prepared by the multidisciplinary team or annual review team that specifies a student's level of functioning and needs; the instructional goals and objectives for the student and how they will be evaluated; the nature and extent of special education, related services, and supplementary aids and services the student will receive; and the initiation date and duration of the services. Each student's IEP is updated annually.

**Individuals with Disabilities Education Act (IDEA)** Federal law, first enacted in 1975, that protects the educational rights of infants, toddlers, children, and youth with disabilities (ages birth to twenty-one).

**integrated related service delivery** Practice of specialists in various disciplines (e.g., occupational therapists, physical therapists, adaptive physical educators) bringing their knowledge, skills, and expertise into students' typical learning environment to assist in the learning process versus removing students to special environments.

**intellectual disabilities (ID)** Contemporary term often used in place of the term *mental retardation.*

**interaction process** Sets of steps professionals use in order to collaborate; interpersonal problem solving is the most often used interaction process.

**internalizing behaviors** Behavior excesses displayed by students with emotional and behavior disorders in which actions are directed inward (e.g., extreme shyness, hypochondria).

**internship** Opportunities for students to work as apprentices in professional settings to gain information about careers and learn from role models in fields of interest.

**interpersonal problem solving** Interaction process in which a group of professionals identifies the problem, generates alternative solutions, implements the agreed-on intervention, and evaluates its outcomes.

**interpreter** Individual who helps people who are deaf or hard of hearing communicate by translating what a hearing person says into signs, spoken words with cues, or some other way of communicating. The interpreter also translates what the deaf person signs or cues into spoken words.

**intervention assistance team (IAT)** Team of teachers, specialists, and administrators that works with a general education teacher to problem solve regarding a student experiencing academic or behavior difficulty and to decide whether referral for possible special education should occur.

**intrinsic motivation** Reason to act on the basis of an incentive that exists within the individual (e.g., a sense of satisfaction).

**iris** Colored portion of the eye with a hole in the middle that is called the pupil.

**job coach** Professional who helps individuals with disabilities to learn behaviors for succeeding in the workplace.

**juvenile diabetes** Metabolic disorder in which the body cannot properly break down sugars and store them.

**juvenile rheumatoid arthritis (JRA)** Type of arthritis diagnosed in children; symptoms include redness, swelling, soreness in one joint or several joints that lasts for more than six weeks.

**knowledge construction** Process by which a particular framework is used to develop, evaluate, and disseminate new information.

**language** Culturally based system of symbols, governed by complex rules, that individuals use for communication.

**language delay** Condition in which children acquire language at slower-than-typical rate; the delay may be mild, moderate, or significant.

**language difference** Variations from standard speech that are considered normal; dialects are an example of a language difference.

**language disorder** Impairments that interfere with language comprehension and use.

***Larry P. v. Riles*** (1972) Federal court case that established that, because of their bias, IQ tests could not be used to identify African American students as having mental retardation.

**learned helplessness** Condition in which an individual who experiences repeated failure expects more failure and loses motivation.

**learning disabilities (LD)** Condition in which a student has a dysfunction in processing information typically found in language-based activities, resulting in interference with learning. Students with LD have average or above average intelligence but experience significant problems in learning how to read, write, and/or compute.

**learning media assessment** Evaluation process that gathers a variety of information to determine the primary and secondary learning media and literacy needs for students with visual impairments; often addresses a student's use of sensory channels and needs for general learning media.

**least restrictive environment (LRE)** Setting most like the one in which other students are educated in which a student with a disability can succeed. The presumption in current law is that the LRE for most students is general education.

**legal blindness** Disability in which distance visual acuity is 20/200 or less in the better eye with the best correction or in which the visual field is restricted to 20 degrees or less; this clinical measurement typically is used for legal purposes and entitlements.

**lens** The part of the eye that changes shape to focus light at the appropriate place at the back of the eye.

**levels of support** AAMR system for classifying individuals with mental retardation based on whether they need intermittent, limited, extensive, or pervasive support. The system deemphasizes reliance on IQ scores and stresses assisting individuals to reach their potential.

**life skills curriculum** A curriculum or learning system that stresses concepts and skills that students with mental retardation or other disabilities need to function independently.

**long-term memory** The brain's mechanism for permanently storing information it takes in.

**low vision** Visual impairment that exists after correction, but one in which the potential exists for the use of vision, with or without low-vision devices, to accomplish daily tasks.

**low-vision devices** Optical and nonoptical devices and strategies that allow an individual with low vision to accomplish near and distant tasks.

**macroculture** Overarching cultural structure of a society represented by the cultural aspects that all members of that society share.

**meaningful curriculum** Chronologically age-appropriate, relevant curriculum provided for each student according to interests, personal goals, and limitations in reaching those goals.

**mediation** Process in which a neutral professional assists parents and school district personnel in resolving disputes concerning any aspect of a student's special education.

**memory** The mental faculty to retain and recall past experience.

**mental disorder** Terminology to describe emotional and behavior disorders as presented in the *Diagnostic and Statistical Manual of Mental Disorders.* These disorders may or may not be included in the IDEA definition of emotional disturbance.

**mental retardation (MR)**   Disability characterized by significantly below average intellectual functioning and deficits in adaptive functioning that occur during the developmental period (that is, prior to age eighteen) that has an adverse effect on education.

**mentor**   Qualified individual who works with students in areas of interest or ability, guiding the students' development and achievement.

**metacognition**   Thinking about thinking, such as the ability to organize thinking before acting or the ability to relate information just learned to other information already stored in the brain.

**microculture**   Subculture within a larger society that demonstrates some cultural characteristics that differ from the larger society.

*Mills v. Board of Education* (1972)   Federal court case based on a class-action lawsuit establishing that all children with disabilities in Washington, D.C., are entitled to public education.

**minimal brain dysfunction**   Early and outdated term that was used to identify children who were thought to have experienced brain injury as evidenced by their learning and behavior characteristics; early term for learning disabilities; also called Strauss syndrome.

**mixed cerebral palsy**   Type of cerebral palsy that includes characteristics of spastic, athetoid, and ataxic cerebral palsy.

**mixed hearing loss**   Hearing loss that is both sensorineural and conductive. A child with mixed loss has problems hearing muffled or quiet sounds. Mixed losses may fluctuate.

**monoplegia**   Type of paralysis involving only one limb.

**mood disorder**   An emotional disorder, described in the *Diagnostic and Statistical Manual of Mental Disorders,* that includes problems with affect. Depression is an example of a mood disorder.

**morpheme**   Smallest unit of a language that has meaning, composed of phonemes, either free (e.g., dad, clock) or bound (e.g., -ing, un-).

**morphology**   Ability to form words using one or more morphemes and using the rules of the language.

**multicultural education**   An approach to education that includes perspectives from and content about diverse groups, embraces diverse cognitive styles, and promotes equity in a diverse society.

**multidisciplinary team**   Team of teachers, specialists, administrators, and parents who assess a student's individual needs, determine eligibility for special education, and develop the IEP.

**Multimodal Treatment Study of Children with ADHD (MTA)**   Large-scale, federally funded research project that explored the effectiveness of various interventions for children with ADHD.

**musculoskeletal disorders**   Physical disabilities that are the result of problems related to the skeleton or muscles.

**mutual goal**   Shared goal that is the basis for collaboration; should clearly be stated to achieve collaboration.

**myelomeningocele**   Type of spina bifida that occurs when the spinal cord and its covering protrude from the opening in the spine.

**myopia**   Visual impairment that occurs when light entering the eye focuses in front of the retina causing individuals to have difficulty seeing items that are far away; also called nearsightedness.

**National Joint Committee on Learning Disabilities (NJCLD)**   Group of representatives from ten professional and parent organizations concerned about and working on behalf of individuals with learning disabilities.

**natural supports**   Existing resources in any environment (e.g., classmates, co-workers) that can provide support to an individual with severe and multiple disabilities.

**neurological disorder**   Disorder that occurs because of a problem in the central nervous system, that is, the brain, spinal cord, or nerve endings.

**neurotransmitter**   Chemical that relays information from one part of the brain to another.

**No Child Left Behind Act of 2001 (NCLB)**   Federal school reform legislation reauthorizing the Elementary and Secondary Education Act of 1965 and including increased school accountability for student learning, more choices for parents and students, greater flexibility for schools in the use of funds, and an emphasis on early reading intervention.

**nondiscriminatory evaluation**   Core principle in IDEA establishing that no instruments and procedures used to assess students for special education services shall be biased.

**nonoptical devices**   Devices or strategies that do not involve optics used to improve visual performance of tasks for individuals with low vision; examples include book stands, writing guides, lighting, and large type materials.

**nonverbal communication**   Use of nonspeech modes to convey a message, for example, facial expressions, body gestures, manual signs, pictures, and objects.

**nonverbal learning disability**   Subgroup of students with learning disabilities who cannot interpret nonverbal communication, such as facial expressions, posture, and eye contact.

**norm-referenced test**   Assessment in which the student taking the test is being compared to a large number of students, or norm group.

**omission**   Articulation disorder in which some of the sounds of a word are omitted.

**open head injury**   Injury in which the brain is damaged when the skull is fractured and the membrane surrounding the brain is penetrated.

**ophthalmologist**   Physician specializing in the care of the eyes and visual system, and in the prevention of eye disease and injury.

**oppositional defiant disorder (ODD)**   A disruptive behavior disorder, as described in the *Diagnostic and Statistical Manual of Mental Disorders,* that is identified when students are defiant with adults and vindictive or blaming with peers to an excessive degree over a long period of time.

**optical devices**   Devices that incorporate lens systems to enhance visual functioning for individuals with low vision; examples include magnifiers, monoculars, and binoculars.

**optic nerve**   The structure that transmits images from the eye to the brain.

**optometrist**   Professional trained to identify eye problems and to prescribe corrective lenses.

**oral approach**   Instruction based on the principle that most children who are deaf or hard of hearing can be taught to listen and speak with early intervention and consistent training to develop their hearing potential.

**orientation and mobility skills**   Competencies used by persons with visual impairments to travel safely and efficiently in the environment.

**orthopedic impairment (OI)**   IDEA term that refers to students with physical disabilities.

**orthoses**   Braces and other devices used to stabilize legs and support the weight of an individual with a physical disability so that the person can walk or maintain balance.

**ossicles**   Linkage of the three tiniest bones in the body (malleus, incus, and stapes sometimes respectively called hammer, anvil, and stirrup) providing the mechanical coupling between the ear drum and the cochlea.

**other health impairment**   IDEA term for students having medical conditions that result in limited strength, vitality, or alertness.

**P. L. 94-142**   Education of the Handicapped Act of 1975, later renamed Education of All Handicapped Children Act and currently called the Individuals with Disabilities Education Act, protecting the educational rights of students with disabilities.

**paraeducator**   Individual employed as a noncertified staff member to assist certified staff in carrying out education programs and otherwise helping in the instruction of students with disabilities; also called a *paraprofessional.*

**paraplegia**   Paralysis involving both legs.

**PARC v. The Commonwealth of Pennsylvania (1972)** Federal court case that established the right of all children with mental retardation in Pennsylvania to a public education.

**parity** Collaboration concept that participants' contributions are equally valued whether those contributions are great or small.

**partial participation** Term given to students' levels of participation in an activity when they are unable to fully perform an activity on their own but can engage in some parts of the activity with supports as needed.

**partial seizure** Type of seizure in which the electrical discharge affects only part of the brain; symptoms may involve twitching or rapid eye blinks.

**peer tutoring** Approach to peer-mediated instruction in which students are partnered, provided with instructional materials that they are to learn, and expected to help each other in accomplishing the learning goal.

**perfectionism** Striving for a self-imposed advanced goal or unrealistic standard; characteristics and behaviors include compulsive work habits, extensive attention to detail, rigid routine, and unrealistically high standards for self and others.

**person-centered approach** Form of authentic assessment that focuses on the unique characteristics and interests of the student and not on any predetermined set of skills, as usually occurs on a formal assessment.

**pervasive developmental disorder (PDD)** Clinically described disorder in which autism is included, characterized by severe and pervasive impairment in several areas of development: reciprocal social interaction skills, communication skills, or the presence of stereotyped behavior, interests, and activities.

**pervasive developmental disorder not otherwise specified (PDD-NOS)** Clinically diagnosed disorder, associated with autism, in which there is a severe and pervasive impairment in the development or reciprocal social interaction association, with impairment in either verbal or nonverbal communication skills or with the presence of stereotyped behavior, interests, and activities, but criteria are not met for a specific pervasive developmental disorder.

**phenylketonuria (PKU)** Inherited metabolic disorder that occurs when the body is unable to produce the chemicals needed to convert other, toxic chemicals into harmless products. Treatment generally includes a lifelong dietary regimen.

**phoneme** Set of sounds on which a language is based.

**phonemic awareness** Ability to distinguish among the subtly different sounds that make up a language.

**phonological awareness** Ability to hear and manipulate the sounds of a language.

**phonology** Ability to hear the sounds used in a language and to use them correctly in words.

**physical restraint** Emergency intervention, generally implemented only when a student presents immediate serious threat of danger to self or others and personnel are appropriately trained, in which a teacher or another professional restricts a students' freedom of movement, physical activity, or access to his body.

**positive behavior supports (PBS)** A functional and data-based approach to responding to student behaviors with an emphasis on skill development.

**postlingual hearing loss** Hearing loss that occurs after a child has learned to speak.

**Prader-Willi syndrome** Form of inherited mental retardation caused by any of several types of mutation on chromosome 15.

**pragmatics** Function or use of language within a social context; each language has a unique set of rules that governs pragmatics.

**precocity** Demonstrating early development or maturity in ways such as early language development, ability to ask complex questions, rapid learning, extensive vocabulary, or unusual attention span.

**prelingual hearing loss** Hearing loss that occurs prior to speech and language development.

**present level of educational performance** Required IEP component comprising information about a student's current level of academic achievement, social skills, behavior, communication skills, and other functioning areas.

**priming** Intervention in which a parent, teacher, other professional, or trusted peer previews with a student the actual materials that will be used in a lesson the day, morning, or evening before the activity occurs in order to prepare the student for that instruction.

**principles of special methods** Instructional techniques and strategies used by VI specialists to assure that learning is optimized for students with visual impairments, including the use of concrete experiences, learning by doing, and unifying experiences.

**progressive condition** Medical disorder that gets worse over time and may lead to death.

**prompt** Cue designed to get a student to perform a specific behavior.

**prosody** Tone and inflection used when speaking; an area of difficulty for many students with autism spectrum disorders.

**proxemics** Study of acceptable spatial distances between people of various cultures and backgrounds; an area of difficulty for many students with autism spectrum disorders.

**psychological processes** Function of the brain, measured indirectly, through which it takes information in, interprets it, and acts on it.

**psychosocial factors** Influences on student's psychological and social development that include the people around them, the events they experience, and their living conditions.

**pupil** Opening in the center of the iris whose size determines the amount of light that enters the eye.

**receptive language** An individual's ability to comprehend language.

**reconstitution** Mental activity that involves the ability to break down what is observed or learned and to combine parts in order to perform new actions.

**refraction** Process of bending light rays that is part of vision.

**related services** Services required through IDEA for students with disabilities that enable them to benefit from special education. May include transportation, speech/language therapy, and adaptive physical education, among others.

**residential program** Service delivery option for students with extremely serious or complicated disabilities when education in a less restrictive setting is determined by the IEP team not to be possible. In residential programs, students live at the school, attending classes and participating in therapeutic and recreational activities.

**resilience** Ability to recover and not experience long-term harm from episodes of stress or single negative experiences.

**resonance** The nasal or oral aspect of sound during speech.

**response to intervention (RTI)** Approach (first authorized in IDEA 2004) to identifying students as having learning disabilities based on the extent to which their learning accelerates or fails to accelerate when provided with increasingly intense instructional interventions.

**retina** Innermost layer of the eye consisting of the light-sensitive membrane that covers the back wall of the eyeball connecting the rest of the eye to the optic nerve.

**retinitis pigmentosa** Group of diseases that includes deterioration of the retina and leads to problems with peripheral vision and night vision.

**retinopathy of prematurity** Disease usually occurring in premature babies in which abnormal blood vessels grow in the retina causing visual impairment.

**rote memory** Ability to easily remember things without necessarily knowing what they mean.

**school counselor** Professional who works with all students, including those with disabilities, to solve problems related to the social or affective domains.

**school nurse** Professional responsible for all students in a school, including those with disabilities, who conducts vision and hearing screenings, ensures all immunization records are on file, provides routine assistance for ill students, manages the distribution of medications students may take, and contributes information to other professionals about students' medical conditions.

**school psychologist** Professional licensed to administer intelligence tests and other assessments that are used to determine whether a student is eligible to receive special education services; also communicates this information to parents and assists teachers in addressing student social and behavior problems.

**school social worker** Professional who coordinates the efforts of educators, families, and outside agency personnel to ensure that students receive all the supports they need.

**sclera** White portion of the eye that helps it maintain its shape.

**seclusion** Intervention, generally implemented only when other behavior strategies have not been successful and only with clear safety procedures in place, in which a student is involuntarily confined to a room, left alone, and prevented from leaving.

**Section 504 of the Rehabilitation Act of 1973** Federal civil rights law protecting individuals with functional disabilities. Provides protection for some students not eligible for services through IDEA.

**seizure disorder** Neurological condition in which damage to the brain leads to sudden, uncontrolled bursts of electrical activity that may be seen as seizures; Epilepsy.

**self-advocacy** Extent to which a student can identify supports needed to succeed and communicate that information effectively to others, including teachers and employers.

**self-determination** Rights of students with disabilities to make plans for their lives that reflect their wishes and those of their families, not just those of professionals.

**self-directed speech** Mental activity that enables individuals to reflect on how they are doing, to problem solve, and to follow instructions; also called self-talk.

**self-esteem** An individual's overall regard for himself or herself as a person.

**self-fulfilling prophecy** The idea that professionals and others create disabilities or learning problems in students who are nondisabled by treating them as though they are disabled.

**self-stimulatory behavior** Repetitive, stereotyped behavior that has no apparent function; examples include rocking and hand flapping.

**semantics** Content of a language, the meaning and precision of the words selected for communication.

**sensorineural hearing loss** Permanent hearing loss caused by failure or damage of auditory fibers in the inner ear (cochlea) and/or damage to the neural system.

**shared accountability** Collaboration concept in which participants jointly accept the outcomes of their decisions, positive or negative.

**shared resources** Collaboration concept in which each participant contributes something in order to foster shared ownership of the goal that is the purpose of the collaboration.

**shared responsibility** Collaboration concept in which participants jointly make critical decisions, but they often divide the labor for achieving them.

**sheltered English** An instructional approach that uses linguistic scaffolding to facilitate comprehension.

**short-term memory** Brain's mechanism for temporarily storing information it takes in; if information in short-term memory is not saved in long-term memory, it is lost.

**short-term objective** Description of a step followed in order to achieve an annual goal on an IEP; sometimes called a benchmark.

**sickle cell disease** Medical disorder that affects the part of the red blood cells that carries oxygen from the lungs to other parts of the body; the most common symptom is pain.

**social maladjustment** A pattern of willful refusal to conform to acceptable standards of conduct that includes conduct disorders and oppositional defiant disorder. Students who are socially maladjusted put their own needs above all others and do not show genuine signs of guilt or remorse.

**social story** Individualized text or story that describes a specific social situation from the student's perspective; its purpose is to help the student know how to respond appropriately to the described situation.

**socioeconomic status (SES)** A measure of an individual's educational and income level.

**spastic cerebral palsy** Most common type of cerebral palsy in children affecting approximately two-thirds of those with this neurological condition; muscles are stiff and movements are awkward.

**spatial ability** Ability to mentally visualize and manipulate objects, translating into adeptness of physical manipulation and creativity.

**special education** Specialized instruction that students with disabilities are entitled to receive as articulated in IDEA.

**special education teacher** Professional who provides day-to-day instruction and other support for students with disabilities.

**specific language impairment (SLI)** Language disorder that cannot be explained by a physical disability, mental retardation, hearing loss, or another disability.

**speech** Use of the oral channel for exchanging information and knowledge.

**speech and language disorders** Collective term for all the disorders that can occur within the IDEA category called *speech and language impairment.*

**speech disorder** Problem with articulation, voice, or fluency.

**speech or language impairment** Term used in IDEA to refer to speech and language disorders.

**speech reading** Interpretation of lip and facial movements in order to understand speech; also called lip reading. Used by people with hearing loss who communicate orally and by some people who become deaf or hard of hearing later in life.

**speech/language pathologist** Specialist with expertise in meeting students' communication needs, including articulation and language development.

**spina bifida** Neurological physical disability in which the bones of the spine do not close properly.

**spinal cord injury** Group of neurological physical disabilities that occur when there is a break, severe bruise, or other damage to the spinal cord that affects motor and sensory functions.

**stereotypic behavior** Repeated behaviors that serve no constructive function; examples include flapping the hands and rocking.

**stimulant medication** The most commonly prescribed medication for students with ADHD; examples include Ritalin, Dexedrine, Cylert, Adderall, and Focalin.

**stimulus overselectivity** Characteristic of students with autism spectrum disorders in which they attend to only one item or object to the exclusion of others and to the detriment of understanding their environments, or a pattern of responding that has little to do with knowledge.

**strabismus** Condition in which an individual cannot align both eyes simultaneously; sometimes colloquially referred to as "crossed eyes."

**strategy instruction** Method of teaching students techniques, principles, or rules applicable in many learning situations that guide them to complete tasks independently.

**strengths-based assessment** Measurement of students' social and emotional strengths, the characteristics that give them confidence, and traits that help them cope with adversity.

**stuttering** Most common fluency disorder occurring when a person's speech is broken by sound repetitions, prolonged sounds, or unanticipated stoppages of sound.

**substitutions** Articulation disorder in which one sound is used when another is correct (e.g., wan for ran).

**supplementary aids and services (SAS)** A range of supports provided in general education classes or other education-related settings that enable students with disabilities to be educated with children who are not disabled to the maximum extent appropriate.

**supported employment** Practice of assisting adults with disabilities to obtain jobs in the competitive market (not a sheltered workshop) and providing the necessary physical, instructional, and social support to ensure success for the employee.

**syntax** Ability to recognize and follow the rules of a language for the correct order of words during communication.

**systemic bias** Favoritism toward a particular group that occurs at multiple levels within a society or institution; such favoritism becomes an implicit part of the functioning of that society or institution.

**systems of care** Approach to interagency collaboration for the benefit of students with emotional and behavior disorders based on a coordinated network of service providers and guided by core values and principles.

**talent** Traditionally defined as extraordinary ability in a specific area, but now used interchangeably with giftedness.

**TASH** Formerly The Association for Persons with Severe Handicaps. International advocacy organization for people with disabilities, which actively promotes the full inclusion and participation of persons with disabilities in all aspects of life.

**task analysis** Instructional process for ensuring systematic learning by breaking lengthy or complex tasks into distinct small steps and teaching those steps to students, separately at first and gradually in combination.

**teacher assistance team (TAT)** See *intervention assistance team.*

**team** Two or more interdependent individuals with unique skills and perspectives who interact directly to achieve their mutual goals of providing students with effective educational programs and services.

**tetraplegia** Paralysis involving both arms, both legs, the trunk of the body, and the neck; formerly called quadriplegia.

**theory of mind** Recent theory of autism spectrum disorder emphasizing that individuals with this disability truly do not understand that other people have their own thoughts or points of view.

**three-tiered intervention approach** Use of research-based and increasingly intense interventions, usually in reading, as part of a response to intervention (RTI) model for identifying students as having learning disabilities.

**three-year reevaluation** Triannual process of reassessing the needs of a student with a disability; carried out by a multidisciplinary team.

**tonic-clonic seizure** Most well known of generalized seizures; person first stiffens, loses consciousness, and falls; then arms and legs jerk or contract; formerly called grand mal seizure.

**toxoplasmosis** Infection caused by a parasite carried by more than sixty million individuals; dangerous usually only to expectant women who can pass it on to their unborn children, causing them to develop mental retardation or blindness.

**traumatic brain injury (TBI)** Acquired injury to the brain caused by an external physical force, resulting in total or partial functional disability or psychosocial impairment.

**trisomy 21** Term used for Down syndrome; the twenty-first chromosome pair has an extra chromosome, or three (tri) parts.

**unilateral hearing loss** Hearing loss in only one ear; now believed to adversely affect the educational process in a significant percentage of students who have it.

**universal design for learning (UDL)** Based on concepts from architecture and product development, an approach for teaching and learning emphasizing the need to address in instructional planning the entire diversity of student needs.

**universal newborn hearing screening** Program for testing babies' hearing soon after they are born.

**uveal tract** Second layer of the eye that provides nutrition to it.

**values** Cultural elements held in great esteem or considered to be of great importance by a society.

**visual acuity** Clarity or sharpness of vision.

**visual efficiency** Extent to which an individual with a visual impairment uses vision to effectively accomplish daily tasks.

**visual field** Range in which an individual can see objects centrally or peripherally.

**visual impairment** Any level of vision loss that has an impact on an individual's ability to complete daily tasks; this term is often used to include both blindness and low vision.

**visual impairment (VI) specialist** Individual with extensive knowledge of visual impairments who usually takes a lead role in the assessment of students with visual impairments, who manages and delivers special education services to these students, and who provides consultation to other school professionals on students with visual impairments.

**vitreous humor** Clear viscous substance that fills the large cavity behind the lens of the eye.

**voice** Dimension of speech that includes pitch (highness or lowness of sound), intensity (loudness of speech sound), and quality (smoothness or hoarseness of speech sound).

**voice disorder** Condition in which an individual has difficulty with pitch, intensity, vocal quality, or resonance.

**working memory** Mental activity that enables students to remember tasks, to determine the amount of time they have to complete the tasks, and to learn from past mistakes.

**wraparound services** An individually designed set of services involving multiple school and community agencies intended to provide the supports necessary for students with emotional or behavior disorders and their families in order to keep students in their homes.

**zero reject** Core principle of IDEA specifying that no student with a disability, regardless of its nature or severity, can be denied an education.

# references

Abel, M. H., & Sewell, J. (1999). Stress and burnout in rural and urban secondary school teachers. *Journal of Educational Research, 92,* 287–293.

Abelev, M. S. (2009). Advancing out of poverty: Social class worldview and its relation to resilience. *Journal of Adolescent Research, 24,* 114–141.

Abell, M. M., Bauder, D. K., & Simmons, T. J. (2006). Access to the general curriculum: A curriculum and instruction perspective for educators. *Intervention in School and Clinic, 41,* 82–86.

Abelson, M. A., & Woodman, R. W. (1983). Review of research on team effectiveness: Implications for teams in schools. *School Psychology Review, 12,* 125–136.

Ableser, J. (2002, January). *Zero tolerance/IDEA 97 and equal educational opportunity—not!.* Paper presented at the Annual Safe Schools Coalition, Inc., and National Alternative Education Association Joint National Conference on Alternatives to Suspension, Expulsion, and Dropping Out of School, Kissimmee, FL. (ERIC Document Reproduction Service No. ED462514)

Abrams, J., Ferguson, J., & Laud, L. (2001). Assessing ESOL students. *Educational Leadership, 59*(1), 62–65.

Achenbach, T. M. (1991a). *Child behavior checklist for ages 4–18, parent form.* Burlington, VT: Department of Psychiatry, University of Vermont.

Achenbach, T. M. (1991b). *Child behavior checklist, teacher's report form.* Burlington, VT: Author.

Achenbach, T. M., & Rescorla, L. A. (2001). *Manual for ASEBA School-Age Forms & Profiles.* Burlington, VT: University of Vermont, Research Center for Children, Youth, & Families.

Achilles, C. M., Finn, F. K., & Pate-Bain, H. (2002). Measuring class size: Let me count the ways. *Educational Leadership, 59,* 24–26.

Achilles, G. M., McLaughlin, M. J., & Croninger, R. G. (2007). Sociocultural correlates of disciplinary exclusion among students with emotional, behavioral, and learning disabilities in the SEELS national dataset. *Journal of Emotional and Behavioral Disorders, 15,* 33–45.

Ackerman, B. (2006). Learning self-determination: Lessons from the literature for work with children and youth with emotional and behavioral disabilities. *Child Youth Care Forum, 35,* 327–337.

Acrey, C., Johnstone, C., & Milligan, C. (2005). Using universal design to unlock the potential for academic achievement of at-risk learners. *Teaching Exceptional Children, 38*(2), 22–31.

Adams, C. M. (2003). An evolving field: Twenty-five years later—Spinning our wheels or moving forward, *Roeper Review, 25,* 116–117.

Adams, M. (1990). *Beginning to read: Thinking and learning about print.* Cambridge, MA: The MIT Press.

Adams, P. F., Hendershot, G. E., & Marano, M. A. (1999). Current estimates from the National Health Interview Survey, 1996 (National Center for Health Statistics). *Vital Health Statistics, 10,* 200.

Adams-Chapman, I. (2009). Insults to the developing brain and impact on neurodevelopmental outcome. *Journal of Communication Disorders, 42,* 256–242.

Adcock, J., & Cuvo, A. (2009). Enhancing learning for children with autism spectrum disorders in regular education by instructional modifications. *Research in Autism Spectrum Disorders, 3,* 319–328.

Addeduto, A., Murphy, M. M., Richmond, E. K., Amman, A., Beth, P., Weissman, M. D., Kim, J. S., Cawthon, S. W., & Karadottir, S. (2006). Collaboration in referential communication: Comparison of youth with Down syndrome or fragile X syndrome. *American Journal on Mental Retardation, 111,* 170–183.

Adler, L. A., Spencer, T., & McGough, J. J. (2009). Long-term effectiveness and safety of dexmethylphenidate extended-release capsules in adult ADHD. *Journal of Attention Disorders, 12,* 449–459.

Advokat, C. (2009). What exactly are the benefits of stimulants for ADHD? *Journal of Attention Disorders, 12,* 495–498.

Agency for Toxic Substances and Disease Registry (ATSDR). (2007, August). *Case studies in environmental medicine (CSEM): Lead toxicity—What are the physiologic effects of lead exposure?* Atlanta: Centers for Disease Control and Prevention. Retrieved July 1, 2009 from http://www.atsdr.cdc.gov/csem/lead/pbphysiologic_effects2.html#child

Agran, M., Blanchard, C., & Wehmeyer, M. L. (2000). Promoting transition goals and self-determination through student self-directed learning: The self-determined learning model of instruction. *Education and Training in Mental Retardation and Developmental Disabilities, 35,* 351–364.

Agran, M., & Hughes, C. (2008). Asking student input: Students' opinion regarding their individualized education program involvement. *Career Development for Exceptional Individuals, 31,* 69–76.

Agran, M., Snow, K., & Swaner, J. (1999). Teacher perceptions of self-determination: Benefits, characteristics, strategies. *Education and Training in Mental Retardation and Developmental Disabilities, 34,* 293–301.

Agresta, J. (2004). Professional role perceptions of school social workers, psychologists, and counselors. *Children and Schools, 26,* 151–163.

Aguirre, N., & Hernandez, N. E. (1999). *Characteristics of the culturally and linguistically diverse gifted and talented child.* Baton Rouge, LA: Project GOTCHA, Academic Excellence Program, International Education Consultants.

Aiken, L. R. (1987). *Assessment of intellectual functioning.* Boston: Allyn & Bacon.

Ainge, D., Colvin, G., & Baker, S. (1998). Analysis of perceptions of parents who have children with intellectual disabilities: Implications for service providers. *Education and Training in Mental Retardation and Developmental Disabilities, 33,* 331–341.

Ajuwon, P. M., & Craig, C. J. (2007). Distance education in the preparation of teachers of the visually impaired and orientation and mobility specialists: Profile of a new training paradigm. *RE:view: Rehabilitation Education for Blindness and Visual Impairment, 39,* 3–14.

Ajuwon, P. M., & Oyinlade, A. O. (2008). Educational placement of children who are blind or have low vision in residential and public schools: A national study of parents' perspectives. *Journal of Visual Impairment & Blindness, 102,* 325–339.

Akrami, N., Ekehammar, B., Claesson, M., & Sonnander, K. (2006). Classical and modern prejudice: Attitudes toward people with intellectual disabilities. *Research in Developmental Disabilities, 27,* 605–617.

Akuffo, P. B., & Hodge, S. R. (2008). Roles and responsibilities of adapted physical education teachers in an urban school district. *Education and Urban Society, 40,* 243–268.

Al Otaiba, S., & Smartt, S. M. (2003). Summer sound camp: Involving parents in early literacy intervention for children with speech and language delays. *Teaching Exceptional Children, 35*(1), 30–34.

Alarcon, M., Pennington, B. F., Filipek, P. A., & DeFries, J. C. (2000). Etiology of neuroanatomical correlates of reading disability. *Developmental Neuropsychology, 17,* 339–360.

Albert, R. S. (1994). The achievement of eminence: A longitudinal study of exceptionally gifted boys and their families. In R. F. Subotnik & K. D. Arnold (Eds.), *Beyond Terman: Contemporary longitudinal studies of giftedness and talent* (pp. 282–315). Norwood, NJ: Ablex.

Alberto, P. A., & Fredrick, L. D. (2000). Teaching picture reading as an enabling skill. *Teaching Exceptional Children, 33*(1), 60–64.

Albritten, D., Mainzer, R., & Zigler, D. (2004). NCLB: Failed schools or failed law—Will students with disabilities be scapegoats for school failures? *Educational Horizons, 82,* 153–160.

Alderman, G. L., & Gimpel, G. A. (1996). The interaction between type of behavior problem and type of consultant: Teachers' preferences for professional assistance. *Journal of Educational and Psychological Consultation, 7,* 305–314.

Alexander, D., Gray, D. B., & Lyon, G. R. (1993). Conclusions and future directions. In G. R. Lyon, D. B. Gray, J. F. Kavanaugh, & N. A. Krasnegor (Eds.), *Better understanding learning disabilities: New views from research and their implications for education and public policies* (pp. 346–360). Baltimore: Paul H. Brookes.

Ali, S., & Frederickson, N. (2006). Investigating the evidence base of social stories. *Educational Psychology in Practice, 22,* 355–377.

Allen, S. K., Smith, A. C., Test, D. W., Flowers, C., & Wood, W. M. (2001). The effects of "self-directed IEPs" on student participation in IEP meetings. *Career Development for Exceptional Individuals, 24,* 107–120.

Allen, T. (1986). A study of the achievement patterns of hearing-impaired students: 1974–1983. In A. Schildroth & M. Karchmer (Eds.), *Deaf children in America* (pp. 161–206). San Diego: College-Hill Press.

Allen-Meares, P. (2007). *Social work services in school* (5th ed.). Boston: Allyn and Bacon.

Al-Yagon, M., & Mikulineer, M. (2004). Patterns of close relationships and socioemotional and academic adjustment among school-age children with learning disabilities. *Learning Disabilities Research & Practice, 19,* 12–19.

American Academy of Audiology. (2001). *Diagnosing auditory processing disorders.* Retrieved January 3, 2004, from www.audiology.org/professional/jaaa/11-9a.php

American Academy of Child and Adolescent Psychiatry. (2009, March). *Child and Adolescent Mental Illness Statistics.* Retrieved October 18, 2009 from http://www.aacap.org/cs/root/resources_for_families/child_and_adolescent_mental_illness_statistics

American Academy of Pediatrics. (2000). Clinical practice guideline: Diagnosis and evaluation of the child with attention-deficit/hyperactivity disorder. *Pediatrics, 105,* 1158–1170.

American Association for Employment in Education. (2000). *Education supply and demand in the United States.* Retrieved April 9, 2004, from www.ub-careers.buffalo.edu/aaee/S_DReport2000.pdf

American Association of Colleges for Teacher Education. (1999). *Teacher education pipeline IV: Schools, colleges, and departments of education enrollments by race, ethnicity, and gender.* Washington, DC: Author.

American Cancer Society. (2005). Cancer in children: What is childhood cancer? Retrieved September 3, 2006, from www.cancer.org/docroot/CRI/content/CRI_2_4_1X_Introduction_7.asp?rnav=cri

American College of Medical Genetics. (1994). *Policy statement: Fragile X syndrome—Diagnostic and carrier testing.* Retrieved October 3, 2003, from www.faseb.org/genetics/acmg/pol-16.htm

American Foundation for the Blind. (2004). *Employment statistics for people who are blind or visually impaired: U.S.* Retrieved May 9, 2004, from www.afb.org/Section.asp?SectionID=7&DocumentID=1529

American Foundation for the Blind. (2006). *Statistics and sources for professionals: Prevalence.* Retrieved September 5, 2006, from www.afb.org/Section.asp?SectionID=15&DocumentID=1367#prev

American Obesity Association. (2005). *AOA fact sheet: Obesity in youth.* Retrieved August 20, 2006, from www.obesity.org/subs/fastfacts/obesity_youth.shtml

American Printing House for the Blind. (1999). *Annual register of legally blind persons in educational settings below the college level.* Retrieved November 23, 2003, from www.afb.org/Section.asp?SectionID=15&DocumentID=1367

American Printing House for the Blind. (2003). *Distribution of eligible students based on the federal quota census of January 7, 2002 (fiscal year 2003).* Retrieved May 9, 2004, from http://sun1.aph.org/fedquotpgm/dist02.html

American Printing House for the Blind. (2006). *Distribution of eligible students based on the federal quota census of January 5, 2004.* Retrieved September 16, 2006, from http://sun1.aph.org/fedauotpgm/dist05.html

American Psychiatric Association. (1980). *Diagnostic and statistical manual of mental disorders* (3rd edition). Washington, DC: Author.

American Psychiatric Association. (1994). *Diagnostic and statistical manual of mental disorders* (4th ed.). Washington, DC: Author.

American Psychiatric Association. (2000). *Diagnostic and statistical manual of mental disorders* (4th ed., Text revision). Washington, DC: Author.

American Psychological Association. (2000, August). *Training for psychologists and other mental health professionals: SAMHSA reauthorization.* Retrieved September 12, 2003, from http://mirror/apa.org/ppo-OLD/psychsamhsa.html

American Speech-Language-Hearing Association Committee on Language. (1982). *Language.* Retrieved December 26, 2003, from www.asha.org/NR/rdonlyres/1F248614-EEF7-4D54-98AD-F3A0692EFC51/0/19_130_1.pdf

American Speech-Language-Hearing Association. (2000). *Guidelines for the roles and responsibilities of school-based speech-language pathologists* (pp. 258–259). Rockville, MD: Author.

American Speech-Language-Hearing Association. (2002). *Early hearing detection and intervention action center.* Retrieved November 11, 2002, from http://professional.asha.org/resources/legislative/ehdi.cfm

American Speech-Language-Hearing Association. (2003). *Tip sheet: Communicating in a diverse society.* Retrieved November 19, 2003, from www.asha.org/about/news/tipsheets/Diverse_society.htm

American Speech-Language-Hearing Association. (2005). *Evidence-based practice in communication disorders* [position statement]. Retrieved October 28, 2006, from www.asha.org/NR/rdonlyres/4837FDFC-576B-4D84-BDD6-8BFF2A803AD3/0/v4PS_EBP.pdf

American Speech-Language-Hearing Association. (2007). *Childhood apraxia of speech* [Position Statement]. Retrieved August 18, 2009 from www.asha.org/policy

Anctil, T. M., Ishikawa, M. E., & Tao Scott, A. (2008). Academic identity development through self-determination: Successful college students with learning disabilities. *Career Development for Exceptional Individuals, 31,* 164–174.

Anderson, J. A. (2000). The need for interagency collaboration for children with emotional and behavioral disabilities and their families. *Families in Society: The Journal of Contemporary Human Services, 81,* 484–493.

Anderson, J. A., Kutash, K., & Duchnowski, A. J. (2001). A comparison of the academic progress of students with EBD and students with LD. *Journal of Emotional and Behavioral Disorders, 9,* 106–115.

Anderson, J. A., & Matthews, B. (2001). We care?. . . for students with emotional and behavioral disabilities and their families. *Teaching Exceptional Children, 33*(5), 34–39.

Anderson, N. B., Hawkins, J., Hamilton, R., & Hampton, J. D. (1999). Effects of transdisciplinary teaming for students with motor disabilities. *Education and Training in Mental Retardation and Developmental Disabilities, 34,* 330–341.

Anderson, S. (2004). *How many languages are there in the world?* Washington, D.C.: Linguistic Society of America. Retrieved August 13, 2009 from www.lsadc.org/info/pdf_files/howmany.pdf

Angell, M. E., Bailey, R. L., & Larson, L. (2008). Systematic instruction for social-pragmatic language skills in lunchroom settings. *Education and Training in Developmental Disabilities, 43,* 342–359.

Angell, M. E., Stoner, J. B., & Sheldon, D. L. (2009). Trust in education: Professionals' perspectives of mothers of children with disabilities. *Remedial and Special Education, 30,* 160–176.

Antia, S., Jones, P., Reed, S., & Kreimeyer, K., (2009). Academic status and progress of deaf and hard-of-hearing students in general education classrooms. *Journal of Deaf Studies and Deaf Education, 14,* 293–311.

Antia, S., & Kreimeyer, K. (1998). Social interaction and acceptance of deaf or hard-of-hearing children and their peers: A comparison of social-skills and familiarity-based interventions. *The Volta Review, 98,* 157–180.

Antia, S., Kreimeyer, K., & Eldredge, N. (1994). Promoting social interaction between young children with hearing impairments and their peers. *Exceptional Children, 60,* 262–275.

Antle, B. J. (2004). Factors associated with self-worth in young people with physical disabilities. *Health and Social Work, 29,* 167–175.

Appendix A, Part B of the Individuals with Disabilities Education Act (20 U.S.C. 1401 et seq.).

Appl, D. J. (2000). Clarifying the preschool assessment process: Traditional practices and alternative approaches. *Early Childhood Education Journal, 27,* 219–225.

Appl, D. J., Troha, C., & Rowell, J. (2001). Reflections of a first-year team: The growth of a collaborative partnership. *Teaching Exceptional Children, 33*(3), 4–8.

Aram, D., Most, T., & Simon, A. B. (2008). Early literacy of kindergartners with hearing impairment: The role of mother-child collaborative writing. *Topics in Early Childhood Special Education, 28,* 31–41.

Arbib, M. A. (2009). Evolving the language-ready brain and the social mechanisms that support language. *Journal of Communication Disorders, 42,* 263–271.

ARC of New Jersey. (2002, October). *Education advocacy: IEP checklist.* North Brunswick, NJ: Author.

Arc, The. (1998, January). Gene therapy and mental retardation. *Genetic Issues in Mental Retardation, 2*(3), 1–6. Retrieved October 10, 2003, from http://thearc.org/pdf/gbr06.pdf

Arc, The. (2004). *Q & A: Introduction to mental retardation.* Retrieved November 1, 2006, from http://www.thearc.org/faqs/intromr.pdf

Archambault, F. X., Westberg, K. L., Brown, S., Hallmark, B., Zhang, W., & Emmons, C. (1993). Classroom practices used with gifted third and fourth grade students. *Journal for the Education of the Gifted, 16,* 103–119.

Arguelles, M. E., Hughes, M. T., & Schumm, J. S. (2000). Co-teaching: A different approach to inclusion. *Principal, 79*(4), 48, 50–51.

Armer, B., & Thomas, B. K. (1978). Attitudes towards interdisciplinary collaboration in pupil personnel service teams. *Journal of School Psychology, 16,* 168–177.

Arndt, J., & Healey, E. C. (2001). Concomitant disorders in school-age children who stutter. *Language, Speech, and Hearing Services in the Schools, 32,* 68–78.

Arndt, S. A., Konrad, M., & Test, D. W. (2006). Effects of the "self-directed IEP" in student participation in planning meetings. *Remedial and Special Education, 27,* 194–207.

Arnold, L. (1995). ADHD sex differences. *Journal of Abnormal Child Psychology, 23,* 555–569.

Arons, B. S., Katz-Leavy, J., Wittig, A. C., & Holden, E. Q. (2002). Too young for ADHD: The potential role of systems of care. *Journal of Developmental and Behavioral Pediatrics, 23,* 57–63.

Arroyos-Jurado, E., & Savage, T. A. (2008). Intervention strategies for serving students with traumatic brain injury. *Intervention in School and Clinic, 43,* 252–254.

Arthritis Foundation. (2004). *Arthritis in children.* Atlanta: Author. Retrieved March 3, 2004, from www.arthritis.org/AFStore/StartRead.asp?idProduct=3369

Arthritis Foundation. (2006). *What is arthritis?* Retrieved August 20, 2006, from www.arthritis.org/resources/gettingstarted/what_is_arthritis.asp

Artiles, A. J. (2003). Special education's changing identity: Paradoxes and dilemmas in views of culture and space. *Harvard Educational Review, 73,* 164–202.

Artiles, A. J., & Bal, A. (2008). The next generation of disproportionality research: Toward a comparative model in the study of equity in ability differences. *Journal of Special Education, 42,* 4–14.

Artiles, A. J., Harris-Murri, N., & Rostenberg, D. (2006). Inclusion as social justice: Critical notes on discourses, assumptions, and the road ahead. *Theory into Practice, 45,* 260–268.

Artiles, A. J., Harry, B., Reschly, D. J., & Chinn, P. C. (2002). Over-identification of students of color in special education: A critical overview. *Multicultural Perspectives, 4*(1), 3–10.

Artiles, A. J., Rueda, R., Salazar, J. J., & Higareda, I. (2005). Within-group diversity in minority disproportionate representation: English language learners in urban school districts. *Exceptional Children, 71,* 283–300.

Artiles, A. J., & Trent, S. C. (1994). Overrepresentation of minority students in special education: A continuing debate. *Journal of Special Education, 27,* 410–437.

Arwood, E. L. (1983). *Pragmaticism.* Rockville, MD: Aspen.

Ashcroft, S. C., Halliday, C., & Barraga, N. C. (1965). *Study II: Effects of experimental teaching on the visual behavior of children educated as though they had no vision.* Nashville: George Peabody College for Teachers.

Ashton, T. M. (2000). Augmentative communication devices: A critical aspect of assistive technology. *Journal of Special Education Technology, 15*(3), 35–38.

Asperger, H. (1944). Die "Autistischen Psychopathen" im Kindesalter [Autistic psychopathy in childhood]. *Archiv fur Psychiatrie und Nervenkrankheiten, 117,* 76–136.

Aspy, R., & Grossman, B. (2006). *The Ziggurat Model: A framework for designing comprehensive interventions for individuals with high-functioning autism and Asperger syndrome.* Shawnee Mission, KS: Autism Asperger Publishing.

Atwater, S. A. C. (2008) Waking up to difference: Teachers, color-blindness, and the effects on students of color. *Journal of Instructional Psychology, 35*(3), 246–253.

Austin, V. L. (2001). Teachers' beliefs about co-teaching. *Remedial and Special Education, 22,* 245–255.

Avoké, S. K. (2003). Make your case . . . Language minority children and youth in special education. *In CASE, 44*(4), 2, 11.

Avoli, M., Rogawski, M. A., & Avanzini, G. (2001). Generalized epileptic disorders: An update. *Epilepsia, 42*(4), 445–457.

Aylward, E. H., Minshew, N. J., Goldsterin, G., Honeycutt, N. A., Augustine, A. M., Yates, K. O., Barta, P. E. et al. (1999). MRI volumes of amygdala and hippocampus in non-mentally retarded autistic adolescents and adults. *Neurology, 53,* 2145–2150.

Bagwell, C. L., Molina, B. S., Pelham, W. E., & Hoza, B. (2001). Attention-deficit hyperactivity disorder and problems in peer relations: Predications from childhood to adolescence. *Journal of American Academy of Child and Adolescent Psychiatry, 40*(11), 1285–1293.

Bahr, M. W., & Kovaleski, J. F. (2006). The need for problem-solving teams: Introduction to the special issue. *Remedial and Special Education, 27,* 2–5.

Bahr, M. W., Walker, K., Hampton, E. M., Buddle, B. S., Freeman, T., Ruschman, N., Sears, J., McKinney, A., Miller, M., & Littlejohn, W. (2006). Creative problem solving for general education intervention teams: A two-year evaluation study. *Remedial and Special Education, 27,* 27–41.

Bailey, I. L., Lueck, A. H., Greer, R. B., Tuan, K. M., Bailey, V. M., & Dornbusch, H. G. (2003). Understanding the relationships between print size and reading in low vision. *Journal of Visual Impairment and Blindness, 97,* 325–334.

Bailey, P. J., & Snowling, M. J. (2002). Auditory processing and the development of language and literacy. *British Medical Bulletin, 63,* 135–146.

Baker, D. J., Horner, R. H., & Sappington, G. (2000). A response to Wehmeyer (1999) and a challenge to the field regarding self-determination. *Focus on Autism and Other Developmental Disorders, 15,* 154–156.

Baker, P. H. (2005). Managing student behavior: How ready are teachers to meet the challenge? *American Secondary Education, 33*(3), 51–64.

Baker, S., Lang, R., & O'Reilly, M. (2009). Review of video modeling with students with emotional and behavioral disorders. *Education and Treatment of Children, 32,* 403–420.

Baldwin, A. Y. (2002). Culturally diverse students who are gifted. *Exceptionality, 10,* 139–147.

Baldwin, A. Y., & Vialle, W. (1999). *The many faces of giftedness: Lifting the mask.* Belmont, CA: Wadsworth.

Baldwin, J. L. (2007). Standards for teachers of students with physical and health disabilities. Physical Disabilities: *Education and Related Services, 26,* 1–7.

Balkany, T., Hodges, A., & Goodman, K. (1996). Ethics of cochlear implantation in young children. *Otolaryngology: Head and Neck Surgery, 114,* 748–755.

Baltodano, H. M., Harris, P. J., & Rutherford, R. B. (2005). Academic achievement in juvenile corrections: Examining the impact of age, ethnicity and disability. *Education and Treatment of Children, 28,* 361–379.

Banda, D. R., Matuszny, R. M., & Therrien, W. J. (2009). Enhancing motivation to complete math tasks using the high-preference strategy. *Intervention in School and Clinic, 44,* 146–150.

Banks, J. A. (1993). Approaches to multicultural curriculum reform. In J. A. Banks & C. M. Banks (Eds.), *Multicultural education: Issues and perspectives* (pp. 195–214). Boston: Allyn & Bacon.

Banks, J. A. (2006). *Cultural diversity and education: Foundations, curriculum, and teaching* (5th ed.). Boston: Allyn & Bacon.

Bardin, J. A., & Lewis, S. (2008). A survey of the academic engagement of students with visual impairments in general education classes. *Journal of Visual Impairment & Blindness, 102,* 472–483.

Barkley, R. A. (1997). *ADHD and the nature of self-control.* New York: Guilford Press.

Barkley, R. A. (1998). Attention-deficit hyperactivity disorder. *Scientific American, 279*(3), 66–71.

Barkley, R. A. (2004). Adolescents with attention-deficit/hyperactivity disorder: An overview of empirically based treatments. *Journal of Psychiatric Practice, 10,* 39–56.

Barkley, R. A. (2006). ADHD in adults: Developmental course and outcome of children with ADHD, and ADHD in clinic-referred adults. In R. A. Barkley (Ed.), *Attention-deficit hyperactivity disorder: A handbook for diagnosis and treatment* (pp. 248–296). New York: Guilford Press.

Barkley, R. A. (2007). School interventions for attention deficit hyperactivity disorder: here to from here, *School Psychology Review, 36,* 279–286.

Barkley, R. A., et al. (2002). International consensus statement on ADHD. *Clinical Child and Family Psychology Review, 5,* 89–111.

Barnes, S. B., & Whinnery, K. W. (2002). Effects of functional mobility skills training for young students with physical disabilities. *Exceptional Children, 68,* 313–324.

Barnett, D. W., Daly, E. J., Jones, K. M., & Lentz, F. E. (2004). Response to intervention: Empirically based special service decisions from single-case designs of increasing the decreasing intensity. *Journal of Special Education, 38,* 66–79.

Barnhill, G., Cook, K., Tebbenkamp, K., & Myles, B. (2002). The effectiveness of social skills intervention: Targeting nonverbal communication for adolescents with Asperger Syndrome and related pervasive developmental delays. *Focus on Autism and Other Developmental Disabilities, 17,* 112–118.

Barnhill, G., Hagiwara, T., Myles, B. S., & Simpson, R. L. (2000). Asperger syndrome: A study of the cognitive profiles of thirty-seven children and adolescents. *Focus on Autism and Other Developmental Disabilities, 15,* 146–153.

Barnhilll, G. (2001). What is Asperger Syndrome? *Intervention in School and Clinic, 36,* 259–265.

Barnhill, G. P. (2005). Functional behavioral assessment in schools. *Intervention in School and Clinic, 40,* 131–143.

Baroff, G. S. (2000). Eugenics, "Baby Doe," and Peter Singer: Toward a more "perfect" society. *Mental Retardation, 38,* 73–77.

Baroff, G. S., & Olley, J. G. (1999). *Mental retardation: Nature, cause, and management* (3rd ed., pp. 1–60). Philadelphia: Taylor & Francis.

Baron-Cohen, S., Ring, H. A., Wheelwright, S., Bullmore, E. T., Brammer, M. J., Simmons, A., & Williams, S. C. (1999). Social intelligence in the normal and autistic brain: An MRI study. *European Journal of Neuroscience, 11,* 1891–1898.

Barraga, N. C. (1964). *Increased visual behavior in low vision children.* New York: American Foundation for the Blind Press.

Bartelt, L., Marchio, T., & Reynolds, D. (1994). *The READS strategy.* Unpublished manuscript, Northern Illinois University.

Barth, R. S. (2006). Improving relationships within the schoolhouse. *Educational Leadership, 63*(6), 9–13.

Barton, M., Robins, D., & Fein, D. (1999). *Modified Checklist for Autism in Toddlers* (M-CHAT). Retrieved October 12, 2009 from http://www.dbpeds .org/articles/detail.cfm?TextID=466

Barton-Arwood, S. M., Wehby, J. H., & Falk, K. B. (2005). Reading instruction for elementary-age students with emotional and behavioral disorders: Academic and behavioral outcomes. *Exceptional Children, 72,* 7–27.

Baruth, L. G., & Manning, M. L. (1992). *Multicultural education of children and adolescents.* Boston: Allyn & Bacon.

Bashir, A. S., Goldhammer, R. F., & Bigaj, S. J. (2000). Facilitating self-determination abilities in adults with LLD: Case study of a postsecondary student. *Topics in Language Disorders, 21,* 52–67.

Bassi, L. J., & Van Buren, M. E. (1999). Sharpening the leading edge. *Training and Development Journal, 53*(1), 23–33.

Bateman, B. D., & Herr, C. M. (2006). *Writing measurable IEP goals and objectives.* Verona, WI: IEP Resources.

Batshaw, M. L. (Ed.). (2002). *Children with disabilities* (5th ed.). Baltimore: Paul H. Brookes.

Batshaw, M. L., Pellegrino, L., & Roizen, N. J. (Eds.). (2007). *Children with disabilities* (6th ed.). Baltimore: Paul H. Brookes Publishing Co.

Bauer, A. M., & Ulrich, M. E. (2002). "I've got a Palm in my pocket": Using handheld computers in an inclusive classroom. *Teaching Exceptional Children, 35*(2), 18–22.

Bauer, W. M., & Piazza, J. G. (1998). Increasing access through assistive technology for people with disabilities in rural areas. In Center on Disability, *Conference Proceedings: Technology and Persons with Disabilities.* Northridge: California State University. Retrieved March 15, 2004, from http://csun.edu/cod/conf/1998/proceedings/csun98_018.htm

Baumberger, J., & Harper, R. E. (2007). *Assisting students with disabilities: A handbook for school counselors.* Thousand Oaks, CA: Corwin Press.

Bauminger, N., Edelsztein, H. S., & Morash, J. (2005). Social information processing and emotional understanding in children with LD. *Journal of Learning Disabilities, 38,* 45–61.

Bayat, M. (2007). Evidence of resilience in families of children with autism. *Journal of Intellectual Disability Research, 51,* 702–714.

Bear, G. G., Kortering, L. J., & Braziel, P. (2006). School completers and noncompleters with learning disabilities: Similarities in academic achievement and perceptions of self and teachers. *Remedial and Special Education, 27,* 293–300.

Beattie, J. R., Anderson, R. J., & Antonak, R. F. (1997). Modifying attitudes of prospective educators toward students with disabilities and their integration into regular classrooms. *Journal of Psychology, 131,* 245–260.

Beers, M. H., & Berkow, R. (2003). *Mental retardation* (Sec. 19, Chap. 262). *Merck manual of diagnosis and therapy* (17th ed.). Retrieved on October 9, 2003, from www.merck.com/pubs/mmanual/section19/chapter262/262e .htm

Begeer, S., Rieffe, C., & Terwogt, M. M. (2003). Theory of mind-based action in children from the autism spectrum. *Journal of Autism and Developmental Disorders, 33,* 479–487.

Beirne-Smith, M., Ittenbach, R. F., & Patton, J. R. (2002). *Mental retardation* (6th ed., pp. 312–357). Upper Saddle River, NJ: Pearson.

Bélanger, J., & Gagné, F. (2006). Examining the size of the gifted/talented population from multiple identification criteria. *Journal for the Education of the gifted, 30,* 131–163.

Bell, S. M., McCallum, R. S., & Cox, E. A. (2003). Toward a research-based assessment of dyslexia: Using cognitive measures to identify reading disabilities. *Journal of Learning Disabilities, 36,* 505–515.

Benbow, C. P. (1992). Academic achievement in math and science between ages thirteen and twenty-three: Are there differences in the top 1 percent of ability? *Journal of Educational Psychology, 84,* 51–61.

Benbow, C. P., & Stanley, J. C. (1996). Inequity in equity. How "equity" can lead to inequity for high-potential students. *Psychology, Public Policy and Policy, 2,* 249–292.

Benner, G. J., Nelson, J. R., & Epstein, M. H. (2002). Language skills of children with EBD: A literature review. *Journal of Emotional and Behavioral Disorders, 10,* 43–59.

Bennett, A. (1932). *Subnormal children in elementary grades.* New York: Columbia University, Teacher's College, Bureau of Publications.

Bennett, C. I. (2003). *Comprehensive multicultural education: Theory and practice* (5th ed.). Boston: Allyn & Bacon.

Bennett, T., Deluca, D., & Bruns, D. (1997). Putting inclusion into practice: Perspectives of teachers and parents. *Exceptional Children, 64,* 115–131.

Bennett, T., Lee, H., & Lueke, B. (1998). Expectations and concerns: What mothers and fathers say about inclusion. *Education and Training in Mental Retardation and Developmental Disabilities, 33,* 108–122.

Ben-Yosef, E. (2003). Respecting students' cultural literacies. *Educational Leadership, 61*(2), 80–82.

Beratan, G. (2008). The son remains the same: Transposition and the disproportionate representation of minority students in special education. *Race, Ethnicity and Education, 11,* 337–354.

Bergeron, R., & Floyd, R. (2006). Broad cognitive abilities of children with mental retardation: An analysis of group and individual profiles. *American Journal on Mental Retardation, 111,* 417–432.

Bergland, M. M. (1996). Transition from school to adult life: Key to the future. In A. L. Goldberg (Ed.), *Acquired brain injury in childhood and adolescence: A team and family guide to educational program development and implementation* (pp. 171–194). Springfield, IL: Charles C. Thomas.

Berglund, E., Eriksson, M., & Johansson, I. (2001). Parental reports of spoken language skills in children with Down syndrome. *Journal of Speech, Language, and Hearing Research, 44,* 179–191.

Berkeley, S., Bender, W. N., Peaster, L. G., & Saunders, L. (2009). Implementation of response to intervention: A snapshot of progress. *Journal of Learning Disabilities, 42,* 85–95.

Bernstein, D. K., & Tiegerman-Farber, E. (2002). *Language and communication disorders in children* (5th ed.). Boston: Allyn & Bacon.

Bertella, L., Girelli, L., Grugni, G., Marchi, S., Molinari, E., & Semenza, C. (2005). Mathematical skills in Prader-Willi syndrome. *Journal of Intellectual Disability Research, 49,* 159–169.

Besnov, K. D., Manning, S., & Karnes, F. A. (2006). Screening students with visual impairments for intellectual giftedness. *RE:view, 37,* 134–140.

Best, S. M., Heller, K. W., & Bigge, J. L. (2010). *Teaching individuals with physical or multiple disabilities* (6th ed.). Columbus, OH: Merrill.

Beukelman, D. R., & Mirenda, P. (2005). *Augmentative and alternative communication: Management of severe communication disorders in children and adults* (3rd ed.). Baltimore: Paul H. Brookes.

Biddle, B., & Berliner, D. C. (2002). Small class size and its effects. *Educational Leadership, 59,* 12–23.

Biederman, G., & Freedman, B. (2007). Modeling skills, signs and lettering for children with Down syndrome, autism and other severe developmental delays by video instruction in classroom setting. *Journal of Early and Intensive Behavior Intervention, 4,* 736–743.

Biederman, J. (2003). Pharmacotherapy for attention-deficit/hyperactivity disorder (ADHD) decreases the risk for substance abuse: Findings from a longitudinal follow-up of youths with and without ADHD. *Journal of Clinical Psychiatry, 64,* 3–8.

Biederman, J., Ball, S. W., & Monuteaux, M. C. (2008). New insights into the comorbidity between ADHD and major depression in adolescent and young adult females. *Journal of the American Academy of Child & Adolescent Psychiatry, 47,* 426–434.

Biederman, J., Faraone, S., Keenan, K., & Tsuang, M. (1991). Evidence of familial association between attention deficit disorder and major affective disorders. *Archives of General Psychiatry, 48,* 633–642.

Biederman, J., Wilens, T., Mick, E., Spencer, T., & Faraone, S. V. (1999a). Clinical correlates of ADHD in females: Findings from a large group of girls ascertained from pediatric and psychiatric referral sources. *Journal of American Academy of Child and Adolescent Psychiatry, 38,* 966–975.

Biederman, J., Wilens, T., Mick, E., Spencer, T., & Faraone, S. V. (1999b). Pharmacotherapy of attention-deficit/hyperactivity disorder reduces risk for substance use disorder. *Pediatrics, 104*(2), 20.

Bigby, L. M. (2004). Medical and health-related services: More than treating boo-boos and ouchies. *Intervention in School and Clinic, 39,* 233–235.

Bigge, J. L. (1991). *Teaching individuals with physical and multiple disabilities* (3rd ed.). New York: Merrill.

Bigge, J. L., Best, S. J., & Heller, K. W. (2000). *Teaching individuals with physical, health, or multiple disabilities* (4th ed.). Upper Saddle River, NJ: Merrill.

Bigge, J. L., Best, S. J., & Heller, K. W. (2001). *Teaching individuals with physical, health, or multiple disabilities* (4th ed.). Upper Saddle River, NJ: Merrill.

Bigler, E. D., Lajiness-O'Neill, R., & Howes, N. (1998). Technology in the assessment of learning disability. *Journal of Learning Disabilities, 31,* 67–82.

Billingsley, B. (2006). *Special education teacher attrition: What we know, what we can do.* Gainesville: University of Florida, Center on Personnel Studies in Special Education. Retrieved May 12, 2009 from http://www.coe.ufl.edu/copsse/questions-answers/index.php#sd

Billingsley, B. S. (2004). Special education teacher retention and attrition: A critical analysis of the research literature. *Journal of Special Education, 38,* 39–55.

Binger, C., & Light, J. (2006). Demographics of preschoolers who require AAC. *Language, Speech, and Hearing Services in Schools, 37,* 200–208.

Bish, C. E. (1961). The academically talented. *National Education Association Journal, 30*(2), 33–37.

Bishop, A. (2000, September). Technology trends and their potential for bilingual education. *Issue Brief: National Clearinghouse for Bilingual Education, 7,* 1–16.

Bishop, D. V. M. (2002). The role of genes in the etiology of specific language impairment. *Journal of Communication Disorders, 35,* 311–328.

Bishop, V. E. (1986). Identifying the components of successful mainstreaming. *Journal of Visual Impairment and Blindness, 80,* 939–946.

Bishop, V. E. (2004). *Teaching visually impaired children* (3rd ed.). Springfield, IL: Charles C. Thomas.

Blacher, J. (2002). Twice-exceptional: Learning disabled and gifted. *Exceptional Parent, 32*(9), 100–103.

Blachman, D. R., & Hinshaw, S. P. (2002). Patterns of friendship among girls with and without attention-deficit/hyperactivity disorder. *Journal of Abnormal Child Psychology, 30*(6), 625–640.

Black, R. S., & Rojewski, J. W. (1998). The role of social awareness in the employment success of adolescents with mild mental retardation. *Education and Training in Mental Retardation and Developmental Disabilities, 33,* 144–161.

Blackman, B. A. (2000). Phonological awareness. In M. L. Kamil, P. B. Mosenthal, P. D. Pearson, & R. Barr (Eds.), *Handbook of reading research: Volume III* (pp. 483–502). Mahwah, NJ: Lawrence Erlbaum Associates.

Blanchard, L. T., Gurka, M. J., & Blackman, J. A. (2006). Emotional, developmental, and behavioral health of American children and their families: A report from the 2003 National Survey of Children's Health. *Pediatrics, 117,* 1202–1212.

Blanchett, W. J. (2002). Voices from a TASH forum on meeting the needs of gay, lesbian, and bisexual adolescents and adults with severe disabilities. *Research & Practice for Persons with Severe Disabilities, 27,* 82–86.

Blanchett, W. J., Mumford, V., & Beachum, F. (2005). Urban school failure and disproportionality in a post–Brown era. *Remedial and Special Education, 26,* 70–81.

Blatt, B., & Kaplan, F. (1974). *Christmas is purgatory.* Syracuse, NY: Human Policy Press.

Bleach, F. (2001). *Everybody is different: A book for young people who have brothers and sisters with autism.* Shawnee Mission, KS: Autism Asperger Publishing.

Blomgren, M., Roy, N., Callister, T., & Merrill, R. M. (2005). Intensive stuttering modification therapy: A multidimensional assessment of treatment outcomes. *Journal of Speech, Language and Hearing Research, 48,* 509–523.

Blood, G. W., Blood, I. M., Maloney, K., Meyer, C., & Qualls, C. D. (2007). Anxiety levels in adolescents who stutter. *Journal of Communication Disorders, 40,* 452–469.

Bloom, B. (Ed.). (1985). *Developing talent in young people.* New York: Ballantine Books.

Blue-Banning, M., Summers, J. A., Frankland, H. C., Nelson, L. L., & Beegle, G. (2004). Dimensions of family and professional partnerships: Constructive guidelines for collaboration. *Exceptional Children, 70,* 167–184.

Blue-Banning, M., Turnbull, A. P., & Pereira, L. (2002). Hispanic youth/young adults with disabilities: Parents' visions for the future. *Journal of the Association for Persons with Severe Handicaps, 27,* 204–219.

Blum, R. W., Resnick, M. D., Nelson, R., & St. Germaine, A. (1991). Family and peer issues among adolescents with spina bifida and cerebral palsy. *Pediatrics, 88,* 280–285.

Body Health Resources. (2005). HIV/AIDS among youth [statistics from the Centers for Disease Control and Prevention]. Retrieved September 3, 2006, from www.thebody.com/cdc/hivteen.html

Boe, E. E., Cook, L. H., Bobbitt, S. A., & Terhanian, G. (1998). The shortage of fully certified teachers in special and general education. *Teacher Education and Special Education, 21,* 1–21.

Bohn, A. P., & Sleeter, C. E. (2000). Multicultural education and the standards movement: A report from the field. *Phi Delta Kappan, 82,* 156–159.

Bond, M. A., & Wasik, B. A. (2009). "Conversations stations": Promoting language development in young children. *Early Childhood Education Journal, 36,* 467–473.

Bonner, F. A. (2003). To be young, gifted, African American, and male. *Gifted Child Today, 26*(2), 26–34.

Bonner, M. J., Gustafson, K. E., Schumacher, E., & Thompson, R. J. (1999). The impact of sickle cell disease on cognitive functioning and learning. *School Psychology Review, 28,* 182–191.

Borich, G. D., & Tombari, M. L. (1997). *Educational psychology: A contemporary approach* (2nd ed.). New York: Longman.

Borland, J. H., & Wright, L. (1994). Identifying young, potentially gifted, economically disadvantaged students. *Gifted Child Quarterly, 38,* 164–171.

Bos, C. S. (1999). Home–school communication. In C. Jones, H. R. Searight, & M. A. Urban (Eds.), *Parent articles for ADHD.* San Antonio, TX: Communication Skill Builders.

Bos, C. S., Nahmias, M. L., & Urban, M. A. (1999). Targeting home–school collaboration for students with ADHD. *Teaching Exceptional Children, 31*(6), 4–11.

Boscardin, M. L. (2005). The administrative role in transforming secondary schools to support inclusive evidence-based practices. *American Secondary Education, 33*(3), 21–32.

Bosman, A. M. T., Gompel, M., Vervloed, M. P. J., & van Bon, W. H. J. (2006). Low vision affects the reading process quantitatively but not qualitatively. *Journal of Special Education, 39,* 208–219.

Boswell, S. (2005, February 8). Tales from a fourth-grade classroom: Collaboration brings personal satisfaction, improves scores. *ASHA Leader,* pp. 18, 20.

Bouck, E. C. (2008). Factors impacting the enactment of a functional curriculum in self-contained cross-categorical programs. *Education and Training in Developmental Disabilities, 43,* 294–310.

Bouck, E. C. (2009). No Child Left Behind, the Individuals with Disabilities Education Act and functional curricula: A conflict of interest? *Education and Training in Developmental Disabilities, 44,* 3–13.

Boulet, S. L., Gambrell, D., Shin, M., Honein, M. A., & Mathews, T. J. (2009). Racial/ethnic differences in the birth prevalence of spina bifida–United States, 1995–2005. *Journal of the American Medical Association, 301,* 2203–2204. http://www.biausa.org/education.htm

Bowe, F. (2000). *Physical, sensory, and health disabilities: An introduction.* Upper Saddle River, NJ: Merrill.

Bowman-Perrott, L. (2009). Classwide peer tutoring: An effective strategy for students with emotional and behavioral disorders. *Intervention in School and Clinic, 44,* 259–267.

Boyd, B. A. (2002). Examining the relationship between stress and lack of social support in mothers of children with autism. *Focus on Autism and Other Developmental Disabilities, 17,* 208–215.

Boys Town National Research Hospital. (n.d.). *Getting started with early intervention.* Retrieved December 2, 2002, from www.babyhearing.org/LanguageLearning/EarlyIntervention/howhelps.asp

Bracey, G. W. (1999). The ninth Bracey report on the condition of public education. *Phi Delta Kappan, 81,* 147–166.

Bracken, B. A., & Brown, E. F. (2006). Behavioral identification and assessment of gifted and talented students. *Journal of Psychoeducational Assessment, 24,* 112–122.

Bracken, B. A., & McCallum, R. S. (1998). *Universal Nonverbal Intelligence Test.* Itasca, IL: Riverside.

Brackenbury, T., Burroughs, E., & Hewitt, L. E. (2008). A qualitative examination of current guidelines for evidence-based practice in child language intervention. *Language, Speech, and Hearing Services in Schools, 39,* 78–88.

Brackett, D. (1997). Intervention for children with hearing impairment in general education settings. *Language, Speech, and Hearing Services in Schools, 28*(4), 355–361.

Braddock, D., Hemp, R., Parrish, S., Westrich, J., & Park, H. (1998). The state of the states in developmental disabilities: Summary of the study. In D. Braddock, R. Hemp, S. Parish, J. Westrich, & H. Park (Eds.), *The state of the states in developmental disabilities,* (5th ed., pp. 23–53). Washington, DC: American Association on Mental Retardation.

Braden, J. P. (1994). *Deafness, deprivation, and IQ.* New York: Plenum.

Bradley, E. A., Thompson, A., & Bryson, S. E. (2002). Mental retardation in teenagers: Prevalence data from the Niagara region, Ontario. *Canadian Journal of Psychiatry, 47,* 652–659.

Bradley, J. F., & Monda-Amaya, L. E. (2005). Conflict resolution: Preparing preservice special educators work in collaborative settings. *Teacher Education and Special Education, 28,* 171–184.

Bradley, R., Danielson, L., & Doolittle, J. (2005). Response to intervention. *Journal of Learning Disabilities, 38,* 485–486.

Brain Injury Association of America. (2004). *Causes of brain injury.* McLean, VA: Author. Retrieved March 13, 2004, from www.biausa.org/Pages/causes_of_brain_injury.html

Brain Injury Association of America. (2009). *Living with brain injury.* Retrieved September 5, 2009 from http://www.biausa.org/education.htm

Bramahm, J., Young, S., & Bikerdike, A. (2009). Evaluation of group cognitive behavioral therapy for adults with ADHD. *Journal of Attention Disorders, 12,* 434–441.

Brambring, M. (2007). Divergent development of verbal skills in children who are blind or sighted. *Journal of Visual Impairment & Blindness, 101,* 749–762.

Brandes, J. A. (2005). Partner with parents. *Intervention in School and Clinic, 41,* 52–54.

Brasel, K., & Qugiley, S. (1977). The influence of certain language and communication environments in early childhood on the development of language in deaf individuals. *Journal of Speech and Hearing Research, 20,* 95–107.

Braun, J., Kahn, R. S., Froehlich, T., Auinger, P., & Lanphear, B. (2006, September). Exposures to environmental toxicants and attention deficit hyperactivity disorder in U.S. children. *Environmental Health Perspectives,* pp. 1904–1909. Retrieved October 15, 2006, from www.ehponline.org/docs/2006/9478/abstract.html

Brauner, C. B., & Stephens, C. B. (2006). Estimating the prevalence of early childhood serious emotional/behavioral disorders: Challenges and recommendations. *Public Health Report, 121,* 303–310.

Bray, M. A., & Kehle, T. J. (2001). Long-term follow-up of self-monitoring as an intervention for stuttering. *School Psychology Review, 30,* 135–142.

Breggin, P. R. (2000). The NIMH multimodal study of treatment for attention-deficit/hyperactivity disorder: A critical analysis. *International Journal of Risk and Safety in Medicine, 13,* 15–22.

Brent, R. L., & Oakley, G. P. (2006). Triumph or tragedy: The present Food and Drug Administration program of enriching grains with folic acid. *Pediatrics, 117,* 930–932.

Brice, A. (2001). *Children with communication disorders: Update 2001* [ERIC Digest E617] (ERIC Document No. ED459549). Retrieved November 19, 2003, from www.edrs.com/members/sp.cfm?AN=ED459549

Brice, A., & Miller, J. J. (2000). Case studies in inclusion: What works, what doesn't. *Communication Disorders Quarterly, 21,* 237–241.

Brice, A. E., Franklin, E., & Ratusnik, D. L. (2008). *Hola, shalom, hello: Adolescent pragmatics from a cross-cultural perspective.* (ERIC Document Reproduction Service No. ED503417). Retrieved August 15, 2009 from http://www.eric.ed.gov/ERICWebPortal/contentdelivery/servlet/ERICServlet?accno=ED503417

Brice, R. G. (2004). Connecting oral and written language through applied writing strategies. *Intervention in School and Clinic, 40*(1), 38–47.

Brieber, S., Neufang, S., Bruning, N., Kamp-Becker, I., Remschmidt, H., Herpertz-Dahlmann, B., Fink, G. R., & Konrad, K. (2007). Structural brain abnormalities in adolescents with autism spectrum disorder and patients with attention deficit/hyperactivity disorder. *Journal of Child Psychology and Psychiatry, 48,* 1251–1258.

Brigance, A. (1999). *Brigance comprehensive inventory of basic skills—Revised.* North Billerica, MA: Curriculum Associates.

Briggs, C. J., Reis, S. M., & Sullivan, E. E. (2008). A national view of promising programs and practices for culturally, linguistically, and ethnically diverse gifted and talented students. *Gifted Child Quarterly, 52,* 131–145.

Bright Futures. (2000). Bright futures for exceptional learners: An action agenda to achieve quality conditions for teaching and learning for every exceptional learner. *Teaching Exceptional Children, 32*(6), 56–69.

Brightman, H. J. (2002). *Group problem solving: An improved managerial approach.* East Lansing: Michigan State University Press.

Brighton, C. M. (2001). Stronger together than apart: Building models through collaboration and interconnection. *Journal of Secondary Gifted Education, 12,* 163–165.

Broer, S. M., Doyle, M. B., & Giangreco, M. F. (2005). Perspectives of students with intellectual disabilities about their experiences with paraprofessional support. *Exceptional Children, 71,* 415–430.

Bromley, K., Irwin-De Vitis, L., & Modlo, M. (1995). *Graphic organizers: Visual strategies for active learning.* New York: Scholastic Professional Books.

Brooks, R. B. (2001). Fostering motivation, hope, and resilience in children with learning disorders. *Annals of Dyslexia, 51,* 9–20.

Browder, D. M., Ahlgrim-Delzell, L., Courtade, G., Gibbs, S. L., & Flowers, C. (2008). Evaluation of the effectiveness of an early literacy program for students with significant developmental disabilities. *Exceptional Children, 75,* 33–52.

Browder, D. M., & Spooner, F. (2006). *Teaching language arts, math, and science to students with significant cognitive disabilities.* Baltimore: Paul H. Brookes Publishing Company.

Browder, D. M., Ahlgrim-Delzell, L., Pugalle, D. K., & Jimenez, B. A. (2006). Enhancing numeracy. In D. M. Browder & F. Spooner (Eds.), *Teaching language arts, math, and science to students with significant cognitive disabilities* (pp. 171–195). Baltimore: Paul H. Brookes.

Browder, D. M., Mims, P. J., Spooner, F., Ahlgrim-Delzell, L., & Lee, A. (2008). Teaching elementary students with multiple disabilities to participate in shared stories. *Research and Practice for Persons with Severe Disabilities, 33*(1-2), 3–12.

Browder, D. M., Spooner, F., Algozzine, R., Ahlgrim-Delzell, L., Flowers, C., & Karvonen, M. (2003). What we know and need to know about alternate assessment. *Exceptional Children, 70,* 45–61.

Browder, D. M., Wakeman, S. Y., Spooner, F., Ahlgrim-Delzell, L., & Algozzine, B. (2006). Research on reading instruction for individuals with significant cognitive disabilities. *Exceptional Children, 72,* 392–408.

Browder, D., Flowers, C., Ahlgrim-Delzell, L., Karvonen, M., Spooner, F., & Algozzine, R. (2004). The alignment of alternate assessment content with academic and functional curricula. *Journal of Special Education, 37,* 211–223.

Brown, A., & Heath, N. (1998). *Social competence in peer-accepted children with and without learning disabilities.* Paper presented at the annual convention of the National Association of School Psychologists, Orlando, FL. (ERIC Documentation Reproduction Service No. ED420024)

Brown, D., Pryzwansky, W. B., & Schulte, A. C. (2006). *Psychological consultation and collaboration: introduction to theory and practice* (6th ed.). Boston: Allyn & Bacon.

Brown, E. F., & Abernethy, S. H. (2009). Policy implications at the state and district level with RtI for gifted students. *Gifted Child Today, 32*(3), 52–57.

Brown, E. L., Fisher, D., Sax, C., & Grove, K. A. (2000). The resilience of changes promoting inclusiveness in an urban elementary school. *The Elementary School Journal, 100,* 213–227.

Brown, F., & Snell, M. (2000). Meaningful assessment. In M. E. Snell & F. Brown (Eds.), *Instruction of students with severe disabilities* (pp. 67–114). Upper Saddle River, NJ: Merrill.

Brown, F., Snell, M., & Lehr, D. (2006). Meaningful assessment. In M. E. Snell & F. Brown (Eds.), *Instruction of students with severe disabilities* (pp. 67–114). Upper Saddle River, NJ: Merrill.

Brown, L., Farrington, K., Knight, T., Ross, C., & Zielger, M. (1999). Fewer paraprofessionals and more teachers and therapists in educational programs for students with significant disabilities. *Journal of the Association for Persons with Severe Handicaps, 24,* 250–253.

Brown, L., & Hammill, D. R. (1990). *Behavior rating profile.* Austin, TX: Pro-Ed.

Brown, M. (1999). America's most wanted j-o-b-s. *Black Enterprise, 29*(17), 109.

Brown, R. T., Armstrong, F. D., & Eckman, J. R. (1993). Neurocognitive aspects of pediatric sickle cell disease. *Journal of Learning Disabilities, 26*, 33–45.

Brown, R. T., & Madan-Swain, A. (1993). Cognitive, neuropsychological, and academic sequelae in children with leukemia. *Journal of Learning Disabilities, 26*, 74–90.

Brown, S. (1987). Predictors of income variance among a group of deaf former college students. *Journal of Rehabilitation of the Deaf, 20*(4), 20–29.

Brown, S. W., Renzulli, J. S., Gubbins, E. J., Siegle, D., Zhang, W., & Chen, C. (2005). Assumptions underlying the identification of gifted and talented students. *Gifted Child Quarterly, 49*, 68–79.

Brownell, M. T., Adams, A., Sindelar, P., Waldron, N., & Vahhover, S. (2006). Learning from collaboration: The role of teacher qualities. *Exceptional Children, 72*, 169–185.

Brownell, M. T., & Walther-Thomas, C. (2002). An interview with Dr. Marilyn Friend. *Intervention in School and Clinic, 37*, 223–228.

Bruce, S., Godbold, E., & Naponelli-Gold, S. (2004). An analysis of communicative functions of teachers and their students who are congenitally deaf-blind. *RE:view, 36*, 81–90.

Bruner, J. S., Oliver, R., & Greenfield, P. (1966). *Studies in cognitive growth.* New York: Wiley.

Bryan, T., & Burstein, K. (2004). Improving homework completion and academic performance: Lessons from special education. *Theory Into Practice, 43*(3), 213–219.

Bryan, T. H., & Bryan, J. H. (1986). *Understanding learning disabilities* (3rd ed.). Palo Alto, CA: Mayfield.

Bryant, B. R., & Bryant, D. P. (2008). Introduction to the special series: Mathematics and learning disabilities. *Learning Disability Quarterly, 31*, 3–8.

Bryant, D. P., & Byant, B. R. (2003). *Assistive technology for people with disabilities.* Boston: Allyn & Bacon.

Buck, L. H., Polloway, E. A., Smith-Thomas, A., & Cook, K. W. (2003). Prereferral intervention processes: A survey of state practices. *Exceptional Children, 69*, 349–360.

Buescher, T. M., & Higham, S. (2001). *Helping adolescents adjust to giftedness.* (ERIC Digest #E489). Retrieved March 3, 2004, from www.kidsource.com/kidsource/content/adjust_to_giftedness.html

Bulgren, J. A., Deshler, D. D., & Schumaker, J. B. (1997). Use of a recall enhancement routine and strategies in inclusive secondary classes. *Learning Disabilities: Research and Practice, 12*, 198–208.

Bullis, M., Yovanoff, P., Mueller, B., & Havel, E. (2002). Life on the "outs"—Examination of the facility-to-community transition of incarcerated youth. *Exceptional Children, 69*, 7–22.

Bullock, L. M., Gable, R. A., & Mohr, J. D. (2005). Traumatic brain injury: A challenge for educators. *Preventing School Failure, 49*(4), 6–10.

Burcroff, T. L., Radogna, D. M., & Wright, E. H. (2003). Community forays: Addressing students' functional skills in inclusive settings. *Teaching Exceptional Children, 35*(5), 52–57.

Burd, L. (2004). Fetal alcohol syndrome. *Addiction Biology, 9*, 115–118.

Burden, R. (2008). Is dyslexia associated with negative feelings of self-worth? A review and implications for future research. *Dyslexia, 14*, 188–196.

Bureau of Labor Statistics. (1998). *Occupational survey.* Washington, DC: Author.

Burnham, J. (2009). Contemporary fears of children and adolescents: Coping and resiliency in the 21st century. *Journal of Counseling & Development, 87*, 28–35.

Burns, B. J., Hoagwood, K., & Maultsby, L. T. (1998). Improving outcomes for children and adolescents with serious emotional and behavioral disorders: Current and future directions. In M. H. Epstein, K. Kutash, & A. Duchnowski (Eds.), *Outcomes for children and youth with behavioral and emotional disorders and their families: Programs and evaluation best practices.* Austin, TX: Pro-Ed.

Burns, G. L., & Kondrick, P. A. (1998). Psychological behaviorism's reading therapy program: Parents as reading therapists for their children's reading. *Journal of Learning Disabilities, 31*, 278–285.

Burns, M. K., Jacob, S., & Wagner, A. R. (2008). Ethical and legal issues associated with using response-to-intervention to assess learning disabilities. *Journal of School Psychology, 46*, 263–279.

Burns, M. S. (2002, February). *Language and reading in the brain.* Retrieved July 9, 2002, from www.brainconnection.com/topics/?main=col/burns00feb

Burstein, N., Sears, S., Wilcoxen, A., Cabello, B., & Spagna, M. (2004). Moving toward inclusive practices. *Remedial and Special Education, 25*, 104–116.

Bussing, R., Schoenberg, N. E., Rogers, K. M., Zima, B. T., & Angus, S. (1998). Explanatory models of ADHD: Do they differ by ethnicity, child gender, or treatment status? *Journal of Emotional and Behavioral Disorders, 6*, 233–242.

Bussing, R., Zima, B. T., Belin, T. R., & Forness, S. R. (2000). Children who qualify for LD and SED programs: Do they differ in level of ADHD symptoms and comorbid psychiatric conditions? *Behavioral Disorders, 23*, 85–97.

Bynoe, P. F. (1998). Rethinking and retooling teacher preparation to prevent perpetual failure of our children. *The Journal of Special Education, 32*, 37–40.

Cahill, S. M., & Mitchell, S. (2008). Forging collaborative relationships to meet the demands of inclusion. *Kappa Delta Pi Record, 44*, 149–151.

California Department of Education. (2000). *Programs for deaf and hard of hearing students: Guidelines for quality standards.* Sacramento, CA: Author.

Callahan, C. M. (2005). Identifying gifted students from underrepresented populations. *Theory into Practice, 44*, 98–104.

Callahan, C. M., & Miller, E. M. (2005). A child-responsive model of giftedness. In R. J. Sternberg & J. E. Davidson (Eds.), *Conceptions of giftedness* (2nd ed.) (pp. 120–146). New York: Cambridge University Press.

Callard-Szulgit, R. (2005). *Teaching the gifted in an inclusion classroom: Activities that work.* Lanham, MD: Scarecrow Education.

Callicott, K. J. (2003). Culturally sensitive collaboration within person-centered planning. *Focus on Autism and Other Developmental Disabilities, 18*, 60–68.

Cambra, C. (1994). An instructional program approach to improve hearing-impaired adolescents' narratives: A pilot study. *The Volta Review, 96*, 237–246.

Cameto, R., & Nagle, K. (2007). Orientation and mobility skills of secondary school students with visual impairments: Facts from NLTS2 [NCSER 2008-3007]. Washington, D.C.: National Center for Special Education Research.

Campbell, D. J., Reilly, A., & Henley, J. (2008). Comparison of assessment results of children with low incidence disabilities. *Education and Training in Developmental Disabilities, 43*, 217–25.

Carlberg, C., & Kavale, K. (1980). The efficacy of special versus regular class placement for exceptional children: A meta-analysis. *The Journal of Special Education, 14*, 295–309.

Carlson, C. L., Tamm, L., & Gaub, M. (1997). Gender differences in children with ADHD, ODD, and co-occurring ADHD/ODD identified in a school population. *Journal of American Academy of Child and Adolescent Psychiatry, 36*, 1706–1714.

Carlson, J. K., Hagiwara, T., & Quinn, C. (1998). Assessment of students with autism. In R. L. Simpson & B. S. Myles (Eds.), *Educating children and youth with autism: Strategies for effective practice* (pp. 25–53). Austin, TX: Pro-Ed.

Carnahan, C., Musti-Rao, S., & Bailey, J. (2009). Promoting active engagement in small group learning experiences for students with autism and significant learning needs. *Education and Treatment of Children, 32*(1), 37–61.

Carnes, S. L., & Quinn, W. H. (2005). Family adaptation to brain injury: Coping and psychological distress. *Families, Systems, and Health, 23,* 186–203.

Carnine, D., Silbert, J., & Kameenui, E. J. (1997). *Direct instruction reading.* Upper Saddle River, NJ: Pearson.

Caron, E. A., & McLaughlin, M. J. (2002). Indicators of Beacons of Excellence schools: What do they tell us about collaborative practices? *Journal of Educational and Psychological Consultation, 13,* 285–313.

Carpenter, L. (2001). Travel card. In B. S. Myles & D. Adreon (Eds.), *Asperger syndrome and adolescence: Practical solutions for school success* (pp. 92–96). Shawnee Mission, KS: Autism Asperger Publishing.

Carper, R. A., & Courchesne, E. (2000). Inverse correlation between frontal lobe and cerebellum sizes in children with autism. *Brain, 123*(4), 836–844.

Carr, E. G., Dunlap, G., Horner, R. H., Koegel, R. J., Turnbull, A. P., Sailor, W., Anderson, J. L., Albin, R. W., Koegel, L. K., & Fox, L., (2002). Positive behavior support: Evolution of an applied science. *Journal of Positive Behavior Interventions, 4,* 1–16, 20.

Carroll, C., & Mather, S. M. (1997). *Movers and shakers: Deaf people who changed the world.* San Diego, CA: Dawn Sign Press.

Carroll, J. M., Maughan, B., Goodman, R., & Meltzer, H. (2005). Literacy difficulties and psychiatric disorders: Evidence for comorbidity. *Journal of Child Psychology and Psychiatry, 46,* 524–532.

Carroll, S. Z., Blumberg, E. R., & Petroff, J. G. (2008). The promise of liberal learning: Creating a challenging postsecondary curriculum for youth with intellectual disabilities. *Focus on Exceptional Children, 40*(9), 1–12.

Carrow-Woolfolk, E. (1999). *Comprehensive Assessment of Spoken Language (CASL).* Circle Pines, MN: AGS.

Carter, E. W., & Hughes, C. (2005). Increasing social interactions among adolescents with intellectual disabilities and their general education peers: Effective interventions. *Research and Practice for Persons with Severe Disabilities, 30,* 179–193.

Carter, E. W., Hughes, C., Guth, C. B., & Copeland, S. R. (2005). Factors influencing social interaction among high school students with intellectual disabilities and their general education peers. *American Journal of Mental Retardation, 110,* 366–377.

Carter, E. W., & Kennedy, C. H. (2006). Promoting access to the general curriculum using peer support strategies. *Research and Practice for Persons with Severe Disabilities, 31,* 284–292.

Carter, E. W., & Pesko, M. J. (2008). Social validity of peer interaction intervention strategies in high school classrooms: Effectiveness, feasibility, and actual use. *Exceptionality, 16,* 156–173.

Carter, E. W., & Wehby, J. H. (2003). Job performance of transition-age youth with emotional and behavioral disorders. *Exceptional Children, 69,* 449–465.

Carter, E. W., Lane, K. L., Pierson, M. R., & Glaeser, B. (2006). Self-determination skills and opportunities of transition-age youth with emotional disturbance and learning disabilities. *Exceptional Children, 72,* 333–346.

Carter, E. W., Lane, K. L., Pierson, M. R., & Stang, K. K. (2008). Promoting self-determination for transition-age youth: Views of high school general and special educators. *Exceptional Children, 75,* 55–70.

Carter, E. W., Sisco, L. G., Brown, L., Brickham, D., & Al-Khabbaz, Z. A. (2008). Peer interactions and academic engagement of youth with developmental disabilities in inclusive middle and high school classrooms. *American Journal on Mental Retardation, 113,* 479–494.

Carter, E. W., Sisco, L. G., Melekoglu, M. A., & Kurkowski, C. (2007). Peer supports as an alternative to individually assigned paraprofessionals in inclusive high school classrooms. *Research and Practice for Persons with Severe Disabilities, 32,* 213–227.

Cartledge, G., & Kourea, L. (2008). Culturally responsive classrooms for culturally diverse students with and at risk for disabilities. *Exceptional Children, 74,* 351–371.

Cartledge, G., Tillman, L. C., & Johnson, C. T. (2001). Professional ethics within the context of student discipline and diversity. *Teacher Education and Special Education, 24,* 25–37.

Casey, J. (2003, July). *Adult ADHD: A difficult diagnosis.* Retrieved September 1, 2003, from http://my.webmd.com/content/Article/66/79905.htm?pagenumber=2

Cash, R. E. (2001). *Depression in children and adolescents.* Bethesda, MD: National Mental Health and Education Center of the National Association of School Psychologists. Retrieved August 12, 2003, from www.naspcenter.org/pdf/social%20template.pdf

Casteel, C. A. (1998). Teacher–student interactions and race in integrated classrooms. *Journal of Educational Research, 92,* 115–120.

Castellano, J. A., & Díaz, E. (Eds.). (2002). *Reaching new horizons: Gifted and talented education for culturally and linguistically diverse students.* Boston: Allyn & Bacon.

Castles, A., Datta, H., Gayan, J., & Olson, R. K. (1999). Varieties of developmental reading disorder: Genetic and environmental influences. *Journal of Experimental Child Psychology, 72,* 73–94.

Castrogiovanni, A. (2002). *Prison population communicative disorders information.* Rockville, MD: American Speech-Language-Hearing Association. Retrieved November 30, 2003, from www.audiologyonline.com/audiology/newroot/associations/userpages/digicare/news/newsdisp.asp?newsid=126

Cates, C. (2009). Using education to improve control of asthma in children. *Canadian Medical Association Journal, 181,* 248–249.

Catts, H. W., Adlof, S. M., & Weismer, S. E. (2006). Language deficits in poor comprehenders: A case for the simple view of reading. *Journal of Speech, Language, and Hearing Research, 49,* 278–293.

Catts, H. W., Fey, M. E., Tomblin, J. B., & Zhang, X. (2002). A longitudinal investigation of reading outcome in children with language impairments. *Journal of Speech, Language, and Hearing Research, 45,* 1142–1157.

Catts, H. W., Gillispie, M., Leonard, L. B., Kail, R. V., & Miller, C. A. (2002). The role of speed of processing, rapid naming, and phonological awareness in reading achievement. *Journal of Learning Disabilities, 35,* 509–524.

Catts, H. W., Hogan, T. P., & Fey, M. E. (2003). Subgrouping poor readers on the basis of individual differences in reading-related abilities. *Journal of Learning Disabilities, 36*(2), 151–164.

Causton-Theoharis, J. N., & Malgren, K. W. (2005). Increasing peer interactions for students with severe disabilities via paraprofessional training. *Exceptional Children, 71,* 431–444.

Cautilli, J., Riley-Tillman, T. C., & Axelrod, S. (2006). Resistance is not futile: An experimental analogue of the effects of consultee "resistance" on the consultant's therapeutic behavior in the consultation process—a replication and extension. *International Journal of Behavioral Consultation and Therapy, 2,* 362–374.

Cavallaro, C. C., & Haney, M. (1999). *Preschool Inclusion.* Baltimore: Paul H. Brookes Publishing Co.

Cavell, T. A., Elledge, L. C., Malcolm, K. T., Faith, M. A., & Hughes, J. N. (2009). Relationship quality and the mentoring of aggressive, high-risk children. *Journal of Clinical Child and Adolescent Psychology, 38,* 185–198.

Cawley, J. F., Parmar, R. S., Yan, W., & Miller, J. H. (1998). Arithmetic computation performance of students with learning disabilities: Implications for curriculum. *Learning Disabilities Research and Practice, 13,* 68–74.

Cawthorn, S. (2001). Teaching strategies in inclusive classrooms with deaf students. *Journal of Deaf Studies and Deaf Education, 6,* 212–225.

Celeste, M. (2006). Play behaviors and social interactions of a child who is blind: In theory and practice. *Journal of Visual Impairment and Blindness, 100,* 75–90.

Celeste, M. (2007). Social skills intervention for a child who is blind. *Journal of Visual Impairment & Blindness, 101,* 521–533.

Center for Assessment and Demographic Studies. (1998). *1996–1997 Annual survey of deaf and hard of hearing children and youth.* Washington, DC: Gallaudet University.

Center for Assistive Technology. (2004). *Environmental control units* [newsletter insert 6]. Buffalo, NY: School of Public Health and Health Professionals, University of Buffalo, State University of New York. Retrieved March 12, 2004, from http://cat.buffalo.edu/newsletters.ecu.php

Center for Innovations in Education (CISE). (2002, April). *Do you know?. . . Parent's role in assistive technology considerations* [information brochure]. Retrieved April 6, 2003, from www.coe.missouri.edu/~mocise

Center for the Evaluation of Risks to Human Reproduction. (2003, August). *Folic acid.* Research Triangle Park, NC: Author. Retrieved March 13, 2004, from http://cerhr.niehs.nih.gov/genpub/topics/folic_acid-ccae.html

Center on Personnel Studies in Special Education. (2009). *Supply and demand.* Gainesville, FL: Author. Retrieved May 12, 2009 from http://www.coe.ufl.edu/copsse/research-focus-areas/supply-demand.php

Centers for Disease Control and Prevention. (2009). *National early hearing detection and intervention program (EHDI) data.* Retrieved August 24, 2009 from http://www.cdc.gov/ncbddd/ehdi/data.htm

Centers for Disease Control and Prevention. (n.d.). *What is attention deficit hyperactivity disorder?* Retrieved June 12, 2003, from www.cdc.gov/ncbddd/adhd/what.htm

Centers for Disease Control and Prevention. (2009). *Attention-deficit/hyperactivity disorder (ADHD): Data and statistics.* Atlanta: Author. Retrieved July 1, 2009 from http://www.cdc.gov/ncbddd/adhd/data.html

Centers for Disease Control and Prevention, (2002, May). *MMR vaccine and autism (measles–mumps–rubella): Fact Sheet.* Retrieved February 6, 2004, from www.cdc.gov/nip/vacsafe/concerns/autism/autism-mmr-facts.htm

Centers for Disease Control and Prevention, (2004, May). *Fact sheet.* Retrieved June 13, 2006, from www.cdc.gov/nip/vacsafe/concerns/autism/autism-mmr-facts.htm

Centers for Disease Control and Prevention. (2002, March). *Young people at risk: HIV/AIDS among America's youth.* Retrieved April 1, 2004, from www.cdc.gov/hiv/pubs/facts/youth.htm

Centers for Disease Control and Prevention. (2003a, March). *Childhood lead poisoning.* Retrieved October 1, 2003, from www.cdc.gov/nceh/lead/factsheets/childhoodlead.htm

Centers for Disease Control and Prevention. (2004, October). *Cerebral palsy.* Atlanta: Department of Health and Human Services. Retrieved September 2, 2009 from http://www.cdc.gov/ncbddd/dd/cp3.htm

Centers for Disease Control and Prevention. (2004a). *Attention-deficit/hyperactivity disorder: A public health research agenda.* Retrieved April 22, 2004, from www.cdc.gov/ncbddd/adhd/dadphra.htm

Centers for Disease Control and Prevention. (2005). *Youth risk behavior.* Retrieved October 25, 2006, from www.cdc.gov/HealthyYouth/yrbs/pdf/trends/2005_YRBS_Alcohol_Use.pdf

Centers for Disease Control and Prevention. (2006, September). *Traumatic brain injury: Overview.* Atlanta: Department of Health and Human Services. Retrieved October 31, 2009 from http://www.cdc.gov/ncipc/tbi/Overview.htm

Centers for Disease Control and Prevention. (2008). *Health topics: Alcohol and drug use.* Washington, D.C.: Author. Retrieved July 10, 2009 from http://www.cdc.gov/HealthyYouth/alcoholdrug/index.htm

Centers for Disease Control and Prevention. (2008, January). *Fact sheet: Toxoplasmosis.* Retrieved July 30, 2009 from http://www.cdc.gov/toxoplasmosis/factsheet.html

Centers for Disease Control and Prevention. (2009, July). *Lead.* Retrieved July 25, 2009 from http://www.cdc.gov/nceh/lead/

Centers for Disease Control and Prevention. (2009, July). *Phenylketonuria* [Genetics Home Reference]. Retrieved July 25, 2009 at http://ghr.nlm.nih.gov/condition=phenylketonuria

Centers for Disease Control and Prevention. (2009a, May). *Faststats: Asthma.* Atlanta: Department of Health and Human Services. Retrieved October 31, 2009 from http://www.cdc.gov/nchs/fastats/asthma.htm

Centers for Disease Control and Prevention. (2009b, February). *HIV/AIDS: Basic statistics.* Atlanta: Department of Health and Human Services. Retrieved October 31, 2009 from http://www.cdc.gov/hiv/topics/surveillance/basic.htm

Centers for Disease Control and Prevention. (n.d.). Cerebral palsy among children. Retrieved September 3, 2006, from www.cdc.gov/ncbddd/factsheets/cp.pdf#search=%22children%20born%20cerebral%20palsy%20year%22

Centers for Disease Control and Prevention, (2004, May). *Fact Sheet.* Retrieved June 13, 2006, from www.cdc.gov/nip/vacsafe/concerns/autism/autism-mmr-facts.htm

Chako, A., Wymbs, B. T., & Flammer-Rivera, L. M. (2008). A pilot study of the feasibility and efficacy of the strategies to enhance positive parenting (STEPP) program for single mothers of children with ADHD. *Journal of Attention Disorders, 12,* 270–280.

Chamberlin, S. A., Buchanan, M., & Vercimak, D. (2007). Serving twice-exceptional preschoolers: Blending gifted education and early childhood special education practices in assessment and program planning. *Journal for the Education of the Gifted, 30,* 372–394.

Chan, J., & O'Reilly, M. (2008). A social stories™ intervention package with students with autism in inclusive classroom settings. *Journal of Applied Behavior Analysis, 41,* 405–409.

Chapman, C. (2009). A smoother acceleration: Addressing transition issues that arise for accelerated gifted students. *Science Teacher, 76*(3), 42–45.

Charge Syndrome Foundation. (2006). About CHARGE. Retrieved November 1, 2006, from www.chargesyndrome.org/about-charge.asp

Charles, J. M., Carpenter, L. A., Jenner, W., & Nicholas, J. S. (2008). Recent advances in autism spectrum disorders. *International Journal of Psychiatry in Medicine, 38,* 133–140.

Chen, D., Downing, J. E., & Peckham-Hardin, K. D. (2002). Working with families of diverse cultural and linguistic backgrounds: Considerations for culturally responsive positive behavior support. In J. M. Lucyshyn, G. Dunlap, & R. W. Albin (Eds.), *Families and positive behavior support: Addressing problem behavior in family contexts* (pp. 133–154). Baltimore: Paul H. Brookes Publishing Co.

Cheney, D., Flower, A., & Templeton, T. (2008). Applying response to intervention metrics in the social domain for students at risk of developing emotional or behavioral disorders. *Journal of Special Education, 42,* 108–126.

Chevallier, C., Noveck, I., Happe, F., & Wilson, D. (2009). From Acoustics to grammar: Perceiving and interpreting grammatical prosody in adolescents with Asperger syndrome. *Research in Autism Spectrum Disorders, 3,* 502–516.

Chiappe, P. (2005). How reading research can inform mathematics difficulties: The search for the core deficit. *Journal of Learning Disabilities, 38*(4), 313–317.

Children and Adults with Attention-Deficit/Hyperactivity Disorder. (2003). *Evidence-based medication management for children and adolescents with AD/HD* [CHADD Fact Sheet #3]. Retrieved April 22, 2004, from www.chadd.org/fs/fs3.htm

Children's Bureau. (2009). *Child maltreatment 2007.* Washington, D.C.: U.S. Department of Health and Human Services.

Children's Partnership, The. (2003). *America's children and the information superhighway.* Los Angeles: Author. Retrieved December 14, 2003, from www.childrenspartnership.org/bbar/techin.html

Chitiyo, M., & Wheeler, J. J. (2009). Challenges faced by school teachers in implementing positive behavior support in their school systems. *Remedial and Special Education, 30,* 58–63.

Cho, H. J., & Palmer, S. B. (2008). Fostering self-determination in infants and toddlers with visual impairments or blindness. *Young Exceptional Children, 11*(4), 26–34.

Christie, C. A., Jolivette, K., & Nelson, C. M. (2000, December). *Youth aggression and violence: Risk, resilience, and prevention.* Arlington, VA: ERIC Clearinghouse on Disabilities and Gifted Education. (ERIC Document Reproduction Service No. ED 449632)

Christie, K. (2003). Even students are what they eat. *Phi Delta Kappan, 84,* 341–342.

Christodoulou, J. (2009). Multiple intelligences defined. *School Administrator, 66*(2), 23.

Churchill, L. R., Mulholland, R., & Cepello, M. R. (2008). *A practical guide for special education professionals.* Upper Saddle River, NJ: Pearson.

Clare, M. M., Jimenez, A., & McClendon, J. (2005). *Toma el timepo:* The wisdom of migrant families in consultation. *Journal of Educational and Psychological Consultation, 16,* 95–111.

Clark, C., & McDonnell, A. P. (2008). Teaching choice making to children with visual impairments and multiple disabilities in preschool and kindergarten classrooms. *Journal of Visual Impairment & Blindness, 102,* 397–409.

Clark, C., & Stoner, J. B. (2008). An investigation of the spelling skills of Braille readers. *Journal of Visual Impairment & Blindness, 102,* 553–563.

Clark, E., Russman, S., & Orme, S. (1999). Traumatic brain injury: Effects on school functioning and intervention strategies. *School Psychology Review, 28,* 242–250.

Clark, S. G. (2000). The IEP process as a tool for collaboration. *Teaching Exceptional Children, 33*(2), 56–67.

Clayton, J., Burdge, M., Denham, A., Kleinhart, H., & Kearns, J. (2006). A four-step process for accessing the general curriculum for students with significant cognitive disabilities. *Teaching Exceptional Children, 38*(5), 20–27.

Cleft Palate Association. (2007, October). *About cleft lip and palate.* Retrieved August 17, 2009 from http://www.cleftline.org/parents/about_cleft_lip_and_palate

Clegg, J., Murphy, E., Almack, K., & Harvey, A. (2008). Tensions around inclusion: Reframing the moral horizon. *Journal of Applied Research in Intellectual Disabilities, 21*(1), 81–94.

Cline, K. P., Spradlin, T. E., & Plucker, J. A. (2005). Child obesity in Indiana: A growing public policy concern. *Center for Evaluation and Education Policy: Education Policy Brief, 3*(1), 1–7.

Cloninger, C. J. (2004). Designing collaborative educational services. In F. P. Orelove, D. Sobsey, & R. K. Silberman (Eds.), *Educating children with multiple disabilities: A collaborative approach* (pp. 1–30). Baltimore: Paul H. Brookes Publishing Co.

Closs, A. (2000). Issues for the effectiveness of children's school education. In A. Closs (Ed.), *The education of children with medical conditions* (pp. 93–106). London: David Fulton.

Cohen, D. (2006). Critiques of the "ADHD" enterprise. In G. Lloyd, J. Stead, & D. Cohen (Eds.), *Critical new perspectives on ADHD* (pp. 12–33). New York: Routledge.

Colangelo, N., Assouline, S. G., & Gross, M. U. M. (2004). *A nation deceived: How schools hold back America's brightest students.* Iowa City, IA: Institute for Research and Policy on Acceleration (IRPA). Retrieved September 12, 2009 from http://www.accelerationinstitute.org/nation_deceived/

Colangelo, N., & Davis, G. A. (Eds.). (2003). *Handbook of gifted education* (3rd ed.). Boston: Allyn & Bacon.

Cole, C. M., Waldron, N., & Majd, M. (2002, April). The academic progress of students across inclusive and traditional settings. *ISEAS Cable, 23*(4), 1–6.

Cole, C. M., Waldron, N., & Majd, M. (2004). Academic progress of students across inclusive and traditional settings. *Mental Retardation, 42,* 136–144.

Coleman, L. J. (2004). Is consensus on a definition in the field possible, desirable, necessary? *Roeper Review, 27*(1), 10–11.

Coleman, L. J. (2005). *Nurturing talent in high school: Life in the fast lane.* New York: Teachers College Press.

Coleman, M. C., & Webber, J. (2002). *Emotional and behavioral disorders: Theory and practice* (4th ed., pp. 1–19). Boston: Allyn & Bacon.

Coleman, M. R. (2001). *Conditions of teaching children with exceptional learning needs: The bright futures report* [ERIC digest E613]. (ERIC Document Reproduction No. ED455660)

Coleman, M. R. (2003). Exploring secondary options: Four variables for success. *Gifted Child Today, 26,* 22–24.

Coleman, M. R. (2005). Academic strategies that work for gifted students with learning disabilities. *Teaching Exceptional Children, 38*(1), 28–32.

Collett-Klingenberg, L. L. (1998). The reality of best practices in transition: A case study. *Exceptional Children, 65,* 67–78.

Collins, B. C., Kleinert, H. L., & Land, L. E. (2006). Addressing math standards and functional math. In D. M. Browder & F. Spooner (Eds.), *Teaching language arts, math, & science to students with significant cognitive disabilities* (pp. 197–228). Baltimore: Paul H. Brookes Publishing Co.

Collins, S. (2003, July 17). Mentally ill children face life without necessary services. *USA Today,* p. 13A.

Colorado Department of Education. (1993). Answers to questions about ADD. *Attention deficit disorders: A handbook for Colorado educators* (pp. 3–19). Denver: Author.

Colorado Department of Education. (2009, July). *Twice-exceptional students: gifted students with disabilities* [level 1: an introductory resource book]. Denver: Author. Retrieved September 10, 2009 from http://www.cde.state.co.us/gt/publications.htm

Colson, S. E., & Brandt, M. D. (2000). Working with families of children with attention-deficit/hyperactivity disorder. In M. J. Fine & R. L. Simpson (Eds.), *Collaboration with parents and families of children and youth with exceptionalities* (2nd ed., pp. 347–367). Austin, TX: Pro-Ed.

Communication Services for the Deaf (CSD). (2001). *Video relay service info.* Retrieved January 18, 2003, from www.covrs.com/VRS2Index.asp

Compton, M. V., Tucker, D. A., Flynn, P. F. (2009). Preparation and perceptions of speech-language pathologists working with children with cochlear implants. *Communication Disorders Quarterly, 30,* 142–154.

Coniglio, S. L., & Blackman, J. A. (1995). Developmental outcome of childhood leukemia. *Topics in Early Childhood Special Education, 15,* 19–31.

Connecticut Special Education Association. (1936). *Development and progress of special classes for mentally deficient children in Connecticut.* New Haven: Author.

Conners, C. K. (1997a). *Conners' Teacher Rating Scale–Revised (CTRS-R).* North Tonawanda, NY: Multi-Health Systems.

Conners, C. K. (1997b). *Conners' Parent Rating Scale–Revised (CPRS-R).* North Tonawanda, NY: Multi-Health Systems.

Conners, C. K. (2003). *Conners' Continuous Performance Test–II* (version 5). North Tonawanda, NY: Multi-Health Systems.

Conners, F. A., Rosenquist, C. J., Atwell, J. A., & Klinger, L. G. (2000). Cognitive strengths and weaknesses associated with Prader-Willi syndrome. *Education and Training in Mental Retardation and Developmental Disabilities, 35,* 441–448.

Connor, C. M., & Craig, H. K. (2006). African American preschoolers' language, emergent literacy skills, and use of African American English: A complex relation. *Journal of Speech, Language, and Hearing Research, 49,* 771–792.

Connor, D. J. (2006). Michael's story: "I get into so much trouble just by walking": Narrative knowing and life at the intersections of learning disability, race, and class. *Equity and Excellence in Education, 39,* 154–165.

Connor, D. J., & Ferri, B. A. (2006). The conflict within: Resistance to inclusion and other paradoxes in special education. *Disability & Society, 22,* 63–77.

Conoley, J. C., & Conoley, C. W. (1992). *School consultation: Practice and training* (2nd ed.). Boston: Allyn & Bacon.

Conroy, M., Sutherland, K., Haydon, T., Stormont, M., & Harmon, J. (2009). Preventing and ameliorating young children's chronic problem behaviors: An ecological classroom-based approach. *Psychology in the Schools, 46,* 3–17.

Conroy, M. A., Katsiyannis, A., Clark, D., Gable, R. A., & Fox, J. M. (2002). State Office of Education practices: Implementing the IDEA disciplinary provisions. *Behavioral Disorders, 27,* 98–108.

Conroy, P. W. (2005). English language learners with visual impairments: Strategies to enhance learning. *RE:view, 37,* 101–108.

Conroy, P. W. (2006). Hmong culture and visual impairment: Strategies for culturally sensitive practices. *RE:view: Rehabilitation Education for Blindness and Visual Impairment, 38,* 55–64.

Conroy, P. W. (2008). Paraprofessionals and students with visual impairments: Potential pitfalls and solutions. *RE:view: Rehabilitation Education for Blindness and Visual Impairment, 39,* 43–55.

Consortium for Appropriate Dispute Resolution in Special Education. (2001). *Frequently asked questions (FAQs) on mediation.* Eugene, OR: Author. Retrieved March 1, 2003, from www.directionservice.org/cadre/mediationfaqs.cfm

Conti-Ramsden, G., Botting, N., & Durkin, K. (2008). Parental perspectives during the transition to adulthood of adolescents with a history of specific language impairment (SLI). *Journal of Speech, Language, and Hearing Research, 51,* 84–96.

Coo, H., Ouellette-Kuntz, H., & Lloyd, J. E. V. (2008). Trends in autism prevalence: Diagnostic substitution revisited. *Journal of Autism and Developmental Disorders, 38,* 1036–1046.

Cook, C. R., Gresham, F. M., Kern, L., Barreras, R. B., Thornton, S., & Crews, S. D. (2008). Socialskills training for secondary students with emotional and/or behavioral disorders: A review and analysis of the meta-analytic literature. *Journal of Emotional and Behavioral Disorders, 16,* 131–144.

Cook, D. G., & Dunn, W. (1998). Sensory integration for students with autism. In R. L. Simpson & B. S. Myles (Eds.), *Educating children and youth with autism: Strategies for effective practice* (pp. 191–240). Austin, TX: Pro-Ed.

Cook, L., & Friend, M. (2010). The state of the art of collaboration on behalf of students with disabilities. *Journal of Educational and Psychological Consultation, 20.*

Cook, L., & Friend, M. (2010). The state of the art of collaboration on behalf of students with disabilities. *Journal of Educational and Psychological Consultation, 20,* 1–6.

Cook, L. H., & Boe, E. E. (2004, March–April). Exploding the myths of the special education teacher turnover: Examining progress made. *In CASE, 45*(5), 1–2.

Coombs-Richardson, R., & Mead, J. (2001). Supporting general educators' inclusive practices. *Teacher Education and Special Education, 24,* 383–390.

Cooney, G., Jahoda, A., Gumley, A., & Knott, F. (2006). Young people with intellectual disabilities attending mainstream and segregated schooling: Perceived stigma, social comparison, and future aspirations. *Journal of Intellectual Disability Research, 50,* 432–444.

Coots, J. J. (2007). Building bridges with families: Honoring the mandates of IDEIA. *Issues in Teacher Education, 16*(2), 33–40.

Copeland, S. R., McCall, J., Williams, C. R., Guth, C., Carter, E. W., Fowler, S. E., et al. (2002). High school peer buddies: A win–win situation. *Teaching Exceptional Children, 35*(1), 16–21.

Copeland, W., Shanahan, L., Costello, E. J., & Angold, A. (2009). Configurations of common childhood psychosocial risk factors. *Journal of Child Psychology and Psychiatry, 50,* 451–459.

Copp, H. L., Bordnick, P. S., Traylor, A. C., & Thyer, B. A. (2007). Evaluating wraparound services for seriously emotionally disturbed youth: Pilot study outcomes in Georgia. *Adolescence, 42*(168), 723–732.

Corbett, W. P., Clark, H. B., & Blank, W. (2002). Employment and social outcomes associated with vocational programming for youth with emotional or behavioral disorders. *Behavioral Disorders, 27,* 358–370.

Corkum, P. V., McKinnon, M. M., & Mullane, J. C. (2005). The effect of involving classroom teachers in a parent training program for families of children with ADHD. *Child and Family Behavior Therapy, 27,* 29–49.

Corn, A. L., Bina, M. J., & DePriest, L. B. (1995). *The parent perspective on schools for students who are blind or visually impaired: A national study.* Alexandria, VA: Association for Education and Rehabilitation of the Blind and Visually Impaired.

Corn, A. L., & Koenig, A. J. (2002). Literacy for students with low vision: A framework for delivering instruction. *Journal of Visual Impairment and Blindness, 95,* 305–321.

Corn, A. L., & Koenig, A. J. (Eds.) (1996). *Foundations of low vision: Clinical and functional perspectives.* New York: American Foundation for the Blind Press.

Corn, A. L., & Spungin, S. J. (2003). Free and appropriate public education and the personnel crisis for students with visual impairments and blindness. Gainesville: University of Florida, Center on Personnel Studies in Special Education. Retrieved September 9, 2006, from www.coe.ufl.edu/copsse/docs/IB-10/1/IB-10.pdf#search=%22visual%20impairment%20personnel%20crisis%20corn%22

Corn, A. L., Wall, R. S., Jose, R. T., Bell, J. K., Wilcox, K., & Perez, A. (2002). An initial study of reading and comprehension rates for students who received optical devices. *Journal of Visual Impairment and Blindness, 96,* 322–334.

Correa, V. I., Fazzi, D. L., & Pogrund, R. L. (2002). Team focus: Current trends, service delivery, and advocacy. In R. L. Pogrund & D. L. Fazzi (Eds.), *Early focus: Working with young children who are blind or visually impaired and their families* (pp. 405–441). New York: American Foundation for the Blind Press.

Correa-Torres, S. M. (2008). The nature of the social experiences of students with deaf-blindness who are educated in inclusive settings. *Journal of Visual Impairment & Blindness, 102,* 272–283.

Correa-Torres, S. M., & Johnson, J. (2004). Facing the challenges of itinerant teaching: Perspectives and suggestions from the field. *Journal of Visual Impairment and Blindness, 98,* 420–433.

Cosbey, J. D., & Johnston, S. (2006). Using a single-switch voice output communication aid to increase social access for children with severe disabilities in inclusive classrooms. *Research and Practice for Persons with Severe Disabilities, 31,* 144–156.

Cotton, K. (1991). *Educating urban minority youth: Research on effective practices.* Portland, OR: Northwest Regional Educational Library.

Council for Children with Behavioral Disorders. (2009a, May). *CCBD position summary: The use of physical restraints procedures in school settings.* Arlington, VA: Council for Exceptional Children.

Council for Children with Behavioral Disorders. (2009b, May). *CCBD position summary: The use of seclusion in school settings.* Arlington, VA: Council for Exceptional Children.

Council for Exceptional Children. (2002, January). *GT-Legal issues.* Arlington, VA: Author. Retrieved July 3, 2006, from http://www.ericec.org/faq/gt-legal.html

Council for Exceptional Children. (2002, October). *No Child Left Behind Act of 2001: Reauthorization of the Elementary and Secondary Education Act—A technical assistance resource.* Retrieved October 30, 2002, from www.cec.sped.org/pp/OverviewNCLB.pdf

Council for Exceptional Children. (2003, April/May). CEC says *all* students must be included in assessments. *CEC Today, 9*(7), 1, 5, 14.

Council for Exceptional Children. (2006). *Evidence-based practice—Wanted, needed, and hard to get.* Arlington, VA: Author. Retrieved July 2, 2006, from www.cec.sped.org/AM/Template.cfm?Section=Home&TEMPLATE=/CM/ContentDisplay.cfm&CONTENTID=6465

Council for Learning Disabilities. (1993). Concerns about the full inclusion of students with learning disabilities in regular education classrooms. *Learning Disability Quarterly, 16,* 126.

Council of State Directors of Programs for the Gifted. (2001). *The 1999–2000 state of the states gifted and talented education report.* Longmont, CO: Author.

Council of State Directors of Programs for the Gifted. (2007). *Gifted education: State of the nation.* Washington, DC: National Association for Gifted Children. Retrieved September 10, 2009 form http://www.nagc.org/index.aspx?id=1051

Council on Interracial Books for Children. (1978). *Identifying sexism and racism in children's books* [Kit]. New York: Author.

Courchesne, E., Karns, C. M., Davis, H. R., Ziccardi, R., Carper, R. A., Tigue, Z. D., Chisum, H. J. et al. (2001). Unusual brain growth patterns in early life in patients with autistic disorder: An MRI study. *Neurology, 57,* 245–254.

Court, D., & Givon, S. (2003). Group intervention: Improving social skills of adolescents with learning disabilities. *Teaching Exceptional Children, 36*(2), 46–51.

Coutinho, M. J., & Oswald, D. P. (2005). State variation in gender disproportionality in special education: Findings and recommendations. *Remedial and Special Education, 26,* 7–15.

Cox, S. G. (2008, May). Differentiated instruction in the elementary classroom. *Education Digest: Essential Readings Condensed for Quick Review, 73*(9), 52–54.

Coyle, J. L., Easterling, C., Lefton-Greif, M. A., & Mackay, L. E. (2006). *Case presentations by board recognized specialists in swallowing disorders: Evidence based clinical practice demonstrations.* BRS evidence based case presentations, ASHA convention. Retrieved October 27, 2006, from http://convention.asha.org/handouts/855_1198Coyle_James_L._089588_100306032745.pdf

Coyner, L. (1993). Academic success, self-concept, social acceptance and perceived social acceptance for hearing, hard of hearing and deaf students in a mainstream setting. *Journal of the American Deafness and Rehabilitation Association, 27*(2), 13–20.

Cramer, S., & Stivers, J. (2007). Don't give up! Practical strategies for challenging collaborations. *Teaching Exceptional Children, 39,* 6–11.

Cramond, B. (2004). Can we, should we, need we agree on a definition of giftedness? *Roeper Review, 27*(1), 15–16.

Crawford, S., & Elliott, R. T. (2007). Analysis of phonemes, graphemes, onsetrimes, and words with Braille-learning children. *Journal of Visual Impairment & Blindness, 101,* 534–544.

Creaghead, N. A. (1999). Evaluating language intervention approaches: Contrasting perspectives. *Language, Speech, and Hearing Services in Schools, 30,* 335–338.

Crow, K. L. (2008). Four types of disabilities: Their impact on online learning. *TechTrends: Linking Research and Practice to Improve Learning, 5,* 51–55.

Communication services for the Deaf. (2001). *Video relay service info.* Retrieved January 18, 2003, from www.covrs.com/VRS2Index.asp

Csikszentmihalyi, M. (1996). *Creativity: Flow and the psychology of discovery and invention.* New York: HarperCollins.

Csikszentmihalyi, M., Rathunde, K., & Whalen, S. (1993). *Talented teenagers: The roots of success and failure.* New York: Cambridge University Press.

Cukrowicz, K., Taylor, J., Schatschneider, C., & Iacono, W. (2006). Personality differences in children and adolescents with attention-deficit/hyperactivity disorder, conduct disorder, and controls. *Journal of Child Psychology and Psychiatry, 47,* 151–159.

Culatta, B., & Wiig, E. H. (2002). Language disabilities in school-age children and youth. In G. H. Shames & N. B. Anderson (Eds.), *Human communication disorders: An introduction* (6th ed., pp. 218–257). Boston: Allyn & Bacon.

Cullen, M., (2007). Voices of leadership: Stronger together. *Educational Leadership, 65*(10), 90–92.

Cullinan, D. (2002). *Students with emotional and behavior disorders: An introduction for teachers and other helping professionals* (pp. 32–65). Upper Saddle River, NJ: Merrill.

Cullinan, D., Evans, C., Epstein, M. H., & Ryser, G. (2003). Characteristics of emotional disturbance of elementary school students. *Behavioral Disorders, 28,* 94–110.

Cumming, J. J. (2008). Legal and educational perspectives of equity in assessment. *Assessment in Education: Principles, Policy & Practice, 15,* 123–125.

Cummings, R., Maddux, C. D., & Casey, J. (2000). Individualized transition planning for students with learning disabilities. *Career Development Quarterly, 49*(1), 60–72.

Cunningham, A., & Schreibman, L. (2008). Stereotypy in autism: The importance of function. *Research in Autism Spectrum Disorders, 2,* 469–479.

Cunningham, M. M., & Wodrich, D. L. (2006). The effect of sharing health information on teachers' production of classroom accommodations. *Psychology in the Schools, 43,* 553–564.

Curtis, S. E. (2005). Parents and litigation: Insights from a special education law clinic. *Phi Delta Kappan, 86,* 510–514.

Cushing, L. S., Clark, N. M., Carter, E. W., & Kennedy, C. H. (2005). Access to the general education curriculum for students with significant cognitive disabilities. *Teaching Exceptional Children, 38*(2), 6–13.

Cushner, K., McClelland, A., & Safford, P. (2000). *Human diversity in education: An integrative approach.* New York: McGraw-Hill.

Cuskelly, M. (2004). The evolving construct of intellectual disability: Is everything old new again? *International Journal of Disability, Development and Education, 51,* 117–122.

D'Arcangelo, M. (1999). Learning about learning to read: A conversation with Sally Shaywitz. *Educational Leadership, 57*(2), 26–31.

Dabkowski, D. M. (2004). Encouraging active parent participation in IEP team meetings. *Teaching Exceptional Children, 36*(3), 34–39.

Dales, L., Hammer, S. J., & Smith, N. J. (2001). Time trends in autism and in MMR immunization coverage in California. *Journal of the American Medical Association, 285,* 1183–1185.

Dalton, B., Sable, J., & Hoffman, L. (2006). *Characteristics of the 100 largest public elementary and secondary school districts in the United States: 2003–2004.* Washington, DC: National Center for Education Statistics, Institute of Education Sciences. Retrieved September 1, 2006, from http://nces.ed.gov/pubs2001/100_largest/discussion.asp#sb

Daly, B. P., Kral, M. C., & Brown, R. T. (2008). Cognitive and academic problems associated with childhood cancers and sickle cell disease. *School Psychology Quarterly, 23,* 230–242.

Danek, M. M., & Busby, H. (1999). *Transition planning and programming: Empowerment through partnership.* Washington, DC: Gallaudet University.

Daniel, P. T. K. (2000). Education for students with special needs: The judicially defined role of parents in the process. *Journal of Law and Education, 29*(1), 1–30.

Dardig, J. C. (200 ). The McClurg monthly magazine and 14 more practical ways to involve parents. *Teaching Exceptional Children, 38,* 46–51.

Darrow, A. A. (2009). Barriers to effective inclusion and strategies to overcome them. *General Music Today, 22*(3), 29–31.

David, J. L. ( 2008). Collaborative inquiry. *Educational Leadership, 66,* 87–88.

Davidson Institute for Talent Development. (2009, April). *Gifted education policies.* Retrieved April 8, 2009 from http://www.davidsongifted.org/db/StatePolicy.aspx

Davidson, M. A. (2008). ADHD in adults—A review of the literature. *Journal of Attention Disorders, 11,* 628–641.

Davies, D. K., Stock, S. E., & Wehmeyer, M. L. (2002). Enhancing independent task performance for individuals with mental retardation through use of a handheld self-directed visual and audio prompting system. *Education and Training in Mental Retardation and Developmental Disabilities, 37,* 209–218.

Davies, D. K., Stock, S. E., & Wehmeyer, M. L. (2002). Enhancing independent time-management skills of individuals with mental retardation: Using a palmtop personal computer. *Mental Retardation, 40,* 358–365.

Davis, E., Shelly, A., Waters, E., MacKinnon, A., Reddihough, D., Boyd, R., & Graham, H. K. (2009). Quality of life of adolescents with cerebral palsy: Perspectives of adolescents and parents. *Developmental Medicine & Child Neurology, 51,* 193–199.

Davis, L. (1996). Equality and education: An agenda for urban schools. *Equity and Excellence in Education, 29*(1), 61–67.

Davison, J. C., & Ford, D. Y. (2001). Perceptions of attention deficit hyperactivity disorder in one African American community. *Journal of Negro Education, 70,* 264–274.

Dawson, G., Meltzoff, A. N., Osterling, J., & Rinaldi, J. (1998). Neuropsychological correlates of early symptoms of autism. *Child Development, 69,* 1276–1285.

Dawson, M. M. (2007). The ideal versus the feasible when designing interventions for students with attention deficit hyperactivity disorder. *School Psychology Review, 36,* 274–278.

Day, J. N., McDonnell, A. P., & O'Neill, R. (2008). Teaching beginning Braille reading using an alphabet or uncontracted Braille approach. *Journal of Behavioral Education, 17,* 253–277.

De Graaf, I., Speetjens, P., Smit, F., de Wolff, M., & Tavecchio, L. (2008). Effectiveness of the Triple P Positive Parenting Program on behavioral problems in children: A meta-analysis. *Behavior Modification, 32,* 714–735.

Deatline-Buchman, A., & Jitendra, A. K. (2006). Enhancing argumentative essay writing of fourth-grade students with learning disabilities. *Learning Disability Quarterly, 29*(1), 39–54.

Dee, T. S. (2005). *Teachers and the gender gaps in student achievement.* Swarthmore, PA: Swarthmore College. Retrieved August 31, 2006, from http://www.swarthmore.edu/SocSci/tdee1/Research/w11660revised.pdf

DeFur, S. (2000, November). Designing individualized education program (IEP) transition plans (ERIC Digest #E598). Reston, VA: ERIC Clearinghouse on Disabilities and Gifted Education. Retrieved April 19, 2003, from http://ericec.org/digests/e598.html

Deidrick, K. K. M., & Farmer, J. E. (2005). School reentry following traumatic brain injury. *Preventing School Failure, 49*(4), 23–33.

del Carmen Salazar, M. (2008). English or nothing: The impact of rigid language policies on the inclusion of humanizing practices in a high school ESL program. *Equity & Excellence in Education, 41,* 341–356.

Delaney-Black, V., Covington, C., Templin, T., Kershaw, T., Nordstrom-Klee, B., Ager, J., Clark, N., Surendran, A., Martier, S., & Sokol, R. J. (2000). Expressive language development of children exposed to cocaine prenatally: Literature review and report of a prospective cohort study. *Journal of Communication Disorders, 33,* 463–481.

Delano, M. E. (2007). Video modeling interventions for individuals with autism. *Remedial and Special Education, 28,* 33–42.

Delcourt, M., & McIntire, J. (1993). An investigation of student learning outcomes: Results of a program satisfaction survey. *National Research Center on the Gifted and Talented Newsletter* (pp. 6–7). Storrs, CT: National Research Center on the Gifted and Talented.

Delgado, C. E. F., Vagi, S. J., & Scott, K. G. (2006). Tracking preschool children with developmental delay: Third grade outcomes. *American Journal on Mental Retardation, 111,* 299–306.

Delpit, L. D. (1992). Education in a multicultural society: Our future's greatest challenge. *Journal of Negro Education, 61,* 237–249.

DeMario, N. C., & Caruso, M. B. (2001). The expansion of outreach services at specialized schools for students with visual impairments. *Journal of Visual Impairment and Blindness, 95,* 488–491.

DeMario, N. C., & Heinze, T. (2001). The status of distance education in personnel preparation programs in visual impairment. *Journal of Visual Impairment and Blindness, 95,* 525–532.

Dembro, M. R. (2003, September). *Five-minute clinical consult: A reference for clinicians* (12th ed.). Retrieved October 9, 2003, from www.5mcc.com/Assets/SUMMARY/TP0583.html

Dempsey, I., Keen D., Pennell, D., J., & Neilands, J. (2009). Parent stress, parenting competence and family-centered support to young children with an intellectual or developmental disability. *Research in Developmental Disabilities: A Multidisciplinary Journal, 30,* 558–566.

Denehy, J. (2006). Just what do school nurses do? *Journal of School Nursing, 22,* 191–192.

Denning, C. B., Chamberlain, J. A., & Polloway, E. A. (2000). An evaluation of state guidelines for mental retardation: Focus on definition and classification practices. *Education and Training in Mental Retardation and Developmental Disabilities, 35,* 226–232.

Denton, C. A., Foorman, B. R., & Mathes, P. G. (2003). Perspective: Schools that "beat the odds"—Implications for reading instruction. *Remedial and Special Education, 24,* 258–261.

Denton, C. A., Hasbrouck, J. E., & Sekaquaptewa, S. (2003). The consulting teacher: A descriptive case study in responsive systems consultation. *Journal of Educational and Psychological Consultation, 14,* 41–73.

Denton, C. A., Vaughn, S., & Fletcher, J. M. (2003). Bringing research-based practice in reading intervention to scale. *Learning Disabilities Research and Practice, 18,* 201–211.

Denton, C. A., Wexler, J., Vaughn, S., & Bryan, D. (2008). Intervention provided to linguistically diverse middle school students with severe reading difficulties. *Learning Disabilities Research & Practice, 23,* 79–89.

DePaepe, P., Garrison-Kane, L., & Doelling, J. (2002). Supporting students with health needs in schools: An overview of selected health conditions. *Focus on Exceptional Children, 35*(1), 1–24.

DePompei, R., Gillette, Y., Goetz, E., Xenopoulos-Oddsson, A., Bryen, D., & Dowds, M. (2008). Practical applications for use of PDAs and smartphones with children and adolescents who have traumatic brain injury. *NeuroRehabilitation, 23,* 487–499.

DeShazo-Barry, T., Lyman, R. D., & Klinger, L. G. (2002). Academic underachievement and attention-deficit/hyperactivity disorder: The negative impact of symptom severity on school performance. *Journal of School Psychology, 40,* 259–283.

Deshler, D. D. (2003). Intervention research and bridging the gap between research and practice. *Learning Disabilities: A Contemporary Journal, 1*(1), 1–7.

Deshler, D. D., Ellis, E. S., & Lenz, B. K. (1996). *Teaching adolescents with learning disabilities: Strategies and methods* (2nd ed.). Denver, CO: Love.

Deshler, D. D., Schumaker, J., Bulgren, J., Lenz, K., Jantzen, J. E., Adams, G., Carnine, D., Grossen, B., Davis, B., & Marquis, J. (2001). Making learning easier: Connecting new knowledge to things students already know. *Teaching Exceptional Children, 33*(4), 82–85.

DeSimone, J. R., & Parmar, R. S. (2006). Middle school mathematics teachers' beliefs about inclusion of students with learning disabilities. *Learning Disabilities Research and Practice, 21,* 98–110.

DeThorne, L. S., Petrill, S. A., Hayiou-Thomas, M. E., & Plomin, R. (2005). Low expressive vocabulary: Higher heritability as a function of more severe cases. *Journal of Speech, Language, and Hearing Research, 48,* 792–804.

Dettmer, P., Dyck, N., & Thurston, L. P. (1999). *Consultation, collaboration, and teamwork for students with special needs* (3rd ed.). Boston: Allyn & Bacon.

Deutscher, B., & Fewell, R. (2005). Early predictors of attention-deficit/hyperactivity disorder and school difficulties in low-birth weight, premature children. *Topics in Early Childhood Special Education, 25,* 71–79.

Dev, P. C. (1997). Intrinsic motivation and academic achievement: What does their relationship imply for the classroom teacher? *Remedial and Special Education, 18,* 12–19.

DeVilliers, P., & Pomerantz, S. (1992). Hearing-impaired students learning new words from written context. *Applied Psycholinguistics, 13,* 409–431.

DeVito, J. A. (2009). *The interpersonal communication book* (12th ed.). Boston: Allyn & Bacon.

Devlin, P. (2008). Create effective teacher-paraprofessional teams. *Intervention in School and Clinic, 44*(1), 41–44.

Dew, A., Balandin, S., & Llewellyn, G. (2008). The psychosocial impact on siblings of people with lifelong physical disability: A review of the literature. *Journal of Developmental & Physical Disabilities, 20*, 485–507.

Diamond, M., & Hopson, J. (1998). *Magic trees of the mind.* New York: Penguin Putnam.

Diana vs. State Board of Education, CA 70 RFT (N.D. Cal. 70).

Dieker, L. A. (2001). What are the characteristics of "effective" middle and high school co-taught teams for students with disabilities? *Preventing School Failure, 46*, 14–23.

Diener, M. B., & Millich, R. (1997). Effects of positive feedback on the social interactions of boys with attention deficit hyperactivity disorder: A test of the self-protective hypothesis. *Journal of Clinical Child Psychology, 26*, 256–265.

Dietz, C. H. (1995). *Moving toward the standards: A national action plan for mathematics education reform for the deaf.* Washington, DC: Gallaudet University Pre-College Programs.

Dietz, S., & Montague, M. (2006). Attention deficit hyperactivity disorder co-morbid with emotional and behavioral disorders and learning disabilities in adolescents. *Exceptionality, 14*, 19–33.

Dillon, R., & Osborne, S. (2006) Intelligence and behavior among individuals identified with attention deficit disorders. *Exceptionality, 14*, 3–18.

Division for Early Childhood. (1999, October). *Division for Early Childhood (DEC) concept paper on the identification of and intervention with challenging behavior.* Retrieved July 30, 2003, from www.dec-sped.org/pdf/positionpapers/Concept_Paper_Chall_Behav.pdf

Doelling, J. E., Bryde, S., Brunner, J., & Martin, B. (1998). Collaborative planning for inclusion of a student with developmental disabilities. *Middle School Journal, 29*(3), 34–39.

Dole, R. L. (2004). Collaborating successfully with your school physical therapist. *Teaching Exceptional Children, 36*(5), 28–35.

Dollaghan, C. A. (2004). Evidence-based practice in communication disorders: What do we know, and when do we know it? *Journal of Communication disorders, 37*, 391–400.

Dominic, J. A. (2001). Anticipating adolescent aggression. *Kappa Delta Phi Record, 37*, 180–182.

Donenberg, G. R., & Pao, M. (2005). Youths and HIV/AIDS: Psychiatry's role in a changing epidemic. *Journal of the American Academy of Child and Adolescent Psychiatry, 44*, 728–747.

Donne, V. J., & Zigmond, N. (2008). An observational study of reading instruction for students who are deaf or hard of hearing in public schools. *Communication Disorders Quarterly, 29*, 219–235.

Donovan, M. S., & Cross, C. T. (Eds.). (2002a). *Minority students in special and gifted education.* Retrieved February 26, 2004, from www.edrs.com/members/sp.cfm?AN=ED469543

Donovan, M. S., & Cross, C. T. (Eds.). (2002b). *Minority students in special and gifted education.* Washington, DC: National Academies Press.

Dooley, E. A., & Perkins, N. (1998, March). *Let's talk about the needs of African American children with sickle cell disease: A recognized "other health impairment."* Charleston, SC: Coming Together—Preparing for Rural Special Education in the Twenty-First Century, *Conference Proceeding of the American Council on Rural Special Education.* (ERIC Document Reproduction Service No. ED417908)

Doré, R., Dion, É, Wagner, S., & Brunet, J. P. (2002). High school inclusion of adolescents with mental retardation: A multiple case study. *Education and Training in Mental Retardation and Developmental Disabilities, 37*, 253–261.

Doskoch, P. (2005). The winning edge. *Psychology Today, 38*(6), 42–52.

Douville, P. (2000). Helping parents develop literacy at home. *Preventing School Failure, 44*, 179–180.

Dowdy, C. A., Patton, J. R., Smith, T. E. C., & Polloway, E. A. (2000). The transition to adult living. In C. A. Dowdy, J. R. Patton, T. E. C. Smith, & E. A Polloway (Eds.), *Attention-deficit/hyperactivity disorder in the classroom: A practical guide for teachers* (pp. 195–208). Austin, TX: Pro-Ed.

Dowker, A. (2005). Early identification and intervention for students with mathematics difficulties. *Journal of Learning Disabilities, 38*, 324–332.

Downey, M. T., & Metcalf, F. D. (1999). *Colorado: Crossroads of the West* (3rd ed.). Boulder, CO: Pruett.

Downing, J. A. (2004). Related services for students with disabilities: Introduction to the special issue. *Intervention in School and Clinic, 39*, 195–208.

Downing, J. E. (2000). Augmentative communication devices: A critical aspect of assistive technology. *Journal of Special Education Technology, 15*(3), 35–38.

Downing, J. E. (2001). Meeting the communication needs of students with severe and multiple disabilities in general education classrooms. *Exceptionality, 9*, 147–156.

Downing, J. E. (2002). *Including students with severe and multiple disabilities in typical classrooms: Practical strategies for teachers* (2nd ed.). Baltimore: Paul H. Brookes.

Downing, J. E. (2005a). *Teaching communication skills to students with severe disabilities.* Baltimore: Paul H. Brookes Publishing Co.

Downing, J. E. (2005b). *Teaching literacy skills to students with significant disabilities.* Corwin Press.

Downing, J. E. (2008). *Including students with severe and multiple disabilities in typical classrooms: Practical strategies for teachers.* (3rd ed.). Baltimore: Paul H. Brookes Publishing Co.

Downing, J. E. (2010). *Teaching students with moderate and severe intellectual disabilities: Academic instruction in inclusive classrooms.* Thousand Oaks, CA: Corwin.

Downing, J. E. (2005a). *Teaching communication skills to students with severe disabilities.* Baltimore: Paul H. Brookes Publishing Co.

Downing, J. E., Cavallaro, C., & Spencer, S. (2003). *The development of an inclusive elementary school: Perceptions from stakeholders.* Manuscript in preparation.

Downing, J. E., & Demchak, M. A. (2002). First steps: Determining individual abilities and how best to support students. In J. E. Downing (Ed.), *Including students with severe and multiple disabilities in typical classrooms: Practical strategies for teachers* (2nd ed., pp. 37–70). Baltimore: Paul H. Brookes.

Downing, J. E., & Demchak, M. A. (2008). First steps: Determining individual abilities and how best to support students. In J. E. Downing (Ed.), *Including students with severe and multiple disabilities in typical classrooms: Practical strategies for teachers* (3rd ed., pp. 49–90).Baltimore: Paul H. Brookes Publishing Co.

Downing, J. E., Eichinger, J., & Williams, L. J. (1997). Inclusive education for students with severe disabilities: Comparative views of principals and educators at different levels of implementation. *Remedial and Special Education, 18*, 133–142.

Downing, J. E., & Peckham-Hardin, K. D. (2007). Inclusive education: What makes it a good education for students with moderate to severe disabilities? *Research and Practice for Persons with Severe Disabilities, 32*, 16–30.

Downing, J. E., Ryndak, D. L., & Clark, D. (2000). Paraeducators in inclusive classrooms: Their own perceptions. *Remedial and Special Education, 21*, 171–181.

Downing, J. E., Spencer, S., & Cavallaro, C. (2004). The development of an inclusive elementary school: Perceptions from stakeholders. *Research and Practice for Persons with Severe Disabilities, 29*, 11–24.

Doyle, M. B., & Giangreco, M. F. (2009). Making presentation software accessible to high school students with intellectual disabilities. *Teaching Exceptional Children, 41*(3), 24–31.

Drasgow, E., & Yell, M. L. (2001). Functional behavioral assessments: Legal requirements and challenges. *School Psychology Review, 30,* 239–251.

Drasgow, E., Yell, M. L., & Robinson, T. R. (2001). Developing legally correct and educationally appropriate IEPs. *Remedial and Special Education, 22,* 359–373.

Dube, S. R., & Orpinas, P. (2009). Understanding excessive school absenteeism as school refusal behavior. *Children & Schools, 31,* 87–95.

Duchan, J. (2001). *History of speech-pathology in America.* Retrieved November 9, 2003, from www.acsu.buffalo.edu/~duchan/1900-1945.html

Duchan, J. (2006). Getting here: A short history of speech pathology in America: The elocution movement. Retrieved December 8, 2006, from www.acsu.buffalo.edu/~duchan/new_history/hist19c/elocution.html

Duchan, J. (2008). *Getting here: A short history of speech-pathology in America.* Retrieved August 13, 2009 from http://www.acsu.buffalo.edu/~duchan/new_history/overview.html

Duchardt, B., Marlow, L., Inman, D., Christensen, P., & Reeves, M. (1999). Collaboration and co-teaching: General and special education faculty. *The Clearing House, 72*(3), 186–190.

Duckworth, S., Smith-Rex, S., Okey, S., Brookshire, M. A., Rawlinson, D., Rawlinson, R. et al. (2001). Wraparound services for young schoolchildren with emotional and behavioral disorders. *Teaching Exceptional Children, 33*(4), 54–60.

Dudley, J. R. (2005). Best friends of people with mental illness and mental retardation. *Psychiatric Services, 56,* 610–611.

DuFour, R. (2007). Professional learning communities: A bandwagon, an idea worth considering, or our best hope for high levels of learning? *Middle School Journal, 39*(1), 4–8.

Duke, D. L. (1991). School policies and educational opportunities for minority students. *Peabody Journal of Education, 66*(4), 17–26.

Dunlap, G., & Koegel, R. L. (1999). Welcoming editorial. *Journal of Positive Behavioral Interventions, 1,* 2–3.

Dunn, L. (1968). Special education for the mildly retarded: Is much of it justifiable? *Exceptional Children, 35,* 5–22.

Dunn, W. (1999). *Sensory Profile.* San Antonio, TX: Psychological Corporation.

Dunst, C., & Trivette, C. M. (2009). Using research evidence to inform and evaluate early childhood intervention practices. *Topics in Early Childhood Special Education, 29,* 40–52.

Dunst, C. J., & Bruder, M. B. (2002). Valued outcomes of service coordination, early intervention, and natural environments. *Exceptional Children, 68,* 361–375.

DuPaul, G., & Weyandt, L. (2006). School-based intervention for children with attention deficit hyperactivity disorder: Effects on academic, social and behavioral functioning. *International Journal of Disability, Development and Education. 53,* 161–176.

Duran, E. (2006). *Teaching English learners in inclusive classrooms* (3rd ed.). Springfield, IL: Charles C. Thomas.

Durand, V. M. (1999). Functional communication training using assistive devices: Recruiting verbal communities of reinforcement. *Journal of the Association of Behavioral Analysis, 32,* 247–267.

Durand, V. M., Christodulu, K. V., & Koegel, R. L. (2004). Description of a sleep-restriction program to reduce bedtime disturbances and night waking. *Journal of Positive Behavior Interventions, 6,* 83–91.

Durando, J. (2008). A survey on literacy instruction for students with multiple disabilities. *Journal of Visual Impairment & Blindness, 102,* 40–45.

Dybdahl, C. S., & Ryan, S. (2009). Inclusion for students with fetal alcohol syndrome: Classroom teachers talk about practice. *Preventing School Failure, 53,* 185–196.

Dye, G. A. (2000). Graphic organizers to the rescue: Helping students link—and remember—information. *Teaching Exceptional Children, 32*(3), 72–76.

Dyson, L. L. (2003). Children with learning disabilities within the family context: A comparison with siblings in global self-concept, academic self-perception, and social competence. *Learning Disabilities Research and Practice, 18,* 1–9.

Dyson, L. L. (2005). Kindergarten children's understanding of attitudes toward people with disabilities. *Topics in Early Childhood Special Education, 25,* 95–105.

Dyson, L. L. (2007). The unexpected effects of inclusion on the families of students with learning disabilities: A focus-group study. *Learning Disabilities: A Multidisciplinary Journal, 14,* 185–194.

Easterbrooks, S., & Baker-Hawkins, S. (Eds.). (1995). *Deaf and hard of hearing students educational service guidelines.* Alexandria, VA: National Association of State Directors of Special Education.

Echaore-McDavid, S. (2006) *Career opportunities in education and related services* (2nd ed.). New York: Ferguson.

Eckstein, M. (2009). Enrichment 2.0: Gifted and talented education for the 21st century. *Gifted Child Today, 32,* 59–63.

Edeh, O. M. (2006). Cross-cultural investigation of interest-based training and social interpersonal problem solving in students with mental retardation. *Education and Training in developmental disabilities, 41,* 163–176.

Edens, R. M., Murdick, N. L., & Gartin, B. C. (2003). Preventing infection in the classroom: The use of universal precautions. *Teaching Exceptional Children, 35*(4), 62–65.

Edmonds, K., & Crichton, S. (2008). Finding ways to teach to students with FASD: A research study. *International Journal of Special Education, 23*(1), 54–73.

Education Commission of the States. (2004). *No Child Left Behind.* Retrieved March 20, 2006, from http://nclb2.ecs.org/Projects_Centers/index.aspx?issueid=gen&IssueName=General

Edyburn, D. L. (1998, February/March). Part III: A map of the technology integration process. *Closing the gap.* Retrieved November 26, 2002, from www.closingthegap.com/library

Egan, G. (2001). *The skilled helper: A problem-management and opportunity-development approach to helping* (7th ed.). Belmont, CA: Wadsworth.

Egger, H. L., & Angold, A. (2006). Common emotional and behavioral disorders in preschool children: Presentation, nosology, and epidemiology. *Journal of Child Psychology and Psychiatry, 47,* 313–337.

Eichinger, J., & Downing, J. E. (2008). Instruction in the general education environment. In J. E. Downing (Ed.), *Including students with severe and multiple disabilities in typical classrooms: Practical strategies for teachers* (3rd ed., pp. 21–48). Baltimore: Paul H. Brookes Publishing Co.

Eisenberg, D., & Schneider, H. (2007). Perceptions of academic skills of children diagnosed with ADHD. *Journal of Attention Disorders, 10,* 390–397.

Eisenbraun, K., Johnstone, C., Lazarus, S., Liu, K., Matchett, D., Moen, R., Quenemoen, M., Quenemoen, R., Thompson, S., & Thurlow, M. (2009). *Reading and students with visual impairments or blindness.* Minneapolis: Partnership for Accessible Reading Assessment, University of Minnesota. Retrieved August 28, 2009 from http://www.readingassessment.info/resources/publications/visualimpairment.htm

Elhoweris, H., Mutua, K., Alsheikh, N., & Holloway, P. (2005). Effect of children's ethnicity on teachers' referral and recommendation decisions in gifted and talented programs. *Remedial and Special Education, 26,* 25–31.

Eli Lilly. (2003). *The history of ADHD.* Retrieved June 28, 2003, from www.strattera.com/1_3_childhood_adhd/1_3_1_1_2_history.jsp

Elias, M. (2006, September 27). ADHD drugs becomes a family matter. *USA Today.* Retrieved October 10, 2006, from http://www.usatoday.com/news/health/2006-9-27-adhd-drugs_x.htm

Elliott, J., Ysseldyke, J., Thurlow, M., & Erickson, R. (1998). What about assessment and accountability? Practical implications for educators. *Teaching Exceptional Children, 31*(2), 20–27.

Elliott, J. L., & Thurlow, M. L. (2006). *Improving test performance of students with disabilities on district and state assessments* (2nd ed.). Thousand Oaks, CA: Corwin.

Elliot, L. B., Stinson, M. S., McKee, B. G., Everhart, V. S., & Francis, P. J. (2001). College students' perceptions of the C-print speech-to-text transcription system. *Journal of Deaf Studies and Deaf Education, 6*(4), 285–298.

Ellis, E. S. (1998). Watering up the curriculum for adolescents with learning disabilities—Part 2: Goals of the affective dimension. *Remedial and Special Education, 19,* 91–105.

Ellis, E. S., & Lenz, B. K. (1987). A component analysis of effective learning strategies for LD students. *Learning Disabilities Focus, 2,* 94–107.

Ely, R., Emerson, R. W., Maggiore, T., Rothberg, M., O'Connell, T., & Hudson, L. (2006). Increased content knowledge of students with visual impairments as a result of extended descriptions. *Journal of Special Education Technology, 21*(3), 31–43.

Emerson, R. W., Corn, A., & Siller, M. A. (2006). Trends in braille and large-print production in the United States: 2000–2004. *Journal of Visual Impairment and Blindness, 100,* 137–151.

Engel, R. G., & Melamed, B. G. (2002). Stress and coping in children at risk for medical problems. In L. L. Hayman, M. M. Mahon, & J. R. Turner (Eds.), *Chronic illness in children: An evidence-based approach* (pp. 171–198). New York: Springer.

English, K. M. (1997). *Self advocacy for students who are deaf or hard of hearing.* Austin, TX: Pro-Ed.

Enhancing numeracy. In D. M. Browder & F. Spooner (Eds.), *Teaching Language Arts, Math, & Science to Students with Significant Cognitive Disabilities* (pp. 17– 195). Baltimore: Paul H. Brookes Publishing Co.

Epanchin, B. C., & Friend, M. (2007). The adolescence of inclusive practices: Building bridges through collaboration. In J. McLeskey (Ed.), *Classic articles and inclusion.* Upper Saddle River, NJ: Merrill.

Ephross, P. S., & Vassil, T. V. (2004). Group work with working groups. In C. D. Garvin, L. M. Gutiérrez, & M. J. Maeda (Eds.), *Handbook of social work with groups* (pp. 400–414). New York: Guilford Press.

Epilepsy Foundation of America. (2009). *First aid.* Retrieved September 6, 2009 from http://www.epilepsyfoundation.org/about/firstaid/

Epilepsy Foundation of America. (2009). Epilepsy and seizure statistics. Retrieved September 5, 2009 from http://www.epilepsyfoundation.org/about/statistics.cfm

Epilepsy Foundation. (2005). Epilepsy in children. Retrieved September 3, 2006, from www.epilepsyfoundation.org/answerplace/Life/children

Epstein, J. N., Erkanli, A., Conners, C. K., Klaric, J., Costello, J. E., & Angold, A. (2003). Relations between continuous performance test performance measures and ADHD behaviors. *Journal of Abnormal Child Psychology, 31,* 543–554.

Epstein, M. H. (2004). *Behavioral and Emotional Rating Scale: A Strength-Based Approach to Assessment* (2nd ed.). Austin, TX: PRO-ED.

Epstein, M. H., & Cullinan, D. (1998). *The scale for assessing emotional disturbance.* Austin, TX: Pro-Ed.

Epstein, M. H., Kutash, K., & Duchnowski, A. (Eds.). (1998). *Outcomes for children and youth with behavioral and emotional disorders and their families: Programs and evaluation best practices.* Austin, TX: Pro-Ed.

Epstein, M. H., & Sharma, J. M. (1998). *Behavioral and emotional rating scale: A strength-based approach to assessment.* Austin, TX: Pro-Ed.

Erchul, W. P. (1987). A relational communication analysis of control in school consultation. *Professional School Psychology, 2,* 113–134.

Erchul, W. P., DuPaul, G. J., Grissom, P. F., Junod, R. E. V., Jitendra, A. K., Mannella, M. G., Tresco, K. E., Elammer-Rivera, L. M., & Volpe, R. J. (2007). Relationships among relational communication processes and consultation outcomes for students with attention deficit hyperactivity disorder. *School Psychology Review, 36,* 111–129.

Erez, F., & Peled, I. (2001). Cognition and metacognition: Evidence of higher thinking in problem-solving of adolescents with mental retardation. *Education and Training in Mental Retardation and Developmental Disabilities, 36,* 83–93.

ERIC Clearinghouse on Disabilities and Gifted Education. (2001, April). *Educating exceptional children: A statistical profile.* Arlington, VA: Council for Exceptional Children.

ERIC Clearinghouse on Disabilities and Gifted Education. (2003, March). *Prader-Willi syndrome.* Retrieved October 9, 2003, from http://ericec.org/faq/praderwl.html

Erickson, M. E. (1987). Deaf readers reading beyond the literal. *American Annals of the Deaf, 132,* 291–294.

Erickson, M. J., Stage, S. A., & Nelson, J. R. (2006). Naturalistic study of the behavior of students with EBD referred for functional behavioral assessment. *Journal of Emotional and Behavioral Disorders, 14,* 31–40.

Erin, J. N., (1988). The teacher–consultant: The teacher of visually handicapped students and collaborative consultation. *Education of the Visually Handicapped, 20,* 57–63.

Erin, J. N., Fazzi, D. L., Gordon, R. L., Isenberg, S. J., & Paysse, E. A. (2002). Vision focus: Understanding the medical and functional implications of vision loss. In R. L. Pogrund & D. L. Fazzi (Eds.), *Early focus: Working with young children who are blind or visually impaired and their families* (pp. 52–106). New York: American Foundation for the Blind Press.

Erwin, E. J., & Soodak, L. C. (2008). The evolving relationship between families of children with disabilities and professionals. In T. C. Jiménez, & V. L. Graf (Eds.), *Education for all: Critical issues in the education of children and youth with disabilities* (pp. 35–69). San Francisco: Jossey-Bass.

Espe-Sherwindt, M. (2008). Family-centered practice: Collaboration, competency and evidence. *Support for Learning, 23,* 136–143.

Espin, C., Wallace, T., Campbell, H., Lembke, E. S., Long, J. D., & Ticha, R. (2008). Curriculum-based measurement in writing: Predicting the success of high-school students on state standards tests. *Exceptional Children, 74,* 174–193.

Esquivel, S. L., Ryan, C. S., & Bonner, M. (2008). Involved parents' perceptions of their experiences in school-based team meetings. *Journal of Educational and Psychological Consultation, 18,* 234–258.

Estes, M. B. (2006). Charter schools: Do they work for troubled students? *Preventing School Failure, 51,* 55–61.

Etscheidt, S. (1991). Reducing aggressive behavior and increasing self-control: A cognitive behavioral training program for behaviorally disordered adolescents. *Behavioral Disorders, 16,* 107–115.

Etscheidt, S. (2005). Paraprofessional services for students with disabilities: A legal analysis of issues. *Research and Practice for Persons with Severe Disabilities, 30,* 60–80.

Etscheidt, S. (2006). Least restrictive and natural environments for young children with disabilities: A legal analysis of issues. *Topics in Early Childhood Special Education, 26,* 167–178.

Etscheidt, S. (2007). The excusal provision of the IDEA 2004: Streamlining procedural compliance or prejudicing rights of students with disabilities? *Preventing School Failure, 51*(4), 13–18.

Etzel-Wise, D., & Mears, B. (2004). Adapted physical education and therapeutic recreation in schools. *Intervention in School and Clinic, 39,* 223–232.

Evans, D., Hearn, M., Uhlemann, M., & Ivey, A. (1984). *Essential interviewing: A programmed approach in effective communication* (2nd ed.). Pacific Grove, CA: Brooks/Cole.

Evans, J. L. (2001). An emergent account of language impairments in children with SLI: Implications for assessment and intervention. *Journal of Communication Disorders, 34,* 39–54.

Evans, S. W., Serpell, Z. N., Schultz, B. K., & Pastor, D. A. (2007). Cumulative benefits of secondary school-based treatment of students with attention deficit hyperactivity disorder. *School Psychology Review, 36,* 256–273.

Evans, S. W., Sibley, M., & Serpell, Z. N. (2009). Changes in caregiver strain over time in young adolescents with ADHD: The role of oppositional and delinquent behavior. *Journal of Attention Disorders, 12*, 516–524.

Evans, S. W., Timmins, B., Sibley, M., White, L. C., Serpell, Z. N., & Schultz, B. (2006). Developing coordinated, multimodal, school-based treatment for young adolescents with ADHD. *Education and Treatment of Children, 29*, 359–378.

Ezrati-Vinacour, R., Platzky, R., & Yairi, E. (2001). The young child's awareness of stuttering-like disfluency. *Journal of Speech, Language, and Hearing Research, 44*, 368–379.

Fad, K. M. (1998). Success through collaboration. In C. A. Dowdy, J. R. Patton, T. E. C. Smith, & E. A. Polloway (Eds.), *Attention-deficit/hyperactivity disorder in the classroom: A practical guide for teachers* (pp. 173–194). Austin, TX: Pro-Ed.

Faggella-Luby, M. N., & Deshler, D. D. (2008). Reading comprehension in adolescents with LD: What we know, what we need to learn. *Learning Disabilities: Research & Practice, 23*, 70–78.

Fahlman, S. (2000). *Actualization of giftedness: Effects of perceptions in gifted adolescents*. Retrieved March 1, 2003, from www.metagifted.org/topics/gifted/giftedAdolescents/researchActualizationOfGiftedness.html

Fairlie, R. W. (2005, September). *Are we really a nation online? Ethnic and racial disparities in access to technology and their consequences* (Report for the Leadership Conference on Civil Rights Education Fund). Retrieved August 12, 2006 from www.freepress.net/docs/lccrdigitaldivide.pdf

Falk-Ross, F., Watman, L., Kokesh, K., Iverson, M., Williams, E., & Wallace, A. (2009). Natural complements: Collaborative approaches for educators to support students with learning disabilities and literacy difficulties. *Reading and Writing Quarterly, 25*, 104–117.

Falvey, M. Z., Givner, C. C., & Kimm, C. (1996). What do I do Monday morning? In S. Stainback & W. Stainback (Eds.), *Inclusion: A guide for educators* (pp. 117–138). Baltimore: Paul H. Brookes.

Faraone, S. V., Biederman, J., Weiffenbach, B., Keith, T., Chu, M. P., Weaver, A., Spencer, T. J., Wilens, T. E., Frazier, J., Cleves, M., & Sakai, J. (1999). Dopamine $D_4$ gene 7-repeat allele and attention deficit hyperactivity disorder. *American Journal of Psychiatry, 156*, 768–770.

Farber, J. G., & Goldstein, M. K. (1998). Parents working with speech-language pathologists to foster partnerships in education. *Language, Speech, and Hearing Services in Schools, 29*, 24–34.

Farmer, J. E., & Peterson, L. (1995). Pediatric traumatic brain injury: Promoting successful school reentry. *School Psychology Review, 24*, 230–243.

Farmer, T. W. (2000). Misconceptions of peer rejection and problem behavior: Understanding aggression in students with mild disabilities. *Remedial and Special Education, 21*, 194–208.

Farmer, T. W., Farmer, E. M. A., Estell, D. B., & Hutchins, B. C. (2007). The developmental dynamics of aggression and the prevention of school violence. *Journal of Emotional and Behavioral Disorders, 15*, 197–208.

Farmer, T. W., Quinn, M. M., Hussey, W., & Holahan, T. (2001). The development of disruptive behavioral disorders and correlated constraints: Implications for intervention. *Behavioral Disorders, 26*, 117–130.

Farnsworth, C. R., & Luckner, J. L. (2008). The impact of assistive technology on curriculum accommodations for a Braille-reading student. *RE:view: Rehabilitation Education for Blindness and Visual Impairment, 39*, 171–187.

Fasbender, C., & Schweitzer, J. B. (2006). Is there evidence for neural compensation in attention deficit hyperactivity disorder? A review of the functional neuroimaging literature. *Clinical Psychology Review, 26*, 445–465.

Fast, D. (2003, April). *What is the molecular cause of Fragile X syndrome?* Retrieved October 8, 2003, from http://fragilex.org/html/molecular.htm

Felsenfeld, S. (2002). Finding susceptibility genes for developmental disorders of speech: The long and winding road. *Journal of Communication Disorders, 35*, 329–345.

Feng, A. X., & Van Tassel-Baska. (2008). Identifying low-income and minority students for gifted programs: Academic and affective impact of performance-based assessment. In J. L. Van Tassel-Baska (Ed.), *Alternative assessments with gifted and talented students* (129–146). Waco, TX: Prufrock.

Fennick, E. (2001). Co-teaching: An inclusive curriculum for transition. *Teaching Exceptional Children, 33*(6), 60–66.

Fenning, P., & Rose, J. (2007). Overrepresentation of African American students in exclusionary discipline: The role of school policy. *Urban Education, 42*, 536–559.

Ferguson, H., Myles, B. S., & Hagiwara, T. (2005). Using a personal digital assistant to enhance the independence of an adolescent with Asperger Syndrome. *Education and Training in Developmental Disabilities, 40*, 60–67.

Ferrell, K. A. (1999). *Goal 3 survey of personnel preparation programs in visual impairments: A status report and national challenge.* (Available from the Division of Special Education, University of Northern Colorado, Greeley, CO 80639)

Ferrell, K. A. (2000). Growth and development of young children. In M. C. Holbrook & A. J. Koenig (Eds.), *Foundations of education: History and theory of teaching children and youths with visual impairments* (2nd ed., pp. 111–134). New York: American Foundation for the Blind Press.

Ferrell, K. A. (2005). The effects of NCLB. *Journal of Visual Impairment and Blindness, 99*, 681–683.

Ferrell, K. A., Buettel, M., Sebald, A. M., & Pearson, R. (2006). *Mathematics research analysis.* Greeley, CO: National Center on Severe and Sensory Disabilities, University of Northern Colorado. Retrieved August 28, 2009 from http://www.unco.edu/ncssd/research/math_meta_analysis.shtml

Ferrell, K. A., Shaw, A. R., & Dietz, S. J. (1998). *Project PRISM: A longitudinal study of developmental patterns of children who are visually impaired* (Final Report, CFDA 84.023C, Grant H023C10188). Greeley: University of Northern Colorado.

Ferrell, K. A., Trief, E., Dietz, S. J., Bonner, M. A., Cruz, D., Ford, E., & Stratton, J. M. (1990). Visually impaired infants research consortium (VIIRC): First-year results. *Journal of Visual Impairment and Blindness, 84*, 404–410.

Ferri, B. A., & Connor, D. J. (2005). Tools of exclusion: Race, disability, and (re)segregated education. *Teachers College Record, 107*, 453–474.

Fewell, R. R. (2000). Assessment of young children with special needs: Foundation for tomorrow. *Topics of Early Childhood Special Education, 20*(1), 38–42.

Fiedler, C. R., & Danneker, J. E. (2007). Self-advocacy instruction: Bridging the research-to-practice gap. *Focus on Exceptional Children, 39*(8), 1–12.

Fiedorowicz, C. (1999, November). Neurobiological basis of learning disabilities: An overview. *Linking research to practice: Second Canadian Forum proceedings report.* Ottawa, Ontario: Canadian Children Care Federation. Retrieved July 9, 2002, from www.ldac-taac.ca/english/research/neurobio.htm

Field, S., & Hoffman, A. (2002). Preparing youth to exercise self-determination: Quality indicators of school environments that promote the acquisition of knowledge, skills, and beliefs related to self-determination. *Journal of Disability Policy Studies, 13*, 113–118.

Field, S., Sarver, M. D., & Shaw, S. F. (2003). Self-determination: A key to success in postsecondary education for students with learning disabilities. *Remedial and Special Education, 24*, 339–349.

Fierros, E. G. (2000). *An examination of restrictiveness in special education.* Paper presented at The Civil Rights Project: Harvard University, Cambridge, MA.

Fiez, J. A. (2001). Neuroimaging studies of speech: An overview of techniques and methodological approaches. *Journal of Communication Disorders, 34*, 445–454.

Figueroa, R. A., & Newsome, P. (2006). The diagnosis of LD in English learners: Is it nondiscriminatory? *Journal of Learning Disabilities, 39*, 206–214.

Filipek, P. A. (1995). Neurobiologic correlates of developmental dyslexia: How do dyslexics' brains differ from those of normal readers? *Journal of Child Neurology, 10* (Suppl. 1), 62–69.

Finlan, T. G. (1993). *Learning disability: The imaginary disease.* Westport, CT: Bergin & Garvey.

Finn, C. E., Rotherham, A. J., & Hokanson, C. R. (2001). Conclusions and principles for reform. In D. E. Finn, A. J. Rotherham, & C. R. Hokanson (Eds.), *Rethinking special education for a new century* (pp. 335–347). Washington, DC: Thomas B. Fordham Foundation and Progress Policy Institute.

Fischer, M., & Barkley, R. (2006). Young adult outcomes of children with hyperactivity: Leisure, financial and social activities. *International Journal of Disability, Development and Education, 53,* 229–245.

Fischer, M., Barkley, R. A., Smallish, L., & Fletcher, K. (2005). Executive functioning in hyperactive children as young adults: Attention, inhibition, response perseveration, and the impact of comorbidity. *Developmental Neuropsychology, 27,* 107–133.

Fish, W. W. (2008). The IEP meeting: Perceptions of parents of students who receive special education services. *Preventing School Failure, 53*(1), 8–14.

Fishbaugh, M. S. E. (1997). *Models of collaboration.* Boston: Allyn & Bacon.

Fishbaugh, M. S. E. (2000). Recognizing models and purposes of collaboration. In M. S. E. Fishbaugh (Ed.), *The collaboration guide for early career educators* (pp. 1–15). Baltimore, MD: Paul H. Brookes.

Fisher, D., & Frey, N. (2001). Access to the core curriculum: Critical ingredients for student success. *Remedial and Special Education, 22,* 148–157.

Fisher, D., & Ryndak, D. L. (Eds.). (2001). *The foundations of inclusive education: A compendium of articles on effective strategies to achieve inclusive education.* Baltimore: TASH: Equity, Quality, and Social Justice for People with Disabilities.

Fisher, D., Pumpian, I., & Sax, C. (1998). High school students' attitudes about and recommendations for their peers with significant disabilities. *Journal of the Association for Persons with Severe Handicaps, 23,* 272–282.

Fisher, D., Sax, C., & Grove, K. A. (2000). The resilience of changes promoting inclusiveness in an urban elementary school. *The Elementary School Journal, 100,* 213–227.

Fisher, D., Sax, C., & Pumpian, I. (1999). *Inclusive high schools: Learning from contemporary classrooms.* Baltimore: Paul H. Brookes.

Fisher, H., & Logemann, J. A. (1971). *Fisher–Logemann Test of Articulation Competence.* Oceanside, CA: Academic Communication Associates.

Fisher, M., & Meyer, L. H. (2002). Development and social competence after two years for students enrolled in inclusive and self-contained educational programs. *Research and Practice for Persons with Severe Disabilities, 27,* 165–174.

Fitch, F. (2003). Inclusion, exclusion, and ideology: Special education students' changing sense of self. *Urban Review, 35,* 233–252.

Fitzpatrick, M., & Knowlton, E. (2009). Bringing evidence-based self-directed intervention practices to the trenches for students with emotional and behavioral disorders. *Preventing School Failure, 53,* 253–266.

Fix, M., & Passel, J. S. (2003). *U.S. immigration: Trends and implications for schools.* Washington, DC: Urban Institute. (ERIC Document Reproduction No. ED480913)

Fleischer, D. Z., & Zames, F. (2001). *The disability rights movement: From charity to confrontation* (pp. 88–109). Philadelphia: Temple University Press.

Fleischmann, A. (2004). Narratives published on the Internet by parents of children with autism: What do they reveal and why is it important? *Focus on Autism and Other Developmental Disabilities, 19,* 35–43.

Fleischner, J. (1993). What is special about urban special education? *Teacher Education and Special Education, 16*(1), iv–v.

Fleith, D. D. (2001). *Suicide among gifted adolescents: How to prevent it.* Retrieved March 3, 2004, from www.sp.uconn.edu/~nrcgt/news/spring01/sprng012.html

Fleming, J. L., & Monda-Amaya, L. E. (2001). Process variables critical for team effectiveness: A Delphi study of wraparound team members. *Remedial and Special Education, 22,* 158–171.

Fletcher, J. M. (2005). Predicting math outcomes: Reading predictors and comorbidity. *Journal of Learning Disabilities, 38,* 308–312.

Fletcher, J. M., Denton, C., & Francis, D. J. (2005). Validity of alternative approaches for the identification of learning disabilities: Operationalizing unexpected underachievement. *Journal of Learning Disabilities, 38,* 545–552.

Fletcher, J. M., Francis, D. J., Boudousquie, A., Copeland, K., Young, V., Kalinowski, S., & Vaughn, S. (2006). Effects of accommodations on high-stakes testing for students with reading disabilities. *Exceptional Children, 72,* 136–150.

Fletcher, J. M., Lyon, G. R., Fuchs, L., & Barnes, M. A. (2007). *Learning disabilities.* New York: Guilford Press.

Flint, L. J. (2001). Challenges of identifying and serving gifted children with ADHD. *Teaching Exceptional Children, 33*(4), 62–69.

Flores, M. (2009). Teaching subtraction with regrouping to students experiencing difficulty in mathematics. *Preventing School Failure, 53,* 145–152.

Florida Center for Reading Research. (2003). *Fast ForWord Language.* Retrieved February 1, 2004, from www.fcrr.org/FCRRReports/PDF/Fast_ForWord_Language_Report.pdf

Flowers, D. L. (1993). Brain basis for dyslexia: A summary of work in progress. *Journal of Learning Disabilities, 26,* 575–582.

Fogt, J. B., George, M. P., Kern, L., White, G. P., & George, N. L. (2008). Physical restraint of students with behavior disorders in day treatment and residential settings. *Behavioral Disorders, 34,* 4–13.

Fontana, J. L., Scruggs, T., & Mastropieri, M. A. (2007). Mnemonic strategy instruction in inclusive secondary social studies classes. *Remedial and Special Education, 28*(6), 345–555.

Ford, D. (2004). A challenge for culturally diverse families of gifted children: Forced choices between achievement of affiliation. *Gifted Child Today, 27*(3), 26–27.

Ford, D. Y. (1996). *Reversing underachievement among gifted black students: Promising programs and practices.* New York: Teachers College Press.

Ford, D. Y., & Harris, J. J., III. (1995). Underachievement among gifted African-American students: Implications for school counselors. *School Counselor, 42,* 196–203.

Ford, D. Y., & Thomas, A. (1997). *Underachievement among gifted minority students: Problems and promises.* (ERIC EC Digest #E544). Arlington, VA: The ERIC Clearinghouse on Disabilities and Gifted Education.

Ford, D. Y., Grantham, T. C., & Whiting, G. W. (2008). Culturally and linguistically diverse students in gifted education: Recruitment and retention issues. *Exceptional Children, 74*(3), 289–306.

Fore, E., Burke, M. D., & Martin, C. (2006). Curriculum-based measurement: An emerging alternative to traditional assessment for African American children and youth. *Journal of Negro Education, 75*(1), 16–24.

Foreman, P., Arthur-Kelly, M., Pascoe, S., & King, B. S. (2004). Evaluating the educational experiences of students with profound and multiple disabilities in inclusive and segregated classroom settings: An Australian perspective. *Research and Practice for Persons with Severe Disabilities, 29,* 183–193.

Forness, S. R. (2001). Special education and related services: What have we learned from meta-analysis. *Exceptionality, 9,* 185–197.

Forness, S. R., & Kavale, K. A. (2001a). ADHD and a return to the medical model of special education. *Education and Treatment of Children, 24,* 224–247.

Forness, S. R., & Kavale, K. A. (2001b). Reflections on the future of prevention. *Preventing School Failure, 45,* 75–81.

Forness, S. R., Kavale, K. A., & Crenshaw, R. M. (1999). Stimulant medication revisited: Effective treatment of children with ADHD. *Reclaiming Children and Youth, 7,* 230–233, 235.

Forness, S. R., & Knitzer, J. (1992). A new proposed definition and terminology to replace "serious emotional disturbance". *School Psychology Review, 21,* 12–20.

Forster, E. M., & Holbrook, M. C. (2005). Implications of paraprofessional supports for students with visual impairments. *RE:view, 36,* 155–163.

Foster, S., & Cue, K. (2009). Roles and responsibilities of itinerant specialist teachers of deaf and hard of hearing students. *American Annals of the Deaf, 153,* 435–449

Fowler, M. (2002, April). *Attention deficit hyperactivity disorder* (NICHCY Briefing Paper 14, 3rd ed.). Washington, DC: National Information Center for Children and Youth with Disabilities. Retrieved June 7, 2003, from www.nichcy.org/pubs/factshe/fs14txt.htm

Fowler, S., Ogston, K., Roberts-Fiati, G., & Swenson, A. (1995). Patterns of giftedness and high competence in high school students educationally enriched during infancy: Variation across educational racial/ethnic backgrounds. *Gifted and Talented International, 10*(1), 31–36.

Fox, L., Dunlap, G., & Cushing, L. (2002). Early intervention, positive behavior support, and transition to school. *Journal of Emotional and Behavioral Disorders, 10,* 149–157.

Fox, L., Vaughn, B. J., Wyatte, M. L., & Dunlap, G. (2002). "We can't expect other people to understand": Family perspectives on problem behavior. *Exceptional Children, 68,* 437–450.

Fox, S., Farrell, P., & Davis, P. (2004). Factors associated with the effective inclusion of primary-aged pupils with Down syndrome. *British Journal of Special Education, 31,* 184–190.

Fraenkel, P. (2006). Engaging families as experts: Collaborative family program development. *Family Process, 45,* 237–257.

Francis, D. J., Fletcher, J. M., Stuebing, K. K., Lyon, G. R., Shaywitz, B. A., & Shaywitz, S. E. (2005). Psychometric approaches to the identification of LD: IQ and achievement scores are not sufficient. *Journal of Learning Disabilities, 38,* 98–108.

Frank, A. R., & Sitlington, P. L. (2000). Young adults with mental disabilities—Does transition planning make a difference? *Education and Training in Mental Retardation and Developmental Disabilities, 35,* 119–134.

Franklin, L. M., & Bender, W. N. (1997). The adult with ADHD. In W. N. Bender (Ed.), *Understanding ADHD: A practical guide for teachers and parents* (pp. 227–261). Upper Saddle River, NJ: Merrill.

Franklin, M. E. (1992). Culturally sensitive instructional practice for African-American learners with disabilities. *Exceptional Children, 59,* 115–122.

Franz, C. (2000, April). *Diagnosis and management of nonverbal learning disorders.* Paper presented at the annual convention of the National Association of School Psychologists, New Orleans. (ERIC Document Reproduction Service No. ED446292)

Frattura, E., & Capper, C. A. (2006). Segregated programs versus integrated comprehensive service delivery for all learners: Assessing the differences. *Remedial and Special Education, 27,* 355–364.

Freebody, P., & Power, D. (2001). Interviewing deaf adults in postsecondary educational settings: Stories, cultures, and life histories. *Journal of Deaf Studies and Deaf Education, 6,* 130–142.

Freeman, J. (2000). Teaching for talent: Lessons from the research. In C. M. F. van Lieshout & P. G. Heymans (Eds.), *Developing talent across the life span* (pp. 231–248). Philadelphia: Psychology Press.

Freeman, S. F. N. (2000). Academic and social attainments of children with mental retardation in general education and special education settings. *Remedial and Special Education, 21,* 3–18.

French, N., & Pickett, A. L. (1997). Paraprofessionals in special education: Issues for teacher educators. *Teacher Education and Special Education, 20*(1), 61–73.

French, N. K. (1999). Paraeducators: Who are they and what do they do? *Teaching Exceptional Children, 32*(2), 69–73.

French, N. K. (2001). Supervising paraprofessionals: A survey of teacher practices. *Journal of Special Education, 35,* 41–53.

French, N. K., & Chopra, R. V. (2006). Teachers as executives. *Theory Into Practice, 45,* 230–238.

Frey, A. (2002). Predictors of placement recommendations for children with behavioral or emotional disorders. *Behavioral Disorders, 27,* 126–136.

Frey, G. C., Stanish, H. I., & Temple, V. A. (2008). Physical activity of youth with intellectual disability: Review and research agenda. *Adapted Physical Activity Quarterly, 25,* 95–117.

Frey, L. M., & Wilhite, K. (2005). Our five basic needs: Application for understanding the function of behavior. *Intervention in School and Clinic, 40,* 156–160.

Frey, N., & Fisher, D. (2004). School change and teacher knowledge: A reciprocal relationship. *Teacher Education and Special Education, 27,* 57–67.

Friend, M. (2000). Perspective: Myths and misunderstandings about professional collaboration. *Remedial and Special Education, 21,* 130–132.

Friend, M. (2007). The co-teaching partnership. *Educational Leadership, 64*(5), 58–62.

Friend, M. (2008). *Co-teach! A handbook for creating and sustaining effective classroom partnerships in inclusive schools.* Greensboro, NC: Marilyn Friend, Inc.

Friend, M., & Bursuck, W. D. (2006). *Including students with special needs: A practical guide for classroom teachers* (4th ed.). Boston: Allyn & Bacon.

Friend, M., & Bursuck, W. D. (2009). *Including students with special needs: A practical guide for classroom teachers* (5th ed.). Columbus, OH: Merrill.

Friend, M., & Cook, L. (2004). Collaborating with parents and other teachers without being overwhelmed: Building partnerships and teams. In J. Burnette & C. Peters-Johnson (Eds.), *Thriving as a special education teacher.* Alexandria, VA: Council for Exceptional Children.

Friend, M., & Cook, L. (2007). *Interactions: Collaboration skills for school professionals* (5th ed.). Boston: Allyn & Bacon.

Friend, M., & Cook, L. (2010). *Interactions: Collaboration skills for school professionals* (6th ed.). Columbus, OH: Merrill.

Friend, M., & Pope K. L. (2005). Creating schools in which all students can succeed. *Kappa Delta Pi Record, 41*(2), 56–61.

Friend, M., & Shamberger, C. (2008). Inclusion. In T. L. Good (Ed.), *Twenty-first century education: A reference handbook* (Volume II, Part XI, Ch. 64; pp. 124–131). Thousand Oaks, CA: Sage.

Friesen, B. J., Giliberti, M., Katz-Leavy, J., Osher, T., & Pullmann, M. D. (2003). Research in the service of policy change: The "custody problem." *Journal of Emotional and Behavioral Disorders, 11,* 39–47.

Frith, U. (Ed.). (1991). *Autism and Asperger syndrome.* Cambridge, UK: Cambridge University Press.

Frostig, M., & Horne, D. (1964). *The Frostig program for the development of visual perception: Teacher's guide.* Chicago: Follett.

Fryxell, D., & Kennedy, C. H. (1995). Placement along the continuum of services and its impact on students' social relationships. *Journal of the Association for Persons with Severe Handicaps, 20,* 259–269.

Fuchs, D., & Fuchs, L. (2006). Introduction to response to intervention: What, why, and how valid is it? *Reading Research* Quarterly, 41, 93–99.

Fuchs, D., & Fuchs, L. S. (1998). Respecting the importance of science and practice: A pragmatic view. *Learning Disability Quarterly, 21,* 281–287.

Fuchs, D., Compton, D. L., Fuchs, L. S., Bryant, J., & Davis, G. N. Making "secondary intervention" work in a three-tier responsiveness-to-intervention model: Findings from the first-grade longitudinal reading study of the National Research Center on Learning Disabilities. *Reading and Writing: An Interdisciplinary Journal, 21,* 413–436.

Fuchs, D., Mock, D., Morgan, P. L., & Young, C. L. (2003). Responsiveness-to-intervention: Definitions, evidence, and implications for the learning disabilities construct. *Learning Disabilities Research and Practice, 18,* 157–171.

Fuchs, L. (2003). Assessing intervention responsiveness: Conceptual and technical issues. *Learning Disabilities Research and Practice, 18,* 172–186.

Fuchs, L. S., & Fuchs, D. (1998). Building a bridge across the canyon. *Learning Disability Quarterly, 21,* 99–101.

Fulk, B. M., Brigham, F. J., & Lohman, D. A. (1998). Motivation and self-regulation: A comparison of students with learning and behavior problems. *Remedial and Special Education, 19,* 300–309.

Fulk, B. M., & King, K. (2001). Classwide peer tutoring at work. *Teaching Exceptional Children, 34*(2), 49–53.

Fullan, M. (2008). *The six secrets of change: What the best leaders do to help their organizations survive and thrive.* San Francisco: Jossey-Bass.

Gabe, J., Bury, M., & Ramsay, R. (2002). Living with asthma: The experiences of young people at home and at school. *Social Science and Medicine, 55,* 1619–11633.

Gabig, C. (2008). Verbal working memory and story retelling in school-age children with autism. *Language, Speech, and Hearing Services in Schools, 39,* 498–511.

Gable, R. A., Quinn, M. M., Rutherford, R. B., Howell, K. W., & Hoffman, C. C. (1998). *Addressing student problem behavior—Part 11: Conducting a functional behavior assessment.* Washington, DC: Center for Effective Collaboration and Practice.

Gagné, F. (1995). From giftedness to talent: A developmental model and its impact on the language of the field. *Roeper Review, 18,* 103–111.

Gagnon, E. (2001). *The power card strategy: Using special interests to motivate children and youth with Asperger syndrome.* Shawnee Mission, KS: Autism Asperger Publishing.

Gagnon, J. C., & Leone, P. E. (2005). Elementary day and residential schools for children with emotional and behavioral disorders: Characteristics and entrance and exit policies. *Remedial and Special Education, 26,* 141–150.

Gallagher, J. J. (2002). *Society's role in educating gifted students: The role of public policy* [senior scholar series]. National Research Center on the Gifted and Talented. Retrieved February 27, 2004, from www.edrs.com/members/sp.cfm?AN=ED476370

Gallagher, J. J. (2006). *Driving change in special education.* Baltimore: Paul H. Brookes.

Gallagher, P. A., Floyd, J. H., Stafford, A. M., Taber, R. A., Brozovic, S. A., & Alberto, P. A. (2000). Inclusion of students with moderate or severe disabilities in educational and community settings: Perspectives from parents and siblings. *Education and Training in Mental Retardation and Developmental Disabilities, 35,* 135–147.

Gallagher, P. A., Vail, C. O., & Monda-Amaya, L. (2008). Perceptions of collaboration: A content analysis of student journals. *Teacher Education and Special Education, 31,* 12–21.

Gallaudet Research Institute. (November 2008). *Regional and national summary report of data from the 2007–08 annual survey of deaf and hard of hearing children and youth.* Washington, DC: Gallaudet Research Institute, Gallaudet University.

Gallegos, A., & McCarty, L. L. (2000). Bilingual multicultural special education: An integrated personnel preparation program. *Teacher Education and Special Education, 23,* 264–270.

Gallimore, L., & Woodruff, S. (1996). The bilingual–bicultural (Bi–Bi) approach: A professional point of view. In S. Schwartz (Ed.), *Choices in deafness: A parents' guide to communication options* (2nd ed., pp. 89–115). Bethesda, MD: Woodbine House.

Garcia, J. N., & deCaso, A. M. (2004). Effects of a motivational intervention for improving the writing of children with learning disabilities. *Learning Disability Quarterly, 27,* 141–147.

Garcia, L. J., Laroche, C., & Barette, J. (2002). Work integration issues go beyond the nature of the communication disorder. *Journal of Communication Disorders, 35,* 187–211.

Garcia, S. B., & Ortiz, A. A. (1988). *Preventing inappropriate referrals of language minority students to special education.* Washington, DC: National Clearinghouse for Bilingual Education.

Gardner, H. (1983). *Frames of mind: The theory of multiple intelligences.* London: Paladin.

Gardner, H. (1991). *Creating minds.* New York: Basic Books.

Gardner, H. (1993). *Multiple intelligences: The theory in practice.* New York: Basic Books.

Gardner, H. (2006). Training others in the art of therapy for speech sound disorders: An interactional approach. *Child Language Teaching and Therapy, 22,* 27–46.

Gardner, J. F. (1993). The era of optimism, 1850–1870: A preliminary reappraisal. *Mental Retardation, 31*(2), 89–95.

Gardner, S. A. (2003). The unrecognized exceptionality: Teaching gifted adolescents with depression. *English Journal, 92*(4), 28–32.

Garrick-Duhaney, L. M., & Salend, S. J. (2000). Parental perceptions of inclusive placements. *Remedial and Special Education, 21,* 121–128.

Garriott, P. P., Wandry, D., & Snyder, L. (2000). Teachers as parents, parents as children: What's wrong with this picture? *Preventing School Failure, 45*(1), 37–48.

Gartin, B. C., & Murdick, N. L. (2001). A new IDEA mandate: The use of functional assessment of behavior and positive behavior supports. *Remedial and Special Education, 22,* 344–349.

Gartin, B. C., & Murdick, N. L. (2005). IDEA 2004: The IEP. *Remedial and Special Education, 26,* 327–331.

Gartin, B. C., & Murdick, N. L. (2009). Children with cancer: School related issues. *Physical Disabilities: Education and Related Services, 27*(2), 19–36.

Gartin, B. C., Murdick, N. L., Thompson, J. R., & Dyches, T. T. (2002). Issues and challenges facing educators who advocate for students with disabilities. *Education and Training in Mental Retardation and Developmental Disabilities, 37,* 3–13.

Gately, S. (2008). Facilitating reading comprehension for students on the autism spectrum. *Teaching Exceptional Children, 40*(3), 40–45.

Gately, S. E., & Gately, F. J. (2001). Understanding co-teaching components. *Teaching Exceptional Children, 22*(4), 40–47.

Gavin, M. K., & Reis, S. M. (2003). Helping teachers to encourage talented girls in mathematics. *Gifted Child Today, 26,* 32–44.

Geary, D. C., Hoard, M. K., & Hamson, C. O. (1999). Numerical and arithmetical cognition: Patterns of functions and deficits in children at risk for a mathematical disability. *Journal of Experimental Child Psychology, 74,* 213–239.

Geenen, S., Powers, L. E., & Lopez-Vaasquez, A. (2001). Multicultural aspects of parent involvement in transition planning. *Exceptional Children, 67,* 265–282.

Geers, A., & Moog, J. (1989). Factors predictive of the development of literacy in profoundly hearing-impaired adolescents. *The Volta Review, 91,* 69–86.

Geisthardt, C. L., Brotherson, M. J., & Cook, C. C. (2002). Friendships of children with disabilities in the home environment. *Education and Training in Mental Retardation and Developmental Disabilities, 37,* 235–252.

Genetics Home Reference. (2009, October). *Phenylketonuria.* Washington, D.C.: National Institutes of Health. Retrieved October 20, 2009 from http://ghr.nlm.nih.gov/condition=phenylketonuria

George, A. L., & Duquette, C. (2006). The psychosocial experiences of a student with low vision. *Journal of Visual Impairment and Blindness, 100,* 152–163.

Gerber, M. M. (2005). Teachers are still the test: Limitations of response to instruction strategies for identifying children with learning disabilities. *Journal of Learning Disabilities, 38,* 516–524.

Gerber, P. J., & Popp, P. (1999). Consumer perspectives on the collaborative teaching model: Views of students with and without LD and their parents. *Remedial and Special Education, 20,* 288–296.

Gerhardt, P. (2001, April). Transition and life after school. *PDD Network, 31,* 2–9.

Gerlach, K. (2001). *Let's team up! A checklist for paraeducators, teachers, and principals* [NEA checklist series]. Washington, DC: National Education Association.

Gersten, R., Baker, S., & Edwards, L. (1999). *Teaching Expressive Writing to Students with Learning Disabilities* (ERIC/OSEP Digest E590). (ERIC Document Reproduction Service No. ED439532). Retrieved July 22, 2002, from www.edrs.com/members/sp.cfm?AN=ED439532

Gersten, R., Brengelman, S., & Jimenez, R. (1994). Effective instruction for culturally and linguistically diverse students: A reconceptualization. *Focus on Exceptional Children, 27,* 1–16.

Gersten, R., & Smith-Jones, J. (2001). Reflections on the research to practice gap. *Teacher Education and Special Education, 24,* 356–361.

Gersten, R., Vaughn, S., & Kim, A. H. (2004). Introduction: Special issue on sustainability. *Remedial and Special Education, 25,* 3–4.

Gersten, R., Williams, J. P., Fuchs, L., Baker, S., & Koppenhaver, D. (1998). Understanding reading comprehension difficulties of students with learning disabilities. In R. Gersten, J. P. Williams, L. Fuchs, S. Baker, D. Koppenhaver, S. Spadorcia, et al. (Eds.), *Improving reading comprehension for children with disabilities: A review of research.* Washington, DC: Office of Special Education Programs, U.S. Department of Education. (ERIC Document Reproduction Service No. ED451650)

Getty, L. A., & Summy, S. E. (2004). The course of due process. *Teaching Exceptional Children, 36*(3), 40–43.

Ghere, G., & York- Barr, J. (2007). Paraprofessionals turnover and retention in inclusive programs: Hidden cost and promising practices. *Remedial and Special Education, 28,* 21–32.

Ghezzi, P. (2007). Discrete trials teaching. *Psychology in the Schools, 44,* 667–679.

Giangreco, M. F. (2001). Interactions among program, placement, and services in educational planning for students with disabilities. *Mental Retardation, 39,* 341–350.

Giangreco, M. F. (2003). Working with paraprofessionals. *Educational Leadership, 61*(2), 50–53.

Giangreco, M. F., & Broer, S. M. (2005). Questionable utilization of paraprofessionals in inclusive schools: Are we addressing the symptoms or causes? *Focus on Autism and Other Developmental Disabilities, 20,* 10–26.

Giangreco, M. F., & Broer, S. M. (2007). School-based screening to determine overreliance on paraprofessionals. *Focus on Autism and Other Developmental Disabilities, 22,* 149–158.

Giangreco, M. F., Broer, S. M., & Edelman, S. W. (1999). The tip of the iceberg: Determining whether paraprofessional support is needed for students with disabilities in general education settings. *Journal of the Association for Persons with Severe Handicaps, 24,* 281–291.

Giangreco, M. F., Cloninger, C. J., & Iverson, V. S. (1998). *Choosing outcomes and accommodations for children (COACH): A guide to educational planning for students with disabilities* (2nd ed.). Baltimore: Paul H. Brookes.

Giangreco, M. F., & Doyle, M. B. (2002). Students with disabilities and paraprofessional supports: Benefits, balance, and Band-Aids. *Focus on Exceptional Children, 34*(7), 1–12.

Giangreco, M. F., Edelman, S. W., Dennis, R., Prelock, P., & Cloninger, C. (1997). Getting the most out of support services. In M. F. Giangreco (Ed.), *Quick-guides to inclusion: Ideas for educating students with disabilities* (pp. 8–112). Baltimore: Paul H. Brookes.

Giangreco, M. F., Edelman, S., Luiselli, T. E., & MacFarland, S. Z. C. (1997). Helping or hovering? Effects of instructional assistant proximity on students with disabilities. *Exceptional Children, 64,* 7–18.

Giangreco, M. F., Edelman, S. W., & Nelson, C. (1998). Impact of planning for support services on students who are deaf-blind. *Journal of Visual Impairment and Blindness, 92,* 18–29.

Giangreco, M. F., Smith, C. S., & Pinckney, E. (2006). Addressing the paraprofessional dilemma in an inclusive school: A program description. *Research and Practice for Persons with Severe Disabilities (RPSD), 31,* 215–229.

Gibb, G. S., & Dyches, T. T. (2007). *Guide to writing quality individualized education programs.* Boston: Allyn and Bacon.

Gibb, G. S., Young, J. R., Allred, K. W., Dyches, T. T., Egan, M. W., & Ingram, C. F. (1997). A team-based junior high inclusion program: Parent perceptions and feedback. *Remedial and Special Education, 18,* 243–249.

Gibb, S. A., Allred, K., Ingram, C. F., Young, J. R., & Egan, W. M. (1999). Lessons learned for the inclusion of students with emotional and behavioral disorders in one junior high school. *Behavioral Disorders, 24,* 122–136.

Gibbons, K. (2008). Evaluating RTI's effectiveness over the long term. *School Administrator, 65*(8), 13.

Gibbs, N. (1998, November 30). The age of Ritalin. *Time,* pp. 86–96.

Gilger, J. W., & Wilkins, M. A. (2008). Atypical neurodevelopmental variation as a basis for learning disorders. In M. Mody & E. R. Silliman (Eds.), *Brain, behavior, and learning in language and reading disorders* (pp. 4–40). New York: Guilford.

Gillberg, C. (1993). Autism and related behaviors. *Journal of Intellectual Disability Research, 37,* 343–372.

Gillberg, C., & Coleman, M. (2000). *The biology of the autistic syndromes* (3rd ed.). London: Mac Keith Press.

Gillette, Y., & DePompei, R. (2008). Do PDAs enhance the organization and memory skills of students with cognitive disabilities? *Psychology in the Schools, 45,* 665–677.

Gillon, G. T. (2005). Phonological awareness: Effecting change through the integration of research findings. *Language, Speech, and Hearing Services in Schools, 36,* 346–349.

Glasberg, B. (2000). The development of siblings' understanding of autism spectrum disorders. *Journal of Autism and Developmental Disorders, 30,* 143–156.

Glazer, S. M. (2001). Communication disorders: How to identify when students are having difficulty connecting. *Teaching PreK–8, 31*(5), 86–87.

Glenn, E. E., & Smith, T. T. (1998). Building self-esteem of children and adolescents with communication disorders. *Professional School Counseling, 2,* 39–46.

Goddard, H. H. (1912). *The Kallikak family: A study in the heredity of feeble-mindedness.* New York: Macmillan.

Goddard, L., Howlin, P., Dritschel, B., & Patel, T. (2007). Autobiographical memory and social problem-solving in Asperger syndrome. *Journal of Autism and Developmental Disorders, 37,* 291–300.

Goddard, R., D., Goddard, Y., L., & Tschannen-Moran, M. (2007). A theoretical and empirical investigation of teacher collaboration for school improvement and student achievement in public elementary schools. *Teachers College Record, 109*(4), 877–896.

Goddard, R. D., Tschannen-Moran, M., & Hoy, W. K. (2001). A multilevel examination of the distribution and effects of teacher trust in students and parents in urban elementary schools. *The Elementary School Journal, 102,* 3–17.

Godwin-Jones, B. (2003). Emerging technologies: E-books and the tablet PC. *Language Learning and Technology, 7,* 4–8.

Goffman, E. (1963). *Stigma.* Upper Saddle River, NJ: Prentice Hall.

Gold, M. E. (2002). The effects of the physical features associated with albinism on the self-esteem of African American youths. *Journal of Visual Impairment and Blindness, 96*, 133–142.

Goldin-Meadow, S., & Mayberry, R. I. (2001). How do profoundly deaf children learn to read. *Learning Disabilities Research and Practice, 16*(4), 222–229.

Goldman, R., & Fristoe, M. (2000). *Goldman–Fristoe Test of Articulation 2.* Circle Pines, MN: AGS.

Goldstein, H., Moss, J. W., & Jordan, L. J. (1965). *The efficacy of special class training on the development of mentally retarded children* (U.S. Office of Education Cooperative Research Program Project No. 619). Urbana: University of Illinois Institute for Research on Exceptional Children. (ERIC Document Reproduction Service No. ED002907)

Goldstein, K. (1942). *Aftereffects of brain injuries in war.* New York: Grune & Stratton.

Gollnick, D. M., & Chinn, P. C. (1998). *Multicultural education in a pluralistic society.* Upper Saddle River, NJ: Merrill.

Golly, A., Sprague, J., Walker, H. M., Beard, K., & Gorham, G. (2000). The First Steps to Success program: An analysis of outcomes with identical twins across multiple baselines. *Behavioral Disorders, 25*, 170–182.

Golly, A., Stiller, B., & Walker, H. M. (1998). First Steps to Success: Replication and social validation of an early intervention program. *Journal of Emotional and Behavioral Disorders, 6*, 243–250.

Gonzalez, V., Brusca-Vega, R., & Yawkey, T. (1997). *Assessment and instruction of culturally and linguistically diverse students with or at-risk of learning problems.* Boston: Allyn & Bacon.

Goor, M. B., & Schwenn, J. O. (1993). Accommodating diversity and disability with cooperative learning. *Intervention in School and Clinic, 29*(1), 6–16.

Gordon, B. M. (1995). Knowledge construction, competing critical theories, and education. In J. A. Banks & C. A. McGee Banks (Eds.), *Handbook of research on multicultural education* (pp. 184–199). New York: Macmillian.

Gordon, E. W., & Brigdlall, B. L. (2005). Nurturing talent in gifted students of color. In R. J. Sternberg & J. E. Davidson (Eds.), *Conceptions of giftedness* (2nd ed., pp. 120–146). New York: Cambridge University Press.

Gottardo, A., & Meuller, J. (2009). Are first- and second-language factors related in predicting second-language reading comprehension? A study of Spanish-speaking children acquiring English as a second language from first to second grade. *Journal of Educational Psychology, 101*, 330–344.

Gottfried, A. W., Cook, C. R., Gottfried, A. E., & Morris, P. E. (2005). Educational characteristics of adolescents with gifted academic intrinsic motivation: A longitudinal investigation from school entry through early adulthood. *Gifted Child Quarterly, 49*, 172–186.

Gottlieb, J., Alter, M., Gottlieb, B. W., & Wishner, J. (1994). Special education in urban America: It's not justifiable for many. *Journal of Special Education, 27*, 453–465.

Graetz, B. W., Sawyer, M. G., Baghurst, P., & Hirte, C. (2006). Gender comparisons of service use among youth with attention-deficit/hyperactivity disorder. *Journal of Emotional and Behavioral Disorders, 14*, 2–11.

Graham, A., & Anderson, K. A. (2008). "I have to be three steps ahead": Academically gifted African American male students in an urban high school on the tension between an ethnic and academic identity. *Urban Review: Issues and Ideas in Public Education, 40*, 472–499.

Graham, S., Harris, K. R., & Fink-Chorzempa, B. (2003). Extra spelling instruction: Promoting better spelling, writing, and reading performance right from the start. *Teaching Exceptional Children, 35*(6), 66–68.

Graham, S., Harris, K. R., & MacArthur, C. (2006). Explicitly teaching struggling writers: Strategies for mastering the writing process. *Intervention in School and Clinic, 41*, 290–294.

Grantham, T. C., Frasier, M. M., Roberts, A. C., & Bridges, E. M. (2005). Parent advocacy for culturally diverse gifted students. *Theory into Practice, 44*, 138–147.

Gravois, T. A., & Rosenfield, S. A. (2006). Impact of instructional consultation teams on the disproportionate referral and placement of minority students in special education. *Remedial and Special Education, 27*, 42–52.

Gray, C. (2000). *Writing social stories with Carol Gray.* Arlington, TX: Future Horizons.

Gray, C. A. (1996). *Social stories and comic strip conversations: Unique methods to improve social understanding* [videotape]. Arlington, TX: Future Horizons.

Gray, C. A., & Garand, J. D. (1993). Social stories: Improving responses of students with autism with accurate social information. *Focus on Autistic Behavior, 8*, 1–10.

Green, T. D., McIntosh, A. S., Cook-Morales, V. J., Robinson-Zanartu, C. (2005). From old schools to tomorrow's schools: Psychoeducational assessment of African American students. *Remedial and Special Education, 26*, 82–92.

Greenberg, M. T., & Kusche, C. A. (1993). *Promoting social and emotional development in deaf children: The PATHS project.* Seattle: University of Washington Press.

Greenberg, M. T., Kusche, C. A., & Speltz, M. (1991). Emotional regulation, self-control, and psychopathology: The role of relationships in early childhood. In D. Cicchetti & S. L. Toth (Eds.), *Internalizing and externalizing expressions of dysfunction* (Vol. 2, pp. 21–55). Mahwah, NJ: Erlbaum.

Greenburg, L. M. (1999). *Test of Variables of Attention Test Manual.* Lost Alamitos, CA: Universal Attention Disorders.

Greene, R. W., Beszterczey, S. K., Katzenstein, T., Park, K., & Goring, J. (2002). Are students with ADHD more stressful to teach? *Journal of Emotional and Behavioral Disorders, 10*, 79–89.

Greenham, S. L. (1999). Learning disabilities and psychosocial adjustment: A critical review. *Child Neuropsychology, 5*, 171–196.

Greenhill, L., Kollins, S., Abikoff, H., McCracken, J., Riddle, M., Swanson, J., McGough, J., Wigal, S., Wigal, T., Vitiello, B., Skrobala, A., Posner, K., Ghuman, J., Cunningham, C., Davies, M., Chuang, S., & Cooper, T. (2006). Efficacy and safety of immediate-release methylphenidate treatment for preschoolers with ADHD. *Journal of the American Academy of Child and Adolescent Psychiatry, 45*, 1284–1293.

Greenwood, C. R. (2001). Science and students with learning and behavioral problems. *Behavioral Disorders, 27*, 35–52.

Greiling, A. K., Boss, L. P., & Wheeler, L. S. (2005). A preliminary investigation of asthma mortality in schools. *Journal of School Health, 75*, 286–290.

Gresham, F. M., Lane, K. L., & Lambros, K. M. (2000). Comorbidity of conduct problems and ADHD: Identification of "fledging psychopaths." *Journal of Emotional and Behavioral Disorders, 8*, 83–89.

Grether, S. M., & Sickman, L. S. (2008). AAC and RTI: Building classroom-based strategies for every child in the classroom. *Seminars in Speech & Language, 29*, 155–163.

Griffer, M., & Perlis, S. M. (2007). Developing cultural intelligence in preservice speech-language pathologists and educators. *Communication Disorders Quarterly, 29*, 28–35.

Griffin, C. C., Jones, H. A., & Kilgore, K. L. (2006). A qualitative study of student teachers' experiences with collaborative problem solving. *Teacher Education and Special Education, 29*, 44–55.

Griffin, C. C., Kilgore, K. L., & Winn, J. A. (2008). First-year special educators' relationships with their general education colleagues. *Teacher Education Quarterly, 35*, 141–157.

Griffin-Shirley, N., Layton, C. A., Koenig, A. J., Robinson, M. C., Siew, L. K., & Davidson, R. C. (2003). *A survey of teachers of students with visual impairments: Responsibilities, satisfactions, and needs.* Manuscript submitted for publication.

Grigal, M., Neubert, D. A., Moon, M. S., & Graham, S. (2003). Self-determination for students with disabilities: Views of parents and teachers. *Exceptional Children, 70*, 97–112.

Groce, N. E., & Zola, I. K. (1993). Multiculturalism, chronic illness, and disability. *Pediatrics, 91*, 1048–1055.

Gross, B., & Hahn, H. (2004). Developing issues in the classification of mental and physical disabilities. *Journal of Disability Policy Studies, 15*, 130–134.

Grosse, S. J. (1999). *Educating children and youth to prevent contagious disease* [ERIC Digest]. Washington, DC: ERIC Clearinghouse on Teaching and Teacher Education. Retrieved March 1, 2004, from www.ericfacility.net/databases/ERIC_Digests/ed437368.html

Grossman, H. (1995). *Special education in a diverse society.* Boston: Allyn & Bacon.

Grossman, H. J. (1983). *Classification in mental retardation.* Washington, D.C.: American Association on Mental Deficiency.

Gruttadaro, D. (2008, Fall). Capitol Hill watch: The federal government focuses on young adults with serious mental illnesses. *NAMI Beginnings* [Issue 1], pp. 2–3. Retrieved July 14, 2009 from http://www.nami.org/Template.cfm?Section=Your_Local_Nami&template=/ContentManagement/ContentDisplay.cfm&ContentID=81640

Guardino, C. A. (2008). Identification and placement for Deaf students with multiple disabilities: Choosing the path less followed. *American Annals of the Deaf, 153*, 55–64.

Gudino, O., Lau, A., Yeh, M., McCabe, K., & Hough, R. (2009). Understanding racial/ethnic disparities in youth mental health services: Do disparities vary by problem type?. *Journal of Emotional and Behavioral Disorders, 17*, 3–16.

Guerra, P. L., & Nelson, S. W. (2009). Changing professional practice requires changing beliefs. *Phi Delta Kappan, 90*, 354–359.

Guess, D. (2000). Serving persons with severe and profound disabilities: A work in progress. In M. Wehmeyer & J. Patton (Eds.), *Mental retardation in the twenty-first century* (pp. 91–111). Austin, TX: Pro-Ed.

Guetzloe, E. (1999). Inclusion: The broken promise. *Preventing School Failure, 43*, 92–98.

Gulchak, D. J. (2008). Using a mobile handheld computer to teach a student with an emotional and behavioral disorder to self-monitor attention. *Education and Treatment of Children, 31*, 567–581.

Gumpel, T. P. (2007). Are social competence difficulties by performance or acquisition deficits? The importance of self-regulatory mechanisms. *Psychology in the Schools, 44*, 351–372.

Gunn, B., Smolkowski, K., Biglan, A., & Black, C. (2002). Supplemental instruction in decoding skills for Hispanic and non-Hispanic students in early elementary school: A follow-up. *Journal of Special Education, 36*, 69–79.

Guralnick, M. J. (2000). An agenda for change in early childhood inclusion. *Journal of Early Intervention, 23*, 213–222.

Guralnick, M. J., Connor, R. T., Neville, B., & Hammond, M. A. (2002). Mothers' perspectives of the peer-related social development of young children with developmental delays and communication disorders. *Early Education and Development, 13*(1), 59–80.

Guteng, S. I. (2005). Professional concerns of beginning teachers of deaf and hard of hearing students. *American Annals of the Deaf, 150*, 17–41.

Guthrie, P. (2006). *Section 504 and ADA: Promoting student access—A resource guide for educators* (3rd ed.). Fort Valley, GA: Council of Administrators of Special Education.

Gutierrez, A., Jr., Hale, M. N., O'Brien, H. A., Fischer, A., Durocher, J., & Alessandri, M. (2009). Evaluating the effectiveness of two commonly used discrete trial procedures for teaching receptive discrimination to young children with autism spectrum disorders. *Research in Autism Spectrum Disorders, 3*, 630–638.

Gutkin, T. B., & Curtis, M. J. (1999). School-based consultation theory and practice: The art and science of indirect service delivery. In C. R. Reynolds & T. B. Gutkin (Eds.), *The handbook of school psychology* (3rd ed., pp. 598–637). New York: Wiley.

Gutstein, S., & Whitney, T. (2002). Asperger Syndrome and the development of social competence. *Focus on Autism and Other Developmental Disabilities, 17*, 161–171.

Haager, D. (2007). Promises and cautions regarding using response to intervention with English language learners. *Learning Disability Quarterly, 30*, 213–218.

Haar, J., Hall, G., Schoepp, P., & Smith, D. H. (2002). How teachers teach to students with different learning styles. *Clearing House, 75*, 142–145.

Hackman, D. G., & Berry, J. E. (2000). Cracking the calendar. *Journal of Staff Development, 21*(3), 45–47.

Hadwin, J., Baron-Cohen, S., Howlin, P., & Hill, K. (1997). Does teaching theory of mind have an effect on the ability to develop conversation in children with autism? *Journal of Autism and Developmental Disorders, 27*, 519–537.

Hagiwara, T. (1998). *Multimedia social story intervention for students with autism.* Unpublished doctoral dissertation, University of Kansas, Lawrence.

Hagiwara, T. (2001–2002). Academic assessment of children and youth with Asperger syndrome, pervasive developmental disorders—not otherwise specified, and high-functioning autism. *Assessment for Effective Intervention, 27*(1 & 2), 89–100.

Hagiwara, T., & Myles, B. S. (1999). A multimedia social story intervention: Teaching skills to children with autism. *Focus on Autism and Other Developmental Disabilities, 14*, 82–95.

Hall, J., Marshall, R., Vaughn, M., Hynd, G. W., & Riccio, C. (1997). Intervention strategies for preschool children with ADHD. In W. N. Bender (Ed.), *Understanding ADHD: A practical guide for teachers and parents* (pp. 123–148). Upper Saddle River, NJ: Merrill.

Hall, J. P. (2002). Narrowing the breach: Can disability culture and full educational inclusion be reconciled? *Journal of Disability Policy Studies, 13*, 144–152.

Hallahan, D. P., & Kauffman, J. M. (1976). *Introduction to learning disabilities: A psycho-behavioral approach.* Upper Saddle River, NJ: Pearson.

Hallahan, D. P., & Mercer, C. D. (2001, August). *Learning disabilities: Historical perspectives.* Paper presented at the Learning Disabilities Summit: Building a Foundation for the Future, Washington, DC. (ERIC Documentation Reproduction Service No. ED458756)

Hamill, L. B. (1999). *One school district's efforts to develop a formal inclusion program at the secondary level.* (ERIC Document Reproduction Service No. ED436 065) Retrieved February 1, 2001, from www.edrs.com/members/sp.cfm?AN=ED436065

Hammill, D. D. (1990). On defining learning disabilities: An emerging consensus. *Journal of Learning Disabilities, 23*, 74–84.

Hammill, D. D. (1993). A brief look at the learning disabilities movement in the United States. *Journal of Learning Disabilities, 26*, 295–310.

Hammill, D. D., Brown, V., Larsen, S., & Wiederholt, J. L. (1994). *Test of Adolescent and Adult Language 3 (TOAL-3).* Austin, TX: Pro-Ed.

Hammill, D. D., & Bryant, B. (1998). *Learning Disabilities Diagnostic Inventory.* Austin, TX: Pro-Ed.

Handwerk, M. L., & Marshall, R. M. (1998). Behavioral and emotional problems of students with learning disabilities, serious emotional disturbance, or both conditions. *Journal of Learning Disabilities, 31*, 327–338.

Hannah, M., & Midlarsky, E. (2005). Helping by siblings of children with mental retardation. *American Journal on Mental Retardation, 110*, 87–99.

Hansen, A. L. (2007). School-based support for GLBT students: A review of three levels of research. *Psychology in the Schools, 44*, 839–848.

Hardin, B., & Hardin, M. (2002). Into the mainstream: Practical strategies for teaching in inclusive environments. *Clearing House, 75*, 175–178.

Hardman, M. L., & Dawson, S. (2008). The impact of federal public policy on curriculum and instruction for students with disabilities in the general classroom. *Preventing School Failure, 52*(2), 5–11.

Hargrove, L. J. (2000). Assessment and inclusion: A teacher's perspective. *Preventing School Failure, 45*(1), 18–22.

Harn, W. E., Bradshaw, M. L., & Ogletree, B. T. (1999). The speech-language pathologist in the schools: Changing roles. *Intervention in School and Clinic, 34,* 163–169.

Harold, C. (Ed.). (2009). *Professional guide to diseases* (ninth edition). Philadelphia: Lippincott, Williams, & Williams.

Harries, J., Guscia, R., Kirby, N., Nettelbeck, T., & Taplin, J. (2005). Support needs and adaptive behaviors. *American Journal on Mental Retardation, 110,* 393–404.

Harris, G. (1986). Barriers to the delivery of speech, language, and hearing services to Native Americans. In O. Taylor (Ed.), *Nature of communication disorders in culturally and linguistically diverse populations* (pp. 219–236). San Diego: College Hill Press.

Harris, J. J., Brown, E. L., Ford, D. Y., & Richardson, J. W. (2004). African Americans and multicultural education: A proposed remedy for disproportionate special education placement and underinclusion in gifted education. *Education and Urban Society, 36,* 304–341.

Harris, K. R., Graham, S., & Mason, L. H. (2003). Self-regulated strategy development in the classroom: Part of a balanced approach to writing instruction for students with disabilities. *Focus on Exceptional Children, 35*(7), 1–16.

Harris, M. S. (2009). School reintegration for children and adolescents with cancer: The role of school psychologists. *Psychology in the Schools, 46,* 579–592.

Harris, S. F., Prater, M. A., Dyches, T. T., & Heath, M. A. (2009). Job stress of school-based speech-language pathologists. *Communication Disorders Quarterly, 30,* 103–111.

Harris, S. L. (1994). *Siblings of children with autism: A guide for families.* Bethesda, MD: Woodbine House.

Harrison, C. (2004). Giftedness in early childhood: The search for complexity and connection. *Roeper Review, 26,* 78–84.

Harrison, M. M. (2007, Fall). "Does this child have a friend?" *Teaching Tolerance, 32,* 26–31.

Harry, B. (1992). Making sense of disabilities: Low-income Puerto Rican parents' theories of the problem. *Exceptional Children, 59,* 27–40.

Harry, B. (2002). Trends and issues in serving culturally diverse families of children with disabilities. *Journal of Special Education, 36,* 131–138.

Harry, B. (2008). Collaboration with culturally and linguistically diverse families: Ideal versus reality. *Exceptional Children, 74,* 372–388.

Harry, B., & Kingner, J. (2007). Discarding the deficit model. *Educational Leadership, 64*(5), 16–21.

Harry, B., Rueda, R., & Kalyanpur, M. (1999). Cultural reciprocity in sociocultural perspective: Adapting the normalization principle for family collaboration. *Exceptional Children, 66,* 123–136.

Hart, B., & Risley, T. R. (1999). *The social world of children learning to talk.* Baltimore, MD: Paul H. Brookes.

Hart, J. E. (2009). Strategies for culturally and linguistically diverse students with special needs. *Preventing School Failure, 53,* 197–208.

Hart, J. E., & Whalon, K. J. (2008). Promote academic engagement and communication of students with autism spectrum disorder in inclusive settings. *Intervention in School and Clinic, 44,* 116–120.

Hartman, M. A. (2009). Step by Step: Creating a community-based transition program for students with intellectual disabilities. *Teaching Exceptional Children, 41*(6), 6–11.

Hartup, W. W. (1992). *Having friends, making friends, and keeping friends: Relationships as educational contexts.* (ERIC Document Reproduction No. ED345854) Retrieved November 18, 2002, from www.edrs.com/members/sp.cfm?AN=ED345854

Harty, S., Miller, C., Newcorn, J., & Halperin, J. (2009). Adolescents with childhood ADHD and comorbid disruptive behavior disorders: Aggression, anger, and hostility. *Child Psychiatry & Human Development, 40,* 85–97.

Harvey, E. A., Youngwirth, S. D., & Thakar, D. A. (2009). Predicting attention-deficit/hyperactivity disorder and oppositional defiant disorder form preschool diagnostic assessments. *Journal of Consulting and Clinical Psychology, 77,* 349–354.

Hasazi, S. B., Furney, K. S., & Destefano, L. (1999). Implementing the IDEA transition mandates. *Exceptional Children, 65,* 555–566.

Hasselbring, T. S., & Bausch, M. E. (2005/2006). Assistive technologies for reading. *Educational Leadership, 63*(4), 72–75.

Hastings, R., Beck, A., Daley, D., & Hill, C. (2004). Symptoms of ADHD and their correlates in children with intellectual disabilities. *Research in Developmental Disabilities, 26,* 456–468.

Hastings, R. P. (2003). Behavioral adjustment of siblings of children with autism engaged in applied behavior analysis early intervention programs: The moderating role of social support. *Journal of Autism and Developmental Disorders, 33,* 141–150.

Hatlen, P. (1996). The core curriculum for blind and visually impaired students, including those with additional disabilities. *RE:view, 28,* 25–32.

Hatlen, P. (2000). Historical perspectives. In M. C. Holbrook & A. J. Koenig (Eds.), *Foundations of education: History and theory of teaching children and youths with visual impairments* (pp. 1–54). New York: American Foundation for the Blind Press.

Hatlen, P. (2002). The most difficult decision: How to share responsibility between local schools and schools for the blind. *Journal of Visual Impairment and Blindness, 96,* 747–749.

Hatlen, P. H., & Curry, S. A. (1987). In support of specialized programs for blind and visually impaired children: The impact of vision loss on learning. *Journal of Visual Impairment and Blindness, 81,* 7–13.

Havey, J. M. (1999). School psychologists' involvement in special education due process hearings. *Psychology in the Schools, 36,* 117–123.

Havighurst, R. J., Stivers, E., & DeHaan, R. F. (1955). *A survey of education of gifted children.* Chicago: University of Chicago Press.

Hawbaker, B. W., Balong, M., Buckwaiter, S., & Runyon, S. (2001). Building a strong BASE of support for all students through co-planning. *Teaching Exceptional Children, 33*(4), 24–30.

Hawks, D. E. Thinking ahead: A special kind of planning. Exceptional Parent, *39*(4), 64–65.

Haycock, K., & Crawford, C. (2008). Closing the teacher quality gap. *Educational Leadership, 65*(7), 14–19.

Hayes, J., & Flower, L. (1986). Writing research and the writer. *American Psychologist, 41,* 1106–1113.

Hazelkorn, M., Packard, A. L., & Douvanis, G. (2008). Alternative dispute resolution in special education: A view from the field. *Journal of Special Education Leadership, 21*(1), 32–38.

Heacox, D. (2002). *Differentiating instruction in the regular classroom.* Minneapolis: Free Spirit.

Head, G., Robison, L. M., Sclar, D. A., Skaer, T. L., & Galin, R. S. (1999). National trends in the prevalence of attention-deficit/hyperactivity disorder and the prescribing of methylphenidate among school-age children: 1990–1995. *Clinical Pediatrics, 38,* 209–217.

Heffner, D. L., & Shaw, P. C. (1996). Assessing the written narratives of deaf students using the six-trait analytical scale. *The Volta Review 98*(1), 147–168.

Heflin, L. J., & Bullock, L. M. (1999). Inclusion of students with emotional/behavioral disorders: A survey of teachers in general and special education. *Preventing School Failure, 43,* 103–111.

Heilbronner, N. (2009). Jumpstarting Jill: Strategies to nurture talented girls in your science classroom. *Gifted Child Today, 32,* 46–54.

Heiman, T., & Margalit, M. (1998). Loneliness, depression, and social skills among students with mild mental retardation in different educational settings. *Journal of Special Education, 32,* 154–163.

Heiman, T., Zinck, L. C., & Heath, N. L. (2008). Parents and youth with learning disabilities: Perceptions of relationships and communication. *Journal of Learning Disabilities, 41,* 524–534.

Heine, C., & Slone, M. (2008). The impact of mild central auditory processing disorder on school performance during adolescence. *Journal of School Health, 78,* 405–407.

Heineman, M., Dunlap, G., & Kincaid, D. (2005). Positive support strategies for students with behavioral disorders in general education settings. *Psychology in the Schools, 42,* 779–794.Hosp, J. L. (2008). A correlated constraints model of risk and resilience for Latino students with emotional/behavioral disorders. *Behavioral Disorders, 33,* 246–254.

Heinze, T. (1986). Communication skills. In G. School (Ed.), *Foundations of education for blind and visually handicapped children and youth: Theory and practice* (pp. 301–314). New York: American Foundation for the Blind Press.

Helenius, P., Parviainen, T., Paetau, R., & Salmelin, R. (2009). Neural processing of spoken words in specific language impairment and dyslexia. *Brain, 132,* 1918–1927.

Heller, K. W., Alberto, P. A., Forney, P. E., & Schwartzman, M. N. (1996). *Understanding physical, sensory, and health impairments: Characteristics and educational implications.* Pacific Grove, CA: Brooks/Cole.

Heller, K. W., Fredrick, L. D., Dykes, M. K., Best, S., & Cohen, E. T. (1999). A national perspective of competencies for teachers of individuals with physical and health disabilities. *Exceptional Children, 65,* 219–235.

Heller, K. W., & Swinehart-Jones, D. (2003). Supporting the educational needs of students with orthopedic impairments. *Physical Disabilities: Education and Related Services, 22*(1), 3–24.

Hellriegel, K. L., & Yates, J. R. (1999). Collaboration between correctional and public school systems serving juvenile offenders: A case study. *Education and Treatment of Children, 22,* 55–83.

Henderson, B. (2003, January–February). Global Focus: Inclusion—A worldwide movement. *In CASE, 44*(4), 9.

Henderson, C. (2001). *College freshmen with disabilities, 2001: A biennial statistical profile.* Washington, DC: HEATH Resource Center, American Council on Education.

Hendrick-Keefe, C. (1995). Portfolios: Mirrors of learning. *Teaching Exceptional Children, 27*(2), 66–67.

Hendricks, D., & Wehman, P. (2009). Transition from school to adulthood for youth with autism spectrum disorders: Review and recommendations. *Focus on Autism and Other Developmental Disabilities, 24,* 77–88.

Henfield, M. S., Moore, J. L., & Wood, C. (2008). Inside and outside gifted education programming: Hidden challenges for African American students. *Exceptional Children, 74,* 433–450.

Henley, M., Ramsey, R. S., & Algozzine, R. F. (2001). *Characteristics of and strategies for teaching students with mild disabilities.* Boston: Allyn & Bacon.

Hernandez, J. E., Harry, B., Newman, L., & Cameto, R. (2008). Survey of family involvement in and satisfactionwith the Los Angeles Unified School District special education processes. *Journal of Special Education Leadership, 21,* 84–93.

Hertzog, N. B., & Bennett, T. (2004). In whose eyes? Parents' perspectives on the learning needs of their gifted children. *Roeper Review, 26,* 96.

Hess, H. L., Morrier, M. J., Heflin, L. J., Ivey, M. L. (2008). Autism treatment survey: Services received by children with autism spectrum disorders in public school classrooms. *Journal of Autism and Developmental Disorders, 38,* 961–971.

Heubert, J. P. (2003). First, do no harm. *Educational Leadership, 60*(4), 26–30.

Heward, W. L. (2006). *Exceptional children* (8th ed.). Uper Saddle River, NJ: Merrill/Pearson.

Hiatt-Michael, D. (2001, October). *Preparing teachers to work with parents* [ERIC Digest]. Washington, DC: ERIC Clearinghouse on Teaching and Teacher Education.

Hickson, L., Blackman, L. S., & Reis, E. M. (1995). *Mental retardation: Foundations of educational programming* (pp. 1–37). Boston: Allyn & Bacon.

Hieneman, M., Dunlap, G., & Kincaid, D. (2005). Positive support strategies for students with behavioral disorders in general education settings. *Psychology in the Schools, 42,* 779–794.

Hill, C. (2003). The role of instructional assistants in regular classrooms: Are they influencing inclusive practices? *Alberta Journal of Educational Research, 49*(1), 98–100.

Hill, K., & Romich, B. (1999a). Choosing and using augmentative communication systems: Part I: The goal, the team, and AAC rules of commitment. *Exceptional Parent, 29*(10), 76–80.

Hill, K., & Romich, B. (1999b). Choosing and using augmentative communication systems: Part II: AAC success stories: Making the rules of commitment work. *Exceptional Parent, 29*(11), 60, 62, 64–67.

Hilliard, A. G. (1992). Behavioral style, culture, and teaching and learning. *Journal of Negro Education, 61,* 370–377.

Hindin, A., Morocco, C., C., Mott, E., A., & Aguilar, C., M. (2007). More than just a group: Teacher collaboration and learning in the workplace. *Teachers and Teaching: Theory and Practice, 13*(4), 349–376.

Hitchcock, C., Meyer, A., Rose, D., & Jackson, R. (2002). Providing new access to the general curriculum: Universal design for learning. *Teaching Exceptional Children, 35*(2), 8–17.

Hitchcock, C., & Stahl, S. (2003). Assistive technology, universal design, Universal Design for Learning: Improved opportunities. *Journal of Special Education Technology 18*(4).

Hitchings, W. E., Luzzo, D. A., Ristow, R., Horvath, M., Retish, P., & Tanners, A. (2001). The career development needs of college students with learning disabilities: In their own words. *Learning Disabilities Research and Practice, 16,* 8–17.

Hobbs, N. (1975). *The futures of children.* San Francisco: Jossey-Bass.

Hobbs, N., Dokecki, P. R., Hoover-Dempsey, K. V., Moroney, R. M., Shayne, M. W., & Weeks, K. H. (1984). *Strengthening families.* San Francisco: Jossey-Bass.

Hocutt, A. M., Martin, E. W., & McKinney, J. D. (1990). Historical and legal context of mainstreaming. In J. W. Lloyd, N. N. Singh, & A. C. Repp (Eds.), *The regular education initiative: Alternative perspectives on concepts, issues and models* (pp. 17–28). Sycamore, IL: Sycamore Publishing.

Hodapp, R. M., Freeman, S. F. N., & Kasari, C. L. (1998). Parental educational preferences for students with mental retardation: Effects of etiology and current placement. *Education and Training in Mental Retardation and Developmental Disabilities, 33,* 342–349.

Hodgens, J. B., Cole, J., & Boldizar, J. (2000). Peer-based differences among boys with ADHD. *Journal of Clinical Child Psychology, 29,* 443–452.

Hoekman, K., & McCormick, J. (1999). *Motivational variables affecting coping resources among gifted adolescents.* Retrieved March 3, 2004, from www.aare.edu.au/99pap/hoe99771.htm

Hoff, E., & Shatz, M. (Eds.). (2007). *Blackwell handbook of language development.* Malden, MA: Blackwell.

Hogansen, J., Powers, K., Geenen, S., Gil-Kashiwabara, E., & Powers, L. (2008). Transition goals and experiences of females with disabilities: Youth, parents, and professionals. *Exceptional Children, 74*(2), 215–234.

Hoge, G., & Dattilo, J. (1999). Effects of a leisure education program on youth with mental retardation. *Education and Training in Mental Retardation and Developmental Disabilities, 34,* 20–34.

Holahan, A., & Costenbader, V. (2000). A comparison of developmental gains for preschool children with disabilities in inclusive settings and self-contained classrooms. *Topics in Early Childhood Special Education, 20,* 224–236.

Holbrook, M. C., & Koenig, A. J. (2000). Basic techniques for modifying instruction. In A. J. Koenig & M. C. Holbrook (Eds.), *Foundations of education: Instructional strategies for teaching children and youths with visual impairments* (2nd ed., pp. 173–195). New York: AFB Press.

Holcomb, R. K., Holcomb, S. K., & Holcomb, T. K. (1994). *Deaf culture our way: Anecdotes from the Deaf Community* (3rd ed.). San Diego: Dawn Sign Press.

Holden-Pitt, L., & Diaz, J. (1998). Thirty years of the annual survey of deaf and hard-of-hearing children and youth: A glance over the decades. *American Annals of the Deaf, 143,* 72–76.

Holdnack, J. A., & Weiss, L. G. (2006). IDEA 2004: Anticipated implications for clinical practice—Integrating assessment and intervention. *Psychology in the Schools, 43,* 871–882.

Holler, R., & Zirkel, P. A. (2008). Legally best practices in Section 504 plans. *School Administrator, 65*(8), 38–41.

Hollingsworth, H. L. (2001). We need to talk: Communication strategies for effective collaboration. *Teaching Exceptional Children, 33*(5), 6–9.

Hollingworth, L. S. (1926). *Gifted children: Their nature and nurture.* New York: Macmillan.

Hollingworth, L. S. (1942). *Children above 180 IQ.* New York: World Book.

Hollins, E. R., & Spencer, K. (1990). Restructuring schools for cultural inclusion: Changing the schooling process for African American youngsters. *Journal of Education, 172,* 89–100.

Hollowood, T. M., Salisbury, C. L., Rainforth, B., & Palombaro, M. M. (1995). Use of instructional time in classrooms serving students with and without severe disabilities. *Exceptional Children, 61,* 242–253.

Holmes, R. B. (1967). *Training residual vision in adolescents educated previously as nonvisual.* Unpublished master's thesis, Illinois State University, Normal, Illinois.

Holowinsky, I. Z. (2000). Learning disorders and learning disabilities: A logical and socio-political puzzle. *Special Services in the Schools, 16,* 135–145.

Holzbauer, J. J. (2008). Disability harassment observed by teachers in special education. *Journal of Disability Policy Studies, 19,* 162–171.

Honmeyer, J. S., Holmbeck, G. N., Wills, K. E., & Coers, S. (1999). Condition severity and psychosocial functioning in pre-adolescents with spina bifida: Disentangling proximal functional status and distal adjustment outcomes. *Journal of Pediatric Psychology, 24,* 499–509.

Honomichl, R. D., Goodlin-Jones, B. L., & Burnham, M. M. (2002). Secretin and sleep in children with autism. *Child Psychiatry and Human Development, 33,* 107–123.

Honomichl, R. D., Goodlin-Jones, B. L., Burnham, M., Gaylor, E., & Anders, T. F. (2002). Sleep patterns of children with pervasive developmental disorders. *Journal of Autism and Developmental Disorders, 32,* 553–561.

Hook, B. R. (2003, October 2). The iBOT, wheelchair for a new era. *TechNews World.* Retrieved March 12, 2004, from www.technewsworld.com/perl/story/31733.html

Hooper, S. R., Roberts, J. E., Zeisel, S. A., & Poe, M. (2003). Core language predictors of behavioral functioning in early elementary school children: Concurrent and longitudinal findings. *Behavioral Disorders, 29,* 10–24.

Hoover, S. M., Sayler, M. F., & Feldhusen, J. F. (1986). Cluster grouping of gifted students at the elementary level. *Roeper Review, 16,* 13–15.

Horn, I. S. (2008). The inherent interdependence of teachers. *Phi Delta Kappan, 89,* 751–754.

Horn, W. F., & Tynan, D. (2001). Time to make special education "special" again. In C. E. Finn, A. J. Rotherham, & C. R. Hokanson (Eds.), *Rethinking special education for a new century.* Washington, DC: Thomas B. Fordham Foundation and Progressive Policy Institute.

Horn, W. F., & Tynan, D. (2001, Summer). Revamping special education. *Public Interest, 144,* 36–53.

Horne, R. L. (1996, October). The education of children and youth with special needs: What do the laws say? *NICHCY New Digest.* (ERIC Document Reproduction Service No. ED401700) Retrieved December 23, 2002, from www.edrs.com/members/sp.cfm?AN=ED401700

Horner, R. H. (2000). Positive behavior supports. *Focus on Autism and Other Developmental Disabilities, 15,* 97–105.

Horner, R. H., Sugai, G., Todd, A. W., & Lewis-Palmer, T. (2000). Elements of behavior support plans: A technical brief. *Exceptionality, 8,* 205–216.

Hosp, J. L., & Reschly, D. J. (2003). Referral rates for intervention or assessment: A meta-analysis of racial differences. *Journal of Special Education, 37,* 67–80.

Hosp, J. L., & Reschly, D. J. (2004). Disproportionate representation of minority students in special education: Academic, demographic, and economic predictors. *Exceptional Children, 70,* 185–199.

Hosterman, S., DuPaul, G., & Jitendra, A. (2008). Teacher ratings of ADHD symptoms in ethnic minority students: Bias or behavioral difference? *School Psychology Quarterly, 23,* 418–435.

Houghton, S. (2006). Advances in ADHD research through the lifespan: Common themes and implications. *International Journal of Disability, Development & Education, 53,* 263-272.

Hourcade, J. (2002, November). *Mental retardation: Update 2002* [ERIC Digest E637]. Arlington, VA: ERIC Clearinghouse on Disabilities and Gifted Education. (ERIC Document Reproduction Service No. ED473010) Retrieved September 29, 2003, from www.edrs.com/members/sp.cfm?AN=ED473010

Houwen, S., Visscher, C., Lemmick, L. A. P. M., & Hartman, E. (2009). Motor skill performance of children and adolescents with visual impairments: A review. *Exceptional Children, 75,* 464–492.

Howell, A., Hauser-Cram, P., & Kersh, J. E. (2007). Setting the stage: Early child and family characteristics as predictors of later loneliness in children with developmental disabilities. *American Journal on Mental Retardation, 112,* 18–30.

Howley, A., Rhodes, M., & Beall, J. (2009). Challenges facing rural schools: Implications for gifted students. *Journal for the Education of the Gifted, 32,* 515–536.

Howlin, P., Magiati, I., & Charman, T. (2009). Systematic review of early intensive behavioral interventions for children with autism. *American Journal on Intellectual and Developmental Disabilities, 114,* 23–41.

Huber, K. D., Rosenfeld, J. G., & Fiorello, C. A. (2001). The differential impact of inclusion and inclusive practices on high, average, and low achieving general education students. *Psychology in the Schools, 38,* 497–504.

Hubl, D., Bolte, S., Feineis-Matthews, S., Lanfermann, H., Federspiel, A., Strik, W., et al. (2003). Functional imbalance of visual pathways indicates alternative face processing strategies in autism. *Neurology, 61,* 1232–1237.

Hudson, R. F., High, L., & al Otaiba, S. (2007). Dyslexia and the brain: What does current research tell us? *Reading Teacher, 60,* 506–515.

Huebner, K. M. (2000). Visual impairment. In M. C. Holbrook & A. J. Koenig (Eds.), *Foundations of education: History and theory of teaching children and youths with visual impairments* (2nd ed., pp. 55–76). New York: American Foundation for the Blind Press.

Huefner, D. S. (2000). The risks and opportunities of the IEP requirements under IDEA '97. *Journal of Special Education, 33,* 195–204.

Huer, M. B., Parette, H. P., & Saenz, T. I. (2001). Conversations with Mexican Americans regarding children with disabilities and augmentative and alternative communication. *Communication Disorders Quarterly, 22,* 197–206.

Huer, M. B., Saenz, T. I., & Diem, J. H. (2001). Understanding the Vietnamese American community: Implications for training educational personnel providing services to children with disabilities. *Communication Disorders Quarterly, 23,* 27–39.

Huff, R. E., Houskamp, B. M., Watkins, A. V., Stanton, M., & Tavegia, B. (2005). The experiences of parents of gifted African American children: A phenomenological study. *Roeper Review, 27,* 215–221.

Hughes, C. A., & Suritsky, S. K. Notetaking skills and strategies for students with learning disabilities. *Preventing School Failure, 38*(1), 7–11.

Hughes, M. T., Schumm, J. S., & Vaughn, S. (1999). Home literacy activities: Perceptions and practices of Hispanic parents of children with learning disabilities. *Learning Disability Quarterly, 22,* 224–235.

Hughes, R. S. (1999). An investigation of coping skills of parents of children with disabilities: Implications for service providers. *Education and Training in Mental Retardation and Developmental Disabilities, 34,* 271–280.

Human Genome Project Information. (2005). *Genetic disease profile: Sickle cell anemia.* Washington, D.C.: Department of Energy, National Institute of Diabetes and Digestive and Kidney Diseases. Retrieved September 5, 2009 from http://www.ornl.gov/sci/techresources/Human_Genome/posters/chromosome/sca.shtm

Humphries, T., Cardy, J. O., Worling, D. E., & Peets, K. (2004). Narrative comprehension and retelling abilities of children with nonverbal learning disabilities. *Brain and Cognition, 56,* 77–88.

Hunt, P., Alwell, M., Farron-Davis, F., & Goetz, L. (1996). Creating socially supportive environments for fully included students who experience multiple disabilities. *Journal of the Association for Persons with Severe Handicaps, 21,* 53–71.

Hunt, P., Doering, K., Hirose-Hatae, A., Maier, J., & Goetz, L. (2001). Across-program collaboration to support students with and without disabilities in a general education classroom. *Journal of the Association for Persons with Severe Handicaps, 26,* 240–256.

Hunt, P., Farron-Davis, F., Beckstead, S., Curtis, D., & Goetz, L. (1994). Evaluating the effects of placement of students with severe disabilities in general education versus special classes. *Journal of the Association for Persons with Severe Handicaps, 19,* 200–214.

Hunt, P. & Goetz, L. (1997). Research on inclusive educational programs, practices, and outcomes for students with severe disabilities. *The Journal of Special Education, 31,* 3–29.

Hunt, P., Soto, G., Maier, J., & Doering, K. (2003). Collaborative teaming to support students at risk and students with severe disabilities in general education classrooms. *Exceptional Children, 69,* 315–332.

Hunt, P., Staub, D., Alwell, M., & Goetz, L. (1994). Achievement by all students within the context of cooperative learning groups. *Journal of the Association for Persons with Severe Handicaps, 19,* 290–301.

Hunt, R. D. (1997). Nosology, neurobiology, and clinical patterns of AD/HD in adults. *Psychiatry Annals, 27,* 572–581.

Hux, K., Marquardt, J., Skinner, S., & Bond, V. (1999). Special education services provided to students with and without parental reports of traumatic brain injury. *Brain Injury, 13,* 447–455.

Hyatt, K. J. (2007). The new IDEA: Changes, concerns, and questions. *Intervention in School and Clinic, 42,* 131–136.

Idol, L. (1997). Key questions related to building collaborative and inclusive schools. *Journal of Learning Disabilities, 30,* 384–394.

Idol, L. (2006). Toward inclusion of special education students in general education: A program evaluation of eight schools. *Remedial and Special Education, 27,* 77–94.

Individuals with Disabilities Education Act Amendments of 1997, P. L. 105-17, 20 U.S.C. §§ 1400 *et seq.*

Individuals with Disabilities Education Improvement Act of 2004, P.L. 108-446, 20 U.S.C. § 1400 *et seq.*

Ingham, R. J. (2001). Brain imaging studies of developmental stuttering. *Journal of Communication Disorders, 34,* 493–516.

Innes, F. K., & Diamond, K. E. (1999). Typically developing children's interactions with peers with disabilities: Relationships between mothers' comments and children's ideas about disabilities. *Topics in Early Childhood Special Education, 19*(2), 103–112.

Irvine, J. J. (1991). Beyond role models: An examination of cultural influences on the pedagogical perspectives of black teachers. *Peabody Journal of Education, 6*(4), 1–63.

Irvine, J. J., & York, D. E. (1995). Learning styles and culturally diverse students: A literature review. In J. A. Banks & C. A. McGee Banks (Eds.), *Handbook of research on multicultural education* (pp. 484–497). New York: Macmillian.

Ishii-Jordan, S. R. (1997). When behavior differences are not disorders. In A. J. Artiles & G. Zamora-Durran (Eds.), *Reducing disproportionate representation of culturally diverse students in special and gifted education* (pp. 27–46). Reston, VA: The Council for Exceptional Children.

Itier, R., & Taylor, M. (2002). Inversion and contrast polarity reversal affect both encoding and recognition processes of unfamiliar faces: A repetition study using ERPs. *NeuroImage, 15,* 353–372.

Itier, R., & Taylor, M. (2004). N170 or N1? Spatiotemporal differences between object and face processing using ERPs. *Cerebral Cortex, 14,* 132–142.

Izzo, A. (2002). Phonemic awareness and reading ability: An investigation with young readers who are deaf. *American Annals of the Deaf, 147*(4), 18–28.

Janney, R. E., Snell, M. E., Beers, M. K., & Raynes, M. (1995). Integrating students with moderate and severe disabilities into general education classes. *Exceptional Children, 61,* 425–439.

Jans, L. (2000). Use of assistive technology: Findings from national surveys. In *Center on Disability, conference proceedings: Technology and Persons with Disabilities.* Northridge: California State University. Retrieved March 15, 2004, from http://csun.edu/cod/conf/2000/proceedings/0049Jans.htm

Janzen, J. (2003). *Understanding the nature of autism: A guide to the autism spectrum disorders* (2nd ed.).San Antonio, TX: Therapy Skill Builders.

Jarosewich, T., & Stocking, V. B. (2003). Talent search: Student and parent perceptions of out-of-level testing. *Journal of Secondary Gifted Education, 14,* 137–150.

Jenkins, J. R., Antil, L. R., Wayne, S. K., & Vadasy, P. F. (2003). How cooperative learning works for special education and remedial students. *Exceptional Children, 69,* 279–292.

Jensen, P. S. (1999, February 23). *Epidemiologic research on ADHD: What we know and what we need to learn.* Paper presented at ADHD: A Public Health Perspective Conference, Atlanta, GA. Retrieved June 12, 2003, from www.cdc.gov/ncbddd/adhd/dadabepi.htm

Jensen, P. S., et al. (2001). ADHD comorbidity findings from the MTA study: Comparing comorbid subgroups. *Journal of American Academy of Child and Adolescent Psychiatry, 40,* 147–158.

Jimenez, T. C., Graf, V. L., & Rose, E. (2007). Gaining access to general education: The promise of universal design for learning. *Issues in Teacher Education, 16*(2) 41–54.

Jitendra, A. K., Edwards, L. L., Sacks, G., & Jacobson, L. A. (2004). What research says about vocabulary instruction for students with learning disabilities. *Exceptional Children, 70,* 299–322.

Jochum, J., Curran, C., & Reetz, L. (1998). Creating individual educational portfolios in written language. *Reading and Writing Quarterly: Overcoming Learning Difficulties, 14,* 283–306.

Johns, B. H., & Guetzloe, E. C. (Eds.). (2004). *Inclusive education for children and youths with emotional and behavioral disorders: Enduring challenges and emerging practices.* Arlington, VA: Council for Exceptional Children.

Johnsen, S. K. (2009). Best practices for identifying gifted students. *Principal, 88*(5), 8–14.

Johnsen, S. K., & Kendrick, J. (2005). *Teaching gifted students with disabilities.* Waco, TX: Prufrock Press.

Johnson, D. D. (2001). *Vocabulary in the elementary and middle school.* Boston: Allyn & Bacon.

Johnson, D. R., & Johnson, F. P. (2009). *Joining together: Group theory and group skills* (10th ed.). Boston: Allyn & Bacon.

Johnson, D. W. (2009). *Reaching out: Interpersonal effectiveness and self-actualization* (9th ed.). Boston: Allyn & Bacon.

Johnson, D. W., & Johnson, R. T. (1992). Social interdependence and cross-ethnic relations. In J. Lynch, C. Modgil, & S. Modgil (Eds.), *Cultural diversity and the schools: Equity or excellence?* (pp. 179–189). London: Falmer.

Johnson, E., Mellard, D. F., & Byrd, S. E. (2005). Alternative models of learning disabilities identification: Considerations and initial conclusions. *Journal of Learning Disabilities, 38,* 569–572.

Johnson, J. A., Dupuis, V. L., Musial, D., Hall, G. E., & Gollnick, D. M. (2002). *Introduction to the foundations of American education* (12th ed.). Boston: Allyn & Bacon.

Johnson, J. R., & McIntosh, A. S. (2009). Toward a cultural perspective and understanding of the disability and deaf experience in special and multicultural education. *Remedial and Special Education, 30,* 67–83.

Johnson, R. C., & Cohen, O. P. (Eds.). (1994). *Implications and complications for deaf students of the full inclusion movement.* Washington, DC: Gallaudet Research Institute.

Johnston, J., Knight, M., & Miller, L. (2007). Finding time for teams. *Journal of Staff Development, 28*(2), 14–18.

Joint Coordinating Committee on Evidence-Based Practice, American-Speech-Language-Hearing Association. (2005). Evidence-based practice in communication disorders [position statement]. Retrieved October 26, 2006, from www.asha.org/members/deskrefjournals/deskref/default

Jolivette, I., Stichter, J. P., Nelson, C. M., Scott, T. M., & Liaupsin, C. J. (2000, August). *Improving post-school outcomes for students with emotional and behavioral disorders* [ERIC/OSEP Digest E597]. Arlington, VA: ERIC Clearinghouse on Disabilities and Gifted Education. (ERIC Document Reproduction Service No. ED447616)

Jolly, A., & Evans, S. (2005). Teacher assistants move to the front of the class: Job embedded learning pays off in student achievement. *Journal of Staff Development, 26*(3), 8–13.

Jolly, J. L. (2005). Foundations of the field of gifted education. *Gifted Child Today, 28*(2), 14–18, 65.

Jolly, J. L. (2008). Lew Terman: Genetic study of genius—Elementary school students. *Gifted Child Today, 31*(1), 27–33.

Jolly, J. L., & Kettler, T. (2008). Gifted education research 1993–2003: A disconnect between priorities and practice. *Journal for the Education of the Gifted, 31,* 427–446.

Jones, H., & Chronis-Tuscano, A. (2008). Efficacy of teacher in-service training for attention-deficit/hyperactivity disorder. *Psychology in the Schools, 45,* 918–929.

Jones, L., & Menchetti, B. M. (2001). Identification of variables contributing to definitions of mild and moderate mental retardation in Florida. *Journal of Black Studies, 31,* 619–634.

Jones, M. (2006). Teaching self-determination empowered teachers, empowered students. *Teaching Exceptional Children, 39*(1), 12–17.

Jones, S. D., Angelo, D. H., & Koskoska, S. M. (1999). Stressors and family supports: Families with children using augmentative and alternative communication technology. *Journal of Children's Communication Development, 20*(2), 37–44.

Jones, T. W., Jones, J. K., & Ewing, K. M. (2006). Students with multiple disabilities. In D. F. Moores & D. S. Martin (Eds.), *Deaf learners: Developments in curriculum and instruction* (pp. 127–144). Washington, DC: Gallaudet University Press.

Jones, V., Dohrn, E., & Dunn, C. (2004). *Creating effective programs for students with emotional and behavior disorders: Interdisciplinary approaches for adding meaning and hope to behavior change interventions.* Boston: Allyn & Bacon.

Jones, V., & Jones, L. S. (1995). *Comprehensive classroom management: Creating positive learning environments for all students* (4th ed.). Boston: Allyn & Bacon.

Jordan, N. C., & Hanich, L. B. (2003). Characteristics of children with moderate mathematics deficiencies: A longitudinal perspective. *Learning Disabilities Research & Practice, 18,* 213–221.

Jordan, R. (1999). Evaluating practice: Problems and possibilities. *Autism, 3,* 411–434.

Jorgensen, C. M. (1998). *Restructuring high schools for all students: Taking inclusion to the next level.* Baltimore: Paul H. Brookes.

Joseph, J. (2000). Not in their genes: A critical view of the genetics of attention-deficit hyperactivity disorder. *Developmental Review, 20,* 539–567.

Joseph, J., Noble, K., & Eden, G. (2001). The neurobiological basis of reading. *Journal of Learning Disabilities, 34,* 566–579.

Joseph, L. M., & Ford, D. Y. (2006). Nondiscriminatory assessment: Considerations for gifted education. *Gifted Child Quarterly, 50,* 42–51.

Judge, S., Floyd, K. M., & Jeffs, T. (2008). Using an assistive technology toolkit to promote inclusion. *Early Childhood Education Journal, 36,* 121–126.

Justice, L. M., & Ezell, H. K. (2001). Written language awareness in preschool children from low-income households: A descriptive analysis. *Communication Disorders Quarterly, 22,* 123–134.

Justice, L. M., & Fey, M. E. (2004, September 21). Evidence-based practice in schools: Integrating craft and theory with science and data. *ASHA Leader, 9*(9), pp. 4–5, 30–32.

Kadesjo, B., Gillberg, C., & Hagberg, B. (1999). Brief report: Autism and Asperger syndrome in seven-year-old children: A total population study. *Journal of Autism and Developmental Disorders, 29,* 327–331.

Kaff, M. S. (2004). Multitasking is multitaxing: Why special educators are leaving the field. *Preventing School Failure, 48*(2), 10–17.

Kaff, M. S., Zabel, R. H., & Milham, M. (2007). Revisiting cost-benefit relationships of behavior management strategies: What special educators say about usefulness, intensity, and effectiveness. *Preventing School Failure, 51*(2), 35–45.

Kalke, T., Glanton, A., & Cristalli, M. (2007). Positive behavioral interventions and supports: Using strength-based approaches to enhance the culture of care in residential and day treatment education. *Child Welfare, 86,* 151–174.

Kallen, R. J. (2003, September). *Unproven treatments.* Retrieved March 29, 2004, from www.autism-biomed.org/unproven.htm

Kalyanpur, M., & Harry, B. (1999). *Culture in special education.* Baltimore: Paul H. Brookes.

Kameenui, E. J., & Simmons, D. C. (1997). *Designing instructional strategies: The prevention of academic learning problems.* Upper Saddle River, NJ: Merrill.

Kamens, M. W. (2004). Learning to write IEPs: A personalized, reflective approach for preservice teachers. *Intervention in School and Clinic, 40,* 76–80.

Kamhi, A. G. (2003). The role of the SLP in improving reading fluency. Retrieved November 11, 2003, from www.asha.org/about/publications/leader-online/archives/2003/q2/030415f.htm

Kamps, D. M., Greenwood, C., Arreaga-Mayer, C., Veerkamp, M. B., Utley, C., Tapia, Y., Bowman-Perrott, L., & Bannister, H. (2008). The efficacy of classwide peer tutoring in middle schools. *Education and Treatment of Children, 31,* 119–152.

Kampwirth, T. J. (2006). *Collaborative consultation in the schools: Effective practices for students with learning and behavior problems* (3rd ed.). Upper Saddle River, NJ: Merrill.

Kanner, L. (1943). Autistic disturbances of affective content. *The Nervous Child, 2,* 217–250.

Kanner, L. (1964). *A history of the care and study of the mentally retarded* (pp. 9–44). Springfield, IL: Charles C. Thomas.

Kaplan, B. J., Crawford, S. G., Dewey, D. M., & Fisher, G. C. (2000). The IQs of children with ADHD are normally distributed. *Journal of Learning Disabilities, 33,* 425–432.

Kaplan, L. (2003). Inuit snow terms: How many and what does it mean? In F. Trudel (Ed.), *Building capacity in arctic societies: Dynamics and shifting perspectives.* [Proceedings from the 2nd IPSSAS Seminar]. Iqaluit, Nunavut, Canada: International Ph.D. School for Studies of Arctic Societies. Retrieved June 1, 2009 from http://www.uaf.edu/anlc/snow.html#citation

Karchmer, M. A., & Allen, T. E. (1999). The functional assessment of deaf and hard of hearing students. *American Annals of the Deaf, 144*(2), 68–77.

Karlsen, B., & Gardner, E. (1995). *Stanford Diagnostic Reading Test* (4th ed.). Orlando: Harcourt Educational Measurement.

Karnes, F. A., & Stephens, K. R. (2000). State definitions for the gifted and talented. *Exceptional Children, 66,* 219–238.

Kasahara, M., & Turnbull, A. P. (2005). Meaning of family-professional partnerships: Japanese mothers' perspectives. *Exceptional Children, 71,* 249–265.

Kassini, I. (2008). Professionalism and coordination: Allies or enemies? *American Annals of the Deaf, 153,* 309–313.

Katsiyannis, A., & Yell, M. L. (1999). Education and the law: School health services: Cedar Rapids Community School District v. Garrett F. *Preventing School Failure, 44*(1), 37–38.

Katsiyannis, A., Zhang, D., & Archwamety, T. (2002). Placement and exit patterns for students with mental retardation: An analysis of national trends. *Education and Training in Mental Retardation and Developmental Disabilities, 37,* 134–145.

Katsiyannis, J., Landrum, T. J., & Vinton, L. (1997). Practical guidelines for monitoring treatment of attention-deficit/hyperactive disorder. *Preventing School Failure, 41,* 131–136.

Katz, J., Mirenda, & Auerbach, S. (2002). Instructional strategies and educational outcomes for students with developmental disabilities in inclusive "multiple intelligences" and typical classrooms. *Research and Practice for Persons with Severe Disabilities, 27,* 227–238.

Kauffman, J. M. (2005). Waving to Ray Charles: Missing the meaning of disabilities. *Phi Delta Kappan, 86,* 520–521.

Kauffman, J. M., & Landrum, T. J. (2006). *Children and youth with emotional and behavioral disorders: A history of their education.* Austin, TX: Pro-Ed.

Kauffman, J. M., McGee, K., & Brigham, M. (2004). Enabling or disabling? Observations on changes in special education. *Phi Delta Kappan, 85,* 613–620.

Kaufmann, F., Kalbfleisch, M. L., & Castellanos, F. X. (2000). *Attention Deficit Disorders and gifted students: What do we really know?* (RM00146). Storrs, CT: The National Research Center on the Gifted and Talented, University of Connecticut.

Kavale, K. A. (2002). Mainstreaming to full inclusion: From orthogenesis to pathogenesis of an idea. *International Journal of Disability, 49,* 201–214.

Kavale, K. A. (2005). Identifying specific learning disability: Is responsiveness to intervention the answer? *Journal of Learning Disabilities, 38,* 553–562.

Kavale, K. A., & Forness, S. R. (1996). Social skill deficits and learning disabilities: A meta-analysis. *Journal of Learning Disabilities, 29,* 226–237.

Kavale, K. A., & Forness, S. R. (1998). The politics of learning disabilities. *Learning Disability Quarterly, 21,* 245–273.

Kavale, K. A., & Forness, S. R. (2000a). History, rhetoric, and reality: Analysis of the inclusion debate. *Remedial and Special Education, 21,* 279–296.

Kavale, K. A., & Forness, S. R. (2000b). What definitions of learning disability say and don't say. *Journal of Learning Disabilities, 33,* 239–256.

Kavale, K. A., & Spaulding, L. S. (2008). Is response to intervention good policy for specific learning disability? *Learning Disabilities Research and Practice, 23,* 169–179.

Kavale, K. A., Spaulding, L. S., & Beam, A. P. (2009). A time to define: Making the specific learning disability definition prescribe specific learning disability. *Learning Disability Quarterly, 32,* 39–48.

Kay, T., Spaulding, J., & Smerdon, L. (2004). *Behavioral challenges in children: Linking school and home.* Redmond, WA: Brain Injury Association of Washington. Retrieved March 12, 2004, from www.biawa.orgpax/children/Behavioral%20Challenges%20in%20Children.doc

Kearns, J., Burdge, M. D., Clayton, J., Denham, A. P., & Kleinert, H. L. (2006). How students demonstrate academic performance in Portfolio Assessment. In D. M. Browder & F. Spooner (Eds.), *Teaching language arts, math and science to students with significant disabilities* (pp. 277–293). Baltimore: Paul H. Brookes.

Keating, D. P. (1976). Intellectual talent, research and development. *Proceedings of the sixth annual Hyman Blumberg symposium on research in early childhood education.* Baltimore: Johns Hopkins University Press.

Keefe, E. B., & Moore, V. (2004). The challenge of co-teaching in inclusive classrooms at the high school level: What the teachers told us. *American Secondary Education, 32*(3), 77–88.

Keene, N. (1997). *Childhood leukemia: A guide for families, friends, and caregivers.* Sebastopol, CA: O'Reilly & Associates.

Keith, R. W. (1999). Clinical issues in central auditory processing disorders. *Language, Speech, and Hearing Services in the Schools, 30,* 339–344.

Kelley-Smith, S. (2000). *Can we talk? Software for language development. TECH-NJ 2000, 11*(1), 7–10. Retrieved January 12, 2003, from www.edrs.com/members/sp.cfm?AN=ED469059

Kellner, M. H., Bry, B. H., & Salvador, D. S. (2008). Anger management effects on middle school students with emotional behavioral disorders: Anger log use, aggressive and prosocial behavior. *Child & Family Behavior Therapy, 30,* 215–230.

Kellner, R., Houghton, S., & Douglas, G. (2003). Peer-related personal experiences of children with attention-deficit/hyperactivity disorder with and without comorbid learning disabilities. *International Journal of Disability, Development and Education, 50,* 119–136.

Kelly, S. M., & Smith, T. J. (2008). The digital social interactions of students with visual impairments: Findings from two national surveys. *Journal of Visual Impairment & Blindness, 102,* 528–539.

Kemper, T. L., & Bauman, M. (1998). Neuropathology of infantile autism. *Journal of Neuropathology and Experimental Neurology, 57,* 645–652.

Kender, J. P., & Kender, M. A. (1998). Education implications relating neuroanatomical research and developmental dyslexia. *Reading Horizons, 38*(3), 217–225.

Kennedy, C. H., Long, T., Jolivette, K., Cox, J., Tang, J., & Thompson, T. (2001). Facilitating general education participation for students with behavior problems by linking positive behavior supports and person-centered planning. *Journal of Emotional and Behavioral Disorders, 9,* 161–171.

Kennedy, C. H., Shukla, S., & Fryxell, D. (1997). Comparing the effects of educational placement on the social relationships of intermediate school students with severe disabilities. *Exceptional Children, 64,* 31–47.

Kennedy, E. (2006). Literacy development of linguistically diverse first graders in a mainstream English classroom: Connecting speaking and writing. *Journal of Early Childhood Literacy, 6,* 163–189.

Kennedy, M. R. T. (2008). Assessment, treatment, and service issues for students with traumatic brain injury. *NeuroRehabilitation, 23,* 455–456.

Kent, R. D. (2006). Evidence-based practice in communication disorders: Progress not perfection. *Language, Speech, and Hearing Services in Schools, 37,* 268–270.

Kephart, N. C. (1960). *The slow learner in the classroom.* Columbus, OH: Merrill.

Kessler, R. C., Adler, L., Barkley, R., Biederman, J., Conners, C. K., Demler, O., Faraone, S. V., et al. (2006). The prevalence and correlates of adult ADHD in the United States: Results from the National Comorbidity Survey replication. *American Journal of Psychiatry, 163,* 716–723.

Ketelaar, M., Vermeer, A., Helders, P. J. M., & Hart, H. (1998). Parental participation in intervention programs for children with cerebral palsy: A review of research. *Topics in Early Childhood Special Education, 18,* 108–117.

Key, D. L. (2000). *Team teaching: Integration of inclusion and regular students.* (ED447140). Retrieved October 23, 2002, from www.edrs.com/members/sp.cfm?AN=ED447140

Keyser-Marcus, L., Briel, L., Sherron-Targett, P., Yasuda, S., Johnson, S., & Wehman, P. (2002). Enhancing the schooling of students with traumatic brain injury. *Teaching Exceptional Children, 34*(4), 62–67.

Khorsheed, K. (2007). Four places to dig deep to find more time for teacher collaboration. *Journal of Staff Development, 28*(2), 43–45.

Kilincaslan, A., & Mukaddes, N. M. (2009). Pervasive developmental disorders in individuals with cerebral palsy. *Developmental Medicine & Child Neurology, 51,* 289–294.

Killu, K., (2008). Developing effective behavior intervention plans: Suggestions for school personnel. *Intervention in School and Clinic, 43,* 140–149.

Kim, K. H., Lee, Y., & Morningstar, M. E. (2007). An unheard voice: Korean American parents' expectations, hopes, and experiences concerning their adolescent child's future. *Research and Practice for Persons with Severe* Disabilities, 32, 253–264.

Kim, O. H., & Kaiser, A. P. (2000). Language characteristics of children with ADHD. *Communication Disorders Quarterly, 21,* 154–165.

Kim, Y. (2003). The effects of assertiveness training on enhancing the social skills of adolescents with visual impairments. *Journal of Visual Impairment and Blindness, 97,* 261–272.

Kinch, C., Lewis-Palmer, T., Hagan-Burke, S., & Sugai, G. (2001). A comparison of teacher and student functional behavior assessment interview information from low-risk and high-risk classrooms. *Education and Treatment of Children, 24,* 480–494.

King, K. A., Kozleski, E. B., & Landsdowne, K. (2009). Where are all the students of color in gifted education? *Principal, 88*(5), 16–20.

King-Sears, M. E. (2008). Facts and fallacies: Differentiation and the general education curriculum for students with special education needs. *Support for Learning, 23*(2), 55–62.

King-Sears, M. E. (2008). Using teacher and researcher data to evaluate the effects of self-management in an inclusive classroom. *Preventing School Failure, 52*(4), 25–36.

Kirchner, C. (1999). Prevalence estimates for visual impairment: Cutting through the data jungle. *Journal of Visual Impairment and Blindness, 93,* 253–259.

Kirchner, C., & Diament, S. (1999a). Estimates of the number of visually impaired students, their teachers, and orientation and mobility specialists: Part 1. *Journal of Visual Impairment and Blindness, 93,* 600–606.

Kirchner, C., & Diament, S. (1999b). Estimates of the number of visually impaired students, their teachers, and orientation and mobility specialists: Part 2. *Journal of Visual Impairment and Blindness, 93,* 738–744.

Kirchner, C., & Smith, B. (2005). Transition to what? Education and employment outcomes for visually impaired youths after high school. *Journal of Visual Impairment and Blindness, 99,* 499–504.

Kirschenbaum, R. J. (1998). Dynamic assessment and its use with underserved gifted and talented. *Gifted Child Quarterly, 42,* 140–147.

Kisor, H. (1990). *What's that pig outdoors? A memoir of deafness.* New York: Penguin.

Klein, A. M. (2008, Winter). Sensitivity to the learning needs of newcomers in foreign language settings. *Multicultural Education, 6*(2), 41–44 Win 2008.

Klein, R. G., & Biederman, J. (1999, June). *ADHD long-term outcomes: Comorbidity, secondary conditions, and health risk behaviors* (ADHD: Workshops). Atlanta, GA: Centers for Disease Control and Prevention. Retrieved June 23, 2003, from www.cdc.gov/ncbddd/ADHD/dadburden .htm#ADHD%20Long-term

Kleinert, H. L., & Kearns, J. F. (2001). *Alternate assessment: Measuring outcomes and supports for students with disabilities.* Baltimore: Paul H. Brookes Publishing Co.

Kleinert, H. L., Kearns, J. F., & Kennedy, S. (1997). Accountability for *all* students: Kentucky's alternative portfolio assessment for students with moderate and severe cognitive disabilities. *Journal of the Association for Persons with Severe Handicaps, 22,* 88–101.

Kliewer, C., & Biklen, D. (2001). "School's not really a place for reading": A research synthesis of the literate lives of students with severe disabilities. *Journal of the Association for Persons with Severe Handicaps, 26,* 1–12.

Klin, A., Jones, W., Schultz, R., & Volkmar, F. (2003). The enactive mind, or from actions to cognition: Lessons from autism. *Philosophical Transactions of the Royal Society of London, Series B, 358,* 345–360.

Klin, A., Jones, W., Schultz, R., Volkmar, F., & Cohen, D. (2002). Visual fixation patterns during viewing of naturalistic social situations as predictors of social competence in individuals with autism. *Archives of General Psychiatry, 59,* 809–816.

Klingner, J. K., & Artiles, A. J. (2003). When should bilingual students be in special education? *Educational Leadership, 61*(2), 66–71.

Klingner, J. K., & Edwards, P. A. (2006). Cultural considerations with response to intervention models. *Reading Research Quarterly, 41,* 108–117.

Klingner, J. K., & Vaughn, S. (1999). Students' perceptions of instruction in inclusion classrooms: Implications for students with learning disabilities. *Exceptional Children, 66,* 23–37.

Klingner, J. K., Vaughn, S., Hughes, M. T., Schumm, J. S., & Elbaum, B. (1998). Outcomes for students with and without learning disabilities in inclusive classrooms. *Learning Disabilities Research and Practice, 13,* 153–161.

Kloo, A., & Zigmond, N. (2008). Coteaching revisited: Redrawing the blueprint. *Preventing School Failure, 52,* 12–20.

Knitzer, J. (2005). Advocacy for children's mental health: A personal journey. *Journal of Clinical Child and Adolescent Psychology, 34,* 612–618.

Knoblauch, B., & McLane, K. (1999). *Rights and responsibilities of parents of children with disabilities: Update 1999* [ERIC Digest #E575]. Washington, DC: Office of Educational Research and Improvement. (ERIC Document Reproduction Service No. ED437766)

Kochhar-Bryant, C. A. (2008). Collaboration and system coordination for students with special needs: From early childhood to the postsecondary years. Upper Saddle River, NJ: Merrill.

Kode, K. (2002). *Elizabeth Farrell and the history of special education.* Arlington, VA: Council for Exceptional Children.

Koegel, R. L., & Koegel L. K. (1995). *Teaching autistic children.* Baltimore: Paul H. Brookes.

Koegel, R. L., Openden, D., Fredeen, R., & Koegel, L. K. (2006). The basics of pivotal response treatment. In R. L. Koegel & L. K. Koegel (Eds.), *Pivotal response treatments for autism: Communicative, social, and academic development* (pp. 4–30). Baltimore: Paul H. Brookes.

Koegel, R. L., Schreibman, L., Loos, L. M., Dirlich-Wilhelm, H., Dunlap, G., Robbins, F. R. et al. (1992). Consistent stress predictors in mothers of children with autism. *Journal of Autism and Developmental Disorders, 22,* 205–216.

Koenig, A. J., & Holbrook, M. C. (1995). *Learning media assessment of students with visual impairments: A resource guide for teachers* (2nd ed.). Austin, TX: Texas School for the Blind and Visually Impaired.

Koenig, A. J., & Holbrook, M. C. (2000). Planning instruction in unique skills. In A. J. Koenig & M. C. Holbrook (Eds.), *Foundations of education: Instructional strategies for teaching children and youths with visual impairments* (2nd ed., pp. 196–221). New York: American Foundation for the Blind Press.

Koenig, A. J., & Rex, E. J. (1996). Instruction of literacy skills to children and youths with low vision. In A. L. Corn & A. J. Koenig (Eds.), *Foundations of low vision: Clinical and functional perspectives* (pp. 280–305). New York: American Foundation for the Blind Press.

Koenig, K., & Tsatsanis, K. (2005). Pervasive developmental disorders in girls. In D. J. Bell, S. L. Foster, & E. J. Mash (Eds.), *Handbook of behavioral and emotional problems in girls* (pp. 211–238). New York: Kluwer.

Koestler, F. A. (1976). *The unseen minority: A social history of blindness in the United States.* New York: David McKay.

Kogan, M. D., Blumberg, S. J., Schieve, L. A., Boyle, C. A., Perrin, J. M., Ghandour, R. M., et al. (2009, October 5 on-line publication). Prevalence of parent-reported diagnosis of autism spectrum disorder among children in the US, 2007. *Pediatrics.* doi:10.1542/peds.2009-1522

Kohnert, K., Windsor, J., & Yim, D. (2006). Do language-based processing tasks separate children with language impairment from typical bilinguals? *Learning Disabilities Research and Practice, 21,* 19–29.

Kollins, S. H., Barkley, R. A., & DuPaul, G. J. (2001). Use and management of medications for children diagnosed with attention deficit disorder. *Focus on Exceptional Children, 33*(5), 1–24.

Kolloff, P. B. (1991). Special residential high schools. In N. Colangelo & G. Davis (Eds.), *Handbook of gifted education* (pp. 209–215). Boston: Allyn & Bacon.

Konrad, M. (2008). Involve students in the IEP process. *Intervention in School and Clinic, 43,* 236–239.

Konrad, M., & Test, D. W. (2007). Effects of GO 4 IT . . . NOW! Strategy instruction on the written IEP goal articulation and paragraph-writing skills of middle school students with disabilities. *Remedial and Special Education, 28,* 277–291.

Koontz, K., Short, A. D., Kalinyak, K., & Noll, R. B. (2004). A randomized, controlled pilot trial of a school intervention for children with sickle cell anemia. *Journal of Pediatric Psychology, 29,* 7–17.

Kopp, L. M., & Beauchaine, T. P. (2007). Patterns of psychopathology in the families of children with conduct problems, depression, and both psychiatric conditions. *Journal of Abnormal Child Psychology, 35,* 301–312.

Koro-Ljungberg, M., Bussing, R., Williamson, P., Wilder, J., & Mills, T. (2008). African American teenagers' stories of attention deficit/hyperactivity disorder. *Journal of Child and Family Studies, 1,* 467–485.

Kortering, J. L., & Christenson, S. (2009). Engaging students in school and learning: The real deal for school completion. *Exceptionality, 17*(1), 5–15.

Kos, J., Richdale, A., & Hay, D. (2006). Children with attention deficit hyperactivity disorder and their teachers: A review of literature. *International Journal of Disability, Development, and Education, 53,* 147–160.

Koutsoftas, A. D., Harmon, M. T., & Gray, S. (2009). The effect of tier 2 intervention for phonemic awareness in a response-to-intervention model in low-income preschool classrooms. *Language, Speech, and Hearing Services in Schools, 40,* 116–130.

Kovaleski, J. F., & Glew, M. C. (2006). Bringing instructional support teams to scale: Implication of the Pennsylvania experience. *Remedial and Special Education, 27,* 16–25.

Kovas, Y., Haworth, C., Dale, P. S., & Plomin, R. (2007). The genetic and environmental origins of learning abilities and disabilities in the early school years. *Monographs of the Society for Research in Child Development, 72*(3), 1–160.

Kozma, R. B., & Croniger, R. G. (1992). Technology and the fate of at-risk students. *Education and Urban Society, 24,* 440–453.

Krain, A. L., & Castellanos, F. X. (2006). Brain development and ADHD. *Clinical Psychology Review, 26,* 433–444.

Krajewski, J. J., & Hyde, M. S. (2000). Comparison of teen attitudes toward individuals with mental retardation between 1987 and 1998: Has inclusion made a difference? *Education and Training in Mental Retardation and Developmental Disabilities, 35,* 284–293.

Krajewski, J. J., Hyde, M. S., & O'Keefe, M. K. (2002). Teen attitudes toward individuals with mental retardation from 1987 to 1998: Impact of respondent gender and school variables. *Education and Training in Mental Retardation and Developmental Disabilities, 37,* 27–39.

Kraska, M., Zinner, B., & Abebe, A. (2007). Employment status of individuals with disabilities. *Journal for Vocational Special Needs Education, 29*(3), 22–29.

Kratochwill, T. R., McDonald, L., Levin, J. R., Scalia, P. A., & Coover, G. (2009). Families and schools together: An experimental study of multi-family support groups for children at risk. *Journal of School Psychology, 47,* 245–265.

Kratochwill, T. R., Volpiansky, P., & Clements, M. (2007). Professional development in implementing and sustaining multitier prevention models: Implications for response to intervention. *School Psychology Review, 36,* 618–631.

Krebs, C. (2006). Using a dialogue journal to build responsibility and self-reliance: A case study. *RE:view, 37,* 173–176.

Kroeger, S. D., Burton, C., Preston, C. (2009). Integrating evidence-based practices in middle science reading. *Teaching Exceptional Children, 41*(3), 6–15.

Kroeger, S. D., Leibold, C. K., & Ryan, B. (1999). Creating a sense of ownership in the IEP process. *Teaching Exceptional Children, 32*(1), 4–9.

Krug, D. A., Arick, J. R., & Almond, P. J. (1993). *Autism Screening Instrument for Educational Planning* (2nd ed.). Austin, TX: Pro-Ed.

Kruger, R. J., Kruger, J. J., Hugo, R., & Campbell, N. F. (2001). Relationship patterns between central auditory processing disorders and language disorders, learning disabilities, and sensory integration dysfunction. *Communication Disorders Quarterly, 22*(2), 87–98.

Kulik, B. J. (Ed.). (2001). *Physical disabilities: Education and related services.* Albany, NY: Boyd. (ERIC Document Reproduction Service No. ED465246)

Kummer, A. W. (2006, February). Resonance disorders and nasal emission: Evaluation and treatment using "low tech" and "no tech" procedures. *ASHA Leader, 11*(2), 4, 26.

Kummerer, S. E., Lopez-Reyna, N. A., & Hughes, M. T. (2007). Immigrant mothers' perceptions of their children's communication disabilities, emergent literacy development, and speech-language therapy programs. *American Journal of Speech-Language Pathology, 16,* 271–282.

Kundert, D. K. (2008). Prader-Willi syndrome. *School Psychology Quarterly, 23,* 246–257.

Kunzman, R. (2008). Homeschooling. In J. A. Plucker & C. M. Callahan (Eds.), *Critical issues and practices in gifted education: What the research says* (253–260). Waco, TX: Prufrock.

Kurtzweil, P. (1999). How folate can help prevent birth defects. *FDA Consumer.* Retrieved August 15, 2006, from www.cfsan.fda.gov/~dms/fdafolic.html

Kurz, S. (2002, May/June). Treating attention-deficit/hyperactivity disorder (ADHD) in school settings. *Child Study Center Letter, 6*(5), 1–6.

Kusché, C. A., & Greenberg, M. T. (1993). *The PATHS Curriculum.* Seattle: Developmental Research and Programs.

Kuttler, S., Myles, B. S., & Carlson, J. K. (1998). The use of social stories to reduce precursors to tantrum behavior in a student with autism. *Focus on Autistic Behavior, 13,* 176–182.

Kutz, G. D. (2009). *Seclusion and restraints: Selected cases of death and abuse at public and private schools and treatment centers* [testimony before the Committee on Education and Labor, House of Representatives; GAO-09-719T]. Washington, D.C.: U.S. General Accountability Office.

La Paro, K. M., Olsen, K., & Pianta, R. C. (2002). Special education eligibility: Developmental precursors over the first three years of life. *Exceptional Children, 69,* 55–66.

Lackaye, T. D., & Margalit, M. (2006). Comparisons of achievement, effort, and self-perceptions among students with learning disabilities and their peers from different achievement groups. *Journal of Learning Disabilities, 39,* 432–446.

LaFee, S. (2005). Another weighty burden: How much responsibility do schools bear for addressing the obesity of their students? *School Administrator, 62*(9), 10–16.

Lahey, B., & Rowland, A. (1999, April 14). *Epidemiologic issues in ADHD* (ADHD: Workshops). Retrieved June 1, 2003, from www.cdc.gov/ncbddd/adhd/dadepi.htm

Laing, S. P., & Kamhi, A. (2003). Alternative assessment of language and literacy in culturally and linguistically diverse populations. *Language, Speech, and Hearing Services in Schools, 34,* 44–55.

Lake, J. F., & Billingsley, B. S. (2000). An analysis of factors that contribute to parent–school conflict in special education. *Remedial and Special Education, 21,* 240–251.

Lamar-Dukes, P., & Dukes, C. (2005). Consider the roles and responsibilities of the inclusion support teacher. *Intervention in School and Clinic, 41,* 55–61.

Lambert, N. M., Nihira, K., & Leland, H. (1993). *AAMR Adaptive Behavior Scale-School* (2nd edition) (ABS-S:2). Austin, TX: Pro-Ed.

Lambie, R. (2000). *Family systems within educational context: Understanding at-risk and special needs students* (2nd ed.). Denver: Love.

Lancioni, G. E., Singh, N. N., O'Reilly, M. F., Oliva, D., Baccani, S., & Canevaro, A. (2002). Using simple hand-movement responses with optic microswitches with two persons with multiple disabilities. *Research and Practice for Persons with Severe Disabilities, 27,* 276–279.

Landrum, M. S. (2001). Resource consultation and collaboration in gifted education. *Psychology in the Schools, 38,* 457–466.

Landrum, M. S., Katsiyannis, A., & DeWaard, J. (1998). A national survey of current legislative and policy trends in gifted education: Life after the National Excellence Report. *Journal for the Education of the Gifted, 21,* 352–371.

Lane, H. (2002). Do deaf people have a disability? *Sign Language Studies, 2*(4), 356–379.

Lane, H., Hoffmeister, R., & Bahan, B. (1996). *A journey into the Deaf-world.* San Diego: Dawn Sign Press.

Lane, K. L., Pierson, M. R., & Givner, C. C. (2004). Secondary teachers' views on social competence: "Skills essential for success." *Journal of Special Education, 38,* 174–186.

Lane, K. L., Wehby, J. H., & Cooley, C. (2006). Teacher expectations of students' classroom behavior across the grade span: Which social skills are necessary for success? *Exceptional Children, 72,* 153–167.

Lane, S., Bell, L., & Parson-Tylka, T. (1997). *My turn to learn: A communication guide for parents of deaf or hard of hearing children.* Burnaby, Canada: Bauhinea Press.

Language Varieties Network. (2004). *Pidgins, creoles, and other stigmatized varieties.* Retrieved February 7, 2004, from www2.hawaii.edu/~gavinm/home.htm

LaParo, K. M., Olson, K., & Pianta, R. C. (2002). Special education eligibility: Developmental precursors over the first three years of life. *Exceptional Children, 69,* 55–66.

Lardieri, L. A., Blacher, J., & Swanson, H. L. (2000). Sibling relationships and parent stress in families of children with and without learning disabilities. *Learning Disability Quarterly, 23,* 105–116.

*Larry P. v. Wilson Riles.* (1979). C-71–2270 FRP. Dist. Ct.

LaRusso, M. D., Romer, D., & Selman, R. L. (2008). Teachers as builders of respectful school climates: Implications for adolescent drug use norms and depressive symptoms in high school. *Journal of Youth and Adolescence, 37,* 386–398.

LaSasso, C., & Davey, B. (1987). The relationship between lexical knowledge and reading comprehension for prelingually, profoundly hearing-impaired students. *The Volta Review, 89,* 211–220.

LaSasso, C., & Lollis, J. (2003). Survey of residential and day schools for deaf students in the United States that identify themselves as bilingual–bicultural programs. *Journal of Deaf Studies and Deaf Education, 8,* 79–91. (ERIC Document Reproduction Service No. ED661030)

Lassen, S. R., Steele, M. M., & Sailor, W. (2006). The relationship of school-wide positive behavior supports to academic achievement in an urban middle. *Psychology in the Schools, 43,* 701–712.

Latimer, W. W., Ernst, J., & Hennessey, J. (2004). Relapse among adolescent drug abusers following treatment: The role of probable ADHD status. *Journal of Child and Adolescent Substance Abuse, 13*(3), 1–6.

Lau, M. Y., Sieler, J. D., & Muyskens, P. (2006). Perspectives on the use of the problem-solving model from the viewpoint of a school psychologist, administrator, and teacher from a large Midwest urban school district. *Psychology in the Schools, 43,* 117–127.

Lauth, G., Heubeck, B., & Mackowiak, K. (2006). Observation of children with attention-deficit hyperactivity (ADHD) problems in three natural classroom contexts. *British Journal of Educational Psychology, 76,* 385–404.

Law, J., & Garrett, Z. (2004). Speech and language therapy: Its potential role in CAMHS. *Child and Adolescent Mental Health, 9*(2), 50–55.

Lawrence, B. K. (2009). Rural gifted education: A comprehensive literature review. *Journal for the Education of the Gifted, 32,* 461–494.

Lawson, H. A., & Sailor, W. (2000). Integrating services, collaborating, and developing connections with schools. *Focus on Exceptional Children, 33*(2), 1–22.

Lazear, K. J., Gomez, A., & Chambers, T. (1998). Looking at success: Experiences of a select group of children and young adults with serious emotional disturbance. In *Proceedings of the Annual Research Conference, a system of care for children's mental health: Expanding the research base,* Tampa, FL. (ERIC Document Reproduction Service No. ED432848)

Le Couteur, A., Lord, C., & Rutter, M. (2003). *Autism Diagnostic Interview-Revised (ADI-R).* Los Angeles: Western Psychological Services.

Leach, D., & Duffy, M. L. (2009). Supporting students with autism spectrum disorders in inclusive settings. *Intervention in School and Clinic, 45*(1), 31–37.

Leaf, R., & McEachin, J. (1999). *A work in progress: Behavior management strategies and a curriculum for intensive behavioral treatment of autism.* New York: DRL Books.

Learning Disabilities Association of America. (2003). *Speech and language milestone chart.* Retrieved November 11, 2003, from www.ldonline.org/ld_indepth/speech-language/lda_milestones.html

LeBovidge, J. S., Lavigne, J. V., Donenberg, G. R., & Miller, M. L. (2003). Psychological adjustment of children and adolescents with chronic arthritis: A meta-analytic review. *Journal of Pediatric Psychology, 228,* 29–39.

Lederberg, A. R., & Mobley, C. E. (1990). The effect of hearing impairment on the quality of attachment and mother-toddler interaction. *Child Development, 61,* 1596–1604.

Lee, H., & Templeton, R. (2008). Ensuring equal access to technology: Providing assistive technology for students with disabilities. *Theory into Practice, 47,* 212–219.

Lee, S., Odom, S. L., Loftin, R. (2007). Social engagement with peers and stereotypic behavior of children with autism. *Journal of Positive Behavior Interventions. 9,* 67–79.

Lee, S., Palmer, S., Turnbull, A., & Wehmeyer, M. (2006). A model for parent–teacher collaboration to promote self-determination in young children with disabilities. *Teaching Exceptional Children, 38*(3), 36–41.

Lee, S., Wehmeyer, M., Palmer, S., Soukup, J., & Little, T. (2008). Self-determination and access to the general education curriculum. *Journal of Special Education, 42*(2), 91–107.

Lee, S. S., Lahey, B. B., & Owens, E. B. (2008). Few preschool boys and girls with ADHD are well-adjusted during adolescence. *Journal of Abnormal Child Psychology, 36,* 373–383.

Lee, S. W., & Guck, T. P. (2000). Parents and families with a chronically ill child. In M. J. Fine and R. L. Simpson (Eds.), *Collaboration with parents of exceptional children* (pp. 257–276). Brandon, VT: Clinical Psychology Publishing.

LeFever, G. B., Villers, M. S., Morrow, A. L., & Vaughn, E. S. (2002). Parental perceptions of adverse educational outcomes among childen diagnosed and treated for ADHD: A call for improved school/provider collaboration. *Psychology in the Schools, 39,* 63–71.

Leffert, J. S., Siperstein, G. N., & Millikan, E. (2000). Understanding social adaptation in children with mental retardation: A social–cognitive perspective. *Exceptional Children, 66,* 530–545.

Lehmkuhl, H. D., Merlo, L. J., Storch, E. A., Heidgerken, A., Silverstein, J. H., & Geffken, G. R. (2008). Cognitive abilities in a sample of youth with multiple episodes of diabetic ketoacidosis. *Journal of Developmental & Physical Disabilities, 21,* 1–8.

Lemanek, K. L. (2004). Adherence. In R. T. Brown (Ed.), *Handbook of pediatric psychology in school settings* (pp. 129–148). Mahwah, NJ: Erlbaum.

Lemanek, K. L., & Hood, C. (1999). Asthma. In R. T. Brown (Ed.), *Cognitive aspects of chronic illness in children* (pp. 78–104). New York: Guilford Press.

Lemkuhl, H., & Nabors, L. (2008). Children with diabetes: Satisfaction with school support, illness perceptions, and HbA1c levels. *Journal of Developmental & Physical Disabilities, 20,* 101–114.

Lenden, J. M., & Flipsen, P. (2007). Prosody and voice characteristics of children with cochlear implants. *Journal of Communication Disorders, 40,* 66–81.

Lensch, C. R. (2000). *Making sense of attention deficit/hyperactivity disorder.* Westport, CT: Bergin & Garvey.

Lenz, B. K., Ellis, E. S., & Scanlon, D. (1996). *Teaching learning strategies to adolescents and adults with learning disabilities.* Austin, TX: Pro-Ed.

Leo, J. (2002). American preschoolers on Ritalin. *Society, 39*(2), 52–60.

Leonard, E. L., & George, M. R. (1999). Psychosocial and neuropsychological function in children with epilepsy. *Pediatric Rehabilitation, 3*(3), 73–80.

Lerman, D., Vorndran, C., Addison, L., & Kuhn, S. (2004). Preparing teachers in evidence-based practices for young children with autism. *School Psychology Review, 33,* 510–526.

Lerner, J. (2003). *Learning disabilities: Theories, diagnoses, and teaching strategies* (9th ed.). Boston: Houghton Mifflin.

Lerner, J., & Kline, F. (2006). *Learning disabilities and related disorders: Characteristics and teaching strategies* (10th ed.). Boston: Houghton Mifflin.

Leroux, J. A., & Levitt-Perlman, M. (2000). The gifted child with attention deficit disorder: An identification and intervention challenge. *Roeper Review, 22,* 171–176.

Levy, F., Hay, D., & Bennett, K. (2006). Genetics of attention deficit hyperactivity disorder: A current review and future prospects. *International Journal of Disability, Development and Education. 53,* 5–20.

Lewis, B. A., Freebairn, L. A., Hansen, A. J., Iyengar, S. K., & Taylor, H. G. (2004). School-age follow-up of children with childhood apraxia of speech. *Language, Speech, and Hearing Services in Schools, 35,* 122–140.

Lewis, B. A., Freebairn, L. A., & Taylor, H. G. (2000). Academic outcomes in children with histories of speech sound disorders. *Journal of Communication Disorders, 33,* 11–30.

Lewis, S. (2002). Some thoughts on inclusion, alienation, and meeting the needs of children with visual impairments. *RE:view, 34,* 99–101.

Lewis, S., & Allman, C. B. (2000). Educational programming. In M. C. Holbrook & A. J. Koenig (Eds.), *Foundations of education: History and theory of teaching children and youths with visual impairments* (2nd ed., pp. 218–259). New York: American Foundation for the Blind Press.

Lewis, S., & Tolla, J. (2003). Creating and using tactile experience books for young children with vision impairments. *TEACHING Exceptional Children, 35*(3), 22–29.

Lewis, T. J., Scott, T. M., & Sugai, G. (1994). The problem behavior questionnaire: A teacher-based instrument to develop functional hypotheses of problem behavior in general education settings. *Diagnostique, 19,* 103–115.

Leyser, Y., & Heinze, T. (2001). Perspectives of parents of children who are visually impaired: Implications for the field. *RE:view, 33,* 37–48.

Lidz, C. S., & Macrine, S. L. (2001). An alternative approach to the identification of gifted culturally and linguistically diverse learners: The contribution of dynamic assessment. *School Psychology International, 22,* 74–96.

Light, J., & McNaughton, D. (2008). Making a difference: A celebration of the 25th anniversary of the International Society for Augmentative and Alternative Communication. *Augmentative and Alternative Communication, 24,* 175–193.

Lighthouse. (1995). *The Lighthouse national survey on vision loss: The experience, attitudes and knowledge of middle-aged and older Americans.* New York: Arlene R. Gordon Research Institute, Lighthouse.

Lignugaris-Kraft, B., Marchand-Martella, N., & Martella, R. C. (2001). Strategies for writing better goals and short-term objectives or benchmarks. *Teaching Exceptional Children, 34*(1), 52–58.

Liljequist, L., & Renk, K. (2007). The relationships among teachers' perceptions of student behavior, teachers' characteristics, and ratings of students' emotional and behavioural problems. *Educational Psychology, 27,* 557–571.

Lim, J., Wood, B., & Cheah, P. (2009). Understanding children with asthma: Trouble and triggers. *Childhood Education, 85,* 307–313.

Lindsey, P., Wehmeyer, M. L., Guy, B., & Martin, J. (2001). Age of majority and mental retardation: A position statement of the division on mental retardation and developmental disabilities. *Education and Training in Mental Retardation and Developmental Disabilities, 36,* 3–15.

Lindstrom, L., Doren, B., Metheny, J., Johnson, P., & Zane, C. (2007). Transition to employment: Role of the family in career development. *Exceptional Children, 73,* 348–366.

Lipman, P. (1997). Restructuring in context: A case study of teacher participation and the dynamics of ideology, race, and power. *American Educational Research Journal, 34,* 3–37.

Little, C. (2002). Which is it? Asperger's syndrome or giftedness? Defining the differences. *Gifted Child Today, 25,* 58–63.

Little, C. A. (2001). Probabilities and possibilities: The future of gifted education. *Journal of Secondary Gifted Education, 12,* 166–169.

Little, J. W. (1993). Teachers' professional development in a climate of educational reform. *Educational Evaluation and Policy Analysis, 15,* 129–151.

Little, M. E., & Dieker, L. (2009). Coteaching: Two are better than one. *Principal Leadership, 9,* 43–46.

Lloyd, G., Cohen, D., & Stead, J. (Eds.). (2006). *Critical new perspectives on ADHD.* Oxford, UK: Routledge.

Lloyd, J. W., Hallahan, D. P., Kauffman, J. M., & Keller, C. E. (1998). Academic problems. In R. J. Morris & T. R. Kratochwill (Eds.), *The practice of child therapy* (pp. 167–198). Boston: Allyn & Bacon.

Lo, L. (2005). Barriers to successful partnerships with Chinese-speaking parents of children with disabilities in urban schools. *Multiple Voices, 8*(1), 84–95.

Lock, R. H., & Layton, C. A. (2001). Succeeding in postsecondary education through self-advocacy. *Teaching Exceptional Children, 34*(2), 66–71.

Logan, K., Jacobs, H. A., Gast, D. A., Murray, A. S., Daino, K., & Skala, C. (1998). The impact of typical peers on the perceived happiness of students with profound multiple disabilities. *Journal of the Association for Persons with Severe Handicaps, 23,* 309–318.

Lohmeier, K. L. (2005). Implementing the expanded core curriculum in specialized schools for the blind. *RE:view, 37,* 126–133.

Lohmeier, K. L. (2007). Integrating expanded core sessions into the K–12 program: A high school scheduling approach. *RE:view: Rehabilitation Education for Blindness and Visual Impairment, 39,* 31–40.

Lohmeier, K., Blankenship, K., & Hatlen, P. (2009). Expanded core curriculum: 12 years later. *Journal of Visual Impairment & Blindness, 103,* 102–112.

Lohmeier, L. L. (2009). Aligning state standards and the expanded core curriculum: Balancing the impact of the No Child Left Behind Act. *Journal of Visual Impairment & Blindness, 103,* 44–47.

London, E., & Etzel, R. A. (2000). The environment as an etiologic factor in autism: A new direction for research. *Environmental Health Perspectives, 108,* 401–404.

Long, C. E., Gurka, M. J., & Blackman, J. A. (2008). Family stress and children's language and behavior problems: Results from the National Survey of Children's Health. *Topics in Early Childhood Special Education, 28,* 148–157.

Longmore, P. K., & Umansky, L. (Eds.). (2001). *The new disability history: American perspectives.* New York: New York University Press.

Lopes, J. (2005). Intervention with students with learning, emotional and behavioral disorders: Why do we take so long to do it? *Education and Treatment of Children, 28,* 345–360.

Lopez-Reyna, N. A., & Bay, M. (1997). Enriching assessments using varied assessments for diverse learners. *Teaching Exceptional Children, 29*(1), 33–37.

Lord, C., Rutter, M., & Le Couteur, A. (1994). *Autism Diagnostic Interview–Revised:* A revised version of a diagnostic interview for caregivers of individuals with possible pervasive developmental disorders. *Journal of Autism and Developmental Disorders, 24,* 659–685.

Lord-Maes, J., & Obrzut, J. E. (1996). Neuropsychological consequences of traumatic brain injury in children and adolescents. *Journal of Learning Disabilities, 29,* 609–617.

Lorenzi, D. G., Horvat, M., & Pellegrini, A. D. (2000). Physical activity of children with and without mental retardation in inclusive recess settings. *Education and Training in Mental Retardation and Developmental Disabilities, 35,* 160–167.

Lortie, D. C. (1975). *Schoolteacher: A sociological study.* Chicago: University of Chicago Press.

Lovaas, O. I. (1987). *Teaching developmentally disabled children: The ME book.* Austin, TX: Pro-Ed.

Lowenfeld, B. (1973). Psychological considerations. In B. Lowenfeld (Ed.), *The visually handicapped child in school.* New York: The John Day Company.

Lucangeli, D., & Cabrele, S. (2006). Mathematical difficulties and ADHD. *Exceptionality, 12*(1), 53–62.

Lucas, C., & Valli, C. (1992). *Language contact in the American Deaf community.* San Diego: Academic Press.

Luckasson, R., et al. (2002). *Mental retardation: Definition, classification, and systems of supports* (10th ed.). Washington, DC: American Association on Mental Retardation.

Luckner, J., & Denzin, P. (1998). In the mainstream: Adaptations for students who are deaf or hard of hearing. *Perspectives in Education and Deafness, 17*(1), 8–11.

Luckner, J., Bowen, S., & Carter, K. (2001). Visual teaching strategies for students who are deaf or hard of hearing. *Teaching Exceptional Children, 33*(3), 38–44.

Luckner, J. L. (2002). *Facilitating the transition of students who are deaf or hard of hearing.* Austin, TX: Pro-Ed.

Luckner, J. L., & Muir, S. (2001). Successful students who are deaf in general education settings. *American Annals of the Deaf, 146,* 450–461.

Luckner, J. L., & Nadler, R. S. (1997). *Processing the experience: Strategies to enhance and generalize learning.* Dubuque, IA: Kendall/Hunt.

Lue, M. S. (2001). *A survey of communication disorders for the classroom teacher.* Boston: Allyn & Bacon.

Lueck, A. H., Bailey, I. L., Greer, R. B., Tuan, K. M., Bailey, V. M., & Dornbusch, H. G. (2003). Exploring print-size requirements and reading for students with low vision. *Journal of Visual Impairment and Blindness, 97,* 335–354.

Luetke-Stahlman, B., & Luckner, J. L. (1991). *Effectively educating students with hearing impairment.* New York: Longman.

Luftig, R. L., & Muthert, D. (2005). Patterns of employment and independent living of adult graduates with learning disabilities and mental retardation of an inclusionary high school vocational program. *Research in Developmental Disabilities: A Multidisciplinary Journal, 26,* 317–325.

Lund, S. K., & Light, J. C. (2001). *Fifteen years later: An investigation of the long-term outcomes of augmentative and alternative communication interventions.* (ERIC Document Reproduction Service No. ED458 727) Retrieved November 19, 2003, from www.edrs.com/members/sp.cfm?AN=ED_458727

Lussenhop, K., & Corn, A. L. (2002). Comparative studies of the reading performance of students with low vision. *RE:view, 34,* 57–69.

Lustig, D. C. (2002). Family coping in families with a child with a disability. *Education and Training in Mental Retardation and Developmental Disabilities, 37,* 14–22.

Lustig, D. C., & Akey, T. (1999). Adaptation in families with adult children with mental retardation: Impact of family strengths and appraisal. *Education and Training in Mental Retardation and Developmental Disabilities, 34,* 260–270.

Ly, T. M. (2008). Asian American parents' attributions of children with Down syndrome: Connections with child characteristics and culture. *Intellectual and Developmental Disabilities, 46,* 129–140.

Lynch, E. W. (1998). Developing cross-cultural competence. In E. W. Lynch & M. J. Hanson (Eds.), *Developing cross-cultural competence: A guide for working with young children and their families* (2nd ed., pp. 57–63). Baltimore: Paul H. Brookes.

Lyon, G. R. (1997). Progress and promise in research in learning disabilities. *Learning Disabilities: A Multidisciplinary Journal, 8*(1), 1–6.

Lyon, G. R. (1998). *Overview of reading and literacy initiatives.* Statement presented to National Institute of Child Health and Human Development. Retrieved October 7, 1999, from www.nichd.nih.gov/publications/pubs/jeffords.htm

Lyon, G. R., Fletcher, J. M., Shaywitz, S. E., Shaywitz, B. A., Torgesen, J. K., Wood, F. B. et al. (2001). Rethinking learning disabilities. In C. E. Finn, A. J. Rotherham, & C. R. Hokanson (Eds.), *Rethinking special education for a new century* (pp. 259–287). Washington, DC: Thomas B. Fordham Foundation and Progressive Policy Institute.

Lytle, R. K., & Bordin, J. (2001). Enhancing the IEP team: Strategies for parents and professionals. *Teaching Exceptional Children, 33*(5), 40–44.

Maag, J. W., & Reid, R. (2006). Depression among students with learning disabilities: Assessing the risk. *Journal of Learning Disabilities, 39,* 3–10.

Maccini, P., & Gagnon, J. C. (2006). Mathematics instructional practices and assessment accommodations by secondary special and general educators. *Exceptional Children, 72,* 217–234.

MacDonald, V., & Speece, D. L. (2001). Making time: A teacher's report on her first year of teaching children with emotional disabilities. *Journal of Special Education, 35,* 84–91.

MacFarland, D. J., & Cacace, A. T. (2006). Current controversies in CAPD: From Procrustes' bed to Pandora's box. In T. K. Parthasarathy (Ed.), *An introduction to auditory processing disorders* (pp. 247–263). Mahwah, NJ: Lawrence Erlbaum.

MacLennan, D. L, & MacLennan, D. C. (2008). Assessing readiness for postsecondary education after traumatic brain injury using a simulated college experience. *NeuroRehabilitation, 23,* 521–528.

Macleod-Gallinger, J. (1992). Employment attainments of deaf adults one and ten years after graduation from high school. *Journal of the American Deafness and Rehabilitation Association, 25*(4), 1–10.

MacMillan, D. L., & Reschly, D. J. (1998). Overrepresentation of minority students: The case for greater specificity or reconsideration of the variables examined. *Journal of Special Education, 32,* 15–24.

MacMillan, D. L., & Siperstein, G. N. (2001, August). *Learning disabilities as operationally defined by schools: Executive summary.* Paper presented at the Learning Disabilities Summit: Building a Foundation for the Future, Washington, DC. (ERIC Document Reproduction Service No. ED458759)

Madaus, J. W., Foley, T. E., McGuire, J. M., & Ruban, L. M. (2001). A follow-up investigation of university graduates with learning disabilities. *Career Development for Exceptional Individuals, 24,* 133–146.

Madaus, J. W., & Shaw, S. F. (2004). Section 504: Differences in the regulations for secondary and postsecondary education. *Intervention in School and Clinic, 40,* 81–87.

Madaus, J. W., & Shaw, S. F. (2006). Disability services in postsecondary education: Impact of IDEA 2004. *Journal of Developmental Education, 30,* 12–21.

Madigan, K. A., Hall, T. E., & Glang, A. (1997). Effective assessment and instructional practices for students with ABI. In A. Glang, G. H. S. Singer, & B. Todis (Eds.), *Students with acquired brain injury: The school's response* (pp. 123–184). Baltimore: Paul H. Brookes.

Madison, C. L., Johnson, J. M., Seikel, J. A., Arnold, M., & Schultheis, L. (1998). Comparative study of the phonology of preschool children prenatally exposed to cocaine and multiple drugs and non-exposed children. *Journal of Communication Disorders, 31,* 231–244.

Maedgen, J. W., & Carlson, C. L. (2000). Social functioning and emotional regulation in the attention deficit hyperactivity disorder subtypes. *Journal of Clinical Child Psychology, 29,* 30–42.

Maggio, E. (2009). *Making it easier for school staff to help traumatized students: research highlights* [RAND Corporation]. Retrieved July 15, 2009 from http://www.rand.org/pubs/research_briefs/RB9443/index1.html

Magiera, K., Smith, C., Zigmond, N., & Gebaner, K. (2005). Benefits of co-teaching in secondary mathematics classes. *Teaching Exceptional Children, 37*(3), 20–24.

Magiera, K., & Zigmond, N. (2005). Co-teaching in middle school classrooms under routine conditions: Does the instructional experience differ for students with disabilities in co-taught and solo-taught classes? *Learning Disabilities Research and Practice, 20,* 79–85.

Magliaro, S. G., Lockee, B. B., & Burton, J. K. (2005). Direct instruction revisited: A key model for instructional technology. *Educational Technology Research and Development, 53*(4), 41–55.

Maguire, M. (2001). The cultural formation of teachers' class consciousness: Teachers in the inner city. *Journal of Education Policy, 16*(4), 1–5.

Maheady, L., Harper, G. F., & Mallette, B. (2001). Peer-mediated instruction and interventions and students with mild disabilities. *Remedial and Special Education, 22,* 4–14.

Maheady, L., Mallette, B., & Harper, G. E. (2006). Four classwide peer tutoring models: Similarities, differences, and implications for research and practice. *Reading and Writing Quarterly, 22,* 65–89.

Maholmes, V., & Brown, F. E. (2002). Over-representation of African-American students in special education: The role of a developmental framework in shaping teachers' interpretations of African-American students' behavior. *Trotter Review: Race, Ethnicity, and Public Education, 14*(1), 45–59.

Mahr, K. (2007, November 12). ADHD kids can get better. *Time* [on-line]. Retrieved July 1, 2009 from http://www.time.com/time/health/article/0,8599,1683069,00.html

Maker, C. J., Nielson, A. B., & Rogers, J. A. (1994). Giftedness, diversity, and problem-solving. *Teaching Exceptional Children, 27*(1), 4–19.

Maker, C. J., & Schiever, S. W. (2005). *Teaching models in education of the gifted* (3rd ed.). Austin, TX: Pro-Ed.

Malian, I., & Nevin, A. (2002). A review of self-determination literature: Implications for practitioners. *Remedial and Special Education, 23,* 68–74.

Malmgren, K., Abbott, R. D., & Hawkins, J. D. (1999). LD and delinquency: Rethinking the "link." *Journal of Learning Disabilities, 32,* 194–200.

Malmgren, K. W., Causton, Theoharis, J. N., & Trezek, B. J. (2005). Increasing peer interactions for students with behavioral disorders via paraprofessional training. *Behavioral Disorders, 31,* 95–106.

Malone, D. M., Gallagher, P. A., & Long, S. R. (2001). General education teachers' attitudes and perceptions of teamwork supporting children with developmental concerns. *Early Education and Development, 12,* 577–592.

Mancini, K. G., & Layton, C. A. (2004). Meeting fears and concerns effectively: The inclusion of early childhood students who are medically fragile. *Physical Disabilities: Education and Related Services, 22*(2), 29–48.

Mandell, D. S., Listerud, J., Levy, S. E., & Pinto-Martin, J. A. (2002). Race differences in the age at diagnosis among Medicaid-eligible children with autism. *Journal of the American Academy of Child Adolescent Psychiatry, 41,* 1447–1453.

Mank, D., Cioffi, A., & Yovanoff, P. (1998). Employment outcomes for people with severe disabilities: Opportunities for improvement. *Mental Retardation, 36,* 205–216.

March of Dimes. (2003). *Quick reference: Birth defects and genetics—Down syndrome* [fact sheet]. New York: National Down Syndrome Society. Retrieved October 8, 2003, from www.marchofdimes.com/printableArticles/681_1214.asp?printable=true

March of Dimes. (2006). *Quick reference and fact sheets: Down syndrome.* Retrieved October 30, 2006 from http://search.marchofdimes.com/cgi-bin/MsmGo.exe?grab_id=0&page_id=2432&query=down%20syndrome&hiword=DOWNER%20DOWNERS%20DOWNI%20DOWNIE%20DOWNING%20DOWNS%20SYNDROM%20SYNDROMES%20down%20syndrome%20

Marino, M. T., Marino, E. C., & Shaw, S. F. (2006). Making informed assistive technology decisions for students with high incidence disabilities. *Teaching Exceptional Children, 38*(6), 18–25.

Markowitz, J., & Linehan, P. (2001). *Traumatic brain injury: A brief analysis of a critical issue in special education.* Alexandria, VA: National Association of State Directors of Special Education. (ERIC Document Reproduction Service No. ED451633)

Marland, S. P., Jr. (1972). *Education of the gifted and talented—Volume 1: Report to the Congress of the United States by the U.S. Commissioner of Education.* Washington, DC: Office of Education.

Marlin, A. E. (2004). Management of hydrocephalus in the patient with myelomeningocele: An argument against third ventriculostomy. *Neurosurgical Focus, 16*(2), 1–3.

Maroney, S. A., Finson, K. D., Beaver, J. B., & Jensen, M. M. (2003). Preparing for successful inquiry in inclusive science classrooms. *Teaching Exceptional Children, 36*(1), 18–25.

Marschark, M. (1997). *Raising and educating a deaf child.* New York: Oxford University Press.

Marschark, M., Convertino, C., & LaRock, D. (2006). Optimizing academic performance of deaf students: Access, opportunities, and outcomes. In D. F. Moores & D. S. Martin, (Eds.), *Deaf learners: Developments in curriculum and instruction* (pp. 179–200). Washington, DC: Gallaudet University Press.

Marshall, J. M., & Marshall, J. (2005). *Walking with grandfather: The wisdom of Lakota elders.* Boulder, CO: Sounds True.

Marston, D. (1997). A comparison of inclusion only, pull-out only, and combined service models for students with mild disabilities. *Journal of Special Education, 30,* 121–132.

Marston, D. (2005). Tiers of intervention in responsiveness to intervention: Prevention outcomes and learning disabilities identification patterns. *Journal of Learning Disabilities, 38,* 539–544.

Martin, D. V. (2002). ADHD: *Fact, fiction and beyond, history and genetics.* Retrieved December 16, 2002, from www.adhdtexas.com/history.htm

Martin, E. J., & Hagan-Burke, S. (2002). Establishing a home–school connection: Strengthening the partnership between families and schools. *Preventing School Failure, 46*(2), 62–65.

Martin, E. W., Martin, R., & Terman, D. L. (1996). The legislative and litigation history of special education. *Future of Children, 6*(1), 25–39.

Martin, J. E., Marshall, L. H., & Sale, P. (2004). A 3-year study of middle, junior high, and high school IEP meetings. *Exceptional Children, 70,* 285–298.

Martin, J. E., Van Dycke, J. L., Christensen, W. R., Greene, B. A., Gardner, J. E., & Lovett, D. L. (2006). Increasing student participation in IEP meetings: Establishing the self-directed IEP as an evidence-based practice. *Exceptional Children, 72,* 299–316.

Martin, L., & Kragler, S. (1999). Creating a culture for teachers' professional growth. *Journal of School Leadership, 9,* 311–320.

Martinez, R., & Sewell, K. W. (2000). Explanatory style as a predicator of college performance in students with physical disabilities. *Journal of Rehabilitation, 66*(1), 30–37.

Martinez-Torteya, C., Bogat, G. A., von Eye, A., & Levendosky, A. A. (2009). Resilience among children exposed to domestic violence: The role of risk and protective factors. *Child Development, 80,* 562–577.

Masia-Warner, C., Nangle, D. W., & Hansen, D. J. (2006). Bringing evidence-based child mental health services to the schools: General issues and specific populations. *Education and Treatment of Children, 29,* 165–172.

Mason, C., Davidson, R., & McNerney, C. (2000). *National plan for training personnel to serve children with blindness and low vision.* Reston, VA: Council for Exceptional Children.

Mason, C. Y., McGahee-Kovac, M., & Johnson, L. (2004). How to help students lead their IEP meetings. *Teaching Exceptional Children, 36*(3), 18–25.

Mason, S., O'Sullivan, A., O'Sullivan, T., & Cullen, M. A. (2000). Parents' expectations and experiences of their children's education. In A. Closs (Ed.), *The education of children with medical conditions* (pp. 51–64). London: David Fulton.

Mastropieri, M., Jenkins, V., & Scruggs, T. (1985). Academic and intellectual characteristics of behavior disordered children and youth. In R. B. Rutherford (Ed.), *Severe behavior disorders of children and youth* (vol. 8, pp. 86–104). Reston, VA: Council for Children and Behavior Disorders, Council for Exceptional Children.

Mastropieri, M. A. (2001). Is the glass half full or half empty? Challenges encountered by first-year special education teachers. *Journal of Special Education, 35,* 66–74.

Mastropieri, M. A., & Scruggs, T. E. (2005). Feasibility and consequences of response to intervention: Examination of the issues and scientific evidence as a model for the identification of individuals with learning disabilities. *Journal of Learning Disabilities, 38,* 525–531.

Mastropieri, M. A., Scruggs, T. E., Graetz, J., Norland, J., Gardizi, W., & McDuffie, K. (2005). Case studies in co-teaching in the content areas: Successes, failures, and challenges. *Intervention in School and Clinic, 40,* 260–270.

Mastropieri, M. A., Sweda, J., & Scruggs, T. E. (2000). Putting mnemonic strategies to work in an inclusive classroom. *Learning Disabilities: Research and Practice, 15,* 69–74.

Mastropieri, M. A., et al. (2001). Can middle school students with serious reading difficulties help each other and learn anything? *Learning Disabilities Research and Practice, 16,* 18–27.

Mather, N., & Goldstein, S. (2001). The learning environment. In *Learning disabilities and challenging behaviors: A guide to intervention and classroom management* (pp. 138–161). Baltimore: Paul H. Brookes.

Matheson, C., Olsen, R. J., & Weisner, T. (2007). A good friend is hard to find: Friendship among adolescents with disabilities. *American Journal on Mental Retardation, 112,* 319–329.

Mathews, R. (2000). Cultural patterns of South Asian and Southeast Asian Americans. *Intervention in School and Clinic, 36,* 101–104.

Mathews, T. J. (2004). *Trends in spina bifida and anencephalus in the United States, 1991–2002.* Hyattsville, MD: National Center for Health Statistics, Centers for Disease Control and Prevention. Retrieved March 9, 2004, from www.cdc.gov/nchs/products/pubs/pubd/hestats/spine_anen.htm

Mathews, T. J. (2009, April). *Trends in spina bifida and anencephalus in the United States, 1991–2006* [Health e-stats]. Atlanta: Centers for Disease Control and Prevention. Retrieved September 3, 2009 from http://www.cdc.gov/nchs/products/hestats.htm

Mathews, T. J., Honein, M. A., & Erickson, J. D. (2002). *Spina bifida and anencephaly prevalence—United States, 1991–2001.* Atlanta, GA: Morbidity and Mortality Weekly, Centers for Disease Control and Prevention. Retrieved March 9, 2004, from www.cdc.gov/mmwr/preview/mmwrhtml/rr5113a3.htm

Mathur, S. R. (2007). Understanding emotional and behavioral disorders: Are we paying the cost of borderline ethics? *Education and Treatment of Children, 30*(4), 11–26.

Matthews, D., Foster, J., & Gladstone, D. (2007). Supporting professionalism, diversity, and context within a collaborative approach to gifted education. *Journal of Educational and Psychological Consultation, 17,* 315–345.

Mattison, R. E., Hooper, S. R., & Glassberg, L. A. (2002). Three-year course of learning disorders in special education students classified as behavioral disorder. *Journal of the American Academy of Child and Adolescent Psychiatry, 41*(12), 1254–1462.

Matuszny, R. M., Banda, D. R., & Coleman, T. J. (2007). A progressive plan for building collaborative relationships with parents from diverse backgrounds. *Teaching Exceptional Children, 39*(4), 24–31.

Maurice, C., Green, G., & Luce, S. C. (1996). *Behavioral intervention for young children with autism: A manual for parents and professionals.* Austin, TX: Pro-Ed.

Mautz, D., Storey, K., & Certo, N. (2001). Increasing integrated workplace social interactions: The effects of job modification, natural supports, adaptive communication instruction, and job coach training. *Journal of the Association for Persons with Severe Handicaps, 26,* 257–269.

Maxon, A. B., Brackett, D., & van den Berg, S. A. (1991). Self perception of socialization: The effects of hearing status, age, and gender. *The Volta Review, 93,* 7–17.

Mayer, G. R. (2001). Antisocial behavior: Its causes and prevention within our schools. *Education and Treatment of Children, 24,* 414–430.

Mayes, S., & Calhoun, S. (2008). WISC-IV and WIAT-II profiles in children with high-functioning autism. *Journal of Autism and Developmental Disorders, 38,* 428–439.

Mayes, S. D., & Calhoun, S. (2009). Variables related to sleep problems in children with autism. *Research in Autism Spectrum Disorders, 3,* 931–941.

Mayes, S. D., Calhoun, S. L., & Crowell, E. W. (2000). Learning disabilities and ADHD: Overlapping spectrum disorders. *Journal of Learning Disabilities, 33,* 417–424.

Mayne, A. M., Yoshinaga-Itano, C., Sedey, A. L., & Carey, A. (2000). Expressive vocabulary development of infants and toddlers who are deaf or hard of hearing. *Volta Review, 100*(5), 1–28.

Mayr, T., & Ulich, M. (2009). Social-emotional well-being and resilience of children in early childhood settings—PERIK: An empirically based observation scale for practitioners. *Early Years: An International Journal of Research and Development, 29*(1), 45–57.

Mazzocco, M. M. (2001). Math learning disability and math LD subtypes: Evidence from studies of Turner syndrome, Fragile X syndrome, and neurofibromatosis type 1. *Journal of Learning Disabilities, 34,* 520–533.

McAllister, B. A., & Plourde, L. A. (2008). Enrichment curriculum: Essential for mathematically gifted students. *Education, 129,* 40–49.

McAllister, R., & Gray, C. (2007). Low vision: Mobility and independence training for the early years child. *Early Child Development and Care, 177,* 839–852.

McBee, M. T. (2004). The classroom as laboratory: An exploration of teacher research. *Roeper Review, 27*(1), 52.

McCabe, H. (2008). Autism and family in the People's Republic of China: Learning from parents' perspectives. *Research and Practice for Persons with Severe Disabilities, 33*(1–2), 37–47.

McCardle, P., & Chhabra, V. (Eds.). (2004). *The voice of evidence in reading research.* Baltimore: Brookes.

McClatchie, A. & Therres, M. (2003). *AuSpLan: A manual for professionals working with children who have cochlear implants or amplification.* Oakland, CA: Children's Hospital & Research Center at Oakland.

McCluskey, K., & McCluskey, A. (1999). The agony and the empathy: A hyperactive child's journey from despair to achievement. *Reclaiming Children and Youth, 7,* 205–212.

McConville, D., & Cornell, D. (2003). Attitudes toward aggression and aggressive behavior among middle school students. *Journal of Emotional and Behavioral Disorders. 11,* 179–187.

McCoy, K., & Hermansen, E. (2007). Video modeling for individuals with autism: A review of model types and effects. *Education and Treatment of Children, 30,* 183–213.

McCrary, D. E. (2000). Addressing challenging behaviors among young children. In L. M. Bullock & R. A. Gable (Eds.), *Addressing the social, academic, and behavioral needs of students with challenging behavior in inclusive and alternative settings* (pp. 15–20). Arlington, VA: Council for Exceptional Children, Council for Children with Behavioral Disorders. (ERIC Document Reproduction Service No. ED457629) Retrieved July 30, 2003, from http://libproxy.uncg.edu:2101/Webstore/Download.cfm?ID-679128

McCurdy, M., Skinner, C., Watson, S., & Shriver, M. (2008). Examining the effects of a comprehensive writing program on the writing performance of middle school students with learning disabilities in written expression. *School Psychology Quarterly, 23,* 571–586.

McDermott, P. A., Goldberg, M. M., Watkins, M. W., Stanley, J. L., & Glutting, J. J. (2006). A nationwide epidemiologic modeling study of LD: Risk, protection, and unintended impact. *Journal of Learning Disabilities, 39,* 230–251.

McDonnell, J. J., Hardman, M. L., & McDonnell, A. P. (2003). *An introduction to persons with moderate and severe disabilities: Educational and social issues* (2nd ed.). Boston, MA: Allyn & Bacon.

McDonnell, J., Johnson, J. W., Polychronis, S., & Risen, T. (2002). Effects of embedded instruction on students with moderate disabilities enrolled in general education classes. *Education and Training in Mental Retardation and Developmental Disabilities, 37,* 363–377.

McDonnell, J., Mathot-Buckner, C., & Thorson, N. (2001). Supporting the inclusion of students with moderate and severe disabilities in junior high school general education classes: The effects of classwide peer tutoring, multi-element curriculum, and accommodations. *Education and Treatment of Children, 24,* 141–160.

McDonnell, J., Thorson, N., McQuivey, C., & Kiefer-O'Donnell, R. (1997). Academic engaged time of students with low-incidence disabilities in general education classes. *Mental Retardation, 35*(1), 18–26.

McGahee, M., Mason, C., Wallace, T., & Jones, B. (2002). Student-led IEPs: A guide for student involvement. Arlington, VA: Council for Exceptional Children. National Center for Education Statistics. (2009). *How did the 100 largest school districts compare with all school districts?* Retrieved May 15, 2009 from http://nces.ed.gov/pubs2008/100_largest/how.asp

McGahee-Kovac, M. (2002). A student's guide to the IEP (2nd ed.). Washington, DC: National Dissemination Center for Children with Disabilities. Retrieved August 27, 2006, from www.nichcy.org/pubs/stuguide/st1book.htm

McGill-Frazen, A., & Allington, R. L. (1991). The gridlock of low reading achievement: Perspectives on practice and policy. *Remedial and Special Education, 12,* 20–30.

McGoey, K. E., Eckert, T. L., & DuPaul, G. J. (2002). Early intervention for preschool-age children with ADHD: A literature review. *Journal of Emotional and Behavioral Disorders, 10,* 14–28.

McGowan, R. S., Nittrouer, S., Chenausky, K. (2008). Speech production in 12-month-old children with and without hearing loss. *Journal of Speech, Language, and Hearing Research, 51,* 879–888.

McGuire, J. M., Scott, S. S., & Shaw, S. F. (2006). Universal design and its application in educational environments. *Remedial and Special Education, 27*(3), 166–175.

McIntosh, K., Campbell, A. L., & Carter, D. R. (2009). Differential effects of a tier two behavior intervention based on function of problem behavior. *Journal of Positive Behavior Interventions, 11,* 82–93.

McIntyre, L. L. (2008). Parent training for young children with developmental disabilities: Randomized controlled trial. *American Journal on Mental Retardation, 113,* 356–368.

McIntyre, T. (1996). Does the way we teach create behavior disorders in culturally different students? *Education and Treatment of Children, 19,* 354–370.

McKenzie, A. R., & Lewis, S. (2008). The role and training of paraprofessionals who work with students who are visually impaired. *Journal of Visual Impairment & Blindness, 102,* 459–471.

McKenzie, H. S. (1972). Special education and consulting teachers. In F. Clark, D. Evans, & L. Hammerlynk (Eds.), *Implementing behavioral programs for schools and clinics.* Champaign, IL: Research Press.

McLaughlin, S. (1998). *Introduction to language development.* Florence, KY: Delmar Learning.

McLeskey, J. (1992). Students with learning disabilities at primary, intermediate, and secondary grade levels: Identification and characteristics. *Learning Disability Quarterly, 15,* 13–19.

McLeskey, J., Henry, D., & Axelrod, M. I. (1999). Inclusion of students with learning disabilities: An examination of data from reports to Congress. *Exceptional Children, 66,* 55–66.

McLeskey, J., Hoppey, D., Williamson, P., & Rentz, T. (2004). Is inclusion an illusion? An examination of national and state trends toward the education of students with learning disabilities in general education classrooms. *Learning Disabilities Research and Practice, 19,* 109–115.

McLeskey, J., Tyler, N. C., & Flippin, S. S. (2004). The supply and demand for special education teachers: A review of research regarding the chronic shortage of special education teachers. *Journal of Special Education, 38,* 5–21.

McLeskey, J., & Waldron, N. L. (2002). Inclusion and school change: Teacher perceptions regarding curricular and instructional adaptations. *Teacher Education and Special Education, 25,* 41–54.

McLeskey, J., & Waldron, N. L. (2007). Comprehensive school reform and inclusive schools. *Theory into Practice, 45,* 269–278.

McLeskey, J., Waldron, N. L., So, T. H., Swanson, K., & Loveland, T. (2001). Perspectives of teachers toward inclusive school programs. *Teacher Education and Special Education, 24,* 108–115.

McMahon, E. (1994). The role of residential schools for the blind in 1990. *RE:view, 25,* 163–172.

McMillen, M. (2002, December 10). Driven to distraction: Experts advise treating kids with ADHD just like other kids in most situations. Evidence shows that following this advice when teens learn to drive can be a dangerous mistake. *Washington Post,* p. F01.

McNamara, J. K., Willoughby, T., Chalmers, H., & Cura, Y. L. (2005). Psychosocial status of adolescents and learning disabilities with and without comorbid attention deficit hyperactivity disorder. *Learning Disabilities Research and Practice, 20,* 234–244.

McNamara, J. K., & Wong, B. (2003). Memory for everyday information in students with learning disabilities. *Journal of Learning Disabilities, 36,* 394–406.

McNaughton, D., Rackensperger, T., Benedek-Wood, E., Krezman, C., Williams, M. B., & Light, J. (2008). "A child needs to be given a chance to succeed": Parents of individuals who use AAC describe the benefits and challenges of learning AAC technologies. *AAC: Augmentative and Alternative Communication, 24*(1), 43–55.

McPhail, J. C., & Freeman, J. G. (2005). Beyond prejudice: Thinking toward genuine inclusion. *Learning Disabilities Research and Practice, 20,* 254–267.

McVilly, K. R., Stancliffe, R. J., Parmenter, T. R., & Burton-Smith, R. M. (2006). "I get by with a little help from my friend": Adults with intellectual disability discuss loneliness. *Journal of Applied Research in Intellectual Disabilities, 19,* 191–203.

Meadan, H., & Halle, J. W. (2004). Social perceptions of students with learning disabilities who differ in social status. *Learning Disabilities Research and Practice, 19,* 71–82.

Mechling, L. C., & Cronin, B. (2006). Computer-based video instruction to teach the use of augmentative and alternative communication devices for ordering at fast-food restaurants. *Journal of Special Education, 39,* 234–245.

Medved, M. (2001, August 8). Good teamwork outshines superstar systems. *USA Today,* 13A.

Mendez-Perez, A. (2000). Mexican American mothers' perceptions and beliefs about language acquisition in infants and toddlers with disabilities. *Bilingual Research Journal, 24,* 277–294.

Menninger, W. C. (1950). Mental health in our schools. *Educational Leadership, 7,* 520.

Meo, B. (2008). Curriculum planning for all learners: Applying universal design for learning (UDL) to a high school reading comprehension program. *Preventing School Failure, 52*(2), 21–30.

Mercer, C. D., Campbell, K. U., Miller, M. D., Mercer, K. D., & Lane, H. B. (2000). Effects of a reading fluency intervention for middle schoolers with specific learning disabilities. *Learning Disabilities Research and Practice, 15,* 179–189.

Mercer, J. (1973). *Labeling the mentally retarded.* Berkeley: University of California Press.

Mercugliano, M. (1999). *The clinician's practical guide to attention-deficit/hyperactivity disorder.* Baltimore: Paul H. Brookes.

Merritt, S. (2001). Clearing the hurdles of inclusion. *Educational Leadership, 59*(3), 67–70.

Metzler, C. W., Biglan, A., Rusby, J. C., & Sprague, J. R. (2001). Evaluation of a comprehensive behavior management program to improve school-wide positive behavior support. *Education and Treatment of Children, 24,* 448–479.

Meyer, F., & Patton, J. M. (2001). On the nexus of race, disability, and overrepresentation: What do we know? Where do we go? *On point: Brief discussions of critical issues in urban education.* Retrieved April 9, 2004, from www.edrs.com/members/sp.cfm?AN=ED462487

Meyer, L. H. (2001). The impact of inclusion on children's lives: Multiple outcomes, and friendship in particular. *International Journal of Disability, 48,* 9–31.

Michael, R. J. (1995). *The educator's guide to students with epilepsy.* Springfield, IL: Charles C. Thomas.

Michaud, L. J., Semel-Concepcíon, J., Duhaime, A. C., & Lazar, M. F. (2002). Traumatic brain injury. In M. L. Batshaw (Ed.), *Children with disabilities* (5th ed., pp. 525–548). Baltimore: Paul H. Brookes.

Mick, E., Biederman, J., Santangelo, S., & Wypij, D. (2003). The influence of gender in the familial association between ADHD and major depression. *Journal of Nervous and Mental Disease, 191,* 699–705.

Mihalas, S., Morse, W. C., Allsopp, D. H., & McHatton, P. A. (2009). Cultivating caring relationships between teachers and secondary students with emotional and behavioral disorders: Implications for research and practice. *Remedial and Special Education, 30,* 108–125.

Miles, S., & Ratner, N. B. (2001). Parental language input to children at stuttering onset. *Journal of Speech, Language, and Hearing Research, 44,* 116–130.

Miles-Bonart, S. (2002, March). A look at variables affecting parent satisfaction with IEP meetings. *No Child Left Behind: The vital role of rural schools.* Annual national conference proceedings of the American Council on Rural Special Education, Reno, NV. (ERIC Document Reproduction Service No. ED463119)

Milian, M. (1999). Schools and family involvement: Attitudes among Latinos who have children with visual impairments. *Journal of Visual Impairment and Blindness, 93,* 277–290.

Millar, D. C., Light, J. C., & Schlosser, R. W. (2006). The impact of augmentative and alternative communication intervention on the speech production of individuals with developmental disabilities: A research review. *Journal of Speech, Language, and Hearing Research, 49,* 248–264.

Millar, D. S. (2003). Age of majority, transfer of rights, and guardianship: Considerations for families and educators. *Education and Training in Developmental Disabilities, 38,* 378–397.

Miller, B. D. (1999). Promoting healthy function and development in chronically ill children: A primary care approach. In R. P. Marinelli & A. E. Dellorto (Eds.), *The psychological and social impact of disability* (4th ed., pp. 67–85). New York: Springer.

Miller, D. (2006). Students with fetal alcohol syndrome: Updating our knowledge, improving their programs. *Teaching Exceptional Children, 38*(4), 12–18.

Miller, K. J. (2008). Closing a resource room for students who are deaf or hard of hearing. *Communication Disorders Quarterly, 29,* 211–218.

Miller, M. (2006). Where they are: Working with marginalized students. *Educational Leadership, 63*(5), 50–55.

Miller, T. W., Nigg, J. T., & Miller, R. L. (2009). Attention deficit hyperactivity disorder in African American children: What can be concluded from the past ten years? *Clinical Psychology Review, 29,* 77–86.

*Mills v. Board of Education of the District of Columbia.* (1972). 348 F. Supp. 866 (D. D. C. 1972).

Mills, C., & Tissot, S. (1995). Identifying academic potential in students from underrepresented populations: Is using the Ravens Progressive Matrices a good idea? *Gifted Child Quarterly, 39,* 209–217.

Mills, G. E., & Duff-Mallams, K. (1999). A mediation strategy for special education disputes. *Intervention in School and Clinic, 35,* 87–92.

Mills, G. E., & Duff-Mallams, K. (2000). Special education mediation—A formula for success. *Teaching Exceptional Children, 32*(4), 72–78.

Mills, J. R., & Jackson, N. E. (1990). Predictive significance of early giftedness: The case of precocious reading. *Journal of Educational Psychology, 82,* 410–419.

Milner, H. R. (2006). Preservice teachers' learning about cultural and racial diversity: Implications for urban education. *Urban Education, 41,* 343–375.

Minnard, C. V. (2002). A strong building: Foundation of protective factors in schools. *Children and Schools, 24,* 233–246.

Miranda, A., Jarque, S., & Tarraga, R. (2006). Interventions in school settings for students with ADHD. *Exceptionality, 14*(1), 35–52.

Miranda, A., Presentación, M. J., & Soriano, M. (2002). Effectiveness of a school-based mulitcomponent program for the treatment of children with ADHD. *Journal of Learning Disabilities, 35,* 546–562.

Missouri State Department of Elementary and Secondary Education. (2002, April). *Do you know . . . Parent's role in assistive technology considerations* [information brochure], *4*(1). (ERIC Document Reproduction Service No. ED466063)

Mitchell, A. (1997). Teacher identity: A key to increased collaboration. *Action in Teacher Education, 19*(3), 1–14.

Mitchell, R. E. (2004). National profile of deaf and hard of hearing students in special education from weighted survey results. *American Annals of the Deaf, 149,* 336–349.

Mitchell, R. E., & Karchmer, M. A. (2004). Chasing the mythical ten percent: Parental hearing status of deaf and hard of hearing students in the United States. *Sign Language Studies, 4,* 138–163.

Mitchell, W. (2008). The role played by grandparents in family support and learning: Considerations for mainstream and special schools. *Support for Learning, 23,* 126–135.

Moeller, M. P. (2000). Early intervention and language development in children who are deaf and hard of hearing. *Pediatrics, 106*(3), 43. Retrieved April 25, 2002, from www.pediatrics.org/cgi/content/full/106/3/e43

Moes, D. R., & Frea, W. D. (2002). Contextualized behavioral support in early interventions for children with autism and their families. *Journal of Autism and Developmental Disorders, 32*(6), 519–533.

Mogharreban, C. C., & Bruns, D. A. (2009). Moving to inclusive prekindergarten classrooms: Lessons from the field. *Early Childhood Education Journal, 36,* 407–414.

Mokher, C. G., & McLendon, M. K. (2009). Uniting secondary and postsecondary education: An event history analysis of state adoption of dual enrollment policies. *American Journal of Education, 115,* 249–277.

Molina, B. S. G., & Pelham, W. E. (2001). Substance use, substance abuse, and LD among adolescents with a childhood history of ADHD. *Journal of Learning Disabilities, 34,* 333–342.

Mondale, S., & Patton, S. B. (2001). *School: The story of American public education.* Boston: Beacon Press.

Monroe, C. R. (2005). Why are the "bad boys" always black? Causes of disproportionality in school discipline and recommendations for change. *Clearinghouse, 79,* 45–50.

Montague, M. (2008). Self-regulation strategies to improve mathematical problem solving for students with learning disabilities. *Learning Disability Quarterly, 31,* 37–44.

Montgomery, D. J. (2005). Communicating without harm: Strategies to enhance parent–teacher communication. *Teaching Exceptional Children, 38,* 50–55.

Montgomery, W. (2001). Creating culturally responsive, inclusive classrooms. *Teaching Exceptional Children, 33*(4), 4–9.

Moon, T. R., Brighton, C. M., & Callahan, C. M. (2003). State standardized testing programs: Friend or foe of gifted education? *Roeper Review, 25*(2), 49–60.

Moon, T. R., Brighton, C. M., Callahan, C. M., & Robinson, A. (2005). Development of authentic assessments for the middle school classroom. *Journal of Secondary Gifted Education, 16,* 119–133.

Moore, I. M. (2002). Cancer in children. In L. L. Hayman, M. M. Mahon, & J. R. Turner (Eds.), *Chronic illness in children: An evidence-based approach* (pp. 80–103). New York: Springer.

Moore, J. B., Kaffenberger, C., Oh, K. M., Goldberg, P., & Hudspeth, R. (2009). School reentry for children with cancer: Perceptions of nurses, school personnel, and parents. *Journal of Pediatric Oncology Nursing, 26,* 86–99.

Moore, J. E., & Wolffe, K. E. (1996). Employment considerations for adults with low vision. In A. L. Corn & A. J. Koenig (Eds.), *Foundations of low vision: Clinical and functional perspectives* (pp. 340–362). New York: American Foundation for the Blind Press.

Moore, J. L., Ford, D. Y., & Milner, H. R. (2005). Underachievement among gifted students of color: Implications for educators. *Theory into Practice, 44,* 167–177.

Moore, M. S., & Levitan, L. (1993). *For hearing people only: Answers to some of the most commonly asked questions about the deaf community, its culture and the "deaf reality."* Rochester, NY: Deaf Life Press.

Moore, M. S., & Panara, R. F. (1996). *Great Deaf Americans* (2nd ed.). Rochester, NY: MSM Productions, Ltd.

Moore, S. (2002, May 25). Special ed. joins the mainstream. *Los Angeles Times,* p. A1.

Moores, D. (2001). *Educating the deaf: Psychology, principles, and practices* (5th ed.). Boston: Houghton Mifflin.

Moores, D., & Meadow-Orlans, K. P. (Eds.). (1990). *Educational and developmental aspects of deafness.* Washington, DC: Gallaudet University Press.

Moores, D. F. (2009). Cochlear failures. *American Annals of the Deaf, 153,* 423–424.

Morgan, P. L., Farkas, G., & Wu, Q. (2009). Kindergarten predictors of recurring externalizing and internalizing psychopathology in the third and fifth grades. *Journal of Emotional and Behavioral Disorders, 17,* 67–69.

Morrier, M. J., Hess, K. L., & Heflin, L. J. (2008). Ethnic disproportionality in students with autism spectrum disorders. *Multicultural Education, 16*(1), 31–38.

Morrison, G. M., Walker, D., Wakefield, P., & Solberg, S. (1994). Teacher preferences for collaborative relationships: Relationship to efficacy for teaching in prevention-related domains. *Psychology in the Schools, 21,* 221–231.

Mortimore, T. (2008). *Dyslexia and learning style: A practitioner's handbook.* West Sussex, England: John Wiley & Sons.

Moule, J. (2009). Understanding unconscious bias and unintentional racism. *Phi Delta Kappan, 90,* 320–326.

Mrug, S., Hoza, B., & Gerdes, A. C. (2009). Discriminating between children with ADHD and classmates using peer variables. *Journal of Attention Disorders, 12,* 372–380.

Mrug, S., Hoza, B., Gerdes, A. C., Hinshaw, S., Arnold, L. E., Hechtman, L., & Pelham, W. E. (2009). Discriminating between children with ADHD and classmates using peer variables. *Journal of Attention Disorders, 12,* 372–380.

Mrug, S., & Wallander, J. L. (2002). Self-concept of young people with physical disabilities: Does integration play a role? *International Journal of Disability, Development and Education, 49,* 267–280.

Muhlenhaupt, M. (2002). Family and school partnerships for IEP development. *Journal of Visual Impairment and Blindness, 96,* 175–178.

Mukherjee, S., & Lightfoot, J. (2000). The inclusion of pupils with a chronic health condition in mainstream school: What does it mean? *Educational Research, 42,* 59–72.

Mukherjee, S., Lightfoot, J., & Sloper, P. (2000). Communicating about pupils in mainstream school with health needs: The NHS perspective. *Child: Care, Health and Development, 28*(1), 21–27.

Mulhern, J. D. (2003). An evolving field: The gifted child in the regular classroom. *Roeper Review, 25,* 112–115.

Multiethnic Pediatric Eye Disease Study Group. (2009). Prevalence and causes of visual impairment in African-American and Hispanic preschool children: The multi-ethnic pediatric eye disease study. *Ophthalmology.* Retrieved August 26, 2009 from http://www.ophsource.org/periodicals/ophtha/article/S0161-6420(09)00291-7/abstract?source=aemf#cor1

Mundschenk, N. A., & Foley, R. M. (2000). Building blocks to effective partnerships: Meeting the needs of students with emotional or behavioral disorders and their families. In M. J. Fine & R. L. Simpson (Eds.), *Collaboration with parents and families of children and youth with exceptionalities* (2nd ed., pp. 369–387). Austin, TX: Pro-Ed.

Munk, D. D., & Bursuck, W. D. (2001). Preliminary findings on personalized grading plans for middle school students with learning disabilities. *Exceptional Children, 67,* 211–234.

Munson, L. J., & Hunt, N. (2005). Teachers grieve! What can we do for our colleagues and ourselves when a student dies? *Teaching Exceptional Children, 37*(4), 48–51.

Murawski, W. W., & Swanson, H. L. (2001). A meta-analysis of co-teaching research: Where are the data? *Remedial and Special Education, 22,* 258–267.

Murdick, N. L., Gartin, B., & Crabtree, T. (2002). *Special education law.* Upper Saddle River, NJ: Merrill/Pearson.

Murray, C. (2004). Clarifying collaborative roles in urban high schools: General educators' perspectives. *Teaching Exceptional Children, 36*(5), 44–51.

Murray, C., & Greenberg, M. T. (2006). Examining the importance of social relationships and social contexts in the lives of children with high-incidence disabilities. *Journal of Special Education, 39,* 220–233.

Murray, D., Goldstein, D. E., Nourse, S., & Edgar, E. (2000). The postsecondary school attendance and completion rates of high school graduates with learning disabilities. *Learning Disabilities Research and Practice, 15,* 119–127.

Murray, F. R. (2005). Effective advocacy for students with emotional/behavioral disorders: How high the cost? *Education and Treatment of Children, 28,* 414–429.

Murray, M. M., & Curran, E. M. (2008). Learning together with parents of children with disabilities: Bringing parent-professional partnership education to a new level. *Teacher Education and Special Education, 31,* 59–63.

Murray, M. M., & Mandell, C. J. (2004). Evaluation of a family-centered early childhood special education preservice model by program graduates. *Topics in Early Childhood Special Education, 24,* 238–249.

Muscott, H. S. (2002). Exceptional partnerships: Listening to the voices of families. *Preventing School Failure, 46*(2), 66–69.

Muscular Dystrophy Association. (2000). *Facts about Duchenne and Becker muscular dystrophies.* Tucson, AZ: Author. Retrieved March 9, 2004, from www.mdausa.org/publications/fa-dmdbmd-what.html

Myers, A., & Eisenman, L. (2005). Student-led IEPs: Take the first step. *Teaching Exceptional Children, 37*(4), 52–58.

Myers, B. J., Mackintosh, V. H., & Goin-Kochel, R. P. (2009). "My greatest joy and my greatest heart ache:" Parents' own words on how having a child in the autism spectrum has affected their lives and their families' lives. *Research in Autism Spectrum Disorders, 3,* 670–684.

Myers, C. (2007). "Please listen, it's my turn": Instructional approaches, curricula and contexts for supporting communication and increasing access to inclusion. *Journal of Intellectual & Developmental Disability, 32,* 263–278.

Myles, B. S., & Adreon, D. (2001). *Asperger syndrome and adolescence: Practical solutions for school success.* Shawnee Mission, KS: Autism Asperger Publishing.

Myles, B. S., Bock, S. J., & Simpson, R. L. (2001). *Asperger Syndrome Diagnostic Scale.* Austin, TX: Pro-Ed.

Myles, B. S., Constant, J. A., Simpson, R. L., & Carlson, J. K. (1989). Educational assessment of students with higher-functioning autistic disorder. *Focus on Autistic Behavior, 4*(1), 1–13.

Myles, B. S., Cook, K. T., Miller, N. E., Rinner, L., & Robbins, L. (2000). *Asperger Syndrome and sensory issues: Practical solutions for making sense of the world.* Shawnee Mission, KS: Autism Asperger Publishing.

Myles, B. S., & Savner, J. L. (2000). *Making visual supports work in the home and community. Strategies for individuals with autism and Asperger Syndrome.* Shawnee Mission, KS: Autism Asperger Publishing.

Myles, B. S., & Simpson, R. (2002). Asperger Syndrome: An overview of characteristics. *Focus on Autism and Other Developmental Disabilities, 17,* 132–137.

Myles, B. S., & Simpson, R. L. (1998). Inclusion of students with autism in general education classrooms: The autism inclusion collaboration model. In R. L. Simpson & B. S. Myles (Eds.), *Educating children and youth with autism: Strategies for effective practice* (pp. 241–256). Austin, TX: Pro-Ed.

Myles, B. S., & Simpson, R. L. (2001). Understanding the hidden curriculum: An essential social skill for children and youth with Asperger syndrome. *Intervention in School and Clinic, 36,* 279–286.

Myles, B. S., & Southwick, J. (2005). *Asperger syndrome and difficult moments: Practical solutions for tantrums, rage, and meltdowns.* Shawnee Mission, KS: Autism Asperger Publishing.

Nabors, L. A., Iobst, E. A., Weisman, J., Precht, B., Chiu, P., & Brunner, H. (2007). School support and functioning for children with juvenile rheumatic diseases. *Journal of Developmental & Physical Disabilities, 19,* 81–89.

Nadeau, K. G. (2002, April). *Is your daughter a daydreamer, tomboy or "Chatty Kathy"? She may have undiagnosed attention deficit disorder.* Retrieved November 15, 2002, from www.ldonline.org/ld_indepth/add_adhd/nadeau.html

Nadeau, K. G., & Quinn, P. (2004). *ADD(ADHD) self-report questionnaire for teenage girls.* Retrieved July 3, 2009 from ADDvance at http://www.addvance.com/help/women/girl_questionnaire.html

Nagle, K., Yunker, C., & Malmgren, K. W. (2006). Students with disabilities and accountability reform: Challenges identified at the state and local levels. *Journal of Disability Policy Studies, 17,* 28–39.

Nahmias, M. L. (1995). Communication and collaboration between home and school for students with ADD. *Intervention in School and Clinic, 30,* 241–247.

Nail-Chiwetalu, B. J., & Ratner, N. B. (2006). Information literacy for speech-language pathologists: A key to evidence-based practice. *Language, Speech, and Hearing Services in Schools, 37,* 157–167.

Nancollis, A., Lawrie, A. A., & Dodd, B. (2005). Phonological awareness intervention and the acquisition of literacy skills in children from deprived social backgrounds. *Language, Speech, and Hearing Services in Schools, 36,* 325–335.

National Alliance of Black School Educators. (2002). *Addressing overrepresentation of African American students in special education: The preferral intervention process.* Arlington, VA: Council for Exceptional Education.

National Alliance on Mental Illness. (2007, October). Mental illness: Facts and numbers [NAMI fact sheet]. Retrieved July 14, 2009 from http://www.nami.org/

National Association for Gifted Children. (2000). *Curriculum and instruction standards introduction.* Retrieved September 1, 2009 from http://www.nagc.org/index.aspx?id=544

National Association for Gifted Children. (2005). *Why we should advocate for gifted and talented children.* Retrieved August 31, 2006, from www.nagc.org/index.aspx?id=538

National Association for Gifted Children. (2008a). *Hot topics: Young gifted-potential and promise.* Retrieved September 10, 2009 from http://www.nagc.org/index.aspx?id=1467

National Association for Gifted Children. (2008b). *Public high schools for advanced students.* Retrieved September 12, 2009 from http://www.nagc.org/index.aspx?id=974

National Association for Gifted Children. (2009). *What is giftedness?* Retrieved September 10, 2009 from http://www.nagc.org/index.aspx?id=574

National Association for the Education of African American Children with Learning Disabilities. (2002). *One child at a time: A parent handbook and resource directory for African American families with children who learn differently.* Columbus, OH: Author.

National Association of State Directors of Special Education. (2006). *Meeting the needs of students who are deaf or hard of hearing: Educational service guidelines.* Alexandria, VA: Author.

National Cancer Institute. (2005). National Cancer Institute research on childhood cancers. Retrieved September 3, 2006, from www.nci.nih.gov/cancertopics/factsheet/Sites-Types/childhood

National Cancer Institute. (2008). *Childhood cancers: Questions and answers.* Retrieved September 5, 2009 from http://www.cancer.gov/cancertopics/factsheet/Sites-Types/childhood

National Center for Education Statistics. (2000a). *Digest of education statistics, 2001.* Washington, DC: Author.

National Center for Education Statistics. (2000b). *Indicators of school crime and safety, 2000.* Washington, DC: NCES, U.S. Department of Education. Retrieved July 29, 2003, from http://nces.ed.gov/pubs2001/crime2000/index.asp

National Center for Education Statistics. (2000c). *Pursuing excellence: Comparisons of international eighth grade mathematics and science achievement from a U.S. perspective, 1995 and 1999.* Washington, DC: U.S. Department of Education.

National Center for Education Statistics. (2000d). *Survey on professional development and training in U.S. public schools.* Washington, DC: U.S. Department of Education.

National Center for Education Statistics. (2002b). *Digest of educational statistics: Definitions* (pp. 541–554). Retrieved April 30, 2004, from http://nces.ed.gov/pubs_2003/2003060h.pdf

National Center for Education Statistics. (2002c). *Supplemental notes.* Retrieved December 19, 2002, from http://nces.ed.gov/programs/coe/2002/notes/n10.asp

National Center for Education Statistics. (2007). *The condition of education: Contexts of elementary and secondary education-charter schools* [Indicator 32]. Washington, D.C.: U.S. Department of Education, Institute of Education Sciences. Retrieved June 8, 2009 from http://nces.ed.gov/programs/coe/2007/section4/indicator32.asp

National Center for Education Statistics. (2008). Table 54: Percentage of gifted and talented students in public elementary and secondary schools, by sex, reac/ethnicity, and state: 2004 and 2006. *Digest of Education Statistics: 2008.* Washington, D.C.: U.S. Department of Education, Institute for Education Sciences. Retrieved September 11, 2009 at http://nces.ed.gov/programs/digest/d08/tables/dt08_054.asp?referrer=list

National Center for Education Statistics. (2009a). *Characteristics of the 100 largest public elementary and secondary school districts in the United States: 2006–2007* [Statistical analysis report]. Washington, D. C.: U.S. Department of Education, Institute of Education Sciences. Retrieved June 8, 2009 from http://nces.ed.gov/pubsearch/pubsinfo.asp?pubid=2009342

National Center for Education Statistics. (2009b). *The condition of education 2009: Contexts of elementary and secondary education: School characteristics and climate: Poverty concentration in public schools by locale and race/*

*ethnicity* [Indicator 25]. Washington, D.C.: U.S. Department of Education, Institute of Education Sciences. Retrieved June 8, 2009 from http://nces.ed.gov/programs/coe/2009/section4/indicator25.asp

National Center for Education Statistics. (2009c). *The condition of education 2009: Participation in education* [Indicator 8]. Washington, D.C.: U.S. Department of Education, Institute of Education Sciences. Retrieved June 8, 2009 from http://nces.ed.gov/programs/coe/2009/section1/indicator08.asp

National Center for Educational Statistics. (2001). *Digest of educational statistics: Definitions.* Retrieved December 19, 2002, from http://nces.ed.gov/pubs2002/digest2001/definitions.asp#H

National Center for Health Statistics. (2004). *Trends in spina bifida and anencephalus in the United States, 1991–1999.* Retrieved March 20, 2004, from www.cdc.gov/nchs/products/pubs/pubd/hestats/folic/folic.htm

National Center for Health Statistics. (n.d.). *Disabilities/impairments.* Retrieved December 19, 2002 from www.cdc.gov/nchs/fastats/disable.htm

National Center for Hearing Assessment and Management (NCHAM). (2006). *State summary statistics: Universal newborn hearing screening.* Retrieved November 24, 2006, from www.infanthearing.org/status/unhsstate.html

National Center on Birth Defects and Developmental Disabilities. (2009, August). Facts about FASDs. Washginton, D.C.: Centers for Disease Control and Prevention. Retrieved October 20, 2009 from http://www.cdc.gov/ncbddd/fasd/facts.html

National Center on Secondary Education and Transition and PACER Center. (2002, May). *Age of majority: Preparing your child for making good choices* [parent brief]. Retrieved April 6, 2003, from http://ici.umn.edu/ncset/new.html

National Clearinghouse for Careers in Special Education. (2009). *Physical therapist* [brochure]. Arlington, VA: Council for Exceptional Children. Retrieved April 15, 2009 from http://www.personnelcenter.org/phy_ther.cfm

National Clearinghouse for Professions in Special Education. (2003, Spring). *School counselor: Making a difference in the lives of students with special needs* [brochure]. Arlington, VA: Author. Retrieved April 19, 2003, from www.special-ed-careers.org/pdf/schcoun.pdf

National Clearinghouse for Professions in Special Education. (2009). CEC career center. Retrieved May 12, 2009 from http://www.cec.sped.org/Content/NavigationMenu/ProfessionalDevelopment/CareerCenter/

National Clearinghouse on Child Abuse and Neglect Information. (2003, May). *Frequently asked questions on child abuse and neglect.* Washington, DC: U.S. Department of Health and Human Services. Retrieved July 30, 2003, from www.calib.com/nccanch/faq.cfm

National Clearinghouse on Child Abuse and Neglect. (2006). *Child maltreatment: 2004.* Washington, DC: Author. Retrieved November 2, 2006, from www.acf.hhs.gov/programs/cb/stats_research/index.htm#can

National Coalition on Auditory Processing Disorders. (2000). *Simulation of auditory processing problems.* Retrieved January 3, 2004, from www.ncapd.org

National Council on Disability. (1995, May). *Improving the implementation of the Individuals with Disabilities Education Act: Making schools work for all of America's children.* Washington, DC: Author. Retrieved July 19, 2003, from www.ncd.gov/newsroom/publications/95school.html

National Council on Disability. (2000, January). *Back to school on civil rights.* Washington, DC: Author. Retrieved April 9, 2009 from http://www.ncd.gov/newsroom/publications/2000/backtoschool_1.htm

National Diabetes Information Clearinghouse. (2003, November). *Diabetes overview.* Bethesda, MD: Author. Retrieved April 19, 2004, from http://diabetes.nlm.nih.gov/medlineplus/juvenilediabetes.html#nlm_nihresources

National Diabetes Information Clearinghouse. (2008, June). *National diabetes statistics, 2007.* Washington, D.C.: National Institutes of Health. Retrieved September 6, 2009 from http://diabetes.niddk.nih.gov/DM/PUBS/statistics/#d_allages

National Dissemination Center for Children with Disabilities. (2002). *Spina bifida.* Washington, DC: Author.

National Dissemination Center for Children with Disabilities. (2003). *Speech and language impairments* [NICHCY Factsheet 11]. Washington, DC: Author. Retrieved January 4, 2004, from www.nichcy.org/pubs/factshe/fs11txt.htm

National Dissemination Center for Children with Disabilities. (2004). *Visual impairments* {fact sheet No. 13). Washington, D. C,: Author. Retrieved August 27, 2009 from http://www.nichcy.org/InformationResources/Pages/NICHCYPublications.aspx#v

National Dissemination Center for Children with Disabilities. (2004, January). *Cerebral palsy fact sheet.* Washington, DC: Author. Retrieved September 3, 2006, from www.nichcy.org/pubs/factshe/fs2txt.htm

National Down Syndrome Society. (2003, October). *Questions and answers about Down syndrome.* Retrieved October 10, 2003, from www.ndss.org/content.cfm?fuseaction=InfoResGeneralArticle&article=194

National Down Syndrome Society. (2006). Information topics. Retrieved November 1, 2006, from www.ndss.org/index.php?option=com_content&task=view&id=1812&Itemid=95

National Eye Institute. (2009, May). *Retinopathy of prematurity.* Washington, D.C.: National Institutes of Health. Retrieved august 27, 2009 from http://www.nei.nih.gov/health/ropindex.asp

National Federation of the Blind. (2006). *Kurzweil–National Federation of the Blind reader.* Retrieved September 16, 2006 from www.knfbreader.com

National Information Center for Children and Youth with Disabilities. (1996, October). *The education of children and youth with special needs: What do the laws say? (News Digest 15).* Washington, DC: Author. Retrieved October 23, 2002, from http://nichcy.org/outprint.asp#nd15

National Information Center for Children and Youth with Disabilities. (1998). *The IDEA Amendments of 1997* (ND26). Washington, DC: Author. Retrieved October 23, 2002, from www.nichcy.org/newsdig.asp#nd26

National Information Center for Children and Youth with Disabilities. (1999a, September). *Individualized education programs* [briefing paper]. Washington, DC: Author. Retrieved April 6, 2003, from www.nichcy.org

National Information Center for Children and Youth with Disabilities. (1999b, September). *Questions often asked by parents about special education services* [briefing paper]. Washington, DC: Author. Retrieved April 6, 2003, from www.nichcy.org

National Institute for Direct Instruction. (2006). Research base for the effectiveness of direct instruction. Retrieved November 2, 2006, from www.nifdi.org/pdfs/Rsearch_Bse.pdf

National Institute of Child Health and Human Development. (2007). *Down syndrome.* Washington, D.C.: National Institutes of Health. Retrieved August 5, 2009 from http://www.nichd.nih.gov/health/topics/Down_Syndrome.cfm

National Institute of Child Health and Human Development. (2007, February). *Learning disabilities: What are learning disabilities?* Washington, D.C.: National Institutes of Health. Retrieved June 10, 2009 from http://www.nichd.nih.gov/health/topics/learning_disabilities.cfm

National Institute of Child Health and Human Development. (2008, September). *National Institutes of Health research plan on Fragile X syndrome and associated disorders.* Washington, D.C.: National Institutes of Health. Retrieved July 20, 2009 from http://www.nichd.nih.gov/search.cfm?search_string=fragile+x+syndrome+prevalence&submitbtn=Search

National Institute of Child Health and Human Development. (2005, May). *Autism overview: What we know.* Retrieved October 13, 2009 from http://www.eric.ed.gov/ERICWebPortal/contentdelivery/servlet/ERICServlet?accno=ED485723

National Institute of Mental Health. (2009, June). *Attention deficit hyperactivity disorder.* Washington, D.C.: Author. Retrieved July 1, 2009 from http://www.nimh.nih.gov/health/publications/attention-deficit-hyperactivity-disorder/complete-index.shtml#pub3

National Institute of Mental Health. (2009, March). *Short-term intensive treatment not likely to improve long-term outcomes for children with ADHD*. Washington, D.C.: Author. Retrieved July 3, 2009 from http://www.nimh.nih.gov/science-news/2009/short-term-intensive-treatment-not-likely-to-improve-long-term-outcomes-for-children-with-adhd.shtml

National Institute of Mental Health. (2009, March). *Improvement following ADHD treatment sustained in most children*. Washington, D.C.: Author. Retrieved July 3, 2009 from http://www.nimh.nih.gov/science-news/2007/improvement-following-adhd-treatment-sustained-in-most-children.shtml

National Institute of Mental Health. (2000b, October). *Depression in children and adolescents*. Bethesda, MD: Author. Retrieved September 1, 2003, from www.nimh.nih.gov/publicat/depchildresfact.cfm

National Institute of Mental Health. (2002, March). *Attention deficit hyperactivity disorder: Questions and answers*. Bethesda, MD: Author. Retrieved November 16, 2002, from www.nimh.nih.gov/publicat/adhdqa.cfm

National Institute of Mental Health. (2003, April). *Suicide facts*. Bethesda, MD: Author. Retrieved August 12, 2003, from www.nimh.nih.gov/research/suifact.cfm

National Institute of Mental Health. (2005, June). *Mental illness exacts heavy toll, beginning in youth* [press release]. Retrieved November 1, 2006, from www.nimh.nih.gov/press/mentalhealthstats.cfm

National Institute of Mental Health. (2006). *Depression in children and adolescents*. Retrieved October 24, 2006, from http://mentalhealth.gov/healthinformation/depchildmenu.cfm

National Institute of Mental Health. (2006). *The numbers count: Mental disorders in America*. Retrieved November 1, 2006, from www.nimh.nih.gov/publicat/numbers.cfm

National Institute of Mental Health. (2006, February). *Attention deficit hyperactivity disorder*. Retrieved October 1, 2006, from www.nimh.nih.gov/publicat/adhd.cfm#intro

National Institute of Mental Health. (2006, October). *Preschoolers with ADHD improve with low doses of medication* [press release]. Retrieved December 10, 2006, from www.nimh.nih.gov/press/preschooladhd.cfm

National Institute of Mental Health. (2008). *The numbers count: Mental disorders in America*. Washington, D.C.: Author. Retrieved July 1, 2009 from http://www.nimh.nih.gov/health/publications/the-numbers-count-mental-disorders-in-america/index.shtml#ADHD

National Institute of Mental Health. (2009a). *How do children and adolescents experience depression?* Retrieved July 6, 2009 from http://www.nimh.nih.gov/health/publications/depression/how-do-children-and-adolescents-experience-depression.shtml_2009

National Institute of Mental Health. (2009b). *Suicide in the U.S.: Statistics and prevention*. Retrieved July 6, 2009 from http://www.nimh.nih.gov/health/publications/suicide-in-the-us-statistics-and-prevention/index.shtml

National Institute of Neurological Disorders and Stroke. (2001). *NINDS muscular dystrophy (MD) information page*. Bethesda, MD: Author. Retrieved March 9, 2004, from www.ninds.nih.gov/health_and_medical/disorders/md.htm#What_is_Muscular_Dystrophy__(MD)

National Institute of Neurological Disorders and Stroke. (2009, June). *Muscular dystrophy: Hope through research*. Washington, D.C.: National Institutes of Health. Retrieved September 3, 2009 from http://www.ninds.nih.gov/disorders/md/detail_md.htm#110183171

National Institute of Neurological Disorders and Stroke. (2009, September). *Autism fact sheet*. Washington, DC: National Institutes of Health. Retrieved October 16, 2009 from http://www.ninds.nih.gov/disorders/autism/detail_autism.htm

National Institute on Deafness and Other Communication Disorders. (2000). *Communication options for children who are deaf or hard-of-hearing*. Retrieved December 19, 2002, from www.nidcd.nih.gov/health/hearing/commopt.asp#what

National Institute on Deafness and Other Communication Disorders. (2002). *Statistics on voice, speech, and language*. Retrieved January 4, 2004, from www.nidcd.nih.gov/health/statistics/vsl.asp

National Institute on Deafness and Other Communication Disorders. (2006). *Ear infections: Facts for parents about otitis media*. Retrieved October 28, 2006, from www.nidcd.nih.gov/health/hearing/otitismedia.htm

National Institute on Deafness and Other Communication Disorders. (2009, June). *Statistics on voice, speech, and language*. Washington, DC: National Institutes of Health. Retrieved August 18 from http://www.nidcd.nih.gov/health/statistics/vsl.asp

National Institutes of Health, National Institute of Child Health and Development. (2006). *Fragile X syndrome*. Retrieved November 1, 2006, from www.nichd.nih.gov/health/topics/fragile_x_syndrome.cfm

National Institutes of Health, National Institute of Child Health and Human Development. (2006). *Facts about Down syndrome*. Retrieved October 30, 2006, from www.nichd.nih.gov/publications/pubs/downsyndrome.cfm#TheOccurrence

National Institutes of Health. (1997). Food fortification plan likely to reduce birth risks [news release]. Retrieved August 15, 2006, from www.nih.gov/news/pr/dec97/nichd-04.htm

National Institutes of Health. (2000, October). *Consensus statement 113. Pheylketonuria (PKU): Screening and management* (Vol. 17, No. 3). Retrieved October 1, 2003, from http://consensus.nih.gov/cons/113/113_statement.htm#3

National Institutes of Health. (2006). *Fact sheet: Mental retardation*. Retrieved October 23, 2006, from www.nih.gov/about/researchresultsforthepublic/MentalRetardation.pdf

National Joint Committee on Learning Disabilities. (1990, January). *Learning disabilities: Issues on definition*. Rockville, MD: Author. Retrieved July 1, 2002, from www.ldonline.org/njcld/defn_91.html

National Joint Committee on Learning Disabilities. (2002). *National Joint Committee on Learning Disabilities fact sheet*. Retrieved June 28, 2002, from www.ldonline.org/njcld/fact_sheet.html

National Joint Committee on Learning Disabilities. (2003). A reaction to full inclusion: A reaffirmation of the right of students with learning disabilities to a continuum of services. Retrieved November 2, 2006, from www.ldonline.org/about/partners/njcld#reports

National Joint Committee on Learning Disabilities. (2004). *Parent guide to IDEA 2004*. Retrieved November 1, 2006, from www.ncld.org/images/stories/downloads/parent_center/idea2004parentguide.pdf

National Joint Committee on Learning Disabilities. (2005, June). *Responsiveness to intervention and learning disabilities*. Retrieved March 3, 2006, from www.ldonline.org/about/partners/njcld#reports

National Joint Committee on Learning Disabilities. (2006). *Member organizations*. Retrieved November 1, 2006, from www.ldonline.org/about/partners/njcld

National Joint Committee on Learning Disabilities. (2009, June). *NJCLD fact sheet*. Retrieved June 10, 2009 from http://www.ncld.org/content/view/500/389/

National Mental Health Association. (2001). *Mental health statistics: Mental illness and the family*. Retrieved September 12, 2003, from www.nmha.org/infoctr/factsheets/15.cfm

National Mental Health Association. (2006). *Children's mental health statistics*. Retrieved October 25, 2006, from www.nmha.org/children/prevent/stats.cfm

National Research Council. (2001). *Educating children with autism*. Washington, DC: National Academy Press.

National Spinal Cord Injury Statistical Center. (2009). *Spinal cord injury: Facts and figures at a glance*. Birmingham, AL: Author. Retrieved September 3, 2009 from http://www.spinalcord.uab.edu/show.asp?durki=119513

National Virtual Translation Center. (2006, October). *The range of world languages*. Retrieved October 25, 2006, from www.nvtc.gov/lotw/months/november/worldlanguages.htm

Navan, J. (2009). *Nurturing the gifted female: A guide for educators*. Thousand Oaks, CA: Corwin.

Neal, L. I., McCray, A. D., Webb-Johnson, G., & Bridgest, S. T. (2003). The effects of African American movement styles on teachers' perceptions and reactions. *Journal of Special Education, 37*, 49–57.

Neihart, M. (2003). An evolving field: Contrasts in children's development: An interview with Nancy Robinson. *Roeper Review, 25*, 106–111.

Nelson, J. R., Benner, G. J., & Cheney, D. (2005). An investigation of the language skills of students with emotional disturbance served in public school settings. *Journal of Special Education, 39*, 97–105.

Nelson, J. R., Benner, G. J., & Gonzalez, J. (2005). An investigation of the effects of a prereading intervention on the early literacy skills of children at risk of emotional disturbance and reading problems. *Journal of Emotional and Behavioral Disorders, 13*, 3–12.

Nelson, J. R., Benner, G. J., & Rogers-Adkinson, D. L. (2003). An investigation of the characteristics of K–12 students with comorbid emotional disturbance and significant language deficits served in public school settings. *Behavioral Disorders, 29*, 25–33.

Nelson, J. R., Benner, G. J., Lane, K., & Smith, B. W. (2004). Academic achievement of K–12 students with emotional and behavioral disorders. *Exceptional Children, 71*, 59–73.

Nelson, J. R., & Roberts, M. L. (2000). Ongoing reciprocal teacher–student interactions involving disruptive behaviors in general education classrooms. *Journal of Emotional and Behavioral Disorders, 8*, 27–37.

Nelson, K. A., & Dimitrova, E. (1993). Severe visual impairment in the United States and in each state, 1990. *Journal of Visual Impairment and Blindness, 87*, 80–85.

Nelson, M. G. (2001, September). Capitalizing on collaboration. *Information Week, 855*, 109–111.

Nettles, M. T., & Perna, L. W. (1997). *The African American education data book, Volume II*. Fairfax, VA: Frederick D. Patterson Research Institute.

Neubert, D., & Redd, V. (2008). Transition services for students with intellectual disabilities: A case study of a public school program on a community college campus. *Exceptionality, 16*(4), 220–234.

Neuman, R. J., Sitdhiraksa, N., Reich, S., Ji, T. H., Joyner, C. A., Sun, L. W., & Todd, R. D. (2005). Estimation of prevalence of DSM-IV and latent class-defined ADHD subtypes in a population-based sample of child and adolescent twins. *Twin Research and Human Genetics, 8*, 392–401.

Neumark-Sztainer, D., Story, M., Falkner, N. H., Beuhring, T., & Resnick, M. D. (1998). Disordered rating among adolescents with chronic illness and disability: The role of family and other social factors. *Archives of Pediatrics and Adolescent Medicine, 152*(9), 871–878.

New York State Education Department. (2009). 2009-10 New York State alternate assessment administration manual and supplemental materials. Retrieved October 26, 2009 from http://www.emsc.nysed.gov/osa/nysaa/nysaa-manual-0910.html

Newcorn, J. H. et al. (2001). Symptom profiles in children with ADHD: Effects of comorbidity and gender. *Journal of American Academy of Child and Adolescent Psychiatry, 40*(2), 137–146.

Newman, M. (2006). Definitions of literacy and their consequences. In H. Luria, D. M. Seymour, & T. Smoke (Eds.), *Language and linguistics in context: Readings and applications for teachers* (pp. 243–255). Mahwah, NJ: Lawrence Erlbaum.

Newport, E. L., & Meier, R. P. (1985). The acquisition of American Sign Language. In D. Slobin (Ed.), *The crosslinguistic study of language acquisition. The data* (Vol. 1, pp. 881–938). Hillsdale, NJ: Lawrence Erlbaum.

Newton, D. W. (2004). *The reality of dialects*. Retrieved January 31, 2004, from www.wetga.edu/~dnewton/eng12000/dialects.html

Nichols, S. M. C., Bicard, S. C., Bicard, D. F., & Casey, L. B.. (2008). A field at risk: The teacher shortage in special education. *Phi Delta Kappan, 89*, 597–600.

Nietfeld, J., & Hunt, A. (2005). Elementary and preservice teachers' strategies for working with students with hyperactivity [On-line]. *Current Issues in Education, 8*(2). Retrieved September 6, 2006, from http://cie.asu.edu/volume8/number2/

Nieto, S. (2009). From surviving to thriving. *Educational Leadership, 66*(5), 8–13.

Nieto, S. M. (2002–2003). Profoundly multicultural questions. *Educational Leadership, 60*(4), 6–10.

Nigg, J. T., Blaskey, L. G., Huang-Pollock, C. L., & Rappley, M. D. (2002). Neuropsychological executive functions and *DSM-IV* ADHD subtypes. *Journal of American Academy of Child and Adolescent Psychiatry, 41*, 59–67.

Nikopoulos, C., & Nikopoulou-Smyrni, P. (2008). Teaching complex social skills to children with autism; Advances of video modeling. *Journal of Early and Intensive Behavior Intervention, 5*(2), 30–43.

Nippold, M. A. (2001). Phonological disorders and stuttering in children: What is the frequency of co-occurrence? *Clinical Linguistics and Phonetics, 15*, 219–228.

Nippold, M. A. (2002). Stuttering and phonology: Is there an interaction? *American Journal of Speech-Language Pathology, 11*, 99–110.

Nippold, M. A., Ward-Lonergan, J. M., & Fanning, J. L. (2005). Persuasive writing in children, adolescents, and adults: A study of syntactic, semantic, and pragmatic development. *Language, Speech, and Hearing Services in Schools, 36*, 125–138.

Nittrouer, S. (2002). From ear to cortex: A perspective on what clinicians need to understand about speech perception and language processing. *Language, Speech, and Hearing Services in the Schools, 33*, 237–252.

No Child Left Behind. (2002, October). *Overview of No Child Left Behind*. Retrieved October 18, 2002, from www.nochildleftbehind.gov/next/overview/index.html

No Child Left Behind Act of 2001. 20 U.S.C. § 6301 *et seq.* (2001).

Norris, C. A., & Solloway, E. M. (2003). The viable alternative: Handhelds. *School Administrator, 60*(4), 26–28.

Nougaret, A. A., Scruggs, T. E., & Mastropieri, M. A. (2005). Does teacher education produce better special education teachers? *Exceptional Children, 71*, 217–229.

Nover, S. M., & Andrews, J. F. (1998). *Critical pedagogy in deaf education: Bilingual methodology and staff development*. Santa Fe: New Mexico School for the Deaf.

Nowacek, E. J., & Mamlin, N. (2007). General education teachers and students with ADHD: What modifications are made? *Preventing School Failure, 51*(3), 28–35.

Nowell, B. L., & Salem, D. A. (2007). The impact of special education mediation on parent–school relationships: Parents' perspective. *Remedial and Special Education, 28*, 304–315.

Nowell, R., & Innes, J. (1997). *Educating children who are deaf or hard of hearing: Inclusion* (ERIC Digest #E557). (ERIC Document Reproduction Service No. ED414675). Retrieved May 3, 2004, from www.edrs.com/members/sp.cfm?AN-ED414675

Nowicki, E. A., & Sandieson, R. (2002). A meta-analysis of school-age children's attitudes towards persons with physical or intellectual disabilities. *International Journal of Disability, Development and Education, 49*, 243–265.

NSW Genetics Education Program. (n.d.). *Genetics fact sheet: Chromosomal disorders I—Down syndrome–Trisomy 21*. Retrieved October 1, 2003, from www.genetics.com.au

Nylund, D. (2000). *Treating Huckleberry Finn*. San Francisco: Jossey-Bass.

O'Brien, L., O'Brien, J., & Mount, B. (1997). Person-centered planning has arrived . . . or has it? *Mental Retardation, 35,* 480–488.

O'Connor, C., Hill, L. D., & Robinson, S. R. (2009). Who's at risk in school and what's race to go do with it? *Review of Research in Education, 33,* 1–34.

O'Neill, J. J. (1987). *The development of speech-language pathology and audiology in the United States.* Retrieved January 3, 2004, from www.mankato.msus.edu/dept/comdis/kuster2/basics/oneill.htm

Oakes, J., & Lipton, M. (2003). *Teaching to change the world.* Boston: McGraw-Hill.

Oakland, T., Black, J. L., Standford, G., Nussbaum, N. L., & Balise, R. R. (1998). An evaluation of the dyslexia training program: A multisensory method for promoting reading in students with reading disabilities. *Journal of Learning Disabilities, 31,* 140–147.

Obasi, C. (2008). Seeing the Deaf in "Deafness". *Journal of Deaf Studies and Deaf Education, 13,* 455–65.

Obiakor, F. E. (1999). Multicultural education: Powerful tool for educating learners with exceptionalities. In F. E. Obiakor, J. O. Schwenn, & A. F. Rotatori (Eds.), *Advances in special education: Multicultural education for learners with exceptionalities* (pp. 1–14). Stamford, CT: JAI Press.

Obiakor, F. E., & Ford, B. A. (Eds.). (2002). *Creating successful learning environments for African American learners with exceptionalities.* Retrieved February 27, 2004, from www.edrs.com/members/sp.cfm?AN=ED471812

Obiakor, F. E., Utley, C. A., Smith, R., & Harris-Obiakor, P. (2002). The comprehensive support model for culturally diverse exceptional learners: Intervention in an age of change. *Intervention in School and Clinic, 38,* 14–27.

Ochoa, T. A., Kelly, M. L., Stuart, S., & Rogers-Adkinson, D. (2004). The impact of PBL technology on the preparation of teachers of English language learners. *Journal of Special Education Technology, 19*(3), 35–45.

Oddo, N. S., & Sitlington, P. L. (2002). What does the future hold? A follow-up study of graduates of a residential school program. *Journal of Visual Impairment and Blindness, 96,* 842–851.

Odom, S., Brown, W., Frey, T., Karasu, N., Smith-Canter, L., & Strain, P. (2003). Evidence-based practices for young children with autism: Contributions for single-subject design research. *Focus on Autism and Other Developmental Disabilities, 18,* 166–75.

Odom, S. L., Brantlinger, E., Gersten, R., Horner, R. H., Thompson, B., & Harris, K. R. (2005). Research in special education: Scientific methods and evidence-based practices. *Exceptional Children, 71,* 137–148.

Office for Civil Rights. (2009). *Office for Civil Rights annual report to Congress, fiscal years 2007–08.* Washington, DC: U.S. Department of Education.

Office of Special Education and Rehabilitative Services, U.S. Department of Education. (2000, July). *A guide to the individualized education program.* Washington, DC: Author. Retrieved April 6, 2003, from www.ed.gov/pubs/edpubs.html

Ogletree, B.T, Oren, T., & Fischer, M.A. (2007). Examining effective intervention practices for communication impairment in autism spectrum disorder. *Exceptionality, 15,* 233–247.

Ogletree, B. T., Pierce, K., Harn, W. E., & Fischer, M. A. (2001–2002). Assessment of communication and language in classical autism: Issues and practice. *Assessment for Effective Intervention, 27*(1–2), 61–71.

Ohtake, Y., & Chadsey, J. G. (2001). Continuing to describe the natural support process. *Journal of the Association for Persons with Severe Handicaps, 26,* 87–95.

Ohtake, Y., & Chadsey, J. G. (2001). Continuing to describe the natural support process. *Journal of the Association for Persons with Severe Handicaps, 26,* 87–95.

Olion, L. (1988). Enhancing the involvement of black parents of adolescents with handicaps. In A. A. Ortiz & B. A. Ramirez (Eds.), *Schools and the culturally diverse exceptional student: Promising practices and future directions* (pp. 96–103). Reston, VA: Council for Exceptional Children.

Olley, J. G. (1992). Autism: Historical overview, definition, and characteristics. In D. Berkell (Ed.), *Autism: Identification, education and treatment* (pp. 3–20). Hillsdale, NJ: Erlbaum.

Olsen, L. Y., Steelman, M. L., Buffalo, M. D., & Montague, J. (1999). Preliminary information on stuttering characteristics contrasted between African American and white children. *Journal of Communication Disorders, 32,* 97–108.

Olson, B. J., Parayitam, S., & Bao, Y. (2007). Strategic decision making: The effects of cognitive diversity, conflict, and trust on decision outcomes. *Journal of Management, 33,* 196–222.

Olson, L. A., Evans, J. R., & Keckler, W. T. (2006). Precocious readers: Past, present, and future. *Journal for the Education of the Gifted, 30,* 205–235.

Olson, R., Wise, B., Conners, F., Rack, J., & Fulkner, D. (1989). Specific deficits in component reading and language skills: Genetic and environmental influences. *Journal of Learning Disabilities, 22,* 339–348.

Olszewski-Kubilius, P. M., & Scott, J. M. (1992). An investigation of the college and career counseling needs of economically disadvantaged minority gifted students. *Roeper Review, 14,* 141–148.

Ophir-Cohen, M., Ashkenazy, E., Cohen, A., & Tirosh, E. (2005). Emotional status and development in children who are visually impaired. *Journal of Visual Impairment and Blindness, 99,* 478–485.

Opp, G. (1994). Historical roots of the field of learning disabilities: Some nineteenth-century German contributions. *Journal of Learning Disabilities, 27,* 10–19.

Orelove, F. P. (1991). Educating all students: The future is now. In L. Meyer, C. A. Peck, & L. Brown (Eds.), *Critical issues in the lives of people with severe disabilities* (pp. 67–92). Baltimore: Paul H. Brookes Publishing Co.

Orfield, G., Frankenberg, E. D., & Lee, C. (2003). The resurgence of school segregation. *Educational Leadership, 60*(4), 16–20.

Orkwis, R. (2003). *Universally designed instruction.* (ERIC/OSEP Digest). Alexandria, VA: Council for Exceptional Children. Retrieved February 27, 2004, from www.edrs.com/members/sp.cfm?AN=ED475386

Orsmond, G., Kuo, H., & Seltzer, M. (2009). Siblings of individuals with an autism spectrum disorder: Sibling relationships and well-being in adolescence and adulthood. *Autism: The International Journal of Research and Practice, 13*(1), 59–80.

Ortiz, A. A., Wilkinson, C. Y., Robertson-Courtney, P., & Kushner, M. I. (2006). Considerations in implementing intervention assistance teams to support English language learners. *Remedial and Special Education, 27,* 53–63.

Osgood, R. (2008). *The history of special education.* Westport, CT: Praeger.

Ostoits, J. (1999). Reading strategies for students with ADD and ADHD in the inclusive classroom. *Preventing School Failure, 43,* 129–132.

Oswald, D. P., Coutinho, M. J., & Best, A. M. (2000). *Community and school predictors of overrepresentation of minority children in special education.* Paper presented at the Civil Rights Project Conference on Minority Issues in Special Education: Harvard University, Cambridge, MA.

Oswald, K., Safran, S., & Johanson, G. (2005). Preventing trouble: Making schools safer places using positive behavior supports. *Education and Treatment of Children, 28,* 265–278.

Otis-Wilborn, A., Winn, J., Griffin, C., & Kilgore, K. (2005). Beginning special educators' forays into general education. *Teacher Education and Special Education, 28,* 143–152.

Overby, M., Carrell, T., & Bernthal, J. (2007). Teachers' perceptions of students with speech sound disorders: A quantitative and qualitative analysis. *Language, Speech, and Hearing Services in Schools, 38,* 327–341.

Overton, T., Fielding, C., & Alba, R. (2007). Differential diagnosis of Hispanic children referred for autism spectrum disorders: Complex issues. *Journal of Autism and Developmental Disorders, 37,* 1996–2007.

Owens, E., Hinshaw, S., Lee, S., & Lahey, B. (2009). Few girls with childhood attention-deficit/hyperactivity disorder show positive adjustment during adolescence. *Journal of Clinical Child and Adolescent Psychology, 3,* 132–143.

Owens, R. E., Metz, D. E., & Haas, A. (2003). *Introduction to communication disorders: A life span perspective* (2nd ed.). Boston: Allyn & Bacon.

Ozonoff, S., & Miller, J. N. (1995). Teaching theory of mind: A new approach to social skill training for individuals with autism. *Journal of Autism and Developmental Disorders, 25,* 415–433.

Ozturk, M. A., & Debelak, C. (2008). Academic competitions as tools for differentiation in middle school. *Gifted Child Today, 31*(3), 47–53.

Padden, C., & Humphries, T. (1988). *Deaf in America: Voices from a culture.* Cambridge, MA: Harvard University Press.

Paden, E. P., & Yairi, E. (1999). Early childhood stuttering II: Initial status of phonological abilities. *Journal of Speech, Language, and Hearing Research, 42,* 1113–1124.

Pagliaro, C. M. (1998). Mathematics reform in the education of deaf and hard of hearing students. *American Annals of the Deaf, 143*(1), 22–28.

Pagliaro, C. M. (2006). Mathematics education and the deaf learner. In D. F. Moores & D. S. Martin (Eds.), *Deaf learners: Developments in curriculum and instruction* (pp. 29–40). Washington, DC: Gallaudet University Press.

Painter, C. A., Prevatt, F., & Welles, T. (2008). Career beliefs and job satisfaction in adults with symptoms of attention-deficit/hyperactivity disorder. *Journal of Employment Counseling, 45,* 178–188.

Palley, E. (2006). Challenges of rights-based law: Implementing the least restrictive environment mandate. *Journal of Disability Policy Studies, 16,* 220–228.

Palmer, S. B., & Wehmeyer, M. L. (2003). Promoting self-determination in early elementary school: Teaching self-regulated problem-solving and goal-setting skills. *Remedial and Special Education, 24,* 115–126.

Panek, P., & Smith, J. (2005). Assessment of terms to describe mental retardation. *Research in Developmental Disabilities, 26,* 565–576.

Pang, V. P. (2001). *Multicultural education: A caring-centered, reflective approach.* Boston: McGraw-Hill.

Parens, E., & Johnston, J. (2009). Facts, values, and attention-deficit hyperactivity disorder (ADHD): An update on the controversies. *Child and Adolescent Psychiatry and Mental Health, 3*(1), 1–17. Retrieved July 1, 2009 from http://www.capmh.com/articles/browse.asp

Parette, H. P. (1997). Assistive technology devices and services, *Education and Training in Mental Retardation and Developmental Disabilities, 32,* 267–280.

Parette, H. P. (1998). Cultural issues and family-centered assistive technology decision-making. In S. L. Judge & H. P. Parette (Eds.), *Assistive technology for young children with disabilities* (pp. 184–210). Cambridge, MA: Brookline.

Parette, H. P., & Peterson-Karlan, G. R. (2007). Facilitating student achievement with assistive technology. *Education and Training in Developmental Disabilities, 42,* 387–397.

Parette, P., & Huer, M. B. (2002). Working with Asian American families whose children have augmentative and alternative communication needs. *Journal of Special Education Technology, 17*(4), 5–13.

Parette, P., & McMahan, G. A. (2002). What should we expect of assistive technology? *Teaching Exceptional Children, 35*(1), 56–61.

Park, J., & Turnbull, A. P. (2001). Cross-cultural competency and special education: Perceptions and experiences of Korean parents of children with special needs. *Education and Training in Mental Retardation and Developmental Disabilities, 36,* 133–147.

Parmar, R. S., & Signer, B. R. (2005). Sources of error in constructing and interpreting graphs: A study of fourth- and fifth-grade students with LD. *Journal of Learning Disabilities, 38,* 250–261.

Parrish, T. (2000, November). *Disparities in the identification, funding and provision of special education.* Paper presented at the Civil Rights Project Conference on Minority Issues in Special Education: Harvard University Cambridge, MA: Retrieved June 10, 2003, from www.gsc.harvard.edu/news/features/soeced03022001.html

Parrish, T. B. (2001). Who's paying the rising cost of special education? *Journal of Special Education Leadership, 14*(1), 4–12.

Parson, M. B., Reid, D. H., Green, C. W., & Browning, L. B. (1999). Reducing individualized job coach assistance provided to persons with multiple severe disabilities in supported work. *Journal of the Association for Persons with Severe Handicaps, 24,* 292–297.

Parsons, M. B., Reid, D. H., & Green, C. (2001). Situational assessment of task preferences among adults with multiple and severe disabilities in supported work. *Journal of the Association for Persons with Severe Handicaps, 26,* 50–55.

Pary, R., Lewis, S., Matuschka, P. R., Rudzinsky, P., Safi, M., & Lippmann, S. (2002). Attention deficit disorder in adults. *Annals of Clinical Psychiatry, 14,* 105–111.

Passarotti, A., Paul, B., Bussiere, J., Buxton, R., Wong, E., & Stiles, J. (2003). The development of face and location processing : An fMRI study. *Developmental Science, 6,* 100–117.

Passow, A. H., & Frasier, M. M. (1996). Toward improving identification of talent potential among minority and disadvantaged students. *Roeper Review, 18,* 198–202.

Passow, A. H., Goldberg, M. L., Tannenbaum, A. I., & French, W. (1955). *Planning for talented youth.* New York: Teachers College Press.

Passow, A. H., & Rudnitski, R. A. (1994). Transforming policy to enhance educational services for the gifted. *Roeper Review, 16,* 271–275.

Pastor, P. N., & Reuben, C. A. (2005). Racial and ethnic differences in ADHD and LD in young school-age children: Parental reports in the National Health Interview Survey. *Public Health Reports, 120,* 383–392.

Pastor, P. N., & Reuben, C. A. (2008). *Diagnosed attention deficit hyperactivity disorder and learning disability: United States, 2004–2006.* Atlanta: National Center for Health Statistics, Vital Health Statistics. Retrieved July 1, 2009 from http://www.cdc.gov/nchs/fastats/adhd.htm

Pastor, P. N., & Reuben, C. A. (2008). *Diagnosed attention deficit hyperactivity disorder and* learning disability*: United States, 2004–2006* [Data from the National Health Interview Survey, Vital and Health Statistics. Series 10, Number 237]. Washington, D. C.: National Center for Health Statistics, Centers for Disease control and Prevention, U.S. Department of Health and Human Services. Retrieved June 10, 2009 from www.cdc.gov/nchs/data/series/sr_10/sr10_237.pdf

Patchell, F., & Hand, L. (1993). *An invisible disability—Language disorders in high school students and the implications for classroom teachers.* Retrieved December 29, 2003, from http://members.tripod.com/Caroline_Bowen/An%20invisible%20disability.pdf

Paton, J. W. (2003). *Central auditory processing disorders (CAPDs).* Retrieved January 2, 2004, from www.ldonline.org/ld_indepth/process_deficit/capd_paton.html

Pau, C. S. (1995). The deaf child and solving problems in arithmetic. *American Annals of the Deaf, 140*(3), 287–291.

Paul, P. V. (1998). *Literacy and deafness: The development of reading, writing, and literate thought.* Boston: Allyn & Bacon.

Paul, R. (1993). Patterns of development in late talkers: Preschool years. *Journal of Childhood Communication Disorders, 15,* 7–14.

Paul, R., Sprangle-Looney, S. S., & Dahm, P. S. (1991). Communication and socialization skills at ages 2 and 3 in "late-talking" young children. *Journal of Speech and Hearing Research, 34,* 858–865.

Pavri, S., & Luftig, R. (2000). The social face of inclusive education: Are students with learning disabilities really included in the classroom? *Preventing School Failure, 45*(1), 8–14.

Pavri, S., & Monda-Amaya, L. (2001). Social support in inclusive schools: Student and teacher perspectives. *Exceptional Children, 67,* 391–411.

Peck, C. A., Staub, D., Gallucci, C., & Schwartz, I. (2004). Parent perception of the impact of inclusion on their nondisabled child. *Research and Practice for Persons with Severe Disabilities, 29,* 135–143.

Peets, K. (2009). The effects of context on the classroom discourse skills of children with language impairment. *Language, Speech, and Hearing Services in Schools, 40,* 5–16.

Pelham, W. E. et al., (2000). Behavioral versus behavioral and pharmacological treatment in ADHD children attending a summer treatment program. *Journal of Abnormal Child Psychology, 23,* 507–525.

Pellegrino, L. (2002). Cerebral palsy. In M. L. Batshaw (Ed.), *Children with disabilities* (5th ed., pp. 443–466). Baltimore: Paul H. Brookes.

Pellowski, M., & Conture, E. G. (2002). Characteristics of speech disfluency and stuttering behaviors in three- and four-year-old children. *Journal of Speech, Language, and Hearing Research, 45,* 20–35.

Pennington, B. F. (1995). Genetics of learning disabilities. *Journal of Child Neurology, 10* (Suppl 1), 69–77.

*Pennsylvania Association for Retarded Children (PARC) v. Commonwealth of Pennsylvania.* (1972). 343 F. Supp. 279 (E. D. Pa. 1972).

Penuel, W., Riel, M., Krause, A., & Frank, K. (2009). Analyzing teachers' professional interactions in a school as social capital: A social network approach. *Teachers College Record* 11(1), 124–163.

Pereles, D. A., Omdal, S., & Baldwin, L. (2009). Response to intervention and twice-exceptional learners: A promising fit. *Gifted Child Today, 32,* 40–51.

Perkins-Gough, D. (2002–2003). Racial inequities in special education. *Educational Leadership, 60*(4), 90–91.

Perra, O., Williams, J., Whiten, A., Fraser, L., Benzie, H., & Perrett, D. (2008). Imitation and "theory of mind" competencies in discrimination of autism from other neurodevelopmental disorders. *Research in Autism Spectrum Disorders, 2,* 456–468.

Pertsch, C. F. (1936). *A comparative study of the progress of subnormal pupils in the grades and in special classes.* New York: Columbia University, Teacher's College, Bureau of Publications.

Peterson, C., & Slaughter, V. (2009). Theory of mind in children with autism or typical development: Links between eye-reading and false belief understanding. *Research in Autism Spectrum Disorders, 3,* 462–473.

Peterson, J. S., & Ray, K. E. (2006). Bullying and the gifted: Victims, perpetrators, prevalence, and effects. *Gifted Child Quarterly, 50,* 148–168.

Pfeiffer, S. I. (2003). Challenges and opportunities for students who are gifted: What the experts say. *Gifted Child Quarterly, 47,* 161–169.

Pfifner, L., Barkley, R. A., & DuPaul, G. J. (2006). Treatment of ADHD in school settings. In R. A. Barkley (Ed.), *Attention-deficit hyperactivity disorder: A handbook for diagnosis and treatment* (3rd ed.). New York: Guilford Press.

Pickett, A. L. (1997). Paraeducators in school settings: Framing the issues. In A. L. Pickett & K. Gerlach (Eds.), *Supervising paraeducators in school settings: A team approach* (pp. 1–24). Austin, TX: Pro-Ed.

Pickles, A., Simonoff, E., Conti-Ramsden, G., Falcaro, M., Simkin, Z., Charman, T., Chandler, S., Loucas, T., & Baird, G. (2009). Loss of language in early development of autism and specific language impairment. *Journal of Child Psychology and Psychiatry, 50,* 843–852.

Pierangelo, R., & Guiliani, G. (2008). *Understanding assessment in the special education process.* Thousand Oaks, CA: Corwin.

Pierce, C. D., Reid, R., & Epstein, M. H. (2004). Teacher-mediated interventions for children with EBD and their academic outcomes: A review. *Remedial and Special Education, 25,* 175–188.

Pierce, K., & Courchesne, E. (2001). Evidence for a cerebellar role in reduced exploration and stereotyped behavior in autism. *Biological Psychiatry, 49,* 655–664.

Pipho, C. (1997). The possibilities and problems of collaboration. *Phi Delta Kappan, 79,* 261–262.

Pisecco, S., Wristers, K., Swank, P., Silva, P. A., & Baker, D. B. (2001). The effect of academic self-concept on ADHD and antisocial behaviors in early adolescence. *Journal of Learning Disabilities, 34,* 450–461.

Pisha, B., & Coyne, P. (2001). Smart from the start: The promise of universal design for learning. *Remedial and Special Education, 22,* 197–203.

Pisha, B., & Stahl, S. (2005). The promise of new learning environments for students with disabilities. *Intervention in School and Clinic, 41,* 67–75.

Piven, J., Arndt, S., Bailey, J., & Andreasen, N. (1996). Regional brain enlargement in autism: Magnetic resonance imaging study. *Journal of the American Academy of Child and Adolescent Psychiatry, 35,* 530–536.

Piven, J., Saliba, K., Bailey, J., & Arndt, S. (1997). An MRI study of autism: The cerebellum revisited. *Neurology, 49,* 546–551.

Pivik, J., McComas, J., & LaFlamme, M. (2002). Barriers and facilitators to inclusive education. *Exceptional Children, 69,* 97–107.

Place, K., & Hodge, S. R. (2001). Social inclusion of students with physical disabilities in general physical education: A behavioral analysis. *Adapted Physical Activity Quarterly, 18,* 389–404.

Plante, E. (2001). Neuroimaging in communication sciences and disorders: An introduction. *Journal of Communication Disorders, 34,* 441–443.

Planty, M., Hussar, W., Snyder, T., Kena, G., KewalRamani, A., Kemp, J., Bianco, K., Dinkes, R. (2009). *The condition of education 2009* (NCES 2009-081). Washington, D.C.: National Center for Education Statistics, Institute of Education Sciences, U.S. Department of Education. Retrieved June 1, 2009 from http://nces.ed.gov/pubsearch/pubsinfo.asp?pubid=2009081

Planty, M., Hussar, W., Snyder, T., Provasnik, S., Kena, G., Dinkes, R., Kewal Ramani, A., & Kemp, J. (2008). *The Condition of Education 2008: Indicator 22-Students with disabilities exiting school with a regular high school diploma* (NCES 2008-031). Washington, DC: National Center for Education Statistics, Institute of Education Sciences, U.S. Department of Education.

Plunkett, S. W., Behnke, A. O., Sands, T, & Choi, B. Y. (2009). Adolescents' reports of parental engagement and academic achievement in immigrant families. *Journal of Youth and Adolescence, 38,* 257–268.

Podmore, R. (1995). *Signs in success: Profiles of deaf Americans.* Hillsboro, OR: Butte Publications.

Pogrund, R. L., & Fazzi, D. L. (Eds.). (2002). *Early focus: Working with young children who are blind or visually impaired and their families* (pp. 405–441). New York: American Foundation for the Blind Press.

Polloway, E. A., Bursuck, W. D., & Epstein, M. H. (2001). Homework for students with learning disabilities: The challenge of home–school communication. *Reading and Writing Quarterly, 17,* 181–187.

Polloway, E. A., Smith, J. D., Chamberlain, J., Denning, C. B., & Smith, T. E. C. (1999). Levels of deficits or supports in the classification of mental retardation: Implementation practices. *Education and Training in Mental Retardation and Developmental Disabilities, 34,* 200–206.

Poon-McBrayer, K. F., & Garcia, S. B. (2000). Profiles of Asian American students with LD at initial referral, assessment, and placement in special education. *Journal of Learning Disabilities, 33,* 61–71.

Porembski, C., Boyko, E., DeCiccio, A., & Haraway, D. (2002). In their own words: The lessons we learn if we hear. *Preventing School Failure, 46*(2), 57–61.

Porter, L. (1999). *Gifted young children.* London: Open University.

Powers, S. (2003). Influences of student and family factors on academic outcomes of mainstream secondary school deaf students. *Journal of Deaf Studies and Deaf Education, 8,* 57–78.

Prader-Willi Association. (2009, July). *What is Prader-Willi syndrome?* Retrieved July 20, 2009 from http://www.pwsausa.org/syndrome/index.htm

Prader-Willi Syndrome Association. (2005). *Basic facts about PWS: A diagnosis and reference guide for physicians and other health professionals.* Retrieved November 1, 2006, from www.pwsausa.org/syndrome/basicfac.htm

Praisner, C. L. (2003). Attitudes of elementary school principals toward the inclusion of students with disabilities. *Exceptional Children, 69*, 135–145.

Prasse, D. P. (2006). Legal supports for problem-solving systems. *Remedial and Special Education, 27*, 7–15.

Pratt, C., Dotting, N., & Conti-Ramsden, G. The characteristics and concerns of mothers of adolescents with a history of SLI. *Child Language Teaching and Therapy, 22*, 177–196.

Presley, J. A., & Hughes, C. (2000). Peers as teachers of anger management to high school students with behavioral disorders. *Behavioral Disorders, 25*, 241–245.

Price, L. A., Wolensky, D., & Mulligan, R. (2002). Self-determination in action in the classroom. *Remedial and Special Education, 23*, 109–115.

Prins, D., & Ingham, R. J. (2009). Evidence-based treatment and stuttering—historical perspective. *Journal of Speech, Language, and Hearing Research, 52*, 254–263.

Proctor, A., Yairi, E., Duff, M., & Zhang, J. (2008). Prevalence of stuttering in African American preschoolers. *Journal of Speech, Language, and Hearing Research, 51*, 1465–1479.

Prout, H. T., & Prout, S. M. (2000). The family with a child with mental retardation. In M. J. Fine & R. L. Simpson (Eds.), *Collaboration with parents and families of children and youth with exceptionalities* (2nd ed., pp. 217–235). Austin, TX: Pro-Ed.

Pruitt, P., Wandry, D., & Hollums, D. (1998). Listen to us! Parents speak out about their interactions with special educators. *Preventing School Failure, 42*, 161–166.

Public Education Network. (2006, May). *Open to the public: The public speaks out on No Child Left Behind: A summary of nine hearings September 2005 to January 2006*. Washington, DC: Author. Retrieved June 14, 2006, from http://publiceducation.org/2006_NCLB/main/2006_NCLB_National_Report.pdf

Pufpaff, L. A. (2008). Barriers to participation in kindergarten literacy instruction for a student with augmentative and alternative communication needs. *Psychology in the Schools, 45*, 582–599.

Pugach, M. C., & Johnson, L. J. (1995). Unlocking expertise among classroom teachers through structured dialogue: Extending research on peer collaboration. *Exceptional Children, 62*, 101–110.

Pugach, M. C., & Johnson, L. J. (2002). A multidimensional framework for collaboration. In *Collaborative practitioners, collaborative schools* (2nd ed., pp. 25–42). Denver: Love.

Pugh, G. S., & Erin, J. (Eds.). (1999). *Blind and visually impaired students: Educational service guidelines*. Watertown, MA: Perkins School for the Blind.

Pugh, K. R., Mencl, W. E., Jenner, A. R., Lee, J. R., Katz, L., Frost, S. J., et al. (2001). Neuroimaging studies of reading development and reading disability. *Learning Disabilities Research and Practice, 16*, 240–249.

Purcell, M. G., Horn, E., & Palmer, S. (2007). A qualitative study of the initiation and continuation of preschool inclusion programs. *Exceptional Children, 74*, 85–100.

Quinn, K. P., & Lee, V. (2007). The wraparound approach for students with emotional and behavioral disorders: Opportunities for school psychologists. *Psychology in the Schools, 44*, 101–111.

Quinn, M. M., Osher, D., Warger, C. L., Hanley, T. V., Bader, B. D., & Hoffman, C. C. (2000). Teaching and working with children who have emotional and behavioral challenges. Washington, DC: Center for Effective Collaboration and Practice. (ERIC Document Reproduction Service No. ED466076)

Radcliff, D. (2000). *Non-drug interventions for improving classroom behavior and social functioning of young children with attention deficit hyperactivity disorder*. (ERIC Document Reproduction Service No. ED445427) Retrieved June 12, 2003, from www.edrs.com/members/sp.cfm?AN=ED445427

Rafalovich, A. (2001). The conceptual history of attention deficit hyperactivity disorder: Idiocy, imbecility, encephalitis and the child deviant, 1877–1929. *Deviant Behavior: An Interdisciplinary Journal, 22*, 93–115.

Rafoth, M. A., & Foriska, T. (2006). administrator participation in promoting effective problem-solving teams. *Remedial and Special Education, 27*, 130–135.

Ramanathan, A. K., & Zollers, N. J. (1999). For-profit schools continue to skimp on special education: A response to Naomi Zigmond. *Phi Delta Kappan, 81*, 284–290.

Rashid, F. L., Morris, R. D., & Sevcik, R. A. (2005). Relationship between home literacy environment and reading achievement in children with reading disabilities. *Journal of Learning Disabilities, 38*, 2–11.

Rayner, C., Denholm, C., & Sigafoos, J. (2009). Video-based intervention for individuals with autism: Key questions that remain unanswered. *Research in Autism Spectrum Disorders, 3*, 291–303.

Raywid, M. A. (1991). Finding time for collaboration. *Educational Leadership, 51*(1), 30–34.

Rea, P. J., McLaughlin, V. L., & Walther-Thomas, C. (2002). Outcomes for students with learning disabilities in inclusive and pullout programs. *Exceptional Children, 68*, 203–222.

Recruiting New Teachers. (2002). *The urban teacher challenge: Teacher demand and supply in the great city schools*. Belmont, MA: Author.

Reddy, L. A., Newman, E., De Thomas, C. A., & Chun, V. (2009). Effectiveness of school-based prevention and intervention programs for children and adolescents with emotional disturbance: A meta-analysis. *Journal of School Psychology, 47*, 77–99.

Reder, S., & Vogel, S. A. (1997). Lifespan employment and economic outcomes for adults with self-reported learning disabilities. In P. Gerber & D. Brown (Eds.), *Learning disabilities and employment* (pp. 371–394). Austin, TX: Pro-Ed.

Reed, P. (1998). Assistive technology: Putting the pieces together. *Disability Solutions, 3*(2), 1–11.

Reed, S., Antia, S. D., & Kreimeyer, K. H. (2008). Academic status of deaf and hard-of-hearing students in public schools: Student, home, and service facilitators and detractors. *Journal of Deaf Studies and Deaf Education, 13*, 485–502.

Reeves, J. B., Wollenhaupt, P., & Caccamise, F. (1995). *Deaf students as visual learners: Power for improving literacy and communication*. Paper presented at the 18th International Congress on Education of the Deaf, Tel Aviv, Israel. (ERIC Document Reproduction Service No. ED390209) Retrieved May 4, 2004, from www.edrs.com/Webstore/Download2 .cfm?ID-405624

Reid, R. (1999). Attention deficit hyperactivity disorder: Effective methods for the classroom. *Focus on Exceptional Children, 32*(4), 1–19.

Reid, R., DuPaul, G. J., Power, T. J., Anastopoulos, A. D., Rogers-Adkinson, D., Noll, M. B., & Riccio, C. (1998). Assessing culturally different students for attention deficit hyperactivity disorder using behavior rating scales. *Journal of Abnormal Child Psychology, 26*, 187–198.

Reis, E. M. (2002). Attention deficit hyperactivity disorder: Implications for the classroom teacher. *Journal of Instructional Psychology, 29*, 175–178.

Reis, S. M. (2002). Social and emotional issues faced by gifted girls in elementary and secondary school. *SENG Newsletter, 2*(3), 1–5. Retrieved August 31, 2006, from www.sengifted.org/articles_social/Reis_ SocialAndEmotionalIssuesFacedByGiftedGirls.shtml

Reis, S. M. (2003). Reconsidering regular curriculum for high-achieving students, gifted underachievers, and the relationship between gifted and regular education. In J. H. Borland (Ed.), *Rethinking gifted education*. New York: Teachers College Press.

Reis, S. M., & Renzulli, J. S. (2004). *Curriculum compacting: A systematic procedure for modifying the curriculum for above average ability students*. Storrs, CT: National Research Center on the Gifted and Talented. Retrieved April 1, 2004, from www.sp.uconn.edu/~nrcgt/sem/semart08.html

Reis, S. M., & Ruban, L. (2005). Services and programs for academically talented students with learning disabilities. *Theory into Practice, 44*, 148–159.

Reis, S. M., & Sullivan, E. E. (2009). Characteristics of gifted learners: Consistently varied, refreshingly diverse. In F. A. Karnes & S. M. Bean (Eds.), *Methods and materials for teaching the gifted* (3rd edition) (pp. 3–35). Waco, TX: Prufrock.

Reis, S. M., Westberg, K. L., Kulikowich, J., Calliard, F., Hébert, T., Purcell, J. H., et al. (1992). *Why not let high ability students start school in January? The curriculum compacting study* (Research Monograph 93106). Storrs, CT: National Research Center on the Gifted and Talented.

Reis, S. M., Westberg, K. L., Kulikowich, J. M., & Purcell, J. H. (1998). Curriculum compacting and achievement test scores: What does the research say? *Gifted Child Quarterly, 42,* 123–129.

Reiter-Purtill, J., Gerhardt, C. A., Vannatta, K., Passo, M. H., & Noll, R. B. (2003). A controlled longitudinal study of the social functioning of children with juvenile rheumatoid arthritis. *Journal of Pediatric Psychology, 28,* 17–28.

Reitman, D. (1998). Assessment of externalizing disorders. *Clinical Psychology Review, 18,* 555–584.

Reitman, V. (2003, February 10). Attention deficit disorder in adults: A new drug could help people who have trouble focusing. But it's likely to sharpen the debate on the prevalence of the disorder and how it's diagnosed. *Los Angeles Times,* part 6, p. 1. Retrieved July 3, 2003, from www.latimes.com/features/health/la-he-srattera10feb10001516,1,5387828.story

Renshaw, D. C. (1974). *The hyperactive child.* Chicago: Nelson-Hall.

Renzulli, J. S. (1996). Schools for talent development: A practical plan for total school improvement. *School Administrator, 53*(1), 20–22.

Renzulli, J. S. (1998). A rising tide lifts all ships: Developing the gifts and talents of all students. *Phi Delta Kappan, 80,* 104–111.

Renzulli, J. S. (2002). Emerging conceptions of giftedness: Building a bridge to the new century. *Exceptionality, 10,* 67–75.

Renzulli, J. S. (2005). Applying gifted education pedagogy to total talent development for all students. *Theory into Practice, 44,* 80–89.

Renzulli, J. S., & Reis, S. M. (2002). What is schoolwide enrichment? How gifted programs relate to total school improvement. *Gifted Child Today, 25*(4), 18–25, 64.

Repp, A. C., & Horner, R. H. (1999). *Functional analysis of problem behavior: From effective assessment to effective support.* Belmont, CA: Wadsworth.

Reschly, D. J., & Hosp, J. L. (2004). State SLD identification policies and practices. *Learning Disability Quarterly, 27,* 197–213.

Rescorla, L., Ross, G. S., & McClure, S. (2007). Language delay and behavioral/emotional problems in toddlers: Findings from two developmental clinics. *Journal of Speech, Language, and Hearing Research, 50,* 1063–1078.

Research and Scientific Affairs Committee, American Speech-Language-Hearing Association. (2004). *Evidence based practice in communication disorders: An introduction* [Technical report]. Retrieved from www.asha.org/members/deskref-journals/deskref/default

Reyes-Blanes, M. (2002, March). *Partnering with Latino migrant families of children with disabilities: A challenge, a mission.* Paper presented at the annual national conference of the American Council on Rural Special Education (ACRES), Reno, NV. (ERIC Document Reproduction Service No. ED463116)

Reynhout, G., & Carter, M. (2009). The use of social stories by teachers and their perceived efficacy. *Research in Autism Spectrum Disorders, 3,* 232–251.

Reynolds, B. H. (2008). Are principals ready to welcome children with disabilities? *Principal, 88*(2), 16–19.

Reynolds, C. R., & Kamphaus, R. W. (2004). *Behavior assessment system for children: Manual* (BASC-2). Circle Pines, MN: American Guidance.

Rhim, L. M., & McLaughlin, M. (2007). Students with disabilities in charter schools: What we now know. *Focus on Exceptional Children, 39*(5), 1–12.

Ribble, M. S., Bailey, G. D., & Ros, T. W. (2004). Digital citizenship: Addressing appropriate technology behavior.*Learning and Leading with Technology, 39*(1), 6–11.

Rice, C. J., & Goessling, D. P. (2005). Recruiting and retaining male special education teachers. *Remedial and Special Education, 26,* 347–356.

Rice, D., & Zigmond, N. (2000). Co-teaching in secondary schools: Teacher reports of developments in Australian and American classrooms. *Learning Disabilities: Research and Practice, 15,* 190–197.

Richissin, T. (1999, June 25). Race predicts handling of many young criminals: Care vs. punishment of mentally ill youth correlates with color. *The Baltimore Sun,* p. 1A.

Rieck, W. A., & Wadsworth, D. E. D. (2005). Assessment accommodations: Helping students with exceptional learning needs. *Intervention in School and Clinic, 41,* 105–109.

Riehl, C. J. (2000). The principal's role in creating inclusive schools for diverse students: A review of normative, empirical, and critical literatures on the practice of educational administration. *Review of Educational Research, 70,* 55–81.

Riggs, C. G. (2004). To teachers: What paraeducators want you to know. *Teaching Exceptional Children, 36*(5), 8–13.

Rinn, A. N., & Nelson, J. M. (2009). Preservice teachers' perceptions of behaviors characteristic of ADHD and giftedness. *Roeper Review, 31*(1), 18–26.

Rios, F. A. (1993). Thinking in urban, multicultural classrooms: Four teachers' perspectives. *Urban Education, 28,* 245–266.

Ritter, C. L., Michel, C. S., & Irby, B. (1999). Concerning inclusion: Perceptions of middle school students, their parents, and teachers. *Rural Special Education Quarterly, 18*(2), 10–16.

Ritzman, M. J., & Sanger, D. (2007). Principals' opinions on the role of speech-language pathologists serving students with communication disorders involved in violence. *Language, Speech, and Hearing Services in Schools, 38,* 365–377.

Robbins, D., Fein, D., Barton, M., & Green, J. (2001). The modified checklist for autism in toddlers: An initial study investigating the early detection of autism and pervasive developmental disorders. *Journal of Autism and Developmental Disorders, 31,* 131–144.

Roberts, C. M., & Smith, P. R. (1999). Attitudes and behaviour of children toward peers with disabilities. *International Journal of Disability, Development, and Education, 46,* 35–50.

Roberts, F. K. (1986). Education for the visually handicapped: A social and educational history. In G. School (Ed.), *Foundations of education for blind and visually handicapped children and youth: Theory and practice* (pp. 1–18). New York: American Foundation for the Blind Press.

Roberts, J., Schaaf, J., Skinner, M., Wheeler, A., Hooper, D., Hatton, D., & Bailey, D. (2005). Academic skills of boys with fragile X syndrome: Profiles and predictors. *American Journal on Mental Retardation, 110,* 107–120.

Roberts, J. E., Hatton, D. D., & Bailey, D. B. (2001). Development and behavior of male toddlers with Fragile X syndrome. *Journal of Early Intervention, 24,* 207–223.

Roberts, J. S. (2007). Gaining self-determination skills through peer mentoring between students with similar physical impairments: A case study. *Physical Disabilities: Education and Related Services, 26,* 9–29.

Robertson, K., Chamberlain, B., & Kasari, C. (2003). General education teachers' relationships with included students with autism. *Journal of Autism and Developmental Disorders, 33,* 123–130.

Robin, A. L. (1998). *ADHD in adolescents: Diagnosis and treatment.* New York: Guilford Press.

Robinette, D. (1990). *Hometown heroes: Successful deaf youth in America.* Washington, DC: Gallaudet University Press.

Robins, D. L. & Dumont-Mathieu, T. (2006). The Modified Checklist for Autism in Toddler (M-CHAT): A review of current findings and future directions. *Journal of Developmental and Behavioral Pediatrics, 27* (Supplement 2), S111–S119.

Robinson, N. M. (2003). Two wrongs do not make a right: Sacrificing the needs of gifted students does not solve society's unsolved problems. *Journal of the Education of the Gifted, 26,* 251–273.

Rock, M. L. (2000). Parents as equal partners: Balancing the scales in IEP development. *Teaching Exceptional Children, 32*(6), 30–37.

Rodekohr, R. K., & Haynes, W. O. (2001). Differentiating dialect from disorder: A comparison of two processing tasks and a standardized language test. *Journal of Communication Disorders, 34,* 255–272.

Rodgers, C. (2007). *Parenting and inclusive education: Discovering difference, experiencing difficulty.* New York: Palgrave MacMillan.

Rodrigue, J. R., Morgan, S. B., & Geffken, G. R. (1990). Families of autistic children: Psychosocial functioning of mothers. *Journal of Clinical Child Psychology, 19,* 371–379.

Rodriguez, D. (2005). A conceptual framework of bilingual special education teacher programs. In J. Cohen, K. T. McAlister, K. Rolstad, & J. MacSwain (Eds.), *ISB4: Proceedings of the 4th International Symposium on Bilingualism.* Somerville, MA: Cascadilla Press. Retrieved April 14, 2009 from www.lingref.com/isb/4/152ISB4.PDF

Rodriguez, D. (2009). Culturally and linguistically diverse students with autism. *Childhood Education. 85,* 313–317.

Rodriguez, D., & Carrasquillo, A. (1997). Bilingual special education teacher preparation: A conceptual framework. *New York State Association for Bilingual Education Journal, 12,* 98–109.

Roellke, C. R., & King, J. (2008). Responding to teacher quality and accountability mandates: The perspectives of school administrators and classroom teachers. *Leadership and Policy in Schools, 7,* 264–295.

Roffman, A. J. (2000). *Meeting the challenge of learning disabilities in adulthood.* Baltimore: Paul H. Brookes.

Rogers, E. M., & Steinfatt, T. M. (1999). *Intercultural communication.* Prospect Heights, IL: Waveland Press.

Rogers, K. B. (2007). Lessons learned about educating the gifted and talented: A synthesis of the research on educational practice. *Gifted Child Quarterly, 51,* 382–396.

Rogers, M. A., Wiener, J., Marton, I., & Tannock, R. (2009). Parental involvement in children's learning: comparing parents of children with and without attention-deficit/hyperactivity disorder (ADHD). *Journal of School Psychology, 47,* 167–185.

Rogers-Adkinson, D. L., Ochoa, T. A., & Delgado, B. (2003). Developing cross-cultural competence: Serving families of children with significant developmental needs. *Focus on Autism and Developmental Disabilities, 18,*(1), 4–8.

Roid, G. (2003). *Stanford-Binet Intelligence Scales* (5th ed.). Rolling Meadows, IL: Riverside.

Rojewski, J. W. (1999). Occupational and educational aspirations and attainment of young adults with and without LD two years after high school completion. *Journal of Learning Disabilities, 32,* 533–552.

Romski, M. A., Sevcik, R. A., Adamson, L. B., & Bakeman, R. A. (2005). Communication patterns of individuals with moderate or severe cognitive disabilities: Interactions with unfamiliar partners. *American Journal on Mental Retardation, 110,* 226–238.

Roosa, J. B. (1995). *Men on the move: Competence and cooperation—Conflict resolution and beyond.* Kansas City, MO: Author.

Rosa-Lugo, L. I., & Fradd, S. H. (2000). Preparing professionals to serve English-language learners with communication disorders. *Communication Disorders Quarterly, 22,* 29–42.

Roschelle, J. M., Pea, R. D., Hoadley, C. M., Gordin, D. N., & Means, B. M. (2000). Changing how and what children learn in school with computer-based technologies. *Future of Children, 10*(2), 76–101.

Rose, D. H., & Meyer, A. (2002). *Teaching every student in the digital age: Universal design for learning.* Alexandria, VA: Association for Supervision and Curriculum Development.

Rose, L. (1999). *Gender issues in gifted education.* Storrs, CT: National Research Center on the Gifted and Talented. Retrieved March 2, 2004, from www.sp.uconn.edu/~nrcgt/news/spring99/sprng994.html

Rose, L. C., & Gallup, A. M. (2002). The thirty-fourth annual Phi Delta Kappa/Gallup poll of the public's attitudes toward the public schools. *Phi Delta Kappan, 84,* 41–56.

Rose, L. C., & Gallup, A. M. (2003). The thirty-fifth annual Phi Delta Kappa/Gallup poll of the public's attitudes toward the public schools. *Phi Delta Kappan, 85,* 41–56.

Rose, L. C., & Gallup, A. M. (2005). The thirty-seventh annual Phi Delta Kappa/Gallup poll of the public's attitudes toward the public schools. *Phi Delta Kappan, 87,* 41–57.

Rose, L. C., & Gallup, A. M. (2006). The thirty-eighth annual Phi Delta Kappa/Gallup poll of the public's attitudes toward the public schools. *Phi Delta Kappan, 88,* 41–53.

Roseberry-McKibbin, C. (2000). Multicultural matters. *Communication Disorders Quarterly, 21,* 242–245.

Roseberry-McKibbin, C., & O'Hanlon, L. (2005). Nonbiased assessment of English language learners: A tutorial. *Communication Disorders Quarterly, 26,* 178–185.

Rosenberg, M. S., Boyer, K. L., & Sindelar, P. T. (2007). Alternative route programs for certification in special education: Program infrastructure, instructional delivery, and participant characteristics. *Exceptional Children, 73,* 224–241.

Rosenberg, M. S., & Sindelar, P. T. (2005). The proliferation of alternative routes to certification in special education: A critical review of the literature. *Journal of Special Education, 39,* 117–127.

Rosenblum, L. P., & Erin, J. N. (1998). Perceptions of terms used to describe individuals with visual impairments. *RE:view, 30,* 15–26.

Rosenfield, S., & Gravois, T. (1996). *Instructional consultation teams.* New York: Guilford Press.

Rosenholtz, S. J. (1989). Workplace conditions that affect teacher quality and commitment: Implications for teacher induction programs. *Elementary School Journal, 89,* 421–439.

Roth, F. P. (2000). Narrative writing: Development and teaching with children with writing difficulties. *Topics in Language Disorders, 20*(4), 15–28.

Rothstein, L. F. (1995). *Special education law.* Reading, MA: Addison-Wesley.

Rourke, J., & Boone, E. (2008). Collaboration: The driving force for success. *Principal Leadership, 8*(10), 4–7.

Rovet, J. F., Ehrlich, R. M., Czuchta, D., & Akler, M. (1993). Psychoeducational characteristics of children and adolescents with insulin-dependent diabetes mellitus. *Journal of Learning Disabilities, 26,* 7–22.

Rowland, A. S., Umbach, D. M., Stallone, L., Naftel, A. J., Bohlig, E. M., & Sandler, D. P. (2002). Prevalence of medication treatment for attention deficit-hyperactivity disorder among elementary school children in Johnston County, North Carolina. *American Journal of Public Health, 92,* 231–234.

Rowley-Kelly, F. L., & Reigel, D. H. (1993). *Teaching the student with spina bifida.* Baltimore: Paul H. Brookes.

Rozalski, M. E., Yell, M. L., & Boreson, L. A. (2006). Using seclusion timeout and physical restraint: An analysis of state policy, research, and the law. *Journal of Special Education Leadership, 19*(2), 13–29.

Rubin, R. (2009, June 15). Sudden death in kids, ADHD drugs linked. *USA Today* [on-line]. Retrieved July 1, 2009 from http://www.usatoday.com/news/health/2009-06-15-fda-adhd_N.htm

Rubinson, F. (2002). Lessons learned from implementing problem-solving teams in urban high schools. *Journal of Educational and Psychological Consultation, 13,* 185–217.

Rucklidge, J. J., & Tannock, R. (2001). Psychiatric, psychosocial, and cognitive functioning of female adolescents with ADHD. *Journal of American Academy of Child and Adolescent Psychiatry, 40,* 530–541.

Rueda, R., & Garcia, E. (1997). Do portfolios make a difference for diverse students? The influence of type of data on making instructional decisions. *Learning Disabilities Research and Practice, 12,* 114–123.

Rueda, R., Klingner, J. K., Sager, N., & Velasco, A. (2008). Reducing disproportionate representation in special education: Overview, explanations, and solutions. In T. C. Jiménez & V. L. Graf (Eds.), *Education for all: Critical issues in the education of children and youth with disabilities* (pp. 131–166). San Francisco: Jossey-Bass.

Rueda, R., Klingner, J., Sager, N., & Velasco, A. (2008). Reducing disproportionate representation in special education: Overview explanations, and solutions. In T. C. Jiménez, & V. L. Graf (Eds.), *Education for all: Critical issues in the education of children and youth with disabilities* (pp. 131–166). San Francisco: Jossey-Bass.

Ruiz, N. T. (1991). *Effective instruction for language minority students with mild disabilities* (ERIC Digest No. E499). Arlington, VA: ERIC Clearinghouse on Disabilities and Gifted Education, Council for Exceptional Children. Retrieved December 26, 2003, from http://ericec.org/digests/darchives/e499 .html

Rupley, W. H., Blair, T. R., & Nichols, W. D. (2009). Effective reading instruction for struggling readers: The role of direct/explicit teaching. *Reading and Writing Quarterly, 25*, 125–138.

Rutter, M. (2000). Genetic studies of autism: From the 1970s into the millennium. *Journal of Abnormal Child Psychology, 28*, 3–14.

Ryan, A. K., Kay, P. J., Fitzgerald, M., Paquette, S., & Smith, S. (2001). Kyle: A case study in parent–teacher action research. *Teaching Exceptional Children, 33*(3), 56–61.

Ryan, A. L., Halsey, H. N., & Matthews, W. J. (2003). Using functional assessment to promote desirable student behavior in schools. *Teaching Exceptional Children, 35*(5), 8–15.

Ryan, J. B., Peterson, R. L., & Rozalski, M. (2007). State policies concerning the use of seclusion timeout in schools. *Education and Treatment of Children, 30*, 215–239.

Ryan, S., & Ferguson, D. (2006). On, yet under, the radar: Students with fetal alcohol syndrome disorder. *Exceptional Children, 72*, 365–379.

Rylance, B. J. (1998). Predictors of post-high school employment for youth identified as severely emotionally disturbed. *Journal of Special Education, 32*, 184–192.

Ryndak, D. L., & Alper, S. (1996). *Curriculum content for students with moderate and severe disabilities in inclusive settings.* Boston: Allyn & Bacon.

Ryndak, D. L., & Alper, S. (2003). *Curriculum and instruction for students with significant disabilities in inclusive settings* (2nd ed.). Boston: Allyn & Bacon.

Ryndak, D. L., Downing, J. E., Jacqueline, L., & Morrison, A. M. (1995). Parents' perceptions after inclusion of their children with moderate or severe disabilities. *Journal of the Association for Persons with Severe Handicaps, 20*, 147–157.

Ryu, Y. H., Lee, J. D., Yoon, P. H., Kim, D. I., Lee, H. B., & Shin, Y. J. (1999). Perfusion impairments in infantile autism on technetium-99m ethyl cysteinate dimmer brain single-photon emission tomography: Comparison with findings on magnetic resonance imaging. *European Journal of Nuclear Medicine, 26*, 253–259.

Saalasti, S., Lepisto, T., Toppila, E., Kujala, T., Laakso, M., Nieminen-von Wendt, T., et al. (2008). Language abilities of children with Asperger syndrome. *Journal of Autism and Developmental Disorders, 38*, 1574–1580.

Sabornie, E. J., Evans, C., & Cullinan, D. (2006). Comparing characteristics of high-incidence disability groups: A descriptive review. *Remedial and Special Education, 27*, 95–104.

Sachs, H., & Barrett, R. P. (1995). Seizure disorders: A review for school psychologists. *School Psychology Review, 24*, 131–145.

Sachs, J. (1999). The hidden conspiracy in our nation's schools. *Behavioral Disorders, 25*, 80–82.

Sacks, S. Z., & Silberman, R. K. (2000). Social skills. In A. J. Koenig & M. C. Holbrook (Eds.), *Foundations of education: Instructional strategies for teaching children and youths with visual impairments* (2nd ed., pp. 616–652). New York: American Foundation for the Blind Press.

Sadker, M., & Sadker, D. (1994). *Failing at fairness: How America's schools cheat girls.* New York: Macmillan.

Sadler, C., & Sugai, G. (2009). Effective behavior and instructional support: A district model for early identification and prevention of reading and behavior problems. *Journal of Positive Behavior Interventions, 11*, 35–46.

Safford, P. L., & Safford, E. J. (1996). *A history of childhood and disability.* New York: Columbia University Teachers College Press.

Safran, S. P. (2008). Why youngsters with autism spectrum disorders remain underrepresented in special education. *Remedial and Special Education, 29*, 90–95.

Sailor, W., & Roger, B. (2005). Rethinking inclusion: Schoolwide applications. *Phi Delta Kappan, 86*, 503–509.

Salend, S. J. (1998). *Effective mainstreaming: Creating inclusive classrooms* (3rd ed.). Upper Saddle River, NJ: Merrill.

Salend, S. J. (2006). Explaining your inclusion program to families. *Teaching Exceptional Children, 38*(4), 6–11.

Salend, S. J., & Duhaney, L. M. (1999). The impact of inclusion on students with and without disabilities and their educators. *Remedial and Special Education, 20*, 114–126.

Salend, S. J., & Duhaney, L. M. (2005). Understanding and addressing the disproportionate representation of students of color in special education. *Intervention in School and Clinic, 40*, 213–221.

Salend, S. J., & Garrick-Duhaney, L. M. (2002). What do families have to say about inclusion?: How to pay attention and get results. *Teaching Exceptional Children, 35*(1), 622–666.

Salend, S. J., Gordon, J., & Lopez-Vona, K. (2002). Evaluating cooperative teaching teams. *Intervention in School and Clinic, 37*, 195–200.

Salend, S. J., & Rohena, E. (2003). Students with attention deficit disorders: An overview. *Intervention in School and Clinic, 38*, 259–266.

Salend, S. J., & Salinas, A. (2003). Language differences or learning difficulties. *Teaching Exceptional Children, 35*(4), 36–43.

Salisbury, C. L., & McGregor, G. (2002). The administrative climate and context of inclusive elementary schools. *Exceptional Children, 68*, 259–274.

Sall, N., & Mar, H. (1999). In the community of a classroom: Inclusive education of a student with deaf-blindness. *Journal of Visual Impairment and Blindness, 93*, 197–210.

Samson, J. F., & Lesaux, N. K. (2009). Language-minority learners in special education: Rates and predictors of identification for services. *Journal of Learning Disabilities, 42*, 148–162.

Samuels, C. A. (2008, September 12). Behavior disorders in teens are focus of new R & D effort. *Education Week, 28*(2), pp. 1–2.

Samuels, C. A. (2009, January). High schools try out RTI. *Education Week, 28*(19), 20–22.

Sanacore, J. (2008). Turning reluctant learners into inspired learners. *Clearing House: A Journal of Educational Strategies, Issues and Ideas, 82*(1), 40–44.

Sanchez Fowler, L. T., Banks, T. I., Anhalt, K., Hinrichs Der, H., & Kalis, T. (2008). The association between externalizing behavior problems, teacher–student relationship quality, and academic performance in young urban learners. *Behavioral Disorders, 33*, 167–183.

Sanders, W. L., & Horn, S. P. (1998). Research findings from the Tennessee Value-Added Assessment System (TVAAS) database: Implications for educational evaluation and research. *Journal of Personnel Evaluation in Education, 12*, 247–256.

Sandieson, R. (1998). A survey on terminology that refers to people with mental retardation/developmental disabilities. *Education and Training in Mental Retardation and Developmental Disabilities, 33*, 290–295.

Sandler, A. (1997). *Living with spina bifida: A guide for families and professionals.* Chapel Hill: University of North Carolina Press.

Sandler, A. G. (1998). Grandparents of children with disabilities: A closer look. *Education and Training in Mental Retardation and Developmental Disabilities, 33,* 350–356.

Sands, D., & Doll, B. (1996). Fostering self-determination is a developmental task. *Journal of Special Education, 30,* 58–76.

Sanford, J. A., & Turner, A. (1995). *Integrated Visual and Auditory Continuous Performance Test.* Richmond: BrainTrain.

Sanford, J. A., & Turner, A. (2006). *Integrated Visual and Auditory Continuous Performance Test+ PLUS.* Richmond: BrainTrain.

Sanger, D., Moore-Brown, B., & Alt, E. (2000). Advancing the discussion on communication and violence. *Communication Disorders Quarterly, 22,* 43–48.

Sanger, D., Moore-Brown, B. J., Montgomery, J. K., & Larson, V. L. (2002). Service delivery framework for adolescents with communication problems who are involved in violence. *Journal of Communication Disorders, 35,* 293–303.

Santangelo, T. (2009). Collaborative problem solving effectively implemented but not sustained: A case for aligning the sun, the moon and the stars. *Exceptional Children, 75*(2), 185–209.

Santos, M. (2002). From mystery to mainstream: Today's school-based speech-language pathologist. *Educational Horizons, 80,* 93–96.

Sapon-Shevin, M. (2003). Inclusion: A matter of social justice. *Educational Leadership, 61*(2), 25–28.

Sarason, S. B. (1982). *The culture of the school and the problem of change* (2nd ed.). Boston: Allyn & Bacon.

Sass-Lehrer, M. (2002, February). *Early beginnings for families with deaf and hard of hearing children: Myths and facts of early intervention and guidelines for effective services.* Retrieved January 11, 2003, from http://clerccenter2gallaudet.edu/KidsWorldDeafNet/e-docs/EI/index.html

Sasso, G., Garrison-Harrell, L., Mahon, C., & Peck, J. (1998). Social competence of individuals with autism: An applied behavior analysis perspective. In R. L. Simpson & B. S. Myles (Eds.), *Educating children and youth with autism: Strategies for effective practice* (pp. 173–190). Austin, TX: Pro-Ed.

Saunders, M. D. (2001). Who's getting the message? Helping your students understand in a verbal world. *Teaching Exceptional Children, 33*(4), 70–74.

Sawyer, K. (2007). *Group genius: The creative power of collaboration.* New York: Basic.

Sax, C., Pumpian, I., & Fisher, D. (1997, March). Assistive technology and inclusion. *Consortium on Inclusive Schooling Practices: Issue Brief,* 1–5.

Sayer, P. (2008). Demystifying language mixing: Spanglish in school. *Journal of Latinos and Education, 7,* 94–112.

Scanlon, D., Deshler, D. D., & Schumaker, J. B. (1996). Can a strategy be taught and learned in secondary inclusive classrooms? *Learning Disabilities Research and Practice, 11,* 41–57.

Scanlon, D., Gallego, M., Duran, G. Z., & Reyes, E. I. (2005). Interactive staff development supports collaboration when learning to teach. *Teacher Education and Special Education, 28,* 40–51.

Scanlon, D., & Mellard, D. F. (2002). Academic and participation profiles of school-age dropouts with and without disabilities. *Exceptional Children, 68,* 239–258.

Scattone, D. (2008). Enhancing the conversation skills of a boy with Asperger's disorder through social stories™ and video modeling. *Journal of Autism and Developmental Disorders, 38,* 395–400.

Scattone, D., Wilczynski, S. M., Edwards, R. P., & Rabian, B. (2002). Decreasing disruptive behaviors of children with autism using social stories. *Journal of Autism and Developmental Disorders, 32,* 535–543.

Schanzenbach, D. W. (2009). Do school lunches contribute to childhood obesity? *Journal of Human Resources, 44,* 684–709.

Schechtman, M. A. (2007). Scientifically unsupported therapies in the treatment of young children with autism spectrum disorders. *Pediatric Annals, 36,* 497–505.

Scheerenberger, R. C. (1983). *A history of mental retardation.* Baltimore: Paul H. Brookes.

Scheetz, N. A. (2001). *Orientation to deafness* (2nd ed.). Boston: Allyn & Bacon.

Schelvan, R., Swanson, T. C., & Smith, S. M. (2005). Making each year successful: Issues in transition. In B. S. Myles (Ed.), *Children and youth with Asperger syndrome: Strategies for success in inclusive settings.* Thousand Oaks, CA: Corwin.

Scheuermann, B., & Johns, B. (2002). Advocacy for students with emotional or behavioral disorders in the twenty-first century. *Behavioral Disorders, 28,* 57–69.

Scheuermann, B., & Webber, J. (2002a). Autism: Teaching DOES make a difference. *Education and Treatment of Children, 25,* 370–372.

Scheuermann, B., & Webber, J. (2002b). *Autism: Teaching does make a difference.* Stamford, CT: Wadsworth.

Schick, B., Williams, K., & Bolster, L. (1999). Skill levels of educational interpreters working in public schools. *Journal of Deaf Studies and Deaf Education, 4,* 144–155.

Schiff, R., Bauminger, N. & Toledo, I. (2009). Analogical problem solving in children with verbal and nonverbal learning disabilities. *Journal of Learning Disabilities, 42,* 3–13.

Schildroth, A. N., & Hotto, S. A. (1993). Annual survey of hearing impaired children and youth. *American Annals of the Deaf, 138*(2), 163–171.

Schilling, S. R., Sparfeldt, J. R., & Rost, D. H. (2006). Families with gifted adolescents. *Educational Psychology, 26,* 19–32.

Schirduan, V., & Case, K. I. (2001, April). *Mindful curriculum leadership for students with attention deficit hyperactivity disorder (ADHD): Leading in elementary schools by using multiple intelligences theory.* Paper presented at the annual meeting of the American Educational Research Association, Seattle, WA. (ERIC Document Reproduction Service No. ED456605)

Schirmer, B. R. (2001). *Psychological, social, and educational dimensions of deafness.* Boston: Allyn & Bacon.

Schirmer, B. R., Bailey, J., & Fitzgerald, S. M. (1999). Using a writing assessment rubric or writing development of children who are deaf. *Exceptional Children, 65,* 383–397.

Schmitz, M. F., & Velez, M. (2003). Latino cultural differences in maternal assessments of attention deficit/hyperactivity symptoms in children. *Hispanic Journal of Behavioral Sciences, 25,* 110–122.

Schneider, J. (2009). Besides Google: Guiding gifted elementary students onto the entrance ramp of the information superhighway. *Gifted Child Today, 32*(1), 27–31.

Schniedewind, N. (2005). "There ain't no white people here!": The transforming impact of teachers' racial consciousness on students and schools. *Equity and Excellence in Education, 38,* 280–289.

Schoenfeld, N. A., Rutherford, R. B., Gable, R. A, & Rock, M. C. (2008). ENGAGE: A blueprint for incorporating social skills training into daily academic instruction. *Preventing School Failure, 52*(3), 17–28.

Scholl, G. T. (1987). Appropriate education for visually handicapped students. *Teaching Exceptional Children, 19*(2), 33–36.

Schopler, E., Lansing, M., Reichler, R., & Marcus, L. (2005). *The Psychoeducational Profile, 3rd Edition (PEP 3).* Austin, TX: Pro-Ed.

Schopler, E., Reichler, R. F., Bashford, A., Lansing, M. D., & Marcus, L. M. (1990). *Psychoeducational Profile—Revised: Volume I.* Austin, TX: Pro-Ed.

Schore, A. N. (2000, June). *Parent–infant communication and the neurobiology of emotional development.* Paper presented at the Head State National Research Conference, Washington, DC. (ERIC Document Reproduction Service No. ED443546) Retrieved May 3, 2004, from www.edrs.com/Webstore/Download2.cfm?ID=468864&PleaseWait=OK

Schorr, E., Roth, F., & Fox, N. (2009). Quality of life for children with cochlear implants: Perceived benefits and problems and the perception of single words and emotional sounds. *Journal of Speech, Language, and Hearing Research, 52,* 141–152.

Schrag, J. A. (2000, October). *Discrepancy approaches for identifying learning disabilities* (Quick Turn Around Project Forum). Alexandria, VA: National Association of State Directors of Special Education. (ERIC Documentation Reproduction Service No. ED449595)

Schroedel, J. G., & Geyer, P. D. (2000). Long-term career attainments of deaf and hard of hearing college graduates: Results of a fifteen-year follow-up survey. *American Annals of the Deaf, 145*(4), 303–313.

Schroedel, J. G., & Watson, D. (1991). *Enhancing opportunities in postsecondary education for deaf students.* Little Rock: University of Arkansas Rehabilitation Research and Training Center on Deafness and Hearing Impairment.

Schroth, S. T., & Helfer, J. A. (2008). Identifying gifted students: Educator beliefs regarding various policies, processes, and procedures. *Journal for the Education of the Gifted, 32*, 155–179.

Schuck, S. E. B., & Crinella, F. M. (2005). Why children with ADHD do not have low IQs. *Journal of Learning Disabilities, 38*, 262–280.

Schuler, P. (2002). *Gifted kids at risk: Who's listening?* New York: Advocacy for Gifted and Talented Education in New York. Retrieved March 3, 2004, from http://washougalhicap.virtualave.net/gifted.htm

Schulte, A. C., & Osborne, S. S. (2003). When assumptive worlds collide: A review of definitions of collaboration in consultation. *Journal of Educational and Psychological Consultation, 14*, 109–138.

Schultz, B. K., Evans, S. W., & Serpell, Z. N. (2009). Preventing failure among middle school students with attention deficit/hyperactivity disorder: A survival analysis. *School Psychology Review, 38*, 14–27.

Schultz, R., Gauthier, I., Klin, A., Fulbright, R., Anderson, A., Volkmar, F., et al. (2000). Abnormal ventral temporal cortical activity during face discrimination among individuals with autism and Asperger's syndrome. *Archives of General Psychiatry, 57*, 331–340.

Schumaker, J. B., & Deshler, D. D. (2009). Adolescents with learning disabilities as writers: Are we selling them short? *Learning Disabilities Research and Practice, 24*, 81–92.

Schumm, J. S., Vaughn, S., & Harris, J. (1997). Pyramid power for collaborative planning. *Teaching Exceptional Children, 29*(6), 62–66.

Schwarte, A. (2008). Fragile X Syndrome. *School Psychology Quarterly, 23*(2), 290–300.

Schwartz, A. A., Jacobson, J. W., & Holburn, S. C. (2000). Defining person centeredness: Results of two consensus methods. *Education and Training in Mental Retardation and Developmental Disabilities, 35*, 235–249.

Schwartz, I. S., Randall, S. R., Garfinkle, A. N., & Bauer, J. (1998). Outcomes for children with autism: Three case studies. *Topics in Early Childhood Special Education, 18*, 132–143.

Schwartz, S. (2007). *Choices in deafness: A parent's guide to communication options* (3rd ed.). Bethseda, MD: Woodbine House.

Schwartz, S. (Ed.). (1996). *Choices in deafness: A parents' guide to communication options* (2nd ed.). Bethesda, MD: Woodbine House.

Schwarz, P. A. (2007). Special education: A service, not a sentence. *Educational Leadership, 64*(5), 39–42.

Schwiebert, V. L., Sealander, K. A., & Dennison, J. L. (2002). Strategies for counselors working with high school students with attention-deficit/hyperactivity disorder. *Journal of Counseling and Development, 80*, 3–10.

Sciutto, M. J., Terjesen, M. D., & Frank, A. S. B. (2000). Teachers' knowledge and misperceptions of attention-deficit/hyperactivity disorder. *Psychology in the Schools, 37*, 115–122.

Scott, F. J., Baron-Cohen, S., Bolton, P., & Brayne, C. (2002). Brief report: Prevalence of autism spectrum conditions in children aged five to eleven years in Cambridgeshire, UK. *Autism, 6*, 231–237.

Scott, S. S., McGuire, J. M., & Shaw, S. F. (2003). Universal design for instruction: A new paradigm for adult instruction in postsecondary education. *Remedial and Special Education, 24*, 369–379.

Scott, T. M., Anderson, C. M., & Spaulding, S. A. (2008). Strategies for developing and carrying out functional assessment and behavior intervention planning. *Preventing School Failure, 52*(3), 39–49.

Scotti, J. R., & Meyer, L. H. (1999). *Behavioral intervention: Principles, models, and practices.* Baltimore: Paul H. Brookes Publishing Co.

Scruggs, T. E., Mastropieri, M. A., & McDuffie, K. A. (2007). Co-teaching in inclusive classrooms: A metasynthesis of qualitative research. *Exceptional Children, 73*, 392–416.

Seal, B. C. (2004). *Educational interpreting: It's more than interpretation.* New York: Pearson.

Segers, E., & Verhoeven, L. (2004). Computer-supported phonological awareness intervention for kindergarten children with specific language impairment. *Language, Speech, and Hearing Services in Schools, 35*, 229–239.

Seidman, L. J. (2006). Neuropsychological functioning in people with ADHD across the lifespan. *Clinical Psychology Review, 26*, 466–485.

Seiffge-Krenke, I. (2001). *Diabetic adolescents and their families: Stress, coping, and adaptation.* New York: Cambridge University Press.

Seligman, M., & Darling, R. B. (2007). *Ordinary families, special children: A systems approach to childhood disability* (3rd ed.). New York: Guilford Publications.

Seligman, M., Goodwin, G., Paschal, K., Applegate, A., & Lehman, L. (1997). Grandparents of children with disabilities: Perceived levels of support. *Education and Training in Mental Retardation and Developmental Disabilities, 32*, 293–303.

Semel, E., Wiig, E. H., & Secord, W. A. (1995). *Clinical Evaluation of Language Fundamentals 3 (CELF-3).* San Antonio, TX: Psychological Corporation.

Semrud-Clikeman, M. (2005). Neuropsychological aspects for evaluating learning disabilities. *Communication Disorders Quarterly, 26*, 242–247.

Semrud-Clikeman, M., & Glass, K. (2008). Comprehension of humor in children with nonverbal learning disabilities, reading disabilities, and without learning disabilities. *Annals of Dyslexia, 58*, 163–180.

Sexson, S. B., & Madan-Swain, A. (1993). School reentry for the child with chronic illness. *Journal of Learning Disabilities, 26*, 115–125, 137.

Shames, G. H., & Anderson, N. B. (2002). *Human communication disorders: An introduction* (6th ed.). Boston: Allyn & Bacon.

Shames, G. H., & Anderson, N. B. (2006). *Human communication disorders: An introduction* (7th ed.). Boston: Allyn & Bacon.

Shapiro, D. R., Lieberman, L. J., & Moffett, A. (2003). Strategies to improve perceived competence in children with visual impairments. *RE:view, 35*, 69–80.

Shapiro, D. R., Moffett, A., Lieberman, L., & Dummer, G. M. (2005). Perceived competence of children with visual impairments. *Journal of Visual Impairment and Blindness, 99*, 15–25.

Shapiro, D. R., Moffett, A., Lieberman, L., & Dummer, G. M. (2008). Domain-specific ratings of importance and global self-worth of children with visual impairments. *Journal of Visual Impairment & Blindness, 102*, 232–244.

Shapiro, E. S., Miller, D. N., Sawka, K., Gardill, M. C., & Handler, M. W. (1999). Facilitating the inclusion of students with EBD into general education classrooms. *Journal of Emotional and Behavioral Disorders, 7*, 83–93.

Shapiro, J., & Rich, R. (1999). *Facing learning disabilities in the adult years.* New York: Oxford University Press.

Shapiro, L. R., Hurry, J., Masterson, J., Wydell, T. N., & Doctor, E. (2009). Classroom implications of recent research into literacy development: From predictors to assessment. *Dyslexia, 15*, 1–22.

Sharpe, M. N., York, J. L., & Knight, J. (1994). Effects of inclusion on the academic performance of classmates without disabilities. *Remedial and Special Education, 15*, 281–287.

Shaunessy, E. (2003). State policies regarding gifted education. *Gifted Child Today, 26*(3), 16–21, 65.

Shaywitz, B. A., Lyon, G. R., & Shaywitz, S. E. (2006). The role of functional magnetic resonance imaging in understanding reading the dyslexia. *Developmental Neuropsychology, 30,* 613–632.

Shaywitz, B. A., Pugh, K. R., Jenner, A. R., Fulbright, R. K., Fletcher, J. M., Gore, J. C., & Shaywitz, S. E. (2000). The neurobiology of reading and reading disability (dyslexia). In M. Kamil, P. Mosenthal, P. D. Pearson, & R. Barr (Eds.), *Handbook of reading research: Volume III* (pp. 229–249). Mahwah, NJ: Lawrence Erlbaum Associates.

Shaywitz, S. E. (2003). *Overcoming dyslexia: A new and complete science-based program for reading problems at any level.* New York: Random House.

Shaywitz, S. E., & Shaywitz, B. A. (2004). Reading disability and the brain. *Educational Leadership, 61*(6), 6–11.

Shea, T. M., & Bauer, A. M. (1993). *Parents and teachers of children with exceptionalities.* Boston: Allyn & Bacon.

Shelby, M. D., Nagle, R. J., Barnett-Queen, L. L., Quattlebaum, P. D., & Wuori, D. F. (1998). Parental reports of psychosocial adjustment and social competence in child survivors of acute lymphocytic leukemia. *Children's Health Care, 27,* 113–129.

Shepard, M. P., & Mahon, M. M. (2002). Family considerations. In L. L. Hayman, M. M. Mahon, & J. R. Turner (Eds.), *Chronic illness in children: An evidence-based approach* (pp. 143–170). New York: Springer.

Sheridan, S. M., Erchul, W. P., Brown, M. S., Dowd, S. E., Warnes, E. D. Marti, D. C., Schemm, A. V., & Eagle, J. W. (2004). Perceptions of helpfulness in conjoint behavioral consultation: Congruence and agreement between teachers and parents. *School Psychology Quarterly, 19,* 121–140.

Shields, J. D., Heron, T. E., Rubenstein, C. L., & Katz, E. R. (1995). The ecotriadic model of educational consultation for students with cancer. *Education and Treatment of Children, 18,* 184–200.

Shippen, M. E., Crites, S. A., Houchins, D. E., Ramsey, M. L., & Simon, M. (2005). Preservice teachers' perceptions of including students with disabilities. *Teacher Education and Special Education, 28,* 92–99.

Shogren, K. A., Faggella-Luby, M. N., Bae, S. J., & Wehmeyer, M. L. (2004). The effect of choice-making as an intervention for problem behavior: A meta-analysis. *Journal of Positive Behavior Interventions, 6*(4), 228–237.

Shriberg, L., Paul, R., McSweeny, J., Klin, A., Cohen, D., & Volkmar, F. (2001). Speech and prosody characteristics of adolescents and adults with high functioning autism and Asperger Syndrome. *Journal of Speech, Language, and Hearing Research, 44,* 1097–1115.

Siegel, L. (1999). Issues in the definition and diagnosis of learning disabilities: A perspective on *Guckenberger v. Boston University. Journal of Learning Disabilities, 32,* 304–319.

Siegel, L. (2000). *The educational and communication needs of deaf and hard of hearing children: A statement of principle regarding fundamental systematic educational changes.* Greenbrae, CA: National Deaf Education Project.

Siegel, L. S., & Smythe, I. S. (2005). Reflections on research on reading disability with special attention to gender issues. *Journal of Learning Disabilities, 38,* 473–477.

Siegel-Causey, E., & Allinder, R. M. (1998). Using alternative assessment for students with severe disabilities: Alignment with best practices. *Education and Training in Mental Retardation and Developmental Disabilities, 33,* 168–178.

Siegel-Causey, E., & Allinder, R. M. (2005). Review of assessment procedures for students with moderate and severe disabilities. *Education and Training in Developmental Disabilities, 40,* 343–351.

Siegle, D. (2005). Six uses of the internet to develop students' gifts and talents. *Gifted Child Today, 28*(2), 30–36.

Siegle, D., & McCoach, D. B. (2005). Making a difference: Motivating gifted students who are not achieving. *Teaching Exceptional Children, 38*(1), 22–27.

Silberman, R. K. (2000). Children and youth with visual impairments and other exceptionalities. In M. C. Holbrook & A. J. Koenig (eds.), *Foundations of education: History and theory of teaching children and youths with visual impairments* (2nd ed., pp. 173–196). New York: American Foundation for the Blind Press.

Sileo, N. M. (2005). Design HIV/AIDS prevention education: What are the roles and responsibilities of classroom teachers? *Intervention in School and Clinic, 40,* 177–181.

Sileo, T. W., Sileo, A. P., & Prater, M. A. (1996). Parent and professional partnerships in special education: Multicultural considerations. *Intervention in School and Clinic, 31,* 145–153.

Silva, M., Munk, D. D., & Bursuck, W. D. (2005). Grading adaptations for students with disabilities. *Intervention in School and Clinic, 41,* 87–98.

Silver, E. J., & Bauman, L. J. (2006). The association of sexual experience with attitudes, beliefs, and risk behaviors on inner-city adolescents. *Journal of Research on Adolescence, 16,* 29–45.

Silver, L. B. (1988). A review of the federal government's Interagency Committee on Learning Disabilities Report to the U.S. Congress. *Learning Disabilities Focus, 3,* 73–80.

Silver, L. B. (2004). Reading and learning disabilities [Briefing paper 17]. Washington, DC: National Dissemination Center for Children with Disabilities. Retrieved November 2, 2006, from www.nichcy.org/pubs/factshe/fs17txt.htm

Silverman, L. (1993). *Counseling the gifted and talented.* Denver, CO: Love.

Simeonsson, N., & Lorimer, M. (1995). Asthma: New information for the early interventionist. *Topics in Early Childhood Special Education, 15,* 32–43.

Simonton, D. K. (1999). *Origins of genius: Darwin perspectives on creativity.* New York: Oxford University Press.

Simpson, R. L. (2008). Children and youth with autism spectrum disorders: The search for effective methods. *Focus on Exceptional Children, 40*(7), 1–14.

Simpson, R. L., de Boer-Ott, S. R., & Smith-Myles, B. (2003). Inclusion of learners with autism spectrum disorders in general education settings. *Topics in Language Disorders, 23,* 116–33.

Simpson, R. L., McKee, M., Teeter, D., & Beytien, A. (2007). Evidence-based methods for children and youth with autism spectrum disorders: Stakeholder issues and perspectives. *Exceptionality, 15,* 203–217.

Simpson, R. L., & Myles, B. S. (1998). Understanding and responding to the needs of students with autism. In R. L. Simpson & B. S. Myles (Eds.), *Educating children and youth with autism: Strategies for effective practice* (pp. 1–24). Austin, TX: Pro-Ed.

Simpson, R. L., & Zionts, P. (2000). *Autism: Information and resources for professionals and parents* (2nd ed.). Austin, TX: Pro-Ed.

Sims, E. (2008). Sharing command of the co-teaching ship: How to play nicely with others. *English Journal, 97*(5), 58–63.

Sinedlar, P. T., Bishop, A. G., Gill, M. G., Connelly, V., & Rosenberg, M. S. (2007). Getting teachers where they're needed most: The case for licensure reciprocity. *Teacher Education and Special Education, 30,* 47–58.

Sindelar, P. T., Shearer, D. K., Yendol-Hoppey, D., & Liebert, T. W. (2006). The sustainability of inclusive school reform. *Exceptional Children, 72,* 317–331.

Sindelar, P. T., Shearer, D. K., Yendol-Hoppey, D., & Liebert, T. W. (2006). The sustainability of inclusive school reform. *Exceptional Children, 72,* 317–331.

Singer, B. D. (1995). Development and disorders: Selected principles, patterns, and intervention possibilities. *Topics in Language Disorders, 16*(1), 83–98.

Singer, G. H. S. (2002). Suggestions for a pragmatic program of research on families and disability. *Journal of Special Education, 36,* 148–154.

Singer, G. H. S., & Irvin, L. K. (1989). Family caregiving, stress, and support. In G. H. S. Singer & L. K. Irvin (Eds.), *Support for caregiving families: Enabling positive adaptations to disability* (pp. 3–25). Baltimore: Paul H. Brookes.

Singh, D. K. (2000, October). *Families of children with mental retardation: Effective collaboration.* Paper presented at the Biennial Meeting of the Division on Mental Retardation and Developmental Disabilities, Baltimore, MD. (ERIC Document Reproduction Service No. ED455636)

Singh, D. K. (2002). Regular educators and students with physical disabilities. *Education, 123*(2), 236–246.

Singh, D. K. (2003). Families of children with spina bifida: A review. *Journal of Developmental and Physical Disabilities, 15*(1), 37–55.

Skiba, R. J. (2002). Special education and school discipline: A precarious balance. *Behavioral Disorders, 27,* 81–97.

Skiba, R. J., Poloni-Staudinger, L., Simmons, A. B., Feggins-Azziz, L. R., & Chung, C. G. (2005). Unproven links: Can poverty explain ethnic disproportionality in special education? *Journal of Special Education, 39,* 130–144.

Skiba, R. J., Simmons, A. B., Ritter, S., Gibb, A. C., Rausch, M. K., Cuadrado, J., & Chung, C. G. (2008). Achieving equity in special education: History, status, and current challenges. *Exceptional Children, 74,* 264–288.

Skiba, R., Poloni-Studinger, L., Gallini, S., Simmons, A., & Feggins-Azziz, R. (2006). Disparate access: The disproportionality of African American students with disabilities across educational environments. *Exceptional Children, 72,* 411–424.

Skiba, R., Simmons, A., Ritter, S., Kohler K., Henderson, M., & Wu, T. (2006). The context of minority disproportionality: Practitioner perspectives on special education referral. *Teachers College Record, 108,* 1424–1459.

Sleeter, C. E. (2001). Preparing teachers for culturally diverse schools: Research and the overwhelming presence of whiteness. *Journal of Teacher Education, 52,* 94–106.

Slomine, B. S., Salorio, C. F., Grados, M. A., Vasa, R. A., Christensen, J. R., & Gerring, J. P. (2005). Differences in attention, executive functioning, and memory in children with and without ADHD after severe traumatic brain injury. *Journal of the International Neuropsychological Society, 11,* 645–653.

Slomkowski, C., Klein, R. G., & Mannuzza, S. (1995). Is self-esteem an important outcome in hyperactive children? *Journal of Abnormal Child Psychology, 23,* 303–315.

Smith, A. (2006). Access, participation, and progress in the general education curriculum in the least restrictive environment for students with significant cognitive disabilities. *Research and Practice for Persons with Severe Disabilities, 31,* 331–337.

Smith, C. J., Lang, C. M., Kryzak, L., Reichenberg, A., Hollander, E., & Silverman, J. M. (2009). Familial associations of intense preoccupations, an empirical factor of the restricted, repetitive behaviors and interests domain of autism. *Journal of Child Psychology and Psychiatry, 50,* 982–990.

Smith, C. M. M. (2006). *Including the gifted and talented: Making inclusion work for gifted and able learners.* New York: Routledge.

Smith, C. R. (1998). History, definitions, and prevalence. In *Learning disabilities: The interaction of learner, task, and setting* (4th ed., pp. 1–51). Boston: Allyn & Bacon.

Smith, C. R. (2004). *Learning disabilities: The interaction of learner, task and setting* (5th ed.). Boston: Allyn & Bacon.

Smith, D., Wilson, B., & Corbett, D. (2009). Moving beyond talk. *Educational Leadership, 66*(5), 20–25.

Smith, D. W., & Kelly, P. (2007). A survey of assistive technology and teacher preparation programs for individuals with visual impairments. *Journal of Visual Impairment and Blindness, 101,* 429–433.

Smith, J. D. (1985). *Minds made feeble: The myth and legacy of the Kallikaks.* New York: Aspen.

Smith, J. D. (2000). The power of mental retardation: Reflections on the value of people with disabilities. *Mental Retardation, 38,* 70–72.

Smith, J. D. (2003, Fall). Granting Monty's wish: From mental retardation to developmental disabilities. *DDD Express, 14*(1), 4.

Smith, J. D., & Polloway, E. A. (2008). Defining disability up and down: The problem of "normality." *Intellectual and Developmental Disabilities, 46,* 234–238.

Smith, S. (2002). Teaching mentoring and collaboration. *Journal of Special Education Technology, 17*(1), 47–48.

Smith, S. D., Pennington, B. F., Boada, R., & Shriberg, L. D. (2005). Linkage of speech sound disorder to reading disability loci. *Journal of Child Psychology and Psychiatry, 46,* 1057–1066.

Smith, S. J., Jordan, L., Corbett, N. L., & Dillon, A. S. (1999). Teachers learn about ADHD on the Web: An online graduate special education course. *Teaching Exceptional Children, 31*(6), 20–27.

Smith, S. M., & Tyler, J. S. (1997). Successful transition planning and services for students with ABI. In A. Glang, G. H. S. Singer, & B. Todis (Eds.), *Students with acquired brain injury: The school's response* (pp. 185–200). Baltimore: Paul H. Brookes.

Smith, S. W. (2001, June). *Involving parents in the IEP process* [ERIC Digest E611]. Arlington, VA: ERIC Clearinghouse on Disabilities and Gifted Education, Council for Exceptional Children. (ERIC Document Reproduction Service No. ED455658)

Smith, T., Groen, A. D., & Wynn, J. W. (2000). Randomized trial of intensive early intervention for children with pervasive developmental disorder. *American Journal on Mental Retardation, 105,* 269–285.

Smith, T. E. C. (2001). Section 504, the ADA, and public schools. *Remedial and Special Education, 22,* 335–343.

Smith, T. E. C. (2002). Section 504: What teachers need to know. *Intervention in School and Clinic, 37,* 259–266.

Smith, T. E. C. (2005). IDEA 2004: Another round in the reauthorization process. *Remedial and Special Education, 26,* 314–319.

Smith, T. E. C., Dowdy, C. A., Polloway, E. A., & Blalock, G. E. (1997). *Children and adults with learning disabilities.* Boston: Allyn & Bacon.

Sneed, R. C., May, W. L., & Stencel, C. S. (2000). Training of pediatricians in care of physical disabilities in children with special health needs: Results of a two-state survey of practicing pediatricians and national resident training programs. *Pediatrics, 105*(3), 554.

Snell, M. E. (2002). Using dynamic assessment with learners who communicate nonsymbolically. *Augmentative and Alternative Communication, 18,* 163–176.

Snell, M. E., & Janney, R. E. (2000). Teachers' problem-solving about children with moderate and severe disabilities in elementary classrooms. *Exceptional Children, 66,* 472–490.

Snell, M. S., & Janney, R. (2005). *Collaborative teaming* (2nd ed.). Baltimore: Paul H. Brookes.

Snider, B. D. (Ed.). (1995). *Conference proceedings: Inclusion? Defining quality education for deaf and hard-of-hearing students.* Washington, DC: College for Continuing Education, Gallaudet University.

Snider, V. E., Busch, T., & Arrowood, L. (2003). Teacher knowledge of stimulant medication and ADHD. *Remedial and Special Education, 24,* 46–56.

Snow, C. E., Burns, M. S., & Griffin, P. C. (1998). *Preventing reading difficulties in young children.* Washington, DC: National Academy Press.

Snow, P. C., & Powell, M. B. (2004). Developmental language disorders and adolescent risk: A public-health advocacy role for speech pathologists? *Advances in Speech Language Pathology, 6,* 221–229.

Snyder, E. P. (2002). Teaching students with combined behavioral disorders and mental retardation to lead their own IEP meetings. *Behavioral Disorders, 27,* 340–357.

Snyder, H. (2008, November). Juvenile arrests 2006. *OJJDP Bulletin.* Washington, D.C.: U.S. Department of Justice. Retrieved July 10, 2009 from http://www.ojjdp.ncjrs.gov/publications/PubResults.asp#2008

Snyder, H. N. (2005). Juvenile arrests 2003. *Juvenile Justice Bulletin.* Washington, DC: Office of Juvenile Justice and Delinquency Prevention, U.S. Department of Justice. Retrieved October 24, 2006, from www.ncjrs.gov/pdffiles1/ojjdp/209735.pdf

Snyder, H. N., & Sickmund, M. (1999). *Challenging the myths: 1999 national report series: Juvenile justice bulletin* [ED 4544351]. Retrieved September 10, 2003, from www.edrs.com/members/sp.cfm?AN=ED454351

Snyder, L. S., & Downey, D. S. (1997). Developmental differences in the relationship between oral language deficits and reading. *Topics in Language Disorders, 17*(3), 27–40.

Sobel, D. M., & Taylor, S. V. (2006). Blueprint for the responsive classroom. *Teaching Exceptional Children, 38*(5), 28–35.

Social Security Administration. (2004). *Annual statistical report on the social security disability insurance program.* Washington, DC: Author.

Society for Neuroscience. (2006, February). Reading failure. *Brain Briefings.* Retrieved November 10, 2006, from www.sfn.org/index.cfm?pagename= brainBriefings_reading_failure

Solomon, O. (2008). Language, autism, and childhood: An ethnographic perspective. *Annual Review of Applied Linguistics, 28,* 150–169.

Sowell, E., Peterson, B., Thompson, P., Welcome, S., Henkenius, A., & Toga, A. (2003). Mapping cortical changes across the human life span. *Nature Neuroscience, 6,* 309–315.

Sowell, E. R., Thompson, P. M., Welcome, S. E., Henkenius, A. L., Toga, A. W., & Peterson, B. S. (2003). Cortical abnormalities in children and adolescents with attention-deficit hyperactivity disorder. *Lancet, 362,* 1699–1707.

Sparrow, S. S., Balla, D. A., & Cicchetti, D. (1985). *Vineland Adaptive Behavior Scales (classroom edition).* Minneapolis: Pearson Assessments.

Sparrow, S., Balla, D., & Cicchetti, D. (2005). *Vineland adaptive behavior scales* (2nd ed.). Bloomington, MN: American Guidance Services.

Speece, D. L. (2005). Hitting the moving target known as reading development: Some thoughts on screening children for secondary interventions. *Journal of Learning Disabilities, 38,* 487–493.

Speechville. (2009, August). *SLP caseloads by state.* Retrieved August 20, 2009 from http://www.speechville.com/advocacy-depot/caseloads-state.html

Spencer, V. G., & Balboni, G. (2003). Can students with mental retardation teach their peers? *Education and Training in Mental Retardation and Developmental Disabilities, 38,* 32–61.

Sperling, R. A. (2006). Assessing reading materials for students who are learning disabled. *Intervention in School and Clinic, 41,* 138–143.

Spiegel, G. L., & Cutler, S. K. (1996). What every teacher should know about epilepsy. *Intervention in School and Clinic, 32*(1), 34–39.

Spiegel, H. M. L., & Bonwit, A. M. (2002). HIV infection in children. In M. L. Batshaw (Ed.), *Children with disabilities* (5th ed., pp. 123–140). Baltimore: Paul H. Brookes.

Spina Bifida Association of America. (2003). *Folic acid information.* Retrieved March 9, 2004, from www.sbaa.org/html/sbaa_folic.html

Spina Bifida Association of Canada. (1996). *Students with spina bifida and/or hydrocephalus: A guide for educators.* Winnipeg, Manitoba: Author.

Spina Bifida Association. (2009). *Folic acid.* Washington, D.C.: Author. Retrieved September 3, 2009 from http://www.spinabifidaassociation.org/ site/c.liKWL7PLLrF/b.2700277/k.2112/Folic_Acid.htm

Spooner, L. (2002). Addressing expressive language disorder in children who also have severe receptive language disorder: A psycholinguistic approach. *Child Language Teaching and Therapy, 18,* 289–313.

Sprague, J., Walker, H., Golly, A., White, K., Myers, D. R., & Shannon, T. (2001). Translating research into effective practice: The effects of a universal staff and student intervention on indicators of discipline and school safety. *Education and Treatment of Children, 24,* 495–511.

Spungin, S. (Ed.). (2002). *When you have a visually impaired student in your classroom: A guide for teachers* (pp. 72–74). New York: American Foundation for the Blind Press.

Spungin, S. J., & Ferrell, K. A. (1999). The role and function of the teacher of students with visual handicaps. In G. S. Pugh & J. Erin (Eds.), *Blind and visually impaired students: Educational service guidelines.* Watertown, MA: Perkins School for the Blind.

Stambaugh, L. F., Mustillo, S. A., Bruns, B. J., Stephens, R. L., Baxter, B., Edwards, D., & DeKraai, M. (2007). Outcomes from wraparound and multisystemic therapy in a center for mental health services system-of-care

demonstration site. *Journal of Emotional and Behavioral Disorders, 15,* 143–153.

Stanley, J. C. (2005). A quiet revolution: Finding boys and girls who reason exceptionally well and/or verbally and helping them get the supplemental educational opportunities they need. *High Ability Studies, 16,* 5–14.

Stanley, J. C., Keating, D. P., & Fox, L. (1974). *Mathematical talent: Discovery, description, and development.* Baltimore: Johns Hopkins University Press.

Stanovich, K., & Siegel, L. S. (1994). Phenotypic performance profile of children with reading disabilities: A regression-based test of the phonological-core variable-difference model. *Journal of Educational Psychology, 86,* 24–53.

Starkweather, C. W. (2002). The epigenesist of stuttering. *Journal of Fluency Disorders, 27,* 269–288.

Starr, E., Szatmari, P., Bryson, S., & Zwaigenbaum, L. (2003). Stability and change among high-functioning children with pervasive developmental disorders: A 2-year outcome study. *Journal of Autism and Developmental Disorders, 33,* 15–22.

Starr, E. M., Foy, J. B., Cramer, K. M., & Singh, H. (2006). How are schools doing? Parental perceptions of children with autism spectrum disorders, Down syndrome, and learning disabilities: A comparative analysis. *Education and Training in Developmental Disabilities, 41,* 315–332.

Staub, D., Spaulding, M., Peck, C. A., Gallucci, C., & Schwartz, I. S. (1996). Using nondisabled peers to support the inclusion of students with disabilities at the junior high school level. *Journal of the Association for Persons with Severe Handicaps, 21,* 194–205.

Stecker, P. M., Lembke, E. S., & Foegen, A. (2008). Using progress-monitoring data to improve instructional decision making. *Preventing School Failure, 52*(2), 48–58.

Steere, D. E., & Cavaiuolo, D. (2002). Connecting outcomes, goals, and objectives in transition planning. *Teaching Exceptional Children, 34*(6), 54–59.

Stein, L., Jabaley, T., Spitz, R., Stoakley, D., & McGee, T. (1990). The hearing-impaired infant: Patterns of identification and habilitation revisited. *Ear and Hearing, 11,* 201–205.

Stein, M., Carnine, D., & Dixon, R. (1998). Direct instruction: Integrating curriculum design and effective teaching practice. *Intervention in School and Clinic, 33,* 227–233.

Steinberg, A., Bain, L., Yuelin, L., Montoya, L., & Ruperto, V. (2002, March). *A look at the decisions Hispanic families make after the diagnosis of deafness.* (ERIC Document Reproduction Service No. ED472086) Retrieved May 3, 2004, from www.edrs.com/Webstore/Download2.cfm?ID=721579

Steinman, B. A., LeJeune, B. J., & Kimbrough, B. T. (2006). Developmental stages of reading processes in children who are blind and sighted. *Journal of Visual Impairment and Blindness, 100,* 36–46.

Steinweg, S. B., Griffin, H. C., Griffin, L. W., & Gingras, H. (2005). Retinopathy of prematurity. *RE:view, 37,* 32–41.

Stephen, V. P., Varble, M. E., & Taitt, H. (1993). Instructional strategies for minority youth. *Clearing House, 67,* 116–120.

Stephens, K. R., & Karnes, F. A. (2000). State definitions for the gifted and talented revisited. *Exceptional Children, 66,* 219–238.

Sternberg, R. J. (1985). *Beyond IQ.* New York: Basic Books.

Sternberg, R. J., & Zhang, L. (1995). What do we mean by giftedness? A pentagonal implicit theory. *Gifted Child Quarterly, 39,* 88–94.

Stewart, D., & Kluwin, T. N. (2001). *Teaching deaf and hard of hearing students: Content, strategies, and curriculum.* Boston: Allyn & Bacon.

Stewart, R. (2001). Essential components of community living: A life span approach. *Indiana Resource Center for Autism Reporter, 5*(1), 18–27.

Stewart-Scott, A. M., & Douglas, J. M. (1998). Educational outcome for secondary and postsecondary students following traumatic brain injury. *Brain Injury, 12,* 317–331.

Stinson, M. S., & Kluwin, T. N. (1996). Social orientations toward deaf and hearing peers among deaf adolescents in local public high schools. In P. C. Higgins & J. E. Nash (Eds.), *Understanding deafness socially: Continuities in* research and theory (2nd ed). (pp. 113–134). Springfield, IL: Charles C. Thomas.

Stinson, M. S., & Liu, Y. (1999). Participation of deaf and hard-of-hearing students in classes with hearing students. *Journal of Deaf Studies and Deaf Education, 4*(3), 191–202.

Stinson, M. S., & McKee, B. (Eds.). (2000). *Development and evaluation of a computer-aided speech-to-print transcription system.* Rochester, NY: National Technical Institute for the Deaf.

Stivers, J. (2008). Strengthen your co-teaching relationship. *Intervention in School and Clinic, 44,* 121–125.

Stodden, R. A., Galloway, L. M., & Stodden, M. J. (2003). Secondary school curricula issues: Impact on postsecondary students with disabilities. *Exceptional Children, 70,* 9–25.

Stoneman, Z., & Gavidia-Payne, S. (2006). Marital adjustment in families of young children with disabilities: Associations with daily hassles and problem-focused coping. *American Journal on Mental Retardation. 3,* 1–14.

Stormont, M. (2001). Social outcomes of children with AD/HD: Contributing factors and implications for practice. *Psychology in the Schools, 38,* 521–531.

Stormont, M. (2008). Increase academic success for children with ADHD using sticky notes and highlighters. *Intervention in School and Clinic, 43,* 305–308.

Stormont, M., & Stebbins, M. (2005) Preschool teachers' knowledge, opinions and educational experiences with attention deficit/hyperactivity disorder. *Teacher Education and Special Education, 28,* 52–61.

Strassman, B. K. (1992). Deaf adolescents' metacognitive knowledge about school-related reading. *American Annals of the Deaf, 137,* 326–330.

Stratton, K., Gable, A., Shetty, P., & McCormick, M. C. (Eds.). (2001). *Immunization safety review: Measles-mumps-rubella vaccine and autism.* Washington, DC: National Academy Press.

Strauss, A., & Lehtinen, L. (1947). *Psychopathology and education of the brain-injured child.* New York: Grune & Stratton.

Stringaris, A., & Goodman, R. (2009). Three dimensions of oppositionality in youth. *Journal of Child Psychology and Psychiatry, 50,* 216–223.

Stronge, J. H., & Tucker, P. D. (2000). *Teacher evaluation and student achievement* [Student assessment series]. Washington, DC: National Education Association. (ERIC Document Reproduction Service No. ED460074) Retrieved July 25, 2003, from www.edrs.com/members/sp.cfm?AN= ED460075

Stroul, B. A. (1996). *Children's mental health: Creating systems of care in a changing society.* Baltimore: Paul H. Brookes.

Stuart, M. E., Lieberman, L., & Hand, K. E. (2006). Beliefs about physical activity among children who are visually impaired and their parents. *Journal of Visual Impairment and Blindness, 100,* 223–234.

Stuebing, K. K., Fletcher, J. M., LeDoux, J. M., Lyon, G. R., Shaywitz, S. E., & Shaywitz, B. A. (2002). Validity of IQ-discrepancy classifications of reading disabilities: A meta-analysis. *American Educational Research Journal, 39,* 469–518.

Stumbo, N. J., Martin, J. K., & Hedrick, B. N. (2009). Personal assistance for students with severe physical disabilities in post-secondary education: Is it the deal breaker? *Journal of Vocational Rehabilitation, 30,* 11–20.

Suarez, S. C., & Daniels, K. J. (2009). Listening for competence through documentation: Assess children with language delays using digital video. *Remedial and Special Education, 30,* 177–190.

Subedi, B. (2006). Preservice teachers' beliefs and practices: Religion and religious diversity. *Equity and Excellence in Education, 39,* 227–238.

Substance Abuse and Mental Health Services Administration. (2003). *Children's mental health facts and adolescents with mental, emotional, and behavioral disorders.* Washington, D. C.: U.S. Department of Health and Human Services. Retrieved July 7, 2009 from http://mentalhealth.samhsa.gov/publications/allpubs/CA-0006/default.asp

Sullivan, N. A., Fulmer, D. L., & Zigmond, N. (2001). School: The normalizing factor for children with childhood leukemia. *Preventing School Failure, 46,* 4–13.

Sullivan, P. F. (2005). The genetics of schizophrenia. *PLoS Medicine, 2*(7), 212.

Summers, J. A., Hoffman, L., Marquis, J., Turnbull, A., Poston, D., & Nelson, L. L. (2005). Measuring the quality of family-professional partnerships in special education services. *Exceptional Children, 72,* 63–81.

Sunderland, L. C. (2004). Speech, language, and audiology services in public schools. *Intervention in School and Clinic, 39,* 209–217.

Sutherland, K. S., Wehby, J. H., & Gunter, P. L. (2000). The effectiveness of cooperative learning with students with emotional and behavioral disorders: A literature review. *Behavioral Disorders, 25,* 225–238.

Suvak, P. A. (2004). What do they really do? Activities of teachers of students with visual impairments. *RE:view, 36,* 22–31.

Svirsky, M. A., Robbins, A. M., Kirk, K. I., Pisoni, D. B., & Miyamoto, R. T. (2000). Language development in profoundly deaf children with cochlear implants. *Psychological Science, 11,* 153–158.

Swaggart, B. L., Gagnon, E., Bock, S. J., Quinn, C., Myles, B. S., & Simpson, R. L. (1995). Using social stories to teach social and behavioral skills to children with autism. *Focus on Autistic Behavior, 10,* 1–16.

Swanson, E. A. (2008). Observing reading instruction for students with learning disabilities: A synthesis. *Learning Disability Quarterly, 31,* 115–133.

Swanson, H. L. (1999). Reading research for students with LD: A meta-analysis of intervention outcomes. *Journal of Learning Disabilities, 32,* 504–532.

Swanson, H. L. (2000a). Are working memory deficits in readers with learning disabilities hard to change? *Journal of Learning Disabilities, 33,* 551–566.

Swanson, H. L. (2000b). Issues facing the field of learning disabilities. *Learning Disability Quarterly, 23,* 37–51.

Swanson, H. L. (2000c). What instruction works for students with learning disabilities? Summarizing the results from a meta-analysis of intervention studies. In R. Gersten, E. Schiller, & S. Vaughn (Eds.), *Contemporary special education research: Syntheses of the knowledge base on critical instructional issues.* Mahwah, NJ: Lawrence Erlbaum.

Swanson, H. L. (2001). Searching for the best model for instructing students with learning disabilities. *Focus on Exceptional Children, 34*(2), 1–15.

Swanson, H. L., & Hoskyn, M. (1998). Experimental intervention research on students with learning disabilities: A meta-analysis of treatment outcomes. *Review of Educational Research, 68,* 277–321.

Swanson, H. L., & Jerman, O. (2006). Math disabilities: A selective meta-analysis of the literature. *Review of Educational Research, 76,* 249–274.

Swanson, H. L., Zheng, X., & Jerman, O. (2009). Working memory, short-term memory, and reading disabilities: A selective meta-analysis of the literature. *Journal of Learning Disabilities, 42,* 260–287.

Swanson, J. M., Flodman, P., Kennedy, J., Spence, M. A., Moyzis, R., Schuck, S., Murias, M., Moriarity, J., Barr, C., Smith, M., & Posner, M. (2000). Dopamine genes and ADHD. *Neuroscience Biobehavioral Review, 24,* 21–25.

Swanson, J., Arnold, L. E., Kraemer, H., Hechtman, L., Molina, B., Hinshaw, S., Vitiello, B., Jensen, P., Steinhoff, K., Lerner, M., Greenhill, L., Abikoff, H., Wells, K., Epstein, J., Elliott, G., Newcorn, J., Hoza, B., & Wigal, T. (2008). Evidence, interpretation, and qualification from multiple reports of long-term outcomes in the multimodal treatment study of children with ADHD (MTA): Part I—executive summary. *Journal of Attention Disorders, 12,* 4–14.

Swanson, M. (2002). *National survey on the state governance of K–12 gifted and talented education: Summary report.* Retrieved February 27, 2004, from www.edrs.com/members/sp.cfm?AN=ED471886

Swanson, T. J., Hodson, B. W., & Schommer-Aikins, M. (2005). An examination of phonological awareness treatment outcomes for seventh-grade poor readers from a bilingual community. *Language, Speech, and Hearing Services in Schools, 36,* 336–345.

Swenson, N. C. (2000). Comparing traditional and collaborative settings for language intervention. *Communication Disorders Quarterly, 22,* 12–18.

Swinth, Y., Chandler, B., & Hanft, B. (2004). Occupational therapy in school-based settings. *Journal of Special Education Leadership, 17*(1), 16–25.

Switsky, H. N., & Greenspan, S. (Eds.). (2006). *What is mental retardation? Ideas for an evolving disability in the 21st century.* Washington, D.C.: American Association on Mental Retardation.

Symons, F. J., Clark, R. D., Roberts, J. P., & Bailey, D. B. (2001). Classroom behavior of elementary school-age boys with Fragile X syndrome. *Journal of Special Education, 34,* 194–202.

Szatmari, P., Jones, M. B., Zwaigenbaum, L., & MacLean, J. E. (1998). Genetics of autism: Overview and new directions. *Journal of Autism and Developmental Disorders, 28,* 351–368.

Sze, S., & Valentin, S. (2007). Self-concept and children with disabilities. *Education, 127,* 552–557.

Tabassam, W., & Grainger, J. (2002). Self-concept, attributional styles and self-efficacy beliefs of students with learning disabilities with and without attention deficit hyperactivity disorder. *Learning Disability Quarterly, 25,* 141–151.

Tager-Flusberg, H., Rogers, S., Cooper, J., Landa, R., Lord, C., & Paul, R. (2009). Defining spoken language benchmarks and selecting measures of expressive language development for young children with autism spectrum disorders. *Journal of Speech, Language, and Hearing Research, 52,* 643–652.

Tannenbaum, A. J. (2000). A history of giftedness in school and society. In K. A. Heller, F. J. Monks, R. J. Sternberg, & R. F. Subotnik (Eds.), *International encyclopedia of giftedness and talent.* Amsterdam: Elsevier.

Tannock, M. T. (2009). Tangible and intangible elements of collaborative teaching. *Intervention in School and Clinic, 44,* 173–178.

Tannock, R., & Martinussen, R. (2001). Reconceptualizing ADHD. *Educational Leadership, 59*(3), 20–25.

Taras, H., & Potts-Datema, W. (2005). Childhood asthma and student performance at school. *Journal of School Health, 75,* 296–312.

Taras, H., & Potts-Datema, W. (2005). Chronic health conditions and student performance at school. *Journal of School Health, 75,* 255–290.

Tarquin, P., & Walker, S. (1997). *Creating success in the classroom: Visual organizers and how to use them.* Englewood, CO: Teacher Ideas Press.

TASH. (2000). *TASH resolution on the people for whom TASH advocates.* Retrieved January 20, 2003, from www.tash.org/resolutions/res02advocate.htm

Taub, D. J. (2006). Understanding the concerns of parents of students with disabilities: Challenges and roles for school counselors. *Professional School Counseling, 10,* 52–57.

Taunt, H. M., & Hastings, R. P. (2002). Positive impact of children with developmental disabilities on their families: A preliminary study. *Education and Training in Mental Retardation and Developmental Disabilities, 37,* 410–420.

Taylor, J. A., & Baker, R. A. (2002). Discipline and special education students. *Educational Leadership, 59*(4), 28–30.

Taylor-Richardson, K. D., Heflinger, C. A., & Brown, T. N. (2006). Experience of strain among types of caregivers responsible for children with serious emotional and behavioral disorders. *Journal of Emotional and Behavioral Disorders, 14,* 157–168.

Telzrow, C. F., & Bonar, A. M. (2002). Responding to students with nonverbal learning disabilities. *Teaching Exceptional Children, 34*(6), 8–13.

Tennison, A. D. (2007). Promoting equity in mathematics: One teacher's journey. *Mathematics Teacher, 101*(1), 28–31.

Terman, L. M., & Oden, M. (1959). *The gifted group at mid-life.* Stanford, CA: Stanford University Press.

Test, D. W., Browder, D. M., Karvonen, M., Wood, W., & Algozzine, B. (2002). Writing lesson plans for promoting self-determination. *Teaching Exceptional Children, 35*(1), 8–14.

Test, D. W., Fowler, C. H., White, J., Richter, S., & Walker, A. (2009). Evidence-based secondary transition practices for enhancing school completion. *Exceptionality, 17*(1), 16–29.

Test, D. W., Mason, C., Hughes, C., Konrad, M., Neale, M., & Wood, W. M. (2004). Student involvement in individualized education program meetings. *Exceptional Children, 70,* 391–214.

Test, D., W., Fowler, C. H., White, J., Richter, S., & Walker, A. (2009). Evidence-based secondary transition practices for enhancing school completion. *Exceptionality, 17,* 16–29.

Tharp, R., & Wetzel, R. (1969). *Behavior modification in the natural environment.* New York: Academic Press.

Therrien, S. J., & Kubiana, R. M. (2006). Developing reading fluency with repeated reading. *Intervention in School and Clinic, 41,* 156–160.

Thoma, C. A., Rogan, P., & Baker, S. R. (2001). Student involvement in transition planning: Unheard voices. *Education and Training in Mental Retardation and Developmental Disabilities, 36,* 16–29.

Thomas, D. D. (2004). Use transportation as a related service. *Intervention in School and Clinic, 39,* 240–245.

Thomas-Stonell, N., Oddson, B., Robertson, B., & Rosenbaum, P. (2009). Predicted and observed outcomes in preschool children following speech and language treatment: Parent and clinician perspectives. *Journal of Communication Disorders, 42,* 29–42.

Thompson, R. J., Armstrong, F. D., Link, C. L., Pegelow, C. H., Moser, F., & Wang, W. C. (2003). A prospective study of the relationship over time of behavior problems, intellectual functioning, and family functioning in children with sickle cell disease: A report from the cooperative study of sickle cell disease. *Journal of Pediatric Psychology, 28,* 59–65.

Thorp, W. N. (2002). Special needs—Special plans: Estate planning considerations for attorneys representing families with members with disabilities. *Journal of Disability Policy Studies, 13,* 24–50.

Thousand Oaks, CA: Corwin Press. Downing, J. E. (2008). *Including students with severe and multiple disabilities in typical classrooms: Practical strategies for teachers* (3rd ed.). Baltimore: Paul H. Brookes Publishing Co.

Thousand, J. S., & Villa, R. A. (2000). Collaborative teaming: A powerful tool in school restructuring. In R. A. Villa & J. S. Thousand (Eds.), *Restructuring for caring and effective education: Piecing the puzzle together* (2nd ed., pp. 254–291). Baltimore: Paul H. Brookes.

Thousand, J. S., Villa, R. A., & Nevin, A. I. (2002). *Creativity and collaborative learning: The practical guide to empowering students, teachers, and families* (2nd ed.). Baltimore: Paul H. Brookes Publishing Co.

Thurlow, M. L., Lazarus, S. S., Thompson, S. J., & Morse, A. B. (2005). State policies on assessment participation and accommodations for students with disabilities. *Journal of Special Education, 38,* 232–240.

Timm, J. T., Chiang, B., & Finn, B. D. (1998). Acculturation in the cognitive style of Laotian Hmong students in the United States. *Equity and Excellence, 31,* 29–35.

Titus, J. C., Schiller, J. A., & Guthmann, D. (2008). Characteristics of youths with hearing loss admitted to substance abuse treatment. *Journal of Deaf Studies and Deaf Education, 13,* 336–350.

Tobey, E. A., & Hasenstab, S. (1991). Effects of a nucleus multichannel cochlear implant upon speech production in children. *Ear and Hearing, 12* (Suppl.), 48S–54S.

Todd, A. W., Horner, R. H., Vanater, S. M., & Schneider, C. F. (1997). Working together to make change: An example of positive behavioral support for a student with traumatic brain injury. *Education and Treatment of Children, 20,* 425–440.

Todis, B., Glang, A., & Fabry, M. A. (1997). Family–school–child: A qualitative study of the school experiences of students with ABI. In A. Glang, G. H. S. Singer, & B. Todis (Eds.), *Students with acquired brain injury: The school's response* (pp. 3–32). Baltimore: Paul H. Brookes.

Tomasi, S. F., & Weinberg, S. L. (1999). Classifying children as LD: An analysis of current practice in an urban setting. *Learning Disability Quarterly, 22,* 31–42.

Tomlinson, C. A. (2001). *How to differentiate instruction in mixed-ability classrooms* (2nd ed.). Alexandria, VA: Association for Supervision and Curriculum Development.

Tomlinson, C. A. (2004). The Möbius effect: Addressing learner variance in schools. *Journal of Learning Disabilities, 37,* 516–524.

Tomlinson, C. A. (2005). Quality curriculum and instruction for highly able students. *Theory into Practice, 44,* 160–166.

Tomlinson, C. A., Kaplan, S. N., Purcell, J. H., Leppien, J. H., Burns, D. E., & Strickland, C. A. (2006). *The parallel curriculum in the classroom book 1: Essays for application across the content areas K–12.* Thousand Oaks, CA: Corwin.

Tomlinson, C. A., Kaplan, S. N., Renzulli, J. S., Purcell, J., Leppien, J., & Burns, D. (2002). *The parallel curriculum: A design to develop high potential and challenge high-ability learners.* Thousand Oaks, CA: Corwin.

Tomlinson, C. A., & McTighe, J. (2006). *Integrating differentiated instruction and understanding by design: Connecting content and kids.* Alexandria, VA: Association for Supervision and Curriculum Development.

Tommerdahl, J. (2009). What teachers of students with SEBD need to know about speech and language difficulties. *Emotional & Behavioural Difficulties, 14,* 19–31.

Toner, M., O'Donoghue, T., & Houghton, S. (2006). Living in chaos and striving for control: How adults with attention deficit hyperactivity disorder deal with their disorder. *International Journal of Disability, Development and Education, 53,* 247–261.

Toole, D. (1996). *Living legends: Six stories about successful deaf people.* Hillsboro, OR: Butte Publications, Inc.

Torres-Burgo, M., Reyes-Wasson, P., & Brusca-Vega, R. (1999). Perceptions and needs of Hispanic and non-Hispanic parents of children receiving learning disabilities services. *Bilingual Research Journal, 23,* 373–388.

Toscano, R. M., McKee, B. G., & Lepoutre, D. (2002). Success with academic English: Reflections of deaf college students. *American Annals of the Deaf, 147,* 5–23.

Towles-Reeves, E., Kearns, J., & Kleinert, H. (2009). An analysis of the learning characteristics of students taking alternate assessments based on alternate achievement standards. *Journal of Special Education, 42,* 241–254.

Townsend, B. L. (2000). The disproportionate discipline of African American learners: Reducing school suspensions and expulsions. *Exceptional Children, 66,* 381–391.

Townsend, B. L., & Patton, J. M. (2000). Reflecting on ethics, power, and privilege. *Teacher Education and Special Education, 23,* 32–33.

Townsend, B. L., Thomas, D. D., Witty, J. P., & Lee, R. S. (1997). Diversity and school restructuring: Creating partnerships in a world of difference. *Teacher Education and Special Education, 19,* 102–118.

Tractman, G. M. (1961). New directions for school psychology. *Exceptional Children, 28,* 159–162.

Trainor, A. A. (2005). Self-determination perceptions and behaviors of diverse students with LD during the transition planning process. *Journal of Learning Disabilities, 38,* 233–249.

Tran, M. T., Young, R. L., & DiLella, J. D. (1994). Multicultural education courses and the student teacher: Eliminating stereotypical attitudes in our ethnically diverse classroom. *Journal of Teacher Education, 45,* 183–189.

Travis, L., Sigman, M., & Ruskin, E. (2001). Links between social understanding and social behavior in verbally able children with autism. *Journal of Autism and Developmental Disorders, 31,* 119–130.

Traxler, C. B. (2000). *The Stanford Achievement Test,* ninth edition: National norming and performance standards for deaf and hard-of-hearing students. *Journal of Deaf Studies and Deaf Education, 5*(4), 337–348.

Treffinger, D. J. (1995). School improvement, talent, development, and creativity. *Roeper Review, 18,* 93–97.

Trenholm, S. (2001). *Thinking through communication: An introduction to the study of human communication* (3rd ed.). Boston: Allyn & Bacon.

Trent, S., Pernell, E., Mungai, A., & Chimedza, R. (1998). Using concept maps to measure conceptual change in preservice teachers enrolled in a multicultural education/special education course. *Remedial and Special Education, 19,* 16–31.

Trent, S. C., Kea, C. D., & Oh, K. (2008). Preparing preservice educators for cultural diversity: How far have we come? *Exceptional Children, 74,* 328–350.

Trout, A. L., Lienemann T. O., Reid, R., & Epsteina, M. H. (2007). Review of nonmedication interventions to improve the academic performance of children and youth with ADHD. *Remedial and Special Education, 28,* 207–226.

Tucker, B. P. (1995). *The feel of silence.* Philadelphia: Temple University Press.

Tulbert, B. (1999). Creating collaborative and inclusive schools. *Remedial and Special Education, 20,* 379–380.

Turk, T. N., & Campbell, D. A. (2003). What's right with Doug: The academic triumph of a gifted student with ADHD. *Gifted Child Today, 26*(2), 40–45.

Tur-Kaspa, H., Weisel, A., & Segev, L. (1998). Attributions for feelings of loneliness of students with learning disabilities. *Learning Disabilities Research and Practice, 13*(2), 89–94.

Turkstra, L. S., Williams, W. H., Tonks, J., & Frampton, I. (2008) Measuring social cognition in adolescents: Implications for students with TBI returning to school. *NeuroRehabilitation, 23,* 501–509.

Turnbull, A. P., Stowe, M., Wilcox, B., & Turnbull, H. R. (2000). *Free appropriate public education: The law and children with disabilities* (5th ed., pp. 11–30). Denver: Love.

Turnbull, A. P., & Turnbull, H. R. (2001). *Families, professionals, and exceptionality: Collaborating for empowerment* (4th ed.). Upper Saddle River, NJ: Pearson.

Turnbull, A. P., Turnbull, H. R., Erwin, E. & Soodak, L. (2006). *Families, professionals, and exceptionality: Positive outcomes through partnerships and trust* (5th ed.). Upper Saddle River, NJ: Pearson.

Turnbull, A., Edmonson, H., Griggs, P., Wickham, D., Sailor, W., Freeman, R., Guess, D., Lassen, S., McCart, A., Park, J., Riffer. L., Turnbull, R., & Warren, J. (2002). A blueprint for schoolwide positive behavior support: Implementation of three components. *Exceptional Children, 68,* 377–402.

Turnbull, A., Summers, J., & Brotherson, M. (1986). Family life cycle: Theoretical and empirical implications and future directions for families with mentally retarded members. In J. Gallagher & P. Vietze (Eds.), *Families of handicapped persons: Research, programs, and policy issues* (pp. 45–66). Baltimore: Paul H. Brookes.

Turnbull, H. R. (2005). Individuals with Disabilities Education Act reauthorization: Accountability and personal responsibility. *Remedial and Special Education, 26,* 320–326.

Turnbull, H. R., Turnbull, A. P., Wehmeyer, M. L., & Park, J. (2003). A quality of life framework for special education outcomes. *Remedial and Special Education, 24,* 67–74.

Turnbull, R., Huerta, N., & Stowe, M. (2006). *The Individuals with Disabilities Education Act as amended in 2004.* Upper Saddle River, NJ: Merrill.

Turner, K. H. (2009). Flipping the switch: Code-switching from text speak to standard English. *English Journal, 98*(5), 60–65.

Tuttle, D. W. (1987). The role of the special education teacher-counselor in meeting students' self-esteem needs. *Journal of Visual Impairment and Blindness, 81,* 156–161.

Tuttle, D. W., & Tuttle, N. R. (1996). *Self-esteem and adjusting with blindness* (2nd ed.). Springfield, IL: Charles C. Thomas.

Twachtman-Cullen, D. (2000). *How to be a para pro: A comprehensive training manual for paraprofessionals.* Higganum, CT: Starfish Specialty Press.

TwiceGifted.net. (2004). *Gender issues: Gifted girls.* Retrieved February 27, 2004, from www.twicegifted.net/gender.htm

Tye-Murray, N. (1994). *Let's converse: A "how-to" guide to develop and expand conversational skills of children and teenagers who are hearing impaired.* Washington, DC: Alexander Graham Bell Association for the Deaf.

Tyler, K. M., Uqdah, A. L., Dillihunt, M. L., Beatty-Hazelbaker, R., Conner, T., Gadson, N., Henchy, A., Hughes, T., Mulder, S., Owens, E., Roan-Belle, C., Smith, L., & Stevens, R. (2008). Cultural discontinuity: Toward a quantitative investigation of a major hypothesis in education. *Educational Researcher, 37,* 280–297.

Tyler, R. S. (1993). *Cochlear implants: Audiological foundations.* San Diego, CA: Singular.

U.S. Department of Education. (2009). *Twenty-eighth annual report to Congress on the implementation of the Individuals with Disabilities Education Act, Parts B and C.* Washington, D.C.: Author.

U.S. Department of Education. (2009). *Twenty-eighth annual report to Congress on the implementation of the Individuals with Disabilities Education Act, Parts B and C.* Washington, D.C.: Author.

U.S. Department of Education. (2009). *Twenty-eighth annual report to Congress on the implementation of the Individuals with Disabilities Education Act, Parts B and C.* Washington, D.C.: Author.U.S. Department of Education. (2008). *Students ages 6 through 21 with emotional disturbance served under IDEA, Part B, by educational environment and state: Fall 2007* [Table 2-2d]. Retrieved July 6, 2009 from https://www.ideadata.org/TABLES31ST/AR_2-2.htm

U.S. Department of Education. (2009). *Twenty-eighth annual report to Congress on the implementation of the Individuals with Disabilities Education Act.* Washington, DC: Author. Retrieved August 31, 2009 from http://www.ed.gov/offices/OSERS/OSEP

U.S. Department of Education. (n.d.). *Jacob K. Javits gifted and talented students education program.* Retrieved September 11, 2009 from http://www.nagc.org/index.aspx?id=974

U.S. Census Bureau. (2001). *The two or more races population: 2000.* Washington, DC: Author.

U.S. Census Bureau. (2002). *Poverty in the United States: 2001.* Washington, DC: Author.

U.S. Census Bureau. (2009, June). Annual estimates of the resident population by sex, race, and Hispanic origin for the United States: April 1, 2000 to July 1, 2008 (NC-EST2008-03). Retrieved June 7, 2009 from http://www.census.gov/popest/national/asrh/NC-EST2008-srh.html

U.S. Department of Education (2001c). *Twenty-third annual report to Congress on the implementation of the Individuals with Disabilities Education Act.* Washington, DC: U.S Government Printing Office.

U.S. Department of Education and Office of Civil Rights. (1999, July). *Free appropriate public education for students with disabilities: Requirements under Section 504 of the Rehabilitation Act of 1973.* Retrieved from www.ed.gov/offices/OCR/docs/FAPES504.html

U.S. Department of Education, Office of Educational Research and Improvement. (1993). *National excellence: A case for developing America's talent.* Washington, DC: Author.

U.S. Department of Education, Office of Special Education Programs Technical Assistance Center on Positive Behavioral Interventions and Supports. (2003, August). *Schoolwide PBS.* Retrieved August 20, 2003, from www.pbs.org/english/Schoolwide_PBS.htm

U.S. Department of Education. (1979). *Progress toward a free appropriate public education: A report to Congress on the implementation of Public Law 94-142.* Washington, DC: Author.

U.S. Department of Education. (1988). *Tenth annual report to Congress on the implementation of the Education of the Handicapped Act.* Washington, DC: Author.

U.S. Department of Education. (1989). *11th annual report to congress on the implementation of the Education of all Handicapped Children Act.* Washington, DC: Author.

U.S. Department of Education. (1992a). Deaf students education services: Policy guidance. *Federal Register, 57*(211), October 30, 1992, 49274–49276.

U.S. Department of Education. (1992b). *Fourteenth annual report to Congress on the implementation of the Individuals with Disabilities Education Act.* Washington, DC: Author.

U.S. Department of Education. (1993). *Fifteenth annual report to Congress on the implementation of IDEA.* Washington, DC: Author.

U.S. Department of Education. (1993). *Fifteenth annual report to Congress on the implementation of the Individuals with Disabilities Education Act.* Washington, DC: Author.

U.S. Department of Education. (1993). *National excellence: A case for developing America's talent.* Washington, DC: Author.

U.S. Department of Education. (1999). *21st annual report to Congress on the implementation of the Individuals with Disabilities Education Act.* Washington, DC: Author.

U.S. Department of Education. (2000a). Policy guidance on educating blind and visually impaired students. *Federal Register, 65*(111), 36,585–36,595. Retrieved January 6, 2004, from http://ocfo.ed.gov/fedreg/other/q200/060800a.txt

U.S. Department of Education. (2000b). *Twenty-second annual report to Congress on the implementation of the Individuals with Disabilities Education Act (IDEA).* Washington, DC: Author.

U.S. Department of Education. (2001a). *Characteristics of the 100 largest public elementary and secondary school districts in the United States: 1999–2000.* Washington, DC: Author.

U.S. Department of Education. (2001b). Policy guidance on educating blind and visually impaired students.*RE:view, 33,* 77–93.

U.S. Department of Education. (2001c). *Twenty-third annual report to Congress on the implementation of IDEA.* Washington, DC: Author.

U.S. Department of Education. (2002a). *The condition of education 2002.* Washington, DC: Author.

U.S. Department of Education. (2002b). *Fact sheet: The No Child Left Behind Act of 2001.* Retrieved November 4, 2002 from www.ed.gov/offices/OESE/esea/factsheet.html

U.S. Department of Education. (2002c). *No child left behind.* Retrieved November 4, 2002, from www.nochildleftbehind.gov

U.S. Department of Education. (2002d). *Twenty-fourth annual report to Congress on the implementation of the Individuals with Disabilities Education Act.* Washington, DC: Author.

U.S. Department of Education. (2002e). *Special education expenditure project: How does spending on special education students vary across districts?: An analysis of spending by urbanicity, district size, median family income, and student poverty levels in 1999–2000.* Washington, DC: Author.

U.S. Department of Education. (2003). *Twenty-fifth annual report to Congress on the implementation of the Individuals with Disabilities Education Act.* Washington, DC: Author.

U.S. Department of Education. (2004). *Twenty-sixth annual report to Congress on the implementation of the Individuals with Disabilities Education Act.* Washington, DC: Author.

U.S. Department of Education. (2006). *28th annual report to congress on the implementation of the Individuals with Disabilities Education Act, Parts B and C.* Washington, DC: Author.

U.S. Department of Education. (2008). *IDEA data: Part B data & notes.* Retrieved June 9, 2009 from https://www.ideadata.org/PartBData.asp

U.S. Department of Education. (2008). *IDEA data: Part B data & notes.* Retrieved May 15, 2009 from https://www.ideadata.org/PartBData.asp

U.S. Department of Education. (2008). *IDEA data: Part B data & notes.* Retrieved October 15, 2009 from https://www.ideadata.org/PartBData.asp

U.S. Department of Education. (2008). *Students ages 6 through 21 served under IDEA, Part B, by disability category and state: Fall 2007* [Table 1-3]. Retrieved August 1, 2009 from https://www.ideadata.org/TABLES31ST/AR_1-3.htm

U.S. Department of Education. (2008). *Table 2-2. Students ages 6 through 21 served under IDEA, Part B, by educational environmentand state: Fall 2007.* Retrieved May 15, 2009 from http://www.ideadata.org/TABLES31ST/AR_2-2.htm

U.S. Department of Education. (2008). Identifying and treating attention deficit hyperactivity disorder: A resource for school and home. Washington, D.C.: Author. Retrieved July 1, 2009 from http://www.eric.ed.gov/ERICWebPortal/contentdelivery/servlet/ERICServlet?accno=ED502959

U.S. Department of Education. (2008*). 26th annual report to Congress on the implementation of the Individuals with Disabilities Education Act.* Washington, DC: Author.

U.S. Department of Education. (2008a, July). *Children with disabilities receiving special education under Part B of the Individuals with Disabilities Education Act* (Data Analysis System, OMB #1820-0043). Washington, DC: Office of Special Education Programs.

U.S. Department of Education. (2008b, July). *Infants and toddlers receiving early intervention services in accordance with Part C B of the Individuals with Disabilities Education Act* (Data Analysis System, OMB #1820-0557). Washington, DC: Office of Special Education Programs.

U.S. Department of Education. (2009). *28th annual report to Congress on the implementation of the Individuals with Disabilities Education Act.* Washington, D.C.: Author.

U.S. Department of Education. (2009). *IDEA data: Part B data & notes.* Retrieved June 9, 2009 from https://www.ideadata.org/PartBData.asp

U.S. Department of Education. (2009). *Twenty-eighth annual report to Congress on the implementation of the Individuals with Disabilities Education Act.* Washington, DC: Author.

U.S. Department of Education. (2009). *Twenty-sixth annual report to Congress on the implementation of the Individuals with Disabilities Education Act, Parts B and C.* Washington, DC: Author.

U.S. Department of Education. (2009). *Twenty-sixth annual report to Congress on the implementation of IDEA.* Washington, DC: Author.

U.S. Department of Education. (2009). Twenty-eighth annual report to Congress on the implementation of the Individuals with Disabilities Education Act, 2006. Washington, DC: Author.

U.S. Department of Health and Human Services. (1999). Children and mental health. In *Mental health: A report of the Surgeon General* (p. 17). Rockville, MD: Author.

U.S. Department of Health and Human Services. (2001, November). *Emotional and behavioral health in persons with mental retardation/developmental disabilities: Research challenges and opportunities.* Retrieved October 10, 2003, from http://ohrp.osophs.dhhs.gov/nhrpac/mtg07-02/nhrpac11.pdf

U.S. Department of Health and Human Services. (2003, August). *Blamed and ashamed: The treatment experiences of youth with co-occurring substance abuse and mental health disorders and their families.* Retrieved August 21, 2003, from www.mentalhealth.org/publications/allpubs/KEN02-0129/execsumm.asp

U.S. Department of Health and Human Services. (2006). *Child maltreatment 2004.* Washington, DC: U.S. Government Printing Office. Retrieved October 21, 2006 from www.acf.dhhs.gov/programs/cb/pubs/cm04/summary.htm

U.S. Food and Drug Administration. (2004). *Cochlear implants: What is a cochlear implant?* Retrieved November 24, 2006, from www.fda.gov/cdrh/cochlear/whatare.html

U.S. Food and Drug Administration. (2006). *Cochlear implants: Benefits/risks.* Retrieved November 24, 2006, from www.fda.gov/cdrh/cochlear/riskbenefit.html

U.S. Office of Special Education Programs. (2002, August). *Facts from OSEP's national longitudinal studies: Minorities among children and youth with disabilities.* Retrieved October 10, 2003, from www.nlts2.org/pdfs/Fact_sheet1_9_03.pdf

Ulster, A. A., & Antle, B. J. (2005). In the darkness there can be light: A family's adaptation to a child's blindness. *Journal of Visual Impairment and Blindness, 99,* 209–218.

United States Congress. *Educational Amendment of 1978* [P.L. 95-561, IX (A)].

United States Congress. *Javits Gifted and Talented Students Education Act of 1988* (P.L. 100-297, Sec. 4130).

University of South Dakota, Center for Disabilities. (2002). *Fetal alcohol syndrome handbook.* Sioux Falls, SD: Author. Retrieved October 1, 2003, from www.usd.edu/cd/fashandbook

Utley, C. A. (2001). Advances in peer-mediated instruction and interventions in the twenty-first century. *Remedial and Special Education, 22,* 2–3.

Utley, C. A., Delquadri, J. C., Obiakor, F. E., & Mims, V. A. (2000). General and special educators' perceptions of teaching strategies for multicultural students. *Teacher Education and Special Education, 23,* 34–50.

Utley, C. A., Reddy, S. S., & Delquadri, J. C. (2001). Classwide peer tutoring: An effective teaching procedure for facilitating the acquisition of health education and safety facts with students with developmental disabilities. *Education and Treatment of Children, 24,* 1–27.

Vallance, D. D., Cummings, R. L., & Humphries, T. (1998). Mediators of the risk for problem behavior in children with language learning disabilities. *Journal of Learning Disabilities, 31,* 160–171.

Valles, E. C. (1998). The disproportionate representation of minority students in special education: Responding to the problem. *The Journal of Special Education, 32,* 52–54.

Van Acker, R., Boreson, L., Gable, R. A., & Potterton, T. (2005). Are we on the right course? Lessons learned about current FBA/BIP practices in schools. *Journal of Behavioral Education, 14,* 35–56.

Van Garderen, D. (2007). Teaching students with LD to use diagrams to solve mathematical word problems. *Journal of Learning Disabilities, 40*(6), 540–553.

van Garderen, D., Scheuermann, A., & Jackson, C. (2009). Supporting the collaboration of special educators and general educators to teach students who struggle with mathematics: An overview of the research. *Psychology in the Schools, 46,* 56–78.

Van Garderen, D., & Whittaker, C. (2006). Planning differentiated, multicultural instruction for secondary inclusive classrooms. *Teaching Exceptional Children, 38*(3), 12–20.

Van Norman, R. K. (2007). "Who's on first?" Using sports trivia peer tutoring to increase conversational language. *Intervention in School and Clinic, 43,* 88–100.

Vannest, K. J., Temple-Harvey, K. K., & Mason, B. A. (2009). Adequate yearly progress for students with emotional and behavioral disorders through research-based practices. *Preventing School Failure, 53*(2), 73–84.

VanTassel-Baska, J. (1983). Profiles of precocity: The 1982 Midwest talent search finalists. *Gifted Child Quarterly, 27,* 139–144.

VanTassel-Baska, J. (1992). *Planning effective curriculum for gifted learners.* Denver, CO: Love.

VanTassel-Baska, J. (1995). The development of talent through curriculum. *Roeper Review, 18,* 98–102.

VanTassel-Baska, J. (1998). *Excellence in educating the gifted* (3rd ed.). Denver, CO: Love.

VanTassel-Baska, J. (2003). *Curriculum planning and instructional design for gifted learners.* Denver, CO: Love.

VanTassel-Baska, J. (2004). Effective curriculum and instructional models for talented students. In J. VanTassel-Baska (Ed.), *Curriculum for gifted and talented students* (pp. 1–12). Thousand Oaks, CA: Corwin.

VanTassel-Baska, J., Johnson, D. T., & Avery, L. D. (2002). Using performance tasks in the identification of economically disadvantaged and minority gifted learners: Findings from Project STAR. *Gifted Child Quarterly, 46,* 110–123.

VanTassel-Baska, J., & Little, C. (Eds.). (2003). *Content-based curriculum for high-ability learners.* Waco, TX: Prufrock Press.

VanTassel-Baska, J., Patton, J. M., & Prillaman, D. (1991). *Gifted youth at risk: A report of a national study.* Reston, VA: Council for Exceptional Children.

VanTassel-Baska, J., & Stambaugh, T. (2005). Challenges and possibilities for serving gifted learners in the regular classroom. *Theory into Practice, 44,* 211–217.

Van Tassel-Baska, J. L., Cross, T., & Olenchak, F. R. (Eds.). (2009). *Social-emotional curriculum with gifted and talented students.* Waco, TX: Prufrock.

Vaughn, B. S., Wetzel, M. W., & Kratochvil, C. J. (2008). Beyond the 'typical' patient: Treating attention-deficit/hyperactivity disorder in preschoolers and adults. *International Review of Psychiatry, 20,* 143–149.

Vaughn, S., & Coleman, M. (2004). The role of mentoring in promoting use of research-based practices in reading. *Remedial and Special Education, 25,* 25–38.

Vaughn, S., & Edmonds, M. (2006). Reading comprehension for older readers. *Intervention in School and Clinic, 41,* 131–137.

Vaughn, S., Elbaum, B. E., Schumm, J. S., & Hughes, M. T. (1998). Social outcomes for students with and without learning disabilities in inclusive classrooms. *Journal of Learning Disabilities, 31,* 428–436.

Vaughn, S., & Fuchs, L. S. (2003). Redefining learning disabilities as inadequate response to instruction: The promise and potential problems. *Learning Disabilities Research and Practice, 18,* 137–146.

Vaughn, S., & Klingner, J. K. (1998). Students' perceptions of inclusion and resource room settings. *Journal of Special Education, 32,* 79–88.

Vaughn, S., & Linan-Thompson, S. (2003). What is special about special education for students with learning disabilities? *Journal of Special Education, 37,* 140–147.

Vaughn, S., Levy, S., Coleman, M., & Bos, C. S. (2002). Reading instruction for students with LD and EBD: A synthesis of observation studies. *Journal of Special Education, 36,* 2–13.

Vaughn, S., Linan-Thompson, S., & Hickman, P. (2003). Response to instruction as a means of identifying students with reading/learning disabilities. *Exceptional Children, 69,* 391–409.

Vellutino, F. R., Scanlon, D. M., Small, S., & Faneule, D. P. (2006). Response to intervention as a vehicle for distinguishing between children with and without reading disabilities: Evidence for the role of kindergarten and first-grade interventions. *Journal of Learning Disabilities, 39,* 157–169.

Veneri, C. M. (1999). Can occupational labor shortages be identified using available data? *Monthly Labor Review, 122*(3), 15–21.

Venkatagiri, H. S. (2005). Recent advances in the treatment of stuttering: A theoretical perspective. *Journal of Communication Disorders, 38,* 375–393.

Vernon, M., & Rhodes, A. (2009). Deafness and autism spectrum disorders. *American Annals of the Deaf, 154,* 5–14.

Vismara, L., & Lyons, G. (2007). Using perseverative interests to elicit joint attention behaviors in young children with autism: Theoretical and clinical implications for understanding motivation. *Journal of Positive Behavior Interventions, 9,* 214–228.

Visser, J., & Stokes, S. (2003). Is education ready for the inclusion of pupils with emotional and behavioral difficulties? A rights perspective. *Educational Review, 55*(1), 65–75.

Vitello, S. J. (1986). The Tatro case: Who gets what and why. *Exceptional Children, 52,* 353–356.

Vitiello, B., & Sherrill, J. (2007). School-based interventions for students with attention deficit hyperactivity disorder: Research implications and prospects. *School Psychology Review, 36,* 287–290.

Vogel, S. A., & Reder, S. (1998). Educational attainment of adults with learning disabilities. In S. A. Vogel & S. Reder (Eds.), *Learning disabilities, literacy, and adult education* (pp. 43–68). Baltimore: Paul H. Brookes.

Volden, J., Coolican, J., & Garon, N. (2009). Brief report: Pragmatic language in autism spectrum disorder—Relationships to measures of ability and disability. *Journal of Autism and Developmental Disorders, 39,* 388–393.

Volonino, V., & Zigmond, N. (2007). Promoting research-based practices through inclusion. *Theory into Practice, 46*(4), 291–300.

Volonino, V., & Zigmond, N. (2007). Promoting research-based practices through inclusion. *Theory Into Practice, 46,* 291–300.

Volpe, R., DuPaul, G., DiPerna, J., Jitendra, A., Lutz, G., Tresco, K., & Junod, R. (2006). Attention deficit hyperactivity disorder and scholastic achievement: A model of mediation via academic enablers. *School Psychology Review, 35,* 47–61.

Voltz, D. L. (1994). Developing collaborative parent–teacher relationships with culturally diverse parents. *Intervention in School and Clinic, 29,* 288–291.

Voltz, D. L. (2003). Professional development for culturally responsive instruction: A promising practice for addressing the disproportionate representation of students of color in special education. *Teacher Education and Special Education, 26,* 62–72.

Voltz, D. L., Brazil, N., & Ford, A. (2001). What matters most in inclusive education: A practical guide for moving forward. *Intervention in School and Clinic, 37,* 23–30.

Voltz, D. L., Sims, M. J., Nelson, B., & Bivens, C. (2006). M²ECCA: A framework for inclusion in the context of standards-based reform. *Teaching Exceptional Children, 37*(5), 14–19.

Voltz, D. L., Sims, M. J., Nelson, B., & Bivens, C. (2008). Engineering successful inclusion in standards-based urban classrooms. *Middle School Journal, 39*(5), 24–30.

Wadlington, E., & Wadlington, P. L. (2008). Helping students with mathematical disabilities to succeed. *Preventing School Failure, 53,* 2–7.

Wadsworth, S., Olson, R. K., Pennington, B. F., & DeFries, J. C. (2000). Differential genetic etiology of reading disability as a function of IQ. *Journal of Learning Disabilities, 33,* 192–199.

Wagner, M. (1991). Sticking it out: Secondary school completion. In M. Wagner, L. Newman, R. D'Amico, E. D. Jay, P. Butter-Nalin, C. Marder, & R. Cox (Eds.), *Youth with disabilities: How are they doing?* First Comprehensive Report from the National Longitudinal Transition Study of Special Education Students (pp. 5-1–5-31). Menlo Park, CA: SRI International.

Wagner, M., & Blackorby, J. (2002). *Disability profiles of elementary and middle school students with disabilities.* Washington, DC: Special Education Elementary Longitudinal Study (SEELS), Office of Special Education and Rehabilitation Services.

Wagner, M., & Davis, M. (2006). How are we preparing students with emotional disturbances for the transition to young adulthood? Findings from the national longitudinal transition study-2. *Journal of Emotional and Behavioral Disorders, 14,* 86–98.

Wagner, M., Friend, M., Bursuck, W. D., Kutash, K., Duchnowski, A. J., Sumi, W. C., & Epstein, M. H. (2006). Educating students with emotional disturbances: A national perspective on school programs and services. *Journal of Emotional and Behavioral Disorders, 14,* 12–30.

Wagner, M., Kutash, K., Duchnowski, A. J., Epstein, M. H., & Sumi, W. C. (2005). The children and youth we serve: A national picture of the characteristics of students with emotional disturbances receiving special education. *Journal of Emotional and Behavioral disorders, 13,* 79–96.

Wagner, M., Kutash, K., Duchnowski, A. J., Epstein, M. H., & Sumi, W. C. (2005). The children and youth we serve: A national picture of the characteristics of students with emotional disturbances receiving special education. *Journal of Emotional and Behavioral Disorders, 13,* 79–96.

Wagner, M., Newman, L., Cameto, R., & Levine, P. (2005). *Changes over time in the early postschool outcomes of youth with disabilities. A report of findings from the National Longitudinal Transition Study (NLTS) and the National Longitudinal Transition Study-2 (NLTS2)*. Menlo Park, CA: SRI International. Retrieved December 19, 2005, from www.nlts2.org/pdfs/str6completereport.pdf

Wagner, R. K., Francis, D. J., & Morris, R. D. (2005). Identifying English language learners with learning disabilities: Key challenges and possible approaches. *Learning Disabilities Research and Practice, 20*, 6–15.

Wagner, S. M., & McNeil, C. B. (2008). Parent-child interaction therapy for ADHD: A conceptual overview and critical literature review. *Child & Family Behavior Therapy, 30*, 231–256.

Wakefield, A. J., Murch, S. H., Anthony, A., Linnell, J., Casson, D. M., Malik, M., Berelowitz, M. et al. (1998). Ileal-lymphoid-nodular hyperplasia, nonspecific colitis, and pervasive developmental disorder in children. *Lancet, 351*, 637–641.

Waldman, H. B., & Perlman, S. P. (2007). Baby fat may be cute, but chubby kids could be in jeopardy, and for children with disabilities . . . *Exceptional Parent, 37*(2), 12–14.

Waldman, I. D., & Gizer, I. R. (2006). The genetics of attention deficit hyperactivity disorder. *Clinical Psychology Review, 26*, 396–432.

Waldron, N. L., & McLeskey, J. (1998). The effects of an inclusive school program on students with mild and severe learning disabilities. *Exceptional Children, 64*, 395–405.

Walker, H. M., & Golly, A. (1999). Developing behavioral alternatives for antisocial children at the point of school entry. *Clearing House, 73*, 104–106.

Walker, H. M., Golly, A., McLane, J. Z., & Kimmich, M. (2005). The Oregon First Step to Success replication initiative: Statewide results of an evaluation of the program's impact. *Journal of Emotional & Behavioral Disorders, 13*, 163–172.

Walker, H. M., Stiller, B., Severson, H. H., Feil, E. G., & Golly, A. (1998). First step to success: Intervening at the point of school entry to prevent antisocial behavior patterns. *Psychology in the Schools, 35*, 259–269.

Walker, H. M., Zeller, Z. W., Close, D. W., Webber, J., & Gresham, F. (1999). The present unwrapped: Change and challenge in the field of behavioral disorders. *Behavioral Disorders, 24*, 293–294.

Walker, L. A. (2001, May 13) They're breaking the sound barrier. *Parade Magazine*, pp. 4–5.

Walsh, J. M. (2001). Getting the "big picture" of IEP goals and state standards. *Teaching Exceptional Children, 33*(5), 18–26.

Walter, G. G., Foster, S. B., & Elliot, L. (1987, July). *Attrition and accommodation of hearing-impaired college students in the U.S.* Paper presented at the tenth national conference of the Association of Handicapped Student Service Programs in Postsecondary Education. Washington, DC.

Walther-Thomas, C., Korinek, L., & McLaughlin, V. L. (1999). Collaboration to support students' success. *Focus on Exceptional Children, 32*(3), 1–18.

Walther-Thomas, C. S. (1997). Co-teaching experiences: The benefits and problems that teachers and principals report over time. *Journal of Learning Disabilities, 30*, 395–407.

Wanzek, J., & Vaughn, S. (2008). Response to varying amounts of time in reading intervention for students with low response to intervention. *Journal of Learning Disabilities, 41*, 126–142.

Ward, M. E. (2000). The visual system. In M. C. Holbrook & A. J. Koenig (Eds.), *Foundations of education: History and theory of teaching children and youths with visual impairments* (2nd ed., pp. 77–110). New York: American Foundation for the Blind Press.

Ward, M. J., & Berry, H. G. (2005, Summer). Students with disabilities and postsecondary education: A tale of two data sets. *Information from HEATH* [quarterly newsletter]. Washington, DC: George Washington University, National Clearinghouse on Postsecondary Education for Individuals with Disabilities. Retrieved September 1, 2006, from www.heath.gwu.edu/newsletter/Issue%2014/Data%20Feature.htm

Warger, C. (2001). *Cultural reciprocity aids collaboration with families* [ERIC/OSEP digest]. Retrieved September 15, 2003, from www.edrs.com.members/sp/cfm?AN-ED_457633

Warikoo, N., & Carter, P. (2009). Cultural explanations for racial and ethnic stratification in academic achievement: A call for a new and improved theory. *Review of Educational Research, 79*, 366–394.

Warren, S. F. (2000). The future of early communication and language intervention. *Topics in Early Childhood Special Education, 20*, 33–37.

Washburn-Moses, L. (2003). What every special educator should know about high-stakes testing. *Teaching Exceptional Children, 35*(4), 12–15.

Washington State University Department of Speech and Hearing Sciences. (2003). *Significance of Native American program at WSU.* Retrieved November 11, 2003, from http://libarts.wsu.edu/speechhearing/academics/nap-significance.html

Wasserstein, J., Wasserstein, A., & Wolf, L. E. (2001). *Adults with attention deficit hyperactivity disorder* (ERIC Digest). (ERIC Document Reproduction Service No. ED461959) Retrieved June 16, 2003, from http://libproxy.uncg.edu:2101/Webstore/Download.cfm?ID=689824&CFID=5160408&CFTOKEN=44519503

Watson, A., & McCathren, R. (2009). Including children with special needs: Are you and your early childhood program ready? *Young Children, 64*(2), 20–26.

Watson, C. S. et al. (2003). Sensory, cognitive, and linguistic factors in the early academic performance of elementary school children: The Benton-IU project. *Journal of Learning Disabilities, 36*, 165–197.

Watterdorf, D. J., & Muenke, M. (2005). Prader-Willi syndrome. *American Family Physician, 72*, 827–830.

Webb, J. T. (2000, August). *Misdiagnosis and dual diagnosis of gifted children: Gifted and LD, ADHD, OCD, Oppositional Defiant Disorder.* Paper presented at the annual convention of the American Psychological Association, Washington, DC (ERIC Document Reproduction Service No. ED448382)

Webb, J. T., & Latimer, D. (1993). *ADHD and children who are gifted* [ERIC Digest #522]. Reston, VA: Council for Exceptional Children.

Webster, P. E., Plante, A. S., & Couvillion, L. M. (1997). Phonologic impairment and prereading: Update in a longitudinal study. *Journal of Learning Disabilities, 30*, 365–375.

Wechsler, D. (2003). *Wechsler intelligence scale for children–IV.* San Antonio, TX: Psychological Corporation.

Wehman, P., & Sherron Targett, P. (1999). *Vocational curriculum for individuals with special needs: Transition from school to adulthood..* Austin, TX: PRO-ED.

Wehman, P., & Sherron Targett, P. (1999). *Vocational curriculum for individuals with special needs: Transition from school to adulthood.* Austin, TX: Pro-Ed.

Wehmeyer, M., Chapman, T. E., Little, T. D., Thompson, J. R., Schalock, R., & Tassé, M. J. (2009). Efficacy of the supports intensity scale (SIS) to predict extraordinary support needs. *American Journal on Intellectual and Developmental Disabilities, 114*, 3–14.

Wehmeyer, M. L. (2002). *Teaching students with mental retardation: Providing access to the general curriculum.* Baltimore: Paul H. Brookes.

Wehmeyer, M. L. (2002). *Teaching students with mental retardation: Providing access to the general curriculum.* Baltimore: Paul H. Brookes Publishing Co.

Wehmeyer, M. L. (2003) Defining mental retardation and ensuring access to the general curriculum. *Education and Training in Mental Retardation and Developmental Disabilities, 38*, 271–282.

Wehmeyer, M. L., Agran, M., & Hughes, C. (2000). A national survey of teachers' promotion of self-determination and student directed learning. *Journal of Special Education, 34*, 58–68.

Wehmeyer, M. L., Lance, G. D., & Bashinski, S. (2002). Promoting access to the general curriculum for students with mental retardation: A multi-level model. *Education and Training in Mental Retardation and Developmental Disabilities, 37,* 223–234.

Wehmeyer, M. L., Lattin, D. L., Lapp-Rincker, G., & Agran, M. (2003). Access to the general curriculum of middle school students with mental retardation: An observational study. *Remedial and Special Education, 24,* 262–272.

Wehmeyer, M. L., & Patton, J. R. (2000). Mental retardation in the twenty-first century: Introduction to the special issue. *Focus on Autism and Other Developmental Disabilities, 15,* 66–67, 79.

Weinstein, S. (2002). Epilepsy. In M. L. Batshaw (Ed.), *Children with disabilities* (5th ed., pp. 493–524). Baltimore: Paul H. Brookes.

Weisner, T. S. (1999). Bringing together variable-based and person-based methods. *Journal of Early Intervention, 22,* 291–293.

Weiss, A. L. (2004). Why we should consider pragmatics when planning treatment for children who stutter. *Language, Speech, and Hearing Services in Schools, 35,* 34–45.

Welch, M., Brownell, K., & Sheridan, S. (1999). What's the score and game plan on teaming in schools? *Remedial and Special Education, 20,* 36–49.

Welch, M., & Tulbert, B. (2000). Practitioners' perspectives of collaboration: A social validation and factor analysis. *Journal of Educational and Psychological Consultation, 11,* 357–378.

Wells, G. (1986). *The meaning makers: Children learning language and using language to learn.* Portsmouth, NH: Heinemann.

Wells, K. C., Pelham, Jr., W. E., Kotkin, R. A., Hoza, B., Abikoff, H. B., Abramowitz, A. A., et al. (2000). Psychosocial treatment strategies in the MTA study: Rationale, methods, and critical issues in design and implementation. *Journal of Abnormal Child Psychology, 28,* 483–505.

Welsh, M., Parke, R. D., Widaman, K., & O'Neil, R. (2001). Linkages between children's social and academic competence: A longitudinal analysis. *Journal of School Psychology, 39,* 463–482.

WEMOVE.org. (2005). Epidemiology of movement disorders (estimated prevalence) [based on data from the Centers for Disease Control and Prevention]. Retrieved September 4, 2006, from www.life-in-motion.org/downloads/pressroom/Epidemiology.PDF#search=%22cerebral%20palsy%20prevalence%20NIH%22

Werner, G. A., Vismara, L. A., Koegel, R. L., & Koegel, L. K. (2006). Play dates, social interactions, and friendships. In R. L. Koegel & L. K. Koegel (Eds.), *Pivotal response treatments for autism: Communication, social, and academic development* (pp. 200–213). Baltimore: Paul H. Brookes.

Werner, G. A., Vismara, L. A., Koegel, R. L., & Koegel, L. K. (2006). Play dates, social interactions, and friendships. In R. L. Koegel and L. K. Koegel (Eds.), *Pivotal response treatments for autism: Communication, social, and academic development* (pp. 200–213). Baltimore: Paul H. Brookes Publishing Co.

Werts, M. G., Mamlin, N., & Pogoloff, S. M. (2002). Knowing what to expect: Introducing preservice teachers to IEP meetings. *Teacher Education and Special Education, 25,* 413–418.

Wesson, L., & Kudlacz, J. M. (2000). Collaboration for change. *Principal Leadership, 1*(3), 50–53.

West, J., Taylor, M., Houghton, S., & Hudyma, S. (2005). A comparison of teachers' and parents' knowledge and beliefs about attention-deficit/hyperactivity disorder (ADHD). *School Psychology International, 26,* 192–208.

West, J. E. (2005). An opportunity slipping away? *Journal of Visual Impairment and Blindness, 99,* 677–679.

Westberg, K. L., Archambault, F., Dobyns, S., Salvin, T. (1993). The classroom practices observation study. *Journal for the Education of the Gifted, 16,* 120–146.

Westling, D. L., & Fox, L. (2000). *Teaching students with severe disabilities* (2nd ed.). Upper Saddle River, NJ: Merrill.

Westling, D. L., & Fox, L. (2004). *Teaching students with severe disabilities* (3rd ed.). Upper Saddle River, NJ: Merrill.

Westling, D. L. & Fox, L. (2009). *Teaching students with severe disabilities* (4th ed.). Upper Saddle River, NJ: Merrill.

Wetzel, R., & Knowlton, M. (2000). A comparison of print and braille reading rates on three reading tasks. *Journal of Visual Impairment and Blindness, 94,* 146–154.

Weyandt, L. L. (2006). Disorders of childhood origin. In *The physiological bases of cognitive and behavioral disorders* (pp. 231–266). Mahwah, NJ: Lawrence Erlbaum.

Weyandt, L. L., Iwaszuk, W., Fulton, K., Ollerton, M., Beatty, N., Fouts, H., Schepman, S., & Greenlaw, C. (2003). The Internal Restlessness Scale: Performance of college students with and without ADHD. *Journal of Learning Disabilities, 36,* 382–389.

What Works Clearinghouse. (2007). *Intervention: Classwide peer tutoring (CWPT).* Retrieved July 12, 2009 from http://ies.ed.gov/ncee/wwc/reports/beginning_reading/cwpt/index.asp

What Works Clearinghouse. (2009). *Assisting students struggling with reading: Response to intervention (RTI) and multi-tier intervention in the primary grades: IES practice guide.* Washington, D.C.: Institute of Education Sciences (ED), National Center for Education Evaluation and Regional Assistance. Retrieved April 16, 2009 from http://www.eric.ed.gov/ERICWebPortal/contentdelivery/servlet/ERICServlet?accno=ED504264

Wheeler, R. S. (2008). Becoming adept at code-switching. *Educational Leadership, 65*(7), 54–58.

White, S., & Roberson-Nay, R. (2009). Anxiety, social deficits, and loneliness in youth with autism spectrum disorders. *Journal of Autism and Developmental Disorders, 39,* 1006–1013.

Whitmire, K. (2002). The evolution of school-based speech-language services: A half century of change and a new century of practice. *Communication Disorders Quarterly, 23,* 68–76.

Whitney, J. (2005). Five easy pieces: Steps toward integrating AAVE into the classroom. *English Journal, 94*(5), 64–69.

Wiener, J., & Mak, M. (2009). Peer victimization in children with attention-deficit/hyperactivity disorder. *Psychology in the Schools, 46,* 116–131.

Wiener, J., & Sunohara, G. (1998). Parents' perceptions of the quality of friendship of their children with learning disabilities. *Learning Disabilities Research and Practice, 13,* 242–257.

Wiener, J., & Tardif, C. Y. (2004). Social and emotional functioning of children with learning disabilities: Does special education placement make a difference? *Learning Disabilities Research and Practice, 19,* 20–32.

Wiggins, L., Robins, D., Bakeman, R., & Adamson, L. (2009). Brief report: Sensory abnormalities as distinguishing symptoms of autism spectrum disorders in young children. *Journal of Autism and Developmental Disorders, 39,* 1087–1091.

Wilde, L. D., Koegel, L. K., & Koegel, R. L. (1992). *Increasing success in school through priming: A training manual.* Santa Barbara: University of California Press.

Wilens, T. E., Biederman, J., & Spencer, T. J. (2002). Attention deficit/hyperactivity disorder across the lifespan. *Annual Review of Medicine, 53,* 113–131.

Wilkinson, c. Y., Ortiz, A. A., Robertson, P. M., & Kushner, M. I. (2006). English language learners with reading related LD: Linking data from multiple sources to make eligibility decisions. *Journal of Learning Disabilities, 39,* 129–141.

Will, M. C. (1986). Educating children with learning problems: A shared responsibility. *Exceptional Children, 52,* 411–416.

Willard-Holt, C. (1999, May). *Dual exceptionalities* (ERIC Digest #574). Arlington, VA: ERIC Clearinghouse on Disabilities and Gifted Education. Retrieved from http://ericec.org/digests/e574.html

Williams, D. (2008). What neuroscience has taught us about autism: Implications for early intervention. *Zero to Three, 28*(4), 11–17.

Williams, D. L., & Ward-Lonergan, J. (2001, April). *Effect of explicit audience on written communication of children with learning disabilities.* Paper presented at the Annual Convention of the Council for Exceptional Children, Kansas City, MO. (ERIC Document Reproduction Service No. ED454663)

Williams, J., & Sharp, G. (1996). Academic achievement and behavioral ratings in children with absence and complex partial epilepsy. *Education & Treatment of Children, 19,* 143–153.

Williams, L. J., & Downing, J. E. (1998). Membership and belonging in inclusive classrooms: What do middle school students have to say? *Journal of the Association for Persons with Severe Handicaps, 23,* 98–110.

Williams, M., Atkins, M., & Soles, T. (2009). Assessment of autism in community settings: Discrepancies in classification. *Journal of Autism and Developmental Disorders, 39,* 660–669.

Williams, V. I., & Cartledge, G. (1997). Passing notes to parents. *Teaching Exceptional Children, 30*(1), 30–34.

Williamson, P., McLeskey, J., Hoppey, D., & Rentz, T. (2006). Educating students with mental retardation in general education classrooms. *Exceptional Children, 72,* 347–361.

Willicutt, E. G., & Pennington, B. F. (2000). Comorbidity of reading disability and attention-deficit/hyperactivity disorder: Differences by gender and subtype. *Journal of Learning Disabilities, 33,* 179–191.

Wilson, B. A. (1999). Inclusion: Empirical guidelines and unanswered questions. *Education and Training in Developmental Disabilities, 34,* 119–133.

Wilson, K. E., Erchul, W. P., & Raven, B. H. (2008). The likelihood of use of social power strategies by school psychologists when consulting with teachers. *Journal of Educational and Psychological Consultation, 18,* 101–123.

Winebrenner, S. (2003). Teaching strategies for twice-exceptional students. *Intervention in School and Clinic, 38*(3), 131–137.

Winebrenner, S., & Devlin, B. (2001). *Cluster grouping of gifted students: How to provide full-time services on a part-time budget.* Washington, DC: U.S. Department of Education, Office of Educational Research and Improvement, Educational Resources Information Center.

Wing, L. (1981). Asperger syndrome: A clinical account. *Psychological Medicine, 11,* 115–129.

Wing, L. (1991). The relationship between Asperger's syndrome and Kanner's autism. In U. Frith (Ed.), *Autism and Asperger syndrome* (pp. 93–121). Cambridge, UK: Cambridge University Press.

Winn, S., & Hay, I. (2009). Transition from school for youths with a disability: Issues and challenges. *Disability & Society, 24,* 103–115.

Winstanley, C. A., Eagle, D. M., & Robbins, T. W. (2006). Behavioral models of impulsivity in relation to ADHD: Translation between clinical and preclinical studies. *Clinical Psychology Review, 26,* 379–395.

Winter, S. M. (2009). Childhood obesity in the testing era: What teachers and schools can do! *Childhood Education, 85,* 283–288.

Winzer, M. A. (1993). *The history of special education: From isolation to integration.* Washington, DC: Gallaudet University Press.

Winzer, M. A. (2007). Confronting difference: An excursion through the history of special education. In L. Florian (Ed.), *The SAGE handbook of special education* (pp. 21–33). Thousand Oaks, CA: Sage.

Winzer, M. A., & Mazurek, K. (1998). *Special education in multicultural context.* Upper Saddle River, NJ: Merrill.

Wirt, J., Choy, S., Provasnik, S., Rooney, P., Sen, A., & Tobin, R. (2003, June). Section 5: Contexts of postsecondary education. *The condition of education 2003.* Retrieved July 2, 2003, from http://nces.ed.gov/pubs_2003/2003067_5.pdf

Wiskochil, B., Lieberman, L. J., & Houston-Wilson, C. (2007). The effects of trained peer tutors on the physical education of children who are visually impaired. *Journal of Visual Impairment & Blindness, 101,* 339–350.

Witte, R. H., Philips, L., & Kakela, M. (1998). Job satisfaction of college graduates with learning disabilities. *Journal of Learning Disabilities, 31,* 259–265.

Witty, P. (1951). *The gifted child.* Boston: Heath.

Witzel, B., Smith, S. W., & Brownell, M. T. (2001). How can I help students with learning disabilities in algebra? *Intervention in School and Clinic, 37*(2), 101–104.

Woblers, K. A. (2008). Using balanced and interactive writing instruction to improve the higher order and lower order writing skills of deaf students. *Journal of Deaf Studies and Deaf Education, 13,* 257–277.

Wolery, M., Anthony, L., Snyder, E. D., Werts, M. G., & Katzenmeyer, J. (1997). Training elementary teachers to embed instruction during classroom activities. *Education and Treatment of Children, 20,* 40–58.

Wolfe, V. (2001). *A look at rural families weighing educational options: Identifying the factors that influence parents as they make educational placement decisions for their children who are deaf. Sharing results.* (ERIC Document Reproduction Service No. ED461243) Retrieved May 4, 2004, from www.edrs.com/Webstore/Download_2.cfm?ID=686825

Wolffe, K. (1996). Career education for students with visual impairments. *RE:view, 28,* 89–93.

Wolffe, K. E. (2000). Career education. In A. J. Koenig & M. C. Holbrook (Eds.), *Foundations of education: Instructional strategies for teaching children and youths with visual impairments* (2nd ed., pp. 679–719). New York: American Foundation for the Blind Press.

Wolffe, K. E., Sacks, S. Z., Corn, A. L., Erin, J. N., Huebner, K. M., & Lewis, S. (2002). Teachers of students with visual impairments: What are they teaching? *Journal of Visual Impairment and Blindness, 96,* 293–304.

Wolffe, K. E., & Spungin, S. J. (2002). A glance at worldwide employment of people with visual impairments. *Journal of Visual Impairment and Blindness, 96,* 246–253.

Wolfram, W., & Schilling-Estes, N. (1998). *American English: Dialects and variations.* Malden, MA: Blackwell.

Wolinsky, S., & Whelan, A. (1999). Federal law and the accommodation of students with LD: The lawyers' look at the BU decision. *Journal of Learning Disabilities, 32,* 286–291.

Wolter, J. A., Wood, A., & D'Zatko, K. W. (2009). The influence of morphological awareness on the literacy development of first-grade children. *Language, Speech, and Hearing Services in Schools, 40,* 286–298.

Wolters, P. L., Brouwers, P., & Perez, L. A. (1999). Pediatric HIV infection. In R. T. Brown (Ed.), *Cognitive aspects of chronic illness in children* (pp. 105–141). New York: Guilford Press.

Wong, B. Y. L. (2000). Writing strategies instruction for expository essays for adolescents with and without learning disabilities. *Topics in Language Disorders, 20*(4), 29–44.

Wood, D., & Wood, H. (1997). Communicating with children who are deaf: Pitfalls and possibilities. *Language, Speech, and Hearing Services in Schools, 28,* 348–354.

Wood, M., & Valdez-Menchaca, M. C. (1996). The effect of a diagnostic label of language delay on adults' perceptions of preschool children. *Journal of Learning Disabilities, 29,* 582–589.

Wood, S., & Gavin, M. K. (2009). Exploring issues and opportunities in gifted students' transitions to college and career. In F. A. Dixon (Ed.), *Programs and services for gifted secondary students: A guide to recommended practices* (55–69). Waco, TX: Prufrock.

Woodbury, A. C. (1991). *Counting Eskimo words for snow: A citizen's guide.* Austin: University of Texas. Retrieved July 25, 2003, from www.ecst.csuchico.edu/~atman/Misc/eskimo-snow-words.html

Woodcock, R. W., McGrew, K. S., & Mather, N. (2001). *Woodcock–Johnson Psychoeducational Battery–III* (tests of achievement). Allen, TX: DLM.

Woodcock, R. W., McGrew, K. S., Schrank, F. A., & Mather, N. (2007). *Woodcock-Johnson III-Normative Update.* Rolling Meadows, IL: Riverside.

Woods, A. M., & Weasmer, J. (2002). Maintaining job satisfaction: Engaging professionals as active participant. *Clearinghouse, 75,* 186–189.

Worcester, J. A., Nesman, T. M., Raffaele Mendez, L. M., & Keller, H. R. (2008). Giving voice to parents of young children with challenging behavior. *Exceptional Children, 74,* 509–525.

Wright, P. W. D., & Wright, P. D. (2005). *Wrightslaw: IDEA 2004.* Hartfield, VA: Harbor House Law Press.

Wright, P. W. D., & Wright, P. D. (2006). *IDEA 2004.* Hartfield, VA: Harbor House Law Press.

Wright, P. W. D., & Wright, P. D. (2009, January). *Special education caselaw: Decisions from U.S. Supreme Court.* Retrieved April 9, 2009 from http://www.wrightslaw.com/caselaw.htm

Wright-Gallo, G. L., Higbee, T. S., Reagon, K. A., & Davey, B. J. (2006). Classroom-based functional analysis and intervention for students with emotional/behavioral disorders. *Education and Treatment of Children, 29,* 421–436.

Wymbs, B. T., Pelham, W. E., Molina, B. S. G., Gnagy, E. M., Wilson, T. K., & Greenhouse, J. B. (2008). Rate and predictors of divorce among parents of youths with ADHD. *Journal of Consulting and Clinical Psychology, 76,* 735–744.

Xin, J. F., & Holmdal, P. (2003). Snacks and skills: Teaching children functional counting skills. *Teaching Exceptional Children, 35*(5), 46–51.

Yeates, K. O., Bigler, E. D., Dennis, M., Gerhardt, C. A., Rubin, K. H., Stancin, T., Taylor, H. G., & Vannatta, K. (2007). Social outcomes in childhood brain disorder: A heuristic integration of social neuroscience and developmental psychology. *Psychological Bulletin, 133,* 535–556.

Yell, M. L. (1998). *The law and special education.* Upper Saddle River, NJ: Merrill.

Yell, M. L. (2006). *The law and special education* (2nd ed.). Upper Saddle River, NJ: Merrill.

Yell, M. L., & Drasgow, E. (1999). A legal analysis of inclusion. *Preventing School Failure, 43,* 118–125.

Yell, M. L., & Drasgow, E. (2007). Assessment for eligibility under IDEIA and the 2006 regulations. *Assessment for Effective Intervention, 32,* 202–213.

Yell, M. L., Katisyannis, A., & Hazelkorn, M. (2007). Reflections on the 25th anniversary of the U.S. Supreme Court's decision in Board of Education v. Rowley. *Focus on Exceptional Children, 39*(9), 1–12.

Yell, M. L., Katisyannis, A., & Ryan, J. B. (2008). Ensure compliance with the Individuals with Disabilities Education Improvement Act of 2004. *Intervention in School and Clinic, 44*(1), 45–51.

Yell, M. L., Katisyannis, A., & Shiner, J. G. (2006). The No Child Left Behind Act, adequate yearly progress, and students with disabilities. *Teaching Exceptional Children, 38*(4), 32–39.

Yell, M. L., Rozalski, M. E., & Drasgow, E. (2001). Disciplining students with disabilities. *Focus on Exceptional Children, 33*(9), 1–12.

Yell, M. L., & Shriner, J. G. (1997). The IDEA amendments of 1997: Implications for special and general education teachers, administrators, and teacher trainers. *Focus on Exceptional Children, 30*(1), 1–19.

Yell, M. L., Shriner, J. G., & Katisyannis, A. (2006). Individuals with Disabilities Education Improvement Act of 2004 and IDEA regulations of 2006: Implications for educators, administrators, and teacher trainers. *Focus on Exceptional Children, 39*(1), 1–12.

Yirmiya, N., Shaked, M., & Erel, O. (2001). Comparison of siblings of individuals with autism and siblings of individuals with other diagnoses: An empirical summary. In E. Schoper, N. Yirmiya, & C. Shulman (Eds.), *The research basis for autism intervention* (pp. 59–73). New York: Kluwer Academic/Plenum Publishers.

Ylvisaker, M., Todis, B., Glang, A., Urbanczyk, B., Franklin, C., DePompei, R., et al. (2001). Educating students with TBI: Themes and recommendations. *Journal of Head Trauma Rehabilitation, 16,* 76–93.

Yoon, S. Y., & Gentry, M. (2009). Racial and ethnic representation in gifted programs: Current status of and implications for gifted Asian American students. *Gifted Child Quarterly, 53,* 121–136.

York-Barr, J., & Kronberg, R. (2002). From isolation to collaboration: Learning from effective partnerships between general and special educators. In W. Sailor (Ed.), *Whole-school success and inclusive education: Building partnerships for learning, achievement, and accountability* (pp. 163–181). New York: Teachers College Press.

Yoshinaga-Itano, C. (2003). From screening to early identification and intervention: Discovering predictors to successful outcomes for children with significant hearing loss. *Journal of Deaf Studies and Deaf Education, 8,* 11–30.

Yoshinaga-Itano, C., & Downey, D. M. (1996). The psychoeducational characteristics of school-aged students in Colorado with significant hearing losses. *Volta Review, 98*(1), 65–96.

Yoshinaga-Itano, C., Sedey, A. L., Coulter, D. K., & Mehl, A. L. (1998). The language of early- and later-identified children with hearing loss. *Pediatrics, 102,* 1161–1171.

Young, S., Gray, K., & Bramham, J. (2009). A phenomenological analysis of the experience of receiving a diagnosis and treatment of ADHD in adulthood: A partner's perspective. *Journal of Attention Disorders, 12,* 299–307.

Youse, K. M., Le, K. N., Cannizzaro, M. S., & Coelho, C. A. (2002, June 28). Traumatic brain injury: A primer for professionals. *The ASHA Leader,* 4–7.

Ysseldyke, J. E., Algozzine, B., & Thurlow, M. L. (2000). *Critical issues in special education.* Boston: Houghton Mifflin.

Ysseldyke, J., & Olsen, K. (1999). Putting alternative assessments into practice: What to measure and possible sources of data. *Exceptional Children, 65,* 175–185.

Yu, J., Newman, L., & Wagner, M. (2009, July). *Secondary school experiences and academic performance of student with mental retardation* [Facts from NLTS2]. Washington, D.C.: Institute of Education Sciences National Center for Special Education Research. Retrieved July 31, 2009 from http://ies.ed.gov/ncser/pubs/20093020.asp

Zabala, J. M. (1999). *Get SETT for successful inclusion and transition.* Retrieved August 19, 2006, from www.ldonline.org/article/6399

Zachor, D. A., Roberts, A. W., Hodgens, J. B., Isaacs, J. S., & Merrick, J. (2006). Effects of long-term psychostimulant medication on growth of children with ADHD. *Research in Developmental Disabilities: A Multidisciplinary Journal, 27,* 162–174.

Zaff, J. F., Calkins, J., Bridges, L. J., & Margie, N. G. (2002). *Promoting positive mental and emotional health in teens: Some lessons from research.* Retrieved April 22, 2004, from http://libproxy.uncg.edu:2101/Webstore/Download2.cfm?ID=715442&PleaseWait_=OK

Zambo, D. (2008). Looking at ADHD through multiple lenses: Identifying girls with the inattentive type. *Intervention in School and Clinic, 44*(1), 34–40.

Zapien, C. (1998, July). *Options in deaf education—History, methodologies, and strategies for surviving the system.* Retrieved October 16, 2003, from www.listen-up.org/edu/options1.htm

Zascavage, V., Schroeder-Steward, J., Armstrong, P., Marrs-Butler, K., Winterman, K., & Zascavage, M. L. (2008). Considerations for the strategic recruitment of special educators. *Teacher Education Quarterly, 35,* 207–221.

Zeanah, C. H. (Ed.). (2000). *Handbook of infant mental health* (2nd ed.). New York: Guilford Press.

Zebehazy, K., & Whitten, E. (1998). Do residential schools and local education agencies collaborate to improve the transitions of students with visual impairments? *Journal of Visual Impairment and Blindness, 92,* 647–655.

Zebehazy, K., & Whitten, E. (2003). Collaboration between special schools and local education agencies: A progress report. *Journal of Visual Impairment and Blindness, 97,* 73–84.

Zentall, S. S., Moon, S. M., Hall, A. M., & Grskovic, J. A. (2001). Learning and motivational characteristics of boys with AD/HD and/or giftedness. *Exceptional Children, 67,* 499–519.

Zepeda, S. J., & Mayers, R. S. (2006). An analysis of research on block scheduling. *Review of Educational Research, 76,* 137–170.

Zera, D. A., & Lucian, D. G. (2001). Self-organization and learning disabilities: A theoretical perspective for the interpretation and understanding of dysfunction. *Learning Disability Quarterly, 24,* 107–118.

Zhang, D., & Stecker, P. M. (2001). Student involvement in transition planning: Are we there yet? *Education and Training in Mental Retardation and Developmental Disabilities, 36,* 293–303.

Zhou, L. (2009). *Revenues and expenditures for public elementary and secondary education: School year 2006–07 (fiscal year 2007)* [NCES 2009-337]. Washington, D.C.: U.S. Department of Education, Institute of Education Sciences, National Center for Education Statistics. Retrieved June 8, 2009 from http://nces.ed.gov/pubsearch/pubsinfo.asp?pubid=2009337

Zigmond, N. (2006). Twenty-four months after high school: Paths taken by youth diagnosed with severe emotional and behavioral disorders. *Journal of Emotional and Behavioral Disorders, 14,* 99–107.

Zionts, L. T., Zionts, P., Harrison, S., & Bellinger, O. (2003). Urban African American families' perceptions of cultural sensitivity within the special education system. *Focus on Autism and Other Developmental Disabilities, 18,* 41–50.

Zionts, L., & Villiers, D. (2003). Standing up and speaking out: Children's mental health policy forecast 2003. *Beyond Behavior, 12*(3), 18–19.

Zirkel, J. P., & Arnold, E. (2001). Putting the I in the IEP. *Educational Leadership, 59*(1), 62–65.

Zirkel, P. A. (2008). A legal roadmap of SBR, PRR, and related terms under the IDEA. *Focus on Exceptional Children, 40*(5), 1–4.

Zirkel, P. A. (2009). Commentary: Legal eligibility of students with learning disabilities: Consider not only RTI but also §504. *Learning Disability Quarterly, 32,* 51–53.

Zirkel, P. A. (2009). Gifted education. *Principal, 88*(5), 57–59.

Zirkel, P. A., & Gischlar, K. L. (2008). Due process hearing under the IDEA: A longitudinal frequency analysis. *Journal of Special Education Leadership, 21*(1), 22–31.

Zirkel, P. A., & Krohn, N. (2008). RTI after IDEA: A survey of state laws. *Teaching Exceptional Children, 40*(3), 71–73.

Zito, J., Safer, D., dosReis, S., & Riddle, M. (1998). Racial disparity in psychotropic medications prescribed for youths with medicaid insurance in Maryland. *Journal of the American Academy of Child and Adolescent Psychiatry, 37,* 179–184.

Zito, J., Safer, D., Riddle, M., Johnson, R., Speedie, S., & Fox, M. (1998). Prevalence variations in psychotropic treatment of children. *Journal of the American Academy of Child and Adolescent Psychiatry, 8,* 99–105.

Zuniga, M. A. (1998). Families with Latino roots. In E. W. Lynch & M. J. Hanson, (Eds.), *Developing cross-cultural competence: A guide for working with children and their families* (2nd ed., pp. 209–250). Baltimore: Paul H. Brookes Publishing Co.

Abebe, A., 421
Abelev, M.S., 203, 204
Abernethy, S., 490
Achenbach, T.M., 176, 177
Achilles, C.M., 92
Achilles, G.M., 74
Acrey, C., 24, 82
Adams, A., 98, 101
Adams, M., 341
Adams-Chapman, I., 404
Adamson, L., 309
Adamson, L.B., 269
Adcock, J., 313
Addeduto, A., 244
Addison, L., 326
Adlof, S.M., 285
Adreon, D., 318, 319
Advokat, C., 181, 191
Agency for Toxic Substances and
    Disease Registry, 169
Agran, M., 150
Agresta, J., 37
Aguilar, C.M., 98, 103
Ahlgrim-Delzell, L., 25, 252,
    442, 444
Ajuwon, P.M., 383, 393, 394
Akrami, N., 235
Akuffo, P.B., 37
Al Otaiba, S., 277, 289
al Otaiba, S., 131
Al-Khabbaz, Z.A., 250, 252
Al-Yagon, M., 138
Alarcon, M., 131
Alba, R., 323
Alberto, P.A., 256
Alessandri, M., 313
Alexander Graham Bell Association
    for the Deaf and Hard of
    Hearing, 332
Algozzine, B., 252, 442
Algozzine, R.F., 152
Ali, S., 316
Allen-Meares, P., 38
Alliance for Technology Access, 94
Allinder, R.M., 447, 448
Allman, C.B., 382, 383, 385, 395
Allsopp, D.H., 224
Almack, K., 251
Alper, S., 349, 442
American Academy of Child and
    Adolescent Psychiatry,
    199, 207
American Academy of Pediatrics,
    175, 176
American Association for the
    Education of the Severely and
    Profoundly Handicapped
    (AAESPH), 437

American Association on
    Intellectual and
    Developmental Disabilities
    (AAIDD), 235, 236, 237, 241
American Association on Mental
    Retardation, 241
American Association on Mental
    Retardation (AAMR), 235
American Council of the Blind, 377
American Foundation for the Blind
    (AFB), 368, 372, 388
American Medical Association
    (AMA), 165
American Obesity Association, 414
American Printing House for the
    Blind (APH), 372, 382
American Psychiatric Association,
    163, 166, 200, 300
American Society for Deaf People
    (ASDC), 347
American Speech-Language-
    Hearing Association, 268,
    273, 276, 279, 293
Anctil, T.M., 151
Anderson, J.A., 227
Anderson, N.B., 271, 280, 291, 463
Anderson, S., 219, 269
Anderson, C.M., 220
Andrews, J.F., 356
Angell, M.E., 45, 244
Angelou, M., 474
Angold, A., 212, 226
Anhalt, K., 217
Antia, S., 343, 357
Antil, L.R., 255
Antle, B.J., 392, 416
Aram, D., 341, 342
Arbib, M.A., 275
Arc, the, 28, 237, 241
Armer, B., 98
Arndt, S.A., 51
Arnold, L., 165
Arrowood, L., 184
Arroyos-Jurado, E., 407, 415
Arthritis Foundation, 406
Arthur-Kelly, M., 450
Artiles, A.J., 21, 68, 76, 78, 79
Ashcroft, S.C., 370
Ashkenazy, E., 380
Asperger Syndrome Coalition, 320
Aspy, R., 312
Association for Educational and
    Rehabilitation of the Blind
    and Visually Impaired, 373
Association for Retarded Children
    (the Arc), 28
Association for the Severely
    Handicapped (TASH), 437

Assouline, S.G., 490
Atkins, M., 325
Attention Deficit Disorder
    Resources, 168
Atwater, S.A.C., 80
Auerbach, S., 450
Autism Society of America, 299
Avanzini, G., 411
Avery, L.D., 483
Avoli, M., 411
Axelrod, S., 122

Bae, S.J., 445
Baghurst, P., 169
Bagwell, C.L., 173
Bahan, B., 333, 362
Bahr, M.W., 106, 110, 121
Bailey, D.B., 238, 249
Bailey, I.L., 378
Bailey, J., 307, 342
Bailey, P.J., 271
Bailey, R.L., 244
Bailey, V.M., 378
Bain, L., 341
Bakeman, R.A., 269, 309
Baker, D.B., 171
Baker, S., 250, 320
Baker, S.R., 260
Bal, A., 76
Balandin, S., 430
Balboni, G., 255
Baldwin, A.Y., 481
Baldwin, J.L., 431
Baldwin, L., 493
Ball, S.W., 174
Balla, D.A., 248
Baltodano, H.M., 27
Banda, D.R., 29, 138
Banks, J.A., 68, 70, 71, 82, 83, 88
Banks, T.I., 217
Bao, Y., 107
Bardin, J.A., 386
Barette, J., 284
Barkley, R.A., 168, 169, 170, 186, 188
Barnes, M.A., 132
Barnes, S.B., 424
Barnhill, G., 305, 321
Baroff, G.S., 257
Baron-Cohen, S., 302
Barraga, N.C., 370
Barth, R.S., 98, 109, 122
Barton, M., 311
Bateman, B.D., 52
Batshaw, M.L., 439
Bauer, A.M., 89
Bauman, L.J., 412
Baumberger, J., 38
Bauminger, N., 133

Bayat, M., 256
Beach Center on Disability, 51
Beachum, F., 74
Beall, J., 488
Beam, A.P., 127
Bear, G.G., 150
Beauchaine, T.P., 202
Beaver, J.B., 252
Beck, A., 170
Beers, M.H., 239
Behnke, A.O., 91
Beirne-Smith, M., 249
Bélanger, J., 472
Bell, A.G., 266, 331
Bell, L., 358
Benbow, C.P., 481
Bender, W.N., 19, 142
Benedek-Wood, E., 286
Benner, G.J., 22, 209, 217, 277, 278
Bennett, A., 9
Bennett, C.I., 71, 72, 89
Bennett, T., 491
Benson, M., 225
Beratan, G., 74
Bergeron, R., 241
Berglund, E., 249
Berkeley, S., 19, 32, 142, 156, 157
Berkow, R., 239
Berliner, D.C., 92
Bernstein, R.R., 492
Bernthal, J., 277
Berry, H.G., 48
Bertella, L., 243
Besnov, K.D., 493
Best Buddies International, 257
Best, A.M., 77
Best, S.M., 425
Besterczey, S.K., 174
Beukelman, D.R., 442, 443
Beytien, A., 326
Bicard, D.F., 62
Bicard, S.C., 62
Biddle, B., 92
Biederman, G., 318
Biederman, J., 174, 181
Bigby, L.M., 38
Bigge, J.L., 403, 404, 425
Biglan, A., 135
Bigler, E.D., 131
Biklen, D., 448
Billingsley, B., 63
Binger, C., 286
Bishop, A., 275
Bishop, V.E., 380, 386
Bivens, C., 81, 86
Blachman, D.R., 173
Black, C., 135
Black, R.S., 253

Blackman, J.A., 201, 278
Blackman, L.S., 234
Blair, T.R., 151
Blanchard, L.T., 201
Blanchett, W.J., 73, 74
Blank, W., 217
Blankenship, K., 390
Bleach, F., 325
Blomgren, M., 273
Blood, G.W., 284
Blood, I.M., 284
Blumberg, E.R., 452
Bock, S.J., 311
Body Health Resources, 412
Boe, E.E., 63
Bogat, G.A., 203
Bolster, L., 352
Bolton, P., 302
Bond, M.A., 276
Bond, V., 407
Bonner, M., 117
Boone, E., 108
Bordnick, P.S., 220
Boreson, L., 221
Borich, G.D., 339
Boscardin, M.L., 23
Bosman, A.M.T., 375
Boss, L.P., 410
Boswell, S., 283, 285
Botting, N., 284
Bouck, E.C., 259
Boulet, S.L., 405
Bowe, F., 404, 406
Bowman-Perrott, L., 223
Boyer, K.L., 63
Boys Town National Research
    Hospital, 346
Bracken, B.A., 481, 483
Brackenbury, T., 293
Brackett, D., 343, 353
Braden, J.P., 339
Bradley, E.A., 252
Bradley, J.F., 104
Braidwood, L.J., 330
Braille, Louis, 369
Brain Injury Association of
    America, 407
Brambring, M., 383
Bramham, J., 191
Brandt, M.D., 189
Brasel, K., 337
Brauner, C.B., 213
Brayboyes, 371
Brayne, C., 302
Braziel, P., 150
Brent, R.L., 405
Brice, A., 134, 280
Brice, A.E., 270
Brickham, D., 250, 252
Bridges, E.M., 492
Bridges, L.J., 174
Bridgest, S.T., 79
Bridglall, B.L., 473
Brieber, S., 168
Brigance, A., 141
Briggs, C.J., 469
Brigham, M., 56

Brightman, H.J., 107
Brighton, C.M., 470, 482
Brilliant, 371
Brittain, K., 395
Broer, S., 250
Broer, S.M., 395, 452
Brouwers, P., 415
Browder, D., 442, 463
Browder, D.M., 25, 252, 442,
    444, 455
Brown, D., 115
Brown, E.F., 481, 490
Brown, F., 446
Brown, F.E., 77
Brown, L., 210, 250, 252
Brown, R.T., 413
Brown, S.W., 483
Brown, V., 280
Brownell, M.T., 98, 101, 102
Browning, L.B., 453
Brozovic, S.A., 256
Bruce, S., 389
Bruder, M.B., 249
Bruner, J.S., 356
Brunet, J.P., 22
Brunner, H., 427
Bruns, D.A., 249
Bry, B.H., 216
Bryan, D., 143
Bryan, T., 155
Bryant, B., 140
Bryant, B.R., 136, 453
Bryant, D.P., 13, 453
Bryant, J., 143
Bryen, D., 431
Bryson, S., 323
Bryson, S.E., 252
Buchanan, M., 483
Buck, L.H., 43
Buescher, T.M., 486
Buettel, M., 387
Bullock, L.M., 407
Burd, L., 239
Burden, R., 137
Burdge, M., 252
Burdge, M.D., 448
Burke, M.D., 81
Burnham, J., 228
Burns, M.K., 63
Burroughs, E., 293
Burstein, K., 155
Burstein, N., 22
Bursuck, W.D., 42, 117, 135, 154,
    155, 187
Burton, C., 223
Burton, J.K., 25
Burton-Smith, R.M., 245
Bury, M., 409
Busby, H., 352
Busch, T., 184
Bussing, R., 174
Byrd, S.E., 156

Cabello, B., 22
Cacace, A.T., 271
Caccamise, F., 356
Cahill, S.M., 111

Calhoun, S., 305, 312
Calhoun, S.L., 133, 139
California Department of Education
    2000, 337
Calkins, J., 174
Callahan, C.M., 470, 472,
    475, 482
Callard-Szulgit, R., 470, 485
Callicott, K.J., 460
Callister, T., 273
Cameto, R., 89, 351
Campbell, A.L., 32
Campbell, D.J., 447
Campbell, N.F., 133
Cannizzaro, M.S., 407
Capizzi 2008, 52
Capper, C.A., 22
Carey, A., 360
Carlberg, C., 147
Carnahan, C., 307
Carnes, S.L., 430
Caron, E.A., 122
Carpenter, L., 318, 319
Carpenter, L.A., 305
Carr, E.G., 459
Carrell, T., 277
Carroll, C., 351
Carroll, J.M., 223
Carroll, S.Z., 452
Carrow-Woolfolk, E., 280
Carter, D.R., 32
Carter, E.W., 137, 150, 151, 215, 217,
    250, 252, 253, 259, 260, 444,
    451, 452
Carter, M., 322
Carter, P., 71
Cartledge, G., 77, 78, 79
Casey, J., 191
Casey, L.B., 63
Casteel, C.A., 77
Castellano, J.A., 469
Castellanos, F.X., 163
Castles, A., 131
Castrogiovanni, A., 285
Cates, C., 410
Catts, H.W., 285
Causton-Theoharis, J.N., 120, 445
Cautilli, J., 122
Cavaiuolo, D., 261
Cavallaro, C., 444, 450
Cavallaro, C.C., 450
Cavell, T.A., 204
Celeste, M., 380, 383
Center for Applied Special
    Technology (CAST), 24
Center for Effective Collaboration
    and Practice, 213
Center for the Evaluation of Risks to
    Human Reproduction, 405
Center of the Study of Autism, 306
Center on Personnel Studies in
    Special Education, 63
Centers for Disease Control and
    Prevention, 165, 181, 209,
    239, 240, 305, 360, 405, 407,
    409, 412
Cepello, M.R., 37

Certo, N., 453
Chadsey, J.G., 453
Chako, A., 184, 185
Chamberlain, B., 325
Chamberlin, S.A., 483
Chan, J., 321
Chandler, B., 39
Chapman, C., 488, 495
Chapman, T.E., 241
Charles, J.M., 305
Charman, T., 316
Cheah, P., 409
Chen, D., 460
Chenausky, K., 337
Cheney, D., 210, 277
Chevallier, C., 308
Childhood Apraxia of Speech
    Association of North
    America, 277
Children's Bureau, 203
Chitiyo, M., 27
Chiu, P., 427
Cho, H.J., 375
Choi, B.Y., 91
Chopra, R.V., 119
Christenson, S., 139
Christodoulou, J., 472
Chronis-Tuscano, A., 185, 186
Chun, V., 217
Churchill, L.R., 37
Cicchetti, D., 248
Claesson, M., 235
Clare, M.M., 118
Clark, C., 375, 383
Clark, H.B., 217
Clark, R.D., 238
Clayton, J., 252, 448
Cleft Palate Foundation, 275
Clegg, J., 251
Clements, M., 63
Clerc, L., 330, 358
Cloninger, C.J., 463
Closs, A., 424
Coelho, C.A., 407
Cohen, A., 380
Cohen, D., 181
Cohen, D., 165
Cohen, O.P., 349
Colangelo, N., 490
Cole, C.M., 243, 451
Coleman, L.J., 472, 485
Coleman, M., 115
Coleman, M.C., 214, 303
Coleman, M.R., 493
Coleman, T.J., 29
Collaborative Programs of
    Excellence in Autism
    (CPEA), 303
Collett-Klingenberg, L.L., 150, 151
Colletti, L.A., 216
Collins, B.C., 444
Collins, S., 228
Colorado Department of Education
    2009, 493
Colson, S.E., 189
Communication Services for the
    Deaf (CSD), 355

Compton, D.L., 143
Connecticut Special Education
    Association, 9
Conners, C.K., 176, 177
Connor, D.J., 22, 73, 76, 149
Connor, R.T., 288
Connor, T., 73, 76
Conroy, M., 213
Conroy, P.W., 385, 388, 392
Conti-Ramsden, G., 270, 284
Convertino, C., 341
Coo, H., 19
Cook, C.R., 208, 477
Cook, K., 321
Cook, K.T., 309, 310
Cook, K.W., 43
Cook, L., 27, 98, 99, 102, 103, 104, 106,
    110, 111, 115, 116, 121, 458
Cook, L.H., 62
Cook-Morales, V.J., 81
Coolican, J., 270
Cooney, G., 237
Coots, J.J., 87
Coover, G., 227
Copeland, S.R., 252
Copeland, W., 226
Copp, H.L., 220
Corbett, D., 108
Corbett, W.P., 217
Corn, A., 375
Corn, A.L., 370, 377, 378, 394
Correa, V.I., 383
Correa-Torres, S.M., 380, 384
Cosbey, J.D., 443
Costello, E.J., 226
Coulter, D.K., 360
Council for Children with Behavior
    Disorders, 205, 229
Council for Exceptional Children
    (CEC), 23, 25, 28, 37, 57,
    194, 259, 487
Council for Exceptional Children,
    Council for Children with
    Behavior Disorders, 205
Council of State Directors of
    Programs for the Gifted
    2001, 472
Council on Interracial Books for
    Children, 78
Courchesne, E., 304
Courtade, G., 25
Coutinho, M.J., 77, 89, 129
Cox, S.G., 489
Coyle, J.L., 293
Coyner, L., 343
Craig, C.J., 394
Cramer, K.M., 155
Cramer, S., 121
Crawford, C., 132
Crawford, S., 377
Crichton, S., 239
Crinella, F.M., 170
Cristalli, M., 214
Crites, S.A., 4
Cronin, B., 286
Croninger, R.G., 74
Cross, C.T., 76, 473

Cross, T., 479
Crow, K.L., 353
Crowell, E.W., 133, 139
Cue, K., 348
Cukrowicz, K., 172
Culatta, B., 284
Cullen, M., 98
Cullen, M.A., 430
Cullinan, D., 208, 209, 210
Cumming, J.J., 46
Cummings, R.L., 139
Cunningham, A., 309
Cunningham, M.M., 415
Curran, C., 141
Curran, E.M., 108
Curtis, S.E., 61
Cuvo, A., 313

D'zatko, K.W., 277
Dale, P.S., 131
Dales, L., 305
Daley, D., 170
Daly, B.P., 414, 415
Danek, M.M., 352
Daniels, K.J., 270
Danneker, J.E., 260
Darling, R.B., 256, 257
Darrow, A.A., 440
Data Accountability Center, 403
Datta, H., 131
Davey, B.J., 221
David, J.L., 121
Davidson Institute for Talent
    Development, 20
Davidson, M.A., 180, 181
Davidson, R., 372
Davis, E., 404
Davis, G.N., 143
Davis, P., 249
Davison, J.C., & Ford, D.Y., 189
Dawson, M.M., 181
Dawson, S., 31
Day, J.N., 376
de Boer-Ott, S.R., 314
De Graaf, I., 227
De Simone, J.R., 147
De Thomas, C.A., 217
de Wolff, M., 227
Deatline-Buchman, A., 154
Debelak, C., 494
DeFries, J.C., 131
DeHaan, R.F., 468
Deidrick, K.K.M., 427
Deidrick, K.M., 428
del Carmen Salazar, M., 85
Delano, M.E., 314
Delgado, B., 119, 460
Delgado, C.E.F., 249
DeMario, N.C., 394
Demchak, M.A., 450, 455
Dempsey, I., 257
Denham, A., 252
Denham, A.P., 448
Denholm, C., 318
Denton, C., 156
Denton, C.A., 122, 143
Denzin, P., 358

DePaepe, P., 412, 413, 414
Department of Special Education
    and Rehabilitation
    Counseling, University of
    Kentucky, 205
DePompei, R., 431
DeShazo-Barry, T., 171
Deshler, D.D., 134, 151, 154, 156
DeSimone, J.R., 147
DeThorne, L.S., 275
Deutscher, B., 179
DeVito, J.A., 103
Devlin, P., 119
Dew, A., 430
Diagnostic and Statistical Manual of
    Mental Disorders, Text
    Revision, Fourth Edition. See
    DSM-IV-TR
Diament, S., 370
Diamond, K.E., 418
Diamond, M., 340
Diana v. State Board of
    Education, 10
Díaz, E., 469
Dieker, L., 111
Diem, J.H., 290
Dietz, S., 174
DiGiovanni, D., 485, 486
Dillon, R., 170
Dion, E., 22
Disabled Peoples' International, 49
Division for Learning
    Disabilities, 127
Division on Developmental
    Disabilities and
    Autism, 258
Division on Mental Retardation
    and Developmental
    Disabilities, 258
Doctor, E., 276
Dodd, B., 276
Doelling, J., 412
Doering, K., 451, 456
Dohrn, E., 208
Dole, R.L., 40
Donenberg, G.R., 412, 415
Donne, V.J., 341
Donovan, M.S., 76, 473
Dooley, E.A., 413
Doré, R., 22
Doren, B., 149
Dotting, N., 270
Douglas, G., 173
Douglas, J.M., 422
Douvanis, G., 15
Dowds, M., 431
Dowdy, C.A., 192
Downey, D.M., 342
Downing, J.E., 442, 443, 444, 450,
    451, 455, 456, 459, 460
Doyle, A., 250
Doyle, M.B., 243, 452
Dral, M.C., 413
Drasgow, E., 47
Dritschel, B., 306
DSM-IV-TR, 163, 164, 166, 174,
    200, 201, 300, 301, 303

Duchan, J., 266, 267
Duchenne, G.B.A., 406
Duchnowski, A.J., 198, 202
Dudley, J.R., 245
Duff, M., 273
Duffy, M.L., 313
Dufour, R., 98
Duhaime, A.C., 407
Duhaney, L.M., 77, 78
Duhaney, L.M.G., 27
Dukes, C., 115
Dummer, G.M., 380
Dumont-Mathieu, T., 311
Dunlap, G., 215, 218, 226
Dunn, C., 208
Dunn, L., 10, 76
Dunn, W., 311
Dunst, C.J., 249
DuPaul, G., 171, 173
DuPaul, G.J., 179, 186, 188
Duquette, C., 390
Duran, E., 85
Durando, J., 375
Durkin, K., 284
Durocher, J., 313
Dwiggins, K., 288, 289
Dybdahl, C.S., 239
Dyches, T., 48, 49, 53
Dyches, T.T., 290
Dyson, L.L., 21

Easterling, C., 293
Echaore-McDavid, S., 40
Eckert, T.L., 179
Eckstein, M., 470
Edens, R.M., 413
Edgar, E., 149
Edmonds, K., 239
Edmonds, M., 134
Education Commission of the
    States, 30
Educators with Disabilities Caucus
    of the Council for
    Exceptional Children, 7
Edwards, L.L., 151
Edwards, P.A., 93
Edwards, R.P., 326
Egan, G., 104
Egger, H.L., 212
Eichinger, J., 450
Eisenberg, D., 172
Eisenbraun, K., 375
Ekehammer, B., 235
Elbaum, B., 148
Elbaum, B.E., 148
Eldredge, N., 343
Eli Lilly, 182
Elledge, L.C., 204
Elliot, L.B., 348
Elliott, J.L., 54
Elliott, L., 352
Elliott, R.T., 377
Elliott, S., 353, 354
Ely, R., 377
Emerson, R.W., 375
English, K.M., 352
Epanchin, B.C., 15

Epanchin, R.W., 15
Ephross, P.S., 102
Epilepsy Foundation of America, 411
Epstein, M.H., 188, 198, 202, 208, 210, 211, 217, 278
Erchul, W.P., 115, 122
Erel, O., 304
Erez, F., 242
Erickson, M.E., 341
Erickson, M.J., 220
Eriksson, M., 249
Erin, J.N., 371, 374, 383
Erwin, E., 456
Erwin, E.J., 12
Espe-Sherwindt, M., 118
Espin, C., 135
Esquivel, S.L., 117, 121
Estell, D.B., 203
Estes, M.B., 93
Etscheidt, S., 51, 449, 452
Etzel, R.A., 304
Evans, C., 208, 209
Evans, J.R., 476
Evans, S., 119
Evans, S.W., 171, 180, 189
Everhart, V.S., 348
Ewing, K.M., 333

Fad, K.M., 190
Faggella-Luby, M.N., 134, 445
Fairlie, R.W., 94
Faith, M.A., 204
Falk-Ross, F., 134
Falvey, M.Z., 54
Faneule, D.P., 157
Fanning, J.L., 288
Faraone, S.V., 181
Farkas, G., 213
Farmer, E.M.A., 203
Farmer, J.E., 427
Farmer, T.W., 203
Farnsworth, C.R., 386
Farrell, P., 249
Fasbender, C., 162
Fazzi, D.L., 370, 374, 375, 381, 383, 470
Fecich, S., 426
Fein, D., 311
Feng, A.X., 483
Fenning, P., 77
Ferrell, K.A., 375, 386, 387, 390
Ferri, B.A., 22, 76
Fewell, R.R., 179, 440
Fey, M.E., 293
Fiedler, C.R., 260
Fielding, C., 323
Figueroa, R.A., 46
Filipek, P.A., 131
Fink-Chorzempa, B., 134
Finn, F.K., 92
Finson, K.D., 252
Fischer, A., 313
Fischer, M., 167
Fischer, M.A., 313
Fish, W.W., 39, 49, 87, 117
Fisher, B., 475

Fisher, D., 49, 451, 455, 459
Fisher, H., 279
Fisher, M., 450, 451
Fitzgerald, S.M., 342
Fitzpatrick, M., 214
Flammer-Rivera, L.M., 184
Fleischer, D.Z., 8, 12, 17
Fleith, D.D., 487
Fleming, J.L., 111
Fletcher, J.M., 132, 133, 137, 156
Flint, L.J., 171
Flipsen, P., 272
Flores, M., 154
Florida Department of Education, 60
Florida Inclusion Network, 120
Flower, A., 210
Flowers, C., 25
Flowers, L., 131
Floyd, J.H., 256
Floyd, K.M., 108
Floyd, R., 241
Foegen, A., 141
Fogt, J.B., 229
Foley, R.M., 226
Fontana, J.L., 154
Food and Drug Administration, 405
Ford, B.A., 493
Ford, D.Y., 76, 473, 481, 485, 490
Fore, E., 81
Foreman, P., 450
Foriska, T., 109
Forness, S.R., 129, 139, 174, 182, 200
Forster, E.M., 395
Foster, J., 491
Foster, S., 348
Foster, S.B., 352
Fowler, C.H., 215, 252
Fowler, M., 174
Fowler, S., 484
Fox, L., 226, 438, 444, 445, 447, 454
Fox, N., 362
Fox, S., 249
Foy, J.B., 155
Fraenkel, P., 117
Frampton, I., 416
Francis, D.J., 156, 157
Francis, P.J., 348
Frank, K., 98
Frankenberg, E.D., 70
Franklin, E., 270
Frasier, M.M., 492
Frattura, E., 22
Frea, W.D., 458
Fredeen, R., 442
Frederickson, N., 316
Freebairn, L.A., 274
Freebody, P., 331
Freedman, B., 318
Freeman, J., 243
Freeman, J.G., 147
French, N.K., 119
French, W., 468
Frey, G.C., 246
Frey, L.M., 221
Frey, N., 49, 455

Friend, M., 13, 15, 21, 22, 27, 42, 98, 99, 102, 103, 104, 106, 110, 111, 114, 115, 116, 117, 120, 121, 135, 146, 154, 187, 458
Friesen, B.J., 228
Fristoe, M., 279
Frith, U., 301
Frostig, M., 126
Fryxell, D., 444
Fuchs, D., 43, 143, 157
Fuchs, L., 132, 143, 156
Fulk, B.M., 255
Fullan, M., 102
Fulmer, D.L., 415

Gabe, J., 409
Gabig, C., 305
Gable, R.A., 208, 221, 409
Gagné, F., 472
Gagnon, E., 321
Gagnon, J.C., 214
Gallagher, J.J., 10
Gallagher, P.A., 103, 256
Gallaudet Research Institute, 331, 333
Gallaudet, T.H., 330
Gallimore, L., 362
Gallucci, C., 451
Gambrell, D., 405
Garcia, L.J., 284
Garcia, S.B., 80, 292
Gardill, M.C., 215
Gardner, E., 141
Gardner, H., 436, 472, 473
Garon, N., 270
Garrison-Kane, L., 412
Gartin, B.C., 412, 413
Gately, S., 319
Gavidia-Payne, S., 256
Gavin, M.K., 473
Gavin, M.K., 487
Gayan, J., 131
Gebaner, K., 122
Geenen, S., 251
Geers, A., 341
Gentry, M., 74, 473, 474
George, A.L., 390
George, M.P., 229
George, N.L., 229
Gerber, M.M., 156
Gerdes, A., 20
Gerhardt, C.A., 417
Gerhardt, P., 316
Geyer, P.D., 351
Ghezzi, P., 320
Giangreco, M.F., 119, 243, 250, 395, 402, 452
Gibb, G.S., 48, 49, 53
Gibbons, K., 157
Gibbs, S.L., 25
Gil-Kashiwabara, E., 251
Gilger, J.W., 130
Giliberti, M., 228
Gillberg, C., 303
Gillett, Y., 431
Gillon, G.T., 285

Gischlar, K.L., 59
Givner, C.C., 54, 208
Gladstone, D., 491
Glaeser, B., 150, 215
Glaeser, B.C., 137
Glanton, A., 214
Glasberg, B., 325
Glass, K., 138
Glazer, S.M., 271
Glew, M.C., 110
Godbold, E., 389
Goddard, L., 306
Goddard, R.D., 71, 89, 121
Goddard, Y.L., 121
Goetz, E., 431
Goetz, L., 438, 450, 451
Goffman, E., 10
Goin-Kochel, R.P., 324
Gold, M.E., 377
Goldberg, M.L., 468
Goldberg, P., 427
Goldin-Meadow, S., 341
Goldman, R., 279
Goldstein, D.E., 149
Goldstein, H., 10
Goldstein, K., 126
Goldstein, S., 152
Gompel, M., 375
Gonzalez, J., 223
Goodman, R., 191
Gordin, D.N., 494
Gordon, E.W., 473
Gordon, R.L., 374
Goring, J., 174
Gottardo, A., 281
Gottfried, A.E., 477
Gottfried, A.W., 477
Graetz, B.W., 169
Graetz, J., 169
Graham, S., 134, 260
Grainger, J., 171
Grandin, Temple, 301, 302
Grant, C.A., 85
Grantham, T.C., 76, 473, 492
Gravois, T.A., 106
Gray, C., 322, 375
Gray, K., 191
Gray, S., 277
Green, C., 452, 453
Green, T., 81
Green, T.D., 81
Greenberg, M.T., 138, 343, 345
Greenburg, L.M., 176
Greene, R.W., 174
Greenfield, R., 356
Greenhill, L., 191
Greenspan, S., 235
Gregory, G.H., 495
Greiling, A.K., 309
Grether, S.M., 290
Griffer, M., 291
Griffin, C.C., 39, 59, 103, 106, 121
Griffin-Shirley, N., 394
Grigal, M., 260
Groce, N.E., 461
Groen, A.D., 249

Gross, B., 236
Gross, M.U.M., 490
Grossman, B., 312
Grossman, H., 73, 94
Grossman, H.J., 441
Grossnicklaus, K., 246
Grove, K.A., 451
Grskovic, J.A., 174
Gruttadaro, D., 228
Guardino, C.A., 333
Guck, T.P., 430
Gudino, O., 215
Guerra, P.L., 72
Guetzloe, E.C., 214
Guiliani, G., 46, 47, 53, 110
Guitar, C., 274
Gumley, A., 237
Gumpel, T.P., 137
Gunn, B., 135
Gunter, P.L., 223
Guralnick, M.J., 288
Gurka, M.J., 201, 278
Guscia, R., 236
Gustafson, K.E., 413
Guteng, S.I., 354
Guth, C.B., 252
Guthmann, D., 343
Guthrie, P., 16
Gutierrez, A., Jr., 313
Gutstein, S., 314, 321

Haager, D., 63
Haar, J., 73, 77
Haas, A., 270, 273
Hagan-Burke, S., 221
Hagiwara, T., 305, 318
Hahn, H., 236
Hale, M.N., 313
Hall, A.M., 174
Hall, G., 73
Hall, G.S., 198
Hallahan, D.P., 126, 127
Halliday, C., 370
Halperin, J., 180
Halsey, H.N., 220
Hamill, D.D., 140
Hamilton, R., 463
Hammer, S.J., 305
Hammill, D.D., 126, 140, 280
Hammill, D.R., 210
Hammond, M.A., 288
Hampton, J.D., 463
Hand, K.E., 385
Handler, M.W., 215
Haney, M., 450
Hanft, B., 39
Hannah, M., 257
Hansen, A.J., 274
Hansen, A.L., 73
Hansen, D.J., 217
Happe, F., 308
Hardman, M.L., 31, 438, 448
Harmon, J., 213
Harmon, M.T., 277
Harold, C., 406
Harper, G.E., 255

Harper, G.F., 224
Harper, R.E., 38
Harries, J., 236
Harris, K.R., 134
Harris, M.S., 427
Harris, P.J., 27
Harris, S.F., 290
Harris-Murri, N., 21
Harris-Obiakor, P., 87
Harrison, C., 484
Harrison, M.M., 417
Harry, B., 28, 39, 76, 88, 89, 100, 117, 118, 258
Hart, B., 340
Hart, J.E., 83, 313
Hartman, E., 375
Hartman, M.A., 453
Harty, S., 180
Harvey, A., 251
Harvey, E.A., 179
Hasbrouck, J.E., 122
Hastings, R., 170, 325
Hastings, R.P., 28
Hatlen, P., 369, 370, 390
Hatton, D.D., 249
Hauser-Cram, P., 245
Havighurst, R.J., 468
Hawkins, J., 463
Hawks, D.E., 258
Haworth, C., 131
Hay, D., 167, 168, 177
Hay, I., 55
Haycock, K., 132
Haydon, T., 213
Hayiou-Thomas, M.E., 275
Hazelkorn, M., 11, 15
Heacox, D., 494
Hearing Loss Association of
    America (HLAA), 347
Heath, M.A., 290
Heath, N.L., 155
Hedrick, B.N., 421
Heflin, L.J., 88, 305, 326
Heflinger, C.A., 26
Heilbronner, N., 473
Heiman, T., 155
Heine, C., 271
Heineman, M., 215, 218
Heinze, T., 377, 392, 393, 394
Helenius, P., 275
Helfer, J.A., 481
Heller, K.W., 403, 404, 425, 430–431
Henderson, B., 157
Henderson, M., 82
Hendricks, D., 314
Henfield, M.S., 473
Henley, J., 447
Henley, M., 152
Hennessey, J., 181
Hermansen, E., 320
Hernandez, J.E., 117
Herr, C.M., 52
Hertzog, N.B., 491
Hess, H.L., 326
Hess, K.L., 88, 305
Heubert, J.P., 92

Heward, W.L., 446
Hewitt, L.E., 293
Hickson, L., 234, 235
Higareda, I., 76, 79
Higbee, T.S., 221
High, L., 131
Higham, S., 486
Hill, C., 170, 452
Hill, L.D., 20
Hindin, A., 98, 103
Hinrichs Der, H., 217
Hinshaw, S., 171
Hinshaw, S.P., 173
Hirte, C., 169
Hitchings, W.E., 150
Hoadley, C.M., 494
Hobbs, N., 10
Hodge, S.R., 37
Hodgens, J.B., 181
Hodson, B.W., 290
Hoff, E., 270
Hoffmeister, R., 333, 362
Hogansen, J., 251
Holbrook, M.C., 237, 377, 381, 382,
    385, 395
Holdnack, J.A., 156
Holler, R., 16
Hollingsworth, L.S., 468
Holmes, R.B., 370
Holzbauer, J.J., 58
Honein, M.A., 405
Hood, C., 409
Hoppey, D., 15, 251
Hopson, J., 340
Horn, E., 450
Horn, I.S., 120
Horn, S.P., 94
Horn, W.F., 129
Horne, D., 126
Horton, J., 307
Horvat, M., 246
Hosp, J.L., 77, 127
Hosterman, S., 173
Hough, R., 215
Houghton, S., 162, 173, 180, 185
Hourcade, J., 237
Houston-Wilson, C., 385
Houwen, S., 375
Howe, S.G., 369
Howell, A., 245
Howes, N., 131
Howley, A., 488
Howlin, P., 306, 316
Hoy, W., 340
Hoza, B., 20, 173
Hubl, D., 304
Hudson, R.F., 131
Hudspeth, R., 427
Hudyma, S., 185
Huebner, K.M., 370, 371
Huer, M.B., 290
Hughes, C., 150, 444
Hughes, J.N., 204
Hughes, M.T., 148, 155, 282
Hughes, R.S., 257

Hughes, T., 73, 74, 154, 252
Hugo, R., 133
Human Genome Project, 414
Humphries, S., 350
Humphries, T., 139, 333
Hunt, A., 182
Hunt, N., 429
Hunt, P., 438, 450, 451, 456, 457
Hurry, J., 276
Hutchins, B.C., 203
Hux, K., 407
Hyde, M.S., 244

Iacono, W., 172
IDEA 20 U.S.C., 127, 199, 371
IDEA Partnership, 25
Idol, L., 23, 24, 148
Ingham, R.J., 273
Innes, F.K., 418
Innes, J., 349, 351
International Council for Learning
    Disabilities, 141
Iobst, E.A., 427
Irvine, J.J., 94
Isaacs, J.S., 181
Isenberg, S.J., 374
Ishii-Jordan, S.R., 74
Ishikawa, M.E., 151
Itard, Jean-Marc-Gaspard
Itier, R., 304
Ittenbach, R., 249
Ivey, M.L., 326
Iyengar, S.K., 274

Jabaley, T., 360
Jackson, C., 114, 121
Jackson, N.E., 476
Jacob, S., 63
Jacobson, L.A., 151
Jahoda, A., 237
Janas, M., 204
Janney, R.E., 110
Jans, L., 431
Janzen, J., 299, 308
Jarque, S., 181
Jeffs, T., 108
Jenkins, J.R., 255
Jenner, W., 305
Jensen, M.M., 252
Jerman, O., 133, 136
Jimenez, A., 118
Jimenez, B.A., 444
Jitendra, A., 173
Jitendra, A.K., 151, 153, 154
Jochum, J., 141
Johanson, G., 218
Johansson, I., 249
Johns, B., 228
Johns, B.H., 214
Johnsen, S.K., 20, 470
Johnson, D.R., 110
Johnson, D.T., 483
Johnson, E., 156
Johnson, F.P., 110
Johnson, J., 120, 165, 384
Johnson, J.R., 68, 257

Johnson, L.J., 101, 106
Johnson, P., 149
Johnson, R.C., 349
Johnson, S.K., 104
Johnston, S., 443
Johnstone, C., 24, 82
Joint Coordinating Committee on
    Evidence-Based Practice,
    American Speech-Hearing
    Association, 293
Jolly, A., 119
Jolly, J.L., 468, 493
Jones, B., 51
Jones, H., 185, 186
Jones, H.A., 106
Jones, J.E., 273
Jones, J.K., 333
Jones, L.S., 319
Jones, P., 357
Jones, T.W., 333
Jones, V., 208, 226, 319
Jones, W., 304
Jordan, L.J., 10
Joseph, J., 167
Joseph, L.M., 481
Judge, S., 108
Justice, L.M., 293
Juvenile Diabetes Foundation, 415

Kaff, M.S., 120, 215
Kaffenberger, C., 427
Kalinyak, K., 414
Kalis, T., 217
Kalke, T., 214
Kamhi, A., 292
Kamhi, A.G., 285
Kamphaus, R.W., 210
Kamps, D.M., 255
Kampwirth, T.J., 115
Kanner, L., 7, 235, 298
Kaplan, L., 69
Karchmer, M.A., 334, 358
Karlsen, B., 141
Karnes, F.A., 470, 493
Kasahara, M., 118
Kasari, C., 325
Kassini, I., 285
Katiskyannis, A., 11, 43, 48
Katsiyannis, A., 401
Katz, J., 450
Katz-Leavy, J., 228
Katzenstein, T., 174
Kauffman, J.M., 22, 56, 127, 198
Kavale, K., 147
Kavale, K.A., 43, 127, 129, 139, 142,
    156, 157, 174, 182
Kay, T., 416, 448
Kea, C.D., 94
Kearns, J., 54, 252, 448
Kearns, J.F., 447, 448
Keckler, W.T., 476
Keefe, E.B., 22
Keen, D., 257
Keener, N., 16
Keller, H., 437
Keller, H.R., 219
Kelley-Smith, S., 287

Kellner, M.H., 216
Kellner, R., 173
Kelly, M.L., 94
Kelly, P., 394
Kelly, S.M., 380
Kendrick, J., 20
Kennedy, C.H., 444, 451
Kennedy, E., 291
Kennedy, M.R.T., 415
Kent, R.D., 293
Kentucky Department of
    Education, 205
Kephart, N.C., 126
Kern, L., 229
Kersh, J.E., 245
Kessler, R.C., 180
Kettler, T., 493
Key, D.L., 22
Keyser-Marcus, L., 407
Khorsheed, K., 120
Kilgore, K.L., 106
Kilincaslan, A., 404
Killu, K., 221
Kim, K.H., 452
Kimbrough, B.T., 375
Kimm, C., 54
Kincaid, D., 215, 218
Kinch, C., 221
King, B.S., 450
King, K., 255
King, K.A., 482, 493
King-Sears, M.E., 25, 81, 242
Kingner, J., 76
Kingsley, E.P., 257
Kirby, N., 236
Kirchner, C., 370, 372, 388
Kirk, K.I., 362
Kisor, H., 342
Klein, A.M., 72, 73
Klein, R.G., 172
Kleinert, H., 54
Kleinert, H.L., 444, 447, 448
Kleinhart, H., 252
Kliewer, C., 448
Klin, A., 304
Kline, F., 126, 130, 133
Klinger, J.K., 93
Klinger, L.G., 171
Klingner, J.K., 10, 80, 148
Kloo, A., 111
Kluwin, T.N., 330, 339, 341,
    343, 356
Knight, M., 120
Knitzer, J., 200, 226
Knowlton, E., 214
Knowlton, M., 377
Kochhar-Bryant, C.A., 98
Kode, K., 7
Koegel, L.K., 318, 442, 444
Koegel, R.L., 318, 442, 444
Koenig, A.J., 237, 366, 370, 377, 381,
    382, 386, 394
Koestler, F.A., 371
Kogan, M.D., 302–303
Kohler, K., 82
Kohnert, K., 280
Kollins, S.H., 182

Konrad, M., 51, 261
Koontz, K., 414
Kopp, L.M., 202
Koro-Ljungberg, M., 174
Kortering, J.L., 139
Kortering, L.J., 150
Kos, J., 177, 185
Kourea, L., 77, 78, 79
Koutsoftas, A.D., 277
Kovaleski, J., 103
Kovaleski, J.F., 110
Kovas, Y., 131
Kozleski, E.B., 482
Krain, A.L., 163
Krajewski, J.J., 244
Kraska, M., 421
Kratochvil, C.J., 162
Kratochwill, T.R., 63, 227
Krause, A., 98
Krebs, C., 380
Kreimeyer, K., 45, 343
Krezman, C., 286
Kroeger, S.D., 223
Krohn, N., 43
Kruger, J.J., 133
Kruger, R.J., 133
Kubiana, R.M., 134
Kuhn, S., 326
Kulik, B.J., 420
Kummer, A.W., 272
Kummerer, S.E., 282
Kundert, D.K., 238
Kunzman, R., 485
Kuo, H., 325
Kurkowski, C., 452
Kurtzweil, P., 405
Kusche, C.A., 343, 344, 345
Kushner, M.I., 43, 121
Kutash, K., 198, 202
Kutz, G.D., 229

La Paro, K.M., 446
LaFee, S., 414
Lahey, B., 171
Lahey, B.B., 173
Laing, S.P., 292
Lajiness-O'Neill, R., 131
Lamar-Dukes, P., 115
Lambert, N.M., 247
Lancioni, G.E., 443, 453
Land, L.E., 444
Landrum, T.J., 198
Landsdowne, K., 482
Lane, H., 333, 362
Lane, K.L., 137, 150, 208, 209, 215,
    253, 260
Lane, S., 358
Lang, R., 320
Lansing, M., 311
LaRock, D., 341
Larsen, S., 280
Larson, L., 244
LaRusso, M.D., 228
Lassen, S.R., 218
Latimer, W.W., 181
Lau, A., 215
Lau, M.Y., 106

Lavigne, J.V., 416
Lawrence, B.K., 483
Lawrie, A.A., 276
Layton, C.A., 151, 394
Lazar, M.F., 407
Le Couteur, A., 311
Le, K.N., 407
Leach, D., 313
Leaf, R., 320, 321
Learning Disabilities Association of
    America, 133
LeBovidge, J.S., 416
Lee, A., 442
Lee, C., 70
Lee, H., 431
Lee, R.S., 77
Lee, S., 171, 191, 260, 261, 305
Lee, S.S., 173
Lee, S.W., 430
Lee, V., 219
Lee, Y., 452
LeFever, G.B., 189
Leffert, J.S., 244
Lefton-Greif, M.A., 293
Lehmkuhl, H.D., 414, 415
Lehr, D., 446
Lehtinen, L., 126
LeJeuen, B.J., 375
Leland, H., 247
Lemanek, K.L., 409, 427
Lembke, E.S., 141
Lemmick, L.A.P.M., 375
Lenden, J.M., 272
Leo, J., 191
Leone, P.E., 214
Lerman, D., 326
Lerner, J., 126, 130, 133
Lesaux, N.K., 74
Levendosky, A.A., 203
Levin, J.R., 227
Levine, P., 351
Levitan, L., 358
Levy, F., 167, 168
Levy, S.E., 320
Lewis, B.A., 274
Lewis, S., 119, 382, 383, 385, 386,
    395, 442
Lewis-Palmer, T., 221
Leyser, Y., 392, 393
Lieberman, L., 380, 385
Lieberman, L.J., 385
Liebert, T.W., 22
Lienemann, T.O., 188
Light, J., 286
Lightfoot, J., 422
Liljequist, L., 198
Lim, J., 409
Linan-Thompson, S., 151
Lindstrom, L., 149, 150
Lipton, M., 76
Listerud, J., 320
Little, M.E., 111
Little, T., 261
Little, T.D., 241
Liu, Y., 351
Llewellyn, G., 430
Lloyd, G., 181

Lloyd, J.E.V., 19
Lloyd, J.W., 181
Lo, L., 117
Lock, R.H., 151
Lockee, B.B., 25
Lockhart, A.L., 99
Loftin, R., 305
Logan, K., 451
Logemann, J.A., 279
Lohmeier, K., 390
Lohmeier, K.L., 390
Lohmeier, L.L., 391
London, E., 304
Long, C.E., 278
Longmore, P.K., 400
Lopez-Reyna, N.A., 282
Lord, C., 311
Lorenzi, D.G., 246
Lortie, D.C., 98
Lovaas, I., 322
Lovaas, O.I., 320
Loveland, T., 22
Lowenfeld, B., 374, 381, 391
Lucian, D.G., 133
Luckasson, R., 237, 242
Luckner, J.L., 351, 352, 353, 354, 356, 358, 359, 386
Lue, M.S., 269, 272
Luftig, R., 137
Luftig, R.L., 150
Lussenhop, K., 377
Lustig, D.C., 29
Ly, T.M., 249, 257
Lyman, R.D., 171
Lynch, E.W., 118
Lyon, G.R., 132, 142, 143
Lyons, G., 307

Maag, J.W., 138
MacFarland, D.J., 271
Mackay, L.E., 293
Mackintosh, V.H., 324
MacLennan, D.C., 421
MacLennan, D.L., 421
Macleod-Gallinger, J., 352, 353
Madan-Swain, A., 412
Madaus, J.W., 151, 158
Maggio, E., 228
Magiati, I., 316
Magiera, K., 112, 122, 148
Magliaro, S.G., 25
Maheady, L., 224
Maholmes, V., 77
Mahon, M.M., 430
Mahr, K., 162
Maier, J., 451, 456
Majd, M., 243, 451
Mak, M., 173
Malcolm, K.T., 204
Mallette, B., 224, 255
Malmgren, K.W., 120, 445
Maloney, K., 284
Mandell, C.J., 419
Mandell, D.S., 320
Manning, S., 493
Mannuzza, S., 172
Mar, H., 384

March of Dimes, 238
Marcus, L., 311
Margie, N.G., 174
Marino, E.C., 53
Marino, M.T., 53
Marlin, A.E., 405
Maroney, S.A., 252
Marquardt, J., 407
Marschark, M., 341, 343, 356
Marshall, J., 69
Marshall, J.M., 69
Marshall, L.H., 100
Martin, C., 81
Martin, J.E., 100, 111, 260
Martin, J.K., 421
Martinez-Torteya, C., 203
Marton, I., 180
Masia-Warner, C., 217
Mason, B.A., 209, 223
Mason, C., 51, 372, 394
Mason, S., 430
Masterson, J., 276
Mastropieri, M.A., 23, 122, 154, 156
Mather, N., 140, 152, 210
Mather, S.M., 351
Matheson, C., 244
Mathews, R., 405
Mathews, T.J., 405
Matrix Parent Network for Parents of Children with Learning Disabilities, 155
Matthews, B., 227, 410
Matthews, D., 491
Matthews, W.J., 220
Matuszny, R.M., 29, 138
Mautz, D., 453
Maxon, A.B., 343
May, W.L., 416
Mayberry, R.I., 341
Mayes, S., 305, 312
Mayes, S.D., 133, 139
Mayne, A.M., 360
Mayr, T., 212
Mazurek, K., 84, 89
McAllister, R., 375
McCabe, K., 215
McCallum, R.S., 483
McCathren, R., 249, 383
McClendon, J., 118
McClintock, B., 474
McClure, S., 277, 278
McCluskey, A., 189
McCluskey, K., 189
McCoach, D.B., 478
McCormick, M.C., 305
McCoy, K., 320
McCray, A.D., 79
McCurdy, M., 134
McDonald, L., 227
McDonnell, A.P., 376, 383, 438, 448
McDonnell, J.J., 438, 448
McDuffie, K., 122
McDuffie, K.A., 23
McEachin, J., 320
McGahee, M., 51
McGee, K., 56

McGee, T., 360
McGoey, K.E., 179
McGowan, R.S., 337
McGrew, K.S., 140, 210
McGuire, J.M., 24, 122, 157, 450
McIntosh, A.S., 68, 81, 257
McIntosh, K., 32
McIntyre, T., 245, 249, 254
McKee, B., 348
McKee, B.G., 348
McKee, M., 326
McKenzie, A.R., 119
McKenzie, H.S., 102
McLaughlin, M.J., 74, 122
McLaughlin, V.L., 148
McLendon, M.K., 488
McLeskey, J., 15, 22, 23, 121, 251
McLesky, J., 24
McNaughton, D., 286
McNeil, C.B., 184
McNerney, C., 372
McPhail, J., 147
McTighe, J., 494
McVilly, K.R., 245
Means, B.M., 494
Mechling, L.C., 286
Mehl, A.L., 360
Meier, R.P., 337
Melekoglu, M.A., 452
Mellard, D., 103
Mellard, D.F., 156
Menninger, W.C., 98
Meo, B., 82
Mercer, C.D., 126
Mercer, J., 10
Mercugliano, M., 175
Merrick, J., 181
Merrill, R.M., 273
Metheny, J., 149
Metz, D.E., 270, 273
Meyer, C., 284
Meyer, L.H., 22, 450, 451, 458, 459
Michael, R.J., 411
Michaud, L.J., 407
Mick, E., 181
Midlarsky, E., 257
Mihalas, S., 224
Mikulineer, M., 138
Milham, M., 215
Miller, C., 180
Miller, D., 21, 239
Miller, D.N., 215
Miller, E.M., 472, 475
Miller, K.J., 348
Miller, L., 120
Miller, M.L., 416
Miller, N.E., 309, 310
Miller, R.L., 165
Miller, T.W., 165
Milligan, C., 24, 82
Millikan, E., 244
Mills v. Board of Education of the District of Columbia (1972), 10
Mills, J.R., 476
Mills, T., 174

Milner, H.R., 485, 490
Mims, P.J., 442
Miranda, A., 181
Mirenda, P., 442, 443, 450
Mitchell, R.E., 334, 336, 358
Mitchell, S., 111
Mitchell, W., 256
Miyamoto, R.T., 362
Mock, D., 43, 157
Moeller, M.P., 360
Moes, D.R., 458
Moffett, A., 380
Mogharreban, C.C., 249
Mohr, J.D., 409
Mokher, C.G., 488
Molina, B.S., 173
Monda-Amaya, L., 103
Monda-Amaya, L.E., 104, 111, 138
Mondale, S., 8
Monroe, C.R., 77
Montague, M., 137, 174
Montgomery, D.J., 121
Montoya, L., 341
Monuteaux, M.C., 174
Moog, J., 341
Moon, M.S., 260
Moon, S.M., 174
Moon, T.R., 470, 482
Moore, J.B., 427
Moore, J.E., 389
Moore, J.L., 473, 485, 490
Moore, M.S., 358
Moore, S.T., 317
Moore, V., 22
Moores, D., 339, 341
Moores, D.F., 362
Morgan, P.L., 43, 157, 213
Morningstar, M.E., 452
Morocco, C., 98, 103
Morrier, M.J., 88, 92, 305, 326
Morris, P.E., 477
Morris, R.D., 132
Morrow, A.L., 189
Morse, W.C., 224
Mortimore, T., 134
Moss, J.W., 10
Most, T., 341, 342
Mott, E., 98, 103
Moule, J., 77
Mount, B., 447
Mozart, L., 475
Mozart, W., 475
Mroz, M., 286
Mrug, S., 20, 173
Mueller, J., 281
Muhlenhaupt, M., 387
Muir, S., 351, 354, 359
Mukaddes, N.M., 404
Mukherjee, S., 422
Mulholland, R., 37
Multiethnic Pediatric Eye Disease Study Group 2009, 372
Mumford, V., 74
Mundschenk, N.A., 226
Munk, D.D., 155
Munson, L.J., 429
Murdick, N.L., 412, 413

Murphy, E., 251
Murray, C., 122, 138
Murray, D., 149
Murray, F.R., 226
Murray, M.M., 108, 419
Muscott, H.S., 29
Muscular Dystrophy Association, 406
Musti-Rao, S., 307
Muthert, D., 150
Muyskens, P., 106
Myers, B.J., 324
Myers, C., 402, 424
Myles, B., 321
Myles, B.S., 298, 305, 306, 308, 309, 310, 311, 318, 319, 321, 322

Nabors, L.A., 414, 427
Nadeau, K.G., 167
Nadler, R.S., 356
NADS (National Association for Down Syndrome), 237
NAGC (National Association for Gifted Children), 475
Nail-Chiwetalu, B.J., 293
Nancollis, A., 276
Nangle, D.W., 217
Naponelli-Gold, S., 389
National Alliance of Black School Educators, 75, 77, 80
National Alliance on Mental Illness, 228
National Association for Bilingual Education, 77
National Association for Down Syndrome, 28
National Association for Down Syndrome (NADS), 237
National Association for Gifted Children (NAGC), 470, 475, 483, 485, 487
National Association of State Directors of Special Education, 333
National Association for the Education of African American Children with Learning Disabilities, 129
National Association of Multicultural Education, 83
National Black Association for Speech-Language and Hearing, 280
National Cancer Institute, 412, 413
National Center for Education Statistics, 37, 69, 83, 92, 93, 332, 472
National Center for Hearing Assessment and Management, 360
National Center for Learning Disabilities, 55
National Center on Birth Defects and Developmental Disabilities, 239

National Center on Secondary Education and Transition and PACER Center, 55
National Clearinghouse for Careers in Special Education, 39
National Clearinghouse for Professions in Special Education, 40
National Coalition on Mental Health and Special Education, 199–200
National Deaf Education Center, 358
National Diabetes Information Clearinghouse, 414
National Dissemination Center for Children with Disabilities, 372, 405
National Down Syndrome Society, 237
National Exchange Carriers Association (NECA), 355
National Eye Institute, 369
National Federation of the Blind, 377
National Fragile X Foundation, 238
National Institute for Direct Instruction, 152
National Institute of Child Health and Development, 238, 303, 304
National Institute of Child Health and Human Development, 131
National Institutes of Health, 238
National Institute of Mental Health, 162, 167, 168–169, 174, 181, 190–191, 192, 206, 207, 209
National Institute of Neurological Disorders and Stroke, 135, 303, 406
National Institute on Deafness and Other Communication Disorders (NIDCD), 270, 274, 275
National Institutes of Health (NIH), 165, 239, 405
National Joint Committee on Learning Disabilities, 127, 156, 158
National Mental Health Association, 207
National Research Council, 312, 316, 326
National Society for Crippled Children, 437
National Spinal Cord Injury Association, 405
National Spinal Cord Injury Statistical Center, 405
*National Survey of Children's Health,* 302–303
National Technical Institute for the Deaf (NTID), 348
National Virtual Translation Center, 269

Navan, J., 473
Neal, L.I., 79
Neilands, J., 257
Nelson, B., 81, 86
Nelson, J.M., 177
Nelson, J.R., 22, 209, 217, 220, 277, 278
Nelson, S.W., 72
Nesman, T.M., 219
Nettelbeck, T., 236
Neubert, D., 253
Neubert, D.A., 260
Neville, B., 288
Nevin, A.I., 456
New Horizons for Learning, 106
New York State Department of Education, 463
Newcorn, J., 180
Newman, E., 217
Newman, L., 89, 117, 252, 351
Newman, M., 269
Newport, E.L., 337
Newsome, P., 46
Newton, D.W., 291
Nicholas, J.S., 305
Nichols, S.M.C., 62, 63
Nichols, W.D., 151
Nietfield, J., 182
Nieto, S., 122
Nieto, S.M., 71, 91
Nigg, J.T., 165
Nihira, K., 247
Nikopoulos, C., 318
Nikopoulou-Smyrni, P., 318
Nippold, M.A., 288
Nittrouer, S., 337
Noll, R.B., 414, 417
North Carolina Partnership Training System for Special Education, 171
Northwest Regional Educational Laboratory, 116
Nourse, S., 149
Noveck, L., 308
Nover, S.M., 356
Nowell, B.L., 118
Nowell, R., 349, 351
Nowicki, E.A., 409

O'Brien, H.A., 313
O'Brien, J., 447
O'Brien, L., 447
O'Connor, C., 20
O'Donoghue, T., 162
O'Hanlon, L., 291
O'Neill, R., 376
O'Reilly, M., 320, 321–322
O'Sullivan, A., 430
O'Sullivan, T., 430
Oakes, J., 76
Oakley, G.P., 405
Obasi, C., 333
Obiakor, F.E., 87, 493
Ochoa, T.A., 94, 119, 460
Oddo, N.S., 388
Oddson, B., 288

Oden, M., 468
Odom, S., 309
Office for Civil Rights, 17
Ogletree, B.T., 313
Ogston, K., 484
Oh, K., 94
Oh, K.M., 427
Ohtake, Y., 453
Olenchak, F.R., 479
Oliver, R., 356
Olley, J.G., 257
Olsen, K., 446
Olsen, R.J., 244
Olson, B.J., 107
Olson, L.A., 476
Olson, R.K., 131
Omdal, S., 493
Openden, D., 442
Ophir-Cohen, M., 380
Opp, G., 126
Orelove, F.P., 456, 460
Oren, T., 313
Orfield, G., 70
Orsmond, G., 325
Ortiz, A.A., 43, 80, 121
Osborne, S., 170
Osborne, S.S., 121
Osgood, R., 8, 9, 11
Osher, T., 228
Oswald, D.P., 77, 89, 129
Oswald, K., 218
Ouellette-Kuntz, H., 19
Overby, M., 277
Overton, T., 323
Owens, E., 171, 173, 191
Owens, E.B., 173
Owens, R.E., 270, 273
Oyinlade, A.O., 383, 393
Ozturk, M.A., 494

Packard, A.L., 15
Padden, C., 333
Paden, E.P., 282
Paetau, R., 275
Pagliaro, C.M., 342, 343
Painter, C.A., 180
Palmer, S., 260, 261, 450
Palmer, S.B., 260, 375
Pang, V.P., 68
Pao, M., 412
Parayitam, S., 107
PARC, 10
Parens, E., 165
Parette, H.P., 26, 53, 290
Parette, P., 290
Park, J., 257
Park, K., 174
Parmar, R.S., 147
Parmenter, T.R., 245
Parrish, R., 5
Parson-Tylka, T., 358
Parsons, M.B., 452, 453
Parvianen, T., 275
Pascoe, S., 450
Passarotti, A., 304
Passo, M.H., 417

Passow, A.H., 468
Pastor, D.A., 180
Pastor, P.N., 139, 165
Pate-Bain, H., 92
Patel, T., 306
Patton, J.R., 192, 235, 249
Patton, S.B., 8
Paul, P.V., 341
Pavri, S., 137, 138
Paysse, E.A., 374
Pea, R.D., 494
Pearson, R., 387
Peaster, L.G., 19, 142
Peck, C.A., 451
Peckham-Hardin, K.D., 444, 459, 460
Peets, K., 269
Peled, I., 242
Pelham, W.E., 173, 182
Pellegrini, A.D., 246
Pellegrino, L., 439
Pennell, D., 257
Pennington, B.F, 131
Penuel, W., 98
Pereles, D.A., 493
Perez, L.A., 415
Perkins, N., 413
Perlis, S.M., 291
Perlman, S.P., 246
Perra, O., 306
Pertsch, C.F., 9
Pesko, M.J., 451
Peterson, C., 306
Peterson, J.S., 479
Peterson, R.L., 229
Peterson-Karlan, G.R., 26, 53
Petrill, S.A., 275
Petroff, J.G., 452
Pfeiffer, S.I., 493
Pfifner, L.J., 186, 188
Pianta, R.C., 446
Pickles, A., 270
Pierangelo, R., 46, 47, 53, 110
Pierce, K., 304
Pierson, M.R., 150, 208, 215, 260
Pinckney, E., 119
Pinto-Martin, J.A., 320
Pisecco, S., 171
Pisha, B., 24, 98
Pisoni, D.B., 362
Pittman, C., 172
Planty, M., 19, 68
Plomin, R., 131, 275
Plunkett, S.W., 91
Pogrund, R.L., 370, 375, 381, 383, 470
Polloway, E.A., 43, 192, 440
Poon-McBrayer, K.F., 292
Potter, S.C.L., 266
Potterton, T., 221
Potts-Datema, W., 410
Powell, M.B., 285
Power, D., 331
Powers, K., 251
Powers, L., 251
Powers, S., 349

Prader-Willi Association, 238
Praisner, C.L., 22
Prasse, D.P., 43, 103
Prater, M.A., 290
Pratt, C., 270
Precht, B., 427
Preston, C., 223
Prevatt, F., 180
Prins, D., 273
Proctor, A., 273
Prout, H.T., 256
Prout, S.M., 256
Pryzwansky, W.B., 115
Pufpaff, L.A., 289
Pugach, M.C., 101, 106
Pugalle, D.K., 444
Pullmann, M.D., 228
Purcell, M.G., 450

Qualls, C.D., 284
Quigley, S., 337
Quinn, K.P., 219
Quinn, M.M., 224
Quinn, P., 167
Quinn, W.H., 430

Rabian, B., 326
Rackensperger, T., 286
Rafalovich, A., 162, 163
Raffaele Mendez, L.M., 219
Rafoth, M.A., 109
Ramsay, R., 409
Ramsey, M.L., 4
Ramsey, R.S., 152
Rashid, F.L., 132
Ratner, N.B., 293
Ratusnik, D.L., 270
Raven, B.H., 122
Ray, K.E., 479
Rayner, C., 318
Rea, P.J., 148
Reagon, K.A., 221
Redd, V., 253
Reddy, L.A., 217
Reed, P., 453
Reed, S., 351, 357
Reetz, L., 141
Reeves, J.B., 356
Reichler, R., 311
Reid, D.H., 452, 453
Reid, R., 138, 188
Reilly, A., 447
Reis, E.M., 174, 234
Reis, S.M., 469, 470, 473, 475, 488, 493
Reiter-Purtill, J., 417
Reitman, V., 180
Renk, K., 198
Renshaw, D.C., 163
Renzulli, J.S., 470, 481, 488, 494
Reschly, D.J., 177
Rescorla, L., 277, 278
Research and Scientific Affairs Committee, 293
Reuben, C.A., 139, 165
Reynhout, G., 322

Reynolds, B.H., 56
Reynolds, C.R., 210
Rhodes, A., 333
Rhodes, M., 488
Rice, C.J., 63, 94
Richdale, A., 177
Richter, S., 215, 252
Riel, M., 98
Riley-Tillman, T.C., 122
Rinn, A.N., 177
Rinner, L., 309, 310
Risley, T.R., 340
Ritter, S., 82
Ritzman, M.J., 217
Robbins, A.M., 362
Robbins, L., 309
Robbins, L.A., 310
Roberson-Nay, R., 321
Roberts, A.C., 492
Roberts, A.W., 181
Roberts, C.M., 427
Roberts, J., 238, 273
Roberts, J.E., 249
Roberts, J.P., 238
Roberts, J.S., 421
Roberts, R., 206
Roberts-Fiati, G., 484
Robertson, B., 288
Robertson, K., 325
Robertson-Courtney, P., 43, 121
Robin, A.L., 180
Robinette, D., 351
Robins, D., 309, 311
Robins, D.L., 311
Robinson, A., 482
Robinson, M.C., 394
Robinson, N.M., 494
Robinson, S.R., 20
Robinson-Zanartu, C., 81
Rock, M.C., 208
Rock, M.L., 139
Rodgers, C., 28
Rodriquez, D., 37, 311
Roellke, C.R., 31
Rogan, P., 260
Rogawski, M.A., 411
Rogers, K.B., 470
Rogers, M.A., 180
Rogers-Adkinson, D., 94
Rogers-Adkinson, D.L., 119, 460
Roid, G., 247
Roizen, N.J., 439
Rojewski, J.W., 253
Romer, D., 228
Romski, M.A., 269
Roosa, J.B., 322
Roschelle, J.M., 494
Rose, J., 77
Roseberry-McKibbin, C., 291
Rosenbaum, P., 288
Rosenberg, M.S., 63
Rosenblum, L.P., 371
Rosenfield, S.A., 106
Rosenholtz, S.J., 98
Ross, G.S., 277, 278

Rost, D.H., 491
Rostenberg, D., 21
Roth, F., 362
Rourke, J., 108
Roy, N., 273
Rozalski, M., 229
Ruban, L., 493
Rubin, K.H., 162
Rubin, R., 162
Rueda, R., 10, 76, 79, 80
Ruperto, V., 341
Rupley, W.H., 151, 152
Rutherford, R.B., 27, 208
Rutter, M., 299, 311
Ryan, A.L., 220
Ryan, C.S., 117
Ryan, J.B., 43, 48, 229
Ryan, S., 239
Ryndak, D.L., 349, 442, 451, 459
Ryser, G., 208

Saalasti, S., 308
Sabornie, E.J., 209
Sachs, J., 228
Sacks, G., 151
Sacks, S.Z., 380, 381
Sadler, C., 218
Saenz, T.I., 290
Safran, S.P., 218, 299
Sager, N., 10, 80
Sailor, W., 218
Salazar, J.J., 76, 79
Sale, P., 100
Salem, D.A., 118
Salend, S.J., 29, 77, 78, 351
Sall, N., 384
Salmelin, R., 275
Salvador, D.S., 216
Samson, J.F., 74
Samuels, C.A., 43, 215
Sanacore, J., 138
Sanchez Fowler, L.T., 217
Sanders, W.L., 94
Sandieson, R., 409
Sandler, A., 405
Sandler, A.G., 256
Sands, T., 91
Sanford, J.A., 176
Sanger, D., 217
Santangelo, J., 268
Santangelo, T., 121
Sapon-Shevin, M., 149
Sarason, S.B., 98
Saunders, L., 142
Saunders, M.D., 286
Savage, T.A., 407, 415
Sawka, K., 215
Sawyer, K., 102
Sawyer, M.G., 169
Sax, C., 451
Sayer, P., 292
Scalia, P.A., 227
Scanlon, D.M., 157
Scattone, D., 318, 326
Schalock, R., 241

Schantzenbach, D.W., 414
Schatschneider, C., 172
Schectman, M.A., 326
Scheerenberger, R.C., 7
Scheetz, N.A., 330, 339
Scheuermann, A., 121
Scheuermann, B., 228, 306, 308
Schick, B., 352
Schiff, R., 133
Schiller, J.A., 343
Schilling, S.R., 491
Schirmer, B.R., 337, 339, 342
Schmitz, M.F., 175
Schneider, H., 172
Schoenfeld, N.A., 208
Schoepp, P., 73
Scholl, G.T., 381
Schommer-Aikins, M., 290
Schopler, E., 311
Schore, A.N., 337
Schorr, E., 362
Schrank, F.A., 140
Schreibman, L., 309
Schroedel, J.G., 351, 352
Schroth, S.T., 481
Schuck, S.E.B., 170
Schulte, A.C., 115, 121
Schultz, B.K., 171, 180
Schultz, R., 304
Schumaker, J.B., 151, 154
Schumm, J.S., 148, 155
Schwarte, A., 238
Schwartz, I., 451
Schwartz, S., 334
Schwarz, P.A., 21
Schweitzer, J.B., 162
Scott, F., 303
Scott, F.J., 302
Scott, K.G., 249
Scott, L., 274
Scott, S.S., 157
Scott, T.M., 220
Scotti, J.R., 458, 459
Scruggs, T., 122, 154
Scruggs, T.E., 23, 122, 156
Seal, B.C., 38
Sears, S., 22
Sebald, A.M., 387
Secord, W.A., 280
Sedey, A.L., 360
Seguin, E., 7
Seidman, L.J., 191
Sekaquaptewa, S., 122
Seligman, M., 256
Selman, R.L., 228
Seltzer, M., 325
Semel, E., 280
Semel-Concepcíon, J., 407
Semrud-Clikeman, M., 138, 156
SENG (Supporting Emotional
        Needs of Children), 491
Serpell, Z.N., 171, 180, 189
Sevcik, R.A., 132, 269
Shaked, M., 304
Shamberger, C., 13, 21, 22
Shames, G.H., 271, 280, 291

Shanahan, L., 226
Shapiro, D.R., 380
Shapiro, E.S., 215
Shapiro, L.R., 276, 277
Shatz, M., 270
Shaw, S.F., 53, 151, 157, 158
Shaywitz, B.A., 130
Shaywitz, S.E., 130, 135
Shea, T.M., 89
Shearer, D.K., 22
Sheldon, D.L., 45
Shepard, M.P., 430
Sheridan, S.M., 122
Shetty, P., 305
Shin, M., 405
Shippen, M.E., 4
Shogren, K.A., 445
Short, A.D., 414
Shriner, J.G., 11
Shriver, M., 134
Sibley, M., 189
Sickle Cell Disease Information
        Center, 414
Sickman, L.S., 290
Siegel, D., 478
Siegel, L., 158, 337
Siegel, L.S., 129
Siegel-Causey, E., 447, 448
Sieler, J.D., 106
Sigafoos, J., 318
Silberman, R.K., 380, 381
Sileo, N.M., 412
Siller, M.A., 375
Silva, P.A., 171
Silver, E.J., 412
Silver, L.B., 133
Simmons, A., 82
Simon, A.B., 341, 342
Simon, M., 4
Simpson, R.L., 298, 304, 305, 309,
        311, 314, 322, 326
Sims, E., 115
Sims, M.J., 81, 86
Sinclair, A., 348, 349
Sindelar, P., 98, 101
Sindelar, P.T., 22, 63, 91, 98, 101
Singh, D.K., 256, 405
Singh, H., 155
Siperstein, G.N., 244
Sisco, L.G., 250, 252, 452
Sitlington, P.L., 388
Skiba, R., 82
Skiba, R.J., 13, 31, 76, 77, 78, 93,
        132, 237
Skinner, C., 134
Skinner, S., 407
Slaughter, V., 306
Sleeter, C.E., 85
Slomine, B.S., 174
Slomkowski, C., 172
Slone, M., 271
Small, S., 157
Smartt, S.M., 277, 289
Smerdon, L., 416
Smit, F., 227
Smith, A., 455

Smith, B., 388
Smith, B.W., 209
Smith, C., 122
Smith, C.J., 303
Smith, C.R., 126, 130, 133
Smith, C.S., 119
Smith, D., 108
Smith, D.H., 73
Smith, D.W., 394
Smith, J.D., 8, 440
Smith, N.J., 305
Smith, P.R., 427
Smith, R., 87
Smith, S., 110
Smith, T., 249
Smith, T.E.C., 192
Smith, T.J., 380
Smith-Myles, B., 314
Smith-Thomas, A., 43
Smolkowski, K., 135
Smythe, I.S., 129
Sneed, R.C., 416
Snell, M.E., 110, 446, 447
Snider, B.D., 349
Snider, V.E., 184
Snow, P.C., 285
Snowling, M.J., 271
Snyder, H., 211
So, T.H., 22
Social Security Administration, 352
Soles, T., 325
Solomon, O., 308
Sonnander, K., 235
Soodak, L., 456
Soodak, L.C., 12
Soto, G., 451, 456
Soukup, J., 261
Southwick, J., 306, 318
Spagna, M., 22
Sparfeldt, J.R., 491
Sparrow, S.S., 248
Spaulding, L.S., 43, 127, 142, 156,
        157, 416
Spaulding, S.A., 220
Speece, D.L., 156
Spencer, S., 444
Spencer, T., 181
Spencer, V.G., 255
Spina Bifida Association of
        America, 405
Spitz, R., 360
Spooner, F., 252, 442, 455
Spungin, S.J., 386, 394
Spurgin, S., 379
Stading, R., 148
Stafford, A.M., 256
Stage, S.A., 220
Stahl, S., 24, 98
Stalcup, K., 193
Stambaugh, T., 485
Stancliffe, R.J., 245
Stang, K.K., 253
Stanish, H.I., 246
Stanley, J.C., 481, 496
Starr, E., 322
Starr, E.M., 155

Staub, D., 451
Stead, J., 181
Stebbins, M., 179
Stecker, P.M., 141, 261
Steele, M.M., 218
Steere, D.E., 261
Stein, L., 360
Steinberg, A., 341
Steinman, B.A., 375
Stencel, C.S., 416
Stephens, C.B., 213
Stephens, K.R., 470
Stewart, D., 330, 339, 341, 343, 356
Stewart, K.R., 315
Stewart, R., 316
Stewart-Scott, A.M., 422
Stinson, M., 348
Stinson, M.S., 348, 351
Stivers, E., 468
Stivers, J., 114, 121
Stoakley, D., 360
Stokes, S., 214
Stoneman, Z., 256
Stoner, J.B., 45, 375
Storey, K., 453
Stormont, M., 177, 179, 213
Stowe, M., 11
Stratton, K., 305
Strauss, A., 126
Stringaris, A., 191
Stronge, J.H., 94
Stroul, B.A., 219
Stuart, M.E., 385
Stuart, S., 94
Studies to Advance Autism Research
        and Treatment
        (STAART), 303
Stumbo, N.J., 421
Suarez, S.C., 270
Subedi, B., 88
Substance Abuse and Mental Health
        Services Administration
        (SAMHSA), 201
Sugai, G., 218, 221
Suicide Awareness Voices of
        Education, 207
Sullivan, Anne, 437
Sullivan, E.E., 469, 475
Sullivan, N.A., 415
Sullivan, P.F., 202
Sumi, W.C., 198, 202
Summers, J.A., 117
Sunderland, L.C., 37
Supporting Emotional Needs of the
        Gifted (SENG), 491
Sutherland, K., 213
Sutherland, K.S., 223
Suvak, P.A., 393
Svirsky, M.A., 362
Swank, P., 171
Swanson, H.L., 133, 136
Swanson, J., 182
Swanson, K., 22
Swanson, T.J., 290
Swenson, A., 484
Swinehart-Jones, D., 430–431

Swinth, Y., 39
Switsky, H.N., 235
Symons, F.J., 238
Szatmari, P., 323
Sze, S., 416

Tabassam, W., 171
Taber, R.A., 256
TAG (The Association for the Gifted), 487
Tager-Flusberg, H., 308
Tannenbaum, A.I., 468
Tannock, M.T., 121
Tannock, R., 180
Tao Scott, A., 151
Taplin, J., 236
Taras, H., 410, 414
Tardif, C.Y., 138
Tárraga, R., 181
TASH (Association for the Severely Handicapped), 437, 438
Tasse, M., 241
Taub, D.J., 430
Taunt, H.M., 28
Tavecchio, L., 227
Taylor, H.G., 149, 274
Taylor, J., 172
Taylor, M., 185, 304
Taylor-Richardson, K.D., 226
TEACCH (Treatment and Education of Austistic and related Communication-handicapped Children), 316
TeacherVision.com, 50
Tebbenkamp, K., 321
Teeter, D., 326
Temple, V.A., 246
Temple-Harvey, K.K., 209, 223
Templeton, R., 431
Templeton, T., 210
Tennison, A.D., 490
Terman, L.M., 468
Test, D.W., 51, 215, 252, 261
Thakar, D.A., 179
Tharp, R., 102
The Association for the Gifted (TAG), 487
The Center for Appropriate Dispute Resolution in Special Education (CADRE), 60
Thead, B.K., 139
Theoharis, J.N., 120
Therrien, S.J., 134
Therrien, W.J., 138
Thoma, C.A., 260
Thomas, D.D., 77
Thomas-Stonell, N., 288
Thompson, A., 252
Thompson, J.R., 241
Thorp, W.N., 258
Thousand, J.S., 456, 457, 463
Thurlow, M.L., 54
Thyer, B.A., 220
Tirosh, E., 380
Titus, J.C., 343

Toledo, I., 133
Tolla, J., 442
Tombari, M.L., 339
Tomlinson, C.A., 82, 471, 489–490, 493, 494
Tommerdahl, J., 277
Toner, M., 162
Tonks, J., 416
Torgerson-Tubiello, R., 153
Towles-Reeves, E., 55
Townsend, B.L., 73, 77
Tractman, G.M., 101
Traxler, C.B., 341, 342, 353
Traylor, A.C., 220
Treatment and Education of Austistic and related Communication-handicapped Children (TEACCH), 316
Trent, S.C., 78, 94
Trezek, B.J., 120
Trout, A.L., 188
Tschannen-Moran, M., 71, 89, 121
Tuan, K.M., 379
Tucker, Matt, 56
Tucker, P.D., 94
Tulbert, B., 107
Turkstra, L.S., 416
Turnbull, A., 117, 260
Turnbull, A.P., 11, 118, 257, 456
Turnbull, H.R., 11, 456
Turner, A., 176
Turner, K.H., 292
Twain, M., 456
Tye-Murray, N., 340
Tyler, K.M., 73, 74
Tyler, R.S., 362
Tynan, D., 129

U.S. Census Bureau, 71, 87
U.S. Department of Education, 4, 19, 19f, 20, 31, 56, 58, 59, 74, 75, 88, 92, 129, 145, 157, 174, 177–178, 180, 200, 201, 213, 217, 236, 249, 251, 274, 282, 283, 302, 303, 313, 314, 333, 346, 347, 359, 369, 372, 387, 394, 402, 421, 437, 439, 469
U.S. Department of Health and Human Services, 202, 217, 227, 246
U.S. Food and Drug Administration, 362
Ulich, M., 212
Ulster, A.A., 392
Umansky, L., 400
United Cerebral Palsy Association (UCP), 28
USDE, 12, 13, 32
Utley, C.A., 87

Vadasy, P.F., 255
Vagi, S.J., 249
Vahhover, S., 98, 101
Vail, C.O., 103
Valentin, S., 416

Vallance, D.D., 139
Van Acker, R., 221
van Bon, W.H.J., 375
van den Berg, S.A., 343
van Garderen, D., 81, 121
Van Norman, R.K., 255
Van Tassel-Baska, J., 49, 471, 483, 485
Vannatta, K., 407, 417
Vannest, K.J., 209, 223
Vassil, T.V., 102
Vaughn, B.J., 226
Vaughn, B.S., 162
Vaughn, E.S., 189
Vaughn, S., 115, 127, 134, 143, 148, 151, 155
Velasco, A., 10, 80
Velez, M., 175
Vellutino, F.R., 157
Venkatagiri, H.S., 273
Vercimak, D., 483
Vernon, M., 333
Vervloed, M.P.J., 375
Villa, R.A., 456
Villers, M.S., 189
Villiers, D., 228
Virginia Assistive Technology System, 26
Vismara, L., 307
Vismara, L.A., 444
Visscher, C., 375
Visser, J., 214
Vitello, S.J., 401
Volden, J., 270
Volkmar, F., 304
Volonino, V., 121, 147
Volpe, R., 171
Volpiansky, P., 63
Voltz, D.L., 81, 86, 94
von Eye, A., 203
Vorndran, C., 326

Wadlington, E., 137
Wadlington, P.L., 137
Wagner, A.R., 63
Wagner, M., 198, 201, 202, 208, 209, 212, 215, 252, 351, 352
Wagner, S., 22
Wagner, S.M., 184
Wakeman, S.Y., 252, 442
Waldman, H.B., 246
Waldron, N., 98, 101, 243, 451
Waldron, N.L., 22, 23, 121
Walker, A., 215, 252
Walker, H.M., 228
Walker, L.A., 351
Wallace, H., 114
Wallace, T., 51
Walter, G.G., 352
Walther-Thomas, C., 102, 148
Wanzek, J., 127
Ward, M.E., 372
Ward, M.J., 48
Ward-Lonergan, J., 135
Ward-Lonergan, J.M., 288
Warikoo, N., 71
Warren, R.P., 483

Wasik, B.A., 276
Wasserstein, A., 180
Wasserstein, J., 180, 191
Watson, A., 249, 383
Watson, D., 352
Watson, S., 134
Wayne, S.K., 255
Webb-Johnson, G., 79
Webber, J., 214, 306, 308
Wechsler, D., 140, 210, 247
Wehby, J.H., 223
Wehman, P., 314, 452
Wehmeyer, M., 241, 260, 261
Wehmeyer, M.L., 235, 260, 445
Weinstein, S., 411
Weisman, J., 427
Weismer, S.E., 285
Weisner, T., 244
Weiss, A.L., 273
Weiss, L.G., 156
Welch, M., 107
Welles, T., 180
Wells, G., 340
Wells, K.C., 185, 186
Werner, G.A., 444
West, J., 185
West, J.E., 390
Westling, D.L., 438, 444, 445, 447, 454
Wetzel, M.W., 162
Wetzel, R., 102, 377
Wexler, J., 143
Weyandt, L., 171
Weyandt, L.L., 132, 167, 168
Whalon, K.J., 313
What Works Clearinghouse, 43, 223
Wheeler, J.J., 27
Wheeler, L.S., 410
Wheeler, R.S., 292
Whinery, K.W., 424
White, G.P., 229
White, J., 215, 252
White, S., 321
Whiting, G.W., 76, 473
Whitney, J., 291
Whitney, T., 314, 321
Whittaker, C., 81
Whitten, E., 385
Wiederholt, J.L., 280
Wiener, J., 138, 173, 180
Wiggins, L., 309
Wiig, E.H., 280, 284
Wilcox, B., 11
Wilcoxen, A., 22
Wilczynski, S.M., 326
Wilde, L.D., 318
Wilder, L., 174
Wilens, T., 181
Wilhite, K., 221
Wilkins, M.A., 130
Wilkinson, C.Y., 43, 121
Will, M., 13
Will, M.C., 13
Williams, D., 304
Williams, D.L., 135

Williams, K., 352
Williams, M., 325
Williams, W.H., 416
Williamson, P., 15, 174, 251
Willis, B., 273
Wilson, B., 108
Wilson, D., 308
Wilson, K.E., 122
Windsor, J., 280
Wing, L., 299, 308
Winn, J.A., 39, 55, 103
Winn, S., 55
Winzer, M.A., 8, 9, 84, 88, 198, 235, 330, 400
Wirt, J., 180
Wiskochil, B., 385
Witty, J.P., 77
Witty, P., 468
Woblers, K.A., 342
Wodrich, D.L., 415
Wolf, L.E., 180
Wolffe, K., 387
Wolffe, K.E., 388, 389
Wollenhaupt, P., 356
Wolter, J.A., 277

Wolters, P.L., 415
Wood, A., 277
Wood, B., 309
Wood, C., 473
Wood, D., 341
Wood, F., 131
Wood, H., 341
Wood, S., 487
Woodcock, R.W., 140, 210
Woodruff, S., 362
Woods, T., 273
Worcester, J.A., 219
Wright, P.D., 11, 12, 14, 15, 24, 51, 55, 59
Wright, P.W.D., 11, 12, 14, 15, 24, 51, 55, 59
Wright-Gallo, G.L., 221
Wristers, K., 171
Wu, Q., 213
Wu, T., 82
Wyatte, M.L., 226
Wydell, T.N., 276
Wymbs, B.T., 184
Wynn, J.W., 249

Xenopoulos-Oddsson, A., 431

Yairi, E., 273, 282
Yeates, K.O., 407, 417
Yeh, M., 215
Yell, M.L., 11, 43, 47, 48, 49, 61, 401
Yellowbird, S., 273
Yendol-Hoppey, D., 22
Yim, D., 280
Yirmyia, N., 304
Yoon, S.Y., 74, 473, 474
Yoshinaga-Itano, C., 337, 342, 360
Young, C.L., 43, 157
Young, S., 191
Youngwirth, S.D., 179
Youse, K.M., 407
Yu, J., 252
Yuelin, L., 341

Zabala, J.M., 54
Zabel, R.H., 215
Zachor, D.A., 181
Zaff, J.F., 174

Zambo, D., 165
Zames, F., 8, 12, 17
Zane, C., 149
Zapien, C., 331
Zebahazy, K., 385
Zentall, S.S., 174
Zera, D.A., 133
Zhang, D., 260, 261
Zhang, J., 273
Zheng, X., 133
Zhou, L., 91
Zigmond, N., 111, 121, 122, 147, 341, 416
Zinck, L.C., 155
Zinner, B., 421
Zionts, L.T., 228
Zionts, P., 304
Zirkel, P.A., 13, 16, 43, 59, 127, 470
Zola, I.K., 461
Zuniga, M.A., 460
Zureich, A., 171, 172
Zwaigenbaum, L., 323

# subject index

*Note:* Bold numbers indicate pages on which key terms are defined.

AAC. *See* Augmentative and alternative communication (AAC)
AAC (augmentative and alternative communication), **286–288**, 290
AAIDD (American Association on Intellectual and Developmental Disabilities), **235**
AAMR Adaptive Behavior Scale, 247
AAVE (African American Vernacular English), 291–292
ABC approach (antecedents, behaviors, consequences), 221
Ability grouping, **484**
ABR (auditory brainstem response), 360
Absence seizure, **411**
Abstract concepts, 441
Abuse and neglect. *See* Child abuse/neglect
Academic achievement
    autism spectrum disorders, 311
    inclusive practices and, 22
Academic characteristics (of individuals with)
    ADHD, 171–172
    autism spectrum disorders and, 305–307
    deafness and hearing loss, 339–343
    emotional and behavioral disorders, 209
    gifted and talented, 477
    intellectual disabilities, 240–241, 243
    learning disabilities, 134–137
    physical and health disabilities, 415
    severe and multiple disabilities, 442–444
    speech and language disorders, 276–277
    visual impairments, 375–378
Acceleration, **488**
Accent, **291**
Access technologies, **378**
Access to education
    physical and health education, 424–428
    in special education, 24–26
Access to technology, 431
Accountability
    collaboration and, 100–101
    diversity and, 92–93
    inclusion and, 24
    intellectual disabilities and, 259
    No Child Left Behind and, 31, 92
    severe and multiple disabilities, 462–463
    shared, 100–**101**
Accountable instruction, 24–26
ACDs (augmentative communication devices), **443**
Achievement tests, 46, 54
Acquired brain injury (ABI), **407**
Acquired hearing loss, **333**
Acquired immune deficiency syndrome (AIDS), **412**
Acquired physical and health disabilities, 403
Acute (health/medical) conditions, **402**

Adapted physical educator, **37**
Adaptive behavior
    assessment of, 247–248
    autism spectrum disorders, 311
    defined, **236**
    of individuals with intellectual disabilities, 244
Adaptive Behavior Scale, 247
ADD. *See* Attention deficit disorder (ADD)
Adderall, 182, 183
Adderrall XR, 183
Additions, **273**
Adequate yearly progress (AYP), 30, 31
ADHD. *See* Attention deficit-hyperactivity disorder (ADHD)
ADHD–combined type, **164**, 166
ADHD–predominantly hyperactive–impulsive type, **164**, 166
ADHD–predominantly inattentive type, **164**, 166
ADI-R (Autism Diagnostic Interview–Revised), 311
Adolescence
    attention deficit-hyperactivity disorder in, 191–192
    gifted and talented, 484–487
Adopted children, language delays in, 289
Adults/adulthood
    with attention deficit-hyperactivity disorder, 191–192
    with learning disabilities, 149–151
    physical and health disabilities in, 421–422
    transition into. *See* Transition planning (for students with)
Adventitious hearing loss, **333**
Adventitious visual impairment, **371**
Aesthetic sensitivity, **480**
Affective disorders, 201
African Americans
    dialect of, 291–292
    disproportionate representation and, 13
    in gifted education, 76
    identified as gifted, 473
    intellectual disabilities among, 237
    with oculocutaneous albinism, 377
    placement of, 77, 78
    with sickle cell disease, 413
    suspension of, 73–74
African American Vernacular English (AAVE), 291–292
Age
    deafness and hearing loss and, 332
    Down Syndrome and, 238
    identification and, 41
    intellectual disabilities and, 237
    traumatic brain injury and, 407

Aides, 39
AIDS (acquired immune deficiency syndrome), **412**
Albinism, 374
Alcohol use, fetal alcohol syndrome, 238–**239**
Alternate assessment, 462–463
Alternative route to licensure, 63
Alternative teaching, 113
Altruism, **478**
Amblyopia, **373**
American Association on Intellectual and Developmental Disabilities (AAIDD), **235**, 236
American Asylum for the Education of the Deaf and Dumb, 330
American Indian/Alaska Native students
    disproportionate representation and, 13
    placement of, 75
American School for the Deaf, 330
American Sign Language (ASL), 37, **333**, 337, 338
Americans with Disabilities Act (ADA)
    of 1973, 15
    of 1990, 17
    telecommunication relay service (TRS) and, 355
    visual impairments and, 371
Amplification (sound), **335**
Anger, 205–206
Anger management training, 215, 216
Aniridia, **373**
Annual goals (IEP), **52**
Annual review, **48**
Anophthalmia, 374
Anoxia, 276
Antidepressant medications, 182
Anxiety, ADHD and, 174
Anxiety disorders, 201
Aphasia, **271**
Applied academic skill, **251**
Apraxia of speech, **273**
Aqueous humor, **372**
Arc, the, 28, 237, 241
*Arlington Central School District v. Pearl Murphy and Theodore Murphy* (2006), 12
Arthritis, 406
Articulation, **272**
Articulation disorders, **273**
Art therapist, 40
ASD. *See* Autism spectrum disorders (ASD)
ASDS (Asperger Syndrome Diagnostic Scale), 311
Asian students
    disproportionate representation and, 13
    in gifted education, 76
    placement of, 75
ASL. *See* American Sign Language (ASL)

Asperger syndrome. *See also* Autism spectrum disorders (ASD)
  diagnostic criteria for, 301
  language problems with, 308
  pervasive developmental disorder (PDD), 299, 300
Asperger Syndrome Diagnostic Scale (ASDS), 311
Asphyxia, cerebral palsy and, 404
Assessment. *See also* Authentic assessment; Multidisciplinary team
  alternative strategies, 81
  of attention deficit-hyperactivity disorder, 175–177
  of autism spectrum disorders, 311–312, 325
  components of, 45–46
  of deafness and hearing loss, 344–345
  decision making by multidisciplinary team, 47–48
  dynamic, **483**
  of emotional and behavioral disorders, 210–211
  functional behavior assessment, **220**–221
  functional–ecological, **447**, 448
  gifted and talented, 481–483
  instruction for diverse students and, 86–87
  of intellectual disabilities, 247–248
  language, 46–47, 280
  of learning disabilities, 140–142
  multidisciplinary team for, **44**–45
  for non native English speakers, 280–281
  parents' rights and, 45
  person-centered approach, **447**
  physical and health disabilities, 418
  portfolio, 448
  procedures, 46–47
  severe and multiple disabilities, 446–448, 462–463
  of speech and language disorders, 279–281
  of visual impairments, 382
Assistive listening devices, **335**
Assistive technology
  for autism spectrum disorders, 318, 320
  in IEP, 53
  for inclusion, **26**
  for physical and health disabilities, 423, 426
  SETT framework, 54
  for severe and multiple disabilities, 443
  for students with severe and multiple disabilities, 452
Asthma, **409**, 415
Asynchronous development, 479
Ataxic cerebral palsy, **404**
Athetoid cerebral palsy, **404**
At risk students, IDEA and, 20–21
Attention deficit disorder (ADD), **163**. *See also* Attention deficit-hyperactivity disorder (ADHD)
Attention deficit-hyperactivity disorder (ADHD), 160–194, 201
  adolescents with, 191–192
  in adulthood, 180, 191–192
  assessment, 175–177
  behavior interventions, 186–188
  causes of, 165, 167–169
  characteristics of individuals with, 169–175
  comorbidity, 174, 333
  defined, **163**–164

development of the field, 162–163, 164, 165
  *DSM-IV-TR* criteria for, 166
  educating students with, 179–180
  elements of, 164
  environmental supports for, 185–186
  gender and, 165, 167
  in girls, 167
  IDEA and, 20, 177–179
  identification of, 175–179, 190–192
  instructional strategies, 188–189
  learning disabilities and, 139
  learning strategies, 171
  medication for, 181–184, 191
  parent and family perspectives on, 189–190
  parent and professional education for, 184–185
  prevalence of, 164–165
  race and, 165
  Section 504 provisions and, 16
  student profiles, 161–162, 172
  teacher advice on working with, 193
  terminology, 163
  treatment effectiveness, 192
  trends and issues, 190–192
  in very young children, 190–191
Attention, learning disabilities and, 133
Audiogram, **344**
Audiological evaluation, **344**
Audiologist, 40–41
Audio perception, learning disabilities and, 133
Auditory brainstem response (ABR), 360
Augmentative and alternative communication (AAC), **286**–288, 290
Augmentative communication devices (ACDs), **443**
Authentic assessment
  of gifted and talented, 482
  severe and multiple disabilities, **447**–448
Autism, 299, 300. *See also* Autism spectrum disorders (ASD)
  comorbidity with ADHD, 174
  sensory issues with, 310
Autism Diagnostic Interview-Revised (ADI–R), 311
Autism inclusion collaboration model, 314
Autism spectrum disorders (ASD), 297–327
  assessment, 311–312, 325
  characteristics of individuals with, 305–310
  defined, **298**
  definitions of, 299–302
  education of, 312–314
  environmental support, 317–318
  history of field of, 298–299
  IDEA and, 11
  identification of, 311–312
  immunizations and, 305
  instructional strategies, 318–321
  parent and family perspective, 323–324
  placement options, 312–314
  prevalence of, 302–303, 325
  research on, 303
  social skill supports, 321–322
  student profiles, 297
  teachers for, 307, 326
  technology for, 318, 320
  transition into adulthood, 314–316
  trends and issues affecting field of, 325–326

Autistic disorder, diagnostic criteria for, **300**
Autoimmune disorder, 406
AWARE strategy, 154
AYP (adequate yearly progress), 30, 31

BASC-2 (Behavior Assessment System for Children), 210
Behavioral and Emotional Rating Scale (BERS–2nd ed), 211
Behavioral functioning, assessment of, 46
Behavior assessment
  of individuals with autism spectrum disorders, 311–312
  physical and health disabilities, 418
Behavior Assessment System for Children (BASC-2), 210
Behavior characteristics (of students with)
  attention deficit-hyperactivity disorder, 173–174
  autism spectrum disorders, 309
  deafness and hearing loss, 343–344
  intellectual disabilities, 243–245
  learning disabilities, 139
  physical and health disabilities, 415
  severe and multiple disabilities, 444–446
  speech and language disorders, 277–278
  visual impairments, 380–381
Behavior, culture and, 73–74
Behavior disordered (BD), 199
Behavior inhibition, **169**
Behavior intervention plan (BIP), **221**–222
Behavior management
  for attention deficit-hyperactivity disorder, 186–188
  classroom strategies for, 60
  for emotional and behavioral disorders, 214, 216, 218
Behavior Rating Profile (BRP-2), 210
Bell-shaped curve (IQ), 241
Benchmarks, 53
BERS–2nd ed (Behavioral and Emotional Rating Scale), 211
Big idea instructional approach, 456
Bilateral hearing loss, **336**
Bilingual–bicultural (Bi–Bi) approach, **362**
Bilingual education, **84**
Bilingual special education teacher, **36**–37
Biochemical causes of learning disabilities, 132
Biological factors. *See also* Heredity
  autism spectrum disorders, 303–304
  emotional and behavioral disorders, 202
  speech and language disorders, 275
Birth injury, intellectual disabilities and, 239
Black-English, 291–292
Blindness, **370**. *See also* Visual impairments
*Board of Education of the Hendrick Hudson Central School District v. Rowley* (1982), 12
Bookshare, 378
Bound morpheme, 269
Boys Town National Research Hospital, 360
Braille, **375**–377
Braille printer, 379
Braille translation software, 379
Braillewriter, 376–377
Brain function, 130, 131, 304

Brain injury. *See also* Traumatic brain injury (TBI)
    aphasia and, 271
    attention deficit-hyperactivity disorder and, 174
    emotional and behavioral disorders and, 202–203
    intellectual disabilities and, 240
    learning disabilities and, 130–131
Brain research
    on ADHD, 168, 169
    learning disabilities and, 130–131
Brain structure, 130
Brigance Comprehensive Inventory of Basic Skills-Revised, 141
*Brown v. Board of Education of Topeka, Kansas* (1954), **9**
Buddy reviews, ADHD and, 171

Cancer, 412–413
CAPDs (central auditory processing disorders), **271**
Career choices, for students with physical and health disabilities, 422
Career education competence, for the visually impaired, 388
Carl D. Perkins Act, 258
CASL (Comprehensive Assessment of Spoken Language), 280
Catapres, 183
Cataract, **373**
Catatonia, 198
CCTV (closed-circuit television), 377, 379
*Cedar Rapids Community School District v. Garrett F.* (1999), 12, 401
CELF-3 (Clinical Evaluation of Language Fundamentals), 280
CENT-eR (Collaborative Early Intervention National Training e-Resource), 342
Central auditory processing disorders (CAPDs), **271**
Central nervous system, 275
Cerebral palsy, **404**
CHARGE syndrome, 5
Charter schools, 93
Child abuse/neglect
    emotional/behavioral disorders and, 203
    speech and language disorders and, 275
Child Behavior Checklist for Ages 4–18, Parent Form (CBCL/4-18-R), 176
Child Behavior Checklist, Teacher's Report Form, 177
Child development, hearing loss and, 337–339
Child find system, **14**
Childhood apraxia of speech, **273**–274
Childhood schizophrenia, 198
Children's literature, bias in, 78
Choroid, **372**
Chronic conditions, **402**
Chronic stress, emotional/behavioral disorders and, 202–203
Ciliary body, **372**
Civil rights, laws for special education related to, 15–17
Civil rights movement, 9, 10
Classroom assessments
    emotional and behavioral disorders, 210
    for learning disabilities, 141

Classroom environment, 86. *See also* Environmental supports
Classroom expectations, setting, 27
Classwide peer tutoring (CWPT), 255
Clean intermittent catherization (CIC), **401**
Cleft lip and/or palate, **275**
Cleveland, Ohio, 7
Clinical Evaluation of Language Fundamentals 3 (CELF-3), 280
Clinical low-vision evaluation, **382**
Clonidine, 182
Closed-circuit television (CCTV), 377, 379
Cluttering, **273**
Cochlea, **335**
Cochlear implants, **360**–361
Code-switching, 292
Cognitive characteristics (of individuals with)
    ADHD, 169–170
    autism spectrum disorders, 305–307
    deafness and hearing loss, 339
    emotional and behavioral disorders, 208–209
    giftedness, 475–477
    intellectual disabilities, 241–243
    learning disabilities, 133–134
    physical and health disabilities, 415
    severe and multiple disabilities, 441
    speech and language disorders, 276–277
    visual impairments, 374–375
Cognitive disability, **235**
Cognitive impairment, **235**, 236
Cognitive styles, **72**
Collaboration, 27–28, 98–123
    applications of, 109–116
    autism inclusion collaboration model, 314
    communication skills and, 103–106
    with culturally diverse families, 89–91
    defined, **98**
    effectiveness of, 121–122
    elements of, 102–109
    emotional and behavioral disorders, 219–220
    in IDEA, 102
    inclusive practices and, 27–28
    interaction processes, **106**–108
    interagency, 219–220
    legislation and litigation, 101–102
    paraeducators and, 119–120
    with parents and families, 117–118
    personal belief system and, 103
    problem solving and, 106–108
    programs and services fostering, 108
    response to intervention and, 102, 103
    severe and multiple disabilities and, 456–458
    speech and language disorders and, 285–286
    supportive context for, 108–109
    through technology, 109
    time for, 120–121
    understanding, 99–101
Collaborative Early Intervention National Training e-Resource (CENT-eR), 342
College. *See* Postsecondary education (for individuals with)
College Board Advanced Placement (AP) program, 488
College students, learning disabilities and, 157–158
Color-coded notes, 171

Common variable immune deficiency (CVID), 410
Communalism, cultural value of, 73–74
Communication. *See also* Language
    aids for physical and health disabilities, 424–425
    Americans with Disabilities Act of 1990 and, 17
    collaboration and, **103**–104
    deafness and hearing loss and, 338–341
    defined, **269**
    effective strategies, 104–105
    habits to avoid, 105–106
    of individuals with autism spectrum disorders, 308
    of individuals with severe and multiple disabilities, 442–443
    listening and, 104, 105
Communication board, 286–287
Communication disorders, **267**. *See also* Speech and language disorders
Communicative intent, **308**
Community-based instruction (CBI), **251**, 454
Community living/membership skills, 314–315, 316
Comorbidity
    attention deficit-hyperactive disorder, 139, **174**
    cerebral palsy, 404
    deafness and hearing loss, 333
    emotional and behavioral disorders, 209
    learning disorders, 139
    speech and language disorders, 278
    visual impairments, 370
Complexity, **490**
Comprehensive Assessment of Spoken Language (CASL), 280
Compulsory public education, 8–9
Concerta, 183
Conduct disorders, **200**
Conductive hearing loss, **335**
Confidentiality, parent and family rights to, 15
Congenital hearing loss, **333**
Congenital physical and health disabilities, 403
Congenital speech and language disorders, 275
Congenital visual impairment, **371**
Conners' Continuous Performance Test + PLUS (IVA+PLUS), 176
Conners' Parent Rating Scale–Revised (CPRS-R), 176
Conners' Teacher Rating Scale–Revised, 177
Consultant model, 383
Consultant teachers, 115
Consultation, **115**–116, 122
Contact Signing/Pidgin Sign English, 338
Continuous performance tests (CPTs), **176**
Continuous progress monitoring, **43**–44
Continuum of placements, **56**–59, 74–75. *See also* Placement options
Contract (behavior intervention strategy), 221–222
Cooperative learning, 223
Cornea, **372**
Correlated constraints, **203**
Cortical visual impairment, **373**
Co-teaching, 86, **111**–115, 148–149
C-print, 348

Creativity, **471**
Criterion-referenced test, **140**–141
Cued speech, 338
Cultural dissonance, **72**
Cultural familial retardation, **237**
Culture. *See also* Diversity; Multicultural
    education
    academic challenges and, 73–74
    cognitive styles and, 72
    content of instruction and, 71–72
    cultural dissonance and, **72**
    defined, **68**
    elements of, 68–69
    families of children with severe and multiple
        disabilities, 460–461
    influences on behavior, 73–74
    intellectual disabilities and, 257
    language differences and, 291–292
    learning process and, 71–74
    macroculture, **69**–70
    microculture, **69**–70
    race and, 70–71
Curiosity, by gifted students, 476
Curriculum
    content of, and culture, 71–72
    for deaf or hard of hearing students, 345
    for emotional and behavioral disorders, 214
    explicit, 21–22
    implicit, 22
    for intellectual disabilities, 259
    for severe and multiple disabilities, 454–456
    system bias and, 77
Curriculum-based assessment, 81
Curriculum-based measurement (CBM), **141**
Curriculum compacting, **488**, 489
Curriculum flexibility, **488**
Curriculum overlapping, 425–426
CVID (common variable immune
    deficiency), 410
CWPT (classwide peer tutoring), 255
Cylert, 182
Cytomegalovirus, 333

Datafolio, 463
Date, IEP, 55
Day treatment programs, **214**
Deaf-blindness, 332
Deaf community, **333**
Deaf culture, **333**
Deaf Education Network, 352
Deaf Linx, 333
Deafness and hearing loss, 329–364
    Americans with Disabilities of 1990 and, 17
    assessment, 344–345
    causes of, 333–336
    characteristics of individuals with, 337–344
    classification of, 336
    comorbidity, 333
    definitions of, **331**–333, **332**
    degrees of, 336
    development of the field, 330–331
    educational services for, 346–351
    educators for, 349, 350, 354
    identification of, 344–346
    inclusive practices for, 349, 351, 352
    instructional strategies and practices, 353–358
    parent and family perspectives, 358–359

    placement options, 347–351
    prevalence of, 333
    student profiles, 329
    technology for, 355
    transition planning, 351–352
    trends and issues affecting field of, 359–363
    types of, 335–336
"Deaf Students Education Services Policy
    Guidance" (U.S. Department of
    Education), 346
Death, student, 428, 429
Decibels (dB), **336**
Dementia praecox, 198
Depression, 202, **206**–207
Developmental delays, 20, 129, 144, 236
Developmental disabilities, **235**
Dexedrine, 182, 183
Diabetes, 414
Diabetic retinopathy, 374
Diagnosis, autism spectrum disorders, 325
Diagnostic and Statistical Manual of Mental
    Disorders (DSM-IV-TR)
    on ADHD, 163–164, 166, 176
    on autism spectrum disorders, 300, 301
    emotional and behavior disorders, 200, 201
Diagnostic and Statistical Manual of Mental
    Disorders-III (DSM-III), 163
Diagnostic and Statistical Manual of Mental
    Disorders-IV (DSM-IV), 63
Diagnostic and Statistical Manual of the
    American Psychiatric Association
    (DSM-IV-TR), 163
Dialectical code-switching, 292
Dialects, 291–292
*Diana v. State Board of Education of California*
    (1970), **10**–11
Differentiated instruction
    defined, **81**
    diverse students and, 82, 86
    for gifted and talented, 485, **489**–490, 494
    IDEA and, 24–25
Digital divide, the, 94
Digital language code-switching, 292
Diplegia, **404**
Direct instruction (DI), 25, **152**, 153
Direct service, **115**
Disability Is Natural (website), 441
Discrete trial training (DTT), **320**
Discrimination, special education and, 10–12
Disproportionate representation, 13, **74**
    factors contributing to, 76–77
    in gifted education, 76
    labeling and, 75–76
    placement and, 74–75
    recommendations for addressing, 78–79
    systemic bias and, 77–78
Dispute resolution, 60–61
Distortions, **273**
Diversity
    disproportionate representation and, 74–77
    emotional and behavioral disorders and,
        200–201
    gifted and talented learners and, 490–491
    increase in, 68
    instructional practices for, 81–87
    issues and trends, 91–94
    parents/family issues, 87–91

    principal's perspective on, 80
    recommendations for addressing
        disproportionality and, 78–79
    referral/identification practices and, 79–81
    speech and language interventions and, 290
    systemic bias and, **77**–79
    technology and, 94
    visual impairments and, 372
Dogs, hearing ear, 336
Domain specific, **482**
Dominant culture, **68**, 69
Down Syndrome, **237**–238, 246, 250
Dual-enrollment courses, 488
Dual exceptionalities, 20
Duchenne muscular dystrophy, **406**
Due process, **61**
Due process hearing, 61–62
Dynamic assessment, **483**
Dyscalculia, **129**, 136
Dysgraphia, **129**
Dyslexia, **129**, 134, 135
Dystrophin, 406

Eardrum, 335
Early childhood
    attention deficit-hyperactivity disorder in,
        179, 190–191
    autism spectrum disorders in, 312–313
    deaf and hearing loss in, 346–347
    emotional and behavioral disorders in, 212–213
    giftedness/talent in, 483–484
    intellectual disabilities in, 249
    learning disabilities in, 144–145
    physical and health disabilities in, 419
    severe and multiple disabilities in, 448–450
    speech and language disorders in, 282
    visual impairments in, 383
Early childhood special educators, **37**
Early Hearing Detection and Intervention
    (EHDI), 360
Early intervention, 81
    emotional and behavior disorders, 217
    of gifted and talented, 484
Easter Seals, 401
Eating disorders, 201
EBDs. *See* Emotional and behavioral disorders
    (EBDs)
Ebonics, 291–292
Echolalia, **308**
Educational diagnostician, 41
Educational interpreter, **38**
Educationally blind, **370**–371
Education for All Handicapped Children Act
    (1974), 11
Education Program for Gifted Youth (EPGY), 494
Educators. *See* School professionals; Special
    education teachers; Teachers
Efficacy studies, 9–10
Electronic braillewriter, 379
Electronic learning assistants, 146
Elementary and Secondary Education Act of
    1965, 11
Elementary and secondary school services
    for attention deficit-hyperactivity disorder,
        179–180
    for autism spectrum disorders, 313
    for deafness and hearing loss, 347–351

for emotional and behavioral disorders, 213–214

for gifted and talented, 484–485

for intellectual disabilities, 249–252

for learning disabilities, 145–149

for physical and health disabilities, 419–420

for severe and multiple disabilities, 450–452

for speech and language disorders, 283–284

for visual impairments, 383–385

ELLs. *See* English language learners (ELLs)

Embosser (braille printer), 379

Emergencies

with emotional and behavioral disorders, 228–229

with physical and health disabilities, 426–427

Eminence, **475**

Emotional and behavioral disorders (EBDs), 198–229

access to treatment, 228

anger management and, 215, 216

assessment of, 210–211

causes of, 202–203

characteristics of individuals with, 203–209

collaboration for, 219–220

comorbidity, 174, 209

defined, **199**–200

development of the field, 198, 199

educating learners with, 212–215

educational practices for students with, 217–225

emergency measures when working with, 228–229

examples of, 201

functional behavior assessment, **220**–221

gender and, 201–202

IDEA and, 220–221

identification of, 210–212

instructional strategies, 222–225

internalizing and externalizing behaviors, **204**–205

medical perspective, 201

parent and family perspective, 206

placement, 212–215

prevalence of, 200–202

prevention of, 217–219

speech and language disorders and, 275, 278

student profiles, 197

teacher perspective on, 225

transition into adulthood, 215, 217

trends and issues affecting field of, 227–229

Emotional characteristics. *See* Social and emotional characteristics (of students with)

Emotional disturbance (ED), **199**

Emotional intensity, **479**

Emotionally disabled (ED), 199

Emotionally impaired (EI), 199

Employment (of individuals with)

ADHD, 180

deafness and hearing loss, 352–353

intellectual disabilities, 253

severe and multiple disabilities, 452–454

visual impairments, 388–389

Enabling Devices (company), 457

Encephalitis, **239**–240

English as a second language (ESL) programs, **84**–85

English language learners (ELLs)

assessment of speech and language for, 280–281

instruction for, **83**–85

Enrichment, **489**

Environmental factors

with ADHD, 168–169

autism spectrum disorders and, 304

learning disabilities and, 132

speech and language disorders and, 275–276

Environmental supports

for attention deficit-hyperactivity disorder students, 185–186

autism spectrum disorders, 317–318

defined, **317**

Epilepsy, **411**–412

Episodic conditions and disorders, **403**

ESL (English as a second language) programs, **84**–85

Ethical issues, on ADHD in young children, 191

Ethnicity. *See* Race/ethnicity

Etiquette, toward people with disabilities, 18

Eugenics movement, 8

Evidence-based practices

autism spectrum disorders, 325–326

direct instruction, 25

for inclusion, 25

speech and language disorders, 293

Executive functions, **169**–170, 171

Expanded core curriculum, 389–**390**

Experiential learning, 339, 354, 356

Explicit curriculum, 21–22

Expressive language, **269**, 271

Externalizing behaviors, **204**–205

Extrinsic motivation, **138**

Eye, structure of, 372–373

FAE (fetal alcohol effect), **239**

Families. *See* Parent and family perspectives; Parents

Family factors, with emotional and behavioral disorders, 203

FAS (fetal alcohol syndrome), 238–**239**

Fast Forward (software), 288

FBA (functional behavior assessment), **220**–221

Fears, 205

Fetal alcohol effect (FAE), **239**

Fetal alcohol syndrome (FAS), 238–**239**

Field independent cognitive style, **72**

Field-sensitive cognitive style, **72**

Fisher-Logemann Test of Articulation Competence, 279

Fluctuating hearing loss, **336**

Fluency (speech element), **272**

Fluency disorders, **273**

Focalin, 182, 183

*Forest Grove School District v. T.A.* (2009), 12

Formal assessments

emotional and behavioral disorders, 210

for learning disabilities, 140–141

Fragile X Syndrome, **238**

Free appropriate public education (FAPE), **14**

Free morpheme, 269

Friendships

of ADHD students, 173

emotional and behavioral disorders and, 214–215

of individuals with intellectual disabilities, 244, 245

of students with severe and multiple disabilities, 444

Functional behavior assessment (FBA), **220**–221

Functional–ecological assessment, **447,** 449

Functionally blind, **370**–371

Functional vision assessment, **382**

Funding, equity issues with, 91

Gay, lesbian, transgender or bisexual students, 73

Gender

ADHD and, 165, 167

autism and, 303

emotional and behavior disorders, 202–203

fragile X syndrome and, 238

giftedness and, 473–474

HIV/AIDS and, 412

intellectual disabilities and, 237

juvenile rheumatoid arthritis and, 406

learning disabilities and, 129–130

speech and language disorders and, 274

spinal cord injuries and, 405

traumatic brain injury and, 407, 409

General education. *See also* Inclusion; Inclusive practices (for students with)

co-teaching and, 111–115

curricula of, 21–23

deaf or hard of hearing students in, 347–348, 351

emotional and behavioral disorders and, 213, 214

initial consideration of student problems by, 41–42

intellectual disabilities and, 249–252

learning disabilities and, 145–146, 215

physical and health disabilities and, 422

as placement option, 56–57

severe and multiple disabilities and, 450–451

General education teachers, 39, 50

collaboration with special education teachers, 102

Generalization, intellectual disabilities and, **242**

Generalized seizures, **411**

Gene therapy, 239

Genetic hearing loss, **334**

Genetics. *See also* Heredity

autism spectrum disorders and, 303–304

Duchenne muscular dystrophy and, 406

phenylketonuria and, 239

Gifted and talented

adolescent, 485–487

assessment, 481–483

attention deficit-hyperactivity disorder and, 177

characteristics of individuals who are, 475–480

definitions, **470**–472

determining factors of, 474–475

development of the field, 468–470

education of, 483–484

in girls, 473–474

IDEA and, 20

Gifted and talented (*continued*)
    identification of, 481–483, 493
    instructional strategies and approaches, 487–491
    parent and family perspectives, 480, 491–492
    prevalence of, 472–474
    racial/ethnic representation and, 76
    recent changes in field of, 469–470
    student profiles, 467, 480
    teachers for, 486
    technology for, 494
    trends and issues affecting students who are, 492–496
    underachievement and, 478
Glaucoma, **373**
Goldman–Fristoe Test of Articulation, 279
Governors' schools, 485
Grand mal seizure, 410
Graphic organizers, 171
Grouping, 484

Handheld computers, 223
Handicapped, 18
Hands and Voices, 347
Handwriting, learning disabilities and, 134–135
Hard of hearing, **333**. *See also* Deafness and hearing loss
Hearing ear dogs, 336
Hearing impairment, **332**. *See also* Deafness and hearing loss
Hearing loss, **331**. *See also* Deafness and hearing loss
Hearing screening, 46
Hemiplegia, **403**, 404
Heredity
    ADHD and, 167–168
    asthma and, 409
    emotional and behavioral disorders, 202
    learning disabilities and, 131–132
    speech and language disorders and, 275
High school. *See also* Elementary and secondary school services
    acceleration in, 488–489
    learning disabilities, 157–158
High-stakes testing, 23, 92, 252, 259
Hispanic students
    disproportionate representation and, 13
    identified as gifted, 473
    parental involvement, 155
    placement of, 74, 75
HIV (human immunodeficiency virus), 411–412
Home base, 318
Home-based services, 383
Homeschooling, 485
*Honig v. Doe* (1988), 12
Hospital school program, 420
Hydrocephalus, 405
Hyperactivity, 163, 166. *See also* Attention deficit-hyperactivity disorder (ADHD)
Hyperkinetic, 163
Hyperopia, 374
Hypertonia, 404

IDEA. *See* Individuals with Disabilities Education Act (IDEA)
Idealism, **478**

Identification
    age and, 41
    approaches to, 43–44
    assessment. *See* Assessment
    of attention deficit-hyperactivity disorder, 175–179, 190–191
    of autism spectrum disorders, 311–312
    of deafness and hearing loss, 344–346, 360
    of emotional and behavioral disorders, 210–212
    of gifted and talented students, 493
    initial consideration of student problems, 41–42
    of intellectual disabilities, 247–248
    of learning disabilities, 140–144, 156–157
    physical and health disabilities, 418
    of speech and language disorders, 279–281
Idiopathic thrombocytopenic purpura (ITP), 410
IEPs. *See* Individualized education programs (IEPs)
Immaturity, in individuals with autism spectrum disorders, 308–309
Immunizations, autism spectrum disorders and, 305
Implicit curriculum, 22
Impulsivity, ADHD and, 166
Inclusion. *See also* Inclusive practices (for students with)
    accessible instruction and, 24
    accountability and, 24
    assistive technology for, 26
    checklist characterizing schools with, 23
    collaboration and, 27–28, 98
    debate on, 21–22
    definition, **21**
    differentiated instruction, 25
    evidence-based practices for, 25
    positive behavior supports, 27
    research on, 22–23
    for the visually impaired, 385–387
Inclusion facilitators, 41
Inclusive practices (for students with)
    autism spectrum disorders, 313–314
    deafness and hearing loss, 348, 352
    emotional and behavioral disorders, 214–215
    giftedness and talent, 485
    intellectual disabilities, 251–252
    learning disabilities, 146–149
    physical and health disabilities, 420–421
    severe and multiple disabilities, 451, 459
    speech and language disorders, 283–284
Indirect service, **115**
Individualized education programs (IEPs), 14
    components of, 51–55
    defined, **48**
    parent participation in, 88
    purpose of, 49
    student involvement in, 51
    team members for, 49–51
Individualized transition plan (ITP), 388
Individual plan for employment, 389
Individuals with Disabilities Education Act (IDEA), 11
    ADHD and, 162, 177–179
    assessment and, 45–46
    on autism, 299, 302, 303
    autism spectrum disorders and, 326

    collaboration and, 102
    on deafness and hearing loss, 344
    emotional and behavioral disorders and, 199, 220–221
    intellectual disabilities and, 235
    issues addressed in, 11–13
    learning disabilities and, 127
    learning disability identification and, 140
    major provisions in, 14–15
    on monitoring, 48
    physical and health disabilities and, 401, 419
    response to intervention provision in, 31–32
    Section 504 compared with, 178
    severe and multiple disabilities and, 438, 448, 462
    speech and language disorders and, 267–268
    students not specifically included in, 20–21
    students served under, 19–20
    teacher assistance teams and, 43
    on traumatic brain injury, 406–407
    visual impairments and, 371
Individuals with Disabilities Improvement Act, 11
Information processing, learning disabilities and, 133–134
Institutionalization, 436–437
Instruction. *See also* Instructional strategies and approaches (for students with)
    accountable, 24–26
    content of, culture and, 71–72
    differentiated. *See* Differentiated instruction
    for diverse students, 81–87
    for non native English speakers, 83–87
    systemic bias and, 77
    universal design, 82
Instructional assistants, 39
Instructional consultation team, 43
Instructional strategies and approaches (for students with)
    attention deficit-hyperactivity disorder, 188–189
    autism spectrum disorder, 318–321
    deafness and hearing loss, 353–358
    emotional and behavioral disorders, 222–225
    giftedness and talent, 471, 487–491
    health and physical disabilities, 424–427
    intellectual disabilities, 253–255
    learning disabilities, 151–154
    severe and multiple disabilities, 441–442, 454–459
    speech and language disorders, 285–288
    students with emotional and behavioral disorders, 222–225
    twice exceptional students, 493
    visual impairments, 386, 389–391
Integrated service delivery, 463–464
Intellectual ability, assessment of, 46
Intellectual disabilities, 233–261
    assessment of, 247–248
    causes of, 237–240
    comorbidity, 174, 333
    curriculum for, 259
    definitions of, **235**–236
    development of the field, 234–235
    education of, 249–252

high-stakes testing and, 259
identifying students with, 247–249
instructional strategies and approaches for, 253–255
parent and family perspectives on, 256–258
placement of, 248, 249–252, 251
prevalence of, 236–237
self-determination and, 259–261
speech and language disorders and, 275
student profiles, 233
teacher advice on working with, 246
transition planning and, 252–253
trends and issues affecting field of, 258–261
Intelligence tests/testing, 247. *See also* Tests/testing
Intensity (voice), 272, 273
Interaction processes, **106–108**
Interagency collaboration, 219–220
Interdependence, cultural values and, 68
Interdisciplinary teams, 111
Internalizing behaviors, **204–205**
International Baccalaureate (IB) program, 488
Internet, the, 489. *See also* Websites
Internships, 496
Interpersonal problem solving, **106**
Intervention. *See also* Behavior management; Evidence-based practices; Instructional strategies and approaches (for students with)
for attention deficit-hyperactivity disorder, 181–189
for emotional and behavior disorders, 217–225
evaluation of, 108
for gifted and economically disadvantaged, 490–491
implementation of, 108
speech and language disorders, 282–283
three-tiered approach to, **43**, 143
Intervention assistance team, **43**
Intrinsic motivation, **138**
IQ scores
bell-shaped curve, 241
intellectual disabilities and, 240–241
of students with severe and multiple disabilities, 441
Iris, **372**
*Irving Independent School District v. Tatro* (1984), 12, 401
Isolated service delivery, 463
Itinerant special education teacher, 36
Itinerant teaching model, 383–384
ITP (individualized transition plan), 388

Jacob K. Javits Gifted and Talented Students Education Act (1988), 469, 470, 473, 493
Job coach, **251**, 453
Job-shadowing, 496
Juvenile diabetes, 413–**414**
Juvenile insanity, 198
Juvenile justice system, 207
Juvenile rheumatoid arthritis (JRA), **406**

Knowledge construction process, **71–72**
Kurzweil–National Federation for the Blind reader, 377

Labels
of individuals with severe and multiple disabilities, 440
negative influence of, 75–76
Language. *See also* Communication; English language learners (ELLs)
assessment and, 46–47
bilingual special education teachers and, **36**–37
deafness and hearing loss and, 339–341
defined, 369
as element of culture, 69
elements of, 269–270
expressive, **269**
intellectual disabilities and, 242–243
receptive, **269**
Language assessments, 280
Language code-switching, 292
Language delays, **270**–271, 289
Language development, of gifted students, 476
Language differences, **291–292**
Language disorders, 270–271. *See also* Speech and language disorders
in individuals with autism, 308
language differences *vs.,* 291–292
Language impairments, 17, 19
Language interpreters, 41
Large-print materials, 377
*Larry P. v. Riles* (1972), **11**
Latino students. *See* Hispanic students
Laureate-Learning-Systems/Talking-Sterling-Edition (software), 287
Lead poisoning, 240
Learned helplessness, **138–139**
Learning, culture and, 71–74
Learning disabilities
assessment for, 140–142
causes of, 130–132
characteristics of individuals with, 132–139
comorbidity, 333
definitions of, **127–129**
development of the field, 126–127
dimensions of, 129
educating students with, 144–151
educational placements of, 144–149
gender and, 129–130
high school, college and, 157–158
identification, 140–144, 156–157
instructional strategies for, 151–154
parent/family perspectives, 155–156
placement options, 144–149
prevalence of, 129–130
response to intervention, 156–157
RTI for identifying students with, 142–144
seatwork and, 139
student profiles, 125, 128, 149
tools for students with, 146
transition into adulthood, 149–151
trends and issues affecting field of, 156–158
Learning Disability Diagnostic Inventory (LDDI), 140
Learning media assessment, **382**
Least restrictive environment (LRE), **14**–15, 146
Legal blindness, **371**
Lens, **372**
Lesson plan, multicultural education, 84, 85

Leukemia, 412–413
Levels of support, **241**
Life skills curriculum, **251**, 454
Listening skills, 104, 105
Literacy skills/instruction. *See also* Reading skills
severe and multiple disabilities and, 442
for speech and language disorders, 285–286
for the visually impaired, 375–378
Locus of control, 138
Long-term memory, **133**
Low vision, **370,** 371. *See also* Visual impairments
Low-vision device, **377**

Macroculture, **69**–70
Magnifiers, 377
Mandatory school attendance, 8–9
March of Dimes, 401
*Marland Report,* 470, 473
Martin-Bell syndrome, 238
Mathematics skills (of students with)
deafness and hearing loss, 342–343
learning disabilities, 136–137
severe and multiple disabilities, 443–444
Matrix Analysis Test, 483
M-CHAT (Modified Checklist for Autism in Toddlers), 311
Meaningful curriculum, **454–456**
Measurement of progress, on IEP, 55
Mediation, **60**
Medical assessment
of attention deficit-hyperactivity disorder, 175–176
emotional and behavioral disorders, 211
intellectual disabilities, 248
Medical characteristics
intellectual disabilities and, 246, 251
Medical perspective, example of emotional and behavior disorders from, 201
Medication, for attention deficit-hyperactivity disorder, 181–184, 191
Memory
attention deficit-hyperactivity disorder and, 169–170
autism spectrum disorders and, 305–306
of gifted and talented, 475–476
intellectual disabilities and, 241–242
learning disabilities and, 133
Mental deficiency, 235
Mental disability, 235
Mental disorders, **200,** 201, 228. *See also* Emotional and behavioral disorders (EBDs)
Mental handicap, 235
Mental health treatment, 215
Mental illness, 198
Mental impairment, 235
Mental retardation, 9–10, 17, 198, 234, 235, **236.** *See also* Intellectual disabilities
Mentors (for gifted and talented), **495**
Metacognition, **133**, 242, 253–254
Metacognitive strategies, for ADHD, 171
Metadate CD, 183
Microculture, **69**–70
Microphthalmia, 374
*Mills v. Board of Education* (1972), **10**
Mixed cerebral palsy, **404**
Mixed hearing loss, **336**

MMR (measles, mumps, and rubella) immunizations, 305
Mobility aids, 424
Modified Checklist for Autism in Toddlers (M-CHAT), 311
Monitoring, of students with disabilities, 48–49
Monoplegia, **403**, 404
Mood disorders, 174, 201
Morphemes, **269**
Morphology, 134, **269**
Motivation
    extrinsic, **138**
    intellectual disabilities, 242
    learning disabilities, 138–139
    severe and multiple disabilities, 442
Motivation (in students with)
    autism spectrum disorders, 306–307
Motor coordination, learning disabilities and, 134–135
MTA (Multimodal Treatment Study of Children with ADHD) Study, 181, 185
Multicultural education, 86
    defined, **82**
    example lesson plan, 84, 85
    five major dimensions of, 82, 83
    language differences *vs.* disorders and, **291–292**
Multidisciplinary team, 111
    assessment for learning disabilities by, 141–142
    decision making by, 47–48
    defined, **44**–45
    redesigning intervention process, 79–80
Multimodal Treatment Study of Children with ADHD (MTA), 181, 185
Multiple disabilities, 17, 19. *See also* Severe and multiple disabilities
Multiple intelligences (MI), 473
Muscular dystrophy, 416–417
Musculoskeletal disorders, **406**
Music therapist, 40
Mutual goals (for collaboration), **100**
Myopia, 374

*National Excellence: A Case for Developing America's Talent* (report), 469
National Joint Committee on Learning Disabilities (NJCLD), **127**–128
National Library Services for the Blind and Physically Handicapped (NLS), 378
National Longitudinal Transition Study-2 (NLTS-2), 351
*Nation Deceived: How Schools Hold Back America's Brightest Students* (report), 490
Native American culture, 69
Native language use
    assessment and, 10–11, 15
    speech and language disorder assessment and, 280–281
Natural supports, **453**
NCLB. *See* No Child Left Behind Act of 2001 (NCLB)
Neurological disorders, 404–405
New England Asylum for the Blind, 369
NLS (National Library Services for the Blind and Physically Handicapped), 378
No Child Left Behind Act of 2001 (NCLB)
    consequences from high-stakes testing and, 92

deaf education and, 353
English proficiency standards, 83
evidence-based practices and, 293
expanded core curriculum and, **390**
gifted education and, 470
inclusive practices and, 23
intellectual disabilities and, 258
overview, **30**–31
special education teachers and, 36
students with disabilities and, 31
Nondiscriminatory evaluation, 15
Nonoptical devices, **382**
Nonverbal communication, **442**
Nonverbal learning disabilities (NLDs), **138**
Norm-referenced tests, **140**, 446–447
Norpramin, 182, 183
Notetakers, audible and braille, 379
Note-taking, AWARE strategy for, 154
Numbered Heads Together method, 223, 224
Nutrition
    emotional/behavioral disorders and, 202
    learning disabilities and, 132
Nystagmus, 374

Observation assessment, 141
Obsessive-compulsive disorder (OCD), 201
Occupational therapist, **38**–39
Oculocutaneous albinism, 377
Off-level testing, 481
OHI. *See* Other health impairments (OHI)
Omissions, **273**
One teach, one assist approach, 113–114
On-line courses, 494
Ophthalmologist, **381**
Oppositional defiant disorder (ODD), 174, **200**, 201
Optical character recognition (OCR), 379
Optical devices, **382**
Optic nerve, **372**
Optic-nerve hypoplasia, 374
Optometrist, **381**
Oral fluency, 134
Oral language
    learning disabilities and, 134
    sign language *vs.*, 331
    of students with severe and multiple disabilities, 442–443
Orientation and mobility skills, **375**
Orientation and mobility specialist, 40
Orthopedic impairments, **404**
Orthoses, **424**
Ossicles, **335**
Other health impairments (OHI), 402
    ADHD and, 162, 178, 409
    defined, **409**
    types of, 409–414
Otoacoustic emissions (OAEs), 360

Paraeducation, 39
Paraeducators, **39**, 119–120
Parallel teaching, 112
Paranoia, 198
Paraplegia, **403**, 404
Paraprofessionals, 39, 445, 452
Parent and family perspectives, 28–29
    on attention deficit-hyperactivity disorder, 189–190

on autism spectrum disorder, 323–324
on deafness and hearing loss, 358–359
on emotional and behavior disorders, 206, 226–227
on gifted and talented, 480, 491–492
on intellectual disabilities, 256–258
on pervasive development disorder, 315
on physical and health disabilities, 429–430
on severe and multiple disabilities, 460–461
on speech and language disorders, 288–290
on traumatic brain injury, 408
Parent assessment, of attention deficit-hyperactivity disorder, 176
Parent education programs, for parents of children with emotional disorders, 227
Parents. *See also* Parent and family perspectives
    advocating for rights of their children, 10, 12
    of children with autism, 307
    collaboration and, 99, 117–118
    conflict between school and, 61–62
    of diverse students with disabilities, 87–91
    educating about ADHD, 184–185
    firsthand account by, 5, 40
    IEP plan and, 49
    involvement by, 155
    learning disabilities and, 155–156
    participation by, 87, 88
    participation in special education, 29–30
    as part of multidisciplinary team, 45
    preparing for IEP meeting, 50
    professional educators working with, 39–40
    reevaluation process and, 48–49
    rights of, 45
    right to confidentiality, 15
    school reentry process and, 427
    of students with learning disabilities, 148
    of the visually impaired, 391–393
Parity, **100**
Partial participation, **451**–452
Partial seizures, **411**
PATHS (Promoting Alternative Thinking Strategies) Curriculum, 345
PBL (problem-based learning), 490
PBS. *See* Positive behavior supports (PBS)
PDAs. *See* Personal digital assistants (PDAs)
PDD. *See* Pervasive developmental disorder (PDD)
Peer-mediated instruction, 223, 254–255
Peers, participation with, 53. *See also* Friendships
Peer tutoring, 223, **255**
*Pennsylvania Association for Retarded Children v. The Commonwealth of Pennsylvania* (1972), **10**
PEP 3 (Psychoeducational Profile 3), 311
PEPNet, 339
Perception, learning disabilities and, 133
Perfectionism, **479**
Performance assessment, 81
Perinatal causes
    of intellectual disabilities, 237, 239
    of severe and multiple disabilities, 439
Perkins School for the Blind, 369
Personal belief system, collaboration and, 103
Personal digital assistants (PDAs), 242, 243, 286
Person-centered approach, **447**
Personnel. *See* Special education professionals